Basic & Clinical Immunology

4th edition

Basic & Clinical Immunology

DANIEL P. STITES, MD

Professor of Medicine and Laboratory Medicine
Director, Immunology Laboratory
University of California, San Francisco

JOHN D. STOBO, MD

Professor of Medicine
Head, Section of Rheumatology and Clinical Immunology
Howard Hughes Medical Institute
University of California, San Francisco

H. HUGH FUDENBERG, MD

Professor of Medicine and Chairman of
Basic and Clinical Immunology and Microbiology,
Medical University of South Carolina, Charleston

J. VIVIAN WELLS, MD, FRACP, FRCPA

Senior Staff Specialist in Clinical Immunology
Kolling Institute of Medical Research
Royal North Shore Hospital, Sydney

LANGE Medical Publications   LMP   Los Altos, California 94022

A Concise Medical Library for Practitioner and Student

Table of Contents

Preface

As the fourth edition of *Basic & Clinical Immunology* goes to the printer, we are pleased to note that it has achieved a wide readership both in the USA and overseas. Spanish, Italian, and Portuguese editions have been published, and translations are going forward in French, German, Japanese, and Serbo-Croatian. We intend to continue biennial editions in order to keep pace with the rapid advances in this vast field.

Major changes have been made in the fourth edition. The book has been reorganized into 3 sections: Basic Immunology, Immunologic Laboratory Tests, and Clinical Immunology. Several new chapters have been added, including Chapter 5, Immunoglobulins II: Gene Organization and Assembly; Chapter 6, The Human Major Histocompatibility HLA Complex; Chapter 8, Cellular Interactions in the Expression and Regulation of Immunity; Chapter 10, Phagocytic Cells: Chemotaxis and Effector Functions of Macrophages and Granulocytes; Chapter 12, Immune Mechanisms in Tissue Damage; Chapter 13, Autoimmunity; Chapter 14, Clinical Transplantation; Chapter 17, Tumor Immunology; Chapter 20, Effects of Sex Hormones, Nutrition, and Aging on the Immune Response; and Chapter 21, Reproductive Immunology.

We continue to solicit comments and suggestions from our readers for improvements and for correction of any errors they may find.

The clinical chapters focus on primary immunologic diseases or on disorders with important immunopathologic characteristics. These discussions are not intended to serve as a manual of clinical treatment; where specific medications or drug dosages are mentioned, the physician should also consult more comprehensive medical texts.

It is hoped that this book will serve as a text for medical students, house officers, graduate students, practicing physicians, and others interested in learning more about the field. Immunologists from both basic and clinical disciplines should find it a comprehensive review.

–The Editors

San Francisco
July, 1982

Authors

Arthur J. Ammann, MD
Professor of Pediatrics and Director of Pediatric Immunology, University of California School of Medicine, San Francisco.

Eli Benjamini, PhD
Professor of Immunology, Department of Medical Microbiology and Immunology, University of California School of Medicine, Davis.

Joseph L. Caldwell, MD
Dallas, Texas.

Françoise Chenais, MD
Research Associate, Blood Transfusion Center, University of Grenoble, France.

Stephen N. Cohen, MD
Clinical Professor of Laboratory Medicine, Medicine, and Microbiology and Director of Clinical Laboratories, University of California School of Medicine, San Francisco.

Edward H. Cole, MD
Research Fellow, Department of Immunopathology, Scripps Clinic and Research Foundation, La Jolla, California.

Neil R. Cooper, MD
Department of Molecular Immunology, Scripps Clinic and Research Foundation, La Jolla, California.

Steven D. Douglas, MD
Professor of Pediatrics and Microbiology, University of Pennsylvania School of Medicine, and Director, Division of Allergy-Immunology, The Children's Hospital of Philadelphia.

David J. Drutz, MD
Professor of Medicine and Microbiology and Chief of Division of Infectious Diseases, Department of Medicine, The University of Texas Health Science Center at San Antonio, and Audie L. Murphy Memorial Veterans Hospital, San Antonio, Texas.

Oscar L. Frick, MD, PhD
Professor of Pediatrics, University of California School of Medicine, San Francisco.

H. Hugh Fudenberg, MD
Professor of Medicine and Chairman of Basic and Clinical Immunology and Microbiology, Medical University of South Carolina, Charleston.

Kenneth H. Fye, MD
Assistant Clinical Professor of Medicine, University of California School of Medicine, San Francisco.

Ira M. Goldstein, MD
Professor of Medicine, University of California, San Francisco, and Chief of Division of Rheumatology and Clinical Immunology, San Francisco General Hospital.

Joel W. Goodman, PhD
Professor of Microbiology and Immunology, University of California School of Medicine, San Francisco.

Pierre Grabar, DSc
Member of the National Academy of Medicine (France), Honorary Chief of Service at the Pasteur Institute (Paris), and Honorary Director of the Institute of Scientific Cancer Research of the National Center of Scientific Research (Villejuif).

John Richard Graybill, MD
Associate Professor of Medicine, Division of Infectious Diseases, Department of Medicine, The University of Texas Health Science Center at San Antonio, and Audie L. Murphy Memorial Veterans Hospital, San Antonio, Texas.

John S. Greenspan, BSc, BDS, PhD, MRCPath
Professor and Chairman of Oral Biology, Department of Oral Medicine and Hospital Dentistry, University of California School of Dentistry, San Francisco, and Professor of Pathology, University of California School of Medicine, San Francisco.

Perrie B. Hausman, PhD
Instructor of Immunology in Medicine, Division of Geriatrics and Gerontology, Department of Medicine, Cornell University Medical College, New York.

Christopher S. Henney, PhD, DSc
Professor of Microbiology and Immunology and Head of Program in Basic Immunology, Fred Hutchinson Cancer Research Center, Seattle.

Donald Heyneman, PhD
Professor of Parasitology and Vice Chairman, Department of Epidemiology and International Health, University of California School of Medicine, San Francisco.

Paul M. Hoffman, MD
Associate Professor of Neurology and Basic and Clinical Immunology and Microbiology, Medical University of South Carolina, Charleston, and Veterans Administration Medical Center, Charleston.

H. Benfer Kaltreider, MD
Chief of Respiratory Care Section, Veterans Administration Medical Center, San Francisco, and Associate Professor of Medicine, University of California School of Medicine, San Francisco.

David H. Katz, MD
President and Director of Medical Biology Institute, La Jolla, California.

Stanley J. Korsmeyer, MD
Senior Investigator, Metabolism Branch, National Cancer Institute, National Institutes of Health, Bethesda, Maryland.

Robert G. Lahita, MD, PhD
Assistant Professor and Physician, The Rockefeller University, New York.

Juhani Leikola, MD
Director of Central Laboratory, Finnish Red Cross Blood Transfusion Service, Helsinki, Finland.

Jay A. Levy, MD
Associate Professor, Department of Medicine, and Research Associate, Cancer Research Institute, University of California, San Francisco.

Mark Lewis, BSc, PhD
Research Associate, Department of Immunology and Microbiology, Wayne State University School of Medicine, Detroit.

Mara Lorenzi, MD
Assistant Professor of Medicine and Director of Diabetes Clinic, University of California Medical Center, San Diego.

Francisco M. Mampaso, MD
Research Fellow, Department of Immunopathology, Scripps Clinic and Research Foundation, La Jolla, California.

John Mills, MD
Associate Professor of Medicine and Microbiology and Chief of Division of Infectious Diseases, University of California Service, San Francisco General Hospital, San Francisco.

G. Richard O'Connor, MD
Director of the Proctor Foundation and Professor of Ophthalmology, University of California, San Francisco.

Charles S. Pavia, PhD
Assistant Member, Trudeau Institute, Inc., Biomedical Research Laboratories, Saranac Lake, New York.

Thomas T. Provost, MD
Associate Professor of Dermatology, Johns Hopkins University School of Medicine, Baltimore.

Donna M. Rennick, PhD
Research Immunologist, Department of Medical Microbiology and Immunology, University of California School of Medicine, Davis.

Curt A. Ries, MD
Associate Clinical Professor of Medicine, University of California School of Medicine, San Francisco.

Ross E. Rocklin, MD
Professor of Medicine, Department of Medicine, Tufts University School of Medicine, New England Medical Center Hospital, Boston.

Noel R. Rose, MD, PhD
Professor and Chairman, Department of Immunology and Infectious Diseases, School of Hygiene and Public Health, and Professor of Medicine, School of Medicine, Johns Hopkins University, Baltimore.

Kenneth E. Sack, MD
Assistant Clinical Professor of Medicine, University of California, San Francisco.

Benjamin D. Schwartz, MD, PhD
Investigator, Howard Hughes Medical Institute, and Associate Professor of Medicine (Rheumatology) and of Microbiology and Immunology, Washington University School of Medicine, St. Louis.

Stewart Sell, MD
Professor and Chairman, Department of Pathology and Laboratory Medicine, University of Texas Medical School, Houston.

Daniel P. Stites, MD
Professor of Medicine and Laboratory Medicine and Director of Immunology Laboratory, University of California School of Medicine, San Francisco.

John D. Stobo, MD
Professor of Medicine and Head of Section of Rheumatology and Clinical Immunology, Howard Hughes Medical Institute, University of California School of Medicine, San Francisco.

Terry B. Strom, MD
Associate Professor of Medicine, Harvard Medical School, and Department of Medicine, Brigham and Women's Hospital and Beth Israel Hospital, Boston.

Keith B. Taylor, MD
George DeForest Barnett Professor of Medicine, Stanford University School of Medicine, Stanford, California.

Abba I. Terr, MD
Clinical Professor of Medicine, Stanford University School of Medicine, Stanford, California.

Argyrios N. Theofilopoulos, MD
Associate Member, Department of Immunology, Scripps Clinic and Research Foundation, La Jolla, California.

Howard C. Thomas, MB, BS, PhD, MRCP
Senior Wellcome Fellow in Clinical Science and Honorable Senior Lecturer and Consultant Physician, Royal Free Hospital Medical School, London.

Thomas B. Tomasi, Jr., MD, PhD
Professor and Chairman, Department of Cell Biology, and Director of Cancer Research and Treatment Center, University of New Mexico, Albuquerque.

Thomas A. Waldmann, MD
Chief of Metabolism Branch, National Cancer Institute, National Institutes of Health, Bethesda, Maryland.

David R. Webb, Jr., PhD
Department of Cell Biology, Roche Institute of Molecular Biology, Nutley, New Jersey.

Marc E. Weksler, MD
Wright Professor of Medicine and Director of Division of Geriatrics and Gerontology, Cornell University Medical College, New York.

J. Vivian Wells, MD, FRACP, FRCPA
Senior Staff Specialist in Clinical Immunology, Kolling Institute of Medical Research, Royal North Shore Hospital of Sydney, St. Leonards, New South Wales, Australia.

Zena Werb, PhD
Associate Professor of Anatomy, Radiology, and Radiobiology, University of California School of Medicine, San Francisco.

Curtis B. Wilson, MD
Member of Department of Immunopathology, Scripps Clinic and Research Foundation, La Jolla, California.

Alan Winkelstein, MD
Head of Clinical Immunology and Professor of Medicine, University of Pittsburgh School of Medicine, Pittsburgh.

Joseph Wybran, MD
Head of Department of Immunology and Hematology, Erasme Hospital, Free University of Brussels, Belgium.

Maurizio Zanetti, MD
Research Fellow, Department of Immunopathology, Scripps Clinic and Research Foundation, La Jolla, California.

Section I. Basic Immunology

The Historical Background of Immunology | 1

Pierre Grabar, DSc

Immunology is a relatively young branch of medical science. Many observations of importance to immunology were made by microbiologists around the turn of this century, usually in the course of active research in bacteriology and infectious diseases. For many years immunology was studied as part of microbiology, and progress in the field consisted mainly of application of what had been learned about immunologic phenomena to the problems of the diagnosis and control of bacterial infections. Some of the most important advances were made possible by the introduction of chemical techniques in the elucidation of the nature of antigens and antibodies.

The explosive increase in fundamental information has made immunology an independent branch of science. *Zeitschrift für Immunitätsforschung* began publication in 1909 and the *Journal of Immunology* in 1916. There are now 27 national member societies in the International Union of Immunological Societies. This chapter will outline some of the contributions by pioneers in immunology which have led to the current state of the art. Where appropriate, reference is made to relevant chapters in this book.

The term **immune** derives from Latin *immunis,* ie, exempt from "charges" (taxes, expenses). However, for nearly a century the term immunity has denoted resistance to possible attack by an infectious agent. Resistance to second attacks of certain diseases had been observed even in ancient times. Attempts to protect against variola (smallpox) were made in ancient China before our era and in western Asia by inoculation (variolation) using vesicle fluid from persons with mild forms of smallpox, or by purposely seeking out contact with diseased individuals. Lady Mary Wortley Montagu (1721) introduced into England from Turkey the process of **variolation,** or inoculation with unmodified smallpox virus. It was quite dangerous, since disease and death often resulted. Similarly, an ancient Greek king of Pontus, Mithridates VI, tried to protect himself against the effects of poison by administering small amounts of poisonous substances on multiple occasions—a procedure that came to be called **mithridatism.**

A Portuguese army officer, Serpa Pinto, who traveled through central Africa in the middle of the last century, related how local "wizards" protected people against snake bites by treatment with a mixture of snake heads and ant eggs. At the beginning of this century, the same procedure was employed by specialists called "djoekas" among the black population of Dutch Guiana. It is interesting that ants contain formol, which is now used for the detoxification of toxins and venoms.

EARLY IMMUNOLOGY

The first effective—though still empirical—immunization was performed by Edward Jenner, an English physician (1749–1823), who observed that persons who got well after infection with cowpox were protected against smallpox. Jenner introduced vaccination with cowpox in 1796 as a means of protecting against smallpox. The term **vaccination** (L *vacca* cow) was introduced to replace the term variolation.

The scientific approach was not applied to the study of immunologic phenomena until almost a century later as a consequence of work on microbes by Louis Pasteur (1822–1895) and his collaborators. They investigated the possibility of protecting against infection by vaccinations with attenuated strains of microorganisms. Their first observation (1878–1880) was that a culture of *Pasteurella aviseptica* (then called chicken cholera) which had been left in the laboratory during vacation lost its virulence for chickens, and that animals inoculated with this culture were protected against the virulent strain. Pasteur concluded that this culture contained attenuated microbes and, to honor the work of Jenner (nearly 100 years before), extended the term vaccination to denote conferring immunity by injection of attenuated strains of organisms. The idea of using attenuated strains of microorganisms was confirmed by Pasteur when he studied vaccination against anthrax (1881). Research on the mechanisms of protective effects led Richet and Héricourt to the observation (1888) that the blood of an animal immunized with staphylococci conferred partial protection against subsequent inoculation with these microorganisms. The next year, Charrin and Roger observed that the serum of an animal immunized with *Pseudomonas aeruginosa* (then called *Bacterium aeruginosum* among other names) agglutinated a suspension of this microbe.

In 1889, Pfeiffer, a pupil of Koch, used cross-

1

immunization of guinea pigs with 2 similar microbes *(Vibrio cholerae* and *V metchnikovii)* to show that it was possible to distinguish them immunologically, since immunization against one did not protect against the other. The specificity of the protective effects of immunization had already been observed, but this example showed how extremely fine the specificity could be in some cases.

"CELLULAR IMMUNITY" THEORY

In 1882 in Messina, the Russian zoologist Elie Metchnikoff (1845–1916) studied the role of motile cells of a transparent starfish larva in protection against foreign intruders. He introduced a rose thorn into these larvae and noted that a few hours later the thorn was surrounded by motile cells. This experiment can be considered the starting point of cellular immunology. It had already been established by Koch and Neisser that bacteria can be found in leukocytes, but it was thought that this was the result of bacterial invasion of the leukocytes. Metchnikoff showed that the leukocytes had in fact engulfed the microorganisms. In 1883, Metchnikoff observed that *Daphnia,* a tiny transparent metazoan animal, can be killed by spores of the fungus *Monospora bicuspidata* and that in some instances these spores are attacked by blood cells and can be destroyed in these cells, thereby protecting the animal against the invaders. In 1884, he extended these observations to the leukocytes of rabbits and humans, using various bacteria. He noted that the engulfment of microorganisms by leukocytes, which he called **phagocytosis,** is greatly enhanced in animals recovering from an infection or after vaccination with a preparation of these microorganisms. He therefore concluded that phagocytosis was the main defense mechanism of an organism. He later showed the existence of 2 types of circulating cells capable of phagocytosis—the polymorphonuclear leukocytes and the macrophages—as well as certain fixed cells capable of phagocytosis for all of these cells, and proposed the general term **phagocytes** for all of these cells (Chapter 7).

The **cellular immunity** theory of Metchnikoff, who worked at the Pasteur Institute in Paris from 1887, was accepted with enthusiasm by some but was criticized by several other pathologists. The inflammatory reaction had been described by Celsus as early as the first century AD, but before Metchnikoff it had been studied only in mammals. Pathologists such as Virchow (1871) agreed that inflammation was due to changes in the connective tissue cells induced by various agents, particularly by abnormal deposits of metabolic products. Cohnheim (1873) and his collaborator Arnold (1875) considered inflammation to be a local vascular lesion due to a noxious agent which allowed blood cells to penetrate into tissues. Metchnikoff, who had observed the same accumulation of motile cells in lower animals with no circulatory vessels, asserted that diapedesis in higher animals was a process of active penetration of these cells through the walls of the vessels (1892). In his opinion, inflammation resulted from an enzymatic digestion process due to ingestion of the noxious agent by the motile phagocytes.

"HUMORAL" THEORY

Metchnikoff's theory came under severe criticism somewhat later by those who observed immunity in the absence of cells. Fodor in 1886 was apparently the first to observe a direct action of an immune serum on microbes during the course of his studies on anthrax bacilli. Behring* and Kitasato (1890) demonstrated the neutralizing antitoxic activity of sera from animals immunized with diphtheria or tetanus toxin, which was considered the first proof of humoral immunity. In 1894, Calmette observed the same neutralizing activity of snake venom antiserum.

An important humoral defense mechanism described by Pfeiffer and Isaeff (1894) has come to be called the **Pfeiffer phenomenon.** Cholera vibrios injected into the peritoneum of previously immunized guinea pigs lose mobility, are clumped, are no longer stainable, and are later phagocytosed by leukocytes, but they are also lysed in the absence of cells.

A theory of immunity due to humoral factors provoked intense debate between Metchnikoff and the supporters of this new theory, mainly from the laboratory of Robert Koch (1843–1910). At the time of Pfeiffer's discovery, a young Belgian, Jules Bordet (1870–1961), was engaged in the study of agglutination reactions in Metchnikoff's laboratory at the Pasteur Institute. He became interested in the Pfeiffer phenomenon and in 1895 showed that both bacteriolysis and lysis of red cells (which he described in 1898) required 2 factors: one, which he called **sensitizer,** was thermostable and specific; the other, which he called **alexine,** was thermolabile and nonspecific. The factor designated alexine by Bordet came to be called **cytase** by Metchnikoff and **complement** by Ehrlich (Chapter 11). Bordet believed that his "alexine" possessed enzymatic activity and that it consisted of several components.

It is of interest that Bordet's studies of humoral factors were performed in Metchnikoff's laboratory and were in contradiction to the master's theories. Later, both theories gained general acceptance and it was established that humoral factors originated from lymphoid cells.

During this period, the term **antigen** was introduced to designate any substance (then mainly microbes or cells) capable of inducing a reaction against itself and the illogical term **antibody** (both being "anti-") to designate the factor present in the serum possessing this activity. At first, various special names were used to indicate each observed antibody activity, such as **agglutinins, precipitins, sensitizers,** and **opsonins.** The first observation of agglutination is de-

---

*The particle von was added later to Behring's name after he became famous—about the time he received the Nobel Prize.

scribed above. The precipitin reaction was described later—in 1897 by Kraus with microbial culture supernates and the serum of immunized animals, and in 1899 by Tchistovitch with serum protein antigens and by Bordet with milk antigens and serum of animals injected with these fluids. The precipitin reaction was introduced by Wassermann and Uhlenhuth into forensic medicine for the identification of blood or meat.

Resolution of Conflicting Theories

In 1895, Denys and Leclef observed the fixation of antibodies present in an antistreptococcus serum by these organisms and called them **bacteriotropins.** Neufeld and Rimpau had also demonstrated similar in vitro fixation. In 1903, Wright and Douglas, after a careful study of Metchnikoff's observation that phagocytosis of microbes is facilitated by the serum of an immunized animal, used washed cells to demonstrate that the immune serum contained an active factor they called **opsonin.** They proposed the term **opsonization** for the activity, and this phenomenon acted as a "bridge" between the apparently contradictory humoral and cellular theories.

During this same period, Paul Ehrlich (1854–1915) studied the neutralization of toxins by immune serum, using the highly toxic vegetable poisons abrin and ricin, which could be extracted easily in sufficient quantity. These studies enabled him to establish a technique for the evaluation of the antitoxic activity of diphtheria antiserum (1897).

EHRLICH'S "SIDE–CHAIN" THEORY

Ehrlich was interested in the theoretic aspects of immunologic phenomena and in 1896 elaborated his **side-chain theory** to explain the appearance of antibodies in the circulation. He considered it an "enhancement" of a normal mechanism and suggested that cells capable of forming antibodies possessed on their surface membranes specific side chains which were receptors for antigens. He proposed that binding of antigen to the side chains provoked new synthesis of these side chains, which were liberated into serum as antibodies. He expressed the specificity of the reaction of antigens and antibodies as a "key [antigen] in a lock [antibody]" and thought that this reaction was of a chemical nature. During the next few years, he tried to substantiate his theory with various arguments, but the theory was not generally accepted. It was criticized by Bordet, who felt that the antigen-antibody reaction was of colloid nature; by Gruber; and particularly by Arrhenius and Madsen, who insisted on the reversibility of the reaction and on different proportions of reactants in specific precipitates. Nevertheless, Ehrlich's general theory, with modifications and additions, has been taken into consideration by many authors, and his hypothesis on the existence of specific receptors on immunocompetent cells has recently been completely vindicated.

Isoantibody

In 1875, L. Landois published his monograph *Blood Transfusion*. He noted the effects of blood transfusions between members of different species and observed it was preferable to work within a single species. He also stated, however, that there were differences within a single species, since a recipient's own cells could be hemolyzed by serum from a nonidentical donor of the same species.

The term **isoantibody** or **isohemagglutinin** was introduced by Bordet, who observed in 1898 that the serum of rabbits injected with red cells of another species agglutinated the red cells whereas rabbit red cells injected into rabbits were not agglutinated. However, in 1902, Landsteiner used the agglutination reaction to demonstrate several different antigenic specificities of red cells in the same species—the blood groups A, B, and O in humans—which became the basis of blood transfusion (Chapter 27). Later, he also discovered Rh specificity, using rhesus monkey blood. The term isoantibody is no longer used for antibodies to antigenic determinants specific for other species. It is now used to indicate antibody in an individual to antigenic determinants in other genetically nonidentical members of the same species, eg, anti-A antibody (isohemagglutinin) in blood group B humans (see Chapter 27).

Ehrlich also observed that the plant toxins abrin and ricin agglutinate red cells. Landsteiner and Raubitchek in 1907 extended these observations, using particularly *Papilionaceae* (a family of beans). These plant-derived hemagglutinins were later termed **lectins** by W.C. Boyd.

Hypersensitivity

At the close of the 19th century, all of the immunologic phenomena observed to that time supported the view that they were defense mechanisms. Apparent contradictions were the observations of Landsteiner and, particularly, the discovery of anaphylaxis by Charles Richet and Portier in 1902. It had already been shown, particularly by Wassermann and von Dugern, that second challenge of a previously immunized organism with the same antigen increased the antibody activity in its serum. Thus, the fact of immunologic memory had to be explained. The discovery of Charles Richet and Portier was absolutely unexpected. They studied the toxic activity of the tentacles of Actinaria by injecting a glycerin extract into dogs. The first injection, in small doses, had no direct observable effect, and they thought the animals were protected. But a second injection resulted in shock—often lethal for the animals. They proposed the term **anaphylaxis** for this phenomenon (Chapters 18 and 28). The next year, Arthus described what is now called the **Arthus phenomenon,** ie, the local necrotic lesion produced by injecting antigen into a previously immunized animal (Chapter 12). This reaction is specific, whereas an analogous but nonspecific reaction was described by Sanarelli and by Shwartzman many years later—the **Shwartzman phenomenon.**

AN

INQUIRY

INTO

THE CAUSES AND EFFECTS

OF

THE VARIOLÆ VACCINÆ,

A DISEASE

DISCOVERED IN SOME OF THE WESTERN COUNTIES OF ENGLAND,

PARTICULARLY

GLOUCESTERSHIRE,

AND KNOWN BY THE NAME OF

THE COW POX.

BY EDWARD JENNER, M.D. F.R.S. &c.

———— QUID NOBIS CERTIUS IPSIS

SENSIBUS ESSE POTEST, QUO VERA AC FALSA NOTEMUS.

LUCRETIUS.

London:

PRINTED, FOR THE AUTHOR,

BY SAMPSON LOW, Nº. 7, BERWICK STREET, SOHO:

AND SOLD BY LAW, AVE-MARIA LANE; AND MURRAY AND HIGHLEY, FLEET STREET.

1798.

Figure 1–1. Face plate from first edition (1798) of Jenner's *Inquiry Into the Causes and Effects of . . . the Cow pox.*

Figure 1–2. Louis Pasteur (1822–1895). (Courtesy of the Museum of the Pasteur Institute, Paris.)

Figure 1–3. Robert Koch (1843–1910). (Courtesy of the Museum of the Pasteur Institute, Paris.)

Figure 1–4. Elie Metchnikoff (1845–1916). (Courtesy of the Rare Book Library, the University of Texas Medical Branch, Galveston.)

Figure 1–5. Paul Ehrlich (1854–1915). (Courtesy of the Museum of the Pasteur Institute, Paris.)

Figure 1–6. Emil von Behring (1854–1917). (Courtesy of the Museum of the Pasteur Institute, Paris.)

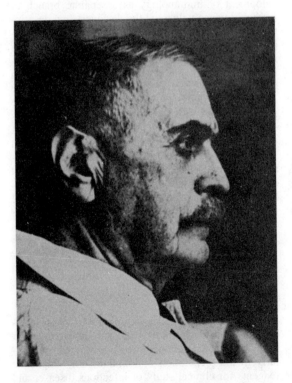

Figure 1–7. Karl Landsteiner (1868–1943). (Courtesy of the Museum of the Pasteur Institute, Paris.)

Figure 1–8. Jules Bordet (1870–1961). (Courtesy of the Museum of the Pasteur Institute, Paris.)

At the beginning of the 20th century, von Pirquet, working in Vienna, studied **serum sickness,** the delayed reaction that occurred following a second injection of a heterologous antistreptococcus serum, and observed that this **hypersensitivity reaction** (von Pirquet and Schick, 1905) sometimes appeared rapidly (Chapter 12). He suggested that this reaction had a direct connection with the presence in the animal of antibodies to the injected serum. In the course of his research on tuberculosis, he observed that a cutaneous reaction appeared more rapidly after a second injection than after the first. He developed the scratch test for tuberculin sensitivity, and in 1906 he proposed the term **allergy** for modified immune reactivity. Since then, this term has been generalized to denote all sensitization phenomena, whereas the better and earlier term **generalized anaphylaxis** is used to denote **anaphylactic shock.**

Another series of investigations on anaphylactic reactions was initiated by Theobald Smith and Otto (1906) and, more successfully, by Rosenau and Anderson in Washington (1909). These investigations showed (1) that the secondary reaction provoked in guinea pigs by the injection of diphtheria toxin and antiserum (this mixture was used at that time for vaccination) was due not to the toxin but rather to antibodies against the antiserum; (2) that the sensitizing time was about 10 days; and (3) that passive sensitization with the serum of a sensitized animal was sufficient to provoke a secondary reaction to the antigen. It was thought that the relatively long time required for sensitization to develop was due to fixation of antibodies to cells. Schultz had demonstrated in 1910 that a contractile reaction occurs in vitro following contact of the antigen with a strip of intestine of a previously sensitized animal. This reaction was also studied by H. Dale with uterine smooth muscle and is now called the **Schultz-Dale reaction** (Chapter 18).

Hay fever was a recognized disease entity for a long time, but until the beginning of this century it was believed to be due to toxic substances in pollen. Experimental "desensitization" was attempted by inoculation of small amounts of pollen to neutralize the supposed toxin (Besredka, 1907; Noon and J. Freeman, 1911). Shortly thereafter, Wolff-Eisner suggested that hay fever might be a hypersensitivity reaction, a concept proved correct in 1921 by Prausnitz and Küstner with different antigens. The term Prausnitz-Küstner (PK) reaction is therefore used to denote the test for passive transfer of reactivity to an allergen (Chapter 18). A similar phenomenon in experimental animals, the **passive cutaneous anaphylaxis (PCA) reaction,** which allows a semiquantitative estimation of antibodies, was described much later—in 1949—by Biozzi, Mene, and Ovary (Chapter 18).

The role of histamine and related substances in inflammatory and anaphylactic reactions is discussed in Chapters 18 and 28, but it is appropriate to cite a few of the more important contributions. Dale and Laidlaw in 1910 showed the similarities between the reactions provoked by histamine and those associated with anaphylaxis. Lewis (1927) explained the "triple response" in skin reactions, and Riley and West (1953) discovered that histamine is present in mast cells and is released by the breakdown of these cells. These observations opened a new field of research into inflammatory and anaphylactic reactions.

ANTITISSUE IMMUNE SERA

Early efforts in the field of transplantation immunology included the production of immune sera against tissue components (Lindemann) and the discovery of tissue and species specificity of antigens. In 1902, Metchnikoff and Besredka prepared antileukocyte antisera and observed that such antisera possessed cytotoxic activity against leukocytes. They also noted that injection of small amounts of antisera induced proliferation of these cells in the injected animal. Metchnikoff envisaged the use of such antisera to enhance the resistance of the organism against infections. Bogomoletz prepared antisera against all lymphoid tissues. The cytotoxic effect of such antisera has been the starting point for the recent use of "antilymphocyte antisera" for inhibition of graft rejection (Woodruff, Starzl). In either case, variable results are obtained because of the multiplicity of antigens on the injected cells and the consequent variety of antibody specificities in the resultant antisera.

The first 3 decades—until 1910—of active development of immunology as a separate branch of medical science witnessed the discovery and description of most of the fundamental immunologic phenomena, although the mechanisms underlying those phenomena were not elucidated. Although Ehrlich postulated that the immune phenomena must represent an "enhancement" of normal mechanisms, they were considered by most immunologists of the time to be part of the organism's "defense apparatus." This opinion gained force from the general assumption that the organism will react only against foreign ("not self") constituents, and Ehrlich's phrase *horror autotoxicus* emphasized his view that the organism would not react against "self" components, though he admitted the possibility of an autoreaction when the "normal regulatory mechanisms" were disturbed (Chapter 13). Actually, at that time, Metalnikoff, in Metchnikoff's laboratory, had demonstrated autosensitization in guinea pigs to their own spermatozoa, and we know now that autoantibodies exist in small amounts even in "normal" sera (see below).

Development of Vaccines

The next 3 decades—until 1940—were concerned mainly with applications and development of knowledge about immunologic phenomena, particularly in the preparation of immune sera, diagnostic reagents for clinical study of infectious disease, and vaccination programs. A few examples are Haffkine's experiments with cholera vaccination in India in 1892, using himself and his collaborators as control subjects;

the use of an attenuated strain of *Mycobacterium tuberculosis,* BCG (bacille Calmette-Guérin, 1908–1921); and vaccination against bacterial toxins using detoxified preparations. Several workers tried to develop a nontoxic but still immunogenic preparation by treating bacterial toxins with various chemicals. Formol was used by Eisler and Löwenstein (1915) for tetanus toxin and by Glenny (1921) for diphtheria toxin, but their preparations were not completely detoxified. Ramon in 1924 developed a method called optimal flocculation for the quantitative measurement of toxins and antitoxins which resulted in a satisfactory method of detoxification. He obtained preparations which he called **anatoxins,** now generally called **toxoids,** as proposed by Ehrlich years before.

In 1916, LeMoignic and Pinoy introduced lipid (as adjuvant) vaccines, and in 1935 Ramon obtained some good results with various other adjuvants to increase the production of antitoxins in horses, although these produced lesions at the site of the injection. These were precursors of the current main adjuvant, Freund's complete adjuvant (1947), used to augment immune responses (Chapter 19).

IMMUNOCHEMISTRY

Important progress was made during the second period of immunologic studies when the principles of chemistry were applied to immunologic research. Although Ehrlich had suggested years earlier that immunologic reactions must have a chemical basis and although Arrhenius, studying antigen-antibody reactions, introduced the term immunochemistry in 1904, the applications of chemical theory and methodology truly began only during this second period.

Among the most productive applications of chemistry to immunology were the studies of Landsteiner and his collaborators (Prasek, Lampl, van der Scheer, Chase). Space does not permit discussion of their many achievements, and only one will be mentioned. In 1903, Obermayer and Pick suggested that antigens possessed the properties of immunogenicity and a capacity to react with antibodies. Subsequently, Landsteiner and his co-workers, as well as others, observed that these properties could be altered by chemical treatment of antigens (Chapter 3). This initiated in 1914 Landsteiner's studies with artificial conjugated antigens. Various chemical groupings were attached to proteins, and the specificity of these groupings was demonstrated in serologic reactions. In 1921, Landsteiner coined the term **haptens** for those specific groupings which by themselves were incapable of provoking the formation of antibodies but were still responsible for specific reaction with antibodies (Chapter 3). Similar studies were later performed by Haurowitz and Breinl (1931), who introduced groupings containing arsonate, which facilitated their recognition. Landsteiner's book *The Specificity of Serological Reactions,* published in German in 1933 and in English in 1936, had a great influence on further research, as did Wells's book *The Chemical Aspects of Immunity* (1925) and Marrack's text *The Chemistry of Antigens and Antibodies* (1935).

Immunologic Tolerance

An important observation made by Felton (1942) showed that if mice are injected with very small amounts of pneumococcal polysaccharide they are protected against infection by the corresponding microbe, but if the injection is made with large quantities of polysaccharide the mice can be infected. This **Felton phenomenon** was also called immunologic unresponsiveness and is now known as **immunologic tolerance.** The multiple mechanisms involved in this phenomenon are discussed in Chapter 13.

Identification of Immunoglobulins

Felton was probably also the first to obtain purified preparations of antibodies, using horse antisera to pneumococci and precipitating the euglobulin fraction rich in antibodies. The practical isolation of pure antibodies from such sera was achieved by Heidelberger and Kendall (1936) by dissociation of specific precipitates with concentrated salt reagents. As a result of studies by Heidelberger and Pedersen with Svedberg's ultracentrifuge (1937) and by Tiselius and Kabat with electrophoresis in liquid media (1938), it became clear that antibodies belong to that globulin fraction of the serum proteins possessing slow mobility, at that time designated γ-globulins (Chapter 4).

In parallel with the development of immunochemistry, studies on the cellular aspects of immunology had been performed mainly by hematologists and pathologists who confirmed the role of white blood cells in the formation of antibodies. Pfeiffer and Marx found that antibodies, which they called sensitizers or fixators, appear earlier in the spleen, lymph nodes, and bone marrow than in the blood. The lymphatic system, which came to be called the reticuloendothelial system, was progressively studied and various cells were described (Chapter 7).

This period of development of the field of immunology also witnessed the isolation of the components of complement, studies on their respective activities, and identification of several specific subgroups among human and animal red cells.

RECENT PERIOD OF IMMUNOLOGY

The period of development of the discipline of immunology beginning just before World War II is characterized by the emergence of an enormous amount of new data. Space limitations preclude even brief mention of much of this work. Moreover, it is not the aim of this chapter to show the recent development and current status of our knowledge. Therefore, only a few examples of some recent fundamental findings are briefly mentioned here.

Owen observed in 1945 that bovine dizygotic twins possess double serologic specificities. Medawar and his collaborators in London (1935) performed careful experiments on mammals, and Hasek performed similar experiments in Prague using coupled eggs of different species. Their studies on transplantation formed the basis for subsequent research on acquired immunologic tolerance and are of fundamental importance for the problem of tissue grafting (Chapters 13 and 14).

In 1948, Astrid Fagraeus showed that it is through the development of plasma cells (described in 1890 by Cajal and more recently by Gormsen and Bjorneboe) that the actual synthesis of antibodies takes place (Chapter 5). In 1953, Grabar and Williams demonstrated that immunoglobulins are heterogeneous and detected the existence of IgA (first called globulin X and then β_{2A}). The nomenclature of the immunoglobulins was established, and the amino acid sequences of many of them were studied.

Rapid progress was due particularly to the work of Porter, Edelman, Hilschman, Putnam, and others. The existence of allotypes and idiotypes of immunoglobulins was established by serologic methods (Grubb, Oudin, Ropartz, Kunkel), and the relationships between the structure of these proteins and genetic information are now being studied in many laboratories (Chapters 3 and 4).

The central role of the thymus in immunologic processes was first clearly established by experimental studies performed by J.F.A.P. Miller in London in 1961–1962 and by Waksman and Yankowic in Boston. These studies were performed with neonatal thymectomy in mice. At that time other groups were studying the role of the thymus, including R.A. Good and his group in Minnesota and N.L. Warner in Melbourne. Their initial observations and studies opened up the whole field of the cellular basis for cooperation between cells responsible for cellular and for humoral immunity, thymus-derived T lymphocytes and bone marrow–derived B lymphocytes.

The last few decades have seen the emergence of new branches of immunology:

(1) **Immunopathology** has made important contributions to our fund of knowledge and has even offered some therapeutic approaches. Studies of pathologic processes have in many ways helped us to understand normal ones, eg, absence of plasma cells in hypogammaglobulinemic children (see Chapter 25).

(2) **Immunogenetics** has included analysis of amino acid sequences in immunoglobulins (Chapter 4), histocompatibility antigens (Chapter 14), genetic markers on immunoglobulins (Chapter 3), and the absence of response to certain antigens in certain strains of animals (Benacerraf, Sela, et al). This contributes to our understanding of the transmission of genetic information and the position on chromosomes of loci controlling histocompatibility antigens.

(3) **Tumor immunology** and the immunochemical analysis of components of various human and animal tumors and leukemic cells have already clarified several important features (Chapter 17). These include the absence of various normal components on tumor cells; the appearance of antigens present normally in fetal life (Abelev; Tatarinov; Gold, Burtin, et al) or in tissues other than the one in which the tumor has developed; and the existence in some tumors of "neoantigens." The latter would imply that new genetic information has been acquired by the cells and might depend on introduction of part of a viral genome into the cell. The intensive studies will result, it is hoped, in effective forms of immunotherapy of cancers, including leukemia (Chapters 17 and 27).

(4) **Transplantation immunology** (Chapter 14) emerged from work on acquired tolerance (mentioned above). Since rejection of grafts is an immunologic phenomenon dependent mainly on the thymus, chemical substances and "antithymocyte" immune sera are being used as immunosuppressive agents. Important information has been obtained in humans and in mice from studies on histocompatibility antigens. The presence of these antigens on leukocytes makes possible histocompatibility typing (Dausset, Snell, Rapaport, 1958). International centers for human histocompatibility typing have been created to establish compatibility between tissues to be grafted (usually kidney) and the recipient. More recently, provocative associations have emerged between certain HLA phenotypes and susceptibility or resistance to disease, particularly immunologic disease.

(5) **Immunologic disorders:** The study of immune disorders is emerging as a separate discipline concerned with both "broad-spectrum" and "antigen-selective" immunodeficiency and with methods of immunotherapy for these disorders, eg, transfer factor, both broad-spectrum and antigen-selective.

Development of Techniques & Instruments

The development of new scientific information is historically related to methodologic advances such as the development of new techniques or instruments. The perfection of the microscope by Leeuwenhoek was important for Pasteur's work in bacteriology and Metchnikoff's studies on phagocytosis. The introduction of chemical methods played a major role in Landsteiner's fundamental studies on immunologic specificity. Later, the quantitative precipitation method described by Heidelberger and Kendall (1935) was the most important factor in the development of modern immunochemistry. The establishment of physical or physicochemical methods such as ultracentrifugation (Svedberg and Pedersen, 1939), ultrafiltration through membranes of graded pore sizes (Elford, Grabar, 1930–1935), electrophoresis in liquid medium (Tiselius, 1937), filtration through absorption columns, particularly through Sephadex and similar materials (Porath, 1950), electron microscopy, radioactive labeling, immunofluorescence, and many other advances have made possible the discovery of entire new fields of study (see Chapters 22 and 23).

Immunologic Methods

Among the purely immunologic methods still in original or modified form we may mention complement fixation (Bordet and Gengou, 1901), passive hemagglutination (Boyden, 1951), rosette formation (Biozzi and Zaalberg, 1964), plaque formation by immunocompetent cells in agar gel (Jerne, Henry, and Nordin, 1963), and the use of antibodies or antigens labeled by fluorescent compounds (Coons, 1942) or by enzymes (Avrameas and Uriel, 1966). Important contributions were made possible by the use of precipitation in gelled media (Chapter 22). At the beginning of the century, Bechold facilitated the observation of ring tests (properly called disk tests and first used by Ascoli in the diagnosis of anthrax) by performing them in gels. Oudin demonstrated in 1946–1948 that each antigen-antibody complex formed an independent precipitation band, and established the simple diffusion method which allows quantitative measurement. The double diffusion method in gels, developed independently by Ouchterlony and by Elek (1948), is particularly useful for qualitative comparisons of antigens and antibodies; immunoelectrophoretic analysis in gels (Grabar and Williams, 1952–1953) and its quantitative modification (Ressler, 1960; Laurell, 1967) have made large contributions to immunology and other branches of science (see Chapter 22).

Other technical advances that have made possible breakthroughs in the investigation of immunologic phenomena include the development of cell or tissue cultures; techniques for separation of various populations of cells, including the use of monospecific antisera, purified antibody solutions, or specific immunoabsorbents; and the advantage of working with pure inbred strains of animals raised under germ-free or at least pathogen-free conditions. Various modifications and improvements of these different methods will be presented in appropriate chapters of this book.

HISTORY OF IMMUNOLOGIC THEORIES: PERSONAL COMMENTS*

Even this brief review of the origins of immunology would lack perspective if we did not urge the reader to consider how much there is yet to be done. Although a considerable body of knowledge has accumulated, many fundamental mechanisms—eg, the induction of antibody formation and the role of immunocompetent cells in cellular immunity—remain to be clarified. Many of the theories proposed to account for these phenomena contain some assumptions or postulates which, in the author's opinion, are either insufficient or superfluous. Since the earliest days of the study of immunologic phenomena, 2 fundamental postulates have persisted: (1) Immunologic phenomena are considered "defense mechanisms." This postulate is historically quite logical because the first observations were of this kind. (2) Under normal conditions, the organism will not react against its own

constituents—a concept to which Ehrlich, as we have already noted, applied the term horror autotoxicus.

Two main theories have been proposed to explain the formation of antibodies and their great variability and multiplicity: (1) The **information theory** holds that it is the antigen which dictates the specific structure of the antibody (Haurowitz and Breinl, 1930). Since it has been shown that antibodies differ in their amino acid sequences, this theory as originally stated has been abandoned. However, other hypotheses have been brought forward, eg, the view that the antigens acting on nucleic acids modify the information (Haurowitz, 1970). (2) The **genetic theory** holds that the information for synthesis of all possible configurations of antibodies exists in the genome and that specific receptors on immunocompetent cells are normally present, as foreseen by Ehrlich. The existence of immunoglobulins on the surfaces of immunocompetent cells has been proved, but this does not mean that all possible configurations for any possible antigenic specificity are really present under normal conditions. It seems difficult to conceive that the total number of immunocompetent cells would be sufficient to account for the enormous numbers of possible antigenic structures. Nevertheless, it would be difficult to imagine a mechanism that would not depend on genetic information.

The cellular aspects of the same problem of antibody formation as envisaged by Jerne (1955) and Burnet (1957–1959) are encompassed in the **clonal selection theory.** The 2 fundamental postulates mentioned above—ie, the "defense mechanism" concept and the prohibition against reaction to "self" constituents—form the basis of this theory. To explain self-recognition and tolerance for endogenous constituents, it has been suggested that cells capable of reacting against self constituents, which must exist in the developing organism, are eliminated or destroyed as **forbidden clones.** On the other hand, if autoantibodies appear, this can only be an abnormal event, as already asserted by Ehrlich, and must be a consequence of **somatic mutations** of certain cells (Burnet, 1965). Several arguments have been advanced both in support of and in opposition to this theory. The idea that all immunologic phenomena are necessarily a part of the organism's defense apparatus has been abandoned by many authors, whereas somatic mutations and **deletion mechanisms** for certain cells are still often taken into consideration. More recently, the existence of both helper and suppressor lymphocytes has been admitted (Gershon, Mitchison), but the mechanisms of their actions are not yet established.

The author considers the 2 fundamental postulates mentioned above unnecessary; in 1947 he proposed a simpler explanation of antibody formation, ie, that antibodies are "transporteurs" of catabolic and metabolic substances. Somatic mutations, being a random phenomenon, may modify some items of genetic information, but this cannot explain the appearance of specific autoantibodies. It is now established that certain autoantibodies are present in normal sera. They

*This section represents the author's personal views concerning the historical development and relative merits of immunologic theories.—*The Editors.*

may also appear in sera from patients with various diseases and can be induced experimentally in animals. At the Microbiology Congress in Rome in 1953, the author suggested that autoantibodies should be regarded as normal physiologic agents which, by their opsonizing activity, serve to help "clean up" the products of dead cells when large numbers of them have been destroyed. Normally, these products can be eliminated after their degradation by the existing autolytic enzymes, and the corresponding immunocompetent cells are therefore not activated to produce antibodies. In cases of massive destruction due to any cause, these enzymes are inhibited by substrate excess, and cells capable of synthesizing autoantibodies, which persist in the normal organism, are induced to form autoantibodies. Thus, for the author, "self-recognition" is at least partially enzymatic, and the formation of antibodies would be a general physiologic mechanism for the elimination of "self" as well as of "not-self" substances. This mechanism would act as a defense system in some cases by eliminating invaders that could not be completely destroyed by the organism's existing enzyme system. The future will show if this line of reasoning explains correctly this fundamental immunologic mechanism.

• • •

CONCLUSION

Immunology started with the work of a few talented scientists using simple methods and instruments and has grown rapidly during the last decades. Thousands of publications, the creation of independent immunology societies with thousands of members in most of the developed countries, the appearance of many special journals or reviews, and the organization of independent International Congresses (the first in Washington in 1971, the second in Brighton in 1974, the third in Australia in 1977, the fourth in Paris in 1980, and the fifth in Japan in 1983) are characteristic of this period. Immunology now ranks as an independent branch of science, and we can hope with some justification that the fundamental problems still unsolved will soon yield to the intense investigative efforts now going forward and that new areas of basic and clinical immunology meriting investigation will continue to emerge.

A SHORT CHRONOLOGY OF IMPORTANT ACHIEVEMENTS IN IMMUNOLOGY

1798   Edward Jenner
Cowpox vaccination.
1880   Louis Pasteur
Attenuated vaccines.
1883   Elie I.I. Metchnikoff
Phagocytosis, cellular defense theory.
1888   P.P. Emile Roux and A.E.J. Yersin
Bacterial toxins.
1890   Emil A. von Behring and Shibasaburo Kitasato
Antitoxins, foundation of serotherapy.
1893   Waldemar M.W. Haffkine
First massive vaccinations in India.
1894   Richard F.J. Pfeiffer and Vasily I. Isaeff
Immunologic lysis of microbes; bacteriolysis.
1894   Jules J.B.V. Bordet
Complement and antibody activities in bacteriolysis.
1896   Herbert E. Durham and Max von Gruber
Specific agglutination.
1896   Georges F.I. Widal and Arthur Sicard
Test for the diagnosis of typhoid (Widal test) on the basis of the Gruber-Durham reaction.
1900   Karl Landsteiner
A, B, O blood groups.
1900   Jules J.B.V. Bordet and Octave Gengou
Complement fixation reaction.
1901   Max Neisser and R. Lubowski
Complement deviation. (This was noted independently by Friedrich Wechsberg in the same year and is known as Neisser-Wechsberg phenomenon.)
1902   Charles R. Richet and Paul J. Portier
Anaphylaxis.
1903   Nicolas M. Arthus
Specific necrotic lesions; Arthus phenomenon.
1903   Almroth E. Wright and Stewart R. Douglas
Opsonization reactions.
1905   Clemens P. von Pirquet* and Bela Schick
Serum sickness.
1906   Clemens P. von Pirquet
Introduced term allergie.
1910   Henry H. Dale and George Barger
Isolated histamine from ergot (and from animal intestinal mucosa in 1911).
1910   Henry H. Dale and Patrick Playfair Laidlaw
Demonstrated allergic contraction of muscle by histamine.
1910   William Henry Schultz
Schultz-Dale test for anaphylaxis.

*Name also appears as Clemens Peter Pirquet von Cesenatico, but common usage is Clemens von Pirquet.

1910   [Francis] Peyton Rous
        Experimental viral cancer immunology.
1921   Albert L.C. Calmette and Camille Guérin
        BCG vaccination. (The vaccine was developed beginning in 1906; it was used experimentally on newborns from 1921 to 1924 and then in mass vaccinations.)
1921   Carl W. Prausnitz and Heinz Küstner
        Cutaneous reactions.
1923   Gaston Ramon
        Diphtheria toxin modified with formaldehyde to produce "anatoxin" (toxoid).
1928   Gregory Shwartzman
        Necrotic reactions; Shwartzman phenomenon.
1930   Friedrich Breinl and Felix Haurowitz
        Template theory of antibody formation.
1935   Alexandre Besredka
        Local immunity; oral immunizations.
1935   Michael Heidelberger and Forrest E. Kendall
–36
        Pure antibodies; quantitative precipitin reactions.
1936   Valy Menkin
–38   *Leucotaxine.*
1938   Arne Wilhelm Tiselius and Elvin A. Kabat
        Demonstrated that antibodies are γ-globulins.
1942   Albert H. Coons et al
        Fluorescein labeling; immunofluorescence.
1942   Jules T. Freund
        Adjuvant.
1942   Lloyd D. Felton
        Immunologic unresponsiveness.
1942   Karl Landsteiner and Merrill W. Chase
        Cellular transfer of sensitivity in guinea pigs. (The investigators had been studying delayed hypersensitivity since the 1930s.)
1944   Peter Brian Medawar and Frank Macfarlane Burnet
        Theory of acquired immunologic tolerance.
1945   Robin R.A. Coombs, R.R. Race, and A.E. Mourant
        Antiglobulin test for incomplete Rh antibodies.
1946   Jacques Oudin
        Precipitin reaction in gels.
1947   Pierre Grabar
        Theory of "globulines transporteurs."
1948   Orjan Ouchterlony and Stephen D. Elek
        Double diffusion (of antigens and antibodies) in gels.
1948   Astrid E. Fagraeus
        Antibodies formed in plasma cells.
1948   Elvin A. Kabat, W.T.J. Morgan,
–49   W.M. Watkins et al
        Structure of ABO blood group antigens.

1952   Ogdon Carr Bruton
        Agammaglobulinemia described in humans.
1952   James F. Riley and Geoffry B. West
        Histamine in mast cells.
1953   Pierre Grabar and C.A. Williams
        Immunoelectrophoretic analysis; heterogeneity of immunoglobulins.
1955   Niels K. Jerne and Frank Macfarlane Burnet
–57   *Clonal selection theory; discovery of human immunodeficiencies.*
1956   Ernest Witebsky and Noel R. Rose
        Induction of autoimmunity in animals.
1957   H. Hugh Fudenberg and Henry G. Kunkel
        Macroglobulins with antibody activity (eg, cold agglutinins, rheumatoid factor).
1958   J. Dausset, F. Rapaport
        Histocompatibility antigens on leukocytes.
1959   R.R. Porter, Gerald M. Edelman, and Alfred Nisonoff
        Structure and formation of antibody molecules.

NOBEL PRIZE WINNERS IN IMMUNOLOGY

1902   Emil von Behring for his work on serum therapy, particularly application against diphtheria.
1908   Paul Ehrlich for his work on fundamental immunology, and Elie Metchnikoff for his discovery of phagocytosis.
1913   Charles Robert Richet for his discovery of anaphylaxis.
1920   (Prize for 1919) Jules Bordet for his discoveries in immunology, particularly complement.
1928   Charles Jules Henri Nicolle for his work on typhus.
1930   Karl Landsteiner for the discovery of human blood groups.
1960   Frank Macfarlane Burnet and Peter Brian Medawar for the discovery of acquired immunologic tolerance.
1972   Gerald Maurice Edelman and Rodney Robert Porter for their discoveries concerning the chemical structure of antibodies.
1977   Rosalyn Yalow for the development of radioimmunoassays of peptide hormones.
1980   Jean Dausset and George Davis Snell for their discoveries on the histocompatibility antigens on human and animal cells, and Baruj Benacerraf for his work on the genetic control of immune responses.

• • •

References

Achalme P: *L'Immunité dans les Maladies Infectieuses*. Rueff (Paris), 1894.

American Council of Learned Societies: *Dictionary of Scientific Biography*. 15 vols. Scribner's, 1970–1976; 1978 (Supplement).

Besredka A: *Les Immunités Locales*. Masson, 1937.

Bloomfield AL: *Bibliography of Internal Medicine: Communicable Diseases*. Univ of Chicago Press, 1958.

Bordet J: *Traité de L'Immunité dans les Maladies Infectieuses*, 2nd ed. Masson, 1937.

Burnet FM, Fenner F: *The Production of Antibodies*. Macmillan (Melbourne), 1949.

Delaunay A: *L'Immunologie*. Presse Universitaire (Paris), 1969.

Ehrlich P: *Gesammelte Arbeiten zur Immunitätsforschung*. Hilschwald (Berlin), 1904.

Foster WD: *A History of Medical Bacteriology and Immunology*. Heinemann, 1970.

Humphrey JH, White RG: *Immunology for Students of Medicine*, 2nd ed. Davis, 1964.

Kelly EC: *Encyclopedia of Medical Sources*. Williams & Wilkins, 1948.

Landsteiner K: *The Specificity of Serological Reactions*. Thomas, 1936.

Metchnikoff E: *L'Immunité dans les Maladies Infectieuses*. Masson, 1901.

Morton LT: *Medical Bibliography: An Annotated Checklist of Texts Illustrating the History of Medicine*, 3rd ed. Lippincott, 1970.

Parish HJ: *A History of Immunization*. Livingstone, 1965.

Rocha e Silva M, Leme JG: *Chemical Mediators in the Acute Inflammatory Reaction*. Pergamon, 1972.

Schmidt JE: *Medical Discoveries: Who and When*. Thomas, 1959.

von Pirquet C, Schick B: *Die Serumkrankheit*. Leipzig, 1905.

Wells HG: *The Chemical Aspects of Immunity*. New York, 1925.

Who's Who in Science in Europe, 2nd ed. 4 vols. Hodgson, 1972.

Wilson D: *Science of Self: A Report of the New Immunology*. Longman, 1971.

Wilson GS: *The Hazards of Immunizations*. Athlone Press, 1967.

Wilson GS, Miles AA (editors): *Topley and Wilson's Principles of Bacteriology and Immunity*, 3rd ed. Arnold, 1946.

World Who's Who in Science: A Biographical Dictionary of Notable Scientists From Antiquity to the Present. Marquis-Who's Who, 1968.

The Immune System: An Overview | 2

David H. Katz, MD

The immune system is an extremely complicated one with a variety of roles in maintaining homeostasis and health. Like the endocrine system, it exerts control within the body by virtue of circulating components capable of acting at sites far removed from their point of origin. The complexity of the system derives from an intricate communications network capable of exerting multiple effects based on a relatively few distinct cell types. The immune regulatory mechanism thus may enormously amplify a given response or markedly diminish it depending on the momentary needs of the organism. A normally functioning immune system is an effective defense against foreign particles such as pathogenic microbial agents and against native cells that have undergone neoplastic transformation. Defective function of the immune system results in disease.

The overview of the immune system presented here emphasizes the immune regulatory mechanisms and how they are genetically controlled. The concepts outlined here are covered in greater detail elsewhere in this text. What I wish to emphasize at the outset is the singular flexibility of response made possible by the complex organization of the cellular and molecular components of the immune system. In almost no instance is the organism limited to one possible pathway in response to an antigenic stimulus.

COMPONENTS OF THE IMMUNE SYSTEM

The genetic, cellular, and molecular components of the immune system are combined in an exquisitely complex communications network. The relationships between these components are reciprocal and circumscribed. Regulatory control of immune mechanisms is a function of their interactions.

Cellular Components of the Immune System

The major cellular components of the immune system are the macrophages and lymphocytes (Chapter 7). Macrophages themselves have a variety of functions in the immune response. Although macrophages are not currently thought to be specific for any given antigen, their role in concentrating and presenting antigens to lymphocytes is a crucial one. In particular, it is apparently the macrophage that determines which T cells (thymus-derived lymphocytes concerned with

cellular immunity) will be induced to stimulation and function by various antigens. Moreover, the macrophages secrete several biologically active mediators capable of regulating the type and magnitude of both T and B lymphocyte responses either by enhancing or suppressing cell division or differentiation. In addition, the macrophage plays a key role in antigen processing, since it is the major phagocytic cell of the monocyte-macrophage system.

Lymphocytes are the antigen-specific cellular components of the immune system, acting via receptors on the surface membrane of every immunocompetent cell. Each receptor is highly specific, and different clones of lymphocytes express their own unique specificity. The origin of lymphocyte specialization is unclear, and debate continues about whether it is genetically transmitted or induced by somatic mutation.

The nature of the antigen receptors on the 2 major classes of lymphocytes appears to differ (see below).

Genetic & Molecular Components of the Immune System

A great many genes and molecules have important roles in the immune system (Table 2–1); only those of major importance are noted here. Section I of Table 2–1 summarizes the structural components and functional activities of immunoglobulin genes and immunoglobulin molecules (Chapter 4). The immunoglobulin gene system is the only one yet known in which 2 discrete structural genes participate in the production of a single polypeptide chain.

Each functional immunoglobulin molecule is composed of 4 chains: 2 identical light (L) chains and 2 identical heavy (H) chains. A single chain is formed by the combination of 2 structural genes to form a variable (V) region and a constant (C) region. On the various chains comprising an immunoglobulin molecule, therefore, one may designate V_L and V_H genes or regions. Proper integration of these regions to make a competent immunoglobulin molecule is an extremely complex task. The genes forming the C region determine the future biologic function of the molecule (eg, whether IgE will bind to mast cells). The H chains determine the immunoglobulin class of the molecule (IgG, IgA, IgM, IgD, IgE). The immunoglobulin molecule's unique antigen receptor site is determined by the primary structure of the V_L and V_H regions. This

Table 2—1. Genes and molecules of the immune system.

Immunoglobulin genes and molecules
  A. Structure:
     1. Variable *(V)* region (antigen-combining site; idiotypes).
     2. Constant *(C)* region (biological function).
     3. Heavy *(H)* chain—$\mu, \gamma, \alpha, \epsilon, \delta$.
     4. Light *(L)* chain—κ, λ.
  B. Function:
     1. Receptors for antigens on B cells.
     2. *V* region also forms part of T cell antigen receptor (remainder still undefined).
     3. Secretory products of plasma cells (antibodies).

Histocompatibility complex genes and molecules
  A. *I*-region *(HLA-D* in man):
     1. Cell interaction *(CI)* genes and molecules control interactions between T cells, B cells and macrophages.
     2. Immune response *(Ir)* genes determine ability of an individual to respond to a given antigen.
     3. Ia antigens are the major antigens responsible for mixed lymphocyte reactivity and GVH reactions.
     4. Biologically active mediators produced by, and active on, T cells, B cells, and macrophages.
     5. Disease susceptibility; resistance to viruses; allergic and autoimmune diseases (may be related to *CI* or *Ir* gene functions or both).
  B. Other regions:
     1. Major and minor transplantation antigens (graft and tumor rejection).
     2. Interactions with infectious viruses *(K/D)*.
     3. Complement components.

Differentiation genes and molecules
  A. Ly (lymphocyte) antigens:
     1. Lyt-1, 2, 3: Distinguish functional subpopulations of T lymphocytes.
     2. Lyb-3, 5, etc: Differentially expressed on certain B lymphocytes; functional correlations still undefined.
  B. Fc receptors:
     1. FcRγ: Present on B lymphocytes, macrophages, and one subpopulation of T lymphocytes (?suppressor T cells).
     2. FcRμ: Present on certain T lymphocytes (?helper T cells) and macrophages.
     3. FcRϵ: Present on B and T lymphocytes and macrophages.
     4. FcRα: Present on T lymphocytes.
  C. Complement receptors: Present on subpopulations of B lymphocytes and T lymphocytes; bind C3b or C3d. Functional significance unclear.

site possesses unique antigenic structures called **idiotypes.** Recently, it has become clear that an individual can develop anti-idiotypic responses to the unique combining sites on his or her own immunoglobulin molecules and that such anti-idiotype responses determine, at least in part, the magnitude and duration of antibody production to a given antigen.

In addition to their biologic role as the products of antigen-secreting plasma cells that have differentiated from precursor B cells, conventional immunoglobulin molecules serve as the antigen-specific receptors on the surface of B lymphocytes. The precise molecular nature of the antigen-specific receptors on T lymphocytes, however, is still unclear. Although the same V-region genes that serve as the antigen-combining sites on conventional immunoglobulin molecules seem to function as the antigen-combining sites on T cells, that portion of the T cell receptor corresponding to the C region of an immunoglobulin molecule has yet to be defined.

The gene system associated with the histocompatibility complex (Chapter 6) and its derivative molecules also play a crucial role in the immune system. The system has been studied most thoroughly where the major histocompatibility gene complexes have been designated as HLA and H-2 in humans and in the mouse, respectively. Both complexes have been shown to consist of several distinct genetic regions responsible for distinct functions. The H-2 complex, located in a small segment of mouse chromosome 17, consists of at least 9 regions and subregions. Within the complex, I-region genes and molecules have been shown to be most versatile with respect to immune responses. In the mouse, 5 I subregions have been well defined: I-A, I-B, I-J, I-E, and I-C. Contained within one or more of these subregions are (1) cell interaction (CI) genes that regulate interactions between macrophages, T cells, and B cells; (2) immune response (Ir) genes that determine an individual's susceptibility to disease by regulating the capacity to respond to certain antigens and viruses; (3) genes encoding Ia antigens, largely responsible for mixed lymphocyte reactivity and graft-versus-host reactions; (4) genes involved in the synthesis of certain biologically active mediators produced by and active on T cells, B cells, and macrophages; and (5) genes that determine susceptibility to allergic and autoimmune diseases and resistance to certain viruses through processes that may be related to the functions of CI or Ir genes (or both). It is not established whether distinct genes are responsible for these various functions or whether they are controlled by relatively few genes. Many of these activities, however, are closely related to one another, suggesting multiple gene control. Similar functional distinctions have been assigned to different regions of the HLA gene complex.

Other immunologically important regions of the H-2 histocompatibility gene complex are the H-2K (and H-2L) and H-2D regions on either end of the complex containing the genes responsible for production of the major transplantation antigens (readily detectable with appropriate antibodies on virtually all cells of the organism). The K, L, and D genes are, in addition, the major antigens attacked by cytotoxic T lymphocytes during rejection of foreign tissue grafts. In recent years, it has also been shown that the products of these genes interact in an undetermined manner with cytopathogenic viruses enhancing recognition of infected cells by cytotoxic T lymphocytes. The S region, also immunologically active, contains structural genes responsible for the synthesis of certain molecules of the complement system, a highly complex network of component molecules performing distinct biologic and chemical functions.

Also highlighted in Table 2–1 are selected differentiation genes and molecules prominently associated with distinct immunologic functions (Chapter 8). The

Ly antigens constitute a family of cell surface antigenic determinations that are differentially expressed on T lymphocytes (Lyt) and B lymphocytes (Lyb). The Lyt antigens are themselves differentially expressed on distinct functional subpopulations of T lymphocytes; an analogous situation appears to hold true for the Lyb antigens. Receptors on the Fc portion of an immunoglobulin molecule have been shown to exist on both T and B lymphocytes as well as on macrophages and are detected by their ability to bind to the Fc regions of aggregated or antigen-complexed immunoglobulin molecules. Certain Fc receptors appear to be specific for IgG molecules (FcRγ) and for the Fc determinants on IgM molecules (FcRμ). FcRγ are present on B lymphocytes, macrophages, and the subpopulation of T lymphocytes that contain suppressor cells (see below). FcRμ are present on macrophages and appear to be differentially expressed on the subpopulation of T lymphocytes containing helper T cells. Lymphocytes (and macrophages) expressing Fc receptors for IgE (FcRε) and IgA (FcRα) have been found in recent years and appear to exert class-specific regulatory effects on antibody responses of the IgE and IgA classes, respectively. Receptor molecules capable of binding certain complement components, notably C3b and C3d, exist on certain subpopulations of B lymphocytes, T lymphocytes, and monocytes, although the functional significance of such complement receptors is still unclear. The appearance of these molecules correlates in time with the ontogenic development of the various lymphocyte classes and of the macrophages on which they appear—hence their designation as differentiation molecules.

FUNCTIONAL SUBPOPULATIONS OF LYMPHOCYTES

The 2 classes of lymphocytes (Table 2–2) have distinct functional capabilities. T lymphocytes neither produce circulating antibodies nor give rise to antibody-secreting cells. The most extensive investigations of these cells have been made in the mouse. Based upon these studies, they can be subdivided into 2 major functional categories: regulatory and effector T lymphocytes.

Table 2–2. Functional subpopulations of lymphocytes.

T lymphocytes
  A. Regulatory T lymphocytes:
    1. Helper cells.
    2. Suppressor cells.
  B. Effector T lymphocytes:
    1. Delayed hypersensitivity (DTH).
    2. Mixed lymphocyte reactivity.
    3. Cytotoxic T lymphocyte (CTL or "killer" cells).
B lymphocytes
  A. Precursors of antibody-forming cells Bμ, Bγ, Bα, Bε.
  B. Memory cells.
  C. ?Regulatory B lymphocytes.

Regulatory T lymphocytes may amplify (as helper cells) or suppress (as suppressor cells) the responses of other T lymphocytes or of B lymphocytes. Distinct subpopulations of T cells appear to be responsible for these activities. Helper T cells are generally of the Lyt-1+ phenotype; suppressor T cells generally express the Lyt-2,3+ phenotype.

Effector T lymphocytes are responsible for such cell-mediated immune reactions as delayed cutaneous hypersensitivity responses (see Chapter 8), rejection of foreign tissue grafts and tumors, and elimination of virus-infected cells. Cytotoxic T lymphocytes (CTL), commonly referred to as "killer" cells, participate in the latter responses. Rejection of foreign tissues also involves T cells that undergo rapid proliferation in mixed lymphocyte reactions (MLR). These cells can be distinguished by their Lyt phenotypes: the MLR cell is of the Lyt-1+ phenotype, the CTL of the Lyt-2,3+ phenotype. Similarly, CTL (Lyt-2,3+) can be distinguished from delayed cutaneous cells, which are also of the Lyt-1+ phenotype.

Thus, T cells performing helper, delayed cutaneous, and MLR functions are all of the Lyt-1+ phenotype. It remains to be established by other criteria, however, whether these functions are performed by distinct subpopulations (although evidence suggests that helper cells and delayed cutaneous cells are discrete entities). Analogously, although CTL and suppressor cells are both of the Lyt-2,3+ phenotype, functional evidence tends to indicate that they represent distinct subpopulations of T cells.

Functional subpopulations of B lymphocytes may be categorized most readily on the basis of the different classes of immunoglobulin molecules they synthesize (Table 2–2). B lymphocytes give rise to cells that synthesize and secrete all classes of circulating immunoglobulin molecules (IgM, IgG, IgA, and IgE). The respective B cell precursors for these antibody-forming cells are designated Bμ, Bγ, Bα, and Bε. Ample evidence now supports the hypothesis that the earliest progenitors of antigen-specific B cells possess receptors of the IgM class; that more mature B cells possess receptors of both IgM and IgD; and that more mature precursor B cells (and perhaps "memory" B cells) express IgG receptors, either alone or in combination with IgD. Although it appears that the B cell precursors of IgM-, IgG-, and IgA-secreting cells may derive from the same subline of B lymphocytes, it is not yet known whether the B cell precursors of IgE-secreting cells derive from that same subline or from a distinct subline. Memory B cells are functionally important for development of rapid secondary (anamnestic) antibody responses upon subsequent antigenic exposure. These cells can be distinguished from "unprimed" B lymphocytes by their distribution in the tissues, size, migratory properties, and surface antigen properties. As yet, there is no hard evidence for the existence of regulatory B lymphocytes functionally analogous to regulatory T lymphocytes, although the future discovery of such cells would not be surprising. The capacity of antibody molecules themselves to spe-

Table 2–3. Genetic control of immune responsiveness.

Cell interaction *(CI)* genes

  A. Control most effective macrophage-lymphocyte interactions.

  B. Control most effective T-T and T-B lymphocyte interactions.

  C. Code for molecules active in enhancing and suppressing
immune responses.

  D. Control most effective lysis of virus-infected and neoplastic target cells by cytotoxic T lymphocytes.

Immune response *(Ir)* and immune suppression *(Is)* genes

  A. *Ir* genes determine ability of an individual to respond to a
given antigenic determinant.

  B. *Is* genes control stimulation of specific suppressor T lymphocytes.

  C. Nature and mechanism(s) of action unknown at present—
could be identical to *CI* genes.

cifically regulate immune response by "antibody feedback" is well documented.

GENETIC CONTROL OF IMMUNE RESPONSIVENESS

The control of immune responsiveness exerted by the genes of the major histocompatibility complex is summarized in Table 2–3. Cell interaction (CI) genes, the most important regulatory genes of the complex, appear to reside in one or more of the I subregions of the H-2 complex. The CI genes control the most effective cell-cell interactions in the immune system. It has been demonstrated that the interactions between macrophages and T cells and between T cells and B cells involve cell surface molecules, termed cell interaction or CI molecules, whose synthesis is controlled by the CI genes located in the I region of the H-2 complex. These genes control the most effective macrophage-lymphocyte interactions and the most effective T-T and T-B lymphocyte interactions. In addition, CI genes control the synthesis of biologically active lymphocyte- and macrophage-derived molecules capable of either enhancing or suppressing immune responses. It is not yet known, however, whether the genes responsible for synthesis of these molecules and the CI genes controlling the most effective cell-cell interactions are identical or distinct. In addition, CI genes located in the K or D regions of the H-2 complex control the most effective lysis of virus-infected and neoplastic target cells by cytotoxic T lymphocytes.

Genetic control of immune responsiveness also involves specific immune response (Ir) and immune suppression (Is) genes. Indeed, the discovery of Ir genes represented the first association between the major histocompatibility complex and regulation of immune responsiveness. Ir genes, inherited in simple mendelian fashion as autosomal dominant traits, have been found in virtually all species and appear to determine an individual's ability to respond to a given antigen. In certain cases, 2 genes are responsible for

the development of an immune response, and the absence of either (or both) results in the inability of the individual to respond to the particular antigen. More recently, investigators have shown that Is genes in the I region also govern the development of specific suppressor T lymphocytes. In contrast to those cases in which absence of one or more Ir genes results in inability of the individual to respond to a particular antigen, the absence of a specific Is gene or genes allows an immune response to occur that is essentially dissociated from the regulatory influence of suppressor T cells. Although considerable work has been done in these areas, we still do not understand the nature or the mechanisms of Ir and Is gene activity. In fact, further investigation is needed simply to determine whether these genes are distinct from CI genes.

REGULATORY INTERACTIONS IN IMMUNE RESPONSES

The discovery of a complex series of regulatory interactions among components of the immune system has proved to be a major breakthrough in our understanding of the system. Work done in the mid 1960s demonstrated that the development of antibody responses depended upon T cell-B cell interactions, and our perspective has now widened to reveal the workings of various genes, molecules, and cells in regulation of the immune system (Table 2–4).

We now know that the genes of the system produce (1) antigen-specific receptors on lymphocyte surface membranes; (2) circulating antibodies that perform effector functions and exert feedback regulation; (3) crucial regulatory effects on various cell-cell interactions necessary for normal immunologic homeostasis; and (4) biologically active molecules capable of enhancing or suppressing T cell or B cell activity. The cells of the system are interdependent. The development of cell-mediated or humoral immunity, therefore, is regulated by a series of essential interactions between macrophages, T cells, and B cells.

Regulatory interactions between constituents of the immune system may be manifested along a spectrum that ranges from enhancement to suppression of

Table 2–4. Regulatory interactions in immune responses.

Genes and molecules

  A. Serve as specific antigen receptors on lymphocyte surface
membranes.

  B. Circulating antibodies perform effector function and exert
feedback regulation.

  C. Regulate cell-cell interactions.

  D. Biologically active molecules enhance or suppress T cell
and/or B cell functions.

Cells

  A. Macrophage ↔ T cell interactions; macrophage ↔ B cell
interactions.

  B. T cell ↔ T cell interactions ↔ cell-mediated immunity.

  C. T cell ↔ B cell interactions ↔ antibody production.

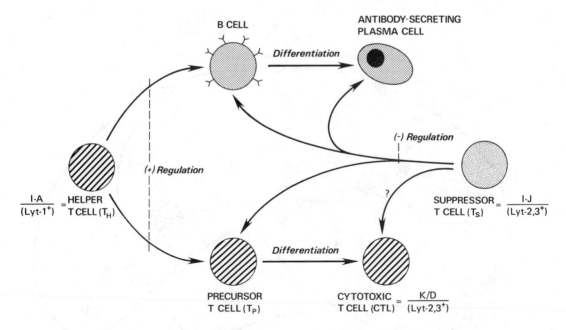

Figure 2–1. Summary of the T lymphocyte regulatory influences in the immune system.

immune responses. The qualitative or quantitative response occurring at any given time, however, will reflect the net effect of the extremely dynamic interplay among the system's components.

Fig 2–1 schematically summarizes our current knowledge of T lymphocyte regulatory influences on the immune system. Depicted to the far left is the helper T cell (T_H), with the surface phenotype Lyt-1+, functionally restricted by CI genes located in the I-A region of the H-2 complex (see above). These cells are capable of exerting positive regulatory effects on B cells (upper portion of Fig 2–1) and stimulating their differentiation into fully mature antibody-secreting plasma cells. Helper T cells also exert positive regulatory influences on precursors of T cells destined to become CTLs (Lyt-2,3+), restricted in their cytolytic function by CI genes located in the K or D regions of the H-2 complex (lower portions of Fig 2–1). The second category of regulatory T lymphocytes, known as suppressor cells (T_S), appears at far right. Suppressor T cells (Lyt-2,3+) are genetically restricted by CI genes located in the I-J region of H-2. As indicated, suppressor T cells can exert negative regulatory effects on the differentiation of B lymphocytes or precursors of CTLs by acting directly on such cells or by interfering with the activity of helper T cells that would normally facilitate their development. Moreover, suppressor T cells have been shown to directly inhibit the secretory function of fully matured plasma cells. Whether a similar direct inhibition can be exerted by suppressor T cells on fully mature CTLs is not known.

A schematic illustration of regulatory cell-cell interactions necessary for the development of a normal antibody response is presented in Fig 2–2. Although the figure specifically represents the induction of IgE

antibody responses, that process is equally applicable to antibody responses of the other immunoglobulin classes. The antigen is a hapten-carrier conjugate. Consequently, the carrier determinants are recognized by T cells and haptenic determinants by B cells. Macrophage presentation of the antigen appears to be particularly favorable for induction of helper T cells, which recognize carrier determinants by virtue of determinant specific receptors and interact in a critical way with macrophage-associated CI molecule. In addition, biologically active macrophage-derived soluble factors may play a role in the induction of helper T cells. Once activated, the helper T cells interact with B cells (that have previously interacted with haptenic determinants via their surface immunoglobulin receptors and are, therefore, specific for the hapten), facilitating the differentiation of such B cells into mature antibody-secreting plasma cells or memory cells. These interactions may occur directly or via the mediation of soluble T cell factors. However, suppressor T cell activity, which can be induced by direct antigen binding in the absence of any macrophage presentation, may interfere with these cell-cell interactions in 3 ways (indicated by the broken arrows in Fig 2–2): (1) by preventing the activation of helper T cells; (2) by hindering helper T cell interactions with B lymphocytes; and (3) by directly inhibiting B cell differentiation.

A virtually parallel scheme can be drawn to depict the regulatory cell-cell interactions essential to the development of effector T cells involved in the various types of cell-mediated immune responses.

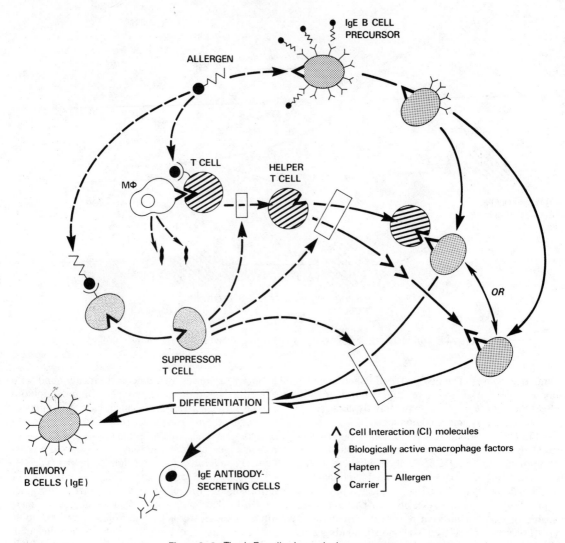

Figure 2–2. The IgE antibody-producing apparatus.

CLINICAL CIRCUMSTANCES REFLECTING ABERRANT GENETIC & REGULATORY CONTROL OF IMMUNE RESPONSES

There is little doubt that our increasing awareness of the many circumstances in which immune functions may be involved in the pathogenesis of disease has contributed substantially to the enormous growth of immunology over the past 20 years. Progressive advances in our knowledge of the immune system have reflected in part the successes of basic immunologic research and in part the perseverance of clinical immunologists who have explored the immune system's involvement in clinical conditions whose primary causes were theretofore unknown. Perhaps in no other area of biomedical science has the interdependence of basic and clinical research been so fruitful. An important consequence of this partnership has been the unusually rapid progress in the development and application of sophisticated laboratory techniques, allowing a more precise examination of the immune system. The earlier, limited techniques for evaluating the molecular components of serum protein have now evolved into technologies that make possible more sensitive and specific tests, not only of blood serum protein but also of serum protein fixed to tissue sites in the body. More recently, the expansion of these techniques has permitted analysis of various aspects of cell-mediated immunity, making possible the construction of immunologic "fingerprints" of a given disease that often reveal a variety of associated abnormalities. The ability to evaluate the association has in certain instances improved the effectiveness of therapy and promises even greater improvements in the years to come.

The importance of developing immunologic fingerprints of disease is perhaps most apparent in the case of immunodeficiency diseases. Not too many years ago, a patient presenting the typical manifestations of immunodeficiency (eg, chronic or recurring infections with pyogenic organisms) was diagnosed under the broad category of "immunodeficiency disorder." Today, immunologic fingerprints make possible the categorization and subcategorization of immunodeficiency disease in a manner that not only makes the diagnosis more precise but also provides a more rational basis for therapy (Chapter 25). Furthermore, recognizing how variable immunologic fingerprints may be from one immunodeficiency disease to another has substantially enlarged our overall understanding of the interactions between components of the immune system. With increased diagnostic proficiency, it has been possible to broaden our awareness of the primary and secondary involvement of the immune system in various diseases of the hematopoietic, gastrointestinal, cardiopulmonary, endocrine, nervous, and other systems. Historically, the rheumatic or autoimmune diseases have been the disorders longest under study and, paradoxically, among the most difficult to unravel in terms of pathogenesis. This seems indicative of the enormous complexity of immunologic events underlying such diseases and the manner in which the internal environment of the individual responds to immunologic abnormalities. Nevertheless, great progress has been made in the diagnosis and management of these diseases. For example, in patients with systemic lupus erythematosus, early diagnosis and initiation of therapy are helpful in preventing severe progressive renal disease (Chapter 31), a complication that 20 years ago was responsible for the high mortality rate in patients with this disorder. Furthermore, acute leukemias are now categorized as B, T, pre-B, and null, and these forms differ in prognosis and response to therapy (Chapter 17).

There is at present a long list of diseases in which primary or associated immunologic abnormalities exist. These disorders are discussed in detail in Chapters 25–40. To provide some general clinical perspectives, the remainder of this chapter will consider possible clinical manifestations associated with aberrations in the genetic and regulatory control of immune responses. Some of these associations have been documented; others are of a speculative nature (Table 2–5). This discussion has been divided into 3 sections based on presumed defects in Ir, Is, or CI gene functions, regulatory T cell functions, and B lymphocyte functions. As previously noted, disturbances in Ir, Is, or CI gene function may determine susceptibility to certain bacterial or viral agents and may predispose an individual to development of certain diseases of unknown cause (Table 2–5).

Excessive or deficient regulatory T cell activity may reflect abnormal cellular activity. In either case, normal homeostasis, usually dependent on the proper balance of suppressor and helper T cell activity, is upset. The existence in humans of excessive suppressor T cell activity has been documented in certain forms of acquired hypogammaglobulinemia. Peripheral blood lymphocytes from a limited number of such patients fail to synthesize and secrete immunoglobulins in tissue culture when stimulated under conditions

Table 2–5. Clinical circumstances possibly reflecting aberrant genetic and regulatory control of immune responses.

Defects in Ir, Is (? C) gene functions
  A. May determine susceptibility to certain etiologic bacterial or viral agents.
  B. May predispose an individual to development of certain diseases of uncertain etiology such as multiple sclerosis, myasthenia gravis, insulin-dependent diabetes, ankylosing spondylitis.

Defects in regulatory T cell function
  A. Excess suppressor and/or deficient helper cell activity.
    1. Certain forms of acquired hypogammaglobulinemia.
    2. Immunodeficiency of aging.
    3. Immunodeficiency associated with certain neoplastic disorders—eg, Hodgkin's disease.
    4. Congenital thymic deficiencies—eg, DiGeorge syndrome.
    5. Susceptibility to certain diseases of viral etiology.
  B. Deficient suppressor cell activity.
    1. IgE-mediated allergic disorders—eg, ragweed hay fever.
    2. Certain malignancies of lymphoid cell clones—eg, leukemia, plasmacytomas.
  C. Excess or inappropriate helper and/or deficient suppressor cell activity.
    1. Certain autoimmune diseases.

Defects in B lymphocyte function
  A. Deficient B cell function.
    1. Certain primary and secondary immunodeficiency diseases.
    2. Immunodeficiency of aging.
  B. Excess B cell function.
    1. Certain autoimmune disorders.

capable of inducing immunoglobulin synthesis in cultures of normal human lymphocytes. The defect is not intrinsic to the B cells, however, since it has been shown that removal of T lymphocytes from the cultured population enables the isolated B cells to synthesize and secrete immunoglobulin. Moreover, addition of patients' T cells to cultures of normal human lymphocytes inhibits the normal cells from synthesizing and secreting immunoglobulin. Hence, the presence and activity of an aberrant population of suppressor T cells in certain patients is phenotypically expressed as hypogammaglobulinemia. The hypothesis that the progressive immunodeficiency of aging (Chapter 20) reflects, at least in part, a similar excess of suppressor T cell activity is more highly speculative still. This aberrancy, however, may be a relative excess based in part on varying degrees of deficiency in helper T cell activity. Similarly, one might envisage the immunodeficiencies associated with certain neoplastic diseases as the result of a relative excess in suppressor T cell activity or a relative deficiency in helper T cell activity. The deficiency in T cell–mediated immunity frequently observed in patients with Hodgkin's disease may reflect such a situation. Indeed, recent studies have indicated that exposure of peripheral blood lymphocytes of patients with active anergic disease to the anthelmintic drug levamisole in vitro respond to certain phytomitogens known to induce DNA synthesis in T cells. This suggests that anergy in these patients reflects the existence of an inhibitory mechanism that prevents T cell responses in vivo rather than any absolute T cell deficiency. It is possible that suppressor T cells may participate in such a mechanism. A primary deficiency of helper (as well as effector) T cell activity is well documented in such congenital abnormalities as DiGeorge syndrome. On the more speculative side, although there is experimental support for the association of susceptibility to certain viral diseases with genetic defects that limit the capacity of the immune system to respond to such agents, the relationship of such defects to the development of malignant diseases of possible viral origin remains to be established.

The consequences of deficient suppressor T cell activity are perhaps best exemplified by the IgE-mediated allergic disorders of humans (Chapter 28). Studies have indicated that following exposure, high titers of IgE antibodies develop under conditions of quite low suppressor T cell activity. In the presence of normal suppressor cell activity, however, the converse is true. Recent studies in our own laboratory have suggested the existence of circulating biologically active molecules in the serum of experimental animals capable of selective positive or negative regulation of IgE antibody production. The character of these regulating processes correlates precisely with the magnitude of IgE antibody response following antigen sensitization. The absence or relative deficiency of suppressor T cell activity may be involved in the pathogenesis of certain malignant diseases of lymphoid cell clones (eg, certain leukemias, multiple myeloma), disorders that could well reflect the "escape" of various immune system constituents from normal regulatory controls.

Similar speculation can be entertained about the existence of inappropriate helper T cell activity in the pathogenesis of certain autoimmune diseases. If one were to entertain such speculation, one could envision nonspecific or cross-reactive helper cell activity generated by exogenous agents or adjuvants resulting in the loss of normal self-tolerance. Defects in B lymphocyte function can certainly be ascribed to some of the primary and secondary immunodeficiency diseases. Deficient B cell function may be important in the pathogenesis of the immunodeficiency of aging. Finally, one might speculate that abnormally excessive B cell activity, alone or in conjunction with abnormal regulatory T cell activity, may play an important role in the pathogenesis of certain autoimmune disorders; indeed, recent evidence supports the existence of hyperactive B cells in experimental animals manifesting spontaneous autoimmune disorders.

CONCLUSIONS

This brief overview of the immune system has stressed the need for a broad understanding of the dynamic interplay among the genes, molecules, and cells of the system that maintain homeostasis between the individual and the external environment. The system is highly complex, and one of the great advantages of this complexity is its inherent flexibility. Because compensatory or alternative routes are available when certain defects, transient or permanent, occur in one or more of the system's components, the immune system can continue to respond to the body's needs. Nevertheless, certain defects, alone or in combination, may result in deleterious primary or secondary consequences. Many of us working in this area are trying to elucidate the nature of these defects and trying to develop therapeutic programs that will restore homeostasis where possible. We believe that this hope can be realized in the near future.

●   ●   ●

References

Benacerraf B, Katz DH: The nature and function of histocompatibility-linked immune response genes. Page 117 in: *Immunogenetics and Immuno-deficiency*. Benacerraf B (editor). Medical and Technical Publishing Co, 1975.

Katz DH: *Lymphocyte Differentiation, Recognition and Regulation*. Academic Press, 1977.

Katz DH: Prospects for the clinical control of IgE synthesis. Page 127 in: *Progress in Clinical Immunology*. Vol 4. Schwartz RS (editor). Grune & Stratton, 1980.

Unanue ER: The regulatory role of macrophages in antigenic stimulation. *Adv Immunol* 1972;**15**:95.

van Rood JJ et al: The genetics of the major histocompatibility complex in man, HLA. Page 31 in: *The Role of Products of the Histocompatibility Gene Complex in Immune Responses*. Katz DH, Benacerraf B (editors). Academic Press, 1976.

Immunogenicity & Antigenic Specificity | 3

Joel W. Goodman, PhD

IMMUNOGENS

Immunogenicity

Immunogenicity is a property of substances that can induce a detectable immune response (humoral, cellular, or, most commonly, both) when introduced into an animal. Such substances are called **immunogens** or **antigens**.

Chemical Nature of Immunogens

The most potent immunogens are macromolecular proteins, but polysaccharides, synthetic polypeptides, and other synthetic polymers such as polyvinylpyrrolidone are immunogenic under appropriate conditions (see below). Although pure nucleic acids have not been shown to be immunogenic, antibodies that react with nucleic acids may be induced by immunization with nucleoproteins. Such antibodies appear spontaneously in the serum of patients with systemic lupus erythematosus (see Chapter 26).

Requirements for Immunogenicity

Immunogenicity is not an inherent property of a molecule, as are its physicochemical characteristics, but is operationally dependent on the experimental conditions of the system. These include the antigen, the mode of immunization, the organism being immunized, and the sensitivity of the methods used to detect a response. For example, it was generally agreed that gelatin was nonimmunogenic until the development of more sensitive methods for detecting antibody proved otherwise. The factors that confer immunogenicity on molecules are complex and incompletely understood, but it is known that certain conditions must be satisfied in order for a molecule to be immunogenic.

A. Foreignness: The immune system somehow discriminates between "self" and "nonself," so that only molecules that are foreign to the circulation of the animal are normally immunogenic. Thus, albumin isolated from the serum of a rabbit and injected back into the same or another rabbit will not generate the formation of antibody. Yet the same protein injected into any other higher vertebrate animal is likely to evoke substantial amounts of antibody depending on the dose of antigen and the route and frequency of injection.

B. Molecular Size: Extremely small molecules such as amino acids or monosaccharides are not immunogenic, and it is generally accepted that a certain minimum size is necessary for immunogenicity. However, there is no specific threshold below which all substances are inert and above which all are active, but rather a gradient of immunogenicity with molecular size. In a few instances, substances with molecular weights of less than 1000 have proved to be immunogenic, but as a general rule molecules smaller than molecular weight 10,000 are only weakly immunogenic or not immunogenic at all. The most potent immunogens are macromolecular proteins with molecular weights greater than 100,000.

C. Chemical Complexity: A molecule must possess a certain degree of chemical complexity in order to be immunogenic. The principle has been illustrated very clearly with synthetic polypeptides. Homopolymers consisting of repeating units of a single amino acid are poor immunogens regardless of size, whereas copolymers of 2 or—even better—3 amino acids may be quite active. Once again, it is difficult to establish a definite threshold, and the general rule is that immunogenicity increases with structural complexity. Aromatic amino acids contribute more to immunogenicity than nonaromatic residues, since relatively simple random polypeptides containing tyrosine are better antigens than the same polymers without tyrosine, and immunogenicity is proportionate to the tyrosine content of the molecule. Also, the attachment of tyrosine chains to the weak immunogen gelatin, which is poor in aromatic amino acids, markedly enhances its immunogenicity.

D. Genetic Constitution of the Animal: The ability to respond to a particular antigen varies with genetic makeup. It has been known for some time that pure polysaccharides are immunogenic when injected into mice and humans but not when injected into guinea pigs. Much additional information has accrued from the use of inbred strains of animals. As one of many examples, strain 2 guinea pigs respond readily in an easily detectable manner to poly-L-lysine, whereas strain 13 guinea pigs do not. The ability to respond is inherited as an autosomal dominant trait. Many similar cases have been described, and the genetic control of the immune response is currently one of the most active areas of investigation in biology (see Chapter 6).

E. Method of Antigen Administration:
Whether an antigen will induce an immune response
depends on the dose and the mode of administration. A
quantity of antigen which is ineffective when injected
intravenously may evoke a copious antibody response
if injected subcutaneously in adjuvant. In general,
once the threshold is exceeded, increasing doses
lead to increasing—but less than proportionate—
responses. However, excessive doses may not only fail
to stimulate antibody formation; they can establish a
state of specific unresponsiveness.

ANTIGENIC DETERMINANTS

Although strong immunogens are large molecules, only restricted portions of them are involved in
actual binding with antibody combining sites. Such
areas, which determine the specificity of antigen-
antibody reactions, are designated **antigenic determinants.** The number of distinct determinants on an
antigen molecule usually varies with its size and chemical complexity. Valence estimates have been made on
the basis of the number of antibody molecules bound
per molecule of antigen. Such measurements provide
minimum values, since steric hindrance may prevent
simultaneous occupation of all sites. Furthermore,
antibody populations from different animals are likely
to vary in specificity, and variations occur also in those
of a single individual at different points in time. This
means that antibodies specific for all determinants of
an antigen molecule may not be present in a particular
antiserum. Typical results using this approach give
about 5 antigenic determinants for hen egg albumin
(MW 42,000) and as many as 40 for thyroglobulin
(MW 700,000).

Haptens

Much of our understanding of the specificity of
antigen-antibody reactions derives from the pioneering
studies of Karl Landsteiner in the early years of the
20th century with small, chemically defined substances which are not immunogenic but can react with
antibodies of appropriate specificity. They are called
haptens, from the Greek word *haptein,* "to fasten."
Landsteiner covalently coupled the diazonium derivatives of a wide variety of aromatic amines to the lysine,
tyrosine, and histidine residues of immunogenic proteins (Fig 3–1). The conjugated proteins raised antibody specific for the azo substituents, demonstrated by
the capacity of the free hapten to bind antibody. The
conjugated hapten therefore behaves like a partial or
complete antigenic determinant. The total determinant
may include amino acids in the protein to which the
hapten is linked. The protein, called the **carrier,** has
its set of native or integral determinants as well as the
new determinants introduced by the conjugated hapten
(Fig 3–2).

Although most haptens are small molecules, macromolecules may also function as haptens. The definition is based not on size but on immunogenicity.

The use of hapten-protein conjugates has spot-
lighted the remarkable diversity of immune mechanisms as well as the exquisite structural specificity of
antigen-antibody reactions. Virtually any chemical entity may serve as an antigenic determinant if coupled to
a suitably immunogenic carrier. Even antibodies with
specificity for metal ions have been produced in this
way.

Landsteiner's studies showed that antibody could
distinguish between structurally similar haptens. In
one series of experiments, antibodies raised to
m-aminobenzenesulfonate were tested for their ability
to bind with other isomers of the homologous hapten
and related molecules in which the sulfonate group was
replaced by arsonate or carboxylate groups (Table
3–1). As expected, the strongest reaction occurred
with the homologous hapten. The compound with the
sulfonate group in the *ortho* position was somewhat
poorer than the *meta* isomer but distinctly better than
the *para* isomer. The substitution of arsonate for sulfonate resulted in very weak binding with antibody.
Although both substituents are negatively charged and
have a tetrahedral structure, the arsonate group is bulk-
ier because of the larger size of the arsenic atom and the
additional hydrogen atom. The benzoate derivatives

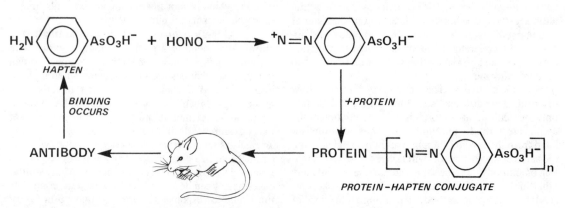

Figure 3–1. The preparation of hapten-protein conjugates and their capacity to induce the formation of antihapten antibody
to the azophenylarsonate group in this example.

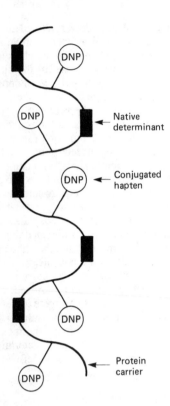

Figure 3–2. Diagrammatic illustration of a hapten-protein conjugate. The protein has several native or integral antigenic determinants denoted by thickened areas. The conjugated dinitrophenyl (DNP) hapten introduces new antigenic determinants.

Table 3–1. Effect of variation in hapten structure on strength of binding to *m*-aminobenzenesulfonate antibodies.

	ortho	*meta*	*para* isomers
R = sulfonate	++	+++	±
R = arsonate	−	+	−
R = carboxylate	−	±	−

Strength of binding is graded from negative (−) to very strong (+++). (From Landsteiner K, van der Scheer J: On cross reactions of immune sera to azoproteins. *J Exp Med* 1936;**63**:325.)

are also negatively charged, but the carboxylate ion has a planar rather than tetrahedral 3-dimensional configuration and shows even less affinity for the antisulfonate antibody.

Another illustration of the exquisite structural specificity of immune reactions is clearly depicted by the work of Avery and Goebel, who prepared antisera against conjugates composed of simple sugars coupled to proteins (Table 3–2). The antisera could readily distinguish between glucose and galactose, which differ only by the orientation of hydrogen and hydroxyl groups on one carbon atom. Similarly, *p*-aminophenol α-glucoside and the corresponding β-glucoside, which present identical surface configurations but differ stereochemically, could be distinguished despite strong cross-reactivity.

Studies of this kind have shown that antibody recognizes the overall 3-dimensional shape of the antigenic determinant group rather than any specific chemical property such as ionic charge. It is believed that antigenic determinants and antibody combining sites possess a structural complementariness which may be figuratively visualized as a "lock-and-key" arrangement (Fig 3–3). The electron cloud box of the antibody site is contoured to match that of the antigenic determinant, with the affinity of binding directly proportionate to the closeness of fit. The startling diversity

Table 3–2. Reactions of antisera with isomeric glucoside protein conjugates.*
(+ represents precipitation)

	p-Aminophenol α-glucoside	*p*-Aminophenol β-glucoside	*p*-Aminophenol β-galactoside
Antisera against:			
α-Glucoside	+++	++	0
β-Glucoside	++	+++	0
β-Galactoside	0	0	+++

*Reproduced, with permission, from Humphrey JH, White RG: *Immunology for Students of Medicine.* Davis, 1970.

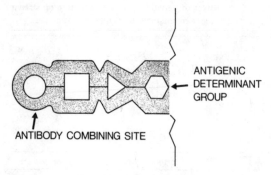

ANTIGENIC
DETERMINANT
GROUP

ANTIBODY COMBINING SITE

Figure 3–3. A view of the "lock-and-key" complementariness between an antigenic determinant group and an antibody combining site. The determinant can be considered to be composed of discrete subunits, which may be amino acids in a peptide chain or sugars in a saccharide chain. The antibody combining site is then composed of subsites, each of which can accommodate a discrete subunit of the antigenic determinant. (Reproduced, with permission, from Goodman JW: Antigenic determinants and antibody combining sites. In: *The Antigens.* Vol 3. Sela M [editor]. Academic Press, 1975.)

of the antibody response is perhaps more comprehensible if antibody specificity is viewed as directed against a molecular shape rather than a particular chemical structure.

Identification of Antigenic Determinants

Much has been learned about the composition, structure, and size of integral (native) determinants of antigen molecules as well as of haptenic determinants from 3 general approaches.

A. Cross-Reaction: This is the reaction of antibody with an antigen other than the one which induced its formation. The former is called a **heterologous** antigen and the latter the **homologous** antigen. The reaction of anti-*m*-aminobenzenesulfonate antibody with any of the other compounds in Table 3–1 is an example of a cross-reaction. Cross-reactions provide a limited amount of information about the composition of antigenic determinants. For example, it was shown that a galactan from the lung thought to be composed only of galactose cross-reacted with horse antiserum against type III pneumococcal polysaccharide, which is composed of glucose and glucuronic acid. A sensitive chemical analysis of this galactan confirmed that it contained a small amount of glucose.

B. Degradation of Complex Antigens: The object is to obtain fragments that represent intact antigenic determinants. It has been applied to a variety of protein and polysaccharide antigens with limited success. The obvious disadvantage of this approach is the improbability of obtaining intact determinants without irrelevant portions of the antigen molecule.

C. Synthetic Antigens: This has proved the most productive approach to delineation of antigenic determinants. A variety of studies have employed natural or synthetic homopolymers of a single amino acid or

sugar, synthetic polypeptides of defined structure, or synthetic haptens coupled to natural protein carriers. An ordered series of haptens may then be synthesized and binding with antibody assessed by inhibition of the quantitative precipitin reaction between antibody and homologous antigen. In this way, the structure of the antigenic determinant can be precisely defined. Homopolymers must usually be of substantial size in order to be immunogenic, and conformational differences between the integral determinant and the synthetic hapten may complicate interpretation. For this reason, recent efforts have concentrated on conjugating haptens to the side chains of protein carriers. Studies have been performed in great detail on the specificity of antibodies to glycosylated antigens, components of nucleic acids conjugated to proteins or polypeptides, and a myriad of other hapten-protein conjugates. The haptens are not integral parts of the molecular superstructure of the carrier, and conformational considerations are minimized. However, very small haptens are incomplete determinants, which limits their usefulness for determining the extent of antigenic determinants. Perhaps the most reliable estimate of the size of an antigenic determinant was derived from a series of peptides of defined size and structure coupled to a protein carrier.

Size of Antigenic Determinants

Antibody complementariness is directed against limited parts of the antigen molecule. Antibodies raised against haptens composed of 2 moieties linked to the same benzene ring, such as glycine and leucine in aminoisophthalylglycylleucine, are specific for one group or the other but not both. Other studies with azoproteins, as well as with dinitrophenylated and penicilloyl proteins, showed that the amino acid in the protein to which the hapten was joined participated in the antigenic determinant.

More precise analysis of determinant group size occurred when it was found that dextrans, which are polysaccharides composed of a single sugar (glucose), are immunogenic. Some dextrans are essentially single chains with very few branch points and provide immunogens for which the size of determinants can be estimated by using an ordered series of oligosaccharides as inhibitors of the dextran-antidextran precipitin reaction. The rationale is based on the premise that each subunit which forms a part of the determinant will contribute binding energy to the reaction with antibody, but enlarging the hapten beyond the size of the determinant will result in no improvement of binding, since the additional subunits will lie outside the antibody combining site (see Fig 3–4). Kabat showed that the hexasaccharide was the best ligand with antidextran antibody, the heptasaccharide being no better on a molar basis. The hexasaccharide was taken to be the size of the antigenic determinant and, by inference, the approximate size of the complementary region of the antibody molecule.

One difficulty that arises in the interpretation of this kind of experiment is that enhanced binding with

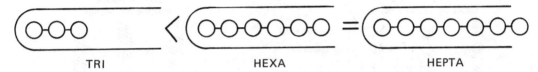

TRI   HEXA   HEPTA

Figure 3–4. Illustration of how hapten binding with antibody permits assessment of the size of antigenic determinants. In the dextran-antidextran system, the hexasaccharide was a better ligand with antibody than smaller oligosaccharides and equal to the heptasaccharide. It was concluded that the hexasaccharide just filled the antibody combining site, providing maximum binding energy. Additional sugar residues lay outside the site, making no contribution to binding.

haptens of increasing size may not necessarily reflect the size of the antigenic determinant but rather the approach to a conformation which is present in the intact antigen and for which the antibody site is complementary. This conformation could involve only a portion of the total hapten in direct binding with antibody, the remainder being essential for the assumption of the required configuration. The results of many studies indicate that antigen conformation is indeed a prominent factor in antibody specificity.

Numerous investigations using homopolymers of amino acids or multichain polymer-protein conjugates as antigens have yielded determinant group sizes in reasonable consonance with the dextran model (Table 3–3). Perhaps the most precise evaluation of determinant size was obtained using immunogens consisting of proteins to which were attached peptides of defined structure. Peptides of the form $(D-Ala)_n-Gly$ (where n varied from 1 to 4) were coupled to proteins, and the conjugates induced peptide-specific antibodies in rabbits. Peptides of the general structure $(D-Ala)_n$ (n = 1 to 4) and $(D-Ala)_n-Gly-\epsilon$-aminocaproic acid (n = 1 to 3) were used as inhibitors of the homologous precipitin reaction. The antigenic determinant in all instances was a tetrapeptide, the lysine residue of the protein carrier participating in the determinant only when the

conjugated hapten was smaller than a tetrapeptide. The consistency of the results and the improbability of conformational complications with such short peptide chains are compelling evidence that the antibody combining site is such as to accommodate 4 amino acid residues. This is in good agreement with other figures in Table 3–3, so we may feel confident that the size of an antigenic determinant has been defined within very narrow limits.

Immunopotency

Even large protein antigens possess a limited number of antigenic determinants. An extreme case in point is tobacco mosaic virus protein, which consists of 158 amino acids. A number of rabbit antisera had specificities limited to an eicosapeptide region of the molecule. As noted above, a given antiserum to ovalbumin has specificity for no more than 5 or 6 distinct determinants. Since the specificity of the immune response is capable of great diversity, there is a selection of determinants in any given situation. The capacity of a region of an antigen molecule to serve as an antigenic determinant and induce the formation of specific antibodies is termed **immunopotency.** Some of the factors involved in immunopotency have been identified.

A. Accessibility: Exposure to the aqueous environment is a cardinal factor in immunopotency. The terminal side chains of polysaccharides represent the most immunopotent regions of that class of antigens. A comparison of multichain synthetic polypeptides with sequences of alanine on the outside and tyrosine closer to the backbone, or the reverse (Fig 3–5), showed that antibodies to the former were largely alanine-specific while the latter evoked antibodies with a predominant specificity for tyrosine. The most exposed sequence was the most immunopotent in each instance.

The conformation of macromolecules determines accessibility to the immune apparatus. Internal sequences within proteins or polysaccharides are not precluded from exposure to the environment. In the case of sperm whale myoglobin, the 3-dimensional structure of which has been elucidated, it was found that peptides from regions which occupied corners of the molecule, and thus were prominently exposed, were important in its immunochemical specificity.

B. Charge: Electrical charge has been considered a dominant factor in specificity since Landsteiner's time, although completely uncharged molecules, such as dextrans, can be immunogenic. As a

Table 3–3. Estimation of the size of sequentially defined antigenic determinants.

Antigen	Species	Determinant
Dextran	Human	Isomaltohexose
Dextran	Rabbit	≥ Isomaltohexose
Poly-γ-glutamic acid (killed B anthracis)	Rabbit	Hexaglutamic acid
Polyalanyl-bovine serum albumin	Rabbit	Pentaalanine
Polylysyl-rabbit serum albumin	Rabbit	Penta- or hexa-lysine
Polylysyl-phosphoryl-bovine serum albumin	Rabbit	Pentalysine
α-Dinitrophenyl–(lysine)$_{11}$	Guinea pig	α-Dinitrophenyl–heptalysine
α-Dinitrophenyl–polylysine	Guinea pig	α-Dinitrophenyl–trilysine
$(D-Ala)_n-Gly-RNase$	Rabbit	Tetrapeptide
Denatured DNA	Human*	Pentanucleotide

*Sera from patients with systemic lupus erythematosus (see Chapter 26).

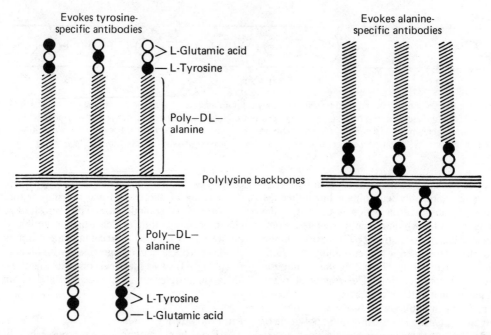

Figure 3–5. *Left:* A multichain copolymer in which L-tyrosine and L-glutamic acid residues are attached to multi-poly –DL – alanyl –poly –L –lysine(poly –[Tyr,Glu] –poly –DL –Ala –poly Lys). *Right:* Copolymer in which tyrosine and glutamic acid are attached directly to the polylysine backbone with alanine peptides on the ends of the side chains. Horizontal lines: poly –L –lysine; diagonal hatching: poly –DL –alanine; closed circles: L-tyrosine; open circles: L-glutamicacid. (From Sela M: Antigenicity: Some molecular aspects. *Science* 1969; **166**:1365. Copyright © 1969 by the American Association for the Advancement of Science.)

general rule, charged residues will contribute strongly to the specificity of immunogens in which they are found. This may be a manifestation of the interdependence of charge and accessibility, since charged groups, being hydrophilic, would be in closer contact with the environment than nonpolar groups subject to other conformational restrictions.

C. Genetic Factors: A growing body of evidence attests to genetic control of the ability to produce antibodies of different specificity against a given antigen. Some of the earliest evidence accrued from a comparison of the specificity of anti-insulin antibodies from strain 2 and strain 13 guinea pigs, which appear to be directed against opposite ends of the insulin molecule. More recent examples have been found primarily in the responses of mice to synthetic polypeptides (see Chapter 6).

Immunodominance

In the preceding section, factors were considered which may determine why a particular region of an antigen molecule acts as an antigenic determinant, immunopotency being a quantitative expression of the strength of an antigenic determinant. Given a particular determinant, which from earlier consideration may be the size of a tetrapeptide, the subunits of that determinant will contribute unequally to reactivity with antibody. The degree of the influence on reactivity is a measure of the "immunodominance" of the component of the antigenic determinant.

Factors which play crucial roles (on a larger scale) in determining immunopotency are also influential in determining immunodominance. The following are important in immunodominance:

A. Conformation: The immunodominant feature of an antigen may be its conformation rather than a particular subunit of its structure. For example, polymers of the tripeptide L-tyrosyl-L-alanyl-L-glutamic acid form an α-helix under physiologic conditions. The same tripeptide can be attached to a branched synthetic polypeptide (Fig 3–6). The tripeptide itself does not possess an ordered configuration. Antibodies to the 2 polymers do not cross-react, and the tripeptide binds antibodies produced against the branched polymer but not those made against the helical polymer. The immunodominant element of the helical polymer is its conformation. Antiserum against human hemoglobin A_1 combines better with the oxygenated form than the reduced form, and this has been attributed to the difference in quaternary structure between the 2 forms. There are many examples of conformation-dependent antibody specificity.

B. Accessibility: Determinants whose specificity is dictated by the sequence of subunits (amino acids or sugars) within the determinant rather than by the macromolecular superstructure of the antigen molecule are designated **sequential determinants.** In such cases, components of the determinant can act as haptens and bind with antibody, the reaction being demonstrable

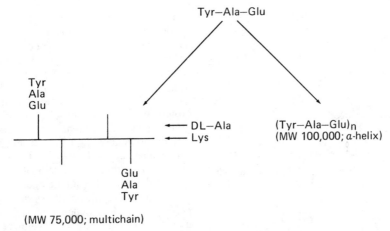

Figure 3–6. A synthetic branched polymer in which peptides of sequence Tyr–Ala–Glu are attached to the amino groups of side chains in multi-poly–DL–alanyl–poly–L–lysine *(left)* and a periodic polymer of the tripeptide Tyr–Ala–Glu *(right)*. (From Sela M: Antigenicity: Some molecular aspects. *Science* 1969;**166**:1365. Copyright © 1969 by the American Association for the Advancement of Science.)

either directly, by such techniques as equilibrium dialysis or fluorescence quenching, or indirectly, by inhibition of the reaction between antigen and antibody. Either sequential determinants may be composed of terminal or internal sequences of macromolecules, or they may be artificially added to carriers, as in the case of the tripeptide Tyr–Ala–Glu.

When the antigenic determinant is a terminal sequence, the terminal residue of the sequence is almost invariably the immunodominant subunit. Again, many examples exist to illustrate this point, which was recognized by Landsteiner when he showed that the terminal amino acid of peptides coupled to a protein carrier exerted a dominant effect on specificity. Goebel made the same observation with glycosides conjugated to protein carriers. In pneumococcal type II polysaccharide, glucuronic acid, which occurs almost exclusively at the terminal nonreducing positions in side chains, is the immunodominant sugar in the specificity of most of the antibodies studied.

Even when specificity is directed toward an internal segment of an antigen, there is a gradient of binding energy for different subunits of the determinant. Dextrans containing very few branch points presumably elicit antibody directed largely or exclusively against interior sequences of glucose. Taking the hexasaccharide as the determinant, the relative contribution to the total binding energy made by each glucose residue was estimated. The results indicated that the first glucose in the determinant contributed 40%, the first 2 glucoses 60%, and the first 3 glucoses 90% of the binding energy of the hexasaccharide. Similar decrements in binding energy were found with other essentially linear polysaccharide and polypeptide antigens.

In general, then, it may be concluded that all determinants exhibit a gradient of immunodominance. When the determinant is comprised of a terminal sequence, the gradient decreases from the most exposed portion inward.

C. Optical Configuration: Antibodies display a pronounced stereospecificity. While amino acid polymers of the D- optical configuration are very weakly immunogenic or nonimmunogenic, D-amino acids can serve as partial or complete determinants when either appended to immunogenic carriers or internally incorporated into synthetic polypeptides. In general, there is little or no cross-reactivity between enantiomorphic determinants. In at least some situations, D-amino acids may be more immunodominant than their stereoisomeric counterparts.

To recapitulate, there is abundant evidence for the existence of antibodies with specificity for conformational features of antigen molecules as well as antibodies whose specificity is directed against sequential determinants. With the latter, antibodies will normally react with small fragments of the antigen, whereas in the former situation disruption of the antigen superstructure results in very weak or negligible activity. Consequently, the determinants of globular proteins, which possess a great deal of ordered structure, have been difficult to delineate in detail, whereas the use of linear or randomly coiled molecules and peptidylprotein conjugates has met with greater success. Such antigens have provided the most solid information concerning the size and nature of antigenic determinants.

IMMUNOGENIC DETERMINANTS

Immunogens are normally large molecules, and immunogenicity is, within limits, a function of molecular size and complexity. A characteristic of immunogens is their capacity to induce cellular immunity mediated by thymus-derived T lymphocytes (see Chapter 8), which haptens are unable to do. It is believed that an immunogen must possess at least 2 determinants in order to stimulate antibody formation,

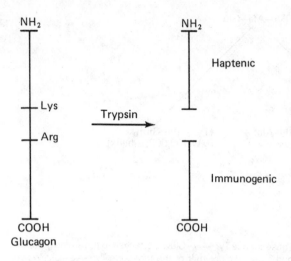

Figure 3–7. The functional dissection of glucagon into immunogenic and haptenic determinants.

which is the function of another line of lymphocytes, bursa-derived B cells. At least one determinant must be capable of triggering a T cell response. These relationships and the concept of cell cooperation are discussed in greater detail in Chapter 8. Our concern here is with structural determinants of immunogens which interact with T and B lymphocytes. It has not been possible to identify such determinants on large proteins, but studies with small, well-defined immunogens support the interpretation that specificities of the 2 cell types may be directed against different determinants of the antigen molecule.

The pancreatic hormone glucagon consists of only 29 amino acids but is immunogenic. It has been functionally dissected into component determinants which interact with T cells (immunogenic determinants) and with antibody (haptenic determinants). Using isolated tryptic peptides of the hormone, it was found that antibodies recognized a determinant or determinants in the amino terminal part of the molecule, whereas T lymphocytes responded only to the carboxyl terminal fragment (Fig 3–7). The latter was therefore identified as the immunogenic or "carrier" portion of the molecule and the former as the haptenic region.

Several synthetic molecules about the size of a single antigenic determinant induce an almost purely cellular immune response, with little or no antibody production, but are capable of acting as carriers for conjugated haptens in much the same fashion as macromolecular immunogens. One such unideterminant immunogen is the compound L-tyrosine-*p*-azobenzenearsonate (ABA-Tyr). Despite its molecular weight of only 409, ABA-Tyr induces cellular immunity with little or no antibody production in a variety of animal species. A hapten such as the dinitrophenyl group can be coupled to ABA-Tyr through a spacer group (6-aminocaproic acid) to produce a bideterminant or bifunctional immunogen (Fig 3–8). This antigen induces antibody specific for the dinitrophenyl haptenic determinant and cellular immunity directed against the ABA-Tyr immunogenic determinant.

Another example is the response of guinea pigs to poly-L-lysine. Responder animals (strain 2 and a fraction of outbred guinea pigs) develop cellular immunity to polymers as small as the heptapeptide. The bifunctional immunogen α-dinitrophenyl-(L-Lys)$_7$ induces antidinitrophenyl antibody responses. Smaller oligomers of lysine do not induce cellular immunity and cannot act as carriers for the dinitrophenyl haptenic determinant.

Experiments with analogs of immunogenic determinants, designed along the lines of Landsteiner's classic studies on the specificity of antihapten antibodies, have shown that cellular (T cell) responses to antigens are as exquisitely specific as antigen-antibody reactions.

Recent findings indicate that in some instances different determinants on a protein antigen may activate different functional subpopulations of T cells (see Chapter 8). For example, different fragments of myelin basic protein induce suppression and immunity in rodents. Immunity is manifested as an autoimmune allergic encephalomyelitis. Animals presensitized with the suppressor-inducing fragment and subsequently challenged with the intact molecule did not develop encephalomyelitis. A determining factor in the selective activation of suppressor or helper T cells by particular determinants appears to be the genetic constitution of the animal. Thus, the same region (though perhaps not the identical determinant) of hen egg lysozyme induces suppression in strain B10 mice but helps in strain B10.A mice. Another example is the induction of suppression or help by a random synthetic copolymer of glutamic acid, alanine, and tyrosine in different inbred strains of mice.

The selective activation of help or suppression is being actively investigated, because it may eventually offer a rationale for manipulating the immune response

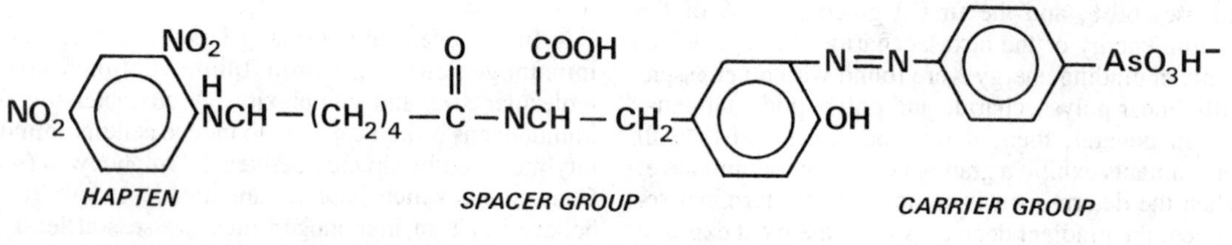

Figure 3–8. The bifunctional antigen dinitrophenyl-6-aminocaproyl-L-tyrosine-*p*-azobenzenearsonate.

in humans to such clinically important antigens as histocompatibility antigens, tumor antigens, and allergens.

THYMUS–INDEPENDENT ANTIGENS

A certain type of molecule may be immunogenic without the apparent participation of T lymphocytes. Such molecules appear to be able to directly trigger B lymphocytes (antibody-producing cells). Their characteristic feature is a structure which consists of repeating units. Bacterial polysaccharides and some polymerized proteins are thymus-independent antigens. However, not all repeating unit polymers behave this way. Poly-L-lysine, for example, is a thymus-dependent antigen in responder guinea pigs despite its simple, repetitive structure.

The mechanism by which thymus-independent antigens act is still unclear, but the immune response to such antigens differs from the response to more typical thymus-dependent antigens in that the antibody produced is largely or exclusively of the IgM class and little or no immunologic memory is engendered.

CONCLUDING REMARKS

The nature and dimensions of haptenic determinants of antigen molecules have received much attention during the past 2 decades, and the problems have now been solved in a reasonably satisfactory way. The use of homopolymers of amino acids or sugars and peptidyl-protein conjugates as antigens has established that a determinant is composed of 4–6 amino acid or sugar residues which contribute unequally to binding with the antibody combining site. The optical configuration and the physical conformation of the determinant weigh heavily in its immunochemical specificity.

These properties bear a strong resemblance to those of the contact regions of enzyme substrates. Six sugar residues entirely fill the combining site of lysozyme. Estimates of the contribution of a given residue in the site to the total free energy of association of a saccharide with the enzyme indicate unequal contribution by the several residues. The proteolytic enzyme papain interacts with a sequence of 7 amino acids in a polypeptide substrate. Here, too, there appears to be an unequal contribution to binding by different subsites in the ligand. The evidence converges toward a coherent image of the dimensions of ligands involved in binding with the active sites of proteins.

In contrast to haptenic determinants, elucidation of the nature and dimensions of immunogenic determinants is still in its infancy. With the exception of thymus-independent antigens, the essential requisite for immunogenicity appears to be recognition by one or more clones of T lymphocytes. A molecule which consists of a single determinant that can trigger a T cell response induces only cellular immunity but can serve as a carrier for a second determinant. The question of why many potent haptenic determinants fail to activate significant T cell responses remains unanswered.

•   •   •

References

Butler VP Jr, Beiser SM: Antibodies to small molecules: Biological and clinical applications. *Adv Immunol* 1973;**17**:255.

Goodman JW: Antigenic determinants and antibody combining sites. Page 127 in: *The Antigens*. Vol 3. Sela M (editor). Academic Press, 1975.

Goodman JW et al: Antigen structure and lymphocyte activation. *Immunol Rev* 1978;**39**:36.

Landsteiner K: *The Specificity of Serological Reactions*. Harvard Univ Press, 1945.

Reichlin M: Amino acid substitution and the antigenicity of globular proteins. *Adv Immunol* 1975;**20**:71.

Sela M: Antigenicity: Some molecular aspects. *Science* 1969; **166**:1365.

Sercarz EE et al: Different functional specificity repertoires for suppressor and helper T cells. *Immunol Rev* 1978;**39**:108.

4 | Immunoglobulins I: Structure & Function

Joel W. Goodman, PhD

The immunoglobulins are the protein molecules that carry antibody activity, ie, the property of specific combination with the substance which elicited their formation (**antigen**). With the possible exception of **natural** antibody, antibodies arise in response to foreign substances introduced into the body. The immunoglobulins comprise a heterogeneous group of proteins which account for approximately 20% of the total plasma proteins. In serum electrophoresis, the majority of the immunoglobulins migrate to the zone designated γ-**globulin,** but significant amounts are also found in the β-**globulin** zone. Different populations of immunoglobulins are also found in varying proportions in extravascular fluids, in exocrine secretions, and on the surface of some lymphocytes. The biologic activities of immunoglobulins can only be understood on the basis of knowledge of their structure, and in this chapter will be described the structure and evolution of immunoglobulin molecules.

BASIC STRUCTURE & TERMINOLOGY

Immunoglobulins are glycoproteins composed of 82–96% polypeptide and 4–18% carbohydrate. The polypeptide component possesses almost all of the biologic properties associated with antibody molecules. Antibodies are bifunctional molecules in that they bind specifically with antigen and also initiate a variety of secondary phenomena, such as complement fixation and histamine release by mast cells, which are independent of their specificity for antigen. Antibody molecules are extremely heterogeneous, as might be expected in view of their enormous diversity with respect to antigen binding and their different biologic activities. This heterogeneity is easily demonstrated by serologic, electrophoretic, and amino acid sequence methods and severely hampered early structural studies.

Two major discoveries ushered in the period of

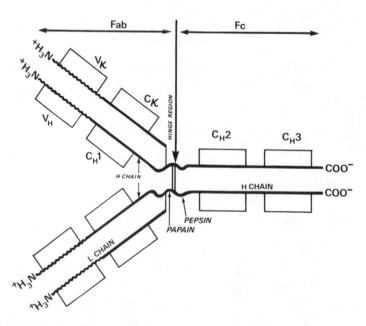

Figure 4–1. A simplified model for an IgG1 (κ) human antibody molecule showing the 4-chain basic structure and domains. V indicates variable region; C, the constant region; and the vertical arrow, the hinge region. Thick lines represent H and L chains; thin lines represent disulfide bonds.

detailed structural study of antibodies. The first was the finding that enzymes and reducing agents could be used to digest or dissociate immunoglobulin molecules into smaller components. The second was the realization that the electrophoretically homogeneous proteins found in serum and urine of patients with multiple myeloma (see Chapter 27) were related to normal immunoglobulins. These myeloma proteins were found to be structurally homogeneous. They are also called monoclonal proteins, since they are synthesized by single clones of malignant plasma cells. A clone here refers collectively to the progeny of a single lymphoid cell.

Our present understanding of immunoglobulin structure is based collectively on studies of monoclonal and normal proteins. The discussion of the details of immunoglobulin structure is introduced with a list of definitions of the relevant terms used here and in Figs 4–1 and 4–2.

List of Definitions

Basic unit (monomer): Each immunoglobulin contains at least one basic unit or monomer comprising 4 polypeptide chains (Fig 4–1).

H and L chains: One pair of identical polypeptide chains contains approximately twice the number of amino acids, or is approximately twice the molecular weight, of the other pair of identical polypeptide chains. The chains of higher molecular weight are designated **heavy (H) chains** (Fig 4–1) and those of lower molecular weight **light (L) chains.**

V and C regions: Each polypeptide chain contains an amino terminal portion, the **variable (V) region;** and a carboxyl terminal portion, the **constant (C) region.** These terms denote the considerable heterogeneity or variability in the amino acid residues in the V region compared to the C region.

Domains: The polypeptide chains do not exist 3-dimensionally as linear sequences of amino acids but

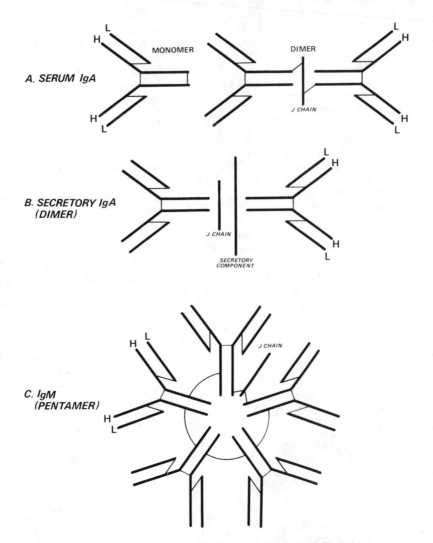

Figure 4–2. Highly schematic illustration of polymeric human immunoglobulins. Polypeptide chains are represented by thick lines; disulfide bonds linking different polypeptide chains are represented by thin lines.

are folded by disulfide bonds into globular regions called domains. The domains in H chains are designated V_H and C_H1, C_H2, C_H3, and C_H4; and those in L chains are designated V_L and C_L.

Antigen-binding site: The part of the antibody molecule which binds antigen is formed by only small numbers of amino acids in the V regions of H and L chains. These amino acids are brought into close relationship by the folding of the V regions.

Fab and Fc fragments: Digestion of an IgG molecule by the enzyme papain produces 2 Fab (antigen-binding) fragments and one Fc (crystallizable) fragment.

Hinge region: The area of the H chains in the C region between the first and second C region domains (C_H1 and C_H2) is the hinge region. It is more flexible and is more exposed to enzymes and chemicals. Thus, papain acts here to produce Fab and Fc fragments.

F(ab')₂ fragment: Digestion of an IgG molecule by the enzyme pepsin produces one $F(ab')_2$ molecule and small peptides. The $F(ab')_2$ molecule is composed of 2 Fab units and the hinge region, with intact inter-H chain disulfide bonds, since pepsin cleaves the IgG molecule on the carboxyl terminal side of these bonds.

Disulfide bonds: Chemical disulfide (–S–S–) bonds between cysteine residues are essential for the normal 3-dimensional structure of immunoglobulins. These bonds can be interchain (H chain to H chain, H chain to L chain, L chain to L chain) or intrachain.

Classes: There are 5 classes of immunoglobulins, designated IgG, IgA, IgM, IgD, and IgE (Table 4–1). They are defined by antigenic differences in the C regions of H chains. IgG, IgA, and IgM have been further subdivided into **subclasses** on the basis of relatively minor antigenic differences in C_H regions.

L chain types: L chains are divided into κ and λ types on the basis of antigenic determinants. Akin to the subclasses of H chains, 4 **subtypes** of λ chains have been found.

Isotypes: The antigenic differences that characterize the class and subclass of H chains and the type and subtype of L chains. Each normal individual expresses all the isotypes characteristic of the species inasmuch as each isotype occupies a distinctive genetic locus in the genome.

Allotypes: Polymorphic (allelic) forms of H and L chains that exhibit a mendelian pattern of inheritance. The antigenic determinants that characterize allotypes are usually localized to C regions. Thus, a particular isotype may have several alternative (allelic) structures.

Idiotypes: Antigenic determinants that distinguish one V domain from all other V domains.

S value: The S value refers to the sedimentation coefficient of a protein, measured by the technique of Svedberg. S values of normal immunoglobulins range from 6S to 19S (Table 4–1). In general, the larger the S value of a protein, the higher its molecular weight.

Polymers: Immunoglobulins composed of more than a single basic monomeric unit are termed polymers. The main examples are IgA **dimers** (2 units) and **trimers** (3 units) and IgM **pentamers** (5 units).

J chain: This is a polypeptide chain which is normally found in polymeric immunoglobulins.

Secretory component: IgA molecules in secretions are most commonly composed of 2 IgA units, one J chain, and an additional polypeptide, the secretory component.

FOUR–CHAIN BASIC UNIT

Immunoglobulin molecules are composed of equal numbers of heavy and light polypeptide chains, which can be represented by the general formula $(H_2L_2)_n$. The chains are held together by noncovalent forces and usually by covalent interchain disulfide bridges to form a bilaterally symmetric structure (Fig 4–1). It has been shown that all normal immunoglobulins have this basic structure, although some, as we shall see, are composed of more than one 4-chain unit.

Each polypeptide chain is made up of a number of loops or domains of rather constant size (100–110 amino acid residues) formed by the intrachain disulfide

Table 4–1. Properties of human immunoglobulin chains.

Designation	H Chains					L Chains		Secretory Component	J Chain
	γ	α	μ	δ	ϵ	κ	λ	SC	J
Classes in which chains occur	IgG	IgA	IgM	IgD	IgE	All classes	All classes	IgA	IgA, IgM
Subclasses or subtypes	1,2,3,4	1,2	1,2	. . .	. . .	. . .	1,2,3,4	. . .	. . .
Allotypic variants	Gm(1)–(25)	A2m(1), (2)	. . .	. . .	. . .	Km(1)–(3)†	. . .	. . .	. . .
Molecular weight (approximate)	50,000*	55,000	70,000	62,000	70,000	23,000	23,000	70,000	15,000
V region subgroups	$V_HI–V_HIV$					$V_\kappa I–V_\kappa IV$	$V_\lambda I–V_\lambda VI$		
Carbohydrate (average percentage)	4	10	15	18	18	0	0	16	8
Number of oligosaccharides	1	2 or 3	5	?	5	0	0	?	1

*60,000 for γ3.

†Formerly Inv(1)–(3).

bonds (Fig 4–1). The N-terminal domain of each chain shows much more variation in amino acid sequence than the others and is designated the variable region to distinguish it from the other relatively constant domains (collectively called the constant region in each chain). The zone where the variable and constant regions join is termed the "switch" region.

Immunoglobulins are rather insensitive to proteolytic digestion but are most easily cleaved about midway in the heavy chain in an area between the first and second constant region domains (C_H1 and C_H2) (Fig 4–1). The enzyme papain splits the molecule on the N-terminal side of the inter-heavy chain disulfide bonds into 3 fragments of similar size: 2 Fab fragments, which include an entire light chain and the V_H and C_H1 domains of a heavy chain; and one Fc fragment, composed of the C-terminal halves of the heavy chains. If pepsin is used, cleavage occurs on the C-terminal side of the inter-H chain disulfide bonds, yielding a large $F(ab')_2$ fragment composed of about 2 Fab fragments. The Fc fragment is extensively degraded by pepsin. The region in the H chain susceptible to proteolytic attack is more flexible and exposed to the environment than the more compact, globular domains and is known as the "hinge" region. Antigen-binding activity is associated with the Fab fragments or, more specifically, with the V_H and V_L domains, while most of the secondary biologic activities of immunoglobulins (eg, complement fixation) are associated with the Fc fragment.

HETEROGENEITY OF IMMUNOGLOBULINS

As already noted, immunoglobulin molecules comprise a family of proteins with the same basic molecular architecture but which exhibit a vast array of antigen-binding specificities and different biologic activities. These different activities are, of course, reflections of structural differences dictated by amino acid sequence of the polypeptide chains. This structural heterogeneity has been an obstacle for protein chemists, but plasmacytomas of human and murine origin provide homogeneous (monoclonal) immunoglobulins which have greatly facilitated the study of the amino acid sequence of antibody molecules.

Light Chain Types

All L chains have a molecular weight of approximately 23,000 but can be classified into 2 types, kappa (κ) and lambda (λ), on the basis of multiple structural differences in the constant regions which are reflected in antigenic differences (Table 4–1). The 2 types of L chains have been demonstrated in many mammalian species. Indeed, the amino acid sequence homologies between human and mouse κ chains are much greater than those between the κ and λ chains within each species, indicating that the 2 types separated during evolution prior to the divergence of mammalian species.

The proportion of κ to λ chains in immunoglobulin molecules varies from species to species, being about 2:1 in humans. A given immunoglobulin molecule always contains identical κ or λ chains, never a mixture of the two.

Heavy Chain Classes

Five classes of H chains have been found in humans, based again on structural differences in the constant regions detected by serologic and chemical methods. The different forms of H chain, designated γ, α, μ, δ, and ϵ (Table 4–1), vary in molecular weight from 50 to 70 thousand, the μ and ϵ chains possessing 5 domains (one V and four C) rather than the 4 of γ and α chains. The δ chain has an intermediate molecular weight which is believed to be due to an extended hinge region. Likewise, the $\gamma3$ chain has an extended hinge region consisting of about 60 amino acid residues, including 14 cysteines, which account for the large number of inter-heavy chain disulfide bonds in IgG3 (Fig 4–3).

The class of the H chain determines the class of the immunoglobulin. Thus, there are 5 classes of immunoglobulins: IgG, IgA, IgM, IgD, and IgE. Two γ chains combined with either two κ or two λ L chains constitute an IgG molecule, the major class of immunoglobulins in serum. Similarly, two μ chains and two L chains form an IgM subunit; IgM molecules are macroglobulins which consist of 5 of these basic 4-chain subunits (Fig 4–2). IgA is polydisperse, comprising 1–5 such units. The other classes (IgD and IgE), like IgG, consist of a single 4-chain unit. The classification and properties of immunoglobulins and their component polypeptide chains are summarized in Tables 4–1 and 4–2.

Subclasses of Polypeptide Chains

Most of the H chain classes have been further subdivided into subclasses on the basis of serologic or physicochemical differences in the constant regions. However, H chains representing the various subclasses within a class are much more closely related to each other than to the other classes. For example, there are 4 subclasses of γ chain in humans, $\gamma1$, $\gamma2$, $\gamma3$, and $\gamma4$ (Table 4–2), which yield IgG1, IgG2, IgG3, and IgG4 subclasses of immunoglobulin G molecules, respectively. The C regions of these γ chains are much more homologous to each other than to those of α, μ, δ, or ϵ chains. In some species, the charge spectra of the IgG subclasses differ sufficiently to permit their isolation by electrophoretic techniques. This is not true in humans, where the subclasses have been recognized by serologic and chemical methods, facilitated by the existence of myeloma proteins.

A noteworthy aspect of the structural differences between the immunoglobulin subclasses is the number and arrangement of interchain disulfide bridges (Fig 4–3). In IgA2, the L chains are covalently linked to each other instead of to the H chains. In other immunoglobulins, the L–H bond may be formed close to the junction of the V_H and C_H1 domains or, alternatively,

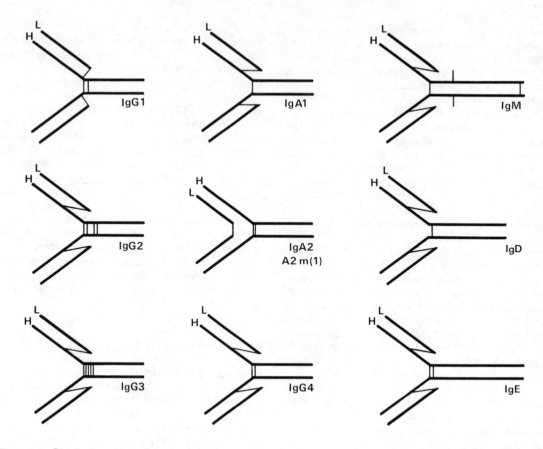

Figure 4–3. Distribution of interchain disulfide bonds in various human immunoglobulin classes and subclasses. H chains are represented by long thick lines and L chains by short thick lines. Disulfide bonds are represented by thin lines. The number of inter–heavy chain disulfide bonds in IgG3 may be as high as 14.

Table 4–2. Properties of human immunoglobulins.

	IgG	IgA	IgM	IgD	IgE
H chain class	γ	α	μ	δ	ϵ
H chain subclass	$\gamma 1, \gamma 2, \gamma 3, \gamma 4$	$\alpha 1, \alpha 2$	$\mu 1, \mu 2$		
L chain type	κ and λ	κ and λ	κ and λ	κ and λ	κ and λ
Molecular formula	$\gamma_2 L_2$	$\alpha_2 L_2{}^*$ or $(\alpha_2 L_2)_2 SC\dagger J\ddagger$	$(\alpha_2 L_2)_5 J\ddagger$	$\delta_2 L_2$	$\epsilon_2 L_2$
Sedimentation coefficient (S)	6–7	7	19	7–8	8
Molecular weight (approximate)	150,000	160,000* 400,000§	900,000	180,000	190,000
Electrophoretic mobility (average)	γ	Fast γ to β	Fast γ to β	Fast γ	Fast γ
Complement fixation (classic)	+	0	++++	0	0
Serum concentration (approximate; mg/dL)	1000	200	120	3	0.05
Serum half-life (days)	23	6	5	2–8	1–5
Placental transfer	+	0	0	0	0
Reaginic activity	?	0	0	0	++++
Antibacterial lysis	+	+	+++	?	?
Antiviral activity	+	+++	+	?	?

*For monomeric serum IgA.
†Secretory component.
‡J chain.
§For secretory IgA.

near the junction between C_H1 and C_H2 in IgG1.

As for L chains, κ chains do not exhibit C region subclasses, but 4 distinct λ chain forms have been discerned in humans which have apparently arisen by tandem gene duplication. These are called **subtypes** to distinguish them from H chain subclasses which determine the subclass of the intact molecule. Since all H chains may be combined with any of the L chains, the latter play no role in determining the class or subclass of immunoglobulin. Put another way, the complete repertoire of κ and λ chains is found in each immunoglobulin subclass.

Allotypic (Allelic) Forms of Heavy & Light Chains

Some H and L chain isotypes bear genetic markers that are inherited in typical mendelian fashion. These alternative forms at a given genetic locus are called **allotypes.** In humans, allelic forms have been found for γ and α H chains and κ L chains. The allotypes associated with γ chains are designated "Gm" (for gamma), those associated with α chains are termed "Am," and those associated with κ L chains are called "Inv" (abbreviation of a patient's name). Thus far, allotypic forms of λ L chains or the H chains of IgM, IgD, and IgE have not been found.

Allotypy has been detected using homologous (same species) antisera that react with antigenic determinants foreign to the immunoglobulins of the host. For example, mothers may become immunized to paternal allotypic determinants on fetal immunoglobulins during the course of pregnancy. Alternatively, immunization may result from blood transfusions. Another source of detecting reagents has been the sera of some patients with rheumatoid arthritis, which contain "rheumatoid factors" reactive with IgG from some (not all) normal individuals (see Chapter 26). Such rheumatoid factors detect allotypic determinants. The structural differences that account for allotypic determinants usually involve only one or, at most, several amino acid substitutions in the constant regions of H and L chains.

SECRETORY COMPONENT & J CHAIN

Immunoglobulins are present not only in serum but also in various body secretions such as saliva, nasal secretions, sweat, breast milk, and colostrum. IgA is the predominant immunoglobulin class in the external secretions of most species. IgA usually exists in human serum as a 4-chain unit of approximately molecular weight 160,000 (7S). This unit may polymerize to give disulfide-bonded polymers with 8-chain, 12-chain, or larger structures. The IgA in secretions consists of two 4-chain units associated with one of each of 2 additional chain types, the secretory component and the J chain (Tables 4-1 and 4-2). The secretory component is associated only with IgA and is found almost exclusively in body secretions. The J chain is associated with all polymeric forms of immunoglobulins which contain 2 or more basic units. Fig 4-2 shows simplified models of secretory IgA and various polymeric serum immunoglobulins. Evidence suggests that binding of an IgA to secretory component or J chain (or both) may promote the polymerization of additional monomeric 4-chain basic units. The secretory component may exist in free form or bound to IgA molecules by strong noncovalent interactions. The binding does not usually involve covalent bonding, although disulfide bonds have been implicated in a small fraction of human secretory IgA molecules. The secretory component is synthesized by nonmotile epithelial cells near the mucous membrane where secretion occurs. Its function may be to enable IgA antibodies to be transported across mucosal tissues into secretions.

The secretory component is a single polypeptide chain of approximately molecular weight 70,000. The carbohydrate content is high but not precisely known (Table 4-1). Its amino acid composition differs appreciably from that of every other immunoglobulin polypeptide chain, including J chain. No close structural relationship exists between the secretory component and any immunoglobulin polypeptide chain. Indeed, secretory component can be found free in secretions of individuals who lack measurable IgA in their serum or secretions. The secretory component has an electrophoretic mobility in the fast β range and shows little tendency to form aggregates in phosphate-buffered saline at pH 7.3.

The J chain is a small glycopeptide with an unusually high content of aspartic acid and glutamic acid. The J chain has a fast electrophoretic mobility on alkaline gels owing to its highly acidic nature. Equilibrium centrifugation in 5.0 M guanidine hydrochloride indicates that the J chain has a molecular weight of approximately 15,000. Physicochemical studies indicate that the J chain molecule is very elongated, with an axial ratio of approximately 18.

Quantitative measurements indicate that there is a single J chain in each IgM pentamer or polymeric IgA molecule. The J chain is covalently bonded to the penultimate cysteine residue of α and μ chains. Whether or not the J chain is required for the proper polymerization of the IgA and IgM basic unit is controversial. Polymeric immunoglobulins of certain lower vertebrates such as nurse shark and paddlefish are apparently devoid of J chain. These observations indicate that J chain is not an absolute requirement for polymerization of the immunoglobulin basic units. Nevertheless, the presence of J chain does facilitate the polymerization of basic units of IgA and IgM molecules into their appropriate polymeric forms.

CARBOHYDRATE MOIETIES OF IMMUNOGLOBULINS

Significant amounts of carbohydrate are present in all immunoglobulins in the form of simple or complex side chains covalently bonded to amino acids in the polypeptide chains (Table 4–1).

The function of the carbohydrate moieties is poorly understood. They may play important roles in the secretion of immunoglobulins by plasma cells and in the biologic functions associated with the C regions of H chains.

The attachment in most cases is by means of an N-glycosidic linkage between an N-acetylglucosamine residue of the carbohydrate side chain and an asparagine residue of the polypeptide chain. However, other linkages have also been observed, including an O-glycosidic linkage between an amino sugar of an oligosaccharide side chain and a serine residue of the polypeptide chain. In general, carbohydrate is found in only the secretory component, the J chain, and the C regions of H chains; it is not found in L chains or the V regions of H chains. Exceptions to this rule have been found in a small number of myeloma proteins. The secretory component has more carbohydrate than either the α chain or the L chain, which accounts for the higher carbohydrate content in secretory IgA than in serum IgA. Studies on monoclonal immunoglobulins indicated that IgM and IgE generally have an average of 5 oligosaccharides each; IgG, one; and IgA, 2 or 3 oligosaccharides. This agrees with the overall carbohydrate content of immunoglobulins, since IgM, IgD, and IgE have the largest amounts of carbohydrate, followed by IgA and then by IgG (Table 4–1). However, these studies were performed on a limited number of monotypic immunoglobulins. In view of the findings that (1) different myeloma proteins of the same class or subclass may differ from one another in carbohydrate content, (2) an individual myeloma protein occasionally exhibits microheterogeneity with respect to its carbohydrate content, and (3) V regions of a small number of immunoglobulin polypeptide chains contain carbohydrate, it is incorrect to assume that all immunoglobulins belonging to a given class or subclass have the same number of oligosaccharide side chains.

BIOLOGIC ACTIVITIES OF IMMUNOGLOBULIN MOLECULES

As we have already noted, immunoglobulins are bifunctional molecules which bind antigens and, in addition, initiate other biologic phenomena which are independent of antibody specificity. These 2 kinds of activity can each be localized to a particular part of the molecule: antigen binding to the combined action of the V regions of H and L chains, and the other activities to the C regions of H chains. These latter activities, some of which are listed in Table 4–2, will be considered in this section.

Immunoglobulin G (IgG)

In normal human adults, IgG constitutes approximately 75% of the total serum immunoglobulins. Within the IgG class, the relative concentrations of the 4 subclasses are approximately as follows: IgG1, 60–70%; IgG2, 14–20%; IgG3, 4–8%; and IgG4, 2–6%. These figures vary somewhat from individual to individual and correlate weakly with the presence of certain H chain C region allotypic markers (Chapter 3). Thus, the capacity of a given individual to produce antibodies of one or another IgG subclass may be under genetic control.

IgG is the only class of immunoglobulin that can cross the placenta in humans, and it is responsible for protection of the newborn during the first months of life (Chapter 21). The subclasses are not equally endowed with this property, IgG2 being transferred more slowly than the others. The adaptive or biologic value of this inequality, if any, is obscure.

IgG is also capable of fixing serum complement (Chapter 11), and once again the subclasses function with unequal facility in the following order: IgG3 > IgG1 > IgG2 > IgG4. IgG4 is completely unable to fix complement by the classic pathway (binding of C1q) but may be active in the alternative pathway. The specific location of the C1q binding site on the IgG molecule appears to reside in the C_H2 domain.

Macrophages bear surface receptors which bind IgG1 and IgG3 and their Fc fragments. The passive binding of antibodies by such Fc receptors is responsible for "arming" macrophages, which can then function in a cytotoxic fashion (Chapters 10 and 12). The specific location of the Fc receptor binding site on IgG1 and IgG3 molecules seems to be in the C_H3 domain.

Immunoglobulin A (IgA)

IgA is the predominant immunoglobulin class in body secretions. Each secretory IgA molecule consists of two 4-chain basic units and one molecule each of secretory component and J chain (Fig 4–2). The molecular weight of secretory IgA is approximately 400,000. Secretory IgA provides the primary defense mechanism against some local infections owing to its abundance in saliva, tears, bronchial secretions, the nasal mucosa, prostatic fluid, vaginal secretions, and mucous secretions of the small intestine. The predominance of secretory IgA in membrane secretions led to speculation that its principal function may not be to destroy antigen (eg, foreign microbial organisms or cells) but rather to prevent access of these foreign substances to the general immunologic system. IgA normally exists in serum in both monomeric and polymeric forms, constituting approximately 15% of the total serum immunoglobulins.

Immunoglobulin M (IgM)

IgM constitutes approximately 10% of normal immunoglobulins and normally exists as a pentamer with a molecular weight of about 900,000 (19S). IgM antibody is prominent in early immune responses to most antigens and predominates in certain antibody responses such as "natural" blood group antibodies. IgM (with IgD) is the major immunoglobulin expressed on the surface of B cells. IgM is also the most efficient complement-fixing immunoglobulin, a single molecule bound to antigen sufficing to initiate the complement cascade (Chapter 11).

Immunoglobulin D (IgD)

The IgD molecule is a monomer, and its molecular weight of approximately 180,000 (7–8S) is slightly higher than that of IgG. This immunoglobulin is normally present in serum in trace amounts (0.2% of total serum immunoglobulins). It is relatively labile to degradation by heat and proteolytic enzymes. There are isolated reports of IgD with antibody activity toward certain antigens, including insulin, penicillin, milk proteins, diphtheria toxoid, nuclear antigens, and thyroid antigens. However, the main function of IgD has not yet been determined. IgD (with IgM) is the predominant immunoglobulin on the surface of human B lymphocytes, and it has been suggested that IgD may be involved in the differentiation of these cells.

Immunoglobulin E (IgE)

The identification of IgE antibodies as reagins and the characterization of this immunoglobulin class marked a major breakthrough in the study of the mechanisms involved in allergic diseases (see Chapter 28). IgE has a molecular weight of approximately 190,000 (8S). It comprises only 0.004% of the total serum immunoglobulins but binds with very high affinity to mast cells via a site in the Fc region. Upon combination with certain specific antigens called allergens, IgE antibodies trigger the release from mast cells of pharmacologic mediators responsible for the characteristic wheal and flare skin reactions evoked by the exposure of the skin of allergic individuals to allergens. IgE antibodies provide a striking example of the bifunctional nature of antibody molecules. "Allergen" is an alternative term used by allergists for any antigen that stimulates IgE production. IgE antibodies bind allergens through the Fab portion, but the binding of IgE antibodies to tissue cells is a function of the Fc portion. Like IgG and IgD, IgE normally exists only in monomeric form.

PROTEIN–CALORIE MALNUTRITION

The thymus was recognized as a barometer of nutrition over a century ago, when thymic atrophy was observed to accompany **protein-calorie malnutrition.** We now know that all the lymphoid organs become smaller during protein-calorie malnutrition, but the thymus, which is replaced by fibrofatty tissue, is the organ most severely affected. The ultimate reason for these histopathologic changes is unknown, but the active cell division characteristic of lymphoid tissues is restricted in protein-calorie malnutrition. Concentrations of other hormones such as epinephrine, corticosteroids, insulin, and thyroxine are altered during protein-calorie malnutrition and its accompanying stress and could have significant effects on lymphoid cells, particularly the thymocyte. Plasma cortisol

levels are often raised in protein-calorie malnutrition, and adrenalectomized animals have been found to survive prolonged protein deficiency without profound involution of lymphoid tissues. Serum samples from individuals with protein-calorie malnutrition also contain increased amounts of other constituents known to inhibit immune responses, such as endotoxins, antigen-antibody complexes, and C-reactive protein. In addition, decreased production of thymic hormones occurs and may be responsible for the larger number of null cells in the blood. Sera from persons with protein-calorie malnutrition appear deficient in a presently undefined low-molecular-weight normal serum component (not albumin) required for optimal lymphocyte activity.

THE VARIABLE REGION

The V regions, comprising the N-terminal 110 amino acids of the L and H chains, are quite heterogeneous. Indeed, no 2 human myeloma chains from different patients have been found to have identical sequences in the V region. However, distinct patterns are discernible, and V regions have been divided into 3 main groups based on degree of amino acid sequence homology. These are the V_H group for H chains, V_κ group for κ L chains, and V_λ group for λ L chains. These V region groups are only associated with the appropriate C region subclasses or subtypes for that particular polypeptide. For example, a V_H sequence will only be found on an H chain, never on a κ or λ light chain, and so forth. However, a particular V_H sequence may associate with any C_H class (γ, α, μ, δ, or ϵ). The genes coding for associated V and C regions are probably linked (see Chapter 5).

V Region Subgroups

When the sequences of the V regions of κ chains are compared, they can be further divided into 4 subgroups which have substantial homologies. The subgroups differ from one another principally in the length and position of amino acid insertions and deletions and bear much closer structural homology to each other than to λ or H chain V regions. Similar subdivisions have been made in H chain V regions and λ chain V regions.

Hypervariable Regions

The V regions are not uniformly variable across their spans but consist of relatively invariant positions, which define the type and subgroup to which the V region belongs, as well as highly variable zones or "hot spots." A plot of the known variations versus position in the sequence reveals 3 or 4 peaks, depending on the chain type (Fig 4–4). These peaks of extreme variability are known as **hypervariable regions** and have been shown to be intimately involved in the formation of the antigen binding site. L chains appear to have 3 hypervariable regions, while H chains have four. The approximate locations of the hypervariable regions in each chain are shown in Fig 4–5.

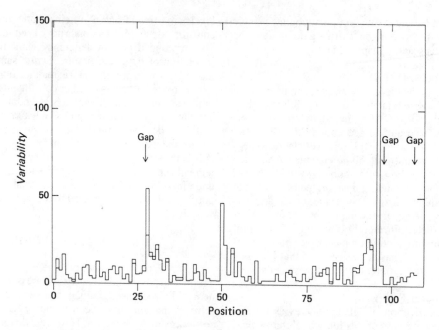

Figure 4–4. The variability at each amino acid residue position in the variable region of human and mouse light chains. Variability was calculated from the following ratio:

$$\frac{\text{Number of different amino acids at a given position}}{\text{Frequency of the most common amino acid at that position}}$$

(Reproduced, with permission, from Wu TT, Kabat EA: *J Exp Med* 1970; **132**:211.)

Idiotypes

The term idiotype denotes the unique V region sequences produced by each clone of antibody-forming cells. Idiotypic antigenic determinants of immunoglobulin molecules were identified by immunizing animals with specific antibodies raised against a particular antigen in genetically similar animals. The only antigenic differences between the immunoglobu-lins of the donor and recipient were the unique V region sequences related to the specificity of the antibody. Thus, responses were restricted to such determinants. It is also possible to immunize across species lines to obtain anti-idiotype antisera, but in this case the antisera must be carefully absorbed with immunoglobulins from the donor species to render them specific for idiotypic markers.

In some cases, the reaction between anti-hapten antibody and anti-idiotypic antisera raised against that anti-hapten antibody can be inhibited by the hapten, indicating that the idiotypic antigenic determinants are close to or within the antigen-binding site of the antibody molecule. An antibody to idiotypic determinants is therefore regarded as an immunologic marker for the antibody combining site. Although it is not yet formally proved, idiotypic determinants are believed to be associated with hypervariable regions which determine antibody specificity.

It seems legitimate to extend the term idiotype to any combination of a particular L chain V region with a particular H chain V region. That is, any such combination will express a unique idiotypic specificity. Since any L chain may combine with any H chain and a common pool of V_H regions is shared by the 5 different classes of H chains, it follows that idiotypic determinants may be shared by different immunoglobulin classes. Idiotypic determinants are heritable, at least in some cases, as observed in certain inbred strains of mice.

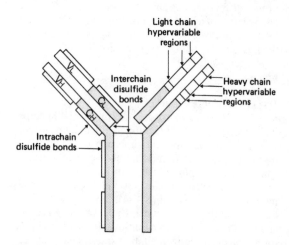

Figure 4–5. Schematic model of an IgG molecule showing approximate positions of the hypervariable regions in heavy and light chains.

THE THREE–DIMENSIONAL STRUCTURE OF IMMUNOGLOBULINS

Although the inference that the polypeptide chains of immunoglobulin molecules are folded into compact globular domains separated by short linear stretches was derived initially from amino acid sequence studies, confirmation of this structural model required examination of crystallized immunoglobulins or their component parts by x-ray diffraction analysis (Fig 4–6). This work has shown that all domains have a characteristic pattern of folding, regardless of their origin. Thus, V region and C region domains from L chains and H chains all have a very similar appearance. In addition, there is close physical approximation between corresponding domains, ie, V_H and V_L, C_H1 and C_L, and the identical H chain domains in the Fc portion. X-ray diffraction analysis of a crystallized myeloma protein complexed with hapten (Chapter 3) revealed that the contact points between antigen and the antibody combining site are located in the hypervariable regions of the H and L chains.

Other evidence in favor of the domain model has come from limited proteolysis of immunoglobulins, in which the major products appear to consist of one or more domains (as expected, based on the model, since the areas between the domains are more exposed and consequently more susceptible to enzymatic attack). It has also been found that some of the proteins present in patients with H chain disease (see Chapter 27) have large deletions involving the entire C_H1 domain.

All domains, including those from the same polypeptide chain, different polypeptide chains, the same molecules, and different molecules, show a significant degree of amino acid homology. This led to the hypothesis that all immunoglobulin polypeptide chains evolved by a process of tandem gene duplication from a common ancestor which was equivalent to one domain.

EVOLUTION OF IMMUNOGLOBULINS

The immune system probably evolved in higher animals in response to the hazards of infection by bacteria, viruses, and other organisms and of the development and spread of aberrant or malignant cells (see Chapter 17). The latter function has been called immunologic surveillance. As mentioned earlier, all immunoglobulin H and L polypeptide chains consist of domains (Fig 4–6). It is generally accepted that all immunoglobulin structural genes have evolved by gene duplication from a common primordial gene which coded for a single domain. Examination of molecular size reveals that each L chain contains 2 domains; γ and α chains contain 4 each; and μ and ϵ chains contain 5 each.

The protein β_2-microglobulin has been isolated from mammalian serum and urine as a polypeptide of 100 amino acids (MW 11,800). It is present on the surface of lymphocytes and many other body cells. It is also a component of the major histocompatibility antigens (HLA) in humans (see Chapter 6). Amino acid sequence analysis shows that β_2-microglobulin has a

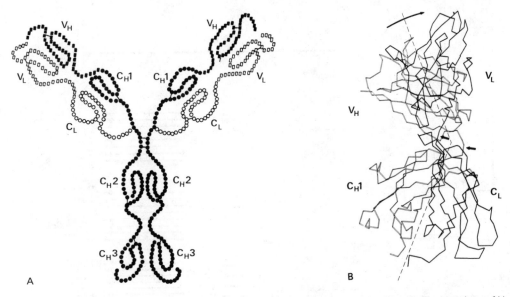

Figure 4–6. Domains of immunoglobulin molecules: *A:* A hypothetical model of an IgG molecule. The V regions of H and L chains (V_H and V_L), the C region of L chains (C_L), and the domains in the C region of H chains (C_H1, C_H2, and C_H3) are folded into compact structures. *B:* A view of the α-carbon backbone of the polypeptide chain of the Fab' domain of a human IgG1 (λ) protein (New) based on x-ray crystallography. The open line indicates the L chain (V_L and C_L) and the solid line indicates the V_H and C_H1 domains of the H chain. The 2 short arrows indicate the V –C switch region of both chains. The longer arrow indicates a possible relative motion of the V and C_1 domains. (Redrawn and reproduced, with permission, from *Proc Natl Acad Sci USA* 1974;71:3440.)

high degree of homology with the C_H3 domain of human IgG and that both β_2-microglobulin and the δ chain have a methionine residue at the carboxyl terminus. A relationship has been postulated between the gene coding for β_2-microglobulin and the primordial gene coding for C regions of immunoglobulins (Fig 4–7).

The ability to mount an immune response has been examined in several invertebrates including the lobster, horseshoe crab (Limulus), starfish, earthworm, and several insect species. The body fluids of many of these species contain substances which agglutinate red cells of other species, sometimes specifically. However, the molecules responsible for this agglutinating activity do not resemble mammalian immunoglobulins in molecular weight, polypeptide chain structure, or stability.

Molecules with the specificity and inducibility of mammalian antibodies have been described to date only for vertebrates. Humoral antibodies have been demonstrated in all major classes of vertebrates. Antibody formation has been demonstrated in a cyclostome (the lamprey) to antigens such as keyhole limpet hemocyanin and T2 bacteriophage. A more primitive

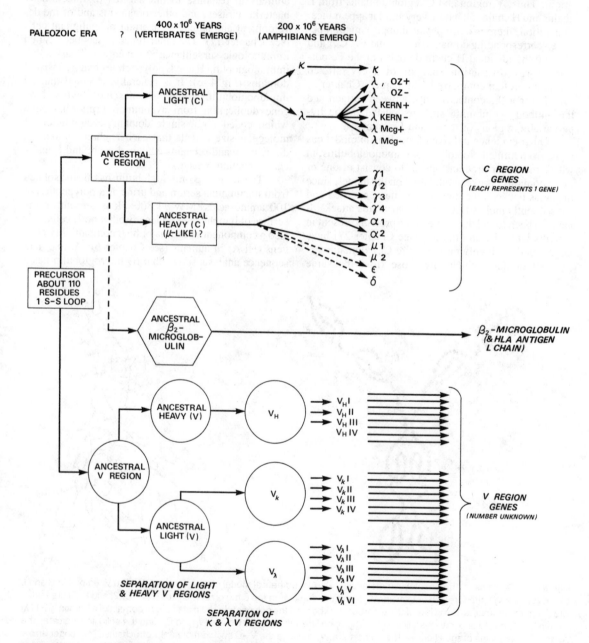

Figure 4–7. A possible scheme for the evolution of genes coding for immunoglobulin polypeptide chains and β_2-microglobulin.

cyclostome, the California hagfish, was found to react to several cellular and soluble antigens with marked antibody production. It appears likely that all vertebrates are capable of producing antibodies.

Chemical analysis of the lamprey antibody indicated that it existed in 2 forms of different sizes: 6.6S and 14S. The 2 forms are antigenically indistinguishable, and both have the basic 4-chain structure (Fig 4–1) with L chains of molecular weight 25,000 and H chains of molecular weight 70,000. The H chains of the lamprey antibody were thought to be homologous to human μ chain. However, other evidence indicates that the lamprey may also have another kind of "antibody" with a unique structure consisting of 4 polypeptide chains of identical size.

Similarly, antibodies isolated from shark, sting ray, bowfin, goldfish, giant grouper, paddlefish, and gar all showed the presence of antigenically indistinguishable 7S (or 8S) and 19S molecules. The H chains of these antibodies were all characterized by a molecular weight of approximately 70,000, high carbohydrate content, and a slower electrophoretic mobility, thus resembling human μ chain. Therefore, it appears likely that μ chain is the most primitive immunoglobulin H chain.

The most primitive animals that possess an immunoglobulin class clearly homologous to human IgG are the amphibians (Table 4–3). Ultracentrifugal analysis of antibodies of frogs and toads demonstrated that a 19S macroglobulin is the early antibody formed after primary immunization with one of a variety of antigens. 7S antibody is formed later in the immune response and is the major immunoglobulin class 2–3 months after immunization. The 19S and 7S antibodies of amphibians are antigenically different. Detailed chemical studies of these molecules indicate that L chains of both forms are similar, with a molecular weight of approximately 23,000, but the H chains differ in molecular weight. The molecular weight of the H chain of the 19S antibody is approximately 72,000 (equivalent to human μ chain). Whether am-

phibians make an immunoglobulin class resembling IgA is unknown; cells resembling plasma cells have been found in the gut of toads but not of fish.

Immunoglobulins in reptiles resemble those in amphibians. During the course of a humoral immune response, early antibody resembling human 19S IgM and later antibody resembling human 7S IgG have been observed in the tortoise, turtle, tuatara, lizard, alligator, and several other species.

In addition to the early 19S and the late 7S immunoglobulins directly homologous to human IgM and IgG, birds also have IgA. All species investigated in the evolutionary scale higher than birds appear to possess all 3 major classes of immunoglobulins—IgM, IgG, and IgA.

Little information is available on the evolution of IgD. The apparent lack of biologic properties, the high susceptibility to degradation, and the low concentration in serum have made its identification difficult. Nevertheless, a molecule cross-reacting with antiserum to human IgD has been detected in the sera of most primates higher than the New World monkeys. Limited amino acid sequence data on the Fc fragment of IgD showed more sequence homology to IgE than to other immunoglobulin classes.

Molecules with properties similar to those of human IgE have been found in the rabbit, dog, monkey, rat, and mouse. Although it is likely that all mammalian species have an immunoglobulin class directly analogous to human IgE, the universal existence of IgE in higher animals has not been firmly established.

A low-molecular-weight immunoglobulin has been observed in lungfish, turtles, and ducks. Its H chain has a molecular weight of approximately 38,000. It is likely that this molecule represents a divergent line of immunoglobulin whose H chain has only 2 instead of 3 or 4 C region domains.

Immunoglobulin polypeptide chains corresponding to human κ and λ type L chains have been found in all mammalian and avian species and possibly reptiles,

Table 4 –3. Immunoglobulin classes and subclasses in various vertebrates.

Species	Class and Subclass				
Human	IgG1, IgG2, IgG3, IgG4	IgA1, IgA2	IgM1, IgM2	IgD	IgE
Ape	IgG	IgA	IgM	IgD	IgE
Monkey	IgG	IgA	IgM	IgD	IgE
Mouse	IgG2a, IgG2b, –*, IgG1	IgA1, IgA2	IgM	IgD	IgE
Rat	IgG2a, IgG2b, IgG2c, IgG1	IgA	IgM	?	IgE
Guinea pig	IgG2, –, –, IgG1	IgA	IgM	?	IGE
Rabbit	IgG2, –, –, IgG1	IgA1, IgA2	IgM	?	IgE
Dog	IgG2a, IgG2b, IgG2c, IgG1	IgA	IgM	?	IgE
Cow	IgG2, –, –, IgG1	IgA	IgM	?	?
Horse	IgGa, IgGb, IgGc, IgGT	IgA	IgM	?	?
Fowl	IgG	IgA	IgM	?	?
Reptile	IgG	?	IgM	?	?
Amphibian	IgG	?	IgM	?	?
Fish	?	?	IgM	?	?
Lamprey	?	?	IgM	?	?

* – indicates the absence of an additional subclass corresponding to that in humans.

bony fish, and sharks. Both types of L chains can associate with H chains of all classes and subclasses for a given antibody specificity. A clear estimate of when the κ/λ divergence took place is impossible to obtain from the available phylogenetic data. Since the degree of sequence similarity between κ and λ is slightly greater than that between μ and γ, it might be expected that the κ/λ divergence took place after the μ/γ divergence, probably after the divergence of the mammalian line from amphibians (Fig 4–7).

Most or all mammalian species have at least 2 IgG subclasses which differ in biologic properties, electrophoretic mobility, and other properties (Table 4–3). The criteria used to subdivide IgG into subclasses in several species have been (1) clear-cut differences between electrophoretic mobilities of different subclasses; (2) antigenic differences; and (3) differences in biologic properties. Since these are probably insufficient criteria on which to build a completely satisfactory definition of all of the IgG subclasses in any one species, other as yet undefined subclasses may well exist in all species except perhaps humans, mice, and rats. Myeloma proteins in these 3 species facilitate the identification of immunoglobulin subclasses.

It is generally accepted that the C regions of H chains belonging to the same subclass are coded for by a single gene. It is noteworthy that subclasses in a species usually do not show immunologic cross-reactions with those of other, even closely related, species. Furthermore, IgG subclasses and their H chain C region allotypes do not always exist in concordance in primates. It has been speculated that more than 10 genes coding for H chain C regions may exist in the genome in all species, with different sets of these genes being expressed in different species. Such mechanisms may also operate in V region genes and may be at least partially responsible for the occurrence of "species-specific" amino acid residues and allotypes involving multiple amino acid substitutions among polypeptide chains coded for by different alleles.

A general hypothetical scheme for the evolution of immunoglobulins is shown in Fig 4–7. The 4 main stages in this evolution may be summarized as follows: (1) formation of V regions and C regions, and H and L chains, in the production of a functional antibody molecule; (2) formation of the major classes of H chains and major types of L chains; (3) formation of the V region subgroups; and (4) the more recent evolution of C region subclasses of many of these chains. The gene coding for β_2-microglobulin probably evolved from the ancestral C region gene. Gene duplication and point mutation are believed to be fundamental processes leading to diversification at each stage.

• • •

References

Amos B (editor): *Progress in Immunology, I.* Academic Press, 1971.

Brent L, Holborow J (editors): *Progress in Immunology, II.* North-Holland Publishing Co., 1975.

Capra JD, Kehoe JM: Hypervariable regions, idiotypy, and the antibody-combining site. *Adv Immunol* 1975;**20**:1.

Cunningham AJ (editor): *The Generation of Antibody Diversity: A New Look.* Academic Press, 1976.

Dayhoff MO (editor): *Atlas of Protein Sequence and Structure.* Vol 5. National Biomedical Research Foundation, 1972.

Eisen HN: *Immunology.* Harper & Row, 1974.

Fudenberg HH et al: *Basic Immunogenetics,* 2nd ed. Oxford Univ Press, 1977.

Gally JA, Edelman GM: The genetic control of immunoglobulin synthesis. *Annu Rev Genet* 1972;**6**:1.

Gergely J, Medgyesi GA (editors): *Antibody Structure and Molecular Immunology.* North-Holland Publishing Co., 1975.

Hill RL et al: The evolutionary origin of the immunoglobulins. *Proc Natl Acad Sci USA* 1966;**56**:1762.

Hilschmann N, Craig LC: Amino acid sequence studies with Bence Jones proteins. *Proc Natl Acad Sci USA* 1965;**53**:1403.

Hood L, Prahl JW: The immune system: A model for differentiation in higher organisms. *Adv Immunol* 1971;**14**:291.

Ishizaka K, Dayton DH Jr (editors): *The Biological Role of the Immunoglobulin E System.* US Department of Health, Education, & Welfare, 1973.

Kochwa S, Kunkel HG (editors): Immunoglobulins. *Ann NY Acad Sci* 1971;**190**:5. [Entire issue.]

Koshland ME: The structure and function of J chain. *Adv Immunol* 1975;**20**:41.

Mestecky J, Lawton AR (editors): *The Immunoglobulin A System.* Plenum Press, 1974.

Metzger H: Structure and function of γM macroglobulins. *Adv Immunol* 1970;**12**:57.

Milstein C, Pink JRL: Structure and evolution of immunoglobulins. *Prog Biophys Mol Biol* 1970;**21**:209.

Möller G (editor): Immunoglobulin D: Structure, synthesis, membrane representation and the function. *Immunol Rev* 1977; No. 37. [Entire issue.]

Natvig JB, Kunkel HG: Immunoglobulins: Classes, subclasses, genetic variants, and idiotypes. *Adv Immunol* 1973;**16**:1.

Nisonoff A, Hopper JE, Spring SB: *The Antibody Molecule.* Academic Press, 1975.

Porter RR: Structural studies of immunoglobulins. *Science* 1973; **180**:713.

Putnam FW: Immunoglobulin structure: Variability and homology. *Science* 1969;**163**:633.

Smith RT, Miescher PA, Good RA (editors): *Phylogeny of Immunity.* Univ of Florida Press, 1966.

Spiegelberg HL: Biological activities of immunoglobulins of different classes and subclasses. *Adv Immunol* 1974;**19**:259.

Tomasi TB, Grey HM: Structure and function of immunoglobulin A. *Prog Allergy* 1972;**16**:81.

Wang AC, Fudenberg HH: Gene expansion and antibody variability. *J Immunogenet* 1974;**1**:303.

Wang AC, Fudenberg HH: IgA and evolution of immunoglobulins. *J Immunogenet* 1974;**1**:3.

Wu TT, Kabat EA: An analysis of the variable regions of Bence Jones proteins and myeloma light chains and their implications for antibody complementarity. *J Exp Med* 1970;**132**:211.

Immunoglobulins II: Gene Organization & Assembly | 5

Stanley J. Korsmeyer, MD, & Thomas A. Waldmann, MD

RECOMBINATIONAL GERMLINE THEORY

The process by which an individual can generate approximately 10^6-10^8 different antibody specificities has been clarified to a great extent in recent years. The first available amino acid sequence data from myeloma proteins revealed that these homogeneous immunoglobulins, composed of light and heavy polypeptide chains, varied markedly in their amino terminal portion (variable regions) but had nearly invariant sequences in their carboxy terminal portions (constant regions). The fact that the amino terminal portions of both the heavy and the 2 light chain immunoglobulin classes (kappa and lambda) appeared to duplicate and diverge over evolutionary time while their carboxy terminal portions remained unchanged posed a molecular genetic dilemma. How could genes coding for these unusual polypeptides undergo numerous changes in part of their sequences while faithfully conserving another portion? This apparent dichotomy prompted Dreyer and Bennett in 1965 to propose that 2 genes would code for a single immunoglobulin polypeptide chain! They further speculated that multiple different variable region genes would exist separated from a single constant region gene and that these segments would be joined together at the DNA level. Such an elegant recombinational model would allow for recognition of a vast array of antigens by the multiple variable regions; yet it would also ensure that the invariant functions provided by the constant regions would be conserved.

DISCONTINUOUS IMMUNOGLOBULIN GENES

Within recent years, investigators using recombinant DNA technology have confirmed the **recombinational germline theory** Dreyer and Bennett had proposed. Direct analysis of immunoglobulin genes by Tonegawa and Leder as well as others revealed that the variable (V) and constant (C) region portions of immunoglobulin were indeed separately encoded and located on different fragments of DNA. However, the variable portion of light chain immunoglobulin proved to be encoded by 2 separate gene segments, not one.

For example, the kappa light chain's initial gene segment, the variable (V_κ) region gene, is fore-shortened, coding for only the first 95 amino acids of the variable region protein (Fig 5–1). The remaining 13 amino acids (positions 96–108) of the variable portion of the molecule are contributed by one of 5 alternative segments termed joining (J_κ) segments. As shown in Fig 5–1, there is but a single constant kappa (C_κ) region gene carried on yet a third segment. The C_κ and J_κ regions are separated within DNA by a long stretch of intervening sequence (IVS). Shorter intervening sequences separate each of the joining (J_κ) segments from each other. Such intervening sequences themselves do not for the most part code for any recognizable protein or function. Many other eukaryotic structural genes are also discontinuous in their organization, being coded for by pieces of structural gene information separated by intervening sequences. These intervening sequences may play a crucial role in determining the evolutionary integrity of structural genes or even in modifying their expression.

SOMATIC ASSEMBLY OF IMMUNOGLOBULIN GENE SEGMENTS CREATES A FUNCTIONAL ANTIBODY GENE

At some point during the differentiation of a pluripotential stem cell into a terminally differentiated kappa-producing plasma cell, a process of DNA rearrangement must occur. This recombination of DNA joins one of many germline variable (V_κ) regions with a particular joining (J_κ) region (Fig 5–1). This rearranged allele is transcribed, and the remaining intervening sequences are removed at a step known as RNA splicing. The final mature mRNA is translated into the complete light chain product. The mRNA, in addition, contains the 19 codons that encode the short hydrophobic leader peptide responsible for the transmembrane passage of this polypeptide. Each germline V_κ region has its own leader sequence (L) separated from the V_κ region by a short intervening sequence. The leader sequence region (L) codes for positions -19 to -4 and is joined to the main V_κ region -3 to 95 by RNA splicing. The leader peptide is present on the cytoplasmic kappa chain but is cleaved off during secretion.

Nucleic acid sequence determinations through recombined and germline variable (V_κ) and joining (J_κ)

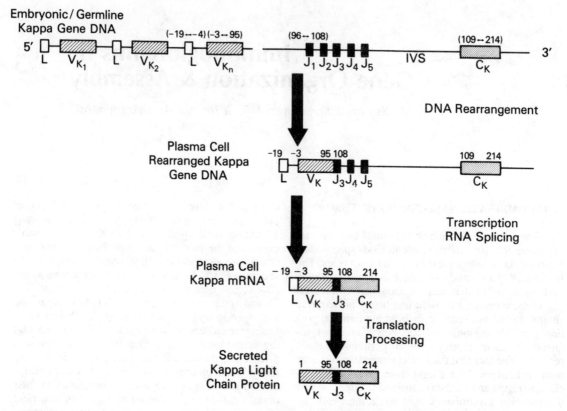

Figure 5–1. Schematic representation of the human kappa gene locus. Multiple germline variable (V$_\kappa$) regions exist, each accompanied by a leader (L) sequence. There are 5 alternative joining (J$_\kappa$) segments, each coding for amino acid positions 96–108. There is but one constant (C$_\kappa$) region per allele. DNA rearrangement joins a single V$_\kappa$ and J$_\kappa$ segment. The remaining intervening sequences (IVS) are removed by RNA splicing.

regions established that the codon for the 96th amino acid was the site at which these 2 fragments usually join. Furthermore, a specific set of nucleic acid bases that flank these germline variable (V) and joining (J) segments appears to mediate V/J joining. At the immediate 3′ side of each germline variable (V$_\kappa$) region and the immediate 5′ side of each germline joining (J$_\kappa$) region is a heptanucleotide, which is an inverted repeat, or so-called palindrome of CAC $\frac{A}{T}$ GTG (Fig 5–2). Following a spacer of 11 or 12 nucleotides on the 3′ side of each V$_\kappa$ gene heptanucleotide is an A,C-rich nonanucleotide. This corresponds to a complementary G,T-rich nonanucleotide that is separated by 22 or 23 nucleotides from its heptanucleotide on the 5′ side of each germline joining (J$_\kappa$) segment. The length of the spacers between the heptanucleotides and nonanucleotides (either 11 or 22 base pairs) is curiously equal to either one or 2 turns of the DNA helix. In both light chain classes, kappa and lambda, it appears that gene segments with 11 base pair spacers always pair with segments having 22 base pair spacers. The fact that both the 7 base pair palindrome and the 9 base pair areas of homology have been remarkably conserved throughout evolution strongly suggests that they are active participants in bringing a V and J region to-

gether. One possibility is that the 2 heptanucleotides and the 2 nonanucleotides would base pair, creating a stemlike structure that would facilitate recombination between the strands (Fig 5–2). Any flanking DNA located between the juxtaposed V$_\kappa$ and J$_\kappa$ segments appears to be deleted from the genome during this process of DNA rearrangement.

The actual nucleotide base within the triplicate codon at which a variable (V) and joining (J) region align can vary and thus generate additional amino acids at this 96th position. It is noteworthy that the 96th amino acid resides within one of the 3 subdivisions of the variable light chain known to have the highest rates of amino acid differences. This subdivision of variable light chain, the third hypervariable region, is also intimately involved in determining an antibody's antigenic specificity. Therefore, the flexible frame of recombination within this 96th codon may well create amino acid substitutions that ultimately generate further antibody diversity.

Thus, this is an elaborate system which utilizes movable gene segments and exploits a flexible frame of recombination at the point of joining to maximize the antibody diversity that can be generated from limited germline information. However, such attempts at gene recombination are frequently imprecise, failing

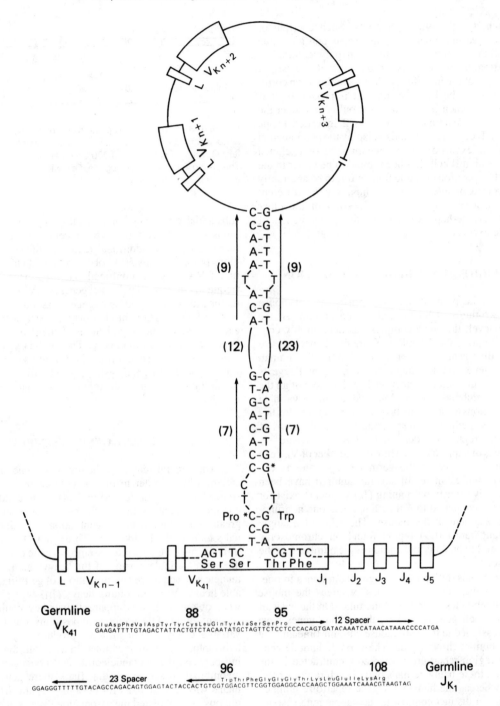

Figure 5–2. Hypothetical recombinational model for V_κ/J_κ joining. A stem structure may form between the palindromic heptanucleotide (CAC $\frac{A}{T}$ GTG) and homologous nonanucleotides (solid arrows) located to the 3′ side of a particular germline variable region ($V_\kappa41$) and those that occur in reverse order on the 5′ side of a germline joining segment ($J_\kappa1$). Spacers of 12 or 23 nucleotides separate the heptanucleotides and nonanucleotides (solid arrows) of the V_κ and J_κ regions, respectively. An asterisk (*) denotes the specific bases at which this particular V_κ and J_κ region are joined together. Any DNA located between the recombining V_κ and J_κ region is apparently deleted.

to properly align these segments. Such aberrant or abortive rearrangements are mistaken events incapable of forming a complete light chain polypeptide. All kappa-producing B cells or plasma cells must, of course, contain one effective V/J recombination corresponding to the kappa chain that is produced. It is known that each B cell expresses only one (either the maternal or paternal copy) of its 2 inherited kappa alleles. B cells are thus said to display the phenomenon of allelic exclusion. The nonexpressed or excluded allele within B cells has been found to be either in the germline position or, quite frequently, to be aberrantly rearranged or even deleted. Thus, several different gene patterns may prevent expression of the other allele and perhaps account for the phenomenon of allelic exclusion.

LIGHT CHAIN GENE ORGANIZATION

The kappa light chain comprises 95% of mouse and two-thirds of human light chain protein. At the DNA level, this gene complex has been highly conserved during the 70 million years the 2 species have been divergent. The general design of the human kappa gene complex diagrammed in Fig 5–1 reveals this to be the simplest functional gene system of all the immunoglobulin classes. Multiple germline variable (V_κ) regions exist within the genome as sets or families of genes, perhaps corresponding to the subgroups of variable regions as defined by the amino acid sequences of kappa chains. The exact number of V_κ gene regions available in the germline repertoire is unknown, but estimates of several hundred have been made. Five functional joining (J_κ) segments exist for humans, compared to 4 functional plus one nonfunctional segment in the mouse. There is but a single constant kappa (C_κ) region found on chromosome number 2 in humans and chromosome number 6 in the mouse.

Humans utilize lambda light chain genes in one-third of their immunoglobulins, whereas the mouse uses lambda less than 5% of the time. On the basis of somatic cell genetic studies, the lambda genes have been assigned to the 16th mouse chromosome and the 22nd human chromosome. The variable lambda gene (V_λ) region repertoire is markedly contracted in the mouse, there being perhaps only 2 such regions present, whereas the human V_λ gene repertoire is much larger. In distinct contrast to the kappa gene system, there are multiple duplicated constant lambda (C_λ) regions with at least 6 such nonallelic C_λ genes present in humans (Fig 5–3). These correspond to the distinct C_λ regions bearing the amino acid markers of Ke$^+$Oz$^-$, Ke$^-$Oz$^+$, Ke$^-$Oz$^-$, and Mcg (Fig 5–3) that were identified by serologic and amino acid analysis of human lambda light chain proteins. The Ke (Kern) and Oz markers actually represent single amino acid differences identified on different lambda Bence Jones proteins. The Mcg subclass of lambda contains only an additional 3 amino acid changes. Thus, the lack of

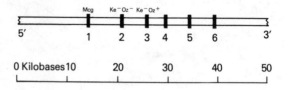

Figure 5–3. Schematic representation of the human lambda constant (C_λ) regions. Six or more separated, nonallelic C_λ regions occupy a 50,000 base pair stretch of DNA. The amino acid markers (Mcg, Ke, Oz) that characterize the identified C_λ regions are indicated.

substantial differences among these separate C_λ regions may reflect a relatively recent duplication of these genes. The additional tandemly linked C_λ regions present on this 50-kilobase stretch of chromosomal DNA may be nonfunctional pseudogenes, infrequently expressed yet intact genes, or even identical duplications of the known genes. As but a single joining lambda segment (J_λ) may be associated with each C_λ gene, the organization of the 2 light chain gene classes varies markedly. The lambda gene system appears to use multiple J_λ C_λ units—in contrast to the kappa gene system, which utilizes a strip of multiple alternative J_κ regions with but a single C_κ gene.

HEAVY CHAIN GENE ASSEMBLY

The general scheme of heavy chain gene organization, while similar to that of light chain genes, is somewhat more complex (Fig 5–4). This additional complexity enables heavy chains to make an even greater contribution to the generation of an individual's total antibody diversity. Three (not 2) segments of DNA must be joined to assemble a gene coding for the entire variable portion of the heavy chain. When nucleic acid sequence determinations of germline variable heavy (V_H) and joining heavy (J_H) gene regions were obtained, it was apparent that they could not account for all of the amino acid positions found in the variable heavy region proteins produced by B cell hybridomas or plasmacytomas. In addition, the spacing between the heptanucleotide and nonanucleotide recombination sequences that flank these gene segments was 22 base pairs for both the V_H and J_H gene regions. This violated the association discussed above of an 11 base pair with a 22 base pair spacer found in all V/J recombinations of light chain genes. This constellation of findings suggested the existence of an additional set of germline gene segments designated the diversity (D_H) gene region. Sets or families of such predicted germline diversity (D_H) gene segments have been demonstrated within the genome. These germline D_H segments are flanked on each side by the same heptanucleotide and nonanucleotide recombination sequences previously discussed. These 2 sequences are themselves separated by the predicted 11 base pair

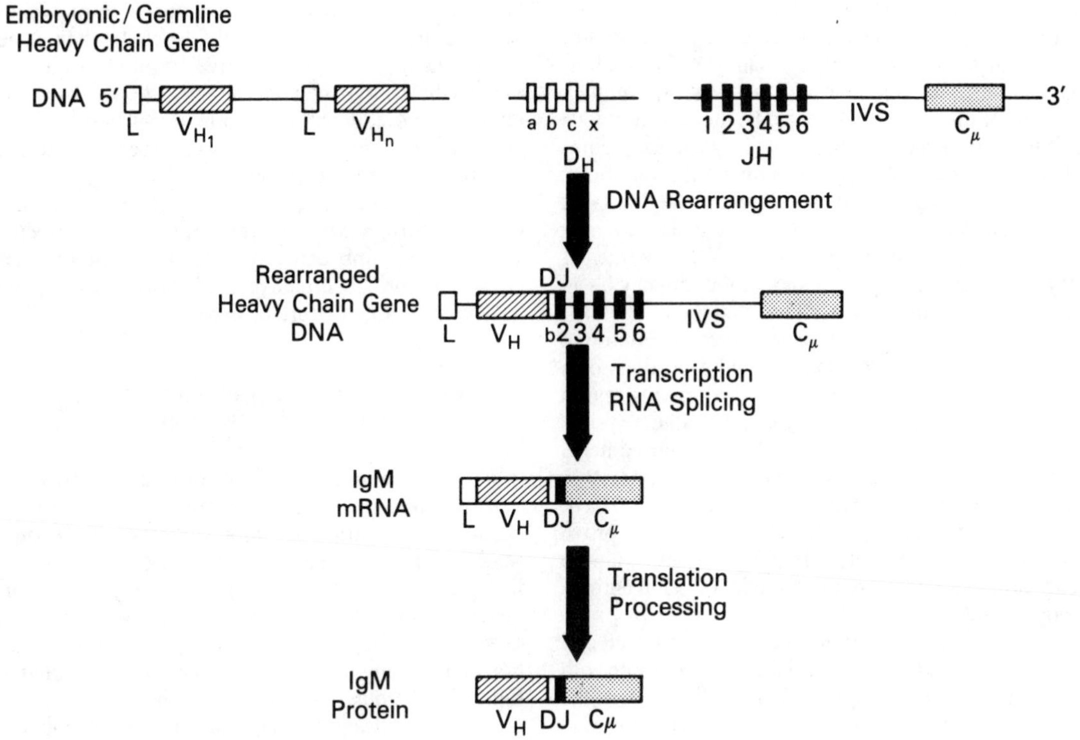

Embryonic / Germline
Heavy Chain Gene

Fig 5–4. Schematic model of the organization and assembly of the human heavy chain gene. In addition to multiple variable (V_H) regions with leader (L) sequences, there are 6 functional joining (J_H) segments and families of diversity (D_H) segments. Single V_H, D_H, and J_H regions are recombined at the DNA level. RNA splicing later removes the residual intervening sequences (IVS).

spacers. These germline D_H segments frequently have more than one open reading frame, and several amino acid sequences can thus be produced by a single gene sequence. The D_H segment accounts for a sizable portion of the heavy chain's third hypervariable or complimentarity-determining region (CDR_3), which is an integral component of an antibody's specificity and frequently its idiotype. As in the V/J joining of light chain genes, these 3 separate germline gene segments ($V_H/D_H/J_H$) of heavy chains can once again utilize several frames of recombination when joining together to generate the variable portion of the heavy chain and thus generate even further diversity.

While the heavy chain gene locus is rich in recombinational opportunities, it appears that the chances of assembling all of these segments correctly is diminished. Thus, aberrant recombinations of these segments (V_H, D_H, and J_H) occur even more frequently in the case of heavy chain gene rearrangements than in the case of light chain rearrangements. Whether the wastage of genetic material that occurs with aberrant recombinations represents the cost of maintaining this wonderfully flexible system or in itself promotes the utilization of alternative gene segments, thus expanding antibody diversity, is an open question.

When active variable heavy (V_H) region genes and their products were compared with the parental germline V_H gene regions from which they presumably originated, an element of somatic mutation was discovered. However, nucleic acid base changes that result in amino acid substitutions are not confined to the complimentarity-determining regions (CDRs) felt to be immediately involved in antigen binding but are actually found scattered throughout the entire V_H region of an actively expressed gene. Of note is the much more frequent occurrence of such point mutations within the V_H regions associated with gamma and alpha heavy chains than with the variable portion of mu chains. Thus, the evidence suggests that the primary IgM response may utilize unmodified germline V_H regions, while heavy chain class switching or continued gene usage might prompt somatic changes within the V_H region. Besides somatic mutation, other mechanisms including clonal selection may play important roles in generating the higher affinity antibodies of the secondary IgG and IgA responses as compared to the lower-affinity primary IgM response.

GENERATION OF ANTIBODY DIVERSITY

Several genetic mechanisms appear to contribute to the generation of an individual's total repertoire of antibody specificities. First of all, both heavy and light chain genes utilize multiple alternative gene segments to assemble a complete variable region. For example, if each germline V_H segment is capable of recombining with any D_H segment and that V_H/D_H complex with any of the available J_H regions, then an enormous amount of diversity can be created by chance recombinatorial joining. Additional amino acid variability can be further generated by allowing the frame of recombination to vary at the sites of juncture of heavy chain V_H/D_H, D_H/J_H and light chain V_L/J_L segments. On top of this purely germline contribution may be an additional component of somatic mutation. The D_H, J_H, and J_L regions in essence represent important "minigenes" that correspond to major portions of a hypervariable or complementarity-determining region (CDR_3) of heavy and light chain variable regions, respectively. However, no further gene subsegments corresponding to the other 2 markedly hypervariable portions of the variable region (CDR_1 and CDR_2) have been identified. Other genetic mechanisms may prove responsible for generating these 2 hot spots of amino acid variation, which are felt to be involved in antigen recognition.

A given heavy chain produced initially by a B cell precursor should theoretically be able to associate with any of a multitude of kappa or lambda light chains the cell could produce. Because the configuration and specificity of the antigen-binding site is affected by both heavy and light chains, alternative combinations of heavy and light chains should markedly enhance diversity.

SEQUENTIAL ACTIVATION OF IMMUNOGLOBULIN GENES

During ontogeny, pre-B cells producing mu chain demonstrable in the cytoplasm but no light chain or surface immunoglobulin clearly precede the appearance of surface IgM-bearing B cells. At the immunoglobulin gene level, several stages of gene recombination have been identified within the B cell precursor series. Early B cell precursors can be identified in which only heavy chain gene recombinations ($V_H/D_H/J_H$) have occurred and all light chain genes remain in their germline configurations. This initial attempt at recombining a V_H, D_H, and J_H segment may be effective, in which case cytoplasmic mu chain will be produced or can be aberrant with no complete heavy chain synthesized. Other cells within the B cell developmental series have been observed which indicate that following heavy chain gene rearrangement, the first attempt at light chain gene rearrangement generally involves the kappa gene class as opposed to the lambda gene class. If a V_κ and a J_κ segment are effectively joined in a cell already possessing an effective $V_H/D_H/J_H$ recombination, a mature mu, kappa-bearing B cell will result. Not infrequently, however, both the maternal and paternal sets of kappa alleles aberrantly rearrange or even delete at this stage of differentiation. This leaves the cell with 2 sets of

lambda genes to recombine in attempts to form a functional light chain. Accordingly, such lambda gene recombinations may be effective, resulting in a mu, lambda–bearing B cell, or might also be mistaken, retaining the cell within the pre–B cell series. This cascade of immunoglobulin gene recombinations, which moves from heavy chain genes to kappa genes and then to lambda, appears to be quite error-prone. Consequently, a sizeable proportion of B cell precursors entering this pathway may waste all of their chances to form an effective heavy or light chain gene and be incapable of further expansion.

HEAVY CHAIN CONSTANT REGION GENE STRUCTURE

The domain and hinge regions that can be identified within immunoglobulin heavy chains are each encoded as a distinct structural gene segment (exons) separated by intervening sequences (introns) at the DNA level. These constant region subunits are assembled together at the level of RNA by a splicing removal of the intervening sequences. The germline organization and splicing pattern of the C_μ region is detailed in Fig 5–5. The other constant heavy chain gene regions are similarly designed. The universal RNA splicing mechanism that assembles these structural subunits depends upon the presence of donor (GT) and acceptor (AG) splice signals located at the respective ends of these intervening sequences. If such signals are not present, RNA splicing cannot occur, and such a gene segment might be nonfunctional and thus classified as a "pseudogene." Examples of such pseudogenes have now been found within various immunoglobulin variable, joining, and constant region gene segments.

IgM exists in 2 forms, either as a monomeric membrane-bound receptor on B cells or in a secreted pentameric form. Initial studies suggested that the mu chain portion of the membrane-bound IgM (μ_m) was larger, containing more hydrophobic amino acids at its carboxy terminal end. Studies of DNA and RNA have shown the molecular basis for the mu membrane (μ_m) and mu-secreted (μ_s) forms of IgM. There are 2 distinct mRNAs, one for μ_m and one for μ_s, that are transcribed from a single C_μ gene locus composed of the 4 separated domains (Fig 5–5). However, the 20 hydrophilic carboxy terminal amino acids of the μ_s chain are contributed by a short μ_s gene segment contiguous with the $C_\mu4$ domain segment. In contrast, the 41 residues of the highly hydrophobic membranous portion of the μ_m chain are provided by 2 exons located 1850 base pairs to the 3' side of the $C_\mu4$ domain segment. Generation of this μ_m mRNA takes advantage of an alternative RNA donor splice site located at the boundary of the $C_\mu4$ and μ_s segments. A splice between this site and an acceptor splice site at the 5' side of the first μ_m exon actually deletes the structural μ_s gene segment and is responsible for joining the $C_\mu4$ segment to the μ_m terminal segment (Fig 5–5). The choice between creating a μ_m versus a μ_s mRNA is

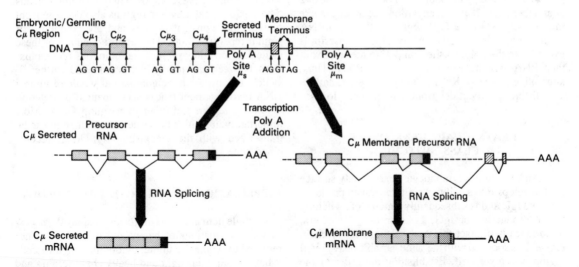

Figure 5–5. Schematic model for creating distinct secreted and membranous forms of IgM from a single constant region locus. Donor (GT) and acceptor (AG) splice sites for RNA splicing border the 4 separated C_μ domains. Alternative sites of poly(A) addition and RNA splicing result in different mRNAs containing either the secreted or the membrane terminus.

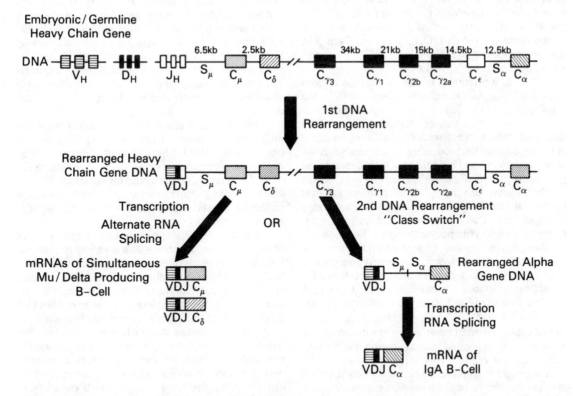

Figure 5–6. Schematic diagram of the mouse heavy chain gene locus, revealing the constant region gene order and spacing. Following the initial DNA rearrangement recombining a V_H, D_H, and J_H region, a B cell can utilize alternative sites of RNA splicing to simultaneously produce IgM and IgD. Alternatively, such a B cell can further differentiate and switch to production of another heavy chain class. For example, a second DNA recombination at the highly homologous switch sites (S_μ and S_α) in front of the C_μ and C_α genes would result in IgA production. Similar homologous switch sites (not shown here) are found in front of each of the constant regions.

probably dictated by the addition of poly(A) to one of 2 alternative sites. If polyadenylation occurs at the site immediately 3' to the $C_\mu 4$ segment, the μ_s mRNA would be produced. Alternatively, if the transcript is extended to the poly(A) site found 3' to the μ_m exon, then RNA splicing would produce μ_m RNA. Thus, alternative modes of RNA splicing create 2 functionally distinct polypeptides from a single gene locus.

HEAVY CHAIN GENE ORDER & CLASS SWITCHING

An immature B lymphocyte bearing only surface IgM develops into a cell that simultaneously produces IgM and IgD and is subsequently capable of switching to the production of IgG, IgA, or IgE. Of central importance is the fact that each of these heavy chain classes is associated with the same variable heavy (V_H) region in a given cell. Establishing the order of the genes in the heavy chain constant region gene locus has helped elucidate the mechanism by which different classes are produced. As can be seen in Fig 5–6, the mu constant (C_μ) region is closely associated with the delta constant ($C\delta$) region. Considerable space separates these 2 genes from the gamma constant ($C\gamma$) region cluster, whose subclass members in the mouse appear in the order of $C\gamma 3$, $C\gamma 1$, $C\gamma 2b$, and $C\gamma 2a$. The epsilon constant region ($C\epsilon$) is located 5' to the terminal alpha constant ($C\alpha$) region.

The close proximity of the C_μ and $C\delta$ regions (only 2500 base pairs apart in the mouse) allows for the simultaneous production of IgM and IgD, which bear the same assembled variable region. Nuclear RNA transcripts from a recombined $V_H/D_H/J_H$ region might undergo differential processing at alternative RNA splice sites to connect a single $V_H/D_H/J_H$ recombined gene with either the C_μ or $C\delta$ region (Fig 5–6). Such a mechanism would be quite analogous to that documented for the mu membrane versus mu-secreted forms of IgM. This could easily account for the capacity of a single lymphocyte to express both of these constant regions (μ and δ) without undergoing any further DNA rearrangements. Conversely, the gamma ($C\gamma$) and alpha ($C\alpha$) constant regions are located a considerable distance 3' to the mu constant (C_μ) region and therefore would be unlikely to co-occupy a single nuclear RNA transcript with C_μ. Initial studies revealed a deletion of all constant regions located to the 5' side of an expressed gamma region subclass or alpha constant region. This suggested that a DNA rearrangement event mediated class switching from mu to either the gamma or alpha constant regions. Nucleic acid sequence analysis has revealed the presence of switch regions located on the 5' side of each constant region that appear to mediate these changes in heavy chain class production. The mu switch region on the 5' side of the C_μ region is a 2000–3000 base pair region comprised of tandemly arranged short repetitive units which are themselves composed of quite homogeneous 5 base pair repeats. Switch regions also occur in front of the other constant regions and are composed of similar repetitive units. The repetitive nature of these switch regions may promote homologous recombinations between the mu switch region and further 3' switch regions. Such recombinations would result in a DNA rearrangement that is accompanied by deletion of the C_μ region and other intervening DNA. Most importantly, it would allow a new constant region to be transcribed with the preexisting $V_H/D_H/J_H$ recombined gene.

APPLICATION TO CLINICAL IMMUNOLOGY

While human B cells uniformly display the necessary recombinations of heavy and light chain genes required to synthesize immunoglobulin, human T cells usually retain their light and heavy chain joining and constant region gene segments in the germline configuration. This marked difference between B and T cells at the immunoglobulin gene level has proved useful in the determination of the cellular origin of human lymphoid malignancies lacking in mature B or T cell surface markers. By such analysis, most cases of common "non-T, non-B" acute lymphocytic leukemias correspond to discrete stages of immunoglobulin gene recombination occurring within the B cell developmental series. Similar studies of other controversial lymphoid malignancies of uncertain phenotypic classification may provide insights into their cellular origins as well.

Human heavy chain disease disorders represent malignant expansions of cells that frequently secrete only a heavy chain which is itself defective, often missing an entire domain or hinge region. Examination of the DNA and RNA that codes for the affected heavy chain immunoglobulin in such cells should provide a molecular genetic explanation for these missing segments.

Analysis of the structure and functional capacity of immunoglobulin genes within a variety of humoral immunodeficiency syndromes may pinpoint the inherited defect within some of these individuals. Considerable genetic polymorphism (variation) exists in the location of certain restriction endonuclease sites that flank human genes. Restriction endonucleases are enzymes that recognize a specific base pair sequence and reproducibly cut DNA only at this site. The variation in restriction endonuclease sites in different individuals thus provides an additional set of genetic markers directly at the gene level. Studying such variations in the location of restriction endonuclease sites within the general population and in affected families should facilitate the assignment of a given defect to a specific chromosome. Such an analysis could ultimately allow prenatal diagnosis and would improve genetic counseling for inherited immunodeficiency states.

•　　•　　•

References

Recombinational Germline Theory

Dreyer WJ, Bennett JC: The molecular basis of antibody formations: A paradox. *Proc Natl Acad Sci USA* 1965; **54:**864.

Discontinuous Immunoglobulin Genes

Chambon P: Split genes. *Scientific American* 1981;**244:**60.

Hozumi N, Tonegawa S: Evidence for somatic rearrangement of immunoglobulin genes coding for variable and constant regions. *Proc Natl Acad Sci USA* 1976;**73:**3628.

Seidman JG et al: Multiple related immunoglobulin variable region genes identified by cloning and sequence analysis. *Proc Natl Acad Sci USA* 1978;**75:**3881.

Tonegawa S et al: Sequence of a mouse germline gene for a variable region of an immunoglobulin light chain. *Proc Natl Acad Sci USA* 1978;**75:**1486.

Somatic Assembly of Immunoglobulin Gene Segments

Brack B et al: A complete immunoglobulin gene is created by somatic recombination. *Cell* 1978;**15:**1.

Early E, Hood L: Allelic exclusion and non-productive immunoglobulin gene rearrangements. *Cell* 1981;**24:**1.

Max EE, Seidman JG, Leder P: Sequences of five potential recombination sites encoded close to an immunoglobulin κ constant region gene. *Proc Natl Acad Sci USA* 1979;**76:**3450.

Max EE et al: Variation in the crossover point of kappa immunoglobulin gene V-J recombination: Evidence from a cryptic gene. *Cell* 1980;**21:**793.

Seidman JG, Max EE, Leder P: A κ-immunoglobulin gene is formed by site specific recombination without further somatic mutation. *Nature* 1979;**280:**370.

Light Chain Organization

Blomberg B et al: Organization of four mouse light chain immunoglobulin genes. *Proc Natl Acad Sci USA* 1981; **78:**3765.

Hieter PA et al: Cloned human and mouse kappa immunoglobulin constant and J region genes conserve homology in functional segments. *Cell* 1980;**22:**197.

Hieter PA et al: The clustered arrangement of immunoglobulin lambda light chain constant region genes in man. *Nature* 1981;**294:**536.

Heavy Chain Gene Assembly

Early P et al: An immunoglobulin heavy chain variable region gene is generated from three segments of DNA: V_H, D_H and J_H. *Cell* 1980;**19:**981.

Sakano H et al: Identification and nucleotide sequence of a diversity DNA segment (D) of immunoglobulin heavy-chain genes. *Nature* 1981;**290:**562.

Schilling J et al: Amino acid sequence of homogeneous antibodies to dextran and DNA rearrangements in heavy chain V-region gene segments. *Nature* 1980;**283:**35.

Siebenlist U et al: Human immunoglobulin D segments encoded in tandem multigenic families. *Nature* 1981; **294:**631.

Ravetch JV et al: The structure of the human immunoglobulin mu locus: Characterization of embryonic and rearranged J and D genes. *Cell* 1981;**27:**583.

Somatic Mutation

Bothwell ALM et al: Heavy chain variable region contribution to the N_p^b family of antibodies: Somatic mutation evident in γ2a variable region. *Cell* 1981;**24:**625.

Gearhart PJ et al: IgG antibodies to phosphorylcholine exhibit more diversity than their IgM counterparts. *Nature* 1981; **291:**29.

Antibody Diversity

Kabat E: Origins of antibody complementarity and specificity-hypervariable regions and the minigene hypothesis. *J Immunol* 1980;**125:**961.

Seidman JG et al: Antibody diversity. *Science* 1978;**202:**11.

Sequential Activation of Immunoglobulin Genes

Alt FW et al: Activity of multiple light chain genes in murine myeloma cells producing a single, functional light chain. *Cell* 1980;**21:**1.

Hieter PA et al: Human immunoglobulin kappa light chain genes are deleted or rearranged in lambda producing B cells. *Nature* 1981;**290:**368.

Korsmeyer SJ et al: A hierarchy of immunoglobulin gene rearrangements in human leukemic pre B-cells. *Proc Natl Acad Sci USA* 1981;**78:**7096.

Heavy Chain Constant Region

Early P et al: Two mRNAs can be produced from a single immunoglobulin mu gene by alternative RNA processing pathways. *Cell* 1980;**20:**313.

Gough NM et al: Intervening sequences divide the gene for the constant region of mouse immunoglobulin mu chains into segments, each encoding a domain. *Proc Natl Acad Sci USA* 1980;**77:**554.

Heavy Chain Gene Order and Class Switching

Davis MM, Kim SK, Hood LE: DNA sequences mediating class switching in immunoglobulins. *Science* 1980; **209:**1360.

Kataoka T, Miyata T, Honjo T: Repetitive sequences in class-switch recombination regions of immunoglobulin heavy chain genes. *Cell* 1981;**23:**357.

Moore KW et al: Expression of IgD may use both DNA rearrangement and RNA splicing mechanisms. *Proc Natl Acad Sci USA* 1981;**78:**1800.

Ravetch JV, Kirsch IR, Leder P: Evolutionary approach to the question of immunoglobulin heavy chain switching: Evidence from cloned human and mouse genes. *Proc Natl Acad Sci USA* 1980;**77:**6734.

Sakano H et al: Two types of somatic recombination are necessary for the generation of complete immunoglobulin heavy chain genes. *Nature* 1980;**286:**676.

Shimizu A et al: Ordering of mouse immunoglobulin heavy chain genes by molecular cloning. *Nature* 1981;**289:**149.

Application to Clinical Immunology

Kan YW et al: Polymorphism of DNA sequence in the globin gene region. *N Engl J Med* 1980;**302:**185.

Korsmeyer SJ et al: Patterns of immunoglobulin gene arrangement in human lymphocytic leukemias. Page 85 in: *Leukemia Markers.* Knapp W (editor). Academic Press, 1981.

6 | The Human Major Histocompatibility HLA Complex

Benjamin D. Schwartz, MD, PhD

The discovery of the human major histocompatibility complex (MHC) dates from the mid 1950s, when leukoàgglutinating antibodies were first found in the sera of multiply transfused patients and in the sera of 20–30% of multiparous women. Analysis of the reaction patterns of these antisera indicated that each antiserum gave a positive reaction with the cells of some but not all individuals and that different antisera reacted with the cells of different but overlapping populations of individuals. This pattern suggested that these antisera were detecting **alloantigens** (ie, antigens present on the cells of some individuals of a given species) which were the products of a polymorphic genetic locus.

The role of these antigens in determining the success of tissue and organ transplants was soon appreciated and provided the initial impetus for studying the genes that determine human leukocyte antigens (HLA). The advent of microcytotoxicity testing to type for specific HLA antigens and the use of computer technology for the codification of the reaction patterns of literally thousands of anti-HLA alloantisera have made possible the delineation of the HLA system. An International Workshop meets every 2–3 years to update the description of the organization and nomenclature of the HLA complex based on findings since the previous Workshop.

In 1973, certain HLA antigens were found to be associated with specific diseases in a high proportion of cases. In addition, in the past decade, it was realized that the HLA complex regulates several aspects of the human immune response. These findings provided a second impetus for the study of the HLA complex.

NOMENCLATURE & GENETIC ORGANIZATION OF THE HLA SYSTEM

The nomenclature of the HLA system is devised by the HLA Nomenclature Committee under the auspices of the World Health Organization. The entire histocompatibility complex is termed the HLA complex. It occupies a segment of approximately 2 centimorgans* (cM) on the short arm of **chromosome 6.** Fig 6–1 schematically depicts our current concept of the HLA complex, showing the genetic regions containing the HLA loci. (A locus is the position on the chromosome where a given gene may be found.) There are 5 officially recognized genetic loci: HLA-A, HLA-B, HLA-C, HLA-D, and HLA-DR (HLA-D-related). The **HLA-D/DR region** contains both the HLA-D and DR loci, which may be identical (see below). The position of the regions with respect to each other and to the centromere, as well as the estimated map distances between regions, is included.

Several additional genetic regions have been linked to the HLA complex. The complement region, which has been mapped between the HLA-B and HLA-D/DR regions, contains genes determining second and fourth components (C2 and C4) of the classic complement pathway and properdin factor B (BF) of the alternative pathway. A series of loci, designated **MB, MT,** and **Te,** which determine **class II or B cell antigens,** are presumed (but not proved) to map within or near the HLA-D/DR region. Finally, a locus that determines antigens identified by primed lymphocyte typing has been termed the **"secondary B cell" (SB) locus** and has been mapped between HLA-DR and glyoxylase.

At each locus, one of several alternative forms (alleles) of a gene may be found. Officially recognized alleles at each locus are designated by the locus and a number; thus, HLA-A1 is the 1 allele at the HLA-A locus. Alleles that have been tentatively assigned to a given locus but are not yet officially recognized are designated by a *w* (for "workshop") placed before the number, eg, HLA-DRw1. Official recognition results in the elimination of the *w*, eg, HLA-DR1.

The HLA system is extremely polymorphic, having multiple different alleles at each known locus. For example, there are at least 18 distinct alleles at the HLA-A locus and at least 32 distinct alleles at the HLA-B locus. Each allele determines a product. The products of the HLA-A, -B, -C, -D, -DR, MB, MT, Te, and SB alleles are cell surface molecules that bear the antigenic determinants. With the exception of

Supported in part by NIH grants AI-13782 and AI-15353 and by the Kroc Foundation.

*A centimorgan is a unit of physical map distance on a chromosome equivalent to a 1% frequency of recombination between linked genes. It is also called a map unit.

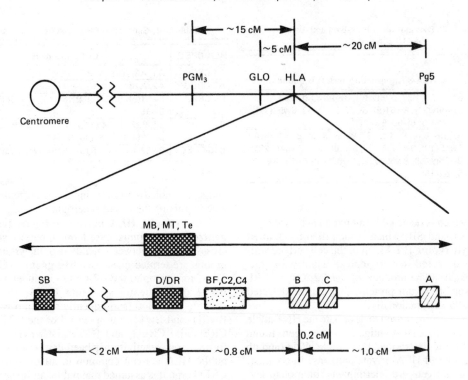

Figure 6–1. The HLA complex on the short arm of chromosome 6. In the upper part of the figure, the position of the HLA complex relative to other markers (PGM₃ = phosphoglucomutase 3; GLO = glyoxylase; Pg5 = urinary pepsinogen) on the short arm of chromosome 6 is shown. Approximate distances are given in centimorgans (cM). The lower part of the figure displays an expanded version of the HLA complex. Class I loci are cross-hatched; class II loci are shaded; and complement loci are stippled. The MB, MT, and Te loci have been linked to HLA but have not been definitively mapped.

Table 6–1. Complete listing of recognized HLA antigens.

HLA-A	HLA-B		HLA-C	HLA-D	HLA-DR
HLA-A1	HLA-Bw4	HLA-Bw42	HLA-Cw1	HLA-Dw1	HLA-DR1
HLA-A2	HLA-B5	HLA-Bw44(12)	HLA-Cw2	HLA-Dw2	HLA-DR2
HLA-A3	HLA-Bw6	HLA-Bw45(12)	HLA-Cw3	HLA-Dw3	HLA-DR3
HLA-A9	HLA-B7	HLA-Bw46	HLA-Cw4	HLA-Dw4	HLA-DR4
HLA-A10	HLA-B8	HLA-Bw47	HLA-Cw5	HLA-Dw5	HLA-DR5
HLA-A11	HLA-B12	HLA-Bw48	HLA-Cw6	HLA-Dw6	HLA-DRw6
HLA-Aw19	HLA-B13	HLA-Bw49(w21)	HLA-Cw7	HLA-Dw7	HLA-DR7
HLA-Aw23(9)	HLA-B14	HLA-Bw50(w21)	HLA-Cw8	HLA-Dw8	HLA-DRw8
HLA-Aw24(9)	HLA-B15	HLA-Bw51(5)		HLA-Dw9	HLA-DRw9
HLA-A25(10)	HLA-Bw16	HLA-Bw52(5)		HLA-Dw10	HLA-DRw10
HLA-A26(10)	HLA-B17	HLA-Bw53		HLA-Dw11	
HLA-A28	HLA-B18	HLA-Bw54(w22)		HLA-Dw12	
HLA-A29	HLA-Bw21	HLA-Bw55(w22)			
HLA-Aw30	HLA-Bw22	HLA-Bw56(w22)			
HLA-Aw31	HLA-B27	HLA-Bw57(17)			
HLA-Aw32	HLA-Bw35	HLA-Bw58(17)			
HLA-Aw33	HLA-B37	HLA-Bw59			
HLA-Aw34	HLA-Bw38(w16)	HLA-Bw60(40)			
HLA-Aw36	HLA-Bw39(w16)	HLA-Bw61(40)			
HLA-Aw43	HLA-B40	HLA-Bw62(15)			
	HLA-Bw41	HLA-Bw63(15)			

Table 6–2. Distribution of HLA-Bw4 and -Bw6 on the HLA-B antigens.

Public Antigen	HLA-B Antigens on Which It Is Found
Bw4	B13, B27, B37, B38(w16), Bw44(w12), Bw47, Bw49(w21), Bw51(5), Bw52(5), Bw53, Bw57(17), Bw58(17), Bw59, Bw63(15)
Bw6	B7, B8, B14, B18, Bw35, Bw39(w16), Bw41, Bw42, Bw45(12), Bw46, Bw48, Bw50(w21), Bw54(w22), Bw55(w22), Bw56(w22), Bw60(40), Bw61(40), Bw62(15)

Table 6–4. Some HLA CREGs and their members.

HLA CREG	CREG Members
A1-CREG	A1, A3, A11, Aw36
A2-CREG	A2, A28
B5-CREG	Bw51(5), Bw52(5), Bw62(15), Bw63(15), B18, Bw35
B7-CREG	B7, B27, Bw54(w22), Bw55(w22), Bw56(w22), Bw60(40), Bw61(40), Bw42
B15-CREG	Bw62(15), Bw63(15), Bw57(17), Bw58(17)

HLA-D, which is detected by a mixed leukocyte reaction (MLR), and SB, which is identified by **primed lymphocyte typing (PLT),** all of the cell surface antigens are detected serologically, usually by microcytotoxicity. The products of the C2, C4, and BF loci are soluble serum proteins that can be detected serologically or functionally.

The same term is used to designate the HLA allele and its product, the HLA antigen. HLA antigens found on the molecule determined by a single allele (and no other) are termed HLA private antigens. In contrast, HLA public antigens are determinants common to several HLA molecules each of which bears a distinct HLA private antigen. HLA-Bw4 and -Bw6 are the best-known examples of HLA public antigens. The entire listing of officially and tentatively recognized HLA antigens determined by the HLA-A, -B, -C, -D, and -DR loci is presented in Table 6–1. The distribution of HLA-Bw4 and -Bw6 on HLA-B antigens is presented in Table 6–2.

In several instances, HLA antigens initially thought to be single private HLA antigens have been subsequently found to be a group of 2 or 3 closely related HLA antigens, each of narrower specificity. These latter antigens are termed "splits" of the original broad specificity. In Table 6–1, HLA antigens that are splits are followed in parentheses by the original broad antigen of which they are splits. Thus, for example, HLA-A25(10) and HLA-A26(10) indicate that HLA-A25 and -A26 are splits of HLA-A10. HLA-A10 could thus be considered a public antigen on the HLA molecules bearing the private HLA-A25 and -A26

antigens. Table 6–3 is a listing of the currently recognized splits of the broad specificities.

Conversely, **HLA private antigens** can be organized into groups based on apparent serologic cross-reactivity between members of the group. These groups are termed **cross-reactive groups (CREGs).** Thus, for example, the B7-CREG includes HLA-B7, Bw22 (subsequently split into Bw54, Bw55, and Bw56), B27, B40 (subsequently split into Bw60 and Bw61), and Bw42. For at least 3 of the CREGs (B5-CREG, B7-CREG, and B15/B17-CREG), the basis for the cross-reactivity has been demonstrated to be a public HLA antigen common to all members of the CREG, and it is assumed that public antigens will also explain the cross-reactivity between members of other CREGs. A listing of some CREGs and their members is presented in Table 6–4.

The MB antigens, MT antigens, and Te antigens are detected serologically and appear to be distinct from HLA-DR antigens but nonetheless are associated with groups of HLA-DR antigens. Thus, for example, MB1 is associated with HLA-DR1, -DR2, and -DRw6; MT2 is associated with HLA-DR3, -DR5, -DRw6, and -DRw8; and Te21 is associated with -DR1 and -DR2. A listing of the MB, MT, and Te antigens and their associations with the DR antigens as given at the Eighth International Workshop is presented in Table 6–5. In the case of the MT antigens, the associa-

Table 6–3. HLA antigen "splits."

Original Broad Specificity	Splits
HLA-A9	Aw23, Aw24
HLA-A10	A25, A26
HLA-B5	Bw51, Bw52
HLA-B12	Bw44, Bw45
HLA-B15	Bw62, Bw63
HLA-Bw16	Bw38, Bw39
HLA-B17	Bw57, Bw58
HLA-Bw21	Bw49, Bw50
HLA-Bw22	Bw54, Bw55, Bw56
HLA-B40	Bw60, Bw61

Table 6–5. MB, MT, and Te antigens and their HLA-DR associations.

MB % DR Included		MT % DR Included		Te % DR Included	
MB1	94% DR1 100% DR2 50% DRw6	MT1	100% DR1 100% DR2 100% DRw6	Te21	22% DR1 57% DR2
MB2	70% DR3 100% DR7	MT2	100% DR3 100% DR5 100% DRw6 100% DRw8	Te24	63% DR3 58%
		MT3	100% DR4 100% DR7 100% DRw9	Te23	61% DR1 36% DR4
MB3	100% DR4 48% DR5 45% DRw6 26% DRw9	MT4	100% DR4 100% DR5 100% DR8	Te22	31% DR4 48% DR5

tion is said to be absolute—so that, for example, an individual with HLA-DR3 has virtually a 100% chance of being MT2-positive. In contrast, the associations of the MB and Te antigens are partial. Thus, for example, an HLA-DR3 individual has only a 70% chance of being MB2-positive. This serologic evidence is consistent with 2 alternative hypotheses. The MB, MT, and Te antigens could be public determinants on the same molecule that bears the HLA-DR antigens, or the MB, MT, and Te antigens may be on molecules that are distinct from the molecules bearing the HLA-DR determinants. Immunochemical studies from several groups appear to indicate that depending on the given MB, MT, and Te antigen and the given HLA-DR antigen, both alternatives are correct. Thus, for example, MB1 appears to be on a molecule distinct from that bearing HLA-DR2, but MT2 appears to be on the same molecule as HLA-DR5. Resolution of this highly complex problem must await further investigation.

The SB antigens are identified by primed lymphocyte typing (see below). The reagents used to define the SB antigens are sets of cryopreserved primed lymphocytes from different donor combinations and include 2 reagents to define each of the SB antigens. Currently, five SB antigens have been defined (SB1–SB5).

The complement components determined by the HLA-linked complement loci also display polymorphism. There are 4 alleles determining the 4 alternative forms of properdin factor B that can be distinguished by their electrophoretic mobility: a common fast form BF*F, a common slow form BF*S, a rare fast form BF*F1, and a rare slow form BF*S1. There are C2 alleles determining the 2 common forms of C2—C2*C and C2*A—and a rare deficiency allele C2*QO. The C4 locus has actually been duplicated, so that there are 2 distinct C4 genetic loci, designated C4A (formerly Rogers), which determines the electrophoretically more acidic group of C4 components; and C4B (formerly Chido), which determines the electrophoretically more basic group of C4 components. There are 7 structural alleles and one deficiency allele at the C4A locus and 3 structural alleles and one deficiency allele at the C4B locus. Table 6–6 presents a listing of the known common alleles at each of the HLA-linked complement loci.

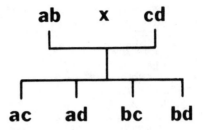

Figure 6–2. Inheritance of HLA haplotypes. A haplotype is the combination of alleles at each locus on a single chromosome that is inherited as a unit. Haplotype designations in the figure are given as a, b, c, and d. The maternal haplotypes are a and b and the paternal haplotypes c and d. Offspring of this mating (ab x cd) inherit one of the 2 possible haplotypes from each parent and so will have haplotypes ac, ad, bc, and bd. There is a 25% chance that 2 offspring will be HLA-identical (eg, ac and ac); a 25% chance that they will be totally HLA-nonidentical (eg, ac and bd); and a 50% chance that they will be HLA-semi-identical (eg, ac and ad).

Haplotype

Because of their close linkage, the combination of alleles at each locus on a single chromosome is usually inherited as a unit. This unit is referred to as the haplotype. Since we inherit one chromosome from each parent, we have two HLA haplotypes. Because all HLA genes are codominant, both alleles at a given HLA locus are expressed, and 2 complete sets of HLA antigens can be detected on cells. By simple mendelian inheritance, there is a 25% chance that 2 siblings will share both haplotypes, a 50% chance that they will share one haplotype, and a 25% chance that they will share no haplotype and will be completely HLA incompatible (Fig 6–2).

Linkage Disequilibrium

Owing to random matings, the frequency of finding a given allele at one HLA locus with a given allele at a second HLA locus should simply be the product of the frequencies of each allele in the population. However, certain combinations of alleles are found with a frequency far exceeding that expected. This phenomenon is termed "linkage disequilibrium" and is quantitated as the difference (Δ) between the observed and expected frequencies. As an example, the HLA-B8 allele and the HLA-DR3 allele are found in the North American white population with frequencies of 0.09 and 0.12, respectively. Thus, the expected frequency with which the HLA-B8-DR3 haplotype should be found is 0.09×0.12, or 0.0108. However, this haplotype is found with a frequency of approximately 0.0740, almost 7 times the expected frequency, for a Δ of $0.740–0.0108 = 0.0632$. Table 6–7 lists some common examples of linkage disequilibrium. Several hypotheses have been offered in an attempt to explain the phenomenon of linkage disequilibrium, including (1) a selective advantage of a given haplotype, (2) migration and admixture of 2 populations, (3) inbreeding, and (4) random drift.

Table 6–6. Common alleles at the HLA-linked complement loci.

BF	C2	C4A	C4B
BF*F	C2*C	C4A*1	C4B*1
BF*S	C2*A	C4A*2	C4B*2
BF*F1	C2*QO	C4A*3	C4B*3
BF*S1		C4A*4	C4B*QO
		C4A*5	
		C4A*6	
		C4A*7	
		C4A*QO	

Table 6–7. Examples of linkage disequilibrium in North American caucasians.

Haplotypes	$\Delta\ (\times 10^3)$
HLA-A1, B8	48.4
HLA-A2, B12	20.2
HLA-B27, Cw1	11.1
HLA-B27, Cw2	19.7
HLA-B7, DR2	39.2
HLA-B8, DR3	63.2

THE HLA ANTIGENS

Based on their tissue distribution and structure, HLA antigens have been divided into 2 classes. **Class I antigens,** also termed the classic histocompatibility antigens, include the HLA-A, -B, and -C antigens. **Class II antigens,** also termed B cell antigens, include the HLA-D, -DR, MB, MT, Te, and SB antigens. **Class III antigens** include the BF, C2, and C4 components of complement and are discussed in Chapter 11.

HLA Typing

A. Class I Antigens: The HLA class I antigens are all defined by serologic reactions, and typing for these antigens is therefore performed using standard serologic techniques. Typing sera are obtained chiefly from multiparous women. These sera tend to have relatively high titers of antibodies directed against a limited number of HLA determinants, since in most cases the woman has been repeatedly immunized with the HLA antigens of a single individual—the father of her children—which are present on the fetuses she carries. Many attempts have been made to produce monoclonal antibodies with high titer and enough specificity for use as typing reagents. Recently, a mouse anti–HLA-B27 monoclonal reagent has been reported. The most widely used method for HLA typing is lymphocyte microcytotoxicity assay (Fig 6–3). Multiple antisera against HLA-A, -B, and -C antigens are placed in the microwells of a typing tray, and the trays are then frozen until needed. For typing, 1000–2000 peripheral blood lymphocytes are added to each microwell. After a short period of incubation, complement is added, and incubation continues. Finally, a vital dye such as eosin is added. Under phase microscopy, cells lysed by an antiserum and complement take up the dye and appear red, whereas live cells exclude the dye and remain unstained. The percentage of cells lysed by each antiserum can be determined, and the HLA-A, -B, and -C phenotype can be assigned on the basis of the reaction patterns.

B. Class II Antigens: HLA-DR, MB, MT, and Te antigens are typed by procedures virtually identical to those just described, with the exception that the

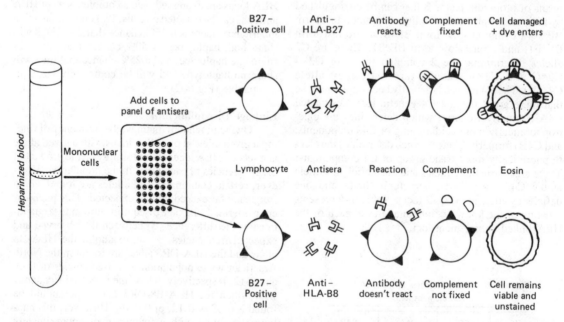

Figure 6–3. Microcytoxicity testing for HLA antigens. The patient's blood is heparinized, and the mononuclear cells (lymphocytes and monocytes) are purified by Ficoll-Hypague gradient centrifugation. The cells are then added to the wells of a microtiter tray containing antisera to HLA antigens. Illustrative examples of a B27-positive cell in wells with anti-B27 antisera (upper part) and anti-B8 antisera (lower part) are shown. Anti-B27 antibodies bind to the HLA-B27 antigens on the cell surface, fix complement, and cause the cell to lyse. Eosin then enters the cell, and the cell appears red under phase microscopy. In contrast, anti-B8 antibodies cannot bind to the cell; complement is not fixed; no lysis ensues; and the live cell excludes eosin and appears unstained under phase microscopy. The reaction patterns allow the cell to be typed as HLA-B27–positive, -B8–negative. This assay is used to type all HLA class I molecules and, with some modifications, to type HLA-DR, MB, MT, and Te antigens.

typing is performed on purified populations of B lymphocytes. The typing sera are pretested to make certain that they cannot be detecting HLA-A, -B, or -C antigens.

The HLA-D antigens are defined and typed by a mixed leukocyte reaction (MLR). In this test, lymphocytes from HLA-D-different individuals mixed in in vitro culture will manifest blast transformation, DNA synthesis, and proliferation in response to the foreign HLA-D antigens on the cells from the other individual. For HLA-D typing (Fig 6–4), a panel of HLA-D-**homozygous typing cells (HTC)** representing all known HLA-D types is used. These "stimulator" cells are irradiated or treated with mitomycin to prevent their DNA synthesis and proliferation in response to the unknown cells, so that a one-way MLR results. The "responder" lymphocytes of the individual to be typed are incubated in microculture with the HTC for 5 days. ^{3}H-thymidine is then added for an additional 12–18 hours, and the incorporation of ^{3}H-thymidine into DNA is used as a measure of DNA synthesis. If the unknown responder cells synthesize DNA after incubation with a particular HTC, then it is concluded that the unknown cells do *not* possess the same HLA-D type as the HTC. If the unknown responder cells show no DNA synthesis, then it is concluded that they do possesses the same HLA-D type as the HTC. If only one HLA-D type can be assigned, it is possible to determine if the unknown cell is heterozygous or homozygous for that HLA-D type by reversing the one-way MLR. The unknown cells are irradiated or treated with mitomycin and

used as stimulator cells. The ability of the HTC, which shares the HLA-D type with the unknown, to synthesize DNA in response to the unknown cell is determined. A lack of DNA synthesis indicates that the unknown cell is HLA-D-homozygous. DNA synthesis by the HTC indicates that it is recognizing a foreign HLA-D antigen and therefore that the unknown cell is HLA-D-heterozygous with one allele not typable with the HTC panel used.

The SB antigens are identified and typed by **primed lymphocyte typing (PLT)** (Fig 6–5). A panel of responding lymphocytes is first primed by stimulator cells matched for HLA-A, -B, -C, -D, -DR, and MB antigens for approximately 10 days in an MLR, and is cryopreserved. Unknown cells are irradiated or treated with mitomycin C and tested for their ability to restimulate the primed responding lymphocytes. The unknown and primed responding lymphocytes are incubated in microculture for 30 hours, ^{3}H-thymidine is added for an additional 12–18 hours, and the incorporation of ^{3}H-thymidine into DNA by the primed lymphocytes is determined. Currently, a set of 2 different responding lymphocytes is used to define each SB antigen. DNA synthesis by a set of responding lymphocytes indicates that the unknown cell has the SB antigen defined by that set.

The HLA type of an individual is usually given as the phenotype and designates all HLA antigens possessed by the individual, eg, HLA-A1, -A2, -B7, -B12, -Cw1, -Cw2, -Dw2, -Dw3, -DR2, -DR3, -MB1, -MB2, -MT1, -MT2, -SB1, and -SB2. To determine the HLA genotype of the individual, ie,

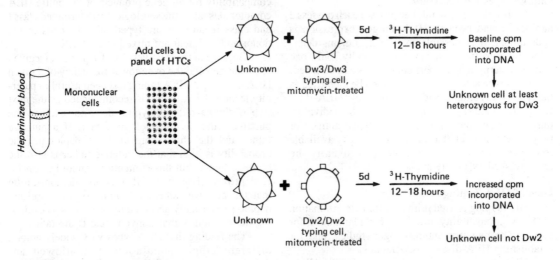

Figure 6–4. HLA-D typing by one-way mixed leukocyte reactions using homozygous typing cells. Mononuclear cells are prepared as described in the legend to Fig 6–3 and added to the wells of a microculture plate containing a panel of mitomycin-treated homozygous typing cells (HTCs) used as stimulator cells. Illustrative examples are given for the unknown responder cells (which are Dw3-positive) reacting with a Dw3/Dw3 HTC (upper part) and with a Dw2/Dw2 HTC (lower part). The cells are incubated for 5 days, after which ^{3}H-thymidine is added and incubation continued an additional 12–18 hours. The amount of ^{3}H-thymidine incorporated by the unknown cells into newly synthesized DNA is then determined. In the upper part of the figure, the unknown cell (which is Dw3-positive) does not recognize the Dw3/Dw3 HTC as foreign, does not proliferate, and does not incorporate ^{3}H-thymidine into DNA. In contrast (lower part), the unknown cell does recognize the Dw2/Dw2 HTC as foreign, does proliferate, and does incorporate ^{3}H-thymidine into DNA. The reaction patterns allow the cell to be typed as Dw3-positive, Dw2-negative.

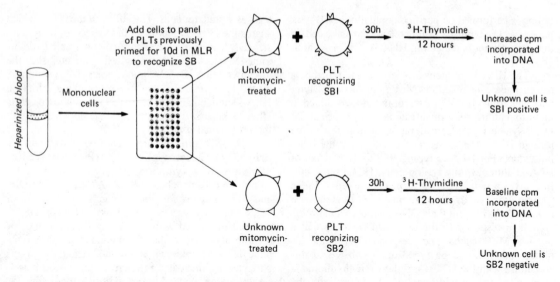

Figure 6–5. SB antigen typing by primed lymphocyte testing. Unknown mononuclear cells are prepared as in the legend to Fig 6–3 and treated with mitomycin. They are then added to the wells of a microculture tray containing lymphocytes previously primed in a 10-day mixed lymphocyte reaction with mitomycin-treated stimulator cells matched for HLA-A, -B, -C, -D, -DR, and MB antigens. The primed cells are known to recognize SB antigens. The cells are incubated for 30 hours, after which ^{3}H-thymidine is added for an additional 12 hours. The amount of ^{3}H-thymidine incorporated by the primed lymphocytes into newly synthesized DNA is then determined. Illustrative examples are given for an unknown cell (which is SB1-positive) incubated with a primed lymphocyte that recognizes SB1 (upper part) and with a primed lymphocyte that recognizes SB2 (lower part). In the upper part, the primed lymphocyte responds to SB1 and incorporates ^{3}H-thymidine into DNA. In the lower part, the primed lymphocyte cannot respond to SB1 and does not incorporate ^{3}H-thymidine into DNA. The reaction patterns allow the cell to be typed as SB1-positive, SB2-negative.

which antigens are determined by which haplotype, family studies are necessary.

C. Blanks: In general, because we each possess 2 haplotypes and because HLA antigen expression is codominant, it is possible to type 2 antigens determined at a particular locus. Occasionally, only one antigen determined at a particular locus can be typed. The HLA type at that locus would then be identified as the typed HLA antigen and a "blank," eg, HLA-B27, B– or HLA-B27,–. In this situation, the individual may either be homozygous for the typed antigen or may have an antigen that cannot be typed by available reagents. These possibilities can usually be distinguished by family studies.

Uses of HLA Typing

HLA typing is used primarily for a determination of HLA compatibility prior to transplantation, for paternity testing, for anthropologic studies, and for establishing HLA-disease associations.

HLA typing was first done to identify HLA-compatible or partially compatible donors and recipients for organ transplantation. The broadest generalization which can be made regarding HLA compatibility and transplantation is that results with closely related living donors matched with the recipient for one or both haplotypes are superior to those obtained with unrelated cadaveric donors matched for a similar number of HLA antigens. This finding derives from the fact that matching for the known HLA determi-

nants within a nuclear family almost always assures compatibility for all gene products of the entire HLA complex. Usually, the serologically determined class I and class II antigens are typed, and the cells of the donor and recipient are mixed in an MLR.

Because of the relatively low frequency of a given HLA antigen and the even lower frequency of a given HLA haplotype, HLA typing has been useful in paternity testing. HLA typing is recommended as the next step if simple red cell typing does not exclude the putative father as the biologic father. If a putative father and the child share an HLA haplotype, the probability is high that the putative father is also the biologic father, but this contention cannot be considered proved. However, HLA typing demonstrating that the putative father and child do not share any haplotype is usually accepted by the courts as excluding the possibility that a given male is the father.

The finding that HLA types vary widely among different ethnic populations has allowed anthropologists to establish or confirm data regarding interrelationships among populations and migration patterns. For example, the finding that HLA-B27 is found in 8% of American whites and 2% of American blacks but is virtually absent from African blacks suggests that the presence of HLA-B27 in American blacks results from an admixture of the American white and African black gene pools.

Finally, HLA typing has been used to establish HLA-disease associations, which are discussed below.

Tissue Distribution, Structure, & Function

A. Class I Antigens: The HLA-A, -B, and -C antigens are found on virtually every human cell (Table 6–8). Structurally, the class I antigens are found on a 2-chain molecule that consists of a polymorphic glycoprotein with a molecular weight of 44,000, determined by genes in the HLA complex, in noncovalent association with a nonpolymorphic 12,000-MW protein, β_2-microglobulin, determined by a gene on chromosome 15 (Fig 6–6). The entire molecule is anchored in the cell membrane by the 44,000-MW chain. Based on extensive structural studies, including determination of the entire amino acid sequence of the HLA-B7 44,000-MW chain, it is known that the 44,000-MW chain contains 337 amino acid residues and can be divided into 3 regions. Starting at the N-terminal end of the molecule, these regions are an extracellular hydrophilic region (residues 1–281), a transmembrane hydrophobic region (residues 282–306), and an intracellular hydrophilic region (residues 307–337). The extracellular hydrophilic region in turn can be divided into 3 domains composed of amino acid residues 1–90, 91–180, and 181–271, respectively. The N-terminal domain (residues 1–90) bears the attachment site for the oligosaccharide side chain. The second and third domains (residues 91–180 and 181–271, respectively) each contain a disulfide loop reminiscent of those seen in immunoglobulin. Based on comparison of the amino acid sequences of HLA-B7 and HLA-A2, it seems likely that the HLA-antigenic determinants will reside in the first or second (or both) of these hydrophilic domains. The 24 residues that comprise the hydrophobic transmembrane region render it long enough to span the hydrocarbon core of the lipid bilayer. The intracellular hydrophilic region can be phosphorylated, and it has been postulated that this reaction may allow extracellular signals to be transmitted to the interior of the cell.

Much of what we know regarding the function of HLA antigens is based on the functions that have been demonstrated for major histocompatibility antigens in other species. Class I antigens are the principal antigens recognized by the host during tissue graft rejection. In cell-mediated cytolysis, the in vitro correlate

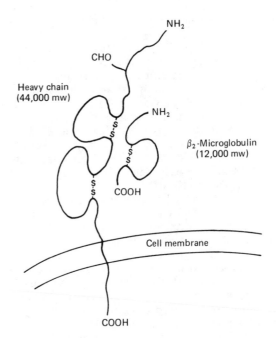

Figure 6–6. A schematic representation of an HLA class I molecule. The molecule consists of a 44,000 MW glycoprotein, the heavy chain, which bears the antigenic determinant, in a noncovalent association with a 12,000 MW nonpolymorphic protein, β_2-microglobulin. NH$_2$ = amino terminal; COOH = carboxy terminal; CHO = carbohydrate side chain; −S−S− = disulfide bond.

of graft rejection, the class I antigens are the target antigens recognized by the killer T lymphocytes. Both private and public HLA antigens can be recognized independently by these T cells. The true physiologic role of class I histocompatibility, however, is probably related to the phenomenon of histocompatibility restriction of cell-mediated lysis (CML) of virus-infected and minor histocompatibility antigen–bearing cells. When T lymphocytes are exposed to a viral (or minor histocompatibility) antigen, they will recognize it in the context of a class I antigen. The cytotoxic T lymphocytes elicited by such an exposure are restricted in their killing to those target cells which bear *both* the same viral (or minor histocompatibility) antigen *and* the same class I antigen as were present on the sensitizing cell. These T lymphocytes will not kill target cells bearing the same viral (or minor histocompatibility) antigen and a different class I antigen, nor will they kill cells bearing the correct class I antigen and a different viral (or minor histocompatibility) antigen. Class I HLA antigens have been shown to restrict the killing of H-Y (male) antigen–bearing cells by autologous female cells and the killing of influenza virus–infected cells. Interestingly, the unexpected finding that a particular influenza virus–infected HLA-A2 target cell was not killed by an appropriate killer T lymphocyte led to the discovery that this HLA-A2 antigen, though serologically indistinguishable from other HLA-A2

Table 6–8. Comparison of class I and class II antigens.

	Class I	Class II
Antigens included	HLA-A, -B, -C.	HLA-D, DR; MB, MT, Te; SB.
Detection	Serologic.	HLA-DR, MB, MT, Te— serologic; HLA-D—MLR; SB—PLT.
Tissue distribution	Wide—virtually on every cell.	Restricted to immunocompetent cells, particularly B cells, and macrophages.
Functions	Target of CML; recognized during graft rejection. Restrict CML of virus-virus-infected cells.	MLR, PLT; D/DR antigens important for antigen presentation, effective interaction between immunocompetent cells.

antigens, was a mutant with an identifiable structural difference.

B. Class II Antigens: Class II antigens are found chiefly on the surfaces of immunocompetent cells, including macrophages/monocytes, resting T lymphocytes (in low amounts), activated T lymphocytes, and particularly B lymphocytes (Table 6–8). HLA-D antigens are the stimulator antigens of the MLR, and it is this reaction that is used to define and detect these antigens (see above). The ability of anti–HLA-DR antisera to inhibit an MLR by interacting with HLA-DR antigens on the stimulating cell suggests that the HLA-DR and HLA-D antigens are at least in close proximity on the cell surface. It is unclear whether HLA-D and HLA-DR antigens are in fact identical but are recognized by different assay systems or whether they are discrete entities. Because HLA-D antigens and SB antigens are not defined by antisera and therefore cannot be isolated serologically, nothing is known about their structure. The remainder of the class II antigens are borne on a 2-chain molecule that consists of a glycoprotein of about MW 34,000 (α chain) and about MW 29,000 (β chain) in noncovalent association (Fig 6–7). Both chains are anchored in the membrane by hydrophobic transmembrane regions and intracellular hydrophilic regions. Structural studies by both 2-dimensional gel electrophoresis and tryptic pep-

tide mapping using murine monoclonal antibodies or rabbit xenoantisera recognizing framework determinants have indicated that the α chains appear extremely similar between molecules bearing different HLA-DR antigens, while the β chains are highly variable. This finding has suggested that the HLA-DR antigenic determinant resides on the β chain and therefore that at least the β chain gene is located within the HLA complex. N-terminal amino acid sequence data have indicated that the HLA-DR molecules are homologous to determinants encoded for by the I-E subregion of the murine I region.

The relationship between the HLA-DR, MB, MT, and Te antigens remains highly controversial at present. The available data suggest that in an HLA-DR2, MB1-positive cell, MB1 is borne on a molecule distinct from the molecule bearing HLA-DR2; and that in an HLA-DRw6, MB1-positive cell, MB1 is on a molecule distinct from the HLA-DRw6–bearing molecule. In contrast, in HLA-DR3, MT2-positive cells and HLA-DR5, MT2-positive cells, at least some class II molecules bear both the HLA-DR3 and MT2 antigens, or HLA-DR5 and MT2 antigens, respectively. Most workers in the field agree that there are at least 2 distinct HLA-encoded class II molecules, each having the basic α-β dimer structure. The complexity of this area will be unraveled during the next several years.

The HLA-D antigens were discovered in 1972 because of their ability to elicit an MLR. They are also thought to be the antigens principally responsible for the in vivo correlate of the MLR, the graft-versus-host reaction. Presumably through this role, the HLA-D/DR region antigens have been implicated in the sensitization phase (ie, the afferent limb) of cell-mediated cytolysis. This is in contrast to the effector phase (efferent limb), where the HLA class I molecules are important as target molecules.

The previously mentioned function relates to the artificial situation in which cells bearing different HLA antigens have been mixed. In the physiologic situation where cells bearing identical HLA antigens are required to interact productively, the HLA-D/DR region antigens have been shown to be involved in antigen presentation by macrophages to T lymphocytes as well as in efficient collaboration between immunocompetent cells. Human suppressor factors that suppress an MLR have been shown to react with anti–HLA-DR alloantisera. In addition, some factors will suppress the MLR response of T cells only if both the factor and the T cell are reactive with the same anti–HLA-DR antiserum.

The SB antigens have been shown to be distinct from all other class II antigens. They can elicit a strong secondary proliferative response and can act as target antigens of cytotoxic T lymphocytes. Their function is presumed (not proved) to be similar to that of the HLA-D/DR antigens.

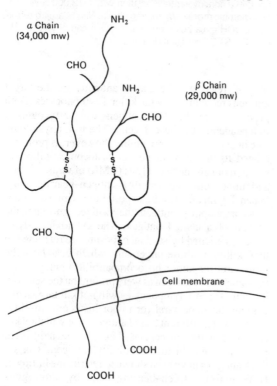

α Chain (34,000 mw)

NH₂

CHO

NH₂

β Chain (29,000 mw)

CHO

CHO

S-S   S-S

S-S

Cell membrane

COOH

COOH

Figure 6–7. Schematic representation of an HLA-DR molecule. The molecule consists of a 34,000 MW glycoprotein (the α chain) in a noncovalent association with a 29,000 MW glycoprotein (the β chain). (Abbreviations as in Fig 6–6.)

IMMUNE RESPONSE GENES

The search for human immune response (Ir) genes has been stimulated by the recognition of the overall homology of the HLA complex with animal major histocompatibility complexes and by the finding that the animal homologs of the HLA-D/DR region are the mapping sites for immune response genes. There is now some evidence that human Ir genes do exist. In humans, allergy to ragweed antigen Ra5 has been found to be highly associated with HLA-DR2 and is almost certainly a manifestation of a human Ir gene. Hyperresponsiveness to collagen has been shown to be associated with HLA-DR4 and appears to be secondary to a lack of collagen-specific suppressor T cells. Low responsiveness to tetanus toxoid and to streptococcal cell wall antigen has been linked to the HLA complex, shown to be dominant, and interpreted as evidence for immune suppressor genes. Possible additional evidence for the presence of Ir genes comes from the HLA-linked disease susceptibility genes and HLA-disease associations discussed below.

HLA & DISEASE

Diseases associated with HLA antigens have several characteristics that should be noted. In general, these diseases (1) are of unknown cause and unknown pathophysiologic mechanism, with a hereditary pattern of distribution but weak penetrance; (2) are associated with immunologic abnormalities; and (3) have little or no effect on reproduction.

Both population and family studies have been used to demonstrate the relationship between marker genes within the HLA complex and various disease states. The 2 types of studies yield different types of information. Population studies permit a statistically significant association between a particular HLA marker gene and a particular disease. Such associations cannot be interpreted as proof of genetic linkage between a **disease susceptibility gene** and the HLA marker gene, since association does not necessarily indicate genetic linkage nor does linkage necessarily indicate association. For example, if a disease susceptibility gene was on a chromosome other than chromosome 6 and therefore not linked to HLA, but the presence of a particular HLA antigen was necessary for the phenotypic expression of that disease susceptibility gene, then an HLA-disease association would be established. Conversely, a gene such as phosphoglucomutase 3 (PGM_3) is on chromosome 6 and therefore linked to HLA, but no HLA-specific association with PGM_3 is found. In contrast, family studies can demonstrate linkage between a disease susceptibility gene and the HLA marker. Because population studies are easier to perform, most of the data on HLA and disease derive from this type of study.

The association of a particular disease with a particular HLA antigen is quantitated by calculating the "relative risk." The relative risk (RR) can be stated as the chance an individual with the disease-associated HLA antigen has of developing the disease compared to an individual who lacks that antigen. It is calculated by the following formula:

$$RR = \frac{p^+c^-}{p^-c^+}$$

where p^+ = the number of patients possessing the particular HLA antigen,

c^- = the number of controls lacking the particular HLA antigen,

p^- = the number of patients lacking the particular HLA antigen, and

c^+ = the number of controls possessing the particular HLA antigen.

The higher the relative risk (above 1), the more frequent is the antigen among the patient population.

In contrast, the absolute risk (AR) is the chance an individual who possesses the disease-associated HLA has of actually developing the disease. It is calculated by the following formula:

$$AR = \frac{p^+}{c^+} \times P$$

where p^+ and c^+ are as above for the relative risk, and

P = prevalence of the disease in the general population.

The prototype of HLA-disease associations, that of **ankylosing spondylitis** with HLA-B27, can be used to illustrate these concepts. Ninety percent of American Caucasian patients with ankylosing spondylitis possess HLA-B27, compared to approximately 9% of American Caucasian controls. The relative risk is therefore $p^+c^- \div p^-c^+ = (90 \times 91) \div (10 \times 9) = 91$. Thus, an HLA-B27–positive individual has 91 times the risk of an HLA-B27–negative individual of developing the disease. The prevalence of clinically apparent severe ankylosing spondylitis is approximately 0.4%. The absolute risk is calculated as $90 \div 9 \times 0.004 = 0.04$. Therefore, of 100 HLA-B27–positive individuals, only 4 will actually develop clinically severe ankylosing spondylitis.

Because there is usually a significant difference in the frequency of a given antigen between different racial groups, it is always necessary to compare a patient group with a control population of the same race. Thus, for example, HLA-B27 is found in 48% of American black patients with ankylosing spondylitis, compared to 2% of American black controls, yielding a relative risk of 37.

In some cases, a disease may be associated with antigens determined by 2 different HLA loci. The actual association is frequently only with one antigen, but an apparent association with the second antigen is seen because of the phenomenon of linkage dis-

Table 6–9. Diseases of known or presumed autoimmunity associated with HLA-DR3.

Systemic lupus erythematosus
Sicca syndrome
Myasthenia gravis
Dermatitis herpetiformis
Insulin-dependent diabetes mellitus
Graves' disease
Idiopathic Addison's disease
Celiac disease
Autoimmune chronic active hepatitis

equilibrium between the genes determining the 2 antigens (see above). The actual or primary association can usually be ascertained by statistically testing each antigen for disease association with the influence of the second antigen removed.

Various diseases have been associated with antigens determined by almost all HLA loci. Thus, for example, idiopathic hemochromatosis has been associated with HLA-A3, ankylosing spondylitis with HLA-B27, rheumatoid arthritis with HLA-DR4, Sjögren's syndrome with MT2, and pauciarticular juvenile rheumatoid arthritis with complement haplotypes. A growing list of diseases has been associated with HLA-DR antigens, and this association has been interpreted by some to indicate that the DR antigens are marker antigens for closely linked immune response genes that somehow predispose to disease. An interesting finding in this regard is that several documented or presumed autoimmune diseases have been found to be associated with HLA-DR3 (Table 6–9). Space considerations preclude a listing of all HLA-disease associations.

Family studies provide an opportunity to establish definite linkage between a disease susceptibility gene and the HLA complex and may provide evidence for simple dominant or recessive inheritance. Thus, for example, a dominant disease susceptibility gene for ankylosing spondylitis with a penetrance of 0.38 has been found to be in very strong linkage disequilibrium with HLA-B27. Other HLA-linked disease susceptibility genes include those for idiopathic hemochromatosis, congenital adrenal hyperplasia, and insulin-dependent diabetes mellitus.

Several hypotheses have been advanced to explain HLA-disease associations. Three of these appear to be most likely. The first hypothesis holds that HLA antigens are merely markers for **immune response genes,** or **immune suppressive genes.** The homology of the HLA-D/DR region with the animal I regions and the increasing evidence for Ir and Is genes in humans make this an attractive theory. An implicit assumption of this hypothesis is that there is an agent responsible for a particular disease and that an Ir or Is gene regulates the ability to respond to the agent. The immunologic response (or lack thereof) to the agent may then predispose to disease. The finding that HLA-DR4 individuals (with or without rheumatoid arthritis) have an abnormally high response to collagen secondary to a lack of suppressor T cells for collagen lends credence to this postulate.

The second postulate suggests that HLA antigens may act as receptors for etiologic agents. If particular HLA antigens act as receptors for viruses, toxins, or other foreign substances and these substances are the etiologic agents for given diseases, then HLA-disease associations would result. The finding that HLA antigens bind Semliki Forest virus has been interpreted to support this postulate.

The third hypothesis is that of molecular mimicry. It postulates that the disease-associated HLA antigen is structurally and immunologically similar to the etiologic agent for the disease and further postulates one of 2 alternatives. The first alternative holds that because of the similarity between the etiologic agent and the HLA antigen, no immune response is mounted, and therefore the etiologic agent produces disease without any interference. The second alternative suggests that a vigorous immune response is mounted against the etiologic agent. Because of the similarity of the agent and the HLA antigen, the immune response is turned against the HLA antigen, and this "autoimmune" response then produces disease. The finding of cross-reactivity between certain microorganisms and certain HLA antigens supports this theory.

Other mechanisms besides those discussed above have also been suggested. It should be emphasized that different mechanisms may be operating in different HLA-disease associations and that more than one mechanism may be operating concurrently to produce disease. Further studies are necessary to clarify these issues.

•   •   •

References

General

Bodmer, WF (editor): *Histocompatibility Testing 1977.* Munksgaard, 1977.

Bodmer WF: The HLA system: Introduction. *Br Med Bull* 1978;**34**:213.

Dausset J, Svejgaard A (editors): *HLA and Disease.* Munksgaard, 1977.

Engleman E et al: Genetic control of the human immune response. *J Exp Med* 1980;**152(2-part 2).** [Entire issue.]

Schwartz BD, Shreffler DC: Genetic influences on the immune response. Page 49 in: *Clinical Immunology.* Parker CW (editor). Saunders, 1980.

Terasaki PI (editor): *Histocompatibility Testing 1980.* UCLA Tissue Typing Laboratory, Los Angeles, CA, 1980.

Nomenclature and Genetic Organization of the HLA System

Awdeh ZL, Alper CA: Inherited structural polymorphism of the fourth component of human complement. *Proc Natl Acad Sci USA* 1980;**77**:3576.

Duquesnoy RJ, Marrari M, Annen K: Association of the B-cell alloantigen MB1 with HLA-DRw1 and HLA-DRw2. *Transplant Proc* 1980;**12**:138.

Duquesnoy RJ, Marrari M, Annen K: Identification of an HLA-DR-associated system of B-cell alloantigens. *Transplant Proc* 1979;**11**:1757.

HLA Nomenclature Committee: Nomenclature for factors of the HLA system, 1980. *Tissue Antigens* 1980;**16**:113.

O'Neill GJ et al: Chido and Rodgers blood groups are distinct antigenic components of human complement C4. *Nature* 1978;**273**:668.

Park MS et al: Evidence for a second B-cell locus separate from the DR locus. *Transplant Proc* 1978;**10**:823.

Raum DD et al: The location of C2, C4 and BF relative to HLA-B and HLA-D. *Immunogenetics* 1981;**12**:473.

Schwartz BD, Luehrman LK, Rodey, GE: Public antigenic determinant on a family of HLA-B molecules: Basis for cross reactivity and a possible link with disease predisposition. *J Clin Invest* 1979;**64**:938.

Schwartz BD et al: HLA serological cross reactivity: HLA-B15 has two public antigens. *Hum Immunol* 1980;**1**:331.

Schwartz BD et al: A public antigenic determinant in the HLA-B5 crossreacting group: A basis for cross reactivity and a possible link with Behçet's disease. *Hum Immunol* 1980;**1**:37.

Shaw S, Johnson AH, Shearer G: Evidence for a new segregant series of B cell antigens that are encoded in the HLA-D region and that stimulate secondary allogeneic proliferative and cytotoxic response. *J Exp Med* 1980;**152**:565.

Shaw S et al: Family studies define a new histocompatibility locus, SB, between HLA-DR and GLO. *Nature* 1981; **293**:745.

HLA Typing

Amos DB, Pool P, Grier J: HLA-A, HLA-B, HLA-C, and HLA-DR. Page 978 in: *Manual of Clinical Immunology.* Rose NR, Friedman H (editors). American Society for Microbiology, 1980.

Carpenter CB, Strom TB: Transplantation immunology. Page 376 in: *Clinical Immunology.* Parker CW (editor). Saunders, 1980.

DeWolf WC, O'Leary JJ, Yunis EJ: Cellular typing. Page 1006 in: *Manual of Clinical Immunology.* Rose NR, Friedman H (editor). American Society for Microbiology, 1980.

Grumet FC, Fendly BM, Engleman EG: Monoclonal anti-HLA-B27 antibody (B27M[1]): Production and lack of detectable typing difference between patients with ankylosing spondylitis, Reiter's syndrome and normal controls. *Lancet* 1981;**2**:174.

National Institute of Health Transplantation and Immunology Branch Staff: NIH lymphocyte microcytotoxicity technique. Page 39 in: *Manual of Tissue Typing Techniques.* Ray JG Jr (editor). NIH Publication No. 80–545. US Department of Health, Education, and Welfare, 1979.

Terasaki PI, McClelland JD: Microdroplet assay of human serum cytotoxins. *Nature* 1964;**204**:998.

Tissue Distribution, Structure, and Function

Bergholtz BO, Thorsby E: HLA-D restriction of the macrophage-dependent response of immune human T lymphocytes to PPD in vitro: Inhibition of anti-HLA-DR antisera. *Scand J Immunol* 1978;**8**:63.

Biddison WE et al: Virus-immune cytotoxic T cells recognize structural differences between serologically indistinguishable HLA-A2 molecules. *Human Immunol* 1980;**1**:225.

Charron DJ, McDevitt HO: Characterization of HLA-D-region antigens by two-dimensional gel electrophoresis: Molecular genotyping. *J Exp Med* 1980; **152(2-Part 2)**:18S.

Corte G et al: Human Ia molecules carrying DC1 determinants differ in both α- and β-subunits from Ia molecules carrying DR determinants. *Nature* 1981;**292**:357.

Eijsvoogel VP et al: Position of a locus determining mixed lymphocyte reaction distinct from the known HL-A loci. *Eur J Immunol* 1972;**2**:413.

Engleman EG, McDevitt HO: A suppressor T cell of the mixed lymphocyte reaction specific for the HLA-D region in man. *J Clin Invest* 1978;**61**:828.

Goulmy E et al: Y antigen killing by T cells of women is restricted by HLA. *Nature* 1977;**266**:544.

Karr RW et al: Molecular relationships of the human B cell alloantigens MT2, MB3, MT4, and DR5. *J Immunol* 1982;**128**:1809.

Kaufman JF, Andersen RL, Strominger JL: HLA-DR antigens have polymorphic light chains and invariant heavy chains as assessed by lysine-containing tryptic peptide analysis. *J Exp Med* 1980;**152(2-Part 2)**:37S.

Kaufman JF, Strominger JL: The light chain of the HLA-DR molecule has a polymorphic N-terminal domain and an immunoglobulin-like C-terminal. *Nature.* [In press.]

Markert ML, Cresswell P: Polymorphism of human B-cell alloantigens: Evidence for three loci within the HLA system. *Proc Natl Acad Sci USA* 1980;**77**:6101.

McMichael AJ et al: HLA restriction of cell-mediated lysis of influenza virus–infected human cells. *Nature* 1977; **270**:524.

Payne R: The HLA complex: Genetics and implications in the immune response. Page 20 in: *HLA and Disease.* Dausset J, Svejgaard A (editors). Munksgaard, 1977.

Ploegh HL, Orr HT, Strominger JL: Major histocompatibility antigens: The human (HLA-A, -B, -C) and murine (H-2K, H-2D) Class I molecules. *Cell* 1981;**24**:287.

Rodey GF, Luehrman LK, Thomas DW: In vitro primary immunization of human peripheral blood lymphocytes to KLH: Evidence for HLA-D region restriction. *J Immunol* 1979;**123**:2250.

Schwartz BD, Luehrman LK, Rodey GE: HLA public determinants are target antigens of cell-mediated cytotoxicity. *J Exp Med* 1980;**152**(2-Part 2):340S.

Shackelford D, Strominger JL: Demonstration of structural polymorphism among HLA-DR light chains by two-dimensional gel electrophoresis. *J Exp Med* 1980;**152**:144.

Shackelford DA et al: Human B-cell alloantigens DC1, MT1, and LB12 are identical but distinct from the HLA-DR antigen. *Proc Natl Acad Sci USA* 1981;**78**:4566.

Immune Response Genes

Marsh DG, Meyers DA, Bias WB: Epidemiology and genetics of atopic allergy. *N Engl J Med* 1981;**305**:1551.

Sasazuki T et al: Association between an HLA haplotype and locus responsive to tetanus toxoid in man. *Nature* 1978;**272**:359.

Sasazuki T et al: An HLA-linked immune suppression gene in man. *J Exp Med* 1980;**152**(2-Part 2):297S.

Solinger AM, Bhatnagar R, Stobo J: Cellular, molecular, and genetic characteristics of T cell reactivity to collagen in man. *Proc Natl Acad Sci USA* 1981;**78**:3877.

Solinger AM, Stobo J: Immune response gene control of T cell reactivity to collagen in man: Association of unresponsiveness with suppressive T cells. *Clin Res* 1981;**29**:531A.

HLA and Disease

Dausset J, Svejgaard A (editors): *HLA and Disease*. Munksgaard, 1977.

Ryder LP, Anderson E, Svejgaard A (editors): *HLA and Disease Registry, Third Report*. Munksgaard, 1979.

Schwartz BD, Shreffler DC: Genetic influence on the immune response. Page 49 in: *Clinical Immunology*. Parker CW (editor). Saunders, 1980.

Terasaki PI (editor): *Histocompatibility Testing 1980*. UCLA Tissue Typing Laboratory, Los Angeles, 1980.

Development & Structure of Cells in the Immune System | 7

Steven D. Douglas, MD

HISTOLOGIC ORGANIZATION OF THE LYMPHORETICULAR SYSTEM

The lymphoid and reticuloendothelial tissues are composed primarily of a network of interlocking reticular cells and fibers with a supporting framework of reticular cells associated with lymphatic vessels. The main cell type that occupies the interstices of the reticular network is the lymphocyte. The other cell types present in various states of differentiation include lymphoblasts, plasma cells, monocyte-macrophages, endothelial cells, and rare eosinophils and mast cells. In mammals, the aggregate of lymphocytes constitutes about 1% of total body weight; the human body contains about 10^{12} lymphocytes. Lymphocytes in the tissues are in dynamic equilibrium with the circulating blood. Most lymphocytes are found in the spleen, lymph nodes, and Peyer's patches of the ileum. For functional purposes, the lymphoid system can be divided into 3 main units (Fig 7–1A and B): (1) the lymphoid precursors (stem cells); (2) T and B cell lineage, including subsets; and (3) antigen-specific clones.

Thymus

The thymus is derived embryologically from the third and fourth branchial pouches and differentiates as ventral out-pocketings from these pouches during the sixth week of fetal life. During vertebrate embryogenesis, the thymus is the first organ to begin the manufacture of lymphocytes. The thymus has the highest rate of cell production of any tissue of the body. Available evidence suggests that the vast majority of cells produced in the thymus die there. The thymus is central to the development and function of the immune system; however, it does not directly participate in immune reactions. In the adult, the thymus consists of many lobules, each containing a cortex and medulla (Fig 7–2). Lymphocytes produced by mitosis in the lobules appear to migrate to the medulla, where they further differentiate and then emigrate from the thymus. The medulla also contains thymic (Hassall's) corpuscles, composed of layers of epithelial cells. The function of thymic corpuscles is not known.

The thymus reaches its maximum size (as a percentage of body weight) in most vertebrates either at birth or shortly thereafter. Subsequently, the gland begins a gradual process of involution. In humans, the thymus decreases from 0.27% of total body weight to 0.02% between the ages of 5 and 15 years.

Neonatal removal of the thymus has profound effects on the immune system in many species of animals. In certain strains of mice, removal of the thymus leads to "wasting disease" (runting) with marked lymphoid atrophy and death. In other strains of mice, severe lymphopenia may occur, with depletion of cells from the paracortical areas of lymph nodes and periarteriolar regions of the spleen. These thymectomized animals have an impaired capacity to mount a humoral antibody response to certain antigens and impaired allograft rejection.

Impaired thymic development may be associated with immunologic deficiency disorders. The thymus also appears to have an endocrine function and to produce a number of thymic hormones. In the "nude" mouse, failure of development of the thymus and marked deficiency of mature T lymphocytes are noted. Histologic abnormalities of the thymus frequently occur in certain autoimmune diseases, particularly systemic lupus erythematosus and myasthenia gravis. These abnormalities include both lymphoid hyperplasia and the development of thymomas. This association between thymomas and autoimmunity suggests a possible relationship between thymic function and disorders of the immune system.

Bursa of Fabricius & Mammalian "Bursa Equivalents"

The bursa of Fabricius, which is present in birds, is a lymphoepithelial organ located near the cloaca. Histologically, the bursa is lined with pseudostratified epithelium and contains within it lymphoid follicles divided into cortical and medullary portions (see below). In chickens, removal of the bursa of Fabricius leads to marked deficiency in immunoglobulins, impairment in development of germinal centers, and absence of plasma cells. The "bursa-dependent" lymphoid system has been shown to be independent of the thymus. The mammalian equivalent of the bursa of Fabricius has not yet been identified.

The lymphoid system can thus be divided into 2 functional compartments: the thymus-dependent (derived, or processed) T lymphocytes and the "bursa equivalent" (non–thymus-processed, or thymus-independent) B lymphocytes.

Using the term B cell should not be taken to mean that the existence of a bursal organ in nonavian verte-

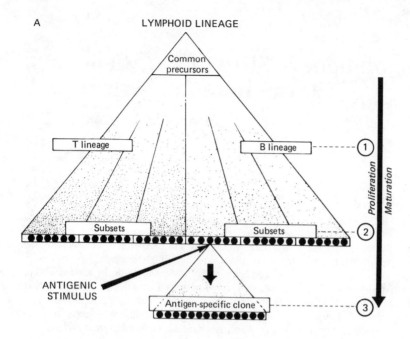

A   LYMPHOID LINEAGE

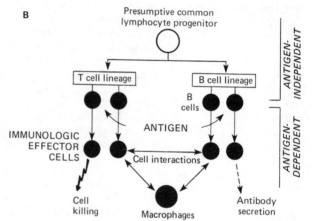

B   Presumptive common
lymphocyte progenitor

Figure 7-1. *A:* Lymphoid lineage. Precursors, T and B lineage, T and B subsets, and antigen-specific clones. *B:* Schematic overview illustrating antigen-independent and antigen-dependent events in the immune response. (Reproduced, with permission, from Zucker-Franklin D et al: *Atlas of Blood Cells: Function and Pathology.* Lea & Febiger, 1981.)

brates is assumed. The "bursa equivalent" may exist in several diffuse sites. Although the term B cell has commonly been interpreted as a reference to a bone marrow lymphocyte, a site of origin in the marrow has not been definitely established. Rodent bone marrow has relatively few B cells. Recent studies have used immunofluorescence staining of membrane and intracellular immunoglobulin to identify the earliest B cells that express immunoglobulin during embryonic development. The earliest cells to appear during development in the mouse occur in the fetal liver between days 10 and 13 of gestation. These **pre-B cells** are large lymphoid cells with diffuse cytoplasmic IgM. Following this (days 15–17 of gestation), smaller lymphoid cells appear with a narrow cytoplasmic rim staining for IgM. By 2 days after birth, lymphocytes which have surface IgM and are capable of mitogenic response to *Salmonella* lipopolysaccharide (LPS) are present in the spleen and bone marrow. Soon thereafter (days 10–20 in the mouse), there is an increase in

splenic lymphocytes which have membrane IgM and IgD. In humans, preliminary evidence indicates similar B cell ontogeny in the fetal liver and neonatal spleen and bone marrow.

Lymph Node Architecture

The lymphoid tissues may show varying degrees of histologic complexity. The lamina propria of the trachea, small intestine, and vaginal mucosa usually contains diffuse lymphoid tissue. Solitary lymph nodules may occur in the submucosa or mucosa of these tissues. The Peyer patches of the ileum (Fig 7–3) and the tonsillar ring of Waldeyer consist of collections of lymphoid nodules in the submucosa.

The lymph nodes are usually located at the junction of major lymphatic tracts. Afferent lymphatics enter the nodes at the subcapsular sinus, from which there is centripetal flow toward the major efferent lymphatic duct, which drains into the thoracic or right lymphatic duct (Fig 7–4). The histologic appearance

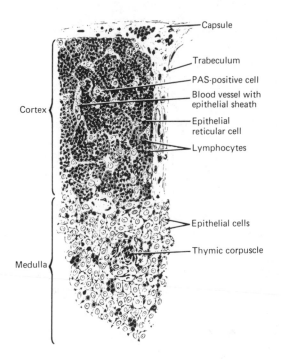

Capsule

Trabeculum

PAS-positive cell

Blood vessel with epithelial sheath

Epithelial reticular cell

Lymphocytes

Cortex

Epithelial cells

Thymic corpuscle

Medulla

Figure 7–2. Histologic organization of the thymus. The cortex is heavily infiltrated with lymphocytes. As a result, the epithelial cells become stellate and remain attached to one another by desmosomes. The medulla is closer to a pure epithelium, although it too is commonly infiltrated by lymphocytes. A large thymic corpuscle consisting of concentrically arranged epithelial cells is seen. The capsule and trabeculae are rich in connective tissue fibers (mainly collagen) and contain blood vessels and variable numbers of plasma cells, granulocytes, and lymphocytes. (Reproduced, with permission, from Weiss L: *The Cells and Tissues of the Immune System: Structure, Functions, Interactions.* Copyright © 1972. Reprinted by permission of Prentice-Hall, Inc., Englewood Cliffs, NJ.)

of the lymph node depends on the state of activity of the node. The "resting" lymph node, which has not been subjected to recent antigenic stimulation, can be morphologically divided into cortex, paracortical areas, and medulla. The margin between the cortex and paracortex may be obscure and contain many "resting" lymphocytes. Within the cortex, there are a few aggregates of lymphocytes called primary follicles. The paracortical areas contain postcapillary venules lined by cuboid epithelium, through which passes the blood supply to the node (Fig 7–5). In the "resting" node, the medulla is composed of connective tissue surrounding the hilum. The antigen-stimulated lymph node (Fig 7–6) shows an increased turnover of lymphocytes. Following antigenic stimulation, the paracortical area is hypertrophied and contains large lymphocytes and blastlike cells and is easily distinguished from the cortex. The cortex contains "germinal" centers composed of metabolically active and mitotic cells and the medulla contains numerous plasma cells which actively secrete antibody.

Spleen

The histologic organization of the spleen (Fig 7–7) reveals areas composed of lymphocytes which are predominantly adjacent to the proximal portion of the splenic arterioles. The "resting" spleen shows masses of lymphocytes surrounding these arterioles (the white pulp). Following antigenic stimulation, blast cells may be seen throughout the splenic follicles and often near the arteriole. The red pulp and marginal area between red and white pulp contain plasma cells. The splenic periarteriolar unit may be functionally similar to the paracortical area of lymph nodes.

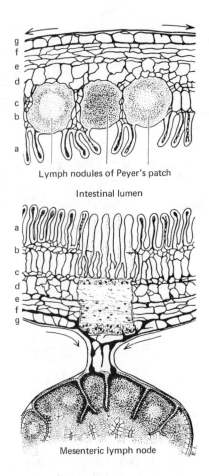

g
f
e
d
c
b

a

Lymph nodules of Peyer's patch

Intestinal lumen

a
b
c
d
e
f
g

Mesenteric lymph node

Figure 7–3. Histologic organization of a Peyer patch. Diagram of magnified sections through ileum: the upper from the area of a Peyer patch, the lower (with histologic structure suggested) from the opposite side of this intestine. The diagram illustrates the disposal of the lymphatic nets (black) in its layers and the direction of flow of chyle and lymph toward mesenteric lymph node. The letters *a, b,* and *c* designate the villi, lamina propria, and muscularis of tunica mucosa; *d,* the tunica submucosa; *e* and *f,* the circular and longitudinal layers of tunica muscularis; and *g,* the tunica serosa. (Reproduced, with permission, from Kampmeier OF: *Evolution and Comparative Morphology of the Lymphatic System.* Thomas, 1969.)

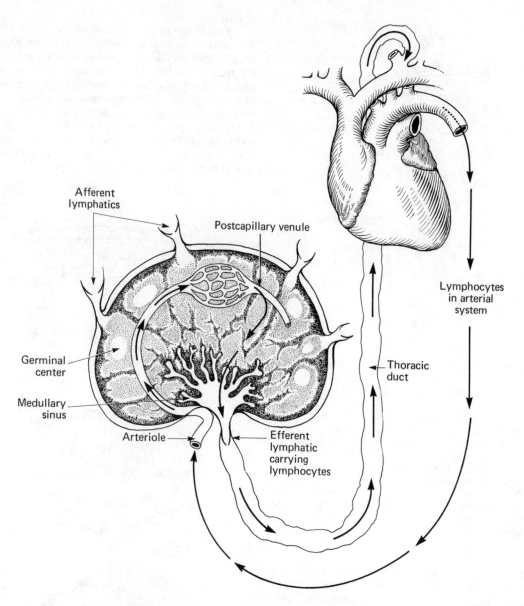

Figure 7–4. Diagrammatic representation of the circulation pathway of lymphoid cells in lymph through lymphatics, vascular system, and lymph nodes.

PHYLOGENY OF IMMUNITY
Daniel P. Stites, MD

The immune response originated in organisms with a nucleus (eukaryotic), probably in response to a need to distinguish self from nonself. Unicellular organisms (protozoa) have undergone evolutionary changes that allow them to differentiate food or invading microorganisms from autologous cell components. Multicellular organisms (metazoa) have also evolved highly complex and functionally integrated cells and tissues which exhibit varying degrees of immunologic individuality. Such cell-specific or tissue-specific antigens arise from a restricted phenotypic expression of the genome. In such organisms specialized cells or immunocytes have developed which protect the entire body from microbial invaders, from incursions of foreign tissue, and from diseases that may be caused by altered or neoplastic cells (immune surveillance).

The steps in the evolution of the immune response in animals cannot be retraced with any certainty. Study of the phylogenetic organization of the animal kingdom as it exists today can at best give only a hazy picture of the many evolutionary events that have resulted in the fantastically complex system of immunity possessed by higher vertebrates. Nevertheless, the study of immunity in extant species has justified the concept of an orderly progression in immunologic development as one ascends the phylogenetic tree.

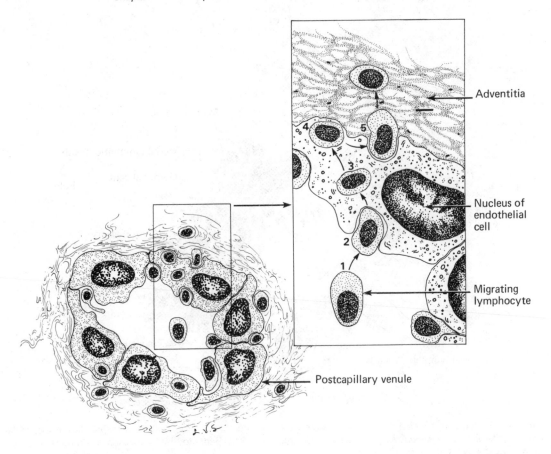

Adventitia

Nucleus of endothelial cell

Migrating lymphocyte

Postcapillary venule

Figure 7–5. Diagrammatic representation of migration of lymphocytes from a postcapillary venule in the paracortical area of a lymph node into the adventitia.

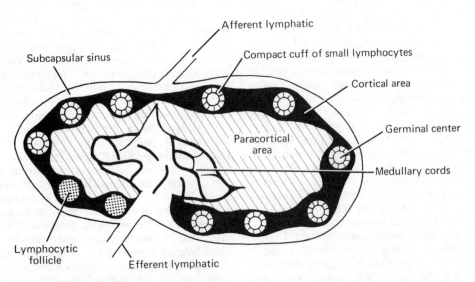

Subcapsular sinus

Afferent lymphatic

Compact cuff of small lymphocytes

Cortical area

Germinal center

Paracortical area

Medullary cords

Lymphocytic follicle

Efferent lymphatic

Figure 7–6. Diagram of immunologically active lymph node. (Reproduced, with permission, from Cottier H, Turk J, Sobin L: A proposal for a standardized system of reporting human lymph node morphology in relation to immunological function. *Bull WHO* 1972;**47**:377.)

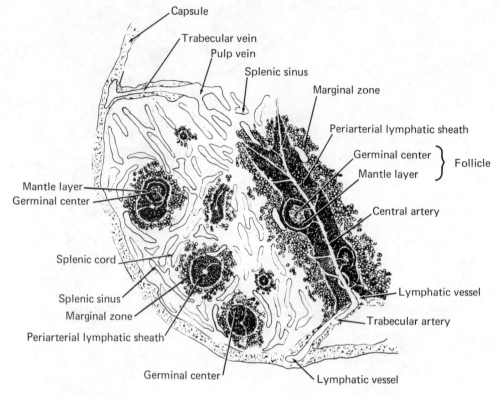

Figure 7–7. Histologic organization of the spleen. (Reproduced, with permission, from Weiss L: *The Cells and Tissues of the Immune System: Structure, Function, Interactions.* Copyright © 1972. Reprinted by permission of Prentice-Hall, Inc., Englewood Cliffs, NJ.)

Furthermore, a great deal has been learned about many of the individual functional units in the immune response by detailed study of lower species that have a limited capacity for immune responses—eg, in invertebrates, one can examine a primitive form of cellular immunity in the absence of specific antibodies.

From an evolutionary standpoint, cellular immunity and particularly phagocytosis preceded the development of antibody production in animals. Invertebrates characteristically demonstrate primitive forms of graft rejection and phagocytosis, but in no invertebrate species have molecules been identified that have a functional or physicochemical structure analogous to vertebrate immunoglobulins. On the other hand, all vertebrate species synthesize antibody, reject grafts, and exhibit immunologic memory. Thus, there is a relatively sharp delineation between the complexity of immunity in invertebrates and vertebrates; no clearly transitional forms have thus far been identified.

The fully developed immune response is characterized by **specificity** and **anamnesis.** These 2 essential criteria should be borne in mind when distinguishing true immunity from primitive or paraimmunologic phenomena in the phylogenetic analysis which follows.

IMMUNITY IN INVERTEBRATES

Survival of unicellular invertebrate species has been achieved to a large degree by their remarkable reproductive capacity rather than by development of specific immune responses to deal with environmental challenges. Perhaps the most primitive type of self-recognition mechanism is the ability of certain protozoa to reject transplantation of foreign nuclei. However, this phenomenon is really quasi-immunologic and probably depends on enzymatic rather than specific antigenic differences among various species.

All invertebrate species do exhibit some form of self-versus-nonself recognition (Fig 7–8). However, true cellular immunity with specific graft rejection and anamnesis has been conclusively demonstrated only in certain earthworms (annelids) and corals (coelenterates) (Table 7–1). Although invertebrates with coelomic cavities possess a variety of humoral substances such as bacteriolysins, hemolysins, and opsonins, none of these have been specifically induced by immunization nor do these rather ill-defined substances have any known physicochemical similarities with vertebrate antibodies. The study of invertebrate immunology has been impeded by the difficult problems of in vivo laboratory cultivation of many species, the unavailability of safe anesthetics, and the relatively

Table 7–1. Evolution of immunity in invertebrates.*

Phylum or Subphylum	Graft Rejection	Immunologic Specificity of Graft Rejection	Immunologic Memory	Phagocytosis	Encapsulation	Nonspecific Humoral Factors	Phagocytic Ameboid Coelomocytes	Leukocyte Differentiation	Inducible Specific Antibodies
Protozoa	Yes. Enzyme incompatibility.	No	No	Yes; whole organism.	No	No	No	No	No
Porifera (sponges)	Yes. Aggregation inhibition; species-specific glycoprotein.	Yes	Yes	No	Yes	No	No	No	No
Coelenterata (corals, jellyfish, sea anemones)	Yes; with graft necrosis.	Yes	Yes, short term.	No	Hyperplastic growth around graft.	No	No	No	No
Annelida (earthworms)	Yes	Yes. First and second set graft rejection.	Short term, either positive or negative.	Yes	Yes	Yes. Nonspecific hemagglutinins, ciliate lysins, bacteriocidins.	Yes. Chemotaxis to bacteria.	Probable PHA response in coelomocyte.	No
Mollusca	Yes	?	?	Yes	Yes	Yes. Hemagglutinins act as opsonins.	Yes	No	No
Arthropoda	Yes	?	?	Yes	Yes	Yes	Yes	No	No
Echinodermata	Yes. Prolonged 4–6 months.	Yes. Specific second set graft rejection.	Short term only.	Yes	Yes	Yes. Hemolysins.	Yes	Yes. Cellular infiltrate in graft rejection.	No
Protochordata (tunicates)	Yes. Genetically determined alloimmunity.	Probable. Tolerance also possible.	Yes	Yes	Yes	Yes	Yes. Macrophage, lymphocyte, and eosinophil.	Yes. Lymphocytes present which form E rosettes and respond to PHA.	No

*Modified from Hildemann WH, Reddy AL: *Fed Proc* 1973;**322**:2188.

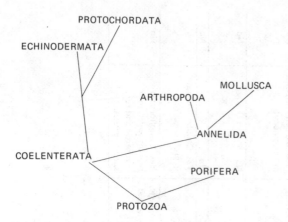

Figure 7–8. Simplified scheme of invertebrate phylogeny.

small amounts of humoral or cellular elements recoverable for in vitro study. Nevertheless, a fascinating array of primitive or quasi-immunologic phenomena have been identified, including the following: (1) self-recognition, (2) phagocytosis, (3) encapsulation, (4) allo- and xenograft rejection, (5) humoral defenses, and (6) leukocyte differentiation.

The most primitive invertebrates, the protozoa, are capable of phagocytosis and rejection of foreign nuclei through enzymatic incompatibilities. Very early experiments (1907) with sponges (porifera) demonstrated species-specific reaggregation of dispersed colonies which could be clearly identified by different colors in individual parent colony members. Failure of different species of sponges to re-form colonies is regulated by specific surface glycoproteins and requires divalent cations, Ca^{2+} and Mg^{2+}. This phenomenon is in a sense a primitive type of graft rejection.

Chronic tissue graft rejection with necrosis of engrafted tissue first appears with the coelenterates (corals, jellyfish, and sea anemones). Allograft rejection with specific recognition and short-term anamnestic response has clearly been demonstrated in *Montipora verrucosa,* the reef-building coral, and recently in a Hawaiian purple marine sponge, *Callysporia diffusa.* Bilateral specific destruction of engrafted tissues occurred when allogeneic foreign colony grafts were attempted. This example of transplantation immunity in a primitive invertebrate also had some degree of alloimmune memory. In corals, allograft rejection results in cellular proliferation in the vicinity of the foreign graft and is reminiscent of proliferation that occurs both in vivo and in vitro in engrafted vertebrate species. There is considerable evidence for specific immune responsiveness with memory in annelids that have received skin allografts or xenografts. However, a curious finding of either enhanced survival or rejection in second set grafts remains unexplained. Coelomocytes, the wandering ameboid phagocytes found in all coelomate (those with a coelom) invertebrates (annelids, mollusks, arthropods, and echinoderms) are capable of transferring immunity to tissue grafts. These cells contain a subpopulation which can

respond to the T cell mitogen PHA with increased DNA synthesis. However, a system of cellular receptors or genetically determined histocompatibility antigens remains to be demonstrated. Mollusks and arthropods appear to lack the form of transplantation immunity demonstrable in annelids, but conclusive experiments on this point are lacking. Hemolymph cells present in some insect larvae are phagocytic and can form rosettes with human or sheep erythrocytes. However, no Fc or C3 receptors have been demonstrated on these cells. Transplantation immunity in echinoderms is partially developed, with both second set rejection and short-term memory for xenografts demonstrable in sea stars and sea cucumbers.

The highest form of invertebrate—the tunicates or protochordates—has a special position in the evolutionary transition from invertebrates to vertebrates. Tunicates possess features which make them close ancestors of the vertebrates, including a notochord, pharyngeal gill slits, dorsal tubular nerve chord, and various self-replicating cell populations. Lymphatic nodules are present, and differentiated leukocytes circulate in hemolymph. Tunicate lymphocytes form sheep red blood cell rosettes and can respond in vitro to PHA. An incompletely understood system of genetically determined antigens responsible for the rejection of fusion between various tunicate species has been described.

In addition to acting as effector cells for graft rejection, the coelomocytes are avid phagocytes. Intracoelomic injections of radiolabeled bacteria or aggregated proteins are cleared at rapid rates by these remarkable cells. There is no accelerated rate of clearance (immune elimination) with subsequent injections. When confronted with particles too large to be engulfed, the coelomocytes are capable of walling them off or encapsulating them. This process of encapsulation of foreign debris is reminiscent of abscess formation in vertebrates and can effectively wall off a noxious substance from contact with host tissues.

Coelomate invertebrates all possess a group of poorly characterized nonspecific humoral substances present in the hemolymph bathing the coelomic cavity. Functionally, these substances agglutinate foreign red blood cells, inactivate ciliary movements, kill some bacteria, and, in mollusks, can enhance phagocytosis by coelomocytes, ie, they are opsonins. These naturally occurring agglutinins probably are best considered lectins similar to those found in plants (eg, PHA or ConA). The action of all of these humoral defense mechanisms is nonspecific, and there is no conclusive evidence for structural or functional homology with vertebrate immunoglobulins.

Leukocyte cellular differentiation appears first with echinoderms and protochordates. Radiosensitive lymphocytes have been identified in tunicates, but their function is unknown. Eosinophilic leukocytes and macrophages are also present. The results of experiments directed at elucidation of the possible diverse immunologic functions of leukocytes in these phyla are awaited with great interest.

IMMUNITY IN VERTEBRATES

The most advanced invertebrates, the protochordates, are probably the ancestors of the true chordates from which all higher vertebrates are descended (Fig 7–9). However, at the level of the most primitive extant vertebrate class, the agnathae, an entirely new component in the immune system is apparent—antibody. Specific antibody synthesis is a property possessed by all vertebrates. Cellular immunity, present in a primitive form in invertebrates, is highly developed and immunologically specific in all vertebrates. Graft rejection is accelerated after primary sensitization, and a true second set rejection phenomenon occurs. However, some difference in the expression of immunologic functions is evident between warm-blooded and cold-blooded animals.

The hallmark of vertebrate immunity is the presence of a truly 2-component immune system, best demonstrated in birds, where 2 independent central lymphoid organs exist—the thymus, which controls cellular immunity, and the bursa, which determines antibody-producing capacity (Table 7–2).

The evolution in vertebrates of immunoglobulins and of humoral immunity is discussed in detail in Chapter 4. Selected aspects of the anatomic organization of lymphatic organs and functional capacity of T cells and cellular immunity will be considered.

Current studies suggest the presence of ''T-like'' and ''B-like'' lymphocytes in teleost fishes based on their physical separability, mitogen responses, and surface characteristics. However, the case for a functional dualism between T and B cells is not as strong for agnathae or elasmobranchs (sharks and rays). The fact that some lymphocytes can respond to PHA and ConA combined with the presence of carrier effects in selected antibody responses suggests that at least a primitive form of T cell immunity exists in fish. Teleost thymus tissue is itself capable of antibody synthesis, and serum antibody in fish is restricted to the IgM class. The T cell–dependent switch from IgM to IgG

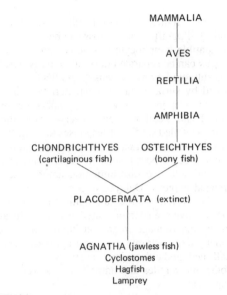

Figure 7–9. Simplified scheme of the vertebrate subphylum. Each major class is represented in capitals.

antibody present in higher vertebrates fails to occur at this phylogenetic stage. Nevertheless, lymphocyte heterogeneity exists in regard to the ability to respond to mitogens and allogeneic cells, at least in the teleosts. Polyclonal activation of ''B-like'' cells from the teleost fish results in proliferation and terminal differentiation to plasma cells. Furthermore, graft rejection with anamnesis and specificity is clearly evident in this as in all other vertebrate classes.

T and B cell lymphocytes are first clearly evident with the amphibia. In this class, the thymus functions as a central lymphoid organ whose cells colonize peripheral lymphatic tissues. Cortical and medullary differentiation of the thymus occurs during larval development. Thymectomy in the *Xenopus* toad results in diminished T cell mitogen responses but preserves B

Table 7–2. Immunologic features exhibited by various vertebrate classes.

Class	Lymphocytes	Plasma Cells	Thymus	Spleen	Lymph Nodes	Bursa	Antibodies	Allograft Rejection
Agnatha (jawless fish)	+	−	PRIM	PRIM	−	−	+	+
Chondrichthyes (cartilaginous fish)								
Primitive	+	−	+	+	−	−	+	+
Advanced	+	+	+	+	−	−	+	+
Osteichthyes (bony fish)	+	+	+	+	−	−	+	+
Amphibia	+	+	+	+	+	−	+	+
Reptilia	+	+	+	+	+(?)	−	+	+
Aves	+	+	+	+	+(?)	+	+	+
Mammalia	+	+	+	+	+	−	+	+

PRIM = primitive.

? = Indicates some question regarding the presence of lymphoid structures under consideration, although such structures or their functional counterparts may have been described.

cell function. Thymectomy also results in loss of ability to reject allografts, and the loss can be restored by histocompatible lymphocyte infusions. Lymphocytes of *Xenopus* can be separated into functionally heterogeneous subpopulations by density gradient centrifugation and by surface marker characteristics. In the salamander, responses of various lymphocyte subclasses to T and B cell mitogens closely parallel those in rodents. Detailed studies of responses to antigens in the newt, *Triturus viridescens,* demonstrate heterogeneous lymphocyte populations in hapten carrier responses and selective discrimination among chemically related haptens. Delayed hypersensitivity reactions in the axolotl, a urodele amphibian, sensitized with DNFB have been demonstrated histologically and in vitro by macrophage migration inhibition. K cell cytotoxicity demonstrable in typical antibody-dependent cell-mediated cytotoxicity reactions is present in poikilothermic reptiles and amphibians as well as in birds and mammals.

Reptiles have T cells with regulatory and helper functions. A molecule similar to IgD has been identified on tortoise B lymphocytes. Studies have demonstrated specificity of T and B cells in alligators to stimulation by mitogens, physical separation on glass wool, and surface markers akin to mammalian and avian lymphocytes. With the exception of a clearcut analog of the bursa of Fabricius, reptiles have a fully differentiated lymphoid system that closely resembles that found in mammals and birds.

Graft rejection occurs in all vertebrate species. However, in agnathae and cartilaginous fish, skin grafts are rejected at a much slower rate than in higher vertebrates. Nevertheless, these relatively primitive vertebrates exhibit typical accelerated second set graft rejection. Bony fish have a highly complex histocompatibility system and consequently exhibit various types of immunologic tissue rejection. Most amphibians are capable of typical graft rejection, but urodeles and apoda seem to have developed only slow, chronic rejection capacities. Reptiles, birds, and mammals show chronic rejection of first set grafts and accelerated rejection of second set grafts. The evident evolutionary trend in vertebrates from slow to accelerated graft rejection may actually reflect weak expression of histocompatibility antigens rather than any inherent deficiency in the effector mechanism of cellular immunity. A highly polymorphic histocompatibility system with strong antigens such as exists in rodents and primates favors accelerated rejection.

An interesting and unique feature of vertebrate immunity is the effect of temperature on immune expression in some species. Cold-blooded (ectothermic) classes of fish, amphibians, and reptiles have no internal regulation of temperature, as contrasted to warm-blooded birds and mammals. Ectotherms have accelerated immune responses at warmer temperatures. In amphibians, the inductive or recognition phases of the immune response are independent of temperature, but the productive phase shows marked temperature dependence. Experimentally, this phenomenon has been demonstrated by the failure of graft rejection in engrafted animals maintained at low temperatures but the immediate onset of rejection when an animal engrafted in the cold is placed in a warmer environment.

Immediate hypersensitivity reactions in vertebrates serve to protect against parasitic infections but also produce atopic diseases. Anaphylactic reactions occur early in phylogeny. Invertebrates, particularly earthworms and crustaceans, can be passively sensitized with heterocytotropic antibody which can cause smooth muscle contractions when presented with sensitizing antigens. Homocytotropic antibodies that sensitize mast cells from the same organism first appear in vertebrates at the level of birds. Both IgG and IgE antibodies function as reagins in many vertebrate species. Much more needs to be learned about the evolution and function of this important aspect of immunity.

Several generalizations regarding phylogenetic emergence of immunity are possible. First, primitive and quasi-immunologic phenomena are present in the simplest forms of extant animal species. Second, cellular immunity precedes humoral immunity in evolution. And third, a truly bifunctional immune system with dual central lymphoid organs in a highly differentiated form is the most recent immunologic evolutionary development.

LYMPHOID CELLS

Morphology

The term lymphocyte refers to a cell type which can be defined by certain morphologic features. Visualized by light microscopy, lymphocytes are ovoid cells 8–12 μm in diameter. They contain densely packed nuclear chromatin and a small rim of cytoplasm that stains pale blue with Romanovsky stains. The cytoplasm contains a number of azurophilic granules and occasional vacuoles. In the area where most cytoplasmic organelles are present (Golgi zone), the cytoplasmic rim is thickened. Phase contrast microscopy of living lymphocytes reveals a characteristic slow ameboid movement which gives a "hand mirror" contour. Histochemical studies have demonstrated nucleolar and cytoplasmic ribonucleoprotein. The cytoplasm contains some glycogen. The lymphocyte contains a number of lysosomal hydrolases. Mitochondrial enzymes are also present in the lymphocyte cytoplasm. By conventional light microscopy, the 2 main lymphocyte subpopulations (T cells and B cells) are indistinguishable.

Electron microscopic examination of the "resting" circulating lymphocyte (Fig 7–10) reveals a dense heterochromatic nucleus which contains some less electron-dense areas referred to as euchromatin. The nucleolus contains agranular, fibrillar, and granular zones. The nucleus is surrounded by the nuclear membrane complex. The cytoplasm of the resting lymphocyte contains organelle systems characteristic of eukaryotic cells (Golgi zone, mitochondria, ribo-

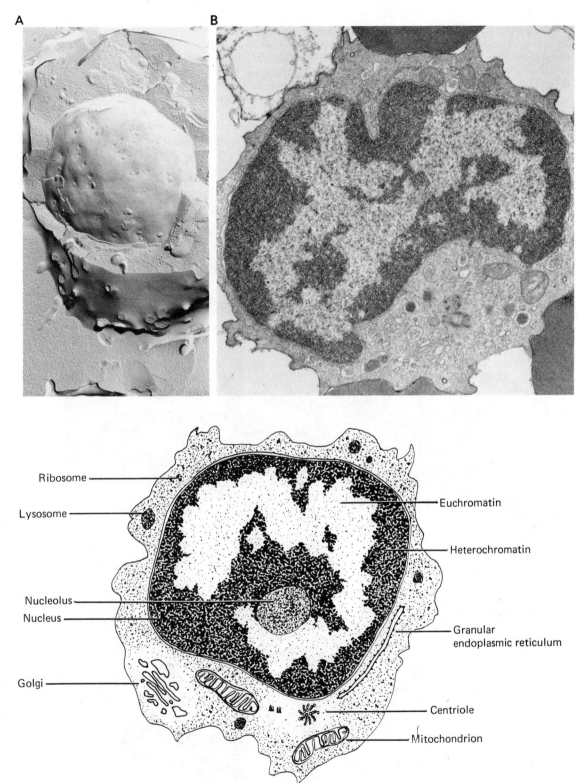

Figure 7–10. *Top: A:* Freeze-fracture electron micrograph of normal human circulating lymphocyte. (× 25,000.) *B:* Transmission electron micrograph of normal circulating human lymphocyte. (× 33,000.) ***Bottom:*** Diagrammatic representation of the micrograph shown at top right.

somes, lysosomes). Many of these organelle systems, however, are poorly developed. There are many free ribosomes, occasional ribosome clusters, and occasional strands of granular endoplasmic reticulum. A small Golgi zone is present which contains vacuoles, vesicles, and occasional lysosomes. Microtubules are often present, and there are frequent typical mitochondria. The cytoplasm usually contains several lysosomes. The plasma membrane of the lymphocyte is a typical unit membrane which may show small projec-

tions and, under some circumstances, longer pseudopodia or uropods. Thus, plasma membrane specialization may be related to cell attachment to surfaces or to cell-cell interaction.

In thin sections of cells examined by transmission electron microscopy, the lymphocyte can be distinguished from cells of the plasma cell series by the extensive development and dilatation of granular endoplasmic reticulum and a well-developed Golgi zone in plasma cells (Fig 7–11). The lymphocyte can be

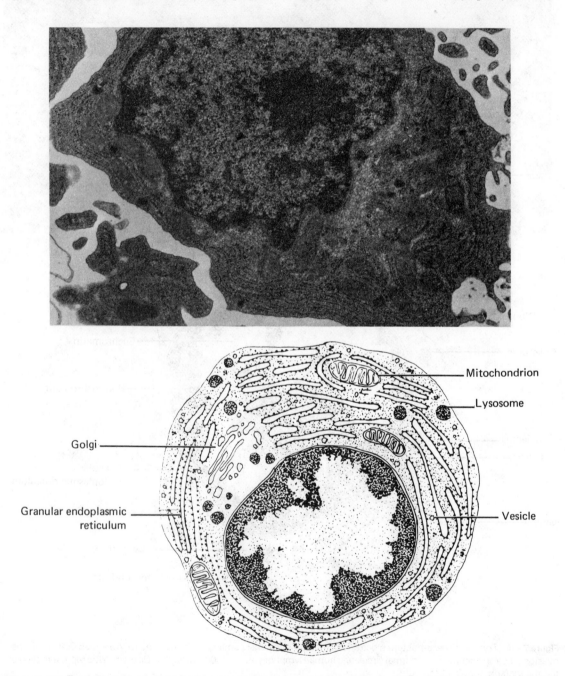

Figure 7–11. *Top:* Electron micrograph of bone marrow plasma cell from patient with multiple myeloma. (× 19,000.) *Bottom:* Diagrammatic representation of cell shown at top.

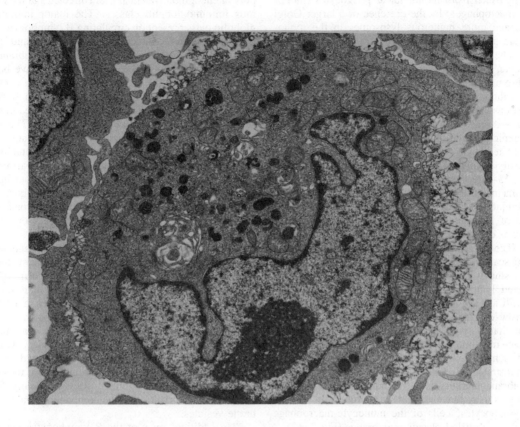

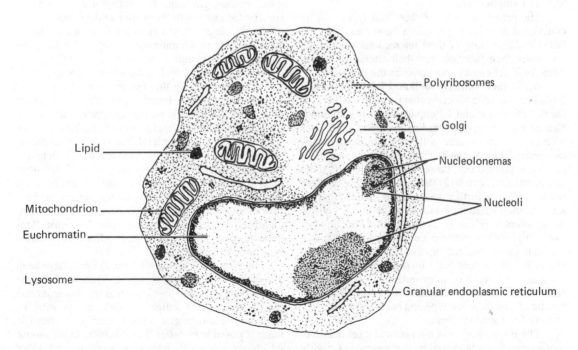

Figure 7–12. *Top:* Electron micrograph of a cell from a 3-day culture of human lymphocytes incubated with phytohemagglutinin (lymphoblast). (× 15,000.) *Bottom:* Diagrammatic representation of lymphoblast.

distinguished from mononuclear phagocytes (mono-cyte-macrophages) by the presence of a larger Golgi zone and more numerous lysosomes in the mono-nuclear phagocyte.

The blast cell, in contrast to the small lym-phocyte, has a nucleus characterized by loosely packed euchromatin, a large nucleolus, and a large cytoplas-mic volume containing numerous polyribosomes and an extensively developed Golgi zone (Fig 7–12). Blast cells are present in lymph nodes in vivo following antigenic stimulation, or in cultures of lymphocytes stimulated in vitro with phytomitogens. The blast cell is easily distinguished by light microscopy and mea-sures 15–30 μm in diameter. It is possible to study the plasma membranes of these cells by the freeze fracture technique; platinum-carbon replicas reveal the pres-ence of intramembranous particles in all membrane systems examined.

The surface topography of cells can be examined using scanning electron microscopy (Fig 7–13). Some early studies reported that thymus cells and thymus-derived lymphocytes have smaller numbers of mi-crovilli and are smoother than the more villous bone marrow–derived B lymphocytes. However, it is now clear that B lymphocytes have a wide spectrum of surface morphologic characteristics, and in some later studies no differences between T and B cells were demonstrable. Scanning electron microscopy, with membrane markers and functional studies of lym-phocytes, may prove valuable in the future. In contrast to lymphocytes, cells of the monocyte-macrophage series have ruffled plasma membranes (Fig 7–13).

T & B Lymphocytes

The general features of these cell types will be considered in order to provide a basic and more de-tailed understanding of their interactions in immune responses, their function, and their alterations in im-munologic deficiency and autoimmune diseases.

A. Surface Markers on B and T Lymphocytes:
It has been possible to define characteristic markers for the detection of B and T lymphocytes using immuno-fluorescence microscopy, radioautography, or rosettes with erythrocytes coated with immunoproteins. Cer-tain generalizations can be made from these studies. It should be pointed out, however, (1) that overlapping cell populations exist; (2) that the specificity of these markers requires further investigation; and (3) that the identification of subpopulations of B and T cells is more complex. There is an important distinction be-tween a plasma membrane **determinant,** which is a macromolecule present on the cell membrane, de-tected by labeled antibody methods and identifying particular cell types or subpopulations, and a **recep-tor,** which is a macromolecule which may be charac-teristic of a specific cell type and has a known binding affinity for a specific ligand.

The B lymphocyte in humans and most mamma-lian species is characterized by the presence of readily detectable surface immunoglobulin. Surface immuno-globulin can be demonstrated using fluoresceinated polyvalent or monovalent antisera directed against var-ious immunoglobulin classes. The major immuno-globulin class present on circulating B lymphocytes is IgM, present in monomeric form. IgD, IgG, and IgA may also be present on B lymphocyte membranes. Under some circumstances, IgM and IgD have both been detected on the same lymphocyte. The occur-rence of various immunoglobulin classes on B cell plasma membranes and intracellularly is related to the sequence of B lymphocyte differentiation. The se-quence of pre-B cell lymphocyte differentiation is initiated from an Ig$^-$ precursor cell present in fetal liver and bone marrow. This cell feeds into a compartment of cells that synthesize μ heavy chains without light chains. These cells subsequently mature to become small surface IgM-bearing B cells. The transition from pre-B cell to B lymphocyte requires accessory cell interactions.

A property of most membrane determinants and receptors which is related to membrane fluidity is their ability to undergo redistribution and **"capping."** When a membrane component combines with its com-plementary molecule, it first undergoes a meta-bolically independent reorganization into patches over the entire cell surface (**"patching"**). It may then undergo a metabolically dependent process by which the marker is topographically redistributed from dispersed patches to localization at one pole of the cell ("capping"). This "capping" event is usually fol-lowed by interiorization of the components via mem-brane vesicles.

In addition, most of the B lymphocytes have a receptor for antigen-antibody complexes, or aggre-gated immunoglobulin. This receptor appears to be specific for a site on the Fc portion of the immunoglob-ulin molecule and is known as the **Fc receptor.** It has been possible to demonstrate a receptor for the third component of complement on some B cells, using erythrocytes coated with antibody and complement. Lymphocytes bearing this receptor have been called complement receptor lymphocytes. The complement receptor is not a single molecular species, and recent evidence indicates distinct membrane binding sites for C3b, C3d, C4, C1q, and B1H. The complement recep-tor has been shown to be distinct from the Fc receptor. Recently, specific alloantibodies (anti-p,23,30) have been described that recognize unique antigens on human B lymphocytes, probably the human counter-part of murine Ia antigens. B cells have also been identified by using antisera prepared against lym-phocytes from patients with the B cell form of chronic lymphocytic leukemia.

In mice, several characteristic antigens have been demonstrated on T lymphocytes. These include the theta (θ) antigen, antigens known as thymus-leukemia (TL) antigens, and antigens known as Lyt antigens (lymphocyte alloantigens). The Lyt antigen system has made it possible to define T cell subsets in the mouse which are related to helper, suppressor, and killer functions. The occurrence of an immunoglobulin-like molecule which has V$_H$ regions on T lymphocytes and

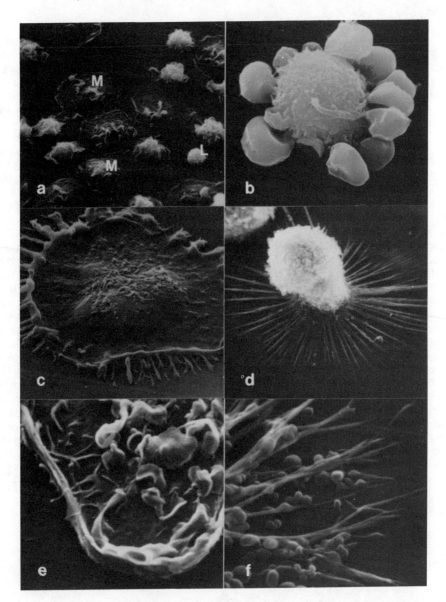

Figure 7–13: Scanning electron micrographs: *a:* Human peripheral blood lymphocytes (L) and spread monocytes (M). (× 750.) *b:* Rabbit pulmonary alveolar macrophage rosetting with sheep erythrocytes coated with IgM antibody and complement (EAC). (× 3800.) *c:* Human peripheral blood monocyte spread on antigen-antibody complexes; prominent microextensions. (×3800.) (Bumol TF, Douglas SD: *Cell Immunol* 1977;**34:**70.) *d:* Human monocyte detached from microexudate-coated surface with EDTA; there is marked ruffling of the cell body in comparison to *c* and prominent cytoplasmic filopodia are evident. (× 1500.) (Ackerman SK, Douglas SD: *J Immunol* 1978;**120:**1372.) *e:* Prominent cytoplasmic rim of human monocyte maintained in culture for 2 weeks. (× 4800.) *f:* Filopodia with bleblike processes, monocyte maintained in culture for 2 weeks. (× 8400.) (Zuckerman SH, Ackerman SK, Douglas SD: *Immunology.* 1979;**38:**401.)

its possible role as the T cell antigen receptor remains a central unanswered question in immunology.

In humans, T lymphocytes have the property of forming rosettes with sheep erythrocytes, and this marker is used to identify human T cells. Many human peripheral T lymphocytes have membrane receptors for the Fc portion of IgG and of monomeric IgM. T cells with receptors for the Fc portion of IgG and IgM

are detected using antisera prepared against ox erythrocytes. Similar to the murine Lyt antigens, these T cell subpopulations alter the differentiation of B cells into immunoglobulin secreting cells. Tμ cells have a helper function, whereas Tγ cells have a suppressor function. In addition, antisera prepared against brain tissue react with T cells, as do antisera prepared in rabbits injected with thymocytes. Various markers

Table 7–3. Lymphocyte distribution in various tissues in humans.

Tissue	Approximate %	
	T Cells	B Cells
Peripheral blood	55–75	15–30
Bone marrow	< 25	> 75
Lymph	> 75	< 25
Lymph node	75	25
Spleen	50	50
Tonsil	50	50
Thymus	> 75	< 25

have been used to determine the distribution of B and T lymphocytes in tissues (Table 7–3).

Flow microfluorimetry and the development of the hybridoma technique for the production of monoclonal antibodies have led to major advances in the analysis of lymphocyte subpopulations. Several monoclonal antibodies have been developed that react with human T cells and their subsets. The reactivity of normal peripheral blood lymphocytes with these reagents indicates that these markers can delineate helper (Th), suppressor (Ts), and cytotoxic (Tc) T lymphocyte subpopulations. These reagents have been applied to the investigation of lymphocyte populations in clinical diseases, and significant population imbalances have been demonstrated.

A series of monoclonal antibodies to T cell membrane markers have been developed in the past few years and used for the delineation of functional subsets of T cells. The reactivity of these antibodies with

human thymocytes at different stages of maturation is shown in Table 7–4. Anti-T1 is a monoclonal antibody reactive with 100% of peripheral T cells but only 10% of thymocytes. The $T1^+$ thymocytes are the only thymocytes capable of reactivity in mixed lymphocyte culture. Anti-T3 has essentially identical reactivity. Anti-T4 reacts with 75% of thymocytes and 60% of peripheral T cells; it appears to identify a helper or inducer subset of peripheral blood T cells, which also are the only peripheral T cells that show a proliferative response to soluble antigens. This $T4^+$ subset is roughly equivalent to the Th_1^+ (Th_2^-) subset defined by heteroantisera. Anti-T5 and anti-T8 react with about 80% of thymocytes and 20–30% of peripheral T cells; anti-T5 identifies a subset with both suppressor and cytotoxic capacity, similar to the Th_2^+ subset. Anti-T6, anti-T9, and anti-T10 react almost exclusively with thymocytes and not with peripheral T cells. The earliest thymocytes bear T9 and T10 markers, or T10 alone; the T10 antigen is apparently lost when the cells leave the thymus for the peripheral compartment. It has been suggested that the $T5^+$ subset in humans is analogous to the murine Lyt-2,3 subset, which mediates both cytotoxic and suppressor functions, and that the human $T4^+$ subset is analogous to the murine Lyt-1 subset, which has helper functions. The $T4^+$ and $T5^+$ subsets make up about 80–90% of the peripheral blood T cells; the remainder appear to be equivalent to the JRA^+ subset defined by autoantisera, which probably has feedback regulatory function. Monoclonal antibodies with specificities similar to those of the anti-T reagents are now available commercially from several manufacturers (anti-OKT, anti-Leu).

Table 7–4. Stages of human thymocytes as defined by reactivity with monoclonal antibodies.*

Cell Stage	Cell Type	Antibody Reactivity
I. Early thymocyte	Thy-1	$T10^+$
	Thy-2	$T10^+, T9^+$
	(Thy-3)†	
II. Common thymocyte	Thy-4	$T10^+, T6^+, T4^+, T5^+, T8^+$
	(Thy-5)†	
	(Thy-6)†	
III. Mature thymocyte	Thy-7	$T10^+, T1^+, T3^+, T4^+$
	Thy-8	$T10^+, T1^+, T3^+, T5^+, T8^+$

*Adapted from Reinherz EL, Schlossman SF: *Cell* 1980;**19**:821.
†Hypothetical transition cell between stages.

Table 7–5. Selectivity of lymphocyte mitogens for T and B cells.

	Human		Mouse	
	T	B	T	B
Phytomitogens (lectins)				
Phytohemagglutinin (PHA)	+	?	+	–
Concanavalin A (ConA)	+	–	+	–
Wax bean	+	–	n.s.	
Pokeweed mitogen (PWM)	+	+	+	+
Insoluble PHA, PWM, ConA	+	+	+	+
Bacterial products				
Lipopolysaccharide (LPS)	–	–	–	+
Aggregated tuberculin	n.s.		–	+
Miscellaneous				
Anti-immunoglobulin sera	–	+	–	?
Dextran polyvinylpyrrolidone	n.s.		–	+
Trypsin	n.s.		–	+

n.s. = Not studied.

Functional studies indicate the presence of lymphocyte populations that serve as natural killer (NK) cells and antibody-dependent killer (K) cells in the surveillance of certain tumors and virus-infected cells. The identification and cell lineage of human NK and K cells is controversial, and these cells have been reported to bear T cell antigens, to have promonocyte features, and to react with monoclonal antibodies that bind to macrophages: OKM-1 and MAC-1. A monoclonal antibody (HNK-1) produced against a membrane antigen from a cultured T cell line may define a differentiation antigen selectively expressed on human NK and K cells.

Studies of tissue distribution demonstrate that T4+ cells of inducer type predominate in the thymic medulla, blood, and T cell traffic areas, including tonsillar paracortex and intestinal lamina propria. Cells of the suppressor-cytotoxic type, T-8, constitute the major T cell population in normal human bone marrow and gut epithelium. In lymph node microenvironments, there is close anatomic proximity between T4+ cells and cells expressing large amounts of Ia antigens, interdigitating cells, and macrophages.

B. Functional Properties: The function of various subpopulations of lymphocytes is discussed in Chapters 8, 9, and 10. Several reagents stimulate lymphocytes in vitro, including plant lectins, bacterial products, polymeric substances, and enzymes. Morphologic transformation occurs following stimulation, with the formation of blast cells or in some instances plasma cells. Lymphocyte transformation may also be assessed biochemically by the measurement of RNA, DNA, or protein synthesis. The specificity of various mitogenic substances for human and murine T and B lymphocytes is shown in Table 7–5. The detailed functional aspects of B and T lymphocytes, their interaction, and their alteration in disease are discussed in subsequent chapters.

MONONUCLEAR PHAGOCYTES (MONOCYTE–MACROPHAGES)

The mononuclear phagocytes include the circulating peripheral blood monocytes, promonocytes, precursor cells in the bone marrow, and tissue macrophages. The tissue macrophages are present in several tissues, organs, and serous cavities. The organization of the mononuclear phagocyte system is shown in Table 7–6. The precursor cell in the mononuclear phagocyte lineage is the monoblast, present in the bone marrow and morphologically similar to the myeloblast. The monoblast gives rise to the promonocyte, a bone marrow cell that is phagocytic and adherent and contains nonspecific esterase. Circulating monocytes are heterogeneous in size, receptor expression, and phagocytic function. The macrophages of the pulmonary alveoli and the peritoneal and pleural cavities are derived chiefly from circulating monocytes; under certain circumstances, however, local proliferation occurs. There is a wide spectrum of morphologic features in the various types of mononuclear phagocytes, but in general these cells have a well-developed Golgi complex and many lysosomes (Figs 7–14 and 7–15). Their surface membranes are characterized by prominent microvilli and ruffles.

Mononuclear phagocytes originate from precursor cells in the bone marrow. They circulate in the peripheral blood as monocytes. The tissue macrophages are derived from both blood monocytes and local proliferation of macrophages.

The major functional properties of monocyte-macrophages are adherence to glass, ingestion of par-

Table 7–6. The mononuclear phagocyte system.*

Stem cell	
↓	
Committed stem cell	
↓	
Monoblasts	Bone marrow
↓	
Promonocytes	
↓	
Monocytes	
↓	
Monocytes	Peripheral blood
↓	
Macrophages	Tissues (listed below)

Normal State	
Connective tissue (histiocyte)	Nervous tissue (microglial cell)
Liver (Kupffer cell)	Skin (histiocyte; Langerhans cell)
Lung (alveolar macrophage)	
Lymph nodes (free and fixed macrophages; interdigitating cell?)	Synovia (type A cell?)
	Other organs (tissue macrophage)
Spleen (free and fixed macrophages)	**Inflammation**
Bone marrow (fixed macrophage)	Exudative macrophage
	Exudate-resident macrophage
Serous cavities (pleural and peritoneal macrophages)	Epithelioid cell
	Multinucleated giant cell (Langerhans type and foreign body type)
Bone (osteoclasts)	

*Reproduced, with permission, from Van Furth R: In, *Mononuclear Phagocytes: Functional Aspects.* Martinus Nijhoff Publishers, 1980.

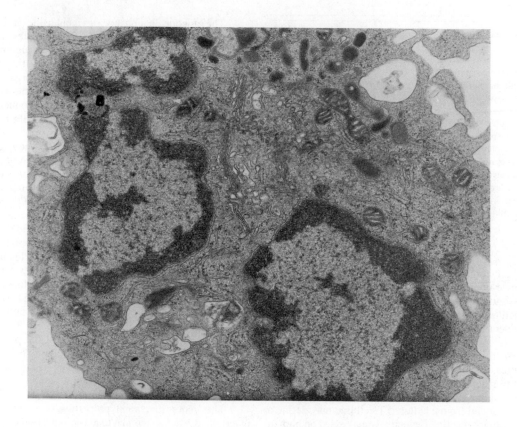

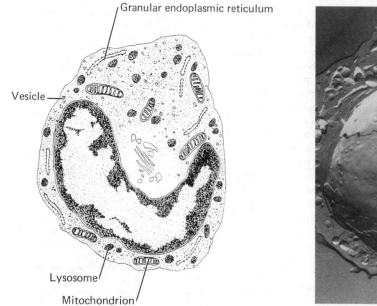

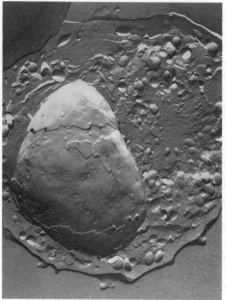

Granular endoplasmic reticulum

Vesicle

Lysosome

Mitochondrion

Figure 7–14. *Top:* Electron micrograph of normal human blood monocyte. (× 34,500.) *Bottom left:* Diagrammatic representation of monocyte. *Bottom right:* Freeze-fracture micrograph of human blood monocyte. (× 10,000.)

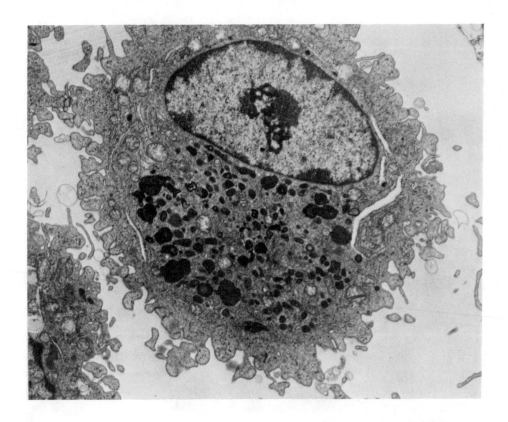

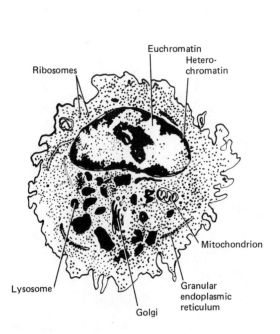

Figure 7–15. *Top:* Electron micrograph of rabbit pulmonary alveolar macrophage. (× 8000.) ***Bottom left:*** Diagrammatic representation of macrophage. ***Bottom right:*** Freeze-fracture micrograph of rabbit pulmonary alveolar macrophage. (× 6000.)

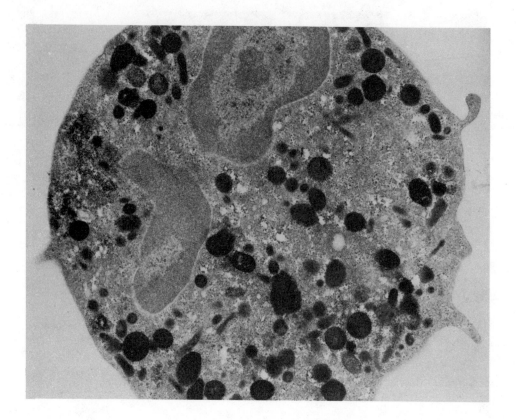

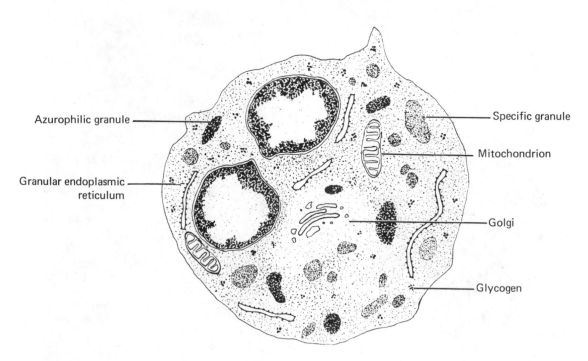

Figure 7–16. *Top:* Electron micrograph of human blood polymorphonuclear neutrophil. (× 30,000.) *Bottom:* Diagrammatic representation of polymorphonuclear neutrophil.

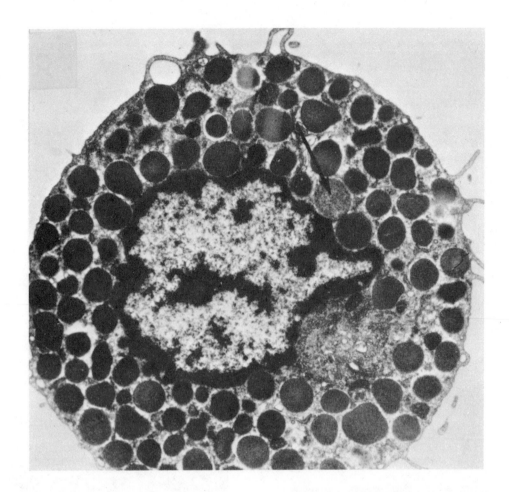

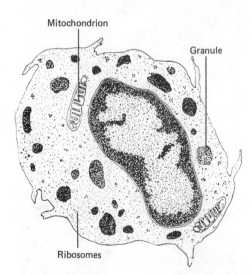

Mitochondrion

Granule

Ribosomes

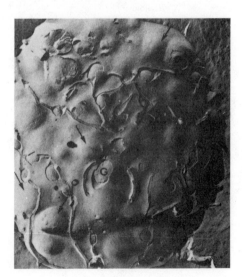

Figure 7–17. *Top:* Unstimulated rat peritoneal mast cell. One granule (arrow) has released its contents. (× 11,000.) ***Bottom left:*** Diagrammatic representation of tissue mast cell. ***Bottom right:*** Freeze-fracture micrograph of rat peritoneal mast cell during degranulation. Granules appear as bulges beneath the membrane (arrows) and, in some areas, granule membrane (G) is exposed by the plane of fracture. (× 7000.) (Reproduced, with permission, from Lawson D et al: Molecular events during membrane fusion: A study of exocytosis in rat peritoneal mast cells. *J Cell Biol* 1977;**72:**242.)

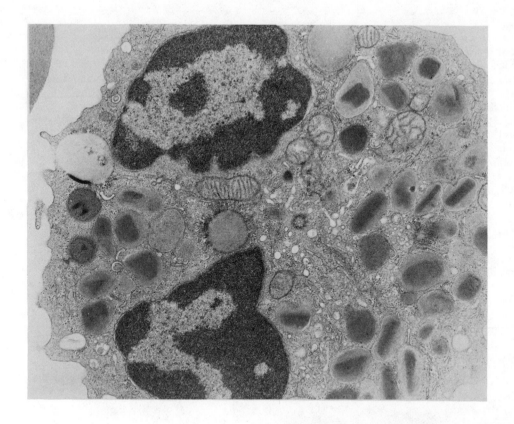

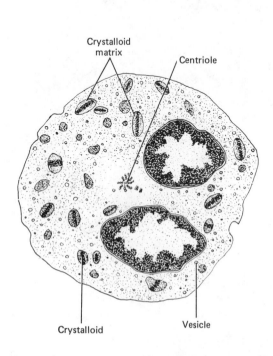

Crystalloid
matrix

Centriole

Crystalloid

Vesicle

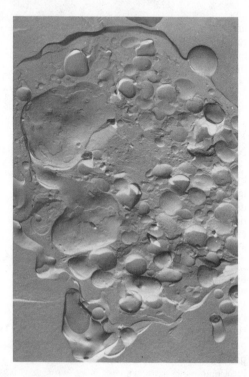

Figure 7–18. *Top:* Electron micrograph of mature human blood eosinophil. (× 12,000.) ***Bottom left:*** Diagrammatic representation of eosinophil. ***Bottom right:*** Freeze-fracture micrograph of human eosinophil. (× 9000.)

ticles smaller than 0.1 μm by pinocytosis, and engulfment of particles larger than 0.1 μm by phagocytosis. During engulfment, the particle first adheres to the plasma membrane of the cell and is then ingested. The monocyte-macrophage is capable of both nonimmunologic and immunologic phagocytosis. Monocyte-macrophages have a plasma membrane receptor which recognizes 2 of the 4 subclasses of human IgG (IgG1 and IgG3); this binding site on the IgG molecule has been localized to the C_H3 domain of the immunoglobulin molecule. The monocyte-macrophage also has an independent receptor system which recognizes the activated third component of complement (C3). Cells of the monocyte-macrophage series are active in killing bacteria, fungi, and tumor cells.

Monoclonal antibodies have been prepared that react with antigens on mononuclear phagocytes. A monoclonal antibody, designated "anti-MAC-1," recognizes a determinant on human monocytes and granulocytes and also on human NK cells, a subset of blood lymphocytes; another monoclonal antibody, 63D3, reacts with blood monocytes but not with T or B lymphocytes. Finally, monoclonal antibodies that react with monocytes and nonmonocyte blood elements include MO1 and OKM1. MO2 and MAC-120 do not react with other cells and are specific for peripheral blood monocytes.

Mononuclear phagocytes have the capacity to bind antigen and antigen-antibody complexes. The monocyte-macrophage frequently degrades antigen which binds to its surface. There is evidence that small amounts of antigen bound to the macrophage surface are important in the induction phase of the immune response. The possible role of the mononuclear phagocyte in interaction with B and T lymphocytes during the immune response is discussed elsewhere.

OTHER CELL TYPES INVOLVED IN IMMUNOLOGIC PHENOMENA

Neutrophils

The polymorphonuclear neutrophil, or granulocyte, comprises approximately 60% of the circulating leukocytes in humans. The neutrophil is 10–20 μm in diameter in smears and 7–9 μm in diameter in sections. The nucleus has 3–5 lobes joined by narrow chromatin threads. The mature neutrophil is primarily a phagocytic cell with 2 distinct types of granules (Fig 7–16). These are known as the primary or azurophilic granules, which contain acid hydrolases, myeloperoxidase, and lysozyme; and the secondary or specific granules, which contain lactoferrin and some lysozyme. Further work is necessary to establish the subcellular localizations of alkaline phosphatase. The primary granules also contain a number of cationic proteins which have antibacterial activity. In the mature neutrophil, 80–90% of the granules are specific granules and 10–20% are azurophilic granules. Neutrophils have a half-life of about 6–20 hours in the peripheral blood, and their survival in tissues under steady state conditions is about 4–5 days. Granulocytes are produced at a rate of 1.6×10^9 cells/kg/d. These cells are capable of migrating toward stimuli (chemotaxis) in the presence of a number of chemotactic factors, including bacterial products, tissue proteases, and complement components. Once localized in inflammatory areas, the neutrophil is capable of binding and ingesting appropriately opsonized materials. Neutrophils have membrane receptors for C3 and for the Fc portion of immunoglobulin. Following phagocytosis, there ensues a complex sequence of morphologic and biochemical events. The major biochemical concomitants of phagocytosis include an increase in phospholipid metabolism, marked stimulation of the hexose monophosphate shunt, and generation of hydrogen peroxide. Clinical disorders related to impaired killing of bacteria by neutrophils are described in Chapter 25; tests of neutrophil function are described in Chapter 23.

Basophils & Mast Cells

The circulating basophil and tissue mast cell are characterized by oval, electron-dense granules which contain biologically active compounds, including heparin and histamine. These cells are often found in connective tissue in the skin surrounding small blood vessels, hair follicles, and adipose tissue. Mast cells are also present in the submucosa of the small intestine and in the sheaths of peripheral nerves and meninges. They are also present in the diffuse connective tissue throughout the reticuloendothelial system. Fig 7–17 shows an electron micrograph of a tissue mast cell. Basophils, mast cells, and mastocytoma cell lines bear receptors which bind the Fc portion of IgE. There are 10^5–10^6 receptor sites per cell, and the receptor is univalent; this receptor is related to triggering of histamine release following interaction of the immunoglobulin with specific antigen. Basophils and mast cells as targets for IgE in anaphylaxis and in allergic phenomena are discussed in Chapters 12 and 18.

Eosinophils

The circulating eosinophils comprise 2–5% of normal peripheral blood leukocytes. They are round cells with a diameter of about 12 μm. Eosinophils are characterized morphologically by a type of granule that stains orange with Romanovsky stains. By electron microscopy, this granule has been shown to contain a characteristic crystalloid (Fig 7–18). Tissue eosinophils are morphologically identical to circulating eosinophils. A second granule type has recently been identified in eosinophils. The eosinophil has been demonstrated to have phagocytic potential, to ingest antigen-antibody complexes, and to have an important role in anaphylactic and allergic phenomena (see Chapters 12 and 18).

• • •

References

Cottier H, Turk J, Sobin L: A proposal for a standardized system of reporting human lymph node morphology in relation to immunological function. *Bull WHO* 1972;**47**:375.

Douglas SD: Electron microscopic and functional aspects of human lymphocyte response to mitogens. *Transplant Rev* 1972;**11**:39.

Douglas SD: Human lymphocyte growth in vitro: Morphologic, biochemical and immunologic significance. *Int Rev Exp Pathol* 1971;**10**:41.

Elves MW: *The Lymphocytes,* 2nd ed. Lloyd-Luke Ltd, 1972.

Gell PGH, Coombs RRA, Lachmann PJ (editors): *Clinical Aspects of Immunology,* 3rd ed. Blackwell, 1974.

Golub ES: *The Cellular Basis of the Immune Response,* 2nd ed. Sinauer Associates, 1981.

Greaves MD, Owen JJT, Raff MC: *T and B Lymphocytes: Origins, Properties and Roles in Immune Responses.* Excerpta Medica, American Elsevier, 1973.

Handwerger BS, Douglas SD: The cell biology of blastogenesis. Page 609 in: *Handbook of Inflammation.* Vol 2. Weissmann G (editor). Elsevier-North Holland, 1980.

Hood LE, Weissman IL, Wood WB: *Immunology.* Benjamin-Cummings, 1978.

Kampmeier OF: *Evolution and Comparative Morphology of the Lymphatic System.* Thomas, 1969.

Kay NE, Ackerman SK, Douglas SD: Anatomy of the immune system. *Semin Hematol* 1979;**16**:252.

Klebanoff SJ, Clark RA: *The Neutrophil –Function and Clinical Disorders.* Elsevier North-Holland, 1978.

Marchalonis JJ: *The Lymphocyte: Structure & Function.* Dekker, 1977.

Möller G (editor): T and B lymphocytes in humans. *Transplant Rev* 1973;**16**:3. [Entire issue.]

Nelson DS: *Immunobiology of the Macrophage.* Academic Press, 1976.

Nelson DS: Macrophages: Progress and problems. *Clin Exp Immunol* 1981;**45**:225.

Nossal GJV, Ada GL (editors): *Antigens, Lymphoid Cells, and the Immune Response.* Academic Press, 1971.

Reinherz EL, Schlossman SF: The differentiation and function of human T lymphocytes. *Cell* 1980;**19**:821.

Roitt I: *Essential Immunology,* 3rd ed. Blackwell, 1977.

Van Furth R (editor): *Mononuclear Phagocytes: Function Aspects.* Martinus Nishoff, 1980.

Weiss L: *The Cells and Tissues of the Immune System: Structure, Functions, Interactions.* Prentice-Hall, 1972.

Zucker-Franklin D et al: *Atlas of Blood Cells: Function and Pathology.* Lea & Febiger, 1981.

Zuckerman SH, Douglas SD: Mononuclear phagocytes: Plasma membrane receptors and dynamics. *Annu Rev Microbiol* 1979;**33**:267.

Cellular Interactions in the Expression & Regulation of Immunity | 8

John D. Stobo, MD

Experiments by Claman et al demonstrating that the antibody response to sheep red blood cells is dependent on the presence of both T cells and B cells provided the first evidence that the expression of immunity requires cooperative interactions between distinct populations of immunocompetent cells. Subsequent studies by many investigators have indicated that both cell-mediated and humoral immunity are crucially dependent on communication among populations of immunocytes. The basic vocabulary used in this communication involves recognition of 2 major classes of self determinants—**major histocompatibility determinants** and **immunoglobulin idiotypes.** This communication can be modified by secreted soluble materials. The subject matter of this chapter is cellular communications necessary for the initiation and controlled expression of immunity.

Although products of genes in the histocompatibility complex (MHC) and immunoglobulin idiotypes are thoroughly discussed in Chapters 6 and 4, respectively, a brief discussion is required here in order to clarify their role in cellular interactions. In mice, the MHC is a genetic locus on the 17th chromosome that can be divided into 5 major subloci: K, I, D, Qa, and Tl. The I region codes for immune response–associated (Ia) determinants and can be further divided into I-A, I-J, and I-E subloci. In humans, the MHC is on the sixth chromosome and consists of 3 well-defined loci—A, B, and D—and 2 newly described and as yet poorly defined loci—MT and SB. Murine K and D are equivalent to human B and A loci, respectively, and code for a 45,000-MW glycoprotein displayed on the surface of all nucleated cells. These glycoproteins are termed class 1 determinants. The murine I and human D region are analogous. Products of these genes are represented by a 2-chain glycoprotein (consisting of a relatively high molecular weight [34,000] α chain and a relatively low molecular weight [29,000] β chain). These class 2 antigens are displayed only on macrophages, B cells, and a small proportion of T cells. Products of genes in the human D region are most analogous to products of the murine I-E subregion. Although it has been suggested that the human MT or SB region is equivalent to the murine I-A subloci, this has not been definitely proved.

Immunoglobulin idiotypes are represented by amino acid sequences inherent in the antigen-combining region of immunoglobulin molecules. Since 2 immunoglobulin molecules with specificity for 2 distinct antigens will have different amino acid sequences in their antigen-combining region, they will therefore have different idiotypes. Idiotypes can serve as antigens that are recognized by the immune system.

Development of T Cells

Antigen-induced activation of cytotoxic T cells, effector T cells that participate in **delayed type hypersensitivity (DTH),** and helper T cells requires that they "see" determinants inherent in the antigen as well as self MHC determinants. Cytotoxic T cells see antigens in conjunction with class 1 MHC determinants, while helper and DTH-reactive T cells see antigen in conjunction with class 2 MHC determinants. Based on this fact, 2 theories have been developed to explain the nature of the recognition unit that serves as the receptor for T cells (Fig 8–1). The **modified self theory** predicts that the T cells will recognize a determinant generated by interactions between antigen and MHC gene products. The **dual recognition theory** suggests that the receptor consists of 2 distinct regions, one that recognizes self MHC determinants and another that recognizes determinants inherent in anti-

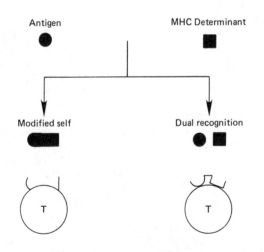

Figure 8–1. Schematic representation of the modified self and dual recognition models used to indicate the nature of the T cell receptor.

gen. Implicit in both of these theories is the supposition that T cells cannot be activated by interactions with either antigen alone or with self MHC gene products alone. The precise physicochemical nature of the T cell receptor has not been delineated; thus, it is not possible to determine which of these 2 theories is correct. There is evidence that at least a portion of the T cell receptor contains idiotypic determinants similar to those displayed by specific antibodies. Molecules similar to those represented by the constant region of immunoglobulins are not synthesized by T cells.

The ability of T cells to recognize self MHC determinants is induced during their development in the thymus. The thymic stroma contains epithelial cells and macrophages that display both class 1 and class 2 MHC determinants. Stem cells that have potential for recognizing any MHC determinant enter the thymus. Physical contact between these stem cells and the MHC-bearing stromal cells results in an ill-defined differentiation process culminating in the generation only of T cells whose receptors have relatively low affinity for self, ie, cells that cannot be activated by interactions with self MHC determinants alone. The inductive nature of this differentiation process is emphasized by the observation that in appropriate experimental models, it is possible to take stem cells from one strain (eg, strain A) of mice, infuse them into a different strain (eg, strain B), and thus "teach" the T cells to recognize MHC determinants of strain B. Similarly, thymectomy of a strain A mouse followed by implantation of thymus from strain B results in T cells that recognize antigens in conjunction with MHC determinants of strain B.

T cell differentiation in the thymus is also accompanied by the development of functional subpopulations of T cells that can be distinguished by differences in the display of certain differentiation antigens. This differentiation is independent of any exposure to antigen and continues after T cells have passed into peripheral lymphoid tissue. In mice, the cell surface antigens that mark functional subpopulations of T cells include the Lyt, Qa, and Ia antigens. In humans, determinants depicted by monoclonal antibodies (OK series, Leu series) mark functional subpopulations of T cells. The usefulness of these reagents in dissecting interactions occurring among functional subpopulations of cells is best explained by first presenting data obtained in mice and then comparing them with data obtained in humans.

In mice, 3 major subpopulations of T cells can be distinguished by display of alloantigens of the Lyt series. The genetic locus coding for the Lyt-1 determinant is on chromosome 19, and genes coding for Lyt-2 and Lyt-3 determinants are closely linked on chromosome 6. The Lyt-1 determinant is present in a polypeptide of approximately 70,000 MW, and the Lyt-2 and Lyt-3 determinants are contained in a macromolecule with subunits of 30,000, 34,000, and 38,000 MW. One population of T cells that comprises approximately 40% of peripheral blood T cells displays a high density of the Lyt-1 determinant (Lyt-1,2^-,3^-, or sim-

ply Lyt-1^+). Included in this T cell population are T cells that help in the differentiation of B cells into immunoglobulin-secreting plasma cells, T cells that help in the development of cytotoxic T cells, and T cells that are effectors for delayed hypersensitivity. A second population of T cells displays only the Lyt-2 and Lyt-3 determinants (ie, Lyt-2,3^+) and represents approximately 20% of T cells. This population contains suppressor cells as well as cytotoxic T cells. (Although these cells lack Lyt-1 determinants when assayed by conventional techniques, they do display small amounts of Lyt-1 when analyzed by the fluorescence-activated cell sorter. [See Chapter 23.]) The third population of T cells (approximately 50% of peripheral blood T cells) displays all 3 Lyt determinants (Lyt-1,2,3^+) and contains the precursors of the Lyt-2,3^+ cells.

The Lyt-1^+ and the Lyt-2,3^+ populations can be further divided into subpopulations based on differences in the display of MHC-encoded determinants. Some Lyt-1^+ cells display determinants encoded for by the I-J and Qa-1 regions (Lyt-1^+, I-J^+, Qa-1^+), while others lack these same determinants. Similarly, some Lyt-2,3^+ T cells also display I-J determinants while others do not.

The ability to depict subpopulations of T cells by differences in their display of these differentiation antigens has been an enormous help in understanding interactions that occur among T cell populations, especially as these interactions are involved in regulating immune reactivity (Fig 8–2). For example, although both the Lyt-1^+,Qa-1^+ and Lyt-1^+,Qa-1^- T cells function to amplify immunoglobulin production, only the Lyt-1^+,Qa-1^+ population is involved also in a feedback regulatory circuit that results in generation of active suppressive influences among the Lyt-2,3^+ cells. In other words, activation of the Lyt-1^+,Qa-1^+ helper cells results in signals transmitted to the Lyt-1,2,3^+ precursor population. These signals, in turn, generate increased suppressive activity by the Lyt-2,3^+ cells that serve to counterbalance helper cell activity and thus control immunoglobulin production. The Lyt-1^+,Qa-1^- cells are therefore referred to as the helper-effector population, while the Lyt-1^+,Qa-1^+ cells are termed the helper-inducer cells.

In an analogous model, the Lyt-2,3^+ cells contain effector and inducer cells. The Lyt-2,3^+,I-J^- are effectors of immunosuppression. The Lyt-2,3^+,I-J^+ cells can mediate feedback signals, again transmitted through the Lyt-1,2,3^+ population, which serve to limit the activity of the Lyt-2,3^+,I-J^- suppressor. This latter circuit has been termed **contrasuppression.** The Lyt-1,2,3 cells contain the contrasuppressors, and this activity is induced by Lyt-2,3^+,I-J^+ cells. Although this circuit may seem unduly complex, it serves to maintain the fine balance required for the controlled expression of immunity.

Several investigators have produced monoclonal antibodies that depict functional subpopulations of human T cells (Table 8–1). The molecules reactive with these antibodies are similar to murine differentia-

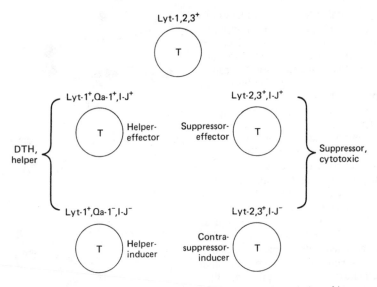

Figure 8–2. Murine T cell populations involved in the expression and regulation of immune reactivity.

tion antigens with regard to their molecular weight, tissue distribution, and sensitivity to proteolysis with trypsin. For example, the monoclonal antibody Leu-1 depicts a molecule with a molecular weight of 67,000 present in relatively large amounts on approximately 80% of peripheral blood T cells. (In a situation analogous to that noted for the display of Lyt-1, a reduced density of the Leu-1 determinant can be detected on the remaining 20% of T cells.) The monoclonal antibodies Leu-2a and Leu-2b detect a molecule with subunits of MW 30,000–33,000 present on 20% of peripheral blood T cells. (The monoclonal antibody OKT5 appears to bind to the same molecules as the Leu-2a and Leu-2b reagents.) The monoclonal antibodies Leu-3 and OKT4 both have specificity for a molecule of MW 55,000–65,000 that is present on approximately 60% of T cells. (To date, it has not been possible to demonstrate a murine equivalent for this determinant.)

These monoclonal antibodies have been useful for depicting functional subpopulations of human T cells. The Leu-3$^+$(OKT4$^+$) subset contains effectors for delayed hypersensitivity, helpers for antibody synthesis, and T cells that can induce generation of suppressor T cells. (These inducers are contained in a radiosensitive population of OKT4$^+$ cells and as yet have not been distinguished by the presence of a

distinctive cell surface marker.) The Leu-2a$^+$,2b$^+$ (OKT5$^+$) subset contains suppressor and cytotoxic T cells. A contrasuppression circuit has not been delineated in humans.

Interactions Between Accessory Cells & T Cells

Activation of helper and DTH-reactive T cells by antigen requires 2 signals each of which is mediated by accessory cells. The first signal requires the presentation of antigen in a manner suitable for recognition by T cells. The second signal involves synthesis of a soluble material by accessory cells and is necessary for full T cell activation to proceed.

The precise events involved in the ability of accessory cells to present antigen to T cells are not completely understood. As indicated, activation of helper and DTH-reactive T cells requires that they see antigen in conjunction with self Ia determinants. Therefore, display of Ia determinants by accessory cells constitutes a minimal requirement for their antigen-presenting capabilities.

Two points concerning the requirement for display of Ia by accessory cells deserve emphasis. First, qualitative display of Ia is important. For example, it has been suggested that in mice only accessory cells that display determinants encoded for by both the I-A and I-E subregions and not accessory cells that display only I-A or I-E determinants can present antigens. Second, accessory cells must display a crucial density of the appropriate Ia antigens. This point is emphasized by the demonstration that stimulation of accessory cells to increase the density of Ia determinants enhances their antigen-presenting function. It has been claimed that accessory cells must also be capable of somehow processing antigen so that it can be properly aligned with Ia determinants. However, exactly which metabolic events are involved in such processing is not known. Clearly, this does not simply

Table 8–1. Monoclonal antibodies to human T cell subpopulations.

Monoclonal Antibody	Molecular Weight of Antigen	Murine Equivalent	Function of T Cell Population
Leu-1	67,000	Lyt-1$^+$	—
Leu-2a,2b, OKT5	30,000–38,000	Lyt-2,3$^+$	Suppressor, cytotoxic
Leu-3, OKT4	55,000–65,000	None known	Helper, DTH-reactive

involve uptake and degradation of antigen by phagocytosis. Ia-bearing phagocytic and nonphagocytic cells are both capable of presenting antigen to T cells. Moreover, the degradation of radiolabeled antigen by accessory cells that can and those that cannot present antigen is similar. Initial studies indicated that metabolic inhibitors could prevent antigen presentation by accessory cells, and this was taken to support the contention that presentation required active metabolic processing. However, subsequent studies indicate that these metabolic inhibitors actually abrogate the second required function of accessory cells, ie, synthesis of soluble materials, and do not affect their presenting capabilities. Finally, although it is assumed that antigen must be displayed in conjunction with Ia on the surface of the accessory cell, this has been difficult to prove. Although antisera directed against accessory cell Ia determinants block antigen presentation, antisera directed against antigen do not. In other words, although activation of T cells requires that they see accessory cell Ia plus antigen, it has not been possible to demonstrate antigen on the surface of antigen-presenting cells.

The second signal required for the activation of helper and DTH-reactive T cells involves the synthesis and release of a soluble material termed interleukin-1 (IL-1). IL-1 appears to exert its effect by stimulating the production of a second distinct interleukin, IL-2, by T cells, and it is IL-2 that then acts in concert with signals mediated by antigen plus Ia to allow full T cell activation to proceed. It is not clear if the T cells that are sensitive to the actions of IL-2 actually synthesize IL-2. To date, only malignant T cell lines have been shown to be capable of both synthesizing and responding to IL-2.

The sequence in which the 2 signals act upon reactive T cells to induce their activation appears to be as follows (Fig 8–3). First, T cells interact with antigen presented in conjunction with Ia. This results in an increase in the expression of receptors for IL-2. Synthesis of IL-1 by accessory cells induces synthesis of IL-2 by the T cells, and it is the action of IL-2 that then allows full T cell activation to proceed.

An obvious missing link in these interactions is represented by the signal that induced IL-1 production by accessory cells. It is possible that no signal is required and that synthesis of sufficient amounts of IL-1 is a constitutive function of accessory cells.

The exact nature of the accessory cells required for full T cell activation in vivo is controversial. Under appropriate in vitro conditions, it is possible to demonstrate that Ia-bearing B cells, T cells, dendritic cells, macrophages, and endothelial cells are all capable of mediating full antigen-induced activation of T cells. It is not clear whether all of these cells can also function as physiologic accessory cells for T cell activation.

The requirement of accessory cells in the activation of suppressor T cells is quite different from that noted for the activation of helper and DTH-reactive T cells. In fact, it has been suggested that in the absence

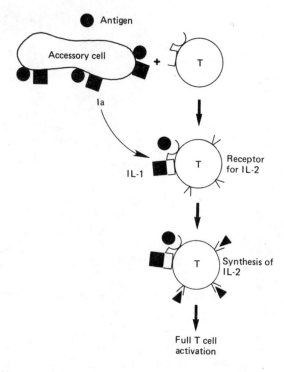

Figure 8–3. Interactions between accessory cells and antigen-reactive T cells required for full T cell activation.

of presentation by accessory cells, antigen is capable of directly activating suppressor T cells. This possibility is supported by 4 observations. First, addition of antigen to T cells completely depleted of antigen-presenting accessory cells results in the preferential activation of suppressor T cells. Second, antigen alone can directly bind to suppressor cells. Third, addition of anti-Ia sera to in vitro mixture of T cells, accessory cells, and antigen, or in vivo infusion of anti-Ia sera followed by immunization with antigen results in the generation of antigen-specific suppressor T cells. Fourth, immunization of mice with large doses of antigen results in activation of specific suppressor T cells. In this situation, it appears that the antigen-presenting capabilities of accessory cells are saturated. The excess antigen is thus able to interact directly with receptors on suppressor T cells and induce their activation. These observations imply an obvious difference between antigen receptors on helper versus suppressor cells; T cell receptors displayed by suppressor cells should be capable of seeing antigen in the absence of self Ia. In fact, it can be demonstrated that suppressor T cells can bind to antigen coupled to a solid support such as sepharose, whereas helper cells cannot. Moreover, soluble materials (presumably receptors) isolated from suppressor cells bind to antigen affinity columns.

Whether or not activation of suppressor T cells requires liberation of a soluble material by accessory cells is not known. It can be demonstrated that neither IL-1 nor IL-2 is sufficient to induce suppressor cell activation. Recently, a third interleukin, IL-3, has been suggested as a requirement for the activation of suppressor T cells.

This difference in the accessory cell requirement for the activation of helper versus suppressor cells may be important in initiating tolerance of self tissue antigens. Ia-bearing accessory cells capable of presenting antigen do not appear in the peripheral lymphoid tissue of mice until 3–4 weeks after birth. Therefore, during the late prenatal and early neonatal period, self antigen will be seen in the absence of antigen-presenting accessory cells and thus will preferentially activate suppressor T cells. Confirmation of this hypothesis awaits proof that absence of reactivity to autologous tissue antigens is in fact due to predominance of specific suppressor T cells (see Chapter 13).

Therefore, it is clear that accessory cells help in the activation of at least some T cells. It is equally clear that T cells can, in turn, facilitate the reactivity and differentiation of at least one population of accessory cells: macrophages. Specific activation of T cells by antigen or nonspecific activation of T cells by mitogens results in the release of soluble materials that can increase the density of Ia determinants expressed by macrophages. T cell–accessory cell interactions required for full T cell reactivity can be represented by a complete circle (Fig 8–4). Antigen presented by accessory cells in conjunction with IL-1 results in the activation of T cells. These T cells are then capable of liberating soluble materials that enhance the antigen-presenting capabilities of macrophages. It is this cooperative interaction that is required for maximal in vivo T cell reactivity.

In some in vitro models, it can be demonstrated that macrophages can also inhibit T cell reactivity. For example, addition of increasing numbers of macrophages to T cells can actually result in diminished antigen or mitogen-induced T cell proliferation. Soluble materials liberated by macrophages (eg, prostaglandins) have been implicated as mediating this immunosuppression. It is not known whether macrophage-mediated immunosuppression represents a physiologic interaction designed to modulate T cell reactivity in vivo.

Cellular Interactions Required for Production of Antibodies

As noted at the beginning of this chapter, the studies of Claman et al demonstrated that antibody production requires interactions between T cells and B cells. Subsequent studies demonstrated that in this interaction, B cells provide the precursors capable of differentiating into antibody-secreting plasma cells, while T cells are required to help this process. From the discussion presented in the previous section, it is clear that accessory cells are also needed for antibody production, since they are required for the activation of helper T cells. In addition to interactions between these 3 cell types, which are necessary to initiate antibody production, a complex series of interactions must also occur among subpopulations of T cells in order for antibody production to be properly regulated. Since purposeful immunization or natural exposure to a single antigen usually results in the production of antibodies to only that and not other antigens, the cellular communication required for the initiation and regulation of antibody production must occur in an antigen-specific fashion. Ia antigens are probably not the determinants that dictate communication. Identical Ia determinants are displayed by clones of cells with specificities for distinct antigens. To account for the specificity involved in cellular interactions involved in antibody production, Jerne proposed the network theory. The essential principles of this theory are as follows: For each of the 10 million different antigens an individual must be prepared to react against, there exists a clone of T cells and B cells that display a receptor demonstrating a best fit for that and not another antigen. The antigen-combining portion of the receptor will therefore display a unique sequence of amino acids that can be distinguished from the amino acid sequence inherent in the receptors of other clones of antigen-reactive cells. These unique amino acid sequences are termed idiotypes. It should be emphasized that a given receptor for antigen can display more than one idiotypic determinant. Amino acid sequences limited to the exact region where antigen combines with the receptor constitute one set of idiotypic determinants. Unique amino acid sequences present in the regions close to but separate from the antigen-combining site constitute another set of idiotypes. These latter determinants are referred to as framework idiotypes.

For each idiotypic determinant inherent in an antigen receptor, there exists another clone of antigen-reactive cells whose receptor contains a com-

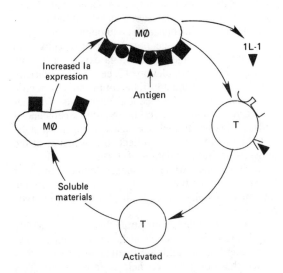

Figure 8–4. Interactions between T cells and macrophages involved in enhancing expression of Ia determinants by macrophages. Activation of T cells results in the synthesis and liberation of soluble materials capable of enhancing the expression of Ia determinants by macrophages. MO = mononuclear phagocyte.

plementary determinant or anti-idiotype. In other words, each clone of T or B cells bears a receptor capable of recognizing not only a determinant inherent in conventional antigen but also an idiotype displayed by the receptor on another clone of T or B cells. Since the number of antigens against which an individual must react is large, the number of clones reactive to a single antigen and the number of clones displaying a specific idiotype is small. Therefore, no one idiotype is present in concentrations sufficient to induce immunologic tolerance. Within this framework, the immune system can be viewed as a large network linked by immunologic recognition of self idiotypes. Perturbations initiated by exposure to antigen result in reverberating interactions between idiotypes, anti-idiotypes, and anti-anti-idiotypes that serve to modulate antibody production (see Chapter 13).

A model that might aid in the understanding of these interactions is provided by interesting observations made about the relationship between cellular receptors for insulin, anti-insulin antibodies, and antibodies directed against idiotypic determinants inherent in anti-insulin antibodies. Since the cellular receptor and anti-insulin antibody are each capable of binding insulin, they will share amino acid sequences that are important in this binding. In other words, they will share certain idiotypes. Antibodies directed against idiotypic determinants inherent in the anti-insulin antibody should also be capable of interacting with the cellular receptor for insulin. Indeed, this can be demonstrated experimentally. In this model, the cellular receptor for insulin is equivalent to the T or B cell receptor for antigen; insulin is equivalent to antigen; and antibodies to insulin are equivalent to antibodies directed against antigen. The anti-idiotypes are represented either by circulating anti-idiotype antibody or antigen receptors on other clones of antigen-reactive cells that have anti-idiotype specificity.

Several observations support the hypothesis that the control of immune reactivity involves the idiotype network. If one immunizes an animal with antigen X, isolates the anti-X antibodies, and then infuses the antibody back into the same animal, it is possible to generate an anti-idiotype response. This supports the view that the immune system is not tolerant to and can recognize self idiotypes. Analysis of the antibodies produced upon immunization with an antigen demonstrates that some have specificity for the antigen while others have specificity for idiotypes inherent in this antibody. (These are termed auto-anti-idiotypes.)

It is possible to manipulate immune reactivity in an antigen-specific fashion by perturbing the idiotypic network. Infusion of antibodies directed against idiotypic determinants in an antibody with specificity for antigen X can specifically modulate the ability of an animal to respond to antigen X and not affect the response to antigen Y, Z, etc. Whether the anti-idiotypic antibody enhances or inhibits immune reactivity depends on the route by which the anti-idiotype is infused (ie, intravenously versus subcutaneously), the species in which the anti-idiotype was raised, the im-

munoglobulin class in which the antibody activity resides, and whether the whole antibody or only F(ab)'$_2$ fragments were used. The ability of anti-idiotypes to modulate immune reactivity represents their ability to interact with immunoregulatory T cells. This is exemplified by the demonstration that immunologic unresponsiveness induced by the infusion of an anti-idiotype can be transferred from one animal to another with T cells.

The network theory implies that antigen receptors on T and B cells will actually manifest dual specificity. One specificity is for determinants inherent in antigen, while the other is for a specific idiotype. This condition is necessary to conserve the diversity of recognition units necessary in a system that must function in the dual capacity of responding to foreign antigen as well as regulating itself. The network theory also suggests that similar idiotypes may be displayed by receptors with specificity for distinct conventional antigens. These cross-reactive idiotypes may be represented by framework idiotypes that are not restricted to the antigen-combining region of the receptor. Indeed, this suggestion can be verified experimentally and is probably responsible for situations in which polyclonal increases in immunoglobulin occur after immunization with a single antigen.

Signals Required for B Cell Activation

As indicated, 2 signals are required for the activation of helper and DTH-reactive T cells. Similarly, 2 signals are required to induce the differentiation of B cells into antibody-secreting plasma cells. One signal is provided by interactions between antigen and B cell immunoglobulin receptors. The second signal is mediated by helper T cells. The bulk of available evidence indicates that helper cell-mediated signals require direct contact between T and B eclls and are not mediated by soluble materials. Although initial studies indicated that only one population of T cells with specificity for antigen plus self Ia existed, it is now clear that another population of T cells with specificity for idiotypic determinants inherent in antigen-specific B cell immunoglobulin receptors also exists. Whether or not interactions between these latter T cells and B cells is also Ia-restricted is not clear. It appears that the initial antibody response reflects the influence of the antigen-specific population of T cells while the subsequent response, which is more restricted in terms of the specificity of the antibody produced, reflects the influence of helper T cells displaying anti-idiotype receptors.

Several studies demonstrate that T cells can only help B cells bearing identical Ia determinants. However, recent studies utilizing T cell clones have demonstrated that not all T cell help is Ia-restricted. This apparent contradiction is perhaps explained by the fact that there are 2 distinct populations of B cells. Help for one population requires matching of Ia determinants, whereas help for the other does not. This latter population of B cells appears in the peripheral lymphoid tissue relatively late during B cell ontogeny (approximately 4 weeks after birth) and displays the B cell differentiation marker Lyb-5. It is possible that it is the human analog of this Lyb-5 population which is activated in in vitro experiments utilizing allogeneic helper T cells.

An important consequence of helper T cell activation is the production of feedback signals, mediated by the Lyt-1^+,Qa-1^+,I-J^+ subpopulation (whether this population manifests specificity for antigen or idiotype is not known), which results in the generation of specific Lyt-$2,3^+$ suppressor T cells. Lyt-$1,2,3^+$ T cells serve as the intermediary for those feedback signals presumably by providing precursors for the Lyt-$2,3^+$ pool.

Suppressor T Cells

A necessary component in the controlled production of antibody is the generation of specific suppressive influences. In a situation analogous to that noted for helper T cells, 2 populations of suppressor cells exist that can be distinguished by differences in their specificity. One population binds antigen, while the other has specificity for idiotypes inherent in the antibody produced and the antigen receptor on T and B cells. The former population is generated in direct response to antigen; the latter presumably is activated in response to expansion of idiotype-bearing B cells. While some investigators have demonstrated Ia restriction in the activity of suppressor cells, others have failed to confirm this. This probably reflects the heterogeneity that exists among the suppressor cell population. The activity of some suppressor cells may indeed require homology at the Ia locus, while the activity of others may not.

In contrast to the requirement for direct cell-to-cell contact necessary for helper T and B cell interactions, it appears that the activity of suppressor cells can be mediated by soluble materials.

Suppressor cells can interrupt circuits involved in antibody production at several different locations, again reflecting the heterogeneity existing among suppressor T cells. For example, some suppressor T cells appear to exert their effect by directly antagonizing the activity of helper T cells; others directly inhibit the differentiation of B cells.

An important feedback loop by which suppressor cells regulate their own activity is the recently described contrasuppression circuit. In this model, the Lyt-$2,3^+$,I-J^+ population of suppressor cells sends feedback signals to Lyt-$1,2,3^+$ cells that result in suppression of activity among the Lyt-$2,3^+$,I-J^- suppressor effector population.

The heterogeneity that exists among suppressor cells and the role that the idiotype network plays in communication among these cells is exemplified by the suppressor system capable of inhibiting murine delayed hypersensitivity to the hapten azobenzenearsonate (ABA) (Fig 8–5). Intravenous infusion of ABA coupled to syngeneic spleen cells activates an Lyt-1^+,2^- population of suppressor T cells (Ts$_1$). These T cells liberate a soluble material bearing both I-J determinants and idiotypes present in antibodies to ABA that activate a second population of Lyt-$1,2,3^+$ suppressor cells (Ts$_2$). These suppressor cells can liberate a soluble material containing anti-idiotype activity that activates a third population of Lyt-$2,3^+$ suppressor T cells (Ts$_3$) whose antigen receptor displays the ABA idiotype. It is this latter population of T cells that constitutes the effector cells which function to inhibit delayed hypersensitivity to ABA.

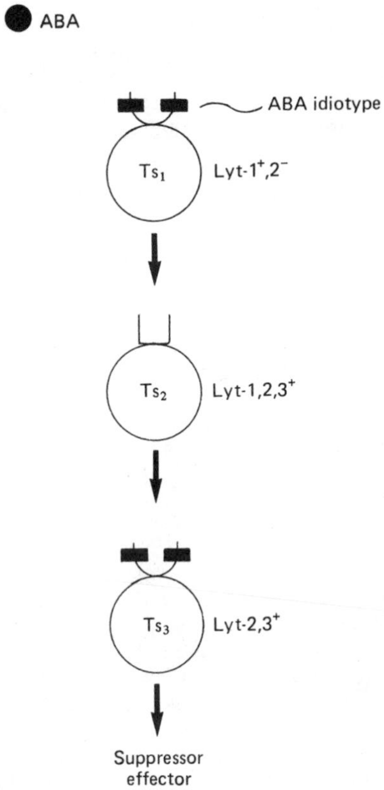

Figure 8–5. Interactions among 3 distinct T cells involved in the suppression of DTH. Antigen, the azobenzenearsonate (ABA) hapten, activates a first-order suppressor cell (Ts$_1$) whose receptor bears an idiotype similar to that present in antibodies directed against ABA. The suppressor T cell in turn activates a second-order suppressor cell whose receptor is specific for the ABA idiotype. This Ts$_2$ then activates a third population of repressor cells that serve as effectors for suppression. ABA = azobenzenearsonate.

Thymus-Independent Antigens

For most antigens, T cells are required to provide the second signal necessary to help B cells differentiate into antibody-secreting plasma cells. However, some antigens can initiate antibody production in the absence of T cell help. These thymus-independent antigens are represented by large molecules, with repeating antigenic units (eg, polymerized flagellin) containing the 2 signals necessary to initiate B cell differentiation. One signal is provided by the antigenic determinants inherent in the molecule, while the other is represented by a portion of the molecule directly capable of activating B cells irrespective of their antigen reactivity. This portion of the T cell–independent antigens therefore acts as a mitogen. Although T cell–ndependent antigens can initiate antibody production in the absence of T cells, substantial production of IgG antibody usually does not occur. This finding indicates that T cells are required for full differentiation of B cells into IgG-secreting plasma cells.

•   •   •

References

General

Eardley D: Feedback suppression: An immunoregulatory circuit. *Fed Proc* 1980;**39:**3114.

Gershon R et al: Contrasuppression: A novel immunoregulatory activity. *J Exp Med* 1981;**153:**1533.

Janeway C, Jason J: How T lymphocytes recognize antigen. *CRC Crit Rev Immunol* 1980;**1:**133.

Raff M: Immunologic networks. *Nature* 1977;**265:**205.

Idiotypes

Adorini L, Harvey M, Sercarz E: The fine specificity of regulatory T cells. 4. Idiotypic complementarity and antigen-bridging interactions in the anti-lysozyme response. *Eur J Immunol* 1979;**9:**960.

Bona C, Paul W: Cellular basis of regulation of expression of idiotype. *J Exp Med* 1979;**149:**592.

Burnet F: A modification of Jerne's theory of antibody production using the concept of clonal selection. *Aust J Sci* 1957; **20:**67.

Eichmann K: Expression and function of idiotypes on lymphocytes. *Adv Immunol* 1978;**26:**195.

Jerne N: The immune system: A web of V-domains. *Harvey Lecture Series* 1975;**70:**93.

Jerne N: The somatic generation of immune recognition. *Eur J Immunol* 1971;**1:**1.

Man-Sun S et al: Antigen- and receptor-driven regulatory mechanisms. 1. Induction of suppressor T cells with anti-idiotypic antibodies. *J Exp Med* 1979;**150:**1216.

Man-Sun S et al: Antigen- and receptor-driven regulatory mechanisms. 3. Induction of delayed-type hypersensitivity to azobenzene-arsonate with anti–cross-reactive idiotypic antibodies. *J Exp Med* 1980;**151:**896.

Ir Genes

Benacerraf B, Germain R: Specific suppressor response to antigen under Ir gene control. *Fed Proc* 1979;**38:**2053.

Katz D: Genetic control and cellular interactions in antibody formation. *Hosp Pract* (May) 1977;**12:**85.

Longa D, Schwartz R: T cell specificity for H-2 and Ir gene phenotype correlates with the phenotype of thymic antigen presenting cells. *Nature* 1980;**287:**44.

McDevitt H: Regulation of the immune response by the major histocompatibility system. *N Engl J Med* 1980;**303:**1514.

Paul W, Benacerraf B: Functional specificity of thymus dependent lymphocytes. *Science* 1977;**195:**1293.

Rosenthal A et al: Macrophage function in antigen recognition by T lymphocytes. Chap 6, pp 131–160, in: *Immunobiology of the Macrophage.* Nelson D (editor). Academic Press, 1976.

Winchester R, Kunkel H: The human Ia system. *Adv Immunol* 1979;**28:**222.

Zinkernagle R, Doherty P: MHC restricted cytotoxic cells: Studies on the biologic role of polymorphic major transplantation antigens determining T cell restriction-specificity, function and responsiveness. *Adv Immunol* 1979;**27:**51.

T Cell Markers

Ledbetter J et al: Evolutionary conservation of surface molecules that distinguish T lymphocyte helper/inducer and cytotoxic/suppressor subpopulations in mouse and man. *J Exp Med* 1981;**153:**310.

Thomas Y et al: Functional analysis of human T cell subsets defined by monoclonal antibodies. 4. Induction of suppressor cells within the OK-T4 population. *J Exp Med* 1981;**154:**459.

Mediators of Cellular Immunity | 9

Ross E. Rocklin, MD

When antigen is injected intradermally into an appropriately sensitized host, a delayed skin reaction may develop over the course of 24–48 hours which is characterized by a mononuclear cell infiltrate. There is ample evidence from experiments involving the transfer of lymphoid cells between laboratory animals (adoptive transfer) that the actual number of antigen-reactive cells present at the site of injection is very small. The great majority of infiltrating cells are apparently immunologically uncommitted, having been attracted to the site by the antigen-responding cells or substances released by these cells. It has been suggested that the initial reaction of antigen with a few specifically sensitized lymphocytes results in the production of soluble mediators, also called lymphokines, which, through their biologic activity, are capable of recruiting host inflammatory cells, activating them, and keeping them at the site. These substances may serve as a means of communication between the cellular reactants which ultimately participate in the cellular hypersensitivity response and may also provide a means by which to amplify this reaction.

A number of in vitro models have been developed which allow investigators to isolate the cells involved in the cell-mediated immune reaction and to study their function and interactions. These experiments basically involve culturing sensitized lymphocytes, activating them with specific stimulants (such as tuberculin PPD, *Candida*) or nonspecific stimulants (such as phytohemagglutinin [PHA] or concanavalin A), and assaying the culture media from these cells for the presence of various biologic activities. A list of some lymphocyte mediators is shown in Table 9–1. These factors affect the behavior of macrophages, polymorphonuclear leukocytes, lymphocytes, and other cell types. By virtue of their biologic effects, one can see how they may play a role in vivo in the expression of cell-mediated immunity in the skin, in resistance to infection by intracellular facultative organisms, and in inflammation.

While these substances exert marked biologic effects on cells in the microenvironment, they are produced in only minute quantities by activated lymphocytes. Few, if any, of the mediators have been purified sufficiently to know their structure so that their detection might be simplified. We do not know, at this writing, how many chemically distinct

Table 9–1. Products of activated lymphocytes.

Mediators affecting macrophages
  Migration inhibitory factor (MIF)
  Macrophage activation factor (indistinguishable from MIF)
  Chemotactic factor for macrophages
Mediators affecting polymorphonuclear leukocytes
  Chemotactic factors for neutrophils, eosinophils, and basophils
  Leukocyte inhibitory factor (LIF)
  Histamine releasing factor
Mediators affecting lymphocytes
  Mitogenic factors
  Factors affecting antibody production
  Transfer factor
Factors affecting other cell types
  Cytotoxic factors—lymphotoxin
  Growth inhibitory factors
      Clonal inhibitory factor
      Proliferation inhibitory factor
  Osteoclast-activating factor
  Interferon
  Tissue factor
  Colony-stimulating activity
  Immunoglobulin binding factor

mediators there are nor how many are actually involved in vivo in cell-mediated immune reactions. However, there is less than total confusion in this field because several lymphocyte mediators have been partially characterized by physicochemical techniques and shown to be distinct entities having effects on different indicator cells. During the next few years further progress will no doubt be made in the isolation and purification of lymphocyte mediators, and it is hoped that more will be learned about their function in cell-mediated immune reactions.

This chapter will describe the known characteristics and functions of soluble lymphocyte factors, their assay systems, possible in vivo effects, pharmacologic modulation, and clinical significance.

FACTORS AFFECTING MACROPHAGES

Macrophage Migration Inhibitory Factor (MIF)

The first of the lymphocyte mediators to be described was MIF. Many years ago it was shown that cells would not migrate out of spleen fragments taken from tuberculous guinea pigs if old tuberculin was present in the culture medium. The migration of mononuclear cells from explants obtained from normal animals was not inhibited when exposed to the same antigen. Explants of normal cells, in the presence of sera from immune animals, were not inhibited in their migration following exposure to old tuberculin, whereas explants from tuberculous guinea pigs in the presence of normal serum were inhibited by old tuberculin. Thus, cells were shown to be directly or inherently antigen-sensitive and not reactive because of the influence of circulating antibody. More recently, the explant system was replaced by a more quantitative and reproducible method that utilizes peritoneal exudate cells obtained from immune animals and placed in small glass capillary tubes. Peritoneal exudate cells consist primarily of macrophages (70–80%) and some lymphocytes (10–20%). The capillary tubes are sealed at one end, centrifuged, and then cut at the cell-fluid interface. The portion of the capillary containing the cells is placed in a chamber, which is then filled with culture medium that may or may not contain antigen. The chambers are then incubated at 37 °C for 18–24 hours. During this period, the cells migrate out of the capillary tube onto the glass surface of the chamber. In the presence of a specific antigen, it can be shown that the sensitized peritoneal exudate cells do not migrate as far as cells which are not exposed to antigen. The areas of cell migration are measured with an instrument called a planimeter, and the ratio of migration inhibition in the presence of antigen to that in the absence of antigen is calculated.

An investigation into the mechanism of migration inhibition of peritoneal exudate cells revealed the involvement of 2 cell types. By separating lymphocytes from macrophages, the role of each cell has been defined in this system. It was shown that the sensitized lymphocyte carried immunologic information and elaborated a soluble factor, MIF, following stimulation by specific antigen. MIF then acted upon the macrophages to inhibit their migration. This latter reaction was immunologically nonspecific in that MIF affected cells from nonimmune as well as immune animals.

Human lymphocytes have also been shown to produce MIF. Human MIF will inhibit the migration of human monocytes or guinea pig macrophages used as indicator cells. The production of antigen-induced MIF by human and animal lymphocytes is closely associated with the presence of in vivo cellular hypersensitivity of the host to that antigen (Fig 9–1). MIF is not found in the culture fluid of lymphocytes cultured either in the absence of antigen or in the presence of an antigen to which the donor is not sensitive. Under some circumstances, however, lymphocytes will release MIF in the absence of a specific immunologic reaction. For example, if lymphocytes have been activated in vitro by mitogens or other nonspecific stimulants, these cells will produce MIF as well as other mediators.

MIF production can be detected 4–6 hours after lymphocytes have been activated in vitro. The cells will continue to release MIF for as long as 4 days provided that a stimulus persists. MIF is stable at 56 °C for 30 minutes and is a nondialyzable macromolecule.

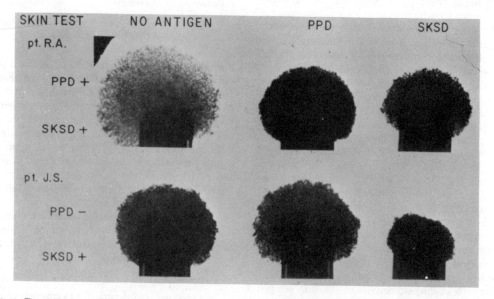

Figure 9–1. The effects of supernates from cultures of lymphocytes from patients RA and JS on normal guinea pig macrophages in capillary tubes. Delayed skin tests in patient RA were positive for both PPD and streptokinase-streptodornase (SK-SD), and MIF was produced in response to both antigens; patient JS was skin test positive for SK-SD but negative for PPD, and MIF was produced only in response to SK-SD. (Reproduced, with permission, from Rocklin RE et al: *J Immunol* 1970;**104**:95.)

Table 9—2. Comparison of the properties of human and guinea pig MIF.

	Guinea Pig MIF	Human MIF
Molecular weight (Sephadex chromatography)	25,000—43,000 (pH5-MIF) 55,000 (pH3-MIF)	23,000—55,000
Chymotrypsin treatment	Sensitive	Sensitive
Neuraminidase treatment	Sensitive	Sensitive
Heat stability (56 °C)	Stable	Stable
Isoelectric point	3.0—4.5 (pH3-MIF); 5.0—5.5 (pH5-MIF)	3.0—4.5 5.0—5.5
Polyacrylamide gel electrophoresis	Prealbumin	Albumin
Buoyant density (CsCl)	Denser than protein	Denser than protein
Salt precipitation ($[NH_4]_2SO_4$)	50-80% saturation	. . .

MIF activity is not diminished when the material is treated with RNase and DNase but is inactivated following enzymatic treatment with trypsin and chymotrypsin. The active synthesis of MIF by cells following stimulation was confirmed by experiments showing that puromycin blocked MIF production. Puromycin is an inhibitor of de novo protein synthesis. In addition, puromycin also affects macrophages in that they no longer respond to preformed MIF. Dactinomycin (actinomycin D), an inhibitor of DNA-dependent RNA synthesis, also prevents lymphocytes from elaborating MIF. Nontoxic doses of corticosteroids do not prevent the lymphocyte from producing MIF in vitro, although they are effective in obliterating the delayed hypersensitivity skin test. Their effect is probably on the macrophage response to preformed MIF.

The properties of guinea pig and human MIF are shown in Table 9–2. Attempts to estimate the size of MIF by sucrose density centrifugation and gel filtration on Sephadex G-100 indicate that guinea pig MIF has a molecular weight of 35–55 thousand and that human MIF is a slightly smaller macromolecule (MW 25,000). Results employing electrophoresis on acrylamide gels demonstrate that guinea pig MIF migrates anodally to albumin, indicating that it is more acidic. Also, the enzyme neuraminidase, which cleaves terminal sialic residues, destroys its activity, suggesting that sialic acid moieties may be necessary for its biologic activity. These results imply that guinea pig MIF is an acidic glycoprotein. Centrifugation of guinea pig MIF in a cesium chloride gradient to determine its buoyant density verifies the glycoprotein nature of this material. Human MIF has similar properties.

Recent experiments indicate that MIF is heterogeneous. Isoelectric focusing of guinea pig and human MIF revealed 2 distinct peaks of activity: one activity with an isoelectric point (pI) of 3.0–4.5 (pH3-MIF) and the other with a pI of 5.0–5.5 (pH5-MIF). pH3-MIF was inactivated by neuraminidase treatment, while pH5-MIF was resistant. Further studies revealed that macrophage-associated esterases can inactivate the pH5-MIF activity, thus identifying a control mechanism for the target cell response to the mediator.

How MIF affects macrophage migration is not known. It would appear that cells which come out of the capillary first are retarded in their migration because they clump together and may physically impede the migration of cells behind them. This could result from membrane changes which cause the cells to become more sticky.

Macrophage Activation Factor

Macrophages obtained from animals made immune by infection exhibit enhanced function when these cells are cultured in vitro. They appear more spread out on glass (Fig 9–2), are more adherent and more phagocytic, and show enhanced bactericidal activity even against organisms antigenically unrelated to those that have infected the host. The in vivo state of activation of macrophages obtained from animals undergoing an active infection can be simulated in vitro by exposing macrophages or monocytes from normal individuals to lymphocyte mediators. It was first shown in the guinea pig that normal macrophages could be "activated" after 72 hours of incubation with a macromolecule similar or identical to MIF. More recent studies indicate that both pH3-MIF and pH5-MIF are capable of causing macrophage activation in vitro. The changes observed included increased adherence to their culture vessel, increased rates of phagocytosis, increased oxidation of glucose through the hexose monophosphate shunt pathway, increased ruffled membrane activity, and increased motility. Monocytes isolated from human blood are plated in monolayers and cultivated with MIF for several days.

Activation of the monocyte monolayers can be measured in a number of ways. One can determine the amount of cellular protein or DNA content per culture dish. This is a measure of cell adherence. The metabolism of monocyte monolayers can be assessed by pulsing them with radioactive ^{14}C-labeled glucose. After a brief incubation period, the amount of $^{14}CO_2$ that has been liberated from the cultures is collected in filter paper and the radioactivity determined. Phagocytosis can be assessed by exposing the monocyte-macrophage monolayers to starch particles and then counting the number of particles which have been ingested per cell. Enhanced bactericidal activity of macrophage monolayers can be determined by exposing the MIF-rich or control monolayers to varying numbers of bacteria and then incubating the monolayers for a short

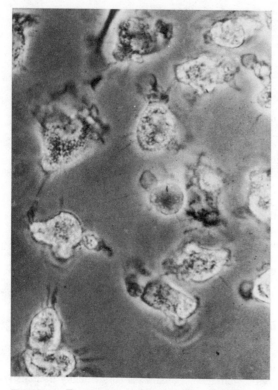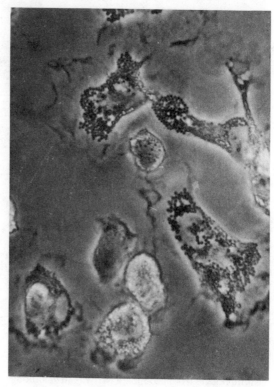

Figure 9–2. The appearance of macrophages after incubation with control supernates *(left)* compared with the appearance of macrophages incubated with MIF-rich fractions *(right).* Note that the latter are more spread out. (Reproduced, with permission, from Nathan DF, David JR, unpublished data.)

time. The cells are then disrupted, the contents plated, and the numbers of surviving bacteria are counted in the MIF-rich monolayers and compared with the counts in the control monolayers.

The tumoricidal capacity of macrophages activated by lymphocyte mediators has been studied in a syngeneic tumor system in strain 2 guinea pigs. Monolayers of normal macrophages were incubated for 3 days in MIF-rich supernates and then co-cultured with radiolabeled hepatoma cells for an additional 24 hours. Cytotoxicity was measured by comparing the number of adherent tumor cells remaining in dishes containing similar numbers of activated and control macrophages. MIF-activated macrophages were cytotoxic for hepatoma and fibrosarcoma cells but not syngeneic fibroblasts or kidney cells. Activation was achieved by supernate preparations devoid of lymphotoxin activity, suggesting that this effect was not due to the adsorption of this mediator onto macrophages.

It is of interest that the activation of macrophages or monocytes takes several days to occur while the inhibition of migration of macrophages may be observed within 24 hours. Just how the inhibition of macrophage migration is related to the later activation of these cells is not known. It has been observed that the inhibition of macrophage migration is a reversible process, ie, that cells initially inhibited in the first 24

hours may again begin to migrate and will actually travel at a faster rate than macrophages in control chambers. It may be that the initial effect of MIF on macrophage function is to change the surface properties of that cell, so that it becomes more sticky. This is observed in one assay as inhibition of migration. Later on, other metabolic changes occur in that cell so that it becomes activated, and in fact its function in general is enhanced. A list of the effects of lymphocyte mediators on macrophage function is shown in Table 9–3.

Macrophage (Monocyte) Chemotactic Factor

As mentioned earlier, the majority of cells infiltrating the site of a delayed hypersensitivity reaction are rapidly dividing, nonsensitive mononuclear cells. This observation has led to the suggestion that the few antigen-activated lymphocytes present might be producing substances which would recruit monocytes. Studies have shown that antigen- or mitogen-activated lymphocytes elaborate a chemotactic substance which selectively attracts macrophages or monocytes. The chemotactic assay is carried out using a chamber which consists of upper and lower compartments separated by a micropore filter of defined pore size. The suspension of macrophages or monocytes is placed in the upper compartment and the chemotactic material in the lower compartment. Usually, one places culture fluid

Table 9–3. Effects of activation of macrophages in vitro by lymphocyte mediators.

Increased adherence to culture vessel

Increased ruffled membrane activity

Increased phagocytosis

Increased pinocytosis

Increased membrane adenylate cyclase

Increased incorporation of glucosamine into membrane components

Decreased electron-dense surface material

Increased glucose oxidation through hexose monophosphate shunt

Increased levels of lactate dehydrogenase in cytoplasm

Decreased levels of certain lysosomal enzymes (acid phosphatase, cathepsin-D, β-glucuronidase)

Increased number of cytoplasmic granules

Enhanced bacteriostasis

Enhanced tumoricidal activity

from unstimulated lymphocytes or from antigen- or mitogen-stimulated lymphocytes in the lower compartment to serve as a chemotactic stimulus. The chambers are incubated at 37 °C for varying times, and the number of cells which migrate through the micropore filter from the top to the bottom are then counted (Fig 9–3). The chemotactic activity of the culture fluid is assessed morphologically by determining the number of cells that have migrated through the micropore filter. A chemotactic index is calculated by subtracting the number of cells which have migrated through the filter, in the presence of the control fluids, from the number of cells migrating through the filter in the presence of the culture fluid obtained from activated lymphocytes. A variation of this assay is one which labels the indicator macrophages with a radioactive substance such as ^{51}Cr and also uses 2 filters instead of one. After the appropriate incubation time, the amount of radioactivity present in the lower filter is determined. This latter modification correlates very well with the morphologic counting of cells, and is perhaps more objective.

The production of macrophage chemotactic factor is antigen-specific. The factor is heat-stable after incubation at 56 °C for 30 minutes (Table 9–4). Its molecular weight in the guinea pig is 35–55 thousand and in humans appears to be 12–25 thousand. On acrylamide gel electrophoresis, the chemotactic activity can be found to migrate in that part of the gel associated with albumin. Its buoyant density is similar to that of pure protein, and it is inactivated by treatment with chymotrypsin but not neuraminidase. Like MIF, the macrophage chemotactic factor is also heterogeneous. Isoelectric focusing experiments revealed peak activities with a pI of 10.1 and 5.6.

The process of chemotaxis or directed migration

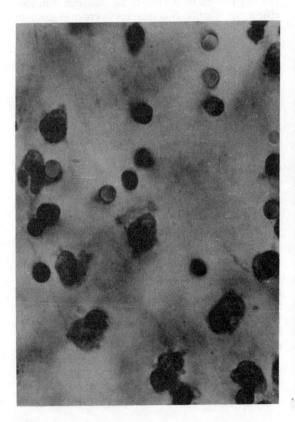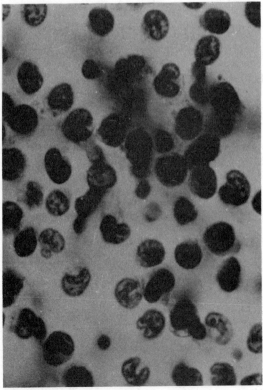

Figure 9–3. The number of cells which have migrated through micropore filters in the absence *(left)* and presence *(right)* of a chemotactic stimulant. (Reproduced, with permission, from Snyderman R et al: *J Immunol* 1972;108:857.)

Table 9—4. Comparison of the properties of human and guinea pig chemotactic factor for macrophages.

	Human	Guinea Pig
Stability at 56 °C	Stable	Stable
Approximate molecular weight determined by gel filtration	12,000– 25,000	35,000–55,000
Disc gel electrophoresis	Albumin	Albumin
Isopyknic centrifugation in cesium chloride	. . .	Like protein
Neuraminidase	Stable	Stable
Chymotrypsin	Sensitive	Sensitive
Isoelectric point	10.1; 5.6	. . .

takes place when the cells are presented with a gradient of the chemotactic material. If the chemotactic material is placed in the upper chamber, as well as being in the lower chamber, then the net result is a loss of directed movement of the cells toward the lower chamber. Furthermore, it has been shown that MIF does not interfere with the activity of chemotactic factor. If MIF is placed in the upper chamber with the cells and the chemotactic factor is placed in the lower chamber, then the net result is an increased movement of the cells toward the lower compartment. When chemotactic factor is placed in the upper chamber with the cells and MIF in the lower chamber, the net result is a loss of directed movement toward the lower chamber.

FACTORS THAT AFFECT POLYMORPHONUCLEAR LEUKOCYTES

Leukocyte Inhibitory Factor (LIF)

The system of polymorphonuclear leukocyte migration inhibition in humans appears to be analogous to that seen in the macrophage system. Polymorphonuclear leukocytes are inhibited in their migration by a soluble material termed leukocyte inhibitory factor or LIF. The effect of LIF is solely on polymorphonuclear leukocyte migration and not upon the migration of macrophages. LIF is produced by sensitized lymphocytes following incubation with specific antigen as well as after stimulation by concanavalin A. LIF can be

Table 9—5. Physicochemical properties of human LIF.

Heat stability	Stable at 56 °C for 30 min Diminished at 80 °C for 30 min
pH stability	4.0–10.0
Molecular weight	60,000–70,000
Buoyant density	Protein
Gel electrophoresis (pH 9.1)	Albumin
Chymotrypsin	Sensitive
Neuraminidase	Resistant
L-Cysteine	Sensitive
2-Mercaptoethanol	Sensitive
Isoelectric point	5.0–5.5; 8.0–8.5
DFP	Sensitive

assayed using human buffy coat cells, as indicated, or by purifying polymorphonuclear leukocytes from the blood and placing them either in capillary tubes, as in the MIF system, or in agar. Cell migration is measured at 18–24 hours, the relative areas of migration are determined, and the amount of inhibition of cell migration is calculated.

The physicochemical properties of human LIF are shown in Table 9–5. Human LIF is nondialyzable, heat-stable at 56 °C for 30 minutes, and has an approximate molecular weight on gel filtration of 68,000. Electrophoretically, LIF has a charge similar to that of albumin and a buoyant density similar to that of pure protein. It is inactivated by enzymatic treatment with chymotrypsin but is resistant to the effects of neuraminidase. LIF appears to be a protease because of its sensitivity to the alkylating effects of diisopropyl fluorophosphate (DFP). In contrast, human MIF is resistant to this compound. It is not known how LIF affects polymorphonuclear leukocyte function in other respects.

Chemotactic Factors for Neutrophils, Basophils, & Eosinophils

Sensitized lymphocytes elaborate chemotactic factors for all 3 types of polymorphonuclear leukocytes. There appear to be 2 factors which affect the directed movement of eosinophils. One of these factors requires the interaction of the mediator with specific antigen-antibody complexes in order to generate the activity, whereas the other factor is active in the absence of antigen-antibody complexes. The chemotactic factors are similar in molecular weight, ranging from 24,000 to 55,000. The chemotactic factor for neutrophils has been separated from that for macrophages. Both of these factors have been found to migrate in different parts of a gel during electrophoresis. It is not clear, however, whether these factors are all distinct materials or the same substance with chemotactic activity for multiple cell types. These chemotactic factors may play a role in various chronic inflammatory disorders or in certain types of delayed hypersensitivity reactions such as the Jones-Mote (cutaneous basophil hypersensitivity) reaction.

Histamine-Releasing Factor

A mediator has recently been described having effects on basophils. This factor, termed histamine releasing factor, is produced by sensitized human lymphocytes in response to antigen and nonspecifically by ConA. It has the capacity to induce histamine release from human basophils in a noncytotoxic manner. The factor is nondialyzable, heat-stable at 56 °C for 30 minutes, and has a molecular weight by gel filtration of 12,000.

MEDIATORS AFFECTING LYMPHOCYTES

Lymphocyte Mitogenic Factor

Following stimulation by specific antigen, sensitized lymphocytes release into the culture fluid a substance which has mitogenic activity for nonsensitized lymphocytes. This material induces normal lymphocytes to undergo blast transformation and incorporate increased amounts of ^{3}H-thymidine into cellular DNA. Lymphocyte mitogenic factor may be detected in the culture fluids of antigen-stimulated lymphocytes after 24–48 hours. These culture fluids are then incubated with nonsensitive lymphocytes for about 6 days. Cell division and transformation are monitored, either by counting the numbers of transformed cells on stained slides or by measuring the incorporation of ^{3}H-thymidine into cellular DNA. Cell division in the cultures that have been incubated with culture fluids obtained from antigen-stimulated lymphocytes is significantly greater than that due to culture fluids from unstimulated lymphocytes.

Lymphocyte mitogenic factor is a nondialyzable macromolecule and is heat-stable at 56 °C for 30 minutes. It is resistant to treatment with RNase and DNase as well as treatment with proteolytic enzymes such as trypsin. It has a molecular weight of approximately 20–30 thousand. This factor is produced within the first 24 hours of culture, and while it is produced by lymphocytes prior to their cell division, it is not clear whether DNA synthesis is required in order for the cells to be able to generate the material.

Mitogenic factors capable of activating or recruiting nonsensitive lymphocytes could furnish a mechanism for expanding a cellular reaction and producing greater amounts of other mediators. The exact role of lymphocyte mitogenic factor in the proliferative response is not clear. It may be that the first stage of proliferation is initiated after activated lymphocytes have released this factor. The second stage would be the nonspecific activation of other lymphocytes by the material. Alternatively, some sensitized lymphocytes may directly proliferate in the absence of lymphocyte mitogenic factor when stimulated by specific antigen.

Factors Affecting Antibody Production

Following stimulation by a specific antigen, lymphocytes from several species produce soluble factors which modulate antibody production. In the mouse, a material has been described that triggers B cells to make 19S IgM class antibody to sheep red cells. In addition, factors have been reported which also increase IgG and IgE antibody production. In humans, a material induces B cells to proliferate, lose their C3 receptors, increase their protein synthesis, and induce production of IgG antibody to specific antigens. On the other hand, there are factors capable of suppressing antibody production.

The factors modulating antibody production have not been well characterized, and it is not known whether they are the same factor acting at a different concentration or several distinct materials. The enhancing factor appears to be a nondialyzable, heat-stable macromolecule. The antibody-suppressing factor appears also to be a nondialyzable material with a molecular weight of 25–55 thousand. This material

may provide a mechanism by which T cells and B cells cooperate in the production of antibody to certain antigens (see Chapter 8).

Transfer Factor

The ability to transfer delayed hypersensitivity in humans can be accomplished by means of a dialyzable material obtained from sensitized individuals. Sensitized lymphocytes contain a substance of low molecular weight called transfer factor which is released either by disrupting the cells or by stimulating them with a specific antigen. This material has the capability of preparing nonsensitive lymphocytes so that they too are then able to respond to specific antigen by undergoing increased DNA synthesis and mediator production.

Transfer factor has a molecular weight of less than 4000, is resistant to treatment by DNase and RNase, but is orcinol-positive. The mechanism by which transfer factor is able to prepare nonsensitized lymphocytes to respond to specific antigen is unknown. There is some indication that the material may be a single-stranded polynucleotide which either is informational or may provide some part of a receptor for antigen. Transfer factor can specifically transfer delayed hypersensitivity without preparing the host to make antibody against the same antigen. It has recently been used as a therapeutic agent in selected patients with immunodeficiency (see Chapter 25).

MEDIATORS AFFECTING OTHER CELL TYPES

Cytotoxic Factors (Lymphotoxin) & Growth Inhibitory Factors

Immune lymphocytes may bring about the cytolysis of certain susceptible target cells in 2 ways. One involves attachment of the lymphocyte directly to the target cell, bringing about lysis of the cell by unknown mechanisms; this is referred to as direct lymphocyte-mediated cytolysis. A second mechanism involves the release of a factor which, in the absence of the lymphocyte, may also bring about the lysis of certain target cells. This material has been referred to as lymphotoxin. This phenomenon was first described in the rat, where lymph node lymphocytes obtained from sensitized rats produced a soluble factor that killed normal rat embryo fibroblasts. Subsequently, lymphotoxic substances have been described in other species, including humans. Sensitized human lymphocytes, in response to specific antigen or in response to mitogens, release a soluble factor or factors which have cytotoxic effects on certain target cells.

There are several assay systems which can detect the activity of lymphotoxin. Lymphocytes are cultured with and without a stimulant for 1–2 days, and the culture fluids are then collected and incubated with the target cells, one of the most susceptible being the mouse L cell or fibroblast. Cytotoxic activity by lymphotoxin on the mouse L cell can be detected in a

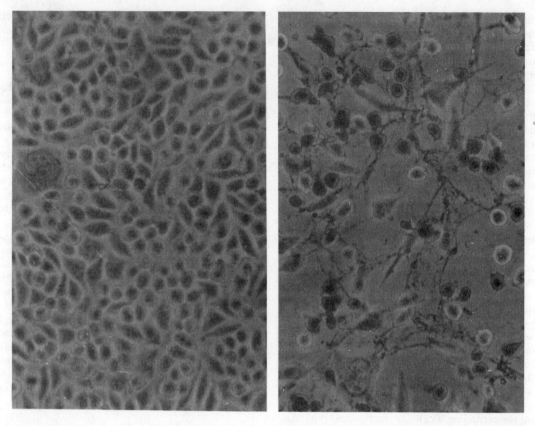

Figure 9–4. Effect on mouse L cell monolayers of incubation for 48 hours with supernates from cultures of lymphocytes. *Left:* Control supernates. *Right:* Supernates containing lymphotoxin. (Reproduced, with permission, from Rosenberg SA et al: *J Immunol* 1973;110:1623.)

number of ways: morphologic counting of the viable remaining cells (Fig 9–4), incorporation of ^{14}C-labeled amino acids into cell protein, or release of ^{51}Cr from labeled target cells.

Guinea pig lymphotoxin is heat-labile, has an estimated molecular weight of 35–55 thousand, migrates with albumin on electrophoresis, has a buoyant density similar to that of protein, and is inactivated by chymotrypsin but not by neuraminidase. The

properties of human lymphotoxin, which has been shown to be heterogeneous, are presented in Table 9–6.

The following mechanism has been postulated for the action of lymphotoxin on susceptible target cells: The lymphocyte, having been activated by intimate contact with target cell membranes, is induced to synthesize the mediator. Following its production, lymphotoxin binds to the target cell membrane, where it

Table 9–6. Physicochemical properties of human lymphotoxins.

	α-LT	β-LT	γ-LT
Molecular weight (molecular sieve chromatography)	75,000–100,000	45,000–50,000	25,000
Trypsin treatment	Stable?	. . .	Sensitive
Pronase treatment	Sensitive	. . .	. . .
DNase, RNase, and neuraminidase treatment	Stable	. . .	. . .
Heat stability at 80 °C	Sensitive	Sensitive	Sensitive
Heat stability at 56 °C	Stable	. . .	. . .
Treatment at pH 5.0–11.0	Stable	. . .	. . .
Storage at 4 °C	Stable	Unstable	Unstable
Isoelectric point	6.8–8.0	. . .	. . .
Polyacrylamide gel electrophoresis	α_2 'β-Globulin	Heterogeneous β-LT$_1$, β-LT$_2$	. . .
Neutralized by anti-α-LT antibodies	Yes	No	No
Peak production after mitogen stimulation	2–3(5) d	8–24 h	< 24 h

effects target cell lysis. Target cell membrane disruption, or physical dislodgment, promotes the lymphocyte's release from the target cell and subsequent cessation of lymphotoxin secretion. This mechanism would inhibit an indiscriminate destruction by lymphocytes which produce the factor and would prevent nonspecific cell damage in the host. The significance of in vivo production of lymphotoxin is unclear. Its role might be related to tumor surveillance, ie, the destruction of neoplastic cells, but how it relates to other delayed hypersensitivity reactions is not clear.

Some activities have been described which, rather than causing the lysis of target cells, inhibit their growth pattern. Such materials have been referred to as proliferation inhibition factor and cloning inhibition factor. These effects are mainly observed on certain target cells such as human HeLa cells. It has recently been shown that all 3 of these activities may be present in the same culture fluid. When present in high concentration, the effect of lymphotoxin may be seen. At lower levels, a permanent growth inhibition may be observed to occur, and at still lower concentrations of mediator only a temporary inhibition of cell growth is noted. It is still not clear whether the effects of lysis and growth inhibition are the result of 3 separate macromolecules or one molecule which can exert diverse effects on different cells depending upon its concentration in the medium.

Interferon

Viruses can induce interferon production in many cell types. Lymphocytes may also produce interferon-like materials when stimulated by either viral or nonviral inducers. Interferon-like activity can be detected in the culture fluid of both antigen- and mitogen-stimulated normal lymphocytes. Interferon stimulated by mitogen takes 3 days to be produced, whereas that induced with antigen takes 7 days. One way in which interferon can be assayed is by taking the culture fluids from unstimulated or stimulated lymphocytes and incubating them in monolayers of neonatal foreskin fibroblasts for 18–24 hours at 37 °C. The monolayers are washed and infected with bovine vesicular stomatitis virus. The number of viral plaques is determined. The interferon titer is defined as that concentration of culture supernate which results in a 50% reduction in the number of viral plaques.

Antigen- or mitogen-induced interferon and virus-induced interferon material share some similarities. They are stable at pH 4.0–10.0, stable at 4 °C for 24 hours, nonsedimentable at 100,000 g for 2 hours, and resistant to DNase and RNase but destroyed by trypsin. Their effect is specific for cells of human origin. Studies in mice suggest that the actual cell which synthesizes interferon is the macrophage, not the lymphocyte. The latter is important, however, in activating monocytes to produce interferon.

Interferon production following or during a specific immunologic reaction is potentially important to the host. Persons who are unable to mount an adequate cellular immune response are plagued by viral infections, and the ability of their lymphocytes to release interferon following stimulation by certain antigens may help determine the level of their resistance to this type of infection.

Osteoclast-Activating Factor

There are several substances which are capable of causing the resorption of bone. These include parathyroid hormone, prostaglandin E_2, and vitamin D metabolites and other sterols. Recently, another mediator of bone resorption has been identified that could be of importance in causing the hypercalcemia seen in neoplastic disease or in the pathogenesis of bone resorption in dental caries. This material is produced by lymphocytes in vitro following stimulation by specific antigen or mitogen and is capable of forming osteoclasts in bone and activating these cells. The technique for measuring bone resorption in organ culture consists of labeling shafts of radius or ulna from 19-day rat fetuses with ^{45}Ca. The culture fluids from lymphocytes are incubated with the organ cultures for 4–6 days. The ratio of ^{45}Ca released into the medium from control and treated bone cultures is used as a measure of bone resorption.

Osteoclast-activating factor has a molecular weight of 13–25 thousand, is heat-labile, and is inactivated by proteolytic enzymes. It can be differentiated from other bone-resorbing material, including parathyroid hormone, vitamin D metabolites, and prostaglandin E_2.

Procoagulant Factor Activity (Tissue Factor)

Antigen- or mitogen-stimulated mononuclear cells produce a procoagulant material that when incubated with factor VIII-deficient plasma is able to correct the prolonged clotting time. This material is antigenically distinct from factor VIII and has been identified as being tissue factor. It is very labile and has not yet been well characterized. The pathophysiologic importance of tissue factor also has yet to be determined, but it is interesting to consider the various entities characterized by both lymphocytic infiltration and pathologic thrombosis, eg, rejection of a transplanted kidney and the delayed hypersensitivity skin test.

Colony-Stimulating Factor

The differentiation of bone marrow cells into granulocytes and mononuclear cells in vitro can be accomplished by the addition of a colony-stimulating factor. While blood monocytes and tissue macrophages appear to be a major source of this material, recent evidence suggests that lymphocytes may also actively produce the material during an immunologic reaction. Mitogen-activated lymphocytes from thymus and spleen elaborate colony-stimulating factor after 4 days in culture. Analysis reveals a heat-stable glycoprotein with a molecular weight of approximately 40–60 thousand.

Immunoglobulin-Binding Factor

This factor was originally described in the guinea

Table 9–7. Properties of immunoglobulin-binding factor.

	Mouse
Temperature (56 °C for 30 min)	Labile
Sieve chromatography	140,000; 300,000
Isoelectric point (pI)	6.30
Polyacrylamide gel electrophoresis (SDS)	80,000
2-Mercaptoethanol	40,000 and 20,000
Trypsin	Sensitive
Pronase	Sensitive
Neuraminidase	Sensitive

pig as having the ability to combine with IgG complexed to antigen and prevent the fixation of C1q. Recent studies in mice suggest that this material may be the Fc receptor shed from T cells. Furthermore, its biologic activity has included a role in regulating antibody formation. Its properties are shown in Table 9–7.

IN VIVO SIGNIFICANCE OF MEDIATORS

Skin Reactive Factor

That products of activated lymphocytes may play a role in the expression of delayed hypersensitivity was shown when lymphocyte mediators were injected into the skin of normal animals. A partially purified preparation of lymphocyte mediators derived from antigen-stimulated cells caused the accelerated development of a delayed hypersensitivity reaction in the skin of normal guinea pigs. The reaction was characterized by the development within 3–5 hours of erythema and induration which reached a peak by 8–12 hours and disappeared by 30 hours. Histologically, the lesion simulated a delayed hypersensitivity reaction in that the infiltrate was comprised primarily of mononuclear cells. The factor or factors responsible for this reaction could be destroyed by trypsin and papain but were resistant to the effects of DNase and RNase. Furthermore, drugs such as puromycin, chlorphenesin, and dactinomycin prevented its production. Cortisone, however, had no effect on its production in vitro by lymphocytes, although it could prevent the expression of this reaction in vivo. Since preparations used to elicit this response contain several mediators, including MIF, chemotactic factor, lymphotoxin, and mitogenic factor, it is not clear at present whether one or a combination of these is responsible for the development of the skin reaction. Some preparations of skin reactive factor also possess vasoactive properties. When injected into the skin, this material will induce the extravasation of Evans blue dye between 20 minutes and 4 hours later. The increased permeability induced by skin reactive factor is not blocked by inhibitors of histamine or 5-hydroxytryptamine but is affected by inhibitors of the kinin system.

Macrophage Disappearance Reaction

If one injects mineral oil intraperitoneally into normal guinea pigs, there ensues over the next few days the development of a peritoneal exudate cell population characterized primarily by macrophages. If specific antigen is injected intraperitoneally along with the oil in an appropriately sensitized guinea pig, then the exudate which forms in that animal contains considerably fewer macrophages. This phenomenon has been termed the macrophage disappearance reaction and is associated with a delayed hypersensitivity state. Moreover, it can be shown that culture fluids derived from antigen-stimulated lymphocytes can substitute for intact cells in eliciting this reaction in vivo. This reaction is mediated by a factor similar to if not identical with MIF. The mechanism responsible for this reaction is unknown but may involve the fact that the macrophages have become sticky and adhere to the peritoneum and thus are not present in the exudate.

Mediator Activity Found in Serum

The usual means for eliciting mediator production is by culturing lymphocytes in vitro. Of particular interest is the observation that MIF and interferon activities can be detected in the serum of animals undergoing an immunologic reaction. Serum collected from animals immunized with BCG and then desensitized by administering a large dose of old tuberculin antigen intravenously was found to contain these activities. When serum from the desensitized animal was filtered on a Sephadex column, both activities were found in the same fraction (MW 45,000).

Effect of Mediators on Lymph Node Architecture

A vasoactive material can be recovered from guinea pig lymph node cells which increases vascular permeability within 30 minutes of injection into normal skin. This material, termed lymph node permeability factor, could be extracted from lymph nodes of immunized animals but could also be obtained in equal amounts from nonimmune animals. Extracts of this material are also obtained from other tissues, including spleen, thyroid, lung, kidney, liver, and muscle. This vasoactive material can be differentiated from other known permeability factors, such as histamine, 5-hydroxytryptamine, bradykinin, and kallikrein. Lymph node permeability factor appears to be different in many respects from the other mediators already discussed. It is released without an immunologic stimulus and is found in numerous tissues, suggesting that it may not play a primary role in the delayed hypersensitivity reaction. It may, however, play a secondary role by contributing to the inflammatory process per se through its release subsequent to cell or tissue damage.

If the efferent lymph is collected from animals undergoing an immunologic reaction, one can detect mediatorlike activity in this fluid. MIF-like and mitogenic factor activity is present in efferent lymph several days after antigen has been injected into the draining lymph nodes. One also observes other changes during this time, including increased vascular permeability, increased flow rate of lymph, and increased output of lymphocytes into the efferent lymph. If preformed mediators are injected into the afferent lymphatics, then one can show changes similar to those that develop in response to antigenic challenge. These changes include increased tissue weight and increased numbers of cells in the efferent lymph as well as paracortical distention and germinal center enlargement. It is thought that the mediators may in some way cause cellular retention by plugging the efferent vessels, thus regulating the rate of efflux of these cells.

CELL TYPES PRODUCING MEDIATORS

Delayed hypersensitivity reactions are generally assumed to be mediated by T cells. It has been further assumed that antigen-induced production of lymphocyte mediators is also a function of the T cell. The recent availability of techniques to separate T and B cells into purified subpopulations has permitted an evaluation of which cell types, in fact, produce these substances. Various studies indicate that both cell types are capable of producing some mediators. For example, both T cells and B cells are capable of producing MIF, chemotactic factor for macrophages, leukocyte inhibitory factor, and interferon. It would appear that lymphocyte mitogenic factor and colony-stimulating factor are produced only by T cells. Several of the lymphocyte mediators from both B and T cells appear to have similar chromatographic patterns. If B cells do produce the same mediators as T cells, then one must reinterpret the role of the B cell in cellular immunity.

PHARMACOLOGIC MODULATION OF MEDIATOR PRODUCTION

Cyclic 3′,5′-adenosine monophosphate (cAMP) plays an important role as a "second messenger" in the regulation of intracellular metabolism. In most normal secretory cells, an increased level of cAMP results in increased production of cell products. In contrast, the immune system is affected differently by cyclic nucleotides. For example, the antigen-induced release of histamine from basophils is abrogated by agents known to raise intracellular levels of cAMP. It has also been shown that immunologic reactions, such as lymphocyte-mediated cytotoxicity and the inhibition of macrophage migration by MIF, are also abrogated by agents which raise cAMP levels. Drugs such as isoproterenol, epinephrine, and prostaglandin E_1, which raise cAMP levels by stimulating adenylate cyclase, and theophylline, which retards its breakdown, interfere with the MIF-induced inhibition of guinea pig macrophages. This effect appears to be on the macrophage response to MIF and not due to inactivation of MIF by the drug. The dibutyryl derivative of cAMP is also effective in blocking MIF activity on macrophages. There is a suggestion that some drugs which elevate levels of cAMP also depress the lymphocyte production of MIF.

The vasoactive amine histamine also appears to play a role in modulating the lymphocyte response to antigen. There is evidence that histamine affects the lymphocyte production of MIF. Histamine has no effect on the macrophage response to preformed MIF. The effects of histamine on the lymphocyte production of MIF can be blocked by certain types of antihistamines (H_2) but not others (H_1). It is not known whether the inhibitory effect on MIF production by histamine acts via its ability to raise cAMP levels or is due to the activation of certain suppressor lymphocytes which may subsequently act upon the MIF-producing cells. Histamine stimulates the production of a lymphokine with immunosuppressive properties.

CLINICAL SIGNIFICANCE

The production of soluble mediators by lymphocytes from normal subjects generally correlates positively with the in vivo state of cellular immunity in that donor. These substances are usually not produced by antigens which fail to elicit a positive delayed skin test. Lymphocytes from some patients with depressed cellular immunity and cutaneous anergy (negative delayed skin tests to multiple antigens) also do not produce these mediators in response to antigenic stimulation. For example, lymphocytes from patients with the DiGeorge syndrome, sarcoidosis, chronic mucocutaneous candidiasis, Wiskott-Aldrich syndrome, Hodgkin's disease, and rheumatoid arthritis do not produce the mediator MIF. In some cases, however, the proliferative response to antigens and mitogens may be normal, even though MIF production is depressed. The cutaneous anergy in these patients may be due to a lack of mediator production (MIF) by their lymphocytes. In other anergic patients, MIF production and proliferative responses are normal, perhaps indicating intact lymphocyte function. Abnormalities in macrophage function or the inflammatory response might explain the anergy observed in these latter patients.

The MIF assay has also been used for the detection of sensitized lymphocytes in patients with certain disease whose pathogenesis may involve an immune mechanism. Lymphocytes from patients with glomerulonephritis produce MIF in response to glomerular basement membrane antigens. Lymphocytes from some of these patients also react to group A streptococci, antigens known to cross-react immunologically with human glomeruli. Although these studies suggest that the lymphocyte may play a significant role in the pathogenesis of certain glomerular lesions, they do not permit one to distinguish whether this involvement is primary to the initiation of tissue damage or secondary, ie, resulting from tissue damage. MIF production has also been found in patients with thyroiditis, pernicious anemia, multiple sclerosis, and Guillain-Barré syndrome when their lymphocytes have been tested with various tissue antigens.

BIOLOGIC SIGNIFICANCE

Lymphocyte mediators might relate to the development of a cellular immune reaction in the following way: Antigen-sensitive lymphocytes, when stimulated by the appropriate antigen, become activated and start synthesizing the various lymphocyte mediators. Chemotactic factors for monocytes and polymorphonuclear leukocytes recruit inflammatory cells to the reaction site. Once there, the macrophages and polymorphonuclear leukocytes might be held at the site by MIF and LIF. Macrophages might be activated to an enhanced state by the action of the activating factor. Other lymphocytes are recruited to participate in the reaction by the mitogenic factor. Lymphocyte mitogenic factor nonspecifically activates other lymphocytes in the area which would perhaps, in turn, start producing lymphocyte mediators. These events have the effect of amplifying an initially small reaction. Once activated, the inflammatory cells become bactericidal or tumoricidal. Furthermore, the vasoactive properties of some of the mediators may account for part of the inflammation. Other protein systems, including the complement system, the kinin system, and the clotting system, are also called into play. If antigen remained at the site, such a reaction would continue, abating as the antigen supply was exhausted. In addition, there may be control systems which inactivate the mediators as they are produced, but these are not well defined at present.

•   •   •

References

Bloom BR: In vitro approaches to the mechanism of cell-mediated immune reactions. *Adv Immunol* 1971;**13**:205.

Bloom BR, Glade P (editors): *In Vitro Methods in Cell-Mediated Immunity.* Academic Press, 1970.

David JR: Macrophage activation by lymphocyte mediators. *Fed Proc* 1975;**34**:1730.

David JR, David RR: Cellular hypersensitivity and immunity: Inhibition of macrophage migration and the lymphocyte mediators. *Prog Allergy* 1972;**16**:300.

David JR, Rocklin RE: Lymphocyte mediators. Pages 307–324 in: *Immunological Diseases,* 3rd ed. Samter M (editor). Little, Brown, 1978.

Lawrence HS: Transfer factor. *Adv Immunol* 1969;**11**:195.

Lawrence HS, Landy M (editors): *Mediators of Cellular Immunity.* Academic Press, 1969.

Nelson DS (editor): *Immunobiology of the Macrophage.* Academic Press, 1976.

Rocklin RE: Clinical applications of in vitro lymphocyte tests. *Prog Clin Immunol* 1974;**2**:21.

Rocklin RE, Bendtzen K, Greineder D: Mediators of immunity: Lymphokines and monokines. *Adv Immunol* 1980;**29**:56.

Phagocytic Cells: Chemotaxis & Effector Functions of Macrophages & Granulocytes | 10

I. MACROPHAGES*
Zena Werb, PhD

It has been a century since Elie Metchnikoff noted that during the inflammatory response leukocytes engulf microorganisms by a process he called **phagocytosis.** There are 2 types of "professional" phagocytes: the **polymorphonuclear leukocytes,** which are circulating cells that migrate into sites of inflammation (see part II of this chapter); and the **mononuclear phagocytes,** which are found circulating in the blood and fixed in tissues and also accumulate in sites of inflammation. Both of these cell types are able to recognize and ingest particles and soluble ligands through receptors on their cell surfaces and to digest these substances within lysosomal compartments. Mononuclear phagocytes, however, show much greater diversity in function and response. This diversity of structure and function is the result of progressive maturation of these cells from their bone marrow precursors, their experiences with endocytosis, and their interaction with T lymphocytes.

Since Metchnikoff coined the term **macrophage,** the chief criterion for identification of these cells has been their phagocytic capacity. From functional and morphologic studies, Aschoff defined the reticuloendothelial system, which, in addition to these phagocytic histiocytes, included a variety of lymphatic and sinusoidal cells. Fibroblasts and endothelial cells, which take up colloidal gold by endocytosis, were added to the list of reticuloendothelial cells by other researchers. It is only in the last 15 years that a new classification of macrophages, monocytes, and their precursor cells has been established. On the basis of their common origin from a hematopoietic stem cell, morphologic features and observed functions, these cells have been grouped together into one system: the mononuclear phagocyte system (Table 10–1). Although the mononuclear phagocytes can be considered to belong to one system, they display functional properties in the environment formed by other systems, including that of lymphatic organs and connective tissue.

*This work was supported in part by the Department of Energy.

LIFE HISTORY & TISSUE DISTRIBUTION OF MONONUCLEAR PHAGOCYTES

Mononuclear phagocytes arise in the bone marrow from a pluripotential stem cell common to all of the hematopoietic cells, including erythrocytes, megakaryocytes, granulocytes, and mononuclear phagocytes. As the stem cell becomes more committed through progressive divisions, the mononuclear phagocytes and the granulocytic series continue to share a common committed stem cell. In culture, these bone marrow cells give rise to mixed colonies of

Table 10–1. Cells of the mononuclear phagocyte system in normal and inflamed tissues.*

Cells	Localization
Stem cells (committed) ↓	Bone marrow
Monoblasts ↓	Bone marrow
Promonocytes ↓	Bone marrow
Monocytes ↓	Bone marrow
Macrophages	Tissues
Normal state	
Histiocytes	Connective tissues
Alveolar macrophages	Lung
Kupffer cells	Liver
Pleural and peritoneal macrophages	Serous cavities
Osteoclasts	Bone
Microglial cells	Nervous system
Synovial type A cells	Joints
Free and fixed tissue macrophages	Spleen, lymph nodes, bone marrow, and other tissues
Inflammation	
Exudate macrophages	Any tissue
Activated macrophages	Any tissue
Elicited macrophages	Any tissue
Epithelioid cells	Any tissue
Multinucleated giant cells (Langerhans types and foreign body type)	Any tissue

*Adapted from Van Furth R (editor): *Mononuclear Phagocytes: Functional Aspects.* Martinus Nijhoff, 1980.

granulocytes and macrophages under some conditions and monocytic colonies under others. The first progenitor cell identifiable as part of the mononuclear phagocyte system is the **monoblast** (Table 10–2), which is a round cell 10–12 μm in diameter with a small rim of basophilic cytoplasm containing a few granules. Monoblasts are capable of phagocytosis and adherence to glass; they display Fc receptors and the esterase cytochemistry typical of the more mature progeny; and they are distinct from myeloblasts, which are the precursors in the granulocytic series. In the mouse, each monoblast divides once, giving rise to the promonocytes with a cycle of about 12 hours.

The promonocytes are about 15 μm in diameter, with an indented nucleus occupying over half the cell. They share with the monoblast the typical features of mononuclear phagocytes, including prominent storage granules that stain azurophilic in smears, some of which are also positive for myeloperoxidase. The azurophil storage granules are synthesized only through this stage of maturation (Table 10–3).

The promonocytes mature into **monocytes,** which have decreased numbers of peroxidase-positive granules and an increased ratio of cytoplasm to nucleus. In contrast to the neutrophils, the marrow reserve of preformed monocytes is small. In humans, they are released into the blood within 2½ days after their formation, where they circulate with a half-life of about 1 day, emigrating randomly from the circulating pool to the extravascular pool. In general, monocytes do not reenter the circulating pool. During inflammation, monocyte production is increased by expansion of the promonocyte pool, a decrease in cell cycle time, and release into the circulation more rapidly. **Tissue macrophages** arise by maturation of monocytes that have emigrated from the blood and by proliferation of immature macrophages in the resident macrophage population that retain their ability to respond to mitogens such as colony-stimulating factor. The relative

predominance of proliferation in phagocytes versus hematopoietic origin is controversial. Most studies favor predominance of the hematopoietic route. In the normal steady state in the mouse, over half of the circulating monocytes settle in the liver as Kupffer cells, with another 15% settling in the pulmonary alveoli. The life span of the mature macrophage is probably months.

With inflammation, both the influx of blood monocytes and the local proliferation of tissue macrophages increase dramatically, and in some granulomas the turnover of the macrophages may also be increased. During inflammation, macrophages in tissues may become activated, leading to structural and functional changes in response to mediators released by antigen-stimulated lymphocytes and complement components. **Giant cells** arise either by fusion of macrophages or failure of cytokinesis during mitosis. **Epithelioid cells**—another form of mature inflam-

Table 10–3. Changes in cellular functional characteristics with maturation of mononuclear phagocytes.

Property	Promono-cyte	Mono-cyte	Immature Macro-phage	Mature Macro-phage
Proliferation	++++	+++	++	0
Azurophil granules (myeloperoxidase-positive)	+++	++	±	0
Lysosomes	+	++	++++	++++
Glass adherence	+	++	+++	+++
Phagocytosis	±	+	+++	++++
Fc receptors	+	++	+++	+++
Lymphocyte interaction	?	++	++++	++++
Nonspecific esterase	+++	+++	+++	+++
Lysozyme secretion	?	++	++	++

+ = representation in the population; ± = small portion of entire population.

Table 10–2. Kinetics of mononuclear phagocytes.

Cell	Property	Human	Mouse
Monoblast	Pool size	?	2.5×10^5
	Cell cycle time	?	12 hours
Promonocyte	Pool size	6×10^8/kg	5×10^5/kg
	Cell cycle time	?	16 hours
	Percentage of nucleated marrow cells	2.9%	0.25%
Monocyte	Pool size in marrow	?	2.5×10^6
	Production rate, basal	7×10^6/kg/h	0.6×10^5/h/kg
	Production rate, inflammation	28×10^6/kg/h	1×10^5/h/kg
	Time in marrow	19–60 hours	2 hours
	Pool size in blood	2.7×10^5/mL	1×10^6/mL
	Half-time in blood	8–71 hours	22 hours
	Pool size marginating in the capillaries	3–4 times circulating pool	
Tissue macrophages Liver	Steady-state distribution from blood (as percentage of monocytes' steady stete)	?	56
Alveoli		?	15
Peritoneum		?	8
Other		?	21
	Turnover time	?	20–60 days

matory mononuclear phagocyte—have decreased phagocytic and digestive capacity and increased endoplasmic reticulum, which suggest that they may have secretory roles.

Macrophages are seen early in development of the lymphoid system and are known to play a role in tissue resorption associated with embryonic development. In parallel with the maturation of the lymphoid system, the mononuclear phagocytes show increasing development during fetal and neonatal life, and a number of their functions are relatively immature at birth. Replication of the tissue macrophages and their precursors appears to be under control of specific growth factors, termed colony-stimulating factors, that are produced by fibroblasts, lymphocytes, and mononuclear phagocytes. The best-characterized colony-stimulating factor is a glycoprotein of MW 60,000 that is recognized by specific receptors found on the surfaces of mononuclear phagocytes.

ENDOCYTOSIS & MACROPHAGE PLASMA MEMBRANE RECEPTORS

The most prominent functional property of the macrophage is its ability to recognize foreign or damaged materials. **Endocytosis** by macrophages may be classified as outlined in Table 10–4. **Pinocytosis** is the ingestion of solutes from the extracellular milieu by the formation of micropinocytic vesicles, which are usually $0.2\ \mu m$ in size, or by the formation of macropinocytic vesicles, which are $1–2\ \mu m$ in size. Although it is likely that both types of pinocytosis are triggered by binding of a soluble ligand to specific receptors, the 2 processes are under different metabolic control, and in the case of macropinocytosis much larger samples of the solutes in the fluid phase of the extracellular medium are included in the vesicle during ingestion. Even without a phagocytic load, macrophages in culture internalize the equivalent of their entire surface area every 30 minutes. **Micropinocytosis,** which is mediated by small vesicles surrounded by a clathrin-rich bristle coat, appears to be constitutive but may be stimulated by specific ligands. **Macropinocytosis** is much more intermittent; is minimal under conditions such as culture in low concen-

trations of serum; and is stimulated by high concentrations of serum and by ionic compounds such as mucopolysaccharides and soluble immune complexes.

During **phagocytosis,** particles are bound to specific or nonspecific membrane receptors, then surrounded by the cell membrane, forming **phagocytic vesicles** (Fig 10–1). The binding and ingestion phases are distinct, and, at low concentrations of specific ligands, particles may bind to the surface of the macrophage without being ingested. The internalization of the particles is a highly organized process that requires circumferential attachment of the macrophage receptors to the ligands attached to the particle, a process called **zippering.** If the ligands are not present at sufficient density for this recognition phenomenon to occur or if the receptors on the macrophage surface are not sufficiently mobile in the fluid phase of the membrane, this process stops at binding. Binding of soluble and insoluble materials to macrophages—and subsequent ingestion of these materials by pinocytosis or phagocytosis—is ascribed to a rapidly increasing number of specific binding activities of the macrophage. While the existence of specific receptors has yet to be demonstrated formally in certain cases, the macrophage of plasma membrane has receptors for a large variety of immune and nonimmune molecules (Table 10–5).

Receptors that bind the Fc portion of immunoglobulins and the C3 components of complement endow the macrophage with its capacity to recognize opsonized particles. There are at least 4 classes of **Fc receptors.** A proteinase-sensitive receptor is able to bind monomers of complexes of IgG of certain subclasses (in humans, IgG1 and IgG3; in the mouse, IgG2a; in the guinea pig, IgG2). Antibodies binding to this receptor are cytophilic, ie, they bind to the mac-

Table 10–4. Types of endocytosis by macrophages.

Type	Vesicle Size	Special Requirements
Pinocytosis		
Micropinocytosis	$0.2\ \mu m$	Receptor-mediated; does not require protein synthesis
Macropinocytosis	$1–2\ \mu m$	Receptor-triggered (?); requires protein synthesis
Phagocytosis		
Immune phagocytosis	$> 0.4\ \mu m$	Mediated by Fc or complement receptors
Nonimmune phagocytosis	$> 0.4\ \mu m$	Mediated by other specific or nonspecific receptors

Table 10–5. Surface receptors of mononuclear phagocytes.

Immune receptors
Fc domain of immunoglobulins
  IgG monomers (proteinase-sensitive receptor)
  IgG complexes (proteinase-insensitive receptors)
  IgE
Complement
  C3b
  C3d
Nonimmune receptors
Hormone receptors
  Colony-stimulating factor
  Lymphokines (migration inhibitory factor)
  Insulin
Mannosyl or fucosyl terminal
α_2-Macroglobulin–proteinase complexes
Lactoferrin
Transferrin
Fibrin/fibrinogen
Fibronectin
Lipoprotein receptors
  Anionic low-density lipoproteins (eg, acetylated)
  Apolipoproteins B and E (chylomicron remnants, β-migrating, very low density lipoproteins)

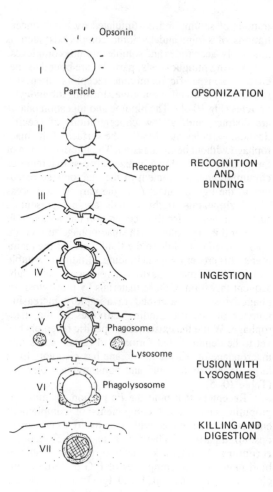

Opsonin

I

Particle   OPSONIZATION

II

Receptor   RECOGNITION
                            AND
                            BINDING

III

IV   INGESTION

V   Phagosome

               Lysosome

                                                FUSION WITH
                                                LYSOSOMES
VI   Phagolysosome

                                                KILLING AND
                                                DIGESTION
VII

rophages first and then interact with antigen. There is a proteinase-resistant Fc receptor that binds to and mediates endocytosis of antigen-antibody complexes or aggregates of IgG subclasses (IgG2 and IgG4 in humans and IgG1 and IgG2b in the mouse) (Fig 10–2). A third type of proteinase-resistant Fc receptor specific for IgG3 has been demonstrated in the mouse. Macrophages also have a receptor that specifically binds IgE. During phagocytosis mediated by these Fc receptors, the receptors are cleared from the membrane, gradually returning over a subsequent period of 6–24 hours. The number or activity of Fc receptors is modified by inflammation and certain disease states, when the number of Fc receptors may quadruple.

The **receptors for complement** are independent of the Fc receptors. In unstimulated macrophages or monocytes, the C3 receptors are much more efficient at mediating binding than at mediating ingestion. It is likely that in vivo, the C3 receptors and Fc receptors function synergistically. With macrophage activation, the complement receptors acquire the ability to mediate ingestion on their own. There are at least 3 complement receptors on mononuclear phagocytes of humans, guinea pigs, and mice. Complement receptor 1 is specific for C3b and complement receptor 2 for C3d. C5a is chemotactic for mononuclear phagocytes, and it is likely that this third complement receptor is expressed on these cells as well as on granulocytes.

Macrophages also have **receptors for lymphokines,** which are involved in macrophage activation; and for colony-stimulating factors, which regulate macrophage proliferation. Receptors for insulin have also been demonstrated on macrophages. Macrophages also have receptors recognizing complex carbohydrates and fucosyl and mannosyl terminal glycoproteins. These receptors may be important to the clearing of glycoproteins and in the recognition of senescent cells, heterologous erythrocytes, yeasts and other fungi, bacteria, and parasites. Macrophages recognize α_2-macroglobulin–proteinase complexes,

Figure 10–1. Events in phagocytosis by phagocytes. *(I)* Particles such as microorganisms and tumor cells can be recognized by the phagocyte only if coated by a molecule for which the phagocyte has a receptor. Substances that make the particle attractive for ingestion have been termed opsonins and include immunoglobulins, complement, fragments, and fibronectin. Once coated with the opsonin *(II)*, the opsonized particle can then be recognized and can bind to specific receptors on the phagocyte surface *(III)*. In the case of some effectors, the binding event does not necessarily lead to subsequent engulfment by the phagocyte. For ingestion to occur, the particle is circumferentially surrounded by the membrane of the phagocyte during sequential zippering between the recognized opsonin on the particle surface and the receptors on the phagocyte surface *(IV)*. The receptors may need to move in the fluid bilayer of the phagocyte membrane in order to make contact with the ligand. Once the circumferential zippering is complete, a membrane-bounded vesicle separated from the plasma membrane (a phagosome) forms *(V)*. At some time during the period of formation of the phagosome, a number of the receptors present on the phagosomal membrane are recycled back to the plasma membrane. The phagosomes then fuse with existing primary and secondary lysosomes to form a phagolysosome *(VI)*, in which the organisms may be killed, with subsequent digestion at acid pH *(VII)*.

Figure 10–2. Scanning electron micrograph of a macrophage in the process of ingesting, by its Fc receptors, IgG-coated sheep erythrocytes. (Courtesy of R Takemura.)

which may be important in in vivo clearance of enzymes such as thrombin, plasmin, kallikrein, and activated complement components. Receptors for proteins containing iron may play a role in the secretion of iron by macrophages. Receptors for fibrin/fibrinogen complexes may play an important role in clearance of fibrin from the circulation or inflammatory sites. The receptor for fibronectin may aid in the adhesion of monocytes to areas containing breaches in the integrity of the endothelial lining of the vessels, and fibronectin may also act as an opsonin for certain particles. Macrophages may play an important role in regulation of triglyceride and cholesterol metabolism through their receptors for normal and altered lipoproteins.

Once formed at the periphery of the cell, pinocytic and phagocytic vesicles flow into the macrophage toward the perinuclear area, guided by microtubules, in an energy-requiring process that utilizes the abundant amount of cytoplasmic contractile proteins. In the perinuclear area, the endocytic vacuoles become secondary lysosomes after fusion with primary lysosomes. Alternatively, the endocytic vacuoles may fuse with preexisting secondary lysosomes. At some stage between the initial formation of the endosomal membrane and the formation of the secondary lysosome membrane, portions of the membrane and its plasma membrane receptors are recycled back to the cell surface. Within the lysosomal compartment, the phagocytosed and pinocytosed contents—as well as some of the plasma membrane proteins—are digested at acid pH by more than 40 hydrolytic enzymes within the lysosomes (Table 10–6). Bacterial macromolecules such as proteins, complex carbohydrates, and lipids are digested to subunits of MW 200 or less that can escape from the lysosome into the cytoplasm.

Chronic intracellular pathogens have evolved a variety of mechanisms designed to subvert the processes of phagocytosis, fusion of phagosomes with lysosomes, and function of lysosomal enzymes. *Trypanosoma cruzi* and certain enveloped viruses penetrate the phagosomal membrane and escape into the cytoplasm. *Mycobacterium tuberculosis* and *Toxoplasma* somehow prevent fusion of lysosomes with phagosomes, a process that can be mimicked by a variety of polyanions, and with lectins such as ConA. *Mycobacterium lepraemurium* is surrounded by a cell wall that is resistant to hydrolysis.

Table 10–6. Lysosomal acid hydrolases of macrophages.

Enzyme	Major Substrates
Phosphatases	Phosphate esters
Aryl sulfatase	Sulfate esters
Cholesteryl esterase	Cholesteryl esters of lipoproteins
Triglyceride lipase	Triglycerides of lipoproteins
Phospholipases	Phospholipids of bacteria, lipoproteins
Glycosidases	Carbohydrates, glycosaminoglycans, etc
Proteinases	
Cathepsin B	Collagen, proteoglycans
Cathepsin D	Hemoglobin

CHEMOTAXIS

Mononuclear phagocytes have the capacity to migrate into and through tissues. This migration may be random or specifically directed toward an inflammatory chemical stimulus, a process called **chemotaxis.** How mononuclear phagocytes find or make a path through the connective tissue is not known. However, macrophages contain on their surfaces—and secrete—proteolytic enzymes active at tissue pH that may be important in their ability to migrate in vivo. Numerous substances generated during inflammation have a capacity to enhance the speed of macrophage movement (chemokinesis) and to orient the movement in the direction of an increased concentration gradient of the agent (chemotaxis). Substances chemotactic for macrophages include factors derived from serum, particularly the C5a anaphylatoxin. C5a is released as a consequence of activation of complement by antibody-antigen complexes, by bacteria, by the classic or alternative pathways, or by the direct action of cell-derived proteolytic enzymes on C5. Other chemotactic substances include bacterial products such as N-formylmethionyl peptides and products from stimulated B and T lymphocytes that attract mononuclear phagocytes to sites of inflammation and delayed hypersensitivity reactions. Factors produced by fibroblasts, fragments of collagen, elastin, and denatured proteins may help attract macrophages to sites of tissue injury. Also important in the consideration of attraction of macrophages to sites of inflammation are substances that inhibit the random migration of macrophages and thus prevent migration away from sites of inflammation. Two chemically distinct classes of substances seem to function in the retention of macrophages: lymphokines (macrophage migration inhibitory factor, macrophage activation factor) and proteolytic enzymes produced during activation of complement (factor Bb) and of the fibrinolytic system (plasmin).

Abnormalities of chemotactic responsiveness of monocytes and macrophages have been noted in individuals with tumors, certain defects in immunity (eg, Wiskott-Aldrich syndrome), and recurrent candidiasis and after infection of macrophages with certain viruses such as influenza and herpes simplex viruses.

METABOLISM DURING PHAGOCYTOSIS

The ingestion of particles by macrophages as well as by neutrophils (see part II of this chapter) is accompanied by a **respiratory burst** observed as a dramatic increase in the consumption of oxygen and activation of a membrane-associated oxidase that is dependent on reduced nicotinamide adenine dinucleotide phosphate (NADPH). This oxidase reduces molecular oxygen to superoxide anion, which in turn dismutates to hydrogen peroxide (Table 10–7). **Superoxide** and **hydrogen peroxide** can interact to give rise to **hydroxyl radical** and, possibly, **singlet oxygen.** Some of the

Table 10–7. Events of the respiratory burst associated with phagocytosis.

Activation of the hexose monophosphate shunt and the glutathione reductase–glutathione peroxidase cycle

Activation of a membrane-associated NADPH oxidase, with increased consumption of oxygen and generation of superoxide anion and hydrogen peroxidase

Formation of hydroxyl radical, singlet oxygen, and other metabolites of reactive oxygen

Chemiluminescence

hydrogen peroxide is destroyed by glutathione peroxidase, with the oxidation of reduced glutathione. Reduced glutathione is regenerated by glutathione reductase and is accompanied by the oxidation of reduced NADPH. This NADPH is derived from the hexose monophosphate shunt, which is also stimulated to accommodate the increased utilization of oxygen. The reactive metabolites of oxygen that are generated at or near the cell surface and within the phagocytic vacuole exert antimicrobial and antitumor cell effects. The macrophage itself is protected from the noxious effects of these oxygen metabolites by its glutathione peroxidase and catalase.

The respiratory burst, although intimately connected with phagocytosis, is not an essential accompaniment to phagocytosis. Many soluble agents, including antigen-antibody complexes, C5a, ionophores, and tumor promoters, can trigger the respiratory burst without phagocytosis. The respiratory burst can also be triggered by opsonized particles or surfaces when phagocytosis is frustrated by the use of a drug such as cytochalasin B. Phagocytosis can also proceed without the respiratory burst. In chronic granulomatous disease, in which an enzyme required for the respiratory burst is missing, phagocytosis occurs normally. In addition to the reactive species of oxygen, such as superoxide anion ($O_2^-\cdot$), hydrogen peroxide (H_2O_2), hydroxyl radical ($OH\cdot$), and singlet oxygen ($^1O_2$), there are a number of other potential microbicidal mechanisms in macrophages. The antimicrobial effects of hydrogen peroxide are augmented by halide ions in the presence of myeloperoxidase (which is found in granules of monocytes but not mature macrophages) or of catalase (which is found in mature macrophages). Other microbicidal mechanisms include hydrogen ion, lysosome, complement components, and lysosomal hydrolases. The relative importance of these mechanisms varies with different microbes. Macrophages may also inhibit the growth of or kill tumor cells by several types of interaction: antibody-dependent cell-mediated cytotoxicity, in which the tumor cells have been coated with antibodies directed to the cell surface; cytostasis, produced by thymidine or by the depletion of arginine by arginase; and mechanisms dependent on the release of reactive species of oxygen from macrophages.

MACROPHAGE SECRETION

Phagocytosis by macrophages has been studied for over a century, but it is only in the last decade that the importance of macrophages as secretory cells has been recognized. Over 50 secretion products of macrophages have been identified (Table 10–8). The role of macrophages as secretory cells may be as important in their interaction with the extracellular milieu as is their role as phagocytic cells. Some of the secretion products of the macrophage influence the inflammatory process at its many steps. This secretion by macrophages is under complex control and varies with the status of the mononuclear phagocytes. Lysosome and complement components appear to be secreted constitutively by macrophages in all states of stimulation. The secretion of other products such as arachidonic metabolites, acid hydrolases, and neutral proteinases is triggered and regulated by engagement of specific receptors, by endocytosis, or by exposure of macrophages to membrane-active drugs, including tumor promoters, ionophores, and endotoxin. Secretion can also be regulated by activated lymphocytes, by tissue pH and oxygen tension, and by other factors influencing the inflammatory activity of macrophages.

Macrophages secrete a number of enzymes active at neutral and acid pH. Plasminogen activator activates the plasma zymogen plasminogen to plasmin, which is of particular interest because of the ability of plasmin to lyse fibrin, activate C1 and C3, and cleave activated Hageman factor into components that convert prekallikrein to kallikrein. Macrophages stimulated by inflammation or activated by endotoxin or infection secrete considerably more plasminogen activator than do resident macrophages, and its secretion is further amplified by phagocytosis of poorly digested materials. **Elastases** and **collagenases,** secreted by macrophages, may be important in the degradation of connective tissue macromolecules such as elastin, collagen, and proteoglycans. Elastase also degrades immunoglobulins, α_1-proteinase inhibitor, fibronectin, and fibrinogen. These enzymes may be present in granulomas and at the site of delayed hypersensitivity reactions and may explain some of the degradation seen in these areas. Lysozyme is able to degrade the cell wall polysaccharide of certain organisms and, in concert with lysosomal hydrolases, which are also released from cells, can contribute to bacterial and tissue breakdown in inflammatory lesions where there is a sufficiently low pH. **Arginase,** an enzyme that degrades arginine, is secreted by inflammatory exudative cells. Because arginine is required for normal metabolism of many cells, its depletion may lead to inhibition of cellular function or cytostasis for tumor cells. Lipoprotein lipase may have an important function in the metabolism of lipoproteins by macrophages.

Macrophages also secrete a variety of plasma proteins. Many of these proteins have previously been identified as secretion products of hepatocytes. α_2-Macroglobulin is a prominent inhibitor of all known

Table 10—8. Secreted products of macrophages.

Enzymes	Reactive metabolites of oxygen
Neutral proteinases	Superoxide anion
Plasminogen activator	Hydrogen peroxide
Metal-dependent elastase	**Bioactive lipids**
Collagenase, specific for interstitial collagens (types I, II, III)	Prostaglandin E_2
Collagenase, specific for pericellular collagen (type V)	6-Ketoprostaglandin F_{1a}
Others	Thromboxane B_2
Lysozyme	Leukotriene C (slow-reacting substance of anaphylaxis)
Lipoprotein lipase	12-Hydroxyeicosatetranoic acid
Arginase	Others
Acid hydrolases	**Nucleotide metabolites**
Proteinases and peptidases	cAMP
Glycosidases	Thymidine
Phosphatases	Uracil
Lipases	Uric acid
Others	**Factors regulating cellular functions**
Plasma proteins	Interleukin-1 (endogenous pyrogen)
a_2-Macroglobulin	Angiogenesis factor
Fibronectin	Interferon
Transcobalamin II	Factors promoting proliferation of—
Apolipoprotein E	Fibroblasts
Coagulation proteins	Endothelial cells
Tissue thromboplastin	T cells
Factor V	B cells
Factor VII	Myeloid cell precursors (colony-stimulating factor)
Factor IX	Factors inhibiting proliferation of—
Factor X	Tumor cells
Complement components	*Listeria monocytogenes*
C1	
C2	
C3	
C4	
C5	
Properdin	
Factor B	
Factor D	
C3b inactivator	
β_1 H (C3b inactivator accelerator)	

proteolytic enzymes and thus may regulate the potential of the macrophages to lyse connective tissue macromolecules and participate in the complement, coagulation, and kinin cascades. It is interesting to note that macrophages contain on their surface a receptor for α-macroglobulin–proteinase complexes. **Fibronectin,** a protein which is opsonic for particles coated with denatured collagen (gelatin) and which also has a structural role in basement membranes and other connective tissue, is secreted in large quantities by the macrophage. Macrophages are able to utilize fibronectin as opsonin and for adhesion to a variety of cells. Macrophages also secrete transcobalamin II, which is involved in the transport of vitamin B_{12}, and apolipoprotein E, a protein involved in lipid transport and metabolism. Macrophages have on their surface a receptor that allows them to recognize and ingest certain lipoproteins containing apolipoprotein E (eg, β-migrating very low density lipoproteins and chylomicron remnants). Macrophages also produce proteins involved in coagulation cascade: tissue thromboplastin and factors V, VII, IX, and X. Because the mac-

rophage also participates in the fibrinolytic system, it has a dual role in clot formation and lysis. Complement components regulate the chemotactic and acidic metabolic and secretory activity of the macrophage; in turn, the macrophage also engages in the synthesis and secretion of complement components. The macrophage synthesizes and secretes virtually all components of the classic and alternative pathways of complement and thus provides additional direct links between acute and chronic hypersensitivity responses.

Nonprotein substances of pharmacologic potency secreted by macrophages certainly play a role in inflammation as important as those of the protein components. The production of reactive metabolites of oxygen have already been commented on. These products are potent oxidizing agents that may inactivate thiol groups of proteins, break bonds in proteins, oxidize lipids and nucleic acids, and initiate free radical chain reactions that may contribute significantly to the tissue damage accompanying inflammation. Macrophages have been shown to produce large amounts of prostaglandin E_2. Prostaglandins affect the functions of macrophages as well as of other cells, including suppression of B cell proliferation, suppression of myeloid stem cell proliferation, and inhibition of mitogen responsiveness. They have also been implicated as the important element in inducing acute-phase reactants in plasma during inflammation. One of the bioactive lipids, leukotriene C, has been identified as the slow-reacting substance of anaphylaxis. Thus, the macrophage may participate in the acute as well as in the chronic inflammatory response.

The macrophage also produces factors, mostly protein in nature, that regulate the functions of other cells. Interleukin-1, which has also been called lymphocyte-activating factor and endogenous pyrogen, is secreted by macrophages. This protein induces T cells to produce interleukin-2, induces fibroblasts to secrete collagenase, and binds to receptors in the hypothalamus, which are then signaled to reset the body temperature to a higher level. During inflammation or hypoxia, macrophages secrete **angiogenesis factor,** which promotes the neovascularization of tissues. They also secrete factors that promote the proliferation of fibroblasts, endothelial cells, and myeloid precursors. Factors including **interferon** inhibit the proliferation of cells, including tumor cells, and proliferation of bacteria. Within the broad spectrum of their states of activity, macrophages may promote or inhibit the same processes and contribute to many facets of the inflammatory response and the regulation of cellular functions.

PROPERTIES OF INFLAMMATORY & ACTIVATED MACROPHAGES

Almost every structural and functional feature of the macrophage has been reported to change when the cells or the host animal are treated in some way. Mackaness demonstrated that lymphocytes recognizing a microbial antigen induced in macrophages an enhanced antimicrobial activity against the specific immunizing pathogen as well as against unrelated pathogens. These cells were observed to spread faster on glass, ruffled their membranes more prominently, contained mitochondrial lysosomes, and were more phagocytic. These macrophages have been termed **activated.** Macrophages from animals treated with nonmicrobial inflammatory stimuli display a similar but not identical pattern of changes (Table 10–9). They show many of the same metabolic, phagocytic, plasma membrane enzyme, and lysosomal changes as activated macrophages, but they lack enhanced antimicrobial and antitumor activity. It is now evident that these macrophages should not be referred to as activated but as inflammatory or elicited. Activation of macrophages occurs as a result of their interaction with mediators from antigen- or mitogen-stimulated lymphocytes, termed lymphokines, or with the products of activation of complement components, or with interferon (Fig 10–3). Activation of macrophages may also occur by direct pharmacologic action of agents such as

Table 10–9. Inflammatory macrophages compared to quiescent resident macrophages.

Nonspecific inflammatory events
Increased size
Increased rate of spreading
Increased adherence to glass
Increased rate and extent of phagocytosis
IgG-coated particles
C3b-coated particles
Modification of plasma membrane ectoenzymes
Decreased 5′-nucleotidase
Increased alkaline phosphodiesterase
Increased rate of fluid phase pinocytosis
Secreted proteins
Increased plasminogen activator
Increased elastase
Increased collagenase
Increased cellular ATP
Increased O_2 consumption, glucose, O_2^- release
Increased prostaglandin release
Decreased leukotriene C production
Lymphokine-mediated events
Increased microbicidal activity
Increased tumor cytostasis and killing
Increased H_2O_2 release
Decreased secretion of apolipoprotein E

endotoxin. In contrast to the specific immunologic activation of T and B cells, the activation of macrophages is not specific to the primary infecting organism. For example, activated macrophages from animals infected with *Trichinella* or *Toxoplasma* are cytotoxic to tumor cells and to unrelated intracellular and extracellular pathogens such as *Listeria* and *Trypanosoma*.

Induction and functional expression of macrophage activation in vivo depend on a complex series of events, and the macrophage is capable of undergoing or expressing a large number of functional and metabolic alterations. The enhancement of microbicidal activity depends on sensitized T cells, which may be native or adoptively transferred in vivo. In culture, unstimulated macrophages may be activated by providing either living sensitized T cells and their antigens or the lymphocyte-derived products from the interaction of viable sensitized T cells and antigen. The substrate for the activation process includes the unstimulated macrophages resident in the tissue spaces as well as newly recruited and mature monocytes migrating from the vascular pool during activation by the immunologically mediated specific event. The properties of the activated macrophages may be understood without necessarily proceeding step by step through the sequence of properties developed during the nonspecific inflammatory response. The number of steps in the activation process and the mechanism by which it is regulated are not fully worked out, and the precise biochemical and metabolic processes that define the activated state are still controversial.

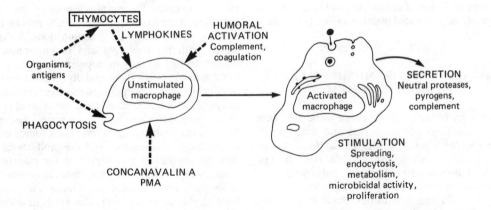

Figure 10–3. Schematic representation of the process of activation of unstimulated macrophages. Macrophages might be activated by interaction with organisms and antigens directly, by interaction with activated T lymphocytes, by interaction with the product of the activation of complement and coagulation systems, or by certain chemicals such as ConA and phorbol diesters (phorbol myristate acetate, PMA). These result in the activation of the macrophage, which is able to phagocytose more readily, secretes neutral proteinases (proteases), pyrogen (interleukin-1), and complement components at a greater rate and is stimulated to spread and undergo other metabolic activities.

THE ROLE OF MACROPHAGES IN REGULATING THE IMMUNE RESPONSE

Macrophages play an important role in initiation and regulation of the immune response, both in vivo and in culture. The macrophage may participate in the immune response in 2 ways. There may be nonspecific roles that depend on the capacity of macrophages to improve the viability of lymphocytes—an action that can be mimicked by the addition of 2-mercaptoethanol in culture. Alternatively, macrophages may suppress the proliferation of lymphocytes nonspecifically

through thymidine, arginase, complement cleavage products, prostaglandin E, and interferon. Macrophages also may alter the function of lymphocytes more specifically. They produce interleukin-1 (formerly called leukocyte-activating factor), which specifically alters T cell function as described in Chapter 8. Another function of macrophages is in the processing and presentation of immunologically active molecules to the lymphocyte. This function requires that the T cell and macrophage display the same major histocompatibility–encoded determinants (Ia antigens) (Fig 10–4). Not all macrophages express Ia antigen;

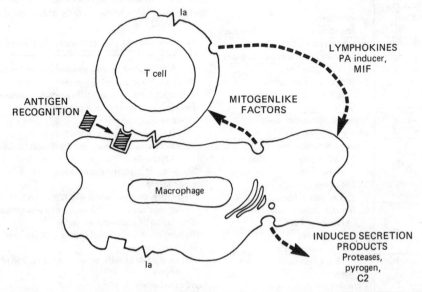

Figure 10–4. Diagrammatic representation of the interaction between macrophages and T cells that is dependent on the compatibility of products (Ia antigens) of genes in the major histocompatibility complex. The interaction depends on recognition of conventional antigens as well as Ia determinants and results in the production of specific mediators capable of activating macrophages.

only a subpopulation of monocytes and macrophages from specifically activated populations are positive for this marker.

DISORDERS OF THE MONONUCLEAR PHAGOCYTE SYSTEM

A variety of human diseases are associated with increased numbers of monocytes and tissue macrophages or with abnormalities in the functions of monocytes and macrophages (Table 10–10). For example, mononuclear phagocytes may proliferate appropriately in response to *Mycobacterium tuberculosis,* producing a monocytosis or reactive hyperplasia manifested by enlargement of organs rich in these cells, such as the spleen and lymph nodes. On the other hand, they may proliferate inappropriately to extents far exceeding normal levels, as in monocytic leukemia or other malignant histiocytic proliferative diseases. Another group of disorders are those in which increased numbers of lysosomes are seen in tissue macrophages or when material taken up by phagocytosis accumulates intracellularly more rapidly than it can be disposed of by metabolic processes. These can be called storage diseases, the result of ingestion of a nondigestible substance, an overloading of iron as in hemosiderosis, or inborn errors of metabolism in which a specific genetic defect of macrophage enzyme function has occurred (eg, Gaucher's disease,

Hurler's disease). There is also a group of macrophage dysfunction syndromes. These include genetic abnormalities such as chronic granulomatous disease, in which both macrophages and polymorphonuclear leukocytes lack an enzyme important in the respiratory burst seen in phagocytosis and do not have the ability to kill pathogens susceptible to reactive metabolites of oxygen. Defects in synthesis and secretion of complement components produce macrophage dysfunction because macrophages are a prominent source of these complement components, and the products of complement activation are important for macrophage, phagocytic, and migratory functions. In osteopetrosis, abnormally low numbers of osteoclasts are found in bone, and bone resorption is abnormal. In addition to these disorders, high concentrations of glucocorticosteroids and ionizing radiation may interfere with the macrophage defense system, including macrophage migration into tissues and macrophage proliferation; thus, opportunistic infections may occur frequently. Another class of macrophage dysfunction has been described in animals in which there are genetically determined differences in macrophage responses to lipopolysaccharides. It is likely that there is heterogeneity in lipopolysaccharide responsiveness in humans as well.

The mononuclear phagocyte system has many functions. It participates in host defense, tissue hygiene, wound healing, and general homeostatic mechanisms, interacting with many other cells and tissue fluids throughout the body (Table 10–11). The chameleonlike adaptations of the macrophages to their tissue environments endow these cells with the ability to influence many processes negatively, positively, or in complex feedback loops. Our challenge is to unravel and reconstruct these mechanisms, so that we can understand how these events are controlled in vivo.

Table 10–10. Participation of mononuclear phagocytes in pathologic processes.

Process	Examples
Inflammatory processes	
Acute inflammation	Monocytosis
	Infectious and parasitic diseases
Chronic inflammation	Reactive hyperplasia
	Infectious and parasitic diseases
Chronic granulomatous	Reactive hyperplasia
inflammation	Intracellular parasites
	Beryllium toxicity
	Sarcoidosis
Destructive granulomas	Wegener's granulomatosis
	Midline granuloma
Storage diseases	Enzyme deficiencies
	Mucolipopolysaccharidoses
	Hurler's disease
	Lipidoses
	Tay-Sachs disease
	Nondigestible substances
	Hemosiderosis
	Xanthomas
	Pneumoconiosis
Mononuclear phagocyte	Chronic granulomatous disease
dysfunctions	Osteopetrosis
	Complement deficiencies
Neoplastic processes	Monocytic leukemia
	Malignant histiocytosis
	Histiocytosis X
	Histiocytic medullary reticulosis

Table 10–11. Functions of macrophages in vivo.

Host defense against microorganisms and tumor cells
  Participation in acute inflammatory response
  Participation in chronic inflammatory response
  Production of endogenous pyrogen
  Immune phagocytosis
  Microbial and cytostatic activities
  Accessory and regulatory cell for T cells, B cells, and natural
    killer cells
  Secretion of complement components
Wound healing
  Regulation of coagulation and fibrinolysis
  Tissue debridement by phagocytosis and secreted enzymes
  Regulation of neovascularization
  Regulation of endothelial cells and fibroblasts
  Bone resorption
  Removal of dead cells, inhaled particles, and effete erythro-
    cytes
Lipid metabolism
  Removal of chylomicron remnants and altered lipoproteins
  Secretion of apolipoprotein E
Regulation of granulocyte and macrophage pools through pro-
    duction of colony-stimulating factors

II. GRANULOCYTES
Ira M. Goldstein, MD

A common feature of most forms of immunologically induced acute inflammation is the accumulation of polymorphonuclear leukocytes (**neutrophils**) at the site of the reaction. These cells are not merely innocent bystanders to events that occur at a focus of inflammation but play an active role in the mediation of these events. Indeed, it has been established that acute inflammation in virtually all multicellular organisms occurs largely as a consequence of a coordinated series of events whereby phagocytic cells attempt to defend the host from "foreign invaders."

In humans as in most higher organisms, the neutrophil is primarily responsible for maintaining normal host defenses against invading microorganisms. Neutrophils are suitably equipped to seek out, ingest, and destroy most "foreign invaders." This requires a series of discrete but coordinated steps which include adherence to endothelium, extravascular emigration, directed migration toward particles to be ingested (**chemotaxis**), membrane recognition of (and attachment to) particles, engulfment of particles (**phagocytosis**), fusion of lysosomes with—and discharge of lysosomal constituents into—phagocytic vacuoles (**degranulation**), and a burst of oxidative metabolism (with generation of oxygen-derived free radicals and hydrogen peroxide).

In the sections that follow, each of these functions of neutrophils will be discussed in some detail. Emphasis will be placed on recent developments in immunology, cell biology, and pathology that have helped to elucidate mechanisms whereby neutrophils promote inflammation. The microbicidal functions of neutrophils are discussed in Chapter 16.

ADHERENCE OF NEUTROPHILS TO VASCULAR ENDOTHELIUM & EXTRAVASCULAR EMIGRATION

The total pool of peripheral blood neutrophils is composed of 2 readily exchangeable subpools. One of these subpools is composed of neutrophils that circulate in the central axial stream within blood vessels. This "circulating pool" of cells represents about half of the total blood neutrophils in humans and is readily measured by the standard clinical leukocyte count and differential. Cells in the "marginal pool," representing the remainder of total blood neutrophils, circulate out of the axial stream and move slowly along the vascular endothelium. Under normal physiologic conditions, neutrophils in the marginal pool adhere to endothelial surfaces only rarely and momentarily.

Regardless of the cause, one of the earliest events accompanying acute inflammation is an increase in the margination of circulating neutrophils (ie, adherence of these cells to vascular endothelium). Adherence is a prerequisite for subsequent diapedesis into the extravascular compartment. Adherence of neutrophils to endothelial cells without subsequent diapedesis and emigration may be the only manifestation of inflammation after minimal damage to tissues.

A number of diverse substances with chemotactic activity for neutrophils (eg, synthetic and complement-derived peptides) have been found capable of augmenting the adhesiveness of these cells. This is manifested in vitro by increased adherence of neutrophils to substrates such as glass, plastic, nylon fibers, and cultured endothelial cells as well as by aggregation of neutrophils in suspension. Administration of chemotactic factors intravenously to experimental animals results in prompt neutropenia, markedly increased margination of neutrophils, and pulmonary vascular leukostasis. Thus, naturally occurring chemoattractants are not only responsible for directed extravascular migration of neutrophils but play a role also in promoting localized adherence of neutrophils to vascular endothelium (Table 10–12).

DIRECTED MIGRATION OF NEUTROPHILS: CHEMOTAXIS

Motile cells such as neutrophils are capable of migrating in a directed fashion along gradients of chemical stimuli. Extravascular emigration of neutrophils most likely is caused by gradients of such chemical attractants that are established between inflamed tissues and blood vessels. There is now abundant evidence that directed migration (**chemotaxis**) of neutrophils is important both in the mediation of inflammation and in the maintenance of normal host defenses against infection. Directed migration of neutrophils in humans is mediated largely by fluid phase components of the complement system (eg, C5a and C5a des Arg) which are generated by cleavage of native complement proteins as a consequence of activation of either the classic or alternative pathways. Other chemoattractants for neutrophils include products of bacteria, products of stimulated leukocytes, products of coagulation or fibrinolysis, oxidized lipids, and synthetic N-formyl methionyl peptides. The precise mechanisms whereby these factors are recognized by neutrophils and thus become capable of initiating directed motility are largely unknown. Only very recently has evidence been obtained that these factors interact with and influence neutrophil membranes. Indeed, struc-

Table 10–12. Factors that influence neutrophil adhesiveness.

Augmenting Factors	Inhibitory Factors
Plasma from patients with diverse forms of inflammation	Plasma from patients receiving anti-inflammatory drugs
cGMP	cAMP
Propranolol	Epinephrine
Deuterium oxide	Colchicine
Chemotactic factors	Ethanol
Divalent cations	Local anesthetics

turally specific receptors for C5a, N-formyl methionyl peptides, and leukocyte-derived chemotactic factors have been demonstrated on the surfaces of both human and rabbit neutrophils.

Chemotactic factors have been shown to be capable of provoking other membrane-dependent neutrophil responses. For example, they stimulate neutrophil oxidative metabolism and provoke selective discharge from neutrophils of lysosomal constituents (Table 10–13). These actions of chemotactic factors are discussed in sections that follow.

RECOGNITION: NEUTROPHIL CELL SURFACE RECEPTOR FUNCTION

There are 2 major constituents of serum (**opsonins**) that act upon certain bacteria, fungi, and other particles to increase their ''palatability.'' One is heat-stable (at 56 °C for 30 minutes) and is found chiefly in serum from animals previously exposed to the test particle (immune serum). The other is heat-labile and is present only in fresh normal serum. The heat-stable constituent is recognized now as immunoglobulin (antibody) of the IgG class (in particular, subclasses IgG1 and IgG3). These molecules—or, more specifically, their Fc portions—are recognized by phagocytic cells by means of what appear to be rather specific **receptors** (''Fc receptors'' or ''IgG receptors''). It has been estimated that 75–90% of human peripheral blood neutrophils bear receptors on their surfaces for IgG-coated particles.

Binding to neutrophils of antigen-antibody complexes, immunoglobulin-coated particles, and aggregated immunoglobulins depends upon the integrity of the Fc regions of the immunoglobulin molecules. Binding to neutrophils of either aggregated or antigen-complexed immunoglobulins exceeds that of the corresponding monomeric immunoglobulin molecules. At least 2 hypotheses have been offered to account for this observation. One hypothesis assumes that although monomeric immunoglobulins have an exposed binding site on their Fc regions available for attachment to neutrophils, such binding is unstable. More stable—and therefore detectable—binding results only from the formation of complexes with multiple sites. Thus, stable binding of polyvalent antigen-antibody complexes or of immunoglobulin aggregates would result from cooperative binding by Fc receptors

of several molecules (which exponentially increases binding of the whole complex). The alternative hypothesis suggests that either aggregation of immunoglobulins or interactions between antibodies and antigens produce allosteric changes in the conformation of immunoglobulin molecules, thereby exposing sites capable of interacting with the neutrophil surface. Thus, the tertiary structure of intact immunoglobulins may influence binding to neutrophils.

Fc receptors on neutrophils have been neither isolated nor identified. They have been observed indirectly, however, by fluorescence microscopy as well as by electron microscopy and shown to be mobile in the plane of the neutrophil plasma membrane. A close correlation has been observed between Fc receptor redistribution and immune complex–induced neutrophil responses, suggesting a relationship between activation of neutrophils and surface receptor mobility.

Heat-labile opsonic activity is attributable principally to a fragment of the third component of complement. Cleavage of C3, as a consequence of activation of either the classic or alternative complement pathways, yields 2 fragments, C3a and C3b. The larger of these fragments, C3b, is capable in its nascent state of becoming fixed to the surfaces of cells and other particles (including bacteria and fungi). C3b renders the particles to which it is attached recognizable by phagocytic leukocytes (including neutrophils) and mediates firm particle-cell adherence by interacting with ''C3b receptors.'' In humans, receptors for fragments of C3 can be demonstrated on over 90% of neutrophils in peripheral blood.

In contrast to receptors for the Fc region of IgG, structurally specific receptors for C3b have been identified on the surface of neutrophils and have been isolated from these cells. There is indirect evidence that optimal expression of C3b receptor activity on the surface of neutrophils is dependent upon the mobility of these receptors in the plane of the lipid bilayer. It has been suggested that aggregation of C3b receptors is a prerequisite for C3-dependent cytoadherence.

It should not be concluded from the foregoing discussion that neutrophils recognize only particles or surfaces coated with fragments of C3 or IgG. Nor should it be concluded that recognition is mediated only by structurally specific surface membrane receptors. Indeed, the term receptor may signify no more than an ability of neutrophils to recognize a given molecule and to be activated by it. Whereas molecular entities within (or on) the neutrophil surface membrane are presumed to mediate these functions, the presence of some of them can only be inferred. Receptors for some ligands have neither been identified nor isolated from human neutrophils. Consequently, it is best to consider neutrophil surface membrane receptors as ''recognition units'' that may or may not be represented by specific single molecules or even by complex intramembranous structures. Recognition units, of necessity, would be linked to ''effector units'' (of similarly vague composition) that trigger or initiate specific cellular functions.

Table 10–13. Chemotactic factor–induced responses of neutrophils.

Directed migration (chemotaxis).

Increased adhesiveness.

Decreased net negative surface charge.

Translocation of monovalent (Na^+ and K^+) and divalent (Ca^{2+}) cations.

Increased oxidative metabolism (generation of superoxide anion radicals).

Degranulation (lysosomal enzyme release).

PHAGOCYTOSIS

When contact is established between a neutrophil and a suitable particle, the particle is ingested by the cell, a process termed **phagocytosis.** Direct observations of phagocytosis by light microscopy and electron microscopy have revealed that attachment of neutrophils to a suitable small particle results in the formation at the site of attachment of pseudopodia that surround the particle and ultimately fuse at its distal pole. The process of particle engulfment by neutrophils requires energy (supplied by anaerobic glycolysis) as well as complex interactions between cytoplasmic contractile proteins (ie, actin and myosin) and the plasma membrane.

Whereas neutrophils appear capable of ingesting seemingly "inert" particles (eg, polystyrene latex beads), particularly under conditions where particle-cell contact is maximized, opsonins such as C3b or IgG clearly increase the rate and extent of particle uptake. Whether they do so merely by promoting particle-cell contact or whether they are indeed capable of activating ingestion is controversial. Several investigators, using erythrocytes coated with IgG or C3b (or both), have demonstrated that the neutrophil C3b receptor is involved chiefly in recognition and attachment and only inefficiently promotes ingestion of bound or adherent particles. In contrast, particle binding to the neutrophil IgG receptor, while less efficient, appears necessary for the induction of optimal phagocytosis. Thus, C3b and IgG have separate but synergistic roles in phagocytosis (Table 10–14). Depending upon the experimental conditions, the presence of particle-bound C3b is able to reduce 100-fold the amount of IgG required to promote engulfment of particles. Under certain conditions, C3b receptors may serve to overcome electrostatic repulsion and permit contact between the neutrophil surface and moieties on particles that promote engulfment. The role of C3b in opsonization is mainly one of establishing contact between particle and phagocyte.

Neutrophils are capable of ingesting certain particles in the complete absence of complement or immunoglobulins. It is likely that such particles have chemical moieties on their surfaces that not only permit attachment by neutrophils but also behave as "surrogate immunoglobulins" and promote ingestion. If this is the case, particles that require only C3b on their surfaces for optimal ingestion by neutrophils might be expected to be ingestible in the native state if particle-cell contact is enhanced. Indeed, such a phenomenon has been demonstrated.

DEGRANULATION

As indicated in the previous sections, phagocytosis by neutrophils requires recognition of the particle to be ingested, adherence or binding of the particle to the cell surface, and, finally, engulfment of the particle within a vacuole and closure of the plasma membrane. Shortly after (or coincident with) these events, lysosomal granules fuse with those portions of the plasma membrane that constitute the phagocytic vacuole. Membrane fusion leads to the discharge of lysosomal enzymes and other granule constituents into the newly formed—or forming—phagosome (**degranulation**). The resultant structure has been termed a **phagolysosome.** Phagolysosome formation underlies many normal cellular functions and is crucial for normal host defenses (see Chapter 16). Degranulation does not appear to be a uniform process. Primary (azurophil) and secondary (specific) granules of neutrophils discharge their contents at different rates during phagocytosis. Secondary granules appear to fuse first with the phagosome membrane.

Under certain conditions, lysosomal enzymes may be released to the outside of the cell. One mechanism whereby lysosomal constituents are extruded from neutrophils is simply "cell death." When neutrophils are exposed to a variety of toxins, injury to the plasma membrane is an early consequence, and all intracellular materials are released from the injured cell, including those ordinarily sequestered with lysosomes. Biologic detergents, for example, act in this manner to cause primary lysis of the cell membrane and, subsequently, disruption of lysosomes.

Under some circumstances, materials gain access to the interior of the cell's vacuolar system, wherein they cause membranes of lysosomes to rupture. Such damage leads to release of cytoplasmic enzymes and other intracellular constituents as the cell dies by a kind of "perforation from within" of its vacuolar system. Crystalline substances such as monosodium urate and silica act on phagocytic cells in this fashion.

Another mechanism of enzyme release from neutrophils involves the discharge of lysosomal hydrolases into the surrounding medium of intact cells engaging in endocytosis. Such release is not accompanied by leakage of cytoplasmic enzymes and appears to be due to the extrusion of lysosomal materials from incompletely closed phagosomes, open at their external borders to the extracellular space but already joined at their internal borders by lysosomes actively discharging their contents into the vacuole. The cell engaging in phagocytosis remains viable, but its released lysosomal contents are free to act upon surrounding tissues. This probably is a common mecha-

Table 10–14. Roles of IgG and C3b in adherence and phagocytosis.*

	Adherence	Phagocytosis
EA (IgM)†	−	−
EA (IgG)	+	+
EA (IgM-C3b)	+++	−
EA (IgG-C3b)	+++	+++

*Adapted from Ehlenberger AG, Nussenzweig V: *J Exp Med* 1977;145:357.
†Sheep erythrocytes (E) sensitized with IgM or IgG antibodies (A).

nism of tissue injury in a variety of disease states.

Phagocytosis per se is not an absolute prerequisite for degranulation of neutrophils. There is substantial evidence that degranulation of neutrophils can be provoked not only by appropriate ligand–surface membrane receptor interactions but also by "nonspecific" membrane perturbation. For example, when neutrophils encounter immune complexes or aggregated immunoglobulins deposited upon solid surfaces, such as Millipore filters or collagen membranes, the cells adhere to these surfaces and selectively release their lysosomal constituents. A similar phenomenon may occur when adherent cells encounter some soluble stimulus such as the complement component C5a. Enzyme release under these conditions occurs by a process called **reverse endocytosis** during which merger of granules with the plasma membrane results in discharge of lysosomal constituents directly to the outside of the cell as though into a phagocytic vacuole. Phagocytosis does not occur, and the viability of adherent cells is not altered. This mechanism of lysosomal enzyme release from neutrophils very likely is pertinent to the pathogenesis of tissue injury in several diseases in which immune complexes are deposited upon cell surfaces or extracellular structures such as vascular basement membranes.

NEUTROPHIL OXIDATIVE METABOLISM

Marked changes in oxidative metabolism ordinarily accompany ingestion by neutrophils of a variety of particles. The cells consume increased amounts of oxygen (by a mechanism insensitive to cyanide) to produce hydrogen peroxide as well as several highly reactive, unstable intermediates such as superoxide anion radicals, hydroxyl radicals, and probably singlet oxygen. Concomitantly, there is stimulation of the hexose monophosphate shunt pathway of glucose oxidation and iodination of proteins (mediated by the lysosomal enzyme myeloperoxidase). The increased ability of phagocytosing neutrophils to reduce nitroblue tetrazolium dye (NBT) is a reflection of enhanced generation of superoxide anion radicals. The importance of these metabolic events to microbial killing by neutrophils has been reviewed extensively and is discussed in Chapter 16.

As is the case with degranulation, these metabolic events can be stimulated in the absence of phagocytosis. For example, neutrophils adherent to certain nonphagocytosable surfaces have been observed to increase their oxidative metabolism, particularly if the surfaces are coated with immune complexes, aggregated IgG, or the opsonic fragment of the third component of complement (C3b). Similarly, neutrophils exposed to certain soluble stimuli have been demonstrated to increase their oxygen uptake, production of superoxide anion, hexose monophosphate shunt activity, and NBT reduction. These soluble stimuli include immune reactants, such as aggregated IgG and complement-derived chemotactic peptides, as well as a variety of nonimmune, surface-reactive compounds such as phospholipase C, phorbol myristate acetate, concanavalin A, and digitonin. The metabolic responses of neutrophils to these soluble stimuli require intact viable cells and closely resemble those observed during phagocytosis.

It appears that cell surface stimulation of neutrophils is sufficient, in the absence of phagocytosis, to provoke the degranulation and the burst of oxidative metabolism that ordinarily accompany ingestion of particles. What is the relation between these 2 responses of neutrophils to stimulation? Whereas it is true that the 2 responses appear to be inseparable when normal neutrophils are allowed to ingest particles, studies with nonphagocytic stimuli indicate that the 2 phenomena can occur independently. For example, it has been demonstrated that there is no significant correlation between the ability of various stimuli to provoke lysosomal enzyme release from neutrophils (degranulation) and their ability to enhance generation of superoxide anion.

Measurements of extracellular superoxide anion, as performed in most studies of stimulated neutrophils, presumably reflect not only the production of this radical but also the activity of endogenous superoxide dismutase and, perhaps, the rate of release of superoxide from the cytoplasm of cells to extracellular fluid. The demonstration that neutrophils contain superoxide dismutase in their cytosol satisfied the requirement for a protective mechanism against the potentially injurious effects of superoxide anion radicals and led to the suggestion that production of superoxide takes place on the outer surface of the cell membrane as well as in phagocytic vacuoles formed by invaginations of this membrane. The hypothesis that the neutrophil superoxide-generating system is localized to the plasma membrane is an attractive one. Surface generation of superoxide (and of its product, hydrogen peroxide) would allow for its concentration within phagocytic vacuoles and provides a convenient explanation for the extracellular recovery of this highly reactive free radical. By conversion to freely diffusible hydrogen peroxide, extracellular or intraphagosomal superoxide anion radicals can mediate all of the biochemical events that ordinarily accompany particle contact, phagocytosis, and microbial killing.

●   ●   ●

References

Macrophages

Adams DO, Edelson PJ, Koren HS (editors): *Methods for Studying Mononuclear Phagocytes.* Academic Press, 1981.

Cohn ZA: The activation of mononuclear phagocytes: Fact, fancy, and future. *J Immunol* 1978;**121**:813.

Forster O, Landy M (editors): *Heterogeneity of Mononuclear Phagocytes.* Academic Press, 1981.

Gallin JI, Quie PG (editors): *Leukocyte Chemotaxis.* Raven Press, 1978.

Johnston RB Jr: Oxygen metabolism and the microbicidal activity of macrophages. *Fed Proc* 1978;**37**:2759.

Karnovsky ML, Lazdins JK: Biochemical criteria for activated macrophages. *J Immunol* 1978;**121**:809.

Metchnikoff E: *Immunité dans les malades infectieuses.* Masson, 1901.

Nathan CF, Murray HW, Cohn ZA: The macrophage as an effector cell. *N Engl J Med* 1980;**303**:622.

Nelson DS (editor): *Immunobiology of the Macrophage.* Academic Press, 1976.

North RJ: The concept of the activated macrophage. *J Immunol* 1978;**121**:806.

Page RC, Davies P, Allison AC: The macrophage as a secretory cell. *Int Rev Cytol* 1978;**52**:119.

Pick E (editor): *Lymphokines, a Forum for Immunoregulatory Cell Products.* Vol 3: *Lymphokines in Macrophage Activation.* Academic Press, 1981.

Silverstein SC, Steinman RM, Cohn ZA: Endocytosis. *Annu Rev Biochem* 1977;**46**:669.

Snyderman R, Goetzl EJ: Molecular and cellular mechanisms of leukocyte chemotaxis. *Science* 1981;**213**:830.

Unanue ER, Rosenthal AS (editors): *Macrophage Regulation of Immunity.* Academic Press, 1980.

van Furth R (editor): *Mononuclear Phagocytes: Functional Aspects.* Parts 1 and 2. Martinus Nijhoff, 1980.

van Furth R (editor): *Mononuclear Phagocytes in Infection, Immunity and Pathology.* Blackwell, 1975.

Zweifach BW, Grant L, McCluskey RT (editors): *The Inflammatory Process,* 2nd ed. 3 vols. Academic Press, 1973–1974.

Granulocytes

Babior BM: Oxygen-dependent microbial killing by phagocytes. (2 parts.) *N Engl J Med* 1978;**298**:659, 721.

Cline MJ: *The White Cell.* Harvard Univ Press, 1975.

Ehlenberger AG, Nussenzweig V: The role of membrane receptors for C3b and C3d in phagocytosis. *J Exp Med* 1977;**145**:357.

Fearon DT, Kaneko I, Thomson GG: Membrane distribution and adsorptive endocytosis by C3b receptors on human polymorphonuclear leukocytes. *J Exp Med* 1981;**153**:1615.

Goldstein IM: Polymorphonuclear leukocyte functions: Role of the plasma membrane. Page 145 in: *Current Topics in Hematology.* Vol 2. Piomelli S, Yachnin S (editors). A. R. Liss, 1979.

Goldstein IM: Polymorphonuclear leukocyte lysosomes and immune tissue injury. *Prog Allergy* 1976;**20**:301.

Henson PM: Pathologic mechanisms in neutrophil-mediated injury. *Am J Pathol* 1972;**68**:593.

Hoover RL, Briggs RT, Karnovsky MJ: The adhesive interaction between polymorphonuclear leukocytes and endothelial cells in culture. *Cell* 1978;**14**:423.

Klebanoff SJ: Antimicrobial mechanisms in neutrophilic polymorphonuclear leukocytes. *Semin Hematol* 1975;**12**:117.

Klebanoff SJ, Clark RA: *The Neutrophil: Function in Clinical Disorders.* North-Holland, 1978.

Snyderman R, Goetzl EJ: Molecular and cellular mechanisms of leukocyte chemotaxis. *Science* 1981;**213**:830.

Stossel TP: Phagocytosis: Recognition and ingestion. *Semin Hematol* 1975;**12**:83.

11 | The Complement System

Neil R. Cooper, MD

MECHANISM OF ACTION OF THE COMPLEMENT SYSTEM

The complement (C) system is the primary humoral mediator of antigen-antibody reactions. It consists of at least 20 chemically and immunologically distinct plasma proteins capable of interacting with each other, with antibody, and with cell membranes. Following activation of the system, these interactions lead to the generation of biologic activity which ranges from lysis of a spectrum of different kinds of cells, bacteria, and viruses to direct mediation of inflammatory processes. In addition, complement is able to recruit and enlist the participation of other humoral and cellular effector systems and induce histamine release from mast cells, directed migration of leukocytes, phagocytosis, and release of lysosomal constituents from phagocytes.

The individual proteins of this system are normally present in the circulation as functionally inactive molecules. Together they comprise approximately 15% (w/w) of the plasma globulin fraction. The native precursor molecules are designated by numerals—C1, C2, C3, etc—or, in the case of certain of the components, by symbols or trivial names—properdin, factor B, factor D, etc. Each complement component must be activated sequentially under appropriate conditions in order for a complement reaction to progress. Thus, activation is not a single event but rather a dynamic process which enables the proteins to become interacting members of a functionally integrated system. Complement enzymes formed during the activation process are designated by a bar placed over the symbol of the component, eg, $\overline{C1s}$, factor $\overline{B}$. An activated, biologically active but nonenzymatic state of a component may also be identified by a bar placed over the term for the component, eg, $\overline{C5b,6,7}$. Fragments of the components arising from enzymatic cleavage are denoted by letters following the term employed for the component, eg, C4a, C4b.

There are 2 parallel but entirely independent mechanisms or pathways leading to activation of the terminal, biologically important portion of the complement sequence (Fig 11–1). These mechanisms of activation, termed the classic and the alternative or properdin pathways, respectively, are triggered by different substances. Each involves several reaction steps. The 2 activation pathways converge at the midpoint of the complement system, and the remainder of the reaction sequence, involving the reactions of C5 through C9, is common to both pathways. The terminal portion of the complement sequence may also be directly activated by certain noncomplement serum and cellular enzymes without participation of the early reacting factors. Among the trypsinlike enzymes capable of activating at the C3 or C5 stage of the reaction are the fibrinolytic enzyme plasmin and certain lysosomal enzymes (Fig 11–1).

THE CLASSIC COMPLEMENT PATHWAY

The classic pathway may be activated by antigen-antibody complexes or aggregated immunoglobulins (Table 11–1). Human immunoglobulins belonging to the IgG1, IgG2, and IgG3 subclasses and IgM class are capable of initiating the classic pathway, whereas the IgG4 subclass and IgA, IgD, and IgE classes are inactive in this regard. Among the IgG subclasses, IgG3 is most active, followed (in order) by IgG1 and IgG2. Immunologic activation occurs via binding of the first complement component (C1) to a site located in the Fc region of the IgG or IgM molecule.

The classic pathway may also be activated nonimmunologically by a number of chemically diverse substances, including DNA, C-reactive protein, and certain cellular membranes and trypsinlike enzymes (Table 11–1). Activation occurs by direct binding of C1 to these substances or, in the case of enzymes such as the fibrinolytic enzyme plasmin, by direct proteolytic attack on the C1 molecule.

Table 11–1. Activation of the complement (C) system.

	Classic	Alternative
Immunologic	IgG, IgM	IgA, IgG
Nonimmuno-logic	Trypsinlike enzymes	Trypsinlike enzymes
	DNA	Lipopolysaccharides
	Staphylococcal protein A	Plant and bacterial poly-saccharides
	C-reactive protein	Cobra venom factor

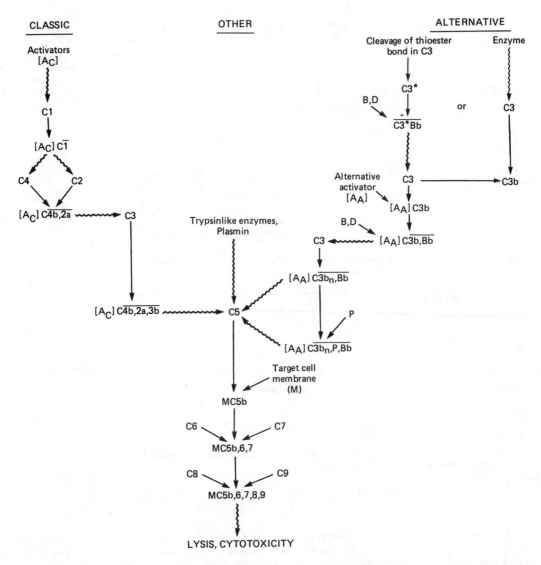

Figure 11–1. Schematic diagram of the mechanisms of assembly of the complement (C) system on the surface of a complement activator. (P= properdin; B = factor B; D = factor D.)

The classic pathway comprises the reaction steps of the first (C1), second (C2), third (C3), and fourth (C4) complement components. The pathway may be subdivided into 2 functional units: first, activation of the first component, C1; and second, generation of 2 related complex complement enzymes, C̄4b,2a and C̄4b,2a,3b.

C1

The steps involved in the activation of C1 following attachment to the activating agent or after proteolytic attack comprise the first functional unit of the classic complement pathway. C1 consists of 3 distinct protein molecules—termed C1q, C1r, and C1s—which are held together by a calcium-dependent bond (Table 11–2). C1 is present in the circulation as a firm C1q-C1r-C1s macromolecule, and individual sub-

units are only found in pathologic conditions. C1 may, however, be readily dissociated and reassociated on removal and restoration of calcium ions. C1q has a molecular weight of 400,000; electrophoretically, it is one of the most cationic proteins of human serum. It is a unique serum protein in that its structure is chemically very similar to that of collagen or basement membrane. Like collagen, it contains large amounts of glycine and the hydroxylated amino acids hydroxylysine and hydroxyproline and a significant carbohydrate content consisting in large part of glucose and galactose residues linked as disaccharide units to the hydroxyl group of hydroxylysine. C1q contains a total of 18 polypeptide chains of 3 distinct types that are organized into a structure, visualized by electron microscopy, consisting of 6 peripheral globular portions connected by fibrillar strands to a central structure. The

Table 11—2. Properties of the complement components and complement regulators.

Name	Synonyms	Molecular Weight	Electro-phoretic Mobility	Approximate Plasma Concentration (μg/mL)
Classic pathway				
C1q	C'O, 11S protein	400,000	γ_2	70
C1r	· · ·	190,000	β	34
C1s	C$\overline{1}$ esterase	87,000	a	31
C2	· · ·	117,000	β_1	25
C3	β_1C	185,000	β_1	1600
C4	β_1E	206,000	β_1	600
Alternative pathway				
C3	Factor A, hydrazine-sensitive factor (HSF)	180,000	β_1	1600
Factor B	C3 proactivator (C3PA), glycine-rich β glyco-protein (GBG), β_2-glycoprotein II	95,000	β_2	200
Factor D	C3 proactivator convertase (C3PAse), glycine-rich β glycoproteinase (GBG)	25,000	a	1
Factor I	C3b inactivator, KAF, C3b INA	88,000	β	34
Factor H	β_1H, C3b inactivator accelerator	150,000	β_1	500
Properdin	· · ·	224,000	γ_2	25
Membrane attack mechanism				
C5	β_1F	180,000	β_1	85
C6	· · ·	128,000	β_2	75
C7	· · ·	121,000	β_2	55
C8	· · ·	153,000	γ_1	55
C9	· · ·	72,000	a	60
Complement regulators				
C$\overline{1}$ inhibitor	C$\overline{1}$ esterase inhibitor, C$\overline{1}$ inactivator	105,000	a_2	180
C4 binding protein	C4bp	>500,000	β	· · ·
Factor I	C3b inactivator, KAF, C3b INA	88,000	β	34
Factor H	β_1H, C3b inactivator accelerator	150,000	β_1	500
Properdin	· · ·	185,000	γ_2	25
S protein	Membrane attack complex inhibitor, MAC INH	80,000	a	>300
Anaphylatoxin inactivator	A1, SCPB, carboxypeptidase N	300,000	a	· · ·
Abnormal proteins				
C3 nephritic factor	C3 NeF, NF	180,000	γ	· · ·

polypeptide chains of the collagenlike portion of each of the 6 subunits form, in all likelihood, a triple helix. A schematic representation of the .C1q molecule is shown in Fig 11–2. The C1q molecule bears the sites which enable the C1 molecule to bind to the Fc region of IgG and IgM molecules and is able to bind approxi-

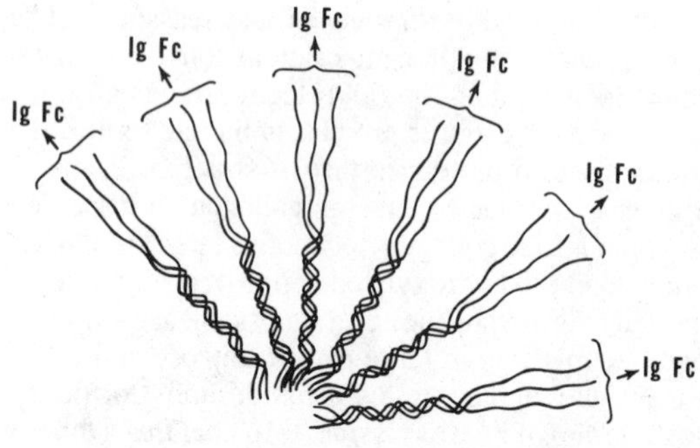

Figure 11–2. Schematic model of the C1q molecule showing the triple helical structure of a portion of each of the 6 subunits. The IgG or IgM binding sites appear to be in the noncollagenous portion of the subunits.

mately 6 IgG molecules. The IgG or IgM binding sites appear to be associated with the peripheral globular subunits of the C1q molecule.

C$\overline{1}$r is a β-globulin with a molecular weight of 190,000 (Table 11–2). Following attachment of C1 via C1q to activators, thus forming [Ac]C1, C1r acquires the ability to enzymatically activate C1s. Integrity of the C1 macromolecule and calcium ions are required for this process.

C1s is an a-globulin with a molecular weight of 87,000 (Table 11–2). Following cleavage of a single peptide bond in the C1s molecule by C1r, C$\overline{1}$s acquires proteolytic enzyme activity. The de novo generated enzyme is of the serine esterase type and thus inhibitable by analogs of diisopropylfluorophosphate. The enzymatic site is located in the smaller of the 2 chains produced on proteolytic activation of the molecules; these chains are linked to each other by disulfide bridges. Upon generation of the C$\overline{1}$s enzyme, the initial phase of the classic complement pathway is completed, and the earlier reactants, including antigen, antibody, C1q, and C$\overline{1}$r, are not necessary for progression of the complement reaction.

Activated C$\overline{1}$s in C1 mediates the next phase of

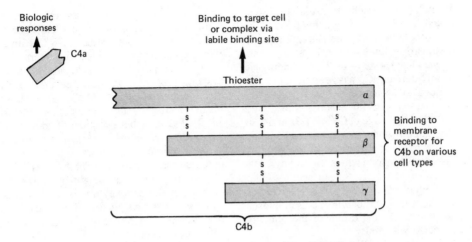

Figure 11–3. Schematic model of the C4 molecule.

the complement reaction: formation of the key complement enzyme [Ac]C$\overline{4b,2a}$ on the activator surface (Fig 11–1). [Ac]C$\overline{4b,2a}$ is formed from the larger fragments of C4 and C2.

C4, C2

C4 is a β_1-globulin with a molecular weight of 206,000, and C2 is a β_1-globulin with a molecular weight of 117,000 (Table 11–2). Formation of the bimolecular complex of C2 and C4 occurs only after both of these molecules have been cleaved by C$\overline{1s}$ or C$\overline{1}$. In the case of C4, C$\overline{1}$ cleaves a single peptide bond located in the larger of the 3 polypeptide chains of this molecule, the α chain (Fig 11–3). This reaction leads to formation or generation of a labile binding site in the larger fragment of C4, C4b, which enables it to bind to activators for a brief period after generation. It has recently been shown that the α chain of C4, like C3 as described below, contains an unprecedented internal thioester bond formed between a glutamyl and a cysteinyl residue. It is probable, in analogy to C3, that C$\overline{1}$-mediated cleavage of the α chain is followed by stress-induced hydrolysis of the thioester bond. This would permit the reactive acyl group of the glutamyl residue to form a covalent bond with a reactive hydroxyl or amino group on the surface of the activator.

C4a, the small peptide produced by C$\overline{1}$ cleavage of C4, has biologic activity. Cleavage of C2 by C1 also generates a labile binding site of unknown chemical composition in the larger C2 fragment, C2a, which allows it to bind to C4b. Magnesium ions are also required for formation of the C$\overline{4b,2a}$ complex. The molecular weight of C$\overline{4b,2a}$ is 280,000. Formation of C$\overline{4b,2a}$ is not an efficient process; the majority of the C2 and C4 molecules entering into this reaction lose their labile binding sites before achieving union with membranes or with each other and diffuse away as inactive reaction products.

C$\overline{4b,2a}$ is a proteolytic enzyme that assumes the role of continuing an ongoing complement reaction, and earlier reacting components are no longer required after it has been formed (Fig 11–1). C$\overline{4b,2a}$, also termed C3 convertase, cleaves and thereby activates the next reacting component of the sequence, C3. The enzymatic site resides in the C2 moiety of the complex.

C3

C3, the substrate of C$\overline{4b,2a}$, is a β_1-globulin with a molecular weight of 185,000. C3 is cleaved at a single site located near the amino terminus of the larger (α) chain of the molecule (Fig 11–4). The smaller of the 2 resulting fragments, C3a, is a biologically potent

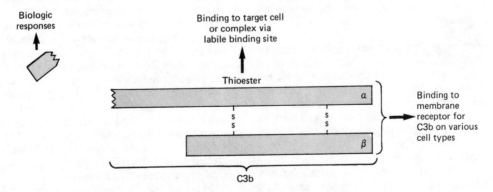

Figure 11–4. Schematic model of the C3 molecule.

peptide which will be discussed later. A labile binding site is generated in the larger fragment, C3b, which enables this molecule to attach to membranes at sites near to but distinct from those utilized by antibody and $\overline{\text{C4b,2a}}$. The chemical nature of the labile binding site has been recently defined. C3 has been found to contain the amino acid sequence –Cys-Gly-Glu-Glu– with the Cys and second Glu residues joined by a thioester bond. With cleavage of C3 into C3a and C3b, the thioester apparently undergoes stress-mediated hydrolysis, and the reactive acyl group of the glutamyl residue forms a covalent bond with a reactive hydroxyl or amino group on the activator surface. A major proportion of C3 molecules undergoing cleavage fails to achieve binding. In all probability, these represent molecules in which the acyl group of the glutamyl residue has reacted with water.

The attachment of C3b to membranes in the vicinity of $\overline{\text{C4b,2a}}$ molecules leads to generation of the last enzyme of the classic pathway, $\overline{\text{C4b,2a,3b}}$. This enzyme has C5, a β_1-globulin with a molecular weight of 180,000, as its natural substrate.

The classic complement pathway thus consists of a series of enzyme-substrate and protein-protein interactions which lead to the sequential formation of several complement enzymes. It should be emphasized that the reactions involved are highly specific, and other molecules have not been found which can substitute for the required complement components. In addition, as the reactions are enzymatically mediated, there is a considerable turnover of molecules of C2, C3, C4, and C5 at the respective steps in the reaction and an accumulation of reaction products free in plasma. Since some of these reaction products have biologic activity, it is evident that a relatively small stimulus to complement activation may lead to considerable generation of these biologically active products.

THE ALTERNATIVE
COMPLEMENT PATHWAY

The alternative complement pathway, or properdin pathway, may be activated immunologically by human IgA and also by some human IgG molecules (Table 11–1). The pathway may also be readily initiated nonimmunologically by certain complex polysaccharides, lipopolysaccharides, and trypsinlike enzymes.

The alternative pathway was originally described as the properdin system, a group of proteins involved in resistance to infection, which was similar to, but distinct from, complement. The properdin system was found to be involved in the destruction of certain bacteria, the neutralization of some viruses, and the lysis of erythrocytes from patients with paroxysmal nocturnal hemoglobinuria. The system did not seem to require specific antibody. Several of the factors involved in the system were identified and isolated in a partially purified state. These included properdin; factor A, a high-molecular-weight protein similar in certain

properties to C4 which was destroyed by treatment of serum with hydrazine; and a heat-labile substance (factor B), similar to but distinct from C2. Investigations indicate that the recently identified alternative pathway of complement activation is identical to the properdin system. Properdin was isolated and found to be a glycoprotein with a molecular weight of 224,000, having the electrophoretic mobility of a γ_2-globulin (Table 11–2). Factor A has been identified as C3. Factor B has several synonyms as a result of its involvement in systems subsequently shown to be different activities of the alternative pathway (Table 11–2); it is a β_2-globulin with a molecular weight of 95,000. The other proteins of the pathway are factor D, an α-globulin with a molecular weight of 25,000; and factors I and H, β-globulins with molecular weights of 88,000 and 150,000, respectively.

Activation of the alternative pathway proceeds in a different manner than the classic pathway. An initial requirement for activation is the presence of C3b, which is undoubtedly continuously generated in small amounts in the circulation. This most likely occurs following water-induced cleavage of the above-described thioester bond in C3, thus forming C3*, which reacts with factors B and D to generate a fluid phase enzyme able to cleave C3 into C3a and C3b (Fig 11–1). It is possible also that C3 in the circulation is cleaved by a loose complex of native C3 and factor B, an enzyme of the coagulation or fibrinolytic systems, or a tissue enzyme. While most of the newly generated C3b remains in the fluid phase, some binds to various cellular surfaces. In either case, this C3b is rapidly inactivated by the control proteins, factors I and H, which cleave it. This steady state condition with low-grade continuous turnover of C3 coupled with rapid inactivation of the newly formed C3b is greatly modified by the introduction of particulate activators of the alternative pathway, such as insoluble polysaccharides and certain cells. As with other cells and tissues exposed to plasma, some of the C3b being continuously generated becomes deposited on the surface of the activator. However, C3b deposited on activators, in contrast to nonactivators, is "protected" from destruction by factors I and H. This surface-bound protected C3b interacts with factors B and D and forms an enzyme termed $\overline{\text{C3b,Bb}}$. This surface-bound enzyme is able to cleave very large amounts of C3. Considerable amounts of this newly generated C3b arrive on the surface of the activator, interact with additional factors B and D, and form more $\overline{\text{C3b,Bb}}$. There is thus at this stage a positive feedback mechanism that amplifies the initial stimulus and leads to increased C3 cleavage (Fig 11–5). Furthermore, the $\overline{\text{C3b,Bb}}$ enzyme molecules are rendered functionally more efficient by properdin, which binds to the complex and stabilizes it by slowing the spontaneous dissociation of factor Bb. The cyclic amplifying system, in conjunction with the crucial protected surface, represents the key events in activation of the alternative pathway.

Many of the C3b molecules generated by the surface-bound $\overline{\text{C3b,Bb}}$ or $\overline{\text{C3b,P,Bb}}$ enzymes bind to

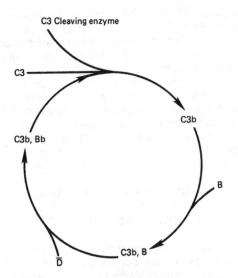

Figure 11–5. The C3b-dependent positive feedback mechanism.

the surface of the activator particle in close proximity to these enzymes. This results in the formation of modified enzymes, $\overline{C3b_n,Bb}$ or $\overline{C3b_n,P,Bb}$ ($n > 1$), which are able to cleave C5 and initiate the membrane attack mechanism. The catalytic site of these enzymes resides in the factor B moiety.

The alternative pathway may also be activated by an isolated protein obtained from cobra venom. This protein appears to represent cobra C3b. This substance has been extensively used to deplete complement activity in vivo for the purpose of studying its biologic function. This protein, cobra venom factor, forms a firm complex with factor B in the presence of magnesium ions. Factor B, altered slightly by incorporation into the complex, is susceptible to cleavage and activation by factor D. A C3 cleaving enzyme is thus generated.

A pathologic member of this pathway, C3 nephritic factor (C3 NeF), is found in the circulation of some patients with hypocomplementemic mesangiocapillary nephritis. This protein forms a fluid phase, C3 converting enzyme, together with native C3 and factors B and D. It is an autoantibody directed to the $\overline{C3b,Bb}$ complex of the alternative pathway.

There are numerous analogies in physicochemical properties of the factors of the alternative and classic complement pathways and the mechanisms of activation of these proteins. $\overline{C1s}$ is similar to factor $\overline{D}$ in that both are serine esterase enzymes. $\overline{C1s}$ cleaves C4 and C2, and the larger fragment of each is incorporated into a new enzyme in the presence of magnesium. Factor $\overline{D}$ cleaves factor B, a molecule very similar in physicochemical properties to C2, in the presence of another protein, C3b, which is physicochemically similar to C4b, and thereby mediates the magnesium-dependent formation of a new proteolytic enzyme. These similar complex enzymes cleave the same single

peptide bond in C3. In each instance, the newly generated C3b modulates the activity of the complex enzyme, enabling it to cleave C5.

THE REACTION OF C5–C9: THE MEMBRANE ATTACK MECHANISM

The terminal portion of the complement sequence is termed the membrane attack system, since C5b–9 must become membrane-bound in order for membrane changes or damage to occur. Following activation, this portion of the complement sequence may become attached to the surface of a cell bearing the activating enzyme of the classic or alternative pathways, or it may become bound to the membrane of a different cell or membrane not bearing any previously reacted complement components. The latter is an example of bystander lysis of cells.

The complement attack mechanism is initiated on cleavage of C5 by $\overline{C4b,2a,3b}$, $\overline{C3b_n,Bb}$, $\overline{C3b_n,P,Bb}$ or certain enzymes such as plasmin (Fig 11–1). The activation reaction results in generation of a small biologically active peptide, C5a (MW 17,000), and a larger fragment, C5b (MW 163,000). C5b has the ability to bind C6 and C7, thus forming a firm trimolecular complex C5b,6,7. This complex has a transient ability to bind to membranes. However, this process is modulated by S protein, a normal serum protein with a molecular weight of 80,000. S protein serves as a natural inhibitor by binding to the membrane binding site of the C5b,6,7 complex. The C5b,6,7 molecules that interact with S protein are inactivated with regard to participation in cytolysis as the SC5b,6,7 complex is unable to attach to membranes. Each membrane-bound C5b,6,7 complex possesses a binding site for a molecule of C8, a γ_1-globulin with a molecular weight

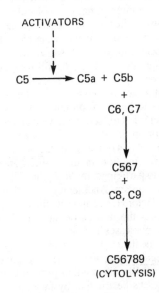

Figure 11–6. Schematic diagram of the membrane attack mechanism.

of 153,000. Membrane leakage begins at this stage; however, the cytolytic process is greatly accelerated by the attachment of C9, an α-globulin with a molecular weight of 72,000, to the membrane bound tetramolecular C5b,6,7,8 complex. The C5b,6,7,8,9 complex represents the fully assembled cytolytic principle of the complement system.

CONTROL MECHANISMS OF THE COMPLEMENT SYSTEM

Uncontrolled activation of the complement system is prevented by the lability of the activated combining sites generated at multiple stages of the complement reaction, including the reaction steps involving C2, C3, C4, and C5, and by time- and temperature-dependent dissociation of some of the active complexes such as the $\overline{C3b,Bb}$, $\overline{C4b,2a}$, and $\overline{C4b,2a,3b}$ complexes. In addition, several serum proteins have been identified which serve to modulate and limit activation of the complement system. These proteins bind to or enzymatically attack only the specifically activated forms of the components.

$\overline{CI}$ inhibitor ($\overline{CI}$ esterase inhibitor) is a multispecific serum enzyme inhibitor with a molecular weight of 105,000 and the electrophoretic mobility of an α_2-globulin. This enzyme inhibitor inhibits not only $\overline{CI}$ but also the fibrinolytic enzyme plasmin, the kinin-forming system enzyme kallikrein, and the coagulation system enzymes Hageman factor (factor XII) and factor XI. $\overline{CI}$ inhibitor inhibits the enzymatic activity of $\overline{CI}$ and its $\overline{CIr}$ and $\overline{CIs}$ subunits by rapidly forming firm, essentially irreversible stoichiometric complexes. $\overline{CI}$ inhibitor does not bind to proenzyme C1 or C1s. The site of attachment is on the light chains of $\overline{CIr}$ and $\overline{CIs}$. Classic pathway activation proceeds past the $\overline{CI}$ inhibitor blockade when the stimulus to activation is so intense that $\overline{CI}$ molecules succeed in forming C4b,2a sites before becoming inactivated by C1 inhibitor molecules or when the available $\overline{CI}$ inhibitor has been consumed. However, activation of the kinin-forming, coagulation, or fibrinolytic systems would also be expected to facilitate activation of the complement system by consuming C1 inhibitor.

Another key control protein of the complement system is factor I. This serum enzyme attacks C3b free in solution or on the surface of cells and cleaves the molecule (Fig 11–4). The C3b degradation products are unable to function in the $\overline{C4b,2a,3b}$ or $\overline{C3b,B}$ enzymes or to participate in the cyclic C3b-dependent feedback mechanism. Another regulator that acts at the C3b stage is factor H, a serum protein that binds to C3b and accelerates the destructive action of factor I on C3b. It also possesses the ability to bind to C3b on various intermediate complexes and, finally, exerts an inhibitory regulatory action on the alternative pathway enzyme $\overline{C3b,P,Bb}$. C4 binding protein binds to C4b and facilitates its destruction by factor I.

Human serum also contains an enzyme, the anaphylatoxin inactivator, an α-globulin with a molecular weight of 300,000, which destroys the biologic activities of the C3a, C4a, and C5a fragments of C3, C4, and C5, respectively. Inactivation is accomplished by cleavage of the carboxyl terminal arginine from each of these molecules.

The S protein binds to the forming C5b,6,7 complex and thus modulates the cytolytic ability of the membrane attack complex, as described earlier. Several other inhibitors or inactivators of activated complement components have been described. These substances have not yet been analyzed in detail.

METHODS OF DETECTION & QUANTITATION OF COMPLEMENT COMPONENTS

Certain precautions are necessary in the handling of blood specimens for complement studies. Preferably, serum should be allowed to clot at room temperature (approximately 22 °C). The serum should be separated from the blood clot as soon as possible and frozen, preferably at −70 °C, to prevent loss of complement activity if the tests are not to be performed within several days.

Some laboratory studies require inactivation of complement in order to avoid hemolysis. This is normally achieved by heating serum at 56 °C for 30 minutes. Although this procedure destroys many of the complement components, several are heat-stable and retain functional activity, although the whole serum is negative in hemolytic complement tests.

Complement activity is generally measured by assessing the ability of serum in limiting dilution to lyse sheep red cells sensitized with rabbit antisheep antibody (hemolysin). Complement titrations of this type provide an overall measure of the integrity of the classic complement pathway and of the membrane attack mechanism. The values are expressed as 50% hemolytic complement units per mL (CH_{50}). One CH_{50} unit is defined as the quantity or dilution of serum required to lyse 50% of the cells in the test serum (see Chapter 22).

A similar assay system is employed to measure the hemolytic activity of individual complement components in isolated form or in serum. In this type of assay system, all the components except the one in question are supplied in excess and certain stringent reaction conditions are employed which are known to be optimal for each component. Under such conditions, the number of hemolytic units may be converted on a weight basis to the absolute concentration of the active complement component. This use of hemolytic activity measurements for absolute quantitation of complement components has a firm theoretical and mathematical basis, since it has been shown that the individual reaction steps of a number of the components conform to a one-hit process. Hemolytic values obtained by such titrations are expressed as site-forming units or effective molecules.

The pattern of depletion of complement compo-

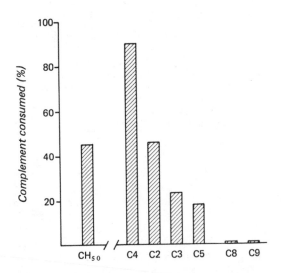

Figure 11–7. Typical component depletion pattern for classic pathway activation.

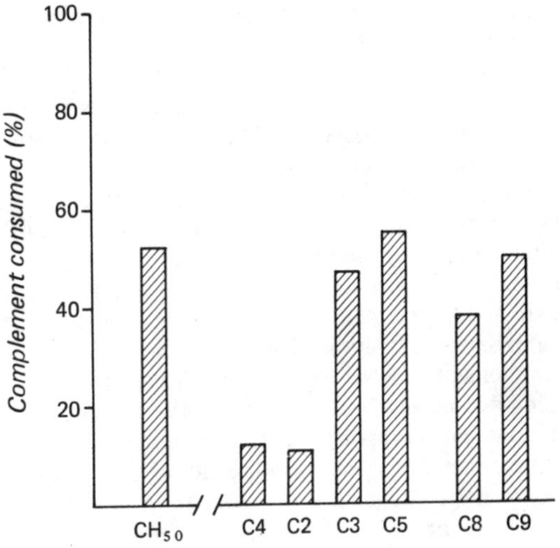

Figure 11–8. Typical component depletion pattern for alternative pathway activation.

nents in patients' sera or following treatment of serum with potential complement-activating agents may indicate the pathway of complement activation involved. Classic pathway activation depletes C1, C4, C2, C3, and C5 and, to a lesser extent, late-acting components as indicated in Fig 11–7. Alternative pathway activation, while depleting only small amounts of C1, C4, and C2, leads to significant consumption of C3–C9 (Fig 11–8).

Many of the complement components can be quantitated in serum or other body fluids by single radial diffusion in agar (Chapter 22). This test is based on the fact that the extent of diffusion of an antigen into agar containing specific antibody is proportionate to the absolute antigen concentration. All of the complement components having serum levels above approximately 20 μg/mL, and for which antiserum is available, can be measured by this technique. However, it should be noted that this method of quantitation, although very useful, does not distinguish between active and inactive complement molecules.

Other methods are available which are not quantitative but which furnish evidence of complement activation. One such technique involves measurement of the physicochemical status of individual complement components by the technique of immunoelectrophoresis. In the case of certain of the components such as $C\overline{1s}$, C2, C3, C4, and factor B, the cleaved activated forms of the components are readily distinguished by an altered electrophoretic mobility. The effect of activation on the mobility of factor B is depicted in Fig 11–9. The native precursor molecule migrates as β_2-globulin on immunoelectrophoresis in agar, while activated factor B migrates as a γ-globulin. Activated C2 also migrates more cathodally than native C2, while activated $C\overline{1s}$, C3, and C4 migrate more anodally than the respective native proteins.

Evidence of complement activation may also be obtained by showing a decrease in the immune adherence titer of the serum being investigated. Immune adherence is an agglutination reaction between a cell bearing $C\overline{4b,2a,3b}$ and an indicator cell, often human erythrocytes, which has a receptor for C3b. The test is generally performed by incubating dilutions of serum with antibody-coated erythrocytes during which time $C\overline{4b,2a,3b}$ attaches to the surface of the cells in proportion to their relative serum concentrations. Subsequently, human erythrocytes are added and the final

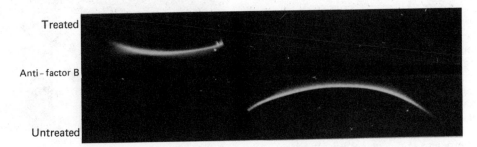

Figure 11–9. Immunoelectrophoretic analysis of factor B (C3PA) in native form *(bottom)* and after activation *(top).* Anti-factor B is in the slot, and the anode is to the right.

dilution of serum giving measurable agglutination is taken as the end point.

Complement may also be demonstrated in diseased tissues at the site of tissue damage by employing specific antibody. An example is the nonimmunoglobulin Coombs test, an agglutination reaction performed with erythrocytes from patients with autoimmune hemolytic anemia and dilutions of antisera to C3, C4, or other complement components. As complement is not normally found on cells, the presence of agglutination with anticomplement sera constitutes evidence for complement activation. In a variant of this technique, complement may be localized in diseased tissues by using fluorescent or radiolabeled antisera to individual complement components. The finding of deposited complement components in the site of tissue damage constitutes evidence for activation of the complement system in the tissue.

Direct evidence of activation of the complement system in vivo may be obtained from metabolic studies with purified radiolabeled complement components. Such studies have been performed with many complement components in normal individuals and in a number of patients with diseases, including glomerulonephritis, rheumatic and autoimmune diseases, hereditary angioedema, and renal allograft rejection. These studies indicate that complement components are normally among the most rapidly metabolized of all plasma proteins, with a mean fractional catabolic rate of approximately 1.4–2% of the plasma pool per hour. Because of the very rapid turnover of complement proteins, static measurements of circulating levels of the complement components often fail to detect in vivo complement activation. Such activation and the pathway involved are, however, readily detected and quantitated by metabolic studies. Hypercatabolism has been found in patients with proliferative glomerulonephritis, systemic lupus erythematosus, seropositive rheumatoid arthritis, hereditary angioedema, and renal allograft rejection. Metabolic studies also reveal reduced synthesis of complement—C3 in some patients with membranoproliferative glomerulonephritis and C4 in some patients with IgG-IgM cryoglobulinemia and Sjögren's syndrome.

BIOLOGIC CONSEQUENCES OF COMPLEMENT ACTIVATION

Cytolytic & Cytotoxic Damage

Complement has been shown to be capable of mediating the lytic destruction of many kinds of cells including erythrocytes, platelets, bacteria, viruses possessing a lipoprotein envelope, and lymphocytes, although with greatly varying degrees of efficiency in each instance. Either complement pathway may produce cytolytic damage. Some species of complement are more efficient in producing lysis of certain cell-antibody combinations. Some cells are quite resistant to destruction by complement even in the presence of

Table 11–3. Consequences of attachment of complement proteins to membranes.

Accumulation of bulk of complement proteins
Changes in membrane environment and charge
Modification of membrane properties and functions
Stimulation of cellular functions
Membrane lesions and swelling
Membrane damage or disruption

marked complement activation on the cell surface. There are many reasons why complement may fail to lyse cells, including the presence of antigenic modulation, a phenomenon whereby antibody alters the distribution of antigen on the cell surface, or a spatial arrangement of antigenic sites which does not facilitate complement activation in a region of the membrane susceptible to lysis. Lack of binding sites for the late-reacting complement components is another possible cause of failure of complement to lyse a cell. Most commonly, however, complement fails to produce lysis because of the nature and structure of the cell wall or membrane or because the cell repairs the complement-mediated damage. Factors in addition to complement may also be required, as in the lysis of gram-negative bacteria.

As the complement components free in serum become attached to the surfaces of cells and other biologic membranes, changes in membrane ultrastructure occur (Table 11–3). There are alterations in membrane electrical charge and membrane environment owing to the accumulation of complement proteins on the cell surface. Membrane swelling also occurs. Complement action produces circular lesions having a diameter of 8–12 nm in many types of membranes (Fig 11–10). These lesions, which are C5b–9 complexes inserted into the cellular membrane, are the sites of lytic membrane damage. The mechanism by which the C5b–9 complex disrupts cellular lipid bilayer mem-

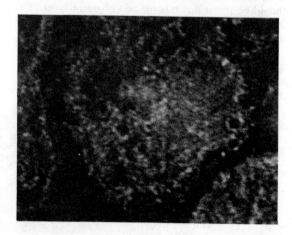

Figure 11–10. Electron micrograph demonstrating the circular lesions produced in the membrane of an enveloped virus by the cytolytic action of complement.

branes, leading to lysis, is not entirely clear. The 2 major theories are (1) that it forms a protein channel ("doughnut") through the lipid bilayer membrane, or, alternatively, (2) that it induces reorganization of the lipids and phospholipids of the bilayer, leading to transmembrane lipid channels. Either type of channel would allow passage of small molecules and initiate osmotic lysis of the cell.

Formation of Complement-Dependent Reactive Sites

New sites are generated or uncovered in the b fragments of C3 and C4 as a consequence of proteolytic cleavage of the molecules during complement activation (Figs 11–3 and 11–4). The labile binding sites which were uncovered or generated by proteolytic cleavage and which permit binding to membranes have been considered earlier. The biologically active α cleavage fragments will be considered below. In addition, however, other reactive sites are generated in C3b and C4b which are recognized by various cells having receptors for C3b or C4b (Figs 11–3 and 11–4). These sites appear to be stable. The secondary or responding cells bind to these sites in C3b or C4b regardless of whether the b fragments are free in solution or attached by the labile binding site to an immune complex or to another cell. In the latter instance, C3b or C4b molecules serve as a bridge between a complex or target cell bearing C3b or C4b bound via the labile binding site and the responding cell having a receptor for C3b or C4b. Attachment of the responding or effector cell to C3b or C4b in this manner may trigger any of several responses by the responding cell.

Many kinds of cells possess receptors for C3b and C4b (Table 11–4). These include phagocytic cells, lymphocytes, primate erythrocytes, and certain nonprimate platelets. The consequences of attachment of C3b or C4b depend on the responding cell type. Phagocytic cells, such as macrophages, monocytes, and polymorphonuclear leukocytes, have C3b receptors. Although phagocytic cells ingest in the absence of complement by any of several mechanisms, the presence of C3b and C4b on the target cell or complex facilitates adherence. In some cases, the complement fragments alone may suffice for ingestion.

C3b receptors are also present on human erythrocytes and platelets from many nonprimate species (Table 11–4). The biologic significance of attachment of complexes or cells bearing C3b to human erythrocytes, a reaction termed immune adherence, is not clear, although it may be an immobilizing mechanism

important in dealing with pathogenic agents. Adherence to nonprimate platelets triggers specific release of vasoactive amines and nucleotides from the platelet. Platelet lysis does not ensue.

In addition, human B lymphocytes have receptors for C3b and C4b (Table 11–4). Although the biologic significance of the presence of these receptors is unclear, it is evident that this reaction brings antigens in direct surface contact with potential antibody-forming cells. It is conceivable that bound complement components play a role in this manner in the induction of an immune response.

Specific receptors for other breakdown products of C3 and for the collagenous portion of the C1q molecule have also been described. The biologic roles played by these complement components are under active investigation.

Biologic Actions of Complement Cleavage Products

The low-molecular-weight fragments of C3, C4, and C5 — C3a, C4a, and C5a, respectively — are known as **anaphylatoxins.** These hormonelike peptides induce smooth muscle contraction, enhance vascular permeability, release vasoactive amines such as histamine from mast cells and basophils, and induce lysosomal enzyme release from granulocytes. In addition, the C5a molecule is chemotactic, ie, it is able to induce the migration of leukocytes into an area of complement activation. The C5a molecule also has numerous other properties, which include granulocyte aggregation and activation of intracellular processes in certain cells, leading to various effects such as release of oxygen metabolites and SRS-A.

Many if not all of the C3a and C4a effects appear to be due to histamine released as a consequence of C3a and C4a interaction with mast cells and basophils. These effects are abrogated by antihistamines and by the action of anaphylatoxin inactivator, or carboxypeptidase N, a serum enzyme that removes the C-terminal arginine residue from these peptides. Although antihistamines and this control enzyme inhibit some of the effects of C5a, C5a des Arg, which lacks the C-terminal arginine, retains significant chemotactic, granulocyte-aggregating, and intracellular activating ability.

C3a, C4a, and C5a have molecular weights of 9038, 8740, and 11,200, respectively. A recently completed comparison of the primary structures of

Table 11–4. Cells possessing C3b and C4b receptors.

B lymphocytes
Neutrophils
Monocytes
Macrophages
Erythrocytes (primates only)
Platelets (rabbit, rodents, cat, dog, but not primates)

Table 11–5. Biologic effects of complement activation peptides.

C3a, C4a, C5a	Cellular release of vasoactive amines.
	Enhanced vascular permeability.
	Contraction of smooth muscle.
	Induced release of lysosomal enzymes.
C5a	Chemotaxis.
	Granulocyte aggregation.
	Stimulation of oxidative metabolism.
	Stimulation of SRS-A release.

these molecules indicates that they are genetically related. They also share a number of the same biologic actions as noted above. Despite these facts, the C3a and C5a anaphylatoxins interact with distinct cell surface receptors and thus are biologically distinct.

There are also other biologic consequences of activation of the complement system mediated by other complement cleavage products. These include the generation of a kinin, possibly a fragment of C2, which increases vascular permeability and contracts smooth muscle. This kinin does not function through release of histamine. It is thought to be involved in the symptomatology of hereditary angioedema. Functional C1 inactivator is genetically lacking in this disease, which is characterized by uncontrolled activation of the complement system.

BIOLOGIC SIGNIFICANCE OF THE COMPLEMENT SYSTEM

The biologic reactions considered above are individual aspects of an integrated system which is able to produce inflammation and facilitate the localization of an infective agent (Fig 11–11). Thus, the kinin and anaphylatoxin activities lead to contraction of smooth muscle, increased vascular permeability, and edema. The chemotactic agents trigger an influx of leukocytes

which remain fixed in the area of complement activation through attachment to specific sites on bound C3b and C4b molecules. Phagocytosis or release of lysosomal and other constituents facilitates the destruction of an infective agent. As is evident from Fig 11–11, there are multiple backup systems which produce similar biologic activities. A minor stimulus to activation of the system produces relatively little of these biologic mediators, while a greater stimulus to activation can be visualized as leading to the generation of additional cleavage products and reactive sites on the components.

Evidence for the biologic importance of this system in host defenses has come from studies of several experimentally induced diseases in animals, from human immunologic disease processes, and from the markedly increased susceptibility to infection which characterizes some congenital or acquired deficiencies of complement components or complement regulators in humans. These disease entities bear certain hallmarks which imply the participation of complement. These include a depression in circulating levels of the complement components, the finding of complement components deposited in the site of tissue damage, and infiltration of polymorphonuclear leukocytes. In animals, it has been possible to further define the pathogenic role of complement in certain conditions. One of the most telling examples is the experimental

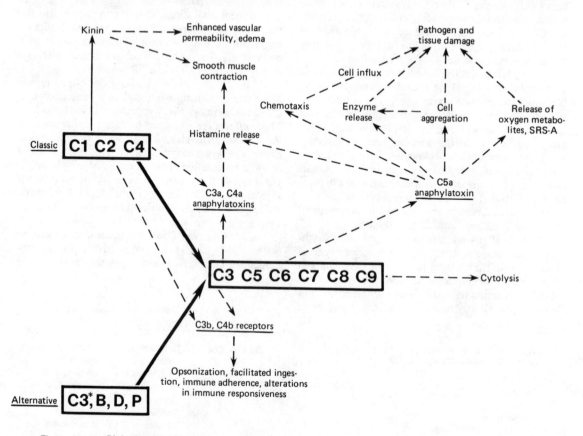

Figure 11–11. Biologic consequences of complement activation. (P = properdin; B = factor B; D = factor D.)

disease nephrotoxic nephritis, which is induced by the injection into an animal of antibody directed against glomerular basement membrane. The injected antibody rapidly fixes to the glomerular basement membrane, and the result is immediate structural and functional injury. Antibody attachment is rapidly followed by activation of complement, which is reflected in a fall in circulating levels and by fixation of complement components to the glomerular basement membrane, where they may be visualized by fluorescence techniques. An influx of polymorphonuclear leukocytes rapidly ensues, followed by destruction of the glomerular basement membrane and proteinuria, which are consequences of the release of degradative enzymes from the leukocytes. The essential role of complement in leading to the influx of leukocytes and facilitating their localization is shown by the fact that infiltration and tissue damage are prevented if the antibody is first rendered unable to fix complement or if the animal is depleted in vivo of C3. Similar mechanisms are involved in the inflammatory component of a number of human diseases, including several types of glomerulonephritis, rheumatoid arthritis, autoimmune hemolytic anemias, and others. Metabolic studies with purified radiolabeled complement components have documented and quantitated in vivo complement activation in these and other diseases as noted earlier.

The physiologic role of complement in the maintenance of a normal state of health is dramatically illustrated by the predisposition to disease or susceptibility to infection which characterizes congenital deficiency of certain of the complement components or their regulators (Table 11–6). Congenital deficiency of C1 inactivator leads to uncontrolled activation of the classic pathway and hereditary angioedema. Over half of the more than 50 reported individuals with hereditary deficiencies of the classic pathway—C1r, C1s, C4, and C2—are clinically ill and suffer from several diseases, including systemic lupus erythematosus, glomerulonephritis, and repeated infections. Most of the relatively few individuals found with genetic deficiencies of C3 or its regulator, C3b inactivator, suffer

Table 11–6. Human disorders associated with congenital complement deficiencies.

C1q	Systemic lupus erythematosus or similar syndrome, hypogammaglobulinemia, nephritis
C1r	Renal disease, systemic lupus erythematosus or similar syndrome, recurrent infections, rheumatoid disease
C1s	Systemic lupus erythematosus
C4	Systemic lupus erythematosus
C2	Arthralgia, systemic lupus erythematosus or similar syndrome, nephritis, susceptibility to infection
C3	Recurrent infections with pyogenic bacteria
C5	Systemic lupus erythematosus, recurrent infections, recurrent gonococcal infections
C6	Recurrent gonococcal and meningococcal infections, Raynaud's phenomenon
C7	Recurrent gonococcal and meningococcal infections, glomerulonephritis, Raynaud's phenomenon
C8	Recurrent gonococcal and meningococcal infections, systemic lupus erythematosus
C1 In	Hereditary angioedema
C3b In	Repeated infections, recurrent infections with pyogenic bacteria

from recurrent life-threatening infections. About half of the 20 individuals with inherited deficiencies of the terminal components—C5, C6, C7, and C8—have recurrent infections with *Neisseria* organisms (gonococcus or meningococcus).

The genes for C2, C4, and factor B (but not other complement components) are coded within the major histocompatibility complex (MHC, HLA) in humans (Chapter 6), but their relationships to other MHC gene products are not known. It is not entirely clear how the absence of a complement component or a regulator predisposes to disease. Most of the genes within this region are of fundamental importance to immune recognition, regulation, and responses (Chapter 6), and these unexplained relationships suggest major but as yet unknown physiologic roles for the complement system in vivo.

• • •

References

Alper CA, Rosen FS: Genetics of the complement system. *Adv Hum Genet* 1976;**7**:141.

Colten HR: Biosynthesis of complement. *Adv Immunol* 1976; **22**:67.

Cooper NR, Ziccardi RJ: The nature and reactions of complement enzymes. Page 167 in: *Proteolysis and Physiological Regulation.* Ribbons DW, Brew K (editors). Academic Press, 1976.

Day NK, Good RA (editors). *Biological Amplification Systems in Immunology.* Vol 2 of: *Comprehensive Immunology.* Plenum Press, 1977.

Hugli TE: The structural basis for anaphylatoxin and chemotactic functions of C3a, C4a and C5a. *Crit Rev Immunol 1981;***4**:321.

Lachmann PJ, Rosen FS: Genetic defects of complement in man. *Springer Semin Immunopath* 1978;**1**:339.

Möller G (editor): Biology of complement and complement receptors. *Transplant Rev* 1976;**32**:1.

Müller-Eberhard HJ: Complement. *Annu Rev Biochem* 1975; **44**:697.

Müller-Eberhard HJ, Schreiber RD: Molecular biology and chemistry of the alternative pathway of complement. *Adv Immunol* 1980;**29**:1.

Opferkuch W, Rother K, Schultz DR (editors): *Clinical Aspects of the Complement System.* G. Thieme, 1978.

Porter RR, Reid KBM: The biochemistry of complement. *Nature* 1978;**275**:699.

12 | Immune Mechanisms in Tissue Damage

I. ANTIBODY–MEDIATED TISSUE INJURY
J. Vivian Wells, MD, FRACP, FRCPA

Traditionally, it has been thought that a major stimulus to the development of immune responses is protection against microorganisms that threaten the welfare of the host. It is now clear, however, that protective immune responses also may prove deleterious to the host, as is the case in autoimmune disorders. Thus, immune responses to an infecting organism may eradicate the organism but at the same time produce significant pathologic or even lethal effects in the host. Pathogenetic mechanisms that can produce both beneficial and deleterious effects will be described in this chapter as immune mechanisms that cause tissue damage.

Various immune mechanisms involved in the production of tissue damage were classified in 1963 by Gell and Coombs into 4 basic types:

Type I: Anaphylactic
Type II: Cytotoxic
Type III: Arthus type and antigen-antibody complexes
Type IV: Delayed hypersensitivity

This classification does not depend on the host species or on the method of antigen exposure. In this chapter the classification of Gell and Coombs will be used as a basis for the discussion of immune mechanisms in tissue damage (Fig 12–1).

TYPE I REACTIONS

Anaphylactic or reagin-dependent reactions are also termed immediate hypersensitivity reactions to distinguish them from reactions associated with delayed hypersensitivity (type IV). Immediate hypersensitivity will be discussed in Chapter 18, but certain aspects will be discussed here for comparison with mechanisms involved in type II, III, and IV reactions.

Type I reactions are produced by pharmacologically active substances released from tissue cells, such as basophils and mast cells, following reaction between antigen and specific antibody adsorbed to the tissue cell membrane. Depending on the mode of administration of antigen, the clinical features may be systemic or local. Generalized anaphylaxis includes the following abnormalities in different systems: (1) Respiratory tract: bronchial obstruction and laryngeal edema. (2) Gastrointestinal tract: nausea, vomiting, cramping pain, and diarrhea (occasionally with blood in the stool). (3) Cardiovascular system: hypotension and shock. (4) Skin: very pruritic, circumscribed, discrete wheals with raised, erythematous serpiginous borders and blanched centers. These may coalesce into giant hives resembling angioedema.

The various factors involved in the production of anaphylactic responses will now be summarized briefly.

Components of Type I Reactions
A. Reaginic Antibodies: Reaginic antibodies are also called **homocytotropic antibodies** because of their autologous tissue–binding properties. Most of the antibodies responsible for type I reactions in humans belong to the IgE class. Studies in lower species have demonstrated a class of antibodies comparable to human IgE. Many lower species also contain specialized IgG antibodies which can bind to tissues and function as reaginic antibodies producing type I reactions. The binding of reaginic antibodies is accomplished via the Fc region of the molecule.

Guinea pig passive cutaneous anaphylaxis is produced by the passive transfer of guinea pig anaphylactic serum antibody by intradermal injection into an area of shaved skin, followed 4–24 hours later by an intravenous injection of specific antigen and Evans blue dye. The site of interaction is demarcated by extravasation of blue dye from the dilated blood vessels. The comparable test in humans is the classic Prausnitz-Küstner (PK) reaction. In this test, serum from a **sensitized** subject is injected into the skin of a **nonsensitive** recipient, and the recipient is challenged with antigen after a latent period of at least 12 hours. The classic wheal-and-erythema response may be elicited up to 6 weeks after the first injection. This test is no longer routinely used because there is a risk of transfer of serum hepatitis and because methods for the measurement of serum concentrations of total IgE and specific IgE class antibody have become available.

The physicochemical characteristics of IgE are

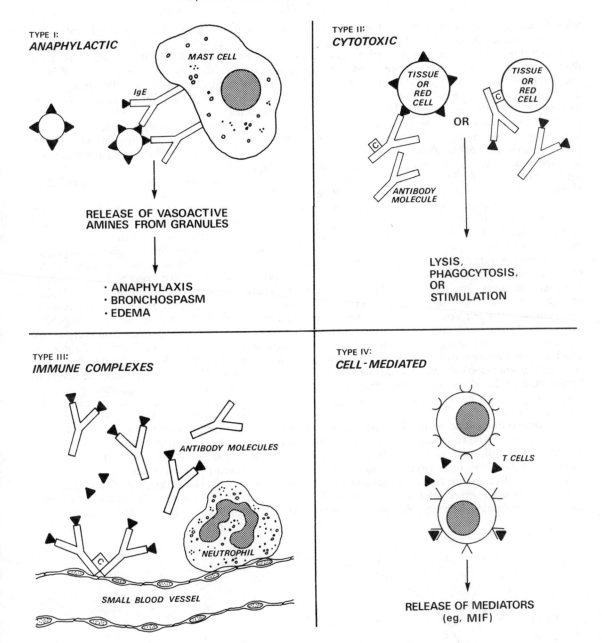

Figure 12–1. Schematic diagrams of the 4 types of immunologic mechanisms that may produce tissue damage. The diagrams are described in the text. C indicates complement; ▲, antigen; U and V, specific receptors for antigens.

summarized in Chapter 4, but it is emphasized that the serum concentration of IgE in normal subjects is approximately 0.004% that of IgG. The Fc region of the IgE molecule is heat-labile, and heating results in loss of the ability of IgE to passively sensitize tissue cells.

B. Antigen (Allergen): Many antigens are capable of inducing IgE antibody under appropriate conditions. Systemic anaphylaxis is most likely encountered following exposure of a sensitized subject to compounds such as heterologous proteins (antisera, hormones, enzymes, Hymenoptera venom, pollen extract, and food), polysaccharides (iron dextran), diag-

nostic agents (iodinated contrast materials, sulfobromophthalein), and therapeutic agents (antibiotics, vitamins). The IgE antibody response to an antigen is T-dependent and is under complex genetic control. For example, the IgE and IgG antibody responses to Ra5, an allergen from ragweed pollen, are clinically associated with histocompatibility antigen HLA-B7.

C. Tissue Cells (Basophils and Mast Cells): A basophil or mast cell possesses membrane receptors capable of binding the Fc region of IgE molecules. Bound IgE molecules are in a state of dynamic equilibrium, since Fc fragments of IgE molecules compete with whole IgE molecules for the receptor. Bridging of adjacent membrane IgE molecules by specific antigen initiates a series of biochemical changes resulting in the release of the active substances stored in mast cells and basophils. It is probable that considerably fewer than 100 IgE molecules must be activated to initiate this exquisitely sensitive process. In experimental conditions, it is possible to induce release of vasoactive amines by the addition of aggregated IgE antibodies to mast cells or basophils. Complement is not involved in this reaction. In humans, as noted above, IgE is the reaginic antibody classically responsible for binding to target cells and inducing anaphylaxis. Rare instances occur, however, where IgG myeloma proteins are capable of inhibiting the binding of IgE reaginic antibodies to monkey lung tissue and the release of histamine.

Conditions other than the reaction between reaginic antibodies and antigen can result in the release of vasoactive amines from target cells. The chemical detergent 48/80 is frequently used in experimental studies to induce the release of vasoactive amines from target cells. Activation of either the alternative or classic pathways of complement can generate a factor which releases histamine from both nonsensitized and sensitized human basophils in the absence of antibody. Complement-mediated release of vasoactive amines consistently occurs more quickly than allergen-mediated release.

D. Intracellular Biochemical Events: The postulated sequence of biochemical events occurring in the target cell following antigen-bridging of IgE molecules on the surface of the target cell and resulting in the release of vasoactive amines is summarized in Fig 12–2. There are several steps in the process with varying requirements for energy, and several factors are known to influence the process at different stages.

(1) Activation of a cellular proesterase requires entry of extracellular Ca^{2+} into the cell. This step is inhibited by diisopropyl fluorophosphate and is associated with contraction of microfilaments.

(2) Additional proesterase is activated autocatalytically.

(3) An energy-requiring stage with microfilaments moving granules alongside microtubules or plasma membrane is inhibited by glucose deprivation (eg, 2-deoxyglucose).

(4) A further step requiring Ca^{2+} is inhibited by ethylenediaminetetraacetic acid.

(5) A step leading to release of amines (perhaps exchanged for Na^+) is inhibited by elevation of the intracellular concentration of cAMP.

Considering the multiple biochemical stages, the multiple levels of inhibition, and, in particular, the importance of intracellular concentrations of cAMP and cGMP, it is not surprising that several pharmacologic agents influence the rate of release of vasoactive amines from target cells. These drugs act at different levels on α-adrenergic, β-adrenergic, and prostaglandin receptors. It was known for almost 40 years that epinephrine could suppress antigen-induced type I reactions. This is now known to be due to its action as a β-adrenergic agent by stimulating adenylate cyclase activity, which leads to an increased intracellular concentration of cAMP. This in turn suppresses the release of vasoactive amines. Conversely, α-adrenergic agents, which produce reductions in intracellular concentrations of cAMP, lead to increased release of vasoactive amines.

The reader is referred to Chapter 18 for a detailed discussion of vasoactive amines and the histochemistry and pharmacology of anaphylactic reactions.

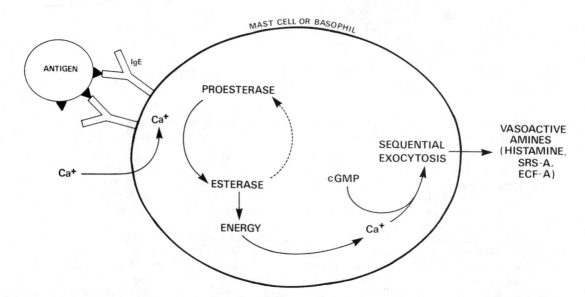

Figure 12–2. Schematic diagram of the major biochemical events in a type I reaction which follows antigen-bridging of IgE molecules on a target cell and results in release of vasoactive amines.

E. Pharmacologically Active Amines:

1. Histamine–Histamine is the most important vasoactive amine, but the observation that antihistamine compounds failed both in experimental situations and in clinical applications to control all the manifestations of type I reactions led to the realization that a mixture of vasoactive amines is generally released from target cells. Histamine exists in a preformed state within granules in mast cells, basophils, platelets, and perhaps other tissue cells. The in vivo effects of histamine in humans are mainly of the erythematous and angioedematous type and are attributed to increased capillary permeability secondary to partial interruption of vascular endothelium. Histamine also produces increased respiratory airway resistance.

2. Slow-reacting substance of anaphylaxis (SRS-A)–SRS-A does not exist in a preformed state, but its production is induced during a type I anaphylactic reaction. Recent studies have confirmed that SRS-A is leukotriene-D (LTD), one of the group of leukotrienes. The latter are prostaglandins formed by the metabolism of arachidonic acid by the lipoxygenase pathway. The leukotrienes display potent biologic effects, including increased vascular permeability and smooth muscle contraction. Their synthesis is not inhibited by antihistamines. However, drugs that inhibit the lipoxygenase pathway do prevent the generation of SRS-A in lung tissue. SRS-A (LTD) has now been synthesized in vitro.

3. Eosinophil chemotactic factor of anaphylaxis (ECF-A)–ECF-A was discovered when it was established that neither histamine nor SRS-A was chemotactic for human eosinophils. ECF-A exists in a preformed state in the mast cell granule as an acidic peptide with a molecular weight of 500–600.

4. Serotonin–Serotonin (5-hydroxytryptamine) exists in a preformed state in the granules of mast cells, platelets, and enterochromaffin cells. It causes capillary dilatation, increased permeability, and smooth muscle contraction (in some species). It is probably not an important vasoactive amine in type I reactions in humans.

5. Heparin–Heparin is an acidic mucopolysaccharide which accounts for metachromatic staining of mast cell granules by basic dyes. It contributes to anaphylaxis in dogs but apparently not in humans.

6. Kinins–Kinins are not primary vasoactive amines in type I reactions but contribute to the clinical features through their secondary involvement. (See humoral amplification systems on p 148.)

7. Prostaglandins–Prostaglandins comprise a number of naturally occurring aliphatic acids with a variety of biologic activities including increased permeability and dilatation of capillaries, smooth muscle contraction, bronchial constriction, and alteration in the pain threshold. Most of their actions appear to be mediated by changes in the intracellular concentration of cAMP. Their exact role in the production of various clinical features in type I anaphylactic reactions in humans has not been defined.

Clinical Features of Type I Reactions

Detailed clinical findings in human subjects are discussed in Chapter 28, but it is emphasized here that the division into general and local type I anaphylactic reactions is artificial. The general reaction is associated with widespread dissemination of the antigen, with systemic symptoms of edema, urticaria, and bronchial constriction. The local reaction is manifested most frequently in diagnostic skin tests, but such a patient should be considered sensitized on a systemic basis; the local administration of an excessive amount of antigen or the intravenous administration of a small amount of antigen to such a patient may be accompanied by generalized anaphylaxis.

TYPE II REACTIONS

Type II reactions are classically considered to be cytotoxic in character and involve the combination of IgG or IgM antibodies with antigenic determinants on a cell membrane. Alternatively, a free antigen or hapten may be adsorbed to a tissue component or cell membrane, and antibody subsequently combines with this adsorbed antigen. Complement fixation frequently occurs in this situation and leads to cell damage. There are situations, however, particularly in experimental studies, where the combination of cell-bound antigen and antibody does not result in damage to the cell membrane. The combination may in fact lead to stimulation of the cell, some examples being long-acting thyroid stimulator (LATS) (see Chapter 34), antilymphocyte antisera, and anti-immunoglobulin antisera. The latter 2 examples are documented in experimental studies, but their role in vivo has not been clarified.

Some authors have proposed the classification of "type V" reactions when the antibodies are cell-stimulating, based mainly on studies with LATS, an IgG antibody that binds to the thyroid-stimulating hormone (TSH) receptor on the thyroid cell and stimulates the cell. Further study has shown, however, that not all anti-TSH receptor antibodies are thyroid-stimulating antibodies. There are 3 other areas where antireceptor antibodies have been studied intensively, ie, the insulin receptor, the acetylcholine receptor, and prolactin and growth hormone receptors. Antibodies to the acetylcholine receptor block normal neuromuscular transmission in myasthenia gravis (Chapter 35). Antibodies to prolactin and growth hormone receptors appear mainly to block the attachment of the homologous hormone. With antibodies to insulin receptors, one may produce blockage of the action of insulin or mimicking of its action.

A recent symposium on the immunopathology of receptors on nonlymphoid cells reported no single consistent response to an antireceptor antibody; the humoral mechanisms included the following: (1) blockade of the recognition site of the receptor; (2) stimulation of the receptor by imitation of the action of the natural ligand; (3) damage to the receptor or cell (or both) either alone or with participation of complement or other cells; (4) accelerated degradation of the receptor; and (5) alteration of the binding affinity of the receptor for its natural ligand.

Gell and Coombs, who originally proposed the classification into type I–IV reactions, argue against the change to establish a "type V" reaction. At present, such a change is unnecessary, and cell-stimulating antibodies are considered type II reactions.

Blocking antibody is another example of the second (cell-stimulating) type of type II reaction. Some antibodies to an antigen competitively inhibit the reaction between that antigen and antibodies of a different class or with different biologic properties. Thus, IgG antibodies to an allergen may competitively inhibit the binding of that allergen with IgE antibody and thereby block the release of vasoactive amines. Other examples include antibodies which mask histocompatibility antigens on tissue cells and permit them to escape rejection and antibodies in cancer patients which bind to tumor-associated antigens on the tumor cell. These antibodies are not complement-fixing, and they permit continued growth of tumor cells despite the availability of lymphocytes cytotoxic for those tumor cells. These special examples will not be discussed further in this section.

The usual sequelae of attachment of circulating antibody to either a tissue antigen or membrane-adsorbed antigen are, therefore, cell lysis or cell inactivation with activation of complement; phagocytosis of the target cells with or without activation of complement; or lysis or inactivation in the presence of effector lymphoid cells.

COMPLEMENT–DEPENDENT ANTIBODY LYSIS

The target for the cytotoxic reaction may be either a formed blood element or a specific cell type within a particular tissue.

Formed Blood Elements

A. Red Blood Cells: Red cell lysis is the most important clinical instance involving type II cytotoxic reactions. The lysis of red blood cells by antibody and complement has been extensively studied in vitro, and there are numerous examples of similar mechanisms operating in vivo. After transfusion with grossly incompatible blood, red cell lysis may occur intravascularly. If antibodies against relatively minor determinants are present, direct cell lysis may not occur but the binding of antibody to the red cell antigen leads to increased phagocytosis by cells of the monocyte-macrophage system, especially in the spleen. Complement is frequently (not always) involved in this process. Similar phenomena also occur when subjects become sensitized to red blood cell antigens following bacterial or viral infection or after interaction with drugs which alter the red cell membrane. The clinical

features of autoimmune hemolytic anemia and drug-induced hemolytic anemia are discussed in Chapter 27.

B. Platelets: Platelets are lysed by a variety of mechanisms which result in the release of biologically active components such as serotonin and factors which operate in the early stages of coagulation. Platelet sensitization may be associated with antibody, as in idiopathic thrombocytopenic purpura, or with anti-drug antibodies, as in Sedormid- or quinidine-induced thrombocytopenia (see below and Chapter 27).

C. Polymorphonuclear Leukocytes: Granulocytopenia may result from type II cytotoxic reactions associated with antibodies specific for granulocytes or antibodies to drugs adsorbed onto the granulocyte surface. This is an uncommon mechanism for the production of granulocytopenia, however, compared to bone marrow suppression or direct toxic effects of drugs on granulocytes.

D. Lymphocytes: Interest in this phenomenon was stimulated by the discovery that certain diseases, such as systemic lupus erythematosus, are associated with cold-reactive serum antibodies specific for lymphocytes. In vitro tests indicate that some of these antibodies can specifically lyse T cells. It has been proposed that human T cells and brain cells possess a cross-reacting antigen, as proved in mice, and that anti-T cell antibody binds to human brain cells. Thus, anti-T cell antibody crossing the blood-brain barrier through the choroid plexus previously damaged by deposition of circulating DNA–anti-DNA complexes may be a key factor in the etiology of the cerebral manifestations of systemic lupus erythematosus. The relevance of these antibodies and T cells to other features of systemic lupus erythematosus is not known (see Chapters 13 and 26).

Kidney

Type II reactions can be produced in almost any tissue by inducing heterologous antibodies to different tissue components and by varying the conditions under which the antibody is introduced into the experimental animal. In practical terms, some tissues or organs have been studied extensively in lower species and are of great importance in humans, eg, the kidney.

Nephrotoxic serum nephritis has been experimentally induced in numerous animal species by the injection of heterologous antibody against a renal extract. The antigen may be either a crude homogenate of kidney or highly purified components of glomerular basement membrane. The main effects are seen in glomeruli and occur in 2 stages. The heterologous phase is seen a few hours after the administration of the antibody and is characterized by proteinuria, reduced glomerular filtration, and polymorphonuclear infiltration of the glomeruli. This stage is due to the administered heterologous nephrotoxic antibody and is short-lived. Within 4–6 days, the autologous stage is reached, with further indications of glomerular damage caused by the host antibody response. An increase in the dose of heterologous antibody increases the severity of the inflammatory reaction and may cause the death of the animal from renal failure within 2–3 weeks. The degree of tissue damage and inflammation is directly related to the degree of involvement of various humoral amplification systems which will be discussed later in this chapter. They include activation of the complement system, in particular C3a and C5a (see Chapter 11), the release of lysosomal enzymes from polymorphonuclear leukocytes, the deposition of fibrinogen or fibrin in the glomeruli, and other as yet undetermined factors. If complement depletion is achieved in an animal by treatment with cobra venom factor, the polymorphonuclear leukocyte inflammatory response does not appear and the glomeruli are generally spared damage. Factors other than complement components chemotactic for polymorphonuclear leukocytes are involved, however, since proteinuria can be produced in animals depleted of complement or polymorphonuclear leukocytes if sufficiently large amounts of injected antibody are deposited along the glomerular basement membrane.

An alternative method of inducing nephritis secondary to antibody reacting with glomerular basement membrane is to inject antigens isolated from glomerular basement membrane. This has been confirmed in several species, including rabbits, monkeys, and sheep. In the sensitized animal, antibodies to glomerular basement membrane may be detected in the serum or may be deposited in a linear pattern along the membrane. Antibodies can be eluted from the affected kidney and produce a similar pattern of nephritis when reinjected into another animal of the same species. Circulating antibodies that are directed against the glomerular basement membrane will persist in the circulation of nephrectomized animals, and these antibodies can even be transferred in cross-circulation experiments to a previously healthy animal of the same species.

Deposition of antibodies in a linear pattern along the human glomerular basement membrane occurs in 3 types of disease states:

(1) Subjects who received renal allografts in the earlier years of renal transplantation were generally treated with antilymphocyte antiserum. Most of these early antilymphocyte antisera are now known to have contained antibodies against glomerular basement membrane antigens. These antibodies were apparently formed in response to lymphocyte membrane antigens which shared antigenic determinants with glomerular basement membrane antigens. The species most often used to prepare the antilymphocyte antiserum were the horse, goat, and sheep. This heterologous antibody was injected into patients and then deposited along the glomerular basement membrane of the transplanted kidney. Its effects in producing renal disease were overshadowed in this situation by the process of graft rejection, but this situation is analogous to classic nephrotoxic serum nephritis.

(2) The classic example of linear deposition of glomerular basement membrane antibodies is Goodpasture's syndrome. The clinical features of this disease are discussed in Chapter 31, and it is men-

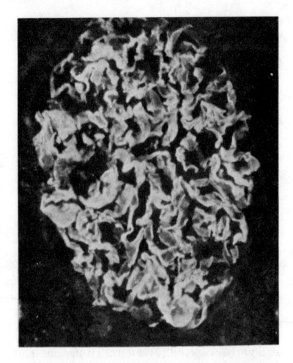

Figure 12–3. Direct immunofluorescence microscopy with fluorescein-labeled anti-IgG antiserum of a renal biopsy specimen demonstrating smooth, linear, ribbonlike deposition of IgG antibodies to glomerular basement membrane. The specimen was taken from a 16-year-old girl with Goodpasture's syndrome.

tioned briefly in this section. This deposition denotes the existence of antibodies with specificity for glomerular and pulmonary basement membranes. The deposition of antibodies in these 2 sites accounts for the main symptoms of hematuria, renal failure, and recurrent hemoptysis. The pattern of linear staining in a patient with Goodpasture's syndrome is shown in Fig 12–3.

(3) Immunofluorescent examination of renal biopsy specimens from patients with renal disease shows that linear deposition of antibodies to glomerular basement membrane may occur in several diseases, including scleroderma, diabetic glomerulonephritis, systemic lupus erythematosus, malignant hypertension, polyarteritis nodosa, or toxemia of pregnancy. The primary disease process leads to renal damage, and this in turn sensitizes the patient to glomerular basement membrane. Antibodies to glomerular basement membrane develop as a secondary phenomenon. These patients show only slight to moderate antibody deposition of the linear type with a coincidental granular deposition of preformed immune complexes and complement (see below). Fibrin deposition is frequently heavy in such cases.

Skin

Type II reactions caused by the deposition of circulating antibody along the basement membrane at the dermal-epidermal junction are termed pemphigoid disorders (see Chapter 32).

Other Tissues

Other tissues which have been studied include muscle, thyroid, myocardium, brain, testis, and ovary. Tissue homogenate is used to sensitize a homologous animal by injection in adjuvant, or an antiserum to the homogenate is prepared in a heterologous species. In each case, the production of tissue damage is thought to reflect the deposition of circulating heterologous or autologous antibody on target cells, with subsequent lysis of the cell or damage to the tissue containing the particular antigen.

ANTIBODY–DEPENDENT CELL–MEDIATED CYTOTOXICITY (ADCC)

Considerable confusion has arisen in the last few years over the terminology, methodology, interpretation, and clinical application of cell lysis studies. In such studies, either circulating cells or tissue cells, such as lymphocytes or monocytes, are tested for their ability to lyse target cells. The test cell is prepared from a subject who may or may not be sensitized to antigens on the target cell, and the target cell may or may not be coated with complement. The roles of antibody and complement vary in different systems. It is appropriate in this section to discuss cell-mediated cytotoxic reactions which are antibody-dependent. These cytotoxicity tests therefore include several variables, including test cells, target cells, source of antibody, source of complement, and the label used to indicate or measure cell damage.

Test cells are most frequently isolated from peripheral blood in human subjects, but in experimental studies with animals they may be isolated from almost any lymphoid tissue. T cells are probably not able to mediate this type of cellular toxicity. The number of macrophages in the test cell population is also important in interpretation of the results.

A wide variety of target cells have been used from syngeneic, allogeneic, and xenogeneic animals. The most frequent target cells used in tests to determine the cytotoxic functions of human cells include chicken red blood cells, normal peripheral blood lymphocytes from other human subjects, human tumor cells, cells from long-term cultures of lymphoblastoid cell lines, and murine mastocytoma cells.

The antibody tested includes specific antibody to antigens on their target cells, antibody to antigens to which the donor of the test cell has been sensitized, and normal IgG. Complement is generally tested in the system by providing fresh serum from a human, rabbit, or guinea pig source.

The 3 main methods used to indicate damage or lysis of the cell are (1) entry of a dye into the cell, (2) loss of the ability of the cell to adhere to surfaces, and (3) loss of cell-bound ^{51}Cr. The measurement of ^{51}Cr released from ^{51}Cr-labeled target cells is now the most common method of measuring cytotoxicity. The mechanism proposed is that antibody or antibody-antigen complexes are attached to the target cell and are bound by their Fc regions to receptors for the Fc region on the membrane of the effector cell; the proximity of the test cell and the target cell then permits lysis of the target cell to occur. It is possible that complement components may be involved in this process, but their role is controversial. Antibody-dependent cell-mediated cytotoxicity requires only very small amounts of antibody to facilitate cell lysis.

Much controversy still surrounds the identity of the main cell type responsible for this type of cytotoxicity. It is generally accepted that cells in the monocyte-macrophage series can lyse cells by this mechanism. The disagreement concerns the identity of the type of lymphocyte which can accomplish antibody-dependent cell-mediated cytotoxicity. The general methods used to characterize these populations of lymphocytes do not yield sufficient data to identify this cell. The view that these lymphocytes required a membrane receptor for the Fc region of antibody molecules to accomplish cell lysis led to the conclusion that these cells were B cells. This conclusion was disputed, since other B cell markers could not be demonstrated consistently on these cells and it was shown that T cells could acquire an Fc receptor during lymphocyte transformation. Similarly, it could not be confirmed that these cells were T cells. The term **killer cell** or **K cell** has therefore been introduced to refer to this type of cell.

TYPE III REACTIONS

These reactions are secondary to localization of antigen-antibody complexes in tissues, and inflammation is the main feature. Classic reactions of this type are the **Arthus reaction** and **serum sickness.** Similar sequences of events occur in both examples and also in immune complex diseases, now increasingly recognized in clinical medicine. The pathogenesis of the characteristic inflammatory lesions in type III reactions is summarized in Table 12–1.

ARTHUS REACTION

The classic Arthus reaction is produced in experimental animals by the local tissue interaction between antigen and circulating antibody. This results in destructive inflammation of small blood vessels, ie, vasculitis. Following intradermal injection of antigen into an appropriately sensitized animal, the area shows local swelling and erythema in 1–2 hours. This reaction increases to a maximum 3–6 hours after injection and disappears within 10–12 hours. Microscopic examination of the tissue shows neutrophils initially, and these cells are replaced by mononuclear cells and

Table 12–1. Pathogenesis of inflammatory
lesions in type III reactions.

(1) Formation of antigen-antibody complexes (generally in antigen excess).
(2) Fixation of complement by the complexes.
(3) Release of complement components chemotactic for leukocytes.
(4) Damage to platelets, causing release of vasoactive amines.
(5) Increased vascular permeability.
(6) Localization of antigen-antibody complexes in vessel walls.
(7) Further fixation of complement and release of chemotactic factors.
(8) Infiltration with polymorphonuclear leukocytes.
(9) Ingestion of immune complexes by neutrophils and release of lysosomal enzymes.
(10) Damage to adjacent cells and tissues by lysosomal enzymes.
(11) Deposition of fibrin.
(12) Regression and healing if the lesion is due to a single dose of antigen, or chronic deposition and inflammation if there is continuing formation of immune complexes.

eosinophils, with degradation of phagocytosed immune complexes and disappearance of the inflammation. When a limited amount of antibody is available for experimental study, the antibody can be injected intradermally and an Arthus reaction can then be induced by injection of the antigen either into the site where the antibody was previously injected or into the bloodstream.

Probable clinical counterparts of Arthus type reactions with local concentrations of antigen are various examples of **hypersensitivity pneumonitis** or **extrinsic allergic alveolitis** from inhalation of organic dusts. In these cases, the inhaled antigens may be fungal in origin, may be associated with insects, or may be heterologous proteins such as avian proteins in bird handler's pneumonitis. Fungi frequently involved are thermophilic actinomycetes and *Micropolyspora faeni*. The clinical features are described in detail in Chapter 30, but a characteristic feature of the acute disease is the onset of symptoms of chills, cough, dyspnea, and fever 4–6 hours after inhalation of the responsible antigen. The usual pattern is resolution of such an attack within 12–18 hours, although some residual pulmonary findings may persist for several days.

SERUM SICKNESS

The term serum sickness classically refers to the combination of symptoms and signs seen in patients 3 days to 3 weeks after the injection of foreign (heterologous) serum. It includes fever, malaise, urticarial and erythematous skin rashes, arthralgia, lymphadenopathy, and splenomegaly. The abnormal findings usually subside within 1–2 weeks. In the first 4 decades of this century, it was not uncommon for up to 50% of patients to develop this reaction after treatment with horse serum as an antiserum to diphtheria, tetanus, or other organisms. It has almost disappeared in these situations since alternative methods of active immunization have been developed for these diseases, but it is still seen in developing countries. In developed countries the reaction now occurs as serum sickness reactions to drugs such as penicillin and in patients after renal allotransplantation who receive heterologous antilymphocyte serum to suppress or prevent graft rejection. A key feature in serum sickness is the formation of antigen-antibody complexes in the bloodstream and their subsequent deposition at various sites throughout the body. Many diseases are now known to be associated with formation of intravascular immune complexes, although these complexes are variably involved in the production of symptoms and signs in different diseases. Diseases associated with significant clinical features secondary to formation and deposition of immune complexes are now collectively termed the **immune complex disorders.**

IMMUNE COMPLEX DISORDERS

Immunologic Pathogenesis

Some of these disorders are listed in Table 12–2. It should be emphasized that pathogenetic mechanisms listed in Table 12–1 operate to varying degrees in these disorders and are influenced by many factors. These factors include the nature of the host, antigen, antibody, antigen-antibody complexes, complement, platelets, and polymorphonuclear leukocytes. In many cases, these factors can only be studied in experimental animals.

A. Host: Animal species vary greatly in their propensity to develop the manifestations of immune complex disorders. Rabbits have been studied in detail as experimental animals, since they develop a variety of pathologic lesions after single or multiple injections of selected foreign antigens. Several species are known to be affected by certain types of persistent long-term virus infections, including lymphocytic choriomeningitis in mice, equine infectious anemia in horses, and Aleutian mink disease. It also appears that genetic factors are important within a species, since different strains of mice show varying degrees of susceptibility to persistent virus infections. Although it is an accepted clinical observation that some families have a greater than normal susceptibility to certain diseases associated with immune complex deposition (eg, rheumatoid arthritis), the level at which these genetic factors operate has not been clarified. Since the various phenomena associated with immune complexes can only develop in the presence of antibody, there must be some form of genetic control at the level of immune response genes, with development of appropriate antibody response to injected antigen (see Chapter 6).

B. Antigen: Almost any injected foreign antigen which elicits a detectable antibody response can lead to the development of immune complex deposition.

Table 12–2. Examples of human diseases associated with immune complexes detectable in plasma and deposited in tissues.

Microbial infections
　Bacterial and spirochetal
　　Acute poststreptococcal glomerulonephritis
　　Syphilis
　　Mycoplasmal pneumonia
　　Subacute bacterial endocarditis
　　Shunt nephritis *(Staphylococcus albus)*
　　Lepromatous leprosy
　Viral
　　Acute viral hepatitis
　　Chronic HBsAg infections
　　HBsAg in polyarteritis nodosa
　　Guillain-Barré syndrome
　　Infectious mononucleosis glomerulonephritis
　　Dengue hemorrhagic fever
Parasitic infections
　Malarial nephrotic syndrome
　Tropical splenomegaly syndrome
　Leishmaniasis
　Trypanosomiasis
　Schistosomiasis
　Onchocerciasis
Disseminated malignancy
　Solid tumors
　　Carcinoma of lung
　　Carcinoma of breast
　　Carcinoma of colon
　　Malignant melanoma
　Leukemia
　　Acute lymphoblastic leukemia
　　Chronic lymphocytic leukemia
　Lymphoma: Hodgkin's disease
Autoimmune disorders
　Systemic lupus erythematosus
　Hashimoto's thyroiditis
　Rheumatoid arthritis
Miscellaneous
　Essential mixed cryoglobulinemia
　Celiac disease
　Dermatitis herpetiformis
　Crohn's disease
　Ulcerative colitis
　Henoch-Schönlein nephritis
　Hepatic cirrhosis
　Sickle cell anemia
Drug reactions
　Serum sickness
　Penicillamine nephropathy

However, the traditional method of producing an immune complex disorder has been injection of serum from a heterologous species. Such a serum contains many different foreign serum proteins, and this was a problem in defining the contributing factors during experimental studies. Accordingly, experiments were done with single foreign serum proteins—eg, BSA—injected into a selected species such as the rabbit. The pathologic effects of injected antigens vary according to the injection protocol. A single injection is likely to be associated with healing, as in serum sickness. However, the intravenous injection of a large dose of antigen to a previously sensitized animal may, if the patient or animal escapes death from immediate type I anaphylactic reaction, exhibit a severe type III reaction with an accelerated onset within 4 days. In this case, the histologic findings are those of an acute Arthus reaction.

Foreign extrinsic antigens other than foreign serum proteins can produce immune complex disorders. These include a variety of bacterial and viral organisms and therapeutic agents such as drugs (see Table 12–2). In many cases, the drugs act as haptens bound to serum proteins to elicit the appropriate antibody responses and thence immune complex deposition.

Persistent or continuous administration of antigen leads to an increased deposition of immune complexes in the renal glomeruli. This may occur with exogenous antigen in experimental animals, with endogenous antigens such as nucleic acid antigens (as in systemic lupus erythematosus), and with infection with persistent replicating viruses. With exogenous antigens, the situation is further complicated by the fact that changes may be observed in the nature of the disease depending on whether the antigen is administered as one injection per day or multiple injections during the day. It is likely that these varying experimental results, in relation to variations in antigen administration, reflect basic differences in antibody responses.

C. Antibody: IgG and IgM are the antibody classes normally involved in the deposition of immune complexes in tissues. There is considerable variation in the affinity or avidity of the antibodies involved in immune complex formation; the genetic makeup of the host and the nature, route, and timing of antigen administration define the nature and affinity of the antibody elicited by that antigen. A general division into precipitating and nonprecipitating antibodies has been suggested in immune complex formation. Precipitating antibodies were thought to be associated with self-limiting forms of disease such as serum sickness, while nonprecipitating antibodies were associated with a longer half-life for circulating immune complexes and with chronic immune complex deposition. Further studies have shown that this division is not strictly correct, and chronic immune complex deposition can be associated with both precipitating and nonprecipitating antibodies.

D. Antigen-Antibody Complexes: Most of our increased understanding of immune complex disorders originated with the realization that they are dynamic processes. There are constantly changing concentrations of antigens, antibodies, and antigen-antibody complexes, and these changes themselves influence the biologic behavior of the complexes. Regional changes in the tissue and serum greatly affect complexes and determine whether they are in antigen excess, equivalence, or antibody excess. These conditions can only be analyzed in detail in experimental animals, and summaries will be given of experimental studies in several laboratories on the relationship between antigen-antibody complexes, their catabolism, and their deposition in different tissues.

One group of experiments showed that small immune complexes formed under conditions of great antigen excess were approximately 11S in size, with the molecular formula Ag_2Ab_2. With low to moderate degrees of antigen excess, small immune complexes were still formed but their size was 8.5S and their molecular formula was Ag_1Ab_1. The antigen-antibody ratio varied from 0.85 to 1.2 for immune complexes formed in the range of 5- to 60-fold antigen excess. If they were formed in higher degrees of antigen excess (eg, up to 500-fold), the antigen-antibody ratio remained in the region of 1.2–1.25. The molecular formulas for such complexes were Ag_2Ab_2, Ag_1Ab_1, and possibly small amounts of Ag_2Ab_1.

In another study, the results of single or repeated injections of 0.5 g of BSA into rabbits were compared. A single injection of the antigen was generally associated with the formation of low-affinity IgG antibodies. These formed poorly aggregating immune complexes with a molecular weight of 300–500 thousand and with the molecular formula Ag_2Ab_1 or Ag_3Ab_2. Rarely, one observed large immune complexes (MW > 1 million) with low-affinity IgM antibody. The histologic feature in the kidney for both groups was that of acute diffuse glomerulonephritis. Animals given repeated injections could be arbitrarily divided into those producing low levels and those producing intermediate levels of antibody. Those producing low levels of antibody produced antibody of high affinity which formed immune complexes with a molecular weight of 500–700 thousand. The renal histologic picture of these animals was that of diffuse proliferative glomerulonephritis. Those that produced intermediate levels of antibody tended to form immune complexes with molecular weights greater than 1 million.

Another experimental approach was to prepare hapten-protein conjugates of defined size and antigenic valency and to examine their behavior in experimental animals (as models for immune reactions to drugs). Antigen with a valency of less than 4 showed restricted activity with antibody in complement fixation or precipitation reactions and formed mainly soluble immune complexes. Thus, complexes with a density less than 19S tended to fix complement poorly and had a prolonged intravascular half-life. Immune complexes with a density greater than 19S generally had a ratio of antigen to antibody of 2:5 or less, fixed complement efficiently, and had a relatively short intravascular half-life. Whereas the antigenic valency appeared to restrict lattice formation and precipitation, in vitro precipitation could be enhanced by the addition of human or rabbit complement, eg, C1q. These observations on the relationship between the composition of the immune complexes and their clearance from plasma have implications in the organ distribution of deposited immune complexes.

Studies of the rate of clearance of radiolabeled immune complexes showed that immune complexes with a molecular size greater than 11S (molecular formula greater than Ag_2Ab_2) were rapidly removed in the liver by the monocyte-macrophage system; less than 1% was deposited in lungs, kidneys, or spleen. This distribution was unchanged in rabbits depleted of complement, but the immune complex had to include 2 or more IgG molecules. If the immune complexes were formed from reduced and alkylated antibodies, then the immune complexes were not cleared by the liver. With the injection of increasing amounts of preformed immune complexes, the monocyte-macrophage system appeared to become saturated and the liver was no longer capable of clearing excess amounts of immune complexes greater than 11S. Increased amounts were therefore found in the circulating plasma, and it was suggested that such complexes were then more likely to lodge in the renal glomeruli. A corollary of this study was that the in vivo interaction of fixed tissue macrophages and IgG antibodies in soluble immune complexes was not mediated by circulating complement components.

Other studies have been done to assess the clearance in experimental animals of complexes between staphylococcal enterotoxin and equine IgA antitoxin. Equine IgA antibodies fix complement poorly and form soluble immune complexes in antibody excess. Three different situations were tested: toxin excess, toxin-antitoxin equivalence, and antibody (antitoxin) excess. In conditions of toxin excess, the clearance of immune complexes from the circulation was slow and was independent of the concentration of antitoxin until there was sufficient antitoxin present in the plasma to bind 80% of enterotoxin. In conditions of equivalence, there was rapid clearance of the immune complexes by the monocyte-macrophage system. In antibody excess, the immune complexes were nonprecipitating complexes of high molecular weight, yet their clearance rate was slow and decreased even further with the addition of more antitoxin. It was concluded that the rapid removal of toxin and its catabolism by the monocyte-macrophage system was not an important mechanism for in vivo detoxification by antibody.

The behavior of circulating immune complexes can be influenced by the administration of certain drugs. Analysis of the survival in mice of injected preformed immune complexes with a molecular formula of Ag_2Ab_2 showed no difference in intravascular survival between control and cortisone-treated mice. However, there was significantly prolonged intravascular survival of immune complexes with a molecular formula greater than Ag_2Ab_2 in cortisone-treated mice compared to controls. This was associated with enhanced and prolonged deposition in renal glomeruli. This observation, if confirmed, has important implications for the role of corticosteroid therapy in immune complex disorders such as systemic lupus erythematosus.

E. Complement: The important role of the complement system in immune complex disorders has been known for some time in terms of the biologic activities of components such as C3a, C5a, and C567 in producing changes such as inflammation and chemotaxis. Recent studies have outlined a further role in terms of the relationship between circulating immune complexes in plasma and the attachment of such complexes to the surfaces of lymphocytes and platelets. The term **complex release activity** refers to the release of immune complexes from the membranes of circulating lymphocytes or platelets and the maintenance of such complexes in a soluble form in the plasma. This activity appears to be mediated by the alternative pathway for complement activation; it relies on the presence of Mg^{2+} ions and functions in C4 and C5 deficiency. This complex-releasing activity appears to increase with age in experimental animals, with the result that a lower percentage of immune complexes is bound to cell membranes immediately after injection of preformed immune complexes. It has yet to be established whether this means that the higher percentage of immune complexes in the plasma in older animals predisposes them to increased tissue deposition of the circulating complexes.

F. Platelets: Immune complexes bind to the platelet membrane, leading to the release of its stored vasoactive amines. In a type III reaction, vasoactive amines are also released from basophils initially attracted to the area by chemotaxis. As indicated earlier in this chapter, the vasoactive amines lead to increased vascular permeability and to small blood vessel damage, resulting in precipitation of immune complexes at the basement membrane. Binding of immune complexes to platelets appears to be more efficient with preformed immune complexes formed in antibody excess rather than at equivalence. Immune complexes formed in antigen excess are frequently inactive in this regard. Absence of the Fc fragment from the antibody slows the reaction but does not affect the final extent of the reaction.

G. Polymorphonuclear Leukocytes: Infiltration by polymorphonuclear leukocytes is a crucial step in the production of the pathologic sequelae of immune complex deposition in tissues. Various factors affect the release of lysosomal enzymes which produce the tissue damage. The binding of immune complexes to neutrophils can lead to the release of lysosomal hydrolases from neutrophils. Phagocytosis need not occur before these lysosomal enzymes are released. Antigen added to fixed nonphagocytosable antibody attached to an insoluble collagen membrane induced the release of lysosomal enzymes from added polymorphonuclear leukocytes. The cells retained their viability after this selective release of lysosomal enzymes, and non–granule-associated cytoplasmic enzymes remained in significant amounts. Agents which increased the intracellular concentration of cAMP— eg, prostaglandin E_1 and theophylline—inhibited this selective exclusion of lysosomal enzymes without affecting cell viability. The complement component C5a induced the selective release of lysosomal enzymes from intact, viable, cytochalasin B-treated human polymorphonuclear leukocytes without requiring phagocytosis or cellular adherence to surfaces. The

extracellular concentration of Ca^{2+} is crucial in this situation, since the addition of increasing amounts of Ca^{2+} enhances the release of enzymes but a Ca^{2+} concentration of greater than 2 mM inhibits secretion of the enzymes.

Detection of Immune Complexes

Tests for the detection of circulating immune complexes in animals or in patients with a suspected immune complex disorder are described in detail in Chapter 22. The fact that several tests are used to detect circulating immune complexes indicates that *no single test* is sufficient for all situations. This is not surprising in view of the dynamic nature of the processes involved in the formation of immune complexes at different stages of antigen administration. Unfortunately, in humans the identity of the antigen is generally unknown and so specific detection of the antigen is not possible. Exceptions to this rule, where the identity of the antigen is known, include nucleic acid antigens in systemic lupus erythematosus, drugs in drug sensitivity, and HBsAg in some cases of polyarteritis nodosa. Immune complexes are generally detected by their behavior as cryoglobulins, their propensity to adhere to cell membranes, their physical characteristics, or their property of interaction with complement components such as C1q.

Clinical Features of Immune Complex Disorders

The clinical features of immune complex disorders are discussed in subsequent chapters in relation to the organ systems they most frequently affect. Some general comments will be made here.

The systemic symptoms and signs of classic serum sickness following a single administration of antigen are likely to result from systemic deposition in blood vessels or clearance by the monocyte-macrophage system. Nevertheless, with repeated antigen administration, persistent viral infection, or continuous availability of an endogenous antigen such as DNA, the renal glomeruli remain the chief site of deposition of circulating immune complexes. In some cases, the predominant microscopic finding is the deposition of IgA and complement in the mesangium (Fig 12–4). The antigen deposited in the kidney in these cases of **IgA nephropathy** is unknown. Recent reports have emphasized that chronic deposition of circulating antigen-antibody complexes frequently involves extraglomerular renal structures, including the interstitium, Bowman's capsule, and the walls of peritubular capillaries. This may occur in patients with advanced malignancy with the renal deposition of circulating tumor antigen-antibody complexes. In patients with systemic lupus erythematosus, examination by direct immunofluorescence of skin biopsies from both clinically normal skin and diseased skin frequently shows the deposition of immune complexes and complement at the dermal-epidermal junction. Marked deposition at this skin site is significantly associated with heavy deposition in the renal glomer-

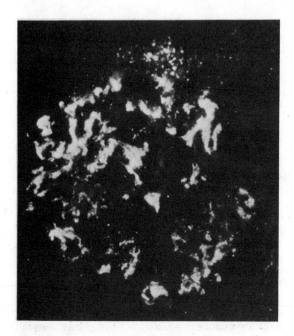

Figure 12–4. Direct immunofluorescence microscopy with fluorescein-labeled anti-IgA serum demonstrating granular deposition of IgA in the mesangium of a glomerulus in a renal biopsy specimen taken from a 30-year-old woman with IgA nephropathy and hematuria.

uli. It has been suggested—but not confirmed—that the deposition of circulating immune complexes in the choroid plexus may be of pathogenetic significance in the development of the cerebral manifestations of systemic lupus erythematosus.

TYPE IV REACTIONS

Cell-mediated immune reactions occur as the result of the interactions between actively sensitized lymphocytes and specific antigens. They are mediated by the release of **lymphokines,** direct cytotoxicity, or both. They occur without the involvement of antibody or complement. The classic lesion of a cell-mediated immune reaction is the delayed skin reaction which develops over a period of 24–48 hours and which has the characteristic mononuclear cell infiltrate (Fig 12–5). The details of delayed skin reactions were discussed in Chapter 8, but a brief outline will be presented here.

The first stage in such a reaction is the binding of antigen by a small number of specific antigen-reactive T lymphocytes. The evidence for and against the role of immunoglobulin in T lymphocyte function as the specific antigen receptor was summarized in Chapter 8. This initial stage is followed by the production and release of soluble mediators with a wide variety of biologic activities. These products of activated lymphocytes, or lymphokines, have various activities on

macrophages, polymorphonuclear leukocytes, lymphocytes, and other cell types (see Chapter 9). Their overall function is to amplify the initial cellular response by recruitment of other lymphocytes (both T and B cells), to induce mitogenesis in these cells, to attract polymorphonuclear leukocytes, and, in particular, to attract, localize, and activate macrophages at the site of the lesion. There are distinct lymphocyte mediators for some of the functions that have been described, and physicochemical characterization of the different factors is confirming this view. However, it is not clear whether there are a small number of molecules with multiple functions at different concentrations or whether a different molecule is specific for each in vitro function (see Chapter 9).

The clotting system is involved in the earlier stages of a delayed hypersensitivity reaction. Macrophages exposed to lymphokines such as MIF (see Chapter 9) become immobilized and activated. A fibrin net has been demonstrated around such macrophages. This fibrin deposition appears to induce the synthesis of plasminogen activator by the macrophage, so that plasmin is available to lyse the fibrin. A lymphokine released from activated lymphocytes induces the release of procoagulant activity from monocytes. This activity has recently been adapted as a sensitive test for cellular immunity to a particular antigen in a patient by measuring the effects of stimulated mononuclear cells on the clotting time of recalcified plasma.

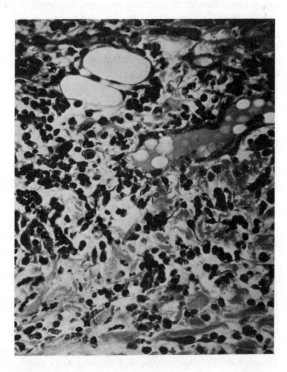

Figure 12–5. Photomicrograph of a skin biopsy of a positive delayed skin test 48 hours after the injection of PPD into a previously sensitized guinea pig. Note the characteristic mononuclear cell infiltrate.

There are normal control mechanisms that lead to resolution of such a lesion, but these have not been clarified. In cases where multiple doses of antigen have been given to a hypersensitive individual, the lesions may progress to the stage of local ulceration and necrosis.

An important corollary to the delayed skin reaction is that activated cells in these lesions can nonspecifically affect cells other than those specific for the initial sensitizing and challenging antigen. Thus, the inflammatory cells that arise may be bactericidal or tumoricidal, and this is the basis of the current trials of immunotherapy in the treatment of tumors with agents which nonspecifically induce delayed skin reactions, eg, BCG and levamisole.

In some cases, the extent and duration of inflammation in the delayed skin reaction are increased by the involvement of other systems, including the complement, clotting, and kinin systems (see below).

Contact sensitivity to a simple defined chemical is an example of a pathologic process which is wholly the result of a delayed skin reaction. It is felt that some human autoimmune disorders characterized by lymphocyte infiltration of the target organ involve type IV reactions (eg, Hashimoto's thyroiditis). Generally, it is difficult in such situations to decide if the cell-mediated immunity is a primary or secondary event. Most other examples of allergic reactions include multiple mechanisms. It is generally the rule that cellular and humoral reactions to an antigen proceed at the same time, though in varying degrees. Emphasis is usually placed on the effects of repeated or prolonged delayed skin reactions and their possible role in producing symptoms. However, it is equally true that disease may be due to or associated with **anergy,** ie, the absence of delayed skin reactivity. It is not uncommon in patients with some forms of tumors, immunodeficiency, and infections. This will not be discussed in detail, but several factors may lead to delayed type anergy, including suppressive factors in plasma. Sarcoidosis, although of unknown cause, is probably the best known disorder with anergy and plasma suppressive factors.

• • •

HUMORAL AMPLIFICATION SYSTEMS

The 4 types of immune mechanisms have been discussed above as distinct entities. It must be emphasized, however, that in the intact animal a typical immune reaction will involve a mixture of the 4 types of reactions. Thus, we see a combination of type II and type III reactions in virus infections. Both the type of immune reaction (its extent and variety) and the type of associated clinicopathologic phenomena are complicated by the involvement in immune reactions of several body systems collectively termed **humoral amplification systems.** Various interrelationships between these systems often lead to involvement of one

or more of them after initial activation of immune processes. Each is composed of a series of proteins, substrates, inhibitors, and enzymes. These systems include the **complement, coagulation, kinin,** and **fibrinolytic** systems (Fig 12–6).

Complement System

This complex system of at least 15 distinct serum proteins is described in detail in Chapter 11. It is reemphasized here that involvement of the complement system can be initiated by a wide variety of stimuli along either the classic or alternative pathways of activation. Recent studies have clearly demonstrated the variety of biologic activities of different complement components apart from the classic observation of the function of cell lysis. Thus, we have the important biologic effects of C3a and C5a, which, as anaphylatoxins, induce the release of histamine from the granules of mast cells, producing increased capillary permeability, edema, and smooth muscle contraction. Both C3a and C5a, together with the trimolecular complex C567, also have chemotactic activity for polymorphonuclear leukocytes. These functions all contribute to the degree of inflammation at the site of an antigen-antibody reaction involving complement activation. Other amplification systems are also involved in the complement system, eg, the fibrinolytic enzyme plasmin can directly attack C1, C3, and C5; the plasma proteolytic enzyme thrombin, which converts fibrinogen to fibrin, can attack C3; and a fragment of C2 has a kininlike activity in causing increased vascular permeability and contraction of smooth muscle.

Coagulation

Studies have not demonstrated a common mode of activation of the coagulation and complement systems, although, as mentioned above, thrombin formed during activation of the later stages of the coagulation system has the ability to act on complement components. It is certainly true, however, that damage to the endothelium of small blood vessels leads to activation of the coagulation pathway by **Hageman factor** (factor XII) and at the same time leads to local changes including the release of tissue enzymes which may then activate the complement system. Obviously, if the damage is produced initially by the deposition of immune complexes or bacteria, then the complement system would be involved.

Factor XII is activated by exposure to collagen, and this leads to the formation of kinins as well as activation of subsequent stages in the coagulation system. In some local immune reactions, histologic examination reveals thrombosed small blood vessels, frequently with associated necrosis.

Kinin System

This system is also known as the **kallikrein system.** It is initiated by activation of factor XII, leading eventually to the formation of kallikrein, which acts on an α-globulin substrate, **kininogen,** to form **bradyki-**

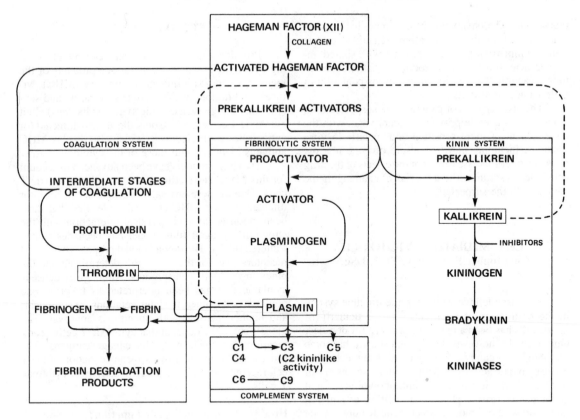

Figure 12–6. Schematic diagram demonstrating the multiple relationships between the coagulation, fibrinolytic, complement, and kinin systems.

nin. Bradykinin is a nonapeptide which produces marked and prolonged slow contractions of smooth muscle. Its activity in plasma is inactivated by kininases. The pathway of formation of bradykinin can be inhibited in at least 3 stages by C1 inactivator (C1 esterase inhibitor), which normally inactivates C1. This α_2-globulin is absent in patients with hereditary angioneurotic edema, and this may result in increased activity of the kinin system during an attack of angioneurotic edema. Involvement of the kinin system in immune reactions is further emphasized by the fact that the enzyme kallikrein, which cleaves kininogen to produce bradykinin, is itself directly chemotactic for polymorphonuclear leukocytes.

The kinins possess a variety of activities, including chemotaxis, smooth muscle contraction, dilatation of peripheral arterioles, and increased capillary permeability.

Fibrinolytic System

This system is also initiated by the activation of factor XII, and it then proceeds through intermediate stages to the formation of plasmin from its precursor plasminogen. Plasmin is a proteolytic enzyme of broad specificity which can digest not only fibrin but also fibrinogen, factor XIIa, clotting factors V and VIII, prothrombin, C1 inactivator, C1, C3, and C5. Clearly, both factor XII and plasmin have several actions rele-

vant to different humoral amplification systems.

These 4 systems are involved in several mechanisms which serve to amplify and to control an initial small stimulus. They are particularly suited to modify the vascular and cellular events in immune and nonimmune reactions in terms of hemostasis, inflammation, and tissue repair.

DRUG REACTIONS

The above discussion of the 4 basic types of immune reactions included isolated examples of drug reactions as a specific immune reaction. It should be appreciated that although a particular drug may induce a single type of immune reaction, it is not uncommon for more than one type of reaction to occur in a sensitized subject. These may occur either simultaneously or at different stages. Thus, penicillin may produce an acute fatal type I anaphylaxis, a type II reaction with hemolytic anemia, a type III reaction clinically resembling serum sickness, or a type IV delayed hypersensitivity reaction.

Since many drugs are relatively simple in structure, they function immunologically as haptens and must be bound to a macromolecular complex or carrier protein to be immunogenic. Drugs which are bound loosely or reversibly to proteins are generally not immunogenic. The phenomenon of immunologic cross-reactivity means that in a patient sensitized to one drug, administration of another drug with shared antigenic determinants may produce a pathologic immune reaction. This occurs with various penicillin or sulfonamide derivatives.

The investigation of patients with suspected drug reactions has been improved in recent years with the development of more sensitive and specific in vitro methods, including in vitro culture of bone marrow cells. This permits assessment of the effects of the drug and patient's serum without the risk of challenging the patient with the suspected drug.

II. CELL–MEDIATED CYTOTOXICITY
Christopher S. Henney, PhD, DSc

The possible involvement of the immune system in the destruction of alien cells and particularly of tumor cells has been a matter of concern for decades. Only recently, however, has it been shown that some lymphoid cells can lyse foreign cells. The mechanism of the cytotoxic activity of lymphocytes remains one of the most intriguing issues of immunobiology, for it encompasses, in the physiologic setting of cell-cell interactions, those most characteristic features of the immune system: antigen recognition and the ability to distinguish self from nonself.

The first indication that lymphoid cells might be cytotoxic followed from observations that the regression of murine mammary carcinomas was often preceded by rapid lymphoid cell infiltration. Later, more direct evidence was obtained by Govaerts, who showed that thoracic duct lymphocytes from dogs that had rejected kidney allografts were capable of destroying donor kidney cells in vitro. The immunologic specificity of this reaction was indicated by the fact that kidney cells from unrelated animals were not destroyed. The observation that lymphoid cells could directly cause tissue damage led to a radical revision of concepts of cell destruction by the immune system, for it had been axiomatic that immune cytotoxicity implied destruction of cells by antibody in concert with proteins of the complement system.

It is now clear that cytotoxic lymphocytes are produced as a normal component of a mammalian host's immune response. Furthermore, as will become apparent, some cytotoxic cells are present in lymphoid tissue even before antigenic stimulation. Indeed, there are several distinctive cell types that can be cytotoxic. Some of these bring about lysis in cooperation with classic IgG antibody, but other lymphocytes, including a subpopulation of thymus-derived (T) lymphocytes, lyse target cells directly. In this section, we will briefly review these different cells and comment on their modes of action and their possible significance.

CYTOTOXIC T CELLS

Prominent among the antigens capable of eliciting cytotoxic T cells are cell surface products of the major histocompatibility gene complex (MHC), viruses, and tumor-specific antigens. Viruses (and several other antigens, including synthetic haptens) elicit cytotoxic T cells that lyse only those virus-infected (or antigen-bearing) target cells which also display MHC antigens identical with those of the cytotoxic cell.

Two basic models have been advanced to account for this **MHC restriction** of the action of cytotoxic T cells. One of these envisages a single T cell receptor directed against MHC-encoded molecules that have been modified by their physical interaction with the "foreign" antigen (this model has been designated "altered self"). The second model proposes two T cell receptors: one for the "foreign" determinant and the other for the MHC gene product. Although evidence is available that has been interpreted as favoring one model over the other, the interpretations are equivocal, and neither has met with unanimous approval. The models share the concept that cytotoxic T cells bear a receptor that can specifically engage antigens. The processes "triggered" by antigen occupation of the T cell receptor account for the lytic activity of cytotoxic T cells.

How Do Cytotoxic T Cells Function?

Much of our current understanding of how cytolytically active T cells function comes from in vitro studies. One widely used system, first described by K.T. Brunner and his collaborators, is shown diagrammatically in Fig 12–7. In this system, cytotoxic T cells are raised in C57BL/6 mice by intraperitoneal injection of an allogeneic tumor (P-815 of the DBA/2 strain). Lymphocyte populations from the immunized animal are then assayed for lytic activity by culturing for a short period (usually about 4 hours) with a ^{51}Cr-labeled sample of the immunizing tumor. Although this system involves lysis of allogeneic cells, mechanistically it is believed to be identical to the means by which cytotoxic T cells destroy virally infected autochthonous tissue or syngeneic tumor cells.

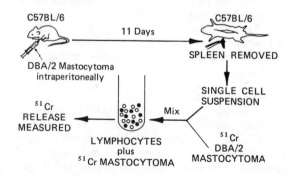

Figure 12–7. General method for induction and assay of cytotoxic T cells.

Thus, the following statements about how cytotoxic T cells function are thought to have general applicability.

T cell-mediated cytolysis in vitro requires intimate contact between a viable effector cell and its target. When killer and target cells are separated either by a semipermeable membrane or by suspension in a viscous medium such as agarose or dextran, cytolysis does not occur. Cytolysis results from single collisions between effector and target cell, so that lysis is a linear function of both time and effector cell incidence.

Except for the observation that the effector cell must be viable, little is known of the metabolic requirements for cytolysis. Drug inhibition studies have suggested, however, that protein synthesis is not a requirement for lysis. Similarly, the effector T cell does not need to proliferate in order to lyse target cells, nor does it need to synthesize either DNA or RNA.

Thus, a viable effector T cell is necessary for lysis. On the other hand, there is no evidence that the target cell needs to be metabolically active in order to be subjected to lytic attack. Indeed, recent studies using both glutaraldehyde-fixed target cells and cytoplasts obtained from cells enucleated by passage through cytochalasin B gradients have shown that both "fixed" and enucleated cells are lysed efficiently. These studies suggest that the target cell is a totally passive partner in the lytic event, serving merely to display antigen. The effector cell, in contrast, survives the interaction that results in the demise of the target-cell and can interact with additional targets. T cell-mediated lysis is thus a **lytic cycle**. A diagrammatic representation of this cycle is shown in Fig 12–8.

Three separate aspects of the lytic cycle can be considered: (1) cell-cell interaction, (2) the events following interaction, and (3) the resulting rupture of the target cell's membrane and loss of cytoplasmic contents. The 3 aspects are considered sequentially below.

A. Cell-Cell Interaction: The initiation of lysis by effector T cells is conceptually a simple one: the interaction of a killer lymphocyte with an antigen-bearing target cell. Cytotoxic T cells bind avidly—and specifically—to cell monolayers bearing antigenic determinants against which the T cell donor is immune. It is widely asserted that this adsorption is analogous to the first stage in T cell-mediated lysis, for cytolysis requires cell-cell interaction. The binding of cytotoxic T cells onto cell monolayers has been shown to be inhibited by low temperatures, by azide, and by dinitrophenyl, implying that the cell-cell interaction is an energy-requiring process. The adhesion of effector cells to their targets has also been shown to be inhibited by cytochalasin B—implying, perhaps, that accommodation of antigen into its T cell receptor site is accompanied by membrane modulatory movement. T cell-target cell interaction has also been shown to require the presence of Mg^{2+}.

B. Lesion Insertion: In contrast to the energy requirements of effector cell-target cell conjugation, the subsequent lytic phase of cytolysis is apparently energy-independent. Membrane permeability changes in the target cell occur within minutes following effector cell addition. It is not known how long the cytotoxic T cell "sits" on the target cell before moving on to cause further damage, but those events which follow lesion insertion—and which occur prior to membrane disruption—can proceed without the lymphocyte. These events are absolutely dependent on the presence of Ca^{2+}.

A number of inhibitors of the lytic activity of cytotoxic T cells do not interfere with effector cell adherence to target cell monolayers. Such inhibitors thus apparently prevent lysis at a stage following cell-cell interaction, and it is customary to suppose that they affect lesion insertion. Chief among these agents are drugs that augment cAMP levels in the cytotoxic T cell. Augmented cAMP levels are associated with diminished lytic activity. This inhibition, however, is reversible; when cAMP concentration falls to resting levels, full cytotoxic function is restored. The mechanism linking cAMP levels to lytic expression has not been defined.

C. Destruction of the Target Cell Membrane: The terminal stages of T cell-mediated lysis are perhaps the best understood. As a result of the collision with a cytotoxic T cell, the target cell undergoes a progressive series of membrane permeability changes ending in rupture of its membrane. The changes in the target cell membrane that herald lysis of the cell have been clearly demonstrated using markers of varying molecular size as indicators of target cell destruction.

Using the P-815 mastocytoma as target cell and cytotoxic T cells from the spleens of alloimmunized C57BL/6 mice (as in Fig 12–7), changes in the permeability of the target cell membrane (as measured by ATP and ^{86}Rb efflux) have been induced within 10 minutes of addition of cytotoxic T cells. Protein-bound ^{51}Cr or ^{3}H-thymidine DNA emigrates from target cells only later, after lag periods related to the effective molecular size of the indicator. These findings suggest that the initial lesion caused by cytotoxic T cells allows rapid exchange of inorganic ions and small molecules

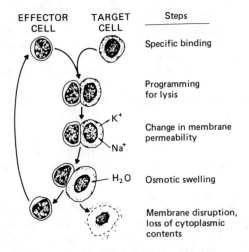

EFFECTOR CELL	TARGET CELL	Steps
		Specific binding
		Programming for lysis
	K^+ Na^+	Change in membrane permeability
	H_2O	Osmotic swelling
		Membrane disruption, loss of cytoplasmic contents

Figure 12–8. Stages in T cell-induced lytic cycle.

but not of macromolecules. It seems likely that the latter become able to pass the cell membrane only after secondary effects on the cell resulting from disordered osmotic regulation have taken place. The eventual demise of the target cell appears to be caused by colloid osmotic forces resulting from water influx.

Despite a fairly good appreciation of the overall events involved in T cell–mediated lysis (depicted in Fig 12–8), the mechanism by which the killer cell gives rise to a lytic lesion has remained elusive. Recent evidence from studies using model membrane systems suggests that cytotoxic T cells lyse their targets by the insertion of proteins which form a hydrophobic "channel" through the plasma membrane of the target cell. This model is reminiscent of that proposed to account for the lytic action of the complement proteins. It seems very unlikely, however, that complement proteins themselves are involved in the lytic action of cytotoxic T cells.

NATURAL KILLER (NK) CELLS

In the mid 1970s, a novel cytotoxic activity was observed in lymphoid tissue from rats and mice. As the activity was present even before purposeful immunization of the animals, it was termed natural killer (NK) activity and the cells responsible for the activity were designated **NK cells.** NK cells have been described in all species so far examined (except, curiously, the cat) and are readily distinguished from T cells on the basis of cell surface markers. For example, murine NK cells lack the characteristic Lyt-2 and Lyt-3 alloantigens present on cytotoxic T cells but do have antigens termed NK-1 and NK-2 which are not present on T cells. Analogous differences exist between human cytotoxic T cells and NK cells.

NK cells share with cytotoxic T cells the ability to lyse certain target cells directly, but here too there are notable distinctions between the 2 types of effector cells. As mentioned above, cytotoxic T cells are characterized by their exquisite immunologic specificity. They can, for example, distinguish between the haptens trinitrophenyl and dinitrophenyl. In contrast, NK cells totally lack classic immunologic specificity and can kill cells across organ, strain, and species barriers. Regardless of the species from which they are derived, NK cells are characterized by their ability to lyse a wide variety of cell types, most notably lymphomas and other tumor cells. Normal tissues— including fibroblasts, thymocytes, and a portion of bone marrow cells—are also lysed, but normal cells are generally much less susceptible than tumor cells to NK cell–mediated lysis.

Two general theories have been advanced to account for the fact that NK cells lyse such a broad spectrum of cell types. One possibility is that NK cells are clonally arrayed. This hypothesis suggests that the ability of a given lymphoid cell population to kill many different target cells is a reflection of clonality and that a given NK cell clone lyses only a limited number of cell types. This hypothesis has not met with experimental support, for recent technologic advances have made possible the long-term growth of NK clones in vitro. Such clones kill as broad a spectrum of target cells as do the parent populations from which they are derived.

These findings have lent support to an alternative proposal: that susceptibility to NK cells lies in the display of a shared membrane component which for the sake of argument we may term an antigen. Search for a common membrane antigen as the potential substrate for NK cell attack is currently under way, and early observations suggest that membrane glycoconjugates may be of determining significance.

We know little of the mechanism of action of NK cells. Drug inhibition studies analogous to those carried out for cytotoxic T cells have been performed with similar results. NK cell–mediated lysis involves—as does that caused by cytotoxic T cells—direct membrane-membrane contact between an effector cell and a susceptible target cell. All of those drugs (cytochalasin B, colchicine, the cAMP-"active" drugs, EDTA) that inhibit T cell–mediated lysis also inhibit NK cell–mediated cytotoxicity at similar concentrations. These findings suggest that although they require separate "triggering" pathways, the mechanisms of action of NK and cytotoxic T cells are similar if not identical.

The ability of several lymphocyte-derived soluble mediators (**lymphokines**) to regulate lytic expression has recently received considerable attention. The observation that one lymphokine, **interferon,** augments the lytic activity of NK cells has formed the scientific foundation from which was recently launched a widely heralded clinical campaign employing interferon as an antineoplastic agent. Interferon, however, also boosts cytotoxic T cell reactivity. Another lymphokine, **interleukin-2 (IL-2),** selectively increases NK reactivity, and although IL-2 also plays an important role in the differentiation of cytotoxic T cells, it does not augment the activity of fully differentiated cytotoxic T cells. It remains to be determined whether this augmentation of cytotoxic activity by lymphokines can be exploited therapeutically.

So far in this section we have confined our attention to cells that exert their cytotoxic effects directly. Other populations of cells are cytolytic only in the presence of antibody. Such cells include polymorphonuclear leukocytes, some macrophage populations, and a population of lymphoid cells termed **K cells.**

K CELLS: ANTIBODY–DEPENDENT CELL–MEDIATED CYTOTOXICITY

Antibody-dependent cell-mediated cytotoxicity was first described by Moller as a pathway by which methylcholanthrene-induced fibrosarcoma cells could be lysed in vitro. Since that time, it has become clear that the phenomenon is a general one, involving a wide range of target cells and several effector cell types.

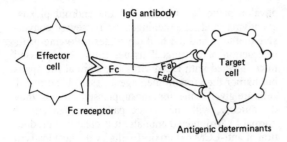

IgG antibody

Effector cell

Fc

Fab
Fab

Target cell

Fc receptor

Antigenic determinants

Figure 12–9. Schema for antibody "bridging" associated with K cell–mediated cytotoxicity.

The common feature of effector cells is display of a membrane receptor for the Fc portion of IgG antibody, although not all cells that display such receptors are cytotoxic. Several morphologically and developmentally distinctive cell types have been shown to exert a cytotoxic capacity in vitro toward antibody-coated target cells. Among these are polymorphs, macrophages, platelets, fetal liver cells, and a mononuclear cell present in lymphoid tissue that lacks characteristic markers of mature T and B cells and has been termed a **K cell.**

The involvement of antibody is a complex one involving both the antigen-binding and Fc portions of the molecule. It is widely believed that antibody serves to "bridge" the effector to the target cell in the manner shown in Fig 12–9. Different target cells seem to be lysed by different effector cells—eg, the cell responsible for lysis of antibody-coated erythrocytes differs from that which lyses antibody-coated tumor target cells. The reasons for this selectivity are not known.

IgG antibody of each of the major isotypes can support K cell–mediated cytotoxicity. This includes, therefore, both those subclasses that can "fix" the first component of complement and those that cannot. Thus, although both K cell–mediated lysis and complement fixation involve the Fc fragment of the antibody molecule, different sites within this domain seem to mediate the 2 activities.

Antibody-dependent cell-mediated cytotoxicity, like NK cell- and T cell–mediated lysis discussed above, requires effector cell–target cell interaction. Drug inhibition studies similar to those described above for T cell–mediated lysis, have indicated that the K cell must be alive in order to be cytotoxic. Thus, x-ray radiation, the presence of sodium azide, or treatment of K cell populations with antimycin A (a potent inhibitor of electron transport processes) all inhibit lysis. Other drugs, including cytochalasin B and the cAMP-"active" drugs, also inhibit lysis, as they do T cell- and NK cell–mediated lysis. These observations support the view that the mechanism of lysis by K cells is the same as that involving T and NK effector cells.

THE BIOLOGIC SIGNIFICANCE OF CYTOTOXIC CELLS

Proponents of the view that the immune system "surveys" against the development of malignant cells have found solace in the demonstration that cytotoxic cells exist in normal lymphoid tissue. They argue that such cells can readily fulfill a surveillance role by lysing cells that are "nonself." Although (teleologically) this argument makes a great deal of sense, there is little experimental evidence to support it. This is not to say that cytotoxic cells do not fill a crucial role in host defenses—simply that it has been difficult to assemble unambiguous experimental evidence that they do.

A series of recent observations collectively argue that NK cells can play a salient role in controlling tumor cell growth in vivo. In one study, Reid and her collaborators showed that nude (athymic) mice that had received systemic administration of anti-interferon antibody became able to support the growth of primary metastatic carcinomas. Such tumors could not be established in untreated animals. As interferon is known to regulate the cytotoxic activity of NK cells, it was argued, circumstantially, that the primary defect of animals receiving anti-interferon antibody was an inability to mount normal NK responses. In a similar vein, Kawase, Urdal, and Henney showed that mice rendered selectively deficient in NK cells were unable to regulate the growth of an NK-susceptible lymphoma cell line that was not tumorigenic in normal mice. Other studies have indicated a potentially important role for NK cells in controlling metastatic spread of tumor cells.

A role for K cells in host defenses has been difficult to establish, although their involvement has been suggested in several disease states. Clearly, any immune response that results in the production of IgG antibody brings with it the feasibility of K cell involvement. Bernstein and others have recently provided evidence that K cell–mediated cytotoxicity may contribute to the eradication of T cell leukemias in AKR mice. Leukemic animals were treated by repeated systemic administration of a monoclonal IgG antibody directed against a cell surface component of the leukemia cells. Treated animals showed evidence of leukemic cell arrest. Since the recipient animals were complement-deficient and an IgM antibody of the same specificity was ineffective therapeutically, these data are most consistent with the involvement of an IgG-dependent, complement-independent pathway of growth retardation. K cell–mediated lysis seems the most likely candidate.

Cytotoxic T cells—the first-characterized and still the best-understood of the categories of cytotoxic cells associated with lymphoid tissue—probably serve principally to control viral replication. This has been elegantly demonstrated in the case of influenza virus infection of the upper respiratory tract, where the T cell–mediated destruction of host cells bearing viral determinants limits virus replication.

Interestingly, while cytotoxic T cells are readily produced in recipients of skin (and other organ) allografts, they do not appear to be the principal effector mechanism of the tissue destruction associated with allograft rejection. Recent studies in a number of murine models suggest that another T cell subpopulation distinct from that to which the cytotoxic cells belong is chiefly responsible for graft rejection, although cytotoxic T cells may play a role.

Although it is conventional to consider cytotoxic T cells as wholly beneficial to their host, there have been several documented examples in which development of cytotoxic T cells results in destruction of host tissues. This has been most clearly demonstrated in mice injected intracranially with lymphocytic choriomeningitis (LCM) virus. Normal animals so infected develop acute inflammation of the choroid plexus, ependyma, and leptomeninges with a severe convulsive diathesis and die 6–8 days later following gross destruction of meningeal tissue. Immunosuppressed mice injected with LCM virus live normal life spans but harbor the virus in meningeal tissue. If normal T cells are given to the immunosuppressed animals, they die quickly, with the classic pathologic features of normal LCM-infected animals. It is clear that production of anti-LCM cytotoxic T cells by the host leads to the destruction of tissues bearing LCM virus.

In sum, there are ample indications that cytotoxic cells are important components of the mammalian host's immune system. Just how crucial they are and in which processes their activity is of significance have yet to be determined.

•   •   •

References

General

Albini B, Brentjens JR, Andres GA: *The Immunopathology of the Kidney*. Edward Arnold, 1979.

Amos HE: Laboratory investigation of an allergic drug reaction. Page 221 in: *Recent Advances in Clinical Immunology*. Vol 2. Thompson RA (editor). Churchill Livingstone, 1980.

Coombs RRA, Gell PGH: Classification of allergic reactions responsible for clinical hypersensitivity and disease. Page 761 in: *Clinical Aspects of Immunology*. Gell PGH, Coombs RRA, Lachmann PJ (editors). Blackwell, 1975.

Dick G (editor): *Immunological Aspects of Infectious Diseases*. MTP Press Ltd, 1979.

Gallin JI et al: Disorders of phagocyte chemotaxis. *Ann Intern Med* 1980;**92**:520.

Henson PM: Mechanisms of exocytosis in phagocytic inflammatory cells. *Am J Pathol* 1980;**101**:494.

McCluskey RT, Andres GA (editors): *Immunologically Mediated Renal Diseases*. Dekker, 1978.

Panayi GS, Johnson PM (editors): *Immunopathogenesis of Rheumatoid Arthritis*. Reedbooks, 1979.

Weller PF, Goetzl EJ: The regulatory and effector roles of eosinophils. *Adv Immunol* 1979;**27**:339.

Anaphylactic Reactions

Holroyde MC et al: Bronchoconstriction produced in man by leukotrienes C and D. *Lancet* 1981;**3**:17.

Hugli TE, Muller-Eberhard HJ: Anaphylatoxins: C3a and C5a. *Adv Immunol* 1978;**26**:1.

Katz DH: Recent studies on the regulation of IgE antibody synthesis in experimental animals and man. *Immunology* 1980;**41**:1.

Seale JP: Prostaglandins, slow-reacting substances (leukotrienes) and the lung. *Aust NZ J Med* 1981;**11**:550.

Cytotoxic Reactions

Briggs WA et al: Antiglomerular basement membrane antibody–mediated glomerulonephritis and Goodpasture's syndrome. *Medicine* 1979;**58**:348.

Kay HD et al: A functional comparison of human Fc-receptor bearing lymphocytes active in natural cytotoxicity and antibody-dependent cellular cytotoxicity. *J Immunol* 1977;**118**:2058.

Lindstrom J: Autoimmune response to acetylcholine receptors in myasthenia gravis and its animal model. *Adv Immunol* 1979;**27**:1.

MacDermott RP et al: Autologous human cellular cytotoxicity induced by mitogenic and non-mitogenic lectins. *J Immunol* 1977;**117**:1402.

MacDonald HR, Bonnard GD: A comparison of the effector cells involved in cell-mediated lympholysis and antibody-dependent cell-mediated cytotoxicity in man. *Scand J Immunol* 1975;**4**:129.

Moller G (editor): Natural killer cells. *Immunol Rev* 1979;**44**. [Entire issue.]

Rachelefsky GS et al: Antibody-dependent lymphocyte killer function in human immunodeficiency diseases. *Clin Exp Immunol* 1975;**19**:1.

Scott R et al: Human antibody-dependent cell-mediated cytotoxicity against target cells infected with respiratory syncytial virus. *Clin Exp Immunol* 1977;**28**:19.

Wands JR, Isselbacher KJ: Lymphocyte cytotoxicity to autologous liver cells in chronic active hepatitis. *Proc Natl Acad Sci USA* 1975;**72**:1301.

Immune Complexes

Barnett EV (moderator): Circulating immune complexes: Their immunochemistry, detection and importance. *Ann Intern Med* 1979;**91**:430.

Inman RD, Day NK: Immunologic and clinical aspects of immune complex disease. *Am J Med* 1981;**70**:1097.

Wager O et al: Evaluation of six tests for circulating IgG complexes with special reference to IgM rheumatoid factors: Analysis of systemic lupus erythematosus and rheumatoid arthritis series. *Clin Exp Immunol* 1981;**46**:149.

Cell-Mediated Reactions

Cohen S, Pick E, Oppenheim JJ (editors): *Biology of the Lymphokines*. Academic Press, 1979.

Geczy CL, Hopper KE: A mechanism of migration inhibition in delayed-type hypersensitivity reactions. *J Immunol* 1981;**126**:1059.

Waksman BH: Immunoglobulins and lymphokines as mediators of inflammatory cell mobilization and target cell killing. *Cell Immunol* 1976;**27**:309.

Cell-Mediated Cytotoxicity

Cerrottini J-C, Brunner KT: Cell-mediated cytotoxicity, allo-graft rejection and tumor immunity. *Adv Immunol* 1974; **18**:67.

Henney CS: Mechanisms of tumor cell destruction. In: *Mechanisms of Tumor Immunity*. Green I, Cohen S, McCluskey RT (editors). Wiley, 1977.

Herberman R, Holden H: Natural cell-mediated immunity. *Adv Cancer Res* 1978;**27**:305.

Perlmann P, Holm G: Cytotoxic effects of lymphoid cells in vitro. *Adv Immunol* 1969;**11**:117.

13 | Autoimmunity

Argyrios N. Theofilopoulos, MD

Recent major advances in cellular immunology, molecular biology, and genetics have strongly influenced current thinking about autoimmunity. These advances have increased our understanding of the basic aspects of antibody diversity, the generation of cellular and humoral immune responses and their interdependence, the mechanisms of tolerance induction, and the means by which reactivity develops against autoantigenic constituents.

Since 1900, the central dogma of immunology has been that the immune system does not normally react to self. This phenomenon, described originally by Ehrlich, is accepted today as immunologic tolerance to self components, an obvious necessity for health. Accordingly, autoimmunity defines a state in which the natural unresponsiveness or tolerance to self terminates. As a result, antibodies or cells react with self constituents, thereby causing disease. The above definition implies that responses against self do not occur normally and that if they do occur with sufficient magnitude and duration, the outcome is harmful to the host. However, it has recently become apparent that autoimmune responses are not as rare as once thought and that not all autoimmune responses are harmful. In fact, current argument emphasizes that certain forms of autoimmune responses such as recognition of cell surface antigens encoded by the major histocompatibility complex (MHC) and of anti-idiotypic responses against self idiotypes, unlike the "horror autotoxicus" responses of Ehrlich, are important, indeed essential, for the diversification and normal functioning of the intact immune system. Therefore, a distinction between "horror autotoxicus" and normal or positive autoimmune responses is in order.

It is now recognized that an abnormal autoimmune response is sometimes a primary cause and at other times a secondary contributor to many human and animal diseases. Clinically, the wide spectrum of autoimmune diseases has been divided into systemic, or "non-organ-specific diseases" and organ-specific

ones (Table 13–1). Types of autoimmune diseases frequently overlap, and more than one autoimmune disorder tends to occur in the same individual, especially in persons with autoimmune endocrinopathies. For unknown reasons, autoimmune syndromes may also be associated with lymphoid hyperplasia, malignant lymphocytic or plasma cell proliferation, and immunodeficiency disorders such as hypogammaglobulinemia, selective IgA deficiency, and complement component deficiencies. Moreover, autoantibodies sometimes develop as part of the aging process. Non-organ-specific autoimmune diseases, epitomized by systemic lupus erythematosus (SLE), are characterized by autoimmune responses directed against widely distributed self-antigenic determinants. Although a given non-organ-specific disease usually involves many self antigens, such diseases may also develop following abnormal immune responses against only one antigenic target which is expressed in different organs. One example of such an antigen is determinants on basement membranes at diverse sites. In contrast to generalized autoimmune diseases, organ-specific diseases (eg, certain forms of thyroiditis) result from abnormal responses directed against an antigen that is confined to a given organ. It is not known what determines the extent of autoimmune responses, the number of autoantigens that elicit them, or the target organ. In many instances, it is not clear whether autoimmune responses are directed against unmodified self antigens or self antigens that have been modified by any of numerous agents such as viruses and haptenic groups.

There is as yet no established unifying concept to explain the origin and pathogenesis of the various autoimmune disorders. Studies in experimental animals support the notion that autoimmune diseases may result from a wide spectrum of genetic and immunologic abnormalities which differ from one individual to another and may express themselves early or later in life depending on the presence or absence, respectively, of many superimposed exogenous (viruses, bacteria) or endogenous (hormones, abnormal genes) accelerating factors.

Publication No. 2644 from the Department of Immunopathology, Scripps Clinic and Research Foundation, 10666 North Torrey Pines Road, La Jolla, CA 92037. The author's work is supported by National Institute of Health Grant AI-07007 and Research Career Development Award CA-00303.

Table 13–1. Autoimmune diseases.

	Autoantibody	Method of Detection
Organ-specific diseases		
Myasthenia gravis	Anti-acetylcholine.	Immunoprecipitation of ^{125}I-α-bungarotoxin–conjugated acetylcholine receptors.
Graves' disease (diffuse toxic goiter)	Thyroid-stimulating immunoglobulin (TSI) or anti-TSH receptor autoantibody.	Bioassay; measurement of adenylate cyclase activity after incubation of thyroid tissue with immunoglobulin from patient's serum, radioreceptor assay for antibodies competing with TSH for the receptor on thyroid membranes.
Hashimoto's thyroiditis	Antibodies to thyroglobulin and to microsomal antigens.	Radioimmunoassay, tanned erythrocyte agglutination, complement fixation, immunofluorescence assay.
Insulin-resistant diabetes associated with acanthosis nigricans	Anti-insulin receptor.	Inhibition of ^{125}I-insulin binding to receptors on monocytes or adipocytes.
Insulin-resistant diabetes associated with ataxia-telangiectasia	Anti-insulin receptor.	
Allergic rhinitis, asthma, functional autonomic abnormalities	Antibodies to β_2-adrenergic receptors.	Binding of ^{125}I–protein A to lung membranes preincubated with sera; ability of plasma to inhibit binding of ^{125}I-iodohydroxybenzylpindolol (IHYP) to calf lung membranes; immunoprecipitation of soluble receptors complexed with ^{125}I-IHYP in the presence of propranolol.
Juvenile insulin-dependent diabetes	Antibodies to islet cells.	Immunofluorescence assay.
Pernicious anemia	Antibody to gastric parietal cells and to vitamin B_{12}–binding site of intrinsic factor.	Immunofluorescence assay, radioimmunoassay.
Addison's disease	Antibodies to adrenal cells.	Immunofluorescence assay.
Idiopathic hypoparathyroidism	Antibodies to antigens of parathyroid cells.	Immunofluorescence assay.
Spontaneous infertility	Antibodies to sperm.	Agglutination and immobilization of spermatozoa.
Premature ovarian failure	Antibodies to interstitial cells and corpus luteum cells.	Immunofluorescence assay.
Pemphigus	Antibodies to intercellular substance of skin and mucosa.	Immunofluorescence assay.
Bullous pemphigoid	Antibodies against basement membrane zone of skin and mucosa.	Immunofluorescence assay.
Primary biliary cirrhosis	Antibodies to mitochondrial antigens.	Immunofluorescence assay.
Autoimmune hemolytic anemia	Anti–red blood cell antibodies.	Direct and indirect Coombs tests.
Idiopathic thrombocytopenic purpura	Antiplatelet antibodies.	Immunofluorescence assay.
Idiopathic neutropenia	Antineutrophil antibodies.	Agglutination, immunofluorescence assay.
Systemic diseases ("non–organ-specific")		
Goodpasture's syndrome	Anti–basement membrane antibodies.	Immunofluorescence assay, radioimmunoassay.
Rheumatoid arthritis and Sjögren's syndrome	Anti-γ-globulin antibodies. Antibodies to EBV-related antigens.	Sensitized-SRBC agglutination, latex-immunoglobulin agglutination, radioimmunoassay, immunofluorescence assay, immunodiffusion.
Systemic lupus erythematosus	Antinuclear antibodies.	Immunofluorescence assay.
	Anti-ds and ss-DNA.	Farr assay, solid phase enzyme and radioimmunoassay, hemagglutination, counterelectrophoresis.
	Anti-Sm antibodies.	Hemagglutination, immunodiffusion, radioimmunoassay.
	Anti-ribonucleoprotein antibodies.	Hemagglutination, radioimmunoassay.
	Antilymphocyte antibodies.	Immunofluorescence assay, cytotoxicity.
	Anti–red blood cell antibodies.	Coombs test.
	Antiplatelet antibodies.	Immunofluorescence assay.
	Anti–neuronal cell antibodies.	Immunofluorescence assay.
	Anti-γ-globulins.	Radioimmunoassay.

IMMUNOPATHOLOGIC MECHANISMS IN AUTOIMMUNE DISEASES

Three main immunopathologic mechanisms act to mediate autoimmune diseases, though in any given disorder more than one may sometimes be in operation:

(1) The first mechanism is the action of autoantibody on unmodified or modified intracellular structures or cell surfaces. Destruction of cells or tissues ensues, usually because of the presence of complement but also sometimes as a result of antibody-mediated cellular cytotoxicity. In some instances, autoantibodies directed against functional cellular receptors stimulate or inhibit specialized cellular functions without associated cell destruction.

(2) Second, autoantigen-autoantibody immune complexes may form in intercellular fluids or in the general circulation and ultimately mediate tissue damage. Such complexes, depending on their size—which is determined primarily by the ratio of the 2 reactants—may circulate widely and be deposited in tissues throughout the body, especially those with large filtering membranes (kidney, joint, choroid plexus). Complement factors as well as granulocytic and monocytic cells are then attracted to the sites of immune complex deposition, and their involvement leads to cell death.

(3) Third, the disease process may be caused by sensitized T lymphocytes. These lymphocytes produce tissue lesions by poorly understood mechanisms which presumably involve the release of destructive lymphokines or which attract other destructive inflammatory cell types to the lesion.

Examples of the first type of autoimmune diseases are autoimmune hemolytic anemias, neutropenias, lymphopenias, and thrombocytopenias as well as anti–basement membrane antibody–caused diseases, a variety of autoimmune endocrinopathies, and anti–receptor-mediated diseases (Table 13–1). The immunopathologic mechanisms of some of these diseases will be summarized below. Hemolytic anemias can be idiopathic or secondary to such factors as viral infections and drugs, and the cause may be warm- or cold-reactive autoantibodies that are detectable bound to red cell surfaces or in serum samples examined by direct and indirect hemagglutination assays. Lymphopenias, neutropenias, and thrombocytopenias are frequent secondary manifestations of autoimmune disorders such as systemic lupus erythematosus and rheumatism in which antilymphocyte, anti-polymorphonuclear cell, and antiplatelet an-

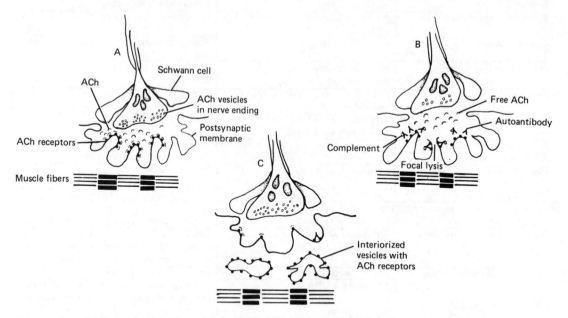

Figure 13–1. Immunopathology of myasthenia gravis. *A:* Normally, acetylcholine (ACh), synthesized and accumulated in vesicles at the motor nerve terminals, is released by exocytosis. Thereafter, it interacts with acetylcholine receptors on the invaginated postsynaptic membrane of the muscle, triggering the transient opening of cation-specific channels through which sodium and potassium flow according to their concentration gradient across the muscle cell membrane. If enough acetylcholine receptors are activated, an action potential is triggered that is propagated along the muscle and activates the contractile machinery. Transmission is terminated and the ion channels close following removal of acetylcholine from the cleft by diffusion and destruction by acetylcholinesterase that is localized over the whole surface of the postsynaptic membrane. *B* and *C:* In myasthenia gravis, there is a reduction of acetylcholine receptors due to focal lysis of the postsynaptic membrane by complement-fixing anti-acetylcholine autoantibodies or antigenic modulation involving crosslinking of acetylcholine receptors, interiorization, and proteolysis. (Modified and reproduced, with permission, from Lindstrom J: Autoimmune response to acetylcholine receptors in myasthenia gravis and its animal model. *Adv Immunol* 1979;**27**:1.)

tibodies often develop. Goodpasture's syndrome, characterized by glomerulonephritis and pulmonary hemorrhage, is caused by anti-basement membrane autoantibodies; these antibodies can be found deposited uniformly along the membrane, resulting in a smooth, continuous linear pattern (Chapters 30 and 31). A variety of endocrinopathies may result from autoantibodies directed against antigens on endocrine glands, hormones produced by them, or receptor sites for the hormones. For example, Addison's disease may be the result of antiadrenal autoantibodies. Most patients with juvenile-onset (insulin-dependent) diabetes have islet cell antibodies in their sera, and patients with Hashimoto's thyroiditis and primary myxedema have antibodies to thyroglobulin, microsomal protein, and other thyroid constituents. It is of interest that over 30% of patients with autoimmune thyroid disease have concomitant gastric parietal cell antibodies in their sera, whereas thyroid antibodies have been demonstrated in up to 50% of pernicious anemia patients. Parietal cells in many ways behave like endocrine cells, since they secrete intrinsic factor in response to stimulation by gastrin. Absence of intrinsic factor leads to malabsorption of vitamin B_{12}. Pernicious anemia may develop as a result not only of autoantibodies against parietal cells but also of autoantibodies specific for intrinsic factor.

A most interesting group of autoimmune endocrinopathies and other autoimmune diseases is caused by autoantibodies against functional cell surface receptors. Antireceptor antibodies are known to underlie the pathogenesis of at least 4 diseases: (1) myasthenia gravis, with antibodies produced against the acetylcholine receptors of neuromuscular junctions; (2) Graves' disease, in which antibodies against the thyroid receptors for thyroid-stimulating hormone (TSH) develop; (3) the syndrome of acanthosis nigricans, in which profound insulin resistance results from the production of anti-insulin receptor antibodies; and (4) ataxia-telangiectasia, another autoimmune disorder in which one finds antibodies against the insulin receptors. In each case, the antibody (usually IgG, but sometimes other immunoglobulins) competes with neurotransmitter or hormone for binding sites on the cell surface. Attachment of antibody to the receptor can result in a variety of biologic effects such as (1) blocking of function by hastening degradation of the receptor; (2) mimicking the action of a normally activated receptor, as in Graves' disease and certain cases of acanthosis nigricans with diabetes; and (3) blocking hormone binding, thereby inducing resistance to the hormone, as in ataxia-telangiectasia.

Myasthenia gravis is a neuromuscular disorder manifested by weakness, fatigue of voluntary muscles, and often remarkable patient responsiveness to anticholinesterase drugs. The functional defect in neuromuscular transmission observed in this disease is localized in the postsynaptic surface of the neuromuscular junction. The structure of the neuromuscular junction is altered, and the number of functional acetylcholine receptors decreases—all brought about by anti-acetylcholine receptor antibodies. These autoantibodies interact with acetylcholine receptors located on the postsynaptic membrane at or near the acetylcholine binding site, and this interaction leads to blockade, greatly increased receptor interiorization, and subsequent degradation as well as focal lysis in the presence of complement (Fig 13–1). The disease can be transmitted to experimental animals by serum IgG of myasthenic patients.

Graves' disease, characterized by overproduction of thyroxine and triiodothyronine, is probably caused by thyroid-stimulating immunoglobulins (TSI), which stimulate the thyroid gland through a reaction with the cell receptor for TSH. This reaction activates adenylate cyclase inside the cell membrane, initiating increased activity by protein kinases, which leads to increased secretion of thyroid hormones (Fig 13–2).

In a few nonobese patients with type B acanthosis nigricans and diabetes, insulin is often present at normal or above-normal levels, but its binding to specific receptors is greatly diminished. The insulin receptors, although present in normal numbers, are almost com-

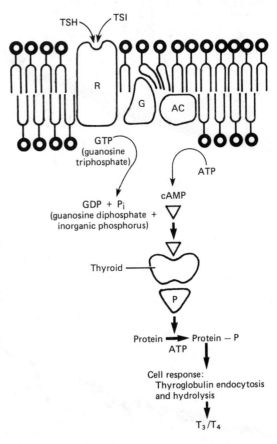

Figure 13–2. Pathogenesis of Graves' disease. TSI mimics the action of TSH, thereby stimulating secretion of thyroid hormones (see text). (Reproduced, with permission, from De Baets M et al: Autoantibodies to the thyrotropin receptor and their significance in autoimmune thyroid disease. In: *Immunologic Analysis: Recent Progress in Diagnostic Laboratory Immunology.* Masson, 1982.)

pletely inactivated by autoantibody directed against them. The antibodies attach themselves to the receptors, probably at some site adjacent to the receptor rather than at the actual insulin-binding site, changing the receptor's total structure in such a way that it can no longer bind insulin tightly (Fig 13–3). Such autoantibodies may not only block and desensitize the receptors, but when bound they can also mimic insulin's action on target cells. Although this insulin-mimicking effect lasts only a short while, it indicates that the information for turning on cells is in the receptor rather than in insulin itself. Insulin-resistant diabetes is found in approximately 60% of patients with ataxia-telangiectasia; this has been attributed to the presence

in serum of blocking anti-insulin receptor antibodies.

Recent findings suggest that antireceptor autoantibodies may be responsible for many other syndromes. For example, autoantibodies to β_2-adrenergic receptors have been identified occasionally in sera of patients with bronchial asthma or allergic rhinitis. Receptor blockade by β_2-receptor antibodies could upset the balance between β-receptor–induced relaxation of airway smooth muscle and the opposing influence of other mediators such as α-receptor agonists, histamine, prostaglandins, and acetylcholine. The β-receptor antibodies might also reduce receptor density on smooth muscle cells by hastening receptor degradation, as with acetylcholine receptor in myas-

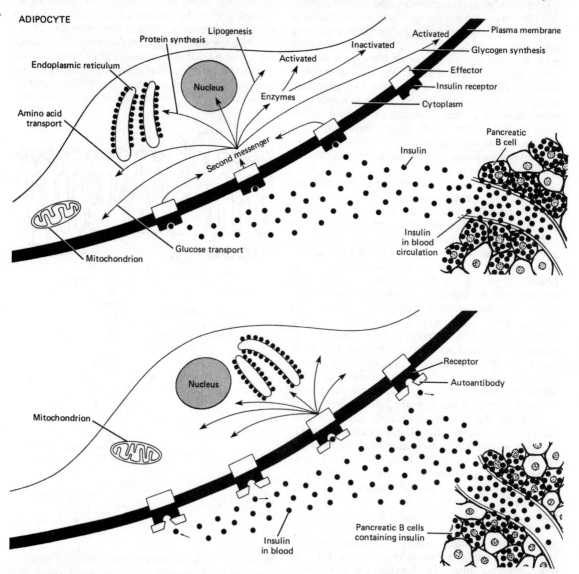

Figure 13–3. Pathogenesis of insulin-resistant diabetes associated with acanthosis nigricans. *Above:* Insulin released from the pancreas normally binds to receptors on sensitive cells, and the hormone-receptor complex activates various intracellular processes. *Below:* In a small number of diabetic patients, insulin secretion is normal but receptor sites are partially blocked by autoantibody; impaired hormone binding means that few sites are activated at any given time. (Reproduced, with permission, from Roth J: Insulin receptors in diabetes. *Hosp Pract* [May] 1980; 15:98. Drawn by Albert Miller.)

thenia gravis. A very recent suggestion is that such autoantibodies may be more prevalent than originally thought and that they may play an important role in the pathogenesis of inherent functional autonomic abnormalities.

Among the non-organ-specific autoimmune diseases, the most prominent is systemic lupus erythematosus. This prototypical autoimmune disease is characterized by a variety of autoimmune responses and manifestations of immune complex disease such as glomerulonephritis, vasculitis, and nonerosive polyarthritis. Among the various autoantibodies encountered, the most notable are those against nuclear components such as DNA, deoxyribonucleohistone, histone, RNA, nucleolar antigens, and components of the soluble nuclear extracts, among which the most prominent are ribonucleoprotein antigen and Sm antigen. High titers of antibody to double-stranded DNA and to Sm are found only in patients with systemic lupus erythematosus and can be considered diagnostic. Some antinuclear antibodies, especially antibodies to single-stranded DNA, occur with various frequencies and titers in other rheumatic diseases as well. In systemic lupus erythematosus, there also may be anti-red cell and antiplatelet antibodies that cause hemolytic anemia and thrombocytopenia, as well as antilymphocyte antibodies directed against T and B cells and anti-neuronal cell antibodies that may play some role in the central nervous system manifestations of systemic lupus erythematosus. Recent studies of monoclonal anti-DNA antibodies derived from the MRL/l strain of mice, which spontaneously develop systemic lupus erythematosus, have suggested to some investigators that the autoantibody spectrum of lupus may not be as broad as once thought, since individual monoclonal antibodies react with numerous substances (cardiolipin, phosphatidic acid, phosphatidylglycerol, lupus anticoagulant factor, polynucleotides) whose backbones contain diester-linked phosphate groups. It was suggested that some of the diverse serologic abnormalities in patients with systemic lupus erythematosus may result from the binding of certain autoantibodies to a phosphodiester-containing epitope present in diverse biologic molecules distributed widely throughout the body. More detailed experiments on specificity must be done to determine whether this is the case.

Recent studies have implied that antinuclear antibodies in sera of humans and mice with systemic lupus erythematosus may have a much more fundamental effect than just complexing with antigen in serum and depositing onto tissues. Thus, experiments in SLE-prone strains of mice have disclosed the presence in sera of autoantibodies directed not only against the classic right-handed helical DNA (B-DNA) but also against left-handed helical DNA (so-called Z-DNA). Z-DNA was proved to be strongly immunogenic in experimental animals—unlike B-DNA, for which such animals exhibit strong tolerance. Theoretically, Z-DNA is an inactive methylated form of DNA that, upon methylation and activation, be-

comes involved in gene regulation. Moreover, in recent research, autoantibodies to Sm and RNP interacted with a type of small RNA complexed with protein. This small RNA was highly conserved among the species tested. The anti-RNP antibodies recognized small nuclear ribonucleoprotein particles (snRNP) that contained U1 RNA, whereas the anti-Sm antibodies recognized, in addition to U1 RNA, particles containing snRNP U2, U4, U5, and U6. Experiments with an in vitro system containing HeLa cells infected with adenovirus revealed that both anti-RNP and anti-Sm antibodies could inhibit the appearance of spliced mRNAs by interfering with the function of the U1 snRNP, thus suggesting that these autoantibodies may inhibit nuclear editing of RNA transcripts. The above findings, although provocative, may have limited importance in the pathologic process of systemic lupus erythematosus if the autoantibodies cannot penetrate living cells. Although some investigators have offered data suggesting penetration of cells by anti-RNP antibodies attached first via Fc surface receptors, these findings remain controversial, and the bulk of evidence so far indicates that such autoantibodies do not internalize within living cells so as to interfere with specific metabolic processes.

Rheumatoid arthritis, another major autoimmune disease, is characterized by the presence in serum of autoantibodies directed against the Fc portion of IgG. Such autoantibodies, usually of IgM or IgG isotype, combine with IgG to form immune complexes that are considered to participate in the associated synovitis and vasculitis via activation of the complement cascade and attraction of polymorphonuclear cells to the sites of their deposition (Chapter 26).

In most of the above-described organ-specific and non-organ-specific autoimmune diseases, not only autoantibodies but also certain cell types such as K cells and T cells have been incriminated as primary or accessory participants in their immunopathology. Of course, as will be discussed in the following sections of this review, abnormalities of regulatory T cells have been considered as one of the primary causes of autoantibody production by B cells.

Although much is known about the immunopathologic mechanisms of autoimmune diseases, their causes are still largely unknown. However, a wealth of information has accumulated in the last few years on such important topics as diversity of the immune system, means of normal immunoregulation, and tolerance induction. Thus, one can now with some confidence design a framework upon which future work concerning such disorders will be arrayed. These aspects are reviewed below.

DIVERSITY OF IMMUNE RESPONSES

Humoral and cellular diversity of the immune system is intimately connected with the question of self-nonself discrimination. The first task of an immune system is to react against virtually any foreign substance. It is well established that an individual can produce specific antibodies to all antigenic determinants in the universe. In fact, the immune system is capable of producing specific antibodies even against all sorts of odd, artificially synthesized chemicals and molecules; in other words, the immune system appears to recognize all antigenic possibilities. Simultaneously with acquisition of immune responsiveness, the immune system must fulfill a second requirement—that it exhibit no or minimal reactivity against self antigens. How such an enormous diversity of immune responses develops accompanied by a very restricted responsiveness to self is not known, although several recent findings have greatly expanded our knowledge in this respect.

Hypothetically, the great diversity of self determinants is what dictates how large the immune repertoire must be. If the repertoire is limited, the possibility for reactivity to self via cross-reactions is high. If the repertoire is large, the possibility for cross-reactivity against self is greatly reduced. Two major theories offer genetic explanations for the enormous diversity of immunoglobulin chain variable (V) regions, which determine the antigen-combining sites. The **germ line theory,** in its most extreme form, postulates that for every V region there must exist a different gene in the germ line. In contrast, the **somatic mutation theory** proposes that a small number of germ line genes diversify either by point mutations or by recombination events during the differentiation of lymphocytes to create the antibody repertoire de novo in each individual. Recent studies by DNA cloning of human and murine cells containing genes for immunoglobulins (Chapter 5) strongly indicate that both germ line and somatically mutated genes contribute to antibody diversity. Thus, it has been clearly demonstrated that although a large number (10^4–10^5) of germ line antibody genes exist, further expansion of antibody repertoire occurs via somatic recombinations and rearrangements of separate segments of DNA coding for particular portions of the antibody molecule (V, variable; J, joining; D, diversity; C, constant). These multiple gene segments scattered along the chromosome of a germ line genome assemble during the development of B lymphocytes and form a complete immunoglobulin gene. By further substitutions and mutations occurring especially in V regions of IgG and IgA isotypes and far less, if at all, in IgM isotype V regions, a vast array of antibodies can be generated. Thereby, the germ line diversity of 10^4–10^5 antibody specificities is expanded to a total diversity of well over a million antibodies. Thus, through a large number of germ line genes, somatic mutations, and selection of useful variant lymphocytes that react against foreign antigens, great diversity is generated. It is unclear at what stage of B cell differentiation—from stem cell to mature B cell—commitment to an ultimate antibody specificity occurs. However, central to understanding B cell expression is the fact that most B cells are relatively short-lived (a few days), and thus the repertoire is generated over and over again, presumably from stem cells within the marrow of mature individuals. It seems that lymphocytes are constantly "learning," in an evolutionary sense, throughout the life of their host, but this accumulated experience is lost when the animal or a particular clonotype dies, and the lymphocytes of the next generation of vertebrates must start again from the baseline "knowledge" of inherited V genes.

In contrast to B cells and despite the large amount of data generated in recent years, little is proved about the mechanisms that determine diversification of the second type of immunocyte—namely, the T cell. This in large part reflects the paucity of our information on such issues as the nature of T cell receptors for antigen and properties such as affinity of antigen-binding by such cells, as well as the great technical difficulty, until recently, in obtaining relatively enriched or clonable antigen-specific T cell populations for analysis. Experiments in murine hematopoietic radiation chimeras strongly suggest that the major organ in which T cells diversify is the thymus, via contact or processing by epithelial and giant nursing cells. Jerne suggested in 1971 that the T cell receptor repertoire is selected by these cells' reactivity with self MHC antigens. In Jerne's model, the starting point is an inherited set of T cell receptor genes each specific for an allelic form of the MHC of the species. That species' total repertoire then reflects the extent of polymorphism for all of its histocompatibility antigens. According to this theory and its later modifications by others (Fig 13–4), in the first stage, T cells initially specific for self MHC gene products are selected in the thymus to differentiate and proliferate. The self MHC antigens expressed in the thymic epithelial cells may be either class I (K, D, L antigen of murine H-2 or -A, -B, and -C antigens of human HLA) or class II (Ia antigens of mice, DR of humans). Stem cells that carry anti-class I receptors are destined to become cytotoxic, whereas those carrying anti-class II receptors eventually become helper T cells (see below). Then, in a second stage, only those T cells that bear low-affinity receptors for self MHC antigens are allowed to mature and leave the thymus as functional T cells, while the high-affinity antiself receptor-bearing T cells are eliminated by an unknown process. Such T cells with low reactivity for self MHC antigens have concomitantly high affinity for allelic variants of self MHC antigens. These clones of cells account for the high frequency of alloreactive T cells present in humans and in animals. Simultaneously and independently, the low-affinity antiself cells modify their receptors, either in the thymus or in the periphery, by rapid mutational events so as to recognize not only self MHC antigens but also determinants on conventional thymus-dependent antigens. Recognition of either antigen (self MHC or nonself MHC antigen) separately is not enough to trigger T cell differentiation to effector cells, whereas simultaneous recognition of both antigens delivers a sufficient signal to allow T cell differentiation. Many modifications of this original postulate as well as new models have been proposed to explain T cell diversification,

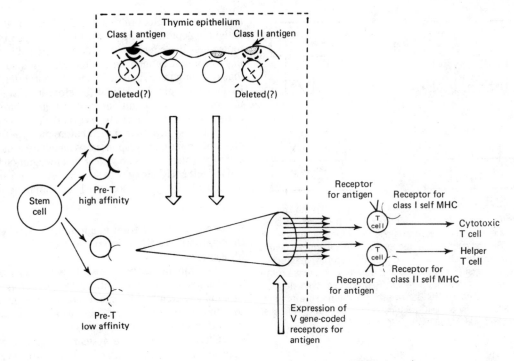

Figure 13–4. Stages in T cell maturation and generation of T cell repertoire.

alloreactivity, and the roles of the thymus and of self MHC determinants in T cell–dependent responses. At present, it is difficult to prove or disprove any of these hypotheses as long as the T cell receptor for antigens and the respective genes for such receptors are not identified. Nevertheless, one fact remains clear, as discussed below: Recognition of self is of extreme importance in diversification of repertoire and efficient T cell–dependent immune responsiveness.

FORMS OF NORMAL AUTORECOGNITION & OF POSITIVE AUTOIMMUNITY

Recognition of Self MHC by T Cells

Numerous studies on colonial marine forms and flowering plants as well as on more sophisticated and diversified higher animals have demonstrated that self recognition mediated by cell surface receptors is a fundamental biologic process concerned with many types of developmental and differentiation events. Examples are the lectinlike cell surface molecules of the cellular slime mold *Dictyostelium discoideum* that determine cellular cohesiveness, the specific cell surface molecules of simple metazoa and of colonial tunicates that allow formation of colonies, and the cellular receptors on vertebrate embryonic cells that allow appropriate cells to aggregate into tissues and organs. Such self recognition may occur between cells having identical receptors (like-like interactions), complementary receptors (lock and key interactions), or receptors interacting via a linker molecule.

It has now been demonstrated beyond any doubt

that certain elements of the vertebrate immune system preserve and express throughout life such a self recognition capacity, which apparently is essential for the normal function and diversification of the immune system. This conclusion is now a fundamental tenet of immunologic theory. The initial finding for most antigens was that collaboration between helper T cells and precursors of effector cells (B cells, cytotoxic T cells, suppressor T cells) is required for antigen-driven differentiation into mature effector cells. In addition, helper T cell differentiation begins only after association with antigen-presenting macrophages or antigen-expressing cells. In contrast, B cells and suppressor T cells can proliferate after contact with free soluble antigen. Significantly, in murine humoral responses, T cell help is initiated and delivered only if the T cells, B cells, and antigen-presenting macrophages are compatible at the MHC, more specifically at the I region. Complete disclosure of the MHC's role and of self recognition in immune responses awaited discovery that T cell–mediated immunity and efficient killing of virus- or hapten-modified cellular targets also required identity of the effector cytotoxic T cells and target cells at the MHC—more specifically, at the K or D region of the murine H-2 (A and B for HLA). This phenomenon, applicable to both helper and cytotoxic T cells, was designated the **MHC restriction phenomenon** and was found to be operative in many species, including humans, and in vitro as well as in vivo. The restriction and interaction of T cells with self MHC-bearing stimulator cells results not from a like-like interaction between T cells and stimulator cells but from a true T cell antiself receptor.

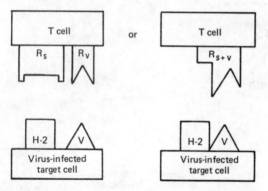

Figure 13–5. The one-receptor, 2-receptor hypothesis for cytotoxic and helper T cell recognition. It is still not clear whether the T cell expresses one receptor specific for self H-2 (R_S) and another that recognizes nonself antigen (in the illustration, viral antigen R_V), or a single receptor that recognizes a complex of self H-2 and non–H-2 antigens (in the illustration, viral [V] antigens). (Reproduced, with permission, from Doherty PC, Bennink JR: Monitoring the integrity of self: Biology of MHC-restriction of virus-immune T cells. *Fed Proc* 1981;**40**:218.)

A key question raised by MHC restriction concerns the nature of the T cell receptor. Two models have been proposed to explain the dual specificity of subsets of T cells for antigen and self MHC products (Fig 13–5): (1) The **2 recognition sites model** expresses the view that helper and cytotoxic T cells possess 2 separate recognition sites that are specific for 2 separate antigens on macrophages or target cells, respectively; one receptor site binds to the restricting self MHC, and the other binds to the cell surface–associated non-MHC antigen. (2) The **single recognition site model** is based on the assumption that T cells express a single receptor site that is specific for a single neoantigenic determinant formed when the self MHC complexes with the foreign antigen on macrophages or target cells. At present, no definite proof exists for either model, and convincing arguments for both models as well as for additional models have been presented. The precise structure of the T cell receptor has not been clearly defined, although strong evidence implicates the V region of immunoglobulin heavy chain as responsible for both the specificity directed to MHC and the specificity for non-MHC antigenic determinants.

It is not known why T cells are MHC-restricted and need to recognize self for optimum participation in humoral and cellular responses. This trait may distinguish them from B cells or antibodies, which do not express such a restriction. Probably this dual recognition is required for efficient stimulation of T cells that might be endowed with low-affinity receptors for antigen only. Such dual recognition would appear to be advantageous for survival of the species. For example, cytotoxic T cells seem to be essential for recovery from some acute viral infections. By recognizing and lysing virus-infected cells displaying viral antigens plus self MHC antigens, before assembly of progeny virus particles, these T cells limit viral multiplication. If their antigen receptors bound avidly to free antigen (viral) molecules, these receptors would be inhibited in binding to foreign antigen on an infected cell's surface, thus reducing the cytotoxic T cell's antiviral function. Evolutionary pressure would therefore lead to retention of the self-recognition capability in cytotoxic T cells, which presumably evolved from a self-recognition system that existed before the appearance of adaptive immune responses. Whatever the models and explanations, it is now clear that recognition by T cells of self MHC along with an extraneous antigen is a prerequisite for generation of effector immune functions.

Recognition of Self Immunoglobulin V Region Determinants & the Idiotype–Anti-Idiotype Network

As summarized above, responses of T cells to self MHC antigens play an essential role in *initiating* both humoral and cellular immune responses. We shall see now that responses to self may also play a role in *regulating* these immune responses.

Clearly, the immune system interacts with antigenic determinants, also called **epitopes,** via antigen-combining sites present in the hypervariable regions of V domains within immunoglobulin molecules either on the surfaces of or secreted by lymphocytes. The B cells probably express the whole immunoglobulin molecule as their receptors, but the T cells appear to express only the combining site derived from the V domains of heavy chains. Important discoveries clearly demonstrate that an antibody molecule has a dual character, acting to recognize a given antigen and, in turn, itself becoming immunogenic, even in the animal that produces this antibody. The hypervariable regions of a given immunoglobulin alone can act as antigenic determinants to generate another set of antibodies which recognize the uniqueness of that immunoglobulin as distinct from antibodies of different specificities. Sets of antigenic or epitopic determinants of immunoglobulin V domains were termed **idiotypes,** and the antibodies elicited against them were termed **anti-idiotypes.** Each single idiotypic epitope located on different portions of the V region was called an **idiotope.** An anti-idiotope antibody does not react with the entire array of idiotypic determinants of an immunoglobulin molecule but only with a single determinant, the idiotope. However, anti-idiotypic antibodies of a single specificity may be represented in different immunoglobulin classes. Idiotypic determinants have been described that are on V_L alone, V_H alone, or both, involving either antigen-binding sites or non-combining sites (framework regions) of the V domains (Fig 13–6). Idiotypes representing antigenic differences of immunoglobulin molecules at the V region differ from **allotypes,** which result from inherited variations (polymorphism) in the genes coding for certain amino acid sequences in the constant (C) region of immunoglobulin molecules, and from **isotypes,**

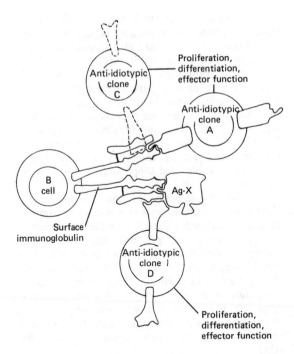

Figure 13–6. Specificity of anti-idiotypic antibodies. In this model, a B cell clone is the predominant clone reacting to an antigenic determinant on antigen X (Ag-X). Having expanded to the point that its antigen-binding receptors reach an immunogenic level, the B clone stimulates 3 separate lymphocyte clones each of which possesses surface receptors that recognize idiotypic determinants on the immunoglobulins expressed by the B clone and its progeny cells. Anti-idiotype clone A recognizes idiotypic determinants within the antibody combining site, whereas clone C recognizes H chain idiotypic determinants outside the combining site, and clone D recognizes L chain idiotypic determinants in combination with determinants on antigen X. Each of these anti-idiotype clones could be in the T or B cell series, and the cells or their products could express helper or suppressor functions, leading (respectively) to idiotype-specific augmentation (positive feedback) or inhibition (negative feedback) of this immune response. In turn, as each anti-idiotype expands to the point that its antigen-specific receptors reach immunogenic levels, anti-(anti-idiotypic) responses of a positive and negative type could be induced. (Modified and reproduced, with permission, from Hood LE, Weissman IL, Wood WB: Page 38, Fig 1–29, in: *Immunology.* Benjamin/Cummings, Menlo Park, California, 1978.)

which depict the different C regions found on immunoglobulin molecules (C_μ, C_δ, $C_{\gamma 3}$, $C_{\gamma 1}$, $C_{\gamma 2b}$, $C_{\gamma 2a}$, C_ϵ, C_α). Both B cells and T cells, as well as their soluble products (antibodies, antigen-specific T cell–derived helper and suppressor factors), express idiotypic determinants. Moreover, in accord with the clonal selection theory of Burnet (see below), the idiotype of immunoglobulin secreted by an antibody-forming B cell is the same as that of the cell surface immunoglobulin receptors for antigen. The number of idiotypes an individual possesses is apparently as large

as its range of antibody specificities or repertoire, actual and potential.

The responses of animals to most antigens involve several clones of reactive cells producing antibodies that have many idiotypic specificities or antigenic differences in the V region. However, after antigenic challenge, only a few clones of lymphocytes expand, resulting in the expression of a dominant idiotype. Idiotypic cross-reactions in inbred animals such as mice are not uncommon, especially among antibodies directed against relatively simple antigenic determinants. In most cases, cross-reactive idiotypes show linkage to allotypic markers present on the C region of the immunoglobulin heavy chains. In contrast, most outbred animals and humans infrequently express cross-reactive idiotypes consistent with the broadly heterogeneous regions that can combine with the different antigenic determinants present on a complex antigen. Nevertheless, even in outbred species, cross-reactive idiotypes are occasionally present as a result either of inheritance of antibody genes among related individuals or of preservation and sharing of certain germ line genes by unrelated individuals within the species.

The dual characteristics of antibody molecules and the apparent presence within an individual's repertoire of V genes with specificities for other V region products stimulated Jerne to propose in 1974 that autoimmune responses to self idiotypes might form the basis of immunoregulatory network systems in which homeostasis is preserved through a functional assembly of idiotype–anti-idiotype interactions. According to this model, an antigen induces the production of an antibody (Ab_1) characterized by its idiotype (Id_1). In turn, the latter stimulates the synthesis of an anti-idiotypic antibody (anti-Id_1 or Ab_2) bearing the idiotype Id_2 that can trigger the production of anti-(anti-idiotypic) antibody (anti-Id_2 or Ab_3), and so on. Initial models of the network system suggested that the network was open-ended and of unlimited extent, whereas more recent studies tend to support a circular configuration of limited sets of idiotypes and anti-idiotypes. According to network theories, for every **paratope** (antibody combining site of an antibody molecule), a complementary fitting idiotope on another antibody molecule can be found, and vice versa. Such an idiotope must be stereochemically similar (3-dimensional) to the epitope on the antigen against which the antibody was originally directed. Jerne calls the subset of immunoglobulin molecules that contain these idiotypes the **internal image set;** Lindenmann calls them **homobodies.**

Jerne assumes that such an idiotypic-anti-idiotypic network is functional, which means that its regulation should account for the various modes of the immune response (steady state, enhancement, suppression). One must infer that suppressive interactions dominate stimulatory ones in order to avoid the aberrant proliferation of clones. Moreover, before antigenic challenge, the system is in a virgin state that can be regarded as a stable reference state. Upon the introduction of antigens, macroscopic perturbation occurs and drives the system toward a new steady state characterized by immune memory or tolerance.

The idiotype network concept is now widely accepted because of a rather impressive accumulation of data in support of its existence and functional importance. Thus, autoanti-idiotypic antibodies as well as operational suppressive and enhancing networks have been described. Autoanti-idiotypic antibodies have been detected in mice immunized with T cell-independent antigens such as phosphorylcholine, bacterial levan, and trinitrophenyl (TNP)-Ficoll. Antibody titers and numbers of specific antibody-secreting plaque-forming cells apparently decrease while the amount of autoanti-idiotypic antibodies increases, which seems to indicate that autoanti-idiotypic antibodies exert a negative feedback on expression of the immune response. Moreover, in agreement with predictions made by the network theory, when experimentally produced anti-idiotypic antibodies are administered passively to animals, suppression or enhancement of the relevant idiotype may ensue. This is accomplished via the interaction of sets of B cells, helper and suppressor T cells bearing complementary idiotypic and anti-idiotypic determinants, identical idiotypic determinants through an antigen bridge or an anti-idiotype bridge, or identical anti-idiotypic determinants through an idiotype bridge. For suppressive effects, the following hypothetical sequence of events could take place (Fig 13–7A). First, antigens (in the illustrated instance, a T cell-independent antigen) induce proliferation of B lymphocytes, whose receptors are characterized by Id_1. In a first step, precommitted precursor pre-B_1 cells differentiate into mature B_1 lymphocytes. The latter proliferate and differentiate into plasma cells (in Fig 13–7A depicted as Z_1) secreting an antibody (Ab_1) characterized by Id_1. Ab_1 recognizes and eliminates the antigen. Its idiotype (Id_1) stimulates the proliferation of anti-idiotypic (anti-Id_1) B_2 cells, which differentiate from the precursor pre-B_2. Presumably, this step is dependent on T cells that carry anti-Id_1 receptors, since it has been established that an immune response to an immunoglobulin molecule requires helper T cells. The B_2 cells differentiate into Z_2 plasma cells secreting αId_1 (Ab_2) antibodies, which act negatively on the Id_1-bearing B_1 cells. Anti-idiotypic antibodies, upon attaining concentrations above a critical threshold, can also exert negative influences on these idiotype-expressing cells by engaging subsets of suppressor T cells that express the relevant anti-idiotype. An intermediate helper T cell whose receptor would express Id_1 idiotype may be necessary for interaction with anti-idiotypic antibodies and induction of anti-Id_1-bearing suppressor T cells (Fig 13–7B). By studying idiotype-induced suppression in mice, suppressor T cells have been subdivided into 3 populations. The first population (Ts_1) is Lyt-1$^+$, bears I-J and idiotypic determinants, and functions in a non-H-2(?) or V_H-restrictive manner during the induction phase of the immune response. The Ts_1 population

secretes a factor (TsF_1) which, together with antigen, induces a second complementary population of suppressor cells (Ts_2) that bear Lyt-2 alloantigen, I-J determinants, and anti-idiotypic receptors. The latter population functions in an H-2 and V_H-restrictive manner during the effector phase of the immune response in previously primed animals. However, this second population does not contain the final suppressor T cells. The available data suggest that the Ts_2 cells via a soluble factor (TsF_2) activate a third population of Lyt-2, I-J, and idiotype-bearing T cells (Ts_3), the possible final suppressors in the immune recipient.

Anti-idiotypic antibodies can also induce enhancement of immune responses instead of suppression. This can result either (1) from the stimulation of idiotype-bearing helper T cells that then induce idiotype-bearing B cells, or (2) from the elimination of specific suppressor T cells. In this last instance, anti-idiotypic antibodies (anti-Id_1, Ab_2) might induce the production of anti–anti-idiotypic antibody (anti-Id_2, Ab_3), which is assumed to suppress the production of anti-Id_1 antibody by B cells on the one hand and to eliminate anti-Id_1-bearing suppressor cells on the other.

Thus, various experimental models seem to indicate that idiotypic interactions, essentially autoimmune in nature, can play an important role in functional regulatory circuits of the immune system and in promoting communications between T and B cells. The system emerges as a self-contained, highly organized network of complementary T and B cell surface–bound and soluble idiotypes that is constantly engaged in recognition of self. If one agrees that idiotypes may sterically represent mirror images of antigens, it would be reasonable to suppose that the immune system accepts the structural diversity in the universe as nothing new or strange since it "sees" these structures continuously in its complementary circuits. According to this somewhat extreme but provocative view, "foreign" determinants are in fact never foreign, and consequently, challenge with non-self antigens is an epiphenomenon that does not set in motion any novel element in the system but only perturbs it until it reaches a new steady state.

THEORIES OF TOLERANCE INDUCTION

What has been said makes it clear that vertebrates have all the genetic information necessary to respond immunologically against self and nonself constituents and the ability to induce and regulate their immunologic apparatus via self recognition processes. Despite these conclusions, however, it is well established that the immune system of a normal individual is in general phenotypically tolerant to self.

Early studies demonstrated that tolerance to self is acquired through an active process that involves a direct contact between self components and specific antigen-reactive cells. For example, removing the

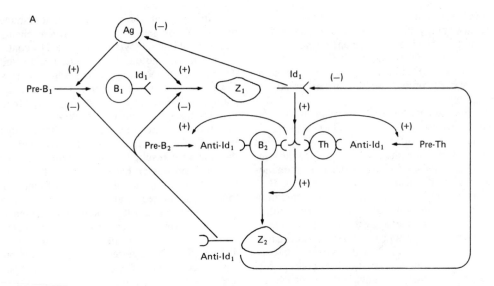

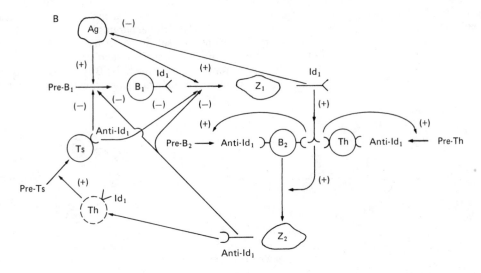

Figure 13–7. *A:* Regulatory interactions leading to the production of autoanti-idiotypic antibodies (anti-Id₁), which suppress the proliferation and differentiation of Id^+_1 clones in the case of a T cell–independent response. Pre-B₁ and Pre-B₂, respectively, are the precursors of B₁ and B₂ cells. Z₁ and Z₂ cells differentiate from the corresponding B cells. Pre-Th is the precursor of the T helper (Th) cells. Id₁ antibodies are specific for the antigen, whereas (anti-Id₁) antibodies are specific for the idiotype Id₁. The sign (+) corresponds to activation and the sign (−) to inhibition. *B:* Regulatory circuit corresponding to a suppressive type of network where idiotype-specific suppressor T (Ts) cells are generated in the course of a T cell–independent response. Pre-Ts is the precursor of the Ts cells. (Reproduced, with permission, from Hiernaux J: Anti-idiotypic networks. *Fed Proc* 1981;**40:**1484.)

hypophysis from a tree frog during early life (tadpole), allowing the gland to differentiate in isolation from its donor, and finally, transplanting the organ back into the mature donor results in rejection instead of acceptance. Moreover, animals genetically deficient in certain proteins still make antibodies when injected with the proteins. After studying responsiveness to exogenous antigens in experimental animals—and assuming

that responses against them are controlled by mechanisms similar to those for endogenous antigens—investigators have advanced several hypotheses to explain the apparent unresponsiveness to self by an individual possessing the genetic information to do so. There are 2 types of tolerance: central and peripheral. In central forms, no antibody is produced at all after antigenic challenge, since the responsible immunocytes are missing (clonal deletion) or are silenced directly (clonal anergy). In peripheral forms, some antibody is initially produced; but then, because of the expression of suppressive mechanisms (suppressor T cells, antibodies, anti-idiotypes, and immune complexes), antibody production diminishes greatly or ceases entirely.

The first serious attempt to explain how unresponsiveness to self might be acquired was undertaken by Burnet as a corollary to his clonal selection hypothesis. Burnet was the first to introduce the concept of the immunologic **clone,** a subset of immunocytes all having identical receptors for antigen. Burnet's clonal selection theory of acquired immunity proposed that virgin clones of immunocytes circulate in the body awaiting contact with their specific antigens, after which they undergo blast transformation and divide repeatedly to produce thousands of descendant cells of the same specificity. This concept followed Jerne's postulation that antibody molecules are not fashioned on a template formed by an invading antigen but are preformed, waiting to be selected by their complementary antigen. In other words, antibodies are made before the exposure to antigens, and their combining site specificity is solely determined by structural genes upon which antigens have no influence other than inducing proliferation of the clone that expresses the specific idiotype or V domain for that antigen.

In any event, Burnet proposed that immune tolerance to self antigens is subserved by a mechanism that causes fetal immunocytes to be deleted by contact with their specific autoantigen (**clonal deletion**) (Fig 13–8). This proposition owes its origin to the work of Owen, who first demonstrated that contact with foreign antigenic substances during early life resulted in immunologic tolerance. He observed that mature dizygotic twin cows tolerated each other's body tissues in that they did not reject mutual grafts. Undoubtedly, the tolerance resulted from embryonic parabiosis in which blood was exchanged between the twins. Subsequently, Billingham and Medawar found that adult mice of an inbred strain tolerated skin grafts of a second inbred strain if, as newborns, animals of the first strain were injected with replicating cells of the second strain. For the development of autoimmune diseases, Burnet suggested that precursor lymphocytes committed to nonself but related to self antigens mutate during their multiplication and accidentally make lymphocytes reactive to self.

The above theory was later redefined and expanded by Nossal and associates, who coined the terms "clonal abortion," "clonal anergy," "clonal silencing," and "clonal purging"—all to describe the same event. Nossal proposed that at some stage in their differentiation from stem cells to mature antibody-forming precursor cells, B lymphocytes go through a phase during which contact with antigen (whether en-

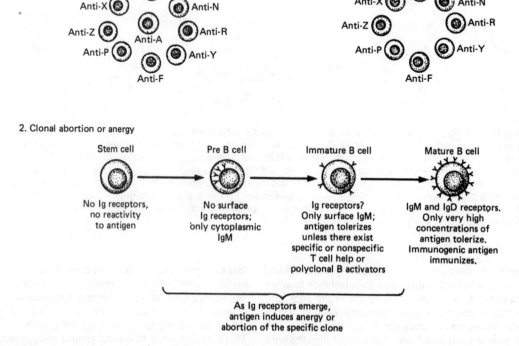

Figure 13–8. The clonal deletion and clonal abortion (anergy) theories of B lymphocyte tolerance. (Modified and reproduced, with permission, from Nossal GJV, Pike BL: Page 136 in: *Immunology 80: Progress in Immunology.* Academic Press, 1980.)

dogenous or exogenous) induces only tolerance and not immunity (Fig 13–8). This phase is referred to as the **tolerance-sensitive** or **obligatory paralyzable phase.** The concept is based on work in vivo and in vitro showing that the amount of antigen required to produce an effective negative signal varies enormously with the B cell's degree of maturity. If a hapten, polyvalently substituted on essentially any carrier moiety, is allowed to act for several days on lymphocytes in vivo and then for a brief time in vitro, a typical situation producing tolerance might be one in which mature B cells need a high antigen concentration (eg, 2×10^{-7} M), immature B cells need 5×10^{-10} M, and cells "caught" in the pre-B to B transition need 5×10^{-13} M for 50% of the cells to become tolerant. There is, then, a severalfold sensitivity difference between the extreme cases, and one should remember that the physiologic circumstance engendering acquisition of tolerance to self is that a B cell first encounters antigen during the pre-B to B transition. Further experiments showed that the early tolerance-inducing encounter between antigen and immature B cells did not lead to death of the tolerant cells. In other words, the immature B cells received and stored some negative signal without having been eliminated. Given that an animal can have antigen-binding B cells incapable of reacting to antigen and present in a functionally silent state, the process whereby such tolerance is induced was more accurately redefined as "clonal anergy" than "clonal abortion" or "clonal deletion."

Since the initial description of these findings, additional studies have clearly demonstrated the ease of inducing tolerance in neonatal spleen cells and bone marrow cells of neonates and adults with a concomitant resistance of tolerance induction in adult splenocytes. Significantly, spleens of adult animals contain a minor subset of immature B cells that can be tolerized as easily as neonatal B cells. This finding suggests that the ease of tolerance induction is not a unique property of neonatal cells but of immature B cells, in general, which are continuously produced throughout life. Additional studies showed that tolerance induction in immature or neonatal B cells requires (1) protein and DNA synthesis, an active process that cannot be explained simply as a passive phenomenon such as receptor blockade; and (2) multivalency of the inducing antigen. This last finding suggests that receptor cross-linking is involved in negative signal generation and that many autologous proteins, present in serum and extracellular fluids in monovalent form, may not induce tolerance to self by this mechanism unless they become associated with certain cell membranes, thereby gaining operational multivalency. Of course, many key self antigens are presented to the developing lymphoid system predominantly in multivalent form, such as the MHC determinants, which exist as cell membrane macromolecules.

Additional strong support for the particular tolerance sensitivity of immature B cells comes from experiments in which fetal and neonatal spleen B lymphocytes, unlike adult splenocytes, were highly sensitive to suppression of cell surface immunoglobulin (antigen receptor) expression after exposure to heterologous anti-immunoglobulin antibodies. Similar susceptibility can be observed in adult bone marrow B lymphocytes, clearly indicating that newly formed B cells are susceptible to ligand-induced inactivation throughout life. These observations strongly suggest that interaction at the cell surface receptors of B lymphocytes at a particularly sensitive stage of the maturation cycle, regardless of this interaction's antigen specificity or nonspecificity, results in functional inactivation of such cells. At least in the case of anti-immunoglobulin modulation, this inactivation is expressed by the inability of such cells to replace receptors on their surface membranes. It is not clear whether this process involves inhibition of further intracellular immunoglobulin synthesis or instead reflects a cell's inability to transfer the intracellular immunoglobulin to the cell surface membrane. Nor has it been determined at the molecular level why immature B cells are so much more easily tolerized and inactivated than their mature counterparts.

Until recently, there was no clear indication that the T lymphocyte class undergoes a central form of tolerance in the sense of classic clonal deletion or anergy described above for B cells. However, the recent development of methods to produce clones of cytotoxic T lymphocytes from single precursor cells has enabled Nossal and Pike to address this question. They find that a profound and long-lasting deficit in activated cytotoxic precursors, first demonstrated by the fifth day of life in the thymus and the eighth to tenth days in the spleen, develops in mice rendered tolerant to semiallogeneic cells when newborn. It remains to be determined whether this represents their destruction through early contact with antigen (clonal deletion), their functional silencing through a mechanism akin to B cell "clonal anergy" described above, the in vivo action of suppressor cells preventing their emergence, or some mixture of these phenomena. Experiments in murine lymphoid populations in vitro indicate that phenotypic deletion of inducer Lyt-1$^+$ cells with specific helper activity and Lyt-1$^+$ cells that induce suppressor cell activity by suppressor T cells may occur, thereby suggesting that clonal deletion of T cell subsets such as helper and cytotoxic cells could result from suppressor T cell activity.

Another major mechanism proposed for centrally induced tolerance is that of antigen- or ligand-induced inactivation of immune responsiveness (Fig 13–9). The term **ligand-induced inactivation** is used in a broadly descriptive sense to indicate the loss of reactivity in a population of specific immunocompetent lymphocytes as a direct consequence of interation between antigenic determinants and the cell surface receptors binding such determinants under circumstances or conditions that are either particularly unfavorable to triggering or are particularly favorable to inactivation of the cell. Monomeric antigens could be incapable of signaling the B cell, in which case, at high molarity, they could occupy the B or T cells'

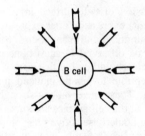

1. Monomeric antigen
blockades B cell receptors.

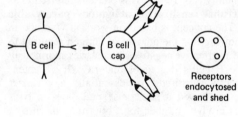

Receptors
endocytosed
and shed

2. Bi- or multivalent antigen
modulates receptors.

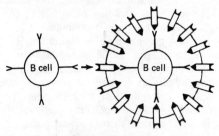

3. Multivalent antigen
"freezes" the membrane.

Figure 13–9. Antigen blockade mechanisms of B lympho-cyte tolerance. (Reproduced, with permission, from Nossal GJV, Pike BL: Page 136 in: *Immunology 80: Progress in Immunology.* Academic Press, 1980.)

antigen receptors so as to prevent macrophage-associated or other immunogenic forms of antigen from gaining access to these cells. It is perhaps relevant that aggregate-free forms of antigens are much more tolerogenic than the aggregated forms. Bivalent to multivalent antigens could, on the other hand, induce tolerance by depriving the cell of its antigen receptors through the patching-capping-endocytosis cycle, a process that has been called modulation. The example of anti-immunoglobulin–induced inactivation of immature B cells discussed above may be related. Finally, a third possibility is that high concen-trations of certain multivalent antigens—especially those that are linear with repetitive units more or less equally spaced along the membrane—can immobilize antigen receptors, thus "freezing" the membrane and inhibiting transmission of stimulatory signals.

Although clonal abortion or anergy as well as antigen blockade may be significant means by which tolerance to self is achieved, additional studies suggest that the absence of autoimmune reactions may result, at least in part, from continuous and active suppression exerted peripherally by subsets of T cells, the so-called **suppressor T cells** (Fig 13–10). In such instances,

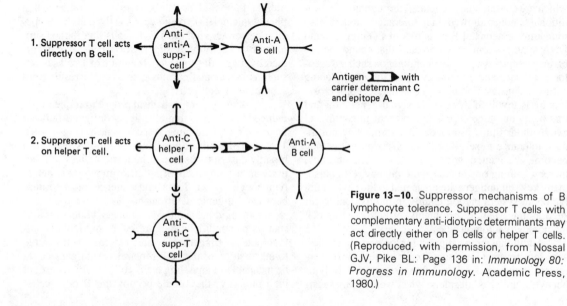

1. Suppressor T cell acts
directly on B cell.

Antigen ▶ with
carrier determinant C
and epitope A.

2. Suppressor T cell acts
on helper T cell.

Figure 13–10. Suppressor mechanisms of B lymphocyte tolerance. Suppressor T cells with complementary anti-idiotypic determinants may act directly either on B cells or helper T cells. (Reproduced, with permission, from Nossal GJV, Pike BL: Page 136 in: *Immunology 80: Progress in Immunology.* Academic Press, 1980.)

suppressor T cells may carry anti-idiotypic determinants for interacting with and silencing a B cell that carries the complementary idiotype, or they may antagonize the action of a helper T lymphocyte as outlined in previous sections and in subsequent ones.

In the mouse, it appears that 3 types of T cells are present: inducer cells, suppressor cells, and an intermediate cell type that acts on both inducer and suppressor cells. These cell types, apart from having separate and distinct physiologic functions, can be identified by characteristic surface markers associated with each. T cells containing the surface glycoprotein Lyt-1$^+$ are known as inducer or initiator cells, since they induce or activate other effector cell sets to fulfill their respective genetic programs. These Lyt-1$^+$ cells act to stimulate B cells to antibody production, induce macrophages and monocytes to participate in delayed hypersensitivity reactions, and stimulate precursors of cytotoxic T cells to differentiate to killer effector cells. Moreover, they induce a set of resting nonimmune T cells of the phenotype Lyt-1,2,3$^+$, a precursor pool of cells that regulate supply and function of the more mature Lyt-1$^+$ inducer and Lyt-2$^+$ suppressors, to generate potent feedback inhibitory activity via the suppressor T cell subset. Depending on the expression of surface alloantigens coded by the J subregion of the I region of the murine MHC, the inducer Lyt-1$^+$ cells, playing a pivotal role in the type of immune response produced, have been subdivided into 2 subsets: Lyt-1$^+$:I-J$^+$ are inducers of suppressors, whereas Lyt-1$^+$:I-J$^-$ are inducers of antibody secretion. The nature of these inducer T and B cell interactions is not completely defined, but one possibility is that the T-inducer antigen receptor structure related to the V region of immunoglobulin heavy chains may trigger only B cells that bind the same antigen and carry similar idiotypic determinants.

In contrast to Lyt-1$^+$ inducer cells, cells of the Lyt-2$^+$ set, representing approximately 10–20% of the T cell pool (current studies with monoclonal antibodies suggest that all murine T cells carry varying densities of Lyt-1$^+$ alloantigen), are specifically equipped (1) to develop cytotoxic activity against alloantigens and hapten- or virus-modified target cells; (2) to suppress both humoral and cellular immune responses after immunization; (3) to amplify suppressor activity; and (4) to induce other cells to countermand suppressor signals (contrasuppression). Suppressor and cytotoxic cells are probably 2 different subsets, and there probably is more than one type of suppressor T cell. Initial suppression of inducer Lyt-1$^+$ T cells is brought about by suppressor T cells secreting antigen-binding protein that expresses MHC determinants (usually I-J) and idiotypic V region determinants. Such suppressor T cells then induce other idiotypically complementary subsets of suppressor T cells that, via complex interactions among themselves and with inducer T cells and B cells, finally diminish an immune response. A simplified version of these types of interactions is given in Fig 13–11. The induction of suppressor cells to many antigens is under the control of immune response (Ir) genes.

From the above description, it becomes apparent that the immune system has evolved complex but sophisticated methods for preventing excessive responses to antigenic stimulation. In fact, the majority

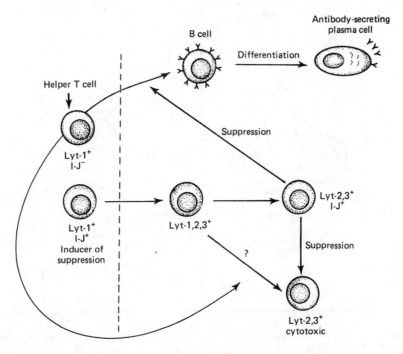

Figure 13–11. Regulatory circuits of murine T cells.

of immunologic cells seem not to be effector cells ready to respond to foreign antigens but regulatory cells that respond to messages originating from within the immune system itself in the form of cell surface-bound and soluble idiotypes and anti-idiotypes. Although the role of suppressor cells in tolerance induction and regulation of responses against conventional antigens, transplantation antigens, allotypes, and idiotypes is well-documented, the importance of these cells in inducing tolerance to autoantigens and in preventing autoimmune responses remains unproved. Newborn animals appear to have an excessive number of suppressor T cells in the thymus and spleen; nevertheless, experimentally induced suppressor T cells are associated more with tolerance induction in adults than in neonates. Certain antigens have been described that carry epitopic determinants endowed with the ability to interact specifically with suppressor but not helper T cells.

Peripheral means of tolerance induction include circumstances in which the antibody alone or in the form of **immune complexes** in antibody excess may act suppressively relative to the ongoing response. Suggested mechanisms (Fig 13–12) of antibody-mediated or immune complex-mediated suppression include (1) antigen shielding or masking by antibody, resulting in blockade of antigen recognition by antigen receptor–bearing lymphocytes; (2) activation of IgG Fc receptor–bearing suppressor T cells, with subsequent release of soluble factors that suppress helper T cells; and (3) direct stimulation of B cells with Fc

receptors to secrete soluble suppressor factors. Although some forms of antibody-induced suppression require the Fc portion of the molecule, others do not. Some investigators suggest that suppressive effects exerted by high concentrations of antibody are independent of the Fc portion, whereas those exerted by low concentrations are Fc-dependent. Antibody or immune complexes may also serve as "blocking factors" that impede an effective immune response to such cell-associated antigens as those on tumor cells. The premise is that such a response requires access of cytolytic T cells to antigenic determinants on the cell surface. However, stimulation of humoral immune responses and subsequent complexing of antibodies with antigen in the circulation may result either in masking of the antigenic determinants or occupation of the antigen receptors on the cytolytic cells, blocking these cells' access to and preventing direct interaction with the target cell (Fig 13–13). Interestingly, autologous anti-idiotypic responses of mice to cytotoxic lymphocytes with specificity for tumor antigens were found to suppress tumor regression, presumably via occupation of the antigen receptors on cytotoxic cells.

As can be seen from the above account, a variety of means exist for induction of tolerance or unresponsiveness. Some inhibit immune responses centrally by paralyzing or silencing the responding cells, others by acting peripherally via suppressor cells or antibodies. Central forms of tolerance appear to be more compatible with the expected mechanisms for induction of tolerance to self. However, the mechanisms described

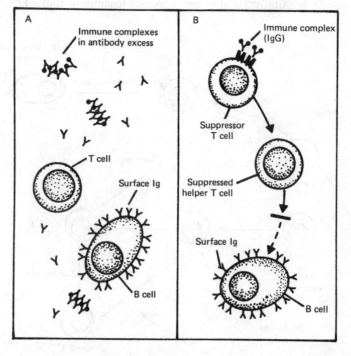

Figure 13–12. Suppression of immune responses by antigen-antibody complexes. *A:* Antigen shielding or masking by antibody (blockade of antigen recognition by antigen receptor–bearing B and T cells). *B:* Activation of IgG, Fc receptor-bearing suppressor T cells with release of factors that suppress helper T cells.

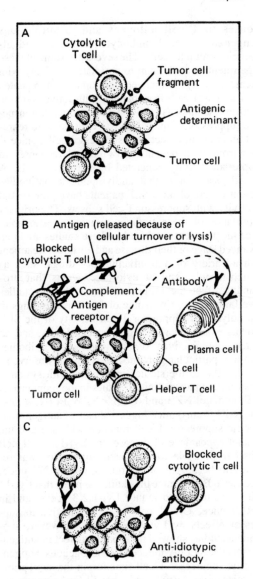

Figure 13–13. Blocking of antitumor cell–mediated immunity by antibodies or antigen-antibody complexes. *A:* Cytolytic T cells with appropriate receptors and access to antigenic determinants on the tumor cell surface induce lysis of the target cells. *B:* Stimulation of humoral immune responses via antigen sensitization of antigen receptor-bearing helper T and B cells will also result in antitumor antibodies. These antibodies, although usually beneficial to the host, may sometimes block anti–tumor cell responses by combining directly with antigen on the tumor cell surface, thereby rendering it inaccessible to cytolytic T cells; or they may combine with tumor antigens (released or shed after tumor cell lysis) in the circulation, form complexes, and then bind to antigen receptor–bearing cytotoxic T cells, thus blocking their access to and preventing their direct interaction with tumor cell determinants. *C:* Antitumor antibodies may also induce anti-idiotypic antibodies directed against the antigen receptors (V region) on cytolytic T cells, thereby inhibiting these cells from interacting with the target tumor cells.

above should not be regarded as mutually exclusive. Indeed, it seems certain that different forms of the tolerant state result from different mechanisms, and a diversity of mechanisms may be operative simultaneously. Because self antigens occur in diverse forms and concentrations, undoubtedly the same is true for physiologic self-tolerance.

ETIOLOGY & PATHOGENESIS OF AUTOIMMUNE DISEASES

Many theories and mechanisms have been proposed for the generation of autoimmune responses (Table 13–2). Their theoretic bases and controversies concerning each are presented below, along with pertinent examples and findings in humans and in appropriate experimental animals, especially murine systemic lupus erythematosus, summarized in parallel. Reviewing the available evidence, one must surmise that such spontaneous diseases have a multifactorial basis, with immunologic, genetic, virologic, hormonal, and other factors playing essential roles, each acting singly or synchronously with the others.

Table 13–2. Theories of origin of autoimmunity.

Release of sequestered antigens
Diminished suppressor T cell function
Enhanced helper T cell activity, T cell bypass
Thymic defects
Presence of abnormal clones, defects in tolerance induction
Polyclonal B cell activation
Refractoriness of B cells to suppressor messages
Defects in macrophages
Stem cell defects
Defects in the idiotype–anti-idiotype network
Abnormal genes: Immune response genes, immunoglobulin genes
Viral factors
Hormonal factors

IMMUNOLOGIC FACTORS IN AUTOIMMUNE DISEASES

Release of Sequestered Antigens

As indicated above, for induction of unresponsiveness to self, contact between autoantigen and the immune system is required early in ontogeny. If an antigen is sequestered within an organ, thus precluding contact with the lymphoreticular system, no immunologic tolerance at the T or B cell level can be established. However, any tissue damage that exposes the antigen later in life would then provide an opportunity for autoantibody formation, since tolerance induction in adults with many mature B cells is much more difficult to achieve than in neonates, whose immature, easily tolerized B cells predominate. Autoantibody production following release of sequestered antigens has been repeatedly demonstrated; eg, autoantibody formation against sperm after vasectomy, against the crystalline lens after eye injury, against heart muscle antigens after myocardial infarct, etc. In most of these instances, the autoimmune response is transient and probably disappears before clinical symptoms are generated. Progressive autoimmune disease appears to require persistent antigen that is presented in an immunogenic form. Not excluded is the possibility that once antigen has been liberated by nonspecific injury, the autoantibody thus induced may secondarily cause chronic release of antigen by participating with complement to mediate tissue injury. In this instance, chronic autoimmune disease may ensue.

Diminished Suppressor T Cell Function

As stated in the preceding sections, immune responses are normally down-regulated by complex interactions between immune response–helping and immune response–suppressing cells and their soluble products. It follows, therefore, that loss of a given autoantigen-specific suppressor T cell subset or nonspecific loss of this class of cells could result in the spontaneous appearance of autoantibodies. Antigen-nonspecific suppressor T cells can be identified numerically by the expression of certain surface alloantigens detected by polyclonal or monoclonal antibodies (OKT-5, OKT-8) against them or by expression of surface Fc receptors for IgG. Functionally, these suppressors are marked by their ability to release soluble products after stimulation with concanavalin A (ConA), which suppresses B mitogen–induced polyclonal activation and immunoglobulin secretion or allogeneic mitogenic responses. With these methods, numerical or functional abnormalities of suppressor T cells have been noted in a variety of organ-specific and generalized autoimmune disorders. However, the validity of ascribing reduced suppressor T cell number or function assessed by the above procedures as causes of organ-specific autoimmune diseases must be questioned for the following reasons: (1) It is very difficult to imagine how a generalized suppressor T cell defect could be expressed as an organ-specific autoimmune disease; and (2) it is equally difficult to imagine how elimination, reduction, or dysfunction of a very minor subset of suppressor T cells that reduces the activity of immunocyte clones responsive to a specific autoantigen could be expressed in the total compartment of suppressor T cells which are enumerated with monoclonal antibodies or assessed functionally by ConA stimulation. Although more acceptable on theoretic grounds, the numerical or functional diminution of total suppressor T cells in generalized autoimmune diseases, such as systemic lupus erythematosus, involving many autoimmune responses also remains controversial. Generally, such subjects have significant lymphopenia and decreases in absolute and relative numbers of T cells. T cell functional studies in humans with systemic lupus erythematosus reveal, in most cases, impaired delayed hypersensitivity to various antigens in addition to decreased proliferative re-

sponses to T cell mitogens and to autologous (syngeneic mixed lymphocyte response) and allogeneic stimulator cells. The severity of some of these impairments was thought to correlate positively with disease activity. Moreover, the subject of repeated claims is that T cells from patients with active systemic lupus erythematosus cannot generate antigen-nonspecific suppressor signals. This was considered to represent an inherent defect of T suppressor cells, since B cells from such patients show normal responses to suppressor activity generated by normal T cells. A related assertion is that antilymphocyte antibodies present in sera of most SLE patients have preferential reactivity with suppressor T cell subsets. The primary importance of these findings remains questionable, since most patients included in these studies are at an advanced stage of their disease and are under treatment with a variety of anti-inflammatory drugs, such as corticosteroids, and of cytostatic agents that profoundly affect the immune system. Recent studies have failed to confirm some of the above findings in that polyclonal suppressor T cell activity of the SLE patients examined was within normal limits, and no preferential reactivity of antilymphocyte antibodies with any particular immunocyte type was observed.

Similar to the studies in humans with systemic lupus erythematosus, initial studies in the spontaneous SLE model of NZB and (NZB × NZW)F_1 (New Zealand [NZ] strains) mice suggested lack of antigen-nonspecific suppressor T cell function with age and the parallel appearance of disease; the Lyt-1,2,3$^+$ T cell subset responsible for feedback suppression was reported to be absent or malfunctioning in NZ mice, whereas in BXSB mice the claim was made that Lyt-1$^+$ cells were unable to induce Lyt-1,2,3$^+$ cells, and in MRL/1 mice, Lyt-1$^+$ cells were insensitive to suppressor effects by Lyt-1,2,3$^+$ cells. However, subsequent studies showed no apparent defect in antigen-nonspecific (ConA-induced) or exogenous antigen-specific suppressor T cell function in the susceptible NZ mice or the 2 newly described SLE murine strains, BXSB and MRL. The origins and the histologic, serologic, and cellular characteristics of these SLE-prone strains of mice are shown in Table 13–3. Additional studies in these and other murine strains have brought into question the primary importance of natural thymocytotoxic antibodies in the development of murine systemic lupus erythematosus, since not all of the above 3 afflicted strains have natural thymocytotoxic antibodies in their sera. Moreover, natural thymocytotoxic antibodies are found in some recombinant NZB inbred strains in the absence of other types of autoantibodies and vice versa, and some strains with natural thymocytotoxic antibodies in their sera do not have detectable disease. Therefore, the above studies cast doubt that a *generalized* defect of suppressor T cells or the presence of natural thymocytotoxic antibodies causes autoimmunity. Furthermore, as discussed in the section on genetic aspects of autoimmunity, studies in murine models of systemic lupus erythematosus have excluded the pres-

Table 13–3. Characteristics of SLE-prone murine strains.

1. Derivation and Genetic Markers

Strain	Derivation	H-2	Lymphocyte Surface Alloantigens	Igh-1(IgG2a) Allotype	Accelerating Gene(s)
NZB	Inbred for color from stock of	$H-2^d$	Thy-1.2, Lyt-1.2, Lyt-2.2, Lyt-3.2,	e	?
NZW	undefined background	$H-2^z$	Qa-1[a], Mls[a], Thy-1.2	e	
BXSB	Derived from (C57BL/6J × SB/Le)F$_1$	$H-2^b$	Thy-1.2, TL⁻, Lyt-1.2, Lyt-2.2, Lyt-3.2, Qa-1[b]	b	Y-linked
MRL	Genome = 75% LG, 13% AKR, 12% C3H, and 0.3% C57BL/6	$H-2^k$	Thy-1.2, TL⁻, Lyt-1.2, Lyt-2.1, Lyt-3.2, Qa-1[b]	a	lpr only in MRL/l (MRL/Mp-lpr/lpr) but not in MRL/n (MRL/Mp-+/+)

2. Mortality Rates

Strain	Sex	50% (months)	90% (months)
NZB	Female	16	21
	Male	17	23
NZW	Female	24	32
	Male	25.5	33.5
(NZB × NZW)F$_1$	Female	8.5	12.8
	Male	15	19
MRL/l	Female	5	7.3
	Male	5.5	8.6
MRL/n	Female	17	23
	Male	23	27
BXSB	Female	20	24
	Male	5.5	8

3. Histoimmunopathologic Characteristics

Strain	Glomerulo-nephritis	Thymic Atrophy	Lymphoid Hyperplasia	Arteritis	Myocardial Infarction	Arthritis
NZB	+	+	+	0	+	0
(NZB × NZW)F$_1$	+++	+	+	0	+	0
MRL/l	+++	+	+++	+	+	+
BXSB	+++	+	++	0	+	0

4. Serologic Characteristics

Common — Hypergammaglobulinemia, antinuclear antibodies, anti-dsDNA, anti-ssDNA, antihapten antibodies, high levels of gp70, immune complexes (DNA–anti-DNA, gp70–anti-gp70), reduced complement levels (NZB is C5-deficient).

Uncommon — Anti-Sm (MRL mice; with sensitive techniques, such antibodies can also be found in the other SLE strains), IgG and IgM rheumatoid factors and intermediate complexes (MRL/l), antierythrocyte (NZB; NZB × NZW), NTA (NZB, NZB × NZW, BXSB).

5. Surface and Functional Characteristics of Lymphoid Cells

B cells — Hyperfunction and polyclonal activation in all strains, autoimmune clones in all strains, increased number in BXSB mice only, normal ontogeny of isotype diversity in all strains, normal capping and interiorization of Ig–anti-Ig complexes, early ontogeny of TI-2 responses in NZ mice, defective antibody-mediated suppression in all strains.

T cells — Generalized suppressor function normal in all strains; T cell number (Lyt-1⁺) and nonspecific T helper function increased in MRL/l only; defects in interleukin-2 production and response in all strains; reduced syngeneic mixed lymphocyte response in all strains; cytotoxicity against H-2 compatible allogeneic cells in NZ mice only.

Tolerance — Defective tolerance induction to some exogenous antigens in all strains.

Thymus — Essential in MRL/l disease but not in NZ and BXSB disease.

Nonlymphoid tissues — Noncontributory to disease development in any SLE-prone strain.

ence in such animals of a unique gene predisposing to autoimmune responses, since the various autoantibodies found in these mice segregate independently in recombinant mice and in F_2 hybrid generations. However, these findings still do not exclude abnormalities of specific subsets of suppressor T cells that control responses to autoantigens, nor do they exclude a secondary role of anti-T cell autoantibodies in accelerating autoimmunity. In general, little current experimental evidence supports the concept that suppressor T cells are important in controlling immune responsiveness to self. Perhaps with the availability of more sophisticated techniques such as experimentally induced specific elimination in vivo of suppressor T cells and the study of autoantigen-specific suppressor T cell function as well as of idiotype-anti-idiotype regulation, clarification of the role of suppressor T cells in autoimmunity will be forthcoming.

Enhanced Helper T Cell Activity, Escape of Tolerance at the T Cell Level, & Other T Cell Abnormalities

As stated, for most immune responses to antigens, collaboration between helper T cells and B cells is required. It has been proposed that unresponsiveness to self is maintained by self-tolerance at the helper T cell level. In activation of such tolerant helper T cells via nonself antigens that cross-react with self—or substitution of helper T cells with certain nonspecific factors—existing B cells not tolerant to self can be activated to produce autoantibodies. This concept derives from the work of Weigle, Chiller, and associates, who found that T and B cells have different antigen concentration requirements for induction of tolerance and that escape from a tolerant state occurs much faster at the B cell level than the T cell level. Thus, after injection of deaggregated human gamma globulin as a tolerogen, tolerance induction in the intact mouse takes 4–5 days for completion. Induction of tolerance in either thymus cells or peripheral T cells is rapid and parallels the kinetics of tolerance induced in the intact animal; peripheral B cells are only slightly slower to assume the tolerant state. Conversely, a latent period of 8–15 days follows injection of the tolerogen before tolerance is noticeable in bone marrow cells, and the tolerant state is not complete in these cells until 21 days have elapsed. Of more importance to self-tolerance is the marked kinetic difference in the spontaneous termination of tolerance in peripheral T and B cells. Peripheral T cells, like intact mice, remain tolerant for 100–150 days, although peripheral B cells return to complete competency 50–60 days after injection of tolerogen. Further studies have shown that the dose of antigen required to induce tolerance in adult thymus cells or peripheral T cells is 100–1000 times less than that required to induce tolerance in adult bone marrow cells or peripheral B cells. Therefore, when central unresponsiveness is induced with small doses of antigen, B cells remain competent or escape very fast from tolerance, whereas T cells become tolerant for a long time. On the basis of these findings, self-tolerance is

apparently maintained despite the presence of self-responding B cells owing to the lack of appropriate help from the tolerant T cell partners. Accordingly, autoimmunity is then inducible either (1) by direct stimulation of autoantigen-reactive B cells with polyclonal activators (see below), and T cell help is not needed; (2) by circumvention of the T cell–unresponsive state to self antigens through nonspecific T cell replacing helper factors; or (3) by induction of helper T cells via altered forms of the tolerated self antigen or with antigen that cross-reacts with the tolerated self antigen. Induction of autoreactivity by certain polyclonal B cell activators will be discussed below. Factors have also been isolated from activated T cells capable of causing competent B cells to differentiate. In theory, such factors that terminate tolerance to certain exogenous and endogenous antigens could be liberated from T cells during responses to allogeneic cells (allogeneic effector factor), presumably because of nonspecific activation of host T cells via a graft-versus-host (GVH) reaction. Presumably, an example of this mechanism is the appearance of autoantibodies, the development of immune complex-mediated glomerulonephritis, and the deposition of immune complexes in the skin of some patients undergoing GVH reactions after bone marrow allotransplantation. However, whether autoimmune responses are indeed induced by such T cell-replacing factors remains to be shown directly. In fact, factors secreted from T cells activated by suboptimal concentrations of ConA failed to induce autoantibodies in recent experiments despite enhancement of polyclonal immunoglobulin synthesis by B cells and induction of antibodies against heterologous serum proteins. This inability of endogenous T cell-replacing factors to collaborate with self-reactive B cells in the generation of autoantibody, if verified further, would suggest that the mechanism of autoimmunity proposed above—ie, the bypass of tolerant T cells by T cell-replacing factors secreted in response to nonspecific stimuli—is unlikely to be of significance in vivo.

Termination of specific immunologic tolerance by immunization either with altered preparations of the tolerated antigen or with antigens that cross-react with the tolerated antigen has been well documented by many investigators. Thus, rabbits made tolerant to bovine serum albumin (BSA) after neonatal injection lose their tolerant state following injection of chemically altered BSA or heterologous albumins that cross-react with BSA. In this situation, the unrelated determinants on the cross-reacting albumins seem to activate T cells, permitting stimulation of B cells competent for both BSA and the unrelated determinants. Presumably, provision of a new carrier determinant for which no self-tolerance has been established bypasses the tolerant T cells and induces them to collaborate with B cells not tolerant to self to produce autoantibodies. A new carrier determinant could arise through some modification of the self molecule—eg, by defects in synthesis or abnormalities in lysosomal breakdown, yielding a split product and exposing new groupings; by combination with a drug; by association with a new antigen that drugs or viruses have induced on cells; or as a result of the presence of exogenous cross-reactive antigens that provide the new carrier with the ability to provoke autoantibody formation. Incorporation of autoantigens into Freund's complete adjuvant frequently endows them with the capacity to stimulate humoral and cellular immune responses in the species from which the antigen originated. Drug-induced autoimmune responses are well documented; for example, autoimmune hemolytic anemia develops in association with the administration of methyldopa, and production of antinuclear antibodies follows treatment with hydralazine, isoniazid, or procainamide. Parenthetically, a genetically controlled polymorphism of the hepatic acetyltransferase enzymes is responsible for different rates of inactivation of these drugs. Slow acetylators are more prone to develop antinuclear antibodies with hydralazine ingestion, but there is no predominance of slow acetylators among systemic lupus erythematosus patients, nor are slow acetylators at greater risk of development of the disease. High titers of cold agglutinins to the I blood group arise as an occasional complication of *Mycoplasma pneumoniae* infections. The autoantibody persists for only a few days but is associated with a short-lived and sometimes severe hemolytic episode. The cold agglutinin is thought to be a cross-reacting autoantibody arising from the response to I-like determinants of the *Mycoplasma*. Anti-I cold agglutinins also develop in rabbits injected with group C streptococcal vaccine, owing to cross-reactivity of the I blood group substance with the immunodominant sugar moiety of the group C carbohydrate. A similar situation probably occurs in rheumatic fever of humans, in which certain streptococci carry antigenic determinants that cross-react with heart muscle or neuronal tissues, resulting in Sydenham's chorea. The brain and nerve damage sometimes occurring in humans after rabies vaccination may develop in much the same way if the rabies vaccine is prepared from heterologous brain tissue, and the same is true of autoantibodies evolving in patients receiving animal hormone replacement therapy, eg, bovine insulin or ACTH. There is also evidence that antigens common to *Trypanosoma cruzi* and cardiac muscle provide some of the immunopathologic lesions seen in Chagas' disease.

Little is known about whether enhanced generalized or autoantigen-specific T helper activity increases in autoimmune diseases. Experiments in murine strains with systemic lupus erythematosus suggest that antigen-nonspecific T helper activity is within normal limits in NZB, (NZB × NZW)F$_1$, and BXSB mice but elevated in MRL/l mice, which are characterized by a profound proliferation of their Lyt-1$^+$ T cell subset. Manipulations such as total lymphoid or whole body irradiation as well as neonatal thymectomy—all of which suppress or completely inhibit the massive T cell proliferation of this strain—result in markedly prolonged survival and reduced levels of autoantibodies.

Notably, MRL/l mice exhibit, even at an early age, a profound progressive defect in ConA-induced T cell proliferation as well as production of and response to exogenous interleukin-2 (IL-2). A similar defect, but less severe, develops in the NZ and BXSB autoimmune mice. IL-2 (formerly called T cell growth factor) is a lymphokine produced by mitogen- or antigen-stimulated T cells. IL-2 has significant T cell regulatory function, since it stimulates thymocyte proliferation, provides helper activity for antibody production, facilitates the induction of cytotoxic T cells, and promotes the proliferation of helper and cytotoxic T lymphocytes in long-term culture. The relationship, if any, of the defect in IL-2 production in SLE strains and their disease remains unclear at this time. It is of interest that despite this defect in vitro, all SLE mice respond well to exogenous and of course to endogenous antigens, including T-dependent antigens, and exhibit normal cytotoxic responses against virus-infected targets as well as allogeneic cells when tested just before the appearance of overt manifestations of disease. These contrasting findings (lack of IL-2 production in vitro but normal or enhanced responsiveness in vivo) suggest either that the in vitro findings do not accurately reflect the in vivo situation; that IL-2 has little influence on the manifestations of immune function in vivo; or that there exist factors other than IL-2 that can induce T cell proliferation as well.

Syngeneic or autologous mixed lymphocyte responses—proliferative reactions that occur after cocultivation of T lymphocytes with autologous or syngeneic non-T cells—are also reported to decrease in both humans and mice with systemic lupus erythematosus. Normally in mice, this response results from the stimulation of Lyt-1$^+$ T cells by antigens, presumably self Ia antigens, expressed on B cells and macrophages. The defect of older affected mice was found to reside in the responder T cell population. The origin of this defect and its primary or secondary importance in the pathogenesis of generalized autoimmunity remain unknown.

Thymic Defects

The thymus, via its epithelial microenvironment and its giant nursing cells, as well as hormones such as thymopoietin and thymosin, is essential for the differentiation of T cells and their helper, suppressor, and cytotoxic subsets. It is unclear whether generalized autoimmunity such as that in systemic lupus erythematosus can result from intrinsic thymic abnormalities, although a variety of related pathologic and hormonal thymic abnormalities have been described. Indeed, all SLE mice develop early thymic atrophy, particularly involving the cortex and, to a lesser extent, the medulla. Such thymic atrophy associated with abnormal fine structure appears by the fourth month in mice, which at 6–7 months of age have lost 70–90% of their cortices. In BXSB and MRL/l mice, which die earlier than the (NZB × NZW)F$_1$ mice, thymic atrophy and cystic necrosis appear by 2 months of age and progress to complete loss of the cortical areas by 4½ and 3½ months of age, respectively. In addition, some have reported that adult NZB mice lack a serum activity, thought to be a thymic hormone, and that administration of thymic hormone (ie, extract of thymic tissue) to NZB mice or transplantation of thymuses or of thymocytes from young NZB mice to the older mice may temporarily prevent some of the immunologic defects and delay the onset of autoimmunity. However, others have failed to inhibit the disease in autoimmune mice treated repeatedly with thymocytes from young counterparts, and attempts to confirm the therapeutic efficacy of thymosin in NZ mice have also failed. Moreover, thymectomy in newborn (NZB × NZW)F$_1$ and BXSB mice has little effect on the time of onset, mortality rate, or development of systemic lupus erythematosus in these strains of mice, and congenitally athymic (NZB × NZW)F$_1$ mice develop disease like their euthymic counterparts. Furthermore, transplantation and exchange of thymuses between the congeneic MRL/l and MRL/n mice, which exhibit markedly differential expressions of systemic lupus erythematosus—the former die by the fifth month of age with severe systemic lupus erythematosus, whereas the latter have very late developing disease, with death occurring at around the second year of life—showed that the genotype of the thymus is not the determining factor in expression of this disease. MRL/l mice thymectomized at birth and then transplanted with either MRL/l or MRL/n thymus developed equally early disease, and MRL/n mice thymectomized and transplanted with MRL/n or MRL/l thymus developed late disease like the thymectomized counterparts. However, in contrast to the situation in NZ and BXSB mice, MRL/l mice expressed the disease only in the presence of a thymus, irrespective of its genotype, and neonatally thymectomized animals did not develop SLE-like disease nor this strain's characteristic massive T cell proliferation. Although these experiments strongly suggest that thymuses of autoimmune mice are not intrinsically abnormal nor necessarily essential for autoimmunity, they do not exclude the possibility that secondary thymic defects or accelerated thymic involution occurring in such mice or humans via a variety of means, including thymocytotoxic antibodies, may accelerate the autoimmune manifestations.

Polyclonal B Cell Activation

The cardinal feature of many—if not all—autoimmune diseases is the production of antibodies against numerous self antigens by the B cells. Although such an abnormality may be secondary to T cell defects (enhanced helper or reduced suppressor function), the alternative possibility that one or more defects at the B cell level are the primary causes of autoimmunity must also be considered. Of course, such B cell defects might secondarily induce T cell abnormalities that could accelerate the disease process. The B cell defects might be intrinsic and genetically imposed—eg, an ability of certain clones of autoreactive B cells to respond without T cell help—or might be extrinsic—eg, activation of B cells by en-

Table 13–4. Polyclonal activators of B lymphocytes.*

Lipopolysaccharide (LPS)
PPD
Staphylococcus aureus protein A
Nocardia water-soluble mitogen
Lipid A - associated protein
2-Mercaptoethanol (2-ME)
a-Thioglycerol (a-TG)
Macrophage- and T cell - derived lymphokines
Fc fragment of immunoglobulins
Proteolytic enzymes, eg, trypsin
Polyanions, eg, dextran sulfate, poly I-C
Antibiotics, eg, nystatin, amphotericin B
Lanatoside C
Mycoplasma
Some viruses and viral components (EBV, gp70, measles)
Parasites *(Trypanosoma brucei, Trypanosoma cruzi, Plasmodium malariae)*

*Reproduced, with permission, from Goodman and Weigle: *Immunology Today* 1981;2:54.

dogenous or exogenous mitogens, the so-called polyclonal activators.

The proposition that polyclonal B cell activators can induce autoantibody production is based on the existence in the body of B cells that are not tolerant to self and the ability of B cell mitogens to stimulate these cells directly or by substituting for helper T cells. Thus, when self antigens are present in low concentrations, B cells with receptor reactivities ranging from low to high avidity are believed to escape tolerance induction and assume competence to interact with autologous antigens while T cells are rendered tolerant. Polyclonal B cell activators may trigger such B cells to produce autoantibody.

A variety of bacterial products, some viruses or viral components, parasites, and other substances may act as polyclonal B cell activators (Table 13–4). The fact that so many exogenous substances can act as polyclonal B cell activators has led to great interest in their ability to induce antibodies directed against the body's own components. Considerable data suggest that this occurs, as indicated by the development of rheumatoid factors and antinuclear, antilymphocyte, antierythrocyte, and anti–smooth muscle antibodies after bacterial, parasitic, or viral infections. Moreover, bacterial lipopolysaccharide induces murine lymphocytes to form a variety of autoantibodies, predominantly IgM class, such as anti-DNA, anti-γ-globulin, antithymocyte, and antierythrocyte autoantibodies. Injection of mice with lipopolysaccharide induces IgM responses against self IgG that account for 25–85% of the total number of IgM-producing cells. Many other bacterial products also provoke polyclonal B cell activation, but their ability to induce autoantibodies remains unknown. Protozoan parasites such as *Trypanosoma brucei, Trypanosoma cruzi,* and *Plasmodium malariae* are also polyclonal B cell activators, and autoimmune responses to DNA, red blood cells, and thymocyte antigens have been observed in animals experimentally infected with *T brucei*. Finally, some viruses act as polyclonal B cell activators, the best known of which is Epstein-Barr virus (EBV). Peripheral mononuclear cells from normal persons and patients with rheumatoid arthritis become activated to secrete polyclonal IgG and IgM anti-γ-globulin antibodies during incubation with EBV, but cells from patients with rheumatoid arthritis produce much greater quantities of antibody with higher affinity than cells from normal persons. EBV activates the B cells directly, without requiring the participation of helper T cells, although T cells can suppress this process. Thus, during EBV-induced infectious mononucleosis, suppressor T cells become activated, preventing B cell activation in vitro by EBV as well as by other polyclonal B cell activators such as pokeweed mitogen. Cultured cells from patients with rheumatoid arthritis generate much less T cell-mediated suppression for EBV-induced polyclonal B cell activation than normal cells. This defect in suppressor T cell function is specific for EBV-induced polyclonal B cell activation, while other T cell suppressor functions such as ConA-induced suppression and even EBV-induced suppression of allogeneically induced polyclonal B cell activation remain within normal limits. In addition, the defective T suppressor function described in patients with rheumatoid arthritis is not a common feature of many other autoimmune diseases, including systemic lupus erythematosus. The relationship of EBV to rheumatoid arthritis is discussed further in the section on viral factors in autoimmunity.

Many other factors such as macrophage- and T cell-derived lymphokines, Fc fragments of immunoglobulins, proteolytic enzymes such as trypsin, polyanions, and certain antibiotics may express properties of polyclonal B cell activators, but whether or not they can induce autoantibodies has not been determined. In general, autoantibodies induced by polyclonal activators are transient, of low affinity, and primarily of the IgM isotype, although induction of IgG type rheumatoid factors and anti-DNA by certain forms of lipopolysaccharide, especially those high in lipid A, has recently been demonstrated. Whether — and, if so, how often — such polyclonal activation occurs in vivo is unclear, but it may be partly responsible for the low levels of autoreactive antibody found in the sera of normal individuals. However, these autoantibodies are usually of such low avidity that they are of little significance. A possible exception may be rheumatoid factor induction by EBV in rheumatoid arthritis.

Polyclonal activation of B cells has also been suggested as a possible contributing factor to the spontaneous SLE-like disease of several murine strains. Indeed, B cells of all of these strains are polyclonally activated very early in life. This polyclonal activation is manifested by hypergammaglobulinemia, large numbers of immunoglobulin-containing or immunoglobulin-secreting cells in their spleens, excessive production of immunoglobulin in splenocyte cultures, and production of anti-hapten antibodies in vitro and in vivo. Neither the role of this polyclonal

activation nor its relationship to specific autoantibody production has been totally clarified. Introduction of the xid mutation of partially immunodeficient CBA/N mice into NZB mice prevents the development of high numbers of spontaneously activated B cells and other autoimmune phenomena. However, studies in recombinant strains of NZB mice as well as their F_2 hybrids showed that the polyclonal B cell activation segregated independently of autoantibody production. Moreover, transfer of autoimmunity with bone marrow of SLE mice into histocompatible normal mice and the absence of autoimmunity after reciprocal transfers of normal bone marrow cells into SLE strains further suggests the irrelevance of polyclonal non-lymphoid cell-associated activators as primary causative agents of murine systemic lupus erythematosus. This conclusion is reinforced by the following observations: (1) known potent polyclonal B cell activators induce primarily IgM autoantibodies, yet the tissue damage that accompanies most autoimmune diseases is mediated by IgG autoantibodies; (2) induction of autoantibodies by polyclonal activators is transient and disappears with elimination of the activator; and (3) no endogenous polyclonal B cell activator has been proved as an exclusive property of sera or tissue extracts of animals or humans with systemic lupus erythematosus. These arguments, of course, do not exclude a secondary role of polyclonal B cell activators as accelerators of autoimmunity in genetically predisposed individuals.

Macrophage Defects

There is general agreement that the mononuclear phagocyte serves an essential role in the cellular and molecular events that underlie immune competence by processing and presenting antigen to lymphocytes and by generating a number of humoral factors that influence the activities of lymphocytes. Moreover, the phagocytic function is important in disposal of immunologically undesirable materials such as immune complexes. Surprisingly, little information is available on the functional state of mononuclear phagocytic cells in autoimmune disorders. Most experiments deal with the capacity of macrophages from mice and humans with generalized autoimmune diseases to process and degrade antigens and the ability of the reticuloendothelial system to remove immune complexes or other particles from sera of such individuals. Most reports on the phagocytic activity of NZB-derived macrophages have shown elevated activity in terms of antigen phagocytosis, although some data suggest that the NZB cells do not effectively degrade the ingested antigen. Studies on the clearance of inert particles or immune complexes by macrophages of NZ mice are inconclusive. Some have shown a reduction in clearance; others portray clearance as increased or normal; and still others claim normal clearance but weak affinity for binding to Fc receptors of Kupffer cells and therefore easy re-release into the circulation. Decreased in vivo clearance of antibody-sensitized red blood cells has been described in humans with autoimmune disorders. Whether this defect is a primary one resulting from a defect in Fc or complement receptor number or function or is secondary to occupation of the receptors by circulating immune complexes formed in vivo is not clear at present.

Phagocytes are essential for the development of various lymphocyte functions, particularly those of the T lymphocytes. As stated above, most T lymphocyte activities require that the macrophage take up and present the antigen in a process modulated by the I region of the MHC. Macrophages from newborn mice, tested at an age when immune responsiveness is low and tolerance is easily induced, present antigen poorly. This defect has been correlated with the small number of macrophages that bear Ia antigens in spleens of neonatal mice compared to adult mice. Whether the ontogenic development of Ia antigens on macrophages of autoimmune and normal mice differ (earlier development in the former than the latter), accounting for the lack of tolerance to self, remains to be determined.

Defects in Tolerance Induction

Studies have been performed in mice with systemic lupus erythematosus to determine whether there are defects in tolerance induction. Indeed, all murine systemic lupus erythematosus strains studied were defective in tolerance induced to deaggregated human gamma globulin, bovine gamma globulin, or hapten-substituted γ-globulin in vitro and in vivo. Some studies attributed this defect to T cells, others to B cells, and yet others to both levels. Whether difficulty in tolerance induction applies to antigens other than deaggregated gamma globulins, both exogenous and endogenous, has not been investigated comprehensively. However, experiments with hapten-modified self cells have shown that MRL/l mice are as easily tolerized as immunologically normal mice, suggesting that the defect might not be universally applicable to all antigens.

Defects of Multipotential Stem Cells, Committed Progenitor Cells of Various Hematopoietic Lineages, & B Cell Precursors

At present, the best way of defining the humoral, cellular, microenvironmental, and viral factors from which autoimmunity develops is to transfer autoimmune disease by using specific tissues or tissue extracts from strains of animals having a genetic predisposition to autoimmunity into recipients without this defect. Such transfer studies have been performed among systemic lupus erythematosus murine strains and their normal counterparts. Thus, NZB autoimmune disease has been transferred with this strain's fetal liver, bone marrow, or spleen cells into lethally irradiated, normal histocompatible strains of mice. Lethally irradiated NZB mice transplanted with H-2-compatible allogeneic normal mouse bone marrow or spleen cells do not develop autoimmunity. In some reverse transfers, NZB bone marrow cell suspensions were depleted of T cells, the H-2-compatible normal recipients were thymectomized, or anti-T cell an-

tibodies were given after transplantation and disease developed nonetheless. These experiments have been cited as evidence that many of the NZB peculiarities may be intrinsic to hematopoietic cells and may develop independently of T cell aberrations. However, non-H-2 incompatibilities between donor and recipient determined by genes in loci other than H-2 potentially complicate these interpretations. Similar experiments have been performed between BXSB male and female SLE mice. The male BXSB mice develop severe early systemic lupus erythematosus with 50% mortality rates at 5–6 months of age, whereas the females develop late systemic lupus erythematosus with 50% mortality rates after 18 months (Table 13–3). Reciprocal transfers of bone marrow or spleen cells between these mice show that male cells can transfer early disease in both lethally irradiated male and female recipients, whereas female cells cause late disease regardless of the recipient's sex. Further experiments indicate that transfers of spleen cells from older male BXSB mice with clear-cut disease produces disease in recipients no faster than transfer of cells derived from premorbid mice. The conclusion is, therefore, that the active cells in these transfers are stem or precursor cells—not autoantibody-secreting B cells—and that the development of BXSB disease does not result from an accumulation of defects among stem cells, which are equally abnormal throughout the animal's life. Like the NZB mice, transfer of BXSB male disease by bone marrow cells can be accomplished in the absence of T cells in the inoculum and in thymectomized female recipients. This finding implies that the defect of this strain of mice is associated with precursors of the B cell lineage.

Defects in Idiotype–Anti-idiotype Network & Idiotype Mimicry of Autoantigen

As stated above, B and T cells and their soluble products may express idiotypic or anti-idiotypic determinants through which regulation of immune responses occurs. Anti-idiotypic antibodies may suppress or enhance immune responses. In most instances of autoanti-idiotypic responses to antibodies against exogenous antigens, the autoanti-idiotypic antibodies suppress the original immune response expressing the corresponding idiotype. In addition to anti-idiotype-mediated suppression, stimulation of Ab_1 by anti-idiotypes representing the "mirror image" of antigens that Jerne postulated has been described in recent experiments. Initial studies provided evidence that expression of idiotypes specific for Ab_1 may reappear on Ab_3, since Ab_4 bound to Ab_1 and Ab_1 itself inhibited the binding of radiolabeled Ab_3 to Ab_4. These results suggest that the immune idiotypic network is not open-ended but somehow circular. In further experiments, animals immunized with Ab_2 (anti-idiotype) developed not only Ab_3 (anti-anti-idiotype) but Ab_1 (idiotype) as well, suggesting that Ab_2 contains antigenic determinants (epitopes) conformationally similar to those on the inciting antigen, thereby fulfilling the predicted hypothesis of an "internal mirror image.'' Together, these observations suggest that a given antibody—as well as an autoantibody—could be viewed as the product both of original stimulation by the antigen and of stimulation by Ab_2 (anti-idiotype) that can internally mimic the antigen. The induction of idiotypes in the absence of antigen has been demonstrated in several systems. For example, monoclonal IgM antibodies directed against sheep erythrocytes, when injected into normal mice, induced direct plaque-forming cells of the same specificity as the injected antibodies. Moreover, induction of anti-tobacco mosaic virus antibodies in mice injected with specific anti-idiotypic antibodies has been observed. In this instance, Ab_2 behaved like the antigen: It reacted with anti-tobacco mosaic virus antibodies and also promoted the synthesis of anti-tobacco mosaic virus antibodies in the total absence of tobacco mosaic virus. Thus, these antibodies may be considered the internal images of tobacco mosaic virus. Furthermore, injection of experimental mice with anti-idiotypic antibodies to the murine MHC ($H-2K^k$ specificity) induced anti-$H-2K^k$ antibodies in the absence of exposure to $H-2K^k$ antigen. Generation of helper and killer T cell subsets via anti-idiotypic antibodies is also known.

In some instances, anti-idiotypic antibodies not only induced the idiotype but also mimicked functional properties of the inciting antigen unrelated to the latter's capacity to stimulate the immune system. For example, anti-idiotypic antibodies prepared against bovine anti-insulin mimicked the action of insulin by interacting with insulin receptors on tissues and stimulating the physiologic action of insulin itself. In this instance, a portion of the anti-idiotype, presumably part of its combining site, apparently resembled the insulin site reactive with insulin receptors. Similarly, anti-idiotypic antibodies against antibodies to retinol-binding protein or to alprenolol (a β-adrenergic antagonist) competed with retinol-binding protein or dihydroalprenolol binding to specific receptors on intestinal epithelial cells or red blood cells, respectively.

From these observations, one can speculate that autoimmune responses may be the result of defects in immunoregulation that allow underproduction or overproduction of anti-idiotypic antibodies. Such defects would permit either unchecked production of autoantibodies or cyclic stimulation of Ab_1 (idiotype) in the absence of the inciting antigen, respectively. Ultimately, such defects must be connected to the B cell–helper T cell–suppressor T cell circuit and their idiotypes and anti-idiotypes.

To summarize: A variety of T and B cell immunologic defects may lead to the expression of transient or permanent autoimmune manifestations. No one of these mechanisms excludes the others; in fact, concerted action is likely, since defects of the T cell component are reflected by B cells and vice versa. Some of these abnormalities, such as in suppressor or helper cells, can be operative in either organ-specific or non–organ-specific autoimmune disease—whereas others, such as polyclonal B cell activators and early

thymic involution, whose effects are non–organ-specific, would relate more closely to generalized diseases.

GENETIC FACTORS IN AUTOIMMUNE DISEASES

In human autoimmune diseases and in many induced or spontaneous animal models of autoimmunity, the role of genetic factors in determining the incidence, onset, and nature of the autoimmune process is clearly evident. However, in the case of most of these conditions, it has not been possible to attribute autoimmune predisposition to the action of a single genetic locus.

Primary candidates suspected of determining susceptibility or resistance to the development of autoimmune and, of course, other types of diseases are those genes that code for the magnitude and nature of immune responses to antigens. These are the MHC genes and the immunoglobulin genes. In regard to autoimmune diseases, associations with both MHC genes and immunoglobulin allotypic genes have been described. After reviewing the large number of studies available, one must conclude that most autoimmune diseases, at least in Caucasian populations, are associated, albeit not to a very satisfactory degree, with the alleles DR2, DR3, DR4, and DR5 (Table 13–5). Seropositive rheumatoid arthritis, which is independent of HLA-ABC, correlates chiefly with DR4, whereas systemic lupus erythematosus, once linked with HLA-B8, is now generally associated with DR2 and DR3. This distinction could imply a very different pathogenetic mechanism for these 2 diseases, usually considered to be closely related. Associations found for Caucasian populations may not apply for other ethnic groups, and vice versa. For example, Graves' disease is closely related to B8/DR3 in Caucasoids but to DR5 and DR8 in Japanese populations. Moreover, no uniform associations are observed among patients classified as having ''organ-specific autoimmune diseases'' or among those having ''generalized autoimmune diseases,'' suggesting that each autoimmune disease has, at least in part, a distinct genetic background, although one frequently sees simultaneous expression of multiple organ-specific autoimmune diseases in a given individual and overlap of serologic findings. For example, there is a high incidence of pernicious anemia in patients with Hashimoto's disease (and vice versa); of Addison's disease in persons with autoimmune thyroid disease; and of rheumatoid factor and arthritis in patients with systemic lupus erythematosus. Furthermore, patients with organ-specific disorders are slightly more prone to develop cancer in the affected organ, whereas generalized lymphoreticular neoplasia shows up regularly along with non–organ-specific disease. The genetic, environmental, and immunologic factors predisposing to these combined abnormalities are not known. A high frequency of generalized autoimmune disease also accompanies

Table 13—5. HLA-DR and diseases.*

	Antigen	Relative Risk
Multiple sclerosis	DR2	4.1
Optic neuritis	DR2	2.4
Goodpasture's syndrome	DR2	15
C2 deficiency	DR2	Linked to A25, B18
Dermatitis herpetiformis	DR3	15.4
Celiac disease	DR3	10.8 (also DR7)
Sicca syndrome	DR3	9.7
Addison's disease	DR3	6.3
Graves' disease	DR3	3
Juvenile diabetes	DR3	5.6 (also DR4)
Myasthenia gravis	DR3	2.5
Systemic lupus erythematosus	DR3	5.8
Idiopathic membranous nephropathy	DR3	12
Rheumatoid arthritis	DR4	4.2
Pemphigus	DR4	14.4
IgA nephropathy	DR4	4
Hydralazine-induced systemic lupus erythematosus	DR4	5.6
Hashimoto's disease	DR5	3.2
Pernicious anemia	DR5	5.4
Juvenile rheumatoid arthritis	DR5	5.2

*Reproduced, with permission, from Dausset J, Contu L: Page 513 in: *Immunology 80: Progress in Immunology.* Academic Press, 1980.

deficiencies in certain complement components. Thus, patients with C2 deficiency, an autosomal recessive trait, often have vasculitis, skin rashes, recurrent infections, and a general picture similar to that of systemic lupus erythematosus. Similarly, a high incidence of systemic lupus erythematosus or similar syndromes characterizes patients with C1r, C1s, or C3 deficiencies. Many autoimmune diseases also affect more females, suggesting a linkage with the X chromosome, although this association may be hormonally related (see below).

In general, typing for MHC specificities, particularly those encoded by the putative immune response D/DR locus of HLA, should eventually provide diagnostic benefits relative to clinical autoimmune disorders. These benefits include better definition of homogeneous subgroups of patients with a given disease, a more accurate prognosis for such patients, and identification of individuals likely to develop the disease—an indication of expected severity and development of preventive measures via genetic counseling. However, considering the clinical spectrum of autoimmune disease and the mode of inheritance, it is unlikely that just one gene alone is responsible for susceptibility to the development of autoimmune disease. How HLA genes might be involved in the susceptibility to disease is not yet clear, but possibilities include effects on the magnitude of humoral and cellular responses and on immunoregulation (helper, suppressor, and cytotoxic T cell functions), metabolic influences especially on steroid hormones, and effects on antigen handling by phagocytic cells. Of particular interest is a recent report describing defects in Fc receptor function associated with the HLA-B8/DR3 haplotype. The possibility also exists that some of

the associations between HLA and disease simply represent strong linkage disequilibrium between susceptibility genes and certain HLA haplotypes.

Certain genes coding for V regions (antigen-binding site) or C regions (effector function such as complement fixation and binding to cellular Fc receptors) of immunoglobulins also have an apparent association with particular diseases, including autoimmune diseases, as the importance of immunoglobulin allotypic markers in determining susceptibility to autoimmune disorders suggests. For example, expression of rheumatoid factors in crosses of 129 and C57BL/6 mice depends in part upon a gene linked to the C locus. Thus, high levels of IgA anti-IgG2a (Igh-1) autoantibodies, like those found in sera of the 129 strain, appear only in Igh-1aa mice, whereas IgM anti-IgG1 of the C57BL/6 type are detectable mainly in Igh-1bb mice, and both types of rheumatoid factors are depressed in heterozygous Igh-1ab animals. In other experimental murine systems, autoimmune manifestations and allotypes have been linked with antibody production against autologous erythrocytes, thyroglobulin, and acetylcholine receptor. Similarly, in humans, Gm allotypic homozygosity has been related to the risk of anti-γ-globulin development, and the presence of certain Gm allotypes was associated with autoimmune chronic active hepatitis, myasthenia gravis, systemic lupus erythematosus, insulin-dependent (juvenile-onset) diabetes with serum anti-insulin antibodies, and Graves' disease. Combined assessment of HLA haplotype and of Gm allotype in Japanese families that had more than 2 first-degree relatives affected by Graves' disease provided an excellent predictor of risk for this disease, since all affected individuals had a given combination of these 2 markers, although siblings who shared the disease-associated haplotypes did not necessarily suffer from the disease. Thus, one may expect that HLA and immunoglobulin allotyping, along with establishing other genetic markers and environmental factors, would allow fairly accurate prediction of autoimmune diseases in the future. In regard to allotypic immunoglobulin markers and diseases, it should be noted that idiotypic determinants coded by V genes have been linked to heavy chain C region allotypic markers of mice. Since idiotypic determinants on lymphocyte membranes appear to have fundamental roles in immune regulation, the development of techniques for their assessment, such as hybridoma technology that makes monoclonal idiotypes and anti-idiotypes available, may provide further means of improving genetic analysis of autoimmune disorders.

The genetic control and mechanisms of gene action in autoimmunity have also been studied in animals with spontaneous or induced autoimmune diseases. The best examples are mice with spontaneous lupus-like syndromes. The H-2 haplotypes, lymphocyte surface alloantigens, and IgG allotypes of this kind of mice are shown in Table 13–3. Unfortunately, no consistency or uniformity in any one of these markers is seen in these strains despite the expression of lupus-like syndromes in all of them. Two additional approaches have been used to determine the genetic factors associated with murine systemic lupus erythematosus: The first model results from crossing the several SLE-prone strains and then analyzing their F_1 hybrids in the hope of finding common genetic denominators among these strains; the second model involves analysis of F_2 hybrids and recombinant inbred strains so as to interrelate the individual immunopathologic and histocompatibility traits of SLE-prone strains. In initial studies by Adams and associates, offspring of (NZB × NZW)F_1 back-crossed with NZB and of (NZB × NZW)F_1 out-crossed with NZC mice were studied, and the genes determining expression of lupus nephritis and of autoimmune anemia, respectively, were assessed. Of the 3 genes necessary for the occurrence of lupus nephritis (lpn genes) in the NZB/NZW hybrid mice, one (lpn-1) is in the NZB strain and 2 (lpn-2, lpn-3) are in the NZW strain. Of the 2 genes governing autoimmune anemia (aia-1, aia-2) in the NZB/NZC hybrid mice, both are in the NZB strain and one (aia-2) is also in the NZC strain. Thus, the autoimmune diseases of these mice clearly depend on combinations of genes that are not pathogenic individually. Of these 5 genes, only one, lpn-2, is tightly linked to the MHC in these investigators' opinion. According to Adams, of the 3 genes governing lupus nephritis, none can be a heavy chain V gene, because these are on the murine chromosome 12 (in humans, on chromosome 14), whereas lpn-1 and lpn-2 are on chromosome 17, and lpn-3 is not linked to the heavy chain allotype, as clearly shown. Moreover, lpn-1 and lpn-2 are not kappa light chain V genes, since these are located on the murine chromosome 6 (in humans, on chromosome 2). The finding that aia-1,

governing autoimmune anemia, is on chromosome 4 again precludes its being a heavy chain or kappa light chain V gene. Similarly, these genes are not related to the murine lambda light chain gene or to the J chain gene, since the former is located on chromosome 16 (in humans on chromosome 22) and the latter is located on chromosome 5 of the mouse. Therefore, the evidence indicates involvement in murine systemic lupus erythematosus of classes of genes additional to MHC and V genes. Studies by Raveche and associates similarly showed that antithymocyte production is controlled by a single codominant gene and that an independent dominant gene controls the production of autoantibodies to ssDNA. Apparently neither gene is H-2–linked. At present, the products of such codominant (ie, producing their effect in the heterozygous state), non-MHC, non-V genes are unknown. Additional studies in F_2 crosses of autoimmune mice performed by Dixon and associates, and in recombinant inbred strains by Raveche, Steinberg, and Riblet and associates, clearly demonstrate that murine systemic lupus erythematosus is not the result of an autoimmune gene that predisposes an individual to a wide variety of autoimmune phenomena but rather of multiple abnormal genes that are independently inherited and independently expressed, free from any link with a particular H-2 haplotype or immunoglobulin genes.

Further analysis of these SLE mice shows that individual accelerating factors characteristic for each strain account for differences in the onset and severity of disease as well as mortality rates among them (Table 13–3). In the BXSB mouse, the accelerating factor is associated with the Y chromosome but not with sex hormones and results in much earlier disease and death in males than in females. In the MRL mice, the accelerating factor is the autosomal recessive lpr gene that accounts not only for proliferation of Lyt-1$^+$ T cells but also for a significantly accelerated onset of disease in homozygous MRL/Mp-lpr/lpr mice compared to congeneic MRL/Mp-+/+ mice that do not have the lpr gene. The significance of these genetically determined accelerating factors in the expression of murine systemic lupus erythematosus is indicated in F_1 hybrids of BXSB mice and in transfers of the lpr gene of MRL/l mice to other SLE and normal strains. When the BXSB mouse is used as mother, it complements the predisposition to lupus in both NZB and NZW strains and produces F_1 hybrids quite similar to the traditional mice, with female offspring dying first; but BXSB females crossed with normal strains produce F_1s with little or no disease. However, when the BXSB is used as father in crosses with all other genetically predisposed SLE strains such as NZB, NZW, and MRL/l, then a male-first early SLE develops. Similarly, establishment of the lpr gene in a homozygous state on NZB or MRL/n late–SLE-developing strains results in acceleration of the onset and course of lupus; for example, in NZB mice, the 50% mortality rate drops from 16 months to less than 5 months, and in MRL/n mice from 17 months to 5 months. However, in spite of inducing lymphoproliferation, the lpr gene does not cause early systemic lupus erythematosus in normal mice with no SLE background to influence. In New Zealand hybrid mice, the female hormones (see below) apparently hasten disease onset and death in females compared to males. Thus, murine systemic lupus erythematosus is caused by many independently segregating genetic factors which in the presence of an endogenous or exogenous accelerator express themselves early, whereas in the absence of the accelerator they appear late in life. Future analysis of certain genetic markers whose location on a given chromosome is known and of their possible segregation or association with autoimmune phenomena and autoantibody production in appropriate recombinant and F_2 mice may pinpoint the exact location of the multiple abnormal genes responsible for this disease and provide the basis for further genetic characterization of humans with such multifactorial disease as systemic lupus erythematosus.

HORMONAL FACTORS IN AUTOIMMUNITY

Sex hormones as well as X chromosome- or Y chromosome-linked genes may influence the expression of autoimmune diseases. It is well known that hormones of the hypophysis, thyroid, parathyroid, adrenals, and gonads affect homeostasis of the lymphoid system and responses to antigens by as yet undefined mechanisms. Within the confines of the complex homeostatic role hormones play in lymphocyte function, the effects of the gonads on the immune response and autoimmune disease are particularly apparent. In general, females are far more susceptible to most connective tissue diseases than males. For example, the incidence of systemic lupus erythematosus in women after puberty is 9 times that in men. There is no apparent explanation for this sex difference, but experimental and clinical studies in humans and animals tend to incriminate, at least in part, female sex hormones rather than X chromosome-associated genes. Consistently, females and castrated males, both in lower animals and in humans, have higher levels of immunoglobulin and higher specific immune responses than sexually normal males, although the direct immunosuppressive effects of testosterone or immunoenhancing effects of estrogens have not been shown conclusively. Recent findings of elevated estriol levels in SLE patients with manifestations of Klinefelter's syndrome and of failure of the castrated female monozygotic twin of a lupus victim to develop the disease suggest further that chronic estrogenic stimulation may play an important role in the prevalence of systemic lupus erythematosus in females (see Chapter 20). Indeed, although the total amount of estrogens recovered from female human SLE subjects is normal, estradiol activity may be enhanced by abnormalities in female hormone metabolic patterns. Thus, Lahita and Kunkel found that women with systemic lupus erythematosus had elevations in the 16α-hydroxylated compounds of 16α-hydroxyestrone and

estriol in their serum compared to normal subjects (see Chapter 20).

As in human systemic lupus erythematosus, studies by Talal and associates in the murine SLE model of (NZB × NZW)F_1 mice implicate sex hormones as accelerating factors in autoantibody levels and the overall earlier mortality rate in females than in males. Castrated NAB × NZW)F_1 males resemble females in that they have an accelerated autoimmune disease detectable at the age of 6 months. However, testosterone or dihydrotestosterone inhibits the onset of this autoimmune disease in female mice and in castrated male (NZB × NZW)F_1 mice following subcutaneous implantation of the androgens in Silastic tubes. On the other hand, although prepubertal castration of female (NZB × NZW)F_1 mice is without effect, estrogen administration accelerates overt disease in both males and females. The mechanisms whereby sex hormones modify disease in (NZB × NZW)F_1 mice are largely unknown, but postulated explanations include effects on antigen presentation and handling by the immune system and androgen-induced enhancement of suppressor T cell activity or of tolerance inducibility.

The accelerating effects of female factors such as estrogens is by no means applicable in all human and animal autoimmune diseases. For example, the incidence of ankylosing spondylitis, possibly an autoimmune disease, is higher in males than females. Moreover, in murine models of spontaneous lupus other than the NZB/NZW, the females are not hardest hit. For example, in the MRL/l mouse, sex hormones appear to have little effect, since the females die only slightly earlier than the males; and, contrastingly, BXSB males develop the disease much earlier (50% mortality rate at 6 months of age) than the females (50% at 18 months). In this last strain, the male sex-determined accelerated autoimmunity is Y chromosome-linked and not hormonally mediated. This conclusion is based on the following: (1) Castration of males has no effect on the course of the disease; (2) the disease is inherited in a Y-linked or holandric (father to son) fashion in F_1 crosses of BXSB males with other autoimmune strains; and (3) transfer of early, severe lupus by male BXSB bone marrow or spleen cells is independent of the lethally irradiated BXSB recipient's sex. Interestingly enough, a human counterpart of BXSB male-predominant disease was recently described by Lahita and Kunkel in familial studies of patients with systemic lupus erythematosus. They observed that full expression of the disease predominated in fathers and sons, whereas females, despite having some autoantibodies, did not develop fully expressed systemic lupus erythematosus with associated glomerulonephritis.

VIRAL FACTORS IN AUTOIMMUNITY

Viruses are frequently associated with autoimmune diseases of humans and animals. Such infectious agents may be acquired by horizontal or vertical transmission, and they may promote autoimmune reactions by many and varied mechanisms—among them, polyclonal activation of lymphocytes, release of subcellular organelles after cellular destruction, associative recognition phenomena in which insertion of viral antigens into cellular membranes may promote reactions against preexisting self components, and direct infection and thus functional impairment of certain subsets of regulatory cells such as suppressor T cells.

Among the human viruses, EBV has been most prominently considered as a cause of autoimmune diseases because of its ubiquity, persistence, and ability to act on the immune system. For example, EBV acts as a polyclonal B cell activator stimulating mitoses and immunoglobulin secretion as well as promoting autoantibody production, especially rheumatoid factor, during the course of primary infection. The sera of rheumatoid patients contain an antibody that recognizes unique EBV-induced antigens (RAP: rheumatoid arthritis precipitation; and RANA: rheumatoid arthritis nuclear antigen) present in extracts of an EBV-carrying B type lymphoblastoid cell line of human origin. Furthermore, T cells from these patients have less capacity to suppress EBV-induced B lymphocyte transformation than their normal counterparts. Based on both of these findings, this virus could be involved in the pathogenesis of rheumatoid arthritis. However, seroepidemiologic studies indicate that (1) as a group, subjects with rheumatoid arthritis have the same exposure to EBV as individuals without the disease; (2) antibodies to EBV-associated antigens are not a unique characteristic of such patients but can be found, albeit less often, in normal persons; (3) no evidence proves that EBV enters the joint space; (4) arthritis does not accompany certain EBV syndromes, such as infectious mononucleosis; and (5) in patients with early (under 6 weeks) rheumatoid arthritis, there is no elevation of anti-EBV antibodies, and in one patient with early rheumatoid arthritis no serologic evidence of prior EBV infection or antibody to RANA antigen was detected. These findings refute a primary role for EBV in the etiology of rheumatoid arthritis.

A variety of other viruses have been incriminated as causative agents of autoimmune diseases in humans: myxoviruses, hepatitis viruses, cytomegaloviruses, coxsackieviruses, retroviruses, and others. Most of these viruses induce autoantibodies during natural infections and also autoimmune disease-like immunopathologic characteristics such as vasculitis and glomerulonephritis—which, however, appear to be caused primarily by specific virus–viral antibody immune complexes rather than by autoantibody-antigen complexes. An oncornavirus-associated origin of human systemic lupus erythematosus, although claimed, has not been proved. Thus, although particles resembling viruses have been observed in lymphocytes and kidneys of SLE patients, it is generally agreed that these particles are artifacts or cell structures that have no relationship to viruses. Moreover, isolation of C type viruses or antigens thereof from spleens and placentas of SLE patients is disputed; C type virus antigens, in spite of claims to the contrary, are not conclusively established as components of glomerular immune complex deposits, and repeated attempts to demonstrate specific antibodies against C type viruses in sera of SLE patients have failed. Although increased titers of antibodies against certain viruses, such as measles, have been found in sera of SLE patients compared to normals, this finding has been considered nonspecific—the result of these patients' hypergammaglobulinemia. Despite these negative results, the search for a virus associated with human systemic lupus erythematosus continues. Interestingly, patients with systemic lupus erythematosus have been found to express, in serum, increased levels of a unique interferon (IFN-α)—produced normally by leukocytes in response to viral and nonviral stimuli—which, unlike regular IFN-α, was inactivated at pH 2. Although increased interferon levels have been observed by some investigators to be more prevalent in patients with active SLE, others have not been able to relate any individual serologic or clinical marker of disease to the presence of interferon. Thus, the importance of this finding is unclear at this time.

For obvious reasons, investigative studies of the relationship between viruses and autoimmune disease are best conducted by using animal models that have characteristics in common with the disease in humans. Thus, a viral origin has been established in the disease of Aleutian minks involving a small DNA virus; in equine infectious anemia associated with a transmissible C type viruslike agent that has been isolated; and possibly in canine systemic lupus erythematosus comprising anti-DNA antibodies, rheumatoid factor, anti-red blood cell antibodies, hypergammaglobulinemia, LE cells, and C type virus.

The best demonstration of a role for viruses and their antigenic components in the pathogenesis of autoimmune disease has been in the murine SLE model. Initial reports that NZB disease could be transferred to normal mice with cell-free extracts and filtrates of NZB splenocytes were unconfirmed. Subsequent research demonstrated that NZB mice express infectious xenotropic type C RNA virus throughout life and in high titer. The virus is not found in the mouse itself but becomes apparent after cocultivation of its tissue homogenates with heterologous cells such as those from cats. The correlation between high titers of xenotropic virus production in vitro by tissue homogenates of NZB mice and autoimmunity then suggested a cause-and-effect relationship. This concept was strengthened when viral antigen–antiviral antibody immune complexes were recovered from renal lesions in NZB and (NZB $\times$ NZW)F$_1$ mice. The failure to transmit autoimmune disease with cell-free filtrates was explained by the fact that xenotropic C viruses cannot productively infect mouse cells, only cells of heterologous species. Subsequently, the magnified expression of xenotropic virus in NZB mice was established by Datta and Schwartz as a genetically determined trait controlled by 2 independently segregating, autosomal dominant loci (Nzn-1 and Nzv-2). This demonstration has facilitated genetic analysis of the relationship between xenotropic virus and autoimmunity. The hybrid chosen for study of this relationship was NZB/SWR, because NZB are homozygous for the dominant alleles of viral expression whereas SWR are homozygous for the recessive alleles and do not spontaneously develop autoimmune disease. Analysis of the F_1, F_2, and back-cross progeny of NZB ×SWR mice demonstrated the following: (1) Some progeny whose tissue homogenates express titers of xenotropic virus as high as those of the NZB parent fail to develop signs of autoimmunity; (2) virus-negative offspring from these crosses still develop autoantibodies; (3) the phenotypic expression of virus does not correlate positively with the incidence of glomerular lesions; and (4) levels of the viral antigen gp70 do not correlate with the development of nephritis in these crosses. No correlation between autoimmunity and xenotropic or ecotropic C type virus levels has been observed by Datta and associates in recombinant lines of NZB and C58 mice. Gp70, the major glycoprotein component of the envelope of type C RNA viruses, is found in tissues and sera of virtually all mice. Structural studies of serum gp70 indicate that it is the same in all strains and resembles the gp70 of the NZB xenotropic virus. Its presence is independent of the expression of complete retrovirus particles, and it appears to be produced primarily in the liver.

Gp70 has also been implicated in the pathogenesis of lupus nephritis in spontaneous murine models, because of the high concentrations of gp70 in the sera of these mice and because gp70 is deposited in diseased glomeruli along with specific antibody, complement, and nuclear antigens and antibodies. However, similarly high levels of identical gp70 have been detected in several immunologically normal strains of mice, indicating that gp70 per se is not the factor that determines disease expression. In contrast to normal strains of mice, only SLE mice produced antibodies against xenotropic gp70 and had gp70-anti-gp70 complexes in their sera. Notably, the presence of such complexes related to the expression of glomerulonephritis in (NZB × NZW)F_2 mice. The gp70 that participates in the formation of immune complexes was no different antigenically or structurally by tryptic peptide map analysis from the free xenotropic gp70 found at varying levels in sera of all murine strains. Thus, the high serum levels of xenotropic gp70 apparently do not in themselves cause murine nephritis; rather, the unique ability of autoimmune mice to respond to this autoantigen is the critical factor. To summarize: These studies indicate that although xenotropic virus and viral antigens may participate secondarily in the formation of immunopathologic lesions in the NZB mouse and its crosses, they are not a primary cause.

Additionally, chronic viral infections may have a secondary role in autoimmune diseases if their superimposition on an autoimmune genetic background accelerates autoimmunity. For example, lymphocytic choriomeningitis virus, polyoma virus, and retrovirus infections have all been observed to induce or elevate antinuclear antibodies and SLE-like disease in mice. Although these viruses probably act in part by causing antivirus antibody and immune complexes to form, their stimulation of antinuclear and other autoantibody formation must be considered as potential means of enhancing systemic lupus erythematosus. Neonatal lymphocytic choriomeningitis virus infection changes the 50% mortality rate point caused by SLE-like disease from 16 months to less than 5 months in the NZB female, from 18 to 9 months in the BXSB female, and from 17 to 12 months in the MRL/Mp-+/+ mice. In contrast, normal C3H and SWR mice infected neonatally with lymphocytic choriomeningitis virus and examined from birth to 2 years of age do not develop the fatal SLE-like disease. The transient appearance of autoreactive splenic T cells within 3 days after injection of lymphocytic choriomeningitis virus has been reported in adult mice, and this phenomenon may account for the expression of enhanced autoimmunity in mice with immune disregulation.

In general, viruses—via their polyclonal B cell-activating potential, their cytolytic capacity, their possible tropisms for certain subpopulations of lymphoid cells, and their possible capacity to associate with and convert autoantigens to foreign antigens—may induce aberrant responses and autoagression, with subsequent development of autoimmune manifestations.

• • •

CONCLUSIONS

The study of autoimmunity brings together a fascinating diversity of fields, including immunology, pathology, endocrinology, virology, genetics, and molecular biology. This chapter describes some of the intellectual terrain that has been explored in the search of what we know at present about autoimmune disorders and the reasons for their occurrence.

The role of self recognition in the immune system has been discussed in light of recent experimental data. These findings indicate that under certain conditions, recognition of self-determinants is not totally forbidden or harmful. Thus, before T cells can differentiate to become effector cells, they must recognize both foreign antigen and self-MHC determinants. Furthermore, homeostasis of immunity and control of immune responses appear to involve a complex web that interconnects all lymphocytes and their antigen receptors via self V–anti-self V domain immunoglobulin determinants, the so-called idiotype–anti-idiotype network. Since autorecognition is apparently a normal event in a functioning immune system, the proposal that autoimmune diseases may result in part from an imbalance or aberration of complementary idiotypic–anti-idiotypic responses is reasonable.

Despite the presence of these functionally important normal forms of autorecognition, the fact remains that an individual generally does not respond to a detectable degree against most of its own constituents. The process of inducing tolerance to self, as suggested by experimental studies of tolerance induction to foreign antigens, could be attributed to numerous mechanisms of which the most acceptable are clonal silencing and engagement of suppressor T cells, the latter mechanism presumably acting by the idiotype–anti-idiotype circuit. It is generally agreed that immature immunocytes are much more susceptible to tolerance induction than mature cells. Since the turnover of B cells is very rapid, one can logically conclude that the process of inducing tolerance to self is a continuous event that occurs repeatedly throughout the life of an individual whenever primitive cells with a genetic commitment to self-reactivity emerge from the hematopoietic organs, where they have the opportunity to meet self antigens in situ. Foreign antigens do not usually induce tolerance, because they pass through a succession of lymph nodes where they have optimal opportunity to meet tolerance-resistant mature immunocytes.

What causes failure of the phenotypically apparent self-tolerance mechanism is unknown. However, genetic factors combined with a variety of primary or secondary immunologic abnormalities—as well as hormonal abnormalities and infectious agents such as viruses—may promote the development of autoimmune diseases. The abnormal genes responsible for expression of autoimmune syndromes have not yet been identified, but studies in animal models of systemic lupus erythematosus have shown that many independently segregating genes could be responsible for the formation of the various autoantibodies. Despite the observed (minimal) association between most autoimmune diseases of humans and certain MHC and immunoglobulin genes, the genes controlling expression of autoantibodies in murine lupus have not been closely linked to any particular H-2 type or allotypic marker. Further studies aiming at the precise chromosomal assignment and location of autoimmunity-promoting genes will be of extreme importance in our attempts to understand the pathogenesis of these disorders and possibly to interfere with their progress through genetic engineering techniques of the future.

The etiologic events as well as the actual immunologic abnormalities leading to autoimmunity remain ill-defined—especially those of organ-specific autoimmune diseases, for which few animal models are available. Studies in humans and mice with systemic lupus erythematosus, perhaps the most extensively studied autoimmune disease, have produced a long list of abnormalities at both the B and T cell levels. Originally, the prevailing view was that the characteristic B cell hyperactivity of this disease was secondary to suppressor T cell abnormalities. However, this explanation now seems doubtful. Transplantation experiments between some SLE murine strains and their normal congeneic or histocompatible counterparts indicate that hematopoietic stem cells and precursors of B cells can transfer the disease in the absence of T cells, thus suggesting a primary B cell defect as the responsible agent for this disease. Some T cell abnormalities of such mice develop independently of associated B cell abnormalities in appropriate crosses and vice versa. Assuredly, the possibility that T cells may exert some inhibitory effects on expression of the primary B cell defect cannot be ruled out. Defects in tolerance induction to foreign antigens have been observed in all SLE strains of mice. The reasons for such defects and the relevance to lack of tolerance to self antigens are not clear, but the rapid transition of immunocytes from the immature, easily tolerized state to one of maturity refractory to tolerization is a possibility worth considering. Evidence is available for such a rapid transition in subsets of B cells from NZB mice.

Whatever the basic genetic and molecular immunologic defects, such defects may not become overt until late in life unless accelerating factors are superimposed. These accelerating factors may be endogenous and genetic in nature. One example is the Y chromosome–linked accelerating genes of BXSB mice that predispose to a much earlier development of systemic lupus erythematosus in male than in female mice; another such example is the lpr gene of MRL mice that predisposes, possibly by inducing proliferation of helper T cells, to the earlier expression of disease in MRL/Mp-lpr/lpr mice compared to late-disease-developing congeneic MRL/Mp-+/+ mice that lack the lpr gene. Accelerating factors of autoimmunity may also be female hormones and some exogenous factors such as viruses and bacteria that may activate polyclonally self-reactive B cells.

In concluding, a noteworthy proposal from some investigators, based on the idiotype–anti-idiotype concept, is that iatrogenically induced autoimmunization may benefit certain patients. This proposition stems from observations in experimental systems that auto-anti-idiotypic immunity may obliterate undesirable immune reactivity—as, for example, in allotransplantation—or may, conversely, induce immunity to particular antigens in the absence of such antigens or even mimic the action of antigens on target organs with the appropriate receptors; for example, anti-idiotypic antibodies to monoclonal antibodies specific for *Trypanosoma rhodesiense* may induce antigen-independent antimicrobial immunity in mice, and anti-idiotypic antibodies to anti-insulin antibodies may mimic the action of insulin. These observations not only enhance our knowledge of autoimmunity but also provide examples in which autoimmune reactions may be used under controlled conditions for beneficial results.

In this very complex subject of autoimmunity, all aspects of modern immunology are involved. By using the framework outlined above, additional studies, especially of related genetic and molecular abnormalities, should provide a quite complete description of these diseases in the not too distant future.

• • •

References

Benacerraf B: Role of MHC gene products in immune regulation. *Science* 1981;**212**:1229.

Blecher M, Bar RS: *Receptors and Human Disease*. Williams & Wilkins, 1981.

Bona CA, Cazenave PA (editors): *Lymphocytic Regulation by Antibodies*. Wiley, 1981.

Cantor H, Gershon RK: Immunological circuits: Cellular composition. *Fed Proc* 1979;**38**:2058.

Goodman MG, Weigle WO: Role of polyclonal B-cell activation in self/non-self discrimination. *Immunology Today* 1981; **2**:54.

Klinman NR, Wylie DE, Teale JM: B-cell development. *Immunology Today* 1981;**2**:212.

Katz DH: Adaptive differentiation of lymphocytes: Theoretical implications for mechanisms of cell-cell recognition and regulation of immune responses. *Adv Immunol* 1980;**29**:137.

Theofilopoulos AN, Dixon FJ: Etiopathogenesis of murine SLE. *Transplant Rev* 1981;**55**:179.

Weigle WO: Analysis of autoimmunity through experimental models of thyroiditis and allergic encephalomyelitis. *Adv Immunol* 1980;**30**:159.

Zinkernagel RM, Doherty PC: MHC-restricted cytotoxic T cell studies on the biological role of polymorphic major transplantation antigens determining T cell restriction: Specificity, function, and responsiveness. *Adv Immunol* 1979;**27**:52.

Clinical Transplantation | 14

Terry B. Strom, MD

Interest in the possibility of replacement of diseased or amputated parts of the body probably dates from ancient times, but it was not until the 20th century that immunologic processes were identified as the mechanism responsible for rejection of tissue grafts. While the goal of achieving donor-specific tolerance to grafted tissues without resorting to broadly immunosuppressive treatments has not been achieved in clinical circumstances, transplantation of tissues between genetically distinct donors and recipients (allografts) has proved useful in several clinical circumstances. In this chapter, several transplant organ models will be discussed. Richly vascularized organ grafts such as heart, kidney, pancreas, and liver elicit similar immunologic responses. Although only clinical kidney grafting will be covered in detail, similar principles of tissue matching and immunosuppressive treatment are used in each of these models. Several distinctive nonvascularized graft models will also be discussed, including bone marrow, skin, and corneal transplants.

KIDNEY TRANSPLANTATION

Although chronic hemodialysis offers prolonged survival for individuals with end stage renal disease, the technique is inconvenient and time-consuming. Dialytic therapy does not produce full rehabilitation, whereas recipients with successful kidney allografts often achieve remarkable rehabilitation. However, until recently, graft survival rates for cadaver donor grafts were low and mortality rates high. Appreciation of the importance of pretransplant blood transfusions, improved cross-matching techniques, and modified immunosuppressive protocols have produced gratifying results in the past several years.

PATIENT SELECTION

Although high-risk recipients of cadaveric grafts (eg, elderly patients or juvenile diabetics) are predisposed to morbid and lethal complications, these problems are greatly minimized when high-risk pa-

tients receive well-matched living related donor grafts. The increased incidence of cardiac and cerebrovascular disease, pulmonary disease, and cancer may exclude some older individuals from consideration. Other individuals usually excluded are those with oxalosis, those with a history of recent cancer or uncontrolled active sepsis, and those in whom chronic infection may be reactivated by treatment with corticosteroids.

TISSUE TYPING & CLINICAL IMMUNOGENETICS

Compatibility for red cell ABH antigens between donor and recipient is of utmost importance, as these antigens are expressed on all tissues. Thus, preformed natural anti-A and anti-B antibodies constitute a strong barrier to successful engraftment.

Evidence that the human HLA complex is the major histocompatibility gene complex is derived from the observed superior success rate in living related donor renal and bone marrow transplantation using HLA-identical sibling donor and recipient pairs. In renal transplantation, the profound impact of HLA matching upon long- and short-term graft survival is seen in Table 14–1.

The MLR (mixed lymphocyte response) is a proliferative response of T cells which is stimulated by class II HLA-D region incompatibilities between individuals. Other HLA antigens are at most weakly stimulatory in the MLR. Intrafamilial MLRs are ex-

Table 14–1. Comparative survival of HLA-identical, semi-identical, and cadaveric renal allografts.

Donors	Actuarial Survival*		
	1 Year	5 Years	Half-Life† (Years)
HLA-identical siblings	85–90%	75–80%	34
HLA-semi-identical, parent to child	70–75%	50–55%	11
Cadaver	~ 55%	30–35%	7.5

*Percentage survival of all grafts transplanted 1 and 5 years later.
†Projected from the second year onward, the rate of graft loss is exponential.

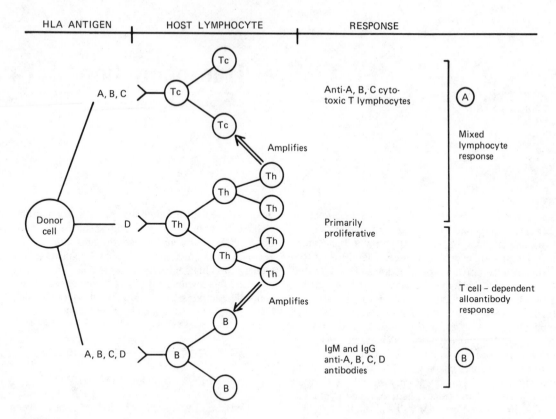

HLA ANTIGEN   HOST LYMPHOCYTE   RESPONSE

Figure 14–1. Helper T lymphocytes (Th cells), stimulated by HLA-D incompatibilities, proliferate (mixed lymphocyte response) and produce amplification signals that trigger the development of cytotoxic lymphocytes from Tc precursor cells and also trigger antibody production from B cells.

tremely useful in choosing a donor among several one-haplotype–matched potential donors. By inference, the one-HLA-A, -B, -C haplotype-matched transplant recipient shares only a single D locus antigen with the donor; hence, the recipient's immune response to the remaining D locus incompatibility becomes a critical factor in eventual graft outcome. Many transplant groups have shown that weak (albeit positive) MLR responses between recipient and donor are associated with 90% 1-year graft survival rates—comparable to those seen among HLA-identical 2-haplotype–matched pairs. However, among one-haplotype–matched pairs with vigorous MLR responses, only a 65% survival rate is observed.

In cadaver donor renal transplantation, matching for alleles of the class I HLA-A, -B, and -C loci yields a small improvement (10%) in 1-year graft survival. Matching for HLA-DR locus antigens appears more important and results in a 15% or more improvement over one or no HLA-DR matches. A rapid MLR that would meet the time constraints of tissue preservation for cadaver donor transplantation is urgently needed and is under development by several groups. As DNA synthesis is a late event in lymphocyte activation, premitotic indices of lymphocyte activation such as the appearance of new proteins upon the membrane of activated lymphocytes may prove useful in this regard.

In summary, evidence suggests a primary role for the D/DR region in the allograft response, since matching for HLA-D in the MLR or HLA-DR by conventional typing is of greater benefit than matching for HLA-A, -B, and -C locus antigens. The reason for the importance of HLA-D/DR matching can probably be ascribed to the capacity of HLA-D/DR but not HLA-A, -B, or -C locus antigens to stimulate helper T lymphocytes (Fig 14–1). Helper cells stimulated by HLA-D/DR incompatibilities proliferate (MLR) and produce amplification signals that facilitate activation of cytotoxic T lymphocytes and other signals that permit B cells to elaborate high-affinity, high-titer alloantibodies. Thus, helper T cells stimulated by HLA-D/DR incompatibilities serve a central role in the generation of cellular and humoral cytodestructive pathways. The target antigens for cytotoxic T lymphocytes are HLA-A, -B, and -C antigens of the sensitizing strain. While the response of helper T cells is primarily proliferative in nature, these cells bind to and lyse cells bearing HLA-D/DR antigens of the sensitizing strain. To date, human antigens have not been identified that selectively stimulate suppressor T lymphocytes. Candidates for such a function might be class II antigens linked to but distinct from HLA-D/DR such as those coded for by genes in the SB locus (see Chapter 6).

PRESENSITIZATION

A positive cross-match of recipient serum (lymphocytotoxic antibody) with donor T lymphocytes is usually predictive of an acute vasculitic form of graft destruction that is not abrogated by immunosuppressive therapy and is designated hyperacute rejection. As the titer of anti-HLA antibodies may wax and wane with time, serum for cross-matching is obtained at regular intervals during the period of pretransplant dialytic therapy preceding transplantation as well as immediately before transplantation. A positive donor-specific cross-match against donor T cells is a contraindication to transplantation. Recent evidence suggests that presensitization against a non-HLA antigen system shared between endothelial cells and monocytes also heralds accelerated rejection. New cross-matching techniques utilizing monocyte target cells are under development.

USE OF BLOOD TRANSFUSION IN RENAL GRAFTS

Nontransfused patients who receive cadaveric renal grafts are at high risk for graft failure. While the number of blood transfusions needed to ensure graft survival is at issue, the bulk of evidence shows that more than 10 units is optimal. The transfusion effect probably consists of 2 major features: First, exposure of a potential recipient to a large number of HLA antigens allows the recipient to select those of greatest interest, and these preferences are detected by monthly screens for antibodies. Future organ donors are thereby selected in a negative fashion. Second, priming with HLA antigens may induce antigen-specific unresponsiveness in some recipients, presumably by induction of suppressor cells, such as that noted in experimental models where pretransplant conditioning with blood products prolongs graft acceptance.

Except for grafts from HLA-identical donors, living donor haplo-identical grafts actually do provide strong histocompatibility barriers—particularly those haplo-identical pairs with a strong MLR; graft survival in this situation also appears to benefit from blood transfusions. In particular, the use of donor-specific blood on 3 occasions before transplantation results in superior graft survival in those 70% of recipients who do not become sensitized to the prospective donor. Again, the effect is one of negative selection of the nonresponders, while an additional degree of specific unresponsiveness may also be induced.

GRAFT REJECTION

Hyperacute Rejection

Allografts transplanted into presensitized recipients may be rejected very quickly. About 80% of patients who have preformed cytotoxic antibodies to donor T lymphocytes in their sera reject their allografts immediately after transplantation. Some episodes of hyperacute rejection are due to the presence of antibodies directed against non-HLA endothelial antigens. Early biopsies of hyperacutely rejecting kidneys show a linear localization of IgG and C3 on the glomerular and peritubular capillary walls, and ultrastructurally there are platelet aggregates in many of the capillary lumens. Polymorphonuclear leukocytes line the capillary walls, and most of the intrarenal capillaries and the arterioles are blocked by microthrombi, resulting in cortical necrosis. Such hyperacute antibody-mediated rejections are refractory to standard immunosuppressive therapy.

Acute Rejection

The classic, typical rejection episode occurs 7–21 days posttransplantation and is associated with fever, chills, oliguria, and a swollen graft. For many years, most investigators believed that transplant rejection was simply a form of cell-mediated immunity. In classic experiments, specific sensitivity to grafts can be transferred by lymphoid cells to syngeneic recipients but not by serum containing antidonor antibody. Convincing evidence that both cellular immunity and humoral immunity are involved in rejection is obtained from pathologic studies and techniques designed to recover infiltrating cells and graft-bound antibodies.

Although a variety of mononuclear cell types are present in the rejection lesion of nonpresensitized hosts, there is evidence that rejection of solid tissue allografts is in fact initiated by T lymphocytes. T lymphocytes have been shown to accumulate in graft infiltrates, and—since allosensitized T cells produce target cell injury when confronted with cells bearing the antigens of the immunizing donor—it has been assumed that this is the primary mode of graft injury. Donor-specific "killer" cytotoxic lymphocytes (CTL) with cytotoxicity against ^{51}Cr-labeled donor target cells have been recovered from cells infiltrating rejected human renal allografts, and the degree of cytotoxic activity correlates with the intensity of cellular rejection. Although "killer" cell activity can be attributed to T cells, these are not the only cell type with cytolytic activity in all situations, since B cells, K cells, and macrophages accumulate within the grafts as the events of rejection proceed. Cell-mediated graft injury is almost certainly due to the combined effects of cytotoxic T cells as well as forms of immunity similar to delayed hypersensitivity reactions. Pathologic studies show a predominant pattern of mononuclear leukocyte infiltration. Cellular rejection episodes are usually reversed by high-dose corticosteroid therapy.

Chronic Rejection

Months or years after renal transplantation, function may gradually deteriorate without there being any clear-cut rejection episode. Kidneys undergoing chronic rejection show severe narrowing of numerous arteries and thickening of the glomerular capillary basement membrane. Arteriolar narrowing is most common in the interlobular and arcuate vessels, with intimal thickening and rupture of the internal elastic lamina, but the endothelial lining remains intact. Serial biopsies of chronically rejecting kidneys have shown that these lesions are formed by continual or intermittent adherence of platelets and fibrin aggregates to the vessel wall. The mural deposits become covered by endothelium and incorporated into the intima, which often contains IgM and complement, emphasizing the role of the humoral system in this form of rejection. Chronic rejection is resistant to traditional immunosuppressive therapy. In fact, recent reductions in mortality rates are related to recognizing this syndrome by renal biopsy and to withholding potentially dangerous and ultimately futile high-dose corticosteroid therapy.

Immunologic Tests for Rejection

The diagnosis of renal allograft rejection is usually based upon the appearance of signs, symptoms, or altered biochemical indices suggesting reduced renal function. These manifestations may be late events in an immunologically mediated process. Immunologic monitoring after transplantation includes 2 basic types of assays: (1) those that reflect specific host antidonor immune activity and (2) those that measure nonspecific host immunologic activation. Antibodies directed against donor HLA-DR antigens and endothelial antigens are frequently measured. Antidonor antibodies may be detected by complement-dependent cytotoxicity or in the antibody-dependent, cell-mediated cytotoxicity assay. Donor-specific cytotoxic T lymphocytes also appear in the host's peripheral blood in temporal association with acute rejection episodes.

Antidonor antibodies are present prior to episodes of rejection. Persistence of antidonor antibodies following therapy designed to halt graft rejection is a very poor prognostic sign even when improvement in graft function is observed immediately following therapy.

Other tests that do not directly assess antidonor responses are also of value. Measurement of the spontaneous rate of DNA synthesis in the recipient's peripheral blood mononuclear cells is useful, because a significant increase in DNA synthesis is associated with either rejection or infection. Identification of T cell subset patterns may be useful. When the normal 2:1 ratio of T helper cells to T suppressor cells is maintained despite immunosuppressive therapy, rejection is highly likely. A diminished T helper/suppressor ratio correlates well with clinical quiescence.

IMMUNOSUPPRESSIVE THERAPY

When histocompatibility differences exist between donor and recipient, the immune response must be modified or suppressed for graft acceptance. Immunosuppressive therapy in general diminishes all immune responses, including those to bacteria, fungi, viruses, and even malignant tumors. Agents used in clinical renal transplantation are discussed below.

Azathioprine

This thioprine, the S-imidazolyl derivative of 6-mercaptopurine, has been the mainstay of antirejection therapy for renal transplantation since 1961, despite its potential for myelosuppression. It can be administered orally and has made clinical renal transplantation an effective and practical therapeutic procedure. Its usefulness is underscored by the high rate of graft failure that accompanies even temporary cessation of therapy during the early postgraft period. Azathioprine competes with inosinic acid for interaction with enzymes required for elaboration of nucleic acids. Rapidly dividing cells such as immunoblasts are especially sensitive to its effects. Because cell division and proliferation occur in response to antigenic stimulation, immune suppression may be mediated by interfering with DNA synthesis and thus inhibiting division among immunologically competent cells.

The major effect of azathioprine is to prevent rejection, but it does not abort ongoing rejection. In several experimental systems, optimal immunosuppression with azathioprine requires about 48 hours of pretreatment. Hence, therapy is generally instituted clinically 2–5 days prior to transplantation in recipients of kidneys from living related donors. The drug is continued at levels of 2–3 mg/kg/d as long as the allograft functions. Because it is rapidly metabolized by the liver, its dose need not be automatically varied directly in relation to renal function. Nonetheless, reduction in dosage may be required because some patients—particularly those with azotemia—are usually sensitive to azathioprine's myelosuppressive effects. Leukopenia is by far the most important parameter by which to identify azathioprine toxicity. Unfortunately, interruption of azathioprine therapy necessitated by leukopenia prejudices graft survival. Excessive doses of the agent may cause jaundice, anemia, and alopecia, and the increased incidence of cancer in transplant recipients may be a toxic effect. Although cyclosphosphamide is often substituted for azathioprine in patients with hepatocellular damage, clinical evidence suggests that patients with active hepatitis do not require cytotoxic drug therapy for maintenance of graft function.

Corticosteroids

Corticosteroids are important adjuncts to immunosuppressive therapy. Cell-mediated alloimmunity is also diminished by corticosteroids as assessed in vitro and in vivo. The production of cytotoxic T lymphocytes from noncytotoxic precursor cells is diminished by corticosteroids in vitro and in vivo, although the cytolytic action of fully differentiated killer cells is not altered in short-term assays. Recent evidence demonstrates that clonal expansion and viability of activated T cells is dependent upon production of T cell growth factor by helper cells. Corticosteroids appear to stop helper cells from secreting T cell growth factor by an indirect effect. Activated macrophages secrete the monokine interleukin-1; interleukin-1 interacts with helper cells, which subsequently elaborate T cell growth factor. Corticosteroids actively preclude macrophages from secreting interleukin-1. As a result, T cell growth factor secretion is abrogated. Corticosteroids, therefore, probably reverse rejection episodes by abrogating secretion of T cell growth factor and thereby denying activated killer T cells an essential trophic factor.

The effect of corticosteroids on humoral immunity is less profound. Although their chronic administration decreases IgG synthesis, primary or secondary antibody responses to antigens given during short courses of steroid treatment are not dampened.

Prednisone in large doses is unquestionably an effective agent for the reversal of cellular rejection. Until recently, 1–1.5 mg/kg/d of prednisone was initiated immediately prior to or at the time of transplantation, with the dosage reduced to maintenance levels over a period of 2–3 months. New evidence suggests that these steroid doses are excessive, and present practice is to administer 50 mg of prednisone per day at the time of transplantation. Six weeks later, the dose is reduced to 25 mg/d of prednisone. The well-known side effects of corticosteroids—especially impairment of wound healing and predisposition to infection—make it desirable to taper the dose as rapidly as possible. Methylprednisolone, 1 g intravenously daily, should be given for 3 days immediately upon diagnosis of acute rejection. When this treatment is effective, the results are usually (not invariably) apparent within 48–96 hours. Such "pulse" doses are less effective in chronic rejection, especially when associated with severe vascular and glomerular lesions. Although most patients with stable renal function at 6 months or 1 year do not require large doses of prednisone, maintenance doses of 7.5–15 mg/d are used most commonly. Several short-term studies have demonstrated that alternate-day steroids provide adequate suppression in some transplant patients, and such treatment reduces steroid toxicity. Only a single long-term study has demonstrated superiority of such treatment in maintaining long-term graft function and reducing late complications. Some workers have suggested that transition to alternate-day steroids predisposes to rejection. There is no proof that corticosteroids are routinely required as prophylactic therapy for rejection; one retrospective analysis suggests that such therapy is unnecessary. Additionally, both high-dose oral prednisone and intravenous methylprenisolone have been utilized effectively to reverse rejection episodes, and controlled studies have not demonstrated any advantage of either route or dose schedule.

It is essential that high-dose steroids be used prudently so as to minimize their potentially lethal side-effects. Not all rejection episodes can be treated, eg, vasculitic or chronic rejection and third or fourth rejection episodes occurring within the first 6 months following transplantation, especially in leukopenic patients. It has become increasingly clear with experi-

ence that patient survival is enhanced by judicious use of immunosuppressive therapy without excessive graft loss.

Antilymphocyte Globulin (ALG) & Antithymocyte Globulin (ATG)

When sera from animals made immune to host lymphocytes are injected into the recipient, a marked suppression of cellular immunity to tissue allografts results, and cellular immunity is dampened considerably. For use in humans, peripheral human lymphocytes, lymphoblastoid cell lines, lymphocytes from cadaver spleens, or lymphocytes harvested from thoracic duct fistulas have been used. These cells are injected into horses, rabbits, or goats to produce antilymphocyte serum, from which the globulin fraction is then separated. Before use, undesired antibodies directed against platelets, erythrocytes, serum proteins, thymic stroma, and glomerular basement membrane are removed by specific absorption.

There is little doubt that in experimental animal models, high-dose ATG administration is a potent suppressor of cell-mediated immunity and allograft responses. Nevertheless, ALG and ATG have had a perplexing history in clinical renal transplantation. Without question, many of the preparations are able to abolish delayed skin hypersensitivity reactions. They can be administered safely intravenously, preferably via large-bore central venous catheters or arteriovenous fistulas. Anaphylactoid responses occur, but lethal reactions are rare. The globulin can also be injected intramuscularly, although patients complain of pain and inflammation at the injected sites. The material is often administered 5–7 days before transplantation and is continued for 2 weeks thereafter.

Clinical opinion varies regarding the efficacy of these agents as immunosuppressive adjuncts; although they may improve early transplant function by preventing acute rejection episodes, long-term benefit is less clear. Some ALG and ATG preparations suppress early posttransplant rejection episodes, while other similarly prepared products are ineffectual. No tests are currently available to predict accurately the in vivo potency of the material. A revival of interest in ATG centers around recent evidence that ATG may reverse some rejection episodes that are refractory to steroid therapy. Heterologous antilymphocyte antibodies undoubtedly contain antibodies directed against a variety of lymphocyte surface determinants. The full clinical potential of ATG and ALG may only be realized after a better understanding is gained of the immunosuppressive moiety present in effective batches of heterologous antilymphocyte antibodies. Alternatively, monoclonal antilymphocyte antibodies are undergoing clinical evaluation. These absolutely pure antibodies produced by immortalized hybridomas offer an attractive means of producing effective antibodies in bulk. At least 2 monoclonal antibodies reacting with all postthymic T lymphocytes are undergoing clinical trial. OKT 3 has been demonstrated to abort acute rejection episodes, although recurrent rejections commonly occur. Antibody T 12, which also reacts against T cells but does not have the immunostimulatory mitogenlike properties of OKT 3, has been used with success for treating steroid-resistant rejection episodes.

Donor Pretreatment

Based on an earlier finding regarding the role of leukocytes in initiating mouse skin allograft rejection and graft-versus-host (GVH) disease, Elkins and Guttmann set out to determine whether rejection of vascularized organ allografts, specifically rat kidney grafts, depended upon the presence of host passenger white blood cells resident within the graft. Since extensive perfusion of the organ graft was ineffective in the removal of all passenger cells, an attempt was made to deplete these cells by alternative means. Brief treatment with antilymphocytic serum (ALS) induced acceptance of histoincompatible renal allografts for prolonged periods in a high percentage of rat recipients. A detailed analysis of this system suggested that prolonged graft survival was dependent upon passenger cell depletion rather than recipient suppression. In another study, the same investigators showed that treatment of the graft donors by ALG prolonged renal allograft survival as effectively as recipient treatment. Subsequently, it was found that the immune response to renal allografts could be largely avoided if the donor's hematopoietic tissue was made compatible with the recipient or depleted by various drugs. Clinically, excellent graft survival has been obtained in programs that administer 3–5 g of cyclophosphamide and 5 g of methylprednisolone by rapid intravenous infusion 4–12 hours prior to organ harvest from cadaver donors. Nonetheless, randomized prospective controlled studies have failed to show differences between the survival of grafts obtained from treated or untreated donors. These studies are especially disappointing in view of the solid experimental support for the passenger leukocyte hypothesis and the benign nature of the treatment protocol. Obviously, further investigations are warranted.

Cyclosporin A

Cyclosporin A is a fungal peptide metabolite with potent antilymphocyte activity. It is only weakly toxic to other hematopoietic cells. Preliminary evidence suggests that lymphoblasts—but not resting lymphocytes—are damaged by this agent. Cyclosporin A acts directly upon helper cells and reduces their capacity to elaborate T cell growth factor. Cyclosporin A is remarkably effective in prolonging experimental allograft survival in a variety of models. A large percentage of rabbit renal allograft recipients tolerate cyclosporin A withdrawal after a month of therapy without suffering graft loss. Assessment of this agent in human renal transplantation is currently under way. Cyclosporin A does effectively suppress clinical rejection episodes in humans. As in the case of azathioprine, cyclosporin A is used as maintenance immunosuppressive therapy rather than as an agent that reverses acute rejection per se. In one clinical trial, cyclosporin A plus small maintenance doses of oral corticosteroids have been remarkably effective in promoting engraftment. Since corticosteroids and cyclosporin A act via discrete mechanisms in their capacity to abort T cell growth factor release, true synergy may be possible.

Nephrotoxicity, hepatotoxicity, lethal fungal infection, and lymphomas have been noted following cyclosporin A therapy. The proper role of this agent is being evaluated at several institutions by randomized clinical trials.

Cyclic Nucleotides & Prostaglandins

The ability of sensitized cytotoxic T lymphocytes to destroy target cells bearing sensitizing alloantigens is regulated by cAMP and cGMP. The ability of cytotoxic T cells to lyse target cells is inhibited by a variety of agents, including prostaglandins, shown to elevate levels of lymphocyte cAMP. Adenylate cyclase activators and theophylline also cause an additive suppression of alloantigen-induced T cell proliferation. Thus, the proliferative and effector arcs of cell-mediated alloimmunity are inhibited by elevations of intracellular cAMP.

Recent trials in experimental animals have indicated that prostaglandins prolong survival of allografts. The potential therapeutic usefulness of natural prostaglandins is severely limited by their very brief biologic half-life. Consequently, prostaglandin E derivatives with prolonged biologic half-lives and the ability to activate adenylate cyclase have been synthesized and tested in models of alloimmunity both in vitro and in vivo. Dimethyl and secroprostaglandin derivatives of prostaglandin E suppress in vivo models of allograft immunity. These agents have been administered postoperatively to rat renal allograft recipients transplanted across major histocompatibility barriers. Daily treatment ensures long-term graft survival.

Total Lymphoid Irradiation

Remarkable tolerance to tissue and marrow grafts has been achieved in experimental animals following total lymphoid irradiation. The radiotherapy protocol is similar to the protocol used in humans for treatment of Hodgkin's disease and consists of 200 rads per day delivered 5 times per week for a total dose of 3400 rads directed to the thymus, spleen, and cervical, axillary, mediastinal, inguinal, and mesenteric lymph nodes. Irradiated animals accepted marrow, skin, and cardiac allografts. Bone marrow recipients were demonstrably chimeras, yet they showed no signs of GVH disease. Heart allografts transplanted 1 day following completion of a course of irradiation demonstrated markedly prolonged graft survival. Tissue graft survival was permanent in animals given irradiation plus marrow and a tissue graft from the same allogeneic strain. Preliminary clinical results using this treatment suggest at least adequate immunosuppression; however, total nodal irradiation plus azathioprine may increase the risk of developing lymphoma. It is ironic that modern research in transplantation biology may have come back full circle to radiotherapy, which was the mode of immunotherapy in the first successful human allograft.

Discontinuance of Immunotherapy

Discontinuance of immunosuppression is not routinely advocated, yet some patients who ceased taking immunosuppressives continue to enjoy satisfactory graft function. Long-term follow-up studies of such patients are needed, since it is not known whether these patients maintain functioning grafts for as long a period as patients taking standard therapy. One possibility is that some fortunate individuals develop suppressor cells specific for the donor and tolerate discontinuation of therapy. Future investigations may be useful in identifying these recipients for drug withdrawal.

BONE MARROW TRANSPLANTATION

Attempts at bone marrow transplantation are based on the assumption that a defect in hematopoietic stem cells rather than the marrow microenvironment is responsible for the disease state. After a period of abysmal failure, bone marrow transplantation is now being used with increasing success for treatment of severe aplastic anemia, acute leukemia, and immunodeficiency states. The real impetus for modern marrow transplantation was provided by evidence that lethal irradiation of experimental animals could be prevented by shielding of the spleen or treated by reconstitution with infused bone marrow. As in all other transplant systems, graft rejection is common; however, bone marrow transplantation has a unique complication owing to the ability of the transplant to mount an immunologic reaction against the host, ie, GVH reaction.

Since animal studies indicate that rejection and GVH disease are minimized when donor and recipient are matched for antigens encoded by genes in the major histocompatibility locus, allogeneic marrow transplantation has been limited almost exclusively to ABO-compatible, HLA-identical sibling combinations (unless an identical twin donor is available). Several recent cases have indicated that HLA-D-matched related donors that are mismatched for some HLA-A, -B, or -C determinants may be utilized as graft donors for treatment of aplastic anemia and combined immunodeficiency disease, while the use of HLA-D-incompatible donors results in lethal GVH disease. Sex compatibility between donor and recipient may facilitate engraftment.

PROCEDURE OF BONE MARROW TRANSPLANTATION

The technical aspects of bone marrow transplantation are simple. Classically, bone marrow cells are aspirated from the donor at multiple sites. The aspirate is heparinized, filtered through screens producing a monodispersed cell suspension, and immediately transfused intravenously into the patient. A dose of approximately 10^9 nucleated cells per kilogram is given to the patient. These methods are likely to soon become antiquated, since recent experimental and preliminary clinical results suggest that GVH reactions can be prevented if mature T lymphocytes are eliminated from the marrow before transplantation. Removal of postthymic T cells from the marrow inoculum can be accomplished by use of a differential agglutination and centrifugation technique that employs peanut agglutinin and soybean agglutinin to separate hematopoietic and lymphopoietic stem cells. Alternatively, anti-T cell antibodies conjugated with toxins, used with complement or bound to immunoaffinity columns, can be utilized to eliminate T cells from the marrow graft.

DONOR SELECTION

Allogeneic bone marrow transplantation is an effective form of therapy for some patients with combined immune deficiency, severe aplastic anemia, leukemia, osteopetrosis, and paroxysmal nocturnal hemoglobinuria. Marrow transplantation is much more successful in persons under 21 years of age than in older patients. Pretransplant blood transfusions prejudice successful engraftment. The deleterious influence of transfusion is likely to be caused by donor-specific sensitization, since a positive recipient antidonor response index in the MLR, lymphocyte-mediated cytotoxicity, or antibody-dependent cell-mediated cytotoxicity tests correlate with bone marrow rejection in HLA-identical donor and recipient pairs.

IMMUNOSUPPRESSIVE THERAPY

In order to facilitate engraftment, the recipient is treated with immunosuppressive agents. In aplastic anemia, cyclophosphamide in high doses has been used with success. Rejection is rare in nontransfused hosts receiving HLA-identical marrow grafts. Since many patients with severe aplastic anemia are of necessity transfused prior to transplantation, total body irradiation is sometimes used as an adjunct to cyclophosphamide in order to achieve engraftment. While hosts treated with cyclophosphamide and irradiation have a higher rate of engraftment than patients receiving cyclophosphamide alone, combination therapy leads to an increased risk of lethal GVH disease. Cyclosporin A is undergoing trial as an alternative to cyclophosphamide combined with total body irradiation. For leukemic recipients, more intensive conditioning is needed to destroy the leukemic cells.

Posttransplantation immunosuppressive therapy is used to prevent GVH disease. Methotrexate, antithymocyte globulin, and prednisone are more effective than methotrexate alone in preventing GVH disease.

GRAFT–VERSUS–HOST DISEASE

Graft-versus-host disease occurs in most bone marrow transplantation recipients who achieve engraftment. This disease is caused by an immunologic attack mounted by immunocompetent donor T cells upon the tissues of an immunologically incompetent host who is unable to reject the marrow graft. Although animal studies have demonstrated that antigens of the major histocompatibility gene complex are potent stimulators of GVH disease, most human transplant recipients are HLA-identical to their donors. Hence, non–HLA-linked genes are obviously capable of provoking GVH disease. Initially, GVH disease involves an antigen-specific stimulation of donor cells producing T cell proliferation. GVH disease is not observed in rodents transplanted with marrow lacking mature T cells. Preliminary trials in humans suggest that depletion of T cells in the graft may radically decrease the incidence of GVH disease. The proliferative response of donor T cells in the host tissue leads to enlargement of host spleen, liver, and lymph nodes. Splenomegaly is caused in large part by a proliferative response of host cells. Subsequently, the host tissues that contain proliferating lymphoid cells develop an invasive and destructive lesion. It is assumed—but not firmly established—that antigen-specific cytotoxic T cells participate in this process. Yet in a rodent model, GVH disease correlates positively with activation of suppressor but not killer T cells. Cutaneous deposition of IgM and complement has been demonstrated in bone marrow recipients undergoing GVH disease, suggesting that humoral mechanisms may participate in tissue injury. The major clinical manifestations of GVH disease result from involvement of skin, liver, and intestinal mucosa. All patients undergoing GVH disease have skin involvement that may progress from a geographically limited maculopapular eruption to a generalized erythroderma to bulla formation and desquamation. Skin biopsy is required for confirmation, since skin eruptions due to other causes may occur. Patients with mild GVH disease (grade I) manifest only skin involvement. The morphologic features of dermatitis associated with GVH disease are heralded by infiltration of basophilic lymphocytes into the dermal-epidermal interface. Subsequently, degeneration of the basal epithelium, spongiosis, and the appearance of occasional mummified cells (necrotic keratinocytes and melanocytes) in the mid and lower dermis typify florid dermatitis of this origin. In extreme examples, necrosis of the entire epidermis is seen. Resolving or quiescent dermatitis is characterized by epidermal atrophy and the disappearance of dermal lymphocytes. In more severe forms of GVH disease (grades II–IV), intestinal disease, liver disease, or both are present. Intestinal disease presents as diarrhea and may progress to cause severe generalized abdominal pain, malabsorption, and ileus, whereas liver disease produces hyperbilirubinemia, elevated serum glutamic-oxaloacetic transaminase, and often elevated alkaline phosphatase. Fever is often noted. Histologically, intestinal GVH disease is typified by the appearance of lymphocytes into the mucosa of large and small bowel. The lesion includes necrosis of varying degrees of intensity. Hepatic disease is initially associated with lymphoid infiltration of the portal region and periportal piecemeal hepatocyte necrosis. GVH enteritis and hepatitis can be distinguished from viral processes. Viral enteritis—but not enteritis associated with GVH disease—is associated with viral inclusions in epithelial and stromal cells, and viral hepatitis typically presents with ballooning degeneration and viral inclusion bodies associated with necrosis. The influence of severe GVH disease is profound. Patients with GVH disease limited to skin survive, whereas only 15% of patients with more advanced GVH disease survive. Posttransplantation immunosuppressive therapy is used to ameliorate GVH disease. Prophylactic measures are far more effective than treatment initiated after the appearance of clinically manifest GVH disease. Following successful engraftment, patients that develop acute GVH disease are treated with corticosteroids, antilymphocyte sera, or, more recently, monoclonal anti–T cell antibodies. Although the rate of progression of GVH disease may decrease, individuals that develop intestinal or liver involvement almost invariably die. Infection is usually the immediate cause of death in individuals afflicted with irreversible graft rejection or severe GVH disease.

SKIN TRANSPLANTATION

The immunologic and pathologic mechanisms of graft rejection have been most extensively studied in animal models of skin rejection. The pivotal importance of immunologically specific alloactivated T cells and the influence of MHC antigens in eliciting vigorous rejection have been clearly elucidated in experimental skin graft models. Skin allografts differ in several important features from many other organ transplant systems. The route and frequency of host sensitization are influenced by the lack of direct vascular donor-to-host anastomoses. In addition, epidermal cells express a high density of class II or class B cell alloantigens, while parenchymal renal, cardiac, and pancreatic cells are relatively deficient in these antigens. It is likely that the differences in the mode of sensitization and differences in antigenic expression account for the vigor of skin allograft rejection.

Skin graft rejection is only modestly controlled by chemical immunosuppression or enhancement protocols. As a consequence, skin allografts, so important to the experimentalist, are of minor clinical importance. Skin allografts have been successfully utilized as a temporary measure in rehabilitating children with massive (70% of the body surface) full-thickness burns. Sequential replacement of the allograft by isograft as healing proceeds has permitted continuous wound closure in patients who almost invariably died before the use of skin allografts became available. In one series, a role has been claimed for azathioprine and tissue typing in prolonging graft survival.

CORNEAL TRANSPLANTATION

Corneal transplantation enjoys an extremely high success rate. The enviable circumstances surrounding human corneal transplantation include the ease of obtaining and storing viable corneas. Furthermore, immunosuppression is not routinely required to maintain avascular human corneal allografts. This situation led to the establishment of the first human corneal eye bank in New York City in 1944.

Corneal grafts are most commonly performed for replacement of nonhealing corneal ulcerations. Penetrating corneal transplants require removal of the entire thickness of the host cornea and subsequent replacement by donor tissue. The cornea does contain HLA-A and -B antigens, albeit in low concentrations, as well as A and B blood group antigens. In contrast, HLA-D/DR antigens have not been found on the cornea. While the cornea can no longer be regarded as an immunologically privileged site, immunization via corneal inoculation often results in activation of antigen-specific suppressor cells.

Immunologically specific corneal rejection does occur on occasion. While avascular corneal grafts exclude lymphocytes, vascularized grafts undergo rejection. Indeed, the incidence of reversible rejection episodes correlates positively with donor and recipient HLA matching. Moreover, the incidence of corneal graft rejection coincides with the appearance of donor-specific cytotoxic T lymphocytes in the recipient's circulation.

In order to avoid rejection, the grafts—as small as possible—are centrally placed in an attempt to avoid contact with the highly vascularized limbic region. Eccentrically placed grafts are subject to a high rate of immunologic failure. Rejection of allogeneic corneal grafts can usually be reversed by corticosteroid therapy.

• • •

References

Kidney Transplants

Morris PJ, Ting A: The crossmatch in renal transplantation. *Tissue Antigens* 1981;**17**:75.

Opelz G, Graver B, Terasaki PI: Induction of high kidney graft survival rate by multiple transfusion. *Lancet* 1981;**1**:1223.

Strom TB, Tilney NL, Carpenter CB: Kidney transplantation in the treatment of terminal uremia. *Ann Clin Res* 1981;**13**:224.

Terasaki PI, Opelz G, Mickey MR: Clinical kidney transplants. *Cell Immunol* 1981;**62**:277.

Ting A, Morris PJ: Powerful effect of HLA-DR matching on survival of cadaveric renal allografts. *Lancet* 1980;**2**:282.

Marrow Transplants

Good RA: Toward safer marrow transplantation. *N Engl J Med* 1982;**306**:421.

Ramsay NKC et al: A randomized study of the prevention of acute graft-versus-host disease. *N Engl J Med* 1982;**306**: 392.

Thomas ED et al: Bone marrow transplantation. (2 parts.) *N Engl J Med* 1975;**292**:832, 835.

15 | The Secretory Immune System

Thomas B. Tomasi, Jr., MD, PhD

INTRODUCTION

The mucosal surfaces of humans are in direct continuity with the external environment and are therefore a major site of antigenic exposure. The external secretions that bathe these surfaces form a unique immunologic system involved in host defense. The importance of immunologic mechanisms functioning locally in the secretions themselves was first suggested by studies during the early part of this century. It was shown that the level of antibodies in mucosal fluids correlated more directly with resistance to certain infections than did serum antibody titers. Subsequent developments permitted quantitation of the immunoglobulin classes in secretions, and IgA was shown to be the predominant immunoglobulin of external secretions, in contrast to serum and internal secretions where IgG predominates. Moreover, the antibody response in secretions appears to be regulated independently from the response in serum. These are critical features of the immunologic system common to mucosal surfaces, now referred to as the secretory or mucosal immune system. This chapter will review the secretory immune system and its structural and biologic characteristics.

IMMUNOGLOBULINS

Fig 15–1 illustrates the concept of external versus internal fluids. External secretions bathe mucosal epithelia that are in continuity with the external environment. There is a predominance of IgA in these fluids, and the IgG/IgA ratio is often less than 1, compared to 4:1 or 5:1 for serum. Internal secretions, on the other hand, are often contained in closed cavities, and IgG is the major immunoglobulin class. In addition to IgA, IgM and IgE are also present in external secretions in larger amounts than can be explained by simple transudation from serum. The IgM, IgE, and IgA in most external secretions are normally produced in large part by plasma cells residing locally in the lamina propria of secretory sites such as gut, nasal mucosa, and salivary glands. In some secretions, significant amounts are transported from serum (eg, bile, discussed below). In the presence of inflammation, however (eg, following invasive infections), increased capillary permeability permits transudation of serum proteins into secretory fluids and their content of IgG increases.

Although differences among species do exist, certain features of external secretions are shared by all mammals that have been studied. We will limit this discussion to humans as much as possible and consider the various mucosal sites as a unit system. Two common characteristics of external secretions can be defined. First, the various immunoglobulin classes are present in mucosal fluids in proportions significantly different from those in serum, and the levels are not explicable by simple transudation. Second, there is independent regulation of the serum and secretory antibody response. This dissociation has considerable

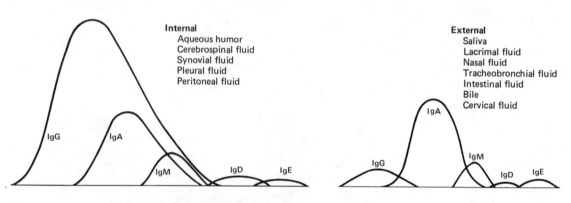

Figure 15–1. Body secretions characterized by immunoglobulin content.

biologic importance, for it is known that natural infection or immunization may stimulate one system without necessarily having any effect on the development of immunity in the other. Furthermore, as discussed below, mucosal immunization may actually be associated with a suppressed systemic response.

Structure of Secretory IgA

There are significant differences in structure between serum and secretory IgA (sIgA). Human serum IgA exists mainly as a 7S monomer, with 10–15% in polymeric form, whereas IgA in external secretions exists mainly, although not exclusively, as a dimer. Small amounts of 7S IgA and higher polymers (trimer, tetramers, and pentamers) are also present in secretions.

The sIgA is a complex molecule composed of an IgA dimer (MW 300,000), a molecule of secretory piece or component (SC) (MW 70,000), and a molecule of J chain (MW 15,000). The entire molecule has a sedimentation coefficient of 11S and molecular weight of 385,000 (Fig 15–2). Secretory component binds to dimeric and polymeric IgA but does not bind to 7S IgA or IgG. The IgM found in secretions has also been shown to have SC bound to it, but IgG and IgE do not. SC is also present in a free or unattached form in most normal mucosal fluids, as well as in the secretions of neonates and patients with IgA deficiency, both of which lack sIgA. Free SC can be shown to bind in vitro to dimeric IgA, and the complex involves disulfide bonds. It has been hypothesized that SC is coiled around the Fc portions of the IgA dimer and extends from one hinge region to the other, with secondary forces interacting between the Fc region and SC. This integral relationship between SC and the IgA dimer may well account for the increased stabilization of sIgA, rendering it less susceptible to attack by various proteolytic enzymes. It has been suggested that

this resistance to proteolysis, compared to other immunoglobulin molecules, gives a selective advantage to sIgA antibodies in secretory fluids.

J Chain

J chain is a glycopeptide of MW 15,000 which is disulfide-bonded to polymeric IgA and IgM. It is not present in 7S monomeric IgA, IgG, IgD, or IgE. Because of its association with polymeric immunoglobulins, it is suggested that J chain functions in vivo by inducing the correct polymerization of the subunits of IgA and IgM. J chain is incorporated into IgA and IgM just prior to their secretion from the plasma cell.

Higher polymers of IgA and IgM are disulfide-bonded to J chain so that only 2 of the monomeric units of IgA or IgM are bound to J chain; the remainder of the subunits are bound directly to each other by disulfide bonds not involving J chain (Fig 15–3). In vitro experiments suggest that the mechanism of polymerization involves linkage of two 7S monomers by J chain to form a stable dimer. Complexing with J chain may alter the conformation of the subunits and enables them to interact directly through noncovalent forces with other subunits not containing J chain. These forces are responsible for bringing the subunits into close enough apposition to allow the remaining intersubunit disulfides (not involving J chain) to form. J chain is bound to the penultimate carboxyl-terminal cysteine of α and μ chains and may confer on IgA and IgM the ability to bind secretory component. Secretory component has been shown to reside on the epithelial cell membrane and may act as a receptor for the trans-epithelial transport of polymeric (mainly dimeric) IgA and IgM synthesized in the lamina propria.

IgA Subclasses

Two subclasses of IgA (IgA1 and IgA2) have been identifiable in serum and secretions. IgA1 ac-

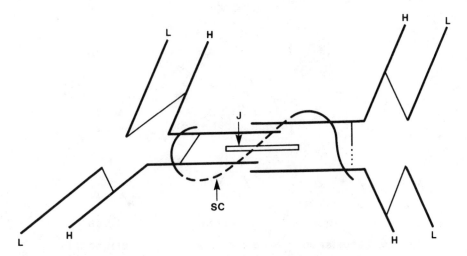

Figure 15–2. Model for secretory IgA. (SC, secretory component; H, heavy chain; L, light chain; J, J chain.) (Modified from Heremans JS: The IgA system in connection with local and systemic immunity. In: *The IgA System.* Mestecky J, Lawton AR [editors]. Plenum Press, 1974.)

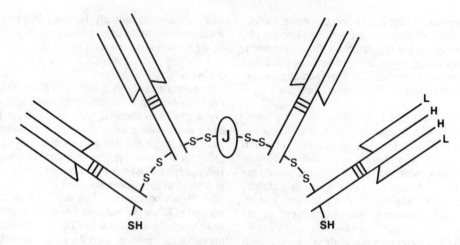

Figure 15-3. Model for polymeric IgA of the tetramer type depicting a linear array. (H, heavy chain; L, light chain; J, J chain.)

counts for approximately 90% of the total serum IgA, whereas in most mucosal secretions, the IgA2 subclass comprises as much as 40–60% of the total IgA (Fig 15–4). The subclasses differ antigenically and exhibit significant differences in galactosamine content, hinge region structure, number of interchain disulfide bonds, and metabolic properties (Table 15–1). The IgA2 subclass may be further subdivided by allotypic markers on their heavy chains. The genetic locus that codes for the heavy chain markers occurs in 2 allelic forms, A2m(1) and A2m(2). These alleles have a varying incidence among different races; eg, the A2m(1) marker is prevalent in Caucasians and the A2m(2) marker in Mongoloid and Negroid populations.

The class and subclass antigens on IgA are re-

sponsible for anaphylactic transfusion reactions in some IgA-deficient patients. Following multiple transfusions, many of these patients develop antibodies against antigenic determinants on IgA. Antibodies to allotype specificity have also been reported to cause urticarial reactions.

A major difference between the subclasses of IgA is related to their dissociability in the presence of nonaqueous solvents (denaturants) such as urea or guanidine. Exposure of the IgA1 subclass to denaturants does not result in dissociation into H and L chains, whereas similar treatment of most (though not all) IgA2 proteins produces disulfide-linked dimer-H and -L chains. This is due to the absence of the L–H disulfide bond in these IgA2 proteins (Fig 15–4). This

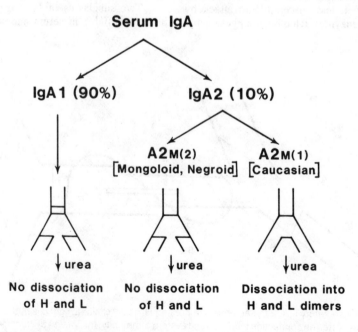

Figure 15-4. Distribution of subclasses of IgA with S—S bonds shown.

Table 15–1. IgA subclass characteristics.

	IgA1	IgA2
Serum (proportion)	90%	10%
Serum (concentration)	1.8 mg/mL	0.22 mg/mL
Milk (proportion)	40%	60%
Electrophoretic mobility (pH 8.6)	Slower	Faster (anode)
Galactosamine	Present	Not present
Hinge region	Duplicated + Carbohydrate	12–13 residue gap No carbohydrate
Serum half-time	5.9 d	4.5 d
Fractional catabolic rate	24%	34%
Synthetic rate	24 mg/kg/d	21.3 mg/kg/d
Genetic marker on Fc (allotypic)	Absent	Present A2m(1) Absent A2m(2)
Dissociability in acid, urea, etc	No	Yes A2m(1) No A2m(2)
Noncovalent interaction	Weak	Strong
Monomer of subclass combines with secretory component	No	Yes A2m(1) No A2m(2)

characteristic is found only with the IgA2 A2m(1) type, whereas the IgA2 A2m(2) proteins, like the IgA1 subclass, do not dissociate in denaturants. The presence or absence of the L–H interchain bridge in human IgA2 is therefore an expression of a particular allotype.

The IgA subclasses are of further importance in that certain pathogenic microorganisms, especially *Neisseria gonorrhoeae, Neisseria meningitidis* (but not nonpathogenic strains of *Neisseria*), *Haemophilus influenzae,* and *Streptococcus pneumoniae,* produce an extracellular enzyme capable of cleaving human IgA1. The enzyme, known as IgA protease, is exquisitely selective and cleaves a single peptide bond (proline-threonine or proline-serine) in the hinge region of the heavy chain of the IgA1 subclass. After cleavage, the IgA1 antibodies lose some of their biologic properties such as their ability to agglutinate. IgA2 is resistant to IgA protease, as are all other proteins which have been examined, even those containing proline-threonine or proline-serine residues. It can be speculated that, through the course of evolution, certain bacteria developed IgA proteases as an effective virulence factor that permitted more successful host invasion. In similar fashion, it has been suggested that IgA2 may have arisen as a protease-resistant variant of IgA1 by a deletion in the hinge region of 13 amino acid residues that includes the bonds cleaved by the IgA protease.

SYNTHESIS & TRANSPORT OF sIgA

Origin of IgA in Secretions

The major portion of sIgA is produced within various secretory tissues. Using fluorescent antibody or in vitro culture techniques, one can demonstrate that submucosal plasma cells residing locally in secretory sites elaborate primarily dimeric IgA that subsequently appears in mucosal fluids. These plasma cells lie in close apposition to the overlying epithelium and are predominantly comprised of cells that produce IgA. For example, the lamina propria of the human gastrointestinal tract contains 20–30 IgA cells per IgG cell. This ratio contrasts with that of peripheral lymph nodes and spleen, where the ratio is 1:5 (IgA:IgG). Under normal physiologic conditions, only small amounts of IgA pass from serum into external secretions. IgM and IgE are also produced locally, although in the normal individual there are far fewer plasma cells containing these immunoglobulins than IgA.

In addition to the previously described mechanism whereby locally produced dimeric IgA is secreted directly across the crypt epithelium, it has been demonstrated in mice and rats that dimeric IgA is transported from serum into bile via the liver. Bile duct obstruction disrupts the transport of IgA, and large increases of dimeric IgA (but not IgG or IgM) appear in the systemic circulation. If the bile duct ligature is released before permanent liver damage ensues, there is a rapid fall in serum IgA to normal. Furthermore, it has been shown that human polymeric IgA from monoclonal and polyclonal sources binds specifically to the plasma membrane of normal human hepatocytes. It appears probable, therefore, that the liver plays an important role in the clearance of polymeric IgA from serum and that the transport of IgA from serum into bile augments the quantity of sIgA arriving at the gut lumen.

Origin of Secretory Component in Secretions

Secretory component is a glycoprotein structurally unrelated to immunoglobulins. Unlike IgA and J chain, which are produced by submucosal plasma cells, SC is synthesized within glandular epithelial cells. Acini and ducts of human salivary and lacrimal glands, respiratory and gastrointestinal tract mucosa (including the biliary tree and gallbladder), and the epithelium of the cervix, uterine tubes, and ureters have all been shown to produce SC. SC can be detected in fetal tissue as early as 8 weeks of age (prior to the appearance of any plasma cells), and free SC is found in the external secretions of neonates (who have no detectable IgA) and in patients with agammaglobulinemia. Isolated case reports suggest that SC deficiency in patients may be associated with absent or markedly diminished sIgA in mucosal fluids despite the presence of normal blood levels of IgA. This has provided indirect evidence that SC is required for transport of IgA across mucosal or glandular epithelium. As mentioned above, SC may also act as a receptor in the transport of IgA across the hepatic parenchymal cell into bile.

IgG, IgM, & IgE in Secretions

IgG in most normal external secretions is derived in large part from nonspecific transudation from serum, although some local synthesis occurs. Studies of intestinal lymphatics in the dog have shown that the lymph:serum concentration of most proteins is related to the molecular sieving property of intestinal capillaries. The concentration of IgG in mesenteric lymph is what would be expected based on its molecular size, and this suggests that relatively little IgG is produced in this species in the intestine itself. Serum IgG reaches the interstitial fluid bathing the gut lamina propria and then permeates the capillary walls, but its precise route of transport across the epithelium is unknown. Some of it probably is extruded into the lumen at the tip of the villus, where cells are normally shed. In addition to transudation from serum, studies with fluorescent antisera have demonstrated that small numbers of IgG-producing cells are present in the lamina propria, but these are few in comparison to IgA. When inflammation occurs in a mucous membrane, there may be both an increase in transudation of IgG from serum and an invasion of the mucosa by IgG-producing plasma cells. These serum-derived antibodies may be of considerable importance in recovery from mucosal infections.

IgE occurs in very small concentrations in secretory fluids. However, greater proportions are present than can be accounted for by simple transudation from serum. The concentration of IgE relative to other proteins is higher in nasopharyngeal fluids than it is in serum. The lamina propria of the respiratory and gastrointestinal mucosa contains approximately 2–5% IgE-producing cells, in contrast to spleen and peripheral lymph nodes, where rare (< 1%) IgE cells are found. The IgE in external secretions does not contain SC and is physicochemically and antigenically similar to serum IgE. The route of transport of IgE into secretions is unknown, but it may follow the same route as IgG and 7S IgA.

IgM is locally synthesized in secretory tissues.

The human gastrointestinal tract has been shown to contain 5 times more IgM-producing cells than IgG cells. IgM is also present in parotid fluid in higher concentration than IgG. Furthermore, individuals with selective IgA deficiency can be shown to have large amounts of IgM in submucosal plasma cells and in secretions. Like IgA, the IgM molecule has the capacity to bind secretory component, and both sIgM and to a lesser extent IgG serve to replace IgA as the predominant secretory immunoglobulin in some but not all patients with selective IgA deficiency. The majority of IgM in secretions contains noncovalently bound SC, while a smaller fraction of the IgM contains covalently (disulfide) bound secretory component.

Route of Transport of sIgA & sIgM

Fig 15–5 illustrates the probable route of transport of secretory immunoglobulins. Dimeric IgA is produced and secreted by the submucosal plasma cells. The quantity of polymer versus monomer synthesized by a mucosal tissue such as the gut lamina propria may depend on the production of cells containing intracellular J chain as well as other factors. Dimeric IgA with complexed J chain diffuses through the interstitium of the lamina propria, crosses the basement membrane, and enters the intercellular space. Since the apical portions of 2 adjacent epithelial cells are in close apposition (tight junction), macromolecules of the size of IgA cannot gain access directly to the lumen. Secretory component, present on the lateral and basal epithelial cell membrane, may act as a receptor. By complexing with dimeric IgA and IgM, it facilitates transport into the epithelial cell by an endocytotic process that involves invagination of the cell membrane and enclosure of the sIgA and sIgM molecules in

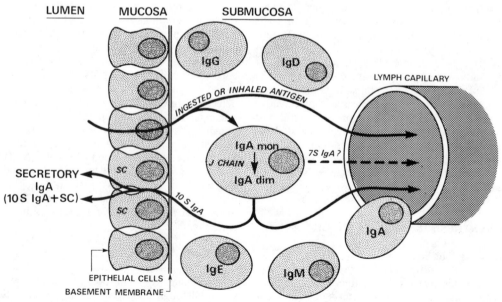

Figure 15–5. Site of synthesis and transport of sIgA. (SC, secretory component; IgA mon, IgA monomer; IgA dim, IgA dimer.)

membrane-bound vesicles. Electron microscopic studies suggest that this is similar to the coated pit–coated vesicle type of transport described for the hepatic uptake of lipoproteins and certain other molecules. The vesicles are transported to the epithelial cell's apical (luminal) membrane or the basal surface of the hepatic cells (bile duct side) and are subsequently extruded, probably by reverse pinocytosis.

Origin of Serum IgA

IgA is synthesized in amounts almost as great as IgG (about 2.5 g/d in adults), but because of its shorter half-life (6 days compared with 22 for IgG1 subclass), the serum concentration is much lower (2 mg/mL for IgA compared with 12 mg/mL for IgG). In humans, neither its origin nor the biologic role of *serum* IgA has been fully elucidated. Several lines of evidence suggest that secretory lymphoid tissue, particularly of the gastrointestinal tract, is a major source of circulating IgA in several animal species. First, oral immunization of mice with certain antigens such as horse spleen ferritin elicits circulating antiferritin antibodies largely of the IgA class. Parenteral immunization with ferritin, on the other hand, results in the production of IgM and IgG antibodies by the spleen and lymph nodes. This observation suggests that serum IgA antiferritin antibodies may be derived from cells originating in the gut. The IgA-secreting cells may reside in the gastrointestinal tract or migrate from the gut to peripheral lymphoid tissues such as the spleen. Second, mice exposed to whole body irradiation rapidly develop a marked deficiency in serum IgA but not IgM or IgG, and shielding the gastrointestinal tract prevents a decrease in serum IgA. Third, studies in several animal species (rat, dog) have revealed that most of the serum proteins found in mesenteric lymph are derived from serum by transudation across the intestinal capillaries. IgA is a striking exception, and it has been calculated that over 80% of lymphatic IgA originates from local synthesis by the plasma cells in the intestinal lamina propria. In the human, however, the contribution of the gut in providing circulating IgA is less clear. It is important to note that in humans, 90% of the total serum IgA is monomeric (7S) and only 10% polymeric, whereas in many animals 10S (dimeric) IgA predominates. There is evidence in several species that most of the IgA synthesized in the gut is dimeric. It is possible that in the human, both monomeric and polymeric IgA are synthesized in intestinal secretory sites and then diffuse or are transported in 2 different directions. Monomeric IgA diffuses into the lymphatics and hence into the circulation, while the dimer is secreted into the intestinal lumen because SC acts as a receptor that preferentially binds polymeric IgA. The smaller size of 7S IgA compared to 10S IgA would also facilitate its diffusion into the lymphatics, although a small amount of dimer could also diffuse into the circulation via this route. Other investigations have suggested that the bone marrow may be a major source of serum IgA; however, a precise measurement of the bone marrow's contribution to the total serum IgA pool

is not available. Thus, the precise origins of serum IgA in humans remain unsettled.

Origin of Gut-Associated Lymphoid Cells

Two types of cells, easily distinguishable by size, are present in thoracic duct lymph. Small lymphocytes, when radiolabeled and injected into syngeneic animals, migrate mainly to the spleen and peripheral lymph nodes. In contrast, large lymphocytes (lymphoblasts) from the duct lymph localize preferentially in the lamina propria of the small gut, with only a few being found in the spleen and virtually none in lymph node. Since the lymphatics of the gut drain into the mesenteric lymph nodes and subsequently to the thoracic duct, it is likely that the lymphoblasts originated in gut-associated lymphoid tissue and that these cells migrate to secretory organs and eventually give rise to the lamina propria plasma cells that secrete IgA. In the rabbit, Craig and Cebra transferred allogeneic donor lymphoid cells (from Peyer's patches and lymph nodes) of one immunoglobulin allotype into lethally irradiated recipients of a different allotype. Using fluorescent antisera to immunoglobulin allotypes to identify cells containing donor immunoglobulin, they showed the preferential migration of cells from Peyer's patches to the intestinal lamina propria. Table 15–2 demonstrates that cells from popliteal lymph nodes migrate almost entirely to the spleen and give rise mostly to IgG cells, whereas Peyer's cells migrate to both spleen and gut and give rise primarily to IgA cells.

Antigen is thought to be transported to the lymphoid cells in Peyer's patches through its overlying M cells—specialized epithelial cells lacking microvilli and containing large numbers of vacuoles that probably are involved in transporting antigens across the gut lumen. Antigen sensitization occurs in lymphoid cells precommitted (by unknown mechanisms) to the production of IgA. The antigen-specific precursors of IgA-producing cells then migrate via the efferent lymphatics to the mesenteric lymph nodes and hence to the thoracic duct and circulation. The migrating cells enter the lamina propria of secretory tissues regardless of whether the initial antigen is present at the local site or not. However, in the absence of an antigenic stimulus, the cells are present only transiently and probably die in situ. If continued antigenic stimulation is present locally, proliferation of the cells occurs and the se-

Table 15–2. Homing properties of Peyer's patch cells.*

Source of Cells	Spleen % of Donor Cells Containing		Gut Lamina Propria Cells Containing	
	IgG	IgA	IgG	IgA
Popliteal lymph nodes	74	8	Few	None
Peyer's patch	13	77	Few	Many

*Data from Craig SW, Cebra JJ: Peyer's patches: An enriched source of precursors for IgA-producing immunocytes in the rabbit. *J Exp Med* 1971;**134**:188.

cretory antibody response is greater and more persistent.

Not only do precursors of IgA-producing cells (eg, B cells) migrate as described above, but T cells possess this property as well. It is important to realize that the IgA antibody response is highly T cell-dependent. This is best illustrated in athymic mice, where serum and intestinal levels of IgA are markedly decreased. There is also some evidence that in certain patients with IgA deficiency the fundamental defect may lie in the absence or malfunction of specific IgA helper T cells—ie, T cells that provide help for IgA B cells but not for B cells of other classes. Approximately 40% of patients with IgA deficiency have class-specific suppressor cells but whether these are responsible for selective deficiency of IgA is unclear. The existence of class-specific helper and suppressor T cells also has been demonstrated for IgE and IgG.

A specialized tissue in the lung with many of the characteristics of Peyer's patches has also been described. This has been referred to as bronchial-associated lymphoid tissue, and cells from these tissues are reported to give rise to IgA cells in both the lung and intestinal lamina propria, suggesting a common receptor mechanism on cells from these secretory sites. At present, the full extent of cell migrations within the secretory system has not been established. However, there is good evidence that cells from gut lymphoid tissue migrate to salivary glands, lacrimal glands, small intestine, and mammary glands. Cell migration to the latter site is under hormonal control and occurs abundantly during lactation, when the antibodies to maternal microorganisms are protective to the newborn. Thus, human breast milk contains large amounts of IgA antibodies, and these are probably derived in large part from cells that received their initial antigenic stimulus in the gut and then migrated to the breast. These cells would be expected to produce antibodies directed against antigens encountered in the maternal gastrointestinal tract, and—reasoning teleologically—this would provide the infant with the very antibodies needed to confront the large and varied number of organisms a newborn encounters immediately after birth. Only IgG passes the human placenta in significant amounts, and this class does not permeate secretory epithelial membranes, so that the only antibodies present on mucous surfaces of the newborn are those derived from milk. This is true of most species and is a compelling (albeit indirect) argument for breast feeding. The importance of breast feeding is well known in veterinary medicine and is best illustrated by the classic studies of Theobald Smith in 1922. He showed that over 75% of calves deprived of colostrum die within a few days of birth of E coli septicemia. More recent investigations have shown that oral immunization of pregnant sows can protect newborn piglets against transmissible gastroenteritis virus and rotavirus infections, both of which produce serious and economically important diseases. Protection is conferred largely by IgA type antibodies present in the milk. In humans, the case for breast feeding is less well established, but a considerable amount of recent data, particularly from studies of populations in developing countries, suggest that breast-fed infants are generally healthier and have less diarrheal disease, although it is difficult to attribute this solely to the immunity received in milk. Artificial formulas contain very low titers of antibodies compared to human breast milk, and of course the antibody spectrum is that of the cow and not the infant's mother.

Biologic Function of the Secretory Immune System

A. Antiviral Activity: The best-established role of secretory immunoglobulins is in resistance to infections with viral agents. The induction of virus-specific secretory antibodies is determined by the type of viral antigen (live virulent, attenuated, or inactivated) and the route and dose of immunization (parenteral or local). This is exemplified by the work with poliovirus. Similar serum levels of IgM, IgG, and IgA antibodies are present after immunization of humans with either oral live attenuated poliovaccine (Sabin) or parenteral inactivated vaccine (Salk). However, a significant secretory antibody response in the alimentary tract and nasopharynx occurred only after oral immunization and persisted for as long as 5 years. In addition, infants with double-barreled colostomies were locally immunized in the distal colon. Only the immunized segments produced antibodies and were capable of preventing colonization with poliovirus. These and other experiments demonstrate that secretory immunoglobulins with virus-neutralizing activity induced by natural infection or immunization are largely sIgA antibodies. Antibody titers in secretions are better correlated than serum titers with resistance to reinfection following subsequent challenge with live virus. Thus, immunity to many respiratory viruses that produce their disease locally in the respiratory mucosa seems to be mediated largely by locally produced sIgA antiviral antibodies. A role for cell-mediated reactions in preventing colonization of mucous membranes has not been established but may also be of importance. As an example of the role of the secretory system in preventing viral infections, the data obtained with a "common cold"-producing rhinovirus is shown in Table 15–3. After immunization and rechallenge with the virus, nasal antibody and protection from illness were seen only after the intranasal immunization of volunteers.

There are 2 general types of virus infections with respect to the importance of serum versus secretory antibody protection (Fig 15–6). Following viral exposure, there is replication of the virus in the mucosa of the portal of entry, ie, the respiratory or gastrointestinal tract. Viruses such as rhinovirus, respiratory syncytial virus, myxoviruses, and certain types of adenovirus remain localized superficially in the mucosa, where they produce disease. The second type of viral infection is exemplified by poliovirus, echovirus, and measles virus, where, following the initial mucous membrane phase, systemic infection occurs. In this

Table 15-3. Neutralizing antibodies in serum and nasal fluids following intramuscular and intranasal immunizations with rhinovirus type 13. Following immunization, volunteers were challenged with the live virus and the development of symptoms recorded. Note that only the group which developed nasal antibody showed significant protection against challenge with the live virus.*

Route of Vaccination	Number in Group	Geometric Mean Titer (Reciprocal)		Illness (%)
		Serum	Nasal	
Intranasal	28	53.8	4.5	36
Intramuscular	11	72.5	1.5	82
Control (no vaccine)	23	4.0	1.3	78

*Data from Perkins JC et al: Evidence for protective effect of an inactivated rhinovirus vaccine administered by the nasal route. *Am J Epidemiol* 1969;**90**:319.

group, circulating antibody is important in preventing viral dissemination and dispersion to peripheral organs. For example, with the Salk poliovaccine (killed virus administered systemically), the major antibody is serum IgG with little or no secretory response. Although immune to systemic infection by virtue of serum antibody, the patient may become a carrier, with the virus persisting at the portal of entry, because of the lack of secretory antibody. With the oral Sabin poliovaccine, secretory antibody is induced and is effective in preventing colonization and the establishment of the carrier state.

An important example of the possible dissociation between systemic and local immunity is seen following infection with respiratory syncytial virus. This virus is a frequent cause of bronchiolitis in infancy despite significant titers of passively acquired maternal IgG antibodies. Obviously, serum antibody is not protective against respiratory syncytial virus, since infection occurs at the height of maternally derived antibody titers. If an inactivated vaccine is given parenterally, even higher levels of IgG antibodies develop in the serum of the infant, but these afford little protection. In fact, more serious disease may occur in previously immunized children. It has been suggested

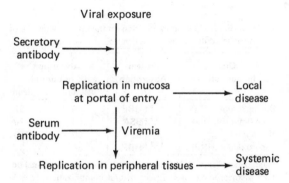

Figure 15-6. Sequence of spread of viral infection.

that the virus multiplies in the lung in the absence of mucosal immunity, and if high titers of IgG antibody are present in the serum, transudation occurs into the local site, and the interaction of serum IgG (complement-fixing) antibody with antigen in the lung produces a hypersensitivity reaction of the Arthus (immune complex) type (Chapter 30). Similarly, a severe form of measles occurs, often complicated by pneumonia, in children and adults previously immunized parenterally with inactivated measles vaccine who subsequently become infected with the live virus. In these cases, measles antigen, antibody, and complement have been found in blood vessel walls in the local skin lesion.

B. Antitoxin Activity: With certain microorganisms that act primarily by secreting exotoxins (eg, cholera), the presence of local antitoxin antibodies contributes significantly to protection against the disease.

C. Antibacterial Activity: Until recently, the function of the secretory system in bacterial infections has been difficult to demonstrate experimentally (other than antitoxin immunity) because of our inability to elucidate a definitive effector mechanism of IgA for bacterial killing such as opsonization and complement fixation. The low levels of several complement components and the apparently small numbers of phagocytes on most mucosal surfaces have contributed to this dilemma. The finding that the adherence of bacteria to mucous membrane surfaces is diminished by specific antibody, including sIgA, has been an important discovery and has opened up a new area for investigation.

Over a decade ago, studies in human volunteers and in animals orally immunized with killed cholera organisms suggested that immunity to cholera was mediated largely by coproantibodies (intestinal immunoglobulins). More recently, it was shown that the adherence of *Vibrio cholerae* in vivo to the walls of the intestinal loops of rabbits was markedly decreased by prior immunization or by the presence of cholera-specific coproantibodies. Adherence of *E coli* to gut and urinary tract epithelial cells, adherence of gonococci to cervical and vaginal cells, and adherence of streptococci to buccal epithelial cells are other examples. Essential to bacterial colonization of mucous membranes is the requirement that bacteria selectively adhere to epithelial surfaces. Selectivity of adherence is exemplified in the pattern of colonization of certain bacterial species, eg, certain strains of streptococci colonize only limited locations within the human oral cavity. Cell surface antigens of bacteria influence their adherence to mucosal surfaces and thus directly affect colonization. Opposing the adherence of bacteria to mucous surfaces are factors related to the cleansing action of these membranes, ie, mucous secretions, cilial beating of epithelial cells in the trachea, intestinal motility and peristalsis in the bowel, rapid fluid flow, and epithelial desquamation. sIgA antibodies augment these effects by binding to glycoproteins critical to adherence on the surface of bacteria, thereby inhibiting

Table 15—4. Inhibition of adherence of *Streptococcus salivarius* to human buccal epithelial cells by parotid fluid sIgA.*

Prior Treatment of Bacteria	Adherence (% of Control)†
Buffer (control)	100
Parotid fluid	56
65 μg of sIgA	24
sIgA + anti-IgA	98

*Data from Williams RC, Gibbons RJ: Inhibition of bacterial adherence by secretory immunoglobulin A: Mechanism of antigen disposal. *Science* 1972;**177**:697. Copyright 1972 by the American Association for the Advancement of Science.

†(Number of bacteria per epithelial cell in test system ÷ Number of bacteria per epithelial cell in control system) × 100.

adherence and colonization. Antibodies directed against cholera and *Salmonella* inhibit intestinal colonization by these organisms. The sIgA isolated from parotid fluid specifically inhibits the attachment of strains of streptococci to human buccal epithelial cells, but only to strains against which it exhibits antibody activity (Table 15–4).

The formation of plaque on teeth appears to be a requirement for caries production. Certain types of *Streptococcus mutans* are cariogenic and produce dextran polymers from sucrose. These polymers enable *S mutans* to adhere to and colonize smooth surfaces of teeth, a necessary requirement for the formation of dental plaque and caries. Antisera directed against *S mutans* cells inhibit the adherence of these organisms to smooth surfaces, independently of bacterial killing. With certain antibodies, rather than directly blocking surface structures involved in adherence, inhibition of adherence correlates with inhibition of the synthesis of the cell-associated polysaccharide dextran by the bacterial enzyme glucosyltransferase (dextran sucrase). High-molecular-weight dextrans are required for adherence to the surface of the tooth. Rats immunized locally with *S mutans* and later orally infected with live *S mutans* developed salivary antibodies of the IgA class that inhibited dextran sucrase activity and decreased caries production when compared to control rats. Thus, immunization against human caries is theoretically possible, and appropriate antigens and routes of immunization are currently being explored with this objective in mind.

Lysis and killing of bacteria involves complement fixation, and IgA does not fix complement via the classic pathway in a manner similar to that of IgG or IgM. IgA does, however, have the capacity to activate complement via the alternative pathway (see Chapter 11). Although very small amounts of classic and alternative pathway components have been found in secretions, it is still not known whether sufficient amounts of these components are present to be biologically significant. Thus, the question of the biologic relevance of activation of complement by sIgA is still unanswered.

The ability of phagocytes to engulf particulate

matter is enhanced in the presence of specific antibody, with or without complement. Although secretory IgA antibodies can combine and coat bacteria in vivo, the evidence that this results in enhanced phagocytosis of bacteria is not conclusive. Some reports claim opsonizing properties for IgA directed against certain bacteria or red cells, although most studies using highly purified preparations of IgA have failed to show opsonizing activity for IgA. Whether IgA is able to mediate antibody-dependent cell-mediated cytotoxicity has not been firmly established. However, a small population of T cells have Fc receptors for IgA, and in at least one study, IgA antibody and human monocytes have been reported to mediate antibody-dependent cell-mediated cytotoxicity against meningococcus.

D. Inhibition of Absorption of Nonviable Antigens by the Gastrointestinal Mucosa: Contrary to earlier opinion, adults of many mammalian species absorb small but significant amounts of macromolecular antigens across the epithelial cells of mucous membranes. Recent studies using an inverted gut sac technique have shown that oral immunization with protein antigens specifically inhibits the uptake of the immunizing protein but not that of an unrelated antigen (Table 15–5). In the rat intestine, absorption of bovine albumin or horseradish peroxidase was decreased if there had been prior immunization of the animal with the corresponding antigen. Thus, local immune reactions may provide a control mechanism for limiting the intestinal absorption of intact macromolecules. It has been postulated, but not proved, that the diminution in absorption is mediated by secretory antibodies. This would protect the organism against harmful antigens by forming nonabsorbable complexes that would be degraded by proteolytic enzymes on the surface of the intestine. Whether similar mechanisms operate in the absorption of inhaled antigens across the respiratory mucosa is not known, but there is initial evidence that this may be the case. The consequences of secretory IgA deficiency are seen in patients with a selective deficiency of IgA. Most of these patients have recurrent infections and have high titers of antibodies directed against milk and food antigens. This is because their gastrointestinal tracts are "leaky" and antigens

Table 15—5. Effect of immunization on the intestinal uptake of antigen in adult rats using the inverted gut sac technique.*

Oral Immunization With:	Protein Absorption Of:	Absorption (% of Control)	
		Jejunum	Ileum
Bovine serum	^{125}I HRP	99	97
albumin (BSA)	^{125}I BSA	50	70
Horseradish	^{125}I BSA	80	110
peroxidase (HRP)	^{125}I HRP	38	33

*Data from Walker WA, Isselbacker KJ, Block KJ: Intestinal uptake of macromolecules: Effect of oral immunization. *Science* 1972;**177**:608. Copyright 1972 by the American Association for the Advancement of Science.

are absorbed that elicit serum antibodies in the IgM and IgG classes. For example, patients with IgA deficiency may have circulating immune complexes within an hour of drinking 100 mL of milk, and these are composed of milk proteins (casein, bovine albumin, etc) complexed with specific antibodies. The occurrence of immune complexes with exogenous antigens may explain the well-known clinical association between IgA deficiencies and certain autoimmune syndromes. Another possible mechanism might involve the excessive and continued absorption of foreign antigens that are cross-reactive with self-antigens (similar to the mechanism postulated by which certain strains of streptococci cause rheumatic fever and glomerulonephritis). A few individuals with IgA deficiency are apparently normal, and it has been found that most of these patients have IgM in their secretions (also to a lesser extent IgG)—in other words, IgM and IgG have replaced IgA.

E. Local Cell-Mediated Immunity: Cell-mediated immunity is important in protection against certain viral and bacterial infections, homograft rejection, and tumor immunity. T cells and macrophages, both of which participate in cell-mediated reactions, have been found in significant numbers in the lamina propria of secretory sites. Nasal immunization of guinea pigs with dinitrophenylated human gamma globulin or influenza virus have shown that lymphocytes obtained by bronchial lavage from the respiratory tract of these animals inhibit macrophage migration (primarily a parameter of cell-mediated immunity) in the presence of specific antigens, while those from parenterally immunized animals show much smaller amounts of activity. Therefore, depending upon the route of immunization, local cell-mediated immunity in the respiratory tract can exist independently from that found systemically. Relatively little work has been done on cell-mediated reactions at various mucosal sites, but they may be of considerable importance, particularly in regard to recovery from certain infections once the mucous membrane is colonized.

F. Oral Tolerance: Peyer's patches contain T cells capable of IgA class-specific helper function, as well as T cells that are responsive to alloantigens in the mixed lymphocyte reaction. Furthermore, animals given antigens by the oral route develop antigen-specific suppressor T cells for IgG and IgM in their spleens that may be derived from Peyer's patches. Thus, enteric immunization can induce an antigen-specific state of nonreactivity (oral tolerance) that lasts a variable period of time, depending on the dose and type of antigen administered. Mice given ovalbumin enterically prior to systemic challenge with the same antigen remain tolerant to ovalbumin for more than 2 months after feeding ovalbumin. Not only is the systemic antibody response abrogated following certain types of oral immunization, but delayed hypersensitivity may also be suppressed. Contact sensitivity may be induced in mice or guinea pigs by painting the skin with oxazolone or picryl chloride and can be measured by determining the increase in skinfold thickness. Prior treatment of the animals with the same chemical via the oral route results in tolerance to the compound. The abrogation of contact sensitivity by prior oral feeding is well recognized in the older literature as the "Sulzberger-Chase phenomenon." Although suppressor cells, which are formed initially in the gut and later migrate to peripheral lymphoid tissues, have been implicated in oral tolerance, so too have soluble circulating suppressor factors. Current investigations may provide answers to the mechanism of oral tolerance that may differ depending on the type of antigen, dose administered enterically, and time at which systemic tolerance is examined after feeding. It is important to note that systemic tolerance may be induced together with an active secretory response. Thus, oral immunization may produce a mucosal immune response concomitantly with an inability to mount a serum antibody response or systemic delayed hypersensitivity to the identical antigen given systemically.

● ● ●

References

Bienenstock J, Johnson N, Perey DYE: Bronchial lymphoid tissue. 1. Morphological characteristics. *Lab Invest* 1973; **28**:686.

Craig SW, Cebra JJ: Peyer's patches: An enriched source of precursors for IgA-producing immunocytes in the rabbit. *J Exp Med* 1971;**134**:188.

Freter R: Parameters affecting the association of vibrios with the intestinal surface in experimental cholera. *Infect Immun* 1972;**6**:134.

Grey HM et al: A subclass of human γA globulins (γA2) which lacks the disulfide bonds linking heavy and light chains. *J Exp Med* 1968;**138**:1223.

Hopf U et al: In vivo and in vitro binding of IgA to the plasma membrane of hepatocytes. *Scand J Immunol* 1978;**8**:543.

Husband AJ, Gowans JL: The origin and antigen-dependent distribution of IgA-containing cells in the intestine. *J Exp Med* 1978;**148**:1146.

Mestecky J et al: Selective induction of an immune response in human external secretions by ingestion of bacterial antigen. *J Clin Invest* 1978;**61**:731.

Mulks MH, Plaut AG: IgA protease production as a characteristic distinguishing pathogenic from harmless Neisseriaceae. *N Engl J Med* 1978;**299**:973.

Ogra PL, Karzon DT: Distribution of poliovirus antibody in serum, nasopharynx and alimentary tract following segmental immunization with poliovaccine. *J Immunol* 1969;**102**:1423.

Orlans E et al: Rapid active transport of immunoglobulin A from blood to bile. *J Exp Med* 1978;**147**:588.

Richman LK et al: Enterically induced immunologic tolerance. 1. Induction of suppressor T lymphocytes by intragastric administration of soluble proteins. *J Immunol* 1978;**121**:2429.

Roux ME et al: Origin of IgA-secreting plasma cells in the mammary gland. *J Exp Med* 1977;**146**:1311.

Tomasi TB Jr: *The Immune System of Secretions.* Osler AG, Weiss L (editors). Prentice-Hall, 1976.

Tomasi TB et al: Mucosal immunity: The origin and migration patterns of cells in the secretory system. *J Allergy Clin Immunol* 1980;**65**:12.

Walker WA, Isselbacher KJ, Bloch KJ: Intestinal uptake of macromolecules: Effect of oral immunization. *Science* 1972;**177**:608.

Williams RC, Gibbons RJ: Inhibition of bacterial adherence by secretory immunoglobulin A: Mechanism of antigen disposal. *Science* 1972;**177**:697.

Immunity & Infection | 16

David J. Drutz, MD, & John Mills, MD

Immunity and infection are inseparable. The scientific discipline of immunology was born of the study of how animals, by natural or artificial means, become immune to microbial infections and toxins. The work of Jenner concerning prophylactic immunization against smallpox was the first successful application of the observation that recovery from an infection is accompanied by acquired immunity to the infecting microorganism.

We live in a world filled with microorganisms; every facet of our existence brings us into contact with bacteria, fungi, viruses, and a diversity of other parasitic or potentially parasitic life forms. We possess a rich natural microflora on all body surfaces, within all orifices, and throughout most of the gastrointestinal tract. Even vital digestive functions are mediated partly by intestinal flora. Considering the continuous nature of our encounters with microorganisms, and notwithstanding the often mutually beneficial relationship, it is surprising that infections are not more common. However, through eons of coexistence, humans have developed sophisticated mechanisms for dealing with potential invading pathogens. Such mechanisms are the essence of **natural resistance,** which can be defined as the combined protective effects of anatomic barriers, baseline cellular phagocytosis, digestion by phagocytic cells, and effector mechanisms (such as complement), all of which are modified by nutritional status, hormonal status, and genetic makeup.

Host defenses against infection are at once local and systemic, nonspecific and specific, and humoral and cellular. It is difficult to identify any infectious agent that fails to challenge multiple host defense mechanisms; indeed, the concept of overlapping host defenses is crucial to our understanding of susceptibility to infection. Thus, ''immunologic redundancy'' may account for a reasonable measure of good health even in the face of an apparently significant host immune defect.

HOST DEFENSES AT
BODY SURFACES

In order for an invading pathogen to produce an infection, it must somehow slip through an impressive barrier of surface defenses which operate wherever intact body tissues confront the environment. Such defenses are potent even though relatively nonspecific. They are seldom accorded the great significance they deserve.

Discharge of Microorganisms From the Body

A variety of normal functions act to continually reduce the body's bacterial burden. The mucociliary escalator of the respiratory tract brings microorganisms and foreign material to the oropharynx, where they may be coughed out or swallowed and excreted in the bowel contents. Desquamation and other forms of epithelial cell turnover at body surfaces remove large numbers of adherent microbes. Defecation results in the elimination of about 10^{12} bacteria daily, and urination eliminates microorganisms colonizing the urethral epithelium. Factors that impede diarrheal elimination of invasive microorganisms (drugs inhibiting gut motility in salmonellosis) or free passage of the urinary stream (prostatic hypertrophy) greatly enhance the risk of serious infection.

Salivation, lacrimation, and sneezing also displace potentially infective microorganisms. Patients with Sjögren's syndrome, which is characterized by severe impairment of lacrimation and salivation, are at risk of ocular and oral sepsis resulting from loss of these vital defense mechanisms.

Local Production of Chemical
Antimicrobial Factors

Lysozyme (muramidase), a cationic low-molecular-weight enzyme present in tears, saliva, and nasal secretions, reduces the local concentration of susceptible bacteria by attacking the mucopeptides of their cell walls. Salivary glycolipids prevent attachment of potentially cariogenic bacteria to oral epithelial cell surfaces through a process of competitive inhibition. Similar substances present on cell surfaces apparently act as the attachment sites for bacteria. Saliva and milk contain a lactoperoxidase-SCN-H_2O_2 system that possesses antibacterial activity in vitro. (Its mechanism of action is similar to that of myeloperoxidase-mediated killing in the neutrophil; see below.) Gastric acidity retards access of *Salmonella* species and *Vibrio cholerae* to the intestine. Achlorhydria and gastric resection increase susceptibility to salmonellosis, cholera, and possibly giardiasis

(Giardia lamblia). Neutralization of gastric contents with bicarbonate greatly increases the susceptibility of human volunteers to cholera and shigellosis. Enveloped viruses are not, as a rule, pathogenic by the enteric route because their lipoprotein surface membranes are susceptible to hydrochloric acid and to enzymatic lysis. Acidity of skin and vaginal secretions retards local colonization by potential pathogens. Spermine, a polyamine present in prostatic secretions, is a potent (and highly pH-dependent) inhibitor of gram-positive microorganisms at concentrations normally encountered in semen. Seminal plasma also possesses potent bactericidal activity related to the presence of zinc.

Bacterial Interference

The normal biota of body surfaces serves an important host defense function. Not only does normal flora serve to stimulate "natural" antibody (eg, absence of a normal flora increases the susceptibility of germ-free animals to infection), but such flora also dictates to some extent the ability of potential pathogens to gain an initial foothold in the body. For example, the skin commensal *Propionibacterium acnes* appears to be capable of retarding skin colonization with *Staphylococcus aureus* and *Streptococcus pyogenes* through the production of antibacterial skin lipids. Mechanical removal of the lipids with acetone permits local multiplication of these pathogenic cocci under experimental conditions.

Anaerobic bacteria in the bowel are able to retard the local growth of *Salmonella* species through the production of fatty acids. Antibiotics which selectively eliminate the responsible anaerobes indirectly predispose to salmonellosis. Resident bowel flora may also prevent acquisition of *Shigella* species by their effect on local pH as well as by producing volatile fatty acids harmful to *Shigella*. Bile acids are excreted as glycine and taurine conjugates and are deconjugated by gut anaerobes. Deconjugated bile salts are inhibitory for a number of microorganisms, including *Bacteroides fragilis, Clostridium perfringens*, lactobacilli, and enterococci.

Viridans streptococci resident in the pharynx appear to prevent the local growth of pneumococci. *Staphylococcus epidermidis* and diphtheroids in the nasal vestibule retard colonization by *S aureus*. The mechanisms of these important microbial interactions are unclear.

Attachment to & Penetration of Epithelial Cells

Because intact skin is not easily infected, most infections in otherwise normal persons begin at mucosal surfaces. For many pathogens, the first step in initiation of infection is attachment to an epithelial surface. Ability to attach may therefore be a prime determinant of virulence. Before a microorganism reaches an epithelial cell, it must traverse a mucous or salivary barrier. These secretions may contain materials that prevent epithelial cell attachment (eg, re-

leased receptor material that competes with receptor sites on the cells themselves). Diet may also interfere with epithelial cell colonization (eg, a meat diet may contain receptors for bacterial adhesion; carbohydrate-binding proteins [lectins] from plant and animal sources, such as concanavalin A, may inhibit attachment of lactobacilli and *E coli* to mucosal cells).

A. Mechanisms of Epithelial Cell Attachment: Epithelial cell attachment is a function partially of microbial surface factors (binding sites) and partially of receptor sites on epithelial cell surfaces. There is considerable evidence that receptor sites on mammalian cells may be composed of sugars, because D-mannose, L-fucose, and D-galactose, among others, can inhibit the attachment of many bacterial species to epithelial cells. The precise nature and location of these epithelial cell receptors is unknown. Bacteria appear to attach to sugar receptors by means of lectin-like binding sites (adhesins). Adhesins often take the form of proteinaceous, hairlike fimbriae (pili). Fimbriae appear to mediate the attachment of gonococci to mucosal epithelial surfaces and, in the urethra, may prevent the washing away of microorganisms by the force of the urinary stream. Similar structures on enteric gram-negative rods are adherent to urinary tract epithelial cells and may play a role in the pathogenesis of certain urinary tract infections. Fimbriae are important in the attachment of strains of *E coli*, salmonellae, and vibrios to the intestinal epithelium in the pathogenesis of diarrhea. In a classic form of enterotoxigenic diarrhea in piglets, toxin-producing *E coli* are unable to produce diarrhea unless K-88 antigen is present on the surface of the bacteria. This antigen is distributed over the *E coli* in the form of fimbriae and mediates attachment of the bacteria to a D-mannose-resistant epithelial cell receptor site. A similar fimbria-borne antigen known as CFA (colonization factor antigen) is important in the pathogenesis of enterotoxigenic *E coli* infections in humans. Finally, attachment by *S pyogenes* to epithelial cells is mediated by lipoteichoic acid which, along with M protein, is located in surface fimbriae. However, fimbriae are not always predictive of microbial virulence; many nonpathogenic bacteria such as the common saprophytic *Neisseria* species are well fimbriated.

Other surface factors may mediate epithelial cell attachment as well. For example, *Streptococcus mutans*, a mouth organism believed to be important in producing dental caries, synthesizes glucans from sucrose which promote adherence of the bacteria to each other and to dental surfaces. (*S mutans* can also attach to teeth by interacting directly with components of the enamel pellicle.) Interestingly, glucans and dextrans serve to bind endocarditis-producing streptococci to cardiac valve tissues and thus behave as virulence factors for infective endocarditis. *Mycoplasma pneumoniae* attaches to the surface of ciliated respiratory mucosal cells by a specialized tip structure. Neuraminic acid receptors may be involved in the adherence process. *Chlamydia* species lack an anatomically identifiable binding site; cell receptor specificity is mediated, at least in part, by N-acetylglucosamine.

Many viruses have surface proteins which allow attachment to specific cell membrane receptors. For example, influenza virus surface hemagglutinin attaches specifically to N-acetylneuraminic acid residues on the cell membrane; removal of these receptors prevents viral attachment. Host specificity of many viruses is determined by cell receptors, eg, whole poliovirus will not replicate in hamster kidney cells, but if infectious RNA is prepared, it circumvents the required attachment phase by direct penetration of the cell, and a single cycle of viral replication occurs.

B. Significance of Epithelial Cell Penetration: Microbial attachment is not necessarily followed by epithelial cell penetration. Infections with *M pneumoniae, Corynebacterium diphtheriae, Bordetella pertussis, V cholerae,* and enterotoxigenic *E coli* take place entirely at the epithelial surface. Other pathogens penetrate into epithelial cells, where they replicate and produce the principal manifestations of disease. This is the mechanism whereby *Shigella* species infect the colon. Finally, there are pathogens which do not stop at the stage of epithelial cell invasion but proceed to systemic spread. This pattern is typical of salmonellosis.

It has become apparent that epithelial cell invasion is an important mechanism of infection for many other potential pathogens, including protozoa, spirochetes, various fungi, *Listeria monocytogenes,* and *Neisseria gonorrhoeae.* In an intraepithelial cell location, pathogens may be protected from antibodies and antibiotics and from ingestion and killing by polymorphonuclear leukocytes and mononuclear phagocytes.

Epithelial cell penetration appears to involve a process of endocytosis similar in many ways to phagocytosis. The factors that determine the "hospitality" of epithelial cells for invading pathogens is unclear. Intraepithelial microbes appear to be viable, but this is not surprising, since epithelial cells lack the comprehensive antimicrobial armamentarium of "professional" phagocytes such as polymorphonuclear leukocytes, monocytes, and macrophages. Some microorganisms, such as *Toxoplasma gondii,* appear capable of actively promoting endocytosis. The mechanism by which this is accomplished is unclear; however, toxoplasmas which are coated with antibody lose this capability even though the antibody is not directly harmful to the protozoon.

C. Host Defenses Against Attachment to Epithelial Cells: It is clearly in the interest of the host to prevent attachment of potential pathogens to epithelial cells. This may be partially accomplished by members of the normal microbial flora that attach to mucosal cells and cover up critical receptor sites. Fibronectin, a high-molecular-weight protein present on the surfaces of oropharyngeal epithelial cells, also appears to cover up epithelial cell receptor sites for bacteria. Finally, attachment may be retarded by local factors such as glycoproteins and pH.

Antibody on mucosal surfaces plays a significant role in dictating the outcome of mucosal invasion. The antibody response at mucosal surfaces is mediated principally by secretory IgA. Secretory IgA consists of IgA antibody (synthesized by plasma cells at the local mucosal surface) covalently bound to "secretory component," a unique protein that is synthesized by mucosal epithelial cells (Chapter 15). Mucosal immunity appears to be highly localized; elevated antibody titers in salivary secretions, for example, may not be associated with similar activity in the tears.

The mechanisms by which secretory IgA operates against microorganisms in the complex environment of secretions is not entirely clear. Secretory IgA binds antigens effectively and can neutralize viruses and bacterial enterotoxins. Mycoplasmas are inhibited in their attachment, motility, and growth. Secretory IgA cannot activate complement by either the classic or alternative pathway and appears not to be capable of promoting phagocytosis. Secretory IgA can potentiate the bacteriostatic effect of the iron-binding protein lactoferrin, which is present in secretions in abundance. As noted below, lactoferrin acts by depriving microorganisms of needed iron. Secretory IgA enhances the effects of lactoferrin by preventing bacteria from releasing their own iron-binding compounds (enterochelins, ferromyns). The clearest role for secretory IgA in bacterial disease is in the prevention of bacterial attachment to mucosal cells. Under experimental conditions, IgA can prevent the attachment of oral streptococci and *V cholerae* to mucosal surfaces. This may be why intraluminal gut antibody (coproantibody) levels are so important in protecting guinea pigs from oral challenge with *V cholerae.* Secretory IgA is believed to be important in retarding the colonization of mucosal surfaces with a variety of other microorganisms as well, including *N gonorrhoeae.* The mechanism by which secretory IgA blocks attachment of bacteria to mucosal cells is uncertain.

Not surprisingly, microorganisms have evolved countermeasures to permit their attachment to mucosal epithelial cells despite the presence of secretory IgA. *Streptococcus sanguis* and *Streptococcus mitior* (bacteria important in dental plaque formation), *Streptococcus pneumoniae, N gonorrhoeae, Neisseria meningitidis* and *Haemophilus influenzae* have all been shown to elaborate an IgA protease in vitro that cleaves and inactivates the IgA1 subclass, yielding intact Fab and Fc fragments. The IgA2 subclass is resistant to cleavage by virtue of the absence of 13 amino acid residues in the hinge region, the site at which IgA1 proteases exert their effects. Some strains of *Bacteroides asaccharolyticus, Bacteroides melaninogenicus,* and *Capnocytophaga* are capable of cleaving not only IgA1 but also IgA2 and IgG. These bacteria are important etiologic agents in human periodontal disease. Immunoglobulin protease activity has been detected in human oropharyngeal secretions, dental plaque, and vaginal secretions. It seems likely that these proteases may play an important role in the interaction of bacteria and epithelial cells.

SYSTEMIC IMMUNITY TO INFECTION

Cellular Systems of Systemic Immunity

Once microorganisms have breached local defense mechanisms, a number of tightly integrated immunologic events are called into play which are predominantly related to the activity of 2 types of phagocytic cells: polymorphonuclear leukocytes and mononuclear phagocytes. These cells have been termed "professional phagocytes" because their membranes possess specialized receptors for the Fc portion of IgG molecules (IgG1 and IgG3 subclasses) and for activated C3. These receptors augment the process of phagocytosis by assisting in the ingestion of microorganisms with IgG or activated C3 on their surfaces. Nonprofessional or facultative phagocytes, in contrast, include endothelial cells, epithelial cells, fibroblasts, and other cells which will ingest microorganisms under specialized conditions but which do not possess specialized membrane receptors for IgG or C3.

Mononuclear phagocytes are the only phagocytic cells of nonvertebrates and subserve a digestive function in at least some of them. Granulocytes are found in animals which possess circulatory systems. Why the need arose for 2 different types of phagocytic cells whose capabilities overlap in many respects is still unknown. However, many consider the polymorphonuclear neutrophil (PMN), by virtue of its peculiarly segmented nucleus, to be especially well designed to traverse tight spaces.

A. Polymorphonuclear Neutrophil Leukocytes: These cells are concerned principally with the destruction of microorganisms that rely upon the evasion of phagocytosis for survival. Once ingested, such microorganisms generally perish. Microorganisms of this type are considered **extracellular pathogens;** their prototype is the pneumococcus.

B. Mononuclear Phagocytes: These cells are concerned principally with the control of microorganisms which are able to survive intracellular residence and against which neutrophils are ineffective. The principal effector cells are monocytes and macrophages. Monocytes are immature circulating forms of mature tissue macrophages. Monocytes may serve as a backup system to neutrophils in acute infections, but they phagocytose less efficiently and lack many of the potent bactericidal systems of the neutrophil. Macrophages are much more important in chronic infections. Sensitized lymphocytes may augment the bactericidal activities of macrophages through direct cell-to-cell contact or by the intervention of soluble mediators or lymphokines. Conversely, macrophages may process ingested or adsorbed microbial antigens preparatory to the sensitization of lymphocytes. Intracellular pathogens such as *Mycobacterium leprae, Mycobacterium tuberculosis, L monocytogenes, Salmonella typhi,* and some viruses and protozoa appear to be under control of lymphocytes and macrophages.

Humoral Systems of Systemic Immunity

The role of humoral factors in systemic infection is largely related to augmentation of phagocytic function through the processes of chemotaxis and opsonization. In many respects, the humoral immune system provides specificity to the phagocytic system. However, some mechanisms of antimicrobial activity are mediated solely by humoral factors.

A. Complement-Mediated Bacteriolysis: In the presence of specific antibody and an intact classic complement pathway, many gram-negative bacteria can be directly lysed by serum. Among these are *N gonorrhoeae, N meningitidis, H influenzae,* and strains of *Salmonella, Shigella,* and *Vibrio.* Endotoxin in the cell membrane of gram-negative bacteria, unless blocked by other membrane constituents, may also directly activate the alternative complement pathway, with the result that bacteriolysis occurs in the absence of antibody. Thus, the alternative complement pathway may serve as an important first line of defense in the nonimmune host—a role that it also plays in regard to phagocytosis (see below). In order for bacteriolysis to occur, activation of the entire terminal attack sequence of the complement cascade is ordinarily required. The importance of terminal complement components is illustrated by the fact that patients with deficiencies of C6, C7, or C8 may suffer repeated episodes of gonococcal or meningococcal sepsis.

Unlike the situation described above, specific antibody and both the classic and alternative complement pathways subserve a predominantly opsonic function for gram-positive bacteria and fungi.

Bacterial variants that have lost cell wall material (L forms) are susceptible to complement-mediated lysis even when the gram-positive and gram-negative microorganisms from which they are derived are resistant to the effects of antibody and complement.

B. Viral Neutralization: Humoral antibodies constitute one of the more important mechanisms of host resistance to viral infections. (See Special Aspects of Viral Immunity, below.)

C. Beta-Lysin: Beta-lysin is a highly reactive heat-stable cationic protein which is bactericidal for gram-positive microorganisms (except streptococci). Its release from platelets during coagulation results in serum levels which are far higher than plasma levels. Beta-lysin acts at the cell membrane of gram-positive bacteria to produce a nonenzymatic destructive effect similar to that of histones. Gram-negative microorganisms are resistant to its effects except under experimental conditions or in the presence of antibody, complement, and lysozyme.

D. Lysozyme: Lysozyme is a basic protein that originates from phagocytic cells and is present in serum in a concentration of $1-2$ μg/mL. It is actively secreted by monocytes and macrophages. Its mechanism of action is discussed later.

Microbial Agglutination & Bloodstream Clearance

Bacteria which gain access to the circulation are

generally cleared from the blood by the fixed tissue macrophages of the mononuclear phagocyte system—especially the Kupffer cells of the liver. Features of opsonization and phagocytosis are presumably the same as for other mononuclear phagocytes (see below). However, there is evidence that the agglutination of microorganisms by serum factors, perhaps on a nonspecific basis, serves to augment the clearance of microorganisms from the bloodstream as well.

POLYMORPHONUCLEAR NEUTROPHIL LEUKOCYTE FUNCTION

The mature human neutrophil is an end-stage cell that, once released from the bone marrow, circulates with a half-life of 6–7 hours before losing functional capability and leaving the body in a random (non–age-related) fashion. About 10^{11} neutrophils enter and leave the body daily. Release of granulocytes into the peripheral blood appears to relate to cell stickiness and deformability and to a releasing factor that may act upon bone marrow sinusoids. The factors controlling maturation and production of granulocytes are poorly understood. Clonal growth in vitro of committed neutrophil precursor cells is dependent upon the presence in the culture system of glycoprotein molecules known collectively as **colony-stimulating activity (CSA).** In humans, the major source of this material appears to be the interaction of monocytes and T lymphocytes. Neutrophil lactoferrin may serve as a feedback regulator of granulopoiesis by blocking the production in monocytes of soluble factors that stimulate T lymphocytes to produce CSA. Other controlling factors may include endotoxin and neutrophil breakdown products.

The total blood neutrophil pool is composed of approximately equal numbers of circulating and marginated cells. Both marginated and bone marrow neutrophil pools are called into play during acute infections. Studies of neutrophil NBT dye reduction in response to endotoxin, rosetting of IgG-coated erythrocytes, and response to stimulation by chemotactic peptides suggest that there is functional heterogeneity among circulating neutrophil populations.

Phagocytosis by neutrophils is composed of 4 interrelated phases: chemotaxis, opsonization, ingestion, and killing.

Chemotaxis

Neutrophils in the circulation are concentrated in areas of inflammation because of increased stickiness of endothelial surfaces, attachment to capillary walls, and migration into the tissues. Granulocyte–endothelial cell adherence can be conveniently estimated by studying the ability of leukocytes in heparinized whole blood specimens to adhere to columns of spun nylon fibers. The kinin and complement systems are involved in changes of capillary permeability; however, once phagocytes are in the tissues, chemotactic factors attract them toward the site of microbial invasion (Fig 16–1).

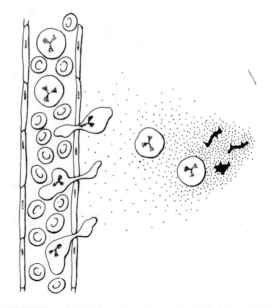

Figure 16–1. A capillary in an area of inflammation. Neutrophils become sticky, attach to capillary endothelium, and migrate between cells of the capillary wall. There is movement toward the area of bacterial invasion as a consequence of the gradient of chemotactic factors, with highest concentration at the site of highest bacterial concentration. (Reproduced, with permission, from Quie PG: The phagocytic system and host resistance to microbial disease. Chapter 18 in: *Clinical Concepts of Immunology.* Waldman RH [editor]. Williams & Wilkins, 1979.)

Chemotaxis can be defined as the ability of motile cells to recognize and respond to a suitable chemical gradient with directional migration. Chemokinesis is the reaction by which chemical substances determine the rate of cellular locomotion. Both factors influence the accumulation of inflammatory cells at an infective focus.

Microorganisms are capable of elaborating chemotactic factors (chemotaxins) in the absence of serum. The best-studied of these is N-formylmethionine, a peptide important in the initiation of bacterial protein synthesis. Formyl-methionyl peptides are unique to bacteria and may signal their presence in the body. A series of formyl di- and tripeptides (F-Met-Phe; F-Met-Leu-Phe) has been synthesized and has been of great value in explaining early events in chemotaxis. The prototype peptide F-Met-Leu-Phe expresses chemotactic activity at concentrations as low as 0.01–0.1 nM. Interaction of monosodium urate or calcium pyrophosphate crystals with neutrophils can also produce a factor (**crystal-induced chemotactic factor; CCF**) of MW 8400 that is directly chemotactic for neutrophils.

Despite these examples of direct stimulation of neutrophil chemotaxis, most chemotactic factors are produced through the mediation of the complement system (Fig 16–2). Following complement activation by either the classic or alternative pathways, C3 and

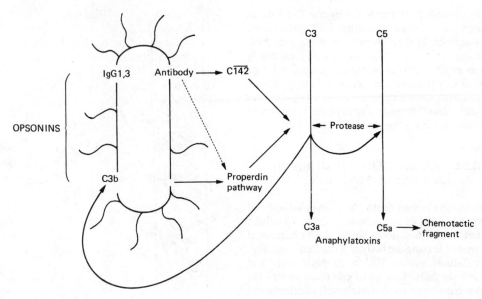

Figure 16–2. Serum-mediated generation of chemotactic factors and opsonization of microorganisms. (Modified and reproduced, with permission, from Stossel TP: Phagocytosis. *N Engl J Med* 1974;**290**:719.)

C5 are cleaved into a and b fragments, respectively. Both C3a and C5a serve as anaphylatoxins, provoking the noncytolytic release of histamine from mast cells and basophils, contracting smooth muscle, and increasing capillary permeability. In addition, C5a is recognized as the most potent chemotactic factor derived from the complement system. Concentrations as low as 5–10 ng/mL will provoke directed migration of neutrophils, monocytes, and eosinophils. C5a also augments the adhesiveness of neutrophils to diverse surfaces, and to themselves in suspension. Other chemotactic complement factors include the trimolecular complex C5,6,7; by-products of this complex produced by trypsin digestion; and digestive products of C5 produced by bacterial proteases and thrombin. Other sequentially reacting protein systems (kallikrein system; fibrinolysis system) also contain factors with leukotactic activity. Leukocytes contain factors that are directly or indirectly chemotactic, and leukotactic factors may arise from sensitized leukocytes following contact of cells with antigen. Finally, a variety of chemotactic lipids have been identified, including HETE (leukotriene LTB$_4$) prostaglandins, and lipid constituents of bacterial chemotactic factors.

When C5a, formyl-methionyl peptides, and (presumably) other chemotactic factors attach to leukocyte receptors, an esterase is activated; arachidonic acid metabolism and the hexose monophosphate shunt are activated; sodium, potassium, and calcium fluxes occur; membrane polarity is altered; and directed cell movement occurs. The moving neutrophil has specific morphologic features. The leading edge of the pseudopod is free of granules; the trailing edge (uropod) exhibits thin retraction fibrils that attach to the sub-

stratum. Actin microfilaments fill the leading edge of the pseudopod, extend as a thin submembranous layer around the cell, and then reappear as dense bundles in the uropod. These microfilaments provide structural support, and in concert with myosins and other regulatory proteins, are capable of contracting, thus providing the dynamic forces needed for cell movement. Microtubules are also present in the cell but have no role in mobility. Rather, they serve as an internal scaffolding, increasing rigidity and maintaining cell shape. They also appear to be the structures responsible for persistence of movement in a specific direction in the absence of a chemotactic gradient.

Additional events reported to occur when chemotactic factors bind to target sites on phagocytes include at least partial initiation of the respiratory burst (with chemiluminescence and superoxide anion production); increased expression of C3b and IgG receptors; cGMP production (which stimulates chemotaxis); and partial degranulation. Many of these phenomena are discussed in greater detail in the section dealing with killing.

Since it is in the interest of microorganisms to avoid stimulating leukocyte chemotaxis, they have developed protective mechanisms. Thus, gonococci that produce disseminated infection activate complement (specifically the C5a fragment) less rapidly than gonococci that produce mucosal infection. *Pseudomonas aeruginosa* elaborates a protease (elastase) that inactivates both classic and alternative complement pathway components. *Capnocytophaga,* an important pathogen in periodontal infection, interferes directly with neutrophil chemotaxis. Finally, enterotoxigenic strains of *E coli* that produce diarrhea through their ability to stimulate cAMP production by the gut mucosa can also stimulate cAMP production by human leukocytes. The ability of leukocytes to undergo chemotaxis can thereby be inhibited.

Opsonization

The function of serum opsonins (Gk *opsonein* to prepare food for) is to react with microorganisms and make them more susceptible to ingestion by phagocytes. The virulence of many pathogens relates in part to their ability to evade phagocytosis by virtue of certain surface antigens. Microorganisms in which antiphagocytic surface factors are of importance include *Streptococcus pneumoniae*, group B streptococci, *Klebsiella pneumoniae*, *H influenzae*, *N meningitidis*, *B fragilis*, and some strains of *P aeruginosa* (capsular polysaccharides); *Bacillus anthracis* (capsular polypeptide); *N gonorrhoeae* (pili composed of protein; other poorly characterized surface factors); *S pyogenes* (capsular hyaluronic acid and M protein); and *S aureus* (protein A, which has the capacity to bind to the Fc portion of IgG, thereby competing with phagocytes for the Fc sites of opsonins).

Van Oss has postulated that nonvirulent bacteria possess relatively hydrophobic surfaces that favor phagocytosis, whereas virulent (especially encapsulated) microorganisms are characterized by hydrophilic surface factors that retard phagocytosis. According to this view, it is the purpose of opsonization to increase hydrophobicity, thereby reducing the charge repulsion between microorganism and neutrophil, both of which are negatively charged.

Opsonization of bacteria may occur by at least one of 3 mechanisms, as noted below. However, no simple scheme can summarize the opsonic requirements of any single genus or species of microorganism.

First, specific antibody alone (subclasses IgG1 and IgG3) may act as an opsonin as shown in Fig 16–3.

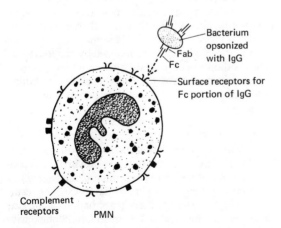

Figure 16–3. Schematic representation of receptors on the surface of a neutrophil (PMN) that interact with complement components and with the Fc portion of IgG molecules. (Reproduced, with permission, from Cline MJ: *The White Cell*. Harvard Univ Press, 1975.)

This mechanism has been explored most thoroughly in studies employing pneumococci under conditions of abundant antibody. Here, anticapsular antibody combines with the surface polysaccharide antigens of the pneumococci through antibody combining sites located on the Fab portion of the immunoglobulin molecule. The Fc portion of the molecule, which is critical to its function as an opsonin, is then free to attach to Fc receptor sites on the surface of phagocytes, thus completing a bridge between bacteria and phagocytic cell.

Second, specific antibody acting in concert with complement via the classic C1, C4, C2 pathway may promote microbial opsonization. Here, a quantity of IgM or IgG apparently insufficient to opsonize on its own may react with bacteria and activate sequentially the hemolytic complement sequence. Receptor sites for activated C3 (C3b) are present on the surface of phagocytes (Fig 16–3). The activated C3 on the bacterial surface apparently serves as a bridge between bacteria and phagocyte, prompting ingestion.

Third, opsonization can be nonspecific, via the alternative complement pathway. Although antibody is absolutely required for opsonic activity mediated by the classic complement pathway, the alternative pathway does not require antigen-antibody interaction. Instead, this pathway is activated directly by bacterial or fungal polysaccharides, resulting in fixation of C3, the crucial opsonic factor, to the surface of the microorganism. Ingestion by phagocytes is therefore mediated by the cellular receptor for activated C3.

Normal 7S immunoglobulin isolated from nonimmune animals has been shown to participate functionally in this system (at least in the case of pneumococci). The immunoglobulin does not appear directed toward the capsule, and its site of binding on the pneumococcus is unknown.

Since the alternative complement pathway is present in nonimmune animals and is not dependent upon the presence of anticapsular antibody for its action, it has been considered to play an important role in the early and critical preimmune stages of infection prior to the production of specific antibody. This is also the stage at which surface phagocytosis is considered most important (see below). The precise role of the alternative complement pathway in human infection is not clear, but it has been suggested that the abnormal susceptibility of patients with sickle cell anemia to fulminating pneumococcal infection may be related to their demonstrably low levels of heat-labile pneumococcal opsonins. Such patients may fail to utilize fully the alternative pathway of complement activation, perhaps because some of the necessary components are synthesized in the spleen. Although levels of factor B and properdin are normal, there is a deficiency of C3 proactivator convertase (C3PA) activity. Patients with sickle cell anemia undergo early autosplenectomy as a result of repeated infarcts.

There are 3 other factors that may promote phagocytosis of microorganisms in association with the above systems.

A. Surface Phagocytosis: As noted, many microbial pathogens may possess antiphagocytic surface components (such as pneumococcal capsular polysaccharide) which protect them from phagocytosis in the absence of specific antibody. Yet there are often no homologous antibodies in the serum before the fifth or sixth day of illness. Survival of a patient during the preantibody stage of infection may depend not only upon the alternative complement pathway but also upon surface phagocytosis. Here, encapsulated bacteria are trapped between leukocytes themselves, between leukocytes and tissue surfaces, or along with leukocytes in the interstices of fibrin clots. Surface phagocytosis may occur with mononuclear phagocytes as well as neutrophils. Heavily encapsulated type 3 pneumococci may resist surface phagocytosis for some time. Surface phagocytosis is much less efficient in areas where leukocytes are not tightly packed (pleural, pericardial, and joint fluids; cerebrospinal fluid).

B. Natural Antibody: Antibodies present in the serum in the absence of apparent specific antigen contact are referred to as natural antibodies. They probably reflect contact with microorganisms possessing related antigens. For example, more than 80% of persons over the age of 1 year have antibody to type 7 pneumococci, although the carrier rate of this microorganism is only about 1%. The antibody appears following exposure to certain viridans streptococci that possess a cross-reacting surface antigen.

Presumably, natural antibodies may participate with the heat-labile opsonin system in preventing infection with microorganisms which do not possess surface factors posing a serious challenge to phagocytosis.

C. Tuftsin: Leukokinin, a γ-globulin moiety which coats the polymorphonuclear neutrophil (PMN), is capable of stimulating phagocytosis by neutrophils under experimental conditions. The biologic activity of leukokinin rests in a single peptide, tuftsin—so called because it was discovered at Tufts University. The peptide (Thr-Lys-Pro-Arg) is apparently produced in the spleen. It has also been prepared synthetically. A membrane enzyme of the neutrophil appears capable of splitting tuftsin from leukokinin. Splenectomy results in a severe deficiency of tuftsin and may be one of several reasons why splenectomized patients are more susceptible to certain infections.

Ingestion (See Fig 16–4)

Once a microorganism has been adequately opsonized, the machinery of membrane locomotion is activated, as described previously. Since energy for this process is provided by anaerobic glycolysis, phagocytosis can take place even in the anaerobic interior of an abscess. The movement of pseudopodia around microorganisms requires actin and myosin microfilament activity identical to that described for chemotaxis. Ingestion is not an all-or-none phenomenon but requires sequential interactions between opsonic ligands distributed homogeneously over the surface of the particles to be ingested and

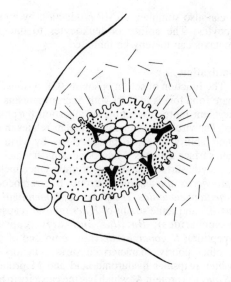

Figure 16–4. A section of the neutrophil is shown engulfing a clump of opsonized bacteria. The neutrophil membrane is "activated" by antibody molecules and complement factor C3b. This causes contractile proteins in the cytoplasm to polymerize and become microfilaments and microtubules and the neutrophil engulfs the bacterial clump. (Reproduced, with permission, from Quie PG: The phagocytic system and host resistance to microbial disease. Chapter 18 in: *Clinical Concepts of Immunology.* Waldman RH [editor]. Williams & Wilkins, 1979.)

receptors on the phagocyte membrane (Fig 16–4). This sequential interaction results in the circumferential flow of phagocyte membrane around the particle, "zipping up" the particle into the forming phagosome. Cell pseudopodia fuse on the distal side of the material being ingested, and the particle becomes encased within a phagocytic vacuole (phagosome). The phagosome buds off from the cell periphery and moves toward the center, apparently through the mediation of microtubules. Recent evidence suggests that rabbit polymorphonuclear leukocytes discharge inert particles by a process of exocytosis at the same time that other particles are being internalized by phagocytosis. If this is shown to occur with bacteria, it may represent a mechanism whereby the PMN amplifies its killing potential by the cycling of microorganisms to be killed.

Respiratory Burst

This term describes a metabolic pathway, dormant in resting cells, the function of which is to produce a group of highly reactive microbicidal agents by the partial reduction of oxygen (Fig 16–5). The respiratory burst occurs with any perturbation of the cell membrane of the neutrophil (including contact with N-formylmethionyl peptides) and is independent of the process of ingestion. There are 4 components to the respiratory burst: increase in oxygen consumption, superoxide ($O_2^-\cdot$) production, H_2O_2 production, and hexose monophosphate shunt activation.

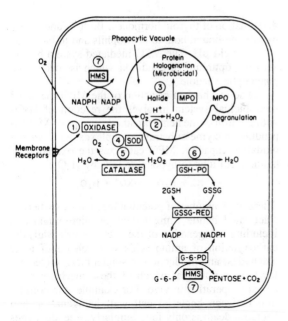

Figure 16-5. Events that occur during oxidative killing. Abbreviations: HMS, hexose monophosphate shunt; MPO, myeloperoxidase; SOD, superoxide dismutase; GSH-PO, glutathione peroxidase; GSH, reduced glutathione; GSSG, oxidized glutathione; G-6-PD, glucose-6-phosphate dehydrogenase; G-6-P, glucose-6-phosphate. (Reproduced, with permission, from Root RK: Page 177 in: *Microbiology, 1981.* Schlessinger D [editor]. American Society for Microbiology, 1981.)

The mechanism of the burst is as follows: (1) Contact of a particle with the neutrophil membrane activates a membrane-associated flavoenzyme system currently referred to as "NADPH oxidase" (some consider the enzyme to be NADH oxidase). NADPH oxidase catalyzes the one-electron reduction of oxygen (O_2) to superoxide ($O_2^-\cdot$), using NADPH as the electron donor. The functional integrity of this step can be tested by the use of nitroblue tetrazolium (NBT) dye—a yellow water-soluble electron acceptor dye that is converted to insoluble blue formazan on reduction. NBT dye reduction in phagocytes occurs by a chemical reaction between the dye and $O_2^-\cdot$ generated during the respiratory burst. (2) Two molecules of superoxide combine in the presence of the enzyme superoxide dismutase to form hydrogen peroxide (H_2O_2):

$$O_2^-\cdot + O_2^-\cdot + 2H^+ \rightarrow O_2 + H_2O_2$$

(3) Myeloperoxidase (MPO) is deposited by degranulation into phagocytic vacuoles, where, in the presence of H_2O_2 and halide it catalyzes microbicidal reactions (see below). (4) Superoxide that escapes from the phagocytic vacuole is reduced by H_2O_2 at an enhanced rate by superoxide dismutase (SOD). (5–7) Cytoplasmic H_2O_2 is detoxified by the catalase and glutathione peroxidase–glutathione reductase systems. Both the superoxide-forming NADPH oxidase and the glutathione systems generate $NADP^+$ in the course of

their activity. This $NADP^+$ is converted back to NADPH by the hexose monophosphate shunt.

Degranulation

The destruction of susceptible microorganisms within neutrophils is intimately associated with the process of degranulation, the release of granule contents into phagosomes. There is slso firm evidence that some degranulation takes place to the cell exterior.

Human neutrophils contain 2 major types of granules. Primary granules contain abundant hydrolytic lysosomal enzymes, large amounts of myeloperoxidase (the green hue of which is largely responsible for the color of pus), lysozyme, elastase, and cationic proteins. (Recent studies suggest that there may be a second population of primary granules that lack myeloperoxidase). Secondary (specific) granules appear as the promyelocyte matures to a myelocyte in the marrow. They are smaller than primary granules, stain poorly (neutrophilic), and later outnumber primary granules in the mature neutrophil. Secondary granules contain lactoferrin and lysozyme.

As the phagosome forms during microbial engulfment, neutrophil granules undergo violent movement in proximity to the phagosome, fuse with the phagocytic vacuole, and disappear from the cytoplasm (degranulate). Somewhere between the stages of attachment and digestion, the membranes of specific granules begin to fuse with the nascent phagosomes. As a result, lactoferrin and lysozyme are allowed to enter the extracellular space. Azurophilic granules fuse with the phagosomes slightly later; the contents of these granules tend to remain in the phagolysosome. As with chemotaxis and ingestion, microfilaments and microtubules appear to be important in the fusion of phagosomes and granules.

Killing

The mechanisms by which neutrophils kill microorganisms are not fully understood. However, it is clear that multiple interlocking microbicidal systems are present, providing considerable redundancy in host defense mechanisms. For example, pneumococci may be killed either by oxidative mechanisms or by the presence of a low pH in the phagocytic vacuole.

The antimicrobial mechanisms of human PMNs may be divided into 2 broad categories: oxygen-dependent and oxygen-independent (Table 16–1).

A. Oxygen-Dependent Systems: Oxidative mechanisms of killing may be divided into those which are myeloperoxidase (MPO)-mediated and those which are not. Of the systems to be described, only the MPO system has definitely been proved to participate in oxygen-dependent killing by phagocytes. However, recent studies reveal that in up to 0.025% of the general population, the neutrophils do not contain myeloperoxidase, and yet these persons do not exhibit predisposition to infection. Therefore, the primacy of MPO in oxidative microbial killing is open to question. Oxygen-dependent killing not dependent on MPO clearly takes place, but its mechanism is unknown.

Table 16–1. Antimicrobial systems of the polymorphonuclear neutrophil.

Oxygen-dependent
  Myeloperoxidase-mediated: Components of this system include the following:
    Myeloperoxidase
    H_2O_2
    Oxidizable cofactor (usually halide)
    Acid
  Myeloperoxidase-independent:
    H_2O_2
    Superoxide anion
    Singlet oxygen
    Hydroxyl radical
Oxygen-independent
  Cationic proteins
  Lactoferrin
  Lysozyme
  Acid pH
  Nuclear histones
  Elastase

---

1. Myeloperoxidase-mediated–The importance of MPO in bacterial killing by phagocytes, reported by Klebanoff in 1967, has been widely confirmed. Incubation of bacteria with H_2O_2, MPO, and a halide ion results in efficient killing at H_2O_2 concentrations as low as 10 μM. Without MPO, similar levels of killing are not achieved until the concentration of H_2O_2 reaches 0.5 mM. Components of the MPO system are as follows:

a. Myeloperoxidase–MPO is found in the primary (azurophil) granules and accounts for up to 5% of the dry weight of the neutrophil. In conjunction with H_2O_2, oxidizable halide cofactors, and an acid pH, a potent antimicrobial system is developed in the phagolysosome which has antibacterial, antifungal, antiviral, and antimycoplasmal capabilities.

b. H_2O_2–Under ordinary circumstances, the H_2O_2 utilized in this system is considered to arise from the respiratory burst. With deficient H_2O_2 production (eg, chronic granulomatous disease), certain microorganisms may paradoxically provide the H_2O_2 which mediates their own destruction. Among these are pneumococci and other streptococci. These microorganisms are classed as Lactobacillaceae; their terminal oxidations are catalyzed by flavoproteins which reduce oxygen to H_2O_2. Because they lack catalase, H_2O_2 accumulates and can be used in the MPO-mediated killing system. This may explain why patients with chronic granulomatous disease show no particular predisposition to streptococcal infections.

c. Halide–Chloride is present in the neutrophil at a level considerably above that required for participation in MPO-mediated killing. Chloride could enter the phagocytic vacuole along with the phagocytosed particle or could be transferred across the membrane of the phagolysosome. The other logical halide participant could be iodide—provided either directly from the serum (serum concentration < 1 μg/dL) or by the

deiodination of thyroid hormones. Both T_3 and T_4 are membrane-bound both to neutrophils and to bacteria.

d. Acid pH–The MPO-mediated system has an acid pH optimum, a condition which is met in the phagocytic vacuole.

The mechanism of action of the MPO-mediated microbicidal system involves the reaction of H_2O_2 with the iron of the heme prosthetic groups of MPO to produce enzyme-substrate complexes with strong oxidative capacity. MPO catalyzes the oxidation of halide (X^-) ions to hypohalite ions by H_2O_2:

$$X^- + H_2O_2 \rightarrow XO^- + H_2O$$

There are a number of potential mechanisms whereby "activated halide" might damage microorganisms, including halogenation of the bacterial cell wall, decarboxylation of amino acids with release of toxic aldehydes, and production of singlet oxygen (see below). It is not clear which of these mechanisms is actually operative in vivo. For example, the correlation between bacterial cell wall halogenation and bacterial death is only fair. Similarly, free aldehydes are not toxic enough to account alone for bacterial killing. Moreover, bacterial death can take place under experimental circumstances that preclude amino acid decarboxylation.

e. Singlet oxygen–Singlet oxygen ($^1O_2$) has the same molecular formula as atmospheric (triplet) oxygen (O_2) but differs in the distribution of electrons around the 2 oxygen nuclei. In atmospheric oxygen, the electrons form a cylindric cloud; in singlet oxygen, the electron cloud is distorted away from a cylindric configuration. This distortion so alters the chemical properties that singlet and atmospheric oxygen must be regarded as distinct chemical species.

The terms singlet and triplet have to do with the magnetic properties of the 2 forms of oxygen, which in turn originate from the magnetism of the electron. The electron possesses a magnetic field resembling that of a bar magnet, with a north and south pole. In most molecules, each electron is paired with another whose magnetic field is oppositely oriented, so that the fields cancel and the molecule is diamagnetic. In atmospheric oxygen, however, 2 of the electrons are unpaired and arrange themselves so that their magnetic fields are oriented in the same direction. For this reason, atmospheric oxygen is paramagnetic. In singlet oxygen, a higher energy species, these 2 electrons pair, abolishing the paramagnetism of the molecule. When heated sufficiently, both singlet and triplet oxygen will radiate light, generating an emission spectrum composed of a series of sharp lines at precisely defined wavelengths. In a magnetic field, each line in the spectrum of atmospheric oxygen splits into 3 closely spaced lines ("triplet"). This splitting results from an interaction between the external field and the unpaired electrons in the oxygen molecule. Singlet oxygen emission lines remain unsplit in a magnetic field ("singlet"). Thus the terms triplet and singlet originate from the magnetic behavior of the spectral emission lines.

There are several potential sources for singlet oxygen during the respiratory burst:

1. OCl^-, a product of the MPO reaction, is known to react with H_2O_2 to produce singlet oxygen:

$$OCl^- + H_2O_2 \rightarrow {}^1O_2 + Cl^- + H_2O$$

2. The reaction of superoxide ($O_2^-\cdot$) with H_2O_2 can produce singlet oxygen and hydroxyl radical (see below). This reaction (Haber-Weiss reaction) is strongly catalyzed by iron and lactoferrin.

$$O_2^-\cdot + H_2O_2 \rightarrow {}^1O_2 + OH\cdot + OH^-$$

3. Spontaneous dismutation of superoxide (in the absence of superoxide dismutase) may produce singlet oxygen:

$$2O_2^-\cdot + 2H^+ \rightarrow {}^1O_2 + H_2O_2$$

The lifetime of singlet oxygen is short, with dissipation of energy by thermal decay, light emission, or chemical reaction. Singlet oxygen has a particular propensity to react with double bonds and would be lethal to any biologic system that is contacted. However, there is little direct proof that singlet oxygen is actually produced in the leukocyte. The production of a low-level burst of light by phagocytosing PMNs (chemiluminescence), detectable in a liquid scintillation counter, was once taken to indicate that singlet oxygen had been produced. However, it is now known that many oxidizing species can oxidize a second molecule to form a light-emitting product. For example, both H_2O_2 and $O_2^-\cdot$ can produce light-emitting reactions, the light emission occurring at all visible wavelengths. In contrast, the singlet oxygen → atmospheric oxygen transition produces a characteristic red light emission. Thus, standard tests of leukocyte chemiluminescence reflect only a nonspecific accompaniment of the respiratory burst and do not prove the presence of singlet oxygen.

2. Myeloperoxidase-independent systems– Numerous persons have been identified whose PMNs and monocytes contain no MPO. The bactericidal activity of MPO-deficient PMNs is characterized by a lag period, but the killing of most ingested microorganisms is eventually complete. Thus, MPO is required for optimal microbicidal activity, but its absence from phagocytes is not necessarily disabling. Obviously, other mechanisms exist in MPO-deficient cells for the destruction of invading pathogens. At least 4 oxygen-dependent systems may continue to function in the PMN in the absence of MPO:

a. H_2O_2– At high concentrations, H_2O_2 has direct antimicrobial activity. In addition, it may act in concert with ascorbic acid and certain metal ions to kill ingested microorganisms by nonenzymatic means. Some microorganisms are more susceptible to H_2O_2 than others, depending on their ability to produce catalase or peroxidase (the latter may subsume the function of catalase).

b. Superoxide anion– A direct toxic effect of superoxide anion on microorganisms has been postulated. However, many microorganisms contain superoxide dismutase and would be expected to resist the action of this radical in the phagocytic vacuole. Actually, the H_2O_2 formed from the superoxide anion has far greater microbicidal potential when employed as a component in the MPO-mediated system. Superoxide anion itself is only weakly bactericidal.

c. Singlet oxygen– Singlet oxygen is reportedly present in reduced amounts in phagocytosing PMNs which are deficient in MPO. It is possible that the radical comes about as a by-product in the spontaneous dismutation of superoxide anion.

d. Hydroxyl radical– Hydroxyl radical, formed by the interaction of H_2O_2 and superoxide anion, may be formed in the leukocyte by the Haber-Weiss reaction, as noted above. Alternatively, superoxide may have to react with an intermediate peroxy compound before $OH\cdot$ is produced. The hydroxyl radical is a highly unstable oxidizing species that reacts almost instantaneously with most organic molecules that it encounters. It is best known as one of the major products resulting from the passage of ionizing radiation through water and has been implicated in the toxicity of radiation for tissues. Recent studies suggest that hydroxyl radical is produced by both PMNs and monocytes.

B. Oxygen-Independent Systems: Systems of microbicidal activity that are independent of the respiratory burst include those based upon cationic proteins, lactoferrin, lysozyme, nuclear histones, elastase, and production of acid in the phagocytic vacuole. Nonoxidative microbicidal mechanisms are of obvious importance, because certain microorganisms can clearly be killed by neutrophils under anaerobic conditions (eg, *P aeruginosa, Candida parapsilosis,* anaerobic bacteria).

1. Cationic proteins– Cationic proteins from azurophilic granules were the first antimicrobial substances defined in the neutrophil. Previous names for these substances have included "phagocytin" and "leukin." Cationic proteins are rich in arginine; are most active at neutral pH; and rapidly affect the ability of microorganisms to replicate without destroying their structural integrity. Separate cationic protein subclasses demonstrate specificity for certain classes of microorganisms. The susceptibility of gram-negative microorganisms to lysis by neutrophils is related to the amount of polysaccharide in the outer cell envelope; smooth strains may be more difficult to kill than rough strains. No clinical examples of impaired cationic protein function in human neutrophils have yet been identified.

2. Lactoferrin– Lactoferrin from specific granules may exert antimicrobial function by binding and withholding required iron from ingested bacteria and fungi. One-third to three-fourths of lactoferrin is discharged into the extracellular medium during phagocytosis, so that lactoferrin may exert a substantial proportion of its effect outside the phagocyte.

Microorganisms appear to defend themselves by the presence of enterochelins (siderophores, ferromyns) that compete with the transferrin or lactoferrin systems for iron. Antibody shifts the balance toward the host by interfering with the production of enterochelin. At least one patient has been described in whom impaired bacterial killing was associated with lactoferrin-deficient neutrophil granules.

3. Lysozyme–Lysozyme, present in both primary and specific granules, attacks mucopeptides in the cell walls of various bacteria. Bacteria intrinsically insensitive to lysozyme become sensitive to it in the presence of hemolytic complement or ascorbic acid and hydrogen peroxide. Because bacterial death often precedes temporally the action of lysozyme, this enzyme may serve in a digestive rather than microbicidal capacity.

4. Low pH–During phagocytosis, the pH in the phagosome falls. In rat macrophages, the increase in acidity has been shown to be dramatic (pH 3.5–4.5) and rapid (20 minutes). In human neutrophils, the fall in pH is less extreme (pH 4.5–6.5) and slower (60 minutes). The mechanism of acidification is unknown, but recent studies suggest that it is coupled in a 1:1 ratio with cellular oxygen consumption. In patients with chronic granulomatous disease, impaired cell respiration leads to inability of cells to generate hydrogen ion release.

Acidification appears to enhance the function of some antimicrobial enzyme systems (eg, MPO-H_2O_2-halide, or lysozyme), but others (eg, cationic proteins) function best at neutral or slightly alkaline pH. Some bacteria are killed directly by organic acids in an acid medium or by lipophilic acids.

5. Nuclear histones–These substances are released into surrounding tissues by death and autolysis of cells. They have direct antimicrobial activity.

6. Proteases–Granulocytes contain a variety of proteases that are active at neutral pH (eg, cathepsin G, serine esterases, elastase). These substances may be more important in microbial digestion than in killing.

7. Serum factors–As noted previously, serum factors promote phagocytic killing of microorganisms chiefly by their opsonic function. However, a recent study has demonstrated that both IgG and complement may augment the ability of human monocytes to kill intracellular *S aureus* and *E coli*. The mechanism by which this occurs has not been elucidated.

Extracellular Release of Granulocyte Constituents

As noted above, the respiratory burst is activated by a perturbation of the neutrophil surface independently of the process of ingestion. Moreover, specific granules may discharge their contents to the outside of the cell during phagosome formation. The best evidence that these mechanisms are operative in antimicrobial host defenses comes from studies of the interaction of neutrophils and fungal mycelia and of eosinophils with metazoan parasites and flagellates. Mycelial elements clearly too large to be completely

ingested by human neutrophils can still be killed by a process that includes the spread of neutrophils over the mycelial surface, respiratory burst activity with iodination of the fungal surface, and partial neutrophil degranulation.

Exocytosis of granulocyte contents is apparently a common phenomenon and may play a more important role than merely the killing of attached, uningested microorganisms. For example, the MPO-halide system is capable of inactivating a variety of chemotactic factors (C5a, synthetic chemotactic peptides, and bacterial chemotactic factors), thus modulating the inflammatory response. The same system also inactivates proteinase inhibitors in the locale of the PMN, thus allowing proteases released from the phagocytes to more readily damage connective tissue structures. Finally, lysozyme, which is continuously secreted by mononuclear phagocytes, appears capable of inhibiting the movement of PMNs into areas of monocyte-macrophage accumulation, thus regulating the types of cells that migrate into an inflammatory focus.

THE MONONUCLEAR PHAGOCYTE SYSTEM & ITS FUNCTION

The mononuclear phagocyte system has its origin in the bone marrow monoblast and promonocyte. Only the intermediate stage cell (the monocyte) is ordinarily encountered in the circulation. The ratio of circulating to marginated monocytes in humans is approximately 1:3. Monocytes circulate with a half-life of 8½ hours, leaving the circulation randomly (ie, unrelated to age). There is a daily monocyte turnover of approximately 7 $\times 10^6$ cells per hour per kg body weight (Chapter 10).

Unlike neutrophils, monocytes do not die when they leave the circulation but mature to macrophages (histiocytes) in the tissues: alveolar macrophages (lung), Kupffer cells (liver), and macrophages of spleen sinusoids, lymph nodes, peritoneum, and other areas. There is good evidence that macrophages in the lung and liver may proliferate locally as well. Macrophage maturation is accompanied by an increase in cell size and in numbers of cytoplasmic organelles including mitochondria and lysosomes (containing hydrolytic enzymes) as well as other morphologic, biochemical, and functional changes. These changes vary from tissue to tissue according to the state of the host (normal, infected, or otherwise stimulated). The synthetic activities of macrophages can also be stimulated in culture, a good example being the increase in lysosomal hydrolases after exposure in vitro to foreign serum. Functional maturity of these cells is shown by increasing phagocytic capability, increased numbers of Fc receptors for IgG on the cell surface, and increased responsiveness to lymphocyte activation. Mature macrophages in unique environments may achieve distinctive cellular physiology. For example, alveolar macrophages, like monocytes (see below), depend predominantly on aerobic metabolism for their energy supply, whereas peritoneal macrophages depend primarily on glycolytic metabolism. In addition, alveolar macrophages contain large amounts of lysozyme, which is at least partially endocytosed from respiratory secretions.

Chemotaxis

Humoral mediators of mononuclear phagocyte chemotaxis are less well understood than are neutrophils. However, monocyte chemotaxis occurs in response to synthetic N-formylated oligopeptides, and C5a provides chemotactic activity from the serum. Recruitment of mononuclear phagocytes is effected to a major degree by chemotactic materials released from sensitized T lymphocytes. Additional lymphocyte-derived substances, such as migration inhibitory factor, encourage the accumulation of chemotactically attracted phagocytes in inflammatory foci.

Opsonization

The membranes of human monocytes and macrophages contain receptors for IgG (subclasses IgG1 and IgG3) and C3. Presumably, therefore, the process of opsonization is similar to that which occurs with neutrophils. *Mycoplasma* species have the interesting ability (in vitro) to attach to macrophages in the absence of antibody or complement. When so attached, they retard ameboid movement of the phagocytic cell. Upon addition of specific antibody, mycoplasmas are phagocytosed and killed. Such experimental observations permit dissection of the attachment and ingestion phases of mononuclear phagocyte function, but their practical significance is uncertain.

Ingestion

Monocytes ingest bacteria more slowly than neutrophils, kill them less efficiently, and utilize predominantly oxygen-dependent metabolic pathways (oxidative phosphorylation) to accomplish phagocytosis. Nevertheless, a respiratory burst clearly accompanies monocyte-microbial encounters, with generation of H_2O_2, $O_2^-\cdot$, and $OH\cdot$ and with chemiluminescence.

Killing

Monocytes possess 2 lysosomal populations. The first appears early in monocyte maturation and contains myeloperoxidase, arylsulfatase, and acid phosphatase. The contents of the second, later-appearing lysosomes are unknown. Monocytes do not possess the bactericidal cationic proteins of neutrophils; lactoferrin is absent. However, the MPO-H_2O_2-halide system is apparently operative, and monocytes from patients with chronic granulomatous disease have impaired microbicidal activity.

As monocytes mature to macrophages in the tissues, additional lysosomal structures develop on a continuing basis reflecting both the prolonged life span of these phagocytic cells and their ability to synthesize new membrane and membrane receptors. Preexisting primary lysosomes may fuse with phagocytic vacuoles or pinocytotic vesicles to produce secondary lysosomes. At least in vitro, their formation and contents are closely related to the extracellular milieu. There is a definite relationship between endocytic activity and the formation of lysosomes; as macrophages mature, there is a progressive rise in lysosomes and their hydrolytic enzyme content.

The mechanisms by which macrophages kill microorganisms are not understood. Myeloperoxidase is not found beyond the monocyte stage of macrophage development, and there is a progressive decline in the ability of maturing macrophages to generate $O_2^-\cdot$ and H_2O_2. Enzymes that are found in mononuclear phagocytes (including acid phosphatase, β-glucuronidase, lipase, lysozyme, hyaluronidase, and others) appear to serve a digestive rather than a microbicidal function. In the presence of oxygen and clofazimine, a phenazine dye used in the treatment of leprosy, H_2O_2 generation in the human macrophage is stimulated and killing is enhanced. Possibly, therefore, macrophages employ an H_2O_2-generating system in microbial killing. Catalase, which is present in macrophages, may substitute for myeloperoxidase, which is not present, and may thus catalyze the oxidation of substrates in the presence of H_2O_2. Under in vitro conditions, catalase can substitute for myeloperoxidase in the myeloperoxidase-H_2O_2-halide microbicidal system. Lipid peroxidation, which occurs in alveolar macrophages and monocytes, may be another mechanism potentiating the antimicrobial action of H_2O_2 because malonyldialdehyde, a catabolite of lipid peroxides, has antibacterial activity.

Secretory Products of Mononuclear Phagocytes

These cells secrete or shed into their environment a variety of biologic products that may be important in terms of mediating the immune response. For example, lysosomal acid hydrolases are produced by mouse peritoneal macrophages even in the absence of a phagocytic stimulus. Lysozyme is secreted in large amounts from a variety of mononuclear phagocytes in the presence or absence of phagocytic stimuli; the source does not seem to be lysosomes. Neutral proteases have been identified as secretory products of macrophages. Other products include prostaglandins, complement and properdin components, fibroblast growth-regulatory agents, regulators of angiogenesis, bone marrow stem cell stimulators, interferon, and blood coagulation-regulating substances.

Fate of Intracellular Microorganisms

Depending upon their ability to survive intracellular conditions, phagocytosed microorganisms may be killed and digested, killed and poorly degraded, or not killed and merely sequestered within the cells. Some microorganisms have apparently developed mechanisms for ensuring their intracellular survival and replication in macrophages. *Mycobacterium tuberculosis* is admirably equipped in this regard. In the absence of immune serum, tubercle bacilli prevent the fusion of lysosomes with phagosomes, apparently through the mediation of a markedly anionic trehalose glycolipid. In the presence of immune serum phagolysosomal fusion occurs, but *M tuberculosis* is resistant to the discharged lysosomal contents. *Mycobacterium lepraemurium* and *Mycobacterium leprae* are also resistant to phagolysosomal contents, and the latter organism is also apparently capable of escaping into the cytoplasm of phagocytes, where it is not recognized as a foreign invader. Typhus-producing rickettsial species also escape from phagolysosomes and multiply freely in the macrophage cytoplasm in the absence of specific antibody. In contrast, antibody-coated rickettsiae are unable to escape the phagolysosome. Some obligate intracellular parasites gain entry to the cytoplasm directly instead of by rupture of the phagosome (eg, *T gondii, Chlamydia* species). Entry is apparently actively mediated by the microorganisms. In the presence of specific antibody. this parasite-mediated endocytosis is blocked while true phagocytosis is facilitated.

Cell-Mediated Immunity
(Lymphocyte-Macrophage Interaction)

Acquired resistance to a broad range of intracellular parasites has its origin in a cell-mediated immune response involving both macrophages and lymphocytes. During the induction of immunity, macrophages probably facilitate the engagement of antigen-sensitive T lymphocytes, although the mechanism by which this is accomplished is unclear. Antigen-activated T cells, the specific mediators of cellular resistance to infection, are generated in regionally stimulated lymphoid tissue and then released into the general circulation.

Interactions between mononuclear phagocytes and sensitized lymphocytes occur during expression of cellular resistance to infection. Sensitized lymphocytes produce soluble factors (lymphokines), one of which, MIF, encourages circulating blood monocytes to localize at sites of microbial invasion. In addition, lymphocytes specifically committed to microbial antigens can be stimulated (at least in vitro) to release products that enhance (activate) the endocytic and microbicidal capacity of macrophages (Fig 16–6). The mechanisms by which lymphokines might augment macrophage killing are unclear. Indeed, whether such factors actually function in vivo is also unclear. The principal role of sensitized lymphocytes may be to encourage accumulation of abundant mononuclear phagocytes at foci of microbial invasion.

A full description of the "activated macrophage" is not yet at hand. Activated macrophages spread out more extensively on glass, exhibit more Fc and Fab receptors, and are more actively phagocytic than unstimulated cells. In addition, there is increased oxidation of glucose, increased lysosomal hydrolase and ectoenzyme activity, and increased antimicrobial and antitumor activity. The reason for the enhanced antimicrobial activity is not clear, ie, whether it is related to increased metabolism or reflects merely increased phagocytosis. There is recent evidence that antimicrobial and antitumor functions can be dissociated,

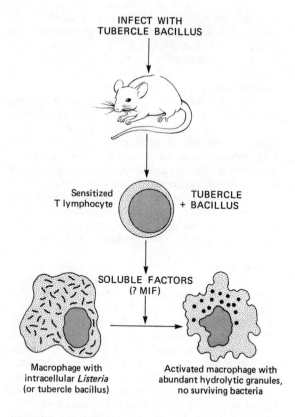

Figure 16–6. Macrophage killing of intracellular bacteria triggered by specific cell-mediated immunity reaction. (The final stage shown is probable but still hypothetical.) (Redrawn and reproduced, with permission, from Roitt IM: *Essential Immunology,* 2nd ed. Blackwell, 1974.)

with the latter requiring a higher degree of macrophage activation than the former.

Although cell-mediated immunity may be induced specifically through the action of sensitized lymphocytes, it is expressed nonspecifically in the sense that macrophages, once stimulated to a state of enhanced microbicidal activity, will perform this function nonspecifically. Thus, animals infected with *T gondii* will more readily limit infection with *L monocytogenes* and other intracellular parasites through the presence of activated macrophages. The practical significance of this observation is unclear, however, since experimental animals appear to eliminate the homologous sensitizing microorganism much more efficiently than the heterologous challenge microorganism.

The importance of lymphocytes in immunity to intracellular infection is well demonstrated by the phenomenon of adoptive immunity, wherein lymphocytes transferred from an animal with immunity to a given infection (such as tuberculosis) confer immunity to the same pathogen upon a normal animal (Fig 16–7). The animals must be closely related genetically to demonstrate this phenomenon; otherwise, a GVH reaction might ensue. The use of transfer factor (an immunolog-

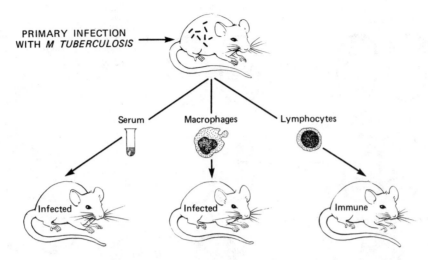

Figure 16–7. Transfer of specific and nonspecific immunity by lymphocytes from an immune animal. The recipient of the lymphocytes resisted simultaneous challenge with *M tuberculosis* combined with *Listeria* organisms. The recipients were not immune to *Listeria* given alone. Serum or macrophages did not transfer immunity. (After Mackaness.)

ically active dialyzable lymphocyte extract) in humans is based upon the principles of adoptive immunity. Since whole lymphocytes are not transferred between individuals, a GVH response is not a problem.

There is a close relationship between cell-mediated immunity and delayed hypersensitivity; skin test reactivity to a given pathogen is generally transferred along with adoptive immunity to that pathogen. These processes are not inseparable, however. Thus, RNA extracted from *M tuberculosis* may transfer immunity but not skin test reactivity. Conversely, mycobacterial lipids may be more important in the delayed hypersensitivity skin test response than in immunity.

SPECIAL ASPECTS
OF VIRAL IMMUNITY

Viral Spread & Replication

Because viruses are obligate intracellular parasites, the mechanism of immune restriction of virus replication differs significantly from that of bacteria. Although extracellular viruses may be removed by the same humoral and cellular mechanisms that remove bacteria, the intracellular replicative steps of viruses and virus-infected cells (that have developed virus-specified antigens on their surface) are also major targets for the host's immune response. The mechanism by which viruses are transmitted also differs considerably from bacteria.

A. At the Cellular Level: At the cellular level, Notkins has defined 3 types of viral transmission (Fig 16–8).

1. Extracellular (type I) spread–Infectious virions are released from the cell to spread in the extracellular milieu. Many types of viruses (eg, influenza, adenoviruses) spread primarily by this route, and most spread by this mechanism at least some of the time.

2. Intercellular (type II) spread–Virions spread from cell to cell through desmosomes of intercellular bridges (cell fusion) without contact with the extracellular milieu. Members of the herpesvirus group (especially cytomegalovirus, EB virus, and varicella-zoster virus) are transmitted primarily by this means.

3. Nuclear (vertical; type III) spread–The viral genome is latent or integrated into the host genome and is passed from parent cell to progeny during meiosis. Phenotypic evidence of viral presence may be striking (many virus-specific antigens on the cell surface) or absent, and the stability of integration is variable. Retroviruses are a classic example of this mechanism.

B. In the Host: Within an animal host, 3 general types of viral spread are recognized:

1. Local–Viral infection is largely confined to a mucosal surface or organ—eg, rhinoviruses (respiratory epithelium), rotaviruses (gastrointestinal epithelium).

2. Primary hematogenous–Virus is inoculated directly into the bloodstream, with subsequent organ dissemination. The best examples are arboviruses and hepatitis B virus.

3. Secondary hematogenous–Initial virus infection and replication occur on a mucosal surface; bloodstream invasion occurs afterward by hematogenous dissemination to target organs. The initial mucosal phase is often relatively asymptomatic. *Examples:* Common viral exanthems, poliomyelitis, mumps.

Properties of Viruses That Allow Them to Escape Immunologic Defense Mechanisms

A. Poor or Absent Cellular or Humoral Immune Response to Viral Antigens: As most viruses are good antigens, the immune response is usually vigorous. However, a viruslike obligate intracellular parasite, the etiologic agent of scrapie, does not induce a detectable immune response.

Type I: Extracellular

Virus

Type II: Intercellular

Type III: Parent to progeny

Meiosis

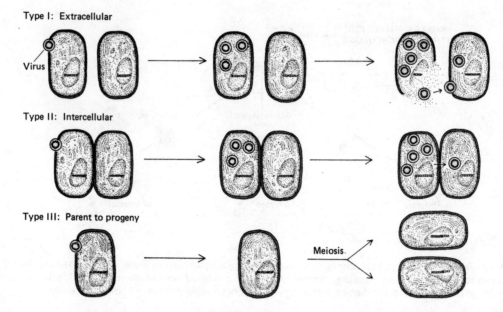

Figure 16–8. Three routes of viral spread are recognized. In type I spread, the infected cell is lysed and the progeny virus particles spread extracellularly to near and distant uninfected cells. Other viruses induce intercellular connections, allowing them to spread from cell to cell without leaving the cytoplasm (type II spread). In type III spread, viral genetic information is incorporated into the cell genome and passes to progeny during meiosis. (Reproduced, with permission, from Notkins AL: Viral infections: Mechanisms of immunologic defense and injury. *Hosp Pract* [Sept] 1974;9:66.)

B. Type II or III (Intracellular) Spread: Although this mechanism of transmission limits exposure of extracellular virus to humoral or cellular host defense mechanisms, the virus-infected cells (with virus-specified surface neoantigens) are themselves susceptible to immunologic attack.

C. Serologic Plasticity (Influenza Virus) or Multiplicity (Enteroviruses, Rhinoviruses): Some viruses, best exemplified by influenza, are capable of rapidly changing their surface antigenic structure by mutation or recombination (or both), allowing sequential infection of human and animal hosts. Thus, a single person may be infected with influenza virus 5 or 10 times or more in a lifetime. These antigenic changes are responsible in part for repeated influenza epidemics. This is in contrast to a structurally related virus, measles, that exhibits extreme serologic stability and elicits lifelong immunity. Other viruses have evolved a large number of serologic variants with little cross-reactivity among them. The best examples are the rhinoviruses ($\geq$ 82 serotypes) and the enteroviruses ($\geq$ 66 serotypes). Sequential infections with these agents are common.

D. Nonneutralizing Virus-Antibody Complexes (eg, Hepatitis B, Lactic Dehydrogenase Virus): This phenomenon probably occurs to some extent with all viruses (as the virus-antibody reaction is reversible), but with some viruses the reaction with antibody seems to have very little effect on infectivity. These antibodies may produce immune complex disease (see Chapter 33).

Immunologic Reactions Involving Viruses

A variety of immunologic reactions involving viruses have been shown to occur in vitro; evidence that they are operative in vivo and are important in host defense against infection is less complete.

A. Humoral Defense Mechanisms: Antibodies constitute one of the important mechanisms of host resistance to viral infection. They appear to be more important in preventing infection or dissemination than limiting an infection that has already begun. Virus-antibody reactions that have been defined in vitro include neutralization (both with and without complement), complement-facilitated lysis of infected cells (Fig 16–9), opsonization, and enzyme inhibition.

1. Complement-independent neutralization–Antibodies of the G, M, and A classes have been shown to neutralize the infectivity of virtually all known viruses; this is the most important virus-antibody interaction. The reaction is highly specific, as the antibody is synthesized in response to viral antigens, but it is only effective against extracellular virus (type I spread). With viruses that disseminate intracellularly (type II or type III spread), neutralizing antibody alone will be ineffective once infection is established, as it has no effect on the virus unless viral antigens are expressed on the cell surface.

In every instance that has been studied, the mechanism of viral neutralization involves combination of antibodies with the virus coat proteins. In most cases the antibodies prevent cellular adsorption and penetration of the virus, but in some instances antibody coat-

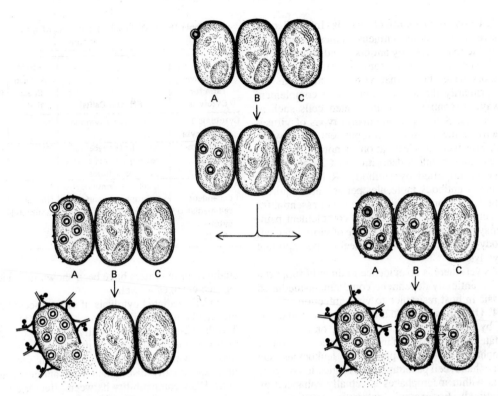

Figure 16–9. Virus-infected cell can be destroyed by antiviral antibody and complement, but whether this halts type II spread depends in part on the speed of transmission. If, for example, infected cell A is immunologically destroyed before the virus is transmitted to cell B, the infection will be stopped *(left)*. If, on the other hand, the virus transmission to cell B occurs before cell A can be destroyed immunologically, the infection will progress *(right)*. (Reproduced, with permission, from Notkins AL: Viral infections: Mechanisms of immunologic defense and injury. *Hosp Pract* [Sept] 1974;9:70.)

ing of extracellular virus may interfere with subsequent intracellular events (eg, uncoating) or may physically aggregate virus particles. The exact mechanism of neutralization is unclear but presumably involves a change in the steric conformation of the virus surface or actual covering of receptor sites, either of which prevents the virus from gaining entry to the cells. The fact that a single antibody molecule can neutralize a large virion with many repeated sequences of surface antigen suggests that conformational changes may be more important than simple interference. Neutralization of this sort is reversible in that the virus-antibody complexes may be dissociated to yield infectious virions.

IgA often plays a role in viral infections which begin on or are confined to mucosal surfaces. In the case of rhinovirus infections and perhaps parainfluenza and respiratory syncytial virus infections of adults, where viral replication may be confined to respiratory epithelium, resistance to infection is determined by surface IgA; serum IgG neutralizing antibody has much less protective value. For viral infections which begin on a mucosal surface and then disseminate by hematogenous spread (eg, poliomyelitis, measles, rubella), local antibody may completely prevent infection. However, disease can also be prevented by serum antibody even though viral

replication still may occur on the mucosal surface. Thus, persons immunized parenterally with inactivated poliovaccine possess serum antibody to poliovirus but not local colonic or oropharyngeal secretory antibody. Although still susceptible to mucosal infection with poliovirus, they are resistant to disease. During such an infection, virus will be found in oropharyngeal secretions and stool but not in blood or neural tissue.

2. Complement-facilitated neutralization– There is good evidence that complement plays an important role in neutralization of extracellular virus. Complement alone can neutralize some enveloped viruses by direct lysis (eg, retroviruses), but it is primarily important as an adjunct to neutralization by specific antibody, in which it may enhance antibody-mediated steric changes or aggregation, thus preventing adsorption of virus to cells, or may directly lyse enveloped viruses. Complement coating of virions may also facilitate binding to and ingestion by phagocytic cells (see below). The importance of complement-facilitated neutralization in determining in vivo resistance to viral infection has not been determined. IgA (in contrast to IgG and IgM) does not fix complement well, and this class of antibody has not been shown to function in complement-dependent neutralization reactions.

3. Lysis of virus-infected cells–Infected cells that have virus-specified antigens on their surfaces are susceptible to cytolysis by antibody and complement. The elegant studies of Sissons, Oldstone, and collaborators have shown that virus-infected cells are lysed primarily through the alternative complement pathway, in contrast to nonnucleated cells such as erythrocytes. Some (perhaps many) types of viruses can activate the alternative complement pathway directly; however, this activation is not sufficient to induce cytolysis unless deposition of C3b on the cell surface is amplified by antibody. Relatively large amounts of antibody molecules per cell are required, and the Fc portion of the molecule is not essential for the reaction. Although the classic complement pathway may be activated on the surface of virus-infected, antibody-coated cells, it does not seem to be important for cytolysis.

As yet, there is no evidence to directly support a role for antibody-dependent complement-mediated cytolysis in host resistance to virus infection.

4. Opsonization–Coating of extracellular viruses by IgG antibody, complement, or both, may facilitate phagocytosis and intracellular destruction by macrophages or polymorphonuclear leukocytes. On the other hand, cell penetration and replication of some viruses within macrophages is actually enhanced by IgG antibody. For example, enteroviruses are susceptible to antibody-mediated opsonization, while replication of arboviruses may be enhanced by antibody.

5. Enzyme inhibition–Influenza virus has a surface protein, neuraminidase, which enzymatically cleaves the viral receptor (N-acetylneuraminic acid) from the host cell membrane. Neuraminidase has no known role in infection of cells but does function by facilitating *release* of progeny virus. Antibody against neuraminidase has been shown to limit viral replication and spread but not to neutralize the virion. Presumably, similar nonneutralizing antigen-antibody interactions may be found for other viruses.

B. Cell-Mediated Defense Mechanisms: Delayed hypersensitivity to many viruses can be identified in the immune host using skin test reactivity (eg, mumps) or in vitro measures such as a blastogenic response of lymphocytes to viral antigens. Some cell-mediated reactions which appear to be important in host resistance to or defense against viral infection are as follows:

1. Cellular cytotoxicity–Virus-infected cells may be lysed by sensitized lymphocytes or in some cases by activated macrophages or even polymorphonuclear leukocytes. Virus-infected cells develop new antigens on their surfaces that are recognized as "nonself" by leukocytes, triggering lysis of the cell. Production of new cell surface antigens is particularly evident with enveloped viruses, such as the herpesviruses and myxoviruses, in which the viral envelope is derived by budding from an altered cell membrane. However, cellular cytotoxicity also has been shown with nonenveloped viruses (eg, reoviruses) that do not mature by budding. Where

Table 16–2. Distinguishing features of antiviral cytolytic reactions.

Descriptive Term for Cytolysis	Effector Cell(s)	Target Antigen Specificity?	HLA Restriction?
Cytotoxic T lymphocytes	Subclass of T lymphocytes	Yes	Yes
Natural cytotoxicity	NK cells (Fc receptor–bearing T lymphocytes and macrophages)	No	No
Antibody-dependent cell-mediated cytotoxicity (ADCC)	K cells—T lymphocytes, macrophages, and perhaps other leukocytes with Fc receptors	Yes (through antibody)	No

studied, these viruses have been shown to induce cell surface changes as well.

Cell-mediated cytolysis of virus-infected cells is mediated through 3 distinct mechanisms: (1) cytotoxic T cells, (2) natural cytotoxicity, (3) antibody dependent cell-mediated cytotoxicity (Table 16–2). Cytotoxic T lymphocytes appear early in virus infection, specifically distinguish viral antigens, and require HLA compatibility between effector and target cells for cytolysis. The effector T cells are of the suppressor-cytotoxic subset, as defined by monoclonal antibodies. The protective effect of cytotoxic T cells has been proved in mice by adoptive transfer experiments, but their role in human virus infections remains speculative.

Natural cytotoxicity is mediated by many types of cells (so-called NK cells) bearing Fc receptors, including some T cells and macrophages. The cytotoxicity is "natural" in that it is present toward antigens to which the animal has not previously been exposed. Susceptible targets include virus-infected autologous or heterologous cells and various transformed and tumor-derived cell lines. There is no requirement for HLA matching of effector and target cells. Antiviral NK activity is enhanced by interferon. The role of NK cells in resistance to virus infection in vivo is unknown.

Antibody-dependent cellular cytotoxicity is mediated by cells similar to NK cells but requires antibody coating of the target cells. The specificity of the reaction is determined solely by the antibody used, with lysis occurring when the effector cells bind the Fc fragment of IgG that is bound to the target cell. There is no requirement for cellular recognition of the antigens or HLA matching between effector and target cells. Although antibody-dependent cellular cytotoxicity has been demonstrated in vitro with human and animal cells, proof of its importance in limiting virus replication in vivo is lacking.

2. Lymphokine production–Sensitized lymphocytes release lymphokines in response to viral antigens. The best characterized of these from a virologic standpoint is **interferon** (see below). Lymphokines also attract effector cells (macrophages and polymor-

Table 16–3. Characteristics of the recognized types of interferon.*

Interferon Type	Experimentally Demonstrated Property		
	Producer Cell	Inducing Stimulus	Major Activity
Leukocyte (Alpha)	Null lympho-cytes	Viruses, foreign cells	Antiviral, activate killer cells
Fibroepithe-lial (Beta)	Fibroblasts, epithelial cells, macrophages	Viruses, nu-cleic acids	Antiviral
Immune (Gamma)	T lymphocytes	Mitogens (in-cluding anti-gens)	Immunoregu-latory

*Adapted, with permission, from Baron S: The interferon system. *Am Soc Microbiol News* 1979;**45**:358.

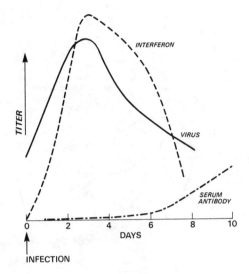

Figure 16–10. Appearance of interferon and serum antibody in relation to recovery from influenza virus infection of the lungs of mice. (From Isaacs A: *New Scientist* 1961; 11:81.)

phonuclear leukocytes) that may nonspecifically destroy viruses or virus-infected cells; some lymphokines are directly toxic to virus-infected cells.

3. Interferon–Interferon is a family of proteins produced by somatic cells in response to a variety of stimuli, including virus infection. These proteins were identified originally by their potent antiviral activity, but more recently they have been shown to affect a multiplicity of cellular functions, including the immune response. Additionally, interferons inhibit the growth of some other intracellular parasites (eg, *Chlamydia*) and certain tumor cells.

Recently, 3 clearly distinct types of interferon have been recognized and the nomenclature codified by an expert committee (Table 16–3). Alpha and beta interferons are primarily antiviral, while the function of gamma interferon is thought to be primarily immunoregulatory. However, these immunoregulatory activities (eg, augmentation of leukocyte cytotoxicity) may affect the outcome of virus infections as well.

Interferon production may be stimulated by infection by viruses, protozoa (eg, *Toxoplasma*), rickettsiae, chlamydiae, and certain bacteria. A variety of bacterial products, such as endotoxins and nucleic acids, also are interferon inducers. In addition, synthetic nucleic acids (especially double-stranded RNA) and some chemicals (eg, tilorone) may stimulate interferon production. Sensitized lymphocytes will make immune interferon in response to specific antigens.

Interferon is produced by and released from cells early in the course of virus infection (in some cases, at the time of adsorption); thus, it is available much earlier than antibody (Fig 16–10). The antiviral action of interferon is mediated indirectly, through effects on host cells. Exposure of cells to interferon triggers intracellular synthesis of antiviral proteins that probably act by selectively inhibiting the synthesis of viral proteins (Fig 16–11). The antiviral activity may be transferred to neighboring cells, without the continued presence of interferon, via an unknown mechanism. The antiviral state persists after interferon exposure

and is lost slowly, probably through cell death or division. The antiviral action of interferon is pathogen-nonspecific but host-specific. Although interferon production is stimulated by many viruses and inhibits the growth of many viruses, the protection it gives is limited to the cells of the producing species. For example, human interferon will protect human and some primate cells but will not protect mouse or chicken cells.

The evidence that interferon is an important host defense against virus infection is summarized in Table 16–4. Perhaps the most persuasive evidence comes from animal models of virus infection in which the interferon response was specifically ablated using anti-interferon antibody. The relative contribution of

Table 16–4. Evidence for role of interferon in host defenses against virus infection.*

Type of Evidence	Example
Time correlation	Interferon produced just before and during arrest of virus replication, before specific response.
Place correlation	Maximal interferon production near site of maximal virus replication.
Quantitative correlations	Concentrations of interferon produced in vivo are comparable to amounts required in vitro for antiviral activity.
Transfer	Exogenous or chemically induced interferon controls virus infections in humans and experimental animals.
Ablation	Deletion of interferon (eg, by specific antibody) in cell culture and experimental animals enhances virus replication.

*Adapted, with permission, from Baron S: The interferon system. *Am Soc Microbiol News* 1979;**45**:358.

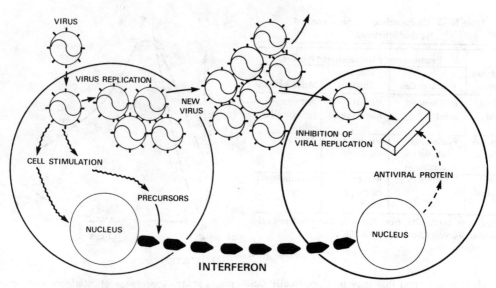

Figure 16–11. Schematic representation of interferon activity.

interferon to host control of virus infection varies with the system studied, but it appears to play a significant role in most.

Recently, techniques for producing large amounts of interferon from human leukocytes have made possible clinical trials in which exogenous human interferon has been administered therapeutically for human viral infections. Promising results have been obtained in infections due to certain herpesviruses, hepatitis B virus, and certain respiratory viruses. Additionally, experiments with subhuman primates indicate that patients infected with rabies and certain togaviruses (eg, St. Louis encephalitis) probably would be benefited by exogenous interferon. Although production of human interferon is presently very expensive, improved cell culture technology and the recent cloning of the interferon genome in bacteria (with synthesis of interferon by the microorganism) will probably lower the cost substantially.

4. Host restriction–In the case of several viruses, virulence has been associated with ability to replicate in macrophages. For example, with mouse hepatitis virus, virulent strains can replicate in macrophages whereas avirulent strains do not. Conversely, macrophages from strains of mice resistant to mouse hepatitis virus infection or illness generally are nonpermissive of viral replication, whereas macrophages from susceptible strains allow virus replication. Host restriction may be mediated in part by the immune response. For example, rabbitpox virus replicates in rabbit macrophages, but if the macrophages are activated (eg, by lymphocyte supernates), virus replication no longer occurs.

5. Phagocytosis–Phagocytosis of viruses by macrophages or, less commonly, by neutrophils (especially in the presence of antibody) may be responsible for resistance to infection and illness (eg, with enteroviruses).

C. Other Host Defenses: Many nonspecific factors have been shown to alter the outcome of virus infection in experimental systems. For example, body temperature (fever or hypothermia) and local hypoxia or acidosis might affect virus replication. Some of these factors may act by affecting host defense mechanisms discussed previously, as well as by directly altering virus replication. In many cases, however, the role these factors play in the intact animal is obscure.

Experimentally, some viral infections (especially herpesviruses) can be shown to be modulated almost entirely by cellular immunity, with antibody playing no demonstrable role. Despite this, the exact component of cellular immunity (cellular cytotoxicity, phagocytosis, lymphokine production) which is responsible for protection has not been defined in most cases.

Virus-Induced Immunopathology

In certain viral infections, some or all of the pathologic changes appear to be due to a response of the host's immune system to viral antigens.

A. Humoral: The best example of antibody-related tissue damage is virus-induced immune complex disease, which has been shown to occur with hepatitis B, Aleutian mink disease, lactic dehydrogenase virus infection, dengue hemorrhagic fever, and others. Nonneutralizing antibody, stimulated by virus replication, combines with virus, and the resulting soluble immune complexes are deposited in tissues and organs. Leukocytes are required for an injurious inflammatory reaction to occur following deposition of these immune complexes (see Chapter 12). Although lysis of infected cells by antibody and complement theoretically could occur during viral infection, this has not been convincingly demonstrated in vivo.

B. Cell-Mediated: Host cell injury has been shown to occur by means of lymphocyte cytotoxicity, although its importance in in vivo infections is not entirely clear. Lymphokine production with non-specific cytotoxicity by leukocytes may also be important.

ANERGY & INFECTION

The mechanisms responsible for cell-mediated immunity are complex and potentially vulnerable to disruption by a variety of processes. Inability to express delayed hypersensitivity to tuberculin has been appreciated in sarcoidosis and Hodgkin's disease for over 50 years. We now know that anergy extends to a variety of antigens and, in the case of Hodgkin's disease, is associated with a predisposition to opportunistic intracellular infection. The mechanism by which these 2 diseases disturb cell-mediated immunity is not known, but both conditions are characterized by a granulomatous reaction that may extensively invade the paracortical areas of lymph nodes and the white pulp of the spleen. It is to these areas that T lymphocytes normally migrate and proliferate when antigenically stimulated.

Viral Diseases

Certain viruses can infect cells of the immune system and thereby impair their function. In 1911, von Pirquet noted that the tuberculin skin test reaction disappeared during the first days of rash with measles infection. In fact, tuberculin anergy may persist up to 2 months beyond the appearance of the rash. Both delayed hypersensitivity and cell-mediated immunity are suppressed by measles; quiescent cases of tuberculosis may be reactivated and existing cases worsened by infection with this virus. This effect may be due to damage to either lymphocytes or mononuclear phagocytes. Although other viral infections (influenza, varicella, type 1 poliovirus vaccine) can depress skin reactivity to tuberculin, at least partly on the basis of lymphocyte cytotoxicity, these infections do not appear to predispose to reactivation of latent infections due to intracellular pathogens.

Immunodepression by mumps virus appears to result from a nonspecific inhibition of sensitized lymphocytes or effector macrophages involved in the delayed hypersensitivity reaction. Thus, skin sensitivity to various antigens can be successfully transferred to normal recipients from previously sensitized guinea pigs with active mumps infection even though the infected guinea pigs are anergic at the time of cell transfer.

Recent studies suggest that development of fatal wild rabies infection may reflect the operation of a selective immunosuppressive mechanism whereby cytotoxic T cells specific for rabies virus–infected target cells fail to develop. Such cells do develop during nonfatal infection with attenuated strains of rabies virus. Wild rabies virus is not known to replicate in the cells of the immune system.

Since recirculation of T cells appears essential to facilitate the induction and expression of cell-mediated immunity, infection by viruses that can disrupt this traffic may damage the immune reactivity of the host. For example, thoracic duct lymphocytes (which are predominantly T cells) have specific receptors for myxo- and paramyxoviruses. Newcastle disease virus (a paramyxovirus) can attach to sialyl residues on the lymphocyte surface and then elute, destroying the receptors and releasing sialic acid. This results in a temporary but severe disruption of lymphocyte recirculation from blood to lymph because cells normally homing to the spleen and lymph nodes are diverted and trapped by the liver. Another mechanism of immunosuppression occurs in infections with lactic dehydrogenase (LDH) virus, which produces cytopathologic changes in thymus-dependent areas of the spleen, the paracortical areas of lymph nodes, and the cortex of the thymus. In addition to depressing cell-mediated immunity, the presence of chronic viremia results in increased numbers of germinal centers (the sites of B cell proliferation) and enhanced antibody response to certain antigens.

Granulomatous Infections

Lepromatous leprosy, miliary tuberculosis, disseminated coccidioidomycosis and other disseminated chronic intracellular infectious diseases are associated with both specific and nonspecific suppression of cell-mediated immunity. Specific immunosuppression is generally marked by failure to respond to antigens derived from the infecting microorganism (eg, lepromin in patients with leprosy; coccidioidin or spherulin in coccidioidomycosis; tuberculin in patients with miliary tuberculosis). Nonspecific immunosuppression is manifested by prolongation of skin homografts, depression of mixed lymphocyte responses, anergy to unrelated skin tests, and decreased sensitization to hapten-sensitizing agents such as DNCB. Whereas antimicrobial therapy can generally reverse the nonspecific immunosuppression, specific anergy to the infecting microorganism is often not reversible (particularly in leprosy). Thus, the nature of the 2 immunosuppressive phenomena may not be identical, and unrestricted proliferation of microorganisms due to the specific immune defect may lead secondarily to the nonspecific defects.

The mechanism of nonspecific immunosuppression is not fully understood. However, there is evidence that the presence of multiple granulomas in the white pulp of the spleen and in paracortical areas of lymph nodes may divert lymphocyte traffic, as in Hodgkin's disease. Alternatively, these diseases may be associated with serum or plasma factors that suppress lymphocyte function in vitro. Such factors tend to disappear when the antigenic load is reduced by chemotherapy. Finally, the defect may result from a suppression of cell-mediated immune responses by monocytes or by non-IgG-bearing, nonphagocytic, sheep red cell rosette–forming cells which appear to be suppressor T cells. Such suppressor T cells might be generated in response to the specific challenge organism.

The mechanism of specific immunosuppression is even less well understood. However, some data suggest that a relationship to Ir genes may exist. For example, variation in susceptibility to acute infection with lymphocytic choriomeningitis virus in adult mice is partially controlled by dominant genes closely linked with the H-2 locus. Recent studies suggest that there is a relationship between coccidioidal dissemination and type 9 histocompatibility specificity. Whether this association is independent of HLA prevalence within racial groups at increased risk (blacks, Filipinos) is unclear at this time.

FEVER

The occurrence of fever in infectious diseases is so universal that its presence generally stimulates a search for an invading pathogen. In only a few infections (eg, gonorrhea, syphilis, lepromatous leprosy) is fever absent. Despite its nearly universal occurrence and its historical association with infection, the true significance of fever remains uncertain. Nevertheless, there is at least some evidence that it plays a role in host defense. For example, human lymphocytes incubated in vitro at 39 °C show a higher uptake of thymidine than lymphocytes incubated at 37 °C. Also, human leukocytes demonstrate maximal phagocytic activity between 38 and 40 °C. Finally, during fever there is a

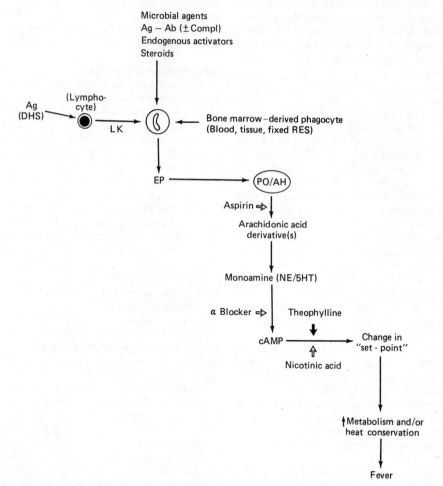

Figure 16–12. Postulated pathway for the pathogenesis of fever. Endogenous pyrogen circulates to the hypothalamus (PO/AH), where it induces the production of a metabolite of arachidonic acid. This substance, in turn, increases the synthesis of norepinephrine, an alpha-adrenergic agonist that increases the production of cAMP. This cyclonucleotide then directly causes alterations in the activity of temperature-sensitive neurons that bring about an increase in heat conservation or production (or both). Ag = antigen; Ag-Ab = antigen-antibody complexes; Compl = complement; cAMP = cyclic 3',5'-adenosine monophosphate; DHS = delayed hypersensitivity; EP = endogenous pyrogen; 5HT = serotonin; LK = lymphokine; NE = norepinephrine; PO/AH = preoptic area of anterior hypothalamus; RES = reticuloendothelial system; ⇨ inhibitors; → activators. (Reproduced, with permission, from Bernheim HA, Block LH, Atkins E: Fever: Pathogenesis, pathophysiology, and purpose. *Ann Intern Med* 1979;**91**:261.)

decrease in circulating levels of iron. This observation, coupled with the fact that the production of bacterial siderophores (iron-binding proteins) is suppressed by elevated temperature, may indicate that fever hinders the ability of microorganisms to obtain and sequester needed supplies of iron. Although fever has never been shown to have frank survival implications for mammals, it has been shown clearly that cold-blooded animals such as the desert iguana will perish from certain infections unless allowed access to elevated environmental temperatures. (Only by moving to a warm environment can such animals raise their body temperature.) Infected febrile lizards become hypoferremic; when injected with exogenous iron, their mortality rate increases significantly despite their being kept at a warm ambient temperature.

Current concepts of fever production indicate that the common stimulus to body temperature elevation is the response of the preoptic area of the anterior hypothalamus (PO/AH) to a circulating substance known as leukocytic pyrogen or endogenous pyrogen (EP). Endogenous pyrogen is a protein that is freshly synthesized or cleaved off from an active precursor in bone marrow–derived phagocytes in response to microbial agents, antigen-antibody complexes, endotoxin (lipid A component), or the pyrogenic steroid etiocholanolone. Human neutrophils and monocytes are capable of generating this pyrogen, whereas lymphocytes are not. However, it is known that lymphocytes may produce soluble factors that enhance pyrogen production by macrophages. The pyrogenic molecules produced by PMNs and monocytes are not identical; further, monocytes produce more endogenous pyrogen than do PMNs, and for a longer period of time. Degranulation of leukocytes is not essential for pyrogen release; indeed, the protein seems to be localized to the cell cytoplasm rather than to granules. There is evidence that the pyrogen's action on the anterior hypothalamus is mediated through the activities of monoamines, sodium, calcium, prostaglandins, and cAMP. Figure 16–12 illustrates one scheme whereby a febrile response is produced.

Endogenous pyrogen has recently been highly purified, and a radioimmunoassay has been developed for its detection. In vitro, the pyrogen is capable of stimulating the respiratory burst in PMNs and stimulating the reduction of NBT dye to formazan. These observations help in understanding the phenomenon of increased spontaneous NBT dye reduction in the leukocytes from patients with a variety of disease processes having fever as their only common feature. In addition, the protein has been shown to cause selective release of specific granule contents (lysozyme and lactoferrin) from human neutrophils in vitro. It is possible that the purpose of lactoferrin release is restriction of iron availability to microorganisms. The function of lysozyme release is less clear, but it is known that neutrophils from patients with acute bacterial infections may contain 50% less lysozyme than control neutrophils.

•   •   •

References

Host Defenses at Body Surfaces

Elliott K et al (editors): *Adhesion and Microorganism Pathogenicity: Ciba Foundation Symposium 1980.* Pitman, 1981.

Hanson LA et al: The biologic properties of secretory IgA. *J Reticuloendothel Soc* 1980;**28(Suppl):**1.

Keusch GT: Specific membrane receptors: Pathogenetic and therapeutic implications in infectious diseases. *Rev Infect Dis* 1979;**1:**517.

Kilian M: Degradation of immunoglobulins A1, A2, and G by suspected principal peridontal pathogens. *Infect Immun* 1981;**34:**757.

Kornfeld SJ et al: Secretory immunity and the bacterial IgA proteases. *Rev Infect Dis* 1981;**3:**521.

Maibach H et al (editors): *Skin Microbiology: Relevance to Clinical Infection.* Springer-Verlag, 1981.

Ratzan KR: The role of surface factors in the pathogenesis of infection. Chap 5, p 145, in: *Seminars in Infectious Disease.* Vol 2. Weinstein L, Fields BN (editors). Stratton, 1979.

Woods DE et al: Role of salivary protease activity in adherence of gram-negative bacilli to mammalian buccal epithelial cells in vivo. *J Clin Invest* 1981;**68:**1435.

Systemic Immunity to Infection

Goldstein IM: *Current Concepts: Complement in Infectious Diseases.* Upjohn, 1980.

Petersen BH et al: *Neisseria meningitidis* and *Neisseria gonorrhoeae* bacteremia associated with C6, C7, or C8 deficiency. *Ann Intern Med* 1979;**90:**917.

Polymorphonuclear Leukocyte Function

Ambrusco DR et al: Lactoferrin enhances hydroxyl radical production by human neutrophils, neutrophil particulate fractions, and an enzymatic generating system. *J Clin Invest* 1981;**67:**352.

Babior BM: Oxygen-dependent microbial killing by phagocytes. (2 parts.) *N Engl J Med* 1978;**298:**659, 721.

Bagby GC Jr et al: Interaction of lactoferrin, monocytes, and T lymphocyte subsets in the regulation of steady-state granulopoiesis in vitro. *J Clin Invest* 1981;**68:**56.

Bergman MJ et al: Interaction of polymorphonuclear neutrophils with *Escherichia coli. J Clin Invest* 1978;**61:**227.

Densen P et al: Phagocyte strategy vs microbial tactics. *Rev Infect Dis* 1981;**2:**817.

Diamond RD et al: Damage to pseudohyphal forms of *Candida albicans* by neutrophils in the absence of serum in vitro. *J Clin Invest* 1978;**61:**349.

Gallin JI et al (editors): *Leukocyte Chemotaxis: Methods, Physiology, and Clinical Implications.* Raven Press, 1978.

Klebanoff SJ, Clark RA: *The Neutrophil: Function in Clinical Disorders.* North-Holland, 1978.

Malech HL: Cellular aspects of neutrophil chemotaxis. Pages 188–190 in: *Microbiology 1981*. Schlessinger D (editor). American Society for Microbiology, 1981.

Parry MF et al: Myeloperoxidase deficiency: Prevalence and clinical significance. *Ann Intern Med* 1981;**95:**293.

Payne SM, Finkelstein RA: The critical role of iron in host-bacterial interactions. *J Clin Invest* 1978;**61:**1428.

Quie PG: The phagocytic system and host resistance to microbial disease. Chap 18, p 173, in: *Clinical Concepts of Immunology*. Waldman RH (editor). Williams & Wilkins, 1979.

Root RK et al: The microbicidal mechanisms of human neutrophils and eosinophils. *Rev Infect Dis* 1981;**3:**565.

Seligmann B et al: Human neutrophil heterogeneity identified using flow microfluorometry to monitor membrane potential. *J Clin Invest* 1981;**68:**1125.

Shurin SB et al: A neutrophil disorder induced by *Capnocytophaga*, a dental micro-organism. *N Engl J Med* 1979;**301:**849.

Tauber AI, Babior BM: Evidence for hydroxyl radical production by human neutrophils. *J Clin Invest* 1977;**60:**374.

Van Epps DE et al: Enhancement of neutrophil function as a result of prior exposure to chemotactic factor. *J Clin Invest* 1980;**66:**167.

Walker RI et al: Neutrophil kinetics and the regulation of granulopoiesis. *Rev Infect Dis* 1980;**2:**282.

Wilkinson PC: Leukocyte locomotion and chemotaxis: Effects of bacteria and viruses. *Rev Infect Dis* 1980;**2:**293.

The Mononuclear Phagocyte System & Its Function

Davies P et al: Secretory and regulatory products of macrophages. (Symposium.) *J Reticuloendothel Soc* 1979; **26:**35.

Elsbach P: Degradation of microorganisms by phagocytic cells. *Rev Infect Dis* 1980;**2:**106.

Frenkel JK, Caldwell SA: Specific immunity and nonspecific resistance to infection: *Listeria*, protozoa, and viruses in mice and hamsters. *J Infect Dis* 1975;**131:**201.

Moulder JW: Intracellular parasitism: Life in an extreme environment. *J Infect Dis* 1974;**130:**300.

Nakagawara A et al: Hydrogen peroxide metabolism in human monocytes during differentiation in vitro. *J Clin Invest* 1981;**68:**1243.

Nelson DS (editor): *Immunobiology of the Macrophage*. Academic Press, 1976.

van Zwieten R et al: Extracellular proton release by stimulated neutrophils. *J Clin Invest* 1981;**68:**310.

Weinberg JB et al: Monocyte chemotactic peptide receptor: Functional characteristics and ligand-induced regulation. *J Clin Invest* 1981;**68:**621.

Special Aspects of Viral Immunity

Allison AC: On the role of mononuclear phagocytes in immunity against viruses. *Prog Med Virol* 1974;**18:**15.

Baron S: The interferon system. *Am Soc Microbiol News* 1979;**45:**358.

Downham MA et al: Breast-feeding protects against respiratory syncytial virus infections. *Br Med J* 1976;**2:**274.

Notkins AL: Viral infections: Mechanisms of immunologic defense and injury. *Hosp Pract* (Sept) 1974;**9:**65.

Oldstone MB: Virus neutralization and virus-induced immune complex disease: Virus-antibody union resulting in immunoprotection or immunologic injury—two sides of the same coin. *Prog Med Virol* 1975;**19:**84.

Sissons JGP, Oldstone MBA: The antibody-mediated destruction of virus-infected cells. *Adv Immunol* 1980;**29:**209.

Sissons JGP, Oldstone MBA: Killing of virus-infected cells by cytotoxic lymphocytes. *J Infect Dis* 1980;**142:**114.

Smith H: Mechanisms of virus pathogenicity. *Bacteriol Rev* 1972;**36:**291.

Starr SE, Allison AC: Role of T lymphocytes in recovery from murine cytomegalovirus infection. *Infect Immun* 1977; **17:**458.

Stiehm ER et al: Interferon: Immunobiology and clinical significance. *Ann Intern Med* 1982;**96:**80.

Woodruff JF, Woodruff JJ: T lymphocyte interaction with viruses and virus-infected tissues. *Prog Med Virol* 1975; **19:**120.

Anergy & Infection

Bullock WE: Anergy and infection. *Adv Intern Med* 1976; **21:**149.

Kleinhenz ME et al: Suppression of lymphocyte responses by tuberculous plasma and mycobacterial arabinogalactan: Monocyte dependence and indomethacin reversibility. *J Clin Invest* 1981;**68:**153.

Stobo JD et al: Suppressor thymus-derived lymphocytes in fungal infection. *J Clin Invest* 1976;**57:**319.

Wiktor TJ et al: Suppression of cell-mediated immunity by street rabies virus. *J Exp Med* 1977;**145:**1617.

Fever

Bernheim HA, Block LH, Atkins E: Fever: Pathogenesis, pathophysiology, and purpose. *Ann Intern Med* 1979; **91:**261.

Dinarello CA, Wolff SM: Mechanisms in the production of fever in humans. Chap 6, p 173, in: *Seminars in Infectious Disease*. Vol 2. Weinstein L, Fields BN (editors). Stratton, 1979.

Dinarello CA et al: *Current Concepts: Fever*. Upjohn, 1980.

Roberts NJ: Temperature and host defense. *Microbiol Rev* 1979;**43:**241.

Tumor Immunology | 17

Eli Benjamini, PhD, Donna M. Rennick, PhD, & Stewart Sell, MD

INTRODUCTION

The cellular events that result in cancer are poorly understood. Four major mechanisms have been postulated: (1) infection with a tumorigenic virus; (2) mutation in genes controlling cell growth; (3) expression of a preexisting "oncogene"; and (4) disturbance in normal growth control mechanisms, so that a genetically normal cell no longer displays normal differentiation.

The carcinogenic process occurs in one of 2 ways: by clonal proliferation or by progressive alterations of cellular growth from a reversible "premalignant" stage to an irreversible malignant stage. The 2 processes are not mutually exclusive; progressive premalignant alterations in a larger cell population could result in malignant "degeneration" of one cell that clonally "outgrows" other cells because it has a selective growth advantage. There is convincing evidence for each carcinogenic pathway, both in naturally occurring human cancers and in experimentally induced cancers of animals. Thus, many cancers appear to arise de novo in otherwise normal tissue, whereas others arise following a well-defined sequence of "premalignant" changes. One of the best examples of the latter is the sequence of metaplasia (squamous) → dysplasia (failure to differentiate) → localized carcinoma (carcinoma in situ) in the epithelium of the uterine cervix, ie, an orderly and predictable series of events leading to invasive squamous cell carcinoma.

The concept of strict clonal origin versus malignant progression is important in considering the possible role of immune control of cancer cells. If tumors arise from a single clone and express relatively fixed properties, then neoplasms that contain autoimmunogenic surface changes will be recognized as foreign and rejected, whereas those that do not express immunogens or are weakly immunogenic may not be recognized and eliminated by the immune system. If a tumor expresses progressive changes in cell surface antigens as well as in biologic behavior, then the time at which a functional immunogenic surface change occurs is critical. Thus, cells which express antigens at a premalignant stage could be eliminated before becoming malignant. On the other hand, cancers that express antigens may be able to change antigen expression under the influence of immune attack (immune

modulation). Whereas there are considerable data supporting a theory of clonal origin of cancer, there is also evidence that somatic mutation or selection of cancer cells for malignant properties and loss of cell surface antigens may be responsible. Thus, the ability of an immune response to control neoplastic growth is complicated by the biologic properties of neoplastic cells. The ability of oncologists and tumor immunologists to comprehend this relationship is further confounded by the fact that each neoplasm is an individual and 2 neoplasms do not necessarily behave in exactly the same way, even when they are morphologically similar.

The goals of tumor immunology are to elucidate the complex immunologic interrelationship between the host and the tumor and to manipulate this relationship for the purpose of diagnosis, prevention, and treatment of cancer.

TUMOR ANTIGENS

It was observed as early as 1910 that serum obtained from mice which had recovered from tumors could inhibit the growth of the same tumor in other mice, presumably because of antibodies directed against tumor antigens. Attempts were then made to treat cancer in experimental animals by immunization methods using various tumor preparations. Because of the promising results obtained with experimental animals, the hope was raised that cancer could be cured by immunologic methods. Unfortunately, it soon became apparent that the results obtained were not immunologic responses against tumor-specific antigens but rather allogeneic responses against histocompatibility antigens present on both normal and tumor tissue. The inability to demonstrate **tumor-specific transplantation antigens (TSTAs)** led to a general loss of interest in the potential application of immunology to oncology. However, interest was renewed following the development of inbred strains of mice that allowed transplantation of tumor cells between histocompatible animals and investigations of the immunologic relationship between host and tumor without the complications arising from histocompatibility antigens.

Studying transplantation of methylcholanthrene (MCA)-induced sarcoma in syngeneic (histocompatible) mice, Gross observed in 1943 that with some transplantable neoplasms, tumor nodules appeared when syngeneic tumor cells were injected into the skin and that the nodules grew for a few days and then regressed. Reinjection of identical tumor cells into the same individual did not produce tumor nodules, implying that the animal that had rejected the tumor was now resistant to it. Gross's observations were confirmed and extended about 10 years later by Foley, who transplanted MCA-induced murine sarcoma cells subcutaneously into syngeneic mice. After allowing the transplanted tumors to grow for a certain period of time, the tumors were strangled by tying sutures around their bases to interrupt the blood supply. Following regression of their tumors, the animals were able to reject a second transplant of the same tumor. These observations were further extended in 1957 by Prehn, who demonstrated that following surgical removal of a transplantable tumor, mice were highly resistant to a subsequent transplantation of the same tumor. The specificity of this immunity to tumor cells was demonstrated by the experiments of Prehn and Main, who showed that immunizations with normal skin grafts or with normal cells from various organs obtained from the donor of the transplanted tumor cells did not confer immunity to subsequent challenge with the tumor. These and other experiments led to the conclusion that tumor cells possessed distinct TSTAs.

While antigenic changes may be detected both intracellularly and on the surfaces of cancer cells, the field of tumor immunology depends almost entirely upon study of antigenic changes on the cell surfaces. Malignant changes may result in a number of antigenic changes that may be expressed in a number of ways (Fig 17–1). One such change is the loss of cell surface structures present in normal tissue. This is exemplified by the loss of A, B, and H isoantigens in lung carcinoma. Conceptually, this loss may be due to regulatory changes of the expression of the genes involved in the AB and H synthesis or due to the appearance of other gene products that "mask" the AB and H antigens on the malignant cell. Changes in the antigenic composition of the cancer cell may also involve the appearance of new antigens not present in normal tissue. Here again, these new antigens may represent new structures arising from gene activation, by the repression of a gene, or by mutation of genes coding for cell surface components. Another example of an antigenic change on the surface of the malignant cell is the appearance of structures present in fetal or embryonic tissue but not in normal adult tissue. Such a change is represented by the oncodevelopmental or oncofetal products (see below).

TYPES OF TUMOR ANTIGENS

Tumor antigens may be classified into 4 major types: (1) those expressed on chemically or physically

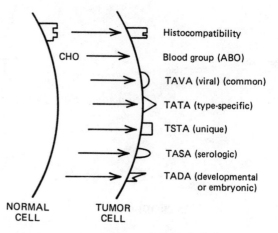

Figure 17–1. Some antigenic features of tumor cells. A number of changes on the cell surfaces of tumor cells have been noted, including loss or gain of histocompatibility antigen, loss of blood group carbohydrates, the appearance of virus-associated antigens (tumor-associated viral antigen [TAVA]), and tumor-associated transplantation antigens (TATA) common for tumors of the same histologic type. Also seen are tumor-specific transplantation antigens present on only one tumor (TSTA), antigens detected only by serologic reactions unique for a given tumor (tumor-associated serologic defined antigens [TASA]), and markers shared by embryonic or developing tumors and established tumors (tumor-associated developmental antigens [TADA]). (After Sell S: *Immunology, Immunopathology and Immunity,* 3rd ed. Harper & Row, 1980.)

induced tumors; (2) those expressed on virally induced tumors; (3) those associated with oncodevelopmental products; and (4) those of "spontaneous tumors," which may exhibit the characteristics of one or more of the above.

A. Antigens of Chemically Induced Tumors: It was recognized over a quarter of a century ago and still holds true today that with some exceptions, each tumor induced by a chemical carcinogen has a distinct antigenic specificity. For example, when the carcinogen methylcholanthrene (MCA) is applied in an identical manner on the skin of 2 syngeneic mice, each of the developing tumors (sarcomas) will exhibit antigenic determinants specific to that tumor, with little or no antigenic cross-reactivity between the tumors. Moreover, even if the carcinogen is applied in an identical manner to 2 similar sites on the same animal, the developing tumors are antigenically distinct. It is important to note that all the cells of a given chemically induced tumor share the same antigenic determinants, implying that they arise from a single transformed cell. This antigenic specificity will be expressed in subsequent generations following propagation in vivo or in vitro.

The appearance of tumor-specific antigens on cells of chemically induced tumors may be explained by 3 major mechanisms: (1) The activation of repressed genes. This mechanism is based on the premise that the genome of the normal cell contains the genetic information for the synthesis of all the tumor antigens. (2) Mutations, wherein the chemical carcinogens that are also mutagens induce somatic mutations during neoplastic transformation. These mutations induce, at random, new genetic configurations capable of coding for new antigenic determinants that would now be expressed in the progenies of the transformed cell. (3) Selection of a preexisting rare clone that arises as a result of normal mutations in normal tissues. Experimentally, there is convincing evidence that random mutations induced by chemical carcinogens are responsible for the diversity of the tumor antigens expressed on chemically induced tumors. This mechanism would account for the observation that the chances of detecting common antigenic determinants among chemically induced tumors are low. The antigens of physically induced tumors (ie, induced by UV light or x-ray radiation) behave like those of chemically induced tumors, exhibiting distinct antigenic specificity with little cross-reactivity between tumors. This is probably due to oncogenic mechanisms similar to those involved in chemically induced cancers.

The generality that chemically or physically induced tumors rarely share common tumor antigens makes the utilization of the immune response for the diagnosis, prevention, or treatment of such tumors difficult if not impossible. This is rather unfortunate in view of the many human tumors attributed to physical and chemical environmental factors such as radiation, tar, and smoke.

B. Antigens of Virally Induced Tumors: Both DNA and RNA viruses have been shown to be associated with oncogenesis (although not necessarily as the etiologic agent). Regarding antigens of experimental tumors caused by DNA viruses, each of the viruses induces unique nuclear antigens (T and μ) and cell surface antigens. A given virus induces the expression of the same antigens regardless of the tissue origin or animal species. Although these antigens are coded for by the virus, they are distinct from virion antigens and are referred to as **tumor-associated antigens.** Virally induced tumors may occasionally express oncofetal antigens coded for by the host genome as a result of deregulation by the transforming event.

While a viral etiology of human cancer is still not established, the association of DNA viruses with cell transformation and cancer in animals is well established and is perhaps the best link of viruses to human oncogenesis. For example, **Epstein-Barr virus (EBV),** one of the herpesviruses, is the cause of human infectious mononucleosis; it is also associated with (but not proved to be the etiologic agent of) Burkitt's lymphoma and nasopharyngeal carcinoma. In the same vein, herpes simplex type 2 has been linked to human cervical carcinoma. In animals, herpesviruses have been shown to be oncogenic, as exemplified by Marek's lymphoma of chickens.

When the oncogenic RNA viruses (**oncornaviruses**) infect the host cell, a set of enzymes coded

for by all oncornaviruses is involved in the synthesis of a double-stranded circular DNA copy of the RNA genome inserted into the host cell genome during cell transformation. The infected cells produce virus progeny by budding, with the core of the virus dome-shaped. Accordingly, these viruses are also referred to as **C type viruses.**

Tumor cells induced by oncornaviruses express antigens coded for by both the viral and host genomes. These include (1) the viral envelope antigens, mostly the envelope glycoprotein gp70, molecular weight approximately 70,000 (there is extensive immunologic cross-reactivity among all gp70 determinants of murine oncornaviruses); (2) intraviral proteins; and (3) cell surface antigens. While antibodies to gp70 will prevent infectivity, immunity against the neoplastic cell surface antigens is mainly responsible for the immunologic rejection of the malignant cell. These cell surface antigens are distinct from the viral antigens and also from the H-2 histocompatibility antigens. The complexity of neoantigens expressed in virally induced tumors is illustrated by the Rous sarcoma system of hamsters: The antigens include **virus envelope antigen (VEA), virus group-specific antigens (gs antigens),** virus-coded nonviral proteins, cell-coded determinants activated by the virus, and oncodevelopmental antigens coded by cellular genes that are activated by virus-induced transformation.

Unlike the unique antigenic specificity exhibited by individual tumors induced by chemical carcinogenesis, virally induced tumors show extensive cross-reactivity. This is true not only for tumors induced by a given virus or even a group of viruses in different individuals of the same species but also for tumors induced by the same virus in different species. For example, DNA viruses such as polyoma, SV40, and Shope papilloma induce tumors that exhibit extensive cross-reactivity within each group. Moreover, many leukemogenic viruses such as Raucher leukemia virus, Gross leukemia virus, and Friend and Maloney viruses cause tumors that not only cross-react within each group but also exhibit cross-reactivity between some groups. Such cross-reactivity strongly suggests that the neoplastic transformation associated with viral infection represents a direct effect of the virus, presumably because of the continuous presence of genetic information derived from the viral genome that determines the antigen and the phenotype of the transformed cell. Alternatively, the cross-reactivity may be due to the fact that the antigenicity is determined by the genome of the host cell, which is consistently activated by the various transforming viruses.

Although the viral etiology of human malignancy has yet to be established, several immunologic features of some human tumors are quite similar to those of tumors induced in experimental animals by viruses. For example, colon carcinoma cells obtained from different patients exhibit immunologic cross-reactivity. Cross-reactivity is also well established for cell surface antigens of Burkitt's lymphoma and of neuroblastoma of different patients. Several other human cancers have been shown to exhibit cross-reactivity to a greater or lesser degree.

C. Oncodevelopmental Tumor Antigens:
Many tumors exhibit on their cell surfaces or secrete into serum a variety of oncodevelopmental products. All of these products are "self" components normally expressed during embryonic and fetal development but present not at all or in very low levels in normal well-differentiated tissue. The components are not immunogenic in the autochthonous host, and their presence has been detected by the use of allogeneic or xenogeneic serum. One of these products is the **carcinoembryonic antigen (CEA)** present chiefly on the wall of the tumor cell and found in cancers of the gastrointestinal tract, particularly of the colon. It may also be shed into the circulation and has been detected in the sera of patients with a variety of neoplastic as well as nonneoplastic diseases. Thus, in humans, high CEA levels (above 2.5 μg/mL) have been found in colonic cancer; in some tumors of the lung, pancreas, stomach, and breast; in nonneoplastic diseases such as emphysema, ulcerative colitis, pancreatitis, and alcoholism; and in serum of heavy smokers. Another oncodevelopmental antigen associated with several tumors is alpha-fetoprotein (AFP), which is not found on the cell wall but is rapidly secreted by tumor cells. It is found in high concentrations in fetal serum, maternal serum, and serum of adults with hepatomas and testicular teratoblastomas. A variety of tumors both of different organs and of different histologic types express high immunologically cross-reactive CEA or oncofetal proteins as assessed by xenogeneic antisera. The use of these products in the diagnosis and treatment of cancer is discussed below.

The appearance of these antigenically similar oncodevelopmental products associated with such a wide variety of tumor types strongly suggests that their presence is the result of gene derepression and loss of synthesis control rather than the appearance of new gene products following mutagenesis.

Following malignant transformation, cells may begin to express certain "inappropriate" or "illegitimate" antigens or may begin to synthesize products such as hormones or enzymes normally elaborated only by other cell types.* For example, in humans, "illegitimate" blood group antigens have been demonstrated—ie, antigens related to A substance and the P system are associated with some stomach cancers, and antigens of the MN group are found in some brain cancers. These observations lend support to the hypothesis that at least with these tumors, the appearance of antigens is due to aberrant control of expression of preexisting genes rather than to random mutations. Not all of these newly or inappropriately expressed "self" constituents are immunogenic in the autochthonous host. Therefore, their expression is not important in the host-tumor relationship, though they may serve as

indicators of malignancy (see section on immunodiagnosis).

D. Antigens of Spontaneous Tumors: There is still controversy over whether the immunologic behavior of "spontaneous" tumors (no known inducing cause) is similar to that of tumors experimentally induced by chemical, physical, or viral carcinogens. It is even questioned whether spontaneous tumors exhibit tumor antigens on their cell surfaces. These questions arise out of our inability, in the case of most spontaneous tumors, to demonstrate tumor-specific antigens and an immunologic response of the autochthonous host to these antigens. In fact, most spontaneous tumor antigens have been identified by the use of allogeneic or xenogeneic antisera following exhaustive absorptions with normal tissue. Moreover, investigations of transplantation antigens of spontaneous tumors in animals demonstrate that they may possess tumor antigens which are only weakly immunogenic. Nevertheless, evidence is accumulating for the presence of antigens on the surfaces of cells of spontaneous tumors. In a recent study, antibodies to autochthonous tumors were present in 56 of 75 patients with malignant melanoma. Antibodies of 4 patients exhibited individually specific melanoma antigens; 5 patients had antibodies recognizing shared melanoma antigens; and 21 had antibodies against widely distributed antigens. This and other reports indicate the presence of tumor antigens on cells of some spontaneous tumors, but the frequency of such antigens on spontaneous tumors and their biologic significance remains unknown. The antigenic specificity of some spontaneous tumors is distinct, with little or no cross-reactivity. In this respect, these spontaneous tumors resemble chemically induced tumors wherein little or no cross-reactivity among tumors is apparent. Other spontaneous tumors share antigenic determinants and in this respect resemble virally induced tumors.

EFFECTOR MECHANISMS IN TUMOR IMMUNITY

In mammals, a complex network of cells and their products interact to perform a variety of diverse functions necessary for the generation, expression, and regulation of many levels of innate and specific immunity. The important role played by both humoral and cellular responses in mediating immunity to infectious disease is well established. Using a variety of experimental conditions, it can be shown that cellular and humoral immune effector mechanisms are capable of destroying tumor cells in vitro (Table 17–1).

Humoral Responses

Antibodies have been demonstrated in serum of many animals bearing a variety of experimentally induced tumors. Although these antibodies have been useful in serologic characterization and in the isolation of tumor-associated antigens, the presence of a humoral response is not consistently correlated with

---

*Not "oncodevelopmental antigens" in the true sense.

Table 17-1. Possible effector mechanisms in tumor immunity.

I. Humoral
Opsonization and phagocytosis
Lysis by complement
Loss of cell adhesion
II. Cellular
Direct lysis by cytotoxic T cells
Antibody-dependent cell-mediated cytotoxicity
Activation of macrophages by factors released by T cells
Non-specifically activated macrophages
Natural killer (NK) cells

increased tumor resistance in the host. Nevertheless, there are several ways in which tumor-specific antibodies could theoretically mediate antitumor activity.

A. Complement-Mediated Lysis: If tumor-associated antigens induce a humoral response, it is likely that the interaction of the tumor cell with some of the antibodies will activate the complement system, leading to lesions in the cell membrane and eventual lysis. Lysis by complement has been shown to be effective in vitro against certain tumor cells in suspension; however, cell death is not usually evident when treating target cells consisting of solid tumor tissue. In general, variation in susceptibility to lysis may be influenced by the ability of the tumor cell to induce high-affinity cytotoxic antibodies (IgM and IgG); by the distribution and density of the antigens present on the cell membrane; by the ability of the tumor cell to repair complement-mediated lesions in its membrane; or by the ability of the antibody to reach the appropriate cell surface antigens.

Studies conducted originally with transplantable tumors in mice have provided some basis for complement-mediated lysis operating in vivo. The presence of cytotoxic antibodies suppresses the growth of murine leukemia and lymphoma cells injected into the blood or growing in ascites fluid; however, the growth of solid lymphoid tumor implants (non-virus shedding) was not affected. A number of studies have also demonstrated that the incidence of tumor spread by metastases was reduced in animals with high levels of cytotoxic antibodies. For example, it has been shown that antitumor antibodies could prevent the establishment of lung metastasis following injection of mammary carcinoma cells into the bloodstream of mice, but that these same antibodies failed to suppress the growth of the same tumor injected subcutaneously. Furthermore, it was noted that a critical tumor dosage threshold exists above which antitumor antibodies are ineffective. Thus, if cytotoxic antibodies provide any tumor resistance at all, they might be expected to be effective against dispersed tumors (leukemia) or against the spread of solid tumors by a small number of metastatic cells via body fluids.

B. Opsonization and Phagocytosis: Opsonization is the binding of specific antibody and complement components with particulate antigen to facilitate its phagocytosis. In vitro studies have demonstrated the ability of macrophages to exert cytotoxic activity against some tumor cells by cytophagocytosis in the presence of immune serum. The relevance of this activity in vivo is difficult to assess.

C. Loss of Cell Adhesion: The ability of antibodies to bind the surface of tumor cells in vivo may be important in antitumor activities other than those mediated by complement-dependent lysis or phagocytosis by macrophages. Antibodies bound to the membranes of malignant cells may modulate surface structures and thereby interfere with cell adhesive properties. This could have a deleterious effect on certain types of tumors, since the ability to adhere to each other and to surrounding host tissue may be essential for successful establishment of the malignant clone by providing cellular organization and support. Furthermore, adherence of circulating tumor cells to the endothelium of blood vessels appears to precede metastatic spread. Antibodies specifically bound to the membranes of tumor cells may result in loss of adhesive properties important to the establishment of blood-borne metastatic foci.

Cell-Mediated Responses

Cell-mediated immunity involves a complex set of reactions that can lead to tissue destruction typified by allograft rejections, various autoimmune disease states, and forms of delayed hypersensitivity. Studies of these reactions have shown that tissue destruction can be highly specific or nonspecific and is mediated primarily by lymphocytes and macrophages. The ability of these cellular components to mediate tumor cell destruction as well was first demonstrated in adoptive transfer studies between syngeneic animals. Since then, the development of several in vitro systems has permitted study of the activity of various cell types and the molecular mechanisms that may be operative in cytotoxic reactions against tumor cells.

A. Direct Lysis by T Lymphocytes: Immune T lymphocytes can specifically recognize and kill target cells that share the same antigens as the immunizing tumor cells. This mechanism, in contrast to specific humoral immunity, is able to destroy solid tissue as well as dispersed tumors. The ability of tumor-immune T lymphocytes to kill homologous tumor cells can be measured by a variety of techniques, including (1) the dye exclusion test—visual estimation of the number of cells killed by counting dead target cells that take up vital stains; (2) colony inhibition—reduction in the number of colonies formed by tumor cells when transferred to tissue culture plates following incubation with immune lymphocytes; (3) ^{51}Cr release cytotoxicity assay—release of labeled intracellular components of the killed target cells (Fig 17-2); and (4) the Winn neutralization assay—reduction in tumor cell growth following transfer of immune donor cells and tumor cells into syngeneic recipients (Fig 17-3).

The exact nature of the cellular and molecular events leading to lysis of tumor cells by cytotoxic T lymphocytes has not been resolved. However, it is

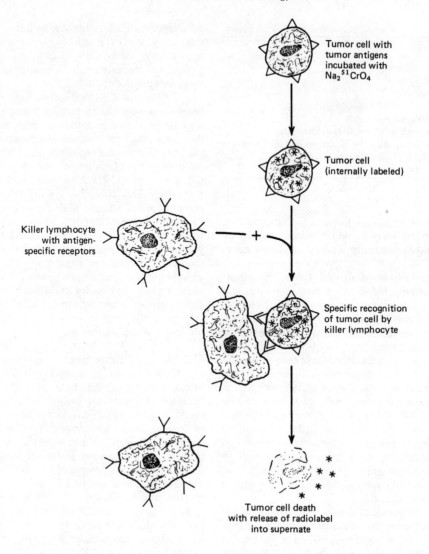

Tumor cell with
tumor antigens
incubated with
$Na_2{}^{51}CrO_4$

Tumor cell
(internally labeled)

Killer lymphocyte
with antigen-
specific receptors

Specific recognition
of tumor cell by
killer lymphocyte

Tumor cell death
with release of radiolabel
into supernate

Figure 17–2. Cytotoxicity assay by chromium release. Target cell death is determined by measuring the radioactivity released into the supernate following incubation of the killer cells and labeled tumor cells. The spontaneous release of the ^{51}Cr isotope is measured in the supernate of labeled tumor cells incubated in the absence of specific killer lymphocytes. Specific lymphocyte-mediated cytolysis of tumor cells can then be calculated. (Experimental ^{51}Cr release minus spontaneous release.)

clear that the first step is recognition of the target cell by an antigen-specific T cell receptor. Following recognition, a series of energy-dependent events occur, leading ultimately to lysis of the target cell. (For a full discussion of these events, see Chapter 12.)

The cytotoxic activity of immune T lymphocytes described above is based on in vitro observations. Evidence that cytotoxic T lymphocytes may play a role in the host's antitumor resistance has been demonstrated mostly in adoptive transfer studies with experimentally induced tumors. For example, spleen cells or lymph node cells transferred from tumor-immune mice into normal or immunologically incompetent syngeneic recipients can confer immunity to a subsequent lethal tumor challenge. The transferred immunity is specific for the tumor used to immunize the donor mice and is mediated by T lymphocytes, since it can be completely abrograted by pretreatment of the donor cells with anti–T cell serum and complement prior to transfer. In a second set of experiments, it was demonstrated that the ability of immune T lymphocytes to transfer specific immunity can be directly correlated with this population's ability to express in vitro cytotoxicity against ^{51}Cr-labeled homologous tumor cells.

B. Antibody-Dependent Cell-Mediated Cytotoxicity (ADCC) (Fig 17–4): Tumor target cells coated with IgG antibody can be destroyed following interaction with several types of effector cells bearing receptors for the Fc portion of these antibodies. ADCC

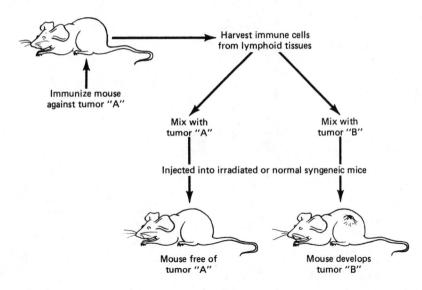

Figure 17–3. The Winn neutralization assay tests the ability of various cell populations (T, B, null, and macrophages) from immune lymphoid tissues to inhibit tumor growth in vivo. The specificity of this antitumor activity can be determined by mixing the immune lymphoid cells with other tumor types not used for immunization of the effector cell donor.

effector cell populations include granulocytes, macrophages (see below), and **K (killer) cells.** K cells are lymphocytes without T or B cell surface markers and are present in the lymphoid tissues and blood of normal animals.

The actual mechanism of tumor cell lysis by ADCC is not known. ADCC is not augmented by the presence of complement and requires close effector cell-target cell contact. This close interaction is facilitated by binding of the effector cell to the Fc portion of the antibody, which is bound to the target cell through its Fab portions. Triggering of the lytic process can be blocked by immune complexes, aggregated immunoglobulins, and protein A, all of which bind to the Fc portion of the specific IgG.

Although antibody-dependent killing of certain tumor cells by K cells and macrophages has been shown to occur in vitro, there remains the fundamental question whether ADCC plays a role in tumor resistance in vivo. Limited studies indicate that this form of cytolysis may enhance tumor resistance in some tumor systems such as murine leukemias and lymphomas wherein tumor-specific antibodies are readily induced. However, sufficient data are not available with which to assess clearly the potential of ADCC as an antitumor mechanism.

C. Killing Mediated by "Activated" Macrophages: Mononuclear phagocytic cells are capable of many effector functions important in the host's innate and specific immunity to infectious diseases. It is evident that macrophages also have tumoricidal capabilities. In general, macrophages from normal donors are noncytotoxic or show only marginal cytotoxicity in vitro against a variety of target cells, including many types of tumor cell lines. The

cytotoxic activity of macrophages is markedly enhanced following infection of the donor with intracellular microorganisms (mycobacteria, *Toxoplasma, Listeria,* etc) or following in vitro sensitization of macrophages from normal donors with killed bacteria or their products. The efficiency of the in vitro cytolysis of tumor target cells by macrophages is also increased by the presence of activated lymphocytes or their lymphokines which activate macrophages (Fig 17–5). The events leading to cytotoxic macrophage killing are currently being exploited as a form of cancer immunotherapy (Chapter 40).

The induction of cytotoxic macrophages by tumor-immune T lymphocytes has been studied in a series of experiments. It has been shown that lymphocytes obtained from mice immunized with irradiated lymphoma cells were not active by themselves against the immunizing tumor cells in vitro. However, macrophages obtained from these same immunized donors were *specifically* cytotoxic to the lymphoma target cells. Furthermore, peritoneal macrophages isolated from normal syngeneic mice could be rendered cytotoxic following incubation with spleen cells from immunized donors. Again, the cytotoxicity was specific for only those tumor cells that were antigenically homologous to the immunizing tumor. Macrophage activation was shown to be induced by a **specific macrophage activation factor (SMAF)** produced by a noncytotoxic population of immune T lymphocytes. The properties of SMAF that lead to activation of macrophages capable of specifically recognizing and killing tumor cells are not clear. It has been suggested that SMAF may be an immunoglobulinlike T cell product that specifically absorbs to macrophages and possesses a recognition site for the immunizing tumor antigen, thereby imparting specificity to the ensuing

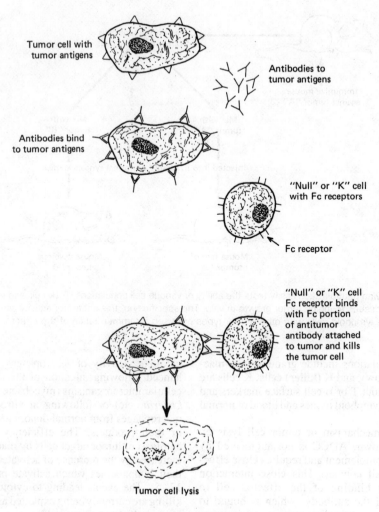

Tumor cell with tumor antigens

Antibodies to tumor antigens

Antibodies bind to tumor antigens

"Null" or "K" cell with Fc receptors

Fc receptor

"Null" or "K" cell Fc receptor binds with Fc portion of antitumor antibody attached to tumor and kills the tumor cell

Tumor cell lysis

Figure 17–4. Antibody-dependent cell-mediated cytotoxicity (ADCC).

cytotoxic events. Another way by which macrophages could specifically kill tumor cells once they have become activated by immune T lymphocytes is through mediation by antitumor antibodies (ADCC).

Activated macrophages isolated from donors infected with certain intracellular microorganisms or exposed to general immunopotentiating agents such as endotoxin and polyinosine-cytosine express nonspecific cytotoxicity for a wide range of tumor types but not against normal cells. Several mechanisms may be involved in generating these cytotoxic macrophages. Agents that consist of endotoxin and polynucleotides may activate macrophages directly. In general, however, many agents that activate macrophages function as specific antigenic stimuli for immune lymphocytes which release a variety of lymphokines. Some of these lymphokines attract macrophages to the site of the immunologic reaction, prevent their migration away (by MIF), and stimulate them with MAF to undergo morphologic changes resulting in enhanced killing capabilities. Since the enhanced killing mediated by these mechanisms can be

demonstrated against a variety of tumor target cells, the macrophage appears to be an important nonspecific effector of an antigen-specific cell-mediated response. The factors that convert macrophages into tumoricidal cells is distinct from SMAF and can be obtained from the supernates of sensitized lymphocytes also containing MIF activity. The recognition system mediating this form of tumor cell killing is unknown. However, the ability of nonspecifically activated cytotoxic macrophages to discriminate between transformed and normal target cells is reproducible. It is still not clear whether the increased lysis of transformed cells is a property of the target cell or due to the discriminative ability of the effector macrophages.

The oncocytolytic process mediated by macrophages appears to be the same whether they are from donors immunized specifically with tumor or with general immunostimulants. Destruction of tumor cells by macrophages requires intimate contact between the 2 cells. Phagocytosis does not appear to be an important mechanism in this type of killing. By labeling secondary lysosomes with indigestible nontoxic

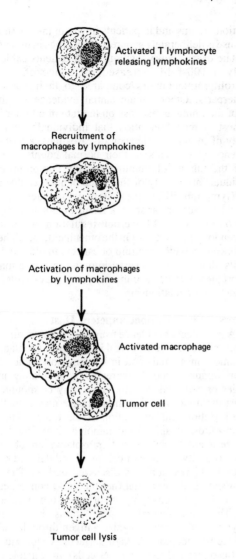

Activated T lymphocyte releasing lymphokines

Recruitment of macrophages by lymphokines

Activation of macrophages by lymphokines

Activated macrophage

Tumor cell

Tumor cell lysis

Figure 17–5. Tumor cell destruction by macrophages.

agents, it was shown that an activated macrophage directly transfers the contents of its lysosomes into the target cell following membrane fusion between the 2 cells. The efficiency of the killing process is dependent on the amount of cytocidal lysosomal enzymes delivered into the target cell. Thus, only fully activated macrophages with increased numbers of lysosomes were capable of mediating significant tumor killing. It has been reported by several investigators that soluble cytotoxic or cytostatic mediators are present in the culture supernates of activated macrophages; however, the nature of these factors and their mechanism of action is not well understood.

Although many in vitro studies have demonstrated the cytotoxicity of appropriately stimulated macrophages, evidence that they play a crucial role in the natural defense of the host against malignant disease is difficult to assess directly. Nevertheless, several animal model systems have been useful in

determining the ability of macrophages to modulate tumor growth in vivo. For example, animals injected with immunostimulants known to enhance in vitro macrophage cytotoxic activity (facultative intracellular pathogens, polynucleotides, pyran copolymer, glucan, and double-stranded RNA) have a reduced incidence or delayed appearance of chemically induced tumors. The enhanced tumor resistance induced by such immunostimulants is abolished by agents known to be cytotoxic for macrophages such as carrageenan, silica particles, and gold salts. Stimulation of the reticuloendothelial system of mice with *Toxoplasma* or Freund's complete adjuvant leads to a reduced incidence of certain kinds of spontaneous tumors. Furthermore, these mice show increased antitumor resistance to implants of syngeneic tumors. Direct correlation between acquired tumor resistance and activated macrophages was provided by the finding that macrophages harvested from these animals showed enhanced in vitro killing of tumor cells and were capable of inhibiting the in vitro growth of these tumors. A role for macrophages in the host's natural antitumor resistance is further indicated by their accumulation at the site of tumor regression. Based on comparative studies of the content of macrophages in different tumors, it has been claimed that a direct relationship exists between the degree of macrophage infiltration and the reduction of metastatic spread, although it has not been ruled out that they are simply involved in the "cleanup" of cellular debris.

D. Lysis by Natural Killer (NK) Cells: Spleen cells from nonimmune rodents as well as peripheral blood lymphocytes from normal humans may lyse a variety of target cells. Among those target cells damaged are a number of tumor cell lines. These "natural killer" (NK) cells have been identified repeatedly in the spleens, lymph nodes, bone marrow, and blood of normal animals using a variety of cellular cytotoxicity assays (see Chapter 12). NK cells are clearly different from immune cytotoxic T lymphocytes and K cells. Murine NK cells have been identified as small lymphocytes that originate in the bone marrow and can develop into cells with full cytotoxic activity in congenitally athymic and neonatally thymectomized mice. They lack surface immunoglobulins and C3 receptors but appear to possess immunoglobulin Fc receptors and have extremely low levels of T cell antigen. NK cells fail to show phagocytic activity and are nonadherent to nylon-wool or glass; however, they do adhere to the glycosphingolipid asialo-GM_2. Hence, NK cells lack the characteristics of mature T lymphocytes, B lymphocytes, or macrophages. NK cells can be functionally distinguished from K cells, since the NK activity is not dependent on the presence of antibody and is not inhibited by the presence of antigen-antibody complexes. The level of NK cytotoxic activity is different in different strains of mice. In general, NK activity can be augmented by exposure to bacterial adjuvants, tumor cells, virally infected cells, and—most notably—interferon. Activation does not induce immunologic memory.

NK cells can recognize and lyse a wide variety of tumor cells and other cell lines in vitro. The nature of the receptor through which the target cell is bound and the degree of specificity in the recognition are unknown. It does appear that glycoproteins on the surface of the target cell are important for recognition by the putative NK receptor. When NK effector function in several strains of mice was assayed against many different target cells, some types of cells were lysed by some murine strains but not by others. The pattern of lytic reactivity to the panel of labeled target syngeneic, allogeneic, and xenogeneic cells was different for each strain. This suggests that a broad specificity in NK effector function exists, and it may be under some form of polygenetic control not presently known to be within the constraints of the histocompatibility system.

The above studies demonstrate the antitumor activity of NK cells in vitro. The role of NK activity in vivo is only circumstantial. It appears that NK activity is influenced by age, increasing from low levels early in life and then declining again to low levels in old age. Aging mice exhibit a marked decline in NK-mediated tumor killing in vitro that coincides with an increasing incidence of spontaneous tumors in age-matched mice. A role for NK cells in the control of tumors is further suggested by the observation that congenitally athymic and neonatally thymectomized mice still exhibit considerable resistance to spontaneously arising tumors and to transplantable tumors. Although these mice have few or no T cells, they possess normal or increased numbers of NK cells. Clearly, more studies are necessary; nevertheless, limited data suggest that NK cells may be important effector cells against the early stages of tumor growth prior to the development of fully activated macrophages and immune T killer cells.

THE ROLE OF THE IMMUNE RESPONSE IN THE HOST–TUMOR RELATIONSHIP

There are 2 major lines of evidence tending to show that the immune response has a profound effect on the host-tumor relationship: One is based on the observation that the incidence of malignant neoplastic disease is higher in immunosuppressed individuals than in their normal counterparts. The other is based on experimental and clinical observations that directly implicate the immune response in the fate of the tumor. In general, the immune response to tumors is of benefit to the host; however, it may under certain circumstances be detrimental (see below).

Tumors in Immunosuppressed Individuals

The importance of the immune response in the host-tumor relationship is indicated by the fact that immunosuppressed individuals are more susceptible to tumors than their normal counterparts. Thus, an increased incidence of tumors, primarily lymphoproliferative, is known to occur in humans immunosuppressed by drugs or radiation. This is best exemplified by the high incidence of leukemias in radiation victims and in patients in whom the immune response is deliberately suppressed by drugs in order to facilitate organ transplantation. Such patients exhibit nearly a 100-fold increased incidence of lymphoproliferative tumors compared to their normal counterparts. Other circumstantial evidence for the role of the immune response on the fate of a tumor in the host is the observation that individuals with a variety of immune deficiency diseases have a higher incidence of cancer than their normal counterparts. Since the tumors of immunologically compromised individuals are mostly of the reticuloendothelial system (lymphoproliferative), it may be questioned whether the tumors arise as a result of immune suppression or because of aberrant regulation of the reticuloendothelial system. On the other hand, the higher incidence of a wide spectrum of cancers in older individuals along with a lowered immune response may support the view that the immune system plays a role in the host-tumor relationship.

Tumors in the Immunocompetent Host

A great deal of evidence from experimental tumor systems as well as from several instances of spontaneous tumors in animals and in humans now indicates that an immune response expressed by circulating antibodies or cell-mediated immunity may be mounted against the tumor and that the response may actually cause rejection and destruction of the tumor. Thus, immunization of animals to tumor antigens renders them resistant to subsequent transplantation of the tumor primarily because of cell-mediated delayed hypersensitivity reactions, as discussed earlier. The T lymphocyte is the essential (not the only) component of delayed hypersensitivity involved in tumor rejection. There are several subpopulations of T lymphocytes all of which recognize antigen through antigen-specific receptors on their surfaces. Cytotoxic T cells (also referred to as T killer cells) are capable of directly destroying tumor cells in vitro. The effect of these cells in vivo is still not clear, although experiments utilizing cell transfers indicate that this T cell subpopulation is operative in vivo. Another subpopulation of T cells is primarily responsible for delayed hypersensitivity reactions. They are activated by antigens to release lymphokines, among which are substances with the ability to recruit macrophages and other monocytes to the area of the antigen (ie, the tumor) and activate macrophages to destroy tumor cells. The appearance of T lymphocytes and macrophages at the site of regressing experimental tumors or of tumors that show spontaneous regression suggests their in vivo role in tumor rejection.

Two other observations point to the importance of the immune response in the host-tumor relationship. First is the observation that highly immunogenic primary tumors induced by viruses in experimental animals are usually rejected by the immunologically competent host but not by immunosuppressed individuals. Second is that which is referred to as "concomitant immunity." This is the phenomenon of the rejection of newly arising tumors in a tumor-bearing individual in spite of the progression of a primary tumor. The phenomenon of concomitant immunity, seen also in humans, is explained by the development of immunity to the primary tumor that causes rejection of that tumor at another site. This is supported by the finding that delayed hypersensitivity components are present at the site of the new tumor. Concomitant immunity in humans is perhaps the closest parallel to the induction of immunity to tumor transplantation in experimental animals.

Immune Surveillance

The belief that immunity plays a beneficial role in the host-tumor relationship can be traced back to Ehrlich, who in 1908 speculated that tumor cells which arise frequently and bear specific antigen could be eliminated by the immune response of the host. In the early 1950s, Lewis Thomas postulated that cell-mediated immunity has evolved as a primary and specific defense mechanism against neoplastic cells which arise continuously through somatic mutations. In the late 1950s, the term "immunological surveillance" was coined by Burnet, who postulated that cell-mediated immunity evolved to recognize and destroy autologous cells with nonself markers such as tumor cells bearing tumor antigens. The theory of immune surveillance, then, hypothesizes that immune mechanisms may eliminate newly appearing tumor cells and thus serve as a surveillance system for cancer. In order to be effective, the immune surveillance system must be able to recognize and react to tumor antigens on the newly arising malignant clones before the tumor mass has obtained a critical size beyond which this controlling mechanism would be ineffective. Some of the requirements for effective immune surveillance are listed in Table 17–2.

Whereas there are ways to explain how immune surveillance may be circumvented by cancer, what is

Table 17–2. Requirements for an effective immune response against tumors.

(1) The tumor clone must express a cell surface antigen, and this tumor antigen must appear early in the development of the tumor.
(2) The tumor antigen must be able to initiate an immune response in the host (ie, be immunogenic).
(3) The host's immune system must be able to recognize and respond to the tumor antigen (ie, the host must be immunologically competent).
(4) The host response must not result in tolerance to the antigen.
(5) The expression of the antigen must not change, and each tumor cell must have a recognizable antigen. (Antigen modulation or somatic mutation must not occur.)
(6) The immune response must result in an appropriate effector mechanism that will affect the viability (cytotoxic) or inhibit the growth (cytostatic) of the tumor cells.
(7) The immune response must not result in production of an effector mechanism that will inhibit specific tumor immunity (ie, enhancement or blocking of tumor immunity).

Table 17–3. Circumstantial evidence of tumor-limiting factors in humans.

Spontaneous regression.
Self-healing melanomas.
Regression of metastases after resection of primary.
Regression of tumor following "non – tumor killing" doses of chemotherapy.
Reappearance of metastases after long latent periods.
Frequent failure of circulating tumor cells to form metastases.
Infiltration of tumors by mononuclear cells.
Higher incidence of tumors after clinical immunosuppression.
High incidence of tumors in immune deficiency diseases.
Increased tumor incidence with aging.

the evidence that there is an immune mechanism for limiting tumor growth? Examples of tumor immunity have been demonstrated in experimental animals, particularly for virally induced tumors and tumors induced by "strong" chemical carcinogens. However, considerable evidence indicates that tumors induced by "weak" carcinogens or those arising "spontaneously" are weakly antigenic or not antigenic at all. Circumstantial evidence for the existence of tumor-limiting factors in humans is set forth in Table 17–3. Although this list is impressive at first glance, individual patients exhibiting effects consistent with tumor immunity are relatively rare, and the effects often can be explained in other ways. Most untreated human tumors grow without evidence of tumor immunity. Documented spontaneous regressions are rare and occur most often with tumors of embryonal tissues such as choriocarcinomas, hypernephromas, and neuroblastomas, suggesting developmental controlling factors other than immunity. Regression of metastases without chemotherapy or irradiation is extremely rare. Reappearance of metastases after a long latent period may be explained by a number of factors controlling dormancy other than immunity. Although infiltration of tumors by mononuclear cells is frequently used to support some role of the immune response in the fate of the tumor, there is limited evidence that such infiltration actually affects the growth of the tumor. The tumors found in immunosuppressed or immunodeficient patients are frequently of lymphoid elements, suggesting an abnormality in lymphocyte controlling mechanism (T suppressor cells?) rather than specific tumor immunity. Finally, a number of immune abnormalities occur in the elderly, including loss of the thymic cortex and the appearance of a variety of autoantibodies. However, there is no directly demonstrable cause-and-effect relationship between abnormalities of the immune response associated with aging and the increased incidence of cancer associated with aging.

In summary, the role of immunity in immune surveillance against newly arising tumors remains controversial. In animal models, both antigen-specific and non–antigen-specific (eg, macrophages, NK cells) reactivity of the immune system can prevent or in selected models even cure cancer. However, these models do not necessarily reflect the situation in humans. As mentioned, in both experimental animals and humans, most spontaneously occurring tumors are weakly antigenic if at all. This lack of antigenicity may reflect the ability of the tumors to escape the surveillance of the immune system, whereas other "more antigenic" tumors would be destroyed.

Limitations on the Effectiveness of the Immune Response Against Tumors

Some of the foregoing experimental evidence and clinical observations indicate that the immune response plays a beneficial role in the host-tumor relationship. On the other hand, there is both experimental and clinical evidence that the immune response may have either a negligible beneficial effect or in some cases even a detrimental effect on the host-tumor relationship.

A. Tumors in Privileged Sites: Certain areas of the body are immunologically "privileged" sites in that they are not reached by effector cells of the immune response (eg, the eyes and tissues of the central nervous system in humans and the cheek pouch in hamsters). Tumors in the eye and the central nervous tissue seldom are infiltrated with "active" mononuclear cells, in contrast to tumor tissue in other parts of the body. Thus, tumors arising in such areas would escape destruction by immune components and could perhaps serve as a sheltered site for the development of primary tumors.

B. Antigenic Modulation: Loss of antigenicity or change in antigenic markers is a means by which tumor cells may avoid immunologic destruction. Antigenic modulation has been demonstrated with murine leukemia cells expressing thymic lymphocyte (TL) antigens. When these tumor cells are grown in the presence of cytotoxic anti-TL antibodies, certain cells lose their TL antigens, perhaps by shedding or internalization. These variants become predominant in the culture. However, removal of the antiserum leads to reappearance of the TL antigens. This indicates that genetic selection has not taken place but that specific antibody suppresses the production of the corresponding antigen.

C. Enhancement and Blocking Factors: Immune enhancement is the progressive growth of tumors in the presence of serum from tumor-immune or tumor-bearing animals (whereas untreated animals usually reject the same tumor). Such enhancement has been attributed to the presence of "blocking" antibodies, soluble tumor-associated antigens, or immune complexes. These humoral factors can enhance tumor survival by interfering with the cellular assault against tumors at several levels. For example, the early production of antibodies may result in their absorption to the surface of tumors that mask tumor antigens and prevent the induction of T killer cell-mediated immunity, thus blocking the afferent arm of the immune response. Central blockage could occur if tumor-specific antibodies or immune complexes regulate or even inhibit sensitization, proliferation, or the functional

capabilities of sensitized lymphocytes. Inhibition of efferent immune mechanisms would apply if blocking antibodies cover the tumor cells and prevent sensitized lymphocytes from recognizing and killing the target antigens. Alternatively, soluble tumor-associated antigens could saturate the receptors of effector lymphocytes, thereby interfering with their ability to interact with the tumor graft. Although the contribution of humoral factors to immune stimulation of spontaneous tumors is unclear, the ability of antibodies to enhance the growth of transplanted tumor cells such as MCA-induced sarcomas, Moloney virus–induced lymphomas, and mammary adenocarcinomas is well known. In most of these studies, enhancement was demonstrated following transfer of tumors to recipients immunized with tumor-derived materials in such a way as to induce the formation of humoral antibody or to recipients transfused with serum from immunized animals.

In general, tumor enhancement has been largely attributed to the presence of "blocking" serum factors; nevertheless, enhancement has been demonstrated by the adoptive transfer of immune lymphocytes. In these studies, lymphocytes sensitized against allogeneic or syngeneic tumors could stimulate rather than inhibit tumor growth. This result appeared to be dependent on the amount of time elapsed between sensitization and lymphocyte transfer as well as on the dose. In agreement with these observations, in vitro cytotoxicity studies revealed that lymphocytes harvested early in tumor development did not mediate significant killing of tumor target cells but actually stimulated tumor growth in vitro if used in low effector cell/target cell ratios. Although these findings need further clarification under more controlled conditions, they suggest that tumors could escape immune surveillance by immunostimulation early in their development, thereby increasing the possibility that tumor growth could outrun the inhibitory capacity of a matured immune response.

D. Immune Capacity Versus Tumor Mass: The immune response has a finite capacity for effectiveness against tumors. Highly immunized animals display a remarkable resistance to tumor implants at several dosage levels compared to normal recipients. However, if the tumor challenge is sufficiently large, the immunized recipient succumbs to the growth of a lethal cancer. The reasons for this breakdown in tumor resistance are not entirely clear, although protection from effector functions afforded by the aggregation of a large number of tumor cells or the release of large amounts of tumor antigens that may block effector cell functions are among the possibilities. It can be reasoned that tumors emerging by first escaping the host's immune surveillance by one of the mechanisms discussed earlier would be assured continued growth once critical mass had been reached. Nevertheless, small metastatic foci may still be effectively rejected by the immune response. In fact, it has been shown that cancer patients or tumor-bearing animals with large primary tumors are resistant to implants of small numbers of the autochthonous tumor cells at a second site (concomitant immunity).

E. Suppressor T Lymphocytes: The induction of antigen-specific suppressor cells plays an important role in the normal regulation of the immune response to that antigen. The suppressive activity can affect the level of both the humoral response and the cell-mediated response. Tumor-specific suppressor T cells have been demonstrated in some tumor-bearing mice and may play a role in the apparent ineffectiveness of the response in tumor-bearing mice. The immunosuppressor cells can be detected within 24 hours of subcutaneous implantations of MCA-induced sarcoma cells and persist throughout the early stages of tumor growth. Furthermore, transfer of suppressor cells can suppress the rejection of immunogenic dosages of transplantable tumor cells when administered simultaneously with or 5 days following tumor implantations.

F. Suppression Mediated by the Tumor: The finding that certain types of tumors synthesize various materials such as prostaglandins which affect the activity of the immune response has led to speculation that some tumors may be able to actively suppress the immune response directed against them. The importance of this mechanism as a means of "tumor escape" is still not well documented.

IMMUNODIAGNOSIS

Immunodiagnosis of cancer may be based on 2 approaches: one deals with the detection of "markers" of tumor cells and the other with assessing the host's antitumor response.

Detection of Tumor Markers

Tumor cells are known to express cytoplasmic, cell surface, or secreted products that are sufficiently different in quantity or quality from products of normal cells to act as "tumor markers." Many of these are termed antigens, because they are identified by antisera raised in another species. However, most such markers have not been convincingly shown to be immunogenic in the animal in which the tumor arose.

Most tumor markers consist of excessive production of a normal product or production of a material normally produced during development but present not at all or only in very low quantities in adults (oncodevelopmental markers) (Table 17–4).

Secreted products released into the bloodstream provide the best diagnostic markers. The most useful of these are myeloma proteins, produced by plasma cell myelomas; alpha-fetoprotein produced by hepatocellular carcinomas, and teratocarcinomas, containing yolk sac elements; and carcinoembryonic antigen, produced by tumors of the gastrointestinal tract.

Secretion of a "monoclonal" immunoglobulin is easily detected by electrophoretic separation of serum proteins. This results in the appearance of a sharp and narrow increase in a band in the β- or γ-globulin zone. Often there is excess secretion of light chains of the monoclonal globulin that appear as Bence Jones proteins in the urine. These were first identified in the 1860s by heating urine to 50–60 °C. At this temperature, a white cloudy precipitate appears that redissolves with further heating. Bence Jones protein is present in about half of myeloma patients and represents the first identified tumor marker used routinely in clinical diagnosis. In a given patient, the amount of serum myeloma protein or urine Bence Jones protein is an accurate reflection of the tumor burden. The effects of therapy can therefore be monitored by following the amount of myeloma protein in the serum or Bence Jones protein in the urine. Monoclonal proteins rarely are found in other diseases, so that this is an important diagnostic procedure.

Alpha-fetoprotein (AFP), the major serum protein in the fetus, falls shortly after birth to the normal serum AFP concentration in humans of about 20 ng/mL but then rises if cancer of liver or yolk sac cells develops (Table 17–5). Since low elevations of serum AFP also occur with noncancerous conditions such as cirrhosis and hepatitis, elevation of serum AFP does not justify a diagnosis of cancer unless levels above 500–1000 ng/mL are reported. However, in over half of patients with hepatocellular carcinoma, AFP elevations of this magnitude are essentially diagnostic of this form of cancer.

Carcinoembryonic antigen (CEA) is a term

Table 17–4. Expression of some oncodevelopmental markers by tumors.*

| Product | Level of Expression by Tumors | | | |
	Fetal or Adult Tissue Normally Producing It	Embryologically Closely Related	Embryologically More Distinctly Related	Different Cell Line
Carcinoembryonic antigen	Colonic carcinoma.	Gastric, pancreatic, liver cancer.	Lung, breast cancer.	Sarcoma, lymphoma.
Alpha-fetoprotein	Hepatoma, yolk sac, teratocarcinoma.	Colonic, gastric, pancreatic cancer.	Lung cancer.	(?) Sarcoma.
Hormone (eg, serotonin)	Carcinoid.	Adrenal (pheochromocytoma).	Oat cell cancer (lung).	Lung cancer.
Placental isoenzymes	Choriocarcinomas.	Testicular-ovarian teratocarcinomas.	Hepatomas.	Lung cancer.

*Reproduced, with permission, from Sell S: *Immunology, Immunopathology and Immunity.* Harper & Row, 1980.

Table 17–5. AFP production by normal fetal and adult tumor tissue.*

Fetal Tissue	AFP† (% of Total)	Adult Tumor Tissue	AFP‡ (% of Patients > 40 ng/mL)
Yolk sac	61	Endodermal sinus	100
Liver	30	Hepatoma	80
Biliary tract	?	Biliary tract	25
Stomach	3	Gastric	15
Colon	3	Colon	3
Small intestine	2	–	–
Lung	<1	Pulmonary carcinoma	7
Breast	<1	Adenocarcinoma	2
Other	<1	Sarcoma	<1

*Reproduced, with permission, from Sell S: *Immunology, Immunopathology, and Immunity.* Harper & Row, 1980.

†Incorporation of radiolabeled amino acids into AFP percent of total AFP synthesized. (Sell S, Skelly H: *Natl Cancer Inst Monogr* 1976;**56**:645).

‡Percent of patients having a serum concentration of AFP > 40 ng/mL (Waldman TA, McIntire KR: *Cancer Res* 1975;**35**:991).

applied to a glycoprotein produced normally by the cells lining the gastrointestinal tract, particularly the colon. Normally, the polarity of these cells dictates that CEA will be secreted into the gastrointestinal lumen. However, if cancer of these cells develops, the polarity of the cells changes and CEA may be secreted into the blood, where it may be detected by a variety of immunochemical assays. Elevations of CEA above the normal serum concentrations of 2.5 ng/mL frequently are found associated with a variety of malignant and nonmalignant diseases, particularly cirrhosis of the liver and inflammatory diseases of the gastrointestinal tract and lung (Table 17–6). For this reason, CEA can be used only as an adjunct to other diagnostic procedures. However, values of CEA above 10 ng/mL are highly suggestive of carcinoma, since elevations of this magnitude are frequently found with lung, pancreas, and breast carcinoma, particularly if metastasis has occurred. CEA elevations cannot be used precisely to identify a tissue of origin of the carcinoma.

As with myeloma proteins, AFP or CEA concentrations in patients with tumors that secrete these markers may be used to monitor the effects of therapy. If AFP or CEA elevations fall to normal and remain there, therapy may be considered successful. However, if serum AFP or CEA continues to rise or re-elevation occurs, regrowth or metastatic spread is likely.

Other changes in serum markers are not as consistently useful in immunodiagnosis of cancer. Elevations in hormones occur in a variety of human cancers. For instance, elevations of human chorionic gonadotropin occur in the following frequencies: lung cancer, 10%; breast cancer, 20%; gastrointestinal cancer, 20%; ovarian cancer, 40%; testicular cancer, 60%; and malignant melanoma, 10%. Thus, although useful, hormone production by a given tumor type is inconsistent and does not clearly identify the tissue of origin.

Isozymes are closely related enzymes but with different physicochemical or immunochemical forms. Usually in normal adult tissues there is a predominant pattern of isozymes or a dominant form of an enzyme. The pattern or form is often different in tumors than in normal tissues. In addition, the amount of enzyme activity usually found in a given tissue may be quite different from that of normal adult differentiated tissue. Unfortunately, such enzyme changes are of more

Table 17–6. CEA concentrations in human sera.*

Type of Patient	Number of Patients Tested	0–2.5 ng/mL (%)	2.6–5 ng/mL (%)	5.1–10 ng/mL (%)	10 ng/mL (%)
Healthy subjects					
Nonsmokers	892	97	3	0	0
Former smokers	235	93	5	1	1
Smokers	620	81	15	3	1
Colorectal carcinoma	544	28	23	14	35
Pulmonary carcinoma	181	34	25	25	26
Pancreatic carcinoma	55	9	31	25	35
Gastric carcinoma	79	39	32	10	19
Breast carcinoma	125	53	20	13	14
Other carcinoma	343	51	28	12	9
Noncarcinoma malignancy	228	60	30	8	2
Nonmalignant disease, benign breast disease	115	85	11	4	0
Rectal polyps	90	81	15	3	1
Cholecystitis	39	77	17	5	1
Severe alcoholic cirrhosis	120	29	44	25	2
Active ulcerative colitis	146	69	18	8	5
Pulmonary emphysema	49	43	37	16	4

*Reproduced, with permission, from Sell S: *Immunology, Immunopathology, and Immunity.* Harper & Row, 1980. (Modified from Go VL: *Cancer* 1976;**37**:562.)

academic than clinical interest, since enzyme or isozyme changes in serum are often not useful in distinguishing between benign and malignant disease. Although elevations or changes may frequently occur in tumor tissue, such elevations are often not seen in the serum. For example, serum amylase is elevated in fewer patients with pancreatic cancer than in those with pancreatitis. On the other hand, elevation of acid phosphatase is useful in diagnosis of carcinoma of the prostate with metastases. If a serum enzyme or isozyme is elevated by cancer production, it may be used to follow the effects of therapy, as with the other serum markers described above.

Application of monoclonal antibodies to detect tumor markers may greatly expand the number of diagnostic tests available. At present, great activity in identification of new cancer markers is under way. Although a number of possibilities have emerged, no definitive marker for any tumor has yet achieved the status of clinical application. However, monoclonal antibodies against common human antigens are proving useful in differentiating various T cell lymphomas in humans. Monoclonal antibodies have also been used to isolate and characterize tumor markers. For example, 2 cell surface glycoproteins of MW 240,000 and 94,000 have been isolated and characterized from malignant melanoma tissue. However, it has not yet been demonstrated that these "antigens" are present on normal melanocytes during development, and the clinical usefulness of these "markers" is not established.

Monoclonal antibodies have also been of use in the classification of tumors of the lymphoid system. Before monoclonal antibodies were recognized, leukemias and lymphomas were classified according to other markers: T cell tumors formed rosettes with sheep red blood cells, B cell tumors had surface immunoglobulin, and null cell tumors had neither marker. This was of some importance, because within a given morphologic classification, B cell tumors responded most favorably to the therapy and null cell tumors responded least favorably. Monoclonal antibodies to different T cell subsets have been developed and are being applied to the classification of human leukemia and lymphomas. Although not yet shown to be related to clinical behavior of the tumor, it is anticipated that such classification will eventually contribute to a more precise definition of prognosis and selection of therapy.

Radiolabeled antibodies have been used to localize antigen-bearing tumors (radioimmunoscintigraphy). Anti-CEA and anti-AFP have been used for this purpose. Following injection of radiolabeled antibodies, the patient is scanned by computer-assisted tomography for localization of radioactivity. Anecdotal reports indicate that in selected patients, occult metastatic tumors have been localized by this procedure. However, the practical usefulness of this procedure remains to be determined. The presence of circulating AFP or CEA does not appear to block tumor localization. This finding makes it difficult to understand how specific antibodies can be localized to tumors under the condition used. It may be that localization is caused by nonspecific trapping of immune complexes in tumors with an increased vascular supply. Additional results with this approach are awaited with interest.

Detection of Tumor-Specific Immunity

Antitumor immunity has been demonstrated many times in experimental animals and in humans. Accordingly, the possibility of using the presence of humoral or cellular antitumor immunity as a clue to the diagnosis of cancer has been assessed. Human antibodies to Epstein-Barr virus (EBV) have been demonstrated in patients with Burkitt's lymphoma and nasopharyngeal carcinoma. Humoral antibodies to some melanomas and osteogenic sarcomas have been detected, and antibodies to herpes simplex have been found in high frequency in patients with cervical carcinoma and epidermoid carcinomas of the oropharynx. Preparations of tumor cell extracts have been shown to be useful for delayed hypersensitivity skin testing to tumor antigens and for the in vitro correlates of delayed hypersensitivity such as microcytotoxicity, MIF production, lymphocyte blastogenesis, and others.

Conceptually, specific immunodiagnosis of cancer is predicated on either detecting the presence of a tumor-specific antigen or on demonstrating the presence of a host's immune response against such an antigen. In the case of many experimentally induced tumors, one or both of these can be accomplished. Thus, in cases where tumor antigens exhibit immune cross-reactivity, a certain tumor antigen might react with immune components (humoral or cellular) of different hosts exhibiting the cross-reactive tumor antigen. Therefore, immunodiagnosis is most promising in cases of virally induced tumors, since they exhibit such immune cross-reactivity. However, there are difficulties in satisfying these requirements in the case of spontaneous tumors that may only express unique antigens. Although antigens prepared from the tumor of a given individual might be used to monitor that individual's immune response to that tumor, it would be useless to employ such antigenic preparations for detecting the immune responses of other individuals if the tumors did not exhibit immune cross-reactivity, as in the case of most chemically induced or spontaneous tumors. It is therefore not surprising that detection of antitumor immune responses for the specific and early diagnosis of human cancer has not been achieved. Furthermore, to date, none of the tumor-specific markers discussed earlier have provided the specificity and sensitivity necessary for the early diagnosis of cancer. However, in some instances tumor markers and antitumor immune responses have proved useful in evaluating the progression (or regression) of disease and thus in evaluating patients' responses to therapy and in determining the recurrence of the disease.

TUMOR IMMUNOPROPHYLAXIS

Conceptually, immunization against a given on-cogenic virus would lead to immunoprophylaxis against the virus and subsequent tumor induction by that virus. Indeed, this approach has been successful in experimental animals and in prophylaxis against Marek's disease in chickens. Furthermore, large-scale experiments are under way to assess the effect of immunization against feline leukemia and feline sarcoma viruses on the incidence of cancer in domestic cat populations. Although attempts to immunize against oncogenic viruses may be faced with some of the same difficulties as those encountered in immunization against other pathogenic viruses, this mode of tumor immunoprophylaxis (ie, immunization against the virus) appears to be a rational means of conferring protection against tumors induced by viruses.

Immunization against the tumor itself depends upon the presence of tumor cell surface antigens. There are literally thousands of reports of immunoprophylaxis against experimentally transplanted tumors. The immunogens used included the following preparations: (1) live tumor cells in sublethal doses, (2) replication-blocked tumor cells, (3) tumor cells with enzymatic or chemically altered surface membranes, (4) extracts of tumor cells that have retained the cell surface antigens, and (5) chemically modified extracts of tumor cells. Such immunogenic preparations have been shown to induce antitumor immunity (humoral, cellular, or both), conferring various degrees of protection against subsequently transplanted dosages of the homologous tumor that result in tumor growth in nonimmunized controls. In this respect, immunoprophylaxis to tumors resembles immunoprophylaxis to infectious agents: protection correlates positively with the induction of humoral or cellular immunity, and it is specific. As is the case with infectious diseases, immunoprophylaxis against transplanted tumors also has a finite capacity—it may be protective against transplantation of a given supralethal dosage of tumor cells but ineffective if this dosage is exceeded.

Prophylaxis against tumors by vaccination would depend upon immunologic cross-reactivity between the immunogen and the tumor. Thus, at least on theoretic grounds, it should be feasible to immunize only against virally induced tumors and other tumors that exhibit immunologic cross-reactivity. For example, cross-reactivity has been demonstrated among patients with Burkitt's lymphoma, nasopharyngeal carcinoma, melanoma, and neuroblastoma, suggesting the possibility of preparing tumor vaccines for prophylactic purposes. However, it should be remembered that immunization would not necessarily result in protection against the tumor: It may lead to the induction of immune components (such as blocking antibodies) that will enhance rather than impede tumor growth and metastasis. Such considerations must be taken into account prior to immunization.

PRESENT & FUTURE STATUS OF IMMUNOTHERAPY

With the realization that the immune response may be recruited for the therapy of tumors, numerous attempts to do so have been made. The various forms of antitumor immunotherapy of cancer are discussed in Chapter 40. So far, the results have been disappointing. Thus, to date, immunotherapy is not the treatment of choice—or, for that matter, an effective treatment—of any type of cancer. This is true both for immunotherapy as the sole form of treatment and when it is used as an adjunct to other forms of treatment such as chemotherapy, radiotherapy, or surgery.

In many instances, strong tumor antigens have been demonstrated under experimental conditions. Such antigens were used for the preparation of highly effective vaccines that could protect immunized animals against supralethal doses of transplanted tumor cells. In fact, the literature contains many examples of successful immunoprophylaxis of experimental animals to transplanted virally and chemically induced tumors. In spite of this protection against cancer implants, the vaccines were largely ineffective in the treatment of established tumors. Such vaccines had either no effect or at best a marginal effect upon the progression of the disease, even though the treated individuals exhibited immunity specific to the tumor. Although it is generally anticipated that immunologic manipulation is of benefit to the host, there are studies that indicate instances where immunologic manipulation is detrimental to the host, leading to tumor enhancement rather than tumor destruction. Various mechanisms may underlie tumor enhancement following immunologic manipulation. For example, enhancement may be due to induction of tumor-specific or generalized suppression of the immune system. It may be due to induction of antibodies that may bind to tumor cells without destroying them, thereby protecting the tumor from destruction by tumor-specific cytotoxic cells or cytotoxic antibodies. These are but a few of several mechanisms proposed to explain tumor enhancement by immunologic intervention.

Even if tumor enhancement is not a factor, it is becoming clear that failure of immunotherapy may be due to many other factors that must be considered when immunotherapy is contemplated. For example, the immune response cannot be expected to be effective against a large tumor mass, since the response has a finite capacity. Consequently, immunotherapy should be tried only following tumor reduction by surgery, chemotherapy, or by other means. Moreover, the recipient of immunotherapy must be immunologically competent if the immunotherapeutic approach is base on augmenting the individual's own immune response. Based on the same rationale, if adoptive immunotherapy is attempted, it is essential to determine that the tumor-bearing individual does not possess factors capable of interfering with the transferred response. There are difficult logistic problems also with attempts to deliver antitumor drugs or radiation by specific antitumor antibodies. For example, large amounts of circulating tumor antigens might combine with antitumor antibodies and thus prevent the antibodies from reaching the target tumor cell. Moreover, it is still not clear what would be the fate of radiation-carrying antibodies or of drug-antibody complexes following their action on the tumor cells. Would they trigger immunopathologic conditions in the recipient? In short, the problems and logistics of tumor immunotherapy are staggering and require a great deal of experimental research.

Much work is currently being done in an attempt to assess the potential use of tumor-specific antibodies in immunotherapy. It is hoped that hybridoma technology will make possible the production of large quantities of antitumor antibodies. These antibodies may themselves lead to destruction of the tumor or may be used as "missiles" for antibody-based chemother-apy or radiotherapy. Some of the reservations noted earlier about using antitumor antibodies for these purposes—namely, specificity and quantity—could perhaps be overcome by utilizing hybridomas. In addition, current advances in immunology and cell biology make possible the cloning of lymphocytes. This will lead to production of large amounts of lymphokines and the construction through genetic engineering of relevant cell lines or microorganisms that will produce large quantities of lymphokines. These lymphokines might be used for tumor cell destruction following their targeting to the tumor or for generalized immune enhancement such as the enhanced activation of NK cells (which preferentially destroy tumor cells) by interferon. The extent to which these new advances will make cancer immunotherapy a reality remains to be seen.

● ● ●

References

Host-Tumor Relationship

Beers RF Jr: The role of immunological factors in viral and oncogenic processes: Introduction. *Johns Hopkins Med J* 1974;**3 (Suppl)**:21.

Cochran AJ: *Man, Cancer and Immunity.* Academic Press, 1978.

Ferrone S et al (editors): *Current Trends in Tumor Immunology.* Garland STPM Press, 1979.

Fink MA (editor): *The Macrophage in Neoplasia.* Academic Press, 1976.

Mitchison NA, Landy M (editors): *Manipulation of the Immune Response in Cancer.* Academic Press, 1978.

Pierce GB, Shikes R, Fink LM: *Cancer: A Problem of Developmental Biology.* Prentice-Hall, 1978.

Waters H (editor): *The Handbook of Cancer Immunology.* Vols 1–9. Garland STPM Press, 1978–1981.

Weiss DW (editor): *Immunological Parameters of Host-Tumor Relationship.* Academic Press, 1971–present.

Woodruff MFA: *The Interaction of Cancer and Host: Its Therapeutic Significance.* Grune & Stratton, 1980.

Tumor Antigens

Baldwin RW: Immunological aspects of chemical carcinogenesis. *Adv Cancer Res* 1973;**18**:1.

Basombrio MA, Prehn RT: Studies on the basis for diversity and time of appearance of antigens in chemically induced tumors. *Natl Cancer Inst Monogr* 1972;**35**:117.

Gotz H, Buchezl ES (editors): *Applied Tumor Immunology: Methods for Recognizing Immune Phenomena Specific to Tumors.* Walter de Gruyter, Berlin, N.Y., 1975.

Helstrom KE, Brown JP, Hellstrom I: Monoclonal antibodies to tumor antigens. *Contemp Top Immunobiol* 1980;**11**:117.

Roseberg SA (editor): *Serologic Analysis of Human Cancer Antigens.* Academic Press, 1980.

Ruddon RW (editor): *Biologic Markers of Neoplasia: Basic and Applied Aspects.* Elsevier, 1978.

Sell S (editor): *Cancer Markers: Developmental and Diagnostic Significance.* Humana Press, 1980.

Immunotherapy

Chirigos MA (editor): *Immune Modulation and Control of Neoplasia by Adjuvant Therapy.* Vol 7 of: *Progress in Cancer Research and Therapy.* Raven Press, 1978.

Terry WD, Windhorst D (editors): *Immunotherapy of Cancer: Present Status of Trials in Man.* Vol 6 of: *Progress in Cancer Research and Therapy.* Raven Press, 1978.

Waters H (editor): *The Handbook of Cancer Immunology.* Vol 5. Garland STPM Press, 1978.

18 | Immediate Hypersensitivity

Oscar L. Frick, MD, PhD

The term immediate hypersensitivity denotes an immunologic sensitivity to antigens that manifests itself by tissue reactions occurring within minutes after the antigen combines with its appropriate antibody. Such a reaction may occur in any member of a species (anaphylaxis) or only in certain predisposed or hyperreactive members (atopy).

In 1890, von Behring discovered the prophylactic use of antiserum against diphtheria toxin. In the search for other prophylactic antisera, Portier and Richet noted an immediate shocklike reaction in a sensitive dog to a sea anemone toxin; this harmful reaction they called **antiphylaxis** (or anaphylaxis), to distinguish it from the helpful **prophylaxis.** Within the next decade, hay fever and asthma were recognized as human counterparts of animal anaphylactic reactions, and histamine was considered to be the primary pharmacologic mediator of such symptoms. Later it was discovered that skin tests could be used for the specific diagnosis of the troublesome antigen and that a prolonged series of injections of these antigens could help relieve allergic symptoms.

ANAPHYLAXIS

Anaphylaxis is a manifestation of immediate hypersensitivity resulting from the in vivo interaction of cellular sites with antigen and specific antibody.

Generalized anaphylaxis is a shocklike state occurring within minutes following an appropriate antigen-antibody reaction. Upon the first exposure of an animal to an antigen, a cytotropic antibody can form which sensitizes mast cells and basophils in tissues and blood, respectively. After a second exposure to the antigen, the sensitized animal reacts to histamine and other mediators released by mast cells as a result of the antigen-antibody reaction. Histamine causes a marked vasodilatation and leakage of intravascular fluids, resulting in shock. There are smooth muscle spasms, especially in certain smooth muscle–containing organs such as guinea pig bronchi and canine liver "vessels." These are the principal specific shock organs in these 2 species. The extreme bronchoconstriction in the guinea pig results in respiratory obstruction, asphyxia, and death. The extreme vasodilatation and leakage of fluids in the dog or in humans causes profound shock and death. Epinephrine may be a lifesaving treatment in anaphylaxis.

Local anaphylaxis may occur in specific target organs such as the gastrointestinal tract, nasal mucosa, or skin. Experimentally, the skin or other tissue may be passively sensitized with serum from a sensitized animal; subsequent intravenous or local injection of antigen will result in a local anaphylactic reaction. This method has been used for the passive cutaneous anaphylaxis (PCA) test, in which the skin of an animal (guinea pig, rabbit, human, rat or mouse, etc) is injected with serum from a sensitive animal of the same or another species. After an appropriate latent period, the antigen is given intravenously along with Evans blue dye, and this will react with the skin-fixed antibody, causing the release of histamine. This results in vasodilatation and leakage of albumin, to which the blue dye is attached, producing a blue spot. This blue spot indicates that an anaphylactic reaction has taken place in the skin.

In Vitro Anaphylaxis

Several tissue models of anaphylaxis have been developed for experimental studies. The Schultz-Dale test uses isolated smooth muscle from a sensitized animal. Ileum, uterus, or a tracheal ring is suspended in a physiologic buffered saline solution. Such smooth muscle strips can also be passively sensitized by bathing them in serum from a hypersensitive animal. After addition of antigen to the bath, smooth muscle contractions occur within seconds or minutes. Alternatively, finely chopped lungs or skin fragments from actively sensitized animals (or such fragments passively sensitized with serum from an immunized animal) are suspended in physiologic buffer. Addition of antigen causes release of histamine and slow-reacting substance of anaphylaxis (SRS-A), which is quantitated by bioassay or chemical means. Peritoneal mast cells from actively or passively sensitized rats, upon addition of antigen, show visible degranulation, and histamine and serotonin release may be measured in the supernate.

Any antigen should be able to elicit anaphylaxis in a properly sensitized animal. These may be proteins, chemical haptens such as drugs attached to proteins, carbohydrates, or, occasionally, nucleic acids. These antigens usually must be soluble antigens. Cellular antigens such as sheep red cells or bacteria cause weak anaphylaxis, which probably indicates that soluble antigens are eluted from the cell surface to participate in such reactions.

Antibody Classes

Cytotropic antibodies, especially of the IgG and IgE classes, are involved in anaphylactic sensitization. In special circumstances, IgA and IgM may also be involved. Homocytotropic antibodies—antibodies that will sensitize an animal of the same species—are usually considered cardinal in such reactions. These are IgE in all species so far examined (γG_1 or γG_α electrophoretic mobility in guinea pigs and rats, respectively). Heterocytotropic IgG antibodies and occasionally IgM and IgA antibodies can passively sensitize tissues (especially skin) of other species. The classic example is rabbit IgG antibody, which can passively sensitize guinea pig skin for PCA. On the contrary, IgG antibodies of ungulates such as sheep, goats, and horses are unable to sensitize guinea pig skin for PCA. Apparently, the former have a specific skin-fixing site on their Fc portions.

Sensitization of Target Tissue for Anaphylaxis

In most cases, 10–14 days are required after immunization before IgG antibodies result in active anaphylactic sensitization; IgE sensitization may occur somewhat earlier. Passive sensitization has a latent period (time between injection of antibody and challenge with antigen) of 3–6 hours for IgG antibodies. This latent period allows antibody to "fix" to the target mast cells. However, the IgG passive sensitization is short-lived; the IgG molecules become detached within 12–24 hours. An antigenic challenge at this later time causes no (or minimal) anaphylaxis. There is an inverse squared relationship between the local IgG antibody concentration (c) and time (t) of the latent period: $c = 1/t^2$. In fact, if there is sufficient antibody concentration, the latent period can be reduced to almost zero and the reaction can occur immediately after passive sensitization.

Passive sensitization with IgE antibody may occur within 6 hours but becomes stronger by 24–72 hours, the usual time at which antigenic challenge is made. Anaphylactic reactions occurring after 48–72 hours are almost exclusively due to IgE antibodies (IgG antibodies are already detached and do not participate in such a reaction). IgE antibodies remain fixed to the target mast cells for many weeks, eg, 3 weeks in rats and 6 weeks in humans.

Molecular Models of Anaphylaxis

Following the first exposure to antigen, the animal responds with antibody formation (Fig 18–1). Cytotropic antibodies such as IgG or IgE fix to the

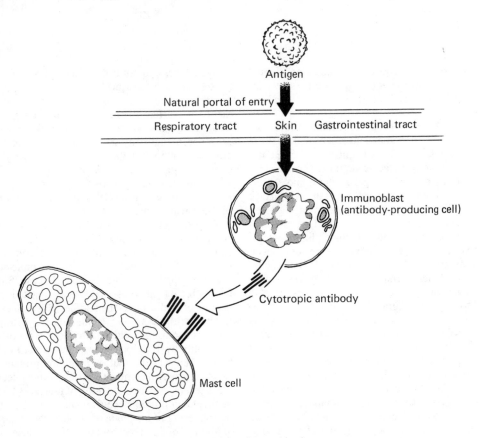

Figure 18–1. Atopic sensitization.

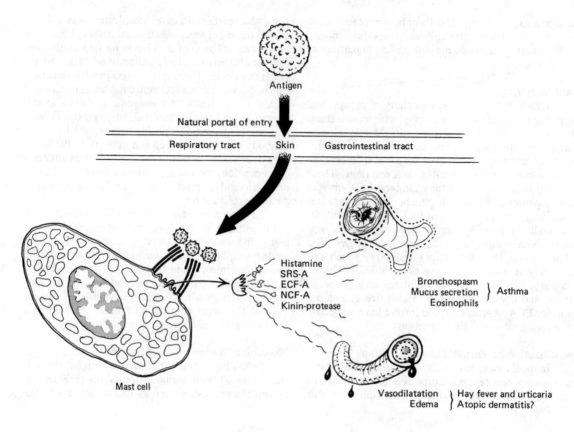

Figure 18–2. Atopic reaction.

surface of mast cells, and the animal is considered sensitized. Such antibodies may also be passively introduced into the general circulation or into local tissues.

With the second exposure, the antigen seeks out these tissue-fixed antibodies and reacts with them at the cell surface (Fig 18–2). An antigen molecule combines with 2 antibody molecules to form a bridge. This bridging brings together 2 IgE receptor molecules, which triggers an enzymatic cascade at the cell surface that causes the dissolution or expulsion of mast cell granules. These granules dissolve and release histamine, serotonin, and heparin, their pharmacologically active agents. Free histamine and serotonin act on adjacent smooth muscle and vascular endothelial cells, causing the clinical symptoms of anaphylaxis (eg, bronchospasm and edema). Other mediators are also released from mast cell granules—SRS-A, eosinophil and neutrophil chemotactic factors of anaphylaxis (ECF-A, NCF-A), and kinin-generating protease. These also exert their pharmacologic effects on neighboring cells. The optimal ratio of antigen to antibody to elicit anaphylaxis is slight to moderate antigen excess. So-called "toxic complexes" of composition Ag_3Ab_2 or Ag_5Ab_3 best trigger such anaphylactic reactions. These are small complexes which best bridge surface receptors in the combining site of sensitizing antibodies. Complexes of Ag_2Ab_1 formed in extreme antigen excess do not trigger anaphylaxis. Such complexes are unable to bridge antibodies because both combining sites on each antibody molecule are attached to 2 different antigen molecules. Large amounts of antibody are complexed by relatively few antigens in zones of antibody excess or at the optimal proportions for precipitation. These are usually insufficient for triggering anaphylactic reactions, but in these zones minimal anaphylaxis can occur.

This molecular model of anaphylaxis can be duplicated with immunoglobulin reacting with antibody molecules fixed to the mast cell. The reaction forms complexes of a composition appropriate to trigger anaphylaxis. Anti-IgE antibodies will complex with the Fc portion of the tissue-fixed IgE molecule, and such bridging will trigger histamine release. Similarly, tissue-fixed antibodies may be aggregated by mild heating or bisdiazotized benzidine. This creates nonantigenic bridges among tissue-fixed cytotropic antibodies and triggers the anaphylactic reaction. IgE or IgG antibody-fixing cell receptors on mast cells may be blocked with normal or myeloma proteins of the same class which compete with antibody molecules for these receptors. Such blocking of receptors by normal or myeloma proteins prevents antibody fixation, and no triggering of anaphylaxis is possible. Antireceptor antibodies bridge receptors directly to cause mediator release.

Target Cells & Mediator Release

Target cells for anaphylaxis are the tissue-fixed mast cells, especially in shock organs such as lung, bronchial smooth muscle, and vascular endothelium. Blood basophils may also act as target cells. Antibody molecules fixed to mast cells are physically distorted by antigen, and this activates serine esterases in a pathway similar to the classic complement cascade (Chapter 11). The speed and completeness of activation of this enzyme cascade are modulated by the cAMP-cGMP "second messenger" balance in the cytoplasm of such target cells. This cascade is energy- and calcium-dependent and causes dissolution or expulsion of mast cell granules. Positively charged histamine and serotonin are electrostatically complexed with negatively charged heparin-proteoglycan. After dissolution of the granule, positively charged sodium ions from extracellular fluid exchange with positively charged histamine and serotonin on heparin and cause their release in a free state. Free histamine and serotonin exert their pharmacologic effects on adjacent smooth muscles and vascular endothelial cells. Similar mechanisms probably exist for the release of other preformed mediators: ECF-A, NCF-A, and proteases. Cromolyn sodium apparently can stabilize mast cell membranes or granules and can prevent the release of mediators.

In summary, anaphylaxis is a reaction found in almost all vertebrate animal species (hamster excepted) which results from sensitization of tissue-fixed mast cells by cytotropic antibodies following exposure to antigen. Subsequent exposure to antigen results in complexing of an antigen molecule with 2 antibody molecules in mild to moderate antigen excess. Complexed antibody molecules are physically distorted and initiate an enzyme cascade ending in the release of pharmacologic mediators which exert their effects upon adjacent target tissue.

ALLERGY & ATOPY

Von Pirquet proposed the term **allergie** (Gk *allos* "other" + *ergon* "work") in 1906 to denote an immune deviation from the original state or a "changed reactivity" of an individual. An allergic individual was one who deviated from the expected immunologic response. Von Pirquet included all forms of altered immunologic responsiveness, encompassing reactions to toxins, bacteria, and other infectious agents; pollen hay fever; and urticaria produced by foods. Coca in 1923 coined the word **atopy** (Gk *atopos* "uncommon") to denote an abnormal state of hypersensitivity as distinguished from hypersensitivity responses in normal individuals, eg, contact dermatitis, serum sickness, anaphylaxis, and infection with tubercle bacilli.

Clinical Types of Atopy

Until recently, atopy was thought to be restricted to humans, but such conditions have now been described in dogs, rats, and even a baby walrus. In genetically susceptible individuals, atopy may affect one or more primary shock organ systems. In humans, atopy involving the respiratory system (the nasal mucosa, bronchioles, and aural mucosa) can cause hay fever, asthma, and serous otitis. With the skin as shock organ, urticaria, angioneurotic edema, and atopic dermatitis (eczema) occur. Sensitized intestinal and urinary systems react with antigen to cause vomiting, abdominal pain, diarrhea, and urinary frequency and pain on urination. Vascular involvement, especially of the central nervous system, may result in headaches, personality changes, and other nervous system manifestations.

Genetic Basis of Atopy

Hay fever and asthma can be familial. If both parents have atopy, there is a 75% chance of the child having atopic symptoms; with one parent involved, there is a 50% chance. Thirty-eight percent of atopic patients have no parental history of atopy.

With the recent discovery of immune response genes associated with HLA haplotypes, a ragweed hay fever haplotype has been postulated. Ragweed-allergic patients in a family tree had the same HLA haplotype, whereas nonallergic members of the family had different haplotypes. The numerical haplotype designation among allergic families varied widely, but within a family, ragweed sensitivity was associated with a single haplotype.

In large Caucasian population samples, there appear to be HLA associations with certain ragweed and grass pollen fractions (Table 18–1). Ragweed Ra3 is associated with HLA-A2 and -A28, strongly associated also with total IgE level; Ra5 with HLA-Dw2 and -B7; and Ra6 with HLA-Dw35. Rye I grass is associated with HLA-B8 and -Dw3; Rye II with HLA-Dw3 and -B8; and timothy A3 with HLA-B7. Negative associations also occur with Ra3 with HLA-A3 and -A11; Rye I with HLA-A9; and timothy A3 with HLA-A9 and -A10. It is suggested that genetic factors control the immune response and perhaps also the pharmacologic regulation and pathologic expression of allergy. The best studies have been done on

Table 18–1. Associations of pollen sensitivity with HLA types.

Pollen Antigen	HLA Association*	
	Positive	Negative
Ra5	Dw2, B7	
Ra3	A2, A28	A3, A11
AγE	0	0
Rye I	B8, Dw3, A1	A9
Rye II	Dw3, B8	
Timothy A3	B7	A9, A10

*A positive association indicates a significant association between positive skin tests or the radioallergosorbent test (RAST) and a given HLA type. A negative association indicates a statistically significant relationship between the absence of positive skin test or RAST reactivity and a given HLA type.

genetic control of immune response, where 2 antigen-specific factors, Ir and Is genes, are linked to HLA loci or controlled by genes associated with the HLA complex. Hyperresponsiveness to particular antigens (cited above) appears associated with alleles of the 2 most common HLA haplotypes. Furthermore, regulation of total IgE concentration is not HLA-linked. Hyperresponsiveness of airways to methacholine has a familial aspect. Much more work is required to establish the genetic components in atopy.

Allergens

Allergens are the antigens that give rise to allergic sensitization of the IgE antibody class. Most natural allergens are somewhat peculiar in that their molecular weight appears to be restricted to the range 10–70 thousand. Smaller molecular antigens, unless polymerized, would be unable to bridge adjacent IgE molecules and receptors. Large allergens (> MW 70,000) might not penetrate mucosal surfaces sufficiently to reach IgE antibodies on cell receptors. These large allergens are extremely polar compounds, induce sensitization in very small amounts (ng to μg), and have many sulfhydryl groups, indicating much cross-linking. Purified allergens were observed to be brownish in color and to contain an enolized sugar-lysine combination. This is characteristic of the "ripening" or "Mailliard reaction" and was suggested as a requirement for allergenicity. However, more recent purifications and amino acid sequencing of ragweed (Ra5) and of bee venom allergen phospholipase A showed that they do not have the enolized sugar-lysine.

An allergen can result in both IgE and IgG antibodies, but mild formalin or glutaraldehyde treatment to form "allergoids" reduces the allergenicity (IgE formation) without affecting the antigenicity (IgG "blocking" antibody formation). Such polymerized pollen antigens greatly enhance IgG blocking antibody production, with little change in IgE antibodies and good clinical improvement, so that frequency of injections can be markedly reduced.

Antibodies

Prausnitz and Küstner used serum to passively transfer the allergic reactivity from an atopic patient to the skin of a normal individual. These antibodies were subsequently called reaginic, or skin-sensitizing, antibody. This reaginic antibody in humans has been identified as IgE. IgE has a molecular weight of 196,000 and a sedimentation coefficient of 8S; it is a fast γ_1-globulin on electrophoresis, has a high carbohydrate content of 12%, and consists of 2 light chains (either type κ or λ) and 2 heavy chains of type ϵ.

The 550-amino-acid sequence of the ϵ heavy chain of myeloma IgE ND* has recently been established and is similar to the μ chain of IgM except for the C-terminal 19 amino acids (Fig 18–3). The ϵ heavy chain consists of one V region and four C domains,

*IgE ND = the IgE myeloma protein from "patient ND."

$C_\epsilon1$, $C_\epsilon2$, $C_\epsilon3$, and $C_\epsilon4$. There are 15 half-cysteines, 10 of which form one intrachain disulfide bond in each of the 5 domains. There is one interchain cysteine binding the light and ϵ heavy chains and 2 inter-ϵ chain bonds just before and after the $C_\epsilon2$ domain. There is a second intrachain disulfide bridge within the $C_\epsilon1$ domain. Rich in carbohydrate (12%), IgE has 6 oligosaccharide side chains of unknown function: 3 in the $C_\epsilon1$, one in the $C_\epsilon2$, and 2 in the $C_\epsilon3$ domains (A–F in Fig 18–3).

The skin-fixing, or mast cell cytotropic, activity resides in the $C_\epsilon3$ or $C_\epsilon4$ domains, and the well-known heat lability of reaginic skin fixation involves these 2 regions. Reduction of disulfide bonds also alters cytotropic activity. A working hypothesis is that firm attachment of the IgE molecule to the mast cell membrane involves at least 2 kinds of sites within the $C_\epsilon3$ and $C_\epsilon4$ regions of the ϵ chain. The primary recognition site for the mast cell surface receptor appears to be located in the $C_\epsilon4$ region. Secondary binding may be located in either $C_\epsilon3$ or $C_\epsilon4$. And, finally, the inter-heavy chain bond assisting half-cysteine 318 may exert an avidity effect which binds the ϵ chain firmly to the mast cell membrane.

The primary biologic property of IgE is tissue fixation, ie, cytotropism for the mast cell and basophil membranes. Like IgA, IgE does not fix complement by the classic pathway. In very large amounts, IgE can fix C3 by the alternative pathway, but this is probably not biologically relevant. IgE does not cross the placenta. Nine patients with IgE myeloma have been discovered, and these have provided sufficient material for the above structural and sequencing data.

Animal antisera to human IgE myeloma proteins have been labeled with fluorescein or ^{125}I, and the labeled antisera used to localize the tissue and cellular distribution of IgE. Plasma cells forming IgE have been found extensively in the secretory surfaces inside the body, eg, the bronchi and bronchioles of the respiratory tract, the gastrointestinal mucosa, and the urinary bladder. The tonsils and adenoids were especially rich in IgE-forming plasma cells. This secretory distribution of IgE-forming cells is similar to that of secretory IgA–producing plasma cells. Thus, both can be considered secretory immunoglobulins. The highest concentrations are found in nasal polyps, particularly in polyps of allergic individuals. The systemic lymphoid organs, such as the spleen, liver, and regional lymph nodes, have only rare IgE-forming lymphocytes (which is also true for the circulating blood). When radiolabeled IgE was injected into monkeys, IgE was found only on blood basophils and tissue mast cells. No other cells contained surface IgE. On electron microscopy, basophils are seen to have IgE in large patches on their surfaces. With high concentrations of antibody, capping occurs, and the cell eventually removes the cap. The number of IgE molecules on a basophil surface has been estimated at 5300–27,000 in nonallergic individuals and at 15,000–41,000 in highly allergic individuals. Passive sensitization with IgE myeloma protein of a normal individ-

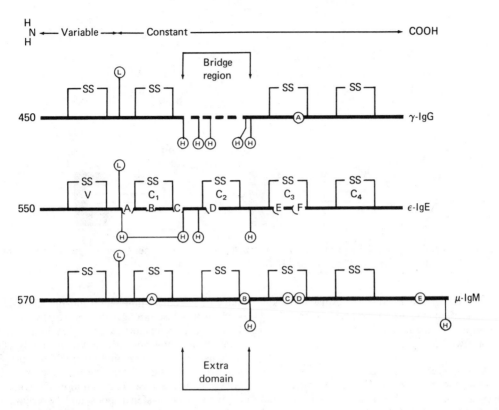

Figure 18–3. Diagrammatic representation of domains, inter–heavy chain bonds (L = light chain, H = heavy chain), and carbohydrate units (A, B, C, etc). Deletion of a counterpart to the $C_\epsilon 2$ and $C_\mu 2$ domains is one possible explanation of the general structure of the bridge region in the γ chain. (Reproduced, with permission, from Bennich H: Structure of IgE. *Prog Immunol* 1974; **2**:49.)

ual's basophils (containing 5300 IgE molecules) raised the number of IgE molecules to 36,000—the same as in the highly allergic individual.

Measurement of IgE

There is so little IgE in the serum that it escaped detection for many decades because the methods for immunoglobulin detection were not sufficiently sensitive. The normal adult IgE level is about 250 ng/mL. In severely allergic individuals, where IgE concentration is about 700 ng/mL, a specific IgE precipitin band is detectable by Ouchterlony immunodiffusion. However, for most studies such sensitivity is not sufficient, and radioisotopic methods are required for IgE quantitation.

A. Radioimmunosorbent Test (RIST) for Total IgE Concentration: This most sensitive of the detection methods detects 1 ng or less of IgE in serum. Rabbit anti-IgE myeloma protein is coupled to cyanogen bromide–activated filter paper disk (PRIST). Dilutions of an IgE-containing standard serum or an unknown patient's serum are reacted with the anti-IgE-coated particles. After thorough washing, the particles are reacted with ^{125}I rabbit anti-IgE myeloma protein. After additional washing, the particles are counted in a gamma counter to determine the amount of bound IgE.

In an alternative assay method, rabbit anti-IgE is coupled to insoluble beads. One aliquot of beads is reacted with radiolabeled IgE myeloma protein, while other aliquots are reacted with either dilutions of a standard IgE-containing serum or dilutions of a patient's serum. The relative inhibition of binding of radiolabeled IgE resulting from IgE in the test sample or standard is determined and graphed. From this plot, the IgE concentration in the sample can be determined with an accuracy of less than 1 ng/mL.

B. Radioallergosorbent Test (RAST) for Specific IgE Concentration: Purified allergen extract is coupled to cellulose particles or paper disks. Patient's serum containing IgE antibody or a standard serum is reacted with the allergen-coupled immunosorbent. After thorough washing, ^{125}I-labeled rabbit anti-IgE is reacted with the immunosorbent (Fig 18–4). After further washing, the radioactivity on the centrifuged sorbent is determined and is a measure of the amount of specific serum IgE antibodies to that allergen. This measures 1 ng of specific IgE antibody.

Specific IgE antibodies in human serum also have been measured by passively sensitizing monkey tissues, such as strips of monkey ileum or finely chopped monkey lung or skin tissues. The passively sensitized monkey smooth muscle preparation is suspended in a buffer bath, and allergen added to the bath will cause contractions of the smooth muscle which can be mea-

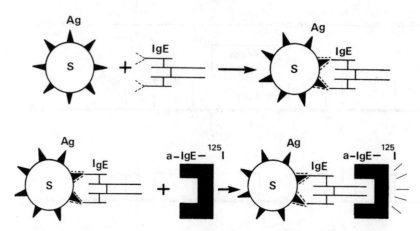

Figure 18–4. Schematic diagram of the radioallergosorbent test (RAST). S is the sorbent, with antigenic determinants (Ag). Human IgE attaches to the antigen and is detected with radiolabeled anti-IgE.

sured by a kymograph. Passively sensitized monkey lung or skin fragments are reacted with allergen and centrifuged. The supernate is then measured for histamine or SRS-A.

Serum Concentrations of IgE

Serum concentrations of IgE can be expressed in international units (IU): 2.3 ng IgE = 1 IU. The normal newborn has virtually no IgE in its cord serum ($\pm$ 1–2 IU/mL). By the age of 1½–4½ months, the mean is 9 IU/mL in healthy children. This increases to 32 IU/mL between 9 months to 3 years of age. The adult level is about 90 IU/mL (with a range of 29–800 IU/mL).

In a group of allergic children, 17 out of 21 children with asthma had elevated serum IgE levels (Fig 18–5). Three of the remaining children had IgE levels in the upper normal range. Only 7 of 21 children with allergic rhinitis had increased IgE, while 14 were in the upper normal range. IgE levels present in nasal secretions mirror those in the serum. IgE levels in nasal secretions ranged from 10–150 ng/mL in a group of normal children and adults to 36–850 ng/mL in a group of asthmatic children. A group of Ethiopian children with active *Ascaris* infection were noted to have a mean serum IgE level of 4400 ng/mL (range, 240–14,300 ng/mL), which is 30 times the normal IgE level. Subsequently, patients with other parasitic infections, especially other roundworms, were found to have extremely high serum IgE levels. Patients with atopic dermatitis had an IgE level 9 times the normal mean, whereas patients with urticaria and other dermatoses had normal IgE levels.

Measurement of total IgE levels may be useful in the early detection of allergy in infants. A survey of 34 infants from allergic families found 11 to have serum IgE levels greater than 20 IU/mL. Ten of these 11 children had allergic symptoms.

The serum IgE level apparently reflects an excess of IgE antibody in a pathophysiologic sense because allergic reactions occur upon sensitized mast cells in tissues. The amount of IgE in skin tissue can be mea-

sured by injecting dilute rabbit anti-IgE serum into the skin. Normal serum IgE concentrations of 65–130 IU/mL gave a threshold skin reaction with a 1:10,000 dilution of rabbit anti-IgE serum. In highly allergic patients, a 1:20 million dilution of rabbit anti-IgE still reacted in the skin. There was a rough correlation between minimal tissue concentration of IgE necessary to give a threshold skin response and the serum concentration of IgE. Measurement of skin IgE in this way is not generally recommended because injecting a foreign animal serum into the skin could sensitize the patient to rabbit proteins.

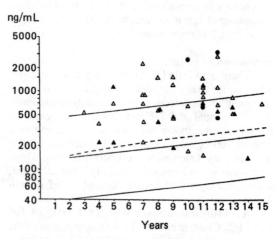

Figure 18–5. Serum IgE concentrations in children with asthma (Δ), asthma plus eczema (▲), and allergic rhinitis (hay fever) during the pollination season (●). The solid lines (—) represent the regression line and 95% confidence limits calculated on the logarithmic IgE values in 132 healthy children; the dotted line (- - -) represents the regression line calculated on the arithmetic IgE values in the same children. (Reproduced, with permission, from Berg T, Johansson SGO: IgE concentrations in children with atopic diseases. *Int Arch Allergy Appl Immunol* 1969;36:220.)

Table 18–2. Changes in symptoms and antibody levels produced by allergy treatment.*

Season	Number of Patients†	Mean Seasonal Symptom Index (SI)	Mean "Postseason" Allergen-Specific IgE Antibody Titer (units)	Mean IgG "Blocking Antibodies" (units)
1967 (control)	8	0.445	2,520	< 10
1967 (treated)	9	0.150	1,150	121
1968 (treated)	17	0.183	1,400	272
1969 (treated)	16	0.136	740	...
1970 (treated)	15	0.126	940	196
1970 (untreated)	12	0.243	1,715	65

*Reproduced, with permission, from Levy DA. In: *Conference on the Biological Role of the IgE System.* Ishizaka K, Dayton DH Jr (editors). US Department of Health, Education, & Welfare, 1973.
†Includes only those patients for whom all 3 sets of data are available.
Note: SI × IgE Ab: $r_s = 0.94$ ($p = 0.02$).   SI × IgG Ab: $r_s = 0.7$ ($p > 0.1$).
IgE Ab × IgG Ab: $r_s = 0.7$ ($p > 0.1$). r_s = symptom index.

Specific IgE Antibodies

The most widely used in vitro method of measuring specific IgE antibodies to a variety of allergens is the radioallergosorbent test (RAST). This assay is used extensively for the diagnostic quantitation of IgE antibodies to a variety of allergens. It is used to measure IgE antibody titers during the treatment of patients and to standardize allergens in a modified test.

A group of 20 children with ragweed hay fever were followed for 5 years and treated with preseasonal ragweed injections for 4 of those 5 years (Table 18–2). Over the 4 years, IgE antibodies against ragweed fell and reached a low plateau. Concomitantly, the symptom index of hay fever fell and reached a plateau. IgG blocking antibodies rose during the therapy. Because the children were doing so well, with minimal symptoms, the preseasonal therapy was omitted in the fifth year. Subsequently, IgE antibodies rose, the symptoms became more severe, and the IgG blocking antibodies fell. This suggested that treatment had been stopped too soon and should be resumed. The radioallergosorbent test will probably find its greatest usefulness in monitoring the course of allergic therapy.

Using a standard allergen coupled to an immunosorbent and a standard patient's serum containing antibodies to that allergen, this allergen assay can be inhibited by similar unknown allergen solutions for standardization purposes. For example, a known system (such as ragweed antigen E) coupled to an immunosorbent and reacted with a known patient's IgE antiserum to ragweed antigen E gives a certain level of binding of radiolabeled anti-IgE. An aliquot of unknown allergen containing the same amount of qualitatively identical antigen E should theoretically inhibit this reaction 100% if added prior to the immunosorbent-bound antigen E. A lesser quantity of antigen E or a partially related antigen would cause less complete inhibition. Therefore, this test can be used to standardize unknown allergen preparations in both quantity and quality. An international effort to establish standardized allergen extracts is now going forward under WHO auspices. Methods of standardization being proposed are a combination of skin test end point titration, RAST inhibition, and isoelectric focusing of extracts to determine whether a minimal number of established important antigens are present.

IgE & Cell-Mediated Immunity

A reciprocal relationship between serum IgE antibody levels and cellular immunity has been demonstrated in rats immunized with dinitrophenyl-*Ascaris* extract. Thymus-derived lymphocytes appear to regulate the production of IgE, and immunization with *Ascaris* antigen and *Bordetella pertussis* vaccine stimulated T cells. A second immunization on day 5 with *Ascaris* protein conjugated with the dinitrophenyl hapten caused high titers of IgE antibody. Neonatally thymectomized or lethally irradiated rats could not make anti-dinitrophenyl IgE antibody. IgE antibody production was not restored with B cells alone but was restored with both T and B cells. Thus, T cells helped B cells turn on the IgE antibody mechanism.

Sublethal whole body irradiation, adult thymectomy and splenectomy, T cell immunosuppression with antithymocyte serum, and radiomimetic drugs (5-bromouridine deoxyriboside and dactinomycin) all enhanced IgE production, which lasted for weeks. It appeared that IgE production persisted in the absence of T cells. IgG and IgM antibodies occurred soon after immunization and did not stop IgE production. Next, thymus (or spleen) cells from hyperimmunized rats were injected into irradiated rats that were producing IgE antibodies. This caused a rapid fall (within 2 days) in IgE. Thus, IgE production by B cells appears to be under regulatory control by T cells.

IgE production in humans may also be under T cell regulatory control. A patient with thymic alymphoplasia, with a high serum IgE level (16 μg/mL) and allergic symptoms, had severe depletion of small lymphocytes in the thymic-dependent paracortical areas of lymph nodes, but lymphoid and plasma cells were normal. Patients with Wiskott-Aldrich syndrome have high serum IgE, eczema, and impairment of cellular immunity. Similarly, eczema also occurs in patients

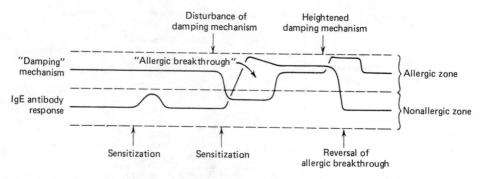

Figure 18–6. Possible pathogenesis of "allergic breakthrough." (Reproduced, with permission, from Katz DH: *J Immunol* 1979; **122**:2191.)

with ataxia-telangiectasia and impaired cellular immunity. Patients with Hodgkin's disease or sarcoidosis, with acquired impairment of cellular immunity, are being reported with high serum levels of IgE. On the other hand, patients with X-linked hypogammaglobulinemia (often with compensatory hyperreactive cellular immunity) commonly have eczema.

Humoral and cellular immune responses were recently evaluated in 10 patients with active atopic dermatitis. IgE levels were elevated (mean, 6420 IU/mL; normal mean, 90 IU/mL), but complement receptor lymphocytes and surface immunoglobulin-positive B cells were normal. T cell function was diminished in that 6 out of 9 patients were unresponsive to concentrated *Candida* (1:10) and streptokinase-streptodornase (1:1) extracts as delayed skin tests. Spontaneous sheep erythrocyte T cell rosettes were below normal, and 2 of 10 patients had reduced PHA responsiveness. Eighteen patients with moderate to severe atopic dermatitis had a mean of only 13.7% active T cell rosetting lymphocytes compared to 29.6% in 30 normal adults. In both of these studies, all patients were being treated with topical corticosteroids, and these drugs could have caused impaired cellular immunity. In summary, there appears to be an inverse relationship between IgE concentration and cellular immunity.

An interesting concept of "allergic breakthrough" has been proposed (Fig 18–6) in which IgE antibody production is minimal in normal nonallergic individuals and maintained at a low level by IgE "damping mechanisms" such as suppressor T cells or their soluble factors. The low level is maintained because the damping affects only the IgE system. In animals, experimental procedures such as low-dose irradiation, cyclophosphamide, and antilymphocyte serum treatments temporarily depress T cells, especially the normal regulatory suppressor T cells. Natural events, such as virus infections, appear to act in a similar manner. This depression permits escape of IgE helper T cells that stimulate IgE-forming B cells. Both T and B cells may then respond by differentiation and proliferation upon contact with a suitable antigen in the environment or diet. Therefore, depression or

failure of the normal damping mechanism may initiate allergic sensitization.

Conversely, stimulation of IgE suppressor T cells may restore this damping mechanism and return IgE antibody levels to normal, ie, below the allergic threshold. In inbred mice, Freund's complete adjuvant has strongly stimulated IgE suppressor T cells to abrogate ongoing IgE antibody production. Other immunotherapy procedures may also stimulate this damping mechanism, as discussed later under immunotherapy.

TARGET CELLS OF IgE–MEDIATED ALLERGIC REACTIONS

Mast Cells

Basophilic cells in connective and subcutaneous tissues were first recognized by Ehrlich, who associated a "feeding" or "mast" function with them. Others described them as "emergency kits" or "sentinal cells" of mediator-effector responses placed at mucous and cutaneous surfaces and around venules to recruit critical factors in homeostasis of the microenvironment (Fig 18–7). The primary function of mast cells appears to be storage of granules containing potent inflammatory and repair materials which are released upon injury to the organism. They contain strong pharmacologically active materials such as heparin, histamine, serotonin, kinin protease, and SRS-A; tissue degradation and repair materials such as chymase and hyaluronic acid; and factors affecting other cells, such as eosinophil and neutrophil chemotactic factors of anaphylaxis (ECF-A, NCF-A) and platelet-aggregating factor. It has been generally accepted that mast cells in all tissues are the same. However, the drug cromolyn sodium prevents the release of mediators from human mast cells in the bronchi and nose but does not affect skin mast cells.

Basophils

Basophilic cells comprise 0.5–2% of circulating

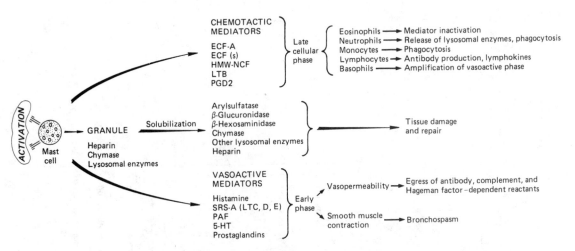

Figure 18–7. Schematic view of relationship between mast cell activation and inflammatory events. (Reproduced, with permission, from Wasserman SI, Soter NA: Page 192 in: *Advances in Allergology and Applied Immunology.* Pergamon Press, 1980.)

white cells. They were once thought to be identical to mast cells, from which they are indistinguishable by light microscopy, but electron microscopy reveals that the structure of granules is different in the 2 types of cells. Basophils contain histamine and SRS-A; their histamine release is not inhibited by cromolyn sodium. The content of other mediators is under study.

Other Target Cells

Blood platelets contain serotonin and possibly other allergic inflammatory mediators. In some species, like the rabbit, platelets also contain heparin and histamine. Histamine released from rabbit platelets is involved in the deposition of IgG immune complexes in the renal tissue of rabbits with acute glomerulonephritis. Such immune complex deposition can be prevented by prior treatment of the rabbit with antihistamine drugs. Furthermore, neutrophils and macrophages participating in the allergic inflammatory response are major sources of SRS-A leukotrienes, prostaglandins, and kinins, and perhaps other secondary mediators.

MEDIATORS OF ALLERGIC REACTIONS

Physiologic Role of Allergic Mediators

The primary role of the mediators of allergic reactions appears to be defense against injury, first by causing inflammation and then by stimulating tissue repair. In the presence of large concentrations of antihistamines, surgical wound healing is considerably impaired. Heparin temporarily suspends blood clotting, which permits inflammatory cells to enter the area of tissue injury. Histamine causes leakage by blood vessel endothelial cells and permits additional inflammatory cells and serum proteins, such as antibody, to enter the area of damaged tissue. There appears to be a role for histamine and perhaps other

mediators in normal growth—especially fetal growth. The highest concentrations of histamine are present during the fetal period. In pregnant rats given chronic high doses of antihistamines, fetal growth and maturation were impaired. Histamine appears to have a role in the control of microcirculation at the capillary level, where there appears to be a homeostatic balance between capillary constriction caused by epinephrine and capillary dilatation caused by histamine.

Although diseases such as acute glomerulonephritis are associated with deposition of antigen-IgG-complement complexes in the kidney or lung, these may be harmful overreactions of a normal defense mechanism. In intestinal parasitic nematode infestations in the rat, IgE on mast cells reacts with parasitic antigens. This causes the release of histamine and serotonin, which results in leakage of serum proteins from intestinal blood vessels. Among such proteins are IgG and IgM antibodies against the parasite, and these antibodies are apparently involved in the normal clearing of parasites from the intestine. Therefore, this is a useful defense mechanism. In animals, the acquisition of IgE antibodies to parasites results in permanent protection against subsequent infection by that parasite. This is known as the "self-cure phenomenon."

Facilitation by mediators of other cells entering the field of reaction may augment inflammation or may function in negative feedback control of the inflammation. The release of ECF-A causes the influx of eosinophils into the area of allergic inflammation. Electron micrographs have shown eosinophil phagocytosis of ferritin-antibody complexes. Eosinophil granules contain arylsulfatase-B, an enzyme that splits SRS-A into 2 inactive fragments. This provides an inactivating control on smooth muscle spasm induced by SRS-A.

Pharmacologic Role of Mediators

Histamine is a bioactive amine (MW 111) which causes smooth muscle contractions of human bron-

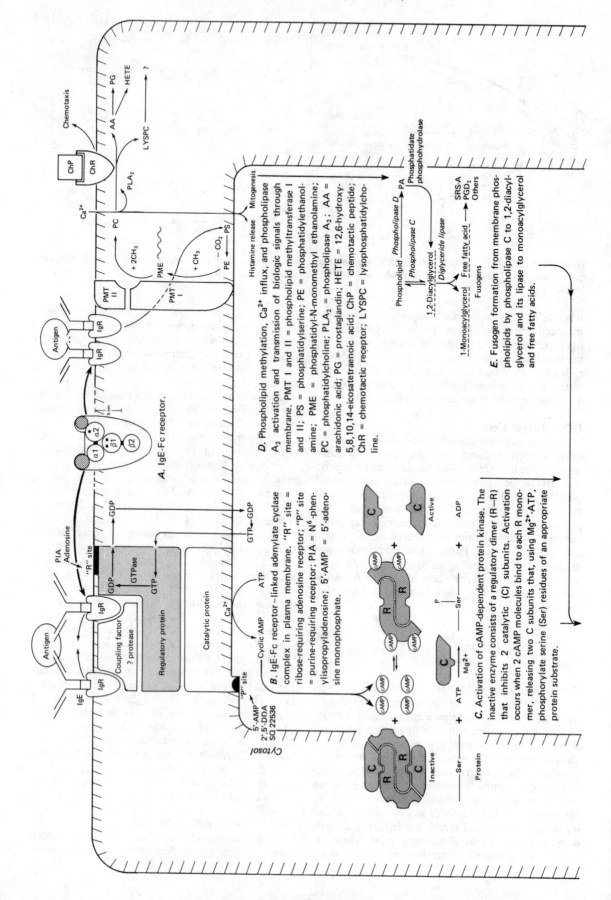

A. IgE-Fc receptor.

B. IgE-Fc receptor–linked adenylate cyclase complex in plasma membrane. "R" site = ribose-requiring adenosine receptor; "p" site = purine-requiring receptor; PIA = N⁶-phenylisopropyladenosine; 5′-AMP = 5′-adenosine monophosphate.

C. Activation of cAMP-dependent protein kinase. The inactive enzyme consists of a regulatory dimer (R–R) that inhibits 2 catalytic (C) subunits. Activation occurs when 2 cAMP molecules bind to each R monomer, releasing two C subunits that, using Mg^{2+}-ATP, phosphorylate serine (Ser) residues of an appropriate protein substrate.

D. Phospholipid methylation, Ca^{2+} influx, and transmission of biologic signals through membrane. PMT I and II = phospholipid methyltransferase I and II; PS = phosphatidylserine; PE = phosphatidylethanolamine; PME = phosphatidyl-N-monomethyl ethanolamine; PC = phosphatidylcholine; PLA_2 = phospholipase A_2; AA = arachidonic acid; PG = prostaglandin; HETE = 12,6-hydroxy-5,8,10,14-eicosatetraenoic acid; ChP = chemotactic peptide; ChR = chemotactic receptor; LYSPC = lysophosphatidylcholine.

E. Fusogen formation from membrane phospholipids by phospholipase C to 1,2-diacylglycerol and its lipase to monoacylglycerol and free fatty acids.

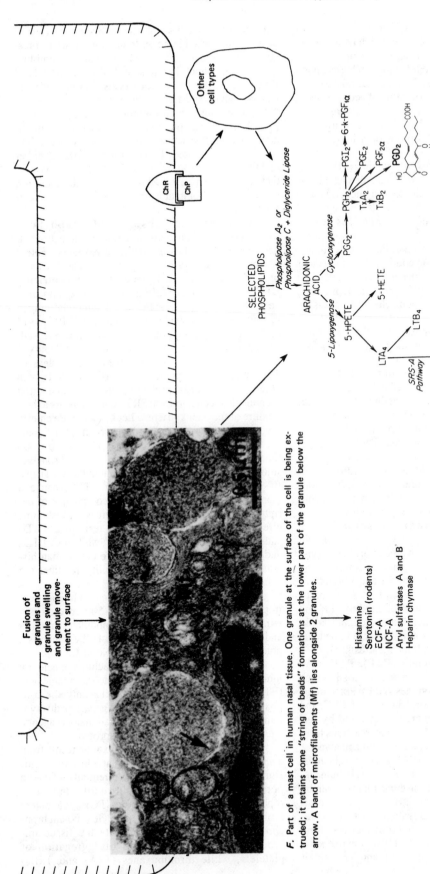

Figure 18–8. Enzymatic activation events in IgE antibody–sensitized mast cells and basophils upon antigen exposure leading to secretion of allergic mediators. (Reproduced, with permission, from [A] Metzger H et al: *Fed Proc* 1982;41:8; [B] Holgate ST, Lewis RA, Austen KF: Page 846 in: *Immunology, 1980. Proceedings of the Fourth International Congress of Immunology, Paris, 1980:* Academic Press, 1980; [C] Winslow CM, Austen KF: *Fed Proc* 1982;41:22; [D] Hirata F, Axelrod J: *Science* 1980; 209:1087; [E] Sullivan TJ: Page 232 in: *Biochemistry of Acute Allergic Reactions.* KROC Foundation, 1981; [F] Trotter CM, Orr TSC: *Clin Allergy* 1973;3:411; [G] Lewis RA, Austen KF: *Nature* 1981;293:103.)

chioles and small blood vessels, increased permeability of capillaries, and increased secretion by nasal and bronchial mucous glands. Histamine is stored in mast cells and in basophil granules and is released upon dissolution of the granules. Its maximal reaction occurs in 1–2 minutes, and its duration of action is about 10 minutes. Therefore, in humans it could be responsible for the symptoms of hay fever, urticaria, angioedema, and the bronchospasm of acute anaphylaxis.

Serotonin, or 5-hydroxytryptamine (MW 176), occurs in murine mast cells and human platelets. It has a pharmacologic role in anaphylaxis in mice, rats, and rabbits but apparently not in humans. It is antagonized by lysergic acid. Serotonin is preformed, is held in mast cell granules, and, similar to histamine, is released as a result of an antigen-antibody reaction.

ECF-A, an acidic tetrapeptide with a molecular weight of about 500, is also released as a result of an antigen-antibody reaction. It is preformed, like histamine and serotonin, and upon release it causes an influx of eosinophils into the area of allergic inflammation. The eosinophils dispose of antigen-antibody complexes and exert a feedback control on SRS-A through their granular enzyme, arylsulfatase B.

HMW-NCF. High-molecular-weight (about 750,000) neutrophil chemotactic factors are formed after bronchial challenge with antigen and in physical urticarias, eg, cold and solar. They attract neutrophils specifically but not eosinophils or mononuclear cells.

Kinin-generating proteases. Three proteases from human basophils and lung fragments cleave and activate Hageman factor to generate kinins from plasma kininogen and by prekallikrein activation. These proteases may link IgE-mediated reactions with Hageman factor–dependent kinin-generating coagulation and fibrinolytic pathways. **Bradykinin** is a 9-amino-acid peptide split by the enzyme kallikrein from a serum α_2-macroglobulin precursor. In humans, it causes slow, sustained contraction of smooth muscles, including those of the bronchi and vessels; increased vascular permeability; increased secretion of mucous glands, including those of the bronchi; and stimulation of pain fibers. Therefore, bradykinin could be responsible for symptoms of hay fever, angioedema (associated with painful swelling), and asthma.

Platelet-activating factors (PAF). PAF (MW 523 and 551) is the common name for a substance identified structurally and synthesized by Pinckard as acetyl glycerol ether phosphorylcholine (AGEPC) and by Benveniste as PAF-acether. It is released by IgE antibody-antigen reactions, by non-IgE reactions from rabbit and human basophils, and from human alveolar macrophages. In guinea pigs, PAF-acether is the most potent bronchoconstrictor described so far. In humans, it is postulated that intrinsic asthma might occur by PAF-acether released by non-IgE reactions from alveolar macrophages that aggregate platelets; these release granules containing potent bronchoconstrictors. Within 15 seconds after AGEPC infusion in baboons, intravascular platelet aggregation and release of

platelet factor 4 (PL4) and thromboxane B_2 (TxB$_2$) occur with marked increase in pulmonary artery pressure and prolonged systemic hypotension resembling anaphylactic shock in humans. AGEPC is 100–1000 times more active on a molar basis than histamine in causing wheal and flare in human skin.

Arachidonic acid metabolites. Cell membrane phospholipids are phosphorylated during IgE-mediated reactions that activate phospholipases A_2 and C to form arachidonic acid. This in turn is oxidized in either of 2 pathways—5-lipoxygenase or cyclooxygenase—that appear interrelated. Slow-reacting substances are generated in inflammatory reactions from several cell sources.

Slow-reacting substance of anaphylaxis (SRS-A) results from antigen-antibody interactions. It has been identified as a mixture of extremely potent spasmogenic and vasodilatory lipoxygenase metabolites of arachidonic acid; these are the **leukotrienes** LTC$_4$, LTD$_4$, and LTE$_4$, (Fig 18–8G). They appear to be generated in 2 phases after an IgE antibody-antigen reaction. Pure human mast cells generate 5–10 units of SRS-A per microgram of cellular histamine released, while human lung fragments generate 40–100 units of SRS-A per microgram of cellular histamine released. This suggests a combined action of mast cells with other activated cells, probably pulmonary interstitial mononuclear cells, to form SRS-A; this appears to be a mixture of the 3 leukotrienes. Leukotrienes are chiefly involved in the continued bronchospasm of asthma.

Leukotrienes have 100 times (LTC$_4$) to 1000 times (LTD$_4$) the potency of histamine as bronchial smooth muscle spasmogens on isolated muscle strips. In vivo, leukotrienes, especially LTD$_4$, cause a marked prolonged fall in dynamic compliance of peripheral airways in guinea pigs, whereas the histamine effect chiefly affects central airway resistance. LTD$_4$ causes hypotension in the guinea pig, while both LTD$_4$ and LTE$_4$ are about 100 times more potent than histamine in causing vascular permeability in guinea pig skin.

From membrane arachidonic acid in human neutrophils, 5-lipoxygenase generates 5-hydroxyeicosatetraenoic acid (5-HETE), which modulates motility and possibly glucose transport; and LTB$_4$ which is a potent chemotactic agent comparable to C5a.

Both oxidative pathways of arachidonic acid are inhibited by an analog, 5,8,11,14-eicosatraynoic acid (ETYA), while benoxaprofen blocks only the 5-lipoxygenase pathway. The cyclooxygenase pathway is inhibited by nonsteroidal anti-inflammatory agents, eg, aspirin, indomethacin, and ibuprofen.

Prostaglandins and **thromboxanes** result from cyclooxygenase metabolism of arachidonic acid. Human lung mast cells form preferentially PGD$_2$, a potent vasodilator. From neutrophils and macrophages, this pathway generates PGF$_{2\alpha}$, a potent bronchoconstrictor, and PGE$_1$ and PGE$_2$, potent broncho- and vasodilators that regulate the tissue microenvironment. PGI$_2$ causes disaggregation of platelets, while thromboxanes (TxA$_2$ and TxB$_2$)

aggregate platelets and thus are potent regulators of blood coagulation and homeostasis.

There appear to be considerable physiologic reinforcing interactions between 5-lipoxygenase and cyclooxygenase pathway reagents. In human skin, PGD_2 causes a transient edema (wheal and flare) which, if given with a subclinical dose of the chemotactant LTB_4, causes prolonged neutrophilic induration. Inhibition of one of the 2 pathways may make more arachidonic acid substrate available for metabolism by the other pathway. It was proposed that cyclooxygenase inhibition by aspirin made more arachidonic acid available to form SRS-A leukotrienes to cause aspirin-induced asthma. However, benoxaprofen, a 5-lipoxygenase inhibitor, did not prevent aspirin-induced bronchospasm. Therefore, the interactions of arachidonic acid metabolites require more study to further elucidate mechanisms of action.

Histamine Release from Sensitized Leukocytes (Basophils)

A practical in vitro miniature allergic reaction is used extensively as an investigative and diagnostic test for allergy. Leukocytes from a heparinized blood sample drawn from an allergic individual are incubated with the allergen for 15 minutes. The leukocyte sample is centrifuged, and the histamine content of the supernate is measured spectrofluorometrically (or by radiolabeled histamine or bioassay). With increasing amounts of antigen, there is increased histamine release. The histamine is expressed as a percentage of the total amount of histamine present in an aliquot of leukocytes. Blood basophils are the only source of

histamine in the blood, and although a buffy coat preparation is used, one is actually measuring basophil histamine release. The degree of sensitivity in a patient is directly proportionate to the amount of histamine released by antigen (Fig 18–9). The degree of sensitivity in different patients may be compared by the relative amounts of antigen required to release 50% of the histamine from their white cells. Fig 18–9 shows that patient J. Mu. is 300 times more sensitive than patient L. Kr. A remarkable correlation between the degree of symptoms and the amount of antigen necessary for 50% release from leukocytes has been noted (Fig 18–10). This test has been useful in following the course of patients during hyposensitization therapy (Fig 18–11). At the start of therapy, this patient required 5 μg of antigen to release 50% of his histamine, whereas after 2½ years of therapy he required 5150 μg of antigen to release the same percentage of histamine. This is a 1000-fold decrease in his cell sensitivity and correlated positively with his clinical improvement.

Eosinophils

Eosinophils are not direct targets in allergic reactions, ie, IgE antibodies do not fix to their surfaces. However, they are intimately associated with allergic reactions, and blood or local tissue eosinophilia is often a useful clinical test for allergy or parasitic infestation. Eosinophils normally comprise about 1–3% of the circulating leukocytes; in allergic patients, 10–20% eosinophilia may occur.

The function of eosinophils in allergic reactions has long been a mystery, but now we have some insights. Both mast cells and basophils in allergic

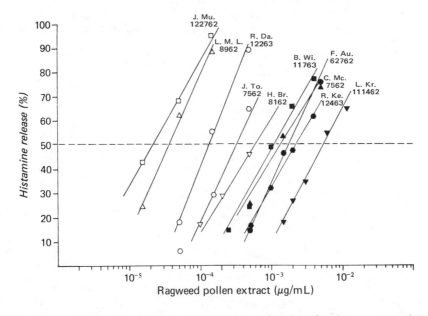

Figure 18–9. Dose-response relationships for histamine release as a function of antigen concentration (cells from 10 ragweed-sensitive donors). (Reproduced, with permission, from Lichtenstein LM, Osler AG: Studies on the mechanism of hypersensitivity phenomena: Histamine release from human leukocytes by ragweed pollen antigen. *J Exp Med* 1964; **120**:507.)

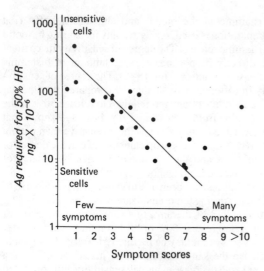

Figure 18–10. Correlation between average seasonal symptom scores of hay fever patients and measurements of cellular sensitivity to antigen E (ng antigen required for 50% histamine release [HR] from a standard suspension of isolated washed leukocytes). (Reproduced, with permission, from Lichtenstein LM, Norman PS: Human allergic reactions. *Am J Med* 1969;**46**:169. Also in: Norman PS: Present status of hyposensitization treatment. Page 46 in: *Proceedings of the Sixth Congress of the International Association of Allergology.* Excerpta Medica Foundation, 1968.)

reactions release eosinophil chemotactic factors (ECF-A and ECF-C) that attract eosinophils to the allergic inflammation area. Eosinophils have been shown by electron microscopy in anaphylactic reactions in rabbits to engulf ferritin-antiferritin complexes which are attached to the eosinophilic granules. Aryl-

sulfatase B and histaminase are released by eosinophils, probably from the granules, during the reaction. These cleave the 2 main allergic mediators, SRS-A and histamine, respectively. Therefore, eosinophils exert a negative feedback control on allergic reactions by limiting the amount of mediators and remove the allergic antibody-antigen complexes by phagocytosis.

Eosinophils have their major role in defense against parasites. In schistosomal infections, after skin penetration by the larval cercaria, the schistosomulum is sensitized by IgG antibody, which activates complement by both classic and alternative pathways. Mast cells adhere to complement-coated schistosomules by their membrane receptors for complement; they activate IgE to release ECF-A and histamine. More eosinophils are recruited, and their complement receptors are enhanced to accelerate eosinophil-mediated parasite killing. Eosinophils position their granules on the parasite surface, which undergoes lysis under the onslaught of the granules' major basic protein. Macrophages activated by IgE antischistosome antibodies also participate in the parasite killing process.

Autonomic Nervous Controls as "Mediators" of Allergic Reactions

The catecholamines (epinephrine, norepinephrine, dopamine) are agonists of the sympathetic nervous system; acetylcholine is the parasympathetic agonist. These substances modulate the severity of the allergic reaction by regulating the amount of mediator release from target cells and the degree of responsiveness of shock organ cells. Catecholamines contain a catechol nucleus (a benzene ring with 2 adjacent hydroxy groups) and an amine group. Epinephrine acts primarily as a hormone, and norepinephrine is a

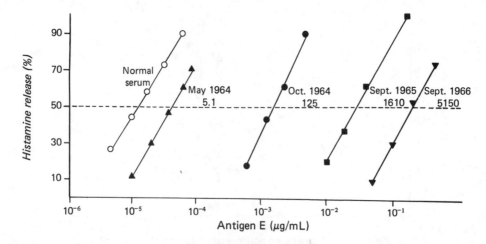

Figure 18–11. Dose-response curves of cells suspended in normal serum or in the patient's own serum obtained before immunotherapy (May 1964) and after approximately 1, 2, and 3 years of immunotherapy. The numbers to the right of the curves in allergic serum indicate the ratio of the antigen concentration required for 50% histamine release in the allergic sera as compared to the normal serum (open symbols). (Reproduced, with permission, from Lichtenstein LM, Norman PS: Human allergic reactions. [Editorial.] *Am J Med* 1969;**46**:170.)

neurotransmitter at both peripheral and central levels. Both compounds occur naturally in mammals. Another synthetic catecholamine, isoproterenol, has important pharmacologic effects on the allergic reaction.

The autonomic nervous system is divided into sympathetic (adrenergic) and parasympathetic (cholinergic) systems, and these exert generally opposing actions on the various organs of the body. These 2 systems maintain homeostasis in bronchial smooth muscle cells; cholinergic stimulation through acetylcholine causes smooth muscle constriction, whereas adrenergic stimulation through epinephrine causes relaxation. Thus, there is constant alternating responsiveness of bronchial smooth muscles to cholinergic and adrenergic stimuli, maintaining smooth muscle tone or homeostasis.

CELL RECEPTORS & ALLERGIC REACTIONS

Biochemical Cellular Events in Release of Allergic Mediators From Mast Cells & Basophils

A. IgE Receptor: The receptors for IgE in basophils and mast cells have been characterized in rat basophil leukemia (RBL) cells, mouse mastocytoma cells, and human basophils. Schematically, Fig 18–8A shows the 2-chain IgE receptor (MW 80,000) composed of α (MW 50,000) and β (MW 30,000) chains, each of which has 2 domains. In the larger α chains, both α_1 and α_2 domains appear on the basophil surface. The smaller α_1 (MW 21,000) is rich in carbohydrate; the larger α_2 (MW 24,000) has little carbohydrate but apparently binds to the IgE molecules. The nonglycosylated intramembranous noncovalently

bound β chain has β_1 (MW 20,000) and β_2 domains; the latter appears exposed on the inner cytoplasmic side of the plasma membrane. Phosphorylation of both the α and β chains has been reported, but whether this actually does occur and if so how are currently under study.

B. Triggering Signals Induced by IgE Receptor Bridging: A rabbit antiserum against IgE receptors of RBL cells (anti-RBL) was produced that reproduced all the effects of antigen-IgE antibody or IgE-anti-IgE reactions in basophils. Fragments F(ab')$_2$ of IgE antibody with antigen, or of rabbit anti-RBL with receptor, or of rabbit anti-IgE with IgE all caused histamine release, whereas their Fab' monomers failed to do so (Fig 18–12). Therefore, bridging of two IgE receptors was needed for histamine release; IgE antibody with antigen or anti-IgE with IgE acted merely as a suprasurface projection of the IgE receptors.

IgE receptors are closely associated with membrane phospholipid methylation by methyl transferases and with adenylate cyclase activation, leading to formation of Ca^{2+} channel and mediator release (Fig 18–8D). Initially, a membrane-associated serine esterase acts on phosphatidylserine (PS in Fig 18–8D) to form phosphatidylethanolamine (PE) on the semiviscous cytoplasmic interior side of the plasma membrane. This activates methyltransferase I, which places one methyl group onto phosphatidylethanolamine. This in turn activates methyltransferase II, which adds 2 more methyl groups to form phosphatidylcholine, now on the outside surface side of the plasma membrane. Phosphatidylcholine causes a calcium channel, permitting Ca^{2+} to enter the cell; Ca^{2+} is necessary for mediator release. Furthermore, Ca^{2+} is needed to activate phospholipase A$_2$ (PLA$_2$), which converts phosphatidylcholine to lysophosphatidylcholine. PLA$_2$ ac-

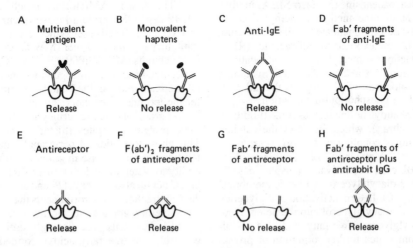

Figure 18–12. Schematic summary of studies on the roles of IgE and IgE receptor in mediator release from mast cells and basophils. *A.* Multivalent or divalent antigens initiate release. *B.* Monovalent haptens do not initiate release. *C.* Anti-IgE initiates mediator release. *D.* Monovalent Fab' fragments of anti-IgE do not initiate release. *E.* Antibodies to IgE receptor initiate release. *F.* Divalent F(ab')$_2$ fragments of antireceptor antibody also cause release. *G.* Monovalent Fab' fragments of the rabbit antireceptor antibody do not initiate release unless *(H)* they become linked by antirabbit IgG antibody. (Reproduced, with permission, from Kulczycki A: *J Allergy Clin Immunol* 1981;**68**:5.)

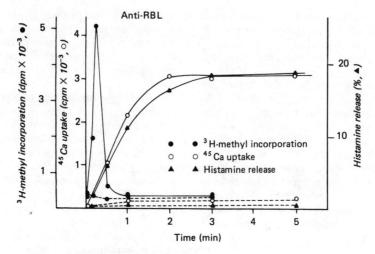

Figure 18–13. Phospholipid methylation, Ca^{2+} influx, and histamine release in rat mast cells. Mast cells were first incubated with [^{3}H]methionine or $^{45}Ca^{2+}$. Incorporation of [^{3}H]methyl groups into phospholipids, $^{45}Ca^{2+}$ influx, and histamine release were measured after various treatments. Cells were treated with either divalent F(ab')$_2$ (—) or monovalent Fab' (---) fragments of antibodies to RBL cells. (Reproduced, with permission, from Ishizaka T: *Fed Proc* 1982;**41**:17.)

tivation also causes membrane phospholipid to release free arachidonic acid and, in neutrophils, stimulation of both cyclooxygenase and lipoxygenase pathways to form prostaglandins (PG) and 5-hydroperoxyeicosatetraenoic acid (5-HPETE), while mast cells preferentially make prostaglandin D$_2$ (PGD$_2$). When anti-RBL serum was added to RBL cells in the presence of preincubated methyl ^{3}H-methionine, methyl ^{3}H-lysophosphatidylcholine appeared within 15 seconds, indicating the speed of the phospholipid methylation upon bridging of IgE receptors. In these stimulated cells, within 2 minutes $^{45}Ca^{2+}$ uptake and within 3 minutes histamine release were maximal (Fig 18–13). S-Isobutyl-3-deazoadenosine (3-deazo-SIBA) inhibits S-adenosyl-L-methionine-mediated methylation. In purified rat mast cells preincubated with 1–100 μmol of 3-deazo-SIBA and exposed to anti-receptor (RBL) serum, all 3 reactions—methyl ^{3}H-lysophosphatidylcholine formation, $^{45}Ca^{2+}$ uptake, and histamine release—were blocked, which suggests that all 3 reactions depend on phospholipid methylation.

Lysophosphatidylcholine increases the fluidity of the plasma membrane, which increases the calcium channel and allows coupling of the IgE receptor to adenylate cyclase. Methylation of membrane phospholipids in RBL cells also activates phospholipase C, which forms 1,2-diacylglycerol, which is membrane fusogen (Fig 18–8E). In turn, activation of diglyceride lipase cleaves 1,2-diacylglycerol into the potent fusogens 1-monoacylglycerol, free fatty acid, and arachidonic acid, from which further formation of prostaglandins and leukotrienes is stimulated.

Concomitantly with membranous phospholipid methylation, membrane adenylate cyclase is stimulated by the bridging of two IgE receptors aided by increased fluidity of the plasma membrane. The bridging of two IgE receptors activates adenylate cyclase by

squeezing down a coupling protein (probably DNP-inhibitable serine esterase), which couples a guanosine 5'-triphosphate (GTP)-dependent mechanism of a regulatory protein (G/F or N protein), which binds with the catalytic protein of adenylate cyclase, inducing a high catalytic state (Fig 18–8B). In the presence of Ca^{2+}, activated catalytic protein converts cytosol ATP to cAMP. This peak rise in cAMP occurs within 15 seconds—concomitantly with phospholipid methylation, described above—and results in feedback suppression of further phospholipid methylation and inhibits further Ca^{2+} influx and histamine release (Fig 18–14).

The burst of cAMP formation activates one or two cAMP-dependent protein kinase isoenzymes (types I and II). The inactive enzymes are tetramers of an inhibitory regulatory dimer (MW 55,000) and 2 catalytic subunits (MW 39,000) (Fig 18–8C). Two cAMP molecules bind to each regulatory monomer, which allosterically releases the 2 catalytic units. These transfer the terminal phosphoryl group of ATP to the hydroxyl group of specific serines and threonines in cationic protein substrates (histones and protamines). This phosphorylation of perigranular membrane proteins causes an increase in granule membrane permeability to water and calcium that cause granule swelling. Calcium also causes ATP- and actomyosin-dependent contraction of microfilaments that move the swollen secretory granules to the mast cell surface (Fig 18–8F). Fusogens (1,2-diacylglycerol, 1-monoacylglycerol, and free fatty acids), formed above, now cause fusion of the mast cell granules to form secretory granules and channels and then fuse with the plasma membrane, which results in secretory expulsion of the granule contents—the preformed mediators histamine, serotonin in rodents, ECF-A, and NCF-A.

Furthermore, phospholipid methylation and

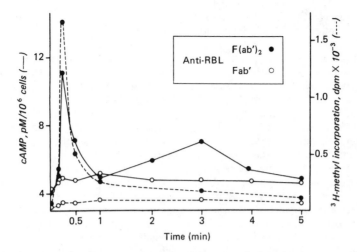

Figure 18–14. Kinetics of changes in cAMP (—) and phospholipid methylation (- - -) induced by either F(ab')₂ fragments (●) or Fab' fragments (○) of anti-RBL. (Reproduced, with permission, from Ishizaka A: *Fed Proc* 1982;41:17.)

phospholipase A_2 activation are necessary for rabbit neutrophil and probably macrophage chemotaxis and release of arachidonate and its metabolites, primarily from the lipoxygenase pathway, especially SRS-A leukotrienes LTC_4, LTD_4, LTE_4 (Fig 18-8G).

Clinical Relevance in Asthma of IgE Receptor Concentration on Mast Cells

In order to explain clinical differences in allergic respiratory diseases, it has been proposed that pollen- or dander-sensitive asthmatics have many IgE receptors on mast cells that react with many high-affinity IgE antibodies directed at multivalent pollen antigens, eg, ragweed antigen E (Fig 18–15). Such reactions would occur even with minute doses of pollens, because of a profusion of ragweed IgE antibodies; these would be bimolecular reactions occurring at a rate dependent upon concentration of antigen and its receptor-bound specific IgE antibodies.

With house dust mite or mold allergens, most cells might contain only a few scattered IgE receptor-bound antibody molecules in which a high concentration of antigen would be necessary to form sufficient bridges to appose two IgE receptors and trigger the reaction. This might proceed as a trimolecular reaction which would be proportionate to

[Antigen] X [Receptor-bound antigen-specific IgE]².

Therefore, in patients with chronic or intrinsic asthma, a specific antigen exposure might be unrecognized because rapid reactions would occur only in times of extremely high antigen exposure, eg, changing a vacuum cleaner bag or bronchial inhalation challenge with house dust. It is suggested that ''idiopathic'' or ''intrinsic'' asthma in the elderly may be related to an increased incidence of house dust or mold allergy in this age group, in which IgE levels usually wane.

Receptors for Autonomic Agonists

Target cells have receptors, presumably on their surfaces, for the autonomic agonists acetylcholine and epinephrine. Adrenergic receptors apparently have a receptive substance with a steric configuration complementary to the amine group in the catecholamine. This interaction initiates a chain of biochemical reactions which culminate in the ultimate reaction of that cell. Although receptors have not as yet been biochemically defined, they are usually described in terms of actions induced by agonists and by blockage of such

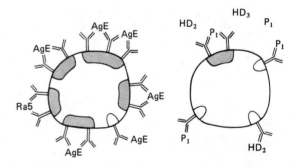

Figure 18–15. Hypothetical schematic model illustrating that clinical differences in chronicity of allergic diseases may be related in part to differences in numbers of receptor molecules bridged by antigen. Unoccupied receptors and receptors occupied by other IgE molecules are not shown. Bridged (or apposed) receptors that initiate mediator release are shaded; unapposed receptors are not. *Left:* Mast cell of ragweed-allergic individual has many receptors occupied by IgE antibodies directed at multivalent ragweed antigens, predominantly antigen E (AgE). *Right:* Mast cell of house dust–allergic individual. In this case fewer antigen-specific IgE antibodies are present that are directed at antigen P_1 and other theoretic house dust (HD) antigens. (Reproduced, with permission, from Kulczycki A: *J Allergy Clin Immunol* 1981;68:5.)

actions by antagonistic agents. On this basis, Ahlquist described adrenergic α and β receptors which often had antagonistic or synergistic effects. α-Adrenergic receptors respond primarily to norepinephrine, with epinephrine or isoproterenol causing a 10- or 100-fold reduced response, respectively. On the other hand, β-adrenergic receptors respond primarily to isoproterenol, with epinephrine and norepinephrine similarly causing a 10- or 100-fold reduced response. Thus, epinephrine is a natural agonist for both α and β receptors, with its ultimate effect probably modulated by other factors. α-Adrenergic receptors are blocked by ergot alkaloids, haloalkylamines (eg, phenoxybenzamine, dibenamine), benzodioxans, and imidazolines. β-Adrenergic receptors are blocked by propranolol, dichloroisoproterenol, and pronethalol.

β-Adrenergic receptors have been further classified, depending upon their action on certain tissues, into β_1 and β_2 receptors. β_1-Adrenergic stimulation causes an increase in heart rate (chronotropic effect) as well as an increased force of cardiac contraction (inotropic effect). Increased mobilization of free fatty acids from fat cells also occurs, producing a rise in blood lipids. β_2-Adrenergic receptors cause relaxation of smooth muscles, especially in the bronchus, uterus, and bladder. They also cause inhibition of peripheral glucose uptake and increased muscle glycogenolysis, both of which cause a rise in blood glucose. The agonist for both β_1 and β_2 receptors is isoproterenol; both are blocked by propranolol. There are, however,

several newly synthesized agonists for β_2 adrenergic receptors, eg, metaproterenol (Alupent, Metaprel), albuterol (Salbutamol), and terbutaline (Bricanyl). These have been developed for treatment of asthma to act primarily as bronchodilators and to avoid the cardiac stimulatory effects of β_1 receptors. The β_2 receptors are blocked specifically by butoxamine, while pronethalol has primarily a β_1 blocking action.

Whether α-adrenergic receptors exist in the human bronchus is a question under current study, and there is some disagreement. In animals such as the guinea pig, α-adrenergic stimulation by norepinephrine or propranolol blocking of β-adrenergic receptors results in bronchoconstriction. Such an effect has not been conclusively demonstrated in humans.

In summary, the allergic shock organ tissues, smooth muscle, and vascular endothelium have responses modulated by the autonomic nervous system (Fig 18–16). Cholinergic stimulation by the action of acetylcholine on a cholinergic or a γ receptor on target cells causes smooth muscle contraction and increased capillary permeability. α-Adrenergic stimulation by norepinephrine acting on the α receptor causes bronchial smooth muscle contraction and vasoconstriction (in the guinea pig). β-Adrenergic stimulation by epinephrine or isoproterenol causes smooth muscle relaxation and decreases capillary permeability. Cholinergic stimulation is blocked by atropine, and α-adrenergic effects are blocked by phenoxybenzamine, while β_2 stimulation is blocked by propranolol. Therefore,

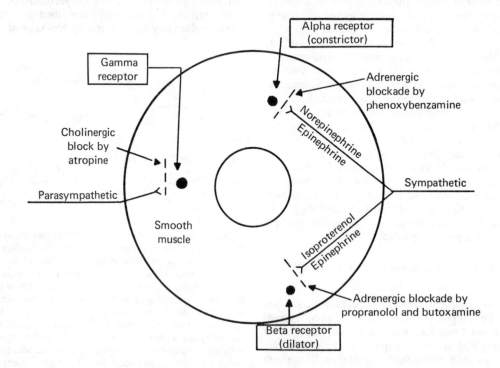

Figure 18–16. Autonomic receptors of smooth muscle of blood vessels and bronchi. (Reproduced, with permission, from Reed CE: The role of the autonomic nervous system in the pathogenesis of bronchial asthma: Is the normal bronchial sensitivity due to beta adrenergic blockade? Page 404 in: *Proceedings of the Sixth Congress of the International Association of Allergology.* Excerpta Medica Foundation, 1968.)

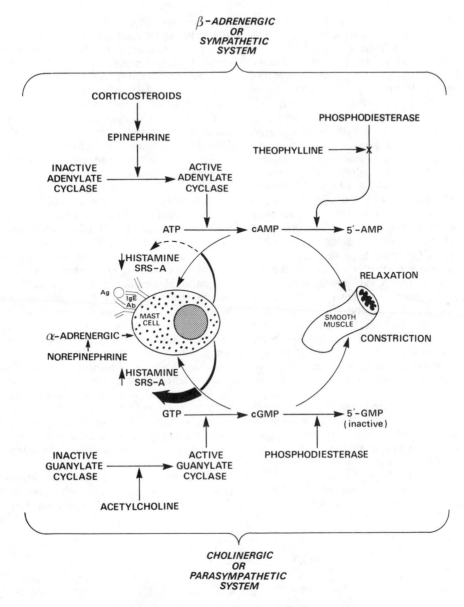

Figure 18–17. The balance theory of sympathetic and parasympathetic regulation.

the use of appropriate agonists and antagonists to these reactions in clinical management provides a pharmacologic basis for control of symptoms resulting from allergic reactions.

Considerable evidence is emerging that the β-adrenergic receptor is a cell membrane enzyme coupled to the catalytic unit of adenylate cyclase. This enzyme is changed from a relatively inactive to an active form by isoproterenol or epinephrine. Activated adenylate cyclase catalyzes the formation of cyclic nucleotide (as shown in Fig 18–17) by acting upon ATP in the cell cytoplasm to form cyclic 3′,5′-adenosine monophosphate (cAMP), which consists of adenylic acid with a diesterified phosphate group at the C3′ and C5′ positions of the attached ribose. cAMP in

the presence of dibasic cations (Ca^{2+} and Mg^{2+}) modulates the activity of cell enzymes and permeability barriers. Furthermore, cAMP is converted to an inactive 5′-AMP by phosphodiesterase.

According to the hypothesis of Sutherland, hormones such as norepinephrine and epinephrine (catecholamines) act as the first messenger, which reacts with a receptor enzyme (such as adenylate cyclase), which in turn activates a second messenger, cAMP. This second messenger induces the cell to perform its physiologic function: the fat cell to undergo lipolysis, the liver cell to undergo glycogenolysis, the smooth muscle cell to relax, and the mast cell to inhibit its release of mediators.

Intracellular concentration of cAMP rises in the

target cell upon external stimulation with prostaglandins PGE₁ and PGE₂ and also increases with histamine itself (Fig 18–18). There appears, therefore, to be a catalytic subunit of adenylate cyclase in the membrane which responds to one of 3 or more independent receptor subunits. Such receptor subunits can be blocked independently by drugs—eg, β-adrenergic receptor is blocked by propranolol; the histamine receptor is of the H₂ type which is blocked by burimamide; and the prostaglandin receptor may possibly be blocked by indomethacin or by aspirin. Basophils, in which the β-adrenergic receptor is blocked by propranolol, will still respond to prostaglandins PGE₁ or PGE₂ with a rise in intracellular cAMP—and also to exogenous histamine in a similar manner—whereas burimamide-treated basophils fail to respond to histamine but will respond with a rise in intracellular cAMP to epinephrine or PGE₁ stimulation. It has been suggested that the release of histamine from mast cells by antigen and antibody will exert a negative feedback control upon other basophils to inhibit further release of histamine. The concept of 3 independent receptors on target cells causing a rise in intracellular cAMP is of possible major therapeutic interest in status asthmaticus, wherein the β-adrenergic receptor appears to be unresponsive to epinephrine but is still apparently responsive to prostaglandin PGE₁.

Lymphocytes which form antibodies or which participate in cellular immune responses by undergoing mitogenesis and enlargement in response to antigen or plant lectins are under similar autonomic and biochemical regulatory controls. A rise in intracellular cAMP induced by epinephrine or prostaglandin PGE₁ in such lymphocytes inhibits mitogenesis and aborts further immune responsiveness. Therefore, hormonal influences upon antibody formation and immune response are under intensive current study.

The α-adrenergic receptor is less well understood. Several workers have suggested that ATPase may function as the α receptor. It may compete for ATP with adenylate cyclase in the direct formation of inactive 5'-AMP without the intermediary cAMP formation step. Norepinephrine may stimulate ATPase to utilize ATP directly to form inactive 5'-AMP; such a diversion of precursor ATP would cause a lowering of the intracellular cAMP, and this in turn would result in an increased mediator release from such a stimulated basophil.

Phosphodiesterase converts cAMP to inactive 5'-AMP. Methylxanthine drugs such as theophylline, theobromine, and caffeine inhibit phosphodiesterase and its destruction of cAMP; therefore, a high cAMP level is maintained. Leukocytes from ragweed-allergic individuals exposed to ragweed antigen E had a dose-dependent release of histamine. This was inhibited by increasing doses of epinephrine and, independently, by increasing doses of theophylline. In fact, the effect of these 2 drugs was synergistic in that an ineffective inhibitory dose either of epinephrine alone or of theophylline alone, when given together, resulted in important inhibition of histamine release. This synergistic effect of catecholamines and theophylline in the treatment of bronchospasm in asthma has been known for many years and was the rationale for using combinations of these drugs in single tablets for bronchodilator therapy of asthma. Currently, they are given individually in dosages calculated according to body weight.

The cholinergic or γ receptor in target cells appears to be guanylate cyclase, which occurs either in the membrane or in the cell cytoplasm. Inactive gua-

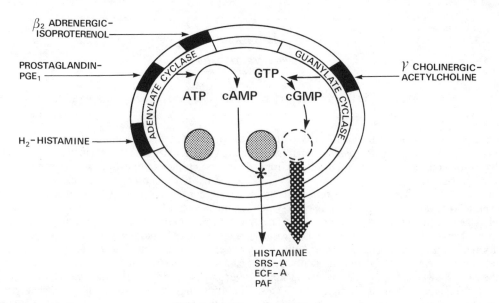

Figure 18–18. Schematic representation of a cell showing the relationships between intracellular cAMP and various independent receptor subunits.

nylate cyclase is converted by acetylcholine to active guanylate cyclase, and this converts guanosine triphosphate (GTP) into a cyclic nucleotide called cyclic 3',5'-guanosine monophosphate (cGMP). In mast cells, the intracellular rise in cGMP is associated with an increase in mediator release. This release can be blocked by atropine. Similarly, in bronchial smooth muscle, a rise in intracellular cGMP is associated with smooth muscle contraction which is blocked by atropine. cGMP is destroyed by phosphodiesterase by conversion to an inactive form, 5'-GMP, or guanyl monophosphate. Although both adenyl phosphodiesterase and guanyl phosphodiesterase are destroyed by the methylxanthines, it has been demonstrated that adenyl phosphodiesterase is about 10 times more susceptible to methylxanthine than is guanyl phosphodiesterase. This may explain the preferential action of methylxanthines on the cAMP system over that on the cGMP system and therefore the effectiveness of methylxanthines in the treatment of asthma.

In summary, the biochemical modulation of mediator release from mast cells has been demonstrated using a preparation of IgE-sensitized cells prepared from minced human lung.

THE BALANCE THEORY OF REGULATION CONTROLS

A balance has been proposed between cAMP and cGMP to maintain homeostatic controls of cell activation. This is illustrated in Fig 18–17. In an asthmatic individual, cholinergic stimulation through acetylcholine acting upon guanylate cyclase causes a rise in cGMP. In the mast cell, mediator release is augmented and the bronchial smooth muscle constricts. This mechanism is blocked by atropine. Guanyl phosphodiesterase inactivates the elevated cGMP, converting it to 5'-GMP and turning off the response. Asthmatic symptoms may be further augmented by norepinephrine, which stimulates the α-adrenergic receptor to decrease cAMP and therefore augments the release of mediators from mast cells and possibly increases smooth muscle bronchoconstriction. This mechanism can be blocked by an α-adrenergic blocking agent such as phentolamine. Opposing these mechanisms is the cAMP system, in which epinephrine, isoproterenol, PGE_1 or PGE_2, and even histamine activate adenylate cyclase, which converts ATP to cAMP. This elevated cAMP level inhibits the release of mediators from the sensitized mast cells and results in bronchial smooth muscle relaxation. Methylxanthines such as theophylline further augment the cAMP level by inhibiting adenyl phosphodiesterase to prevent the destruction of cAMP. One action of corticosteroid hormones appears to be the improvement of epinephrine function on the β-adrenergic receptor to augment cAMP levels. This schema of a balance between cGMP and cAMP in asthma suggests that there are points in the mechanism which are likely to respond to pharmacologic control and could thus be of significance in treatment.

THE β-ADRENERGIC BLOCKADE THEORY OF ATOPY

It has been proposed that the basic problem in asthmatic individuals is a partial β-adrenergic blockade. This may be an inherited or acquired (ie, infectious) lesion of the receptor–transducer–adenylate cyclase complex, resulting in its defective function. Such a blockade would interfere with the homeostatic control of bronchi and target cells (mast cells and basophils).

The Hypothalamically "Imbalanced" Anaphylactic Guinea Pig

The anterior hypothalamus mediates parasympathetic responses, and the posterior hypothalamus mediates sympathetic responses. Electrolytic removal of one hypothalamic division, or electric stimulation of the antagonistic division, caused an autonomic imbalance in the guinea pig. Such a guinea pig, when sensitized for anaphylaxis, had markedly altered responses to antigen. There was only mild anaphylaxis when the anterior hypothalamus (parasympathetic) was removed, and there was great augmentation of anaphylaxis when the posterior hypothalamus (sympathetic) was removed. Correspondingly, similar effects were noted with electric stimulation of the appropriate hypothalamic area.

The *Bordetella pertussis*-Induced Hypersensitive State of Mice & Rats

The normal mouse or rat is a poor experimental animal in which to demonstrate anaphylaxis because these animals are relatively insensitive to histamine and serotonin. They form, primarily, IgG antibodies to soluble protein antigens. However, they are quite sensitive to catecholamines, with a marked rise in blood glucose following epinephrine injection.

B pertussis inoculation alters the responsiveness of mice and rats to the chemical mediators of anaphylaxis. Five days after *B pertussis* injection, these animals become extremely hypersensitive to histamine, serotonin, bradykinin, and, in one strain, to acetylcholine. They also become quite hypersensitive to cold, barometric pressure changes, and respiratory irritants. They become much less sensitive to catecholamines, responding with no rise in blood glucose after epinephrine injection. There is enhanced antibody formation, especially of the IgE class. *B pertussis* causes reduced functioning of the β-adrenergic receptors and therefore an autonomic imbalance. A similar β-adrenergic defect might account for the symptoms of asthma in humans.

In humans, such an autonomic imbalance would result in a disturbed homeostatic control of bronchi and target cells, resulting in a weak β-adrenergic response and an overactive cholinergic control. Such an imbalance could account for many of the nonimmunologic "triggers" of asthma attacks in humans. These triggers include emotional upset, which is vagally mediated and inhibits the sympathetics; hyperirritable airways to cold, smoke, and irritant chemicals, which are cholinergically mediated and reversed by atropine; and nocturnal attacks, when histamine levels in the blood are highest and catecholamine and corticosteroid levels are lowest. The recumbent position also enhances cholinergic responsiveness. Furthermore, β-adrenergic blockade diverts the normal protein antigen-induced antibody formation from IgG and IgM classes to the IgE pathway. These features are all characteristic of human patients with asthma.

Hyperreactivity of the airways to inhaled small doses of methacholine is observed in asthmatic individuals and can be used as a differential diagnostic test for asthma. Both patients with hay fever and patients with asthma histories (up to 22 years without an attack) show increased airway responsiveness to methacholine. This observation suggests a basic β-adrenergic defect in such patients. However, the same findings could be explained by a hyperreactive cholinergic receptor system. A defective response to isoproterenol (10 mM) has been demonstrated in mixed leukocytes of asthmatic individuals where there was no rise in cAMP level. On the contrary, in patients with hay fever and in normal control patients, there was a 3- or 4-fold rise in cAMP. Although a genetic defect in β-adrenergic receptors is postulated, most asthmatics have been treated with catecholamines and methylxanthines for long periods of time. This may have caused iatrogenic unresponsiveness of the β-adrenergic receptor.

Radioactive adrenergic ligands—[^{3}H]dihydroalprenolol ([^{3}H]DHA) for β-adrenergic receptors and [^{3}H]dihydroergocryptine ([^{3}H]DHE) for α-adrenergic receptors—made direct binding studies possible. Lymphocytes of atopic asthmatic patients had significantly reduced numbers of β-adrenergic receptors even during periods without symptoms or medications. Similarly, patients with atopic dermatitis, in whom β-adrenergic agonists had never been used, had decreased numbers of lymphocyte β-adrenergic receptors. In patients undergoing thoracotomy for suspected lung cancer, lung specimens of inactive asthma patients had significantly reduced cAMP levels compared to those in nonasthmatics. Furthermore, in asthmatics, both lung tissue and lymphocytes had increased [^{3}H]DHE binding and decreased [^{3}H]DHA binding, which indicated a significant and mutually reciprocal shift in numbers of adrenoreceptors from beta to alpha. Similarly, an α-adrenergic shift was also observed in lymphocytes of atopic dermatitis patients, but not with other chronic dermatoses. Overall, there was a general reduction in number of both α- and β-adrenergic receptors in asthmatics. Finally, preincubation with hydrocortisone of lymphocytes from atopic individuals restored the normal ratio between α- and β-receptor numbers. Thus, atopic patients appear to be a clinical example of "receptor interconversion."

In summary, either β-adrenergic blockade or cholinergic overreactivity could produce an autonomic imbalance and could account for increased airway irritability, for hypersensitivity to allergic mediators, for reduced sensitivity to catecholamines, and possibly for increased IgE production in certain allergic individuals.

Central Nervous System Reflexes in Patients With Asthma

Central neural control of bronchi is superimposed upon the biochemical sympathetic and parasympathetic agents acting upon target cells and smooth muscle cells. There are superficial irritant receptors in bronchi of animals and of humans. These receptors are stimulated by inhalation of irritating chemicals, such as sulfur dioxide and histamine, and by physical irritants such as cold air. Afferent fibers via the vagus nerve reach the brain stem, where they synapse with efferent vagal fibers returning to the bronchial smooth muscle. Stimulation of irritant receptors leads to a vagal reflex arc via the brain stem that results in reflex bronchial smooth muscle contraction and bronchospasm. In asthmatic individuals, these irritant receptors are hyperreactive, which is apparently the basis for the methacholine test. Asthmatic patients usually respond with bronchoconstriction to inhalations of 0.25 mg methacholine, whereas the nonallergic individual will rarely react to even 25 mg of this compound. A positive methacholine inhalation test is used as a differential diagnostic test for asthma.

In a dog model of asthma, which responds with bronchoconstriction after exposure to inhaled antigen, deposition of antigen into one bronchus via a tube caused bronchospasm in both lungs. This indicates that a reflex arc controlling bronchospasm exists. As a result of an antigen-antibody reaction on the surface of a mast cell in the bronchus, histamine is released which acts upon irritant receptors to initiate the vagal reflex, resulting in bronchospasm. This is an alternative to the direct effect of histamine on bronchial smooth muscles. Parenteral or locally administered atropine blocks the bronchospasm following an antigen inhalation challenge in such asthmatic dogs and in similar allergic humans. Cooling blocks vagus impulses. In an asthmatic dog with the vagi surgically exposed and cooled with ice water, antigen-induced bronchospasm could be stopped within seconds by cooling the vagus. When the vagus was warmed, bronchospasm returned promptly, only to be terminated on recooling the vagus. The relative degree of the importance of the vagal reflex bronchospasm versus direct histamine-induced bronchospasm in asthma is currently under study by several groups.

APPROACHES TO THE TREATMENT OF ALLERGY BASED UPON THE MECHANISM OF THE REACTION

The first point of attack on the allergic mechanism is identification of the specific allergen by a careful history and skin test, with subsequent avoidance of the allergen (Fig 18–19). This approach is frequently suc-

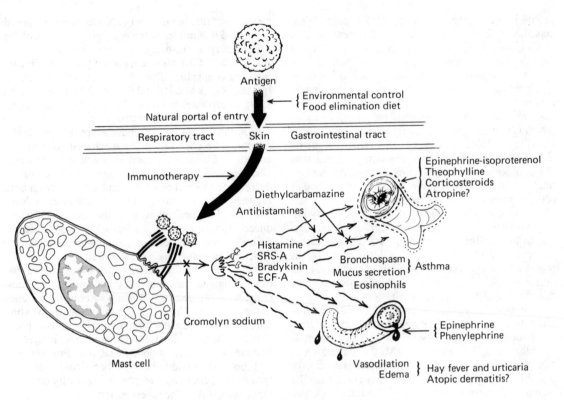

Figure 18–19. Therapeutic approaches to atopic reaction.

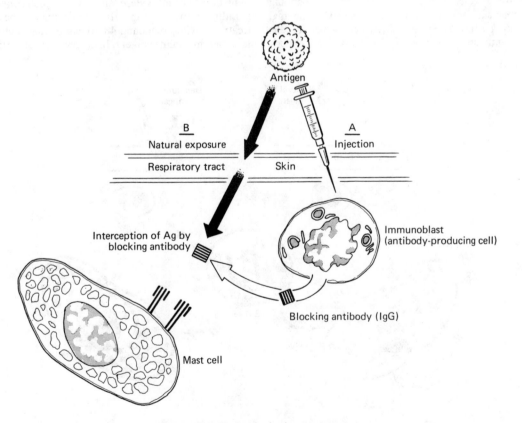

Figure 18–20. Immunization treatment.

cessful in the treatment of allergy due to animal danders, house dust, molds, or foods. The next point of
attack is the antigen-antibody reaction on the surface of
the mast cell. Immunotherapy or hyposensitizing injection of the allergen stimulates the formation of an
IgG blocking antibody, which remains in the circulation or tissues. Upon exposure to antigen, these antibodies react with the antigen, forming a complex
which is then removed by the reticuloendothelial system (Fig 18–20). If the antigen cannot reach the IgE on
the target cells, the allergic reaction does not take
place. In some patients, the clinical improvement correlates well with the degree of blocking antibodies
present; in others, there is no correlation.

A second protective mechanism achieved by immunotherapy is the induction of IgE immune tolerance, in which IgE antibody production is suppressed
by continued immunotherapy. If little or no IgE is
produced, then continued sensitization of the mast cell
does not occur. (See Chapter 28 for a discussion of the
beneficial effects of allergen injections.)

In mice, allergens that have been partially denatured with mild urea treatment appear to preferentially stimulate IgE suppressor T cells, and this results
in reduction of IgE antibodies. Mild denaturation of
allergen during ether-glycerinated saline extraction or
possibly glutaraldehyde treatment may act in a similar
manner. Therefore, injections of denatured allergen
(Fig 18–21) may preferentially stimulate IgE suppressor T cells to reestablish the normal damping
mechanism for IgE. This is in contrast to the IgG
blocking antibody system, in which helper T cells
apparently are stimulated preferentially. New experi-

mental immunotherapy methods are being proposed
and tested that influence the regulatory controls of the
IgE and IgG antibody systems, eg, D-glutamic
acid-lysine (DGL)-ragweed, and polyethylene glycol-
ragweed conjugates. These have successfully reduced
IgE antibodies in mice and dogs and have diminished
allergic responses in dogs. These methods are undergoing clinical trials in humans.

A third action of immunotherapy is nonspecific
target cell desensitization, the mechanism of which is
unknown. Children with both ragweed and *Alternaria*
allergies, when treated with ragweed alone, had a
decrease in the leukocyte histamine release with both
ragweed and *Alternaria*. In fact, histamine release
with anti-IgE antibodies was also dramatically reduced, indicating that the basophils were "desensitized." There are perhaps additional mechanisms by
which immunotherapy works as well.

The next area of allergy therapy is the enzyme
cascade leading to release of histamine from mast
cells, with attempts to stabilize lysosomal membranes
in the mast cell. Cromolyn sodium acts by preventing
the release of mediators from mast cell granules, probably by stabilizing lysosomal membranes. It does not
prevent the antigen-antibody reaction. Previously it
had been suggested that glucocorticoids stabilize
lysosomal membranes; whether this actually occurs in
humans is still under investigation.

Another action of corticosteroids is the inhibition
of histidine decarboxylase, an enzyme which converts
histidine into histamine. In guinea pigs, repeated
treatment with compound 48/80 causes mast cells to
lose their histamine content. In the presence of cortico-

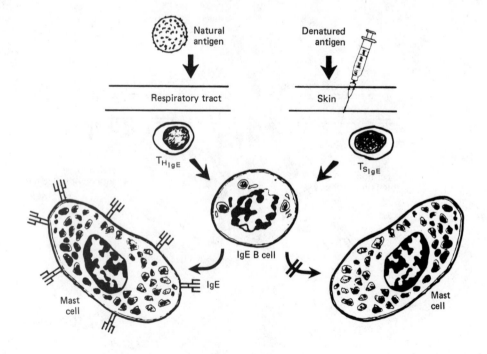

Figure 18–21. Immunotherapy stimulates IgE-specific suppressor T cells to abrogate IgE antibody production.

steroids, mast cells fail to reaccumulate histamine until corticosteroids are withdrawn. Huge concentrations of corticosteroids in humans (eg, 300 mg prednisone) could conceivably inhibit antibody formation, but this is not an effect found with the usual dosage of corticosteroids given to humans.

The next area of therapeutic attack is interference with the action of the mediators of allergy. Prior administration of antihistamines, which resemble histamine in chemical structure, blocks histamine receptors on shock organ cells. When histamine is subsequently released, the receptors are occupied, and histamine is unable to act and is promptly destroyed by monoamine oxidases. Diethylcarbamazine appears to have a similar action for SRS-A. Furthermore, the enzyme arylsulfatase A can destroy SRS-A.

Finally, one can attempt to treat allergic diseases by counteracting the effects of the allergic reaction on the shock organ. As outlined above, biochemical control of mediator release and smooth muscle contraction can be counteracted both by appropriate blocking agents (atropine to block the cholinergics, phentolamine to block the α-adrenergics) and by reinforcement of the β-adrenergic system with isoproterenol, exogenous epinephrine, and corticosteroids.

• • •

References

Ahlquist RP: A study of the adrenotropic receptors. *Am J Physiol* 1948;**153**:586.

Bennich H: Structure of IgE. *Prog Immunol* 1974;**2**:49.

Benveniste J et al: Platelet-activating factor (PAF-acether): Molecular aspects of its release and pharmacological actions. *Int Arch Allergy Appl Immunol* 1981;**66 (Suppl 1)**:121.

Berg TLO, Johansson SGO: Allergy diagnosis with the radioallergosorbent test (RAST). *J Allergy Clin Immunol* 1974; **54**:209.

Berg TLO, Johansson SG: IgE concentration in children with atopic diseases. *Int Arch Allergy Appl Immunol* 1969;**36**:219.

Berrens L: The chemistry of atopic allergens. *Monogr Allergy* 1971;**7**:1.

Butterworth AE et al: Damage to schistosomula of *Schistosoma mansoni* induced directly by eosinophil major basic protein. *J Immunol* 1979;**122**:221.

Caulfield JP et al: Secretion in disassociated human pulmonary mast cells. *J Cell Biol* 1980;**85**:299.

Frick OL, German DF, Mills J: Development of allergy in children. 1. Association with virus infections. *J Allergy Clin Immunol* 1979;**63**:228.

Gleich GJ et al: Measurement of the potency of allergy extracts by their inhibitory capacities in the radioallergosorbent test. *J Allergy Clin Immunol* 1974;**53**:158.

Gold WM, Kessler GF, Yu DYC: Role of vagus nerves in experimental asthma in allergic dogs. *J Appl Physiol* 1972; **33**:719.

Hirata F, Axelrod J: Phospholipid methylation and biological signal transmission. *Science* 1980;**209**:1082.

Holgate ST, Lewis RA, Austen KF: The role of cyclic nucleotides in mast cell activation and secretion. Page 846 in: *Progress in Immunology IV*. Fougereau M, Dausset J (editors). Academic Press, 1981.

Ishizaka K, Ishizaka T: Physicochemical properties of reaginic antibody. 1. Association of reaginic activity with an immunoglobulin other than γA or γG globulin. *J Allergy* 1966;**37**:169.

Ishizaka T: Biochemical analysis of triggering signals induced by bridging of IgE receptors. *Fed Proc* 1982;**41**:17.

Ishizaka T, Soto CS, Ishizaka K: Mechanisms of passive sensitization. 3. Number of IgE molecules and their receptor sites on human basophil granulocytes. *J Immunol* 1973;**111**:500.

Johansson SGO: Raised levels of a new immunoglobulin class (IgND) in asthma. *Lancet* 1967;**2**:951.

Katz DH: The allergic phenotype: Manifestation of "allergic breakthrough" and imbalance in normal "damping" of IgE antibody production. *Immunol Rev* 1978;**41**:77.

Kay AB: The role of the eosinophil. *J Allergy Clin Immunol* 1979;**64**:90.

Kulczycki A Jr: Role of immunoglobulin-E and immunoglobulin-E receptors in bronchial asthma. *J Allergy Clin Immunol* 1981;**68**:5.

Lee WY, Sehon AH: Suppression of reaginic antibodies. *Immunol Rev* 1978;**41**:200.

Levine BB et al: Ragweed hay fever: Genetic control and linkage to HL-A haplotypes. *Science* 1972;**178**:1201.

Levy DA: Manipulation of the immune response to antigens in the management of atopic disease in man. Page 239 in: *Conference on the Biological Role of the IgE System*. Ishizaka K, Dayton DH Jr (editors). US Department of Health, Education, & Welfare, 1973.

Lewis RA, Austen KF: Mediation of local homeostasis and inflammation by leukotrienes and other mast cell–dependent compounds. *Nature* 1981;**293**:103.

Lichtenstein LM, Norman PS: Human allergic reactions. *Am J Med* 1969;**46**:163.

Liu FT et al: Immunologic tolerance to allergenic protein determinants: Properties of tolerance induced in mice treated with conjugates of protein and a synthetic copolymer of D-glutamic acid and D-lysine (D-GL). *J Immunol* 1979;**123**:2456.

Marsh DG, Meyers DA, Bias WB: The epidemiology and genetics of atopic allergy. *N Engl J Med* 1981;**305**:1551.

May CD et al: Significance of concordant fluctuation and loss of leukocyte sensitivity to two allergens during injection therapy with one nonspecific desensitization. *J Allergy Clin Immunol* 1972;**50**:99.

Metzger H et al: Structure of the high affinity mast cell receptor for IgE. *Fed Proc* 1982;**41**:8.

Norman PS: An overview of immunotherapy. *J Allergy Clin Immunol* 1980;**65**:87.

Orange RP, Murphy RC, Austen KF: Inactivation of slow reacting substance of anaphylaxins (SRS-A) by arylsulfatases. *J Immunol* 1974;**113**:316.

Pinckard RN et al: Acetyl glyceryl ether phosphorylcholine: Platelet-activating factor. *Int Arch Allergy Appl Immunol* 1981;**66 (Suppl 1)**:127.

Samuelsson B: Leukotrienes: Mediators of allergic reactions and inflammation. *Int Arch Allergy Appl Immunol* 1981;**66 (Suppl 1)**:98.

Sullivan TJ: Diacyl glycerol metabolism and release of mediators from mast cells. Pages 229–238 in: *Biochemistry of Acute Allergic Reactions, Fourth International Symposium.* Becker EL, Austen KF (editors). Liss, 1981.

Sutherland EW: On the biological role of cyclic AMP. *JAMA* 1970;**214**:1281.

Szentivanyi A: The beta-adrenergic theory of the atopic abnormality in bronchial allergy. *J Allergy* 1968;**42**:201.

Szentivanyi A: The conformational flexibility of adrenoreceptors and the constitutional basis of atopy. *Triangle* 1979;**18**:109.

Szentivanyi A, Williams JF: The constitutional basis of atopic disease. Pages 173–210 in: *Allergic Diseases of Infancy, Childhood, and Adolescence.* Bierman CW, Pearlman DS (editors). Saunders, 1980.

Tada T, Ishizaka K: Distribution of IgE-forming cells in lymphoid tissues of humans and monkeys. *J Immunol* 1970; **104**:377.

Townley RG, Ryo UY, Kang B: Bronchial sensitivity to methacholine in asthmatic subjects free of symptoms for one to 21 years. *J Allergy* 1971;**47**:91.

Tse KS, Kepron W, Sehon AH: Effects of tolerogenic conjugates in a canine model of reaginic hypersensitivity. 1. Suppression of hapten-specific IgE antibody response. *J Allergy Clin Immunol* 1978;**61**:303.

Widdicombe JG, Kent DC, Nadel JA: Mechanism of bronchoconstriction during inhalation of dust. *J Appl Physiol* 1962;**17**:613.

Wildbolz U, Sehon AH, Kepron W: A canine model for specific suppression of IgE-mediated bronchial, hemodynamic and cutaneous hypersensitivity. *Am Rev Respir Dis* 1979;**119**:86.

Winslow CM, Austen KF: Enzymatic regulation of mast cell activation and secretion by adenylate cyclase and cyclic AMP–dependent protein kinases. *Fed Proc* 1982;**41**:22.

Immunosuppression, Immunopotentiation, & Anti-Inflammatory Drugs | 19

David R. Webb, Jr., PhD, & Alan Winkelstein, MD

Since the time of Ehrlich and Landsteiner, scientists studying immunochemistry and the biology of the immune response have been interested in how such responses might be modified. Although the initial impetus for such interest resulted from studies on the rejection of transplanted tissue, more recent interest in immunosuppression and immunopotentiation has centered on the use of such methods to more clearly define the mechanisms by which the immune system works.

In the broadest sense it could be said that interest in immunopotentiation developed first with the work of Jenner. A more systematic approach resulted from the work of Pasteur and Koch in their attempts to "vaccinate" or otherwise protect both humans and animals from disease. In this sense, any inoculation may be regarded as immunopotentiation.

Suppression or destruction of lymphoid cells had been observed as early as 1899 by Metchnikoff. Shortly thereafter Smith, in 1909, demonstrated that passively administered specific antibody given concomitantly with antigen would lead to a suppression of the immune response. Thus, immunosuppression, like immunopotentiation, was a recognized immunologic phenomenon long before anything was known about the underlying mechanisms.

IMMUNOSUPPRESSION

Given this brief introduction, it is apparent that broad definitions of both immunosuppression and immunopotentiation could include virtually all aspects of the immune response. However, for the purposes of discussion it is possible to delineate more strictly the various aspects of immunosuppression under 3 general headings: (1) natural immunologic unresponsiveness or tolerance, (2) artifically induced unresponsiveness, and (3) pathologically induced unresponsiveness (Table 19–1).

Natural Immunologic Unresponsiveness or Tolerance

Since this subject is considered in Chapter 13, little will be said about it here. Suffice it to say that many of the current concepts of immunology developed from a consideration of the failure of the host to respond to "self" antigens. The existence of a

Table 19–1. Types of immunosuppression.

Class	Mechanism of Induction
Natural immunologic unresponsiveness	Tolerance to self-antigens induced during ontogeny
Artificially induced unresponsiveness	Paralysis by antigen Use of specific antisera (antilymphocyte serum, antithymocyte serum, anti-Ig, Thy-1, etc) Excess of antigen-specific antibody Cytotoxic drugs or hormone therapy Radiation Surgery
Pathologically induced immunosuppression	Immunodeficiency disease, resulting in enhanced tumor growth, and frequent viral, bacterial, and fungal infections

natural mechanism of immunosuppression has lent much impetus to attempts to artificially manipulate the immune response.

Artificially Induced Unresponsiveness

As previously noted, as early as the 1900s experiments suggested that it was possible to artificially alter or suppress the immune response. Parker has suggested that artificially induced immunosuppression be divided into 6 general categories: (1) administration of antigen, (2) administration of specific antisera or antibody, (3) use of other "biologic" reagents such as antilymphocyte antisera, (4) use of cytotoxic drugs, (5) radiation, and (6) surgical ablation of lymphoid tissue. These areas will be considered when we examine how immunosuppression may be induced.

Pathologically Induced Immunosuppression

This subject might at first appear to be an offshoot of natural tolerance. However, the observation that many disease states can alter immunoresponsiveness has led to considerable research into the mechanisms responsible. This warrants, then, separate consideration. It has been known for many years that patients suffering from a variety of infectious diseases are more susceptible to infection with other pathogens. Proliferative disorders involving immunocompetent cells (eg, lymphomas, multiple myeloma, leukemia), as well as chronic infectious diseases such as syphilis, tuberculosis, and leprosy, may induce both specific and nonspecific suppression of responsiveness. This immunosuppression results from specific interaction of the host's immune system and the disease, leading to ablation of the "normal" immunologic function of the host. The process may be active or passive; an invading organism may produce a substance which suppresses the host's immune response or, alternatively, the host's normal mechanisms of resistance may be blocked.

Induction of Immunosuppression

A. Immunoparalysis by Antigen: The use of specific antigen as a method of inducing suppression in humans has been employed successfully for many years for allergen desensitization. This method is not infallible, however, as anyone who has ever undergone allergic desensitization will attest.

The ability of a given antigen to induce an immunosuppressive state depends on many factors. These include the antigen's chemical nature and molecular size, the route of injection, the timing of injection, and the nature of the immune response to be affected. Generally speaking, it is easier to induce both responsiveness and nonresponsiveness to moderately large antigens (MW 10^4–10^5). In addition, proteins are by far the most effective antigens and therefore are the most effective in the induction of suppression. Antigen suppression is also critically dependent on the route of injection, the most common routes being subcutaneous or intramuscular. There are many modifications of these methods, however. Two closely related antigens can be injected together, resulting in antigen competition and subsequent suppression. Antigen fragments or nonmetabolizable antigens (such as some synthetic polypeptides of D-amino acids) can also result in immune suppression. The problems of using antigen-induced suppression relate to our lack of understanding of the mechanism of suppression induced in this way. Thus, it is possible to induce hyperreactivity or sensitivity using a protocol which, theoretically, should induce suppression. This is especially dangerous if such hypersensitization leads to possible anaphylaxis.

B. Induction by Antisera or Specific Antibody: Experimental immunologists have known for some time that the development and control of some immune responses were related to changes in levels of circulating antibody. It is possible to show, for example, that the injection of specific antibody against the immunizing antigen will suppress the immune response to that antigen. The mechanism of such suppression is thought to be related to a homeostatic feedback mechanism, ie, once the immune system has produced sufficient antibody, it can shut itself off. It has been shown that antibody-producing cells will bind antigen-antibody complexes via an Fc receptor on their surface, and this may in part account for the mechanism of this mode of suppression. However, such suppression can be induced using antibody fragments minus their Fc portion. This suggests that simple

blocking of the relevant antigenic determinants, thus preventing stimulation of the relevant lymphocyte, may be the more general mechanism of action.

In practical terms, the usefulness of specific antibody has been proved by preventing Rh(D) sensitization in potentially susceptible pregnant women. This inhibition of initial sensitization serves to prevent the development of erythroblastosis fetalis in a subsequent pregnancy with an Rh-positive fetus. Since fetal cells enter maternal circulation at the time of delivery, an Rh-negative mother may be sensitized to D antigen by an Rh-positive child. If such sensitization occurs, Rh-positive antibodies are formed in subsequent pregnancies with an Rh-positive fetus. These antibodies can traverse the placenta and react with fetal red cells to produce erythroblastosis fetalis. However, the administration of specific antibodies to D antigen (RhoGAM) to the mother within 72 hours of delivery prevents sensitization and consequently inhibits the development of erythroblastosis fetalis during the next pregnancy. RhoGAM will not suppress antibody production if the mother is already sensitized to Rh antigens.

C. Antilymphocyte Serum: While the administration of specific antibody is directed at suppressing only certain specific antigen-sensitive cells, the use of antibodies directed against the lymphocytes themselves attempts to produce indiscriminate immunosuppression. When thymocytes, spleen cells, lymph node cells, or thoracic duct lymphocytes from one animal species are injected into another animal species, specific antilymphocyte serum may be generated. Such specific antiserum can be subsequently injected into the animal from which the immunizing lymphocytes are derived. This will induce a nonspecific decrease in immunoresponsiveness. For example, following injection of antilymphocyte serum, lymphocytopenia occurs, and there follows a decrease in cellular immunity. The effect on humoral responses is variable. With lymphocytes in culture, the serum can be demonstrated to lyse lymphocytes in the presence of complement or, in its absence, to cause agglutination or blast transformation. Antilymphocyte serum is effective in suppressing cellular immunity against a variety of tissue graft systems (ie, heterografts, xenografts, secondary allograft rejection). This may be related to the fact that antilymphocyte serum can suppress the response to histoincompatible antigens and thereby interfere with the ability of antigen-sensitive cells to respond to these antigens.

Interestingly, it appears that certain thymus-derived or T lymphocytes are resistant to antilymphocyte serum both in vitro and in vivo. This may account for its restricted action on the immune response.

In terms of mode of administration and therapy, the usual regimen calls for treatment with antilymphocyte serum prior to exposure to antigen as well as continued treatment following antigen exposure. Such treatment does not lead to irreversible suppression, since when the serum is discontinued a cellular immune response may be expressed. Choice of a therapeutic regimen is also frustrated by the fact that the mechanism of action of antilymphocyte serum is poorly understood. At this juncture there are no definitive data which explain all of the effects which potent sera are known to produce. A choice of regimen must be dictated by what is known about the efficiency—in terms of titer, cytotoxicity, and effects on the immune response—of a particular batch of serum. Furthermore, since antilymphocyte serum is an antiserum raised in a heterologous species, the question of serum sickness arises; there may be complications due to nephritis resulting from repeated injections of a foreign serum. However, it appears that at least some of the danger can be abated by the concomitant use of corticosteroids.

Antithymocyte globulin (ATG), prepared by immunizing horses with human thymus cells, is now being clinically evaluated to treat renal allograft rejection reactions. This preparation is also used experimentally to treat GVH disease after bone marrow transplantation and in selected cases of aplastic anemia. In the latter condition, it is thought that impaired hematopoiesis in some individuals represents inhibition of stem cell differentiation by suppressor T cells.

In addition to specific antibody and antilymphocyte serum, there appears to be an inhibitory serum factor present in the α-globulin fraction of serum. Its usefulness, however, remains to be determined.

D. Cytotoxic Drugs or Hormone-Induced Immunosuppression: The immunosuppressive properties of both cytotoxic agents and corticosteroids have been defined in animal studies; these agents are effective in inhibiting both humoral and cellular responses to a variety of test antigens. They do not inhibit all immune responses equally, however. Several factors combine to determine their potency with respect to a selected immune response. These factors, which also affect their clinical usefulness, can be summarized as follows:

(1) A primary immune response is more readily inhibited than a secondary or anamnestic reaction. Drugs that are effective in suppressing an immune response in an unsensitized animal generally show little or no activity in a sensitized animal. The same effect is observed in patients. For example, the primary immune response elicited by a renal transplant is impaired by a combination of azathioprine and corticosteroids. However, if the recipient has been presensitized to donor histocompatibility antigens, these agents are not capable of inhibiting the transplant rejection reaction.

(2) The stages of an immune response differ markedly in their susceptibility to immunosuppressants. The cellular events associated with an antigenic challenge can be subdivided into 2 phases (Fig 19–1), designated the induction phase and the established or effector phase. The former is the interval between sensitization and generation of the final immune effec-

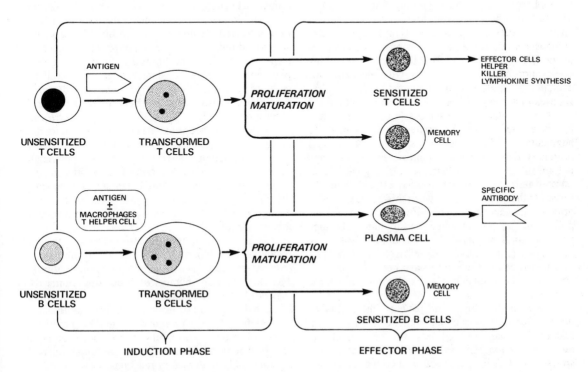

Figure 19–1. The development of an immune response. The period from antigenic challenge through the proliferative expansion of transformed lymphocytes is considered the **induction phase**. The period following cellular expansion is defined as the **established (effector) phase**.

tors; it is characterized by the rapid proliferative expansion of precursor cells. Once the final effectors have been formed, the reaction is considered to have entered an established phase. Most immunosuppressive agents are effective if used either immediately before the antigen or during the induction phase; they are much less active once the reaction has entered the established phase. Furthermore, once a population of memory lymphocytes has been generated, it is almost impossible to erase immunologic memory.

(3) The effectiveness of immunosuppressive agents in a primary response is highly dependent on the timing of their administration relative to initial antigenic challenge. Based on their effective interval, immunosuppressive agents are divided into 3 groups: **Group I:** Agents which elicit their maximum immunosuppressive activity when administered just prior to the antigen. These agents are considerably less effective if used after the immunologic challenge. Included in this group are corticosteroids, irradiation, and the alkylating agent mechlorethamine. **Group II:** Agents which exert immunosuppressive properties only if administered in the period immediately following the immunologic challenge. Specifically, these compounds do not block reactions if used prior to the antigen. Agents in this group include the cytotoxic metabolites such as mercaptopurine (6-MP) and its derivative azathioprine. **Group III:** Agents which show inhibitory activity if administered either prior to or after antigenic stimulation. However, these drugs are more immunosuppressive following the challenge. Cyclophosphamide is the major drug in this category.

(4) Immunosuppressive drugs may exert a differential toxicity for T and B lymphocytes. Cyclophosphamide causes a proportionately greater reduction in the number of B cells than T cells. This observation correlates positively with the ability of cyclophosphamide to suppress humoral antibody responses to a greater extent than cellular reactions.

(5) In certain circumstances, a paradoxic effect may be elicited by immunosuppressive drugs, namely, augmentation of a particular response. It was noted originally that irradiation administered several days before an antigenic challenge led to a greater than normal antibody response. Similar effects were observed with mercaptopurine when this agent was used prior to antigen challenge. With selected treatment protocols, cyclophosphamide can simultaneously suppress humoral responses and augment delayed hypersensitivity responses to the same antigen. The heightened cellular reactions have been attributed in part to cyclophosphamide's toxicity for suppressor lymphocytes.

(6) In both animals and patients, the ability to inhibit manifestations of an immune response may result from pharmacologic activities other than immunosuppression. Expression of most immune responses involves the participation of both immunologically competent cells and nonspecific effectors such as neutrophils and monocytes. The numbers or functions of these effectors can be altered by immunosuppressive drugs, an effect which can lessen or obliterate the expression of a particular response. Thus, apparent immunosuppression can result from the anti-inflammatory properties of a particular agent.

1. Corticosteroids–Adrenocortical hormones are widely used to treat disorders of aberrant immunity. Many different corticosteroid preparations are available and differ in potency as anti-inflammatory and salt-retaining agents. However, in equivalent quantities, the effects of all steroid preparations on immunity and inflammation appear similar.

Until recently the immunosuppressive activities of corticosteroids in humans were poorly defined. This resulted partly from failure to recognize differences between species in the susceptibility of lymphocytes to steroid-induced lysis. Lymphoid cells in the mouse, rat, and rabbit are very susceptible to these hormones, and drug administration leads to pronounced cell destruction. By contrast, normal lymphocytes from guinea pigs, monkeys, and humans are more resistant to steroids, and therapy does not cause massive lympholysis. Not all human lymphocytes are resistant; the malignant cells in acute lymphoblastic leukemia are very sensitive to steroids, and chronic lymphatic leukemia cells are moderately sensitive.

A prompt but transient reduction in blood lymphocytes occurs following a single large dose of steroids (Fig 19–2). Maximum lymphopenia occurs 4–6 hours after drug administration. Both T and B cells are affected, and the magnitude of the T cell reduction is significantly greater. However, the acute reduction in circulatory cells does not result from lympholysis. Rather, lymphopenia is due to a redistribution or altered circulation, and within 24 hours after steroid administration blood lymphocytes have returned to normal concentrations. Studies in guinea pigs, another steroid-resistant species, suggest that T cells are temporarily sequestered in the bone marrow.

Steroids also markedly affect the distribution of other circulating leukocytes. There is a temporary increase in blood neutrophils. This effect is due to 2 factors: an increased release of cells from the marrow and demargination of those cells which are adherent to the endothelium of small blood vessels. Since neutrophils in the marginal pool are potentially able to leave the vascular compartment, this reduction may adversely affect the host's ability to respond to inflammatory stimuli.

In parallel with the decrease in circulating lymphocytes, both blood monocytes and eosinophils are reduced, primarily as a result of redistribution of cells. The changes in the number of circulating monocytes may adversely affect their ability to participate in delayed hypersensitivity reactions. Other studies have shown that steroids profoundly alter the functional activities of both neutrophils and monocytes; this effect further limits their ability to participate in both immune and inflammatory reactions.

The effects of corticosteroids on human immune responses are still incompletely defined. Administration of these agents for several days is associated with a

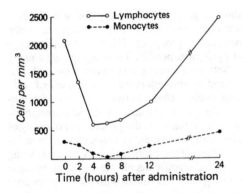

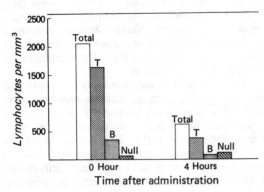

Figure 19–2. The effect of hydrocortisone administration on circulating lymphocytes and monocytes. Hydrocortisone, 400 mg, was administered intravenously in a single dose to a normal volunteer. The upper panel shows the effect on the total lymphocyte and monocyte counts. The lower panel shows the effect on circulating thymus–derived (T) and bone marrow–derived (B) lymphocytes as well as lymphocytes without detectable surface markers (null cells) 4 hours after drug administration. T lymphocytes were measured by the sheep erythrocyte rosette assay; and B lymphocytes were measured by the complement receptor assay. (Reproduced, with permission, from Fauci AS, Dale DC, Balow JE: Glucocorticosteroid therapy: Mechanisms of action and clinical considerations. *Ann Intern Med* 1976; 84:304.)

modest decrease in serum immunoglobulin concentrations. In one study, IgG concentration was modestly reduced; IgA and IgM levels were only minimally depressed. This effect may be due, in part, to an increased rate of immunoglobulin catabolism. However, in vitro studies using cultured spleen cells indicated that steroids can directly inhibit the synthesis of IgG.

Short-term human experiments suggest that the immediate effects of corticosteroids on humoral immune responses do not result from a decrease in specific antibody titers. In immunologic disorders such as idiopathic thrombocytopenic purpura (ITP) and autoimmune hemolytic anemia (AIHA), the early beneficial effects accrue from a reduction in the amount of antibody bound to the target cell or interference with the ability of reticuloendothelial cells to bind and

phagocytose antibody-coated cells. Both activities serve to reduce the rate of excessive cell destruction.

In disorders caused by the pathologic effects of immune complexes, steroids may also inhibit the release of lysosomal enzymes by neutrophils. This process is the final step in producing tissue damage. Similarly, allergic reactions may be inhibited by stabilization of intracellular membranes in mast cells and basophils, which impairs the cellular release of vasoactive mediators.

Cell-mediated immune responses are also inhibited by corticosteroids. Patients may manifest an inability to express cutaneous hypersensitivity despite previous sensitization (anergy). This effect is not immediately apparent. It generally requires 10–14 days of steroid therapy before skin test reactivity is impaired.

Several different effects of steroids may contribute to impaired cellular immunity. These include (1) inhibiting the migration of T cells to the sites of antigen deposition; (2) preventing lymphocytes from releasing lymphokines which are needed to recruit additional cells to participate in the reaction; (3) interfering with lymphocyte-induced target cell lysis; (4) reducing the number of monocytes available to nonspecifically affect the response; and (5) blocking the local interaction between lymphocytes and monocytes. This inhibition in cell-mediated responses can lead to overwhelming infections, including those due to intracellular organisms which do not usually cause disease in normal subjects.

In many disorders with an apparent immunologic basis, corticosteroids have proved effective inhibitors of disease activity. They are more effective in controlling acute inflammatory processes than in preventing chronic complications. For example, they can inhibit the acute manifestations of rheumatic fever and rheumatoid arthritis but are of limited value in preventing chronic valvular heart disease or deforming arthritis. Long-term steroid therapy is not innocuous. Although a discussion of the many toxic effects of steroids is beyond the scope of this section, it is important to recognize that, in many situations, high-dose corticosteroid therapy administered for prolonged periods can cause more morbidity than the underlying disease.

In an attempt to increase the ability of corticosteroids to inhibit expressions of aberrant immune responses, several investigators have employed "megadose" quantities of these agents, eg, methylprednisolone, 1–2 g intravenously. Despite several encouraging (uncontrolled) reports, this form of therapy has not been clearly shown to be more efficacious than conventional therapy. Megadose therapy and conventional therapy exert comparable effects on immune function.

2. Cytotoxic drugs–Immunosuppression can also be achieved with the use of cytotoxic agents designed to kill immunologically competent cells. These agents are not selectively toxic for competent lymphocytes but are potentially able to kill any cell which has the capacity to replicate. Although originally developed for their anticancer effects, animal studies indicated that these drugs possessed significant immunosuppressive activity. Clinically, these drugs were used initially to inhibit transplantation rejection reactions. Their use was later extended to the treatment of autoimmune diseases. Although most cytotoxins possess immunosuppressive properties, only 2, azathioprine and cyclophosphamide, have been used extensively in treating patients.

The ability of a cytotoxic drug to reduce the number of immunologically reactive cells depends on several interacting factors. Two important determinants are the proliferative status of the target cell and the cell cycle specificity of the agent. The latter refers to the phase of the cell's mitotic cycle in which a particular drug can exert its toxic effect. The mitotic cycle has been divided into 4 components, termed G_1, S, G_2, and M (Fig 19–3). G_1 is the stage during which the cell is actively preparing to reduplicate its DNA content. This is followed by the S, or DNA synthetic, phase. Once the cell has completed this synthesis, the cell enters a G_2, or premitotic, stage during which it is preparing to divide. The final phase is the M, or mitotic, period, in which there is equal nuclear and cytoplasmic division.

Cytotoxic drugs have been categorized into 3 groups based on their ability to kill cells in different phases of the mitotic cycle: (1) **Phase-specific drugs** are selectively toxic during a discrete period of the mitotic cycle. Most of the drugs in this group are S phase toxins; they specifically interfere with DNA synthesis. Azathioprine, mercaptopurine, methotrexate, and cytarabine are examples of phase-specific immunosuppressants which are primarily S phase toxins. (2) **Cycle-specific drugs** show broader toxicities. They can kill both intermitotic and cycling cells.

They show a preferential toxicity for actively proliferating elements, and cyclophosphamide is the major drug in this group. (3) The third group is designated as **cycle-nonspecific**. These agents are equally toxic to both proliferating and intermitotic cells. Irradiation and mechlorethamine have this effect.

These cycling characteristics are major determinants of both lymphocytotoxic and immunosuppressive activities of cytotoxic drugs. The vast majority of immunologically competent lymphocytes are in an intermitotic phase of the proliferative cycle, and during this time phase-specific agents are not toxic to these cells. Consequently, treatment with these agents does not acutely reduce the number of blood or tissue lymphocytes. By contrast, cycle-specific and cycle-nonspecific agents are effective against intermitotic lymphocytes and will cause a generalized depletion of immunologically competent cells. This lympholysis is a dose-related phenomenon.

Similar considerations also apply to the ability of cytotoxic agents to inhibit immune responses. The proliferative activities of lymphocytes in an immune response can be related to the previously described phases of the reaction (Fig 19–1). Prior to antigen stimulation, potentially responsive lymphocytes are in an intermitotic phase of their cycle. These cells remain in this dormant period until they contact the appropriate antigen, when they transform into actively proliferating cells. They undergo several successive mitotic divisions after which they mature into nonproliferating effector cells. In cell-mediated reactions the effector cells are intermitotic lymphocytes, while in humoral responses they are plasma cells programmed to secrete antibodies specifically reacting with the antigen. Plasma cells are end-stage cells and lack the capacity to replicate further.

In animal models, the cell cycle–cytotoxic

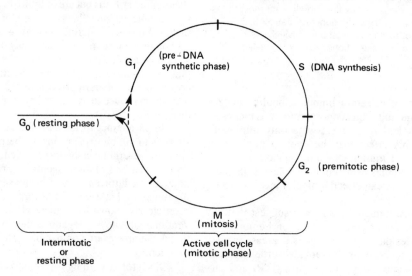

Figure 19–3. Mitotic cycle: Drugs which are selectively toxic for cells in a discrete phase of their cycle are designated **phase-specific agents**; most exert their toxicity for cells in the S phase. **Cycle-specific agents** are toxic for both intermitotic and proliferating cells but show greater toxicity for those in active cycle. **Cycle-nonspecific agents** show equal toxicity for all cells regardless of the mitotic activity.

Table 19–2. Disorders in which cytotoxic drugs are probably effective or of doubtful value.

I. **Disorders in which cytotoxins are probably effective**
   Rheumatoid arthritis
   Systemic lupus erythematosus
   Lipoid nephrosis
   Membranous glomerulonephritis
   Wegener's granulomatosis
   Chronic active hepatitis
   Inflammatory bowel disease
   Autoimmune hemolytic anemia
   Immune thrombocytopenia
   Circulating anticoagulants
II. **Disorders in which cytotoxins are of doubtful value**
   Membranoproliferative (hypocomplementemic) glomerulo-
      nephritis
   Progressive systemic sclerosis
   Sjögren's syndrome

characteristics of drugs closely correlate with their effective immunosuppressant intervals. The cycle-nonspecific agents are maximally inhibitory when employed immediately prior to antigenic challenge. They correspond to the group I agents as defined previously. These agents exert their immunosuppressive activities by depleting intermitotic lymphocytes, including those potentially responsive to the test antigen. Phase-specific drugs belong to group II agents and are active only in the period after antigenic challenge when the responding cells are in a replicating phase. Because of the restrictive toxicity, these agents are ineffective if administered before the immunologic challenge. Cycle-specific drugs correspond to group III agents and are effective both before and after antigenic challenge. This can be attributed to their toxicity for both intermitotic and proliferating cells. Their maximum activity as immunosuppressants occurs when they are administered after antigen challenge. This agrees with their increased cytotoxic activity for replicating cells.

Cytotoxic drugs have been used widely to treat autoimmune disorders. A partial list is shown in Table 19–2. It is difficult to ascertain their true effectiveness, since there are few controlled trials. Many of these diseases show an unpredictable course with both spontaneous remissions and exacerbations, and one must interpret cautiously claims regarding the beneficial effects of cytotoxic agents. Another limitation is the lack of specific laboratory tests which can accurately monitor changes in the undesired or pathologic immune response. Despite these limitations, it appears that cytotoxins are potentially useful in several disorders.

a. Azathioprine–Azathioprine, a nitroimidazole derivative of the purine antagonist mercaptopurine (6-MP), is classified as a phase-specific compound. In vivo, it is rapidly converted into the parent compound. Although there are conflicting data, most investigators believe that the addition of the imidazole side chain improves the immunosuppressive potency and increases the therapeutic:toxic ratio.

Biochemically, both azathioprine and 6-MP act by competitive enzyme inhibition to block synthesis of inosinic acid, the precursor of the purine compounds adenylic acid and guanylic acid. These effects are manifested primarily by a decrease in the rate of cell replication. Although immunosuppression may result from the drug's toxicity for antigen-responsive cells in an active phase of the replicative cycle, there is evidence suggesting alternative modes of action. It has been suggested that azathioprine may bind to and inactivate antigen receptor sites present on T lymphocytes. Evidence from other studies indicates that azathioprine may also markedly reduce the number of K lymphocytes, which are those cells believed responsible for antibody-dependent cellular cytotoxicity reactions. In addition to their immunosuppressive activities, both azathioprine and 6-MP have potent anti-inflammatory properties.

Azathioprine and the corticosteroids in combination are the prime drugs to inhibit rejection of organ transplants. More recently, they have been employed to suppress manifestations of several autoimmune disorders. A significant number of patients with severe rheumatoid arthritis experienced clinical improvement in their disease. Remissions have also been reported in patients with autoimmune blood dyscrasias, Wegener's granulomatosis, and systemic lupus erythematosus. Azathioprine may permit the use of reduced amounts of corticosteroids in the treatment of diseases such as chronic active hepatitis. Azathioprine is administered orally, and the maximum beneficial effects generally require continuous therapy for several weeks.

The primary lymphocytotoxic effects of azathioprine are directed against actively replicating cells, and short therapeutic courses do not reduce the number of small T or B cells in the peripheral blood. The number of large lymphocytes is decreased, and these are believed to be transformed cells which have entered an active proliferative cycle following exposure to appropriate antigens. Azathioprine also reduces the number of circulating neutrophils and monocytes. This effect results from cytotoxic activity against hematopoietic precursors.

b. Cyclophosphamide–Cyclophosphamide is the other cytotoxic drug used extensively for immunosuppression. Animal studies indicate that this cycle-specific agent is a highly effective immunosuppressant. Immunosuppression for many antigens can be induced readily, and its therapeutic ratio is very high. This alkylating agent has more sustained suppressive activity for humoral antibody responses, an observation which is in accord with its greater effect on B lymphocytes. The effect on cell-mediated responses is variable; some responses are inhibited, whereas others are augmented. Enhanced cellular responses may be due to the drug's toxicity for suppressor lymphocytes.

Cyclophosphamide is not highly effective in preventing transplant rejection reactions and thus is not

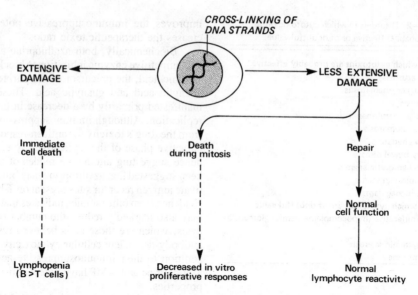

Figure 19–4. The effect of cyclophosphamide on lymphocytes appears primarily due to cross-linking DNA strands. As shown, this can result in lympholysis and decreased in vitro proliferative response. In cells which are not extensively damaged, repair can occur and the lymphocyte regains its full proliferative capacity. Because of their slow rate of recovery, the effect on B cells is more pronounced than that on T cells.

used extensively in these circumstances. By contrast, it has been employed successfully in the treatment of several disorders believed to result from aberrant immunity. The most convincing evidence for beneficial effects has been reported in patients with Wegener's granulomatosis, in selected patients with severe rheumatoid arthritis, in children with nephrotic syndrome (who are either unresponsive to steroids or who relapse if corticosteroids are discontinued), and in patients with autoimmune blood disorders such as idiopathic thrombocytopenic purpura. Its effectiveness in other diseases, such as systemic lupus erythematosus, is more controversial. There is considerable dispute as to its value in lupus nephritis.

Cyclophosphamide can be administered either orally or intravenously. Cyclophosphamide is inactive until metabolized by the liver. Although the active moiety has not been identified, it is present in the circulation for only a few hours after administration. The predominant cytotoxic effects are due to the ability of the drug to cross-link DNA. This effect may immediately kill an affected cell, render it susceptible to death during mitosis, or, if DNA repair can be effected, permit normal cellular activities (Fig 19–4). In patients treated with large doses of cyclophosphamide, these changes are manifested by lymphopenia and a transient impairment in the ability of residual cells to proliferate in vitro. Both T and B cells are susceptible to this alkylating agent. The drug's selectivity for B cells appears to result from a slower rate of recovery by these cells. Studies in patients with connective tissue diseases indicate that therapy for several weeks will significantly reduce immunoglobulin concentrations and autoantibody titers.

c. Cyclosporin A–Cyclosporin A, a cyclic polypeptide, has received wide attention as a new and promising immunosuppressant. This drug differs from conventional agents in that it is not cytotoxic for lymphocytes and has no antimitotic activity. Furthermore, it exhibits a high degree of selectivity; its principal activities appear to be directed at a specific subpopulation of T lymphocytes called T helper (inducer) cells. To date, most investigators have concentrated on assessing its ability to suppress allograft rejection reactions. In virtually every model tested, treatment markedly prolongs graft survival; this includes skin, organ (kidney, liver, heart, pancreas), and bone marrow transplants. Comparative studies indicate that cyclosporin A is more potent than azathioprine, the agent usually employed to suppress rejection reactions. The immune inhibitory activities of cyclosporin A are usually reversible; once therapy is discontinued, most transplants are rapidly rejected.

In addition to inhibiting allograft rejection reactions, cyclosporin A also suppresses expression of several experimental autoimmune syndromes, including adjuvant-induced arthritis, experimental allergic encephalomyelitis, and experimental uveitis. It is also a potent inhibitor of GVH disease. Cyclosporin A's effects on humoral immune responses are variable. It suppresses antibody production to thymus-dependent antigens such as sheep erythrocytes in mice. Examination of cellular components of this reaction, however, indicates that this inhibitory activity is primarily due to an effect on T helper cells. Other experiments have shown that only minimal reduction of antibody synthesis occurred in cyclosporin-treated mice challenged with thymus-independent antigens such as bacterial endotoxin.

Table 19–3. Summary of effects of immunosuppressive drugs.*

	Cyclophosphamide	Azathioprine and Mercaptopurine	Methotrexate
Decreased primary immune response	+++	+++	+++
Decreased secondary immune response	++	+	+
Decreased immune complexes in NZB mice	++	0	0
Anti-inflammatory effect	+	+++	++
Decreased delayed hypersensitivity	± to ++	+	±
Lymphopenia	+++	+	±
Inhibition of mitogenic responses	+++	0	0
Selectivity for B cells	++	0	0

*Adapted in part from Hurd ER: Immunosuppressive and anti-inflammatory properties of cyclophosphamide, azathioprine and methotrexate. *Arthritis Rheum* 1973;16:84.

The mechanisms by which cyclosporin A exerts its immunosuppressive activities are not fully known. It appears that one effect is to inhibit the initial phases of lymphocyte transformation. The primary targets of the drug are T helper cells; T suppressor cells are generally spared. Recent studies suggest that at low doses, cyclosporin A may act by blocking lymphocyte receptors for T cell growth factor (TCGF); this lymphokine is important in the proliferative expansion of antigen-sensitive cells. Higher drug quantities also impair TCGF release.

In many respects, cyclosporin A has distinct advantages as an immunosuppressant. It minimally suppresses hematopoiesis; therefore, treated patients do not become neutropenic or thrombocytopenic. Furthermore, preliminary data suggest that the incidence of infection in cyclosporin-treated transplant recipients is less than that seen in a comparable group of patients receiving azathioprine and prednisone. Nevertheless, there are significant toxicities associated with therapy. The agent causes hepatic dysfunction, including abnormal liver function tests, focal hepatic necrosis, and cholestasis. It also has toxic effects on the kidney. Most disturbing, initial studies suggest that there is a high incidence of lymphoma in treated patients; this frequency may approach 10% during the first year after renal transplantation. Thus, more thorough clinical trials, including long-term studies, are required before this agent can be accepted for widespread clinical use.

d. Other agents–Two other cytotoxic drugs, chlorambucil and methotrexate, have been occasionally used as immunosuppressants. Chlorambucil, an alkylating agent, might prove to be an acceptable alternative to cyclophosphamide, since the major pharmacologic effects of both are similar. In addition, chlorambucil does not cause certain severe side-effects sometimes associated with cyclophosphamide. These include hemorrhagic cystitis and alopecia (see below). Unfortunately, the lymphocytotoxic effects of chlorambucil occur at a slow rate, and its potency as an immunosuppressant is considerably less than cyclophosphamide. Current therapeutic trials with chlorambucil in patients with autoimmune disorders are too preliminary to permit accurate assessment of its clinical effectiveness.

Methotrexate is a phase-specific compound which acts by inhibiting folate metabolism. The drug specifically blocks the enzyme dihydrofolate reductase, which catalyzes an essential reaction in DNA biosynthesis. Methotrexate is a potent immunosuppressant which can inhibit both humoral and cellular reactions. It has not been used extensively in treating autoimmune diseases. This may be due to the numerous side-effects associated with its administration, which include megaloblastic anemia, mucositis, and progressive liver fibrosis. Table 19–3 summarizes the comparative properties of cyclophosphamide, azathioprine, and methotrexate.

New immunosuppressive drugs showing considerable promise in animal studies but not yet fully evaluated clinically include procarbazine, oxisuran, and niridazole. All of these agents appear to exhibit some specificity for immune responses mediated by T lymphocytes. Of these, niridazole appears to be the most promising. In animal studies, this agent, in combination with azathioprine and prednisone, is highly effective in preventing graft rejection reactions.

Another group of compounds with immune-modulating properties are the E series of prostaglandins. There are considerable data from in vitro experiments indicating that prostaglandins may be normal regulatory substances. Studies in animals have shown that prostaglandin E_1 (PGE$_1$) administered in pharmacologic quantities (100–1000 times endogenous amounts) alters both immune responsiveness and the course of autoimmune disease. Depending upon the immune response evaluated, PGE$_1$ can enhance or suppress test reactions. More significantly, this compound can prolong survival in NZB/NZW mice, an animal model of SLE, and can ameliorate adjuvant arthritis in the rat. Whether these studies have clinical applicability is not presently known.

e. Toxicity of cytotoxic drugs–As a group, the cytotoxic agents cause multiple and potentially serious side-effects. The major toxic effects of this group of agents are listed in Table 19–4. These drugs are toxic to any rapidly dividing cell population, but the 3 tissues most severely affected are the bone marrow, the gastrointestinal epithelium, and the germinal cells of the gonads. Bone marrow suppression is potentially

Table 19–4. Undesired effects of cytotoxic immunosuppression.

1. Bone marrow depression (neutropenia, thrombocytopenia, anemia).
2. Gastrointestinal disturbances.
3. Sterility.
4. Infections resulting from generalized depression of immune responses.
5. Increased risk of malignancies, especially lymphomas.
6. Selective toxicities of individual drugs.
   a. Azathioprine–Hepatic dysfunction.
   b. Cyclophosphamide–Hemorrhagic cystitis, alopecia.

the most serious toxic reaction and is a dose-related phenomenon. Since there is a delay between the destruction of proliferating precursors and the appearance of cytopenias, the effect on bone marrow does not manifest itself immediately. Typical gastrointestinal manifestations may be quite severe and include transient symptoms such as nausea and vomiting, abdominal pain, and diarrhea. Administration of cytotoxic drugs or other alkylating agents also interferes with gonadal function, leading to sterility in both males and females. Cyclophosphamide can also cause hemorrhagic cystitis and alopecia.

Long-term complications of cytotoxic therapy include susceptibility to infections—particularly those due to opportunistic organisms—and an increased risk of cancer. Studies in renal transplant patients suggest that a typical timetable characterizes the infectious complications. In particular, the period between 1 and 6 months posttransplantation is the most critical in terms of life-threatening infections. This interval coincides with maximum use of immunosuppressive drugs. During this period, transplantation patients are particularly susceptible to infection with a wide range of opportunistic organisms. One common infecting organism is cytomegalic inclusion virus (CMV); clinical or laboratory evidence of CMV infection can be found in 60–96% of transplanted patients. A lower risk is seen in a late transplant period (after 6 months); this probably relates to the lesser amounts of immunosuppression required for graft survival. However, these individuals are still prone to chronic viral infections, particularly hepatitis and CMV, and opportunistic organisms, especially *Cryptococcus neoformans*.

There is a greatly increased risk of cancer in transplant patients receiving immunosuppressive drugs—approximately 100 times that of age-matched controls. Furthermore, the frequency increases with the length of time from transplantation. One series reported an 11% incidence at 1 year and a 24% rate after 5 years.

The types of cancer seen in transplant patients differ considerably from those in the general population. Skin cancers are most common—typically squamous cell, often multicentric, and usually of low-grade malignancy. Lymphomas account for about one-third of nondermatologic malignancies in transplant patients. Several features of these tumors are

unusual. They are usually of the histiocytic or immunoblastic cell types. In contrast, Hodgkin's disease, the most common lymphoma in the general population, accounts for less than 2% of transplant-related tumors. In the graft recipients, the interval between transplantation and the appearance of lymphoma is short, averaging 27 months. Another unique feature is their tendency to involve the central nervous system; this site was affected in more than 40% of patients with lymphoma. Frequently, the central nervous system was the only area of involvement. To date, the pathogenic basis for the increased risk of lymphoid neoplasms is not defined. However, both the chronic antigenic stimuli resulting from the organ graft and the continued need for suppression of the recipient's immune system undoubtedly are of importance.

Unfortunately, comparative data have not been compiled in patients with autoimmune diseases receiving immunosuppressive therapy. The incidence of lymphoma may be particularly difficult to calculate, as these patients appear to be predisposed to these neoplasms even in the absence of therapy designed to inhibit immune responses.

Another potential problem in patients receiving immunosuppressives, particularly those treated with alkylating agents such as cyclophosphamide, is the occurrence of acute myeloblastic leukemia (AML). This disease is uncommon in transplant patients, but high incidences have been reported in many groups of cancer patients receiving these cytotoxic drugs. In several series, the incidence approaches 10%. Speculation about the factors leading to leukemia includes consideration of the radiomimetic properties of the cell cycle–specific compounds, their ability to cause chromosomal breaks and other genetic injuries, and the chronic suppression of the immune defense system. Although the risk of AML in treated patients with nonmalignant diseases has not been defined, it must be considered a serious risk.

E. Plasma Exchange: The advent of mechanical blood cell separators has led to the introduction of plasma exchange as a potential means of treating some immunologically related disorders. These instruments function by continuously removing and centrifuging large volumes of blood; the cellular elements are then returned to the patient. Plasma containing either pathogenic autoantibodies or toxic immune complexes is discarded, and the blood volume is restored with volume expanders, (eg, fresh frozen plasma, 5% albumin). A typical exchange procedure will replace 50–60% of the plasma volume.

Although trials of plasma exchange therapy have been initiated in several centers, the overall effectiveness has not been evaluated. Typically, this form of therapy is reserved for the management of patients with severe immunologic disorders, usually during acute exacerbations. Uncontrolled studies suggest that it can produce striking clinical responses in a variety of disorders, including Goodpasture's syndrome, myasthenia gravis, lupus nephritis, and rheumatoid arthritis.

The major advantage of plasma exchange is its ability to rapidly decrease the serum concentrations of pathogenic factors. Because of its predominantly intravascular location, IgM is more effectively removed than IgG, which is distributed throughout extracellular spaces. The concentration of circulating immune complexes can also be effectively lowered. Because immunoglobulin synthesis is not altered, reductions are transient, and it is usual to administer a cytotoxic immunosuppressant concomitantly.

F. Radiation: Suppression of the immune response also occurs when animals or humans are subject to stress following surgical manipulation or x-ray irradiation. Immune suppression induced by trauma is a poorly defined area of study which has not been systematically explored; however, some information is available on the suppression following irradiation.

In experimental animal models, irradiation with x-rays has long been used to suppress immune responses or to study lymphocytic cells required for developing immune responses. The sum of this evidence indicates that most lymphocytes are sensitive to x-rays. Radiation induces profound lymphopenia in lymphoid organs and in the general circulation and suppresses most immunocompetent cell functions. However, there does exist a population of lymphocytes which are radiation-resistant and which have specialized functions in the immune response.

G. Total Nodal Irradiation: Fractionated irradiation, administered to all major lymph node areas, has proved to be a highly effective means of treating patients with disseminated Hodgkin's disease. In the course of patient follow-up studies, it was observed that these individuals showed evidence of long-lasting immunosuppression. Among the findings were a prolonged period of lymphopenia, decreased numbers of circulating T cells, B cell lymphocytosis, and impaired reactivities to both polyclonal T cell mitogens and allogeneic cells. Many of these abnormalities persisted for as long as 10 years following treatment.

In order to more systematically evaluate this means of achieving therapeutic immunosuppression, correlative animal studies were undertaken. In rodents, this type of divided, low-dose radiation to the major lymph node–bearing areas proved to be highly inhibitory to all components of the immune system. Treated animals showed profound decreases in humoral responses and prolonged survival of skin allografts. One of the most interesting phenomena was the ability to transplant bone marrow across major histocompatibility barriers. In murine studies, the recipients were treated with 3400 rads (17 treatments); this was followed by marrow infusion from allogeneic donors. Not only was the marrow accepted, but the recipients did not develop GVH disease. It appears that the conditioning regimen produced a change in the host's immune system such that immunologically competent cells in the donor's marrow were prevented from reacting against the recipients' antigens. These animals proved to be true chimeras in that they accepted skin grafts from mice of the marrow donor strain but rejected third-party grafts.

Other studies indicate that total nodal irradiation can be used to treat the lupus-like syndromes which occur in NZB/W and MRL/l mice. In fact, this immunosuppressive regimen shows distinct advantages over many other forms of therapy in that it can reverse established disease; it serves both to suppress disease manifestations and to greatly prolong survival.

The basis for the sustained immunosuppressive activities of total nodal irradiation has not been fully defined. Comparative studies indicate that it acts differently than conventional whole body irradiation, in which the entire dose is administered at one time. For example, marrow recipients after whole body irradiation develop fatal GVH disease; this complication is not seen after total nodal irradiation. One concept used to explain its effectiveness is the induction of suppressor cells. Both nonspecific and antigen-specific suppressor cells have been identified in treated animals.

Preliminary clinical trials of total nodal irradiation are now in progress. It is being tested in the treatment of severe rheumatoid arthritis and systemic lupus erythematosus with nephritis and in the prevention of renal transplantation rejection reactions. Further controlled trials are needed before its clinical potential can be adequately evaluated, but initial results are encouraging.

IMMUNOPOTENTIATION

The obvious counterpoint to immunosuppression is immunopotentiation or enhancement of the immune response. By enhancement we may mean an increase in the rate at which the immune response develops, an increase in the intensity or level of the response, a prolongation of the response, or the development of a response to an otherwise nonimmunogenic substance.

The agents which enhance immune responses are generally termed adjuvants and may be divided into 2 categories: (1) general potentiation refers to substances which may enhance both cellular and humoral immune responses to wide variety of antigens; (2) specific potentiation deals with a special class of molecules which enhance specific responses to certain antigens only (Table 19–5).

In concert with studies on immunosuppression, experiments dealing with potentiation have added significant contributions to our understanding of how the immune system functions. As suggested earlier, everything—including vaccination—which involves a stimulation of a previously nonimmune state could be termed potentiation. For purposes of this discussion, however, we consider immunopotentiation to be limited to those states in which there is an increase in the immune response above that which can be achieved by injection of antigen alone.

General Potentiation

A wide variety of compounds are capable of

Table 19–5. Classification of immunopotentiators.

Class	Compounds	Mechanism
General potentiation (nonspecific)	Water and oil emulsions and inorganic compounds	Not clear. Possibly delayed or slow release of antigen, or enhancement of inflammatory response
	Synthetic polynucleotides	Stimulates antigen processing and helper T cell function; may enhance effector function
	Hormones, cyclic nucleotides, and drugs which affect cyclic nucleotide levels	Affect all cell types and all aspects of the immune response
	Bacterial endotoxins	Seem to stimulate B cells but may also affect T cells and macrophages
	Allogeneic effect	Specific stimulation of T cells to release "factors" active in the immune response
Possible specific potentiation	Transfer factor	Unknown but suspected to be information transfer
	Immunogenic RNAs	Appear to transfer specific genetic information

potentiating immune responses, ie, acting as adjuvants. These can be grouped into several categories: (1) water and oil emulsions (Freund's adjuvant); (2) synthetic polynucleotides; (3) hormones, drugs, and cyclic nucleotides; (4) endotoxins; (5) lymphokines and monokines. In addition to studying the mechanisms and modes of action of adjuvants, a substantial effort has been directed toward finding immunopotentiating agents which stimulate only a particular kind of response, ie, cellular immunity or humoral immunity. Selective adjuvants would allow tumor immunologists to stimulate the most efficacious arm of the immune response to augment tumor rejection. It should be noted, however, that the mechanism of action of virtually all known adjuvants is poorly understood. This hampers attempts to use adjuvants in patient care.

A. Water and Oil Emulsions and Inorganic Compounds (Freund's Adjuvant): The use of mineral oil preparations to intensify immune responses was introduced by Freund in the 1940s. His particular mixture consisted of mineral oil, lanolin, and killed mycobacteria (Freund's complete adjuvant). This adjuvant, mixed with aqueous antigen, became very popular with experimental immunologists over the years. It is prohibited for human use because it produces severe local granulomatous reactions.

Although Freund's complete adjuvant has been in extensive use for 20 years, its mechanism of action is poorly understood. At least part of its potentiating capacity appears to be due to the slower release of antigen to the appropriate target cells. This is not its sole mechanism of action, however, since Freund's incomplete adjuvant (minus the bacteria) is a poor substitute for the complete form. Recent evidence suggests that certain components of the mycobacterium itself, such as cell wall lipids and mucopolysaccharides as well as mycobacterial RNA, may be potent adjuvants which in themselves provide a possible explanation for the efficiency of Freund's complete adjuvant.

A variety of inorganic compounds such as alum (potassium aluminum sulfate), aluminum hydroxide, and calcium phosphate have been used as adjuvants. Alum-precipitated antigen preparations are frequently employed to aid in desensitization of allergic individuals. Presumably, they induce high titers of circulating antibody and result in antibody-mediated suppression of the allergic response. Once again, the mechanism of action of these compounds is poorly understood. It may relate both to the slow release of antigen by these compounds and to their ability to cause inflammation, thereby intensifying the general reaction to antigen exposure. A combination of these factors probably accounts for their activity.

B. Synthetic Polynucleotides: Nucleic acids can have biologic effects other than those related to their genetic informational role. As synthetic polyribonucleotides in double- and single-stranded form became available, Braun showed these compounds to be potent stimulators of virtually all aspects of immunoresponsiveness. The most studied synthetic polynucleotide is a double-stranded homoribopolymer consisting of one strand of polyadenylate and one strand of polyuridylate, usually abbreviated poly A·U. In contrast to water and oil emulsions, much more is known about the mode of action of this compound. Its primary target is apparently the thymus-derived T cell. The addition of poly A·U concomitantly with antigen will stimulate helper T cell function, delayed hypersensitivity, and cell-mediated cytotoxicity. There is evidence that it also acts directly on B cells (antibody-forming cells) to increase production of antibody and possibly to enhance cellular proliferation. The mechanism of action of the polynucleotides appears to be at the level of the cell membrane and to be related in some way to changes in cyclic nucleotide metabolism. The usefulness of synthetic polynucleotides as immune potentiators in humans is still under study, and it remains to be seen whether they will prove useful in a clinical setting.

C. Hormones, Cyclic Nucleotides, and Prostaglandins: As discussed in the section on immunosuppression, lymphocytes are sensitive to a wide variety of drugs. Much of this sensitivity can be attributed to the fact that these cells when stimulated by antigens are very active metabolically. Thus, any drug known to be an effective metabolic inhibitor or stimulator will probably influence immunocompetent cells. Evidence is accumulating that lymphocytes, particularly T cells, are remarkably sensitive to hormonal modification. It is possible to demonstrate direct effects on T lymphocyte activation by using biogenic amines, cholinergic agents, growth hormone, insulin, corticosteroids, prostaglandins, progesterone, testosterone, and possibly hormones from the pituitary.

Many of the drugs and hormones—particularly the biogenic amines, cholinergic agents, and prostaglandins—appear to be linked to changes in cyclic nucleotide metabolism in lymphocytes. The addition of drugs which raise cyclic nucleotide levels can enhance or suppress various aspects of the immune response. The usefulness of such drugs is already being exploited in the treatment of allergic asthma, general allergic responses, immunodeficiency disease, cancer, and benign proliferative disorders such as psoriasis. The future of such compounds looks quite promising.

An area of research that is receiving a great deal of attention involves the study of nonsteroidal anti-inflammatory drugs—indomethacin, aspirin, fulfanamic acid, etc—on immune responses. These drugs have been shown to act by interfering with the generation of prostaglandins and other fatty acid derivatives related to prostaglandins. As is obvious in their description, these drugs block inflammation. However, they have also been shown to affect immune responses in both humans and experimental animals. In general, the presence of nonsteroidal anti-inflammatory drugs enhances specific immune responses. This conclusion is complicated somewhat by the presence of subpopulations of lymphocytes that vary in their response to prostaglandins as well as inhibitors of prostaglandin synthesis. It is important to take note of recent studies in patients with Hodgkin's disease. Several groups have obtained data suggesting that the immune depression observed in these patients is related to the presence of prostaglandin-producing suppressor cells. Recent studies suggest that the decline in immune competence observed in old people may be linked to alterations in the prostaglandin sensitivity of lymphocyte subpopulations.

D. Bacteria and Bacterial Products: Other nonspecific stimulants include BCG, the methanol-extracted residue (MER) of BCG, *Corynebacterium parvum,* and levamisole. The latter is a potent anthelmintic drug which is also an effective immunostimulant. To date, clinical experiences with these agents are inconclusive. There is suggestive evidence that BCG may have beneficial effects in malignant melanoma and may act as an adjuvant to chemotherapy of acute myeloblastic leukemia. Original reports of dramatic prolongations in remissions of acute lymphoblastic leukemia have not been confirmed.

Studies in melanoma provide insight into the potency of BCG as a therapeutic modality. When BCG is injected directly into metastatic skin tumor nodules, about 60% of these nodules regress. Significantly, regression occurs almost exclusively in those individuals who can develop a positive delayed hypersensitivity skin test to PPD. Most anergic patients show no response. In the reactive patient, a small number of uninjected tumors will also regress, and this suggests some distal effects. Nonetheless, large visceral metastases are not affected. It appears that the predominant activity of BCG is a local one and is highly dependent on the individual's capacity to develop a cell-mediated response to tuberculin protein.

Studies of the systemic activities of BCG in patients with advanced forms of melanoma are too preliminary to assess accurately its potential beneficial effects. There are data that suggest that this agent may be effective in eliminating micrometastases, and it may become a useful adjunct to systemic chemotherapy in patients with visceral metastatic disease.

BCG and the other immunostimulatory agents have been tested in many other forms of cancer; unfortunately, the results to date must be considered highly preliminary and inconclusive. These adjuvants may prove of value in specific clinical uses, but such conclusions must await further trials.

One of the most exciting recent developments has been the synthesis of muramyl dipeptide (MDP). This molecule, an analog of part of the streptococcal peptidoglycan subunit, is the minimal structure that can elicit adjuvant effects in guinea pigs similar to those seen with mycobacteria in Freund's adjuvant. Using this compound, workers have established the T cell as the primary cell target. Additionally, this substance and its analogs do not elicit the unpleasant side-effects often observed with the more complex bacterial products.

Bacterial endotoxins—cell wall components from gram-negative bacteria (eg, *Escherichia coli, Shigella, Salmonella*—have long been known to produce a variety of effects on the immune response and immunocompetent cells. For example, they nonspecifically stimulate proliferation of B cells as well as induce the nonspecific appearance of anti-red blood cell antibody (particularly anti-sheep red blood cell antibody). In addition, these compounds serve as potent adjuvants of immune responses. Their principal limitation is that, by themselves, they are immunogenic. This is particularly undesirable in an agent of potential therapeutic use. In addition, these compounds are quite pyrogenic. Their principal usefulness has been in elucidating the mechanism of development of immune responses and the method of control.

E. Lymphokines and Monokines: The lymphokines and monokines (substances produced by lymphocytes or monocytes that modulate immunocompetent cell functions) are not yet clinically useful entities. However, rapid developments in this field suggest that some of these naturally occurring immune modulators may take their place on the pharmacist's shelf by the end of the 1980s. For this reason, we will consider briefly some of the more prominent substances now being studied.

1. Interleukins–These proteins have been known since the early 1970s and were called lymphocyte- or thymocyte-activating factors, T cell growth factors, etc. Since 1980, they have been grouped under the generic title "interleukins." **Interleukin-1** (IL-1; lymphocyte-activating factor) is produced by macrophages and can stimulate the growth of thymocytes and T cells. Its importance clinically may relate to its capacity to maintain chronic inflammatory reactions in damaged joints where macrophages have been shown to produce large quantities of this substance. It has also been identified as an endogenous pyrogen. This molecule of 15,000 MW has been purified, and studies are under way to determine its precise structure and mode of action. **Interleukin-2 (IL-2; T cell growth factor)** is a protein produced by T lymphocytes (which may require a prior signal from IL-1) in response to antigenic or mitogenic stimuli. It has the capacity to stimulate the growth of T lymphocytes. It has already proved useful in the growth and maintenance of long-term T lymphocyte cultures in both human and mouse studies. This may allow some rather specialized clinical procedures to be used in treatment. For example, cytotoxic T lymphocytes specific for tumors could be grown in large quantities and subsequently injected into a tumor-bearing patient

for specific immunotherapy. IL-2 has already proved useful in animal models of immune deficiency in restoring immunologic responsiveness. These results are being extended to other animal models. It is expected that IL-2 may be useful as a general restorative of immune competence in immunosuppressed individuals.

In addition to IL-1 and IL-2, which affect primarily T lymphocytes, several substances that appear to affect B lymphocytes are currently being identified and studied. It is possible that in the future, entire families of T cell- and B cell-specific substances will be available to the clinician.

2. Interferons–Although these proteins are known primarily as antiviral substances, the recent cloning of interferon genes into bacterial plasmids has provided for the first time the potential for large-scale

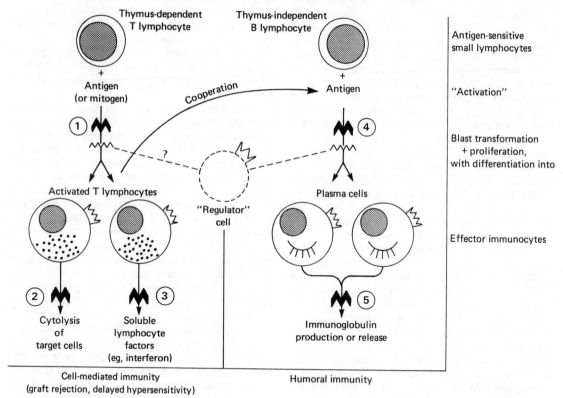

Figure 19–5. Simplified scheme illustrating sites at which immunosuppressors or immunopotentiators may act in regulating immune responses. Antigen-specific thymus-dependent (T) or thymus-independent (B) lymphocytes are thought to be "activated" by contact with antigen to produce either specific tolerance (not shown) or blast transformation, followed by proliferation of differentiated clones of effector immunocytes capable of producing antibody- or cell-mediated immunity. The sawtooth symbols on the surfaces of effector cells indicate that the appearance of hormone receptors may be one result of their differentiation. The heavy wave symbols indicate steps at which experimental evidence suggests *(1)* inhibition or stimulation of mitogen- or antigen-induced blast transformation and proliferation of T lymphocytes; *(2)* inhibition or stimulation of specific immune cytolysis of allogeneic target cells; *(3)* inhibition or stimulation of production (or release) of soluble lymphocyte products such as interferon; *(4)* reversal of antigen-induced immune suppression when lymphocytes are exposed to cAMP-active drugs during initial contact with antigen, prevention of humoral (agglutinating) antibody response to allogeneic cells by cholera enterotoxin, or inhibition of proliferation of antibody-forming cells; or *(5)* inhibition or stimulation of production (or release) of antibody to heterologous erythrocytes. A hypothetical "regulator" cell is also shown, although its relation to the other cells is not clearly defined. (Redrawn and reproduced, with permission, from Bourne HR et al: *Science* 1974;**184**:19. Copyright © 1974 by the American Association for the Advancement of Science.)

production and study of this important family of proteins. It is clear that interferons can influence immunocompetent cell function in both positive and negative ways. Indeed, one class of interferons—immune interferon or interferon γ—is a product of T lymphocytes. Clinical trials are now under way with both naturally occurring interferon and the bacterially produced recombinant interferons. It is estimated that these proteins will be available for clinical use by the mid 1980s. By that time, we should have a better idea of their clinical utility in treating diseases other than virus infections, particularly cancer.

Specific Immunopotentiation

In addition to nonspecific potentiators of immune responses, one material capable of specifically potentiating the response is **transfer factor,** a dialyzable extract obtained from human peripheral white blood cells. This substance was first described 25 years ago. Since its discovery, it has largely remained a novel clinical entity despite extensive attempts to characterize its active component or mode of action and to develop an animal model. The original experiments demonstrated that a dialyzable, DNase-resistant human white blood cell extract could transfer specific skin test sensitivity (to PPD, for example) from donor to recipient in the apparent absence of antigenic exposure.

Much of the subsequent research was directed toward possible clinical applications of such a preparation, but it remains to be studied in a clinical setting in a systematic way (ie, double-blind studies). In part this has had to await the development of satisfactory models to test its effects objectively. International studies are in progress to evaluate its effectiveness, particularly in immune-deficient disease states. Reports to date indicate some effectiveness in children with immunodeficiencies and possible effectiveness in cancer patients and patients with limited immunodeficiencies (the suspected situation in patients who have certain fungal diseases).

New animal models have been developed recently in which transfer factor preparations can be made and tested. These offer the potential for gaining a better understanding of transfer factor and its mode of action.

CONCLUSIONS

It is clear that much remains to be done before the varied facets of immunosuppression and immunopotentiation are understood. The use of agents which enhance or suppress specific immune responses is increasingly important in our attempts at dissecting the immune system. The points at which an immune response might be altered by drugs affecting cAMP levels are outlined in Fig 19–5.

The development of methods of specific immunosuppression remains a major task for the clinical immunologist, particularly in relation to graft rejection. The possible utility of potentiation may lie in its role as therapy for patients with suppressed responses, as in some forms of cancer.

● ● ●

References

General References

Bach JF: *The Mode of Action of Immunosuppressive Agents.* North-Holland, 1975.

Braun W: Pages 4–23 in: *Cyclic AMP, Cell Growth, and the Immune Response.* Braun W, Lichtenstein LM, Parker CW (editors). Springer, 1974.

Decker JL et al (editors): Cytotoxic drugs in rheumatic diseases. (Symposium.) *Arthritis Rheum* 1973;**16**:79.

Heppner GH, Calabresi P: Selective suppression of humoral immunity by antineoplastic drugs. *Annu Rev Pharmacol Toxicol* 1976;**16**:367.

Kaplan SR, Calabresi P: Immunosuppressive agents. (2 parts.) *N Engl J Med* 1973;**289**:952, 1234.

Lawrence HS, Landy M (editors): *Mediators of Cellular Immunity.* Academic Press, 1969.

Lin H: Differential lethal effect of cytotoxic agents on proliferating and nonproliferating lymphoid cells. *Cancer Res* 1973;**33**:1716.

Makinodan T, Santos GW, Quinn RP: Immunosuppressive drugs. *Pharmacol Rev* 1970;**22**:189.

Parker CW, Sullivan TJ, Wedner HJ: Cyclic AMP and the immune response. Pages 1–79 in: *Advances in Cyclic Nucleotide Research.* Greengard P, Robinson GA (editors). Raven Press, 1974.

Parker CW, Vaura JD: Immunosuppression. *Prog Hematol* 1974;**6**:1.

Rubin RH et al: Infection in renal transplant recipient. *Am J Med* 1981;**70**:405.

Schein PS, Winokur SH: Immunosuppressive and cytotoxic chemotherapy: Long term complications. *Ann Intern Med* 1975;**82**:84.

Sercarz EG, Williamson AR, Fox CF (editors): *The Immune System.* Academic Press, 1974.

Smith RT, Landy M (editors): *Immune Surveillance.* Academic Press, 1970.

Spreafico F, Anaclerio A: Immunosuppressive agents. Page 245 in: *Immunopharmacology.* Hadden JW, Coffey RG, Spreafico F (editors). Plenum Press, 1977.

Strober S et al: Allograft tolerance after total lymphoid irradiation (TLI). *Immunol Rev* 1979;**46**:87.

Winkelstein A: The effects of azathioprine and 6 MP on immunity. *J Immunopharm* 1979;**1**:429.

Winkelstein A: Effects of cytotoxic immunosuppressants on tuberculin-sensitive lymphocytes in guinea pigs. *J Clin Invest* 1975;**56**:1587.

Winkelstein A: Effects of immunosuppressive drugs on T and B lymphocytes in guinea pigs. *Blood* 1977;**50**:81.

Winkelstein A: The role of immunosuppressants in lymphocyte function. Pages 33–66 in: *The Handbook of Cancer Immunology*. Vol 6. Waters H (editor). Garland STPM Press, 1981.

Corticosteroids

Claman HN: Corticosteroids and lymphoid cells. *N Engl J Med* 1972;**287**:388.

Fauci AS: Mechanisms of the immunosuppressive and anti-inflammatory effects of glucocorticosteroids. *J Immunopharm* 1979;**1**:1.

Fauci AS, Dale DC, Balow JE: Glucocorticosteroid therapy: Mechanisms of action and clinical considerations. *Ann Intern Med* 1976;**84**:304.

Symposium on corticosteroids. *Transplant Proc* 1975;**71**:130.

Cytotoxic Drugs

Cooperating Clinics Committee of the American Rheumatism Association: A controlled trial of cyclophosphamide in rheumatoid arthritis. *N Engl J Med* 1970;**283**:883.

Decker JL et al: Cyclophosphamide or azathioprine in lupus glomerulonephritis. *Ann Intern Med* 1975;**83**:606.

Elion GB, Hitchings GH: Azathioprine. Page 404 in: *Antineoplastic and Immunosuppressive Agents, Part II*. Sartorelli AC, Johns DG (editors). Springer-Verlag, 1975.

Gerber NL, Steinberg AD: Clinical use of immunosuppressive drugs. (2 parts.) *Drugs* 1976;**11**:14, 90.

Gershwin ME, Goetzl EJ, Steinberg AD: Cyclophosphamide: Use in practice. *Ann Intern Med* 1974;**80**:531.

Hahn BH, Kantor OS, Osterland CK: Azathioprine plus prednisone compared with prednisone alone in the treatment of systemic lupus erythematosus. *Ann Intern Med* 1975;**83**:597.

Novak SN, Pearson CM: Cyclophosphamide therapy in Wegener's granulomatosis. *N Engl J Med* 1971;**284**:938.

Penn I: Leukemias and lymphomas associated with the use of cytotoxic and immunosuppressive drugs. *Recent Results Cancer Res* 1979;**69**:7.

Penn I: Tumor incidence in human allograft recipients. *Transplant Proc* 1979;**11**:1047.

Phillips SM, Zweiman B: Mechanisms in the suppression of delayed hypersensitivity in the guinea pig by 6-mercaptopurine. *J Exp Med* 1973;**137**:1494.

Skinner MD, Schwartz RS: Immunosuppressive therapy. (2 parts.) *N Engl J Med* 1972;**287**:221, 281.

Steinberg AD et al: Cytotoxic drugs in treatment of nonmalignant diseases. *Ann Intern Med* 1972;**76**:619.

Turk JL, Parker D: The effect of cyclophosphamide on the immune response. *J Immunopharm* 1979;**1**:127.

Turk JL, Poulter LW: Selective depletion of lymphoid tissue by cyclophosphamide. *Clin Exp Immunol* 1972;**10**:285.

Cyclosporin A

Borel JF: Cyclosporin A: Present experimental status. *Transplant Proc* 1981;**13**:344.

Calne RY: Cyclosporin. (Editorial.) *Nephron* 1980;**26**:57.

Antilymphocyte Sera

Najarian JS, Simmons RL: The clinical use of antilymphocyte globulin. *N Engl J Med* 1971;**285**:158.

Spreafico F: Biological activities of anti-lymphocytic serum. *Adv Pharmacol Chemother* 1972;**10**:257.

Specific Antibodies

Freda VJ et al: Prevention of Rh hemolytic disease: Ten years' clinical experience with Rh immune globulin. *N Engl J Med* 1975;**292**:1014.

Immunostimulation

Bluming AZ: Current status of clinical immunotherapy. *Cancer Chemother Rep* 1975;**59**:901.

Fahey JL et al: Immunotherapy and human tumor immunology. *Ann Intern Med* 1976;**84**:454.

Gutterman JU: Immunology and immunotherapy of human malignant melanoma: Historic review and perspectives for the future. *Semin Oncol* 1975;**2**:155.

Lymphokines, Monokines, & Interferon

DeWeck A (editor): *Second International Lymphokine Workshop*. Academic Press, 1980.

Friedman RM: *Interferons: A Primer*. Academic Press, 1981.

Prostaglandins

Goodwin JS (editor): *Suppressor Cells in Human Disease States*. Vol 14 of: *Immunology Series*. Dekker, 1981.

Effects of Sex Hormones, Nutrition, & Aging on the Immune Response | 20

I. SEX HORMONES AND IMMUNITY
Robert G. Lahita, MD, PhD

The sex steroids are potent regulators of metabolic processes and are known to affect functions as diverse as social behavior and resistance to infection. They are also active metabolites at extremely low concentrations. For these reasons, careful investigation of the role of sex steroids in immunology will undoubtedly reveal important functions. Clearly, the determination of sex and the later development of secondary sexual characteristics are accompanied by distinct immunologic capabilities such as the capacity of females of various mammalian species to outperform males in terms of immune responsiveness. Though this has been documented many times, the process remains enigmatic to most immunologists. Examples of this sexual difference are the ease with which immune tolerance is produced in males; the fact that overall cell-mediated immunity seems to be greater in females than in males; and the fact that homografts and tumors are rejected with greater efficiency by females. Women have the capacity to maintain a 9-month period of gestation with a fetus who might be antigenically dissimilar, and their host resistance has been repeatedly shown to vary with cyclic hormonal shifts during pregnancy and menses. Lastly, there are great differences in the sex incidence of many common diseases with immunologic features. These observations strongly suggest that the sex steroids play an important role in disease processes.

SEX STEROIDS & THE NORMAL IMMUNE RESPONSE

Androgens

Little is known about the direct role of androgens such as testosterone on immune responsiveness. Few studies have dealt with the direct effects of these compounds on in vitro or in vivo metabolism in humans; indeed, most experimental work has been restricted to murine systems. Testosterone is generally thought to be immunosuppressive. The data are inconsistent: Syngeneic grafts of testes in female mice had almost no influence on allograft rejection; however, actual injection of testosterone ($650 \mu g$ 3 times a week) in rodents delayed graft rejection in castrates, further implying that testosterone was a potent immunosuppressant. Testosterone has been shown to reduce resistance to viral infections and is known to enhance or reduce immune responsiveness to a variety of antigens. Therefore, its only accepted consistent effect in animals is its ability to immunosuppress chickens by retarding the function and development of the bursa. The discrepancy of observed effect might be due to a variety of factors. A role for the male hormones as immunosuppressive agents, however, might add to their known clinical usefulness as stimulants of formation of erythrocytes and other marrow-derived cell populations. The erythropoietic effect of androgens is probably due to their capacity for triggering pluripotential stem cells to divide and ultimately to differentiate into compartments of cells that contain lymphoid elements, whereas estrogens do not have this effect. Additionally, the recent finding of receptors for estrogen and dihydrotestosterone on the thymus gives added importance to their roles in lymphoid maturation. Androgens have recently been found also to modify the activities of regulatory genes that influence the function of structural genes. It is currently suggested that this mechanism may explain the immunoregulatory roles of androgenic hormones. Another hypothesis is that the weakness of the male immune system (compared to the female) could be due to variability in sensitivity to androgen and not the actual concentration of plasma androgen, thus explaining the wide variety of effects observed. Actual experimentation with inbred normal and diseased mice, for example, might show that the immune responses of diseased mice are the direct effects of lower or higher gene sensitivities. Much information about the regulatory effect of androgens comes from recent work with mice with autoimmune disease. An androgen-sensitive cell or biochemical event seems responsible for immune tolerance and significant differences in the manifestations of disease when males are compared to females.

Estrogens

Estrogens have been studied more extensively than androgens and, like androgens, have been assigned the dual roles of immunosuppressants and stim-

293

ulants. As is the case with androgens also, the actions of estrogen are probably concentration-dependent. As an example, estradiol in selected concentrations has been shown to prolong first- and second-set skin grafts in mice and to inhibit corneal graft acceptance in preimmunized rabbits. In mice, estrogenic compounds cause thymic involution and decrease the total numbers of small lymphocytes that reside there. This effect is opposite to that of testosterone with regard to the success of bone marrow transplants, because primary failure of such transplants is known to occur if estrogen is given before or after the transplant.

Estradiol and diethylstilbestrol present in supraphysiologic doses of 10–50 μg/mL reduce the peripheral blood lymphocyte proliferative response to phytohemagglutinin (PHA) and concanavalin A (ConA). In mixed lymphocyte reactions, as little as 200 ng of estradiol could stimulate peripheral blood lymphocyte activity, while 2000-ng amounts inhibited this response (as judged by tritiated thymidine uptake). Washing the lymphocytes prevented this inhibitory effect, and the evidence indicates that the estrogen must be present in the culture from the outset. In humans and in animals, fluctuations of lymphocyte responses have also been observed during the normal menstrual cycle and during pregnancy (see below). In addition, castrated male and certain female mice often display hyperplastic spleens and thymuses after challenge with thymus-dependent antigens, indicating that estrogens have an effect on thymic cell activity that might account for the often observed enhanced immune responsiveness to such antigens in the presence of hormone. Sustained levels of estrogens in mice have also led to a reduction in natural killer cell activity. The effects of estrogens on macrophages are unknown but thought to be minimal, since concentrations of 2–20 μg/mL of estradiol do not inhibit the response to macrophage inhibition factor (MIF). The effects of estrogens on humoral responses are also unclear, since in some studies they are shown to enhance immune responsiveness and in others they have a suppressive effect. Enhanced immune responses to SRBC have been reported in estrogen-treated mice, while in some studies estrogens have been shown to protect mice against bacterial infection. In one experiment, injection of mice with 2.5 μg of estradiol resulted in increased numbers of splenic antibody-producing cells in animals sensitized to E coli. In another study, the presence of lower concentrations of estradiol (500–5000 pg/mL) in cultures of peripheral blood lymphocytes increased their uptake of thymidine and increased the numbers of antibody-secreting cells, as judged by plaque-forming ability. Such increases in antibodies are also observed for mice treated with diethylstilbestrol, where anaphylactic antibody responses were greater. Immune suppression, on the other hand, has been seen with regard to host response to type III pneumococcal polysaccharide, tumor cells, graft rejection, PHA response, and cell-mediated immunity against Toxoplasma gondii. The reasons for much of this apparent suppression are unclear; as is the

case with other sex hormones also, the critical factor probably is the concentration of hormone used or the cell population affected. Confusing immune effects with actual shifts in cell populations can result in misinterpretation of results. As an example, the granulocytopenia, lymphopenia, and failure of bone marrow transplants induced by some large doses of estrogen are in actuality the result of lympholysis and osteoproliferation. It is hoped that the confusion surrounding the true effects of varying concentrations of estrogen on immune responses in humans and animals will in time be resolved with a better understanding of hormonal metabolism, interactions, and tissue specificity.

Progesterone

Another sex steroid that has been shown to affect the immune response is progesterone. In concentrations of 10–15 μg/mL, it reduces the peripheral blood lymphocyte response to PHA and ConA. Unlike estradiol, it can be added to a cell culture on the fifth day of a mixed lymphocyte culture (MLC) and will inhibit the incorporation of tritiated thymidine, a marker for cellular proliferation. Therefore, it appears that this compound inhibits only the uptake of tritiated thymidine and not cell activation.

Progesterone seems also to have an active role in thymic function, since the murine thymus is able to metabolize the compound by 20α-hydroxylation. (This is greater than observed for lung and kidney, which also have this enzyme.) Isolated thymocytes metabolize this compound, suggesting even a greater role for this hormone in thymic function. Such a role might be important during pregnancy, when progesterone is synthesized and secreted by trophoblastic cells into maternal blood in large amounts (886 μg/mL in intervillous blood and 160 μg/ml in late pregnancy in peripheral blood). Recent experiments suggest that progesterone extended the viability of homologous skin grafts in rhesus monkeys or of heart grafts in rats. The steroid is thought by many to be a potent immunosuppressant, probably because in concentrations of 50–200 μg/mL it suppressed the expected inflammatory reaction to cotton threads and prolonged the survival of skin xenografts and allografts in rats. As in the case of estrogens, progesterone had no effect on macrophages. In general, as with estrogens, low doses of the compound stimulate the production of antibody and high doses significantly inhibit its formation.

SEX HORMONES, IMMUNITY, & DISEASE

Immune Disease in Animals

A fair amount of data implicate the sex steroids in the pathologic processes of autoimmune diseases in animals. Animal models are selected because of the similarities of their disease to that in humans. Several inbred strains of mice, for example, develop a disease similar to human systemic lupus erythematosus (SLE). Unlike the disease in humans, however, there is a

Table 20–1. Murine data suggesting importance of estrogens in systemic lupus erythematosus.

1. Immunologic tolerance better produced in male of species.
2. Female rodent has enhanced susceptibility to autoimmune disease and development of immune complexes.
3. Thymocytotoxic antibodies develop in NZB mouse by 3 months (more so in females than in males).
4. More anti-DNA antibodies in females.
5. Greater morbidity in females.
6. Androgen therapy or castration decreases mortality rate in the mouse.
7. Gonadectomy of young male mice increases morbidity and mortality rate from disease.

relentless progression of disease in all members of the strains. The disease in the mouse is associated with rising titers of antinuclear antibodies and, in some strains, rheumatoid factor. The mice may develop autoimmune hemolytic anemia and, like humans, go on to die of renal disease. In some strains of these mice, there is—as in the human illness—a higher incidence in females. Two strains of mice where females are involved early are the (NZB × NZW)F$_1$ hybrid and the MRL/l varieties. These strains are studied widely from a genetic, sexual, and immunologic point of view in the hope that obscure aspects of the human illness might be better understood (Table 20–1). The importance of sex incidence is increased by careful genetic engineering. Recently, for example, careful inbreeding resulted in development of a strain of mouse (BXSB) in which the males acquire an autoimmune illness and die earlier than females. The disease in this murine species is said to be dependent on the Y chromosome. As will be seen for human disease, however, a whole series of illnesses of immune nature tend to affect females in preference to males.

In these animals with systemic lupus erythematosus, as in humans, the development of antibodies to DNA is associated with increased morbidity and mortality rates. Such antibodies occur spontaneously and undergo a regulated "switch" from IgM to IgG during the course of the disease. In the (NZB × NZW)F$_1$ hybrid, the females have higher titers of antibody and undergo the "switch" from IgM to IgG earlier. Sex hormones such as estrogens, when given repeatedly, influenced the survival, formation of antibodies to DNA, and development of immune complex nephritis. The estrogens apparently alter the disease in stages. Generally, male sex hormones suppressed and female hormones accelerated the disease. Experiments where females were given testosterone or 5α-dihydrotestosterone showed a retarded progression of the autoimmune disease. This was due not merely to the anabolic effects of the hormone, since the synthetic androgen danazol, known for its anabolic effects, did little to prolong the survival of such mice. Castration of male (NZB × NZW)F$_1$ hybrid mice resulted in an increased mortality rate and the earlier appearance of IgG, while such changes were almost absent in castrated females of this strain.

It is generally agreed that many factors might affect the disease process in the mouse. Among these are X-linked genes, metabolism of estrogen relative to that of testosterone, dose of hormone, age of mouse at time of administration, and the effects of agents on various antibodies in addition to those directed against double-stranded DNA. Regarding the latter, anti-T cell and anti–single-stranded DNA antibodies have also been found earlier in NZB females and castrated NZB males. Males produced lower titers of these antibodies than did females. This was not Y-chromosomally related, since females given testosterone had the same response as males. Some investigators have described an X-linked response of mice to certain natural and synthetic polynucleotides, and this is a subject of active investigation. There is no doubt that many of these antibody responses are genetically controlled, but just how the hormones modify these control processes remains the central question. Many investigators feel that the estrogens simply decrease suppressor T cell function, while androgens increase suppressor cell function and decrease immune complex clearance and formation.

In animals such as the mouse, dosage of hormone is a problem, since large doses of either estrogen or testosterone can be lympholytic and immunosuppressive, while small doses can have the opposite effect. The range of action is most important, and generalizations based on a few experiments in animals can be misleading.

New data from investigations of murine lupus suggest a role for androgens in the development of immune tolerance. All strains of SLE mice are reported to have defective immune tolerance, and this defect is reported to be the effect of an absence of androgens or perhaps, as mentioned previously, an absence of responsive cells. The site of action of the androgens is reported to be the thymocyte, since androgens modulate cells in transition from marrow to thymus. Using 20α-hydroxysteroid dehydrogenase as a T cell marker, several investigators have noted a decrease in thymocytes and an increase in T suppressor cells after androgen administration. This androgen responsiveness has been invoked as a reason for the frequency of autoimmune disease in females of inbred mice and remains an attractive hypothesis to be tested in all species.

Immune Disease in Humans

A host of factors are influential in the etiology and pathogenesis of immune disorders in humans. What is curious, however, is the large number of diseases in females that have as part of the pathologic picture a disordered immune system manifested chiefly by the formation of autoantibodies. Diseases occurring predominantly in females in which the immune system is affected are listed in Table 20–2. Many factors might account for this association. Females have higher baseline levels of IgM than males, whereas no such difference has been observed for IgG levels. Black females also have higher levels of either IgM or IgG

Table 20–2. Some diseases that predominate in females (female:male).

Systemic lupus erythematosus (10:1)
Scleroderma (3:1)
Rheumatoid arthritis (3:1)
Myasthenia gravis (3:1)
Sjögren's syndrome (9:1)
Idiopathic thrombocytopenic purpura (chronic) (4:1)
Chronic active hepatitis (9:1)
Primary biliary cirrhosis (9:1)

Table 20–3. Evidence incriminating estrogens in the pathogenesis of human systemic lupus erythematosus.

1. Improvement of disease following ovariectomy.
2. Worsening of disease following the use of oral contraceptives and during pregnancy.
3. The documented greater than expected frequency of systemic lupus erythematosus in individuals with Klinefelter's syndrome.

than either white females or males. Estrogens appear to have important effects on certain aspects of diseases such as lupus in humans, since excesses of estrogen in the form of oral contraceptives appear to worsen the illness, and depletion of estrogen by procedures such as gonadal extirpation have been associated with amelioration of the disease process. In addition, a subset of males with Klinefelter's syndrome (XXY genotype) has been described in which systemic lupus erythematosus is also present, and it is likely from clinical data that feminization of males results in an increase in the incidence of autoimmune diseases in the males. While considerable work has been done in animal systems on sexual influences on mortality and morbidity rates, only recently have these influences on human disease come under systematic scrutiny (Table 20–3).

Recent work in humans with systemic lupus erythematosus has shown that there is an accumulation of 16-hydroxylated or highly estrogenic metabolites. Such compounds (Fig 20–1), like 16α-hydroxyes-

trone, are being studied for their in vivo feminizing properties and their in vitro and in vivo effects on the immune system. Elevation of 16α-hydroxyestrone has been reported in both males and females with systemic lupus erythematosus. This compound appears to be significantly estrogenic by all standard parameters, such as its tight binding to the cytosol receptor and its potent uterotrophic activity in the rat after sustained administration. It is unique in that it does not bind tightly to testosterone-estrogen–binding globulin (TEBG), which might be of significance during times when such protein binding exerts a modulating effect on these hormones. One such time is during normal pregnancy. 16α-Hydroxyestrone also has unique chemical properties, which would indicate that unlike other estrogens, it can covalently bind to a variety of serum proteins and membrane components. Several other hormone metabolites important in diseases similar to systemic lupus erythematosus are being investigated. What is obvious, however, is that there are differences in sex hormone hydroxylation which are

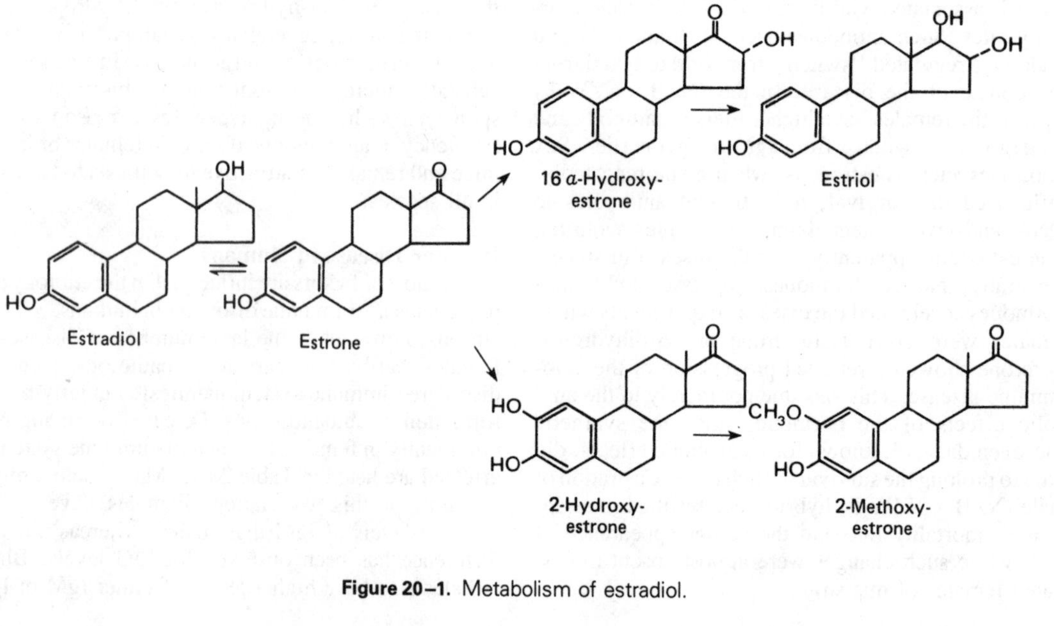

Figure 20–1. Metabolism of estradiol.

quite noticeable in systemic lupus erythematosus and perhaps other immune disorders such as rheumatoid arthritis and chronic liver disease. Different mechanisms are operable, since patients with rheumatoid arthritis have a different response to estrogenic compounds.

Systemic lupus erythematosus is not the only rheumatic disease in which sex hormones have been of interest. The severity of rheumatoid arthritis has been shown to be less in patients using oral contraceptives. Although such effects are small, it is nevertheless possible that distinct processes such as the previously described nonspecific suppression of adjuvant arthritis by estrogens in animals might be operative.

As mentioned previously, the androgens might also be important modulators of immune reactivity. It might also be said that the androgens act along with estrogens to achieve an effective ratio. Recent studies have suggested that the plasma androgens of females with systemic lupus erythematosus are abnormally low, and our data also indicate that the oxidation of testosterone in systemic lupus erythematosus may not be normal. Further examination of androgen and estrogen metabolism in systemic lupus erythematosus might better explain the much higher incidence in females, which remains unaccounted for. Sex differences are not limited to women with arthritic disease, since there are other immune arthritic diseases in which the incidence is higher in males, eg, Reiter's syndrome. As in the murine models, testosterone and other androgens might play a role in the induction of specific cell populations, and insight into these diseases might follow from an understanding of this inductive process.

Study of the metabolism of all of the male and female hormones and their influences on the immune system might even lead to new and effective modes of therapy for these diseases and perhaps a variety of other unrelated illnesses.

THEORIES CONCERNING
THE ROLE OF SEX HORMONES
& THE IMMUNE RESPONSE

From what has been said, the sex steroids clearly appear to have a direct role in the immune response. The target cells and tissues of such hormones are undoubtedly complex and require a great deal of investigation. Much confusion exists about the quantity of metabolite or metabolites needed to evoke a stimulatory or inhibitory response. This has been a formidable problem, since in many species tested the true physiologic dose of hormone and the sexual cyclicity of the animal are not taken into account.

Evidence to date supports the concept of immunostimulation by estrogens and inhibition by androgens, compounds which in cyclic concentrations in females might account for their so-called immune superiority. It is likely, however, that it is the balance or ratio of both of these classes of compounds depen-

dent on gender that accounts for the observations and that these compounds act in balance. An imbalance of hormones would explain the threshold differences seen in human diseases where sexual phenotype is preserved but subtle immune aberrations occur. Certain trace intermediate metabolites (eg, 16α-hydroxyestrone) with no previously identified role might play a significant role in immune regulation.

It is also probable that the chronology of sexual maturation is related to substantial change in the character of the immune response. Puberty is such a time of metabolic change. Such shifts might influence the prognosis and severity of a whole host of diseases, some with sexual prevalence (eg, systemic lupus erythematosus), and perhaps certain lymphoid malignancies such as acute lymphoblastic leukemia, where age is an important factor in estimating prognosis. Even the period of sexual senescence characterized by sex hormone shifts might be important in producing abnormalities of the immune system, such as circulating immune complexes and the presence of antinuclear antibodies in the "normal" aged population.

Lastly, it is likely that our knowledge of transplantation immunology and problems of fertility will be enhanced by research into the phenomenon of gestation and abnormalities that occur in pregnant women with diseases such as systemic lupus erythematosus. The relative risk of acquiring a host of diseases might be amplified by the sex steroids, and there may be a relationship to HLA type. The actual molecular role of hormones (intra- and extracellularly) is of major importance in normal and abnormal processes occurring in every organ system of the host. Knowing how such natural substances work on the immune system might enable us to engineer changes in immune regulation and perhaps such different functions as sexual preference, longevity, and even social behavior.

II. NUTRITION & THE
IMMUNE SYSTEM
Jay A. Levy, MD

Humans require 6 basic dietary components to support growth and maintain life and health: proteins, carbohydrates, fats, vitamins, minerals, and water. The first 3 are the major nutrients supplying energy for growth and metabolism (4, 4, and 9 calories per gram, respectively). In the USA and most Western countries, approximately 15% of these calories come from proteins and the rest are derived about equally from carbohydrates and fats. While each of the 6 nutrients is essential for the efficient functioning of the body, there are obvious differences in the relative quantities required for well-being. Moreover, a suitable combination of these food constituents is needed for the regulation of normal body activities.

Adequate nutrition is necessary for proper functioning of the immune system. Malnutrition is a major cause of immunodeficiency, affecting not only populations with limited food supplies but also individuals living in overcrowded ("slum") conditions and those suffering from chronic illness. Malnutrition appears to have a particularly significant influence on cell-mediated immunity, but the humoral response, phagocytosis, and the complement system are also affected. More recently, an excess of nutrients — notably fats and carbohydrates — has been found to have a detrimental effect on the immune system. The information reviewed in this chapter comes from empirical observations on individuals with protein and calorie malnutrition, clinical studies, and animal experiments in which the effect of specific nutrients on immunity could be evaluated.

PROTEIN–CALORIE MALNUTRITION

The thymus was recognized as a barometer of nutrition over a century ago, when thymic atrophy was observed to accompany **protein-calorie malnutrition.** We now know that all the lymphoid organs become smaller during protein-calorie malnutrition, but the thymus, which is replaced by fibrofatty tissue, is the organ most severely affected. The ultimate reason for these histopathologic changes is unknown, but the active cell division characteristic of lymphoid tissues is restricted in protein-calorie malnutrition. Concentrations of certain hormones such as epinephrine, corticosteroids, insulin, and thyroxine are altered during protein-calorie malnutrition and its accompanying stress and could have detrimental effects on lymphoid cells, particularly the thymocyte. In addition, decreased production of thymic hormones occurs and may account for the large number of null cells in the blood. Plasma cortisol levels are often raised, and adrenalectomized animals have been found to survive prolonged protein deficiency without profound involution of lymphoid tissues. Part of the cortisol effect could result from the low serum albumin present in this state, since a large proportion of the hormone is unbound and physiologically active. Serum samples from individuals with protein-calorie malnutrition also contain increased amounts of other constituents known to inhibit immune responses, such as endotoxins, antigen-antibody complexes, and C-reactive protein. Moreover, these sera appear deficient in a presently undefined low-molecular-weight normal serum component (not albumin) required for optimal lymphocyte activity.

Individuals with protein-calorie malnutrition have a high incidence of infection, particularly with mycobacteria, viruses, and fungi, and show lymphopenia and a decreased **delayed cutaneous hypersensitivity** reaction to several antigens. Their lymphocytes produce less interferon in response to viruses. In addition, PHA-induced lymphocyte transformation is significantly impaired. These observations have indicated their substantial reduction in cell-mediated immunity.

An effect of protein-calorie malnutrition on humoral immunity has not been generally observed. Most studies have shown that B cell numbers and immunoglobulin levels are not depressed, and antibody response varies according to the type and form of antigen presented. For instance, malnourished children may react adequately to poliomyelitis and smallpox vaccines but poorly to yellow fever and typhoid vaccines. Generally, only responses to antigens requiring the help of T lymphocytes, macrophages, or both are affected. Secretory IgA is also low in individuals with protein-calorie malnutrition, and this may be of clinical significance because of the increased incidence in such persons of gram-negative septicemia and food allergies. Since serum IgA levels are normal, synthesis of secretory component by epithelial cells is probably reduced. Some of these abnormalities probably reflect concomitant vitamin deficiencies (see below). In many cases of protein-calorie malnutrition, hypergammaglobulinemia is present, accompanied by detectable IgE levels, which are normally nil in individuals with adequate dietary intake. These observations probably reflect decreased T cell response, recurrent infections, and increased gastrointestinal permeability to food antigens. With severe protein-calorie malnutrition, reduction in all antibody-producing cells occurs. For example, children with **kwashiorkor,** which is characterized by hypoproteinemia and hypoalbuminemia, usually have high immunoglobulin values, whereas children suffering with nutritional **marasmus** (a chronic condition with muscle wasting and extreme weight reduction) have reduced levels of serum immunoglobulins.

Individuals with protein-calorie malnutrition also have impaired killing by polymorphonuclear neutrophils (PMNs) and macrophages; phagocytosis is usually normal, but the oxidative and glycolytic activities of these cells are reduced. Since myeloperoxidase is an iron-dependent enzyme, some decrease in intracellular killing could be due to iron deficiency (see below). Moreover, NADPH oxidase may be reduced by high levels of plasma cortisol, a substance that inhibits the activity of this enzyme in human leukocytes. Levels of lysozyme are also low in PMNs, plasma, and tears of patients with protein-calorie malnutrition. In addition, a defect in macrophage function has been considered the cause, in malnourished subjects, of low-affinity antibodies. This observation could explain the frequent occurrence of immune complexes in serum samples of children with protein-calorie malnutrition. Furthermore, the abnormal processing of antigen by macrophages and the reduced production of lymphokines and chemotactic factors contribute to the ineffective delayed hypersensitivity observed with protein-calorie malnutrition. All these factors as well as decreased complement and transferrin levels play a role in the high incidence of infection in affected individuals. Complement abnormalities occur secondary to enhanced consumption of its components during activation (eg, from infection); decreased synthesis seems less involved, although there are histopathologic changes in complement-synthesizing tissues such as liver, lymph nodes, and intestinal mucosa.

The immune system can also be influenced by the time and extent of protein-calorie deprivation. Australian aboriginal children under conditions of moderate *chronic* protein deprivation had increased T cell-mediated immune responses but reduced B cell function rather than the expected compromise of cell-mediated immunity. This observation is unexplained but could reflect increased production of thymic hormone in response to chronic protein deprivation, concurrent infection, or some limited nutritional replacement. Some experiments have indicated that lymphoid tissues are extremely vulnerable to acute severe starvation but adapt to dietary restriction if it is less severe and occurs over a long period of time.

Malnourishment of the mother can lead to intra-uterine deficiencies in nutrients that affect the ability of the infant at birth to respond to infections. Long-term effects of this intrauterine malnutrition include marked suppression of both cellular and humoral immunity. Maternal protein deficiency in animals decreases development of thymus and brain in the progeny. Similarly, calorie restriction in young pregnant rats profoundly affected postnatal immunocompetence of the offspring. Reduced protein and calorie intakes early in life also have deleterious effects on the normal development of the thymus.

In severe protein-calorie malnutrition, the antibody response is the first to return to normal after introduction of an adequate diet, but prior sensitization to a foreign antigen may not be recalled by the previously malnourished individual. For example, children exposed to *Candida albicans* but who lack a skin response to its antigen do not respond to skin testing after nutritional deprivation has been corrected. Moreover, experiments have shown that the successful attainment and maintenance of a satisfactory amnestic response to certain antigens requires adequate nutrition during both the primary and secondary phases of the process. If it is deficient during the primary phases and is then restored, the secondary phase is still depressed. Thus, an adequate nutritional state is required at the time of immunization, and concomitant nutritional therapy may not ensure a good response.

A discussion of protein-calorie malnutrition must also consider vitamin, mineral, and other nutrient deficiencies that occur concomitantly and may have equally important roles in the malfunction of the immune system. Moreover, infection, a common burden of undernourished individuals, compromises the immunologic response. These variables are probably responsible for some differences in measurements of immune function by various investigators of malnutrition.

Many observations on the effects of malnutrition on immune responses are not fully explained scientifically but obviously indicate an effect of specific nutrients on the proliferation of immune cells, their enzymes, and their natural enhancing and suppressing serum factors. Attempting to define more precisely the possible influence of each dietary constituent on immune responses, researchers have turned to animal experimentation. Their results are reviewed below, but the reader must bear in mind that a selective deficiency of one dietary nutrient is rarely encountered clinically. It should also be emphasized that no animal model can simulate the complex interaction of nutrition, hormones, and cultural factors in human malnutrition.

NUTRIENT DEFICIENCIES

PROTEIN DEFICIENCY

Investigations into the importance of proteins for the normal functioning of the immune system have included animal studies in which animals are subjected to acute and **chronic protein insufficiency.** These experiments confirmed observations in humans that the immune response is greatly influenced by the timing and severity of nutrient deprivation. Animals severely deprived of protein, particularly at a young age, had a persistent defect in cytotoxic T cell-mediated function, suggesting an interruption in the normal development of the thymus. Lymphoid follicles in the lymph nodes lacked the normal cuff of small T lymphocytes but had adequate numbers of plasma cells. Primary delayed hypersensitivity, BCG response, skin allograft rejection, and in vitro mixed lymphocyte culture activity were all markedly depressed. In addition, the antibody response to T cell-dependent antigens such as sheep red blood cells (SRBC) was decreased and could be restored by injection of normal syngeneic thymocytes. The primary immunologic response was increased, whereas the secondary response, which depends on T cells, was depressed. These results explain the diminished amount of tumor-blocking antibodies detected in animals deprived of proteins or certain amino acids (see below). Severe protein deficiency has facilitated the development of tolerance in mice and suggests that processing of antigens by macrophages is also impaired. In contrast, intrinsic B cell function in these animals fed low-protein diets was intact, as demonstrated by normal levels of immunoglobulins and the successful induction of antibodies to *Brucella abortus*, a B cell-dependent antigen. Yet all animals fed extremely low amounts of protein had a decrease in both humoral and cellular immunity.

Adult animals chronically fed limited amounts of protein showed a different response. Their serum antibodies were profoundly reduced, but their cell-mediated immune function was enhanced. In these animals with chronic protein insufficiency, the total number and immunocompetence of T cells were increased, as reflected by the enhanced GVH reaction, rejection of skin allografts, T cell mitogenic response, and phagocytic activity of peritoneal macrophages. One explanation for this result has been the possible outpouring of thymic hormones (see above). However, the increased number of null cells with high terminal deoxynucleotidal transferase activity, indicative of thymocyte precursors, observed in chronic protein insufficiency has not been supported this suggestion. The depressed humoral response in chronic protein insufficiency was indicated by the reduction in serum antibodies and a sensitivity to bacterial infections. The size of the spleen and the number of antibody-forming cells were principally affected, since immunoglobulin production per antibody-forming cell was unchanged.

AMINO ACID DEFICIENCY

As noted above, the quality and quantity of protein have profound effects on immune function, and deficiencies of specific amino acids are particularly important in this respect. However, the association of a single amino acid deficiency with reduction of immune function has not been reported in humans; these observations have been made only in experimental animals. Diets markedly deficient in phenylalanine and tryptophan, for example, cause marked reduction in humoral antibody synthesis with little influence on cellular responses. The effect of tryptophan loss appears related to its role in maintaining ribosomal aggregates. Other amino acids whose deficiencies can decrease antibody production are tyrosine, valine, threonine, cysteine, and isoleucine. Restricted intake of arginine, histidine, and lysine has induced a slight depression in humoral immune response.

Marked deficiencies of the branched-chain amino acids isoleucine and (particularly) valine have also impaired some T cell responses. Similarly, limited amounts of the sulfur-containing amino acids methionine, cysteine, and cystine in the diet have marked deleterious effects on all lymphoid tissues. Leucine is an exception, since its restriction results chiefly in depression of cell-mediated immunity. In excess, it can cause depression of B cell activity by activating enzymes involved in the catabolism of valine and isoleucine.

FATTY ACID DEFICIENCY

Two polyunsaturated fatty acids, linoleic acid and arachidonic acid, have been shown to be required nutrients for experimental animals and young children, but an essential fatty acid deficiency is rare in human adults. Cells responsible for the immune response, like other cells of the body, have lipid membranes whose fatty acid concentrations are influenced by serum lipids. Therefore, dietary fats, which play an important role in modifying the plasmalemma, could affect lymphocyte responses. During stimulation of lymphocytes, for example, marked changes in lymphocyte membrane fatty acid turnover take place with increased incorporation of polyunsaturated fatty acids. Consequently, a decrease in membrane polyunsatu-

rated fatty acid concentration would result in a diminution in membrane fluidity, which is important in antigen capping and surface events associated with lymphocyte stimulation. Observations in animals with polyunsaturated fatty acid deficiencies have indicated that an absence of corn oil (linoleate) causes a significantly reduced humoral response within 1 month. Primary and secondary antibody responses against both T cell–dependent and T cell–independent antigens are also decreased. In contrast, a relative polyunsaturated fatty acid deficiency may potentiate cell-mediated immunity, perhaps secondary to reduced prostaglandin production (see below).

Saturated fatty acids and cholesterol are also important components of the cell membrane, and their reduced intake could affect immune responses (see below). Diets low in fat have an additional significance, because dietary lipid is the vehicle for absorption of other fat-soluble nutrients, especially certain vitamins and carotenes. Finally, dietary fatty acids are particularly important in the prenatal period, as exemplified by experiments with mice fed low-fat diets shortly after birth, who showed a decrease in the development of lymphoid organs (particularly spleen, thymus, and liver) and an overall reduction in immunologic response.

VITAMIN DEFICIENCIES

As mentioned above, some of the immunodeficiencies observed in malnourished individuals may result from a lack of adequate vitamins and minerals. The limited experiments conducted thus far have indicated that any vitamin responsible for synthesis of DNA and protein (eg, vitamin B_{12}, vitamin B_6, folic acid, vitamin A) has an effect on the immune system. These studies of isolated vitamin deficiencies demonstrate that a single nutrient deficit can result in a substantial impairment of an immunologic process (Table 20–4). In patients with vitamin B_{12} deficiency (primary pernicious anemia), for example, lymphocyte responses to mitogens are impaired, and a modest reduction in the phagocytic and bactericidal capacity of PMNs may be found. Peripheral lymphocytes from patients with folic acid deficiency also are not stimulated by mitogens in vitro, and these individuals have decreased delayed hypersensitivity responses, but their PMN functions remain intact.

Those vitamin deficiencies that have most dramatically disturbed antibody production are deficiencies of vitamin B_6, vitamin A, pantothenic acid, biotin, and folic acid. Their effect has been attributed to a marked reduction in the number of individual antibody-forming cells in the spleen, not immunoglobulin production per cell. Thiamine, riboflavin, and vitamin D have limited effects on antibody production.

Vitamin B_6 (Pyridoxine) Deficiency

The role of vitamin B_6 in immunity is linked to its

Table 20–4. Influence of vitamin and mineral deficiencies on immune function.

	T Cells	B Cells	Macro-phages	Neutro-phils
Vitamins				
A	+++	+++		
Thiamine		++		
Riboflavin		++		
B_6	+++	+++		++
B_{12}	++	+		
Biotin		+++		
Pantothenic acid		+++		
Folic acid	++	+++		
C			++	++
D			++	++
E	++	++	++	
Niacin and tryptophan		++		
Minerals				
Zinc	+++			
Iron	+++	+		+++
Copper			++	++
Magnesium		++		
Selenium	++			++

The data are summarized from observations on animals and human subjects. (+ = minimal effect of nutrient deficiency on immune mechanism; ++ = limited effect; +++ = marked effect; blank = no known effect.)

ability to catalyze the biosynthesis of nucleic acids required for cellular proliferation and production of specific immune proteins. Vitamin B_6 deficiency is accompanied by a reduction in number and function of both T and B lymphocytes. Vitamin B_6-deficient animals have reduced delayed hypersensitivity responses and prolonged survival time of skin homografts. Their response to antigenic challenge is greatly diminished and reflects a reduction primarily in antibody-forming cells, not actual antibody synthesis. Nevertheless, recent work has suggested that deficiency of this vitamin can lead to a decreased secretion of newly synthesized proteins (eg, immunoglobulins). Thymic epithelial cell function is also reduced in vitamin B_6-deficient animals. Lymphoid precursors from neonatally thymectomized vitamin B_6-deficient donors are converted to functional T lymphocytes when exposed only to normal thymic epithelial cells, not those from vitamin B_6-deficient animals. This effect probably results from lack of production of one of the thymic hormones, since the number of lymphoid precursors in vitamin-deficient mice is not markedly decreased. Pyridoxine deficiency has also been associated with reduced phagocytic activity of neutrophils. Finally, mothers deprived of vitamin B_6 during pregnancy have fetuses with much smaller spleens and thymuses than control mothers. Likewise, cell-mediated immune responses in newborn children are markedly reduced.

Vitamin A Deficiency

Besides being important in maintaining the structural and functional integrity of epithelial lining cells (along with ascorbic acid), vitamin A has been found to be needed for the mitogenic response of both T and B cells. Vitamin A–deficient animals have a defect in the synthesis of membrane glycoproteins, which are crucial for mitogen binding and cell proliferation. Thus, they have poor T and B cell responses to certain antigens. Moreover, the epithelial cell damage resulting from vitamin A deficiency can impair secretory IgA production. Severe vitamin A deficiency also leads to atrophy of the thymus and spleen and a marked decrease in circulating leukocytes and lymphocytes. Levels of serum thymic factor are not usually lowered. Vitamin A–deficient children have been shown to have depressed delayed hypersensitivity reactions, which in part explains the high incidence of infection in this group. Modest increases in dietary vitamin A can enhance cell-mediated immunity, including natural killer (NK) cell activity, but an excess of vitamin A depresses these immune responses.

Vitamin C & Vitamin E Deficiency

Vitamin C is required for maintenance of epithelial cells and the function of PMNs, in which high concentrations of this vitamin are found. No substantial effect of vitamin C deficiency on antibody production or T cell function has been reported. However, a reduced delayed hypersensitivity response has been observed that appears to be caused by an inability to develop a local inflammatory response rather than by an immunologic defect in lymphocytes. Macrophages also contain large amounts of ascorbic acid, particularly those in the peritoneum and lung. During infection, levels of this vitamin rapidly decrease in leukocytes along with a reduction in their phagocytic activity, which returns to normal after recovery.

Vitamin E deficiency in animals has produced depressed delayed hypersensitivity and lymphocyte responses and decreased immunoglobulin production. Supplemental doses of this vitamin have caused enhanced primary and secondary immune responses, probably by increasing the number of antibody-forming cells. This effect is not related to its antioxidant property but perhaps results from an induction of cell proliferation; there is an accumulation of vitamin E in lymphoid cells. Increased intake of vitamin E also enhances cell-mediated responses, including the delayed hypersensitivity reaction, and the clearance function of reticuloendothelial cells. Massive doses, however, have inhibited immune functions in healthy volunteers and can impair PMN bactericidal function.

MINERAL DEFICIENCIES

Zinc Deficiency

The mineral deficiency most frequently encountered in humans is deficiency of zinc, which, like iron deficiency, often occurs in protein-calorie malnutrition. Reduced intake of these minerals may explain some of the immune abnormalities observed in undernourished individuals. Zinc is necessary for several cellular processes, eg, interactions at the membrane, steps in the cell cycle, mRNA metabolism, and the function of certain enzymes (thymidine kinase, DNA polymerase) involved in DNA synthesis. Thus, this metal has a stimulating effect on all replicating cells, including those involved in the immune response. It is essential for lymphocyte transformation. In general, a restriction of zinc intake leads to a breakdown in cell-mediated immunity, particularly that of helper and cytotoxic T cells. The thymus involutes, and there is a deficiency in circulating thymic hormones. The latter result could explain the large proportion of null cells in the peripheral blood, but zinc could also be involved, since it is necessary for the function of **terminal deoxynucleotidal transferase.** Primary and secondary antibody responses to thymus-dependent antigens are also decreased. Very little effect on B cell and macrophage function is observed. Antibody-dependent cell-mediated cytotoxicity is largely unchanged or slightly increased. Zinc deficiency, however, is accompanied by loss of appetite, so a decrease in energy stores could be responsible for some of the effects on T cell function observed with low zinc intake. As has been observed with massive doses of certain vitamins, excess zinc can inhibit phagocytosis by PMNs and macrophages.

Iron Deficiency

Iron deficiency is well documented in protein-calorie malnutrition and is probably an important factor contributing to the high infection rate. Iron is required for maintenance of lymphoid tissue and for enzymes involved in the bactericidal activity of PMNs. Moreover, many of the iron-activated enzymes, including cytochrome c, catalase, cytochrome oxidase, and peroxidase, are necessary for normal cell function. In addition, the iron-binding proteins transferrin and lactoferrin have direct bacteriostatic effects and are more markedly reduced than total protein in subjects with protein-calorie malnutrition. These proteins bind iron avidly and thus sequester it from pathogens that require the nutrient for multiplication. However, massive increases in serum iron can saturate transferrin and enhance susceptibility to infection.

In iron deficiency, cell-mediated immunity is primarily affected. The delayed hypersensitivity response is impaired, and T cells have a decreased mitogenic response and definite diminution in lymphokine production. Bactericidal activity of PMNs is depressed because of the reduced function of iron-requiring enzymes. In rare cases, antibody production is also reduced. These changes in immune response can be noted with as little as a 10% decrease in dietary iron, but some effects of this mineral deficiency on the immune system could reflect an interference with folate metabolism.

Copper, Magnesium, & Selenium Deficiency

Copper deficiency, presumably because of decreased dietary intake, impaired intestinal absorption,

and reduced synthesis of ceruloplasmin, occurs frequently in association with kwashiorkor. Deficiency of this metal prevents normal function of the reticuloendothelial system.

Magnesium is required for transphosphorylation and activates enzymes critical to the production of ATP. Along with calcium, it participates in the activation of complement. Magnesium-deficient animals appear to have primarily a reduction in antibody-forming cells. Immunoglobulin levels are decreased, and the humoral response to particular antigens is diminished. Thymic atrophy can also take place. The divalent cations are required as well for cellular membrane function.

With selenium deficiency, cell-mediated immunity is principally affected, especially when vitamin E levels are also reduced. Phagocytosis is decreased, and T cells appear to be coated by factors that suppress their response to mitogens and antigens. These inhibitors apparently result from lipid peroxidation, which is prevented by the antioxidant activity of selenium as well as of vitamin E.

Several trace elements, including cadmium, chromium, lead, manganese, and silica, have also been reported to influence immune responsiveness.

NUTRIENT EXCESS

OBESITY

The detrimental effects of massive amounts of certain vitamins and minerals have been mentioned. Clearly, moderation and balance in dietary intake of nutrients are essential for normal immune function. Thus, just as a deficiency in proteins, fats, and calories can influence the immune response, so can an excessive intake of nutrients alter normal immunologic function. Clinical surveys, epidemiologic data, and observations at autopsy have shown that the incidence and severity of infectious disease is considerably higher in obese people than in lean controls. Obese individuals have impairment of cell-mediated immune response as measured in vivo and in vitro and a reduction in intracellular killing of bacteria by neutrophils. Likewise, an increased incidence of breast, prostate, and colon cancer is associated with obesity and chronic intake of high-fat diets. Similarly, animals made obese by large caloric intake show a poor host response to infection and readily develop breast, colon, and chemically induced tumors. The dietary lipids appear to be promoters rather than initiators of these cancers. Fat-enriched diets also enhance autoimmune sequelae in lupus-prone mice. Thus, excess dietary lipids can adversely affect the immune system in profound ways.

Experiments with genetically obese mice have demonstrated that a reduction in thymus and spleen weight occurs concomitantly with a decrease in the number of mononuclear cells and T lymphocytes in these organs. Furthermore, the proportion of different subsets of immunocompetent cells is changed in the obese animals. As with chronic protein insufficiency, the number of antibody-forming cells and not immunoglobulin production is affected. Obese mice immunized in vivo with lymphoma cells show a diminished capacity to generate cytotoxic cells, although their NK cell activity is increased. Serum lipid appears to be the immunosuppressive agent, because outside the animal the lymphocyte response is normal. Lipemic serum, frequently associated with obesity, suppresses in vitro cell-mediated responses. In contrast, changes in antibody-dependent cell-mediated cytotoxicity are not commonly seen in obese animals. Finally, the effect of iron and zinc deficiencies in obesity must be considered, since—perhaps because of dietary imbalance or alterations in carrier proteins—these micronutrients are often found in reduced amounts in obese individuals.

CHOLESTEROL EXCESS

Hypercholesterolemia is associated with impaired lymphocyte and reticuloendothelial cell function. Cholesterol is a critical membrane component of cells, and its de novo synthesis plays a substantial role in lymphocyte proliferation. High levels of this lipid turn off the incorporation of acetate into cholesterol and therefore could suppress immune function by inhibiting the cholesterol synthesis required for the lymphocyte response to antigens. Moreover, the extent of inhibition by lipoproteins of lymphocyte proliferation in response to mitogens correlates positively with the cholesterol content rather than triglyceride, phospholipid, or total lipid content of the lipoproteins (see below). However, a decrease in membrane fluidity, resulting from a high cholesterol content, is associated with enhanced T cell activity. Thus, the balance between plasma, membrane, and intracellular cholesterol content (and synthesis) appears to determine optimal lymphocyte responses.

FATTY ACID EXCESS

Generally, diets high in polyunsaturated fatty acids are more immunosuppressive and greater promoters of tumorigenesis than diets high in saturated fats. High levels of polyunsaturated fats have been shown to decrease rejection of skin grafts in animals and suppress delayed hypersensitivity reactions in cancer patients and control subjects. Polyunsaturated fats can inhibit the lymphocyte response to mitogenic stimulation and depress reticuloendothelial cell function. Nevertheless, high levels of circulating saturated fats are associated with decreased resistance to infection and transplantable tumors and a diminished host response to SRBC and other antigens. Incubation of PMNs with saturated fatty acids reduces chemotaxis and bacterial killing. Cholesterol oleate and ethyl palmitate have been reported to reduce antibody response when given before immunization with antigen. They have no effect when administered at the same time. Thus, these lipids may impair the initiation of antigen recognition or processing or may directly inhibit antibody-forming cells.

The reason for an effect of polyunsaturated fats on cellular immunity is not clear. Mertin and associates have proposed that since the polyunsaturated fats linoleic and arachidonic acids are precursors of prostaglandins, these immunoregulatory substances (specifically PGE_2) could depress the cell-mediated (T cell) response. Similarly, the immunosuppression caused by diets high in saturated fat could be explained by the associated polyunsaturated fat, although direct effects of the saturated fats must be considered. A serum factor has been found responsible for T cell suppression in rats fed high-fat diets, since lymphocytes from animals on this diet responded efficiently only when cultured in serum from rats on a low-fat diet. One of the serum inhibitors appeared to be lipoprotein (see below), but other factors such as free fatty acids could also be responsible.

In examining any distinct differences in the effects of saturated and unsaturated fatty acids on immunity, newborn mice were fed high levels of either type of fat. Those receiving polyunsaturated fats had more serum immunoglobulins—particularly IgG (not IgM or IgA)—than those fed saturated fat, which had a decreased number of B cells. High levels of both kinds of fatty acids diminished T cell blastogenesis. Thus, whereas adequate amounts of oleic and linoleic acids are important for a good mitogenic response of T cells, inhibition occurs when high concentrations of these and other fatty acids are present. Recently, we have observed a selective expression of certain immunoglobulin subtypes with diets differing in content of saturated versus unsaturated fatty acids. The type of fat ingested appeared to influence the subclass of antibody produced.

A balance of saturated and unsaturated fatty acids is also important for normal blastogenic response. Human peripheral lymphocytes cultured in the presence of saturated (palmitate, stearate) or unsaturated (oleate, linoleate, arachidonate) fatty acids bound to albumin (as they are in normal serum) had decreased mitogenic responses. However, when these fatty acids were present simultaneously, this inhibition was less pronounced or absent. Even at very high levels of fatty acid intake, inhibition was prevented if there was a balance between these 2 types of lipids. The results probably reflect the need for an appropriate concentration of these fatty acids in the cell membrane. In this regard, corticosteroids, which can raise serum free fatty acid levels via a hormone-sensitive lipase, can influence the content of membrane fatty acid. This action, which could enhance lysis of the cells, may be one mechanism by which this hormone modulates the immune response.

LIPOPROTEIN EXCESS

Work in several laboratories has indicated that plasma lipoproteins can have a regulatory effect on lymphocytes and influence the immune response. Among the normal effects attributed to lipoproteins are the following:

(1) **Low-density lipoproteins (LDL)** transport cholesterol and regulate its biosynthesis in human lymphocytes. Cholesterol is essential for proliferation of lymphocytes, and interruption in its synthesis can thus affect lymphocyte response (see above).

(2) **High-density lipoproteins (HDL)** combine with lymphocytes and facilitate cholesterol removal. This activity changes membrane fluidity and can also influence proliferation of the cells via cholesterol synthesis.

(3) **Very low density lipoproteins (VLDL)** specifically inhibit the initiation of protein synthesis and subsequent DNA synthesis in certain cells, including lymphocytes.

(4) Some lipoproteins inhibit the attachment of certain complement components to cell surfaces and therefore can modulate immune attack.

Certain lipoproteins have been implicated in the reduced frequency of rosetting T cells and the reduced blastogenic response of T cells in patients with hepatitis virus infections and Hodgkin's disease. In some cases, C-reactive protein or amyloid protein A, associated with lipoproteins, appeared responsible, but in others the lipoproteins were themselves probably involved. In normal serum, a minor subset of LDL has been identified that reduces blastogenesis of T cells. The mechanism is unknown, but the cell membrane seems involved, since calcium uptake at the surface of lymphocytes is decreased. High concentrations of lipoproteins greatly inhibit lymphocyte response and the tumoricidal capacity of activated macrophages. These studies probably reflect an exaggeration of their normal regulatory role and result from the enrichment of cell membranes with cholesterol and other lipids.

We are just beginning to appreciate the dynamic role lipids can play in regulating immune responses. All of the experimental studies are subject to criticism, because of the variables involved in the testing. Nevertheless, the results indicate that—as vital components of the cell membrane, interactants with the cell surface, or precursors for serum suppressor factors—the relative availability of lipids to the body can influence normal immune function (Table 20–5).

CARBOHYDRATE EXCESS

It is well known that diabetic patients are more susceptible to infections than normal controls and have greater morbidity when they do become ill. **Hyperglycemia** significantly impairs both lymphocyte and phagocyte function and thus modifies the host response to infection. During hyperglycemia, the

Table 20–5. Influence of lipids on immune function.*

Fatty acid deficiency
  Depresses humoral immune responses to various antigens
  Decreases development of lymphoid organs in newborns with overall reduction in immunologic response
Obesity
  Alters susceptibility to some infections
  Associated with high incidence of certain cancers
Cholesterol excess
  Alters susceptibility to some infections
  Alters humoral and dermal hypersensitivity responses to antigens
  Alters lipid content of cells and the composition of cellular membranes, leading to impaired phagocytic activity or altered surface binding by lipid haptens
  Alters reticuloendothelial clearance of particulate matter
Saturated fatty acid excess
  Inhibits primary and secondary humoral immune responses to some antigens
  Depresses in vitro lymphocyte response to certain antigens and mitogens
  Inhibits chemotactic and phagocytic functions of neutrophils
  Alters reticuloendothelial clearance of particulate matter
Polyunsaturated fatty acid excess
  Suppresses delayed cutaneous hypersensitivity reactions
  Inhibits or delays GVH responses and allograft rejection
  Depresses in vitro lymphocyte responses to certain antigens and mitogens
  Inhibits neutrophil chemotactic and phagocytic functions
  Alters reticuloendothelial clearance of particulate matter
Lipoproteins
  Binds to specific lymphocyte surface receptors and modulates lymphocyte activities

*Adapted from Beisel WR: *Cancer Res* 1981;41:3797. Data were obtained from studies of animals and human subjects.

cell-mediated response to bacteria is depressed, graft survival is significantly prolonged, and the response of spleen cells to mitogens is suppressed. In experimental animals, a markedly diminished cell-mediated cytotoxicity of spleen cells for tumor cells has been noted. Since these observations did not occur in vitro, the immune defects must result from the altered metabolic environment in diabetic animals and not abnormal lymphocytes. Insulin does not appear to be important, since insulin levels were normal in the animals examined.

The metabolic environment also appears to influence antibody production, which is reduced during in vivo but not in vitro immunization. Phagocytosis is decreased as well during hyperglycemia, but this effect seems to be caused by the hyperosmolality of the serum rather than the sugar content itself. Sugars other than glucose can also have substantial effects on immune function. Children with galactosemia are at greater than normal risk of bacterial infection. Inhibition of glycolytic activity and not simple hyperosmolality appears responsible, since intracellular ATP is reduced in leukocytes exposed to high galactose concentrations. Low carbohydrate levels have also been shown to depress phagocytosis by neutrophils.

INFLUENCE OF NUTRITION ON HUMAN DISEASE

Both under- and overnutrition are associated with an increased incidence of infectious illness and altered immune responses. Changes in cell-mediated immunity and complement may in fact be an early sign of protein-calorie malnutrition and precede changes in body shape. Likewise, the response of lymphocytes to mitogens may predict certain trace metal and vitamin deficiencies. Thus, nutritional manipulation of immunity could have wide-ranging clinical, biologic, and therapeutic implications, and changes in the diet might modify the host's ability to withstand certain diseases.

AUTOIMMUNITY

Evidence from several laboratories has indicated that diets high in calories (particularly fat) will enhance autoimmunity in autoimmune-prone mice; suppression of their cell-mediated immunity is the most prominent feature. At the same time, it has been noted that marked protein and calorie reduction can protect these animals from the development of autoimmune sequelae, especially immune complex glomerulonephritis. The reason for this effect is not certain, but since antibodies to DNA and other autoantigens are generally decreased and T cell responses increased, either activation of suppressor T cells or a direct reduction in hyperactive B cell activity must be involved. Zinc deficiency also reduces the immune abnormalities in these mice, probably via its effect on the thymus. Moreover, diets low in fat alone (not calories) can significantly reduce the incidence and severity of the disease. The mechanism for this protective effect is still unknown, but it does not appear to involve the immunoinhibitory substance PGE_2. The low-fat diets maintain the mitogenic response of T cells and enhance the rejection of skin homografts and the mixed lymphocyte reaction. Evidently, a reduction in dietary lipids alone can alter certain regulatory immunocytes in these animals to permit the expression of normal immune function. These observations suggest that dietary changes could be used to modify autoimmunity in humans.

CANCER

Studies in animals have indicated that nutritional manipulation can enhance or depress tumor-specific immunity. The overall result depends on the degree of dietary restriction and its differential effect on cellular and humoral immunity. Protein-calorie malnutrition, which generally leads to an unwanted compromise in the immune system, can increase the antitumor response of the host. One suggested explanation for this effect is reduction in the synthesis of blocking antibodies, which appears to be more sensitive to protein deficiency than other immunologic activities. Diets deficient in valine, isoleucine, cysteine, methionine, and threonine have also been effective in inhibiting tumor growth. In contrast, deficiencies of lysine, leucine, histidine, and arginine have little influence on tumor growth but result in extreme weight loss. Diets low in fat and relatively high in protein have also been shown to enhance cell-mediated cytotoxicity and to increase tumor rejection by animals. Moreover, some protective and immune-enhancing effects of supplemental doses of vitamins A and C in animals have been reported but need further study. Similar manipulations of diet in human subjects have not been adequately evaluated.

OTHER DISEASES

Significant impairment of both humoral and cellular immune responses has been observed in surgical patients and hospitalized chronically ill individuals. Protein-calorie malnutrition could be involved secondary to malabsorption or cancer, and nutrition must be an important consideration for recovery from these clinical disorders. Moreover, one must look for subclinical vitamin or trace metal deficiencies, such as zinc, in patients with chronic infection. In addition, the effects of hyperglycemia on phagocytic function and perhaps other immune responses support the known necessity to control serum glucose levels in patients. In multiple sclerosis, there is some evidence that supplementation of the diet with polyunsaturated fatty acids benefits the clinical course. This effect could result from the suppressive action of certain fatty acids (perhaps via PGE_2) on cellular immunity. Finally, as mentioned earlier, individuals receiving renal transplants may benefit from diets high in certain amino acids such as leucine which in animal experiments have reduced allograft rejection. Furthermore, linoleic acid could be used in transplant patients, since the rejection of skin allografts has been prolonged in animals by oral or intraperitoneal administration of this polyunsaturated fatty acid. Preliminary reports on patients given daily supplements of sunflower seed oil state that they have an increased ability to retain renal transplants.

These and other observations emphasize the potential for using individual nutrients to modify clinical disorders. Clearly, our growing understanding of nutrition and its influence on the immune system should offer new approaches in the future for controlling both inherited and acquired illness.

III. EFFECTS OF AGING ON THE IMMUNE RESPONSE
Marc E. Weksler, MD, & Perrie B. Hausman, PhD

The genes that control immune reactivity are located within the major histocompatibility complex (MHC). Genes linked to this complex not only regulate immune responses but also influence maximal life span in mice. This has been taken as support for the contention that there is a link between immune function and aging. Differences in inherited and acquired (ie, environmental) influences on immune function explain the increasing heterogeneity in immune reactivity observed in individuals of an identified population as they age. The coefficient of variation of nearly all immunologic parameters, which is relatively small in young people, increases dramatically as people age.

Although the effects of age on immune function may not be apparent in every elderly subject, most immune functions in elderly populations differ from those in young populations. Age-associated changes in the immune system have been studied in humans and in experimental animals. Thymic involution and decline in serum thymic hormone activity are universally associated with aging; ie, they are found in all aging individuals in all species studied at the same relative age. Other changes in immune reactivity are expressed by elderly populations but not by every elderly subject (eg, autoantibody production). Documenting age-associated change in immune function depends upon a proper selection of subjects for study. Certain changes in immune function occur in the first quarter of the life span and can be identified only if young and adult subjects are compared. Other age-associated changes in the immune system do not occur until the last quarter of the life span and can be identified only if young adult and aged subjects are compared. Finally, the great variability of changes in immune parameters due to aging requires that large numbers of individuals be compared so that the results will be statistically significant.

THYMIC INVOLUTION & IMMUNE SENESCENCE

Involution of the thymus gland is a universal accompaniment of aging in both humans and experimental animals. Long before the immune function of the thymus was recognized, anatomic studies showed that the human thymus gland attained maximum mass at sexual maturity (puberty). After puberty, there is a striking involution in the size of the thymus, so that humans 45–50 years of age retain only 5–10% of the cellular mass of the thymus gland. Studies in experimental animals have confirmed this pattern of thymic involution in other species also. Thus, the maximum weight of the thymus in mice—approximately 70 mg—occurs at 6 weeks of age, the time of sexual maturation in mice. By 6 months of age, when the

mouse has completed only one-quarter or less of its life span, the weight of the thymus has decreased to only 5 mg. The work of Good, Miller, and Waksman in the early 1960s revealed the crucial role of the thymus in the immune system. It is reasonable, therefore, to relate the involution of the thymus during the first half of life to the altered form and function of the immune system during the second half of life.

The thymus gland functions both as an endocrine organ and as a site of cellular differentiation. Thymic polypeptide hormones are synthesized in the thymus and released into the blood. These hormones are important in the differentiation of pre- and postthymic lymphocytes. The level of thymic hormones in the serum of humans and experimental animals begins to fall soon after the morphologic involution of the thymus gland. Thus, in humans between the ages of 20 and 30, the serum level of thymic hormone begins to fall, and after the age of 60, thymic hormone is no longer detectable in serum (Fig 20–2). Comparable studies in mice reveal that thymic hormone levels fall during young adulthood and become undetectable after 6 months of age.

The thymus gland also functions as a site of differentiation of immature lymphoid cells. A large number of immature lymphocytes from the bone marrow enter the cortex of the thymus gland. Some of these lymphocytes migrate to the thymic medulla before leaving the gland as mature T lymphocytes. Only 5% of the lymphocytes that enter the thymus are released into the blood. With age, there is a decreased entry of immature lymphocytes into the thymus. Lymphoid cells of early T lineage, identified by expression of terminal deoxynucleotidal transferase activity, migrate from the bone marrow to the thymus early in the life span. By age 20 years in humans and age 6 months in mice, the migration of terminal deoxynucleotidal transferase–positive lymphocytes from the bone marrow into the thymus has declined significantly.

Although fewer immature lymphocytes enter the thymus with age, the percentage of immature lymphocytes within the thymus gland actually increases with age. This observation is explained by the decreasing capacity of the thymus gland to effect the differentiation of immature lymphocytes. One step in the differentiation of immature lymphocytes within the thymus is the acquisition of the surface receptor for sheep erythrocytes. The presence of this surface receptor permits mature T lymphocytes to form rosettes with sheep erythrocytes. In humans under 20 years of age, only 5% of thymic lymphocytes do not express this receptor. With age, however, there is a steady increase in the percentage of thymic lymphocytes that do not express the surface receptor for sheep erythrocytes (E rosettes; Fig 20–3). By age 60 or 70 years, nearly half of thymic lymphocytes fail to express this receptor. Thus, the increased percentage of immature lymphocytes in the thymus gland of older persons reflects the decreased capacity of the thymus gland to modulate the differentiation of immature lymphocytes.

The failure of immature lymphocytes to become

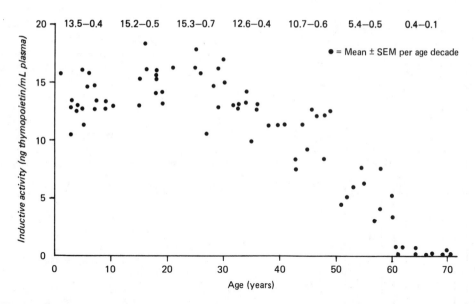

Figure 20–2. Plasma thymic hormone activity from 0 to 70 years of age. (Reproduced, with permission, from Lewis VM et al: *J Clin Endocrinol Metab* 1978; **47**:145.)

differentiated in the thymus is manifested both by an increasing number of immature lymphocytes within the gland and by the appearance of increasing numbers of immature T lymphocytes in peripheral blood. Mature T lymphocytes bind sheep erythrocytes. Immature T lymphocytes bind autologous erythrocytes (autorosetting). With age there is an increase in immature T lymphocytes in the blood that form autorosettes. Thus, the loss of thymic function with age is manifested by a decrease in serum thymic hormone and an increased number of immature T lymphocytes in the thymus and in the peripheral blood.

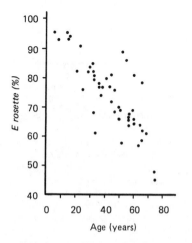

Figure 20–3. Relationship between age and the frequency of thymic lymphocytes capable of forming E rosettes. (Modified and reproduced, with permission, from Singh AK et al: *Clin Exp Immunol* 1979; **37**:507.)

Although the thymus gland was first recognized to be responsible for the establishment and maintenance of cell-mediated immunity, during the 1970s, it became clear that T lymphocytes derived from the thymus gland also influence the expression of humoral immunity mediated by B lymphocytes. Thus, thymus-dependent regulatory lymphocytes with helper or suppressor activity play an important role in humoral immunity (see Chapter 8). The effect of age on the capacity of the thymus gland to regulate lymphocyte differentiation has also been studied in experimental animals. Lethally irradiated and thymectomized young animals have been reconstituted with bone marrow cells and thymus grafts from donors of varying ages (Fig 20–4). The rates of recovery and activity of thymus-dependent immune functions have been followed in these animals. Thymus grafts from newborn animals permit the most rapid reconstitution of the T lymphocyte population and the most complete recovery of responsiveness to T cell mitogens and to T-dependent antigens. When thymus grafts are taken from older animals, the pace of recovery is delayed, and in many cases the level of thymus-dependent immune function never reaches that seen in intact animals or in animals reconstituted with neonatal thymus glands. Thus, the capacity of the thymus to affect the maturation of immature T lymphocytes decreases with age. This probably explains the finding that increasing numbers of immature lymphocytes reside within the thymus of old subjects.

It has now been established that the thymus gland is important in the maturation of B as well as T lymphocytes. Transfer studies similar to those described have measured the influence of thymus gland age on the differentiation of immature B cells. The capacity to

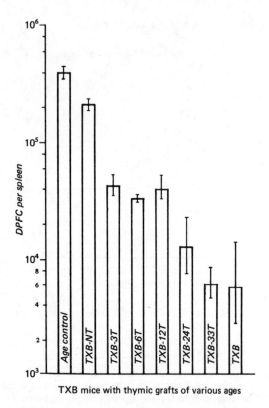

TXB mice with thymic grafts of various ages

Figure 20–4. Influence of age of the thymic graft on the splenic T cell–dependent anti-SRBC response of TXB recipient mice 4 weeks after thymic transplantation. Thymus-grafted TXB mice were given 10^9 SRBC intraperitoneally, and their spleens were assessed for direct plaque-forming cells (DPFC) 4 or 5 days later. Vertical bars, one standard error; sample size per group, 3–7 mice. (Reproduced, with permission, from Hirokawa K, Makinodan T: *J Immunol* 1975; **114**:1659.)

number of lymphocytes or in the number of T or B lymphocytes in the peripheral blood of humans or in lymphoid organs of animals. A few studies report that the total numbers of blood lymphocytes as well as the numbers of T lymphocytes are lower in older humans. Normal strains of mice do not show a loss of splenic T cells with age, although autoimmune strains do. Because elderly individuals have an increased frequency of autoantibodies such as rheumatoid factor and anti-nuclear antibodies, it is possible that, like autoimmune-prone mice, they have decreased numbers of T lymphocytes. In contrast, it has been reported in a few studies that the number of B lymphocytes is increased in old people.

Most studies have quantitated lymphocytes from one or only a few lymphoid compartments. With age, there is a significant redistribution of lymphocytes. There is an age-associated decrease in germinal centers in lymph nodes and an increase in plasma cells and lymphocytes in the bone marrow. Thus, changes in the number of lymphocytes in any one compartment may not reflect the total complement of lymphocytes within the organism. Even if the total number of T lymphocytes is maintained with age, it is possible that these long-lived cells continue to circulate in a postma-

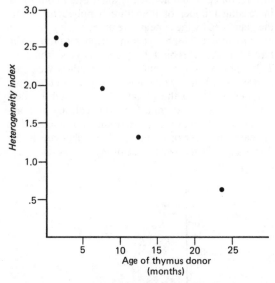

Figure 20–5. Lethally irradiated thymectomized mice were reconstituted with neonatal liver as the source of B lymphocytes. In addition, they received 2×10^7 syngeneic thymus cells intravenously from donors of the age indicated. Six or 7 days later, all animals received 1×10^8 syngeneic thymus cells intravenously from 6- to 8-week-old donors and were immunized with DNP-BCG in CFA a day later. Splenic anti-DNP PFC were assayed 20 days after immunization. The Shannon heterogeneity index was used to describe the degree of heterogeneity of affinity of the indirect anti-DNP PFC population of individual animals. The average value of the index is presented. The larger the index, the greater the heterogeneity. (Reproduced, with permission, from Szewczuk MR et al: *Eur J Immunol* 1980; **10**:918.)

generate a heterogeneous immune response with respect to affinity is one marker of B lymphocyte maturation. Thymocytes from mice under 2 months of age have maximal capacity to trigger the maturation of B lymphocytes, whereas thymocytes from mice 6 months of age or older show a progressive loss of ability to do so (Fig 20–5).

In summary, involution of the thymus gland during the first half of the life span is followed by a decline in levels of thymic hormone and an increase in percentage of immature T lymphocytes. Studies in experimental animals have revealed that thymus cells from mice as young as 3–6 months of age have already begun to lose their capacity to differentiate immature T and B lymphocytes.

AGE–ASSOCIATED CHANGES IN LYMPHOCYTES

It may be surprising that despite thymic involution, most studies have found no decrease in the total

Table 20—6. Increase in autorosette-forming cells (AR-FC) with age.*†

Age of Subject (Years)	ARFC/10³ Lymphocytes	
	Male	Female
22—29	6.7 (7)	7.5 (5)
54—79	19.5 (4)	16.7 (16)

*Reproduced, with permission, from Moody CE et al: *Immunology* 1981;44:431.

†Mononuclear lymphocytes were incubated with autologous erythrocytes in the absence of serum for 16 hours. Cells binding 3 or more erythrocytes were scored as ARFC-positive. The numbers in parentheses indicate the number of subjects studied.

ture state in which they are viable but lack the replicative capacity required for immune competence.

While it appears that the total number of T or B lymphocytes in the peripheral blood in humans does not change significantly with age, evidence now indicates that the proportion of T lymphocyte subpopulations changes with age. Thus, an increase in T lymphocytes that form rosettes with autologous erythrocytes is observed in elderly humans and old experimental animals (Table 20–6). The number of suppressor or cytotoxic T lymphocytes identified by the monoclonal OKT-8 antibody or by an antibody present in the serum of patients with juvenile rheumatoid arthritis declines with age. The modest changes in the proportion of T lymphocyte subsets may be crucial to the regulation of immune reactivity but appear relatively small compared to the large changes in immune function that accompany aging.

The cell surface characteristics of lymphocytes from older animals differ from those of young animals. New antigenic determinants are expressed by lymphocytes from old animals that are recognized by young syngeneic mice. The density of the theta determinant, the receptor for T cell growth factor on the surfaces of T cells, and the density of surface immunoglobulin on B cells decrease with age. Furthermore, the rate of capping of these surface receptors decreases with age. Colchicine, which increases the number of caps and the rate of capping in lymphocytes from young donors, has no effect on lymphocytes from old donors. The number of surface receptors, their affinity, and their mobility probably are important factors in immune reactivity, and changes in these functions with age may contribute to immune senescence.

The enzymatic complement of lymphocytes also changes with age. Lymphocyte adenylate cyclase increases and guanylate cyclase decreases with age. Paradoxically, the content of cAMP falls while cGMP rises in lymphocytes from old humans and experimental animals. Some enzymes, deficient in certain immunodeficiency states, have been found to be decreased in lymphocytes from old donors. The activities of purine nucleoside phosphorylase and ecto-5' nucleotidase are reduced in lymphocytes from old donors. No change in adenosine deaminase activity

was found in lymphocytes from old donors. Finally, lymphocytes from both experimental animals and humans are more susceptible to damage induced by ionizing radiation, ultraviolet light, and mutagenic drugs. These findings suggest that DNA repair enzymes may be altered with age.

CHANGES IN HUMORAL IMMUNITY WITH AGING

The steady state of the immune system can be measured by the number of lymphocytes and the concentration of immunoglobulins in serum. As indicated, there is a subtle change in the proportion of lymphocyte populations with age. There are also small but statistically significant changes in the concentration of immunoglobulins in serum. The concentration of IgA and IgG in human serum rises with age, while the concentration of IgM tends to decrease. In one study, the limited number of humans whose serum IgG concentrations fell had a reduced life expectancy. It is of interest that the concentrations of IgA and IgG in cerebrospinal fluid also increase with age.

The first suggestion that the humoral immune response was altered with age came from measurement of natural antibodies in the sera of humans of different ages. It was found that the concentrations of isoagglutinins and of antibodies to sheep erythrocytes and to *Salmonella* flagellin were lower in elderly humans. In contrast to this decline in natural antibodies with age, there is an increase in autoantibodies and monoclonal immunoglobulins with age (Fig 20–6). Autoan-

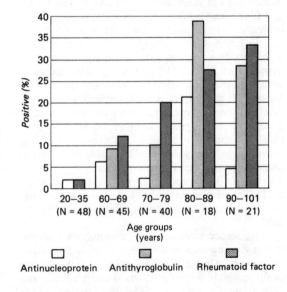

Figure 20–6. Studies of 3 circulating autoimmune antibodies—antinucleoprotein, antithyroglobulin antibody, and rheumatoid factor—show that all increase with age. The reversal of the trend in the very old could, of course, reflect selection by survival. (Modified and reproduced, with permission, from Hallgren HM et al: *J Immunol* 1973; 111:1101, in Weksler ME: *Hosp Pract* [Oct] 1981.)

tibodies to nucleic acids, smooth muscle, mitochondria, lymphocytes, gastric parietal cells, immunoglobulins, and thyroglobulin have all been found with increased frequency in elderly people. When human sera were tested for antinuclear antibody, antithyroglobulin antibody, and rheumatoid factor, approximately one-third of humans over the age of 60 had one or more of these autoantibodies. Some elderly subjects have autoantibodies to a suppressor subset of T lymphocytes. Thus, these autoantibodies might contribute to the disordered immunoregulation of the immune system that accompanies aging. The appearance of autoantibodies results from changes in the lymphoid system. Thus, polyclonal activation of human B lymphocytes showed that there were more autoantibody-secreting lymphocytes in old as compared to young controls.

One class of autoantibodies, auto-anti-idiotypic antibodies, plays an important role in the "down" regulation of the immune response. Anti-idiotypes inhibit the secretion of idiotype-containing antibody. Old animals have been shown to produce excessive auto-anti-idiotypic antibody during the immune response (Fig 20–7). The presence of this anti-idiotype can be demonstrated by the addition of the specific hapten. The hapten inhibits interactions between the idiotype and anti-idiotype, and thus leads to enhanced secretion of idiotype-bearing anti-hapten antibody.

The appearance of autoantibodies has been related to a loss of self-tolerance. Loss of self-tolerance is also suggested by the capacity of lymphocytes from old animals to induce a GVH reaction in syngeneic animals. Furthermore, as has been found in autoimmune strains of mice, the induction of B lymphocyte and T lymphocyte tolerance to exogenous antigens has been shown to be much more difficult in old mice.

In contrast to an increase in the production of autoantibodies, the response of elderly humans and experimental animals to foreign antigens decreases with age. For example, the antibody response to Japanese B encephalitis and parainfluenza virus vaccines was lower in old as compared to young humans. Similarly, the response to pneumococcal polysaccharide, *Salmonella* flagellin, and tetanus toxoid was depressed in elderly people. The character of the immune response was also altered in elderly subjects. The IgG antibody response was more impaired than the IgM response, and the antibody titers were maintained for a shorter time in old as compared to young individuals.

Age-associated changes in the antibody response to foreign antigens have also been studied in experimental animals. Almost all studies revealed that a decline in the antibody response occurs with age. Peak antibody responses were observed during the first third of the life span (in mice between the ages of 2 and 12 months). Subsequently, the antibody response, usually measured as the concentration of serum antibody or the number of splenic plaque-forming cells, declined during the last quarter of the animal's life span so that the aged humoral response was less than 25% of

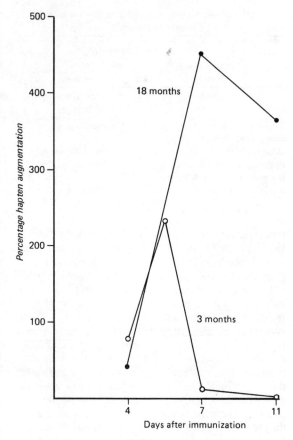

Figure 20–7. C57BL/6 mice, 3 and 18 months of age, were immunized intravenously with 10 μg of TNP-Ficoll and killed at various times after immunization. Their spleens were assayed for direct anti-TNP PFC in the presence and the absence of various concentrations of hapten. The percentage of hapten augmentation is the average obtained from 5 individual mice and is the result of comparing the PFC obtained in the presence of hapten to that obtained in the absence of hapten. (Reproduced, with permission, from Goidl EA et al: *Proc Natl Acad Sci USA* 1980;**77**:6790.)

the maximal response. In general, the primary response was more compromised than the secondary response. The dose of antigens required for a maximal antibody response was 10-fold greater in old mice.

This decline might be related to decreases in the number or affinity of surface receptors for antigen. There is a preferential loss of the IgG and high-affinity antibody response in elderly mice. IgG and high-affinity antibody are highly thymus-dependent, and their loss in old animals reflects the involution of the thymus gland. The finding that thymectomy accelerates the onset of these age-associated changes and the fact that young thymocytes or thymic hormones can augment the IgG and high-affinity antibody response of old mice support this conclusion. Additional support for the contribution of thymic involution to immune senescence is the greater impairment in the response of old animals to thymus-dependent as contrasted with thymus-independent antigens.

The age-associated changes in the immune system discussed so far do not distinguish between an immune system impaired by age and an immune system compromised by the environment within an elderly host. Proof that the lymphocytes from elderly donors and not the aged milieu are responsible for a depressed immune response was derived from transfer studies in which lymphocytes from young or old donors were used to reconstitute syngeneic, thymectomized, lethally irradiated young recipients and from in vitro studies of lymphocytes from young and old donors.

The transfer of lymphocytes from old mice to young, syngeneic recipients revealed an intrinsic functional defect. Thus, thymectomized recipients of old lymphocytes displayed the characteristic impairment manifested by intact old animals: a reduced immune response to foreign antigens with a preferential loss of high-affinity and IgG antibodies. If recipients had an intact thymus gland, the age-associated immune defects were significantly ameliorated. Mixed transfer studies in which B lymphocytes and T lymphocytes from old and young mice were combined in various combinations revealed that the principal defect in lymphocytes from old animals resided in the T lymphocyte preparation. Thus, helper T cell activity in old spleen cells was only one-tenth to one-third that found in spleen cell preparations from young mice. The immune responses of recipients of old lymphocytes were, to a considerable extent, reversed if thymocytes from young animals were mixed with old lymphocytes. When lymphocytes were transferred to young recipients with intact thymus glands, the immune response of these recipients was augmented. This suggests that the thymus of the young recipient was able to facilitate the development of immunologically competent lymphocytes transferred from old animals. Finally, it has been found that lymphocytes from old animals incubated in vitro with thymic hormones also had improved immunologic competence when transferred to young recipients (Table 20-7). In addition to impaired helper T cell activity, mixed transfer studies revealed that suppressor activity in spleen cell preparations increased by 12 months of age.

The humoral immune response can also be studied in vitro. Specific antibody, total antibody, and the number of antibody-forming cells can be determined after incubation of human lymphocytes with polyclonal B cell activators. Lymphocytes from elderly people produced significantly less specific antibody following in vivo immunization or in vitro activation with polyclonal B cell activators. However, there was no decrease in the total amount of immunoglobulin produced or in the total number of antibody-forming cells. The major defect in specific antibody secretion in vitro by lymphocyte preparations from elderly people was due to impaired T lymphocyte function. As was observed in cell transfer studies, a deficiency of helper T cells or an increase in suppressor

Table 20-7. Effect of thymopoietin administration on the anti-DNP PFC response of old mice.*†

Age of Mice (Months)	Thymopoietin-Treated	Indirect Anti-DNP PFC/Spleen	Heterogeneity Index
2 (9)	No	5916 ± 213	2.78 ± 0.20
24 (7)	No	385 ± 79	1.09 ± 0.05
24 (8)	Yes	977 ± 102	2.48 ± 0.33

*Reproduced, with permission, from Weksler ME et al: *J Exp Med* 1978;**148**:996.
†Twenty-four-month-old mice were given 1 µg of thymopoietin by the intraperitoneal route for 5 days before and 10 days after immunization. The thymopoietin-treated 24-month-old mice and untreated 2- and 24-month-old mice were all immunized with DNP-BCG in CFA. The number of splenic anti-DNP PFC was determined 2 weeks after immunization. The number of animals in each group is given in parentheses. The data presented are the mean ± the SEM.

T cell activity was found. B cell function appeared to be less affected by age. When human B cells were purified from young and old subjects and specific antibody response measured after polyclonal B cell activation, no significant difference in response was observed.

Recently, it has been found that the decrease in T lymphocyte function in elderly people and old animals may be in part related to their decreased capacity to produce and bind T cell growth factor. Although the proliferative response of T lymphocytes from old humans was not augmented by exogenous T cell growth factor, the plaque-forming cell response of spleen cells from old animals was augmented if T cell growth factor was added to cultures.

In summary, the humoral immune response is impaired in old subjects. This is chiefly due to a decrease in helper T cell activity, although increased suppressor activity and defects in B lymphocyte function also play a role. It is important to note that while specific antibody responses are greatly impaired with age, the total number of antibody-producing cells and the total amount of antibody formed following antigenic stimulation may be altered only slightly. These observations are reminiscent of the finding that the level of natural antibody and antibody to foreign determinants following immunization are reduced in old animals, while the total immunoglobulin response and serum immunoglobulin concentration are not affected by age. This suggests that the production of other immunoglobulins, eg, autoantibodies including auto-anti-idiotypic antibody, by the aged subject makes up for the deficiency of specific antibody production. Expressed in terms of the immunologic network theory of Jerne, during the life span of the organism there is a progressive shift in balance between idiotypic and auto-anti-idiotypic reactions. In the first half of the animal's life span, idiotypic reactions dominate the immune response, but with increasing age the production of auto-anti-idiotypic antibodies and other autoantibodies becomes dominant.

CELL–MEDIATED IMMUNITY

The maintenance of cell-mediated immunity depends upon the functional integrity of thymus-dependent lymphocytes. As thymic involution is a universal accompaniment of aging, many studies of immune senescence have centered on the functional capacity of T lymphocytes from individuals of different ages. Delayed hypersensitivity and graft rejection are 2 classic manifestations of cell-mediated immunity in vivo. Elderly humans have less vigorous delayed hypersensitivity reactions to common skin testing antigens such as *Candida* and mumps than do young individuals. The impaired responses of elderly people to these antigens might reflect either an altered response to antigenic challenge or the loss of immunologic memory or both. Differences in the interval between sensitization and challenge can be eliminated by sensitizing individuals of different ages to a new antigen, eg, dinitrochlorobenzene (DNCB) and then challenging all subjects after the same interval. Using this protocol, 30% of humans over age 70 failed to respond to DNCB, while only 5% of subjects under age 70 failed to respond.

Ethical constraints prevent the direct assessment of graft-versus-host (GVH) reaction or tissue and tumor graft rejection in normal humans. However, the lymphocyte transfer test, a cutaneous model of the GVH reaction, has been studied in individuals of different ages. Lymphocytes from old donors were less able to induce a positive transfer reaction than lymphocytes from young donors.

Graft rejections depend upon an integrated series of immune reactions, including alloantigen recognition, helper T lymphocyte proliferation, and the generation of cytotoxic T lymphocytes. Cytotoxic T lymphocytes are effector cells in graft rejection. The impaired rejection of grafts reflects a defect in the generation of cytotoxic T lymphocytes. Immunity to viral infection also depends upon the generation of cytotoxic T lymphocytes. Old mice showed a delayed generation of cytotoxic T lymphocytes with specificity to virus-infected cells, a lower peak cytotoxic response, and a shorter duration of cytotoxic activity. Older mice are also impaired in their capacity to generate T cell–mediated immunity to *Listeria monocytogenes*. Older mice infected with *Listeria* develop only one-thousandth the level of T cell immunity found in young mice.

A syngeneic GVH reaction follows the transfer of lymphocytes from old animals to syngeneic recipients. This reaction does not occur when lymphocytes from young animals are transferred to syngeneic recipients. This observation suggests the presence of "autoimmune" T lymphocytes in old animals. Thus, the increase in autoimmune reactivity seen with age is manifested by both humoral and cell-mediated immunity.

The function of T lymphocytes has also been studied in vitro. The proliferative response of lymphocytes from elderly humans is impaired by a variety of T lymphocyte mitogens, eg, phytohemagglutinin

(PHA) and concanavalin A (conA), as well as by antigens to which the lymphocyte donor had been previously sensitized. The lymphocytes of elderly persons sensitized to *Mycobacterium tuberculosis* or varicella virus did not proliferate to the same degree as lymphocytes of young donors cultured with these antigens. The proliferative defect observed in cultures from old humans was not due to a deficiency in the number of T lymphocytes, because the impaired proliferative response was also manifested when purified T lymphocytes from old subjects were used.

The cellular basis of the impaired proliferative responses of T lymphocytes of old subjects has been studied in detail. There is no defect in the capacity of lymphocytes from old persons to bind plant lectins. The number and affinity of receptors for PHA are the same in lymphocytes from old and young donors. However, lymphocyte activation following the binding of PHA is impaired in lymphocytes from old donors. A number of independent techniques have revealed that T lymphocyte preparations from elderly people contain only one-fifth to one-half as many mitogen-responsive cells as do similar preparations from young humans. Not only are there fewer mitogen-responsive T lymphocytes in the blood of elderly people, but their capacity to divide sequentially in culture is impaired. Thus, after 96 hours in culture with PHA, the number of lymphocytes from old subjects dividing for the third time is only one-fourth that found in cultures containing lymphocytes from young subjects. The number of cells dividing for the second time in cultures from old subjects is only one-half that found in cultures from young subjects, although the number of cells dividing for the first time is the same in cultures of lymphocytes from old or young donors (Table 20–8).

In summary, the impaired response of lymphocytes from old humans cultured with PHA reflects a decreased number of mitogen-responsive T lym-

Table 20–8. Sister chromatid analysis of lymphocytes from young or old individuals cultured with PHA.*†

Donor Age (Years)	Number of Lymphocytes Dividing For the First, Second, or Third Time in Culture			Thymidine Incorporation (cpm/Culture $\times 10^{-1}$)
	First	Second	Third	
23–32 (5)	895	2376	4200	47.7 ± 9.6
65–86 (7)	935	1045	815	25.9 ± 6.1

*Reproduced, with permission, from Hefton J et al: *J Immunol* 1980;**125**:1007.

†Lymphocytes were cultured for 72 hours with or without bromodeoxyuridine and PHA. After 94 hours, 1 μg of demecolcine (Colcemid) was added for the final 2 hours before the preparation of cells for sister chromatid analysis. The cells were stained with 10^{-4} M Hoechst stain 33258. These preparations were counterstained with Giemsa stain and analyzed for labeled sister chromatids. Thymidine incorporation was measured during the last 24 hours of cultures not containing bromodeoxyuridine. Data represent the mean percent of dividing cells completing one, two, or three divisions.

phocytes as well as an impaired proliferative capacity of the mitogen-responsive cells in culture. Comparable studies performed in mice have produced similar results. In addition to impaired responses of lymphocytes from old animals to plant lectins, the allogeneic and autologous mixed lymphocyte reactions have been found to be impaired when lymphocytes from old animals are used. Finally, the generation of cytotoxic T lymphocytes in the allogeneic mixed lymphocyte reaction is impaired. In addition to the defects in responsive T lymphocytes, lymphocyte preparations from old animals appear to possess suppressor activity that depresses the proliferative response. A variety of cell types, T lymphocytes, non–T lymphocytes, and macrophages have been reported to mediate suppressor activity.

CONCLUSION

The immune system changes with age. Both cell-mediated and humoral immune responses to foreign antigens and an increased response to autologous antigens are observed in old subjects. These defects can be related to the involution of the thymus and the alteration in the balance among regulatory T lymphocytes and the altered balance between idiotypic and anti-idiotypic activity. The increased susceptibility of elderly people to infectious and neoplastic disease may be a consequence of immune senescence. The contribution of autoantibodies to the pathobiology of aging is less certain. It has been suggested that autoantibodies and circulating immune complexes, which can damage tissues and organs, contribute to the pathologic changes that occur with age.

If the pathobiology of aging were related to the loss of immune competence with age, the survival of individuals with impaired immune responses would be expected to be shorter than that of individuals in whom immune competence was well maintained. Three studies have examined this thesis. In one study, more humans with severely impaired delayed hypersensitivity reactions died within a 2-year period than did age-matched controls who had well-maintained delayed hypersensitivity responses. In another study, humans with autoantibodies had a shorter survival than did age-matched individuals without autoantibodies. A third study showed that elderly humans with reduced suppressor cell activity had shorter survival than did age-matched subjects with normal suppressor activity. These studies failed to distinguish between alterations in the immune response causing shortened survival and alterations resulting from factors that lead to shortened survival. Prospective studies in animals have not revealed any correlation between immune competence measured early in life with subsequent survival. However, long-lived strains generally maintain immune competence for a longer time than do short-lived ones.

During the 1970s, many of the changes in the immune system that accompany aging were defined and related to the involution of the thymus gland. The potential contribution of immune senescence to the diseases of aging has been studied. Whether immune senescence is a primary or secondary contributor to the pathology of aging, it is likely that increased knowledge of immune senescence and the increasing ability to modulate the immune defects that occur in old subjects will offer considerable promise for the control of diseases associated with aging.

• • •

References

SEX HORMONES & IMMUNITY

General References

Carter J: The effect of progesterone, estradiol, and hCG on cell-mediated immunity in pregnant mice. *J Reprod Fertil* 1976;**46**:211.

Castro JE: Orchidectomy and the immune response. 2. Response of orchidectomized mice to antigens. *Proc R Soc Lond* [*Biol*] 1974;**185**:437.

Cohn DA: High sensitivity to androgen as a contributing factor in sex differences in the immune response. *Arthritis Rheum* 1979;**22**:1218.

Eidinger D, Garrett TJ: Studies of the regulatory effects of the sex hormones on antibody formation and stem cell differentiation. *J Exp Med* 1972;**136**:1098.

Kenny JF, Pangburn PC, Trail G: Effect of estradiol on immune competence: In vivo and in vitro studies. *Infect Immun* 1976;**13**:448.

Sex factors, steroid hormones, and the host response: Proceedings of the Kroc Foundation Conference, February

12–16, 1979, Santa Ynez Valley, California. *Arthritis Rheum* 1979;**22**:1153. [Entire issue.]

Thompson JS et al: Effect of estradiol on bone marrow transplantation in lethally irradiated mice. *Nature* 1964;**203**:265.

Wyle FA, Kent JR: Immunosuppression by sex steroid hormones. 1. The effect upon PHA- and PPD-stimulated lymphocytes. *Clin Exp Immunol* 1977;**27**:407.

Sex Steroids & Immune Disease in Animals

Raveche E, Klassen LW, Steinberg AD: Sex differences in formation of anti–T-cell antibodies. *Nature* 1976;**263**:415.

Roubinian JR, Papoian R, Talal N: Androgenic hormones modulate autoantibody responses and improve survival in murine lupus. *J Clin Invest* 1977;**59**:1066.

Sex Steroids & Immune Disease in Humans

Fuks AS, Weinstein Y: 20 alpha hydroxysteroid dehydrogenase (20 alpha SHD) activity in New Zealand mice T lymphocytes and marrow cells: Effect of age, sex, and castration. *J Immunol* 1979;**123:**1266.

Lahita R et al: Alterations of estrogen metabolism in SLE. *Arthritis Rheum* 1979;**22:**1195.

Lahita R et al: Increased 16 alpha hydroxylation of estradiol in SLE. *J Clin Endocrinol Metab* 1981;**53:**174.

Laskin CA et al: Studies of defective testosterone in murine lupus. *J Immunol* 1981;**127:**1743.

NUTRITION & THE IMMUNE SYSTEM

Axelrod AE: Immune processes in vitamin deficiency states. *Am J Clin Nutr* 1971;**24:**265.

Beisel WR et al: Single-nutrient effects on immunologic functions. *JAMA* 1981;**245:**53.

Chandra RK: *Immunology of Nutritional Disorders.* Edward Arnold, 1980.

Chandra RK: Symposium: Nutritional deficiency, immune responses, and infectious illness. *Fed Proc* 1980;**39:**3086.

Erickson KL et al: Influence of dietary fat concentration and saturation on immune ontogeny in mice. *J Nutr* 1980; **110:**1555.

Good RA: Nutrition and immunity. *J Clin Immunol* 1981;**1:**3.

Gross RL, Newberne PM: Role of nutrition in immunologic function. *Physiol Rev* 1980;**60:**188.

Levy JA et al: Dietary fat affects immune response, production of antiviral factors and immune complex disease in NZB/NZW mice. *Proc Natl Acad Sci USA* 1982;**79:**1974.

Mertin J, Hunt R: Influence of polyunsaturated fatty acids on survival of skin allografts and tumor incidence in mice. *Proc Natl Acad Sci USA* 1976;**73:**928.

Newberne PM, Thurman GB: Symposium: Lipids and the immune system. *Cancer Res* 1981;**41:**3783.

Suskind RM (editor): *Malnutrition and the Immune Response.* Raven Press, 1977.

Worthington BS: Effect of nutritional status on immune phenomena. *J Am Diet Assoc* 1974;**65:**123.

EFFECTS OF AGING ON
THE IMMUNE RESPONSE

General References

Doggert D et al: Cellular and molecular aspects of immune system aging. *Mol Cell Biochem* 1981;**37:**156.

Makinodan T, Kay MM: Age influence on the immune system. *Adv Immunol* 1980;**29:**287.

Siskind GW, Weksler ME: The effect of aging on the immune response. *Annu Rev Gerontol Geriat.* [In press.]

Walford RL et al: The immunopathology of aging. *Annu Rev Gerontol Geriat.* [In press.]

Weksler ME: The senescence of the immune system. *Hosp Pract* (Oct) 1981;**16:**53.

Thymic Involution & Immune Senescence

Bach JF et al: Evidence for a serum factor secreted by the human thymus. *Lancet* 1972;**2:**1056.

Boyd E: The weight of the thymus gland in health and in disease. *Am J Dis Child* 1932;**42:**116.

Hirokawa K, Makinodan T: Thymic involution: Effect of T cell differentiation. *J Immunol* 1975;**114:**1661.

Lewis VM et al: Age, thymic involution and circulating thymic hormone activity. *J Clin Endocrinol Metab* 1978; **48:**145.

Singh F, Singh AK: Age-related changes in human thymus. *Clin Exp Immunol* 1979;**37:**507.

Age-Associated Changes in Lymphocytes

Fournier C, Charreire T: Increases in autologous erythrocyte binding by T cells with aging in man. *Clin Exp Immunol* 1977;**29:**468.

Gilman SC, Woda BA, Feldman JD: T lymphocytes of young and aged rats. *J Immunol* 1981;**127:**149.

Gupta S, Good RA: Subpopulation of human T lymphocytes. *J Immunol* 1979;**122:**1214.

Moody CE et al: Lymphocyte transformation induced by autologous cells. *J Immunol* 1981;**44:**431.

Scholar EM, Rashidian M, Heidrick ML: Adenosine deaminase and purine nucleoside phosphorylase activity in spleen cells of aged mice. *Mech Ageing Dev* 1980;**12:**323.

Strelkouskas AJ, Andrew JA, Yunis EJ: Autoantibodies to a regulatory T cell subset in human aging. *Clin Exp Immunol* 1981;**45:**308.

Tam CF, Walford RL: Cyclic nucleotide levels in resting and mitogen-stimulated spleen cell suspensions from young and old mice. *Mech Ageing Dev* 1981;**7:**309.

Humoral Immunity

DeKruyff RH et al: Effect of aging on T cell tolerance induction. *Cell Immunol* 1980;**56:**58.

Dobken J, Weksler ME, Siskind GW: Effect of age on ease of B cell tolerance induction. *Cell Immunol* 1980;**55:**66.

Goidl EA, Innes JB, Weksler ME: Immunological studies of aging. 2. Loss of IgG and high avidity plaque-forming cells and increased suppressor cell activity in aging mice. *J Exp Med* 1976;**1445:**1037.

Goidl EA et al: Production of auto–anti-idiotypic antibody during the normal immune response: Changes in the auto–anti-idiotypic antibody response and the idiotype repertoire associated with aging. *Proc Natl Acad Sci USA* 1980; **77:**6788.

Meredith PA, Kristie JA, Walford RL: Aging increases expression of LPS-induced antibody-secreting B cells. *J Immunol* 1979;**123:**87.

Radl J et al: Immunoglobulin patterns in humans over 95 years of age. *Clin Exp Immunol* 1975;**22:**84.

Thoman ML, Weigle WO: Lymphokines and aging: Interleukin-2 production and activity in aged animals. *J Immunol* 1981;**127:**2102.

Cell-Mediated Immunity

Fournier C, Charreire J: Autologous mixed lymphocyte reaction in man. *Cell Immunol* 1981;**60:**212.

Gozes Y et al: Syngeneic GvH induced in popliteal lymph nodes by spleen cells of old C57BL/6 mice. *J Immunol* 1978;**121:**2199.

Hefton JM et al: Immunological studies of aging. 5. Impaired proliferation of PHA responsive human lymphocytes in culture. *J Immunol* 1980;**125:**1007.

Inkeles B et al: Immunological studies of aging. 3. Cytokinetic basis for the impaired response of lymphocytes from aged humans to plant lectins. *J Exp Med* 1977;**145:**1176.

Zharhary D, Gershon H: T cytotoxic reactivity of senescent mice: Affinity for target cells and determination of cell number. *Cell Immunol* 1981;**60:**470.

Reproductive Immunology | 21

Charles S. Pavia, PhD, & Daniel P. Stites, MD

The immune and reproductive systems interact at many levels. Impregnation of the female by sperm represents an intrusion that must be accepted in order to produce progeny. Fertilization itself must occur in a relatively hostile immunologic environment, since it involves intimate association of the histoincompatible sperm and ovum. Implantation of the zygote with its full complement of paternal and maternal genes and the subsequent development of the placenta are events that should theoretically evoke antagonistic maternal immune responses. However, gestation in all outbred species is a fact that appears to transgress the laws of transplantation. The parturition process has many similarities to immune rejection, but currently there is no evidence that birth is a consequence of the termination of immunologic tolerance between fetus and mother.

Infertility can be induced experimentally by immunization with sperm. Potentially adverse consequences of immunity to sperm in vasectomized males with autoimmunity to sperm is a subject of great interest. Seminal plasma constituents appear to be capable of regulating local immune responses that might otherwise be harmful. Derangements of these physiologic processes in which immune and reproductive systems interact can cause disease. New knowledge regarding pathologic events in this interaction will continue to provide insights into both reproduction and immunology.

REPRODUCTIVE IMMUNOLOGY IN THE FEMALE

Periodic preparations for fertilization and pregnancy occur at monthly intervals when the human female undergoes a physiologic cycle involving maturation and ovulation of an oocyte. The ovum exists temporarily in the reproductive tract unless fertilized by spermatozoa following copulation. After successful fertilization, various components of the uterine (fallopian) tubes begin to nourish and transport the zygote to the uterine cavity; and, upon maturation to the blastocyst stage, the embryo implants itself into the uterine endometrium. The outer layer of cells of the implanted blastocyst, the syncytiotrophoblast, which consists of a multinucleate mass without discernible cell boundaries, now begins to actively invade and penetrate deeply into the neighboring uterine connective tissue and—together with embryonic cells derived from the inner cell mass—gives rise to the more complex fetoplacental unit. These events of viviparous reproduction represent a highly successful evolutionary process whereby the problems of transplant rejection response have been largely circumvented.

IMMUNOREGULATION OF MATERNAL RECOGNITION OF THE FETAL ALLOGRAFT

A central unresolved question is why the developing fetus, which possesses paternal transplantation antigens foreign to the mother and is therefore similar to an allograft, is able to implant and grow in the uterus. The evasion of immune destruction is even more striking, since both humoral and cellular components of the immune system of the pregnant female are activated presumably as a consequence of natural immunization induced by the embryo. Various theories have been advanced to explain the protection of the fetus against expected immune destruction. These include (1) surrounding the fetus by a physical or anatomic barrier (the trophoblast) that prevents passage of maternal lymphoid cells; (2) lack of a full complement of immunogenic paternally derived histocompatibility antigens on the intervening layer of trophoblastic cells, which are thereby incapable of eliciting maternal immune effector mechanisms; and (3) suppressor activity by fetal lymphoid cells, placental cells, and hormones. Any or all of these could enable the fetus to inhibit or circumvent immunologic attack. Other possibilities such as the uterus as a privileged immunologic site and a nonspecific weakening of the maternal immune system during pregnancy have been largely discarded in recent years.

THE UTERUS AS A SITE FOR IMMUNE REACTIVITY

Although the uterus was once considered an immunologically privileged site, most current evidence indicates that both afferent and efferent limbs of the immune response are operative in the area of this reproductive organ. Placement of experimental allografts of normal noninvasive tissue into the nonpregnant uterus usually results in their prompt rejection, similar to the fate of foreign skin grafts. Introduction of allogeneic epidermal cells, leukocytes, or spermatozoa into the uterus immunizes the recipient, resulting in hypertrophy of the draining para-aortic lymph nodes as well as a state of alloimmunity. It appears that antigenic material is capable of passing through the endometrium and is taken up by the neighboring lymphatic vessels. Washed rodent spermatozoa have a priming effect after instillation into the uterine cavity, whereas extrauterine placement is usually ineffective in evoking transplantation immunity. These examples of intrauterine sensitization against alloantigens using skin grafts or injections of cell suspensions can lead to a secondary response when there is a local challenge with tissue material of the same antigenic specificity. In addition, local alloimmunization in the uterine environment has a dramatic effect on subsequent reproductive capabilities. Increased numbers of embryos develop in pregnant animals whose uterine horns have been presensitized against paternal histocompatibility antigens and have already expressed the local "recall flare," a delayed hypersensitivity reaction. The immunologic basis for this unexpected result is unknown, although it suggests that maternal immune reactivity has a beneficial effect and may play a vital role in maternal-fetal coexistence.

Following sexual intercourse, allogeneic spermatozoa are not ordinarily recognized as foreign and are therefore not rejected in the immunocompetent maternal host. This phenomenon may be related to the presence of nonspecific immunosuppressive factors in semen. A high-molecular-weight component present in human seminal plasma has a strong suppressive effect on mitogen, antigen, and allogeneic cell activation of human lymphocytes, while other substances in semen have been shown to interfere with the microbicidal activity of antibody, complement, and granulocytes.

The events of implantation of the fertilized egg and ensuing invasion of uterine tissue by the trophoblast evoke an inflammatory reaction resulting in the formation of a highly specialized gestational tissue called the decidua. Besides possessing endocrinologic activity, decidual tissue may act as a selective barrier by preventing released fetal or trophoblastic antigens from reaching the neighboring afferent lymphatic vessels and by preventing access of sensitized maternal lymphocytes to the conceptus. The decidua may also release immunosuppressive factors. Experimental induction of the decidual reaction affords increased survival of skin allografts that have been inserted in the uteri of pseudopregnant animals. The well-known fact that ectopic pregnancy can elicit decidual reactions in extrauterine sites suggests that this locally evoked reaction at the site of implantation and the later development of the placenta play key roles in maintaining the integrity of the fetus.

MATERNAL IMMUNE RESPONSE DURING PREGNANCY

During pregnancy, there is enlargement of the lymph nodes draining the uterus, presumably in response to foreign fetal antigens or to the protein or steroid hormones produced in relatively high concentrations by the fetoplacental unit. Maternal-fetal incompatibilities can stimulate immune responses in pregnant women, resulting in the production of anti-Rh antibodies in Rh-negative women and in the formation of antihistocompatibility antibodies. These maternal antibodies react relatively specifically with both fetal and paternal leukocyte antigens, thus enabling pregnancy sera to be used as a convenient source of HLA antibodies. This humoral response appears to be augmented with increasing parity. Antibodies also arise that agglutinate leukocytes, are cytotoxic to lymphocytes, and react with antigens contained in the cytoplasm of the syncytiotrophoblast. These pregnancy-induced antibodies have a wide range of activities in vitro. They are capable of inhibiting the mixed lymphocyte reaction and the production of MIF and can interfere with the killing of trophoblast cells by maternal lymphocytes. Antibodies in pregnancy sera that inhibit the mixed lymphocyte reaction are directed primarily against HLA antigens. Of clinical interest is the lack of correlation between the formation of anti-HLA antibodies by the mother and the incidence of congenital disorders.

In addition, a significant number of women express cell-mediated immunity to fetoplacental antigens. When maternal and newborn lymphocytes are mixed together, the production of MIF for guinea pig macrophages was observed in 50% of the mothers studied immediately after delivery. MIF was not detected when maternal cells were cultured with lymphocytes from unrelated donors. In a larger study using the MIF assay, it was demonstrated that pregnant women develop cellular immunity against placental antigens during the fourth month of pregnancy, and this immunity can be maintained for several months. These experiments may measure the response to specific trophoblast antigens not present on cord blood lymphocytes. Human maternal lymphocytes can kill fetal-placental target cells in vitro. However, convincing evidence that this phenomenon occurs in other species is lacking or has been obscured because of inhibitors in pregnancy serum.

Another in vitro indicator of cellular immunity, the mixed lymphocyte reaction, measures allogeneic differences between 2 cell populations and correlates well with the genetic disparity between fetus and mother. Lymphocyte responses of pregnant hosts to paternal or unrelated alloantigens in the mixed lymphocyte reaction do not seem to differ greatly when compared to the responses of nonpregnant controls. Similar results have been reported when responses to PHA were evaluated, indicating that maternal lymphocyte activity during pregnancy is functionally intact. However, substances present in pregnancy serum substantially alter these otherwise normal immune responses. Clinical studies have shown that these inhibitors were absent from the sera of women who were prone to idiopathic spontaneous abortions.

ALLOANTIGENICITY OF THE FETOPLACENTAL UNIT & AN IMMUNOLOGIC ROLE FOR THE PLACENTA

The placenta is a unique and complex organ by virtue of the brief duration of its biologic existence and the heterogeneous composition of structural elements and functionally active cell types belonging to the trophoblastic, lymphocytic, and erythroid series. Like the fetus, the placenta consists of tissue derived from 2 different parental genotypes. The production of protein and steroid hormones that regulate the physiologic activities of pregnancy has long been recognized as a crucial function of the placenta. Concurrently, it acts as the fetal lung, kidney, intestine, and liver. It is becoming increasingly evident that an immunologic role for this organ may be of paramount importance for the successful maintenance of mammalian pregnancy.

That both the maternal and paternal components of fetal transplantation antigens are expressed on cellular elements within the placenta seems unquestionable. However, from an immunologic standpoint, the key question is whether transplantation antigens can be demonstrated on trophoblast membranes. These membranes are the interface in direct apposition to the maternal circulation in hemochorial placentas (such as in humans). As such, they present a direct challenge for both the afferent and efferent limbs of the immune response and could serve as the site of immune attack by immunologically competent maternal lymphocytes.

Whether or not transplantation antigens are expressed on trophoblasts has become a matter of intense controversy. The answer seems to be dependent upon the ontogenetic and phylogenetic expression of these antigens at various stages of gestation. It has been reported that placental antigens may be masked by histocompatibility or specific trophoblast antibodies, fibrinoid, fibrinomucoid, or immune complexes. It has been difficult to demonstrate HLA antigens on human trophoblast cells. Serologic and transplantation studies show that H-2 antigens are expressed weakly on early-stage murine trophoblast, while significant levels of these antigens have been found on late gestational trophoblast material. Whether transplantation antigens are present in an immunogenic form on mammalian trophoblast cells is an important key to our understanding of the many aspects of the immunologic interaction between mother and fetus. The demonstration that maternal lymphocytes are capable of killing cultured human trophoblast cells from their own placenta and that late gestational placental trophoblast cells from mice can induce specific cell-mediated immunity for the relevant paternal alloantigenic determinants suggests that trophoblast cells do display transplantation antigens. Extrauterine placental allografts are usually rejected by allogeneic recipients and provoke a state of alloimmunity, while transplants of trophoblast from early gestational tissue proceed to grow and develop unimpeded without eliciting a detectable allograft rejection response.

A variety of hormonal and immunologic events occurring during pregnancy could modulate maternal transplantation immunity against paternal antigens expressed on the placenta and trophoblast. Circulating substances such as alpha-fetoprotein, placental-ovarian steroids, protein hormones, and antibody have widely different concentrations in pregnancy serum than at their sites of production. These factors have been proposed as naturally occurring immunosuppressive factors. However, there is currently no firm evidence that any of these circulating factors adequately explain the cell regulatory events that occur in the maternal immune system. Although the individual concentrations of a variety of gestational steroid and protein hormones in maternal serum never achieve a level that will suppress immunity in vivo, these substances taken together could exert a potent immunosuppressive effect at the fetal-maternal interface, where they are made and maintained at high levels throughout most stages of pregnancy. Interestingly, the trophoblast produces most of the major pregnancy-associated hormones that have been implicated as immunomodulators, which is consistent with evidence that trophoblastic cells themselves or soluble extracts or eluates of placental tissue inhibit various expressions of cell-mediated immunity.

Other immunologic properties have been ascribed to cells derived from placenta. Trophoblastic tissue serves as an anatomic barrier between fetal and maternal tissues and thereby serves as the first line of defense against maternal antifetal alloimmunity. During early gestation, the trophoblast actively invades and proliferates within the maternal decidua, and—similar to the macrophage—it phagocytoses erythrocytes and other soluble as well as particulate material of maternal origin. Different stages of the trophoblast are highly phagocytic and capable of engulfing pathogenic microorganisms (Fig 21–1). Additional examples of placental immunocompetence include the ability of lymphoid cells from murine placentas to mediate GVH reactions, respond to mitogenic lectins, and synthesize antibodies. The expression of immunelike function by both trophoblastic elements and lymphoid stem cells may be one of several processes enabling the fetoplacental unit to protect itself from injury. This is accomplished by preventing harmful infectious agents and certain maternal antigens and antibodies from reaching the embryo and by limiting passage of cells from mother to fetus. These defense mechanisms could be especially important during the early stages of in utero development, when the fetus is quite vulnerable, since it has not yet acquired complete immune competence.

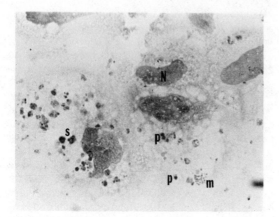

Figure 21–1. Cultured mouse ectoplacental cone tropho-blast was exposed for 18 hours to the blood stage form of the rodent malaria parasite *Plasmodium berghei*. Mature intracellular forms, the schizonts (s), and extracellular merozoites (m) are readily phagocytosed along with pig-ment granules (p). The large and irregularly shaped nuclei (N) and highly vacuolated cytoplasm of the syncytial trophoblast can also be clearly seen.

FETAL–MATERNAL EXCHANGE OF HUMORAL & CELLULAR COMPONENTS

In humans, the placenta is hemochorial which means that there is direct apposition between the ma-ternal circulation and the syncytiotrophoblast that lines the chorionic villi of the placenta. Although fetus and mother are grossly separated, cells as well as soluble substances can pass through the placenta during gesta-tion, particularly at the time of placental separation (Fig 21–2).

That such transplacental traffic results in allosen-sitization to transplantation antigens has been extrapo-lated from observations rather than proved by rigor-ously documented experiments. Syncytial trophoblast (more than 200,000 cells per day) is continuously released from the placenta and has been shown to circulate in human maternal blood from the 18th week of gestation. Various blood elements that undoubtedly contain transplantation antigens can pass bidirection-ally. This establishes adequate conditions for sensitiza-tion of the mother by fetal (paternal) transplantation antigens. Under experimental circumstances—or clin-

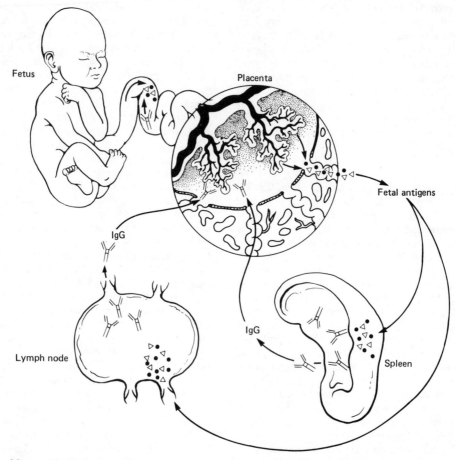

Figure 21–2. Maternal-fetal-placental complex. The anatomic features of the fetal-maternal relationship during pregnancy are depicted, with the placenta acting as a selective filter of leaking fetal or trophoblastic antigens that may sensitize maternal immune effector mechanisms. The passage of maternal immunity to the fetus is likewise regulated by the intervening layer of trophoblastic cells (where fetal and maternal tissues are in intimate proximity).

ically after intrauterine blood transfusion—immuno-competent cells that gain entrance to the fetus can rarely cause GVH disease and runting. The placenta, then, provides only a partial barrier to transport of soluble or cellular elements and certainly should not be viewed as an absolute impediment to their traffic.

In addition, whereas under normal physiologic conditions the trophoblast seems to be invulnerable to immune attack, it is quite probable that some maternal reactivity to this tissue does arise primarily to protect the pregnant host from extensive and otherwise unchecked growth and invasion of the trophoblast, as occurs in choriocarcinoma.

In the early stages of fetal development in primates, immune protection of the fetus is provided by maternally derived antibodies acquired exclusively by placental transmission. In other species, immunoglobulins are transferred via the yolk sac or via intestinal absorption of colostrum during suckling. During gestation, only antibodies belonging to the IgG class are readily transferred from mother to fetus, and this process is most likely facilitated by the interaction of immunoglobulin molecules with Fc receptors shown to be present on the surface of trophoblastic membranes and other extraembryonic membrane components. With intrauterine infection, the fetus is capable of synthesizing IgM and IgA. The presence of high levels of these immunoglobulins in cord serum at birth is presumptive evidence of such infection.

The neonate is exposed to an environment that presents much greater risk of infection than was the case in the uterine shelter. Unless in utero infection has occurred, the newborn is usually not capable of mounting a quick and effective reaction against pathogenic organisms. Maternally acquired antibody provides initial protection against infection. The presence of maternal immunoglobulins in sufficiently high titer should protect against the initial invasion of certain pathogens that would otherwise multiply and disseminate without hindrance.

IMMUNOLOGIC CONSEQUENCES OF TRANSPLACENTALLY PASSED SUBSTANCES

Under certain circumstances, transferred maternal antibody is not beneficial to the fetus. This is most evident in the classic case of hemolytic disease of the newborn mediated by either ABO or Rh blood group fetal-maternal incompatibilities. Situations involving ABO incompatibilities arise more frequently than Rh hemolytic disease but usually take a milder course, with cases requiring transfusion being extremely rare. The disorder occurs primarily in blood group O mothers bearing fetuses of type A or B and is believed to be the result of the transfer of IgG anti-A or anti-B antibodies from mother to fetus. Although blood group A and group B women have antibody to type B and type A erythrocytes, respectively, these naturally occurring isoagglutinins are usually of the IgM class and therefore do not readily cross the placenta and cannot

harm the potentially susceptible fetus.

The more serious condition that can adversely affect fetal development results from Rh isoimmunization, which resembles the pathophysiology of ABO incompatibility yet manifests important immunologic differences. Rh antigens are expressed on blood cells only, whereas antigenic specificities related to A and B blood group determinants are widely distributed in nature and in the human body. During a pregnancy in which an Rh-negative mother is bearing an Rh-positive fetus, sensitization may occur if fetal red blood cells cross into the maternal circulation via the placenta or when there is transplacental hemorrhage following the birth of the child or after an abortion. Alternatively, the mother could already be primed as a result of receiving an earlier transfusion of Rh-positive blood. Less than 1 mL of fetal blood can elicit a response. Maternal antibodies pass through the placenta, gain access to the fetal bloodstream, and cause the destruction of red blood cells. Rh disease occurs rarely during the first pregnancy, with the vast majority of Rh-negative mothers becoming sensitized with increasing parity. The deleterious effects of isoimmunization can be prevented conveniently by administering Rh_0 (D) immune globulin to the mother immediately after delivery of her first Rh-positive child or following an abortion. The major suggested explanation for the action of anti-Rh immunoglobulins is that fetal erythrocytes present in the maternal circulation as a result of fetal detachment are destroyed and rapidly cleared, so that they are not available long enough to sensitize the mother effectively. Treatment must be administered after subsequent Rh-incompatible pregnancies, since there is no apparent development of tolerance following prophylactic therapy.

In certain situations, simultaneous ABO and Rh incompatibilities between mother and fetus may prevent the more destructive effects of Rh isoimmunization. The naturally occurring anti-A or anti-B antibodies in a group O, Rh-negative mother will effectively destroy Rh-positive erythrocytes crossing the placenta if the fetus is also of either group A or B blood type. The rapid removal of these cells by the already primed maternal immune system would make sensitization against Rh factor highly unlikely.

REPRODUCTIVE IMMUNOLOGY IN THE MALE

Since males are not exposed to histoincompatible gametes during reproduction, immune alterations involving the male reproductive system are necessarily autoimmune in nature. Experimentally, auto- or alloimmunization to spermatozoa can in fact result in relative infertility either in the female or male. Naturally occurring autoimmune reactions to sperm are rare but have become increasingly recognized as a consequence of vasectomy. Recent findings suggest that potentially harmful immune responses associated with spermatozoa as antigens are inhibited by naturally occurring immunoregulatory substances in seminal plasma.

ANTIGENS ON SPERMATOZOA

The expression of antigens on sperm is central to the consideration of their immunogenicity in the reproductive tract, much the same as is the presence of antigens on placental trophoblast. Sperm antigens could theoretically elicit either auto- or alloimmunity, and either type could result in partial or complete infertility. Alternatively, these antigens could be nonimmunogenic in the normal environment of the reproductive tract.

With the possible exception of LDH-X, an isoenzyme of LDH restricted mainly to sperm, there do not appear to be any truly tissue-specific antigens on sperm. ABO blood group antigens are expressed on sperm only in secretors, and this important fact suggests that they are absorbed from seminal plasma. Whether these antigens are expressed in the absence of such absorption is currently moot, and no evidence for antibodies to ABO antigens in infertility has been found. The presence of Rh antigens and the haploid expression of the genes determining these blood group antigens remains controversial.

Histocompatability antigens are most likely intrinsically expressed on sperm and not absorbed from seminal plasma. Ia antigens in the mouse are clearly detectable on sperm from epididymis and ductus deferentes, the regions of the male reproductive tract where seminal plasma has not yet been formed. Whether both parental haplotypes are expressed in sperm remains unresolved. HLA-A, -B, -C, and -D antigens all appear to be present on sperm. Evidence for the presence of HLA-D antigens, the probable human analogs of murine Ia antigens, has been derived primarily from the ability of sperm to stimulate lymphocytes in allogeneic mixed sperm lymphocyte cultures. Conclusions from these experiments have been criticized by some because the sperm stimulator cell population was contaminated with small numbers of other cells from the reproductive tract, especially leukocytes known to express HLA-D antigens. However, the weight of evidence at present favors the presence of MHC-determined alloantigens on spermatozoa.

H-Y antigen, which is encoded as a male-specific antigen by a gene on the Y chromosome and is central to primary sex differentiation, appears to be expressed on sperm. If sperm expressed exclusively either Y- or X-determined antigens, the potential for sex determination by antibodies directed at either X- or Y-bearing sperm would be possible. However, most investigators have not been able to show haploid expression of genes determining H-Y or H-X antigens on sperm. Thus, the possibility of exploiting haploid gene expression for sex determination appears remote.

Unresolved questions in the important area of sperm antigens include (1) whether transplantation antigens are expressed in a haploid or diploid mode, (2) the identity of a sperm-specific antigen, and (3) the definition of antigens that give rise to antibodies which cause infertility in males or females.

METHODS OF DETECTING SPERM ANTIBODIES

Many techniques have been described over the years for detection of sperm antibodies in serum and other body secretions. Only 2 have stood the test of time, because they produce results that correlate well with immunologically induced clinical infertility: sperm immobilization tests and sperm agglutination tests. Immunofluorescence and cytotoxicity assays are quite nonspecific and do not usually produce results relevant to the clinical study of immunologic infertility.

Sperm Immobilization Tests

Antibodies absolutely dependent on complement to produce immobilization of sperm were initially described by Fjällbrant (1965) and Isojima (1968). In these assays, donor sperm from the male to be tested—or from a normal control—are washed and incubated with serial dilution of heat-inactivated test serum or other secretions. These can be derived from the male to be tested or from female partners. A source of complement (usually fresh guinea pig serum) is added. A time end point for immobilization (Fjällbrant) of 90% sperm—or a percentage of motile sperm at a standard time (Isojima)—is compared microscopically with sperm incubated in control sera and complement alone. Results obtained from immobilization tests have a definite relationship to immunologic infertility. However, correlation of sperm-immobilizing antibodies with agglutinating antibodies is not perfect.

Sperm Agglutination Tests

Agglutination tests are a sensitive and specific means of detecting sperm antibodies. The 2 main procedures for sperm agglutination are the gelatin agglutination test of Kibrick and the microagglutination test read macroscopically. In the Franklin-Dukes method, no gelatin is used, and agglutination is read on slides or in a microtiter tray in the microscope. Agglutination may be primarily head-to-head or tail-to-tail, rarely head-to-tail. Tail-to-tail agglutination usually occurs in female sera and head-to-head in male sera. The antigens detected by this test are not fully characterized.

Failure to give careful attention to controls in sperm antibody tests has often led to misleading results. Obviously, obtaining a standard source of viable human sperm presents difficulties. Known positive and negative control sera must be included. Other methods, especially immunofluorescence, enzyme-tinted immunoassays, and RIA show promise and would seem to justify further development as reliable clinically relevant antibody assays for human spermatozoa.

ROLE OF ANTISPERM ANTIBODIES IN INFERTILITY

Antisperm Immunity in the Male

There is little doubt that antibodies directed toward various sperm antigens can result in reduced fertility in men. Nevertheless, the precise nature of the immune response against sperm antigens and the particular type of antibody responsible—ie, an agglutinating or immobilizing antibody—remain problematic. Results from several large series on the presence of sperm agglutinins in fertile and infertile men are presented in Table 21-1.

The conclusion from such studies places the cutoff point for a significant titer of sperm-agglutinating antibodies at approximately 1:32. In most such studies, the correlation between sperm agglutinins and complement-dependent immobilizing antibodies is reasonably high. However, the tendency is toward lower titers and fewer fertile individuals with positive immobilizing antibodies. Thus, immobilizing antibodies are mainly specific. Although agglutinating antibodies are a sensitive index for infertility, their specificity is poor.

A likely mechanism for decrease in fertility produced by antisperm antibody is reduction in mobility of the sperm, making it difficult to penetrate cervical mucus. Experimentally, sperm coated with antibody fail to move well through cervical mucus in vitro, when observed in the cervical mucus in a postcoital examination. Thus, antisperm antibody present in seminal plasma or in cervical secretions could prevent the normal penetration of the sperm into the uterus. In fact, direct instillation of sperm in the uterine cavity, after carefully washing them free of antibody, has resulted in fertilization in some instances of antibody-mediated infertility.

Most agglutinating antibodies to sperm in seminal plasma are of the IgA class, and immobilizing antibodies are predominantly IgG. IgM rarely gains access to seminal plasma without a significant inflammatory lesion in the reproductive tract.

The mechanism by which antisperm antibodies

reduce male fertility is related neither to orchitis nor oligospermia. The presence of cytotoxic antisperm antibody correlates poorly with both conditions. It is true that 30% of infertile men with sperm agglutinins have oligospermia, but the majority also have blockage of the efferent ducts in the testes, and a physical explanation thus exists for reduced sperm counts. It is likely that as in vasectomy, resorption of sperm from blocked ducts results in the formation of autoantibodies to sperm.

Autoimmune orchitis can develop in some animals with a permeable blood-testis barrier. This complication is more likely a result of cellular immunity, since in experimental animals it can be transferred with lymphocytes but not antibody. There is no convincing evidence for orchitis as a consequence of vasectomy in men.

Several studies using in vitro correlates of cellular immunity to sperm in infertile individuals have been performed. These have for the most part given conflicting results. Neither lymphocyte transformation nor leukocyte inhibitory factor production has given consistent evidence for cellular sensitization in individuals with sperm immunity. Clearly, this is an important area requiring additional study.

Various forms of therapy have been employed to reduce antibodies to sperm in the male. These include systemic administration of adrenal corticosteroids, attempts at artificial insemination with washed sperm, and, in the case of antibodies in the female, condoms to reduce antibody titers by reducing exposure to sperm. The success of all of these forms of treatment is limited. Further studies are needed to fully confirm their efficacy, especially in controlled clinical trials.

Antisperm Immunity in the Female

Despite the clear-cut experimental production of infertility in sperm-immunized female mice or rabbits, no convincing pathologic role for antisperm antibodies in women has been demonstrated. The effect of antisperm antibodies in immunized women is mainly embryo loss and thus occurs after fertilization. In some studies in women, approximately 75% of patients with primary infertility had serum sperm agglutinins. However, 11–15% of pregnant women also had the same titers of sperm antibody. Many of these false-positive reactions are due to the presence of nonantibody sperm agglutinins, particularly β-globulins and lipoproteins. Nevertheless, the presence of sperm agglutinins in cervical mucus could perhaps interfere with the penetration of sperm into the uterus. Studies meticulously delineating the presence of local versus serum antibody to sperm are needed.

IMMUNOLOGIC CONSEQUENCES OF VASECTOMY

About a million vasectomies are performed annually in the USA. As a result of this procedure, antibodies and probably cellular immunity to sperm

Table 21-1. Sperm-agglutinating antibodies.*

Study	Infertile Men		Fertile Men	
	Number of Subjects	Percent With Ab	Number of Subjects	Percent With Ab
1	400	6.8	500	None
2	1913	3.2	416	2.6
3	2015	3.3	416	None

*Adapted from Mettler L, Scheidl P, Shirwani D: *Int J Fertil* 1974;**19**:7.

develop in most men as a result of interaction of extravasated sperm antigens with the immune system. Sperm are autoimmunogenic, mainly because of their normal sequestration behind a blood-testis barrier and their late development relative to the establishment of self tolerance. The potential adverse consequences of this immune response to sperm include (1) systemic effects on other organ systems and (2) interference with fertility after reanastomosis of the vasa deferentia (vasovasostomy).

There is no doubt that vasectomy in humans leads to production of sperm antibodies. Most studies indicate a 60–70% incidence of sperm agglutinins in serum and a 30–40% incidence of immobilizing antibodies by 1 year following the procedure. There does not appear to be any significant decline in incidence of titer after 5 years, and fragmentary evidence exists for persistence of antibody for 15–20 years.

Granuloma formation due to local extravasation of sperm is relatively common, but the presence of granulomas correlates poorly with antibody to sperm. The antibodies that develop after vasectomy are tissue-specific and do not react with HLA or Ia antigens. A recent study showed a strong association of HLA-A28 with production of sperm antibodies following vasectomy, suggesting a genetic predisposition.

Little is known about cellular immunity to sperm following vasectomy. Several studies in animals immunized with sperm or undergoing vasectomy have shown inconstant development of T lymphocyte responsiveness to sperm. In vitro cellular immune studies in humans are still inconclusive. The well-recognized in vitro immunoinhibitory action of seminal plasma may in fact prevent such responses in vivo. Much more needs to be learned about other components of the immune response to sperm following vasectomy.

There are no established adverse systemic immune effects of vasectomy in humans. In 1968, a few patients with vasectomy were reported with either thrombophlebitis, glomerulonephritis, or multiple sclerosis, but these sequelae have not been observed in larger series. Sex hormone levels are not influenced by vasectomy. A slight increase in antinuclear and anti-smooth muscle antibodies has been demonstrated in a few individuals. There is fragmentary evidence for circulating immune complexes composed of sperm antigens and antibody following vasectomy in men.

A surgical method for reanastomosis of ligated vasa deferentia, termed vasovasostomy, has been successfully developed. The presence of sperm antibodies in 60–70% of vasectomized men represents a potential threat to restoration of full fertility. There are conflicting studies about whether the presence of sperm an-

tibodies results in decreased fertility in such individuals. However, the well-documented antifertility effects of high-titered sperm antibody make it likely that fertility may not be fully restored.

IMMUNOLOGIC FEATURES OF SEMINAL PLASMA

Seminal plasma contains a variety of potentially antigenic substances, particularly enzymes, on enzymatic proteins and nonproteinaceous substances. Immunoglobulins are also present but at much lower concentrations than in serum (IgG, 7–13 mg/dL; IgA, 2–6 mg/dL). IgM is not normally detectable. Other substances with potential regulatory effects in the immune system include transferrin, zinc, prostaglandins, and polyamines.

Several potentially important immunoinhibitory substances have been detected in seminal plasma. One of these has broad-spectrum immunosuppressive effects on T lymphocyte function in vitro, including proliferation induced by mitogen, antigen, and allogeneic cells and in vitro mouse antibody production to T cell–independent and T cell–dependent antigens. Although this factor is apparently a macromolecule present in several species, direct evidence of an in vivo immunosuppressive effect is lacking.

Seminal plasma interferes with a variety of microbicidal functions. Bactericidal and opsonic activity of serum or granulocytes was blocked for a variety of microorganisms, including *Neisseria gonorrhoeae* and *Escherichia coli* but not *Staphylococcus aureus*. The precise mechanism by which this inhibitory activity is mediated has not yet been determined. Complement activation is reduced by incubation with seminal plasma, which contains a large variety of proteases and protease inhibitors. It is interesting to speculate that the various immunoinhibitors in seminal plasma have a role in protecting sperm from immunologic attack in the female reproductive tract. In pathologic states, infectious agents may escape destruction in the reproductive tract as a consequence of inhibition of microbicidal action.

Anaphylaxis due to components of semen (either sperm or seminal plasma) has been rarely described. Symptoms occur immediately following sexual intercourse and include urticaria, angioedema, and occasionally hypotension. Immediate hypersensitivity to intrinsic seminal plasma antigens has been demonstrated. Therapy consists of either abstinence or use of a condom to prevent contact with semen and has proved somewhat successful.

References

General

Beer AE, Billingham RE: *The Immunobiology of Mammalian Reproduction.* Prentice-Hall, 1976.

Scott JS, Jones WR: *Immunology of Human Reproduction.* Academic Press, 1976.

The Uterus as a Site for Immune Reactivity

Beer AE, Billingham RE: Host response to intra-uterine tissue of cellular and fetal allografts. *J Reprod Fertil [Suppl]* 1974;**21:**59.

Stites DP, Erickson RP: Suppressive effect of seminal plasma on lymphocyte activation. *Nature* 1975;**253:**727.

Maternal Immune Response During Pregnancy

Carr MC, Stites DP,Fudenberg HH: Cellular immune aspects of the human fetal-maternal relationship. 3. Mixed lymphocyte reactivity between maternal and cord blood lymphocytes. *Cell Immunol* 1974;**11:**332.

Hetherington CM, Humber DP: The effect of pregnancy on lymph node weight in the mouse. *J Immunogenet* 1977; **4:**271.

Rocklin RE et al: Maternal-fetal relation: Absence of an immunologic blocking factor from the serum of women with chronic abortions. *N Engl J Med* 1976;**295:**1209.

Terasaki PI et al: Maternal-fetal incompatibility. 1. Incidence of HL-A antibodies and possible association with congenital anomalies. *Transplantation* 1970;**9:**538.

Youtananukorn V, Matangkasombut P: Specific plasma factors blocking human maternal cell-mediated immune reaction to placental antigens. *Nature* 1973;**242:** 110.

Immunoregulation of Maternal Recognition of the Fetal Allograft

Kasakura S: A factor in maternal plasma during pregnancy that suppresses the reactivity of mixed leukocyte cultures. *J Immunol* 1971;**107:**1296.

Pavia CS, Stites DP: Humoral and cellular regulation of alloimmunity in pregnancy. *J Immunol* 1979;**123:**2194.

Siiteri PK et al: Progesterone and maintenance of pregnancy: Is progesterone nature's immunosuppressant? *Ann NY Acad Sci* 1977;**286:**384.

Stites DP et al: Immunologic regulation in pregnancy. *Arthritis Rheum* 1979;**22:**1300.

Alloantigenicity of the Fetoplacental Unit & an Immunologic Role for the Placenta

Chatterjee-Hasrouni S, Lala PK: Localization of H-2 antigens on mouse trophoblast cells. *J Exp Med* 1979;**149:**1238.

Faulk WP et al: Antigens of human trophoblasts: A working hypothesis for their role in normal and abnormal pregnancies. *Proc Natl Acad Sci USA* 1978;**75:**1947.

Pavia CS, Stites DP: Transplantation antigen expression on murine trophoblast: Detection by induction of specific alloimmunity. *Cell Immunol* 1981;**64:**162.

Pavia CS, Stites DP: Trophoblast regulation of maternal-paternal lymphocyte interactions. *Cell Immunol* 1981; **58:**202.

Siiteri PK, Stites DP: Immunologic and endocrine interrelationships in pregnancy. *Biol Reprod* 1982;**26:**1.

Fetal-Maternal Exchange of Humoral & Cellular Components

Brambell FWR: *The Transmission of Passive Immunity from Mother to Young.* Vol 18 of: *Frontiers of Biology.* North-Holland, 1970.

Jenkinson EJ, Billington WD, Elson J: Detection of receptors for immunoglobulin on human placenta by EA rosette formation. *Clin Exp Immunol* 1976;**23:**456.

Solomon JB: *Foetal and Neonatal Immunology.* Vol 20 of: *Frontiers of Biology.* North-Holland, 1971.

Immunologic Consequences of Transplacentally Passed Substances

Scott JR, Beer AE: Immunological factors in first-pregnancy Rh isoimmunization. *Lancet* 1973;**1:**717.

Scott JS: Immunological diseases in pregnancy. *Prog Allergy* 1977;**23:**321.

Woodrow JG: Rh-immunisation and its prevention. *Nord Med* 1971;**85:**704.

Antigens on Spermatozoa

Erickson RP, Lewis SE, Butley M: Is haploid gene expression possible for sperm antigens? *J Reprod Immunol* 1981; **3:**195.

Festenstein H, Halim K, Arnaiz-Villena A: HLA antigens on sperm. Page 11 in: *Spermatozoa, Antibodies and Infertility.* Cohen J, Hendry WF (editors). Blackwell, 1978.

Ohno S, Wachtel SS: On the selective elimination of Y-bearing sperm. *Immunogenetics* 1978;**7:**13.

Methods of Detecting Sperm Antibodies

Rose NR et al: Techniques for detection of iso- and auto-antibodies to human spermatozoa. *Clin Exp Immunol* 1976; **23:**175.

Shulman S: Human sperm antibodies and their detection. Page 907 in: *Manual of Clinical Immunology.* Rose NR, Friedman H (editors). American Society for Microbiology, 1980.

Role of Antisperm Antibodies in Infertility

Fjällbrant B: Autoimmune human sperm antibodies and age in males. *J Reprod Fertil* 1975;**43:**145.

Kremer J, Jager S, Kuiken J: The clinical significance of antibodies to spermatozoa. Page 47 in: *Immunologic Influences on Human Fertility.* Boettcher B (editor). Academic Press, 1977.

Mettler L, Scheidel P, Shirwani D: Sperm antibody production in female sterility. *Int J Fertil* 1974;**19:**7.

Rümke P: Autoantibodies against spermatozoa in infertile men. *J Reprod Fertil [Suppl]* 1974;**21:**169.

Immunologic Consequences of Vasectomy

Alexander NJ: Immunological aspects of vasectomy. Page 25 in: *Immunological Influences on Human Fertility.* Boettcher B (editor). Academic Press, 1977.

Clarkson TB, Alexander NJ: Long-term vasectomy: Effects on occurrence and extent of atherosclerosis in rhesus monkeys. *J Clin Invest* 1980;**65:**15.

Lepow IH, Crozier R (editors): *Vasectomy: Immunologic and Pathophysiologic Effects in Animal and Man.* Academic Press, 1979.

Linnet L, Hjort T, Fogh-Andersen P: Association between failure to impregnate after vasovasostomy and sperm agglutinins in semen. *Lancet* 1981;**1:**117.

Lucas PL, Rose NR: Immunological consequences of vasectomy: A review. *Ann Immunol* 1978;**129:**301.

Safety of vasectomy. (Editorial.) *Lancet* 1979;**2:**1057.

Immunologic Features of Seminal Plasma

Brooks GF et al: Human seminal plasma inhibition of antibody complement-mediated killing and opsonization of *Neisseria gonorrhoeae* and other gram-negative organisms. *J Clin Invest* 1981;**67**:1523.

Lord EM, Sensabaugh GF, Stites DP: Immunosuppressive activity of human seminal plasma. 1. Inhibition of in vitro lymphocyte activation. *J Immunol* 1977;**118**:1704.

Mathias CG et al: Immediate hypersensitivity to seminal fluid and atopic dermatitis. *Arch Dermatol* 1980;**116**:209.

Section II. Immunologic Laboratory Tests

Clinical Laboratory Methods for Detection of Antigens & Antibodies | 22

Daniel P. Stites, MD

One of the major challenges for modern medical science is the translation of basic advances in immunochemistry and immunobiology into diagnostic and therapeutic procedures that will be useful in the practice of clinical medicine. Much of this work is done in the clinical immunology laboratory, where tests that utilize a great many of the recently elucidated principles of basic immunology can be performed on a wide variety of samples taken from patients. The results of these laboratory procedures are then utilized by practicing physicians in the diagnosis and treatment of clinical disorders. Furthermore, qualitative and quantitative analysis of several features of the immune response has led to better understanding of the pathogenesis of many clinical disorders. In turn, this understanding has stimulated further basic scientific research in immunology. In fact, observations made by clinical investigators in immunology have frequently dramatically changed the course of basic research in immunology and related fields. An example is the impetus given to research on T cell and B cell immune systems by careful clinical descriptions of patients with thymic aplasia and hypogammaglobulinemia.

In the past 2 decades, immunologic laboratory methods have gradually become increasingly more refined and simplified. Because of their inherent specificity and sensitivity, these methods have now achieved a central role in modern clinical laboratory science. The goals of laboratory medicine are to improve the availability, accuracy, and precision of a body of medically important laboratory tests, to assure correct interpretation, and to assess the significance of new tests introduced into clinical medicine. With the marked proliferation of new laboratory tests employing immunologic principles, these methods of laboratory diagnosis have often been uncritically applied to clinical situations. A better understanding of the methods used in the immunology laboratory should provide the student and practitioner of medicine with a useful guide for correct application and interpretation of this body of knowledge.

In the present chapter, tests for the detection of antigens and antibodies are discussed. Most of the techniques described involve application in the clinical laboratory of the principles of immunochemistry discussed in detail in Section I. This chapter and the next one are not meant to be comprehensive laboratory manuals. Rather, the principles of the various immunologic methods and their application to selected clinical problems are reviewed. It is hoped that careful study of these 2 chapters in conjunction with the first section of this book will provide the reader with a solid background for an enhanced understanding of the detailed discussions of clinical immunology presented in Section III.

The topics covered in this chapter include the following:

(1) Immunodiffusion
(2) Electrophoresis and immunoelectrophoresis
(3) Immunochemical and physicochemical methods
(4) Radioimmunoassay
(5) Immunohistochemical techniques (immunofluorescence)
(6) Agglutination
(7) Complement function

IMMUNODIFFUSION

The purpose of all immunodiffusion techniques is to detect the reaction of antigen and antibody by the precipitation reaction. Although the formation of antigen-antibody complexes in a semisolid medium such as agar is dependent on buffer electrolytes, pH, and temperature, the most important determinants of the reaction are the relative concentrations of antigen and antibody. This relationship is depicted schematically in Fig 22–1. Maximal precipitation forms in the area of equivalence, with decreasing amounts in the zones of antigen excess or antibody excess. Thus, formation of precipitation lines in any immunodiffusion system is highly dependent on relative concentrations of antigen and antibody. The **prozone phenomenon** refers to suboptimal precipitation which occurs in the region of antibody excess. Thus, dilutions of antisera need to be reacted with fixed amounts of antigen in order to obtain maximum precipitin lines. The prozone phenomenon is a common cause of misinterpretation of immunoelectrophoresis patterns in the diagnosis of paraproteinemias.

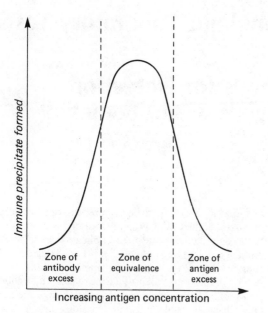

Figure 22–1. Antigen-antibody precipitin curve. Typical precipitin curve resulting from titration of increasing antigen concentration plotted against amount of immune precipitate formed. Amount of antibody is kept constant throughout.

Immunoprecipitation is the simplest and most direct means of demonstrating antigen-antibody reactions in the laboratory. The application of immunoprecipitation to the study of bacterial antigens launched the field of serology in the first part of the 20th century. In 1946, Oudin described a system of single diffusion of antigen and antibody in agar-filled tubes. This important advance was soon followed by Ouchterlony's classic description of double diffusion in agar layered on slides. This method is still in widespread use today and has many applications in the detection and analysis of precipitating antigen-antibody systems.

Immunodiffusion reactions may be classified as single or double. In single immunodiffusion, either antigen or antibody remains fixed and the other reactant is allowed to move and complex with it. In double immunodiffusion, both reactants are free to move toward each other and precipitate. Movement in either form of immunodiffusion may be linear or radial. Specific examples are discussed in the remainder of this section.

Immunodiffusion has its most important clinical application in the quantitation of serum immunoglobulins. In fact, most serum proteins (or antigens) can be accurately determined by single radial diffusion in agar as long as one has specific precipitating antibody directed against the particular serum protein in question.

METHODOLOGY & INTERPRETATION

Double Diffusion in Agar

This simple and extremely useful technique (also called **Ouchterlony analysis**) is based on the principle that antigen and antibody diffuse through a semisolid medium (eg, agar) and form stable immune complexes which then can be analyzed visually.

The test is performed by pouring molten agar onto glass slides or into Petri dishes and allowing it to harden. Small wells are punched out of the agar a few millimeters apart. Samples containing antigen and antibody are placed in opposing wells and allowed to diffuse toward one another in a moist chamber for 18–24 hours. The resultant precipitation lines that represent antigen-antibody complexes are analyzed visually in indirect light with the aid of a magnifying lens. When antigen and antibody are allowed to diffuse in a radial fashion, an arc which approximates a straight line is formed at the leading edges of the diffusing antigen and antibody. The types of patterns produced in simple double diffusion are shown in Fig 22–2.

Double diffusion is commonly performed by placing antigen and antibody wells at various angles for comparative purposes. The 3 basic characteristic patterns of those reactions are shown in Fig 22–3. In addition to these 3 basic patterns, more complex interrelationships may be seen between antigen and antibody. The formation of a single precipitation line between an antigen and its corresponding antiserum can be utilized as a rough qualitative estimation of antigen or antibody purity. However, the relative insensitivity of the test and the limitation of immunodiffusion to *precipitating* antigen-antibody reactions partly restrict the applications of this technique.

Double immunodiffusion in agar can also be used for semiquantitative analysis in human serologic systems where the specificity of the precipitation lines has already been determined. Such an analysis is performed by placing antibody in a central well surrounded circumferentially by antigen wells (Fig 22–4). Serial dilutions of antigen are placed in the surrounding wells, and the development of precipitation lines can be taken as a rough measure of antigen concentration. Alternatively, this form of analysis is

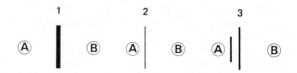

Figure 22–2. Reactions in simple double diffusion. In *(1)* antigen A and antibody B react equidistantly and intensely at equivalence. In *(2)* antigen A is present in reduced concentration or has not diffused as rapidly owing to size or charge, forming a precipitin line closer to the antigen well. In *(3)* a contaminant or impurity present in antigen A is reacting with antibody B.

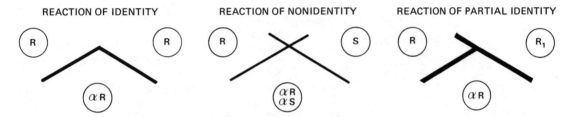

Figure 22–3. Reaction patterns in angular double immunodiffusion (Ouchterlony). R = antigen R, S = antigen S, R₁ = antigen R_1, αR = antibody to R, αS = antibody to S. **Reaction of identity:** Precisely similar precipitin lines have formed in the reaction of R with αR. Note that the lines intersect at a point. **Reaction of nonidentity:** Precipitin lines completely cross owing to separate interaction of αR with R and αS with S when R and S are non–cross-reacting antigens. **Reaction of partial identity:** αR reacts with both R and R_1 but forms lines that do not form a complete cross. Antigenic determinants are *partially* shared between R and R_1.

very useful in determining the approximate precipitating titer of an antiserum by simply reversing the location of antigen and antibody in the pattern (Fig 22–4).

Single Radial Diffusion

The double immunodiffusion system is only semiquantitative. In 1965, Mancini introduced a novel technique employing single diffusion for accurate quantitative determination of antigens. This technique grew out of the simple linear diffusion technique of Oudin by means of the incorporation of specific antibody into the agar plate. Radial diffusion is based on the principle that a quantitative relationship exists between the amount of antigen placed in a well cut in the agar-antibody plate and the resulting ring of precipita-

tion. The technique is performed as diagrammed in Fig 22–5.

In the method described originally by Mancini, the *area* circumscribed by the precipitation ring was proportionate to the antigen concentration. This end point method requires that the precipitation rings reach the maximal possible size, which often requires 48–72 hours of diffusion. Alternatively, the single radial diffusion method of Fahey allows measurement of the rings prior to full development. In this modification, the logarithm of the antigen concentration is proportionate to the *diameter* of the ring.

A standard curve is experimentally determined with known antigen standards, and the equation which describes this curve can then be used for the determina-

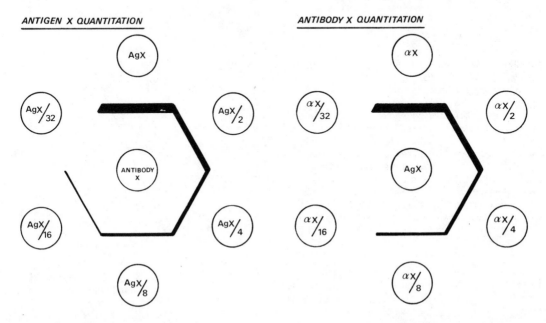

Figure 22–4. Semiquantitative analysis of antigen and antibody by double immunodiffusion. Antigen X is serially diluted and placed circumferentially in wells surrounding the central well containing antibody against antigen X. Precipitin lines form with decreasing thickness until no longer visible at dilution of 1:32 of antigen X. On the right, a similar pattern is generated but with serial 2-fold dilutions of antibody X. Formation of a single precipitin line indicates that a single antigen-antibody reaction has occurred.

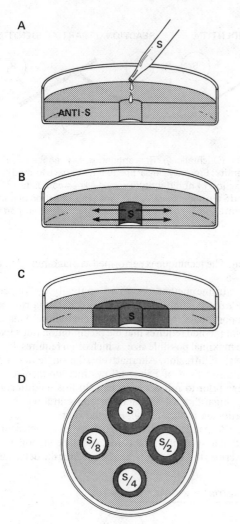

the agar in order to determine immunoglobulin concentrations. Owing to the relatively low concentrations of IgD and IgE in human serum, this technique is used primarily to determine the other 3 immunoglobulin classes, IgG, IgA, and IgM. However, by decreasing the amount of specific anti-immunoglobulin antiserum placed in the agar, so-called "low level" plates can be produced which have increased sensitivity for detection of reduced levels of serum immunoglobulins.

There are a number of common pitfalls in the interpretation of single radial diffusion tests for immunoglobulin quantitation: (1) Polymeric forms of immunoglobulin such as occur in multiple myeloma or Waldenström's macroglobulinemia diffuse more slowly than native monomers, resulting in underestimation of immunoglobulin concentrations in these diseases. (2) High-molecular-weight immune complexes which may circulate in cryoglobulinemia or rheumatoid arthritis will result in falsely low values by a similar mechanism. (3) Low-molecular-weight forms such as 7S IgM in sera of patients with macroglobulinemia, systemic lupus erythematosus, rheumatoid arthritis, and ataxia-telangiectasia may give falsely high values. This phenomenon results from the fact that 7S IgM diffuses more rapidly than the 19S IgM parent molecule, which is used as the standard. (4) Reversed precipitation may occur in situations where the test human serum contains anti-immunoglobulin antibodies. In such a circumstance, diffusion and precipitation occur in 2 directions simultaneously and may result in falsely high values. This

Figure 22–5. Single radial diffusion in agar (radial immunodiffusion). *A:* Petri dish is filled with semisolid agar solution containing antibody to antigen S. After agar hardens, the center well is filled with a precisely measured amount of material containing antigen S. *B:* Antigen S is allowed to diffuse radially from the center well for 24–48 hours. *C:* Where antigen S meets corresponding antibody to S in the agar, precipitation results. After reaction proceeds to completion or at a timed interval, a sharp border or a ring is formed. *D:* By serial dilution of a known standard quantity of antigen S—S/1, S/2, S/4, S/8—rings of progressively decreasing size are formed. The amount of antigen S in unknown specimens can be calculated and compared with standard in the timed interval (Fahey) method (Fig 22–6).

tion of antigen concentration corresponding to any diameter size (Fig 22–6). The sensitivity of these methods is in the range of 1–3 μg/mL of antigen.

The most important clinical application of single radial diffusion is in the measurement of serum immunoglobulin concentrations. A monospecific antiserum directed only at Fc or H chain determinants of the immunoglobulin molecule must be incorporated into

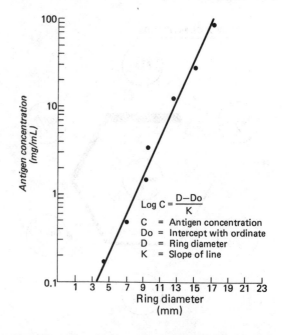

Figure 22–6. Standard curve for single radial diffusion. Relationship between ring diameter and antigen concentration is described by the line constructed from known amounts of antigen (Fig 22–5). Equation and curve for timed interval (Fahey) method.

The equation shown in the figure:

$$\text{Log } C = \frac{D - Do}{K}$$

C = Antigen concentration
Do = Intercept with ordinate
D = Ring diameter
K = Slope of line

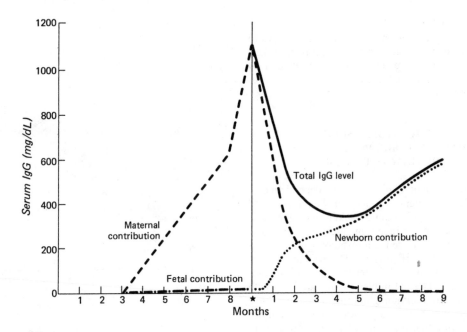

Figure 22–7. Development of IgG levels with age. Relationship of development of normal serum levels of IgG during fetal and newborn stages and maternal contribution. (Modified from Allansmith M et al: *J Pediatr* 1968;72:289.)

Table 22–1. Levels of immune globulins in serum of normal subjects at different ages.*

Age	Number of Subjects	Level of IgG† mg/dL (Range)	% of Adult Level	Level of IgM† mg/dL (Range)	% of Adult Level	Level of IgA† mg/dL (Range)	% of Adult Level	Level of Total γ-Globulin† mg/dL (Range)	% of Adult Level
Newborn	22	1031 ± 200 (645–1244)	89 ± 17	11 ± 5 (5–30)	11 ± 5	2 ± 3 (0–11)	1 ± 2	1044 ± 201 (660–1439)	67 ± 13
1–3 months	29	430 ± 119 (272–762)	37 ± 10	30 ± 11 (16–67)	30 ± 11	21 ± 13 (6–56)	11 ± 7	481 ± 127 (324–699)	31 ± 9
4–6 months	33	427 ± 186 (206–1125)	37 ± 16	43 ± 17 (10–83)	43 ± 17	28 ± 18 (8–93)	14 ± 9	498 ± 204 (228–1232)	32 ± 13
7–12 months	56	661 ± 219 (279–1533)	58 ± 19	54 ± 23 (22–147)	55 ± 23	37 ± 18 (16–98)	19 ± 9	752 ± 242 (327–1687)	48 ± 15
13–24 months	59	762 ± 209 (258–1393)	66 ± 18	58 ± 23 (14–114)	59 ± 23	50 ± 24 (19–119)	25 ± 12	870 ± 258 (398–1586)	56 ± 16
25–36 months	33	892 ± 183 (419–1274)	77 ± 16	61 ± 19 (28–113)	62 ± 19	71 ± 37 (19–235)	36 ± 19	1024 ± 205 (499–1418)	65 ± 14
3–5 years	28	929 ± 228 (569–1597)	80 ± 20	56 ± 18 (22–100)	57 ± 18	93 ± 27 (55–152)	47 ± 14	1078 ± 245 (730–1771)	69 ± 17
6–8 years	18	923 ± 256 (559–1492)	80 ± 22	65 ± 25 (27–118)	66 ± 25	124 ± 45 (54–221)	62 ± 23	1112 ± 293 (640–1725)	71 ± 20
9–11 years	9	1124 ± 235 (779–1456)	97 ± 20.	79 ± 33 (35–132)	80 ± 33	131 ± 60 (12–208)	66 ± 30	1334 ± 254 (966–1639)	85 ± 17
12–16 years	9	946 ± 124 (726–1085)	82 ± 11	59 ± 20 (35–72)	60 ± 20	148 ± 63 (70–229)	74 ± 32	1153 ± 169 (833–1284)	74 ± 12
Adults	30	1158 ± 305 (569–1919)	100 ± 26	99 ± 27 (47–147)	100 ± 27	200 ± 61 (61–330)	100 ± 31	1457 ± 353 (730–2365)	100 ± 24

*Reproduced, with permission, from Stiehm ER, Fudenberg HH: *Pediatrics* 1966;37:717.
†Mean ± 1 SD.

phenomenon has been well documented in the case of subjects with IgA deficiency who have antibodies to ruminant proteins in their serum. The problem of IgA quantitation in this circumstance can be avoided by using anti-immunoglobulin from rabbits (ie, a nonruminant species).

APPLICATIONS: SERUM IMMUNOGLOBULIN LEVELS IN HEALTH & DISEASE

Serum immunoglobulin levels are dependent on a variety of developmental, genetic, and environmental factors. These include ethnic background, age, sex, history of allergies or recurrent infections, and geographic factors (eg, endemic infestation with parasites results in elevated IgE levels). The patient's age is especially important in the interpretation of immunoglobulin levels. Normal human infants are born with virtually no serum immunoglobulins which they have synthesized; the entire IgG portion of cord serum has been transferred transplacentally from the mother (Fig 22–7). After birth, this IgG decays, resulting in a falling serum IgG level. This trend is reversed with the onset of significant autologous IgG synthesis. There is a gradual and progressive increase in IgG, IgA, and IgM levels until late adolescence, when nearly normal adult levels are achieved (Fig 22–8). Furthermore, it is clear that there is a great deal of variability in immunoglobulin levels in the normal population (Fig 22–8 and Table 22–1).

In routine clinical laboratory practice, only IgG, IgA, and IgM levels are ordinarily measured. Abnormalities of serum IgD concentrations have not been associated with specific disease states. In fact, this immunoglobulin is the major B cell receptor and may play only a minor role as a circulating antibody. IgE levels, on the other hand, are useful in differential diagnosis of allergic (see Chapters 18 and 28), parasitic, and rare immunodeficiency states (Chapter 25). Measurement of serum IgE levels requires sensitive methods such as RIA or enzyme-linked immunoassay.

Individual changes in serum immunoglobulins have been recorded in many diseases. A partial list of the instances of quantitative abnormalities in immunoglobulins is listed (Table 22–2). For a detailed discussion of immunoglobulin disorders, the reader is referred to Chapter 25.

ELECTROPHORESIS

Analysis of the heterogeneity in individual proteins is most readily accomplished by electrophoresis. The separation of proteins in an electrical field was perfected in 1937 by Tiselius, who used free or moving boundary electrophoresis. However, owing to the relative complexity of this method, zone electrophoresis in

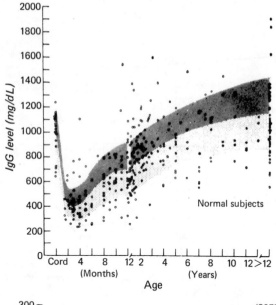

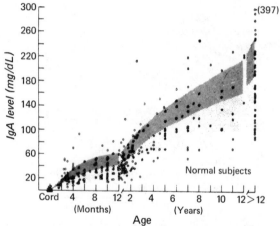

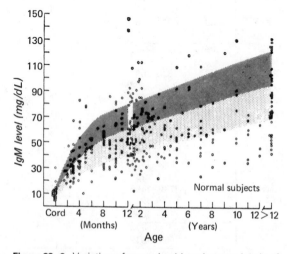

Figure 22–8. Variation of normal subjects' serum levels of IgG, IgA, and IgM with age. Scattergrams of levels of IgG, IgA, and IgM in normal subjects. Shaded areas are ± 1 SD of the mean; each point represents one subject. (From Stiehm ER, Fudenberg HH: *Pediatrics* 1966; **37**:718.)

Table 22–2. Serum immunoglobulin levels in disease.*

Diseases	IgG	IgA	IgM
Immunodeficiency disorders			
Combined immunodeficiency	↓↓ ↔ ↓↓↓	↓↓ ↔ ↓↓↓	↓↓ ↔ ↓↓↓
X-linked hypogammaglobulinemia	↓↓ ↔ ↓↓↓	↓↓ ↔ ↓↓↓	↓↓ ↔ ↓↓↓
Variable common immunodeficiency	↓ ↔ ↓↓↓	↓ ↔ ↓↓↓	↓ ↔ ↓↓↓
Selective IgA deficiency	N	↓↓↓	N
Protein-losing gastroenteropathies	N ↔ ↓↓↓	N ↔ ↓↓↓	N ↔ ↓↓↓
Acute thermal burns	N ↔ ↓↓↓	N ↔ ↓↓↓	N ↔ ↓↓↓
Nephrotic syndrome	N ↔ ↓↓↓	N ↔ ↓↓↓	N ↔ ↓↓↓
Monoclonal gammopathies (MG)			
IgG (eg, G-myeloma)	N ↔ ↑↑↑	N ↔ ↓↓↓	N ↔ ↓↓↓
IgA (eg, A-myeloma)	N ↔ ↓↓↓	N ↔ ↑↑↑	N ↔ ↓↓↓
IgM (eg, M-macroglobulinemia)	N ↔ ↓↓↓	N ↔ ↓↓↓	N ↔ ↑↑↑
L chain disease (ie, Bence Jones myeloma)	N ↔ ↓↓↓	N ↔ ↓↓↓	N ↔ ↓↓↓
Chronic lymphocytic leukemia	N ↔ ↓↓↓	N ↔ ↓↓↓	N ↔ ↓↓↓
Infections			
Infectious mononucleosis	↑ ↔ ↑↑	N ↔ ↑	↑ ↔ ↑↑
Subacute bacterial endocarditis	↑ ↔ ↑↑	↓ ↔ N	↑ ↔ ↑↑
Tuberculosis	↑ ↔ ↑↑	N ↔ ↑↑↑	↓ ↔ N
Actinomycosis	↑↑↑	↑↑	↑↑↑
Deep fungus diseases	N	N ↔ ↑	N
Bartonellosis	↑	↓ ↔ N	↑↑ ↔ ↑↑↑
Liver diseases			
Infectious hepatitis	↑ ↔ ↑↑	N ↔ ↑	N ↔ ↑↑
Laennec's cirrhosis	↑ ↔ ↑↑↑	↑ ↔ ↑↑↑	N ↔ ↑↑
Biliary cirrhosis	N	N	↑ ↔ ↑↑
Chronic active hepatitis	↑↑↑	↑	N ↔ ↑↑
Collagen disorders			
Lupus erythematosus	↑ ↔ ↑↑	N ↔ ↑	N ↔ ↑↑
Rheumatoid arthritis	N ↔ ↑↑↑	↑ ↔ ↑↑↑	N ↔ ↑↑
Sjögren's syndrome	N ↔ ↑	N ↔ ↑	N ↔ ↑↑
Scleroderma	N ↔ ↑	N	N ↔ ↑
Miscellaneous			
Sarcoidosis	N ↔ ↑↑	N ↔ ↑↑	N ↔ ↑
Hodgkin's disease	↓ ↔ ↑↑	↓ ↔ ↑	↓ ↔ ↑↑
Monocytic leukemia	N ↔ ↑	N ↔ ↑	N ↔ ↑↑
Cystic fibrosis	↑ ↔ ↑↑	↑ ↔ ↑↑	N ↔ ↑↑

N = normal, ↑ = slight increase, ↑↑ = moderate increase, ↑↑↑ = marked increase, ↓ = slight decrease, ↓↓ = moderate decrease, ↓↓↓ = marked decrease, ↔ = range.

*Modified and reproduced, with permission, from Ritzmann SE, Daniels JC (editors): *Serum Protein Abnormalities: Diagnostic and Clinical Aspects.* Little, Brown, 1975.

a stabilizing medium such as paper or cellulose acetate has replaced free electrophoresis for clinical use.

In 1952, a two-stage method was reported which combined electrophoresis with immunodiffusion for the detection of tetanus toxoid by antiserum. Shortly thereafter, the now classic method of immunoelectrophoresis (IEP) was introduced by Williams and Grabar and by Poulik. In this technique, both electrophoresis and double immunodiffusion are performed on the same agar-coated slide. During the past 20 years, immunoelectrophoresis has become the cornerstone of clinical paraprotein analysis as well as a standard method for immunochemical analysis of a wide variety of proteins. More recently, radioimmunoelectrophoresis and electroimmunodiffusion methods have been introduced. Various electrophoretic methods and examples of their uses in clinical immunodiagnosis are described in the following paragraphs.

ZONE ELECTROPHORESIS

Proteins are separated in zone electrophoresis almost exclusively on the basis of their surface charge (Fig 22–9). The supporting medium is theoretically inert and does not impede or enhance the flow of molecules in the electrical field. Generally, paper, agarose, or cellulose acetate strips are employed as supporting media. However, a major advantage of cellulose acetate is the speed of completion of electrophoretic migration (ie, 60–90 minutes compared to hours for paper). Additionally, cellulose acetate is optically clear; microquantities of proteins may be applied; and it is adaptable to histochemical staining procedures. For these reasons, cellulose acetate or agarose are commonly used as the supporting medium for clinical zone electrophoresis.

In the technique itself, serum or other biologic fluid samples are placed at the origin and separated by

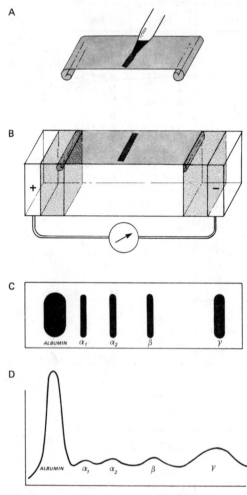

Figure 22–9. Technique of cellulose acetate zone electrophoresis. *A:* Small amount of serum or other fluid is applied to cellulose acetate strip. *B:* Electrophoresis of sample in electrolyte buffer is performed. *C:* Separated protein bands are visualized in characteristic position after being stained. *D:* Densitometer scanning from cellulose acetate strip converts bands to characteristic peaks of albumin, α_1-globulin, α_2-globulin, β-globulin, and γ-globulin.

diagnosis of human paraprotein disorders such as multiple myeloma and Waldenström's macroglobulinemia (Fig 22–10). In these disorders, an electrophoretically restricted protein spike usually occurs in the γ-globulin region of the electrophoretogram. Since in zone electrophoresis the trailing edge of immunoglobulins extends into the β region and occasionally the α region, spikes in these regions are also consistent with paraproteinemic disorders involving immunoglobulins.

A decrease in serum γ-globulin concentration such as occurs in hypogammaglobulinemia can also be detected with this technique (Fig 22–10). Free light chains are readily detectable in urine when present in increased amounts such as in Bence Jones proteinuria of myeloma (Fig 22–11). Zone electrophoresis has also been useful in the diagnosis of certain central nervous system diseases with alterations in cerebrospinal fluid proteins (Fig 22–12).

Recently, oligoclonal bands in cerebrospinal fluid with restricted electrophoretic mobility have been detected in about 90% of clinically definite cases of multiple sclerosis. Agarose electrophoresis gel in conjunction with measurement of cerebrospinal fluid IgG/albumin ratios makes possible a very high degree of specificity for diagnosis of multiple sclerosis (see Chapter 35).

Abnormalities in serum proteins other than immunoglobulins may also be detected by serum protein electrophoresis. Hypoproteinemia involving all serum fractions occurs during excessive protein loss, usually in the gastrointestinal tract. Reduction in albumin alone is a common abnormality which occurs in many diseases of the liver, kidneys, or gastrointestinal tract or with severe burns. Alpha$_1$-globulin decrease may indicate α_1-antitrypsin deficiency, and an increase reflects acute phase reactions occurring in many inflammatory and neoplastic disorders. Increase in α_2-globulins usually reflects the nephrotic syndrome or hemolysis with increased hemoglobin-haptoglobin in the serum. It should be emphasized that zone electrophoresis is almost always a presumptive screening test for serum protein abnormalities. Specific quantitative biochemical or immunologic tests must be performed to definitively identify the protein in question.

IMMUNOELECTROPHORESIS (IEP)

Immunoelectrophoresis combines electrophoretic separation diffusion and immune precipitation of proteins. Both identification and approximate quantitation can thereby be accomplished for individual proteins present in serum, urine, or other biologic fluid.

In this technique (Fig 22–13), a glass slide is covered with molten agar or agarose in a buffer solution (pH 8.2, ionic strength 0.025). An antigen well and antibody trough are cut with a template cutting device. The serum sample (antigen) is placed in the antigen well and is separated in an electrical field with a potential difference of 3.3 V/cm for 30–60 minutes. Antiserum is then placed in the trough, and both serum

electrophoresis for about 90 minutes, using alkaline buffer solutions. The strips are then stained for protein and scanned in a densitometer. In the densitometer, the stained strip is passed through a light beam. Variable absorption due to different serum protein concentrations is detected by a photoelectric cell and reproduced by an analog recorder as a tracing (Fig 22–9). Scanning converts the band pattern into peaks and allows for quantitation of the major peaks. Normal human serum is separated into 5 major electrophoretic bands by this method, ie, albumin, α_1-globulin, α_2-globulin, β-globulin, and γ-globulin.

Applications

Zone electrophoresis is extremely valuable in the

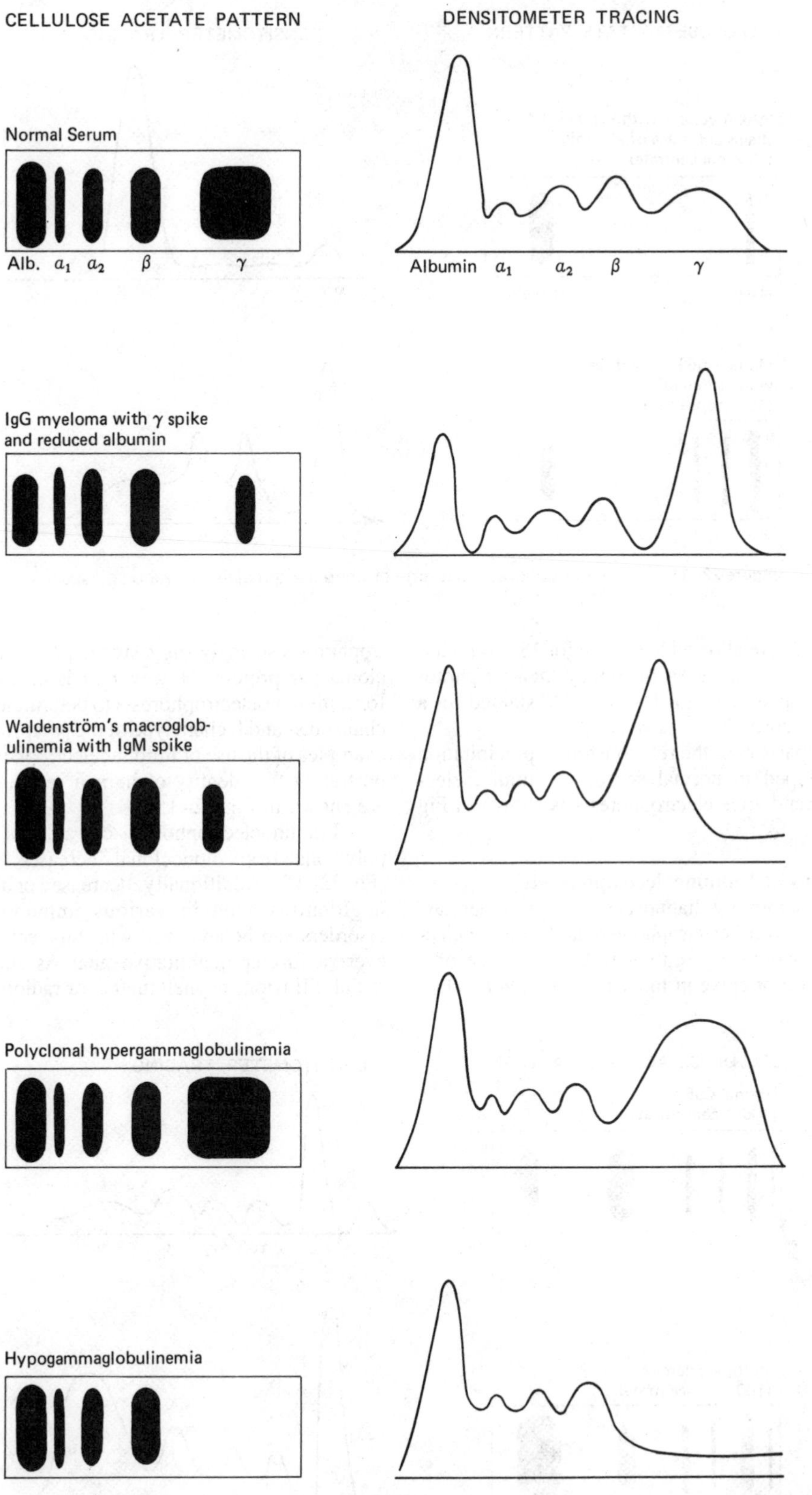

CELLULOSE ACETATE PATTERN   DENSITOMETER TRACING

Figure 22–10. Zone electrophoresis patterns of serum immunoglobulin abnormalities in various diseases.

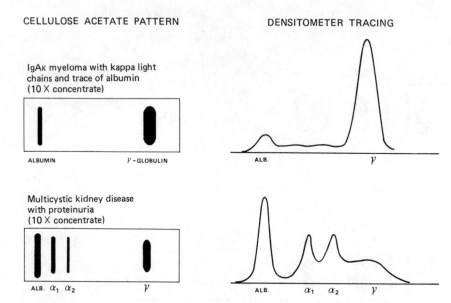

Figure 22–11. Zone electrophoresis patterns of urine abnormalities in various diseases.

and antibodies are allowed to diffuse for 18–24 hours. The resulting precipitation lines may then be photographed or the slide washed, dried, and stained for a permanent record.

A comparison of the relationship of precipitation lines developed in normal serum by immunoelectrophoresis and zone electrophoresis is shown in Fig 22–14.

Applications of Immunoelectrophoresis

In the laboratory diagnosis of paraproteinemias, the results of zone electrophoresis and immunoelectrophoresis should be combined. The presence of a sharp increase or spike in the γ region on zone elec-

trophoresis strongly suggests the presence of a monoclonal paraprotein. However, it is necessary to perform immunoelectrophoresis to determine the exact H chain class and L chain type of the paraprotein. Several examples of the use of immunoelectrophoresis in demonstrating the identity of human serum paraproteins are shown in Fig 22–15.

Immunoelectrophoresis can aid in distinguishing polyclonal from monoclonal increases in γ-globulin (Fig 22–15). Additionally, decreased or absent immunoglobulins seen in various immune deficiency disorders can be analyzed with this technique. However, a further quantitative analysis such as single radial diffusion, nephelometry, or radioimmunoassay

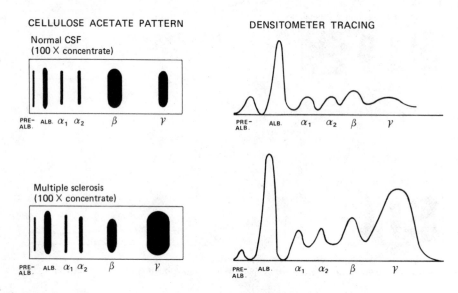

Figure 22–12. Zone electrophoresis patterns of cerebrospinal fluid from normal subject and multiple sclerosis patient.

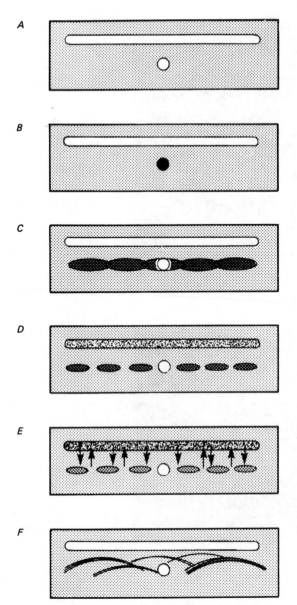

Figure 22–13. Technique of immunoelectrophoresis. *A:* Semisolid agar poured onto glass slide and antigen well and antiserum trough cut out of agar. *B:* Antigen well filled with human serum. *C:* Serum separated by electrophoresis. *D:* Antiserum trough filled with antiserum to whole human serum. *E:* Serum and antiserum diffuse into agar. *F:* Precipitin lines form for individual serum proteins.

should be performed for measurement of immunoglobulin levels.

Immunoelectrophoresis is also of great practical benefit in identifying L chains in the urine of patients with plasma cell dyscrasias or autoimmune disorders. Thus, with specific anti-κ and anti-λ antisera, the monoclonal nature of Bence Jones protein in myeloma can be confirmed.

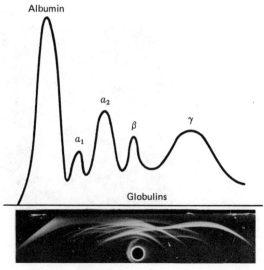

Figure 22–14. Comparison of patterns of zone and immunoelectrophoresis of normal human serum.

Antisera to "free light chains" (kappa or lambda) obtained from urine of myeloma patients may occasionally reveal antigenic determinants not present on light chains "bound" to heavy chains. In H chain diseases, fragments of the immunoglobulin H chain are present in increased amounts in the serum (Chapter 27). It was by careful analysis of immunoelectrophoretic patterns that Franklin initially discovered the existence of this rare but extremely interesting group of disorders. Finally, immunoelectrophoresis is helpful in identifying increased amounts of proteins present in the cerebrospinal fluid in patients with various neurologic diseases.

RADIOIMMUNOELECTROPHORESIS

Radioimmunoelectrophoresis combines immunoelectrophoresis and radioautography for the detection of radiolabeled antigens. It has been applied most often to the study of proteins or immunoglobulins that are intrinsically labeled with radioactive ^{14}C or ^{3}H amino acids during cellular biosynthesis in tissue culture. Plasma cells or lymphoblastoid cells from continuous cell lines are grown in tissue culture with radioactive amino acids. The resultant supernate fluid contains radioactive proteins that are actively synthesized by the cultured cells. Concentrated culture supernates are then subjected to electrophoresis in standard immunoelectrophoresis plates. The troughs are filled with antiserum to human serum as well as with specific antisera for L and H chains. After the precipitation lines have developed, the plate is dried and overlaid with high-speed x-ray film. After a period of exposure, the film is developed and the resultant pattern compared with the normal serum proteins present on the stained immunoelectrophoresis plate.

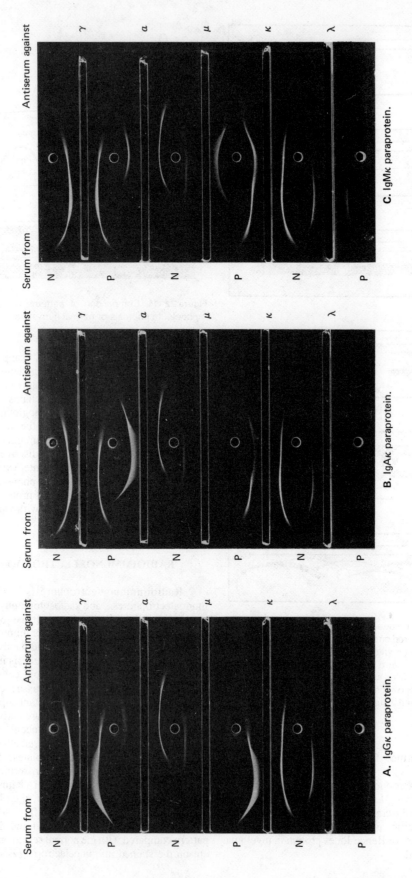

A. IgGκ paraprotein.

B. IgAκ paraprotein.

C. IgMκ paraprotein.

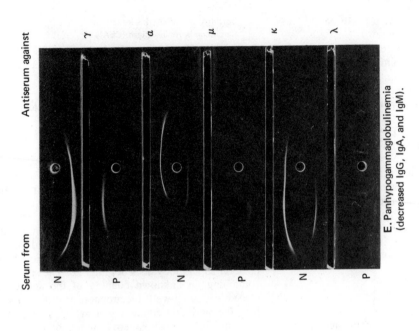

E. Panhypogammaglobulinemia
(decreased IgG, IgA, and IgM).

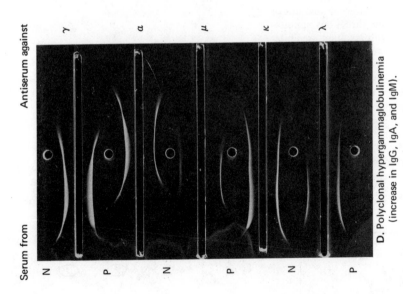

D. Polyclonal hypergammaglobulinemia
(increase in IgG, IgA, and IgM).

Figure 22–15. Immunoelectrophoresis patterns of serum in various diseases. *A:* IgGκ paraprotein. *B:* IgAκ paraprotein. *C:* IgMκ paraprotein. *D:* Polyclonal hypergammaglobulinemia. *E:* Panhypogammaglobulinemia. Individual patterns of serum from normal individual (N) and patient with various serum protein abnormalities (P). In each case, N and P sera are reacted against antisera which are monospecific for γ, α, and μ heavy chains and κ and λ light chains.

This technique can be extremely useful in the investigation of paraproteinemias. Its chief function is to confirm a specific serum protein as the biosynthetic product of a particular organ, tissue, or cell population (Chapter 4).

ELECTROIMMUNODIFFUSION

In immunodiffusion techniques described earlier in this chapter, antigen and antibody are allowed to come into contact and to precipitate in agar purely by diffusion. However, the chance of antigen and antibody meeting—and thus the speed of development of a precipitin line—can be greatly enhanced by electrically driving the 2 together. There has recently been renewed interest in the techniques of electroimmunodiffusion, especially in the serologic diagnosis of infectious diseases by serum **antigen** detection. Although numerous variations have been described coupling electrophoresis with diffusion, only 2 have as yet achieved any degree of clinical applicability. These are **one-dimensional double electroimmunodiffusion** (counterimmunoelectrophoresis) and **one-dimensional single electroimmunodiffusion** (Laurell's rocket electrophoresis).

One-Dimensional Double Electroimmunodiffusion

This method is also known as countercurrent immunoelectrophoresis, counterimmunoelectrophoresis, and electroprecipitation. The basic principle of the method involves electrophoresis in a gel medium of antigen and antibody in opposite directions simultaneously from separate wells, with resultant precipitation at a point intermediate between their origins (Fig 22–16).

The principal disadvantages of double diffusion without electromotive force are the time required for precipitation (24 hours) and the relative lack of sensitivity. Double electroimmunodiffusion in one dimension can produce visible precipitin lines within 30 minutes and is approximately 10 times more sensitive than standard double diffusion techniques. However, this technique is only semiquantitative. Some of the

Table 22–3. Examples of clinical applications of double electroimmunodiffusion.

Cryptococcus-specific antigen in cerebrospinal fluid
Meningococcus-specific antigen in cerebrospinal fluid
Haemophilus-specific antigen in cerebrospinal fluid
Fibrinogen
Cord IgM in intrauterine infection
Carcinoembryonic antigen (CEA)
a_1-Fetoprotein
Fungal precipitins

antigens and antibodies detected by double electroimmunodiffusion are listed in Table 22–3.

One-Dimensional Single Electroimmunodiffusion

This method is also known as "rocket electrophoresis" or the Laurell technique. The principal application of this technique has been to quantitate antigens other than immunoglobulins. In this technique, antiserum to the particular antigen or antigens one wishes to quantitate is incorporated into an agarose supporting medium on a glass slide in a fixed position so antibody does not migrate. The specimen containing an unknown quantity of the antigen is placed in a small well. Electrophoresis of the antigen into the antibody-containing agarose is then performed. The resultant pattern of immunoprecipitation resembles a spike or rocket—thus the term rocket electrophoresis (Fig 22–17).

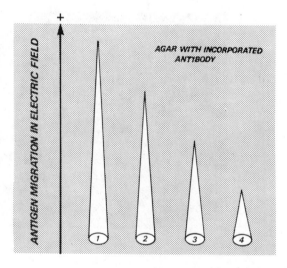

Figure 22–17. Single electroimmunodiffusion in one dimension (rocket electrophoresis, Laurell technique). Antigen is placed in wells numbered 1–4 in progressively decreasing amounts. Electrophoresis is performed and antigen is driven into antibody-containing agar. Precipitin pattern forms in the shape of a "rocket." Amount of antigen is directly proportionate to the length of the rocket.

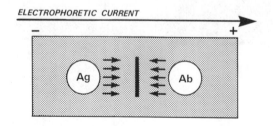

Figure 22–16. Double electroimmunodiffusion in one dimension. Antigen and antibody are placed in well and driven together with an electric current. A precipitin line forms within a few hours after beginning electrophoresis.

This pattern occurs because precipitation occurs along the lateral margins of the moving boundary of antigen as the antigen is driven into the agar containing the antibody. Gradually, as antigen is lost through precipitation, its concentration at the leading edge diminishes and the lateral margins converge to form a sharp point. The total distance of antigen migration for a given antiserum concentration is linearly proportionate to the antigen concentration. The sensitivity of this technique is approximately 0.5 μg/mL for proteins. Unfortunately, the weak negative charge of immunoglobulins prevents their electrophoretic mobility in this system unless special electrolytes and agar are employed. Recently, several commercially available systems have been introduced for quantitating serum immunoglobulins and complement components with this technique.

IMMUNOCHEMICAL & PHYSICOCHEMICAL METHODS
Françoise Chenais, MD

Evaluation of serum protein disorders can usually be effectively accomplished by immunodiffusion and electrophoretic methods. Occasionally, more detailed study of immunologically relevant serum constituents is necessary. In this section, a number of the more complex immunochemical and physicochemical techniques are described that have proved to be important adjuncts in the characterization of serum protein disorders. These techniques have become increasingly available in the clinical laboratory and include ultracentrifugation, column chromatography, measurement of serum viscosity, and methods to detect cryoglobulins, pyroglobulins, and immune complexes.

ULTRACENTRIFUGATION

Ultracentrifugation was the first method developed which clearly demonstrated the existence of several classes of immunoglobulins. Human immuno-globulins were initially subdivided according to their sedimentation coefficients, ie, 7S or 19S. Although other simpler techniques are now available, ultracentrifugation is still used for isolation and characterization of immunoglobulins. The application of centrifugal force to molecules in solution gives them a sedimentation velocity depending on their size, mass, and density relative to the solvent.

In moving boundary ultracentrifugation, the sample is initially uniformly layered in the tube. During centrifugation, the molecules move in the solvent and a concentration boundary develops between the top and the bottom of the tube. Multiple boundaries will develop in complex solutions (Fig 22–18). An important application of analytical ultracentrifugation is the determination of the sedimentation coefficient of abnormal serum proteins (Fig 22–19).

In moving zone ultracentrifugation, the sample is layered over a density gradient. When a centrifugal force is applied to a complex mixture, moving bands of different sedimentation velocity appear (Fig 22–20). The density gradient is used to prevent radial convection currents and thus stabilize the moving zones. It is then possible to obtain a good resolution of the different components. Individual components can be obtained after separation with preparative ultracentrifugation by collecting several fractions layer by layer.

COLUMN CHROMATOGRAPHY

Chromatographic techniques are currently the most widely used methods for protein fractionation and isolation of immunoglobulins. In these techniques, a sample is layered on the top of a glass cylinder or column filled with a synthetic gel and is allowed to flow through the gel. The physical characteristics of protein molecules result in retention in the gel matrix to differing degrees, and subsequent elution under appropriate conditions permits protein separation.

Ion Exchange Chromatography
Ion exchange chromatography separates proteins by taking advantage of differences in their electrical

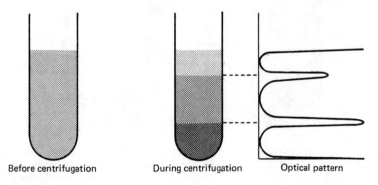

Before centrifugation   During centrifugation   Optical pattern

Figure 22–18. Principle of moving boundary analytical ultracentrifugation.

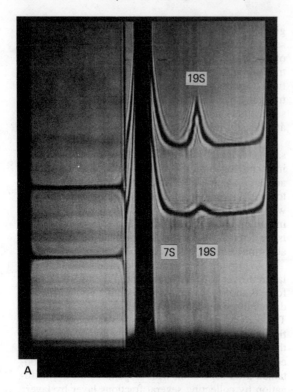

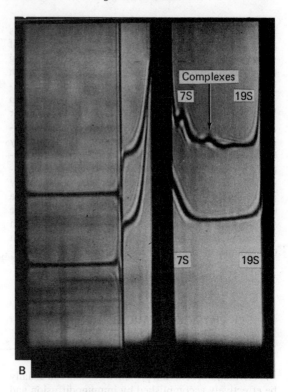

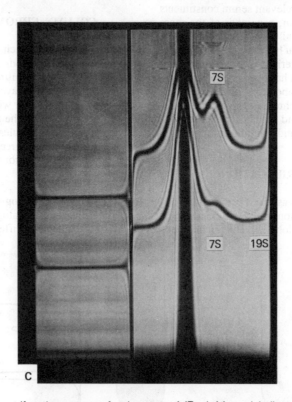

Figure 22–19. Analytic ultracentrifugation patterns of various sera. *A (Top):* Macroglobulinemic serum with increased 19S (IgM) component. *A (Bottom):* Normal serum. *B (Top):* Serum containing immune complexes between 7S and 19S sedimentation coefficients. *B (Bottom):* Normal serum. *C (Top):* Serum with increased 7S molecules. *C (Bottom):* Normal serum. In each case, sedimentation is from left to right.

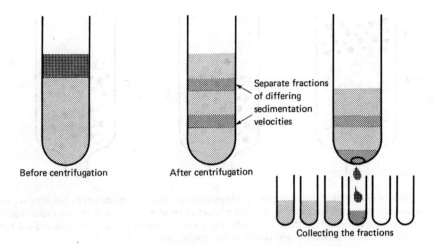

Figure 22–20. Principle of moving zone ultracentrifugation.

charges. The functional unit of the gel is a charged group absorbed on an insoluble backbone such as cellulose, cross-linked dextran, agarose, or acrylic copolymers. Diethylaminoethyl (DEAE), a positively charged group, is the functional unit of anion exchangers used for fractionation of negatively charged molecules (Fig 22–21). Carboxymethyl (CM), negatively charged, is the functional unit of cation exchangers used for fractionation of positively charged molecules. Changing the pH of the buffer passing through the column affects the charge of the protein molecule. Increasing the molarity of the buffer provides more ions to compete with the protein for binding to the gel. By gradually increasing the molarity or decreasing the pH of the elution buffer, the proteins are eluted in order of increasing number of charged groups bound to the gel. For example, Table 22–4 gives the molarity and pH required to elute serum immunoglobulins. DEAE-cellulose chromatography is an excellent technique for isolation of IgG, which can be obtained nearly free of all other serum proteins.

Table 22–4. Molarity of NaCl and pH required to elute human plasma protein from DEA-cellulose. (Adapted from Oh & Sanders, 1966.)

NaCl Molarity	pH	Proteins Eluted
0.025	7.8	IgG
0.045	7.0	Transferrin, fibrinogen
0.050	7.0	a_2-Globulin, albumin, IgA
0.080	6.5	Albumin, a_2-globulin, β-lipoprotein
0.100	6.5	a_2-Globulin, β-globulins, haptoglobin
0.150	6.5	IgM, β-lipoprotein, β-globulin

Gel Filtration

Gel filtration separates molecules according to their size. The gel is made of porous dextran beads. Protein molecules larger than the largest pores of the beads cannot penetrate the gel pores. Thus, they pass through the gel in the liquid phase outside the beads and are eluted first. Smaller molecules penetrate the

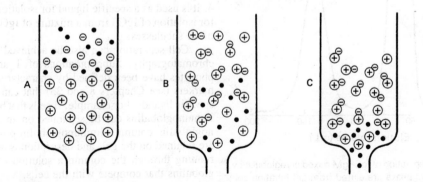

Figure 22–21. Principles of ion exchange chromatography. Three stages of protein separation by ion exchange chromatography are shown: *A:* The column bed is made up of a matrix of positively charged cellulose beads $\oplus$. *B:* The negatively charged molecules $\ominus$ in the protein mixture bind to the column and are retained. *C:* The neutral molecules $\bullet$ pass between the charged particles and are eluted.

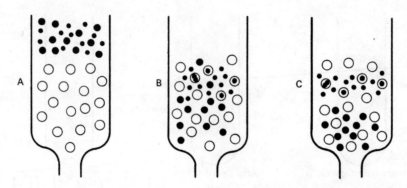

Figure 22–22. Principles of gel filtration chromatography. Three stages of protein separation by gel filtration are shown: *A:* Open circle ○ represents polymerized beads onto which a mixture of small ● and large ⬤ protein molecules is layered. *B:* The molecules enter and pass through the column at different rates depending primarily on size and are separated by a simple sieving process. *C:* Larger molecules are eluted while smaller ones are retained.

beads to a varying extent depending on their size and shape. Solute molecules within the gel beads maintain a concentration equilibrium with solute in the liquid phase outside the beads; thus, a particular molecular species moves as a band through the column. Molecules therefore appear in the column effluent in order of decreasing size (Fig 22–22).

IgM can be easily separated from other serum immunoglobulins by gel filtration. Fig 22–23 shows the separation of the IgM and the IgG components of a mixed IgM-IgG cryoglobulin. Gel filtration is widely used also to separate H and L chains of immunoglobu-

lins or to isolate pure Bence Jones proteins from the urine of patients with multiple myeloma.

Affinity Chromatography

Affinity chromatography uses specific and reversible biologic interaction between the gel material and the substance to be isolated. The specificity of the binding properties is obtained by covalent coupling of an appropriate ligand to an insoluble matrix, such as agarose or dextran beads. The gel so obtained is able to adsorb from a mixed solution the substance to be isolated. After unbound substances have been washed out of the column, the purified compound can be recovered by changing the experimental conditions, such as pH or ionic strength.

Antigen-antibody binding is one of the reactions that can be applied to affinity chromatography. When the gel material is coupled to an antigen, a specific antibody can be purified. Alternatively, when a highly purified antibody can be coupled to the gel, the corresponding antigen can be isolated.

Protein A is a protein isolated from the cell wall of some strains of *Staphylococcus aureus* that specifically reacts with IgG molecules of subclasses 1, 2, and 4. It is used as a specific ligand for isolation of IgG or for isolation of IgG3 from a mixture of IgG molecules of all subclasses.

Cell separation can also be achieved by affinity chromatography. Subpopulations of T and B lymphocytes have been defined by characteristic surface markers (see Chapters 8 and 23) that can react with specific ligands. For example, B cells that bear surface immunoglobulins can be separated on an anti-immunoglobulin column. Immunoglobulin-positive cells are retained on the gel, and desorption is achieved by running through the column a solution of immunoglobulins that compete with the cells.

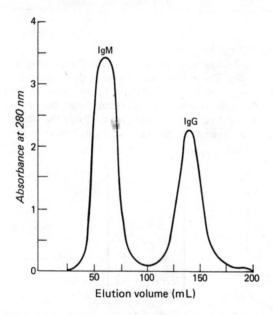

Figure 22–23. Separation of IgG-IgM mixed cryoglobulin by gel filtration. Two peaks are eluted from gel filtration column. The larger IgM molecules precede the smaller IgG molecules which were dissociated by dissolving the cryoprecipitate in an acidic buffer prior to application to the column. The absorbance at 280 nm measures relative amount of protein in various eluted fractions.

SERUM VISCOSITY

The measurement of serum viscosity is a simple and valuable tool in evaluation of patients with paraproteinemia. Normally, the formed elements of the blood contribute more significantly to whole blood viscosity than do plasma proteins. However, in diseases with elevated concentrations of serum proteins, particularly the immunoglobulins, the serum viscosity may reach very high levels and result in a characteristic symptom complex—the hyperviscosity syndrome. Serum viscosity is determined by a variety of factors including protein concentration; the size, shape, and deformability of serum molecules; and the hydrostatic state (solvation), molecular charge, and temperature sensitivity of proteins.

Serum viscosity is measured in clinical practice in an Ostwald viscosimeter. A few milliliters of serum are warmed to 37 °C and allowed to descend through a narrow bore capillary tube immersed in a water bath at 37 °C. The rate of descent between calibrated marks on the capillary tube is recorded. The same procedure is repeated using distilled water. The relative serum viscosity is then calculated according to the following formula:

$$\text{Relative serum viscosity} = \frac{\text{Rate of descent in seconds of serum sample}}{\text{Rate of descent in seconds of distilled water}}$$

Normal values for serum viscosity range from 1.4 to 1.9. Similar measurements can be performed using plasma instead of serum. However, fibrinogen present in plasma is a major determinant of plasma viscosity, and variations in this protein, especially in the presence of nonspecific inflammatory states, can markedly affect the results. For this reason, measurement of serum viscosity is preferred.

Serum viscosity measurements are primarily of use in evaluating patients with Waldenström's macroglobulinemia, multiple myeloma, and cryoglobulinemia. In myeloma, aggregation or polymerization of the paraprotein in vivo often results in hyperviscosity. In general, there is a correlation between increased serum viscosity and increased plasma volume. However, the correlation between levels of relative serum viscosity and clinical symptoms is not nearly as direct. Increased serum viscosity may interfere with various laboratory tests which employ flow-through devices such as Coulter counters and Technicon analyzers in clinical chemistry. A detailed discussion of the hyperviscosity syndrome is presented in Chapter 27. Disorders with increased serum viscosity are listed in Table 22–5.

CRYOGLOBULINS

Precipitation of serum immunoglobulins in the cold was first observed in a patient with multiple myeloma. The term "cryoglobulin" was introduced to designate a group of proteins which had the common property of forming a precipitate or a gel in the cold. This phenomenon was reversible by raising the temperature. Since those initial descriptions, cryoglobulins have been found in a wide variety of clinical situations. Purification and immunochemical analysis have led to classification of this group of proteins (Table 22–6). Type I cryoglobulins consist of a single monoclonal immunoglobulin. Type II cryoglobulins are mixed cryoglobulins; they consist of a monoclonal immunoglobulin with antibody activity against a polyclonal immunoglobulin. Type III cryoglobulins are mixed polyclonal cryoglobulins, ie, one or more immunoglobulins are found, none of which are monoclonal.

Technical Procedure for Isolation & Analysis

Blood must be collected in a warm syringe and kept at 37 °C until it clots. Serum is separated by

Table 22–5. Disorders with increased serum viscosity.

Waldenström's macroglobulinemia
Essential macroglobulinemia
Multiple myeloma
Cryoglobulinemia
Hypergammaglobulinemic purpura
Rheumatoid diseases associated with immune complexes or paraproteinemias
    Rheumatoid arthritis
    Sjögren's syndrome
    Systemic lupus erythematosus

Table 22–6. Classification of types of cryoglobulins and associated diseases.

Type of Cryoglobulin	Immuno-chemical Composition	Associated Diseases
Type I Monoclonal cryoglobulin	IgM IgG IgA Bence Jones protein	Myeloma, Waldenström's macroglobulinemia, chronic lymphocytic leukemia
Type II Mixed cryoglobulin	IgM-IgG IgG-IgG IgA-IgG	Myeloma, Waldenström's macroglobulinemia, chronic lymphocytic leukemia, rheumatoid arthritis, Sjögren's syndrome, mixed essential cryoglobulinemia
Type III Mixed polyclonal cryoglobulin	IgM-IgG IgM-IgG-IgA	Systemic lupus erythematosus, rheumatoid arthritis, Sjögren's syndrome, infectious mononucleosis, cytomegalovirus infections, acute viral hepatitis, chronic active hepatitis, primary biliary cirrhosis, poststreptococcal glomerulonephritis, infective endocarditis, leprosy, kala-azar, tropical splenomegaly syndrome

centrifugation at 37 °C and then stored at 4 °C. When a cryoglobulin is present, a white precipitate or a gel appears in the serum after a variable period, usually 24–72 hours. However, the serum should be observed for 1 week to make certain that unusually late cryoprecipitation does not go undetected. The reversibility of the cryoprecipitation should be tested by rewarming an aliquot of precipitated serum.

Quantitation of the cryoprecipitate can be done in several ways. Centrifugation of the whole serum in a hematocrit tube at 4 °C allows determination of the relative amount of cryoglobulin (cryocrit). Alternatively, the protein concentration of the serum may be compared before and after cryoprecipitation. The precipitate formed in an aliquot of serum may be isolated and dissolved in an acidic buffer and the cryoglobulin level estimated by the absorbance at 280 nm.

After isolation and washing of the precipitate, the components of the cryoglobulin are identified by immunoelectrophoresis or by double diffusion. These analyses are performed at 37 °C, using antiserum to whole human serum and antisera specific for γ, α, μ, κ, and λ chains. In this way, cryoglobulins can be classified into the 3 types described above.

Clinical Significance

Type I and type II cryoglobulins are usually present in large amounts in serum (often more than 5 mg/mL). In general, they are present in patients with monoclonal paraproteinemias, eg, they are commonly found in patients with lymphoma or multiple myeloma. However, some are found in patients lacking any evidence of lymphoid malignancy, just as are "benign" paraproteins (see Chapter 27). Type III cryoglobulins indicate the presence of circulating immune complexes and are the result of immune responses to various antigens. They are present in relatively low concentrations (usually less than 1 mg/mL) in rheumatoid diseases and chronic infections (Table 22–6).

All types of cryoglobulins may be responsible for specific symptoms that occur as a result of changes in the cryoglobulin induced by exposure to cold. The symptoms include Raynaud's phenomenon, vascular purpura, bleeding tendencies, cold-induced urticaria, and even distal arterial thrombosis with gangrene.

Since type II and type III cryoglobulins are circulating soluble immune complexes, they may be associated with a serum sickness–like syndrome characterized by polyarthritis, vasculitis, glomerulonephritis, or neurologic symptoms (see Chapter 26). In patients with mixed essential IgM-IgG cryoglobulinemia, a rather distinctive syndrome may occur that is associated with arthralgias, purpura, weakness, and frequently lymphadenopathy or hepatosplenomegaly. This syndrome may be a sequela of hepatitis B infection. Glomerulonephritis is a common finding. In some instances, it occurs in a rapidly progressive form and is of ominous prognostic significance.

Cryoglobulins may cause serious errors in a variety of laboratory tests by precipitating at ambient temperatures and thereby removing certain substances from serum. Complement fixation and inactivation and entrapment of immunoglobulins in the precipitate are common examples. Redissolving the cryoprecipitate usually does not restore activity to the serum, especially when measuring complement activity.

PYROGLOBULINS

Pyroglobulins are monoclonal immunoglobulins that precipitate irreversibly when heated to 56 °C. This phenomenon is different from the reversible thermoprecipitation of Bence Jones proteins and seems to be related to hydrophobic bonding between immunoglobulin molecules, possibly due to decreased polarity of the heavy chains. Pyroglobulins may be discovered incidentally when serum is heated to 56 °C to inactivate complement before routine serologic tests. Half of them are found in patients with multiple myeloma. The remainder occur in macroglobulinemia and other lymphoproliferative disorders, systemic lupus erythematosus, carcinoma, and occasionally without known associated disease. They are not responsible for any particular symptom except hyperviscosity and have no known significance.

DETECTION OF IMMUNE COMPLEXES

The factors involved in the deposition of immune complexes in tissues and the production of tissue damage are discussed in Chapter 12. Subsequent chapters will deal with the clinical manifestations of diseases associated with immune complexes, including rheumatic diseases (Chapter 26), hematologic diseases (Chapter 27), and renal diseases (Chapter 31). These clinical situations have in common the presence of detectable immune complexes in tissues or in the circulation.

Detection of Immune Complexes in Tissues

Detection of immune complexes in tissues is performed by immunohistologic techniques using immunofluorescence or immunoperoxidase staining. The antisera used are specific for the immunoglobulin classes, complement components, fibrin or fibrinogen, and, in selected cases, the suspected antigen.

By analogy with animal findings, granular deposits of immunoglobulins usually accompanied by complement components are considered to represent immune complexes. The antigen moiety is rarely detected, since it is unknown in most cases.

Detection of Immune Complexes in Serum & Other Biologic Fluids

Until recent years, the presence of circulating immune complexes could only be indirectly inferred when complement levels measured by C3 or CH_{50} were low or when serum was found to be anticomple-

Table 22–7. Methods for detection of circulating immune complexes.

Physical methods
 Ultracentrifugation
 Gel filtration
 Cryoprecipitation
 Precipitation with polyethylene glycol
Interaction with rheumatoid factor or complement
 Precipitin reactions
 Inhibition of agglutination of IgG-coated latex particles
 Anticomplementary activity
 Solid phase radioassay
 C1q binding test
 C1q deviation test
 Conglutinin binding test
Interaction with cell receptors
 Platelet aggregation test
 Inhibition of phagocytosis of labeled aggregates
 Inhibition of EAC rosette formation
 Raji cell test

mentary during the performance of a serologic test using complement fixation. The availability of more selective means for detection of circulating immune complexes has become increasingly necessary in clinical immunology. Immune complex determination is used as a diagnostic criterion for various diseases as an estimate of their severity, as an index to monitor the results of treatment in patients with immune complex diseases, and as a research tool in the investigation of the pathogenetic basis of immunologic diseases. A variety of methods has been developed recently in an attempt to achieve maximum sensitivity, specificity, and reproducibility while keeping the technical procedure simple enough to be used as a routine test.

Methods currently in use are based on different biologic or chemical properties of immune complexes. As a result, they detect complexes of various sizes and properties, and none of the methods are satisfactory for all types. When possible, detection of circulating immune complexes should be done by several techniques.

A. Physical Methods: Ultracentrifugation and gel filtration can be used, although they are not very sensitive methods and are usually used for separation rather than detection of immune complexes.

Cryoglobulins of types II and III, when detected in biologic fluids, represent immune complexes which can be easily isolated and characterized. However, cryoprecipitation is not a universal property of antigen-antibody complexes.

Owing to their large size, immune complexes can be precipitated by high-molecular-weight polymers such as polyethylene glycol even at low concentrations of complexes which may leave soluble antigen or antibody as a residual in the reaction. Precipitated immune complexes are quantitated by measuring the protein content of the resolubilized precipitate (absorbance at 280 nm) or its concentration of immunoglobulins or complement components (radial diffusion).

B. Interaction With C1q, Rheumatoid Factor, or Conglutinin: Precipitin reactions were first used to detect interaction of immune complexes with C1q or rheumatoid factor. They have been superseded by more sensitive methods.

Rheumatoid factor and C1q are able to agglutinate latex particles coated with aggregated IgG. When mixed with immune complexes, active sites on the latex particles are blocked, thereby preventing their subsequent agglutination by rheumatoid factor or C1q. Inhibition of the latex agglutination test can therefore be used for detection of immune complexes.

Binding of immune complexes to C1q leads to activation of complement system, thereby depressing its hemolytic activity. This is the principle of the measure of anticomplementary activity of immune complexes in serum. The sample to be tested is freed from autologous complement activity by heat inactivation. It is then mixed in various dilutions with fresh normal serum which serves as a source of normal complement activity. Hemolytic activity (CH_{50}) of the fresh normal serum is measured with and without the addition of the sample. The anticomplementary activity is expressed as the percentage of reduction of CH_{50}.

Several techniques use radioisotopes either in solid or liquid phase to measure C1q binding. For **solid phase radioassay,** C1q is adsorbed on plastic polystyrene tubes. The sample is incubated in the coated tube, then washed out. The amount of immune complexes bound to C1q is estimated by binding of radiolabeled anti-immunoglobulin antibody or by binding of radiolabeled aggregated IgG onto free C1q. In the **liquid phase assay,** the sample is incubated with soluble radiolabeled C1q. In the C1q binding test, bound C1q is precipitated by polyethylene glycol and radioactivity measured in the precipitate. In the C1q deviation test, remaining free C1q is fixed on sensitized erythrocytes in such conditions that hemolysis does not occur. Radioactivity is measured in the erythrocyte pellet.

Conglutinin, a bovine serum protein, is known to react with fixed C3. This property is used in the **conglutinin binding test.** The sample is incubated with conglutinin, which is adsorbed onto plastic tubes. After washing, conglutinin-bound immune complexes are measured by the uptake of enzyme-conjugated or radiolabeled anti-immunoglobulin antibody.

C. Interaction With Cell Receptors: Antigen-antibody complexes can interact with the membrane of platelets. This interaction produces changes on the platelets which can be revealed by platelet aggregation (**platelet aggregation test**).

Immune complexes can be phagocytosed in vitro by macrophages, as can other large molecular complexes. This is used in a **phagocytosis inhibition test.** Peritoneal macrophages are incubated with the sample to be tested and with radiolabeled aggregated IgG. The presence of immune complexes in the sample is revealed by a decrease in the uptake of radioactivity by the cells compared to a control where incubation takes place with aggregates alone.

B cells have surface receptors for the third component of complement (C3) through which they can bind complement-fixing immune complexes. When peripheral blood lymphocytes are used as a source of B cells, fixation of immune complexes to their surface is revealed by a reduction of the number of EAC rosette-forming cells (see Chapter 23). Cultured lymphoblastoid B cell lines can also be used. The cells from the Raji line have receptors for C3 but lack surface immunoglobulins. Immune complexes bound to their surface can thus be estimated by secondary fixation of a radiolabeled anti-immunoglobulin antibody without interference by surface immunoglobulins.

NEPHELOMETRY

Nephelometry is the measurement of turbidity or cloudiness. In dilute solutions the precipitation reaction between antigen and antibody produces increased turbidity that can be measured by the scattering of an incident light source. Devices to measure light scattering produced by reaction of diphtheria toxin and antitoxin were introduced by Libby in 1938, and this technique has recently received increasing application in the clinical laboratory.

Nephelometric determination of antigens is performed by addition of constant amounts of highly purified and optically clear specific antiserum to varying amounts of antigen. The resultant antigen-antibody reactants are placed in a cuvette in a light beam of various wavelengths and the degree of light scatter measured in a photoelectric cell as the optical density (Fig 22–24). Accurate measurement of antigens can only be made in the ascending limb of the precipitin curve (Fig 22–1), since at equivalence and in antibody excess there is no direct linear relationship between antigen concentration and optical density. Thus, for accurate determination of solutions with high antigen concentrations, dilutions of the sample must be performed.

There are several different approaches to applying nephelometry in the clinical laboratory. Automated immunoprecipitation employs a fluorometric nephelometer in line with a series of flow-through channels that allow for the measurement of multiple samples simultaneously. Laser nephelometers employ a helium-neon laser beam as a light source and sensitive detection devices to measure forward light scatter. Introduction of various electronic filters near the detection device assures a high ''signal-to-noise'' ratio and a relatively high degree of sensitivity. Manual determination of turbidity can also be performed with an ordinary spectrophotometer or fluorimeter. A modified centrifugal fast analyzer equipped with a laser light source has also been employed for turbidity measurements. This method has the potential advantages of speed, low amounts of reagents required, and versatility for other assays.

Nephelometry is theoretically a rapid and simple method for quantitation of many antigens in biologic fluids. Disadvantages of the technique include rela-

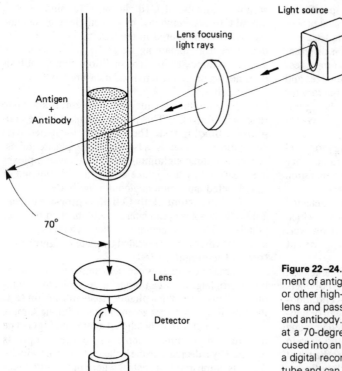

Figure 22–24. The principle of nephelometry for measurement of antigen-antibody reactions. Light rays from a laser or other high-intensity source are collected in the focusing lens and pass through the sample tube containing antigen and antibody. Light passing through the tube and emerging at a 70-degree angle is collected by another lens and focused into an electronic detector. This signal is converted to a digital recording of the amount of turbidity in the sample tube and can be mathematically related to either antigen or antibody concentration in the sample.

tively high cost of optically clear, potent antisera of similar specifications; high background resulting from sera containing lipids or hemoglobin; and the need for multiple dilutions, especially for high antigen concentrations. However, some of these potential sources of error are inherent in other immunoquantitative methods. Many of these inherent disadvantages can be overcome by the use of **rate nephelometry.** In this technique, a nephelometer electronically subtracts background signals. More precise measurement of turbidity is achieved by taking several measurements rapidly during the ascending phase of the precipitation reaction. Nephelometers that combine many of these features are now commercially available. The widespread use of such instruments—and nephelometric grade reagents—has made this method cheaper and applicable to many immunochemical determinations.

RADIOIMMUNOASSAY (RIA)

Radioimmunoassay (RIA) was introduced into clinical medicine in 1960 by Berson and Yalow, who first described its use as a practical method for the quantitation of plasma insulin levels. Since then, radioimmunoassay has achieved widespread use as a sensitive and specific method for the quantitation of microquantities of a large number of clinically relevant compounds. Radioimmunoassay has enjoyed a central role in clinical endocrinology and has largely supplanted the more expensive, cumbersome, and relatively imprecise bioassays of hormones. In fact, radioimmunoassay has profoundly altered clinical endocrinology, since virtually all hormones can now be measured accurately. Some new hormones have been described as a result of analysis of anomalies in radioimmunoassay tests. Recently, radioimmunoassay has been applied to microdetermination of drugs, eg, digoxin, and other small molecules, eg, steroid hormones, which immunologically are classified as haptens. The field of tumor immunology owes much of its growth to application of radioimmunoassay techniques in measuring carcinoembryonic antigen. The radioimmunoassay of HBsAg has provided blood banks with an excellent method for detecting hepatitis antigen in blood and thereby minimizing transmission of the disease by transfusion. In the diagnosis of allergy, the RAST (radioallergosorbent test) has proved useful for detecting specific IgE antibody to allergens (Chapter 18). In the coming decades, one can expect further applications of radioimmunoassay and other sensitive methods in the detection of levels of many drugs and the presence of other immunologically relevant molecules in virtually all tissue fluids. Through the use of automated techniques and computer analysis, radioimmunoassay has become established as an important tool in laboratory medicine. However, an intensifying controversy is developing regarding potential hazards of radiation and disposal of radioactive wastes, the relative instability of some radiolabeled compounds, and the expense of both gamma and beta spectrometers. Alternative methods, including quantitative immunofluorescence, enzyme immunoassay, and laser nephelometry are undergoing rapid development and in some instances have already become applicable for use in clinical laboratories.

Radioimmunoassay methods derive their fundamental and general applicability as laboratory tools in clinical medicine from 2 separate but related properties: great sensitivity and specificity. Virtually any compound to which an antibody can be produced may be measured by radioimmunoassay down to the picogram $(10^{-12}$ g) range. With proper manipulation, radioimmunoassay can be designed to distinguish between molecules which differ by only one amino acid or which are stereoisomers. Furthermore, the ability of molecules to be measured by radioimmunoassay is independent of their biologic activity. This fact has led to some rather surprising discoveries. For example, in classic hemophilia, a disease caused by deficiency of factor VIII, radioimmunoassay as well as hemagglutination inhibition assay has demonstrated normal levels of antigenically reactive but biologically inert procoagulant activity (see Chapter 27). Thus, radioimmunoassay has led to important insights into basic mechanisms of disease and has served as a clinically useful diagnostic tool in many areas of medicine and biology.

RADIOIMMUNOASSAY METHODOLOGY & INTERPRETATION

Summary of Radioimmunoassay Procedure

The general methodology of radioimmunoassay is, in theory, relatively simple. An outline of the steps required to establish a radioimmunoassay for a hypothetical human protein hormone "X" is as follows:

(1) Antiserum to X is raised in heterologous species, eg, rabbit or guinea pig.

(2) If the hormone X is itself nonimmunogenic, ie, a hapten, it is first coupled to a macromolecular carrier, eg, bovine γ-globulin, and the hapten and carrier complex is then used to raise an antiserum.

(3) X is then radiolabeled, usually with ^{125}I (*X).

(4) Labeled antigen *X reacts with enough antibody to bind about 70% of *X.

(5) Various known amounts of unlabeled hormone X are added to a mixture of *X and anti-X and compete for antibody combining sites.

(6) After an appropriate incubation period, labeled *X bound to antibody is separated from unbound *X.

(7) From the amount of *X bound at various X concentrations (Fig 22–25), a curve can be constructed that will allow computation of any unknown X concentration desired (Fig 22–26).

(8) Since the curve is linear over a relatively limited range, dilution of the sample containing an un-

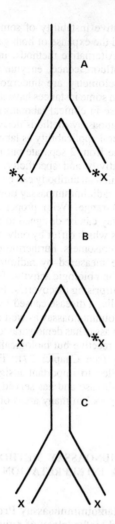

Figure 22–25. General scheme of radioimmunoassay. Schematic representation of competitive binding of antigen X or antigen *X (radioactive) to antibody against X. *A:* No X added and antibody binds only *X. *B:* Approximately equal amounts of X and *X added, with equal binding to antibody. *C:* Excess of X compared to *X displaces radiolabeled antigen from antibody binding sites.

known amount of hormone X is necessary to adjust its concentration to within this measurable range.

Antisera for Radioimmunoassay

In general, large protein or polypeptide hormones such as parathyroid hormone, growth hormone, and insulin are good immunogens, and suitable antisera to these hormones can be prepared in rabbits, goats, or guinea pigs. Many of these hormone antisera are now commercially available, and the cost of purchase may be justified because of the expense of maintaining animal colonies for local antiserum production. High avidity is a desirable feature of antibody, and this can be achieved by prolonged immunization schedules, beginning with the hormone emulsified in Freund's complete adjuvant followed by antigen in Freund's

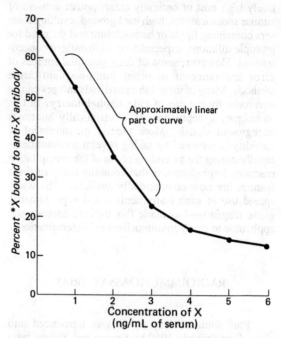

Figure 22–26. Standard curve for radioimmunoassay of hormone X. Theoretic standard curve for estimating amount of hormone X in sera with unknown concentration of X. As amount of X is increased over narrow range (1–6 ng/mL), the percentage of *X bound to anti-X diminishes. This relationship is linear over part of the range, which allows estimation of the amount of X in various serum samples.

incomplete adjuvant. If one wishes to develop an antiserum for radioimmunoassay of a small nonimmunogenic compound, ie, a hapten such as digoxin or a corticosteroid, coupling of the hapten to a larger macromolecule carrier prior to immunization will result in a suitable antiserum directed at free hapten as well as the carrier.

Radiolabeling of X (Antigen)

A generally accepted method is iodination with ^{125}I or ^{131}I, in which the iodine molecule is covalently bound to the tyrosine group in the case of protein antigens.

This reaction is facilitated by the presence of an oxidizing agent such as chloramine-T. If the antigen to be labeled lacks tyrosine groups, alternative iodination procedures have been devised. For example, intrinsic labeling by organic synthesis with ^{3}H can be accomplished with steroid hormones. The advantages of iodination are that it usually does not affect the an-

Table 22–8. Methods of separation of antibody *X from free *X in radioimmunoassay.

Physicochemical
  Electrophoresis on paper or cellulose acetate
  Chromatography
  Gel diffusion
  Ammonium sulfate
  Staphylococcal protein A
  Adsorption
  Talc   ⎫ Precipitate free *X and leave
  Activated charcoal ⎬ antibody *X in supernate.
  Zirconyl phosphate ⎭

Immunologic
  Double antibody method: Addition of second antibody directed at Fc region of anti-X so that antigenic sites of first antibody are bound by second antibody.

tigenic properties of the molecule and that it achieves high specific activity with relatively long isotope half-life, eg, ^{125}I with a 60-day half-life. However, radiation damage, oxidation, and changes in physicochemical structure of the antigen may be deleterious to its reactivity in radioimmunoassay.

Separation of Antibody-Bound Antigen From Free Labeled Antigen

After incubation of labeled antigen *X with specific antibody in the presence of varying amounts of unlabeled free X, separation of bound antibody from free *X must be accomplished to estimate the amount of X present in the competitive binding reaction (Fig 22–25). In general, separation can be accomplished by either physicochemical or immunologic means (Table 22–8). The double antibody method is preferred in most laboratories. It has the advantage of being applicable to any test volume. It is gentle, thus avoiding dissociation of (anti-X)-*X complex, and is relatively simple. One must confirm that the second antibody does not react with any substance in the test material other than antigenic sites on the first antibody. Possible disadvantages include the relatively high cost of the method and the large amount of second antibody required.

Standard Curve & Radioimmunoassay Procedure

After reacting *X and X with anti-X and subsequent separation of the free *X from (anti-X)-*X complex, a standard curve relating bound *X to free *X can be constructed (Fig 22–26). Thus, the amount of X in any tissue fluid sample can be calculated, based on the slope of the standard curve within its linear range.

SOLID PHASE RADIOIMMUNOASSAY SYSTEMS

In recent modifications of the previously described liquid or soluble phase radioimmunoassay, antibody is either adsorbed onto tubes or covalently

linked to a solid matrix. In the coated method, antibody is simply adsorbed to polystyrene tubes, and free antibody is then removed by washing. Unlabeled antigen is added, followed by labeled antigen. After equilibration, the tubes are washed and dried, and radioactivity is measured in a gamma spectrometer. In the covalently linked antibody method, antibody is covalently bound to cross-linked dextrans, eg, Sepharose or Sephadex, and separation of the bound labeled antigen is accomplished by centrifugation. Alternatively, the second antibody in the double antibody method can be covalently bound to Sepharose and separation of labeled complex performed by centrifugation.

APPLICATIONS OF RADIOIMMUNOASSAY

Table 22–9 lists some of the substances currently measured by radioimmunoassay. Radioimmunoassay can also be employed as a general method for a competitive binding inhibition system. Thus, in the case of cAMP, cGMP, or vitamin B_{12}, specific (nonantibody) binding proteins supplant antibody. Otherwise, the principles are identical to those described in the discussion of standard radioimmunoassay.

Table 22–9. Substances measurable by radioimmunoassay.

Steroid hormones	Peptide hormones (cont'd)
Aldosterone	Oxytocin
Androstenedione	Parathyroid
Corticosterone	Placental lactogen
Cortisol	Renin
Cortisone	Secretin
Deoxycorticosterone	Thyroglobulin
Deoxycortisol	Thyrotropin (TSH)
Dehydroepiandrosterone	Thyroxine (T_4)
Dehydrotestosterone	Triiodothyronine (T_3)
Estradiol-17β	Vasopressin
Estriol	**Drugs**
Estrone	Digitoxin
Progesterone	Digoxin
Testosterone	Morphine
Peptide hormones	Ouabain
ACTH	**Other**
Angiotensin I	Anti-DNA antibodies
Angiotensin II	Carcinoembryonic antigen (CEA)
Bradykinin	
Calcitonin	Cyclic AMP (cAMP)
Follicle-stimulating hormone (FSH)	Cyclic GMP (cGMP)
	Fibrinopeptide A
Gastrin	Folic acid
Glucagon	Hepatitis B antigen (HBsAg)
Growth hormone	
Human chorionic gonadotropin (hCG)	IgE
	Intrinsic factor
Insulin	Prostaglandins
Luteinizing hormone (LH)	Vitamin B_{12}
α- and β-Melanocyte-stimulating hormones	

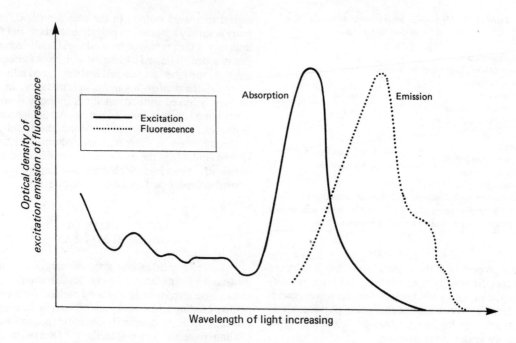

Figure 22–27. Absorption and emission spectra for a fluorescent compound.

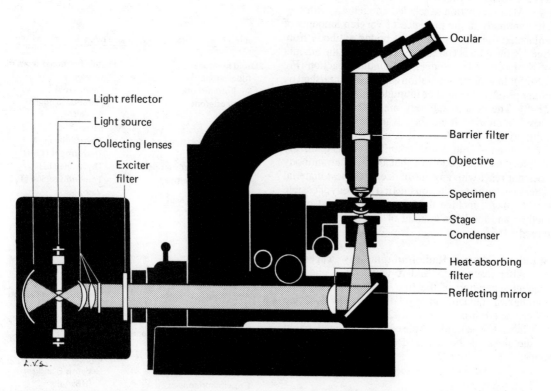

Figure 22–28. Fluorescence microscope with transmitted light. Light beam is generated by a mercury vapor lamp, reflected by a concave mirror, and projected through collecting lenses to the exciter filter which emits a fluorescent light beam. A reflecting mirror directs the beam from underneath the stage, through the condenser into the specimen. A barrier filter removes wavelengths other than those emitted from the fluorescent compound in the specimen, and the fluorescent pattern is viewed through magnification provided by the objective and ocular lenses.

IMMUNOHISTOCHEMICAL TECHNIQUES

IMMUNOFLUORESCENCE

Immunofluorescence is essentially a histochemical or cytochemical technique for detection and localization of antigens. Specific antibody is conjugated with fluorescent compounds, resulting in a sensitive tracer with unaltered immunologic reactivity. The conjugated antiserum is added to cells or tissues and becomes fixed to antigens, thereby forming a stable immune complex. Nonantibody proteins are removed by washing, and the resultant preparation is observed in a fluorescence microscope. This adaptation of a regular microscope contains a high-intensity light source, excitation filters to produce a wavelength capable of causing fluorescence activation, and barrier filters to remove interfering wavelengths of light. When observed in the fluorescence microscope against a dark background, antigens bound specifically to fluorescent antibody can be detected by virtue of the bright color of the latter.

The technique of immunofluorescence was introduced in 1941 by Coons, who employed β-anthracene, a blue fluorescing compound, coupled to pneumococcus antiserum to detect bacterial antigens in tissue sections. Shortly thereafter, his group employed fluorescein-conjugated antisera which emitted a green light that could be differentiated from the blue autofluorescence of many tissues.

Fluorescence is the emission of light of one color, ie, wavelength, while a substance is irradiated with light of a different color. The emitted wavelength is necessarily at a lower energy level than the incident or absorbed light (Fig 22–27). Fluorochromes such as rhodamine or fluorescein used in clinical laboratories have characteristic absorption and emission spectra. Fluorescein isothiocyanate (FITC) is a chemical form of fluorescein which readily binds covalently to proteins at alkaline pH primarily through ϵ amino residues of lysine and terminal amino groups. Its absorption maximum is at 490–495 nm, and it emits its characteristic green color at 517 nm. Tetramethylrhodamine isothiocyanate, which emits red, has an absorption maximum at 550 nm and maximal emission at 580 nm (for rhodamine-protein conjugates). Consequently, different excitation and barrier filters must be employed to visualize the characteristic green or red color of these fluorescent dyes. Generally, one wants to achieve an exciting wavelength nearly equal to that of the excitation maximum of the dye. Similarly, the barrier filter should remove all but the emitted wavelength spectrum. In practice, the actual brightness of fluorescence observed by the eye depends on 3 factors: (1) the efficiency with which the dye converts incident light into fluorescent light; (2) the concentration of the dye in the tissue specimen; and (3) the intensity of the exciting (absorbed) radiation.

Microscopes used for visualizing immunofluorescent specimens are simple modifications of standard transmitted light microscopes (Fig 22–28). In 1967, Ploem introduced an epi-illuminated system that employs a vertical illuminator and a dichroic mirror. In this system (Fig 22–29), the excitation beam is focused directly on the tissue specimen through the lens objective. Fluorescent light emitted from the epi-illuminated specimen is then transmitted to the eye through the dichroic mirror. A dichroic mirror allows passage of light of selected wavelengths in one direction through the mirror but not in the opposite direction.

There are several distinct advantages to the Ploem system. Fluorescence may be combined with transmitted light for phase contrast examination of the tissues, thereby allowing better definition of morphology and fluorescence. Also, interchangeable filter systems permit rapid examination of the specimen at different wavelengths for double fluorochrome staining, eg, red and green (rhodamine and fluorescein, respectively). This advantage in technique has resulted in superior sensitivity for examining cell membrane fluorescence in living lymphocytes.

Methodology & Interpretation

Virtually any antigen can be detected in fixed tissue sections or in live cell suspensions by immunofluorescence. It is the combination of great sensitivity and specificity together with the use of histologic techniques that make immunofluorescence so useful. The steps involved in immunofluorescence include preparation of immune antiserum or purified γ-globulin, conjugation with fluorescent dye, and finally the staining procedure.

For immunofluorescence, an antiserum to the antigen one wishes to detect is raised in heterologous species, eg, goat or rabbit. Potent antisera are needed which should be prepared to contain milligram amounts of antibody per milliliter of antiserum. The potency of antisera is usually assessed by quantitative precipitation or passive hemagglutination. Specificity must be assured at a level which exceeds that detectable in ordinary double diffusion or immunoelectrophoretic techniques. Several more sensitive methods are available, including hemagglutination inhibition and radioimmunoassay. Unwanted antibodies present in either conjugates or antiglobulin reagents for the test can be removed with insoluble immunoabsorbents.

After one is assured of a direct antiserum of high potency and appropriate specificity, the γ-globulin fraction can be prepared by ammonium sulfate precipitation or a combination of salt precipitation and DEAE-cellulose ion exchange chromatography. It is necessary to partially purify serum immunoglobulin, since subsequent conjugation should be limited to antibody as much as possible. This will increase the efficiency of staining and avoid unwanted nonspecific staining by fluorochrome-conjugated nonantibody serum proteins which can adhere to tissue components.

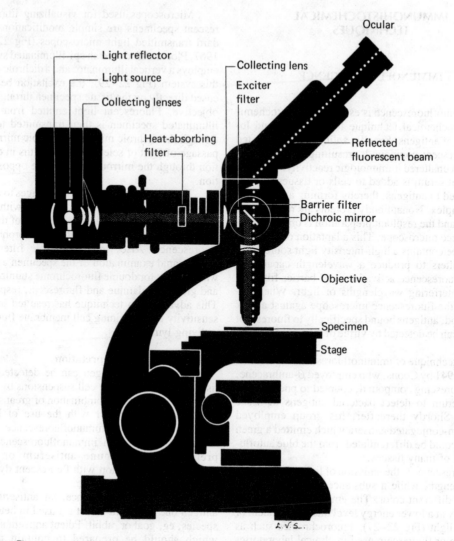

Figure 22–29. Fluorescence microscope with epi-illumination. The light beam is directed through the exciter filter and down onto the specimen. A dichroic mirror allows passage of selected wavelengths in one direction but not another. After reaching the specimen, the light is reflected through the dichroic mirror and emitted fluorescent light is visualized at the ocular.

Conjugation of γ-globulin depends largely on the particular dye one wishes to combine with the antibody molecule. From a clinical standpoint, only fluorescein and rhodamine have been used widely. Fluorescein in the form of FITC, or rhodamine as tetramethylrhodamine isothiocyanate, is either reacted directly with γ-globulin in alkaline solution overnight at 4 °C or dialyzed against γ-globulin. Unreacted dye is then removed from the protein-fluorochrome conjugate by gel filtration or exhaustive dialysis. If necessary, the resultant conjugate can be concentrated by lyophilization, pressure dialysis, or solvent extraction with water-soluble polymers. Thereafter, one must determine both the concentration of γ-globulin and the dye/protein or fluorescein/protein ratio of the compound. This is usually done spectrophotometrically with corrections for the alteration in absorbance of

γ-globulin by the introduced fluorochrome. Fluorochrome-labeled compounds are best stored in the dark, frozen at −20 °C.

Staining Techniques

A. Direct Immunofluorescence: (Figs 22–30 and 22–31.) In this technique, conjugated antiserum is added directly to the tissue section or viable cell suspension.

B. Indirect Immunofluorescence: This technique allows for the detection of antibody in unlabeled sera and is especially useful in the clinical laboratory. It eliminates the need to purify and individually conjugate each serum sample. The method is basically an adaptation of the antiglobulin reaction (Coombs test) or double antibody technique (Figs 22–30 and 22–31). Specificity should be checked as

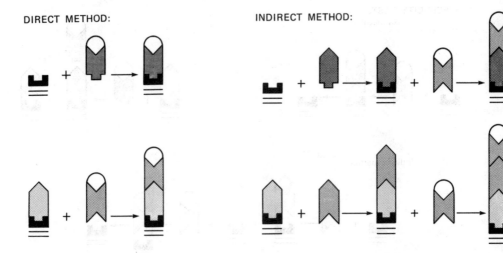

DIRECT METHOD: INDIRECT METHOD:

Figure 22–30. Mechanism of immunofluorescence techniques. **Direct Method.** *(Top):* Antigen in substrate detected by direct labeling with fluorescent antibody. *(Bottom):* Antigen-antibody (immune) complex in substrate labeled with fluorescent antiglobulin reagent. (Modified and reproduced, with permission, from Nordic Immunology, Tilburg, The Netherlands.)

Figure 22–31. Mechanism of immunofluorescence techniques. **Indirect Method.** *(Top):* Incubation of antigen in substrate with unlabeled antibody forms immune complex. Labeling performed with fluorescent antiglobulin reagent. *(Bottom):* Immune complex in substrate reacted with unlabeled antiglobulin reagent and then stained with fluorescent antiglobulin reagent directed at unlabeled antiglobulin. (Modified and reproduced, with permission, from Nordic Immunology, Tilburg, The Netherlands.)

LEGEND

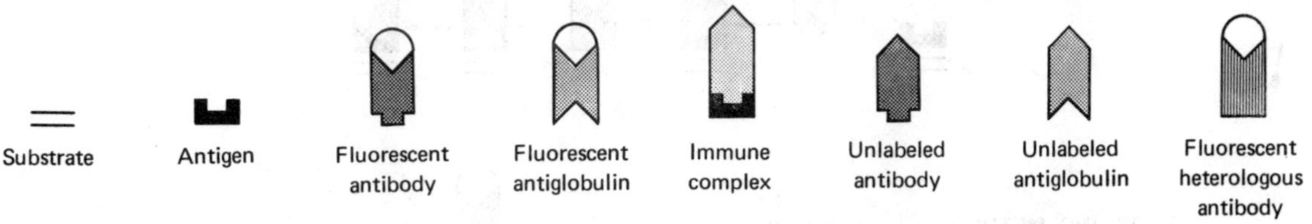

Substrate	Antigen	Fluorescent antibody	Fluorescent antiglobulin	Immune complex	Unlabeled antibody	Unlabeled antiglobulin	Fluorescent heterologous antibody

diagrammed and further established by blocking and neutralization methods (Fig 22–32).

Several additional variations in staining techniques have been used. These include a conjugated anticomplement antiserum for the detection of antigen-antibody-complement complexes and double staining with both rhodamine and fluorescein conjugates.

Immunofluorescence employing routine serologic procedures for the detection of antibody in human serum specimens has been widely accepted. Sensitivity levels are generally higher than is the case with complement fixation and lower than with hemagglutination inhibition. Methods for detecting antibody by immunofluorescence include (1) the antiglobulin method, (2) inhibition of labeled antibody-antigen reaction by antibody in test serum, and (3) the anticomplement method.

C. Biotin-Avidin System: Avidin, a basic glycoprotein derived from egg albumin of MW 68,000, has a remarkably high affinity (10^{15} kcal/mol) for the vitamin biotin. Biotin can easily be coupled covalently to a protein (antibody) and then reacted with fluorochrome-coupled avidin. After reaction of antigen with unlabeled antibody, the biotin-labeled second antibody is added. Since many molecules of biotin can be coupled to an antibody, the subsequent addition of fluorochrome-labeled avidin results in a firm bond with exceedingly bright fluorescence. Other advantages are lack of nonspecific binding of fluorochrome-coupled avidin to various substrates and general use of avidin conjugates in binding to biotin-labeled antibodies regardless of their derivation.

Quantitative Immunofluorescence

Quantitative immunoassays using fluorochrome-labeled antigens and antibodies have recently been developed. The amount of light of a given wavelength emitted from a fluorescent specimen can be precisely measured by a microfluorometer. A number of assay methods have been introduced commercially in the field of quantitative immunofluorescence. The fluorescent immunoassay system (FIAX) can be used to measure IgG, IgA and IgM, C3 and C4, and antinuclear and anti-DNA antibodies. Measurement of immunoglobulins is done by competitive binding of labeled specific antiserum for free and solid phase antigen. The free antigen is present in patients' serum, whereas the bound immunoglobulin is fixed to a polymeric hydrophobic surface. The amount of

SPECIFICITY TESTS
Direct method:

Indirect method:

BLOCKING METHOD (indirect method):

NEUTRALIZING METHOD:

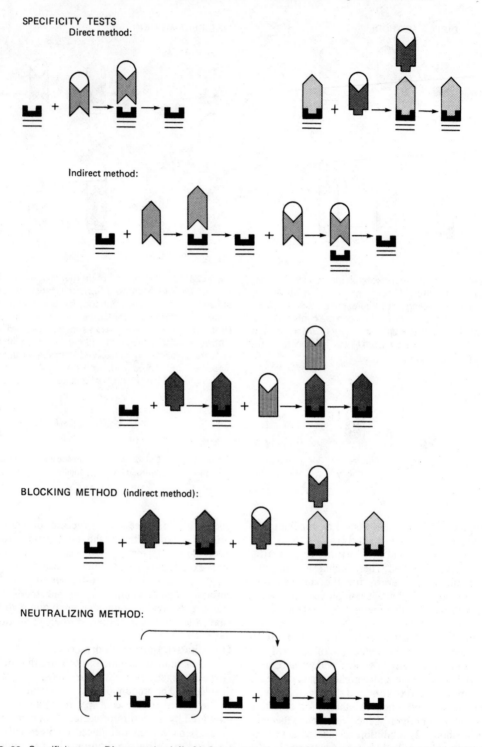

Figure 22–32. Specificity tests. **Direct method.** *(Left):* Substrate antigen fails to react with fluorescent antiglobulin reagent. No fluorescence results. *(Right):* Immune complex–substrate fails to react with fluorescent antibody directed against unrelated antigen. No fluorescence results. **Indirect method.** *(Top):* Unlabeled specific antiglobulin is replaced by unrelated antibody. In second step, fluorescent antiglobulin cannot react directly with antigen in substrate which has not bound specific antiglobulin. No fluorescence results. *(Bottom):* First step performed by reacting specific antibody with substrate antigen. In second stage, the specific conjugate is replaced by unrelated fluorescent heterologous antibody. No fluorescence results. **Blocking method.** Substrate antigen is incubated with unlabeled specific antibody prior to addition of specific fluorescent antibody. Decreased fluorescence results. **Neutralizing method.** Substrate antigen is incubated with specific fluorescent antibody after it is absorbed with specific antigen in substrate. No fluorescence results.

Table 22–10. Clinical applications of immunofluorescence.

Identification of T and B cells in blood
Detection of autoantibodies in serum, eg, ANA
Detection of immunoglobulins in tissues
Detection of complement components in tissues
Detection of specific, tissue-fixed antibody
Rapid identification of microorganisms in tissue or culture
Identification of chromosomes of specific banding patterns
Identification of tumor-specific antigens on neoplastic tissues
Identification of transplantation antigens in various organs
Localization of hormones and enzymes
Quantitation of serum proteins and antibodies

fluorescent antibody bound to the solid phase antigen is measured in a specially designed microfluorometer and converted to mg/dL by reference to a standard curve.

Serum antibodies to various cellular antigens such as DNA or nuclei can also be measured by an indirect fluorescence technique. Substrate (eg, DNA) is fixed to the polymer surface in solid phase and incubated with test sera. A second fluorescein anti-immunoglobulin reagent is then bound to the first antigen-antibody complex and the amount of bound fluorescence measured fluorometrically.

This technique has many of the same advantages as enzyme immunoassay, and additional tests are being developed.

Clinical Applications of Immunofluorescence

Direct and indirect immunofluorescence staining techniques have achieved widespread use in many areas of clinical medicine. In general, immunofluorescence has been of greatest usefulness as a sensitive and specific diagnostic tool. A partial list of its applications in clinical immunology is presented in Table 22–10.

OTHER IMMUNOHISTOCHEMICAL TECHNIQUES

Enzyme-Linked Antibody

This method depends on conjugation of an enzyme to antibody which is directed at a cellular or tissue antigen. The resulting conjugate is then both immunologically and enzymatically active. Thereafter, the principles are entirely analogous to those underlying the direct or indirect immunofluorescence techniques described above.

Horseradish peroxidase is usually the enzyme chosen for coupling to antibody. Tissues are first stained directly with antibody-enzyme conjugate or directly with enzyme-linked antiglobulin reagent following incubation with unlabeled immune serum. Thereafter, the tissue is incubated with the substrate for the enzyme. The enzyme in this case is detected visually by formation of a black color after incubation with hydrogen peroxide and diaminobenzidine. One advantage of this method is that ordinary light microscopes may be utilized for analysis of tissue sec-

tions. Furthermore, enzyme-coupled antibody can be used for ultrastructural studies in the electron microscope.

Quantitative Enzyme Immunoassays

Enzyme immunoassays have emerged as quantitative techniques for detection of antigens, haptens, and antibodies. They all employ various enzymes linked to either antigen or antibody as a label which can easily be detected by measurement of enzyme activity. The multiple variations of enzyme immunoassays are nearly all completely analogous to radioimmunoassays and quantitative immunofluorescence, the obvious difference being use of the enzyme label. An exception is the so-called enzyme multiple immunoassay technique (EMIT), which does not require separation of free and bound enzyme-labeled hapten because the assay depends on direct inactivation of enzyme activity by antibody.

The 2 most widely employed variants of enzyme immunoassay are the competitive enzyme immunoassay and the enzyme-linked immunosorbent assay (ELISA). In the competitive enzyme immunoassay, labeled and unlabeled antigen compete for small amounts of antibody which is then precipitated with a second soluble or soluble phase antibody. Enzyme activity in the bound or free fraction is determined and related by a standard curve to an unknown amount of antigen in the original sample. The ELISA assay can be used to measure either antigen or antibody and is analogous to the radioallergosorbent (RAST) test. To measure antibody, antigen is fixed to a solid phase, incubated with test serum, and then incubated with anti-immunoglobulin tagged with enzyme. Enzyme activity adherent to the solid phase is then related to amount of antibody bound. To measure antigen, antibody is bound to the solid phase, a test solution containing antigen is added, and then a second enzyme-labeled antibody is added. This test requires that at least 2 combining sites be present on the antigen. Substrate is then added, and enzyme activity is related to antigen concentration.

Enzymes that have been frequently used include horseradish peroxidase, alkaline phosphatase, lysozyme, and glucose-6-phosphate dehydrogenase. These enzymes are coupled to antigens or antibodies by various cross-linking agents, particularly glutaraldehyde and dimaleimide. Virtually any enzyme can be used as long as it is soluble, stable, and not present in biologic fluids in quantities that would interfere with serum determinations.

Enzyme immunoassay has been applied to measurement of many substances, including carcinoembryonic antigen (CEA), steroid hormones, immunoglobulins, antibodies to bacteria, viruses, and DNA, and allergens. Using EMIT, small molecules such as morphine, digoxin, and many other drugs can be detected. Advantages of enzyme immunoassays include sensitivity (ng/mL range), simplicity, stability of reagents, lack of radiation hazard, potential for automation, and relatively inexpensive equipment.

Ferritin-Coupled Antibody

Ferritin, an iron-containing protein, is highly electron-dense. When coupled to antibody, it can be used for either direct or indirect tissue staining. Localization of ferritin-coupled antibody-antigen complexes in fixed tissue can then be achieved with the electron microscope. Other electron-dense particles such as gold or uranium can also be introduced chemically into specific antitissue antibodies. These reagents have also been applied in immunoelectronmicroscopy.

Autoradiography

Radioactive isotopes such as ^{125}I which can be easily introduced into immunoglobulins by chemical means provide highly sensitive probes for localization of tissue antigens. The antigens are detected visually after tissue staining by overlaying or coating slides with photographic emulsion. The appearance of silver grains as black dots has been used for subcellular localization of antigen both at light microscopic and ultrastructural levels. Autoradiography has also been applied to detection of proteins or immunoglobulins synthesized by cells in tissue culture.

Miscellaneous Methods

A variety of other methods have been described for localization of antigens in tissues. Many have not found widespread clinical application. In most cases, these techniques depend on secondary phenomena which occur as a result of the antigen-antibody interaction. These methods include the following:

(1) Complement fixation
(2) Conglutinating complement absorption test
(3) Antiglobulin consumption test
(4) Mixed hemadsorption
(5) Immune adherence
(6) Hemagglutination and coated particle reaction
(7) Immunoprecipitation

AGGLUTINATION

Agglutination and precipitation reactions are the basis of the most commonly used techniques in laboratory immunology. Whereas precipitation reactions are quantifiable and simple to perform, agglutination techniques are only semiquantitative and somewhat more difficult. The agglutination of either insoluble native antigens or antigen-coated particles can be simply assessed visually with or without the aid of a microscope. Important advantages of agglutination reactions are their high degree of sensitivity and the enormous variety of substances detectable through use of antigen- or antibody-coated particles.

According to Coombs, the 3 main requirements in agglutination tests are the availability of a stable cell or particle suspension, the presence of one or more antigens close to the surface, and the knowledge that

"incomplete" or nonagglutinating antibodies are not detectable without modifications, eg, antiglobulin reactions.

Agglutination reactions may be classified as either direct or indirect (passive). In the simple direct technique, a cell or insoluble particulate antigen is agglutinated directly by antibody. An example is the agglutination of group A red blood cells by anti-A sera. Passive agglutination refers to agglutination of antigen-coated cells or inert particles which are passive carriers of otherwise soluble antigens. Examples are latex fixation for detection of rheumatoid factor and agglutination of DNA-coated red cells for detection of anti-DNA antibody. Alternatively, **antigen** can be detected by coating latex particles or red blood cells with purified **antibody** and performing so-called reversed agglutination. Another category of agglutination involves spontaneous agglutination of red blood cells by certain viruses. This viral hemagglutination reaction can be specifically inhibited in the presence of antiviral antibody. Thus, viral hemagglutination can be used either to quantify virus itself or to determine by homologous inhibition the titer of antisera directed against hemagglutinating viruses.

Inhibition of agglutination, if carefully standardized with highly purified antigens, can be used as a sensitive indicator of the amount of antigen in various tissue fluids. Hemagglutination inhibition using passive hemagglutination reactions has recently been semiautomated in microtiter plates and is sensitive for measuring antigens in concentrations of $0.2-9~\mu g/mL$. With appropriate modification, passive hemagglutination with protein-sensitized cells can detect antibody at concentrations as low as $0.03~\mu g/mL$.

AGGLUTINATION TECHNIQUES

Direct Agglutination Test

Red blood cells, bacteria, fungi, and a variety of other microbial species can be directly agglutinated by serum antibody. Tests to detect specific antibody are carried out by serially titrating antisera in 2-fold dilutions in the presence of a constant amount of antigen. Direct agglutination is relatively temperature-independent except for cold-reacting antibody, eg, cold agglutinins. After a few hours of incubation, agglutination is complete and particles are examined either directly or microscopically for evidence of clumping. The results are usually expressed as a titer of antiserum, ie, the highest dilution at which agglutination occurs. Because of intrinsic variability in the test system, a titer usually must differ by at least 2 dilutions ("2 tubes") to be considered significantly different from any given titer. Tests are carried out in small test tubes in volumes of 0.2–0.5 mL or in microtiter plates with smaller amounts of reagents, resulting in greater sensitivity.

Indirect (Passive) Agglutination

The range of soluble antigens that can be pas-

Table 22—11. Substances that spontaneously adsorb to red blood cells for hemagglutination.

Escherichia coli antigens
Yersinia antigens
Lipopolysaccharide from *Neisseria meningitidis*
Toxoplasma antigens
Purified protein derivative (PPD)
Endotoxin of *Mycoplasma* species
Viruses
Antibiotics, especially penicillin
Ovalbumin
Bovine serum albumin
DNA
Haptens, eg, DNCB

Table 22—12. Methods used to coat fresh and aldehyde-treated red blood cells with various antigens and antibodies for passive hemagglutination assay.*

Coupling Agent	Comments on Coupling	Antigens Commonly Coated
None	Simple adsorption	Penicillin, bacterial antigens including endo- and exotoxins, viruses, and ovalbumin.
Tannic acid	Adsorption possibly caused by changes analogous to enzymes. Most popular; usually satisfactory, but often difficult and unreliable.	A wide spectrum of antigens: serum proteins, microbial and tissue extracts, homogenates, thyroglobulin, and tuberculin proteins.
Bisdiazotized benzidine (BDB)	Chemically stable covalent azo bonds.	Proteins and pollen antigens.
1,3-Difluoro-4,6-dinitrobenzene (DFDNB)	Adsorption after modification of cell membrane.	Purified proteins and chorionic gonadotropin.
Chromic chloride (CrCl₃)	Proteins bound to red cells by the charge effect of trivalent cations.	Proteins.
Glutaraldehyde, cyanuric chloride, tetrazotized O-dianisidine	Cross-linking and covalent coupling.	Various proteins and certain enzymes.
Tolylene-2,4-diisocyanate	Covalently bound.	Proteins.
Water-soluble carbodiimide	Covalently bound.	Proteins.

*Modified and reproduced, with permission, from Fudenberg HH: Hemagglutination inhibition: Passive hemagglutination assay for antigen-antibody reactions. In: *A Seminar on Basic Immunology.* American Association of Blood Banks, 1971.

sively adsorbed or chemically coupled to red blood cells or other inert particles has dramatically extended the application of agglutination reactions. Many antigens will spontaneously couple with red blood cells and form stable reagents for antibody detection (Table 22–11). When red blood cells are used as the inert particles, serum specimens often must be absorbed with washed, uncoated red blood cells to remove heterophilic antibodies that would otherwise nonspecifically agglutinate the red blood cells. The advantages of using red blood cells for coating are their ready availability, sensitivity as indicators, and storage capabilities. Red blood cells can be treated with formalin, glutaraldehyde, or pyruvic aldehyde and stored for prolonged periods at 4 °C. Although not applicable to all coating antigens, treatment with these preservatives may often be performed either before or after antigen coupling.

Coupling techniques vary greatly in their applicability and success in individual laboratories. A list of general methods available for coating antigens on red blood cells is presented in Table 22–12. Perhaps the most widely used method is the tanned cell technique. Treatment of red blood cells with tannic acid increases the amount of most protein antigens subsequently adsorbed. This higher density of coated antigen greatly increases the sensitivity of the agglutination reaction. Although highly purified antigens are required for immunologic specificity, slightly denatured or aggregated antigens coat tanned red blood cells best.

Agglutination tests may be performed in tubes or microtiter plates. In antisera with very high agglutination titers, a prozone phenomenon may obscure the results. The prozone phenomenon produces falsely negative agglutination reactions at high concentrations of antibody as a result of poor lattice formation and steric hindrance by antibody excess. However, the use of standard serial dilutions eliminates this difficulty. Since IgM antibody is about 750 times as efficient as IgG in agglutination, the presence of high amounts of IgM may markedly influence test results.

HEMAGGLUTINATION INHIBITION

The inhibition of agglutination of antigen-coated red blood cells by homologous antigen is a highly sensitive and specific method for detecting small quantities of soluble antigen in blood or other tissue fluids. The principle of this assay is that antibody preincubated with soluble homologous or cross-reacting antigens will be "inactivated" when incubated with antigen-coated red blood cells. Thus, the test proceeds in 2 stages (Fig 22–33). Antibody in relatively low concentration is incubated with a sample of antigen of unknown quantity. After combination with soluble antigen, antigen-coated cells are added and agglutinated by uncombined or free antibody. (The degree of inhibition of agglutination reflects the amount of antigen present in the original sample.) Controls, including samples of known antigen concentration and uncoated red blood cells, must be employed. This

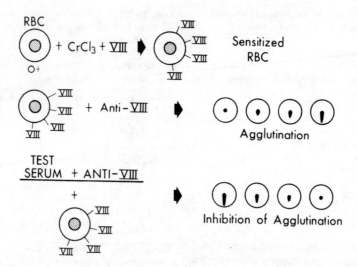

Figure 22–33. Hemagglutination inhibition. Human O+ red blood cells (RBC) are conjugated with coagulation factor VIII antigen by chromic chloride. The sensitized red blood cells are reacted with specific antibody to factor VIII and are agglutinated. In the well of a V-shaped microtiter plate, agglutinated red blood cells appear as discrete dots. Nonagglutinated cells form a streak when the plate is incubated at a 45-degree angle. Agglutination of sensitized red blood cells can be inhibited by the presence of homologous factor VIII antigen present in the test serum. With decreasing amounts of serum added to the test, the specific antibody agglutinates sensitized cells and forms a dot in the microtiter well. A semiquantitative estimation of the amount or titer of antigen in a test serum can be made in this way.

hemagglutination inhibition method has proved very useful in the detection of HBsAg in hepatitis and in the detection of factor VIII antigen in hemophilia and related clotting disorders.

CLINICALLY APPLICABLE TESTS THAT EMPLOY AGGLUTINATION REACTIONS

Antiglobulin Test (Coombs Test)

The development of this simple and ingenious technique virtually revolutionized the field of immunohematology, and in various forms it has found widespread application in all fields of immunology. Antibodies frequently coat red blood cells but fail to form the necessary lattice which results in agglutination. A typical example is antibody directed at the Rh determinants on human red blood cells. However, the addition of an antiglobulin antiserum produced in a heterologous species (eg, rabbit anti-human γ-globulin) produces marked agglutination. Thus, the antiglobulin or Coombs test is used principally to detect subagglutinating or nonagglutinating amounts of antierythrocyte antibodies of any γ-globulin molecule. However, more specific Coombs reagents directed at specific immunoglobulin classes, eg, anti-IgG, anti-IgA, or anti-L chains, may also be employed to detect cell-bound immunoglobulin. So-called "non-gamma Coombs" reagents which are directed against various complement components, eg, C3 or C4, may also produce red cell agglutination in the case of autoimmune hemolytic anemia. In some instances of this disorder, only complement components are bound to the red cell and the classic antiglobulin reaction is negative. The **direct Coombs test** detects γ-globulin or other serum proteins which are adherent to red blood cells taken directly from a sensitized individual. The **indirect Coombs test** is a 2-stage reaction for detection of incomplete antibodies in a patient's serum. The serum in question is first incubated with test red blood cells, and the putative antibody-coated cells are then agglutinated by a Coombs antiglobulin serum. The major applications of Coombs tests include red cell typing in blood banks, the evaluation of hemolytic disease of the newborn, and the diagnosis of autoimmune hemolytic anemia.

Bentonite Flocculation Test

Passive carriers of antigen other than red blood cells have been widely used in serology for the demonstration of agglutinating antibody. Wyoming bentonite is a form of siliceous earth which can directly adsorb most types of protein, carbohydrate, and nucleic acid. After adsorption, many antigens are stable on bentonite for 3–6 months. Simple flocculation on slides with appropriate positive and negative control sera indicates the presence of serum antibody. Bentonite flocculation has been employed to detect antibodies to *Trichinella*, DNA, and rheumatoid factor.

Latex Fixation Test

Latex particles may also be used as passive carriers for adsorbed soluble protein and polysaccharide antigens. The most widespread application of latex agglutination (fixation) has been in the detection of rheumatoid factor. Rheumatoid factor is a 19S IgM antibody directed against 7S IgG (see Chapter 26). If 7S IgG is passively adsorbed to latex particles, specific determinants on the IgG are revealed which then react with IgM rheumatoid factors. This method is more sensitive but less specific for rheumatoid factor than the Rose-Waaler test (see below). Latex fixation has also been used to detect urine hCG in pregnancy testing.

Rose-Waaler Test

This passive hemagglutination test is also used for the detection of rheumatoid factor. Tanned red blood cells (usually sheep) are coated with subagglutinating amounts of rabbit 7S IgG antibodies specific for sheep red blood cells. Human rheumatoid factor will agglutinate these rabbit immunoglobulin-sensitized sheep red blood cells by virtue of a cross-reaction between rabbit IgG and human 7S IgG. The use of this test and latex fixation in the diagnosis of rheumatoid diseases (especially rheumatoid arthritis) is discussed in Chapter 26.

COMPLEMENT FUNCTION

Complement is one of the main humoral effector mechanisms of immune complex-induced tissue damage (see Chapters 11 and 12). Clinical disorders of complement function have been recognized for many decades, but their mechanism and eventual treatment have awaited elucidation of the complement sequence itself. The 9 major complement components (C1–C9) and various inhibitors can now be measured in human serum. Clinically useful assays of complement consist primarily of CH_{50} or total hemolytic assay and specific functional or immunochemical assays for various components. Immunochemical means are available for determining serum concentrations of selected components, but these assays do not provide data regarding the functional integrity of the various molecules.

It is worth emphasizing that the collection and storage of serum samples for functional or immunochemical complement assays present special problems as a result of the remarkable lability of some of the complement components. Rapid removal of serum from clotted specimens and storage at temperatures of −70 °C or lower are required for preservation of maximal activity.

Finally, complement fixation or utilization, which occurs as a consequence of the antigen-antibody reaction, provides a sensitive and highly useful means of detecting antigens or antibodies and has been of particular use in serology.

HEMOLYTIC ASSAY

Specific antibody-mediated hemolysis of erythrocytes in the presence of the intact complement sequence can be used as a crude screening test for complement activity in human serum. However, it has limited usefulness, since a drastic reduction in components is necessary to produce a reduction in the hemolytic assay. Classically, the hemolytic assay employs sheep erythrocytes (E), rabbit antibody (A) to sheep red blood cells, and fresh guinea pig serum as a source of complement (C). Hemolysis is measured spectrophotometrically as the absorbance of released hemoglobin and can be directly related to the number of red blood cells lysed. The amount of lysis in a standardized system employing E, A, and C describes an S-shaped curve when plotted against increasing amounts of added complement (Fig 22–34).

The curve is S-shaped, but in the mid region, near 50% hemolysis, a nearly linear relationship exists between the degree of hemolysis and the amount of complement present. In this range, the degree of red blood cell lysis is very sensitive to any alteration in complement concentration. For clinical purposes, measurement of total hemolytic activity of serum is taken at 50% hemolysis level. The CH_{50} is an arbitrary unit which is defined as the quantity of complement necessary for 50% lysis of red cells under rigidly standardized conditions of red blood cell sensitization with antibody (EA). These results are expressed as the reciprocal of the serum dilution giving 50% hemolysis. Many test variables can influence the degree of

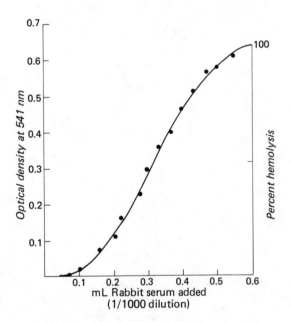

Figure 22–34. Relationship of complement concentration and red blood cells lysed. Curve relating the percentage of hemolysis that results from increasing amounts of fresh rabbit serum (diluted 1:1000) as complement source is added to sensitized sheep red blood cells (erythrocyte amboceptor [EA]). Hemolysis can be precisely determined by measuring the optical density of hemolysis supernates at 541 nm, the wavelength for maximal absorbance by hemoglobin.

hemolysis. These include red cell concentration, fragility (age) of red blood cells, amount of antibody used for sensitization, nature of antibody (eg, IgG or IgM), ionic strength of the buffer system, pH, reaction time, temperature, and divalent cation (Ca^{2+} or Mg^{2+}) concentrations.

The value for CH_{50} units in human serum may be determined in several ways. Usually, one employs the von Krogh equation which converts the S-shaped complement titration curve into a nearly straight line.

The S-shaped curve in Fig 22–34 is described by the von Krogh equation:

$$X = K \left(\frac{Y}{1-Y}\right)^{1/n}$$

where X = mL of diluted complement added,
Y = degree of percentage lysis,
K = constant,
n = 0.2 ± 10% under standard E and A conditions.

It is convenient to convert the von Krogh equation to a log form that renders the curve linear for plotting of clinical results (Fig 22–35):

$$\log X = \log K + \frac{1}{n}\log\frac{Y}{1-Y}$$

The values of $Y/1-Y$ are plotted on a log-log scale against serum dilutions. The reciprocal of the dilution of serum that intersects the curve at the value $Y/1-Y = 1$ is the CH_{50} unit. Values for normal CH_{50}

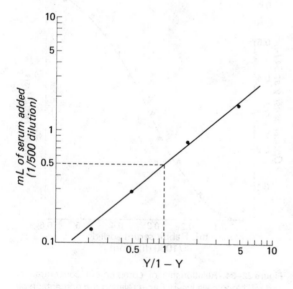

Figure 22–35. Determination of CH_{50} units from serum. Standard curve relating mL of serum 1:500 dilution to $Y/1-Y$ from von Krogh equation. When $Y/1-Y = 1.0$, the percentage of lysis equals 50%. In the example shown, 0.5 mL of 1:500 serum dilution has produced $Y/1-Y = 1.0$, or 50% lysis. The CH_{50} value for this serum equals 1000, since 1 mL of serum would have 1000 lytic units.

units vary greatly depending on particular conditions of the test employed. It should again be emphasized that the CH_{50} (hemolytic) assay is relatively insensitive to reduction in specific complement components and may in fact be normal or only slightly depressed in the face of significant reductions in individual components.

MEASUREMENT OF INDIVIDUAL COMPLEMENT COMPONENTS

Functional Assays

Activation of the entire complement sequence of C1–C9 must occur to produce lysis of antibody-coated erythrocytes (EA). Thus, a general scheme can be proposed to determine the level of activity of individual complement components. Initially, one must obtain pure preparations of each of the individual components. These pure components are then added sequentially to EA until the step is reached just prior to the component to be measured. The test sample is added and the degree of subsequent erythrocyte lysis is then related to the presence of the later-acting components. Of course, all proximal components must be supplied in excess in order to measure more distally acting intermediates. Alternatively, the presence of genetically defined complement deficiencies has made available to the laboratory a further source of specifically deficient reagents for estimating individual component activity. A description of the technique of functional assays for complement components is found in the monograph of Rapp and Borsos.

Immunoassays for Complement Components

Antibodies can be prepared against most of the major complement components, thereby allowing for simple and precise immunochemical determinations of complement components. Techniques that have been utilized for this purpose include electroimmunodiffusion (Laurell rocket electrophoresis), single radial diffusion, and quantitative immunofluorescence. Although immunologic assay of complement components is independent of their biologic function, alterations in chemical composition of complement components during storage may alter their behavior in these immunoassays. For example, in storage, C3 spontaneously converts to C3c, which has a smaller molecular size than native C3. Thus, when single radial diffusion of timed interval variety is used, stored serum will give falsely high estimates because more rapid diffusion produces a larger ring diameter. Crucial to accuracy in clinical laboratory tests for complement is reliability of standards. In general, commercial sera prepared from large normal donor pools are adequate. However, since complement components are thermolabile when stored above −70 °C, great care must be taken to assure adequate refrigerated storage. In fact, the major source of error in complement determination is poor sample handling.

Significance of CH₅₀ Units

A. Reduced Serum Complement Activity: Reduced amounts of serum complement activity have been reported in a variety of disease states (Table 22–13). The reduction in serum complement activity could be due to any one or a combination of (1) complement consumption by in vivo formation of antigen-antibody complexes, (2) decreased synthesis of complement, (3) increased catabolism of complement, or (4) formation of an inhibitor. Although complement has been demonstrated fixed to various tissues, eg, glomerular basement membrane, in association with antibody, tissue fixation of complement is apparently not an important mechanism in lowering serum complement activity. In addition, hemolytic activity (CH_{50}) may be relatively unaffected by major changes in concentration of individual complement components. Isolated reduction in human serum levels of C1, C2, C3, C6, or C7 to 50% of normal only slightly reduces hemolytic activity. For this reason, many laboratories have switched from classic hemolytic assay to a more simple immunochemical determination of C3. In general, the reduction of C3 correlates positively with CH_{50} activity reduction.

B. Elevated Complement Levels: Although complement levels are elevated in a variety of diseases (Table 22–14), the significance of this observation is not clear. The most likely mechanism is overproduction.

The development of specific functional and immunologic methods for detecting complement components has led to the discovery of a variety of genetically determined disorders of the complement system. A discussion of the specific disease states which result from selective deficiency of the various complement components is found in Chapter 25.

C. Abnormalities of the Alternative Pathway of Complement: Conceivably, either deficiencies or excesses in amount or function of the 6 plasma proteins

Table 22–13. Diseases associated with reduced hemolytic complement activity.

Systemic lupus erythematosus with glomerulonephritis
Acute glomerulonephritis
Membranoproliferative glomerulonephritis
Acute serum sickness
Immune complex diseases
Advanced cirrhosis of the liver
Disseminated intravascular coagulation
Severe combined immunodeficiency
Infective endocarditis with glomerulonephritis
Infected ventriculoarterial shunts
Hereditary angioneurotic edema
Hereditary C2 deficiency
Paroxysmal cold hemoglobinuria
Myasthenia gravis
Infective hepatitis with arthritis
Allograft rejection
Mixed cryoglobulinemia (IgM-IgG)
Lymphoma

Table 22–14. Diseases associated with elevated serum complement concentrations.

Obstructive jaundice
Thyroiditis
Acute rheumatic fever
Rheumatoid arthritis
Polyarteritis nodosa
Dermatomyositis
Acute myocardial infarction
Ulcerative colitis
Typhoid fever
Diabetes
Gout
Reiter's syndrome

of the alternative pathway could lead to disease. Clinically relevant abnormalities in this system are so rare that testing for their components is usually of little value. A few patients with increased bacterial infection and inherited deficiencies of C3b or factor B have been described. Possible abnormalities in paroxysmal nocturnal hemoglobinuria, membranoproliferative glomerulonephritis, and some immune complex diseases are currently being investigated.

COMPLEMENT FIXATION

The fixation of complement occurs during the interaction of antigen and antibodies. Thus, the consumption of complement in vitro can be used as a test to detect and measure antibodies, antigens, or both. The test depends on a 2-stage reaction system. In the initial stage, antigen and antibody react in the presence of a known amount of complement and complement is consumed (fixed). In the second stage, hemolytic complement activity is measured to determine the amount of complement fixed and thus the amount of antigen or antibody present in the initial mixture (Fig 22–36). The amount of activity remaining after the initial antigen-antibody reaction is back-titrated in the hemolytic assay (see above). Results are expressed as either the highest serum dilution showing fixation for antibody estimation or the concentration of antigen which is limiting for antigen determinations.

Extremely sensitive assays for antigen or antibody concentrations have been developed using microcomplement fixation. However, these assays are too cumbersome and complex for routine clinical laboratory use.

Complement Fixation Tests

Complement fixation tests (Fig 22–36) have received widespread application in both research and clinical laboratory practice. Table 22–15 lists some of the applications of complement fixation for either antigen or antibody determination. It should be recalled that all complement assay systems involving functional tests can be inhibited by anticomplementary action of serum. This may result from antigen-anti-

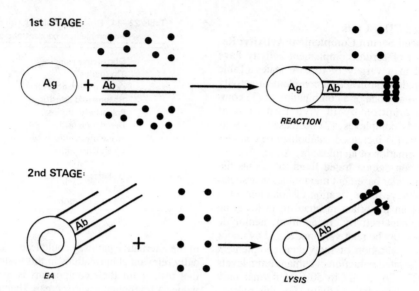

Figure 22–36. Principles of complement fixation. In the first stage, antigen (Ag) and antibody (Ab) are reacted in the presence of complement (●). The interaction of Ag and antibody fixes some but not all of the complement available. In the second stage, the residual or unfixed complement is measured by adding EA (erythrocyte amboceptor), which is lysed by residual complement. Thus, a reciprocal relationship exists between amounts of lysis in second stage and antigen present in the first stage.

Table 22–15. Applications of complement fixation tests.

Hepatitis-associated antigen (HBsAg)
Antiplatelet antibodies
Anti-DNA
Immunoglobulins
L chains
Wassermann test for syphilis
Coccidioides immitis antigen

body complexes, heparin, chelating agents, and aggregated immunoglobulins, eg, as in multiple myeloma.

MONOCLONAL ANTIBODIES

The production of monoclonal antibodies by somatic cell hybridization of antibody-forming cells and continuously replicating cell lines has created a revolution in immunology. The technique of hybridoma formation described by Köhler and Milstein in 1975 has allowed immunologists to prepare virtually unlimited quantities of antibodies that are chemically, physically, and immunologically completely homogeneous. These molecules are then unencumbered by nonspecificity and cross-reactivity. Many examples of their potential and current uses in immunology have been discussed (see Chapters 8 and 13). In laboratory immunology, monoclonal antibodies are already being made to detect cellular and soluble antigens with RIA, ELISA, and IFA. Some well-established immunochemical methods such as

immunodiffusion and immunoelectrophoresis probably do not require the degree of specificity afforded by monoclonal antibodies.

Technique of Monoclonal Antibody Production (Fig 22–37).

Hybridomas or somatic cell hybrids can readily be formed by fusing a single cell suspension of splenocytes or lymphocytes from immunized mice or rats to cells of continuously replicating tumor cells, eg, myelomas or lymphomas. The replicating cell line is selected for 2 distinct properties: (1) lack of immunoglobulin production or secretion, and (2) lack of hypoxanthine phosphoribosyl transferase (HPRT) activity. The cells are fused by rapid exposure to polyethylene glycol. Thereafter, 3 cell populations remain in culture: splenocytes, myeloma cells, and hybrids. The hybrids have the combined genome of the parent lines and eventually extrude chromosomes and acquire a diploid state. Selection for the hybrids is accomplished by awaiting natural death of the splenocytes. The myeloma cell line is killed because in HAT medium, which contains hypoxanthine, aminopterin, and thymidine, HPRT cells cannot use exogenous hypoxanthine to produce purines. Aminopterin blocks endogenous synthesis of purines and pyrimidines, and the cells die. Hybrids begin to double every 24–48 hours, and colonies rapidly form.

The hybridoma cells are then cloned by limiting dilution methods and supernates assayed for antibody production, usually by ELISA or RIA. Recloning is performed to assure monoclonality, and large numbers of cells are grown for antibody production. Extensive immunochemical and serologic studies are performed

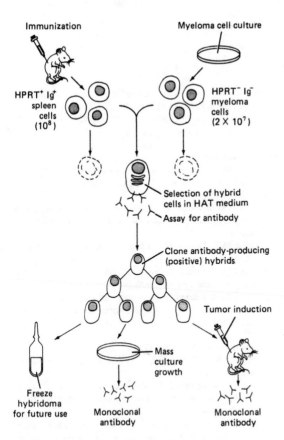

Figure 22–37. Formation of hybridomas between mouse cells and myeloma cells. Mouse myeloma cells that do not produce their own immunoglobulins and lack hypoxanthine phosphoribosyl transferase (HPRT) are fused to splenocytes from an immunized mouse with polyethylene glycol. The hybrid cells are selected in hypoxanthine-aminopterin-thymidine (HAT) medium. Unfused myeloma cells are killed by HAT and unfused splenocytes die out. The hybridomas are cloned and antibody is produced in tissue culture or by ascites formation. (Reproduced, with permission, from Diamond BA, Yelton DE, Scharff MD: Monoclonal antibodies: A new technique for producing serologic reagents. *N Engl J Med* 1981;**304**:1344.)

to assure antibody specificity. Production of large quantities of antibody can be done in tissue culture or by ascites formation in syngeneic mice. Storage of cells in liquid nitrogen for further use is easily accomplished.

Table 22–16. Application of monoclonal antibodies.

Typing T and B cells
Typing T cell subsets
Detecting Ia antigens
Detecting HLA antigens
Detecting serologic differences in viruses
Typing leukemias and lymphomas
Experimental treatment of lymphoid malignancies

Table 22–17. Advantages and disadvantages of monoclonal antibodies.

Advantages	Disadvantages
Exquisite sensitivity	Too specific
Unlimited supply	Decreased affinity
High degree of sensitivity	Decreased immune complex lattice
Immunochemical properties of antibody are defined	Decreased complement fixation
	Relatively high cost to develop new reagents

Some examples of application of monoclonal antibodies in immunology and potential advantages and disadvantages of this type of reagent are listed in Tables 22–16 and 22–17, respectively. As with any new clinical laboratory methodology, all such factors must be assessed in the specific context of the needs of individual laboratories.

COMPARATIVE SENSITIVITY OF QUANTITATIVE IMMUNOASSAYS

A major limitation of all quantitative immunoassays is their sensitivity. Exact lower limits of sensitivity vary with avidity, concentration, lots of antisera, temperature, length of reaction, and other individual laboratory practices. Nevertheless, it is useful to consider the approximate limits of sensitivity of various methods available in the clinical immunology laboratory. The most commonly employed techniques are listed in Table 22–18 in order of increasing sensitivity.

Table 22–18. Relative sensitivity of assays for antigens and antibodies.*

Technique	Approximate Sensitivity (per dL)
Total serum proteins by (biuret or refractometry)	100 mg
Serum protein electrophoresis (zone electrophoresis)	100 mg
Analytic ultracentrifugation	100 mg
Immunoelectrophoresis	5–10 mg
Single radial diffusion	< 1–2 mg
Double diffusion in agar (Ouchterlony)	< 1 mg
Electroimmunodiffusion (rocket electrophoresis)	< 0.5 mg
One-dimensional double electroimmunodiffusion (counterimmunoelectrophoresis)	< 0.1 mg
Nephelometry	0.1 mg
Complement fixation	1 μg
Agglutination	1 μg
Enzyme immunoassay	< 1 μg
Quantitative immunofluorescence	< 1 pg
Radioimmunoassay	< 1 pg

*Modified and reproduced, with permission, from Ritzmann SE: *Behring Diagnostics Manual on Proteinology and Immunoassays,* 2nd ed. Behring Diagnostics (New Jersey), 1977.

• • •

References

General

Hudson L, Hay FC: *Practical Immunology,* 2nd ed. Blackwell, 1980.

Ritzmann SE, Daniels JC (editors): *Serum Protein Abnormalities: Diagnostic and Clinical Aspects.* Little, Brown, 1975.

Rose NR, Friedman H: *Manual of Clinical Immunology,* 2nd ed. American Society for Microbiology, 1980.

Vyas GN, Stites DP, Brecher G (editors): *Laboratory Diagnosis of Immunologic Disorders.* Grune & Stratton, 1975.

Weir DM (editor): *Handbook of Experimental Immunology,* 3rd ed. 3 vols. Blackwell, 1978.

Immunodiffusion

Crowle AJ: *Immunodiffusion,* 2nd ed. Academic Press, 1973.

Deverill I, Reeves WG: Light scattering and absorption developments in immunology. *J Immunol Methods* 1980; **38:**191.

Gilliland BC, Mannik M: Immunologic quantitation of proteins in serum, urine, and other body fluids. Pages 13–30 in: *Laboratory Diagnosis of Immunologic Disorders.* Vyas GN, Stites DP, Brecher G (editors). Grune & Stratton, 1975.

Ouchterlony O, Nilsson LA: Immunodiffusion and immunoelectrophoresis. Chapter 19 in: *Handbook of Experimental Immunology.* Weir DM (editor). Blackwell, 1973.

Stiehm ER, Fudenberg HH: Serum levels of immune globulins in health and disease: A survey. *Pediatrics* 1966;**37:**715.

Electrophoresis

Cawley LP et al: *Basic Electrophoresis, Immunoelectrophoresis and Immunochemistry.* American Society of Clinical Pathologists Commission on Continuing Education, 1972.

Crowle AJ: *Immunodiffusion,* 2nd ed. Academic Press, 1973.

Franklin EC: Electrophoresis and immunoelectrophoresis in the diagnosis of dysproteinemias. Chapter 1 in: *Laboratory Diagnosis of Immunologic Disorders.* Vyas GN, Stites DP, Brecher G (editors). Grune & Stratton, 1975.

Gilliland BC, Mannik M: Immunologic quantitation of proteins in serum, urine, and other body fluids. Chapter 2 in: *Laboratory Diagnosis of Immunologic Disorders.* Vyas GN, Stites DP, Brecher G (editors). Grune & Stratton, 1975.

Jeppsson JO, Laurell CB, Franzen B: Aganese gel electrophoresis. *Clin Chem* 1979;**25:**629.

Ouchterlony O, Nilsson LA: Immunodiffusion and immunoelectrophoresis. Chapter 19 in: *Handbook of Experimental Immunology.* Weir DM (editor). Blackwell, 1978.

Immunochemical & Physicochemical Methods

Brouet JC et al: Biological and clinical significance of cryoglobulins: A report of 86 cases. *Am J Med* 1974;**57:**775.

Fahey JL, Terry EW: Ion exchange chromatography and gel filtration. Chapter 7 in: *Handbook of Experimental Immunology.* Weir DM (editor). Blackwell, 1973.

Grey HM, Kohler PF: Cryoimmunoglobulins. *Semin Hematol* 1973;**10:**87.

Somer T: Hyperviscosity syndrome in plasma cell dyscrasias. *Adv Microcirculation* 1975;**6:**1.

Trautman R, Cowan KM: Preparative and analytical ultracentrifugation. Pages 81–118 in: *Methods in Immunology and Immunochemistry.* Vol 2. Williams CA, Chase MW (editors). Academic Press, 1968.

Radioimmunoassay

Berson SA, Yalow RS: Radioimmunoassay: A status report. Page 287 in: *Immunobiology.* Good RA, Fisher DW (editors). Sinauer Associates, 1971.

Hunter WM: Radioimmunoassay. Chapter 14 in: *Handbook of Experimental Immunology.* Weir DM (editor). Blackwell, 1978.

Newton WT, Donati RM (editors): *Radioassay in Clinical Medicine.* Thomas, 1974.

Parker CW: *Radioimmunoassay of Biologically Active Compounds.* Prentice-Hall, 1976.

Yalow RS: Radioimmunoassay methodology applied to problems of heterogeneity of peptide hormones. *Pharmacol Rev* 1973;**25:**161.

Immunohistochemical Techniques

Goldman M: *Fluorescent Antibody Methods.* Academic Press, 1968.

Guesdon JL, Ternynck T, Avrameas S: The use of avidin-biotin interaction in immunoenzymatic techniques. *J Histochem Cytochem* 1979;**27:**1131.

Hijmans W, Schaeffer M (editors): Fifth International Conference on Immunofluorescence and Related Staining Techniques. *Ann NY Acad Sci* 1975;**254.** [Entire issue.]

Nairn RC: *Fluorescent Protein Tracing,* 4th ed. Longman, 1975.

Wisdom GB: Enzyme immunoassay. *Clin Chem* 1976; **22:**1243.

Agglutination

Fudenberg HH: Hemagglutination inhibition. Pages 101–110 in: *A Seminar on Basic Immunology.* American Association of Blood Banks, 1971.

Gell PGH, Coombs RRA, Lachmann PJ (editors): *Clinical Aspects of Immunology,* 3rd ed. Blackwell, 1975.

Herbert WJ: Passive hemagglutination with special reference to the tanned cell technique. Chapter 20 in: *Handbook of Experimental Immunology.* Weir DM (editor). Blackwell, 1978.

Complement Function

Alper CA, Rosen FS: Complement and clinical medicine. Chap 4 in: *Laboratory Diagnosis of Immunologic Disorders.* Vyas GN, Stites DP, Brecher G (editors). Grune & Stratton, 1975.

Fearon DT, Austen KF: The alternative pathway of complement: A system for host resistance to microbial infection. *N Engl J Med* 1980;**303:**259.

Mayer MM: The complement system. *Sci Am* (Nov) 1973; **229:**54.

Osler AG: *Complement Mechanisms of Function.* Prentice Hall, 1976.

Rapp JH, Borsos T: *Molecular Basis of Complement Action.* Appleton-Century-Crofts, 1970.

Ruddy S, Gigli I, Austen KF: The complement system of man. (4 parts.) *N Engl J Med* 1972;**287**:489, 545, 592, 642.

Schultz DR (editor): *Monographs in Allergy.* Vol 6: *The Complement System.* Karger, 1971.

Monoclonal Antibodies

Diamond B, Yelton D, Scharff MD: Monoclonal antibodies: A new technology for producing serologic reagents. *N Engl J*

Med 1981;**304**:1344.

Kennatt RH, McKearn TJ, Bechtol KB (editors): *Monoclonal Antibodies: Hybridomas—A New Dimension in Biologic Analysis.* Plenum, 1980.

Melchers F, Potter M, Warner NL: Lymphocyte Hybridomas: Second Workshop on Functional Properties of Tumors of T and B Lymphocytes. (Preface.) *Curr Top Microbiol Immunol* 1978;**81**.

23 | Clinical Laboratory Methods of Detection of Cellular Immune Function

Daniel P. Stites, MD

INTRODUCTION

The immune system in humans can be divided into 2 major parts, one involving humoral immunity (antibody and complement) and the other immunocompetent cells. In many ways this separation is artificial, and many examples of the interdependence of cellular and humoral immunity could be cited (see Chapter 8). Nevertheless, dividing the immune system into parts in this way has provided a conceptual and practical framework for the laboratory evaluation of immunity in clinical practice.

In the preceding chapter we reviewed methods of detecting antibodies and methods that employ antibodies for antigen detection. The role of a variety of distinct cell types (Chapter 8) in immune mechanisms in normal and diseased persons has become measurable in the clinical laboratory. Immunocompetent cells, including lymphocytes, macrophages, and granulocytes, are all involved in the delayed hypersensitivity reactions that are so important in immunity to intracellular infection, tumor immunity, and transplant rejection. The clinical laboratory investigation of the number and function of these cells is still beset by difficulties in test standardization, biologic variability, the imprecise nature of many assays, and the complexity and expense of the procedures. Nevertheless, several tests that are of value in assessing cellular function have become available for clinical use. Many of these assays employ sophisticated immunochemical methods for detecting cellular antigens or markers. Thus, we are witnessing an increasing fusion of immunochemistry with cellular immunology.

The present chapter reviews the tests that have medical application in the detection of cellular immune function. The intention is not to provide a comprehensive laboratory manual but to familiarize the reader with the principles, applications, and interpretation of these assays. Our understanding of cellular immunity continues to expand and technologic advances in methods for its assessment have been developed.

The subject matter of this chapter includes (1) delayed hypersensitivity skin tests, (2) lymphocyte activation, (3) assays for T and B lymphocytes, and (4) neutrophil function.

DELAYED HYPERSENSITIVITY SKIN TESTS

Despite the development of a multitude of complex procedures for the assessment of cellular immunity, the relatively simple intradermal test remains a useful tool, occasionally serving to establish a diagnosis. Delayed hypersensitivity skin testing detects cutaneous hypersensitivity to an antigen or group of antigens and, when one is testing for an infectious disease, does not necessarily imply active infection with the agent being tested for. Delayed hypersensitivity skin tests are also of great value in the overall assessment of immunocompetence and in epidemiologic surveys. Inability to react to a battery of common skin antigens is termed **anergy,** and clinical conditions associated with this hyporeactive state are listed in Table 23–1.

Technique of Skin Testing

(1) Lyophilized antigens should be stored sterile at 4 °C, protected from light, and reconstituted shortly before use. The manufacturer's expiration date should be observed.

(2) Test solutions should not be stored in syringes for prolonged periods before use.

(3) A 25- or 27-gauge needle usually assures intradermal rather than subcutaneous administration of antigen. Subcutaneous injection leads to dilution of the antigen in tissues and can lead to a resultant false-negative test.

(4) The largest dimensions of both erythema and induration should be measured with a ruler and recorded at both 24 and 48 hours.

(5) Hyporeactivity to any given antigen or group of antigens should be confirmed by testing with higher concentrations of antigen or, in ambiguous circumstances, by a repeat test with the intermediate dose.

Contact Sensitivity

Direct application to the skin of chemically reactive compounds results in systemic sensitization to various metabolites of the sensitizing compound. The precise chemical fate of the sensitizing compound is not known, but sensitizing agents such as dinitrochlo-

Table 23–1. Clinical conditions associated with anergy.*

I. **Technical errors in skin testing**
  Improper dilutions
  Bacterial contamination
  Exposure to heat or light
  Adsorption of antigen on container walls
  Faulty injection (too deep, leaking)
  Improper reading of reaction
II. **Immunologic deficiency**
  Congenital
    Combined deficiencies of cellular and humoral immunity
      Ataxia-telangiectasia
      Nezelof's syndrome
      Severe combined immunodeficiency
      Wiskott-Aldrich syndrome
    Cellular immunodeficiency
      Thymic and parathyroid aplasia (DiGeorge syndrome)
      Mucocutaneous candidiasis
  Acquired
    Sarcoidosis
    Chronic lymphocytic leukemia
    Carcinoma
    Immunosuppressive medication
    Rheumatoid diseases
    Uremia
    Alcoholic cirrhosis
    Biliary cirrhosis
    Surgery
    Hodgkin's disease and lymphomas
III. **Infections**
  Influenza
  Mumps
  Measles
  Viral vaccines
  Typhus
  Miliary and active tuberculosis
  Disseminated mycotic infection
  Lepromatous leprosy
  Scarlet fever

*Modified from Heiss LI, Palmer DL: *Am J Med* 1974;**56**:323.

robenzene (DNCB) probably form dinitrophenylprotein complexes with various skin proteins. Sensitization with DNCB can be used in skin testing for delayed hypersensitivity in a few selected patients with suspected anergy. It is not a routine procedure and should be reserved for instances in which thorough delayed hypersensitivity testing with other antigens is negative. Furthermore, its use as a diagnostic reagent is not currently approved by the FDA. Following application of DNCB to the skin, a period of about 7–10 days elapses before contact sensitivity can be elicited by a challenge dose applied to the skin surface. This sensitivity persists for years. The ability of a subject to develop contact sensitivity is a measure of cellular immunity to a new antigen to which the subject has not been previously exposed. Thus, the establishment of a state of cutaneous anergy in various disease states may be confirmed and extended by testing with DNCB.

Interpretation of contact sensitivity reactions depends on development of a flare or vesicular reaction at the site of challenge. Induration rarely occurs, since the test dose is not applied intradermally. In some clinical situations, a nonspecific depression in the inflammatory response can result in apparent anergy. A local irritant such as croton oil is occasionally employed to test the ability to mount a nonspecific inflammatory response.

Interpretation & Pitfalls

The inflammatory infiltrate which occurs 24–48 hours following intradermal injection of an antigen consists primarily of mononuclear cells. This cellular infiltrate and the accompanying edema result in induration of the skin, and the diameter of this reaction is an index of cutaneous hypersensitivity. A patient may also demonstrate immediate hypersensitivity to the same test antigen, ie, a coexistent area of erythema (wheal and flare) which usually fades by 12–18 hours but may occasionally persist longer (see Chapter 18). Induration of 5 mm or more in diameter is the generally accepted criterion of a positive delayed skin test. Smaller but definitely indurated reactions suggest sensitivity to a closely related or cross-reacting antigen. There is no definitive evidence that repeated skin testing can result in conversion of delayed hypersensitivity skin tests from negative to positive. However, with some antigens, intradermal testing can result in elevations of serum antibody titers and confuse a serologic diagnosis. For this reason, blood for serologic study should always be obtained before skin tests are performed.

Delayed hypersensitivity skin testing is of relatively little value in establishing the diagnosis of defective cellular immunity during the first year of life. Infants may fail to react because of lack of antigen contact, with resultant sensitization to various test antigens. Consequently, in vitro assay for T cell numbers and function is much more useful in the diagnosis of congenital immunodeficiency disease (see Chapter 25).

In late 1977, an FDA panel submitted a highly critical report to the Commissioner of the FDA on the safety and efficacy of several microbial skin test antigens. The evaluation considered various manufacturers' preparations of histoplasmin, tuberculin (PPD), coccidioidin, *Trichinella* extract, old tuberculin, diphtheria toxin for Schick test, lymphogranuloma venereum antigen, and mumps skin test antigen. The Panel on Review of Skin Test Antigens found only 5 of the 23 tested products to be safe and effective. Immediate removal of 12 and temporary licensing of the remaining 6 were implemented by the Commissioner. The details of this report are published in *Federal Register* 1977;**42**(Sept 30):52, 674, which is published by the US Government Printing Office, Washington, DC.

Possible Adverse Reactions to Skin Tests

Occasional patients who are highly sensitive to various antigens will have marked local reactions to skin tests. These are most likely to occur with second strength and more concentrated doses. Reactions include erythema, marked induration, and, rarely, local necrosis. Systemic side-effects such as fever or anaphylaxis are uncommon. Injection of corticosteroids locally into hyperreactive indurated areas may modify the severity of the reaction. Similarly, the painful blistering and inflammation that sometimes occur following surface application of DNCB can be reduced by topical corticosteroids.

LYMPHOCYTE ACTIVATION

Lymphocyte activation or stimulation refers to an in vitro correlate of an in vivo process which regularly occurs when antigen interacts with specifically sensitized lymphocytes in the host (see Chapters 8 and 9). Lymphocyte transformation is a nearly synonymous term first used by Nowell in 1960 and later by Hirschhorn and others to describe the morphologic changes that resulted when small, resting lymphocytes were transformed into lymphoblasts on exposure to the mitogen phytohemagglutinin (PHA). Blastogenesis refers to the process of formation of large pyroninophilic blastlike cells in cultures of lymphocytes stimulated by either nonspecific mitogens or antigens.

Lymphocyte activation is an in vitro technique commonly used to assess cellular immunity in patients with immunodeficiency, autoimmunity, infectious diseases, and cancer. A myriad of complex biochemical events occurs following incubation with mitogens. These are substances that stimulate large numbers of lymphocytes and do not require a sensitized host, as is the case with antigens. These biochemical events include early membrane-related phenomena such as increased synthesis of phospholipids, increased permeability to divalent cations, activation of adenylate cyclase, and resultant elevation of intracellular cAMP. Synthesis of protein, RNA, and finally DNA occurs shortly thereafter. It is this latter phenomenon, the increase in DNA synthesis, that eventually results in cell division and is the basis for most clinically relevant assays for lymphocyte activation. Convenience and custom have led clinical immunologists to use DNA synthesis rather than earlier events, eg, cAMP or phospholipid metabolism, as a marker for lymphocyte activation.

Although the relationship between lymphocyte activation and delayed hypersensitivity is not always absolute, the method has found widespread use in clinical immunology. The in vivo delayed hypersensitivity skin test is actually the result of a series of complex phenomena including antigen recognition, lymphocyte-macrophage interaction, release of soluble lymphocyte mediators, and changes in vascular permeability. In vitro methods such as lymphocyte activation are useful for studying cellular hypersensitivity, since they permit analysis of specific stages in the immune response. In addition, they avoid challenge of the patient with potentially detrimental anti-

Table 23—2. Examples of lymphocyte suppressive factors in serum.

Serum proteins
Albumin (high concentration)
Specific antibodies to stimulating antigens
Immunoregulatory globulin
Alpha-1-acid glycoprotein
Pregnancy-associated serum globulins
C-reactive protein (CRP)
Serum alpha globulin of amyloid (SAA)
Alpha globulins in cancer, chronic infection, inflammatory diseases
Alpha-fetoprotein (AFP)
Low-density lipoprotein
Antigen-antibody complexes
HLA antibodies
T cell antibodies
Normal serum inhibitors (poorly characterized)

Hormones

Glucocorticoids	Androgens
Progesterone	Prostaglandins
Estrogens	

Drugs

Aspirin	Chloroquine
Cannabis	Ouabain

Others

Interferon	Chalones
Cyclic nucleotides	

gens such as drugs, transplantation antigens, or tumor antigens. Lymphocyte activation measures the *functional* capability of lymphocytes to proliferate following antigenic challenge and is therefore a more reliable test of immunocompetence than merely counting types of lymphocytes (ie, T and B cell assays).

Lymphocyte responses can be suppressed or even augmented by a variety of nonspecific factors present in human serum. This humoral modulation of responses to antigens or mitogens should be clearly differentiated from intrinsic suppression of cellular reactivity. Therefore, it is essential to avoid culture of lymphocytes in serum that may contain inhibitory substances. Their presence can usually be excluded by careful questioning of serum donors. If it is suspected that an individual's serum contains an inhibitor of lymphocyte activation, controls should be done utilizing carefully washed cells from that individual cultured in normal serum. A partial list of serum suppressive factors and drugs that may influence in vitro lymphocyte responses is presented in Table 23–2. A note of caution is warranted regarding the significance of this heterogeneous group of substances. Despite clear demonstration of substances with in vitro effects on lymphocyte responses, their in vivo action, particularly in view of the high concentrations often used in tissue culture, remains a matter of speculation.

METHODS & INTERPRETATIONS

Mitogen Stimulation

A number of plant lectins and other substances have been employed in assessing human lymphocyte function (Table 23–3). In contrast to studies in mice, there is no incontrovertible evidence that T or B lymphocytes are selectively activated by nonspecific mitogens. As discussed in Chapter 7, PHA and concanavalin A are predominantly T cell mitogens, whereas pokeweed mitogen stimulates principally B cells. Neither lipopolysaccharide nor anti-immunoglobulin antibody appears to be a potent B cell stimulant in humans. Staphylococcal protein A from *Staphylococcus aureus* cell walls may be a specific stimulant of human B cells, possibly by triggering cells into DNA synthesis via the Fc receptor for IgG.

Lymphocyte Culture Technique

Lymphocytes are purified from heparinized peripheral blood by density gradient centrifugation on Ficoll-Hypaque. Cultures are set up in triplicate in test tubes or microtiter trays at a cell concentration of approximately 1×10^6 lymphocytes per mL. The culture medium is supplemented with 10 to 20% serum—either autologous, heterologous, or pooled human sera. Mitogens are added in varying concentrations on a weight basis, usually over a 2–3 log range. Cultures are incubated in a mixture of 5% CO_2 in air for 72 hours, at which time most mitogens produce their maximal effect on DNA synthesis. The rate of DNA synthesis was originally estimated by morphologic assessment of the percentage of lymphoblasts present in the culture. However, this method has been largely abandoned owing to the extreme variability and subjectivity of the results. A more accurate measure of DNA synthesis is accomplished by pulse-labeling the cultures with tritiated thymidine (^{3}H-Tdr), a nucleoside precursor which is incorporated into newly synthesized DNA. The amount of ^{3}H-Tdr incorporated—and therefore the rate of DNA synthesis—is determined either by autoradiography and grain counts or by scintillation counting in a liquid scintillation spectrophotometer. The latter method is currently the generally accepted one in most clinical immunology laboratories.

Scintillation counting yields data in counts per minute (cpm) or corrected for quenching to disintegrations per minute (dpm), which are then used as a standard measure of lymphocyte responsiveness. The cpm in control cultures are either subtracted from or divided into stimulated cpm, which yields a ratio commonly referred to as the stimulation index.

Obviously there are a multitude of technical as well as conceptual variables which can affect the results of this sensitive assay system. These include the concentration of cells, the geometry of the culture vessel, contamination of cultures with nonlymphoid cells or microorganisms, the dose of mitogen, the incubation time of cultures, and the techniques of harvesting cells.

The degree of lymphocyte activation is also a function of the cellular regulatory influences present in the culture. Suppressor or helper T, B, and mononuclear cells are all capable of modifying the final degree of proliferation in the specifically stimulated cell population. Some mitogens, particularly ConA, are known to activate suppressor T cells, which may profoundly reduce the proliferative response in such cultures.

Of additional importance in lymphocyte activation are culture time and dose-response kinetics. Since clinically important defects in cellular immunity are rarely absolute, quantitative relationships in lymphocyte activation are of crucial importance. This is especially true when comparing the reduction of responsiveness of normal control subjects with a group of patients with altered lymphocyte function. With the use of microtiter culture systems and semiautomated harvesting devices, an attempt can be made to determine both dose- and time-response kinetics of either mitogen- or antigen-stimulated cultures (Figs 23–1 and 23–2).

Altered lymphocyte function can result in shifts in either time- or dose-response curves to the left or right. These shifts determine the optimal dose and optimal time of the lymphocyte response. Without such detailed analyses, it is usually impossible to accurately observe partial or subtle defects in lymphocyte responsiveness in various disease states. Cultures assayed at a single time with a single stimulant dose period are often grossly misleading.

Confusion may result from a nonstandardized format for presentation of data. Many laboratories present results of lymphocyte stimulation as a ratio of cpm in stimulated culture to those in control cultures—the so-called stimulation index. Others report "raw" cpm or dpm as illustrated in Figs 23–1 and 23–2. Neither method is entirely satisfactory. The stimulation index is a ratio, and marked changes can therefore result from changes in background or control

Table 23–3. "Nonspecific" mitogens that activate human lymphocytes.

Mitogen	Abbreviation	Biologic Source	Relative Specificity
Phytohemagglutinin	PHA	*Phaseolus vulgaris* (kidney bean)	T cells
Concanavalin A	ConA	*Canavalia ensiformis* (jack bean)	T cells (different subset from PHA)
Antithymocyte globulin	ATG	Heterologous antisera	T cells
Staphylococcus protein A	SpA	*S aureus* (Cowan I strain)	B cells, ?T cells
Pokeweed mitogen	PWM	*Phytolacca americana*	T and B cells (primarily B)
Streptolysin S	SLS	Group A streptococci	?

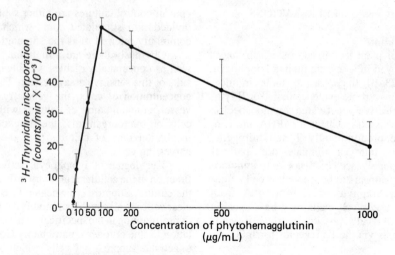

Figure 23-1. Dose-response curve for mitogen stimulation of 10^6 lymphocytes. Dose-response curve of a group of 10 normal adults whose peripheral blood lymphocytes were stimulated with varying concentrations of phytohemagglutinin for 72 hours. Lymphocytes were pulse-labeled with 2 μCi of tritiated (^{3}H) thymidine 6 hours prior to harvesting. Counts per minute of ^{3}H-thymidine incorporation were determined by liquid scintillation spectrometry and are plotted as the mean of 10 individual determinations $\pm$ the range. A maximal response occurred at approximately 100–200 μg/mL of phytohemagglutinin.

cpm of the denominator. It is perhaps best to report data in both ways to permit better interpretations.

Antigen Stimulation

Whereas mitogens stimulate large numbers of lymphocytes, antigens stimulate far fewer cells which are specifically sensitized to the antigen in question. In most instances, only T cells respond to antigens in this test. A wide variety of antigens have been employed in lymphocyte activation, many of them also being used for delayed hypersensitivity skin testing (Table 23–4).

Table 23–4. Antigens commonly used to assess human cellular immunity in vitro.

PPD
Candida
Streptokinase/streptodornase
Coccidioidin
Tetanus toxid
Tumor antigens
Histoincompatible cells (mixed lymphocyte culture)
Vaccinia virus
Herpes simplex viruses

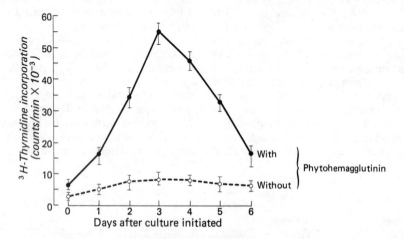

Figure 23–2. Time-response curve for mitogen stimulation of 10^6 lymphocytes. Time-response curve of peripheral blood lymphocytes from 10 normal adults stimulated in tissue culture for various lengths of time with an optimal concentration of phytohemagglutinin (100 μg/mL). Cultures were pulse-labeled with tritiated thymidine for 6 hours on the day of harvest. Maximal response occurred at 3 days after initiating the culture. Results are plotted as mean $\pm$ the range of counts per minute.

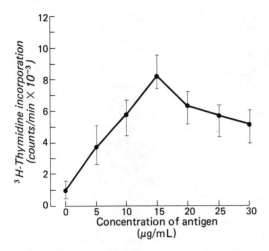

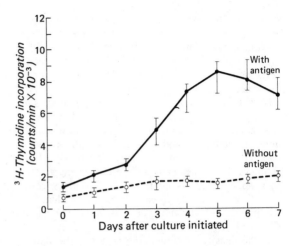

Figure 23–3. Dose-response curve for antigen stimulation of 10⁶ lymphocytes. Dose-response curve of lymphocytes from 15 normal individuals with delayed hypersensitivity to the antigen. Cultures were harvested at 120 hours of culture after a 6-hour pulse with tritiated (³H) thymidine. Counts per minute were determined by scintillation spectrometry. Results are plotted as mean ± the range from 15 skin test–positive subjects at various antigen concentrations. Maximum response is at 15 μg/mL of antigen.

Figure 23–4. Time-response curve for antigen stimulation of 10⁶ lymphocytes. Responses of peripheral blood lymphocytes from 15 normal adults with delayed hypersensitivity to the antigen. Cells were cultured as described in Fig 23–3. Antigen concentration for all cultures was 15 μg/mL. Maximal response occurred from days 5–7 of culture. Results plotted as mean ± the range for 15 individual determinations.

In general, normal subjects show agreement between the results of skin tests and antigen-induced lymphocyte activation. However, in many conditions, the in vitro technique is apparently a more sensitive index of specific antigen-mediated cellular hypersensitivity.

Culture Technique

Culture methods are virtually identical to those described for mitogen stimulation. Additional factors to be considered include the possible presence in serum supplements of antibody directed against stimulating antigens. Antigen-antibody complexes may block or occasionally nonspecifically stimulate lymphocytes.

As in the case of mitogen-induced activation, time- and dose-response kinetics are of crucial importance in generating reliable data. Representative examples of such curves are shown in Figs 23–3 and 23–4. In contrast to mitogen-induced lymphocyte activation, antigen stimulation results in lower total DNA synthesis. Furthermore, the time of maximal response does not occur until the culture has been allowed to continue for 5–7 days. Fig 23–4 clearly illustrates both the usefulness and the necessity of performing careful time- and dose-response kinetics in assessing human lymphocyte function.

MIXED LYMPHOCYTE CULTURE & CELL–MEDIATED LYMPHOLYSIS

Mixed lymphocyte culture (MLC) is a special case of antigen stimulation in which lymphocytes respond to foreign histocompatibility antigen on unre-lated lymphocytes. This test is performed either as a "one-way" or "2-way" assay (Fig 23–5). In the one-way MLC, the stimulating cells are treated with either irradiation (~ 2000 R) or mitomycin to prevent DNA synthesis without killing the cell. The magnitude of the response is then entirely the result of DNA

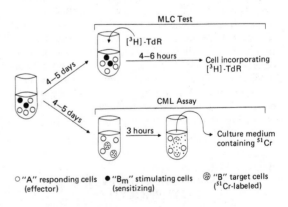

Figure 23–5. MLC and CML assays schematically represented. Cells (black and white balls) from separate individuals are cultured. In MLC, DNA synthesis in responding (noninactivated) cell is measured. In CML assay, the ability of "A" cells to kill ⁵¹Cr-labeled "B" cells is measured. See text for further explanation. (Reproduced, with permission, from Bach FH, Van Rood JJ: The major histocompatibility complex: Genetics and biology. *N Engl J Med* 1976; 295:806, 872.)

synthesis in the nonirradiated or nonmitomycin-treated cells. In the 2-way MLC, cells from both individuals are mutually stimulating and responding, and DNA synthesis represents the net response of both sets of cells and the individual contributions cannot be discerned. The culture conditions, time of exposure, ^{3}H-Tdr pulse labeling, and harvesting procedures are usually identical to those for antigen stimulation. Controls include co-culture of syngeneic irradiated and nonirradiated pairs and co-culture of allogeneic irradiated pairs. The first control provides baseline DNA synthesis and the second assures adequate inactivation by irradiation (or mitomycin) of the stimulator cells.

There is currently great interest in the identity of stimulating and responding cells as well as the responsible cell-associated antigens in the MLC. It appears that the density of stimulating antigens (Ia-like) on human cells is higher on B lymphocytes and that these may be identical to HLA-D locus antigens (Chapter 6). Responding cells are primarily T lymphocytes with obligate macrophage cooperation. B cells can also respond in MLC, since a marked increase in immunoglobulin synthesis can be detected. MLC may be used as a histocompatibility assay (Chapters 6 and 14) and as a test for immunocompetence of T cells, particularly in immunodeficiency disorders (Chapter 25).

Cell-mediated lympholysis (CML) is an extension of the MLC technique in which cytotoxic effector cells generated during MLC are detected (Fig 23–5). This test involves an initial one-way MLC culture followed by exposure of stimulated cells to ^{51}Cr-labeled target cells specifically lysed by sensitized killer lymphocytes. These target cells are HLA-identical to the stimulator cells in MLC. Cytotoxicity is measured as percentage of ^{51}Cr released in specific target cells compared to percentage of ^{51}Cr released from control (nonspecific) target cells. Several lines of evidence indicate that cells which proliferate in MLC and killer cells which participate in CML assay are not identical. Killer cells are generated that have specificity for HLA-A, HLA-B, or HLA-C antigens on target cells, whereas in MLC, HLA-D antigen differences determine the reaction. CML assays provide an additional measure of T cell function and can be used to estimate presensitization and histocompatibility in clinical transplantation. (See also Chapter 14.)

ASSAYS FOR HUMAN T & B LYMPHOCYTES

The era of modern cellular immunology began with the discovery that lymphocytes are divided into 2 major functionally distinct populations. Evidence for the existence of T (thymus-derived) and B (bursa-derived) lymphocytes in humans consists principally of analogic reasoning from studies of other mammalian and avian species and analysis of lymphocyte populations in immunodeficiency diseases (see Chapter 25).

The terms T lymphocyte and B lymphocyte usually denote the functional entities of the 2 major classes of immunocompetent cells in peripheral blood. T lymphocytes arise in the thymus and migrate to peripheral lymphoid organs—lymph nodes, spleen, and blood—during embryonic life (see Chapter 7). B lymphocytes mature during embryogenesis by a functional—but as yet anatomically undefined—equivalent of the avian bursa of Fabricius. T lymphocytes function as effector cells in cellular immune reactions, cooperate with B cells to form antibody (helper function), and suppress certain B cell functions (suppressor function). After appropriate antigenic stimulation, B lymphocytes differentiate into plasma cells which eventually secrete antibody. The notion that there is only one type of T cell or B cell has been found to be an oversimplification, since subclasses of T and B cells are now recognized. Furthermore, rigid assignment of lymphocytes to one or the other of these classes or subclasses is not always possible.

Assays for T and B cells are currently in wide use in clinical immunology. Precise counting of T and B cells in human peripheral blood has made important contributions to our understanding of (1) immunodeficiency disorders, (2) autoimmune diseases, (3) tumor immunity, and (4) infectious disease immunity. It should be emphasized, however, that mere counting of T or B cells does not necessarily correlate with the functional capacity of these cells. At best, these assays provide a nosologic classification of immunocompetent cells; further evaluation of lymphocyte function usually should be performed to fully assess immunologic competence in clinical practice.

Separation of Peripheral Blood Lymphocytes for T & B Cell Assays

Tests for human T and B cells are ordinarily performed on purified suspensions of mononuclear blood cells. An accepted procedure for obtaining cell suspensions is density gradient centrifugation on Ficoll-Hypaque. This method results in a yield of 70–90% mononuclear cells with a high degree of purity but may selectively eliminate some lymphocyte subpopulations. Mononuclear preparations obtained by this method are relatively enriched in *monocytes*. These cells must be distinguished from lymphocytes by morphologic characteristics, phagocytic ability, or endogenous enzymatic activity.

In order to avoid misinterpretation, results of tests for T and B cell markers on separated populations should be expressed as the number of cells per microliter of whole blood. Many published studies have indicated only the percentages of lymphocytes carrying a particular marker. Such a result could be due to an increase in the particular cell population or, alternatively, a decrease in other populations. Thus, it is important that each laboratory establish standard absolute numbers of T and B cells per microliter of whole blood from normal individuals.

T LYMPHOCYTE ASSAYS

E Rosette-Forming Cells

Human lymphocytes that bind sheep red blood cells to form rosettes are T cells (Fig 23–6). This marker is termed the E (erythrocyte) rosette and is currently the most widely accepted means of identifying human T lymphocytes. The nature and exact binding specificity of the T cell receptor for sheep red blood cells is unknown. However, it does not appear to involve immunoglobulin or complement receptors but may be specific for glycoprotein or carbohydrates on the sheep red cell membranes.

A. Performance of E Rosette Test: Sheep red blood cells are mixed in ratios of 100:1 to 50:1 with purified peripheral blood lymphocytes suspended in a balanced salt solution supplemented with 10–25% serum. After brief incubation at 37 °C and gentle centrifugation to pellet the cells, the tubes are incubated overnight at 4 °C. The cells are then gently resuspended and the absolute number of E rosettes counted in a hemacytometer chamber.

B. Interpretation: Lymphocytes which bind at least 3 sheep red blood cells in normal peripheral blood are generally considered T lymphocytes. Dead cells do not form rosettes and can be excluded by vital staining

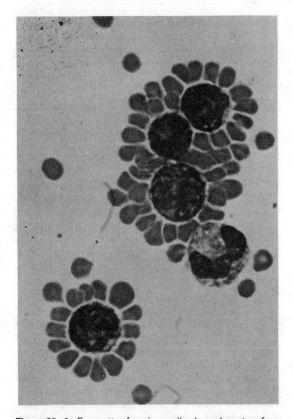

Figure 23–6. E rosette–forming cells. Lymphocytes from human peripheral blood which have formed rosettes with sheep erythrocytes. Such cells are T lymphocytes. A granulocyte has failed to form a rosette. (Courtesy of M Kadin.)

with trypan blue. The percentage of E rosette-forming cells in normal blood is approximately 65–75%. Results in each laboratory test should be expressed in absolute numbers of T cells per microliter by calculation from the lymphocyte count in the original blood sample.

A modification of the E rosette test, called the "active" E rosette test, has been developed. Active E rosettes are those formed after a brief period of incubation of lymphocytes and sheep erythrocytes. The percentage of active E rosettes appears to correlate better with in vivo cellular immunity than the total number of E rosettes. These high-affinity rosettes detected in the "active" E rosette test comprise 20–30% of total peripheral blood mononuclear cells. They may represent a subpopulation of T cells that functions primarily as effector lymphocytes in cellular immunity.

Fc Rosette Assays for Subpopulations of T Cells

Human T cells do not express easily detectable surface immunoglobulins but do appear to have surface receptors for Fc fragments of IgG, IgM, and possibly IgA. Previously, Fc receptors had been demonstrated on B cells and null cells (K cells) as well as nonlymphoid cells, eg, platelets and granulocytes. T lymphocytes bearing Fc-IgG receptors or Fc-IgM receptors are termed Tγ or Tμ cells, respectively. The presence of such Fc receptors has been demonstrated by rosette formation with ox red blood cells coated with either purified IgM or IgG antibody to the erythrocyte membrane. Approximately 20% of T cells are Tγ, and up to 75% are Tμ. These are distinct subpopulations and can be physically separated by density gradient centrifugation after forming rosettes with appropriately coated ox cells. Functional tests have indicated that Tγ cells are suppressors and Tμ cells are helpers. However, some doubt exists regarding the stability of the expression of these Fc receptors. The development of monoclonal antibodies for T cell subsets (see below) has nearly supplanted this technique for detecting T cells.

Human T Cell Antigens

Production of heteroantisera to normal and malignant human T cells created the potential for direct immunochemical detection of cellular subpopulations by immunofluorescence and other sensitive techniques. However, with few exceptions, conventional antisera raised in animals to T cell subsets have lacked sufficient specificity owing to extensive cross-reactivity and broad response to species-specific rather than lineage-specific antigens on the immunizing cells. Some degree of improvement in the quality of these reagents is achieved by use of naturally occurring human antibody derived from sera of patients with various autoimmune diseases, or by use of purified or continuously cultured T cell subpopulations. However, with the advent of monoclonal antibodies produced by murine hybridomas (see Chapter 22), a major breakthrough was achieved in identification of human T cells.

Table 23—5. Human T cell antigens.*

Antigen	Hybridoma Clone	Class	Reactivity With			Molecular Weight	Comment
			Thymocytes	Peripheral Blood T Cells	Functional Subset		
Leu-1	L17F12	IgG2a	90%	95%	Pan-T		Weak expression on cortical thymocytes.
	OKT1	IgG1					
	10.2	IgG2a					
	T101	IgG2a					
	SK5	IgG1					
Leu-2	OKT5	IgG1	90%	30%	Suppressor T cells	32,000	The 2 polypeptide chains are disulfide linked.
	OKT8	IgG2				43,000	
	SKI	IgG1					
Leu-3	OKT4	IgG2	95%	60%	Helper T cells	55,000	Leu-2 and Leu-3 are expressed by mutually exclusive peripheral blood T cells but co-expressed by most thymocytes.
	SK3	IgG1					
Leu-4	OKT3	IgG2a	30%	95%	Pan-T	22,000	The antibodies are mitogenic for T cells. Thymocyte expression is weak on cortical cells and strong on medullary cells.
	SK7	IgG1					
Leu-5	OKT11	IgG1	>90%	100%	Pan-T	55,000	Sheep red blood cell receptor.
	9.6	IgG2					
	OKT6	IgG1	75%	<2%	Thymocyte-specific	49,000	Noncovalent association between the 45,000 MW chain and the 12,000 MW chain β_2-microglobulin. Reactivity with thymocytes is restricted to cells in the cortex.
						12,000	
	OKT9		10%	<2%	Transferrin receptor	44,000	Expressed on activated peripheral T cells.
	OKT10		95%	<2%		45,000	Expressed on activated peripheral T cells.
	12E7	IgG1	100%	100%		28,000	Very high expression by cortical thymocytes. Gene controlling expression is on the X chromosome.
DR	L203	IgG1	<2%	<5%	Self-recognition antigen processing	28,000	Thymic epithelial cells and dendritic cells express DR, but thymic lymphocytes do not. T cells express these antigens when they are stimulated.
	L227	IgG1				34,000	
	L243	IgG2a					

*Courtesy of R Levy, MD.

Monoclonal antibodies have been produced in many laboratories to class-specific and subclass-specific T cell antigens. These antibodies are highly specific and provide sensitive reagents for detecting cells in suspensions or fixed tissue sections. An enormous proliferation of abbreviations for these sera has occurred simultaneously with their commercial availability. Caution should be exercised in assuming equivalence in specificity of various clones that detect the Leu antigens listed in Table 23–5. There are no studies comparing the fine specificity of many of these clones. It is likely that the different clones produce monoclonal antibodies which recognize different determinants present on the same major T cell (Leu) antigens. Further discussion of the role of these T cell subsets in normal and diseased individuals is presented in Chapters 8, 13, 25, 26, and 27.

A. Performance of Test:

1. Production of T cell antibodies–T cells from various sources—especially thymocytes, purified peripheral blood T cells, T leukemia cells, or T cells from continuous culture—can be used for immunization of either goats or rabbits. The resulting antisera have both species-specific and T cell–specific antibodies. The former may be removed by absorption with B cells, liver, or kidney cells. Specificity must be shown by positive reaction with E rosette–forming cells and negative reaction with B cells. Monoclonal antibody can also be produced from murine hybridomas.

2. Detection of T cell markers with specific antisera–Immunofluorescence of either live lymphocytes or frozen tissue sections is possible. Direct immunofluorescence is performed with fluorochrome-labeled γ-globulin fractions from anti–T cell serum.

In vitro cytotoxicity of human T cells by specific antisera may also be used to estimate T cell populations. Methods for assessing T cell killing include trypan blue vital staining or ^{51}Cr release assay.

B. Interpretation: The number of T cells can be determined by their ability to bind specific anti–T cell antibody. This technique has the disadvantage of requiring a relatively expensive fluorescence microscope, whereas counting E rosette–forming cells requires only a simple light microscope. However, specific anti–T cell antisera can prove extremely valuable in identifying T cells in frozen tissue sections or inflammatory exudates. A fluorescence-activated cell sorter has the potential for large-scale separation of human T cells from impure or mixed populations.

Terminal Transferase (TdT)

Terminal deoxynucleotidyl transferase (TdT) is an enzyme that catalyzes the polymerization of deoxynucleoside triphosphates in the absence of a template. The enzyme is a marker for immature cells in the hematopoietic system. It is present in approximately 90% of cortical thymocytes and about 2% of bone marrow cells. Although transiently present in blood and other lymphoid organs during embryogenesis, it is not present in normal tissues (except marrow and thymus) in adult life.

TdT is a useful clinical marker for the presence of immature T cells in patients with leukemias and lymphomas. It can be detected by either enzyme assay or cellular homogenates or in fixed smears by immunofluorescence. There are increased numbers of TdT-containing, cells in the marrow of nearly all patients with acute lymphocytic leukemia and in many cases of T cell lymphoma. Frequently the marker is present in the leukemic population that occurs in blast crisis of chronic myelogenous leukemia. It is not present in mature peripheral T cells and thus can best be considered a marker for pre-T cells and possibly other immature hematopoietic cells.

Common Acute Lymphoblastic Leukemia Antigen (CALLA)

This antigen, to which both monoclonal and conventional antisera have been prepared, is found on the tumor cells in approximately 80% of patients with acute lymphoblastic leukemia and 40–50% of patients with chronic myelogenous leukemia in blast crisis. It has a molecular weight of 100,000 and is not present on normal lymphoid cells from blood or lymph nodes. A few cells in fetal liver and bone marrow appear to express this antigen. It has approximately the same clinical value as terminal transferase (TdT), since most large series show striking concordance between presence of CALLA and TdT in many leukemias and lymphomas.

B LYMPHOCYTE ASSAYS

Surface Immunoglobulin

Lymphocytes with readily demonstrable surface immunoglobulin are B cells. This surface immunoglobulin is synthesized by the lymphocyte and under ordinary conditions does not originate from serum, ie, it is not cytophilic antibody. Lymphocytes generally bear monoclonal surface immunoglobulin, ie, immunoglobulin of a single H chain class and L chain type.

A. Performance of Test: Polyspecific antisera against all immunoglobulin classes permit detection of total numbers of B cells in a blood sample. Alternatively, a mixture of anti-κ and anti-λ antisera will detect total numbers of B cells. Monospecific antisera

Table 23–6. Surface immunoglobulin–bearing B lymphocytes in normal adult blood.[*]

Surface Immunoglobulin	Mean %	Range
Total Ig	21	16—28
IgG	7.1	4—12.7
IgA	2.2	1—4.3
IgM	8.9	6.7—13
IgD[†]	6.2	5.2—8.2
IgE[‡]	. . .	. . .
κ	13.9	10—18.6
λ	6.8	5—9.3

[*]From: WHO Workshop on Human T & B Cells. Scand J Immunol 1974;3:525.

[†]IgD and IgM are frequently expressed on the same cell.

[‡]IgE B cells are extremely rare.

are developed by immunization with purified paraproteins and appropriate absorptions.

Tests for surface immunoglobulin–bearing B cells are performed by direct immunofluorescence with fluorochrome-labeled γ-globulin fractions derived from heterologous anti-immunoglobulin antisera. A major difficulty is to ensure the absence of all aggregated immunoglobulin in these test reagents (see below).

Generally, small amounts of anti-immunoglobulin antisera are mixed with purified lymphocyte suspensions for 20–30 minutes at 4 °C. After removal of unbound immunoglobulin, the presence of surface immunoglobulin is determined by counting in a fluorescence microscope.

Table 23–6 summarizes data on the numbers of surface immunoglobulin–bearing B cells in normal subjects. In certain disease states, eg, systemic lupus erythematosus, antilymphocyte antibody may be bound to B or T cells in vivo. In order to prove that surface immunoglobulin is a metabolic product of that cell, enzymatic removal and resynthesis of surface immunoglobulin may be performed in vitro.

B. Interpretation: The percentages of IgG-bearing lymphocytes are in fact considerably lower than previously reported. Falsely high levels are detected owing to formation of IgG–anti-IgG complexes at the cell surface with bonding to B cells via the Fc receptor. When F(ab')$_2$ anti-IgG reagents were prepared, the percentage of IgG-bearing cells was reduced from 5% to less than 1%.

The problem of binding of anti-immunoglobulin reagents to Fc receptors on B cells and monocytes is particularly a problem with rabbit anti-human antisera. A recent study suggests that nonspecific binding is almost eliminated by use of goat or sheep antisera to human immunoglobulins. Most investigators agree that IgM and IgD are the predominant surface immunoglobulins on human peripheral B lymphocytes.

Cytoplasmic Immunoglobulins

In some lymphoid malignancies, particularly

Waldenström's macroglobulinemia, chronic lymphocyte leukemia, or B cell lymphomas with leukemia, circulating lymphocytes with monoclonal intracytoplasmic immunoglobulins are detected. This immunoglobulin is usually identical to the molecule found on the surface of these cells and is occasionally present as a paraprotein in serum. Rarely, the intracellular immunoglobulin forms distinct crystals that appear as spindles or spicules within cytoplasm.

Recently, a group of patients with acute lymphocytic leukemias have been described with "pre-B cells" that express only intracytoplasmic IgM and no surface immunoglobulins at all. It is important to test for intracellular IgM particularly in so-called null cell acute lymphocytic leukemia patients, since the group with pre-B cell leukemia is probably a distinct clinical subgroup with a different course and prognosis.

Detection of intracellular immunoglobulins is done by direct immunofluorescence with specific anti-heavy chain or light chain sera on acetone- or ethanol-fixed cytocentrifuged preparations of purified lymphocytes.

Table 23–7. Surface markers of human T and B cells.

Marker	Method
T cells	
SRBC receptor	E rosette formation with SRBC*
T cell antigens	Immunofluorescence or cyto-toxicity
Fc receptors for IgG or IgM	Rosette formation with IgG- or IgM-coated ox cells
Terminal transferase (TdT) (pre–T cells)	Immunofluorescence
B cells	
Ig receptor	Direct immunofluorescence
C3 receptor	Rosette formation with EAC-, SRBC-, or C3-coated yeast cells.
Fc receptor	Binding of fluorescent aggregated IgG
B cell antigen	Direct immunofluorescence cytotoxicity or with anti-Ia serum
Cytoplasmic IgM (pre–B cells)	Immunofluorescence

*SRBC = sheep red blood cells.

EAC Rosettes (Erythrocyte-Amboceptor-Complement)

A certain percentage of lymphocytes contain surface receptors for complement. This B cell marker is most readily demonstrated by a rosetting technique similar to E rosette assay (see above). However, to avoid confusion with T cell rosettes, ox cells may be used which do not bind spontaneously to human lymphocytes. Ox red blood cells are coated with IgM antibody to red blood cells in the presence of complement which is deficient in C5 to avoid red cell lysis. These C- and antibody-coated erythrocytes are called EAC. The EAC are then incubated with separated lymphocytes, and rosetted cells surrounded by 3 or more EAC cells are considered positive. Fresh serum-treated yeast cells or zymosan particles can also be used to detect C3 receptors on B cells.

The mean value for EAC rosette–forming cells from various laboratories is 15.4%, with a reported range of 10–19%. Since monocytes and polymorphonuclear leukocytes may also form EAC rosettes, other procedures are necessary to identify these cells. However, this test has the advantage of not requiring fluorescence microscopy.

Fc Receptor

B cells also have receptors for the Fc region of immunoglobulin. This receptor is capable of binding antigen-antibody complexes but not Fc regions of native immunoglobulin. Heat-aggregated immunoglobulin is also bound to the Fc receptor and forms the basis of this assay.

Human immunoglobulin is fluorochrome-labeled and then aggregated by heating at 63 °C. The large aggregates are then incubated with separated lymphocytes and counted with aid of fluorescence microscopy. However, monocytes and polymorphonuclear leukocytes are also positive in this test. Normal values

are 17.2%, with a range of 11–22%. Since a subpopulation of T cells, granulocytes, macrophages, and platelets also bind aggregated immunoglobulin, this test is of doubtful value as a selective B cell assay.

Anti-B Cell Antibody

Purified B cells can be used to develop heterologous antisera for B cell detection. Large numbers of homogeneous B cells can be obtained from the blood of patients with chronic lymphocytic leukemia. After appropriate absorption to remove anti-T cell and species-specific antibodies, this reagent is employed in either immunofluorescence or cytotoxicity assays as described above for anti-T cell antigens. Naturally occurring antibodies from pregnant women or multiply transfused patients can react with Ia-like determinants or B cells. These antisera are useful in detecting HLA-D antigens and as class-specific reagents for B cell detection. Monoclonal antibodies to Ia antigen (HLA-DR) have been produced and are useful in detecting B cells. Tests for T and B cells are summarized in Table 23–7.

FLOW CYTOMETRY & CELL SORTING

Biochemical and biophysical measurements of single cells have been performed for years, primarily using visual analysis in various types of microscopes. Many of the immunohistochemical methods described in Chapter 22—and the cellular analysis methods discussed above—have become increasingly refined through the development of a new class of instruments called flow cytometers. A detailed description of the myriad applications of this general technique is beyond the scope of our discussion. In brief, flow cytometers are instruments capable of analyzing properties of single cells as they pass through an orifice at high velocity. Examples of measurements that can be made include physical characteristics such as size, volume, refractive index, and viscosity and chemical features such as content of DNA and RNA, proteins, and enzymes. These properties are detected by measuring light scatter, Coulter volume, and fluorescence. Instruments have been designed solely to analyze these properties and are combined with sophisticated electronics and computers. However, another class of even more sophisticated instruments—cell sorters—combine analytic capacity with the ability to sort cells based on various preselected properties. One type of sorter, the fluorescence-activated cell sorter (FACS), has found many applications in immunologic research. Since this type of machine is currently being introduced into clinical laboratory immunology, particularly for analysis of T, B, and other lymphoid cells, a description of the principles of its operation is presented here.

Fluorescence-Activated Cell Sorters (Fig 23–7)

A single cell suspension is isolated from blood and labeled either with fluorescent antibody or another fluorochrome dye such as ethidium bromide, which specifically stains DNA. The cells are forced through a nozzle in a liquid jet surrounded by a sheath of saline or water. Vibration at the tip of the nozzle assembly causes the stream to break up into a series of droplets, and the size of the droplets can be regulated so that each will contain exactly one cell. The droplets are illuminated by the monochromatic laser beam and electronically monitored by fluorescence detectors. Droplets that emit appropriate fluorescent signals are electrically charged in a high-voltage field between deflection plates and are then sorted into collection tubes. Rapid, accurate, and highly reproducible separation of cells is thereby accomplished. Viability and sterility can be maintained, so that cells can be not only analyzed but also cultured or assayed functionally.

The flow cytometer has had many applications in immunology. A partial list would include the following: (1) analysis and sorting of subpopulations of T cells by monoclonal fluorescent antibodies; (2) separation of various classes of lymphoid cells through sorting by size or antibody marker; (3) separation of live from dead cells; (4) cloning of individual cells by introducing microtiter plates in place of collection tubes; and (5) analysis of cell cycle kinetics by various DNA stains. Computers are used to analyze multiple parameters measured simultaneously by the flow cytometer, including 2-color fluorescence, forward-angle light scatter, and 90-degree-angle light scatter. It is anticipated that many of the assays described for T and B cells will soon be performed in clinical laboratories with the aid of microfluorimetry in flow cytometers.

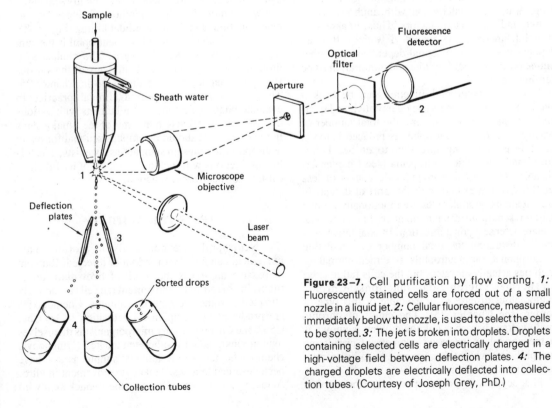

Figure 23–7. Cell purification by flow sorting. *1:* Fluorescently stained cells are forced out of a small nozzle in a liquid jet. *2:* Cellular fluorescence, measured immediately below the nozzle, is used to select the cells to be sorted. *3:* The jet is broken into droplets. Droplets containing selected cells are electrically charged in a high-voltage field between deflection plates. *4:* The charged droplets are electrically deflected into collection tubes. (Courtesy of Joseph Grey, PhD.)

CLINICAL APPLICATION OF B & T CELL ASSAYS

Counting of B and T cells in peripheral blood and tissue specimens has widespread application in both the diagnosis and investigation of pathophysiologic mechanisms of many disease states. Current applications include the following:

(1) Diagnosis and classification of immunodeficiency diseases (Chapter 25).

(2) Determination of origin of malignant lymphocytes in lymphocytic leukemia and lymphoma (Chapter 27).

(3) Evaluation of immunocompetence and mechanisms of tissue damage in autoimmune disease, eg, systemic lupus erythematosus and rheumatoid arthritis (Chapter 26).

(4) Detection of changes in cellular immune competence in cancer that may be of prognostic value (Chapter 17).

NEUTROPHIL FUNCTION

Polymorphonuclear neutrophils (PMNs) are bone marrow–derived white blood cells with a finite life span which play a central role in defense of the host against infection. For many types of infections, the neutrophil plays the primary role as an effector or killer cell. However, in the bloodstream and extravascular spaces, neutrophils exert their antimicrobial effects through a complex interaction with antibody, complement, and chemotactic factors. Thus, in assessing neutrophil function, one cannot view the cell as an independent entity; its essential dependence on other immune processes, both cellular and humoral, must be taken into account.

Defects in neutrophil function can be broken down into 2 general categories: quantitative and qualitative. In quantitative disorders, the total number of normally functioning neutrophils is reduced below a critical level, allowing infection to ensue. Drug-induced and idiopathic neutropenia (see Chapter 27) with absolute circulating granulocyte counts of less than 1000/μL are examples of this sort of defect. In these situations, granulocytes are functionally normal but are present in insufficient numbers to maintain an adequate defense against infection. In qualitative neutrophilic disorders, the total number of circulating polymorphonuclear neutrophils is either normal or sometimes actually elevated, but the cells fail to exert their normal microbicidal functions. Chronic granulomatous disease is an example of this type of disorder (see Chapter 25). The cause of chronic granulomatous disease is unknown; what is known is that the normal or increased numbers of circulating neutrophils in such patients are unable to kill certain types of intracellular organisms.

Phagocytosis by polymorphonuclear neutrophils

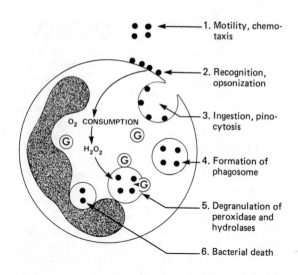

Figure 23–8. Steps in progress of phagocytosis. Schematic representation of phagocytosis by a granulocyte. **1:** Bacteria attract phagocytic cells by chemotactic stimulus. **2:** Presence of opsonins (immunoglobulin and complement) facilitates recognition and surface attachment. **3:** Invagination of cell membrane with enclosed opsonized bacteria. **4:** Intracellular organelle, the phagosome, forms. **5:** Granules fuse with phagosomes and release enzymes into the phagolysosome. **6:** Bacterial death and digestion result. (Modified from Baehner: Chronic granulomatous disease. Page 175 in: *The Phagocytic Cell in Host Resistance.* Bellanti JA, Dayton DH [editors]. Raven Press, 1975.)

can be divided into 5 distinct and temporally sequential stages: (1) motility, (2) recognition, (3) ingestion, (4) degranulation, and (5) intracellular killing (Fig 23–8). The microbicidal activity of the neutrophil is the sum of the activity of these 5 phases. The clinical syndromes resulting from defects in many of the various stages in phagocytosis are discussed in Chapter 25. The laboratory tests used in clinical practice to evaluate phagocytic function in humans with various diseases will be discussed in terms of the 5 major steps in the process. It should be emphasized that for many neutrophil functions no standard assay exists. The following sections will include examples of useful clinical tests of neutrophil function.

TESTS FOR MOTILITY

Neutrophils are constantly in motion. This movement can be either random or directed. Random or passive motion is the result of **brownian movement.** In **chemotactic movement** the cells are actively attracted to some chemotactic stimulus. Chemotaxins are produced by complement activation (C3a, C5a, C567; see Chapter 11), by microorganisms themselves (endotoxins), and by other leukocytes (lymphocyte chemotactic factor). Relatively simple assays have been designed to assess leukocyte movement in vitro. Actually, an in vivo technique, the Rebuck skin window, preceded the development of in vitro assays and was one of the earliest methods developed for assessing leukocyte function.

Test for Random Motility

Random motility is tested for by the **capillary tube method.** Purified neutrophils in 0.1% human albumin solution at a concentration of 5×10^6/mL are placed in a siliconized microhematocrit tube. The tube is enclosed in a chamber specially constructed from microscope slides and embedded in adhesive clay. After being filled with immersion oil, the entire chamber is placed on the stage of a microscope. Motility is assessed by observing the leading edge of the leukocyte column in the microscope at hourly intervals. Measurements are expressed in millimeters of movement from the starting boundary of the packed leukocyte layer.

Test for Chemotaxis

Quantitation of directional locomotion of neutrophils toward various chemotactic stimuli is accomplished by use of a Boyden chamber. Cells to be tested are placed in the upper chamber and are separated from the lower chamber containing a chemotactic substance by a filter membrane of small pore size. Neutrophils can enter the filter membrane but are trapped in transit through the membrane. After a suitable incubation period, the filter is removed and stained and the underside is microscopically examined for the presence of neutrophils.

Although this method is theoretically simple, there are numerous technical difficulties. These include nonavailability of filters of standard pore size, observer bias in quantitation of migrating neutrophils in the microscope, loss of cells which fall off or completely traverse the filter, and failure of many workers to standardize cell numbers and serum supplements.

An additional method for measuring chemotaxis and random motility has been recently developed. This technique involves the radial migration of leukocytes from small wells cut into an agarose medium in a Petri dish. In many respects, the method is similar to single radial diffusion (see Chapter 22). Generally, 3 wells are cut into agarose. The cell population in question is placed in the center well. A chemo-attractant is placed in an outer well, and a control nonattractant is placed in the remaining well. After several hours of migration, the distance from the center of the well originally containing cells to the leading edges of the migrating cells is measured. In this way, the directed motility and the random motion can be quantitated. This method has achieved widespread application and in many laboratories has supplanted the somewhat more cumbersome Boyden chamber technique.

TESTS FOR RECOGNITION

As the neutrophil in an immune host approaches its target, either by random or directed motility, it recognizes microorganisms by the presence of antibody and complement fixed to the surface of the microorganisms. Enhancement of phagocytosis (opsonization) occurs under these circumstances.

Tests to detect the presence of complement and antibody Fc receptors on neutrophils are research tools and have no direct clinical applications. The need for either antibody or complement (opsonins) coating of microorganisms for phagocytosis can be determined by employing sera devoid of either or both of these factors followed by an assay for ingestion and subsequent intracellular killing. Furthermore, IgG and complement receptors on neutrophils as well as mononuclear phagocytes can be readily detected by rosette formation with IgG-coated or complement-coated erythrocytes. Such assays have not been widely applied clinically in the study of failure of host defenses against infection but have considerable promise for elucidating defects in the recognition phase of phagocytosis.

TESTS FOR INGESTION

Ingestion of microorganisms by neutrophils is an active process which requires energy production by the phagocytic cell. Internalization of antibody-coated and complement-coated microorganisms occurs rapidly following their surface contact with neutrophils. Since subsequent intracellular events—ie, degranulation and killing—depend on the success of ingestion, tests for ingestion provide a rapid and relatively simple means of assessing the overall phagocytic process. Unfortunately, the term phagocytosis has often been used to denote *only* the ingestion phase of the process. Thus, terms such as phagocytic index which refer to the average number of particles ingested really should be considered measurements of ingestion rather than of phagocytosis.

All tests to measure the ability of neutrophils to ingest either native or opsonized particles employ 2 general approaches. Either a direct estimate is made of the cellular uptake of particles by assaying the cells themselves, or the removal of particles from the fluid or medium is taken as an indirect estimate of cellular uptake.

Methods for quantitation of the ingestion of particles by cellular assays include (1) direct counting by light microscopy; (2) estimation of cell-bound radioactivity after ingestion of a radiolabeled particle; and (3) measurement of an easily stained lipid, eg, oil red O, after extraction from cells.

One disadvantage of many of these assays is that particles adherent to the neutrophil membrane are included as ingested particles. Other elements that influence results in performing ingestion assays include the presence of humoral factors (opsonins) which enhance uptake, the presence of serum containing acute phase reactants which depress uptake, the need for constant agitation or tumbling of cells and particles to maximize contact and subsequent uptake, the type or size of the test particle used, and, finally, the ratio of particles to ingesting cells. No well-standardized assay is currently available for estimating particle ingestion.

TESTS FOR DEGRANULATION

Following ingestion of particles or microorganisms, the ingested element is bound by invaginated cell surface membrane in an organelle termed the **phagosome.** Shortly thereafter, lysosomes fuse with the phagosome to form a structure called the **phagolysosome.** Degranulation is the process of fusion of lysosomes and phagosomes with the subsequent discharge of intralysosomal contents into the phagolysosome.

Degranulation is an active process and requires energy expenditure by the cell. Thus, impairment of normal metabolic pathways of the neutrophil—especially oxygen consumption and the metabolism of glucose through the hexose monophosphate shunt—interferes with degranulation and subsequent intracellular killing.

A test for degranulation called frustrated phagocytosis has recently been developed and applied to the study of some neutrophil dysfunction syndromes. The frustrated phagocytosis system (Fig 23–9) allows for examination of degranulation independently of ingestion. Heat-aggregated γ-globulin or immune complexes are fixed to the plastic surface of a Petri dish so that they cannot be ingested. Neutrophils are placed in suspension in Petri dishes with and without attached aggregated γ-globulin. The cell membranes of the neutrophils are stimulated by contact between γ-globulin and appropriate cell membrane receptors. This process results in fusion of intraleukocyte granules (lysosomes) with the cell membrane. As a result, intralysosomal contents are discharged into the suspending medium. The rate of release of lysosomal enzymes, particularly β-glucuronidase and acid phosphatase, is taken as an estimate of the rate of degranulation. Nonspecific cell death or cytolysis can be esti-

mated by measuring the discharge of lactate dehydrogenase (a nongranule enzyme) into the medium. This assay system has been used to demonstrate retardation in the degranulation rate by neutrophils from patients with chronic granulomatous disease.

TESTS FOR INTRACELLULAR KILLING

The primary function of the neutrophil in host resistance is intracellular killing of microorganisms. This final stage of phagocytosis is dependent on the successful completion of the preceding steps: motility, recognition, ingestion, and degranulation. A variety of intraleukocytic systems make up the antimicrobial armamentarium of the neutrophil (Table 23–8). Obviously, a defect in intracellular killing could be the result of any one or a combination of these functions. However, in clinical practice only 2 assays have received widespread use, ie, the nitroblue tetrazolium dye reduction test and the intraleukocytic killing test. It is hoped that specific metabolic and antimicrobial assays for other intraleukocytic events will also become available in future.

Table 23–8. Antimicrobial systems of neutrophils.*

Acid pH of phagolysosome
Lysozyme
Lactoferrin
Cationic proteins
Myeloperoxidase-halogenation system
Hydrogen peroxide
Superoxide radical
Hydroxyl radical
Singlet oxygen

*For a further description of these systems, see Klebanoff SJ: *Semin Hematol* 1975;**12**:117 and Cheson BD et al: *Prog Clin Immunol* 1977;**3**:1.

Nitroblue Tetrazolium Dye Reduction Test

Nitroblue tetrazolium (NBT) is a clear, yellow, water-soluble compound that forms formazan, a deep blue dye, on reduction. Neutrophils can reduce the dye following ingestion of latex or other particles subsequent to the metabolic burst generated through the hexose monophosphate shunt. The reduced dye can be easily measured photometrically after extraction from neutrophils with the organic solvent pyridine. The reduction of NBT to a blue color thus forms the basis of the quantitative NBT test. The precise mechanism of NBT reduction is not known, but the phenomenon is closely allied to metabolic events in the respiratory burst following ingestion, including increased hexose monophosphate shunt activity, increased oxygen consumption, and increased hydrogen peroxide and superoxide radical formation. Since the generation of reducing activity in intact neutrophils parallels the metabolic activities following ingestion, NBT reduction is a useful means of assaying overall metabolic

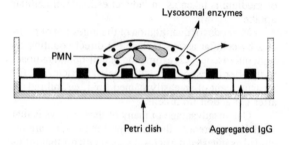

Lysosomal enzymes

PMN

Petri dish   Aggregated IgG

Figure 23–9. Assay of granulocyte degranulation by the "frustrated phagocytosis" method. Neutrophil is attached to aggregated IgG fixed to bottom of Petri dish. Lysosomal enzymes are discharged into supernate as the cell attempts to phagocytose the IgG but is "frustrated." (Courtesy of S Gold.)

integrity of phagocytosing neutrophils. Failure of NBT dye reduction is a consistent and diagnostically important laboratory abnormality in chronic granulomatous disease. Neutrophils from these patients fail to kill certain intracellular microbes and fail to generate H_2O_2 or the superoxide radical.

Quantitative NBT Test

Isolated neutrophils are incubated in a balanced salt solution with latex particles and NBT. After 15 minutes of incubation at 37 °C, the reduced dye (blue formazan) is extracted with pyridine and measured spectrophotometrically at 515 nm. The change in absorbance between cultures of cells that actively phagocytose latex particles and those that do not is taken as an index of neutrophil function. The test is strikingly abnormal in chronic granulomatous disease (see Chapter 25). Various modifications of the quantitative NBT test have been developed as screening tests for chronic granulomatous disease. Prominent among these are so-called slide tests in which neutrophils, latex, and NBT are placed in a drop on a glass slide and the reduction to blue formazan assayed under the microscope. It can be performed on a single drop of blood, but abnormal results should be confirmed with the more precise quantitative method described above.

NBT Tests in Diagnosis of Bacterial Infection

Since NBT dye reduction is enhanced by ingestion of latex particles, it has been reasoned that dye reduction should also be enhanced by phagocytosis of bacteria in infected humans. However, initial enthusiasm for the use of simple spontaneous NBT dye reduction assays, usually performed by the slide method, has been tempered by reports of false-positive or false-negative results in numerous diseases (Table 23–9). (The many factors responsible for these inappropriate results have been summarized by Segal in *Lancet* 1974;**2**:1250.) It is not currently recommended that NBT tests be employed for the diagnosis of bacterial infection.

The NBT test performed by quantitative assay should be reserved for the diagnosis of chronic granulomatous disease, for the study of factors involved in phagocytosis, and for the detection of patients with intraleukocytic killing defects.

Chemiluminescence

Neutrophils emit small amounts of electromagnetic radiation following ingestion of microorganisms. This energy can be detected as light by sensitive photomultiplier tubes, such as those in liquid scintillation counters. During the respiratory burst, H_2O_2, superoxide radicals, and singlet oxygen are generated. Singlet oxygen, a highly unstable and reactive species, combines with bacteria or other intralysosomal elements to form electronically unstable carboxyl groups. As these groups relax to ground state, light energy is emitted. This entire process has been termed **chemiluminescence** and forms the basis of an important assay of neutrophil function. Similar to NBT, it re-

Table 23–9. Diseases in which false-negative and false-positive NBT tests have been reported.*

False-Negative	False-Positive
Pyogenic bacterial infection	Nonpyogenic infections
Arthritis	Fungal infection
Appendicitis	Malaria
Meningitis	*Mycoplasma*
Streptococcal pharyngitis	Parasitic disease
Systemic bacterial infection	Leprosy
	Toxoplasmosis
	Viral infections
Drug therapy	Drug therapy
Antibiotics	Oral contraceptives
Glucocorticoids	
Phenylbutazone	
Salicylates	
Immune deficiency diseases	Immune deficiency disease
Chronic granulomatous disease	Chédiak-Higashi syndrome
Glucose-6-phosphate dehydrogenase deficiency	
Hypogammaglobulinemia	
Lipochrome histiocytosis	
Myeloperoxidase deficiency	
Other conditions	Other conditions
Nephrosis	Behçet's syndrome
Premature infants (infected)	Hemophilia
Sickle cell disease	Inflammatory bowel disease
Systemic lupus erythematosus	Lymphoma
	Myelofibrosis
	Myocardial infarction
	Neonatal period
	Neoplasia
	Osteogenesis imperfecta
	Polycythemia vera
	Pregnancy
	Psoriasis
	Postoperative period
	Typhoid vaccination

*From Segal AW: Nitroblue tetrazolium tests. *Lancet* 1974;**2**:1250.

quires all steps prior to actual bacterial killing to be intact. The oxidative steps in the biochemical pathways present in the neutrophil generate the chemiluminescence, which is easily detected in a liquid scintillation spectrometer with the coincidence circuit excluded.

In the test, neutrophils are incubated in clear, colorless balanced salt solution in the presence of an ingestible particle, eg, latex or zymosan, in a scintillation vial. Luminol, an intermediate fluorescent compound, can be added to intensify the light emissions. The emission of photons of light is measured as cpm in a scintillation counter over the next 10 minutes at 2-minute intervals. Studies with this technique have revealed markedly reduced chemiluminescence in chronic granulomatous disease (patients and carriers) and in myeloperoxidase-deficient patients. This method appears to be somewhat more sensitive than the quantitative NBT test and can probably be performed on very small numbers of cells. Many laboratories are substituting it for NBT reduction as a screening test for neutrophil dysfunction and in detection of carriers of chronic granulomatous disease.

Neutrophil Microbicidal Assay

Many strains of bacteria and fungi are effectively engulfed and killed by human neutrophils in vitro. Assuming that all of the stages of the phagocytic process that precede killing within the phagolysosome are intact, microbicidal assays are extremely useful tests for neutrophil function. As an example, the bactericidal capacity of neutrophils for the common test strain 502A of *Staphylococcus aureus* will be described in some detail.

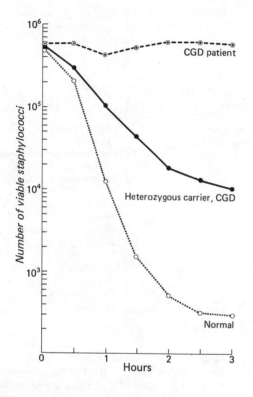

Figure 23–10. Bactericidal assay of granulocytes. Curves represent number of viable intracellular organisms which survive after being ingested by granulocytes. Note marked decline in bacterial survival in normal cells compared to reduced to absent killing by cells from patients and relatives with CGD (chronic granulomatous disease).

Bacteria are cultured overnight in nutrient broth to make certain that they will be in a logarithmic growth phase. They are then diluted to give about 5 bacteria per neutrophil in the final test. Neutrophils are separated from whole heparinized blood by dextran sedimentation and lysis of red blood cells with 0.84% NH_4Cl. Opsonin is provided as a 1:1 mixture of pooled frozen serum (−70 °C) and serum from freshly clotted blood. Bacteria, neutrophils, and opsonin are incubated in tightly capped test tubes and tumbled end over end at 37 °C. An aliquot of the entire mixture is sampled at 0 time. After 30 minutes of incubation, antibiotics are added to kill extracellular bacteria. Aliquots of neutrophils with ingested organisms are sampled at 30, 60, and 120 minutes. Intracellular microorganisms are liberated by lysis of neutrophils by sterile water and the number of *viable* intracellular bacteria is estimated by serial dilutions and plating of lysed leukocytes. Results plotted as in Fig 23–10 show that normal neutrophils result in an almost 2-log reduction in viable intracellular *S aureus* 1 hour after incubation. Killing is virtually absent in cells from patients with chronic granulomatous disease and intermediate in heterozygous carriers of these inherited diseases.

By varying the test organism or the source of opsonin, this assay can be effectively used to measure a wide range of microbicidal activities and serum-related defects. Obviously, falsely ''normal'' killing will be the interpretation of the results if cells fail to ingest organisms normally. Thus, an independent assay for microbial ingestion must be performed prior to the neutrophil microbicidal test.

Some diseases with defective microbicidal activity demonstrable with this assay are listed in Table 23–10. For further details, see Chapter 25.

Table 23–10. Disorders of neutrophil function.

Chronic granulomatous disease (X-linked or autosomal recessive)
Job's syndrome
Chédiak-Higashi syndrome
Myeloperoxidase deficiency
Glucose-6-phosphate dehydrogenase deficiency
Acute leukemia
Down's syndrome
Premature infants
Transient neutrophil dysfunction
    Acute infections
    Ataxia-telangiectasia
    Cryoglobulinemia

References

General

Bloom BR, David JR (editors): *In Vitro Methods in Cell Mediated and Tumor Immunity.* Academic Press, 1976.

Natvig JB, Perlmann P, Wigzell H: Lymphocytes: Isolation, fractionation and characterization. *Scand J Immunol* 1976;**Suppl 5.** [Entire issue.]

Rose NR, Friedman H: *Manual of Clinical Immunology,* 2nd ed. American Society for Microbiology, 1980.

Weir DM (editor): *Handbook of Experimental Immunology,* 3rd ed. 3 vols. Blackwell, 1978.

Delayed Hypersensitivity Skin Tests

Catalona WJ, Taylor PT, Chretien PB: Quantitative dinitrochlorobenzene contact sensitization in a normal population. *Clin Exp Immunol* 1972;**12:**325.

Heiss LI, Palmer DL: Anergy in patients with leukocytosis. *Am J Med* 1974;**56:**323.

Palmer DL, Reed WP: Delayed hypersensitivity skin testing: 1. Response rates in a hospitalized population. 2. Clinical correlates and anergy. *J Infect Dis* 1974;**130:**132, 138.

Lymphocyte Activation

Bach FH, Van Rood JJ: The major histocompatibility complex: Genetics and biology. (2 parts.) *N Engl J Med* 1976; **295:**806, 872.

Douglas SD: Human lymphocyte growth in vitro: Morphologic, biochemical, and immunologic significance. *Int Rev Exp Pathol* 1971;**10:**41.

Ling NR: *Lymphocyte Stimulation.* North-Holland, 1968.

Oppenheim JJ et al: Use of lymphocyte transformation to assess clinical disorders. Page 87 in: *Laboratory Diagnosis of Immunologic Disorders.* Vyas GN, Stites DP, Brecher G (editors). Grune & Stratton, 1975.

Stobo JD: Mitogens. Page 55 in: *Clinical Immunobiology.* Vol 4. Bach FH, Good RA (editors). Academic Press, 1980.

Wedner HJ, Parker CW: Lymphocyte activation. *Prog Allergy* 1976;**20:**195.

Assays for Human T & B Lymphocytes

Aisenberg A: Cell surface markers in lymphoproliferative disorders. *N Engl J Med* 1981;**304:**331.

Aiuti F & others: Identification, enumeration and isolation of B and T lymphocytes from human peripheral blood. *Scand J Immunol* 1974;**3:**521.

Bollum FJ: Terminal deoxynucleotidyl transferase: A hematopoietic cell marker. *Blood* 1979;**54:**1203.

Greaves MF, Owen JJT, Raff MC: *T and B Lymphocytes: Origins, Properties and Roles in Immune Responses.* Elsevier North-Holland, 1973.

Knapp W: *Leukemia Markers.* Academic Press, 1981.

Loor F, Roelants GE (editors): *B and T Cells in Immune Recognition.* Wiley, 1977.

Reinherz EL, Schlossman SF: Current concepts in immunology: Regulation of the immune response: Inducer and suppressor T-lymphocyte subsets in human beings. *N Engl J Med* 1980;**303:**370.

Reinherz EL, Schlossman SF: The differentiation and function of human T lymphocytes. *Cell* 1980;**19:**821.

Flow Cytometry & Cell Sorting

Fulwyler MJ: Flow cytometry and cell sorting. *Blood Cells* 1980;**6:**173.

Herzenberg LA, Sweet RG, Herzenberg LA: Fluorescence-activated cell sorting. *Sci Am* (March) 1976;**234:**108.

Horan PK, Wheelis LL: Quantitative single cell analysis and sorting. *Science* 1977;**198:**149.

Neutrophil Function

Bellanti JA, Dayton DH (editors): *The Phagocytic Cell in Host Resistance.* Raven Press, 1975.

Cheson BD, Curnutte JT, Babior BM: The oxidative killing mechanisms of the neutrophil. *Prog Clin Immunol* 1977;**3:**1.

Miller ME: Assays of phagocytic function. Page 127 in: *Laboratory Diagnosis of Immunologic Disorders.* Vyas GN, Stites DP, Brecher G (editors). Grune & Stratton, 1975.

Quie PG, Mills EL, Holmes B: Molecular events during phagocytosis by human neutrophils. *Prog Hematol* 1977;**10:**193.

Juhani Leikola, MD

Although blood transfusion has become routine in clinical practice, it still imposes definite immunologic and infectious hazards. Most of the risks can be avoided by careful testing of both blood donor and recipient before the transfusion. Hepatitis remains the most important complication despite advances in detection of antigens related to hepatitis B virus. Careful attention to the immunologic and infectious problems of blood transfusion reduces the inherent risks, but the hazards of transfusion cannot be totally eliminated. It is therefore necessary to weigh the therapeutic benefits against the potential hazards before proceeding with the transfusion.

BLOOD GROUPS

The surface of red blood cells contains large numbers of antigenic determinants that are direct or indirect products of genes. These antigenic determinants are classified into blood groups. Within each blood group system, antigens appear to be inherited as products of a single gene or group of closely linked genes. The number of recognized blood groups increases every year (Table 24–1).

The chemical structure of most of these antigens remains unknown, although the nature of some erythrocyte membrane proteins has been established by

Table 24–1. Blood group systems.*

System	Antigens Detected By	
	Positive Reactions With Specific Antibody	**Positive Reaction With One Antibody, Negative With Another†**
$A_1 A_2 BO$	A_1, B, ‡H	A_2, A_3, A_X, and other A and B variants
MNSs	M, N, S, s, U, M^g, M_1, M′, Tm, Sj, Hu, He, Mi^a, Vw (Gr), Mur, Hil, Hut, M^v, Vr, Ri^a, St^a, Mt^a, Cl^a, Ny^a, Sul, Far	M_2, N_2, M^c, M^a, N^a, M^r, M^z, S_2
P	P_1, P^k, ‡Luke	P_2
Rh	D, C, c, C^w, C^x, E, e, e^s (VS), E^w, G, ce(f), ce^s(V), Ce, CE, cE, D^w, E^T, Go^a, hr^s, hr^H, hr^B, $\overline{\overline{R}}^N$, Rh33, Rh35, Be^a, ‡LW	D^u, C^u, E^u, and many other variant forms of D, C, and e
Lutheran	Lu^a, Lu^b, Lu^aLu^b (Lu3), Lu6, Lu9, §Lu4, Lu5, Lu7, Lu8, Lu10–17	
Kell	K, k, Kp^a, Kp^b, Ku, Js^a, Js^b, Ul^a, Wk^a, K11, §KL, K12–16	
Lewis	Le^a, Le^b, Le^c, Le^d, Le^x	
Duffy	Fy^a, Fy^b, Fy3, Fy4	
Kidd	Jk^a, Jk^b, Jk^aJk^b (Jk3)	
Diego	Di^a, Di^b	
Yt	Yt^a, Yt^b	
Auberger	Au^a	
Dombrock	Do^a, Do^b	
Colton	Co^a, Co^b, Co^aCo^b	
Sid	Sd^a	
Scianna	Sc1, Sc2 (Bu^a)	
Very frequent antigens	Vel, Ge, Lan, Gy^a, At^a, En^a, Wr^b, Jr^a, Kn^a, El, Dp, Gn^a, Jo^a, and many unpublished examples	
Very infrequent antigens	An^a, By, Bi, Bp^a, Bx^a, Chr^a, Evans, Good, Gf, Heibel, Hey, Hov, Ht^a, Je^a, Jn^a, Levay, Ls^a, Mo^a, Or, Pt^a, Rl^a, Rd, Re^a, Sw^a, To^a, Tr^a, Ts, Wb, Wr^a, Wu, Zd, and many unpublished examples	
Other antigens	I, i, Bg (HL-A), Chido, Cs^a, Yk^a	
Xg	Xg^a	

*Reproduced, with permission, from Race RR, Sanger R: *Blood Groups in Man,* 6th ed. Blackwell, 1975.
†Recognizable only in favorable genotypes.
‡A genetically independent part of the system.
§Place in system not yet genetically clear.

recent work. The research has focused mainly on substances called sialoglycoproteins or glycophorins. Of these, glycoprotein-α (glycophorin A) carries the blood group M and N antigens and glycoprotein-δ (glycophorin B) the Ss and U antigens. Other glycoproteins have A and B activity. The complete amino acid sequence and carbohydrate composition of glycoprotein-α is now known, and studies to establish the detailed structure of glycoprotein-δ are well under way. Some antigens of cold-reacting autoantibodies reside also in the various membrane glycoproteins.

The clinical significance of a blood group system depends on 2 factors: the frequency of antibodies in the population and their relative potency. Even if many blood groups are not important in clinical transfusion practice, they are objective, simply inherited genetic markers useful in anthropologic studies and in disputed paternity cases.

Table 24–2. Blood group antigens and antibodies in ABO system.

Blood Group	Antigen on Red Cells	Antibodies in Plasma	Frequency*		
			Caucasian	Black	Oriental
A_1	$A + A_1$	anti-B			
A_2	A + H	anti-B (anti-A_1)	41	28	38
B	B (+H)	anti-A	11	17	22
O	H	anti-A anti-B	45	51	30
A_1B	$A + A_1 + B$	. . .	3	4	10
A_2B	A + B (+ H)	(anti-A_1)			

*Frequencies vary in different populations, and the given figures have to be considered as examples.

ABO & LEWIS GROUPS

ABO Antigens

In 1901, Landsteiner published his observation of a consistent pattern in agglutination of human blood cells by other human sera. Cells from group A persons were agglutinated by serum from group B individuals and vice versa (Table 24–2). Cells from others (group O) were not agglutinated by any sera. These people had antibodies to both A and B. Soon after Landsteiner's original discovery, the fourth group, AB, was found with no antibodies to other human cells.

A and B are carbohydrate antigens. The antigenic specificity resides in the terminal sugars of an oligosaccharide. On cell membrane, the majority of A and B antigens are on glycoproteins, but some of the carbohydrate is also bound on membrane lipids. A and B antigens may also appear in body fluids as soluble glycoproteins.

The structure of A and B is schematically shown in Fig 24–1. The last 3 sugars in this stem chain—called H substance—are N-acetylglucosamine, galactose, and fucose. N-Acetylgalactosamine in blood group A and galactose in blood group B are bound to the last galactose of the stem chain.

The ABO blood groups are determined by allelic genes A, B, and O. These genes produce transferase enzymes that conjugate the terminal sugars to the stem carbohydrate. These transferases are specific for their

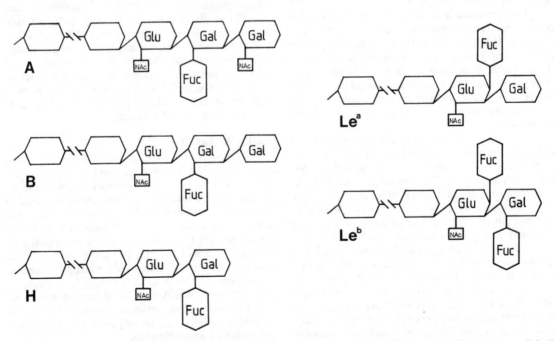

Figure 24–1. Diagrams of proposed chemical structure of blood group antigens A, B, H, Le^b, and Le^a. The sugars are linked by carbohydrate chains to either a peptide chain or a lipid. Glu = glucose; Gal = galactose; Fuc = fucose; NAc = N-acetyl group.

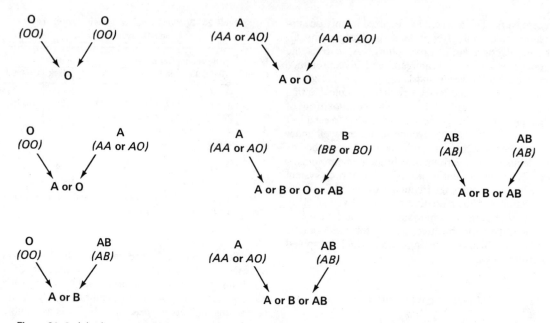

Figure 24–2. Inheritance of ABO groups. Blood group phenotype is printed in nonitalics and genotype in italics.

substrates: A transferase for N-acetylgalactosamine, and B transferase for galactose. O-gene produces no transferase that would modify the blood group substance. Group O persons have only the stem substance, H antigen. In the absence of direct transferase determinations or family studies, it is not possible to determine whether a person who belongs to group A is homozygous, with two A genes, or is heterozygous, with one A and one O gene (Fig 24–2).

The stem chain is influenced by a transferase that conjugates fucose to galactose. This transferase is a product of H gene that is inherited independently of the ABO system. There are rare persons who lack H genes (genotype hh), thus being unable to synthesize a complete stem chain. This phenotype is called Oh or Bombay type. Because of deficient stem chain, A and B substances cannot be formed despite functional A and B transferases.

Blood group A can be divided into subgroups A_1 and A_2 on the basis of the number of A antigenic sites on the cell. About four-fifths of A and AB persons belong to subgroup A_1. The high antigen density on A_1 cells results in formation of a new but relatively weak antigenic specificity, perhaps as a result of the interaction of 2 closely adjacent A-oligosaccharides. A_2 and especially A_2B persons may have antibodies to A_1.

There are rare subtypes of A that have much less A substance than even A_2 cells. A_3 cells react characteristically with anti-A with very small agglutinates surrounded by a large number of nonagglutinated cells. These individuals probably have a heterogeneous red cell population, some cells with nearly normal amounts of A, and many cells with no detectable antigen. A_x cells are not agglutinated by anti-A derived from group B persons; however, serum from group O individuals may produce a weak reaction. To

be able to detect A_x and some other still rarer subgroups of A, blood grouping laboratories often use O serum (called anti-A,B) in addition to anti-A and anti-B. Weak forms of A give an irregular pattern in blood typing and cause grouping difficulties. Blood group B cannot be divided into subgroups, but there are some very rare forms of weak B.

Since the antibodies to A_1 are weak, they are not always practical for differentiating between A_1 and A_2. The distinction is usually made by using substances called lectins. These plant seed extracts selectively react with some carbohydrate blood group antigens. The lectin from *Dolichos biflorus*, in appropriate dilution, clumps only A_1 cells. It is often used simultaneously with lectin from *Ulex europaeus*, which reacts with H substance, since A_2 cells have plenty of H substance compared to A_1 cells.

Anti-A & Anti-B

The biochemical structures of the blood group oligosaccharides occur commonly in nature. Substances derived from intestinal bacteria and some ingested vegetables can trigger an immune response in man. This stimulation is thought to produce anti-A and anti-B in A, B, and O people. Infants start producing anti-A or anti-B (sometimes called isoagglutinins) after a few months of life. In patients with humoral immune deficiency, like hypogammaglobulinemia, the amount of anti-A or anti-B may be reduced to undetectable levels. Anti-H (in addition to anti-A and anti-B) is always present in the serum of the rare O_h individuals, and it is a relatively common specificity in cold-reacting autoantibodies.

Anti-A and anti-B are usually IgM, but a sufficient immunologic stimulus can result in formation of IgG anti-A and anti-B. IgG antibodies can cross the placenta and may cause destruction of fetal red cells. Attempts have been made at antenatal screening of maternal IgG anti-A and anti-B, but the correlation with clinical hemolytic disease of the newborn is not very good (see Chapter 27).

Anti-A and anti-B may be hemolyzing, and they are stronger in group O persons than in A or B individuals. Group O plasma should not be transfused into A or B patients in larger amounts. Therefore, group O red cell concentrate containing only small volumes of plasma should be used instead of whole blood if there is not time to type the patient or if blood of the patient's own group is not available.

Secretors

In about 80% of people, soluble blood group antigens appear in saliva, milk, and other body fluids. The secretion of ABH substances is regulated by allelic genes Se and se that are independently inherited from the ABO system. Secretor status is a mendelian dominant character.

Blood group substances in saliva are detected by hemagglutination inhibition after boiling and centrifugation to remove enzymes and other proteins. ABH antigens are very stable, and the demonstration of blood group substances in cigarettes, sweat spots, etc, is used as evidence in criminal prosecutions. Except for Lewis- and Sda-antigens, other blood groups are not present in saliva.

Lewis Groups

Although the genes regulating the Lewis blood group system are not linked to ABO or Sese systems, the Le antigens are structurally closely related to ABH substances. The stem carbohydrate is essentially the same in ABH and Le. In the presence of Le gene, a transferase is formed that conjugates a fucose to N-acetylglucosamine in the stem chain (Fig 24–3). Whether the resulting antigen is Lea or Leb depends on the secretor status of the individual. If the subject secretes blood group substances, the antigen is Leb; if a nonsecretor, the antigen is Lea. About 20% of people are group Le(a+), 75% are Le(b+), and the rest are Le(a−b−).

Soluble Lewis substances occur in saliva and plasma. In fact, the antigens on red cells have been passively absorbed from the surrounding plasma. Le(a−b−) erythrocytes can be rendered Lewis posi-

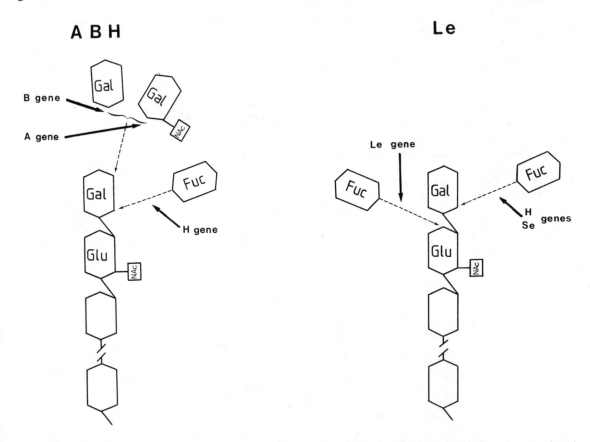

Figure 24–3. Proposed modification of blood group precursor substance by genes of ABO−, Hh−, Secretory (Se−), and Lewis (Le−) systems. Dashed arrows indicate the action of specific transferases, coded by polymorphic genes. For attachment of fucose to galactose in secretory and Lewis substances, function of both H and Se genes is probably needed. Lewis substance is passively adsorbed by red cells. Gal = galactose; GalNAc = N-acetylgalactosamine; GluNAc = N-acetylglucosamine; Fuc = fucose.

tive by incubating them in Le(a+) or Le(b+) plasma. The expression of Le^b on red cells is influenced by the ABO group so that O and B persons have more Le^b than A$_1$ individuals. This variation of antigenic strength makes saliva more suitable for Le^b typing than red blood cells.

Lewis antibodies can occur naturally without antigenic stimuli from other persons' red cells. The antibodies are usually weak and almost exclusively IgM class. A strong anti-Le^a may cause transfusion problems, but anti-Le^b is generally harmless. They do not cause hemolytic disease of the newborn. Only Le(a−b−) persons are able to form anti-Lewis antibodies.

Rh GROUPS

In 1939 and 1940, two remarkable observations were published. Levine and Stetson found that the serum of a mother who had delivered a dead baby agglutinated erythrocytes of about 85% of human adults. Landsteiner and Wiener immunized guinea pigs and rabbits with rhesus monkey blood and obtained, after appropriate absorptions, an antibody that would agglutinate a similar proportion of human erythrocytes. The group was given the name Rh, although the rhesus monkey antigen was much later shown to differ slightly from the human red cell antigen and was renamed LW to honor Landsteiner and Wiener.

Rh Antigens

With the discovery of new antibodies and antigens, the immunology and genetics of Rh groups have become very complicated—over 30 different specificities have been found. The precise chemical nature of these antigens remains unknown.

There are 2 genetic theories to explain the multispecificity of the Rh antigen complex. According to the theory of Fisher and Race, the Rh antigens are determined by 3 pairs of closely linked genes; the theory proposed by Wiener suggests a high number of allelic genes at one locus determining the whole complex. Unfortunately, the proponents of these 2 competing theories used different nomenclatures. It has also been suggested that the different Rh antigenic specificities should be expressed as numerals. Over 40 years after the discovery of the Rh blood group system, considerable confusion still exists in the field because of conflicting systems of terminology.

In practice, many laboratories use a compromise between the nomenclatures. The original Rh antigen is called D, and it is accompanied by the gene products of Cc and Ee loci. The counterpart of D is probably not antigenic, or the gene d is amorphic, since antibodies to d have never been found. In any population, these antigens do not occur at random but have preferential combinations. By using different antisera to determine the Rh phenotype, the probable genotype can be inferred. The genotype is described by 2 sets of letters, eg, CDe/cDE, or more commonly by using only 2 letters, eg, R$_1$R$_2$ (Table 24–3). If only anti-D serum is used in testing, it is not possible to distinguish between homozygous and heterozygous Rh-positive persons. This distinction is clinically important when the father's blood is typed in a case of Rh hemolytic disease of the newborn.

Of the various Rh antigens, D is the strongest immunogen and therefore the most important. It provokes antibody response about 50 times more frequently than the antigens c and E. If one unit of D-positive blood is transfused to an Rh-negative recipient, anti-D will be produced in 60–80% of cases. Therefore, only the D antigen is determined in routine blood banking, and its presence determines the designation Rh-positive or Rh-negative.

Antigen D can appear on the red cell membrane in weak forms which complicate Rh typing. These variants are called D^u, and they differ from "normal" D by having a smaller number of antigenic sites. The detection of D^u requires a strong antiserum and Coombs technique (see Chapter 22). If D^u is detected, the blood is considered Rh-positive.

In rare cases, the red blood cells do not react with

Table 24–3. Common genes and gene combinations in Rh system.

	Genes		Expressed Antigens		Gene Frequency		
	Fisher-Race	Wiener	Fisher-Race	Wiener	Caucasian*	Black*	Chinese†
Rh-positive	cDe	R^0	c, D, e	Rh$_0$, hr', hr''	0.026	0.29	0.03
	CDe	R^1	C, D, e	Rh$_0$, rh', hr''	0.42	0.18	0.73
	cDE	R^2	c, D, E	Rh$_0$, rh'', hr'	0.14	0.11	0.19
	CDE	R^z	C, D, E	Rh$_0$, rh', rh''	Rare	Rare	0.004
Rh-negative	cde	r	c, e	hr', hr''	0.39	0.26	0.02
	Cde	r'	C, e	rh', hr''	0.01	0.008	0.019
	cdE	r''	c, E	rh'', hr'	0.01	0.002	NI††
	CdE	r^y	C, E	rh', rh''	Rare	Rare	0.004

*From Giblett ER: *Genetic Markers in Human Blood.* Davis, 1969.

†From Mourant AE, Kopec AC, Domaniewska-Sobczak K: *The Distribution in the Human Blood Groups and Other Polymorphisms.* Oxford, 1976.

††NI = Not included.

any Rh antisera. The whole Rh substance is lacking, and the group is called Rh_{null}. The antibodies in autoimmune hemolytic anemia (see Chapter 27) often react with all other cells except for Rh_{null}. Therefore, the antibody is said to have Rh specificity.

Rh Antibodies

Since Rh antigens occur only on red cells, there are no "natural" Rh antibodies. An immune response is elicited only after exposure to incompatible blood, either in pregnancy or by transfusion. An exception is anti-e that may occur as an autoantibody.

Anti-D is the commonest and strongest Rh antibody. As little as 0.01 mL of Rh-positive blood may be enough to arouse antibody formation. Since Rh antigens appear early in ontogeny, immunization after abortion of an Rh-positive fetus is possible, although the risk is 10–20 times less than after full-term pregnancy.

Rh antibodies may be IgM initially after a strong immunization, but usually they are IgG. There are only 10–30 thousand Rh antigen sites on each red cell, compared to about 1 million A_1 sites. Because of this low density of antigenic sites, relatively few antibody molecules can be bound onto the cell surface. If the antibodies are IgG class, the cells are not agglutinated in normal physiologic saline since there cannot be enough Rh antibody molecules to counteract the repulsive forces that hold the cells as a suspension. In contrast, the larger IgM antibodies can bridge the cells together. IgG anti-Rh antibodies are called **incomplete** and IgM anti-Rh **complete** or saline-agglutinating antibodies.

Agglutination by IgG antibodies can be enhanced in 3 ways: (1) by using antiserum to IgG (Coombs technique, Chapter 22); (2) by adding 20–30% bovine serum albumin (BSA) to the reaction mixture; and (3) by treating the cells with a proteolytic enzyme (eg, papain). Addition of BSA changes the dielectric constant of the reaction solution, and this is believed to be (at least partially) responsible for the agglutination enhancement. The proteolytic enzymes split off sialic acid–containing glycoproteins from the red cell membrane, resulting in reduction of the negative electric charge and weakening of repulsive forces, thus enabling IgG antibody molecules to bridge the cells. However, other mechanisms may be involved.

Prevention of Rh Immunization

In the early 1960s, American and British groups independently reported that Rh immunization could be prevented by passive administration of anti-D antibody in volunteers. Extensive clinical trials followed, and anti-D antibody has been used for about 10 years to prevent active immunization of Rh-negative mothers by Rh-positive fetal blood.

The mechanism of prevention is still somewhat unclear. The IgG anti-D may specifically inhibit the activation of a B cell response. Rapid clearance of the antigenic cells probably also plays an important role, as it has been known for a long time that mothers who have isoagglutinins against the fetus's cells (eg, mother group O, baby group A) do not form anti-D as readily as women with compatible blood groups. It was shown experimentally that passively administered anti-Kell could inhibit Rh immunization of Kell-negative Rh-negative subjects when challenged with Rh-positive Kell-positive erythrocytes.

It has been calculated that approximately 20 μg of anti-D (Rh_0) per milliliter of red cells is enough to prevent immunization. A single dose of 150–300 μg of Rh immune globulin given within 72 hours after delivery covers the vast majority of cases.

Only a small proportion (3–7%) of mothers at risk would form anti-D antibodies even without administration of immune globulin, which further reduces the number of immunized women by about 85%. There are various reasons for failure to prevent sensitization, including a large volume of fetal blood released into the mother's circulation, immunization occurring during pregnancy before delivery, erroneous typing of the baby as Rh negative, simply forgetting the injection, etc. Anti-D antibodies are not able to prevent a secondary response to D or an immune response to other blood group antigens.

If Rh-positive blood is transfused in error to an Rh-negative recipient, the patient is likely to make anti-D antibodies. If the recipient is a girl or a woman of fertile age, prevention of immunization may be tried if the error is found within 1 or 2 days. A suitable dose is about 4000 μg of anti-D per unit (450 mL) of transfused blood. This dose may be divided and given over a period of 2 days.

OTHER BLOOD GROUPS

There are over 20 blood group systems with almost 200 well-described antigens. Another 200-odd antigens have been reported, but they are very rare or have not been established as independent blood group antigens. In addition to ABO and Rh, only a few have clinical significance.

Kell System

The original Kell antigen has been given the symbol K, and its allelic counterpart is k (sometimes called Cellano). K occurs in about 8% of the white population. There are a number of other antigens belonging to the Kell system (Kp^a, Kp^b, Js^a, Js^b, Ul^a, etc), but antibodies other than anti-K are rare. Anti-K is about as common as the Rh antibodies anti-c and anti-E, and it may cause hemolytic transfusion reactions and isoimmunization during pregnancy. The antibody, if present, is usually strong and easily detected by Coombs technique.

There is a rare variant where all the Kell-related antigens are very weakly expressed on erythrocytes. This variant is associated with chronic granulomatous disease (see Chapter 25). The changes in Kell antigens probably reflect some basic failure in the structure of both red and white cell membranes.

Duffy System

About two-thirds of the white population have the antigen Fy^a. The antigen is destroyed upon enzyme treatment, and the antibodies can be shown only with Coombs technique. Compared to other blood group antibodies, anti-Fy^a is a relatively common cause of hemolytic transfusion reactions. In the laboratory, the antibody is often weak and may be missed in compatibility testing.

The majority of blacks are of phenotype Fy(a−b−), which is extremely rare in whites; these people are also resistant to *Plasmodium vivax* malaria. The membrane structure that carries the polymorphic antigens of the Fy system is apparently a receptor for *P vivax*, and without it the parasite cannot invade the erythrocyte. This natural selection in Africa has resulted in the common occurrence of Fy(a−b−) phenotype in areas of malarial endemicity. In other forms of malaria, the same receptor is not involved, and Fy(a−b−) people are susceptible to *Plasmodium falciparum, Plasmodium ovale,* and *Plasmodium malariae* infection.

Other Systems

Antibodies to Kidd antigens Jk^a and Jk^b are not very common, but they activate complement, causing rapid hemolysis in vivo of incompatible red blood cells. Anti-Jk^a may be very weak in vitro, and the detection of this antibody is the main reason for the inclusion of anti-complement in Coombs reagents to test compatibility.

HLA antigens may sometimes be present on erythrocyte membrane, but they are always weak (see Chapter 6). The blood group antigens of Bg system have in fact been found to be HLA antigens, probably passively adsorbed onto red cell membrane. HLA antibodies do not destroy red cells even if they are positive with anti-Bg antisera.

Some complement components have polymorphic structures that may cause alloantibody formation in suitable subjects (see Chapter 11). The component C4 attaches on normal red cells to a variable degree, and the cells with sufficient C4 of an appropriate type are agglutinated by these antibodies. Anti-C4 alloantibodies, called anti-Rogers and anti-Chido in blood group serology, do not cause clinical ill effects.

Cold agglutinins are common, but they are seldom strong enough to cause anemia in the patient (see Chapter 27). The specificity is usually anti-H, anti-I, anti-A$_1$, or a combination of these. They may cause problems in compatibility testing, but usually they are biologically insignificant. Moderately strong anti-I antibodies occur in connection with *Mycoplasma pneumoniae* infection, and anti-i antibodies are formed as a result of infectious mononucleosis. The antigen i occurs in fetal cells and is rendered I within the first 2 years of life. Rare adults have only i-antigen, and this property is inherited as a recessive trait.

COMPLICATIONS OF TRANSFUSIONS

Blood transfusion can be complicated by immunologic reaction to the contents of the transfused unit or contamination by infectious agents. Faulty transfusion technique can result in a variety of adverse reactions such as circulatory overload, air embolism, hypothermia, bleeding, and metabolic problems after massive transfusion. These reactions will not be discussed further.

Among the transfusion-associated fatalities, hemolysis still seems to be the predominant cause. Among the 70 fatal cases that were reported to United States Bureau of Biologics in 1976–1978, 44 patients died of acute hemolysis. Transfusion hepatitis was the second most important cause of death (10 cases). The rest of the reactions could not be attributed to blood transfusion, or they were caused by various isolated mishaps like bacterial contamination of the blood bag.

Immunologic Reactions

When careful cross-matching and antibody screening are done prior to transfusion, reactions from red cell incompatibility are rare. Serious reactions are usually due to clerical errors in labeling the test tubes or identifying the patient correctly. When a patient with a strong red cell antibody that activates complement by the classic pathway is transfused with incompatible blood, (eg, ABO incompatibility), intravascular hemolysis occurs, often triggering disseminated intravascular coagulation. The severity of the hemolytic reaction depends on the strength of the antibody and the amount of cells that have been transfused. The immediate symptoms include malaise, anxiety, backache, chest pain, and chills. In a severe reaction, the blood pressure may fall. The situation may be complicated by acute renal failure. The clinical signs can be masked by general anesthesia.

If the antibodies do not activate complement (eg, Rh and most other blood group antibodies), the transfused cells become coated by immunoglobulin and are captured by spleen macrophages via Fc receptors. The efficiency of this clearance depends on the number of antibody molecules on the red cells. Abundant anti-D antibodies may cause rapid extravascular destruction of the red cells, resulting in clinical symptoms, whereas weak antibodies against some other blood groups may cause a delayed transfusion reaction with shortened survival of the incompatible cells.

Reactions caused by antibodies against white blood cells are the most common immunologic complications of blood transfusion, occurring in 1–2% of all transfusions. Patients with a history of many transfusions or pregnancies are more prone to these reactions. Fortunately, the reactions are almost never severe. The main symptoms are fever and chills, but nausea, vomiting, and hypotension sometimes occur. Before it is concluded that the reaction is caused by white cell antibodies, the possibility of a hemolytic reaction should be ruled out.

Class-specific or allospecific antibodies to IgA

can cause severe anaphylactoid reactions, and these antibodies have been reported to occur in over 20% of individuals with IgA deficiency, which has a prevalence of about 1:800–1:400 in a healthy population (see Chapter 25). Nevertheless, these reactions are very rare in clinical practice. The reason for their scarcity is not yet known. There are some reports that antibodies to other plasma proteins may be responsible for occasional transfusion reactions, but these findings need confirmation.

Patients sometimes experience allergic reactions during or after the transfusion, commonly urticaria. The transfused blood may have contained traces of substances to which the recipient is hypersensitive, or the donor's allergy in form of reaginic IgE antibodies may have been temporarily transferred to the recipient. Studies to determine the cause of these reactions are usually unrewarding.

Treatment

If a transfusion reaction is suspected, the first step is to stop the transfusion. In hemolytic reactions, maintaining satisfactory kidney function is the most important part of therapy. Since the renal failure appears to be primarily due to ischemia, improvement of renal blood flow may be more useful than just increasing urinary output. Volume replacement with saline solutions, plasma fractions, or albumin is therefore essential. Diuretics such as furosemide should also be given. Hemodialysis or peritoneal dialysis may be needed. If the acute phase is successfully managed, the long-term prognosis is generally good.

Reactions due to leukocyte antibodies do not usually occur until a considerable amount of blood has been transfused, in contrast to hemolytic reactions, which may become obvious with small amounts of transfused blood. In mild fever-chill reactions, antipyretics often suffice. The transfusion may be continued if the possibility of a hemolytic reaction has been ruled out and if the blood is given at a reduced rate with careful observation of the patient, but usually it is better to transfuse leukocyte-poor blood.

Anaphylactoid reactions may require rapid measures to correct the fall of blood pressure and bronchospasm. Epinephrine is given subcutaneously or, in emergency cases, even intravenously. Corticosteroids may be useful, but otherwise the therapy is symptomatic. Reactions due to anti-IgA can occur after administration of only a few milliliters of IgA-containing plasma.

Investigation & Prevention

Laboratory investigations of a suspected hemolytic reaction are aimed at demonstrating hemolysis and antibodies incompatible with the transfused blood. In severe reactions, there is enough free hemoglobin to change the color of plasma and urine. The normal level of plasma hemoglobin is 20–30 mg/L; when it increases to approximately 200 mg/L, it will become visible to the naked eye. Hemoglobin is bound to haptoglobin, reducing its plasma levels to nearly zero.

Table 24–4. Some laboratory investigations in suspected immunologic transfusion reaction.

Tests to detect hemolysis
Color of plasma and urine
Plasma and urine hemoglobin
Plasma: Bilirubin
       Haptoglobin
       LDH
       Methemalbumin
Tests to detect antibodies
Retyping of patient's and donor's blood
Repeating of cross-matches
Antibody screening of patient's serum
Direct antiglobulin on patient's cells
Tests for cytotoxic white cell antibodies
Determination of IgA level and tests for anti-IgA antibodies

The breakdown product of heme, bilirubin, appears in plasma a few hours after the reaction. Determination of lactic dehydrogenase (LDH) may help in the diagnosis. In severe hemolysis, hemoglobin is bound to albumin to make methemalbumin, which has a characteristic dirty brownish color. Some of the laboratory investigations are listed in Table 24–4.

In serologic studies, the blood group of the patient and of the transfused blood unit are retyped, and the cross-match is repeated. Because the reaction may consume all of the antibodies, it is important to test both pre- and posttransfusion samples. The samples are examined for irregular antibodies, and a direct Coombs test is done on the posttransfusion sample.

The hemolytic reaction may be delayed if there were no antibodies at the time of transfusion or the antibodies were very weak and escaped detection. A delayed reaction is usually found by noticing fever and decreasing hemoglobin levels in the patient 3–21 days after transfusion. Determination of bilirubin and haptoglobin and performance of a direct Coombs test and antibody screening help in the diagnosis.

Serious hemolytic reactions are prevented if care is taken to properly identify the patient from whom the samples are drawn and to whom the blood is transfused. Test tubes should be adequately labeled and well-controlled methods used in blood grouping, compatibility testing, and screening for unexpected antibodies. Samples for blood grouping and cross-matching should be taken at different times, since faulty identification of the patient may lead to a severe reaction despite correct laboratory tests.

The practice of screening blood recipients for unexpected red cell antibodies (like anti-K, anti-Fy^a, etc) has increased the safety of transfusion and reduced the absolute need for a cross-match before transfusion. The blood banks should scrutinize transfusion practice in their own surgical services and derive a list of procedures that very seldom require blood. For such procedures, it is not necessary to hold cross-matched blood for individual patients. The patient is ABO and Rh typed, and if the antibody screening is negative, emergency release of ABO-compatible blood is permissible in the unlikely event that transfusion should become necessary. The cross-match is done afterwards.

If the patient's temperature rises over 1 °C during or immediately after the transfusion and there are no signs of hemolysis, the reaction is likely to be due to leukocyte antibodies. HLA antibodies can be screened with the cytotoxicity test (see Chapter 23). In some instances, the reaction is caused by granulocyte antibodies, and the cytotoxicity test then employed on lymphocytes may be negative. The agglutination tests for demonstration of antigranulocyte antibodies are not always reliable and are difficult to standardize.

Febrile reactions can be eliminated or at least made less severe by using leukocyte-poor blood. Theoretically, these patients should receive HLA-matched blood, but because of the large number of different HLA-antigens, this is usually not feasible even in well-equipped blood banks with tissue typing laboratories.

Patients with anaphylactoid reactions should be investigated for the presence of IgA and possible anti-IgA antibodies. Immunodiffusion is not sensitive enough to determine lack of IgA, but more sensitive methods such as hemagglutination inhibition, radioimmunoassay, or enzyme immunoassay should be used. Anti-IgA antibodies can be measured by passive hemagglutination if isolated IgA myeloma proteins are available for the assay. A patient with class-specific anti-IgA should be transfused with either IgA-deficient blood or with thoroughly washed red cell concentrate.

Changing Group of Transfused Blood

As a rule, only blood of the patient's own ABO and Rh group should be given. In emergency cases, or if the blood bank cannot provide a particular blood type, ABO-dissimilar red cell concentrate can be given if the cross-match is negative. Whole blood should not be given, since it contains antibodies that react with the patient's own red cells. Even in emergencies, the transfusion can often be started with infusion of salt solutions and plasma substitutes, and meanwhile the patient's blood group can be typed. If blood of the patient's group is not available, group O red cell concentrate should be given to A and B persons, whereas AB people can be transfused either with A or B red cell concentrate. A is to be preferred, since it is more widely available.

Rh-negative blood may be given to Rh-positive recipients, whereas Rh-positive blood causes anti-D antibody formation in Rh-negative patients. This immunization does not cause immediate ill effects (provided the patient does not already have Rh antibodies), but synthesized antibodies shorten the survival time of the transfused cells. The age of the patient, acute and future needs for blood, and the prognosis of the disease should be considered before deciding to change from Rh-negative to Rh-positive blood. Rh-negative girls and women of fertile age should not be transfused with Rh-positive blood.

INFECTIONS

The most common disease transmitted by blood transfusion is hepatitis, which may be hepatitis B surface antigen (HBsAg)-positive or -negative. In the latter case, it is called non-A non-B hepatitis (see Chapter 29). Hepatitis A is apparently not transmitted by blood, but cytomegalovirus may occasionally be the cause of hepatitis after multiple use of fresh blood, eg, after open heart surgery. The incidence of posttransfusion hepatitis varies greatly with different blood donor populations and is generally higher when donors are paid. Screening of blood units for HBsAg has greatly reduced the incidence of posttransfusion hepatitis B, so that non-A non-B hepatitis is now the most common infectious transfusion complication in the USA.

The incubation time for posttransfusion hepatitis is highly variable, but it is generally agreed that it is not shorter than 2 weeks and not longer than 6 months. Since serologic tests are not yet available for non-A non-B hepatitis, the cause-effect relationship is not always clear-cut. Other causes of hepatic dysfunction must be excluded before the diagnosis of posttransfusion hepatitis is established.

All blood units must be tested for absence of HBsAg. Only so-called third generation tests (based on radioimmunoassay, enzyme immunoassay, or reversed passive hemagglutination) are acceptable, since the less sensitive methods miss some positive samples. Prophylaxis with anti-HBsAg hyperimmune globulin is recommended in connection with accidental exposure to HBsAg-positive blood (needle scratches, minor wounds, etc), but it is not effective if a whole unit of HBsAg-positive blood has been erroneously transfused to the patient.

Screening of syphilis antibodies is also required before blood is transfused. However, blood stored for 48–72 hours does not transmit syphilis, and the usefulness of screening the blood donors in a modern society has recently been questioned.

Malaria and some other infectious diseases may be transmitted via blood transfusion. The risk of these diseases is increasing with more tourists visiting endemic areas. Visitors to these places are usually not permitted to donate blood for at least 6 months. Donors with a history of malaria are rejected permanently or at least for several years.

Occasionally, the blood unit may be contaminated by microbes which grow in the cold. Transfused bacterial endotoxin can trigger shock and disseminated intravascular coagulation, with high mortality rates.

BLOOD COMPONENT THERAPY

In modern transfusion practice, the different cellular and plasma components of blood should be used selectively. Blood component therapy results in fewer complications and optimal utilization of blood. Since there is a worldwide shortage of available blood, rational use of blood components should be greatly encouraged.

Packed Red Blood Cells (Red Cell Concentrates)

Packed red blood cells are indicated for the treatment of most anemias where transfusion is necessary, except for anemia associated with hypovolemic shock. This includes all chronic anemias, subacute and chronic blood loss, and surgical patients who require less than 2 or 3 units of blood replacement at surgery. Compared to whole blood, packed red blood cells have the following advantages: (1) ability to process whole blood more efficiently to obtain other valuable blood components from the same unit; (2) more oxygen-carrying capacity with less risk of circulatory overload; and (3) less infusion of sodium, potassium, ammonia, lactate, citrate, and donor antibodies.

Leukocyte-poor red blood cells are packed cells with the buffy coat containing most of the leukocytes and platelets removed. They are indicated for treatment of patients who have febrile transfusion reactions caused by leukocyte or platelet antibodies. It is not possible to make the blood units completely free of leukocyte antigens.

Frozen red cells are prepared from packed red cells by freezing them in a cryoprotective agent and then thawing and washing them prior to transfusion. Frozen red cells are currently indicated for transfusion of patients with rare blood types when blood is not available in any other form; for patients with leukocyte or platelet antibodies that are so potent that they react to leukocyte-poor red blood cells; and for patients who need washed red cells because they react to plasma proteins. Additional uses of frozen red blood cells are currently under investigation.

Platelet Concentrates

Platelets can be separated from whole blood by differential centrifugation. They may be given to stop or prevent bleeding in thrombocytopenic patients with aplastic anemia or acute leukemia. They may also be given following massive transfusion of stored blood, but they have only limited usefulness in ITP, DIC, and other thrombocytopenias due to increased platelet destruction. In patients with antibodies to histocompatibility antigens, HLA-matched platelets may be given, but this requires a well-equipped blood bank with a tissue typing laboratory and a large selection of HLA-typed donors.

White Cell Concentrate

Large amounts of white cells are useful and perhaps lifesaving in certain granulocytopenic patients with serious septic infections. The granulocytes survive only a short time in the circulation, and to be effective this type of therapy should be given daily. Many histocompatibility antigens are good immunogens, and prolonged random therapy may result in the development of anti-HLA antibodies that reduce granulocyte survival. HLA-matched leukocytes may ameliorate this problem.

Coagulation Factors

When fresh plasma is rapidly frozen and then thawed, the resulting cryoprecipitate contains about 50% of the factor VIII activity of the plasma. In addition, there is a fair amount of fibrinogen. Cryoprecipitate is used for treatment of hemophilia A and von Willebrand's disease and can also be used when fibrinogen is needed. Factor VIII can be further purified and concentrated. Factor VIII concentrates are especially suitable for home therapy. Factor II, VII, IX, and X concentrates are also available for the rare patients who lack these coagulation factors. The commercial concentrates are made from large blood donor plasma pools and have a high risk of hepatitis transmission.

Other Plasma Proteins

Albumin is the most widely used plasma derivative. It is prepared by Cohn's cold ethanol fractionation procedure. Plasma protein fraction (PPF) contains small amounts of other proteins in addition to albumin. The different albumin preparations are used as plasma substitutes for blood volume expansion. Their main advantage over plasma is the avoidance of transmission of hepatitis and the lack of blood group antibodies. They are useless for parenteral nutrition.

The immunoglobulins are also separated in the fractionation process and after concentration may be used as antibody source for passive immunization against some infectious diseases. Immunodeficient patients with hypogammaglobulinemia may need regular immunoglobulin injections as prophylactic therapy (see Chapter 25). Immunoglobulin prepared from Rh-immunized mothers or male volunteers is widely used for prevention of hemolytic disease of the newborn.

• • •

References

Cash JD (editor): Blood transfusion and blood products. *Clin Haematol* 1976;**5**:1. [Entire issue.]

Dodd BE, Lincoln PJ: *Blood Group Topics*. Vol 3 of: *Current Topics in Immunology Series*. Turk JL (editor). Arnold, 1975.

Goldfinger D: Acute hemolytic transfusion reactions: A fresh look at pathogenesis and considerations regarding therapy. *Transfusion* 1977;**17**:85.

Goudemand M, Delmas-Marsalet Y: *Principles of Immunohematology*. Ann Arbor Science, 1975.

Greenwalt TJ et al: *Blood Banking*. Handbook Series in Clinical Laboratory Science. CRC, 1977.

Honig CL, Bove JR: Transfusion-associated fatalities: Review of Bureau of Biologics reports 1976–1978. *Transfusion* 1980; **20**:653.

Huestis DW et al: *Practical Blood Transfusion*, 2nd ed. Little, Brown, 1976.

Koistinen J: Selective IgA deficiency in blood donors. *Vox Sang* 1975;**29**:192.

Leikola J et al: IgA-induced anaphylactic transfusion reactions: A report of four cases. *Blood* 1973;**42**:111.

Marcus D (editor): Blood group immunochemistry and genetics. *Semin Hematol* 1981;**18**:1. [Entire issue.]

Miller WV (editor): *Technical Manual of the American Association of Blood Banks,* 8th ed. American Association of Blood Banks, 1981.

Mollison PL: *Blood Transfusion in Clinical Medicine,* 6th ed. Blackwell, 1979.

Moore BPL: *Serological and Immunological Methods*. Canadian Red Cross Society, 1980.

Moore SB et al: Delayed hemolytic transfusion reactions: Evidence of the need for an improved pretransfusion compatibility test. *Am J Clin Path* 1980;**74**:94.

Race RR, Sanger R: *Blood Groups in Man,* 6th ed. Blackwell, 1976.

Schwartz L et al: *Blood Bank Technology,* 2nd ed. Williams & Wilkins, 1977.

Simmons A: *Problem Solving in Immunohematology*. Year Book, 1977.

Vyas GN, Cohen SN, Schmid R (editors): *Viral Hepatitis*. Franklin Institute Press, 1978.

Wallace J: *Blood Transfusion for Clinicians*. Churchill Livingstone, 1977.

Zmijewski CM: *Immunohematology*, 3rd ed. Appleton-Century-Crofts, 1978.

Section III. Clinical Immunology

Immunodeficiency Diseases | 25

Arthur J. Ammann, MD, & H. Hugh Fudenberg, MD

Four major immune systems assist the individual in the defense against a constant assault by viral, bacterial, fungal, protozoal, and nonreplicating agents that have the potential of producing infection and disease. These systems consist of antibody-mediated (B cell) immunity, cell-mediated (T cell) immunity, phagocytosis, and complement. Each system may act independently or in concert with one or more of the others.

Deficiency of one or more of these systems may be congenital (eg, X-linked infantile hypogammaglobulinemia) or acquired (eg, acquired hypogammaglobulinemia). Deficiencies of the immune system may be secondary to an embryologic abnormality (eg, the DiGeorge syndrome), may be due to an enzymatic defect (eg, chronic granulomatous disease), or may be of unknown cause (eg, Wiskott-Aldrich syndrome).

In general, the symptomatology of immunodeficiency is related to the degree of deficiency and the particular system that is deficient in function. General features are listed in Table 25–1 parts A and B. Features associated with specific immunodeficiency disorders are listed in Table 25–1 part C. The types of infections that occur often provide an important clue to the type of immunodeficiency disease present. Recurrent bacterial otitis media and pneumonia are common in hypogammaglobulinemia. Patients with defective cell-mediated immunity are susceptible to infection with fungal, protozoal, and viral organisms that may present as pneumonia or chronic infection of the skin and mucous membranes or other organs. Systemic infection with uncommon bacterial organisms, normally of low virulence, is characteristic of chronic granulomatous disease. Other phagocytic disorders are associated with superficial skin infections or systemic infections with pyogenic organisms. Complement deficiencies are associated with recurrent infections with pyogenic organisms.

Numerous advances have recently been made in the diagnosis of specific immunodeficiency disorders (Table 25–2). Screening tests are available for each component of the immune system (Table 25–3). These tests enable the physician to diagnose over 75% of immunodeficiency disorders. The remainder can be diagnosed by means of more complicated studies that may not be available in all hospital laboratories.

In addition to antimicrobial agents for treatmen of specific infections, new forms of immunotherapy are available to assist in the control of immunodeficiency or perhaps even to cure the underlying disease (Table 25–4). The usefulness of some of these treatment methods, such as bone marrow transplantation, may be limited by the availability of suitable donors. The discovery of enzyme deficiencies (eg, adenosine deaminase) in association with immunodeficiency offers a potential new avenue of therapy.

Immunodeficiency disorders are discussed below under 4 main categories: antibody or B cell deficiency, cellular or T cell deficiency, phagocytic dysfunction, and complement deficiency. In general, the terminology used for specific deficiencies agrees with the classification recently proposed by a committee of the World Health Organization (Table 25–2).

Table 25–1. Clinical features associated with immunodeficiency.[*]

A. **Features frequently present and highly suspicious:**
   1. Chronic infection
   2. Recurrent infection (more than expected)
   3. Unusual infecting agents
   4. Incomplete clearing between episodes of infection or incomplete response to treatment

B. **Features frequently present and moderately suspicious:**
   1. Skin rash (eczema, *Candida*, etc)
   2. Diarrhea (chronic)
   3. Growth failure
   4. Hepatosplenomegaly
   5. Recurrent abscesses
   6. Recurrent osteomyelitis
   7. Evidence of autoimmunity

C. **Features associated with specific immunodeficiency disorders:**
   1. Ataxia
   2. Telangiectasia
   3. Short-limbed dwarfism
   4. Cartilage-hair hypoplasia
   5. Idiopathic endocrinopathy
   6. Partial albinism
   7. Thrombocytopenia
   8. Eczema
   9. Tetany

[*]Reproduced, with permission, from Ammann A, Wara D: Evaluation of infants and children with recurrent infections. *Curr Probl Pediatr* 1975;5:3. [Entire issue.]

Table 25—2. Classification of immunodeficiency disorders.

I. **Antibody (B cell) immunodeficiency diseases**
    X-linked hypogammaglobulinemia (congenital hypogamma-
        globulinemia)
    Transient hypogammaglobulinemia of infancy
    Common, variable, unclassifiable immunodeficiency
        (acquired hypogammaglobulinemia)
    Immunodeficiency with hyper-IgM
    Selective IgA deficiency
    Selective IgM deficiency
    Selective deficiency of IgG subclasses
    Secondary B cell immunodeficiency associated with drugs,
        protein-losing states
    B cell immunodeficiency associated with 5'-nucleotidase de-
        ficiency
II. **Cellular (T cell) immunodeficiency diseases**
    Congenital thymic aplasia (DiGeorge syndrome)
    Chronic mucocutaneous candidiasis (with or without endo-
        crinopathy)
    T cell deficiency associated with purine nucleoside phospho-
        rylase deficiency
III. **Combined antibody-mediated (B cell) and cell-mediated (T
        cell) immunodeficiency diseases**
    Severe combined immunodeficiency disease (autosomal re-
        cessive, X-linked, sporadic)
    Cellular immunodeficiency with abnormal immunoglobulin
        synthesis (Nezelof's syndrome)
    Immunodeficiency with ataxia-telangiectasia
    Immunodeficiency with eczema and thrombocytopenia
        (Wiskott-Aldrich syndrome)
    Immunodeficiency with thymoma
    Immunodeficiency with short-limbed dwarfism
    Immunodeficiency with adenosine deaminase deficiency
    Episodic lymphopenia with lymphotoxin
    GVH disease
IV. **Phagocytic dysfunction**
    Chronic granulomatous disease
    Glucose-6-phosphate dehydrogenase deficiency
    Myeloperoxidase deficiency
    Chédiak-Higashi syndrome
    Job's syndrome
    Tuftsin deficiency
    "Lazy leukocyte syndrome"
    Elevated IgE, defective chemotaxis, eczema, and recurrent
        infections
V. **Complement abnormalities and immunodeficiency diseases**
    C1q, C1r, and C1s deficiency
    C2 deficiency
    C3 deficiency (type I, type II)
    C4 deficiency
    C5 dysfunction, C5 deficiency
    C6 deficiency
    C7 deficiency
    C8 deficiency
    C9 deficiency

Table 25—3. Initial screening evaluation.

Antibody-mediated immunity
    Quantitative immunoglobulin levels: IgG, IgM, IgA
    Schick test: measures specific IgG antibody response
    Isohemagglutinin titer (anti-A and anti-B): measures IgM
        function
Cell-mediated immunity
    White blood count with differential: measures total lym-
        phocytes
    Delayed hypersensitivity skin tests: measures specific T
        cell and macrophage response to antigens
Phagocytosis
    White blood count with differential: measures total neu-
        trophils
    NBT, chemiluminescence: measure neutrophil metabolic
        function
Complement
    Hemolytic complement quantitation (CH_{50}): quantitates
        complement activity
    C3 level: measures amount of important complement com-
        ponent

lins ranging from complete absence of all classes to
selective deficiency of a single immunoglobulin class.
The degree of symptoms found in patients with antibody immunodeficiency disorders is chiefly dependent
on the degree of antibody deficiency. Patients with
hypogammaglobulinemia become symptomatic earlier
and experience more severe disease than patients with
selective immunoglobulin deficiency. Screening tests
for the specific diagnosis of antibody deficiency disorders are readily available in most hospital laboratories (see Table 25–3 and Chapter 22) and usually
afford early diagnosis with prompt institution of appropriate treatment. Newer procedures such as counting B cells in peripheral blood, determination of in
vitro immunoglobulin production, and suppressor cell
assays permit more precise diagnosis as well as a
greater understanding of the causes (Table 25–5).

ANTIBODY (B CELL) IMMUNODEFICIENCY DISORDERS

Antibody immunodeficiency disorders comprise
a spectrum of diseases with decreased immunoglobu-

X–LINKED INFANTILE HYPOGAMMAGLOBULINEMIA

Major Immunologic Features

- Symptoms of recurrent pyogenic infections usu-
  ally begin by 5–6 months of age.
- IgG less than 200 mg/dL with absence of IgM,
  IgA, IgD, and IgE.
- Absence of B cells in peripheral blood.
- Patients respond well to treatment with γ-glob-
  ulin.

General Considerations

In 1952, Bruton described a male child with hypogammaglobulinemia, and this is now recognized as
the first clinical description of an immunodeficiency
disorder. The disorder is easily diagnosed using standard laboratory tests which demonstrate marked deficiency or complete absence of all 5 immunoglobulin

Table 25—4. Treatment of immunodeficiency.

Treatment	B Cell Disorders	T Cell Disorders	Phagocytic Disorders	Complement Disorders
Gamma globulin	X-linked hypogamma-globulinemia. Acquired hypogammaglobulinemia. Secondary hypogamma-globulinemia when associated with infection. Do not use in selective IgA deficiency.	Use only when absent antibody response is demonstrated. Not recommended for Wiskott-Aldrich syndrome. The new intravenous preparation may be used.	Not recommended.	Not recommended.
Hyperimmune gamma globulin	Use in above disorders when specific exposure has occurred.	May be used when specific exposure has occurred.	May be used when specific exposure has occurred.	May be used when specific exposure has occurred.
Frozen plasma by intravenous infusion	X-linked hypogamma-globulinemia and acquired hypogammaglobulinemia when intramuscular administration is not tolerated or is ineffective.	Use only when absent antibody response is demonstrated. Irradiate to prevent GVH.	Not recommended.	Use with caution. Plasma may exacerbate autoimmune disease.
Infusions of white cells	Not recommended.	Not recommended.	Questionable value.	Not recommended.
Infusions of red cells	Not recommended.	May be of benefit in certain enzyme deficiencies associated with immunodeficiency (adenosine deaminase, purine nucleoside phosphorylase). Irradiate to prevent GVH.	Not recommended.	Not recommended.
Bone marrow transplant	Not recommended.	Use only when impaired T cell function is present. Must have histocompatible donor.	Not recommended.	Not recommended.
Fetal thymus transplantation	Not recommended.	DiGeorge syndrome. Severe combined immunodeficiency without suitable bone marrow donor. Selective use in other combined immunodeficiency disorders.	Not recommended.	Not recommended.
Cultured thymus epithelium	Not recommended.	Selective cases of T cell disorders where no suitable bone marrow donor is available.	Not recommended.	Not recommended.
Fetal liver transplantation	Not recommended.	Sometimes used in severe combined immunodeficiency in absence of suitable bone marrow donor.	Not recommended.	Not recommended.
Transfer factor	Not recommended	May be successful in chronic candidiasis when combined with antifungal agent. Highly debatable effect in other disorders.	Not recommended.	Not recommended.
Thymosin and other thymic factors	Not recommended.	Limited evaluation to date. May enhance T cell function in a variety of T cell disorders, including DiGeorge syndrome. No effect in chronic candidiasis or severe combined immunodeficiency.	Not recommended.	Not recommended.

classes. Male infants with this disorder usually become symptomatic following the natural decay of transplacentally acquired maternal immunoglobulin at about 5–6 months of age. They suffer from severe chronic bacterial infections which can be controlled readily with γ-globulin and antibiotic treatment. The incidence of this disorder in the USA is not precisely known, but estimates in the United Kingdom suggest an overall incidence of one case per 100,000 population. Recently, 2 female siblings with congenital hypogammaglobulinemia have been reported.

Immunologic Pathogenesis

Extirpation of the bursa of Fabricius in avian species results in complete hypogammaglobulinemia. Several investigators think that the bursa equivalent in humans consists of gastrointestinal tract-associated lymphoid tissue, ie, tonsils, adenoids, Peyer's patches, and appendix. Other investigators consider that the bursa equivalent in humans exists in the bone marrow, which provides a source of stem B cells. In X-linked infantile hypogammaglobulinemia, it is felt that this stem cell population is absent, resulting in

Table 25—5. Evaluation of antibody-mediated immunity.

Test	Comment
Protein electro-phoresis	Use to presumptively diagnose hypogam-maglobulinemia or to evaluate for parapro-teins.
Radial immuno-diffusion	Best procedure for quantitation of IgG, IgM, IgA, and IgD.
Radioimmuno-assay	IgE quantitation.
Schick test	DTP immunization must be complete. Use to evaluate IgG function.
Isohemagglutinins	Use to evaluate IgM function. Titer > 1:4 after 1 year of age.
Specific antibody response	Use to evaluate immunoglobulin function. Tetanus, diphtheria, typhoid, etc. Do not immunize with live virus if immunodefi-ciency is suspected.
B cell quantitation	Measurement of the number of circulating B cells. Normal is 10—25% (total IgG-, IgM-, IgD-, and IgA-bearing cells).
In vitro immuno-globulin synthesis	Determines helper/suppressor T cell func-tion in hypogammaglobulinemia.

complete absence of plasma cells and peripheral blood B lymphocytes. Recent investigations have provided evidence of pre-B cells in the marrow and peripheral blood of patients. These pre-B cells fail to secrete immunoglobulin.

Clinical Features

A. Symptoms and Signs: Patients with X-linked infantile hypogammaglobulinemia usually remain asymptomatic until 5–6 months of age, when pas-sively transferred maternal IgG reaches its lowest level. The loss of maternal immunoglobulin usually coincides with the age at which these children are increasingly exposed to pathogens. Initial symptoms consist of recurrent bacterial otitis media, bronchitis, pneumonia, meningitis, dermatitis, and occasionally arthritis or malabsorption. Many infections respond promptly to antibiotic therapy, and this response occasionally will delay the diagnosis of hypogamma-globulinemia. The most common organisms respon-sible for infection are *Streptococcus pneumoniae* and *Haemophilus influenzae;* other organisms such as streptococci and certain gram-negative bacteria are occasionally responsible. Although patients nor-mally have intact cell-mediated immunity and respond normally to viral infections such as varicella and measles, there have been reports of paralytic polio-myelitis and progressive encephalitis following immunization with live virus vaccines or exposure to wild virus. Fatal echovirus infection has been reported in patients with congenital hypogammaglob-ulinemia. The encephalitis in a few patients has responded to treatment with intravenous γ-globulin or plasma. A relationship of echovirus infection, der-matomyositis, and hypogammaglobulinemia has been proposed. These observations suggest that some patients with hypogammaglobulinemia

may also be unusually susceptible to some viral ill-nesses.

An important clue to the diagnosis of hypogam-maglobulinemia is the failure of infections to respond completely or promptly to appropriate antibiotic therapy. In addition, many patients with hypogamma-globulinemia have a history of continuous illness, ie, they do not have periods of well-being between bouts of illness.

Occasionally, patients with hypogammaglobu-linemia may not become symptomatic until early childhood. Some of these patients may present with other complaints, such as chronic conjunctivitis, ab-normal dental decay, or malabsorption. The malab-sorption may be severe and may cause retardation of both height and weight. Frequently the malabsorption is associated with infestation by *Giardia lamblia*. A disease resembling rheumatoid arthritis has been re-ported in association with hypogammaglobulinemia. This occurs principally in untreated infants or is an indication for more intensive therapy with γ-globulin.

Physical findings usually relate to recurrent pyo-genic infections. Chronic otitis media and externa, serous otitis, conjunctivitis, abnormal dental decay, and eczematoid skin infections are frequently present. Despite the repeated infections, lymphadenopathy and splenomegaly are absent.

B. Laboratory Findings: The diagnosis of in-fantile X-linked hypogammaglobulinemia is based on the demonstration of absence or marked deficiency of all 5 immunoglobulin classes. Although a diagnosis can be established utilizing immunoelectrophoresis, specific quantitation of immunoglobulins is recom-mended, especially during early infancy. Total immu-noglobulins are usually less than 250 mg/dL. IgG is usually less than 200 mg/dL, while IgM, IgA, IgD, and IgE are extremely low or absent. Rarely, patients have complete hypogammaglobulinemia except for the presence of normal amounts of IgE. It is unusual for patients with hypogammaglobulinemia to have de-pressed levels of IgG and normal levels of IgM or IgA. Before a diagnosis of hypogammaglobulinemia is es-tablished, there should be a demonstration of failure to make antibody following antigenic stimulation.

Isohemagglutinins that result from natural im-munization are present in normal infants of the appro-priate blood group by 1 year of age. Titers of anti-A and anti-B should be greater than 1:4 in normal indi-viduals. Individuals who have received the complete series of DTP immunizations should react negatively to the Schick test. Previous γ-globulin therapy (within 1 month) may result in a nonreactive Schick test in a patient with hypogammaglobulinemia. Antibody to a specific antigen may be measured following immuni-zation, but a patient suspected of having an im-munodeficiency disorder should never be immunized with live attenuated viral vaccine. Although lymph node biopsies have been recommended in the past, with currently available diagnostic studies this would appear to be an unnecessary procedure. Rarely, in difficult cases, an intestinal biopsy may be necessary to assist in the diagnosis. In X-linked infantile hypogammaglobulinemia, there is a complete absence of plasma cells in the lamina propria of the gut. Studies of peripheral blood lymphocytes indicate a complete absence of circulating B cells, with normal to increased numbers of T cells. Studies of T cell immunity indicate that this system is intact. Delayed hypersensitivity skin tests are usually positive; isolated peripheral blood lymphocytes respond normally to PHA and allogeneic cells (MLC); and there are normal numbers of circulating peripheral blood T cells.

C. Other Studies: X-ray of the lateral nasopharynx has been suggested as a method of demonstrating the lack of lymphoid tissue. It is doubtful that this information adds significantly to the findings on physical examination. X-rays of the sinuses and chest should be obtained at regular intervals to follow the course of the patient and to determine adequacy of treatment. Pulmonary function studies should also be performed on a regular basis, beginning as soon as patient cooperation can be obtained. Patients with hypogammaglobulinemia who have gastrointestinal tract symptoms should be investigated for the presence of *G lamblia* and other causes of malabsorption.

Immunologic Diagnosis

Total immunoglobulins are less than 250 mg/dL; IgG is less than 200 mg/dL; and IgM, IgA, IgD, and IgE are markedly reduced or absent. B cells are absent in peripheral blood, and there are no plasma cells containing immunoglobulins in tissue and lymph nodes. Lymph nodes are markedly depleted in B cell-dependent areas. No antibodies are formed following specific immunization. T cell immunity is intact.

Differential Diagnosis

A diagnosis of X-linked infantile hypogammaglobulinemia may be difficult to establish in the age range of 5–9 months. By this time most infants have lost their maternal immunoglobulins and are susceptible to recurrent infections. The majority of normal infants during this time have levels of IgG less than 350 mg/dL but usually show some evidence of IgM and IgA production (usually greater than 20 mg/dL). If the diagnosis appears uncertain, several approaches may be utilized. Immunoglobulin levels may be determined again 3 months after the initial values. If there is an increase in IgG, IgM, or IgA, it is highly unlikely that the patient has hypogammaglobulinemia. Alternatively, the patient may be immunized with killed vaccines and specific antibody levels determined. The most difficult diagnostic problem is the differentiation of prolonged physiologic hypogammaglobulinemia from X-linked infantile hypogammaglobulinemia. In the former instance, the hypogammaglobulinemia may be severe enough to require treatment, and immunoglobulin levels may be identical to those of patients with congenital hypogammaglobulinemia. Normal production of immunoglobulins may not occur until as late as 18 months of age in patients with physiologic hypogammaglobulinemia. However, in most instances, these patients will begin to produce their own immunoglobulin despite concurrent γ-globulin administration. This is manifested by increasing levels of IgG as well as IgM and IgA. Since commercial γ-globulin contains less than 10% of IgM or IgA, a gradual increase in these values argues strongly against congenital hypogammaglobulinemia. The best way to avoid mistaking congenital hypogammaglobulinemia for prolonged physiologic hypogammaglobulinemia in infants is to carefully compare immunoglobulin levels with age-matched controls (see Chapter 22) and to obtain sequential measurements of immunoglobulins at 3-month intervals during the first year of diagnostic uncertainty.

Patients with severe malabsorption—particularly protein-losing enteropathy—may have severely depressed levels of immunoglobulins. In most instances, a diagnosis of protein-losing enteropathy can be established by the demonstration of a concomitant deficiency of serum albumin. Occasionally, however, patients with severe malabsorption and primary hypogammaglobulinemia may also lose albumin through the intestinal tract. Under these circumstances, a diagnosis can best be made by obtaining an intestinal biopsy. Patients with protein-losing enteropathy have normal numbers of plasma cells in the gut which contain intracellular immunoglobulins.

Polyarthritis may be a presenting feature in patients with hypogammaglobulinemia. Most patients with juvenile rheumatoid arthritis have elevated levels of immunoglobulins. Patients with arthritis and hypogammaglobulinemia usually respond promptly following institution of γ-globulin therapy.

Patients with chronic lung disease should also be suspected of having cystic fibrosis, asthma, α_1-antitrypsin deficiency, or immotile cilia syndrome.

Treatment

Treatment schedules have varied. Commercial γ-globulin is the mainstay of therapy and is usually given in starting doses of 0.2–0.4 mL/kg as a single intramuscular dose. The final amount given and the frequency of injections should be regulated by the control of symptoms rather than a calculated amount or a particular serum level, since metabolism of IgG varies in different individuals. Following the administration of an initial dose once a month, the amount given can be increased by 2–3 mL per injection. If the amount injected into a single site becomes too large, it may be divided and given in 2 sites at the same time. As amounts continue to increase, injections may be given every 2 weeks or every week. Some patients prefer weekly injections of smaller amounts rather than large monthly injections.

Anaphylactoid reactions to γ-globulin administration have been observed. These are not mediated through the classic IgE allergic pathway, since most patients with hypogammaglobulinemia lack IgE. The chief causes of these reactions are aggregate formation in the γ-globulin preparation and inadvertent intravenous administration. Patients who have repeated reactions to γ-globulin should be treated with an alternative preparation obtained from a different commercial source. If patients continue to have reactions, it may be necessary to ultracentrifuge the preparation to remove aggregates prior to administration. Intravenous γ-globulin is now licensed for routine clinical use. Appropriate clinical application would be in patients who fail to respond to intramuscular γ-globulin or who might benefit from large amounts of antibody.

Additional therapy may be necessary in patients who fail to respond to maximum doses of γ-globulin. Because commercial γ-globulin contains primarily IgG and little IgM or IgA, some immunologists consider that there is a beneficial effect of monthly intravenous infusions of fresh-frozen plasma. The dose of plasma used is 10 mL/kg. In adult patients, 1–2 units may be used. To avoid the risk of hepatitis, a "buddy system" has been devised whereby the patient receives plasma from a single reliable donor. Alternatively, screening of plasma for HBsAg should be done. γ-Globulin therapy should be continued if frozen plasma is used. Fresh-frozen plasma therapy may provide other antibacterial substances in addition to IgG, IgM, and IgA.

Continuous use of antibiotics may be necessary. Broad-spectrum antibiotics such as ampicillin in low to moderate doses may be effective in controlling recurrent infection. Physical therapy with postural drainage should be utilized in patients with chronic lung disease or bronchiectasis.

Occasionally, a patient with hypogammaglobulinemia may be discovered who has no symptoms. These patients should receive γ-globulin therapy even though they have not experienced repeated infection. Avoidance of infection with subsequent permanent complications is an important part of treatment in these patients.

Malabsorption, which is occasionally found in patients with hypogammaglobulinemia, usually responds to treatment with γ-globulin or intravenous fresh-frozen plasma (or both). If *Giardia* is found, it should be treated with metronidazole in doses of 35–50 mg/kg/24 h in 3 divided doses for 10 days in children and 750 mg orally 3 times a day for 10 days in adults.

Complications & Prognosis

Although patients with congenital hypogammaglobulinemia have survived to the second and third decades, the prognosis must be guarded. Despite what may appear to be adequate γ-globulin replacement therapy, many patients develop chronic lung disease. The presence of severe infection early in infancy may result in irreversible damage. Patients who recover from meningitis may have severe neurologic handicaps. Patients with severe pulmonary infection frequently develop bronchiectasis and chronic lung disease. Regular examinations and prompt institution of therapy are necessary to control infections and prevent complications. Fatal echovirus infections of the central nervous system have been reported even in patients receiving γ-globulin therapy. Some of these infections have been associated with dermatomyositis. Some patients may develop leukemia or lymphoma.

TRANSIENT HYPOGAMMAGLOBULINEMIA OF INFANCY

Almost all infants go through a period of hypogammaglobulinemia at approximately 5–6 months of age. Under normal circumstances, maternal IgG is passively transferred to the infant beginning at the 16th week of gestational life. At the time of birth the serum IgG value of the infant is usually higher than that of the mother. IgA, IgM, IgD, and IgE are not placentally transferred under normal circumstances. In fact, the presence of elevated values of IgM or IgA in cord blood suggests premature antibody synthesis, usually as a result of intrauterine infection. Over the first 4–5 months of life, there is a gradual decrease in serum IgG and a gradual increase of serum IgM and IgA. The IgM usually rises more rapidly than the IgA. At 5–6 months, serum IgG reaches its lowest level (approximately 350 mg/dL). At this point, many normal infants begin to experience recurrent respiratory tract infections. Immunoglobulin values obtained at this age must be compared to those of normal infants of the same age. Occasionally, an infant may fail to produce normal amounts of IgG at this time, resulting in transient hypogammaglobulinemia or so-called physiologic hypogammaglobulinemia. The presence of normal serum levels of IgM or IgA argues strongly against a diagnosis of X-linked hypogammaglobulinemia. However, some infants with transient hypogammaglobulinemia may also fail to produce normal amounts of IgM or IgA.

Additional studies may be of no diagnostic usefulness, since many infants fail to respond to immunization at this age and isohemagglutinin titers may be low. Under these circumstances, a lymph node or intestinal biopsy may assist in establishing the diagnosis. Patients with congenital hypogammaglobulinemia lack plasma cells containing immunoglobulins in the intestinal tract and in peripheral lymph nodes. In addition, patients with congenital hypogammaglobulinemia lack circulating peripheral blood B cells. If the patient is not experiencing severe recurrent infection, it is best to wait 3–5 months and repeat immunoglobulin measurements rather than perform invasive procedures. In the presence of an increasing IgG, IgM, or IgA level, congenital hypogammaglobulinemia is unlikely. If the patient has been treated with γ-globulin to prevent severe or recurrent infection, then measurement of IgM and IgA assumes greater importance. Because commercial γ-globulin contains primarily IgG, the administration of γ-globulin will not affect serum levels of IgM and IgA. Increasing levels of these immunoglobulin classes indicate that the patient had transient hypogammaglobulinemia. Hypogammaglobulinemia may persist for as long as 2 years.

The cause of transient hypogammaglobulinemia is not known. In some cases, IgG anti-Gm antibodies have been demonstrated during the last trimester of pregnancy in women who have had infants with transient hypogammaglobulinemia. It is postulated that these antibodies cause suppression of endogenous immunoglobulin production in a manner similar to the suppression of normal red cell production in infants with passive transfer of antibody against Rh factors. Recent studies indicate that patients with transient hypogammaglobulinemia have normal numbers of B cells associated with a deficiency of number and function of helper T cells. Helper T cells have become normal with time.

Occasionally, these infants become sufficiently symptomatic so that they must be treated just like those with X-linked hypogammaglobulinemia. γ-Globulin therapy may be required for as long as 18 months. Routine immunization should not be given during the period of transient hypogammaglobulinemia. Once a normal immune system has been established, the complete series of pediatric immunizations should be administered (see Chapter 39).

COMMON, VARIABLE, UNCLASSIFIABLE IMMUNODEFICIENCY
(Acquired Hypogammaglobulinemia)

Major Immunologic Features
- Recurrent pyogenic infections with onset at any age.
- Increased incidence of autoimmune disease.
- Total immunoglobulins less than 300 mg/dL, with IgG less than 250 mg/dL.
- B cells usually normal in number.

General Considerations
Patients with acquired hypogammaglobulinemia present clinically like patients with X-linked hypogammaglobulinemia except that they usually do not become symptomatic until 15–35 years of age. In addition to increased susceptibility to pyogenic infections, they have a high incidence of autoimmune disease. These patients also differ from patients with congenital hypogammaglobulinemia in that they have a higher than normal incidence of abnormalities in T cell immunity, which in most instances shows progressive deterioration with time. Acquired hypogammaglobulinemia affects both males and females and may occur at any age.

Immunologic Pathogenesis
The cause of acquired hypogammaglobulinemia is unknown. Most patients have an intrinsic defect in B cells. Recent studies have demonstrated an inhibitory effect of peripheral blood lymphocytes from patients with acquired hypogammaglobulinemia on the immunoglobulin synthesis of cells from normal patients. A suggested increase in suppressor T cells has been postulated as a cause of this disorder. Other patients have diminished helper T cells. Two enzymatic abnormalities have been described. In some patients there is a failure of heavy chain glycosylation of IgG. In others, a deficiency of 5'-nucleotidase has been described. The latter abnormality is most likely due to alterations in T/B cell ratios rather than a primary defect. An X-linked lymphoproliferative disorder associated with acquired hypogammaglobulinemia has been described following EB virus infection. Genetic studies of acquired hypogammaglobulinemia have demonstrated an autosomal recessive mode of inheritance in certain families in which abnormal lymphocyte metabolism has been shown to be inherited. In most instances, however, no clear-cut genetic transmission can be demonstrated. An increased incidence of other immunologic disorders, including autoimmune disease, has been observed in families of patients with acquired hypogammaglobulinemia. The presence of normal numbers of circulating peripheral blood B cells in most of these patients suggests that the disorder is a result of diminished synthesis or release of immunoglobulin rather than production of fewer immunoglobulin-synthesizing cells.

Clinical Features
A. Symptoms and Signs: In most instances, the initial presentation of acquired hypogammaglobulinemia consists of recurrent sinopulmonary infections. These may be chronic rather than acute and overwhelming, as in X-linked hypogammaglobulinemia. Infections may be caused by pneumococci and *Haemophilus influenzae* as well as other pyogenic organisms. Chronic bacterial conjunctivitis may be an additional presenting complaint. Some patients develop severe malabsorption prior to the diagnosis of hypogammaglobulinemia. The malabsorption may be severe enough to cause protein loss, with the subsequent development of edema.

Autoimmune disease has been a presenting complaint in some patients with acquired hypogammaglobulinemia. A rheumatoid arthritis–like disorder, systemic lupus erythematosus, idiopathic thrombocytopenic purpura, dermatomyositis, hemolytic anemia, and pernicious anemia have been reported in association with acquired hypogammaglobulinemia.

In contrast to patients with infantile X-linked hypogammaglobulinemia, patients with acquired hypogammaglobulinemia may have marked lymphadenopathy and splenomegaly. Intestinal lymphoid nodular hyperplasia has been described in association with malabsorption. Other abnormal physical findings relate to the presence of chronic lung disease or intestinal malabsorption. Leukemia, lymphoma, and gastric carcinoma occur with increased frequency.

B. Laboratory Findings: Immunoglobulin measurements may show slightly higher IgG values than are reported in infantile X-linked hypogammaglobulinemia. Total immunoglobulins are usually less than 300 mg/dL, and IgG is usually less than 250 mg/dL. IgM and IgA may be absent or may be present in significant amounts. The Schick test is useful to demonstrate lack of normal antibody response, but it should be performed following booster immunization with diphtheria antigen. Isohemagglutinins are absent or present in low titers (less than 1:10). The failure to produce antibody following specific immunization establishes the diagnosis in patients who have borderline immunoglobulin values. Live attenuated vaccines should not be utilized for immunization. Peripheral blood B lymphocytes are usually present in normal numbers in patients with acquired hypogammaglobulinemia—in contrast to patients with infantile X-linked hypogammaglobulinemia.

Although most patients with acquired hypogammaglobulinemia have intact cell-mediated immunity, a significant number demonstrate abnormalities as evidenced by absent delayed hypersensitivity skin test responses, depressed responses of isolated peripheral blood lymphocytes to PHA and allogeneic cells, and decreased numbers of T cell rosettes. Patients should be followed sequentially, as the immunodeficiency appears to progressively involve cell-mediated immunity, resulting in additional immunologic deficiencies.

Biopsy of lymphoid tissue demonstrates a lack of plasma cells. Although some lymph node biopsies demonstrate lymphoid hyperplasia, there is a striking absence of cells in the B cell–dependent areas.

C. Other Studies: Other tests which may be abnormal in these patients relate to associated disorders. The chest x-ray usually shows evidence of chronic lung disease, and sinus films show chronic sinusitis. Pulmonary function studies are abnormal. Patients with malabsorption may have abnormal gastrointestinal tract biopsies, with blunting of the villi similar to that seen in celiac disease. Studies for malabsorption may indicate a lack of normal intestinal enzymes and an abnormal D-xylose absorption test. Occasionally, autoantibodies may be found in patients who have an associated autoimmune hemolytic anemia or systemic lupus erythematosus. In pernicious anemia, autoantibodies are not found, but biopsies of the stomach demonstrate marked lymphoid cell infiltration. Associated lymphoreticular malignancies and thymomas have been described.

Immunologic Diagnosis

The total immunoglobulin level is less than 300 mg/dL, with IgG less than 250 mg/dL. IgM and IgA may be absent or present in significant amounts. The antibody response following specific immunization is absent. Isohemagglutinins are depressed, and the Schick test is reactive. Circulating peripheral blood B cells are usually present in normal numbers but may be depressed.

Cell-mediated immunity may be intact or may be depressed, with negative delayed hypersensitivity skin tests, depressed responses of peripheral blood lymphocytes to PHA and allogeneic cells, and decreased numbers of circulating peripheral blood T cells. B cells may be normal or diminished in number in the peripheral blood. There is occasionally an increased number of null cells, ie, lymphocytes lacking surface markers for either T or B cells.

Differential Diagnosis

Occasionally the diagnosis of hypergammaglobulinemia in patients with infantile X-linked hypogammaglobulinemia may be delayed as long as 10 years. Because the treatment of infantile X-linked hypogammaglobulinemia and of acquired hypogammaglobulinemia is identical, this does not present a major clinical problem. Severe malabsorption associated with protein-losing enteropathy may be associated with hypogammaglobulinemia. These patients always have a simultaneous deficiency of serum albumin. A diagnosis of protein-losing enteropathy versus acquired hypogammaglobulinemia may be difficult under circumstances where protein-losing enteropathy is also associated with loss of lymphoid cells. In both groups of patients, depressed antibody responses and deficient cell-mediated immunity have been described. When the presenting feature of acquired hypogammaglobulinemia is an autoimmune disease, the diagnosis may be delayed, to the patient's detriment. In most instances, however, patients with autoimmune disease have normal to elevated immunoglobulin values. Patients with chronic lung disease should also be suspected of having cystic fibrosis, chronic allergy, α_1-antitrypsin deficiency, or immotile cilia syndrome.

Treatment

The treatment of acquired hypogammaglobulinemia is identical to that of infantile X-linked hypogammaglobulinemia. γ-Globulin in a dose of 20–40 mL/mo, fresh-frozen plasma (1–2 units/mo), and continuous antibiotics may be required in various combinations. Patients should be followed at regular intervals with chest x-rays and pulmonary function tests to determine adequacy of therapy. Pulmonary physical therapy is an essential part of treatment in patients with chronic lung disease.

Specific treatment of malabsorption problems may be required. Some patients respond to treatment with γ-globulin or with fresh-frozen plasma. Intravenous γ-globulin is now licensed for routine clinical use. Appropriate clinical application would be in patients who fail to respond to intramuscular γ-globulin or who might benefit from large amounts of antibody. In others, the malabsorption may be associated with secondary enzymatic deficiencies that resemble celiac disease. These patients may respond to dietary restrictions. If the malabsorption is associated with *Giardia* infection, metronidazole therapy should be as for infantile X-linked hypogammaglobulinemia.

Caution should be exercised in the treatment of associated autoimmune disorders. The use of corticosteroids and immunosuppressive agents in a patient with immunodeficiency may result in markedly increased susceptibility to infection. Splenectomy has been used in the treatment of hypogammaglobulinemia and hemolytic anemia, but the mortality rate from overwhelming infection was high.

Complications & Prognosis

Patients with acquired hypogammaglobulinemia may survive to the seventh or eighth decade. Women with this disorder have had normal pregnancies and delivered normal infants (albeit hypogammaglobulinemic until 6 months of age). The major complication is chronic lung disease, which may develop despite adequate γ-globulin replacement therapy. An increased incidence of malignant disease has also been observed, including leukemia, lymphoma, and gastric carcinoma. Patients who develop acquired T cell deficiencies have increasing difficulty with infection characteristic of both T and B cell deficiencies. (See Table 25–1 parts A and B).

IMMUNODEFICIENCY WITH HYPER–IgM

This syndrome, characterized by an increased level of IgM (ranging from 150 to 1000 mg/dL) associated with a deficiency of IgG and IgA, is relatively rare and in most instances appears to be inherited in an X-linked manner. However, several cases have been reported of an acquired form which affects both sexes. The cause is not known. It has been postulated that in the normal individual there is a sequential development of immunoglobulins initiated by IgM production and subsequently resulting in the production of IgG and IgA (Chapter 5). Arrest in the development of immunoglobulin-producing cells after the formation of IgM-producing cells would be a possible cause.

Patients present with recurrent pyogenic infections, including otitis media, pneumonia, and septicemia. Some patients have recurrent neutropenia, hemolytic anemia, or aplastic anemia.

Laboratory evaluation reveals a marked increase in serum IgM, with absence of IgG and IgA. Isohemagglutinin titers may be elevated, and the patient may form antibodies following specific immunization. Detailed studies of cell-mediated immunity have not been performed, but some reports indicate that it is intact. Patients with this disorder may develop an infiltrating malignancy of IgM-producing cells.

Treatment is similar to that of infantile X-linked hypogammaglobulinemia. Because few cases have been reported, it is difficult to determine the prognosis.

SELECTIVE IgA DEFICIENCY

Major Immunologic Features

- IgA less than 5 mg/dL with other immunoglobulins normal or increased.
- Cell-mediated immunity usually normal.
- Increased association with allergies, recurrent sinopulmonary infection, and autoimmune disease.

General Considerations (See also Chapter 12.)

Selective IgA deficiency is the most common immunodeficiency disorder. The incidence in the normal population has been estimated to vary between 1:800 and 1:600. Considerable debate exists about whether individuals with selective IgA deficiency are "normal" or have significant associated diseases. Studies of individual patients and extensive studies of large numbers of patients suggest that absence of IgA predisposes to a variety of diseases. The diagnosis of selective IgA deficiency is established by finding an IgA level in serum of less than 5 mg/dL.

Immunologic Pathogenesis

The cause of selective IgA deficiency is not known. An arrest in development of B cells has been suggested based on the observation that B cells with both surface IgA and IgM or IgA and IgD are increased. An IgG2 subclass deficiency has been described in some patients and has been used to explain the varied clinical manifestations. The presence of normal numbers of circulating IgA B cells suggests that this disorder is associated with decreased synthesis or release of IgA rather than absence of IgA B lymphocytes. Utilizing the concept of sequential immunoglobulin production (IgM → IgG → IgA) discussed in Chapter 5, selective IgA deficiency could result from an arrest in the development of immunoglobulin-producing cells following the normal sequential development of IgM to IgG. The variety of diseases associated with selective IgA deficiency may be the result of enhanced or prolonged exposure to a spectrum of microbial agents and nonreplicating antigens as a consequence of deficient secretory IgA. The continuous assault by these agents on a compromised immune system could result in an increased incidence of infection, autoantibody, autoimmune disease, and cancer. Recently, an increased prevalence of HLA-A1, HLA-B8, and Dw3 has been found in patients with IgA deficiency and autoimmune disease.

Lymphocyte culture studies in IgA-deficient patients have demonstrated that IgA cells synthesize but fail to secrete IgA. Some individuals have suppressor T cells that selectively inhibit IgA production by normal lymphocytes.

Acquired IgA deficiency occurs frequently in patients treated with phenytoin or penicillamine and is frequently associated with sinopulmonary tract infection. In at least some instances, the IgA level returns to normal when the drug therapy is stopped.

Clinical Features

A. Symptoms and Signs:

1. Recurrent sinopulmonary infection–The most frequent presenting symptoms are recurrent sinopulmonary viral or bacterial infections. Patients may occasionally present with recurrent or chronic right middle lobe pneumonia. Pulmonary hemosiderosis occurs with increased frequency and may be confused with chronic lung disease.

2. Allergy–In surveys of atopic populations the incidence of selective IgA deficiency is 1:400–1:200, as compared to an incidence of 1:800–1:600 in the normal population. Although the reasons for this association are not known, the absence of serum IgA may result in a significant reduction in the amount of antibody competing for antigens capable of combining with IgE. It is also possible that patients who lack IgA in their secretions may absorb intact proteins with an enhanced susceptibility to the formation of allergic responses. Allergic diseases in patients with selective IgA deficiency are often more difficult to control than the same allergies in other patients. It has also been the impression of several immunologists that these patients' symptoms are "triggered" by infection as well as by other environmental agents.

An increased incidence of antibody to bovine proteins, sometimes associated with circulating immune complexes, including bovine immunoglobulin, has been found in patients with selective IgA deficiency. This has been interpreted as providing additional evidence for abnormal gastrointestinal tract absorption. However, removal of milk from the diet has not been clearly associated with amelioration of symptoms.

A unique form of allergy exists in these patients. Certain patients with selective IgA deficiency develop high titers of antibody directed against IgA. Following the infusion of blood products, a few of these patients develop anaphylactic reactions. The incidence of antibodies directed against IgA in patients is much higher (30–40%) than the incidence of anaphylactoid transfusion reactions. Most patients who have anti-IgA antibodies have not had a history of γ-globulin or blood administration. Whether these antibodies are "autoantibodies" or antibodies resulting from sensitization is not certain. Possible sources of sensitization include breast milk feeding, passive transfer of maternal IgA, and cross-reaction with bovine immunoglobulin.

3. Gastrointestinal tract disease–An increased incidence of celiac disease has been noted. The disease may present at any time and is similar to celiac disease unassociated with IgA deficiency. Intestinal biopsies demonstrate an increase in IgM-producing cells. An anti-basement membrane antibody has been found with increased incidence.

Ulcerative colitis and regional enteritis have also been reported in association with selective IgA deficiency. Pernicious anemia has been reported in a significant number of patients. These patients have antibodies against both intrinsic factor and gastric parietal cells, which is not the case in hypogammaglobulinemia.

4. Autoimmune disease–A significant number of autoimmune disorders have been described in association with selective IgA deficiency. The disorders include systemic lupus erythematosus, rheumatoid arthritis, dermatomyositis, pernicious anemia, thyroiditis, Coombs-positive hemolytic anemia, Sjögren's syndrome, and chronic active hepatitis. Although the association of IgA deficiency and certain autoimmune disorders may be fortuitous, the increased incidence of IgA deficiency in systemic lupus erythematosus and rheumatoid arthritis is statistically significant (1:200–1:100).

The clinical presentation of patients with selective IgA deficiency and autoimmune disease does not appear to differ significantly from that of individuals with the identical disorder and normal or elevated levels of IgA. Because patients with selective IgA deficiency are capable of making normal amounts of antibody in the other immunoglobulin classes, they usually have characteristic autoantibodies associated with the specific autoimmune disease (antinuclear antibody, anti-DNA antibody, anti-parietal cell antibody, etc).

5. Selective IgA deficiency in apparently healthy adults–Because patients with selective IgA deficiency are capable of making normal amounts of antibody of the IgG and IgM classes, it is not surprising that many are entirely asymptomatic. However, long-term follow-up of some of these patients indicates that they may develop significant disease with time. There may be additional reasons why some patients remain asymptomatic. A small percentage of patients with selective IgA deficiency have normal amounts of secretory IgA and normal numbers of plasma cells containing IgA along the gastrointestinal tract. Some patients have increased amounts of low-molecular-weight (7S) IgM in their secretions. Finally, patients with selective IgA deficiency may have different exposures to pathogens and noxious agents in the environment.

6. Selective IgA deficiency and genetic factors–Both an autosomal recessive and an autosomal dominant mode of inheritance of IgA deficiency have been postulated. IgA deficiency appears with greater than normal frequency in families with other immunodeficiency disorders such as hypogammaglobulinemia. Partial deletion of the long or short arm of chromosome 18 (18q syndrome) or ring chromosome 18 have been described in selective IgA deficiency. However, many patients with abnormalities of chromosome 18 have normal levels of IgA in their serum. Selective IgA deficiency has been reported in one identical twin but not the other. In a study of familial IgA deficiency, an association with HLA-A2, B8, Dw3 was described. Other studies have shown an increase in HLA-A1, B8.

7. Selective IgA deficiency and malignancy–Selective IgA deficiency has been reported in association with reticulum cell sarcoma, squamous cell carcinoma of the esophagus and lung, and thymoma. Several patients with IgA deficiency and malignancy also had concomitant autoimmune disease and recurrent infection.

B. Laboratory Findings: Selective IgA deficiency has been defined as a serum level of less than 5 mg/dL of IgA, with normal or increased values of IgG, IgM, IgD, and IgE. As there are a number of methods for measuring immunoglobulin levels, each laboratory should establish standards for detection of low values.

Studies of B cell immunity indicate that these patients are capable of forming normal amounts of antibody following immunization. In most instances, absence of IgA in the serum is associated with absence of IgA in the secretions and with the presence of normal secretory component. Increased amounts of 7S IgM may be found in the serum and secretions. Abnormal κ/λ ratios are found. Evidence of abnormal antibody formation consists of an increased incidence of autoantibody, including antibodies directed against IgG, IgM, and IgA. The number of circulating peripheral blood B cells (including IgA-bearing B cells) is normal. Increased numbers of suppressor T cells have been reported in some patients.

Cell-mediated immunity is normal in most patients. Delayed hypersensitivity skin tests, the response of isolated peripheral blood lymphocytes to PHA and allogeneic cells, and the number of circulating T cells are normal. In a few patients, a depressed level of T cells, diminished production of T cell interferon, and decreased lymphocyte mitogenic responses have been found.

Other laboratory abnormalities are those typical of the associated diseases. Individuals who have chronic sinopulmonary infection may have abnormal x-rays and abnormal pulmonary function studies. Patients with IgA deficiency and celiac disease have abnormal gastrointestinal tract biopsies, abnormal D-xylose absorption, and an increased incidence of antibody directed against basement membrane. Patients with IgA deficiency and autoimmune disease have characteristic autoantibodies—eg, anti-DNA, antinuclear, anti-parietal cell, a positive Coombs test. An increase in circulating immune complexes has been described.

Immunologic Diagnosis

Serum IgA and secretory IgA are absent in most patients. Some individuals have normal levels of secretory IgA. Other individuals have increased amounts of serum and secretory 7S IgM. A patient has been described with normal serum IgA levels and diminished secretory IgA, with absent secretory component. The antibody response to specific antigens is normal. Studies of cell-mediated immunity, including delayed hypersensitivity skin tests, response of peripheral blood lymphocytes to PHA and allogeneic cells, and numbers of circulating T cells, are usually normal.

Differential Diagnosis

Selective IgA deficiency must be distinguished from other, more severe immunodeficiency disorders associated with IgA deficiency. Forty percent of patients with ataxia-telangiectasia have selective IgA deficiency. These patients usually have cellular immunodeficiency as well. If IgA deficiency is found during the first years of life, a definitive diagnosis may not be possible because the complete ataxia-telangiectasia syndrome may not be present until the patient is 4–5 years old. Other immunodeficiency

disorders that have been associated with selective IgA deficiency are chronic mucocutaneous candidiasis and cellular immunodeficiency with abnormal immunoglobulin synthesis (Nezelof's syndrome). A careful history should be obtained to rule out IgA deficiency secondary to drugs, eg, anticonvulsants or penicillamine.

Treatment

Patients with selective IgA deficiency *should not* be treated with γ-globulin therapy, since they are capable of forming normal amounts of antibody of other immunoglobulin classes and may recognize injected IgA as foreign. The use of γ-globulin in these patients enhances the risk of development of anti-IgA antibodies and subsequent anaphylactoid transfusion reactions. There is as yet no means by which the deficient IgA can be safely replaced. Patients with recurrent sinopulmonary infection should be treated aggressively with broad-spectrum antibiotics to avoid permanent pulmonary complications. Patients with systemic lupus erythematosus, rheumatoid arthritis, celiac disease, etc, respond to treatment (or not) in the same way as patients with the same diseases but no IgA deficiency. Transfusion reactions in patients with selective IgA deficiency may be minimized by several means. If the patient requires a blood transfusion, packed washed (3 times) red cells may be utilized. Although this does not completely eliminate the possibility of a transfusion reaction, it will decrease the risk. Alternatively, patients may be given blood from an IgA-deficient donor whose blood type matches the recipient's. Some immunologists have suggested frozen storage of the patient's own plasma and red cells for future use.

Complications & Prognosis

Patients have survived to the sixth or seventh decade without severe disease. Most individuals, however, become symptomatic during the first decade of life. Recognition of the potential complications and prompt therapy for associated diseases will increase longevity and reduce the morbidity rate. Regular follow-up examination is necessary for early detection of associated disorders and complications. A very few patients have developed normal IgA levels after years of IgA deficiency.

SELECTIVE IgM DEFICIENCY

Selective IgM deficiency is a rare disorder associated with the absence of IgM and normal levels of other immunoglobulin classes. Some patients are capable of normal antibody responses in the other immunoglobulin classes following specific immunization, whereas others respond poorly. Cell-mediated immunity appears to be intact, but detailed studies have not been reported in a sufficient number of cases.

The cause of selective IgM deficiency is not known. The absence of IgM with presence of IgG and

IgA appears to contradict the theory of sequential immunoglobulin development (see Chapter 5). The disorder has been described in both males and females.

Patients are susceptible to autoimmune disease and to overwhelming infection with polysaccharide-containing organisms (pneumococci, *H influenzae*). Insufficient data are available to determine appropriate therapy. It would appear logical to manage these patients in a manner similar to the way an infant is managed following splenectomy, with immediate antibiotic (penicillin or ampicillin) treatment of all infections or with continuous antibiotic treatment. If patients are unable to form antibody to specific antigens, γ-globulin therapy should be given.

SELECTIVE DEFICIENCY OF IgG SUBCLASSES

Patients have been described with varying combinations of deficiency of the 4 IgG subclasses (IgG1, IgG2, IgG3, IgG4). Depending on the severity of the defect, the total serum IgG level may be normal or decreased. Serum levels of IgM and IgA are normal. Some patients respond with normal antibody production following immunization whereas others do not. All of the patients described suffered from repeated pyogenic sinopulmonary infections with pneumococci, *H influenzae,* and *Staphylococcus aureus.* Several patients reached the second decade of life before a diagnosis was established. All responded to treatment with intramuscular γ-globulin. The diagnosis is suggested by demonstrating an abnormal electrophoretic migration of IgG or by specific quantitation of IgG subclasses. The latter is not routinely available.

Table 25—6. Evaluation of cell-mediated immunity.

Test	Comment
Total lymphocyte count	Normal at any age: >1200/μL.
Delayed hypersensitivity skin test	Used to evaluate specific immunity to antigens. Suggest *Candida,* mumps, PPD, and streptokinase-streptodornase. (4 units per 0.1 mL).
Lymphocyte response to mitogens (PHA), antigens, and allogeneic cells (mixed lymphocyte culture, MLC)	Used to evaluate T cell function. Results expressed as stimulated counts divided by resting counts equals stimulation index.
T cell rosettes (E rosettes)	Used to quantitate the number of circulating T cells. Normal: >60%.
Monoclonal antibody to T cells	Determines total number of T cells as well as T cell subsets, eg, helper/suppressor.
Migration inhibitory factor (MIF)	Used to detect lymphokine released from sensitized lymphocytes, which causes inhibition of macrophage migration.
Helper/suppressor T cell function	Determines helper/suppressor T cell function in vitro.

X–LINKED LYMPHOPROLIFERATIVE SYNDROME
(Duncan's Syndrome)

The X-linked lymphoproliferative syndrome is associated with Epstein-Barr virus (EBV) infection. Following infection with EBV, several outcomes are possible: (1) fatal infectious mononucleosis, (2) fatal infectious mononucleosis with lymphoma, (3) infectious mononucleosis with immunodeficiency, and (4) lymphoma (possibly). Some patients may lack antibody to EBV in spite of documented infection. Others have an impaired antibody response especially to Epstein-Barr virus nuclear antigen (EBNA). The immunodeficiency consists chiefly of acquired hypogammaglobulinemia. Other findings include agranulocytosis and cardiovascular or central nervous system birth defects.

CELLULAR (T CELL) IMMUNODEFICIENCY DISORDERS

Immunodeficiency disorders associated with isolated defective T cell immunity are rare. In most patients, defective T cell immunity is associated with abnormalities of B cell immunity as well. This reflects the necessary collaboration between T and B cells before normal antibody formation can occur. Almost all patients with complete T cell deficiency have some impairment of antibody formation. Some patients with T cell deficiency have normal levels of immunoglobulin but fail to produce specific antibody following immunization. These patients are considered to have a qualitative defect in antibody production.

Patients with cellular immunodeficiency disorders are susceptible to a variety of microbial agents including viral, fungal, and protozoal infections. The infections may be acute or chronic.

Screening tests utilized to evaluate T cell immunity are listed in Table 25–3. The availability of newer techniques for the evaluation of T cell immunity has resulted in more precise diagnosis (Table 25–6) in many instances. (See also Chapter 23.)

CONGENITAL THYMIC APLASIA
(DiGeorge Syndrome, Immunodeficiency With Hypoparathyroidism)

Major Immunologic Features
- Congenital aplasia or hypoplasia of the thymus.
- Lymphopenia reflects decreased numbers of T cells.
- Absent T cell function in peripheral blood.
- Variable antibody function.
- Successfully treated with thymus graft.

General Considerations

The DiGeorge syndrome is one of the few immunodeficiency disorders associated with symptoms immediately following birth. The complete syndrome consists of the following features: (1) abnormal facies consisting of low-set ears, "fish-shaped" mouth, hypertelorism, notched ear pinnae, micrognathia, and an antimongoloid slant of eyes; (2) hypoparathyroidism; (3) congenital heart disease; and (4) cellular immunodeficiency. Initial symptoms are related to associated abnormalities of the parathyroids and heart which may result in hypocalcemia and congestive heart failure. If the diagnosis of the DiGeorge syndrome is suspected because of these early clinical findings, then confirmation may be obtained by demonstrating defective T cell immunity. The importance of early diagnosis is related to the complete reconstitution of T cell immunity which can be achieved following a fetal thymus transplant.

Immunologic Pathogenesis

During the sixth to eighth weeks of intrauterine life, the thymus and parathyroid glands develop from epithelial evaginations of the third and fourth pharyngeal pouches. The thymus begins to migrate caudally during the 12th week of gestation. At the same time, the philtrum of the lip and the ear tubercle become differentiated along with other aortic arch structures. It is likely that the DiGeorge syndrome is the result of interference with normal embryologic development at approximately 12 weeks of gestation. In some patients, the thymus has not been absent but is in an abnormal location or is extremely small, though the histologic appearance is normal. It is possible that such patients represent "partial" DiGeorge syndrome in which hypertrophy of the thymus may take place with subsequent development of normal immunity. Following thymic transplantation, there is rapid T cell reconstitution, lack of GVH reaction, and lack of cellular chimerism, suggesting that patients lack a thymic humoral factor capable of expanding their own T cell immunity.

There is no inherited pattern associated with the DiGeorge syndrome. Recently, we have observed 4 DiGeorge patients with a history of maternal alcoholism. It is of interest that the fetal alcohol syndrome is associated with T cell deficiency.

Clinical Features

A. Symptoms and Signs: The most frequent presenting sign in patients with the DiGeorge syndrome is hypocalcemia in the first 24 hours of life which is resistant to standard therapy. Various types of congenital heart disease have been described, including interrupted aortic arch, septal defects, patent ductus arteriosus, and truncus arteriosus. Renal abnormalities may also be present. Some patients have the characteristic facial appearance described above. Patients who survive the immediate neonatal period may then develop recurrent or chronic infection with various viral, bacterial, fungal, or protozoal agents. Pneumonia, chronic infection of the mucous membranes with *Candida,* diarrhea, and failure to thrive may be present.

Spontaneous improvement of T cell immunity occasionally occurs. These patients are considered to have "partial" DiGeorge syndrome, but the reason for the spontaneous improvement in T cell immunity is not known. Patients have also been suspected of having the DiGeorge syndrome on the basis of hypocalcemia and congenital heart disease with or without the abnormal facies but have been found to have normal T cell immunity. Subsequently, these patients may develop severe T cell deficiency.

B. Laboratory Findings: Evaluation of T cell immunity can be performed immediately after birth in a patient suspected of having the DiGeorge syndrome. The lymphocyte count is usually low (less than 1200/μL) but may be normal or elevated. In the absence of stress during the newborn period, a lateral view of the anterior mediastinum may reveal absence of the thymic shadow, indicating failure of normal development. Delayed hypersensitivity skin tests are of little value during early infancy because sufficient time has not elapsed for sensitization to occur. T cell rosettes are markedly diminished in number, and the peripheral blood lymphocytes fail to respond to PHA and allogeneic cells.

Studies of antibody-mediated immunity are of little value in early infancy because immunoglobulins consist primarily of passively transferred maternal IgG. Although it is felt that some of these patients have a normal ability to produce specific antibody, the majority have some impairment of antibody formation. Sequential studies of both T and B cell immunity are necessary, since spontaneous remissions and spontaneous deterioration of immunity with time have been described.

A diagnosis of hypoparathyroidism is established by the demonstration of low serum calcium associated with an elevated serum phosphorus and an absence of parathyroid hormone. Congenital heart disease may be diagnosed immediately following birth and may be mild or severe. Other congenital abnormalities include esophageal atresia, bifid uvula, and urinary tract abnormalities.

Immunologic Diagnosis

T cell immunity is usually absent at birth as indicated by lymphocytopenia, depressed numbers of T cell rosettes, and no response of peripheral blood lymphocytes to PHA and allogeneic cells. Rarely, normal T cell immunity may develop with time, or previously normal T cell immunity may become deficient. In some patients, studies of T cell function are variable and range from depressed T cell numbers with normal function to a complete absence of T cell immunity.

Some patients have normal B cell immunity as indicated by normal levels of immunoglobulins and a normal antibody response following immunization. However, some patients with the DiGeorge syndrome have abnormal immunoglobulin values and fail to make specific antibody following immunization. Live attenuated viral vaccines should be used for immunization.

Rarely, a patient may present with the immunologic features of severe combined immunodeficiency, ie, absent T and B cell immunity. The presence of hypocalcemia or congenital abnormalities of the third and fourth aortic arch establishes the diagnosis.

Differential Diagnosis

Many infants with severe congenital heart disease and subsequent congestive heart failure develop transient hypocalcemia. These infants should be suspected of having the DiGeorge syndrome. When the characteristic facial features are found, in addition to the hypocalcemia and congenital heart disease, an even stronger suspicion is present. Studies of T cell immunity will usually establish a diagnosis except in those infants with the DiGeorge syndrome who have developed effective T cell immunity with time. It is essential that all infants with congenital heart disease and hypocalcemia be followed until they are at least 1 year of age. The hypocalcemia associated with the DiGeorge syndrome is usually permanent, in contrast to that seen in congenital heart disease with congestive heart failure. Congenital hypoparathyroidism is usually not associated with congenital heart disease. However, both in this disorder and in the DiGeorge syndrome, low to absent levels of parathyroid hormone are present and the patients are resistant to the standard treatment of hypocalcemia. Low parathyroid hormone levels may also be found in transient hypocalcemia in infancy. Two patients with DiGeorge syndrome are known to have had spontaneous remissions of hypoparathyroidism.

Immunologic studies in a patient with the DiGeorge syndrome and in one with severe combined immunodeficiency disease may be identical in the newborn period. The presence of hypocalcemia, congenital heart disease, and an abnormal facies differentiates the DiGeorge syndrome from severe combined immunodeficiency disease.

Patients with the fetal alcohol syndrome may have similar facial and cardiac abnormalities as well as recurrent infections associated with decreased T cell immunity.

Treatment

A fetal thymus transplant should be given as soon as possible following diagnosis. This can result in permanent reconstitution of T cell immunity. The technique of thymus transplantation varies from local implantation in the rectus abdominis muscle to implantation of a thymus in a Millipore chamber. The thymus may also be minced and injected intraperitoneally. Because patients with the DiGeorge syndrome have been observed to develop a GVH reaction following administration of viable immunocompetent lymphocytes, fetal thymus glands older than 14 weeks' gestation should not be utilized. Thymocytes from glands younger than 14 weeks' gestation may lack

cells capable of GVH reaction but can provide needed stem cells or thymic epithelial cells for further T cell development. Patients have been successfully treated with thymosin and thymus epithelial transplants.

The hypocalcemia is rarely controlled by calcium supplementation alone. Calcium should be administered orally in conjunction with vitamin D or parathyroid hormone.

Congenital heart disease frequently results in congestive heart failure and may require immediate surgical correction. If surgery is performed prior to the availability of a fetal thymus transplant, any blood given should be irradiated with 3000 R to prevent a GVH reaction.

Complications & Prognosis

Prolonged survivals have been reported following successful thymus transplantation or spontaneous remission of immunodeficiency. Sudden death may occur in untreated patients or in patients initially found to have normal T cell immunity. Congenital heart disease may be severe, and the infant may not survive surgical correction. Death from GVH disease following blood transfusions has been observed in patients in whom a diagnosis of the DiGeorge syndrome was not suspected.

CHRONIC MUCOCUTANEOUS CANDIDIASIS
(With & Without Endocrinopathy)

Major Immunologic Features

- Onset may be either with chronic candidal infection of the skin and mucous membranes or with endocrinopathy.
- Delayed hypersensitivity skin tests to *Candida* antigen are negative in spite of chronic candidal infection.

General Considerations (See also Chapter 32.)

Chronic mucocutaneous candidiasis affects both males and females. A familial occurrence has been reported, suggesting an autosomal recessive inheritance. The disorder is associated with a selective defect in T cell immunity, resulting in susceptibility to chronic candidal infection. B cell immunity is intact, resulting in a normal antibody response to *Candida* and, in some patients, the development of autoantibodies associated with idiopathic endocrinopathies. The disorder may appear as early as 1 year of age or may be delayed until the second decade.

Various theories have been proposed to explain the association of chronic candidal infection and the development of endocrinopathy. Initially it was felt that hypoparathyroidism predisposed to candidal infection. Subsequently it was found that many patients developed severe candidal infection without evidence of hypoparathyroidism. A basic autoimmune disorder has been postulated with the suggestion that the thymus also functions as an endocrine organ and that the thymus and other endocrine glands are involved in an autoimmune destructive process.

Clinical Features

A. Symptoms and Signs: The initial presentation of chronic mucocutaneous candidiasis may be either chronic candidal infection or the appearance of an idiopathic endocrinopathy. If candidal infection appears first, several years to several decades may elapse before endocrinopathy occurs. Other patients may present with the endocrinopathy first and subsequently develop candidal infection. Candidal infection may involve the mucous membranes, skin, nails, and, in older patients, the vagina. In severe forms, infection of the skin occurs in a "stocking and glove" distribution and is associated with the formation of granulomatous lesions. Patients are usually not susceptible to systemic candidal infection. Rarely, they may develop infection with other fungal agents.

Other symptoms are related to the development of a specific endocrinopathy. Hypoparathyroidism is the most common and is associated with hypocalcemia and tetany. Addison's disease is the next most common. A variety of other endocrinopathies have been reported, including hypothyroidism, diabetes mellitus, and pernicious anemia. Occasionally, there is a history of acute or chronic hepatitis preceding the onset of endocrinopathy.

B. Laboratory Findings: Studies of T cell immunity reveal a specific though variable defect in T cell immunity. Patients usually have a normal total lymphocyte count; isolated peripheral blood lymphocytes respond to PHA and to allogeneic cells and to antigens other than *Candida*. The least severe T cell defect is an absent delayed hypersensitivity skin test response to *Candida* antigen in the presence of documented chronic candidiasis. Other patients may have additional defects, including the inability to form migration inhibitory factor (MIF) in response to *Candida* antigens or inability of lymphocytes to be activated by *Candida* antigens. B cell immunity is intact, as demonstrated by the presence of normal or elevated levels of immunoglobulins, increased amounts of antibody directed against *Candida,* and autoantibody formation. Plasma inhibitors of T cell function and increased numbers of suppressor T cells have been reported in some cases. Isolated cases have been reported with chemotaxis or macrophage abnormalities.

Other laboratory abnormalities are related to the presence of endocrinopathies. Hypoparathyroidism is associated with decreased serum calcium, elevated serum phosphorus, and low or absent parathyroid hormone. Increased skin pigmentation may herald the onset of Addison's disease prior to disturbances in serum electrolytes. An ACTH stimulation test is useful to document the presence of Addison's disease. Other abnormalities of endocrine function include hypothyroidism, abnormal vitamin B_{12} absorption, and diabetes mellitus. Abnormal liver function studies may indicate chronic hepatitis. Occasionally, iron deficiency is present which, when treated, results in improvement in the candidal infection. Autoantibodies associated with specific endocrinopathy are usually present before and during the development of endocrine dysfunction. They may be absent when complete endocrine deficiency is present. Patients should be evaluated on a yearly basis for endocrine function because the endocrinopathies are progressive.

Immunologic Diagnosis

Major aspects of T cell immunity are normal, as indicated by a normal response of peripheral blood lymphocytes to PHA and allogeneic cells. Activation of lymphocytes and MIF production in response to antigens other than *Candida* is normal. T cell rosettes are present in normal numbers. In some patients, only the delayed hypersensitivity skin test response to *Candida* antigens is absent. Other patients have an absence of MIF production or an absence of lymphocyte activation by *Candida* antigens. Plasma inhibitors of cellular immunity may also occur. B cell immunity is intact, with normal production of antibody to *Candida.*

Differential Diagnosis

Children with chronic candidal infection of the mucous membranes may have a variety of immunodeficiency disorders. Detailed studies of B and T cell immunity differentiate between chronic mucocutaneous candidiasis, in which there is a selective deficiency of T cell immunity to *Candida* antigens, and other disorders where T cell immunity may be completely deficient. Patients with the DiGeorge syndrome (thymic aplasia and hypoparathyroidism) present early in infancy, whereas chronic mucocutaneous candidiasis with hypoparathyroidism is a disorder of later onset and progressive nature. Patients with late-onset idiopathic endocrinopathies should be considered to have chronic mucocutaneous candidiasis even though candidal infection is not present at the time of diagnosis. These patients may develop chronic candidal infection as late as 10–15 years after the onset of endocrinopathy.

Treatment

There is no treatment to prevent the development of idiopathic endocrinopathy. The physician must be alert to the gradual development of endocrine dysfunction—particularly Addison's disease, which is the major cause of death. Chronic skin and mucous membrane candidal infection is difficult to treat. Topical treatment with a variety of antifungal agents has been attempted but has usually been unsuccessful. Local miconazole therapy has provided control in some patients in recent trials. This drug has also been used intravenously on an experimental basis with some success. Courses of intravenous amphotericin B have resulted in improvement in a significant number of patients, but this form of treatment is limited by the renal toxicity of the drug. Oral clotrimazole is occasionally of benefit. Oral ketoconazole, a new experimental antifungal agent, offers additional promise.

The combination of transfer factor therapy subcutaneously and amphotericin B intravenously has been successful in approximately 50% of patients. Transfer factor is obtained from normal *Candida* skin test-positive donors and administered before or during—or both before and during—amphotericin therapy. Two patients refractory to all other forms of therapy were successfully treated with fetal thymus transplants.

Complications & Prognosis

Patients may survive to the second or third decade but usually experience extensive morbidity. Individuals with severe candidal infection of the mucous membranes and skin develop serious psychologic difficulties. Systemic infection with *Candida* usually does not occur. Rarely, patients may develop systemic infection with other fungal agents. Hypoparathyroidism is difficult to manage, and complications are frequent. Addison's disease is the major cause of death and may develop suddenly without previous symptoms.

COMBINED ANTIBODY–MEDIATED (B CELL) & CELL–MEDIATED (T CELL) IMMUNODEFICIENCY DISEASES

Combined immunodeficiency diseases are due to various causes and are of variable severity. Defective T cell and B cell immunity may be complete, as in severe combined immunodeficiency disease, or partial, as in ataxia-telangiectasia. The association of distinct clinical features in ataxia-telangiectasia serves to further differentiate the disorder from severe combined immunodeficiency disease and also suggests that the causes of these disorders are not the same. Enzymatic deficiencies in the purine pathway have been described in association with combined immunodeficiency disease. This discovery has provided additional evidence for a diverse origin of combined immunodeficiency diseases.

Studies of both T and B cell immunity are necessary to completely evaluate patients with combined immunodeficiency disorders (Tables 25–3, 25–5, and 25–6). In addition, analysis of red and white cell enzymes (adenosine deaminase and nucleoside phosphorylase) may provide additional information for appropriate classification.

The onset of symptoms in patients with combined immunodeficiency diseases is usually early in infancy. They are susceptible to a very wide spectrum of microbial agents. Immunotherapy is frequently difficult and often not available.

SEVERE COMBINED IMMUNODEFICIENCY DISEASE

Major Immunologic Features
- Onset of symptoms by 6 months of age, with recurrent viral, bacterial, fungal, and protozoal infection.
- Occurs in X-linked, autosomal, and sporadic forms.
- Complete absence of both T and B cell immunity.

General Considerations

The immunologic deficiency includes complete absence of T and B cell immunity, resulting in early susceptibility to infection with virtually any type of microbial agent. Patients rarely survive beyond 1 year of age before succumbing to one or more opportunistic infections. The disease is inherited in 2 forms: an X-linked recessive form (X-linked lymphopenic agammaglobulinemia) and an autosomal recessive form (Swiss type lymphopenic agammaglobulinemia). The exact incidence of this disorder is not known, and many patients die before the diagnosis is made. Because the immune system of patients with this disorder may be made completely normal by bone marrow transplantation, early diagnosis is urgent to prevent irreversible complications.

Immunologic Pathogenesis

The basic defect is not known, but it has been postulated that severe combined immunodeficiency disease is a result of failure of differentiation of stem cells into T and B cells. The successful use of histocompatible bone marrow transplantation has provided support for the concept of a basic stem cell defect. However, some authors argue that the defect may reside in failure of the thymus and bursa equivalent to develop normally. Normal stem cells would not be processed into T and B cells under these circumstances. Others argue for an intrinsic defect within the thymus based on in vitro maturation of patients' T cells when cultured in the presence of thymus epithelium, immature T cells defined by monoclonal antibody, and significant numbers of B cells (primarily X-linked form).

Clinical Features

A. Symptoms and Signs: Patients with severe combined immunodeficiency disease usually succumb to overwhelming infection within the first year of life. Early findings include failure to thrive, chronic diarrhea, persistent thrush (oral candidiasis), pneumonia, chronic otitis media, and sepsis. The microbial agents which result in acute and chronic infection include viruses, bacteria, fungi, and protozoa. Infants with this disease are particularly susceptible to *Candida*, cytomegalovirus, and *Pneumocystis carinii* infection. When smallpox immunization was administered routinely, many of these infants developed progressive vaccinia. Death from progressive poliomyelitis following attenuated viral immunization has been documented. During the first several months of life, patients may be partially protected from bacterial infections by the passive transfer of maternal IgG. They subsequently develop susceptibility to a wide variety of gram-positive and gram-negative organisms.

As these patients entirely lack T cell immunity, they are susceptible to GVH reactions which may develop following maternal infusion of cells during gestation or delivery, infusion of viable cells in the form of blood transfusions, or attempts at immunotherapy. (See section on GVH disease.) The presence of an acute or chronic GVH reaction may complicate the diagnosis of severe combined immunodeficiency disease. Some of these patients have been misdiagnosed as having an acute viral illness, histiocytosis X, or other chronic disorders.

Physical findings relate to the degree and type of infections present. Pneumonia, otitis media, thrush, dehydration, skin infections, and developmental retardation may be present. Lymphoid tissue and hepatosplenomegaly are absent unless the disease is complicated by a GVH reaction.

B. Laboratory Findings: All tests of T cell immunity are abnormal. The thymus shadow is absent, lymphopenia is usually present, T cell rosettes are markedly depressed, and the response of isolated peripheral blood lymphocytes to PHA and allogeneic cells is absent. Rarely, some patients have a proliferative response to allogeneic cells. Delayed hypersensitivity skin tests are not useful for diagnosis because in most cases insufficient time has elapsed for cellular sensitization to occur. During the first 5–6 months of life, a diagnosis of severe combined immunodeficiency disease may be difficult to establish because of the presence of maternal IgG. However, most normal infants who have had repeated infection will develop significant amounts of serum IgM or IgA (or both). If the diagnosis is doubtful, it may be necessary to specifically immunize a patient and determine specific antibody responses. Patients suspected of having immunodeficiency diseases should never be immunized with attenuated live virus vaccines. In the majority of patients with severe combined immunodeficiency, B cells are absent or markedly reduced from birth. A subgroup of patients exists in which B cells may be elevated. Adenosine deaminase activity is normal.

Biopsy of lymphoid tissue is rarely necessary to establish a diagnosis. If biopsies are obtained, they should be performed cautiously because secondary infection is frequent. Biopsy of lymph nodes (if they can be found) demonstrates lymph nodes severely depleted of lymphocytes, without corticomedullary differentiation, and without follicle formation. Biopsy of the intestinal tract shows a complete absence of plasma cells.

Patients who have pulmonary infiltrates that do not respond to antibiotic therapy or which are associated with rapid respiration and a low P_{O_2} should be suspected of having *P carinii* infection. Because this disorder can be treated, it is important to establish an early diagnosis. Some debate exists about whether the diagnosis is best made by means of concentrated sputum examination, bronchoscopy, needle biopsy, or open lung biopsy. In most instances, open lung biopsy provides the most complete information. Cytomegalovirus infection should be considered in all patients. Cultures of blood, mucous membranes, and stool for predominant bacterial organisms may be important in determining subsequent treatment. Individuals who have been inadvertently immunized with live poliovaccine should have stools cultured for poliovirus.

Patients frequently have anemia and lymphopenia. Complications such as chronic systemic infection and GVH reaction may result in multiple abnormalities including elevation of liver enzymes, jaundice, chronic diarrhea with subsequent electrolyte abnormalities and dehydration, pulmonary infiltrates, cardiac irregularities, and abnormal cerebrospinal fluid analysis.

Immunologic Diagnosis

Severe combined immunodeficiency disease is associated with complete absence of T and B cell immunity. Evaluation of T cell immunity reveals lymphopenia, absence of thymus shadow, depressed T cell rosettes, absence of peripheral blood lymphocyte responses to PHA, allogeneic cells, and antigens, and absence of response to delayed hypersensitivity skin tests. Evaluation of B cell immunity reveals hypogammaglobulinemia, absence of antibody response following immunization, and depressed or absent numbers of circulating B cells (rarely, elevated B cells).

Differential Diagnosis

Severe combined immunodeficiency disease must be differentiated from other immunodeficiency disorders with defects in T and B cell immunity. The early onset of symptoms and the complete absence of both T and B cell immunity found in severe combined immunodeficiency disease usually result in a specific diagnosis. Combined immunodeficiency associated with absence of an enzyme in the purine pathway (adenosine deaminase) has been described. This disorder is usually less severe initially clinically and immunologically. The presence of a GVH reaction in severe combined immunodeficiency may complicate the diagnosis. If chronic dermatitis is present in association with hepatosplenomegaly and histiocytic infiltration, a mistaken diagnosis of Letterer-Siwe syndrome may be made. Some patients may present with chronic diarrhea and pigmentary skin changes resulting in an erroneous diagnosis of acrodermatitis enteropathica. (See discussion of GVH disease.)

Treatment

Aggressive diagnostic measures are necessary to establish the cause of chronic infection before treatment can be instituted. Open lung biopsy should be performed if *P carinii* infection is suspected. The treatment of choice for *Pneumocystis* consists of pentamidine. Recently, trimethoprim-sulfamethoxazole has been used, but experience is limited and there are no studies to indicate that it is effective in combined immunodeficiency. Specific antibiotic treatment is necessary for suspected bacterial infection. Superficial candidal infection is treated with topical antifungal agents, but systemic infection requires intravenous amphotericin B therapy.

Complications must be avoided. Live attenuated viral immunization should not be performed. Blood products containing potentially viable lymphocytes should be irradiated with 3000–6000 R prior to administration. (See section on GVH disease.)

During the initial period of evaluation, γ-globulin may be administered in doses of 0.2–0.4 mL/kg given once each month or as frequently as once each week. Definitive treatment consists of transplantation of histocompatible bone marrow. Because of the inheritance of the histocompatibility antigens, the usual donor for a bone marrow transplant is a histocompatible sibling. The bone marrow must be matched by both the HLA and MLC tests. (See Chapters 6, 14, and 23.) Despite careful matching, a GVH reaction may develop. Several techniques have been utilized in performing bone marrow transplantation, including intraperitoneal injection and intravenous infusion of filtered bone marrow. The dose of bone marrow cells administered has varied, but as few as 1000 nucleated cells per kilogram have resulted in successful immunologic reconstitution. Transplantation of unmatched marrow has always resulted in a fatal GVH reaction. Recently, some investigators have utilized HLA-nonidentical, MLC-identical bone marrow from nonsibling donors, or MLC-nonidentical marrow prepared by lectin separation of cells to reduce GVH potential. Insufficient data exist about the efficacy of this method.

In the absence of a histocompatible bone marrow donor, other forms of therapy have been utilized. Long-term survivors of fetal liver transplants (less than 8 weeks' gestation) and of fetal thymus transplantation (less than 14 weeks' gestation) have been observed. In both of these techniques, the use of older fetal liver or thymus will result in a fatal GVH reaction, probably because of the presence of mature immunocompetent cells. Thymus epithelial transplants and combined fetal liver and thymus transplants have also been used.

Complications & Prognosis

Patients with severe combined immunodeficiency disease are unusually susceptible to infection with many microbial agents and will succumb prior to 1 year of age if untreated. If the diagnosis is not made immediately, the patient may receive live attenuated viral immunization and succumb to progressive vaccinia or poliomyelitis. In other instances, patients may receive unirradiated blood products and die from complications of GVH disease. Following successful bone marrow transplantation, 10-year survivals with maintenance of normal T and B cell function have been recorded. Patients have survived as long as 1 year

following fetal liver transplantation and as long as 6 years following fetal thymus transplantation. The reconstitution of immunity in patients receiving fetal organ transplantation has not been complete.

CELLULAR IMMUNODEFICIENCY WITH ABNORMAL IMMUNOGLOBULIN SYNTHESIS
(Nezelof's Syndrome)

Major Immunologic Features
- Susceptibility to viral, bacterial, fungal, and protozoal infection.
- Absent to depressed T cell immunity.
- Various degrees of B cell immunodeficiency associated with various combinations of increased, normal, or decreased immunoglobulin levels.

General Considerations
The disorders included in this classification are diverse and probably do not all have the same cause. Consistent features include marked deficiency of T cell immunity and varying degrees of deficiency of B cell immunity. Disorders with specific clinical symptomatology such as ataxia-telangiectasia and Wiskott-Aldrich syndrome or associated with enzyme deficiency such as adenosine deaminase are excluded. Part of the difficulty in defining disorders in this category relates to recent developments in the diagnosis of T cell immunity which were not available when some of these cases were first reported. Most of the cases included in this category are sporadic and do not have a definite inherited pattern.

Immunologic Pathogenesis
The cause is not known. There appears to be no specific genetic pattern, and the disease is sporadic in distribution and occurs in both males and females. The presence of moderate to severe deficiencies of T cell immunity with varying degrees of B cell immunodeficiency suggests that the primary defect is within the thymus. It is possible that this disorder is the result of thymic hypoplasia with deficient interaction of T and B cells and subsequent abnormal antibody formation.

Clinical Features
A. Symptoms and Signs: Patients are susceptible to recurrent fungal, protozoal, viral, and bacterial illnesses. The spectrum of infection is similar to that found in patients with congenital hypogammaglobulinemia and other forms of combined immunodeficiency. Patients frequently have marked lymphadenopathy and hepatosplenomegaly, in contrast to patients with congenital hypogammaglobulinemia and severe combined immunodeficiency disease.

B. Laboratory Findings: Studies of T cell immunity are abnormal, but the degree of deficiency may vary. Lymphopenia may be present, but occasionally a normal lymphocyte count is obtained. T cells are moderately to markedly decreased. The lymphocyte response to PHA and specific antigens may be absent or slightly depressed, and the lymphocyte response to allogeneic cells may vary from nil to normal. B cell immunity is abnormal. The 5 immunoglobulin classes may be present in varying combinations of increased, normal, or decreased amounts. Total circulating B cells are usually present in normal numbers, although the distribution among various types of surface immunoglobulin–bearing B cells may vary. Despite the presence of normal or elevated levels of immunoglobulin, there is no antibody response following specific immunization. Antibody to specific substances may be found, however, indicating that at one time some of these patients may have been able to form antibody. Isohemagglutinins may be absent or normal, and the Schick test may be reactive or nonreactive.

Biopsy of lymphoid tissue in these patients may reveal the presence of plasma cells. The lymph nodes may be large and may contain numerous histiocytes and macrophages with granuloma formation.

Immunologic Diagnosis

The principal immunologic features in this group of disorders consist of moderate to marked reductions in numbers of total lymphocytes and T cells and a diminished response of peripheral blood lymphocytes to PHA, allogeneic cells, and specific antigens. There is usually no response to delayed hypersensitivity skin tests. Variable degrees of B cell deficiency are present, consisting of varying combinations of elevated, normal, or low levels of specific immunoglobulin classes. The antibody response to specific antigens is usually absent. Some evidence of prior antibody formation may be found, eg, nonreactive Schick test, isohemagglutinins. The number of total circulating B cells is usually normal.

Differential Diagnosis

Because there is a lack of uniformity in the clinical and laboratory presentation of these patients, it is necessary to rule out other disorders with definite clinical or laboratory associations. The clinical features of ataxia-telangiectasia are usually present by 3–4 years of age, and an elevated alpha-fetoprotein is usually present by 1 year of age. Patients with Wiskott-Aldrich syndrome have thrombocytopenia from birth and can be excluded on this basis. Patients with severe combined immunodeficiency disease have complete absence of T and B cell immunity. Immunodeficiency disorders associated with enzyme deficiencies may have a similar presentation and are excluded on the basis of enzyme analysis of red or white blood cells. Patients with short-limbed dwarfism are excluded on the basis of characteristic clinical and radiologic features. Patients with cellular immunodeficiency and abnormal immunoglobulin synthesis do not develop endocrine abnormalities and can therefore be distinguished from patients with the DiGeorge syndrome and chronic mucocutaneous candidiasis who are capable of normal antibody synthesis.

Treatment

Aggressive treatment of infection is necessary. Patients failing to show an antibody response after immunization (even if immunoglobulin levels are normal) should receive monthly γ-globulin administration. (See treatment section, congenital hypogammaglobulinemia.) Continuous broad-spectrum antibiotic coverage may be useful. Postural drainage is important to prevent chronic lung disease.

Although histocompatible bone marrow transplantation would appear to be curative in these patients, few successful cases have been reported. This appears to be due to lack of histocompatible donors rather than the complications of transplantation. Transfer factor therapy has been utilized with some success. Thymus transplantation has been reported to provide reconstitution of T cell immunity and partial reconstitution of B cell immunity.

Patients should not be immunized with attenuated viral vaccines. All blood products should be irradiated with 3000 R.

Complications & Prognosis

Patients do not develop the severe complications observed in severe combined immunodeficiency disease. GVH reaction has not been reported. Some of these patients, however, may develop progressive encephalitis following live attenuated viral immunization. Chronic lung disease, chronic fungal infection, and later development of malignancy are long-term complications. Survival until age 18 has been reported.

IMMUNODEFICIENCY WITH ATAXIA–TELANGIECTASIA

Major Immunologic Features

- Clinical onset by 2 years of age.
- Complete syndrome consists of ataxia, telangiectasia, and recurrent sinopulmonary infection.
- Selective IgA deficiency present in 40% of patients.

General Considerations

Ataxia-telangiectasia is inherited in an autosomal manner. It is associated with characteristic features, including ataxia, telangiectasis, recurrent sinopulmonary infection, and abnormalities in both T and B cell immunity. The disorder was first considered to be primarily a neurologic disease and is now known to involve the neurologic, vascular, endocrine, and immune systems.

Immunologic Pathogenesis

There is no unifying theory which explains the multisystem abnormalities present in ataxia-telangiectasia. A defect in the development of mesoderm has been postulated but not confirmed. Other abnormalities described that may account for some of the multisystem disorders are an abnormal collagen deficient in hydroxylysine, elevated alpha-fetoprotein indicative of a defect in organ maturation, enhanced susceptibility of cells to radiation damage, and defective DNA repair. Clones of lymphocytes with structural rearrangement of the long arm (q) of chromosome 14 have been consistently found. The disorder is progressive, with both the neurologic abnormalities and the immunologic deficiency becoming more severe with time.

Clinical Features

A. Symptoms and Signs: Ataxia may have its onset at 9 months to 1 year of age or may be delayed as long as 4–6 years. Telangiectasia is usually present by 2 years of age but has been delayed until 8–9 years of age. As patients become older, additional neurologic symptoms develop, consisting of choreoathetoid movements, dysconjugate gaze, and extrapyramidal and posterior column signs. Telangiectasia may develop first in the bulbar conjunctiva and subsequently appear on the bridge of the nose, the ears, or in the antecubital fossae. Recurrent sinopulmonary infections may begin early in life, or patients may remain relatively symptom-free for 10 years or more. Susceptibility to infection includes both viral and bacterial infections. Secondary sexual characteristics rarely develop in patients at puberty, and most patients appear to develop mental retardation with time.

B. Laboratory Findings: Varying degrees of abnormalities in T and B cell immunity have been described. Lymphopenia may be present, T cells may be normal or decreased, and the response of lymphocytes to PHA and allogeneic cells may be normal or decreased. There may be no response to delayed hypersensitivity skin tests. Serum IgA is absent in approximately 40% of patients. In still other patients, IgE may be absent. Antibody responses to specific antigens may be depressed. The number of circulating B cells is usually normal.

Other laboratory abnormalities relate to associated findings. Abnormalities have been shown on pneumoencephalography, electromyography, and electroencephalography. Endocrine studies have shown decreased 17-ketosteroids and increased FSH excretion. An insulin-resistant form of diabetes has been described. Liver function tests are abnormal. An increased incidence of autoantibodies has been found. Cytotoxic antibodies to brain and thymus have been found. Increased levels of alpha-fetoprotein have been described in all patients tested and may be specific for this disease. Unfortunately, alpha-fetoprotein levels are high in normal infants until 1 year of age. Many patients have elevated titers to EB virus antigens.

Immunologic Diagnosis

Selective IgA deficiency is found in 40% of patients. IgE deficiency and variable deficiencies of other immunoglobulins may also be found. The antibody response to specific antigens may be depressed. Variable degrees of T cell deficiency are observed

which usually become more severe with advancing age.

Differential Diagnosis

If the onset of recurrent infection occurs before the development of ataxia or telangiectasia, it may be difficult to differentiate this disorder from cellular immunodeficiency with abnormal immunoglobulin synthesis. If a patient has a gradual onset of cerebellar ataxia unassociated with telangiectasis and immunologic abnormalities, one may have to wait years before a diagnosis can be established with certainty. Usually, by age 4, the characteristic recurrent sinopulmonary infections, immunologic abnormalities, ataxia, and telangiectasia are present concomitantly. Because selective IgA deficiency is the most common immunodeficiency disorder detected and many patients with selective IgA deficiency have no associated symptomatology, one may have to wait several years before a diagnosis of ataxia-telangiectasia can be excluded. Alpha-fetoprotein levels are normal in patients with IgA deficiency.

Treatment

Early treatment of recurrent sinopulmonary infections is essential to avoid permanent complications. Some patients may benefit from continuous broad-spectrum antibiotic therapy. In patients who develop chronic lung disease, physical therapy with postural drainage is of benefit. Transfer factor has been utilized in some patients without apparent benefit. Successful bone marrow transplantation has not been performed, but this is probably related to the lack of histocompatible bone marrow donors. Fetal thymus transplantation has provided some benefit in a limited number of patients. Thymosin therapy has been used to treat a limited number of patients. Monthly infusions of frozen plasma have been suggested as a source of passively administered antibody.

Attenuated viral vaccines should not be given. All blood products should be irradiated with 3000 R prior to administration.

Complications & Prognosis

Patients who survive for long periods of time develop progressive deterioration of neurologic and immunologic functions. The oldest patients have reached the fifth decade of life. The chief causes of death are overwhelming infection and the development of lymphoreticular or epithelial cell malignancies. Leukemias with associated abnormalities of chromosome 14 have been reported. As these patients reach the second decade, morbidity becomes severe, with chronic lung disease, mental retardation, and physical debility the principal problems. Heterozygote carriers as well as family members have an increased incidence of malignancy.

IMMUNODEFICIENCY WITH THROMBOCYTOPENIA, ECZEMA, & RECURRENT INFECTION
(Wiskott-Aldrich Syndrome)

Major Immunologic Features
- Complete syndrome consists of eczema, recurrent pyogenic infection, and thrombocytopenia.
- Can be diagnosed at birth by demonstration of thrombocytopenia in a male infant with a positive family history.
- Serum IgM usually low with elevated serum IgA and IgE.

General Considerations
Patients may become symptomatic early in life, with bleeding secondary to thrombocytopenia. Subsequently they develop recurrent bacterial infection in the form of otitis media, pneumonia, and meningitis. Eczema usually appears by 1 year of age. The disease appears to be progressive, with increasing susceptibility to infection. It is inherited in an X-linked manner.

Immunologic Pathogenesis
The earliest abnormalities found in patients are thrombocytopenia and hypercatabolism of immunoglobulin. A hypothesis linking thrombocytopenia, eczema, and recurrent infection is not available. It has been suggested that the α granules of platelets and macrophages of patients and carriers are abnormal. Another suggestion is that the inability of patients to respond to polysaccharide antigens results in immunologic attrition. This does not explain the thrombocytopenia or eczema.

Clinical Features
A. Symptoms and Signs: Recurrent infection usually does not start until after 6 months of age. Patients are susceptible to infection with capsular polysaccharide-type organisms (eg, pneumococcus, meningococcus, and *H influenzae*) and may develop meningitis, otitis media, pneumonia, and sepsis. As they become older, they become susceptible to infection with other types of organisms and may have recurrent viral infection.

Eczema is usually present by 1 year of age and is typical in distribution. It may be associated with other allergic manifestations. Frequently, it is secondarily infected.

Thrombocytopenia is present at birth and may result in early manifestations of bleeding. Bleeding usually increases during episodes of infection and is associated with a decrease in the platelet count. The bleeding tendency becomes less severe as the child becomes older.

B. Laboratory Findings: Thrombocytopenia is present at birth. The platelet count may range from 5000 to 100,000/μL. Platelets are small in Wiskott-Aldrich syndrome, in contrast to other disorders associated with thrombocytopenia, eg, idiopathic thrombocytopenia, where they are increased in size.

Anemia is frequently present and may be Coombs-positive. An increased incidence of chronic renal disease has been reported. Studies of B cell immunity demonstrate normal IgG, decreased IgM, increased IgA and IgE, low to absent isohemagglutinins, normal numbers of B cells, and an inability to respond to immunization with polysaccharide antigen. Paraproteins are frequently observed. T cell immunity is usually intact early in the disease but may decline with advancing years.

Immunologic Diagnosis
The earliest detected immunologic abnormality consists of hypercatabolism of immunoglobulins. The typical pattern of low to absent isohemagglutinins, low IgM, and elevated IgA and IgE may not be present until 1 year of age. B cells are normal in number. Patients fail to form antibody following immunization with polysaccharide antigens. T cell immunity may be normal initially and show gradual attrition with advancing age.

Differential Diagnosis
When the complete syndrome is present, there is little confusion in diagnosis. Idiopathic thrombocytopenia in a male child may be difficult to differentiate from Wiskott-Aldrich syndrome. In idiopathic thrombocytopenia, the immunoglobulins, isohemagglutinins, and response to polysaccharide antigens are normal. Male patients with eczema and recurrent infection have normal immunologic studies and normal platelet counts, although they may have elevated IgA and IgE.

Treatment
Infections should be treated promptly and aggressively with antibiotics to cover the most common organisms. Corticosteroids should not be used to treat the thrombocytopenia as they will enhance the susceptibility to infection. Splenectomy has been fatal in virtually all patients. Treatment of immunodeficiency is difficult. Infusions of frozen plasma have been utilized on a monthly basis as a source of passive protection. γ-Globulin is not used because of the thrombocytopenia and potential bleeding at injection sites. Transfer factor has been advocated, but controlled studies have not been performed. Successful bone marrow transplantation has been performed.

Complications & Prognosis
With aggressive therapy, the long-term prognosis has improved. Immediate complications are related to bleeding episodes and acute infection. As patients become older, they become susceptible to a wider spectrum of microbial agents. Chronic keratitis secondary to viral infection is frequent. Lymphoreticular malignancies, especially of the central nervous system, occur in older patients. Myelogenous leukemia occurs more frequently in this disorder than in other immunodeficiency disorders.

IMMUNODEFICIENCY WITH THYMOMA

Recurrent infection may be the presenting sign if the thymoma is associated with immunodeficiency. Infection takes the form of sinopulmonary infection, chronic diarrhea, dermatitis, septicemia, stomatitis, and urinary tract infection. Thymoma has also been associated with muscle weakness (when found in conjunction with myasthenia gravis), aregenerative anemia, thrombocytopenia, diabetes, amyloidosis, chronic hepatitis, and the development of nonthymic malignancy.

Patients with acquired hypogammaglobulinemia should be followed at regular intervals for the development of thymoma, usually detected on routine chest x-rays. Occasionally, the thymoma may be detected prior to the development of immunodeficiency. Marked hypogammaglobulinemia is usually present. The antibody response following immunization may be abnormal. Some patients have deficient T cell immunity as assayed by delayed hypersensitivity skin tests and response of peripheral blood lymphocytes to PHA. Increased suppressor cell activity has been described in some patients. In patients who have aregenerative anemia, pure red cell aplasia is seen on marrow aspiration. Thrombocytopenia, granulocytopenia, and autoantibody formation are occasionally observed. In 75% of cases, the thymoma is of the spindle cell type. Some tumors may be malignant.

In no instance has the removal of the thymoma resulted in improvement of immunodeficiency. This is in contrast to pure red cell aplasia and myasthenia gravis, which may improve following removal of thymoma. γ-Globulin is of benefit in controlling recurrent infections and chronic diarrhea. (See treatment section under X-linked hypogammaglobulinemia.)

The overall prognosis is poor, and death secondary to infection is common. Death may also be related to associated abnormalities such as thrombocytopenia and aregenerative anemia.

IMMUNODEFICIENCY WITH SHORT–LIMBED DWARFISM

Three forms of immunodeficiency with short-limbed dwarfism exist. Type I is associated with combined immunodeficiency, type II with T cell immunodeficiency, and type III with B cell immunodeficiency.

The clinical features of each type vary with the degree of immunodeficiency. In short-limbed dwarfism associated with combined immunodeficiency, symptoms of infection are identical to those seen in severe combined immunodeficiency disease. Susceptibility to viral, bacterial, fungal, and protozoal infection is observed. Patients usually die in the first year. Patients with short-limbed dwarfism and T cell immunodeficiency are susceptible to recurrent sinopulmonary infection, fatal varicella, and progressive vaccinia and may develop a malabsorptionlike syn-

drome. Patients with short-limbed dwarfism and B cell immunodeficiency experience recurrent pyogenic infections in the form of pneumonia, sepsis, otitis media, and meningitis. In all patients, short-limbed dwarfism is characterized by short, pudgy hands and extremities. The head is normal in size, which distinguishes this disorder from achondroplasia. During infancy, redundant skin folds are often seen around the neck and large joints of the extremities. Patients with short-limbed dwarfism and T cell immunodeficiency may also have cartilage-hair hypoplasia manifested by light, thin, and sparse hair.

Abnormal immunologic studies vary with the degree of immunodeficiency. In short-limbed dwarfism associated with combined immunodeficiency, there is complete absence of T and B cell immunity. In short-limbed dwarfism associated with T cell immunodeficiency, T cell immunity is deficient as measured by delayed hypersensitivity skin tests and responsiveness of peripheral blood lymphocytes to PHA, allogeneic cells, and varicella antigens. B cell immunity is intact. In short-limbed dwarfism associated with B cell immunodeficiency, B cell immunity is absent and T cell immunity is intact.

Radiologic abnormalities consist of scalloping, irregular sclerosis, and cystic changes in the metaphyseal portions of long bones. Aganglionic megacolon has been reported. Patients with cartilage-hair hypoplasia have reduced hair diameters and lack the pigmented central core.

Treatment of these disorders is individualized to the associated immunodeficiency (eg, severe combined immunodeficiency, cellular immunodeficiency, and antibody immunodeficiency).

The prognosis varies with the degree of immunodeficiency. There have been no survivors with severe combined immunodeficiency. Patients with T cell immunodeficiency may survive to the fourth or fifth decade only to succumb to overwhelming varicella infection. The prognosis in patients with antibody immunodeficiency is similar to that of X-linked hypogammaglobulinemia, but loss of T cell function may occur with time.

IMMUNODEFICIENCY WITH ENZYME DEFICIENCY

Adenosine Deaminase & Nucleoside Phosphorylase Deficiency

Patients with enzyme deficiency and immunodeficiency may have clinical and laboratory abnormalities identical with those of patients with immunodeficiency with normal enzyme activity. Enzyme deficiency as a cause of immunodeficiency probably accounts for less than 15% of immunodeficiency disorders at present. It is almost certain that additional enzyme deficiencies will be discovered.

Adenosine deaminase and purine nucleoside phosphorylase are enzymes necessary for the normal catabolism of purines (Fig 25–1). Adenosine deami-

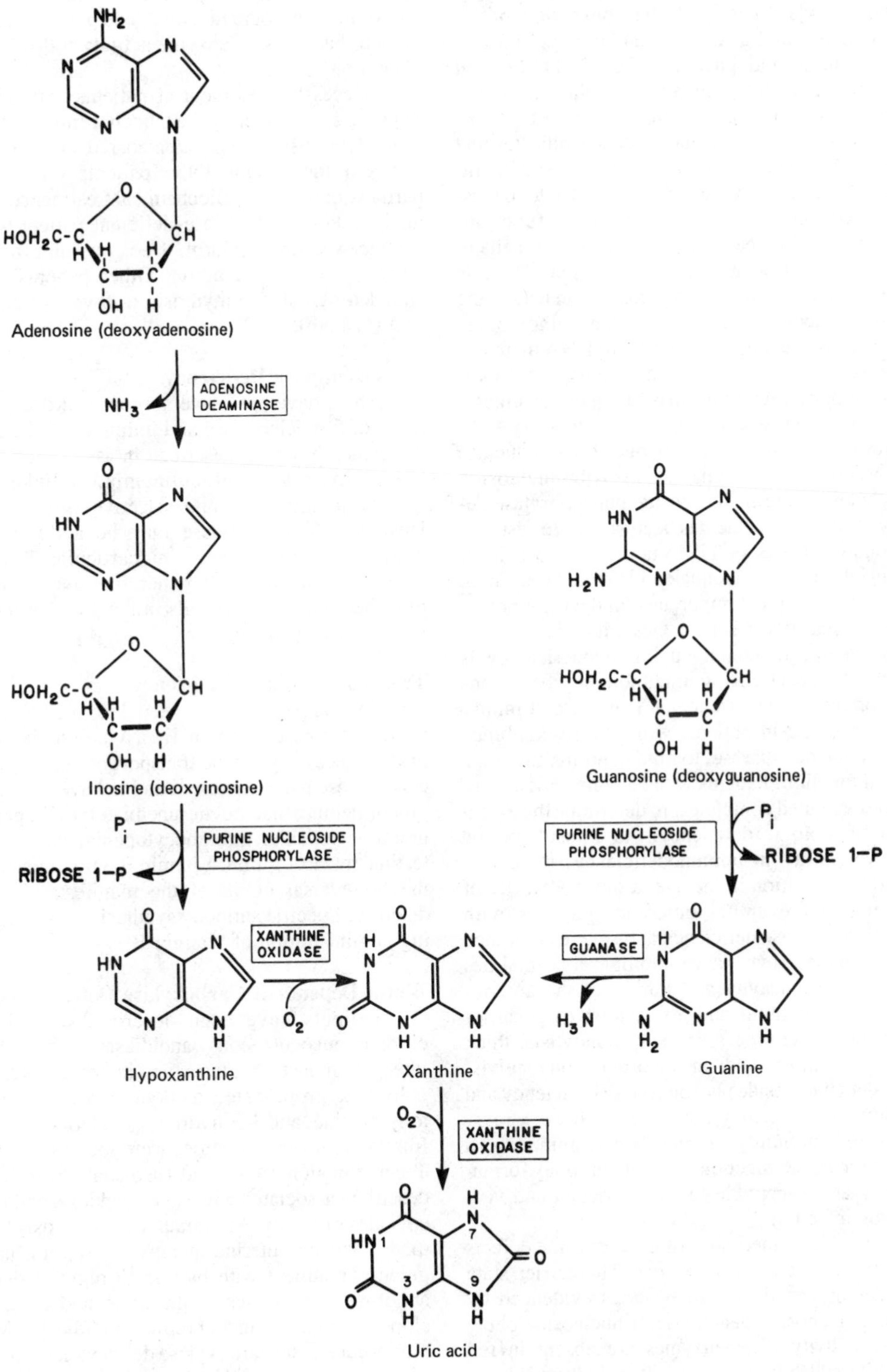

Figure 25–1. Generation of uric acid from purine deoxyribonucleosides by way of the purine bases hypoxanthine, xanthine, and guanine. (Reproduced, with permission, from Martin DW, Mayes PA, Rodwell VW: *Harper's Review of Biochemistry*, 18th ed. Lange, 1981.)

nase catalyzes the conversion of adenosine and deoxyadenosine to inosine and deoxyinosine. Nucleoside phosphorylase catalyzes the conversion of inosine, deoxyinosine, guanosine, and deoxyguanosine to hypoxanthine and guanine (Fig 25–1). Several mechanisms have been postulated to explain the means whereby these enzyme deficiencies result in immunodeficiency. Experimental evidence indicates that adenosine, in increased amounts, may result in increased cAMP activity, which is known to be associated with inhibition of lymphocyte function. Adenosine has also been shown to be toxic to cells in culture as a result of pyrimidine starvation. There is also evidence that exogenous adenosine can lead to the intracellular accumulation of S-adenosylhomocysteine, which acts as a potent inhibitor of DNA methylation. However, the most likely mechanism of inhibition of lymphocyte function is a result of the accumulation of deoxyadenosine and subsequently deoxyATP, which results in inhibition of ribonucleotide reductase and subsequent depletion of deoxyribonucleoside triphosphates. In purine nucleoside phosphorylase deficiency, deoxyguanosine has been shown to result in accumulation of deoxyGTP. Again, this most likely results in inhibition of ribonucleotide reductase. These mechanisms have great importance in devising potential biochemical treatment for these disorders.

The degree of combined immunodeficiency is variable. The spectrum of immunologic aberrations varies from complete absence of T and B cell immunity, as observed in patients with severe combined immunodeficiency disease, to mild abnormalities of T and B cell function. Patients with enzyme deficiencies should be evaluated completely to determine the extent of the immunologic deficiency. As a result of the marked variability in immunodeficiency, there is a considerable variation in the age at onset, severity of symptoms, and eventual outcome. Patients with adenosine deaminase deficiency and severe combined immunodeficiency may have radiologic abnormalities which include concavity and flaring of the anterior ribs, abnormal contour and articulation of posterior ribs and transverse processes, platyspondylisis, thick growth arrest lines, and an abnormal bony pelvis. Patients with nucleoside phosphorylase deficiency and T cell immunodeficiency have normal bone x-rays, absent T cell immunity, normal B cell immunity, a history of recurrent infection, and autoantibody formation. They are susceptible to fatal varicella and vaccinia virus infection.

The mode of inheritance of these enzyme defects appears to be autosomal recessive. The carrier state can be demonstrated in both sexes as evidenced by diminished adenosine deaminase or nucleoside phosphorylase activity. The enzymes are absent in red cells, white cells, tissue, and cultured fibroblasts in these patients. An intrauterine diagnosis of adenosine deaminase deficiency has been made. Patients may not be immunodeficient at birth.

Treatment of this disorder is similar to that of severe combined immunodeficiency or combined immunodeficiency. Several successful bone marrow transplants have been performed, with subsequent return of immunologic function. The patient's cells continue to have absent enzyme activity following transplantation.

Successful treatment of patients with adenosine deaminase deficiency has been reported utilizing monthly infusions of irradiated red blood cells as a source of the enzyme. Other patients have responded partially or not at all. Biochemical treatment of a single nucleoside phosphorylase–deficient patient with oral uridine was unsuccessful. Deoxycytidine therapy is currently under evaluation. Other patients have responded partially to thymosin or thymus transplantation (or both).

5'-Nucleotidase Deficiency

There have been several reports of decreased activity of 5'-nucleotidase and immunodeficiency. This deficiency has been described in association with acquired hypogammaglobulinemia, X-linked hypogammaglobulinemia, and selective IgA deficiency. However, 5'-nucleotidase may be a differentiation marker of lymphocytes—in particular B lymphocytes—and the deficiency therefore may reflect a diminished number of B cells in the peripheral circulation of these patients.

Transcobalamin II Deficiency

Several patients have been described with a deficiency of transcobalamin II, a vitamin B_{12}–binding protein necessary for the transport of vitamin B_{12} into cells. These patients were found to have hypogammaglobulinemia, macrocytic anemia, lymphopenia and granulocytopenia, thrombocytopenia, and severe intestinal malabsorption. Vitamin B_{12} treatment resulted in the reversal of all of the manifestations of the disorder. Specific antibody synthesis occurred following administration of vitamin B_{12}.

Biotin-Dependent Carboxylase Deficiencies

Patients have been described with infantile chronic mucocutaneous candidiasis, ataxia, alopecia, intermittent lactic acidosis, and increased excretion of β-hydroxypropionate, methylcitrate, β-methylcrotonylglycine, and 3-β-hydroxyisovalerate in the urine. Immunologic abnormalities were found in both B and T cell function. A second (neonatal) form has been described associated with severe acidosis and multiple episodes of sepsis. An intrauterine diagnosis has been made, and intrauterine therapy with biotin has been given. Treatment with biotin, 10 mg/d, reduced the abnormal metabolites in the urine and reversed the alopecia, ataxia, and chronic candidiasis. Multiple biotin-dependent carboxylase deficiencies may be one of several causes of the chronic mucocutaneous candidiasis syndrome with abnormal T cell function or severe recurrent sepsis.

EPISODIC LYMPHOPENIA WITH LYMPHOTOXIN

This is a poorly defined disorder in which approximately 12 patients, both males and females, have been reported. The major features include abnormal T and B cell immunity, recurrent viral and bacterial infections, eczema, and the presence of a circulating lymphotoxin. No specific treatment is available. Therapy should be directed toward treatment of bacterial infections. γ-Globulin may be useful. Other forms of immunotherapy have not been tried. The prognosis is uncertain. One patient survived to 11 years of age.

GRAFT–VERSUS–HOST (GVH) DISEASE

GVH disease occurs when there is an unopposed attack of histo*in*compatible cells on an individual who is unable to reject foreign cells. The requirements for the GVH reaction are (1) histocompatibility differences between the graft (donor) and host (recipient), (2) immunocompetent graft cells, and (3) immunodeficient host cells. A GVH reaction may result from the infusion of any blood product containing viable lymphocytes, as may occur in maternal-fetal blood transfusion, intrauterine transfusion, therapeutic whole blood transfusions, or transfusions of packed red cells, frozen cells, platelets, fresh plasma, or leukocyte-poor red cells; or transplantation of fetal thymus, fetal liver, or bone marrow. The GVH reaction may have its onset 7–30 days following infusion of viable lymphocytes. Once the reaction is established, little can be done to modify its course. In the majority of immunodeficient patients, a GVH reaction is fatal. The exact mechanism whereby a GVH reaction is produced is not known. All cells of the body have histocompatibility antigens with the exception of red blood cells. Biopsy of active GVH lesions usually demonstrates infiltrations by mononuclear cells as well as phagocytic and histiocytic cells. The GVH reaction may appear in 3 distinct forms: acute, hyperacute, and chronic.

In the **acute form**, the initial manifestation is a maculopapular rash which is frequently mistaken for a viral or allergic rash. Initially, it blanches with pressure and then becomes diffuse. If the rash is persistent, it will begin to scale. Diarrhea, hepatosplenomegaly, jaundice, cardiac irregularity, central nervous system irritability, and pulmonary infiltrates may occur during the height of the reaction. Enhanced susceptibility to infection is also present and may result in death from sepsis.

In the **hyperacute form** of GVH reaction, the rash may also begin as a maculopapular lesion but then rapidly progresses to a form resembling toxic epidermal necrolysis, usually associated with severe diarrhea. This has not been associated with staphylococcal infection. Clinical and laboratory abnormalities similar to those found in the acute form may be observed. Death occurs shortly after the onset of the reaction.

The **chronic form** of GVH disease may be a result of maternal-fetal transfusion or attempts at immunotherapy with histocompatible bone marrow transplantation. The clinical and laboratory features may be markedly abnormal or only slightly so. Chronic desquamation of the skin is usually present. Hepatosplenomegaly may be prominent along with lymphadenopathy. Chronic diarrhea and failure to thrive are usually present. Secondary infection is a frequent complication. On biopsy of skin or lymph nodes, histiocytic infiltration may be found, leading to an erroneous diagnosis of Letterer-Siwe disease. Patients with Letterer-Siwe disease have normal immunoglobulin values and normal T cell immunity, but patients with chronic GVH disease have severe immunodeficiency. Chronic GVH disease has also been confused with acrodermatitis enteropathica.

The diagnosis is suggested by the diffuse clinical abnormalities present in a patient known to have cellular immunodeficiency and who has received a transfusion of potentially immunocompetent cells in the preceding 5–30 days. The diagnosis is established by the demonstration of sex chromosome or HLA chimerism.

There is no adequate treatment of GVH disease once it is established. Use of corticosteroids only enhances the susceptibility to infection. Antilymphocyte globulin also results in further suppression of immunity. The only treatment is prevention. Any infant suspected of having cellular immunodeficiency who requires the administration of a blood product should receive cells that have been subjected to 3000–6000 R of radiation to destroy viable lymphocytes and thus prevent GVH disease. Blood products to be irradiated include whole blood, packed red blood cells, leukocyte-poor red blood cells, and fresh plasma.

PHAGOCYTIC DYSFUNCTION DISEASES

Phagocytic disorders may be divided into extrinsic and intrinsic defects. Included in the extrinsic category are deficiencies of opsonins secondary to deficiencies of antibody and complement factors; suppression of the total number of phagocytic cells by immunosuppressive agents; interference of phagocytic function by corticosteroids; and suppression of the number of circulating neutrophils by autoantibody directed specifically against neutrophil antigens. Other extrinsic disorders may be related to abnormal neutrophil chemotaxis secondary to complement deficiency or abnormal complement components. Intrinsic phagocytic disorders are related to enzymatic deficiencies within the metabolic pathway necessary for killing of bacteria. These include chronic granulomatous disease with a deficiency of NADPH or NADH oxidase, myeloperoxidase deficiency, and glucose-6-phosphate dehydrogenase deficiency.

Susceptibility to infection in phagocytic dysfunction syndromes may range from mild recurrent skin infections to severe overwhelming, fatal systemic infection. Characteristically, all of these patients are susceptible to bacterial infection and have little difficulty with viral or protozoal infections. Some of the more severe disorders may be associated with overwhelming fungal infections.

Numerous tests can now be performed to evaluate phagocytic dysfunction (see Chapter 23). Screening tests are listed in Table 25–3, and definitive studies in Table 25–7.

Table 25–7. Evaluation of phagocytosis.

Test	Comment
Quantitative nitro-blue tetrazolium (NBT)	Used for diagnosis of chronic granulomatous disease and for detection of carrier state.
Quantitative intracellular killing curve	Used for diagnosis of chronic granulomatous disease. Can be performed using organisms isolated from individual.
Chemotaxis	Abnormal in a variety of disorders associated with frequent bacterial infection. Does not provide a specific diagnosis. Performed using a Boyden chamber utilizing a microscopic or radioactive technique. Rebuck skin window provides a qualitative result in vivo.
Random migration	Abnormal in "lazy leukocyte syndrome." Tests nonchemotactic migration of leukocytes.
Chemiluminescence	Abnormal in chronic granulomatous disease and myeloperoxidase deficiency.

CHRONIC GRANULOMATOUS DISEASE

Major Immunologic Features

- Susceptibility to infection with unusual organisms normally of low virulence, eg, *Staphylococcus epidermidis, Serratia marcescens, Aspergillus.*
- X-linked inheritance (female variant occurs).
- Onset of symptoms by 2 years of age: draining lymphadenitis, hepatosplenomegaly, pneumonia, osteomyelitis, abscesses.
- Diagnosis established by quantitative nitroblue tetrazolium test, quantitative killing curve, or chemiluminescence.

General Considerations

Chronic granulomatous disease is inherited as an X-linked disorder with clinical manifestations appearing during the first 2 years of life. A female variant of the disease has been described. Patients are susceptible to infection with a variety of normally nonpathogenic and unusual organisms. Characteristic abnormal laboratory studies will detect both patients and female carriers of the disease. Female carriers are usually asymptomatic. Early diagnosis and aggressive therapy have improved the prognosis in these patients.

The enzymatic deficiency in chronic granulomatous disease is felt to be either NADH or NADPH oxidase or NADH reductase. The exact location of the enzyme deficiency must await further studies. Absence of cytochrome b has also been described. In the female variant, glutathione peroxidase is felt to be deficient. As a result of these enzymatic deficiencies, the intracellular metabolism of neutrophils and monocytes is abnormal, resulting in decreased oxygen consumption, decreased utilization of glucose by the hexose monophosphate shunt, decreased production of hydrogen peroxide, diminished iodination of bacteria, and decreased superoxide anion production. The net result is decreased intracellular killing of certain bacteria and fungi.

Clinical Features

A. Symptoms and Signs: In the majority of patients, the diagnosis can be established before 2 years of age. The most frequent abnormalities consist of marked lymphadenopathy, hepatosplenomegaly, chronic draining lymph nodes, and at least one episode of pneumonia. Other symptoms include rhinitis, conjunctivitis, dermatitis, ulcerative stomatitis, perianal abscess, osteomyelitis, chronic diarrhea with intermittent abdominal pains, and intestinal obstruction. Chronic and acute infection occurs in lymph nodes, skin, lung, intestinal tract, liver, and bone. A major clue to early diagnosis is the finding of a normally nonpathogenic or unusual organism. Organisms responsible for infection include *S aureus, S epidermidis, S marcescens, Pseudomonas, Escherichia coli, Candida,* and *Aspergillus.*

B. Laboratory Findings: The most readily available study for diagnosis is the quantitative nitroblue tetrazolium test. (See Chapter 23.) Patients have absent nitroblue tetrazolium dye reduction, whereas carriers may have normal or reduced nitroblue tetrazolium reduction. Patients with chronic granulomatous disease are unable to kill certain bacteria at a normal rate. The killing curves for organisms to which these individuals are susceptible usually indicate little or no killing in a period of 2 hours. Other abnormal studies include decreased oxygen uptake during phagocytosis and abnormal bacterial iodination.

The peripheral white cell count is usually elevated even if the patient does not have active infection. Hypergammaglobulinemia is present, and antibody function is normal. Cell-mediated immunity is normal, and complement factors may be elevated. During episodes of pneumonia, the chest x-ray is frequently severely abnormal. Liver function tests may be abnormal as a result of chronic infection. Pulmonary function tests are usually abnormal following episodes of pneumonia and may not return to normal for several months. Several patients have been reported to have a rare Kell blood group, the "McLeod" phenotype.

Immunologic Diagnosis

A diagnosis can be established utilizing the quantitative nitroblue tetrazolium dye reduction assay or quantitative chemiluminescence. Confirmation is obtained utilizing specific bactericidal assays. These assays may also be utilized to identify the carrier state and to establish an intrauterine diagnosis. Both male and female variants of chronic granulomatous disease have abnormal studies. B cell immunity, T cell immunity, and complement are normal. Chemiluminescence is the best method for detecting the carrier state. An intrauterine diagnosis has been made using fetal blood and a nitroblue tetrazolium test.

Differential Diagnosis

Few clinical disorders are easily confused with chronic granulomatous disease. Two other disorders with abnormal enzymatic function are associated with clinical symptoms and laboratory features similar to those of chronic granulomatous disease. One of these is the female variant of chronic granulomatous disease associated with deficient glutathione peroxidase; the other is associated with deficient glucose-6-phosphate dehydrogenase. Any child presenting with osteomyelitis, pneumonia, liver abscess, or chronic draining lymphadenopathy associated with a normally nonpathogenic or unusual organism should be suspected of having chronic granulomatous disease.

Treatment

Aggressive diagnostic measures and therapy are necessary for long-term survival and diminished morbidity. Blood cultures, aspiration of draining lymph nodes, liver biopsy, and open lung biopsy should be utilized to obtain a specific bacterial diagnosis. Therapy should be instituted immediately while results of cultures are pending. The choice of antibiotics should be one which covers the spectrum of infectious agents. An appropriate choice would be penicillin and gentamicin or penicillin and chloramphenicol. These agents cover the majority of organisms with the exception of *Candida* and *Aspergillus*. For these latter organisms, amphotericin is the treatment of choice. Amphotericin therapy should be given intravenously, starting with high doses in the range of 1 mg/kg/d. The ultimate survival of the patient is dependent upon early and intensive therapy. Treatment of the patient with antibiotics may be prolonged, requiring 5–6 weeks of total therapy. Additional therapy has included the use of white blood cell infusions, but experience has been extremely limited. Several investigators have utilized continuous anti-infective therapy with sulfisoxazole. A single successful bone marrow transplant has been performed.

Complications & Prognosis

Chronic organ dysfunction may result from severe or chronic infection. Examples are abnormal pulmonary function, chronic liver disease, chronic osteomyelitis, and malabsorption secondary to gastrointestinal tract involvement. The mortality rate in chronic granulomatous disease has been considerably reduced by early diagnosis and aggressive therapy. Survivals into the second decade and beyond have been recorded. Female carriers have an increased incidence of systemic and discoid lupus erythematosus.

GLUCOSE–6–PHOSPHATE DEHYDROGENASE DEFICIENCY

Glucose-6-phosphate dehydrogenase deficiency is inherited in an X-linked manner. Complete absence of leukocyte glucose-6-phosphate dehydrogenase activity has been associated with a clinical picture similar to that of chronic granulomatous disease. Some investigators have demonstrated decreased hexose monophosphate shunt activity and decreased hydrogen peroxide production in the white blood cells. Leukocytes are unable to kill certain organisms at a normal rate in a manner similar to that found in chronic granulomatous disease. The susceptibility of these patients to microbial agents is similar to that of patients with chronic granulomatous disease. Glucose-6-phosphate dehydrogenase deficiency differs in that the onset is later, both males and females are affected, and hemolytic anemia is present. The laboratory diagnosis is based on the demonstration of deficient white blood cell glucose-6-phosphate dehydrogenase. The nitroblue tetrazolium test, the killing curve, the production of H_2O_2, and O_2 consumption are abnormal. Treatment and prognosis are similar to those of chronic granulomatous disease.

MYELOPEROXIDASE DEFICIENCY

Several patients with complete deficiency of leukocyte myeloperoxidase have been described. Myeloperoxidase is one of the enzymes necessary for normal intracellular killing of certain organisms. The leukocytes of these patients have normal oxygen consumption, hexose monophosphate shunt activity, and hydrogen peroxide production. The intracellular killing of organisms is delayed but may reach normal levels with increased incubation times. Susceptibility to candidal and staphylococcal infections has been the chief problem. The diagnosis can be established utilizing a peroxidase stain of peripheral blood. Chemiluminescence is abnormal. No specific treatment is available other than appropriate antibiotic therapy.

ALKALINE PHOSPHATASE DEFICIENCY

Several patients have been reported who have recurrent bacterial infection associated with absent leukocyte alkaline phosphatase activity. There is a modest reduction in bactericidal activity.

CHÉDIAK–HIGASHI SYNDROME

Chédiak-Higashi syndrome is a multisystem autosomal recessive disorder. Symptoms include recurrent bacterial infections with a variety of organisms, hepatosplenomegaly, partial albinism, central nervous system abnormalities, and a high incidence of lymphoreticular malignancies.

The characteristic abnormality of giant cytoplasmic granular inclusions in white blood cells and platelets is observed on routine peripheral blood smears under ordinary light microscopy. Additional abnormalities include abnormal neutrophil chemotaxis and abnormal intracellular killing of organisms (including streptococci and pneumococci as well as those organisms found in chronic granulomatous disease). The killing defect consists of delayed killing time. Oxygen consumption, hydrogen peroxide formation, and hexose monophosphate shunt activity are normal. Abnormal microtubule function, abnormal lysosomal enzyme levels in granulocytes, and protease deficiency in granulocytes have been described. Correction of abnormal leukocyte function in vitro has been accomplished utilizing ascorbate, but the results of treatment in vivo are contradictory. Improved granulocyte function in vitro has also been observed using anticholinergic agents.

There is no treatment other than specific antibiotic therapy for infecting organisms. The prognosis is poor because of increasing susceptibility to infection and progressive neurologic deterioration. Most patients die during childhood, but survivors to the second and third decade have been reported.

JOB'S SYNDROME

Job's syndrome was originally described as a disorder of recurrent "cold" staphylococcal abscesses of the skin, lymph nodes, or subcutaneous tissue. The first patients were fair-skinned, red-headed girls of Italian descent. Initial descriptions also included eczematoid skin lesions, otitis media, and chronic nasal discharge. Few signs of systemic infection or inflammatory response occurred in association with the infection. Additional reports of Job's syndrome indicated that the disorder might be a variant of chronic granulomatous disease. However, most of the patients studied do not have abnormal immunologic tests.

Treatment consists of appropriate antibiotic therapy. The prognosis is uncertain.

TUFTSIN DEFICIENCY

Tuftsin deficiency has been reported as a familial deficiency of a phagocytosis-stimulating tetrapeptide which is cleaved from a parent immunoglobulin (termed leukokinin) molecule in the spleen. Tuftsin also appears to be absent in patients who have been splenectomized. Local and severe systemic infections occur. Organisms include *Candida, S aureus,* and *S pneumoniae.* Tuftsin levels are determined only in a few specialized laboratories.

There is no treatment, and the prognosis is uncertain. γ-Globulin therapy appeared to be beneficial in the 2 families reported.

LAZY LEUKOCYTE SYNDROME

Patients have been described who have a defective chemotactic response of neutrophils in association with neutropenia. These individuals also have an abnormal in vivo inflammatory response as determined by the "Rebuck window," and they fail to demonstrate an increased number of peripheral blood neutrophils following epinephrine or endotoxin stimulation. The random migration of peripheral leukocytes is abnormal as determined by the vertical migration of white blood cells in a capillary tube. Patients are susceptible to severe bacterial infections.

Treatment with specific antibiotics is indicated. The prognosis is unknown.

ELEVATED IgE, DEFECTIVE CHEMOTAXIS, ECZEMA, & RECURRENT INFECTION

These patients—both males and females—have an early onset of eczema and recurrent bacterial infections in the form of abscesses. Structures involved include the skin, lungs, ears, sinuses, and eyes. Systemic infection may involve other areas. Organisms causing infection include *S aureus, Candida, H influenzae, S pneumoniae,* and group A streptococci. Laboratory findings consist of eosinophilia, IgE concentrations in excess of 5000 IU/mL, diminished antibody response following immunization, and normal lymphocyte response to PHA and ConA but reduced response to antigens and allogeneic cells (MLC). Abnormalities of chemotaxis are present in some but not all patients. Antibiotic therapy is indicated for specific infections. The prognosis is unknown, although patients have survived to adulthood.

LEUKOCYTE MOVEMENT DISORDERS

A number of patients have been described with decreased leukocyte chemotaxis and recurrent infections (usually bacterial). In some, deficiency of IgG and an IgG inhibitor of chemotaxis have also been found. Defective actin polymerization was found in association with defective neutrophil phagocytosis and locomotion. Abnormal chemotaxis has been found in congenital ichthyosis. Mannosidosis, a storage disease manifested by mental retardation and recurrent infections, is associated with abnormal chemotaxis and delayed phagocytosis. Mannose, which accumulates within leukocytes, may interfere with cell function.

Similar abnormalities have been described in type 1B glycogen storage disease.

COMPLEMENT ABNORMALITIES & IMMUNODEFICIENCY DISEASES

A variety of complement deficiencies and abnormalities of complement function have been associated with increased susceptibility to infection (Table 25–8). Complement factors are necessary for normal opsonization, bacterial killing, and neutrophil chemotaxis. Despite the participation of complement components in the phagocytic process, a number of complement deficiencies are unassociated with enhanced susceptibility to infection. Many of these disorders are associated with increased susceptibility to autoimmune disease (see Chapter 26). Hereditary angioneurotic edema as a result of deficiency of C1 esterase inhibitor is discussed elsewhere (see Chapter 28).

Table 25–8. Evaluation of complement disorders.

C1q, C1r, C1s	Deficiency initially suspected by decreased hemolytic complement (CH_{50}). Specific assays required for confirmation.
C2, C4, C5, C6, C7, C8, C9	Deficiency initially suspected by decreased CH_{50}. Specific assays required for confirmation.
C3, C4	Deficiency detected using quantitative assay available in most hospital laboratories.
C5 dysfunction	Present in normal amounts but abnormal in function in "C5 dysfunction" syndrome.

C1q DEFICIENCY

A deficiency of C1q has been reported in patients with X-linked hypogammaglobulinemia and severe combined immunodeficiency disease. The cause of this deficiency is not certain, but it may be related to hypercatabolism as a result of enhanced susceptibility to infection in patients with primary immunodeficiency disorders. The degree to which C1q deficiency increases the susceptibility to infection in patients with other primary immunodeficiency disorders is not known. C1q deficiency has also been described in patients with a systemic lupus erythematosus-like syndrome and increased susceptibility to bacterial infection. C1q deficiency has also been reported in patients with urticarialike lesions and cutaneous vasculitis, sometimes associated with precipitins to C1q.

C1r & C1s DEFICIENCY

Familial deficiencies of C1r and C1s have been described in patients with susceptibility to autoimmune disease. Most of these patients had a systemic lupus erythematosus-like syndrome. In addition, these patients appeared to have an increased susceptibility to bacterial infection. No specific treatment of this disorder has been proposed. The infusion of complement components might theoretically result in enhanced immune complex disease and worsening of the lupus erythematosus-like disorder.

C2 DEFICIENCY

C2 deficiency has been reported in several patients with systemic lupus erythematosus-like disorders, anaphylactoid purpura, dermatomyositis, and increased susceptibility to infection. The patients have chronic renal disease and antibody directed against DNA. An autosomal recessive mode of inheritance is suggested by familial studies. The patients are susceptible to bacterial infection. Recently, C2 deficiency has been associated with the HLA haplotype A10, B18.

Treatment is directed toward the underlying autoimmune disease, with specific antibiotic therapy for infections. In one patient who received a blood transfusion, the levels of serum C3, C5, C6, and C7 decreased dramatically. This observation suggests that complement replacement therapy might result in increased activation of the complement components and increased immune complex disease.

C3 DEFICIENCY

Two forms of C3 deficiency exist. In type I, a marked decrease of C3 is present in the serum. However, C3 is probably deficient as a result of a deficiency of C3 inactivator. In the single patient reported, increased susceptibility to bacterial infection was present throughout life. The patient also had Klinefelter's syndrome. Infusion of normal plasma corrected the abnormalities in the patient and resulted in diminished susceptibility to infection.

A second form of C3 deficiency (type II) has been reported in several patients. Partial lipodystrophy was present in association with an increased susceptibility to bacterial infection and nephritis. The decreased level of C3 was found to be associated with increased destruction and decreased synthesis. The abnormalities were partially explained by the demonstration of an enzyme, C3 convertase, capable of cleaving C3 in vitro and in vivo.

C4 DEFICIENCY

C4 deficiency has been described in several individuals who were asymptomatic. The deficiencies were detected in routine screening of normal blood donors. In another family, C4 deficiency was associated with a systemic lupus erythematosus-like syndrome. Linkage to the histocompatibility antigens A2, B12, and D2 (maternal) and A2, Bw15, and LD108 (paternal) has been noted. C4-deficient patients have diminished chemotactic and opsonic activity and impaired antibody responses.

FAMILIAL C5 DYSFUNCTION & C5 DEFICIENCY

C5 dysfunction has been described as a familial defect in patients presenting with failure to thrive, diarrhea, seborrheic dermatitis, and susceptibility to infection with bacterial organisms.

Laboratory studies usually demonstrate leukocytosis and hypergammaglobulinemia. The total hemolytic complement and C5 levels are normal. Despite the normal levels of C5, chemotaxis is ineffective and can be corrected by adding normal C5 to the testing procedure.

Treatment consists of appropriate antibiotic therapy for infecting organisms. Fresh plasma has been recommended as a potential source of normal C5. Fresh-frozen plasma is not believed to contain sufficient amounts for therapy. However, some of the clinical findings in patients with familial C5 dysfunction closely resemble those found in patients with cellular immunodeficiency disorders. The use of fresh irradiated plasma is recommended to prevent a GVH reaction if the diagnosis has not been established with certainty. Ideally, patients should have studies of T cell immunity performed prior to the institution of treatment.

C5 deficiency has been described in a child with systemic lupus erythematosus. C5 levels in other family members were either normal or 50% of normal.

C6 DEFICIENCY

Several patients with C6 deficiency have been described. In one case, parents of the patient and 5 of 6 siblings had C6 values that were 50% of normal. A male child with repeated episodes of meningococcal meningitis and C6 deficiency has been described. The parents had C6 levels that were 50% of normal. In others, either recurrent meningococcal or gonococcal bacteremia was present.

C7 DEFICIENCY

Several patients with C7 deficiency have been described. Associated diseases include Raynaud's phenomenon, sclerodactyly, telangiectasia, and ankylosing spondylitis. Partial deficiency of C7 was found in the patient's parents and children, suggesting an autosomal inheritance. Increased susceptibility to meningococcal and gonococcal infections was also noted.

C8 DEFICIENCY

Patients with deficiency of C8 and prolonged disseminated gonococcal and meningococcal infections have been described. One patient lacked both functional and immunochemical presence of C8, but no inhibitors for C8 could be identified. Bactericidal activity against Neisseria gonorrhoeae was absent from her serum but could be completely restored by the addition of purified C8. Earlier complement functions such as opsonization and chemotactic factor generation were normal. A family study suggested an autosomal co-dominant mode of inheritance for this disorder. Another family has been reported with C8 deficiency and xeroderma pigmentosa.

C9 DEFICIENCY

Several patients have been described with C9 deficiency. Hemolytic complement activity is reduced but not absent. Patients have not had clinical abnormalities.

SECONDARY IMMUNODEFICIENCY

A variety of disorders are associated with secondary immunodeficiency (Table 25–9). In some, the immunodeficiencies may be transient and may become normal with adequate treatment of the primary disease, eg, tuberculosis, leprosy. In others, the immunodeficiency may be permanent, eg, congenital rubella. Many of the secondary immunodeficiencies may be due to multiple factors. Those observed in malignancies may be secondary to the tumor, associated with therapy, or secondary to malnutrition. The importance of secondary immunodeficiency is in the recognition that such states exist and result in enhanced susceptibility to opportunistic infection. In the future, the recognition of secondary immunodeficiency may assume greater importance as newer forms of immunologic reconstruction become available.

An example of severe acquired immunodeficiency is found among certain homosexual populations. Young males may develop a syndrome of severe T cell immunodeficiency associated with decreased T cell numbers, decreased helper cells, impaired lymphocyte response to mitogens and allogeneic cells, and decreased NK activity. Clinically, this has been associated with opportunistic infections with organisms such as Pneumocystis carinii and Candida. Chronic infection with cytomegalovirus and herpesvirus is also present. There is an increased incidence of neoplastic disease, including Kaposi's sarcoma, Burkitt's lymphoma, and squamous cell carcinoma.

Table 25—9. Secondary immunodeficiency.

Clinical Setting	T Cell	B Cell	Phagocytosis	Complement	Comments
Infection					
Rubella (congenital)	May have decreased T cells, PHA, MLC.	May have hypogamma-globulinemia or selective immunoglobulin deficiencies; no response to rubella immunization; decreased response to multiple antigens.	Normal	Normal	Defects vary with severity of disease.
Measles	Transient suppression of delayed hypersensitivity; decreased PHA.	Normal immunoglobulins; normal antibody response.	Normal	Normal	Similar effect may be seen with measles immunization.
Leprosy	Decreased delayed hypersensitivity; decreased response to M leprae; decreased PHA, T cells.	Decreased B cells in some; increased in others; increased antibody.	Unknown	Unknown	Immunologic deficiency greater in lepromatous form.
Tuberculosis	Decreased delayed hypersensitivity; decreased T cells; decreased MIF.	Immunoglobulins normal	Unknown	Unknown	Severe infection may be associated with anergy.
Coccidioidomycosis	Decreased delayed hypersensitivity; lymphocyte blastogenesis, MIF to coccal antigen.	Normal	Unknown	Unknown	Usually specific decreased immunity. Generalized depression may be present.
Chronic infection	Usually normal	Increased immunoglobulins	Decreased chemotaxis	Increased components	Increased autoantibody.
Acute viral infection	Lymphopenia; decreased T cells; decreased PHA in some.	Normal	Normal	Normal	Defect may vary with severity of illness.
Cytomegalovirus	Specific unresponsiveness to cytomegalovirus.	Elevated IgM, IgA	Unknown	Unknown	
Multiple or repeated viral infection	Decreased T cells, PHA, MLC, helper cells.	Elevated immunoglobulins, IgA, antibody to virus.	Unknown	Unknown	Occurs in selected homosexual individuals. Cause unknown.
Malignant neoplastic disease					
Hodgkin's disease	Suppression of delayed hypersensitivity; decreased PHA; serum factors suppress T cells.	Immunoglobulins normal to increased; decreased antibody response to certain antigens.	Frequent pneumococcal and H influenzae infection; decreased chemotaxis.	Unknown	Some abnormalities may be due to treatment or splenectomy.
Acute leukemia	Decreased delayed hypersensitivity, PHA.	Variable immunoglobulin levels	Normal	Unknown	Some abnormalities due to treatment.
Chronic leukemia	Serum factors inhibit PHA.	Variable immunoglobulin levels	Normal	Unknown	Some abnormalities due to treatment.
Nonlymphoid malignancy	Variable decrease in delayed hypersensitivity; suppression of PHA, MLC, T cells; immunosuppressive factors.	Variable immunoglobulin levels	Normal	Some tumors associated with decreased components.	Some abnormalities of T cells related to severity of disease, others to immunosuppression or radiation.
Myeloma	Increased suppressor T cells (? macrophages).	Impaired antibody response; decreased immunoglobulins.	Normal	Decreased complement components.	
Autoimmune disease					
Systemic lupus erythematosus	Decreased delayed hypersensitivity; decreased T cells, PHA, MLC; decreased suppressor cells in animal models and in humans.	Immunoglobulins usually elevated; increased antibody titers to multiple antigens.	Normal	Certain congenital complement deficiencies (C1q, C1r, C1s) associated with SLE; secondary complement deficiencies frequent.	Some T cell defects may be secondary to treatment.

PHA = phytohemagglutinin stimulation of lymphocytes; MLC = allogeneic cell stimulation of lymphocytes.

Table 25–9 (cont'd). Secondary immunodeficiency.

Clinical Setting	T Cell	B Cell	Phagocytosis	Complement	Comments
Autoimmune disease (cont'd)					
Rheumatoid arthritis	Decreased delayed hypersensitivity; decreased PHA, MLC.	Immunoglobulin levels usually increased; normal antibody response to antigens.	Normal	Increase in complement levels.	Some patients with hypogammaglobulinemia have arthritis.
Chronic active hepatitis	Decreased delayed hypersensitivity; decreased lymphocyte cytotoxicity; decreased T cells; mitogen response normal to decreased.	Immunoglobulins increased	Unknown	Decreased values in some patients.	Steroids increase some abnormalities.
Protein-losing states					
Nephrotic syndrome	Normal	Decreased IgG; IgM and IgA may be decreased; antibody response decreased.	Unknown	Normal in idiopathic lipoid nephrosis, may be decreased in other forms.	
Protein-losing enteropathy	Decreased delayed hypersensitivity; decreased T cells, PHA, MLC.	Hypogammaglobulinemia frequent	Unknown	Unknown	
Other disorders					
Diabetes	Decreased PHA; MLC normal.	Normal	Decreased chemotaxis; poor bacterial ingestion.	Unknown	
Alcoholic cirrhosis	Decreased PHA	Unknown	Abnormal chemotaxis	Some components decreased	
Malnutrition	Lymphopenia; decreased T cells; decreased delayed hypersensitivity.	Immunoglobulins normal; normal antibody response.	Abnormal bacterial killing	Decreased CH_{50}	
Burns	Decreased delayed hypersensitivity; lymphopenia.	Decrease in all immunoglobulins; normal antibody response.	Decreased phagocytic function; decreased chemotaxis.		
Sarcoidosis	Decreased delayed hypersensitivity; decreased PHA; inhibitory plasma factor.	Increased immunoglobulins; normal antibody response.	Unknown	Unknown	
Splenectomy	Normal	Immunoglobulins normal; decreased antibody response to whole organisms; normal antibody response to purified antigens.	Normal	Normal	Tuftsin deficiency found in some patients.
Sickle cell disease	Normal	IgM may be decreased; decreased antibody response to whole organisms with normal response to purified antigens.	Decreased phagocytosis; decreased opsonization; defect in properdin.	Some defects in alternative pathway described.	
Uremia	Decreased delayed hypersensitivity; serum blocking factors suppress PHA, MLC.	Immunoglobulins normal; normal antibody response.	Normal	Levels may be reduced in certain diseases.	
Aging	Decreased delayed hypersensitivity; decreased mitogen response; decreased T cells.	Increased IgG (IgA in some); increased B cells; decreased IgG response to certain antigens.	Unknown	Unknown	Increased autoantibodies.
Subacute sclerosing panencephalitis	Specific unresponsiveness to measles antigen; blocking factor present in some.	Increased antibody to measles	Unknown	Unknown	

PHA = phytohemagglutinin stimulation of lymphocytes; MLC = allogeneic cell stimulation of lymphocytes.

Table 25—9 (cont'd). Secondary immunodeficiency.

Clinical Setting	T Cell	B Cell	Phagocytosis	Complement	Comments
Other disorders (cont'd)					
Down's syndrome	Decreased lymphocyte response to PHA.	Impaired primary and secondary antibody responses.	Unknown	Unknown	Increased susceptibility to infection.
Newborns and premature infants	Increased suppressor cells.	Diminished IgM IgA; impaired ability to form antibody to a variety of antigens.	Decreased killing	Decreased complement factors; abnormal chemotaxis.	Decreased placental transfer of IgG in prematures.
Immunosuppressive treatment					
Corticosteroids	Transient decrease due to sequestration.	Transient decrease; late: reduced immunoglobulin synthesis.	Inhibits release of lysosomal enzymes, decreases phagocytosis of IgG-coated particles.	No effect	Actions of steroids differ in humans and mice.
Cytotoxic drugs (alkylating agents, antimetabolites)	Variable decrease in numbers and functions; responses suppressed or enhanced.	Variable decrease in numbers and function (primary antibody responses impaired).	Decreased production of neutrophils and monocytes.	No effect	Effects depend upon multiple factors (see Chapter 19).
Antithymocyte globulin	Decrease in T cell numbers and functions.	Unknown (some T cell–dependent reactions are impaired).	Unknown	Unknown	Activity against other cells (eg, platelets).
Radiation	Decrease in T cell numbers and functions (may be prolonged).	Impaired antibody production.	Transient decrease in blood monocytes.	Unknown	Total nodal irradiation produces long-lasting immunosuppression.
Cyclosporin A	No change in T cell number; profound depression of allograft rejection reaction.	Inhibition of T cell–dependent antibody responses.	Unknown	Unknown	
Phenytoin, penicillamine	Unknown	IgA deficiency, hypogammaglobulinemia.	Unknown	Unknown	May or may not be reversible.
Anesthesia	Inhibits function.	Inconclusive	Reduced phagocytosis	Unknown	Effect may last for weeks.

PHA = phytohemagglutinin stimulation of lymphocytes; MLC = allogeneic cell stimulation of lymphocytes.

● ● ●

References

X-Linked Hypogammaglobulinemia

Good RA, Zak SJ: Disturbances in gammaglobulin synthesis as "experiments of nature." *Pediatrics* 1956;**18**:109.

Rosen FS, Janeway CA: The gammaglobulins. 3. The antibody deficiency syndromes. *N Engl J Med* 1966;**275**:709.

Siegel RL et al: Deficiency of T helper cells in transient hypogammaglobulinemia of infancy. *N Engl J Med* 1981; **305**:1307.

Acquired Hypogammaglobulinemia

Geha RS et al: Heterogeneity of "acquired" or common variable agammaglobulinemia. *N Engl J Med* 1974;**291**:1.

Good RA et al: Clinical investigations of patients with agammaglobulinemia and hypogammaglobulinemia. *Pediatr Clin North Am* 1960;**7**:397.

Hermans PE, Diaz-Buxo JA, Stobo JD: Idiopathic late-onset immunoglobulin deficiency: Clinical observations in 50 patients. *Am J Med* 1976;**61**:221.

Ochs H: Intravenous immunoglobulin therapy of patients with primary immunodeficiency syndromes. Pages 9–14 in: *Immunoglobulins: Characteristics and Uses of Intravenous Preparations.* U.S. Department of Health and Human Services, 1981.

X-Linked Immunodeficiency With Hyper-IgM

Stiehm ER, Fudenberg HH: Clinical and immunologic features of dysgammaglobulinemia type 1. *Am J Med* 1966; **40**:805.

Selective IgA Deficiency

Ammann AJ, Hong R: Selective IgA deficiency: Presentation of 30 cases and a review of the literature. *Medicine* 1971; **50**:223.

Oxelius VA et al: IgG subclass deficiency in selective IgA deficiency. *N Engl J Med* 1981;**305**:1476.

Selective IgM Deficiency

Hobbs JR, Milner RDG, Watt PJ: Gamma-M deficiency pre-disposing to meningococcal septicaemia. *Br Med J* 1967; **2**:583.

Selective IgG Deficiency

Schur PH et al: Selective gamma-G globulin deficiencies in patients with recurrent pyogenic infections. *N Engl J Med* 1970;**283**:631.

Thymic Aplasia With Hypoparathyroidism

Barrett DJ et al: Clinical and immunologic spectrum of the DiGeorge syndrome. *J Clin Lab Immunol* 1981;**6**:1.

DiGeorge AM: Congenital absence of the thymus and its immunologic consequences: Concurrence with congenital hypoparathyroidism. In: *Immunologic Deficiency Diseases in Man.* Bergsma D, McKusick FA (editors). National Foundation–March of Dimes Original Article Series. Williams & Wilkins, 1968.

Chronic Mucocutaneous Candidiasis

Arulanantham K, Dwyer JM, Genel M: Evidence for defective immunoregulation in the syndrome of familial candidiasis endocrinopathy. *N Engl J Med* 1979;**300**:164.

Kirkpatrick CH, Rich RR, Bennett JE: Chronic mucocutaneous candidiasis: Model building in cellular immunity. *Ann Intern Med* 1971;**74**:955.

Lehner T: Chronic candidiasis. *Trans St Johns Hosp Dermatol Soc* 1964;**50**:8.

Severe Combined Immunodeficiency Disease

Hitzig WH: Congenital thymic and lymphocytic deficiency disorders. In: *Immunologic Disorders in Infants and Children.* Stiehm ER, Fulginiti V (editors). Saunders, 1973.

Pahwa SG, Pahwa RN, Good RA: Heterogeneity of B lymphocyte differentiation in severe combined immunodeficiency disease. *J Clin Invest* 1980;**66**:543.

Cellular Immunodeficiency With Abnormal Immunoglobulin Synthesis

Lawlor GJ et al: The syndrome of cellular immunodeficiency with immunoglobulins. *J Pediatr* 1974;**84**:183.

Ataxia-Telangiectasia

Boder E, Sedgwick RP: Ataxia-telangiectasia: A familial syndrome of progressive cerebellar ataxia, oculocutaneous telangiectasia and frequent pulmonary infection. *Univ Southern Calif Med Bull* 1957;**9**:15.

Bridges BA, Harnden DG: Untangling ataxia-telangiectasia. *Nature* 1981;**289**:222.

Peterson RDA, Cooper MD, Good RA: Lymphoid tissue abnormalities associated with ataxia-telangiectasia. *Am J Med* 1966;**41**:342.

Wiskott-Aldrich Syndrome

Blaese RM et al: The Wiskott-Aldrich syndrome: A disorder with a possible defect in antigen processing or recognition. *Lancet* 1968;**1**:1056.

Cooper MD et al: Wiskott-Aldrich syndrome: Immunologic deficiency disease involving the afferent limb of immunity. *Am J Med* 1968;**44**:489.

Parkman R et al: Complete correction of the Wiskott-Aldrich syndrome by allogeneic bone marrow transplantation. *N Engl J Med* 1978;**298**:921.

Immunodeficiency With Thymoma

Waldmann TA et al: Thymoma, hypogammaglobulinemia and absence of eosinophils. *J Clin Invest* 1967;**46**:1127.

Immunodeficiency With Short-Limbed Dwarfism

Ammann AJ, Sutliff W, Millinchick E: Antibody mediated immunodeficiency in short-limbed dwarfism. *J Pediatr* 1974;**84**:200.

Lux SE et al: Chronic neutropenia and abnormal cellular immunity in cartilage-hair hypoplasia. *N Engl J Med* 1970; **282**:234.

Combined Immunodeficiency With Enzyme Deficiency

Cowan MJ, Ammann AJ: Immunodeficiency associated with inherited metabolic disorders. *Clin Haematol* 1981; **10**:139.

Cowan MJ et al: Multiple biotin-dependent carboxylase deficiencies associated with defects in T-cell and B-cell immunity. *Lancet* 1979;**1**:115.

Giblett ER et al: Nucleoside phosphorylase deficiency in a child with severely defective T cell immunity and normal B cell immunity. *Lancet* 1975;**1**:1010.

Hirschhorn R, Martin DW: Enzyme defects in immunodeficiency diseases. *Semin Immunopathol* 1978;**1**:299.

Meuwissen HJ, Pollara B, Pickering RJ: Combined immunodeficiency disease associated with adenosine deaminase deficiency. *J Pediatr* 1975;**86**:169.

Episodic Lymphopenia With Lymphotoxin

Kretschmer R et al: Recurrent infections, episodic lymphopenia and impaired cellular immunity. *N Engl J Med* 1969;**281**:285.

Chronic Granulomatous Disease

Cheson BD, Curnutte JT, Babior BM: The oxidative killing mechanism of the neutrophil. *Prog Clin Immunol* 1977;**3**:1.

Cohen MS et al: Fungal infection in chronic granulomatous disease. *Am J Med* 1981;**71**:59.

Johnston RB, Baehner RL: Chronic granulomatous disease: Correlation between pathogenesis and clinical findings. *Pediatrics* 1971;**48**:730.

Glucose-6-Phosphate Dehydrogenase Deficiency

Cooper MR et al: Complete deficiency of leukocyte glucose-6-phosphate dehydrogenase with defective bactericidal activity. *J Clin Invest* 1972;**51**:769.

Myeloperoxidase Deficiency

Lehrer RI, Cline MJ: Leukocyte myeloperoxidase deficiency and disseminated candidiasis: The role of myeloperoxidase in resistance to *Candida* infection. *J Clin Invest* 1969; **48**:1478.

Chédiak-Higashi Syndrome

Haliotis T et al: Chédiak-Higashi gene in humans. 1. Impairment of natural-killer function. *J Exp Med* 1980;**151**:1039.

Stossel TP, Root RK, Vaughan M: Phagocytosis in chronic granulomatous disease and the Chédiak-Higashi syndrome. *N Engl J Med* 1972;**286**:120.

Tuftsin Deficiency

Constantopoulos A, Najjar VA, Smith JW: Tuftsin deficiency: A new syndrome with defective phagocytosis. *J Pediatr* 1972;**80**:564.

Lazy Leukocyte Syndrome

Miller ME, Oski FA, Harris MB: Lazy-leukocyte syndrome: A new disorder of neutrophil function. *Lancet* 1971;**1**:665.

Increased IgE, Abnormal Chemotaxis, & Recurrent Infections

Hill HR, Quie PG: Raised serum IgE levels and defective neutrophil chemotaxis in three children with eczema and recurrent bacterial infections. *Lancet* 1974;**1**:183.

Leukocyte Movement

Boxer LA, Henley-Whyte ET, Stossel TP: Neutrophil action dysfunction and abnormal neutrophil behavior. *N Engl J Med* 1974;**291**:1093.

Gallin JL: Abnormal chemotaxis: Cellular and humoral components. Pages 227–248 in: *The Phagocytic Cell in Host Resistance*. Bellanti JA, Dayton DH (editors). Raven Press, 1975.

C1q,r,s Deficiency

Day NK et al: C1r deficiency: An inborn error associated with cutaneous and renal disease. *J Clin Invest* 1972;**51**:1102.

Wara DW et al: Persistent C1q deficiency in a patient with a systemic lupus-like syndrome. *J Pediatr* 1975;**86**:743.

C2 Deficiency

Day NK et al: C2 deficiency: Development of lupus erythematosus. *J Clin Invest* 1973;**52**:1601.

C3 Deficiency

Alper CA, Bloch KJ, Rosen FS: Increased susceptibility to infection in a patient with type II essential hypercatabolism of C3. *N Engl J Med* 1973;**288**:601.

Alper CA et al: Studies in vitro and in vivo on an abnormality in the metabolism of C3 in a patient with increased susceptibility to infection. *J Clin Invest* 1970;**49**:1975.

Familial C5 Dysfunction

Miller ME, Nilsson UR: A familial deficiency of the phagocytosis-enhancing activity of serum related to a dysfunction of the fifth component of complement (C5). *N Engl J Med* 1970;**282**:354.

C6 Deficiency

Leddy JP et al: Hereditary deficiency of the sixth component of complement in man. 1. Immunochemical, biologic and family status. *J Clin Invest* 1974;**53**:554.

Petersen BH et al: *Neisseria meningitidis* and *Neisseria gonorrhoeae* bacteremia associated with C6, C7, or C8 deficiency. *Ann Intern Med* 1979;**90**:917.

C7 Deficiency

Boyer JT et al: Hereditary deficiency of the seventh component of complement. *J Clin Invest* 1975;**56**:905.

Petersen BH et al: *Neisseria meningitidis* and *Neisseria gonorrhoeae* bacteremia associated with C6, C7, or C8 deficiency. *Ann Intern Med* 1979;**90**:917.

C8 Deficiency

Petersen BH et al: *Neisseria meningitidis* and *Neisseria gonorrhoeae* bacteremia associated with C6, C7, or C8 deficiency. *Ann Intern Med* 1979;**90**:917.

Secondary Immunodeficiency

Chandra RK: Immunodeficiency in undernutrition and overnutrition. *Nutr Rev* (June) 1981;**39**:225.

Gottlieb MS et al: *Pneumocystis carinii* pneumonia and mucosal candidiasis in previous healthy homosexual men. *N Engl J Med* 1981;**305**:1426.

26 | Rheumatic Diseases

Kenneth H. Fye, MD, & Kenneth E. Sack, MD

Many of the major rheumatologic disorders are autoimmune in nature. Therefore, a thorough understanding of the mechanisms of the immune response is essential to the rheumatologist. In this chapter we shall discuss the rheumatologic diseases with proved or hypothesized immunologic pathogenesis. It might be helpful to refer to the previous chapter on autoimmunity if questions arise during the study of the rheumatic diseases.

SYSTEMIC LUPUS ERYTHEMATOSUS (SLE)

Major Immunologic Features
- Positive LE phenomenon.
- High-titer antinuclear antibodies (diffuse or outline pattern on immunofluorescence).
- Anti–single-stranded and anti–double-stranded DNA antibodies.
- Depressed serum complement levels.
- Deposition of immunoglobulin and complement along glomerular basement membrane and at the dermal-epidermal junction.
- Numerous other autoantibodies.

General Considerations
The systemic manifestations of systemic lupus erythematosus were first described by Osler in 1895. Prior to that time, lupus was considered to be a disfiguring but nonfatal skin disease. It is now known to be a chronic systemic inflammatory disease that follows a course of alternating exacerbations and remissions. Multiple organ system involvement (eg, arthritis, nephritis, pleuritis) characteristically occurs during periods of disease activity. The cause is not known. The disease affects predominantly females (4:1) of childbearing age; however, the age at onset ranges from 2 to 90 years. The incidence is higher among nonwhites (particularly blacks) than whites.

Immunologic Pathogenesis
The discovery of the LE cell phenomenon marked the start of the modern era of research into the pathogenesis of systemic lupus erythematosus. This initial clinical observation led to the finding of antinuclear factors and antibodies to DNA in the sera of patients with systemic lupus erythematosus. Further studies of renal eluates from patients with systemic lupus erythematosus established the importance of DNA-containing immune complexes in the causation of lupus glomerulonephritis. Reduced serum complement and the presence of antibodies to double-stranded (ds) DNA have become routine correlates of active systemic lupus erythematosus, distinguishing this entity from other lupus variants. The cause of antibody formation to DNA is uncertain. Antibodies to ds-DNA cannot be provoked by experimental immunization and occur almost exclusively in systemic lupus erythematosus and in New Zealand black (NZB) mice, an animal model for systemic lupus erythematosus (see Chapter 13). It is not known whether viral or host DNA is the immunogen for anti-DNA antibody formation. The presence of antibodies to viral surface antigens, to single-stranded DNA, and to DNA:RNA hybrids is indirect evidence that immunization to viral antigens may be occurring in the disease.

Additional autoantibody activity is also intimately associated with the pathogenesis of systemic lupus erythematosus. Lymphocytotoxic antibodies (with predominant specificity for T lymphocytes) occur in many patients with systemic lupus erythematosus and in NZB mice. Such antibodies are capable of killing T lymphocytes in the presence of complement and of coating peripheral blood T cells so as to interfere with HLA typing and with certain functional activities such as the proliferative response to alloantigens. These antibodies have specificity for T cell surface antigens and can be released from the lymphocyte cell surface in the form of specific antigen-antibody complexes. Such complexes may themselves attach to and block the function of other lymphocytes or may contribute to immune complex deposition, leading to vasculitis and nephritis.

The overall immune status in patients with systemic lupus erythematosus and in NZB mice can generally be summarized as an imbalance in which T cell activity is depressed and B cell activity is often enhanced. Delayed hypersensitivity responses may be impaired, in part because of the action of lymphocytotoxic antibodies. Antibody formation is both qualitatively and quantitatively excessive, with unusual and higher-titered antibody responses occurring.

Autoantibody formation is normally prevented

through the action of T regulatory lymphocytes called suppressor T cells. Although the mechanism of suppression is unknown, such suppressor T cells probably play an important role in immunologic tolerance and self/nonself discrimination (see Chapter 13). A deficiency of suppressor T cells has been demonstrated in NZB mice. This deficiency is related to a decrease in concentration of circulating thymic hormone. Administration of thymic hormone to NZB mice can prevent this loss of suppressor T cells and slightly delay the onset of autoimmunity. As NZB mice age and clinical autoimmune disease becomes apparent, there is a marked loss of other T cell effector functions. Such mice are immunologically impaired and susceptible to various infectious agents, including oncogenic viruses. Lymphomas and monoclonal macroglobulinemia commonly develop at this stage.

A number of human family studies have suggested a genetic susceptibility to the development of systemic lupus erythematosus. It has now been clearly demonstrated that lupus patients share common B cell alloantigens. What role these alloantigens play in the pathogenesis of systemic lupus erythematosus has yet to be determined.

Systemic lupus erythematosus, like many rheumatic disorders, occurs predominantly in women. Studies have demonstrated that estrogens enhance anti-DNA antibody formation and increase the severity of renal disease in NZB/NZW mice. Androgens have an opposite effect on both anti-DNA antibody production and renal disease. The mechanisms by which sex hormones influence immunologic phenomena are unknown.

Clinical Features

A. Symptoms and Signs: Systemic lupus erythematosus presents no single characteristic clinical pattern. The onset can be acute or insidious. Constitutional symptoms include fever, weight loss, malaise, and lethargy. Every organ system may become involved.

1. Skin–The most common skin lesion is an erythematous rash involving areas of the body chronically exposed to ultraviolet light. Relatively few patients with systemic lupus erythematosus develop the classic "butterfly" rash or the characteristic erythematous rash over the fingertips and palms. In some cases, the rash is similar in appearance to that of discoid lupus erythematosus. The rash may resolve without sequelae or may result in scar formation, atrophy, and hypo- or hyperpigmentation. In addition, bullae, patches of purpura, urticaria, angioneurotic edema, patches of vitiligo, subcutaneous nodules, and thickening of the skin may be seen. Vasculitic lesions are common and can lead to ischemic ulceration or pyoderma gangrenosum. Alopecia, which may be diffuse, patchy, or circumscribed, is also common. Mucosal ulcerations, involving both oral and genital mucosa, are present in about 15% of cases. Raynaud's phenomenon also occurs in about 15% of patients with systemic lupus erythematosus.

2. Joints and muscles–Polyarthralgia is the most common manifestation of systemic lupus erythematosus (90%). The arthritis is symmetric and can involve almost any joint. It may resemble rheumatoid arthritis, but bony erosions and ulnar deviation are unusual.

Tenosynovitis seldom occurs. Avascular necrosis of bone is a frequent occurrence in systemic lupus erythematosus. The femoral head is most frequently affected, but other bones may also be involved. Corticosteroids, which are a major therapeutic resource in systemic lupus erythematosus, may play a role in the pathogenesis of this complication. Myalgias, with or without frank myositis, are common.

3. Polyserositis–Pleurisy is a frequent manifestation. Although one-third of cases have pleural fluid, massive effusion is rare. Involvement of the pleura produces pleuritic chest pain and shortness of breath. Pericarditis is the commonest form of cardiac involvement and can be the first manifestation of systemic lupus erythematosus. The pericarditis is usually benign, with only mild chest discomfort and a pericardial friction rub, but severe pericarditis leading to tamponade may be seen. Peritonitis alone is extremely rare, although 5–10% of patients with pleuritis and pericarditis have concomitant peritonitis. Manifestations of peritonitis include abdominal pain, anorexia, nausea and vomiting, and, rarely, ascites.

4. Lungs–Lupus pneumonitis is an unusual manifestation. When a pulmonary infiltrate develops in a patient with systemic lupus erythematosus, particularly one being treated with corticosteroids or immunosuppressive drugs, infection must be the first diagnostic consideration. The commonest form of lupus pulmonary involvement is restrictive interstitial lung disease, which may be asymptomatic and detectable only by pulmonary function tests. The chest x-ray is usually normal but may show "platelike" atelectasis or interstitial fibrosis with "honeycombing." Other pulmonary manifestations include alveolar hemorrhage, pneumothorax, hemothorax, and vasculitis.

5. Heart–Clinically apparent myocarditis occurs rarely in systemic lupus erythematosus, but when present may result in congestive heart failure, with tachycardia, gallop rhythm, and cardiomegaly. Arrhythmias are unusual and are considered a preterminal event. The endocarditis of systemic lupus erythematosus is very difficult to diagnose. The verrucous endocarditis of systemic lupus erythematosus, with the characteristic Libman-Sacks vegetations, is usually diagnosed only at autopsy. Thickening of the aortic valve cusps with resultant aortic insufficiency can occur.

6. Kidney–Renal involvement is a frequent and serious feature of systemic lupus erythematosus. Seventy-five percent of patients have nephritis at autopsy. With the extensive use of percutaneous renal biopsy and the study of renal tissue by light microscopy, immunofluorescence, and electron microscopy, 4 histologic lesions associated with rather distinctive clinical features can be distinguished: (1) Mesangial glomerulonephritis is characterized by hypercellularity and the deposition of immune complexes in the mesangium. This is a benign form of lupus nephritis. (2) In focal glomerulonephritis, segmental proliferation occurs in less than 50% of glomeruli. Immune complexes are deposited in the mesangium and in the subendothelium of the glomerular capillary. Focal glomerulonephritis is usually a benign process, but on occasion it may progress to a diffuse proliferative lesion. (3) Diffuse proliferative glomerulonephritis is characterized by extensive cellular proliferation in more than 50% of glomeruli. Immune complexes are deposited largely in subendothelial distribution. This process frequently leads to renal failure. (4) In membranous glomerulonephritis, glomerular cellularity is normal, but the capillary basement membrane is thickened. Immune complexes are deposited mainly in subepithelial and intramembranous areas. This lesion may be associated with the development of renal failure.

It must be emphasized that in individual patients, a benign renal lesion may evolve into a more serious one.

Systemic hypertension is a common finding in acute or chronic lupus renal disease.

7. Nervous system–Cerebral involvement is a life-threatening complication of systemic lupus erythematosus. Disturbances of mentation and aberrant behavior, such as psychosis or depression, are the commonest manifestations of central nervous system involvement. Convulsions, cranial nerve palsies, aseptic meningitis, migraine headache, peripheral neuritis, and cerebrovascular accidents may also occur.

8. Eye–Ocular involvement, both retinal and corneal, is present in 20–25% of patients. The characteristic retinal finding (the cytoid body) is a fluffy white exudative lesion caused by focal degeneration of the nerve fiber layer of the retina. Corneal ulceration occurs in conjunction with Sjögren's syndrome (see below).

9. Gastrointestinal system–Gastrointestinal ulceration due to vasculitis can occur in systemic lupus erythematosus but is uncommon. Pancreatitis is not unusual, and acute and chronic hepatitis may occur.

10. Hematopoietic system–See Laboratory Findings, below.

11. Sjögren's syndrome–Five to 10% of patients with systemic lupus erythematosus develop the sicca complex (keratoconjunctivitis sicca, xerostomia).

12. Drug-induced lupuslike syndrome–Certain drugs may provoke a lupuslike picture in susceptible individuals. The most commonly implicated drugs, hydralazine and procainamide, can induce arthralgias, arthritis, skin rash, and, less commonly, fever and pleurisy. Nephritis and central nervous system involvement are thought not to occur. The serologic picture is similar to that of systemic lupus erythematosus, but antibody to native ds-DNA occurs only rarely. The disease usually remits when the drug is discontinued. The list of agents that produce a lupuslike syndrome is increasing rapidly and includes phenytoin, trimethadione, mephenytoin, isoniazid, aminosalicylic acid, penicillin, tetracyclines, penicillamine, sulfonamides, streptomycin, griseofulvin, phenylbutazone, oral contraceptives, methyl- and propylthiouracil, methyldopa, and levodopa.

B. Laboratory Findings: Anemia is the commonest hematologic finding in systemic lupus erythematosus. Eighty percent of patients present with a normochromic, normocytic anemia due to marrow suppression. A few develop Coombs-positive hemolytic anemia. Leukopenia is common, but the white count rarely falls below 2000/μL. Thrombocytopenia is commonly seen. Urinalysis may reveal hematuria, proteinuria, and red and white cell casts. The sedimentation rate is high in almost all cases. Serologic abnormalities are described in the section on immunologic diagnosis (below). The synovial fluid in systemic lupus erythematosus is yellow and clear, with a low viscosity. The white cell count does not exceed 4000/μL, most of which are lymphocytes. Complement levels are low. The pleural effusion of systemic lupus erythematosus is a transudate with a predominance of lymphocytes and a total white cell count of no more than 3000/μL. A hemorrhagic pleural effusion is very rare. In central nervous system lupus, the cerebrospinal fluid protein concentration is sometimes elevated, and there is occasionally a mild lymphocytosis.

There are numerous characteristic pathologic changes in systemic lupus erythematosus:

(1) The verrucous endocarditis of Libman-Sacks consists of ovoid vegetations, 1–4 mm in diameter, which form along the base of the valve and, rarely, on the chordae tendinea and papillary muscles.

(2) A peculiar periarterial concentric fibrosis results in the so-called "onion skin" lesion seen in the spleen.

(3) The pathognomonic finding in systemic lupus erythematosus, the "hematoxylin body," consists of a homogeneous globular mass of nuclear material which stains bluish purple with hematoxylin. Hematoxylin bodies have been found in the heart, kidneys, lungs, spleen, lymph nodes, and serous and synovial membranes. It should be emphasized that patients with fulminant systemic lupus erythematosus involving the central nervous system, skin, muscles, joints, and kidneys may not have any distinctive pathologic abnormalities at autopsy.

C. X-Ray and Other Findings: Chest x-ray may reveal cardiomegaly (due either to pericarditis or myocarditis), pleural effusion, platelike atelectasis, or interstitial fibrosis with a "honeycomb" appearance. Joint x-rays may show soft tissue swelling and mild osteopenia but rarely show erosions. The lumbar puncture, cerebrospinal fluid, EEG, and radionuclide brain scan are abnormal in many cases of central nervous system involvement.

Immunologic Diagnosis

A. Proteins and Complement: Most patients with systemic lupus erythematosus (80%) present with elevated α_2- and γ-globulins. Hypoalbuminemia is occasionally present. The serum complement is frequently reduced in the presence of active disease, probably because of increased utilization due to immune complex formation, to reduced synthesis, or to a combination of both factors. The serum of patients with active systemic lupus erythematosus occasionally contains circulating cryoglobulin complexes of IgM/IgG aggregates and complement that will precipitate in the cold. The concentration of free urinary light chains correlates positively with the activity of renal disease.

B. Autoantibodies:

1. LE cell phenomenon–This phenomenon was first described in the bone marrow of patients with systemic lupus erythematosus. It reflects the presence of 7S IgG antinuclear antibodies. However, this relatively cumbersome and insensitive technique is largely of historic interest and should be abandoned.

2. Antinuclear antibodies (ANA)–Immunoglobulins of all classes may form antinuclear antibodies. Friou in 1957 introduced the indirect immunofluorescence technique. Six different morphologic patterns of immunofluorescent staining have been described, 4 of which have clinical significance (Fig 26–1).

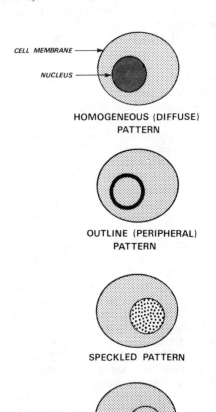

HOMOGENEOUS (DIFFUSE)
PATTERN

OUTLINE (PERIPHERAL)
PATTERN

SPECKLED PATTERN

NUCLEOLAR PATTERN

CELL MEMBRANE

NUCLEUS

Figure 26–1. Patterns of immunofluorescent staining for antinuclear antibodies.

a. The "homogeneous" ("diffuse" or "solid") pattern is the morphologic expression of antideoxyribonucleoprotein antibodies and is strongly associated with active systemic lupus erythematosus. In this pattern, the nucleus shows diffuse and uniform staining.

b. The "outline" ("shaggy" or "peripheral") pattern is the morphologic expression of anti-ds-DNA antibodies and antibodies to soluble nucleoprotein. The outline pattern is best seen when human leukocytes are used as substrate. It is characteristic of active systemic lupus erythematosus.

c. The "speckled" pattern reflects the presence of antibodies directed against non-DNA nuclear constituents. The antigens to which these antibodies are directed can be extracted from the nucleus using saline. The anti-ENA (extractable nuclear antigen) assay detects antibodies against the extractable nuclear antigens, the Sm (Smith) antigen and RNP (ribonucleoprotein) antigen. Antibodies against the Sm antigen are characteristic of systemic lupus erythematosus. High titers of anti-RNP antibodies are the hallmark of mixed connective tissue disease. Other antinuclear antibodies have been described in Sjögren's syndrome, rheumatoid arthritis, scleroderma, and polymyositis-dermatomyositis.

d. The "nucleolar" pattern is caused by the homogeneous staining of the nucleolus. It has been suggested that this antigen may be the ribosomal precursor of ribonucleoprotein. This pattern is most often associated with scleroderma or polymyositis-dermatomyositis.

All the nuclear staining patterns must be interpreted with caution for the following reasons: (1) The serum of a patient with any rheumatic disease may contain many autoantibodies to different nuclear constituents, so that a "homogeneous" pattern may obscure a "speckled" or "nucleolar" pattern; (2) different antibodies in the serum can be present in different titers, so that by diluting the serum one can change the pattern observed; (3) the stability of the different antigens is different and can be changed by fixation or denaturation; and (4) the pattern observed appears to be influenced by the types of tissues or cells used as substrate for the test.

The ANA determination is occasionally positive in normal individuals, in patients with various chronic diseases, and in the aged. However, high titers are most often associated with systemic lupus erythematosus. Absence of ANA is strong evidence against a diagnosis of systemic lupus erythematosus.

3. Anti-DNA antibodies–Three major types of anti-DNA antibodies can be found in the sera of lupus patients: (1) anti–single-stranded or "denatured" DNA (ss-DNA); (2) anti–double-stranded or "native" DNA (ds-DNA); and (3) antibodies that react to both ss-DNA and ds-DNA. These antibodies may be either IgG or IgM immunoglobulins. High titers of anti–ds-DNA antibodies are essentially seen only in systemic lupus erythematosus. In contrast, anti-ss-DNA antibodies are not specific and can be found in other autoimmune diseases, eg, rheumatoid arthritis, chronic active hepatitis, and primary biliary cirrhosis. Furthermore, antibodies to ss-DNA occur in drug-induced lupuslike syndrome and can be induced in experimental animals by the injection of DNA complexed to protein and emulsified in Freund's complete adjuvant. Antibodies to DNA can be quantitatively measured by a radioimmunoassay using labeled DNA. Complement-fixing and high-avidity anti-ds-DNA antibodies are closely associated with the development of renal disease. The amount of antibody correlates well with disease activity, and the antibody titer frequently decreases when patients enter remission.

4. Anti-RNA antibodies–Anti–double-stranded RNA (ds-RNA) antibodies and antibodies against DNA:RNA hybrid molecules are found in 70% of patients with systemic lupus erythematosus. Anti-ds-RNA antibodies react to viral as well as synthetic ds-RNA (eg, poly I · C, poly A · U). Antibodies to ds-RNA are not as specific for systemic lupus erythematosus as anti–ds-DNA antibodies, but they are more specific than anti–ss-DNA antibodies. They are not necessarily associated with lupus nephritis and are not generally found in the renal immune complexes. Because ds-RNA is commonly associated with certain types of viruses, it is possible that anti–ds-RNA reflects viral infection.

5. Antierythrocyte antibodies–These antibodies belong to all major immunoglobulin classes and can be detected by the direct Coombs test. The prevalence of these antibodies among systemic lupus erythematosus patients is not precisely known but ranges from 10–65%. Hemolytic anemia is, however, rare. When present, it is associated with a complement-fixing warm antierythrocyte antibody.

6. Circulating anticoagulants and antiplatelet antibodies–A circulating anticoagulant that prolongs the partial thromboplastin and prothrombin times develops in 10–15% of patients with systemic lupus erythematosus. It appears to be an antibody directed against phospholipid, and for this reason it occurs with increased frequency in patients with a false-positive VDRL. Hemorrhagic complications are rare, but paradoxic thrombotic states may develop, possibly from inhibition of prostacyclin formation or from low levels of antithrombin III. Specific anti-factor VIII antibodies have also been described. These antibodies are potent anticoagulants and may be associated with bleeding. Antiplatelet antibodies are found in 75–80% of patients with systemic lupus erythematosus. These antibodies inhibit neither clot retraction nor thromboplastin generation in normal blood. They probably induce thrombocytopenia by direct effects on platelet surface membrane.

7. False-positive serologic test for syphilis–A false-positive VDRL test is seen in 10–20% of patients with systemic lupus erythematosus. The serologic test for syphilis can be considered an autoimmune reaction, because the antigen is a phospholipid present in many human organs (see above).

8. Rheumatoid factors–Almost 30% of patients with systemic lupus erythematosus have a positive latex fixation test for rheumatoid factors.

9. Anticytoplasmic antibodies–Numerous anticytoplasmic antibodies (antimitochondrial, antiribosomal, antilysosomal) have been found in patients with systemic lupus erythematosus. These antibodies are not organ- or species-specific. Antiribosomal antibodies are found in the sera of 25–50% of patients. The major antigenic determinant is ribosomal RNA. Antimitochondrial antibodies are more common in other diseases (eg, primary biliary cirrhosis) than in systemic lupus erythematosus.

C. Tissue Immunofluorescence Studies:

1. Kidney–(See Chapter 31.) Irregular or granular accumulation of immunoglobulin and complement occurs along the glomerular basement membrane and in the mesangium in patients with lupus nephritis. On electron microscopy, these deposits are seen in subepithelial, subendothelial, and mesangial sites.

2. Skin–Almost 90% of patients with systemic lupus erythematosus have immunoglobulin and complement deposition in the dermal-epidermal junction of skin which is *not* involved with an active lupus rash. Patients with discoid lupus erythematosus show deposition of immunoglobulin and complement only in involved skin (see Chapter 32).

Differential Diagnosis

The diagnosis of systemic lupus erythematosus in patients with classic multisystem involvement and a positive ANA test is not difficult. However, the onset of the disease can be vague and insidious and can therefore present a perplexing diagnostic problem. When polyarthritis is the major complaint, viral infections, bacterial endocarditis, mixed connective tissue disease, rheumatoid arthritis and rheumatic fever have to be considered. When Raynaud's phenomenon is the predominant complaint, progressive systemic sclerosis must be considered. Systemic lupus erythematosus can present with a myositis similar to that of polymyositis-dermatomyositis. The clinical constellation of arthritis, alopecia, and a positive VDRL should suggest secondary syphilis.

Felty's syndrome (thrombocytopenia, leukopenia, splenomegaly in patients with rheumatoid arthritis) can simulate systemic lupus erythematosus. Sometimes the diagnosis of systemic lupus erythematosus can be facilitated by finding anti-ds-DNA or a high titer of ANA (outline pattern) in serum. Some patients with discoid lupus erythematosus may develop leukopenia, thrombocytopenia, hypergammaglobulinemia, a positive ANA, and an elevated sedimentation rate. Ten percent of patients with discoid lupus erythematosus have LE cells and associated mild systemic symptoms. Although the exact relationship between systemic lupus erythematosus and discoid lupus erythematosus is uncertain, the frequent presence of anti-ds-RNA in discoid lupus erythematosus suggests that they are parts of a single disease spectrum.

Treatment

The efficacy of the drugs used in the treatment of systemic lupus erythematosus is difficult to evaluate, since spontaneous remissions occur in the disease. There are few controlled studies, because it is difficult to withhold therapy in the face of the life-threatening disease which can develop in fulminant systemic lupus erythematosus. Depending on the severity of the disease, no treatment, minimal treatment (aspirin, antimalarials), or intensive treatment (corticosteroids, cytotoxic drugs) may be required.

When arthritis is the predominant symptom and other organ systems are not significantly involved, aspirin in high doses is the treatment of choice. When the skin or mucosa is predominantly involved, antimalarials (hydroxychloroquine or chloroquine) and topical corticosteroids are very beneficial. Because high-dosage antimalarial therapy may be associated with irreversible retinal toxicity, these drugs should be used judiciously and in low doses.

Systemic corticosteroids in severe systemic lupus erythematosus can suppress disease activity and prolong life. The administration of systemic corticosteroids in the absence of fulminant or life-threatening systemic lupus erythematosus is unnecessary and dangerous. The mode of action is unknown, but the immunosuppressive and anti-inflammatory properties of these agents presumably play a significant role in their therapeutic efficacy. High-dosage corticosteroid treatment (eg, prednisone, 1 mg/kg/d orally) decreases γ-globulin levels and autoantibody titers and suppresses immune responses. High-dosage corticosteroid therapy is recommended in acute fulminant lupus, acute lupus nephritis, acute central nervous system lupus, acute autoimmune hemolytic anemia, and thrombocytopenic purpura. The course of corticosteroid therapy should be monitored by the clinical response and meticulous follow-up of laboratory and immunologic parameters—complete blood count with reticulocyte and platelet counts, anti–ds-DNA titer, complement levels, etc.

If the clinical and immunologic status of the patient fails to improve or if serious side-effects of corticosteroid therapy develop, immunosuppressive therapy with cytotoxic agents such as cyclophosphamide, chlorambucil, or azathioprine is indicated. Because of serious complications (malignancy, marrow suppression, infection, and liver and gastrointestinal toxicity), immunosuppressive agents should be used with discretion.

Complications & Prognosis

Systemic lupus erythematosus may run a very mild course confined to one or a few organs, or it may be a fulminant fatal disease. Renal failure and central nervous system lupus were the leading causes of death until the corticosteroids and cytotoxic agents came into widespread use. Since then, steroid-induced atherosclerosis, infection, and cancer have become common causes of death. The 5-year survival rate of patients with systemic lupus erythematosus has markedly improved over the past decade and now approaches 80–90%.

RHEUMATOID ARTHRITIS

Major Immunologic Features

- 7S and 19S IgM and 7S IgG rheumatoid factors in serum and synovial fluid.
- Decreased complement and elevated β_2-microglobulin in synovial fluid.

General Considerations

Rheumatoid arthritis is a chronic recurrent, systemic inflammatory disease primarily involving the joints. Constitutional symptoms include malaise, fever, and weight loss. The disease characteristically begins in the small joints of the hands and feet and progresses in a centripetal and symmetric fashion. Deformities are common. Extra-articular manifestations are characteristic of the rheumatoid process and often cause significant morbidity. Extra-articular manifestations include vasculitis, atrophy of the skin and muscle, subcutaneous nodules, lymphadenopathy, splenomegaly, and leukopenia.

The disease affects 1–3% of Americans, with a female to male ratio of 3:1.

Immunologic Pathogenesis

The antigenic stimulus that initiates the immune response and subsequent inflammation in rheumatoid arthritis is unknown. Increased prevalence of HLA-Dw4 and HLA-DRw4 occurs in patients with rheumatoid arthritis. The genetic mechanism that promotes the development of rheumatoid arthritis is unknown, but HLA-Dw4 may impart a genetic susceptibility to an unidentified environmental factor, such as a virus, that initiates the disease process. Although no virus particles have ever been identified, it is likely that an antigenic stimulus leads to the appearance of an abnormal IgG that results in the production of rheumatoid factor and the eventual development of rheumatoid disease (Fig 26–2).

Recent studies have suggested a possible relationship between EB virus and rheumatoid arthritis. Rheumatoid patients have a high frequency of precipitating serum antibody (RA precipitin, RAP) that reacts specifically with a nuclear antigen from an EB virus containing human lymphoblastoid cell line. This antigen (RA nuclear antigen, RANA) is only expressed in EB virus infected cells. The EB virus is a polyclonal stimulator of B cells and can lead to the in vitro production of rheumatoid factor by human B cells. However, because of the high frequency of RAP in normal controls, any causal relationship of EB virus with rheumatoid arthritis remains speculative.

Synovial lymphocytes produce IgG that is recognized as foreign and stimulates an immune response within the joint, with production of 7S IgG, 7S IgM, and 19S IgM anti-immunoglobulins, ie, rheumatoid factors. The presence of IgG aggregates or IgG-

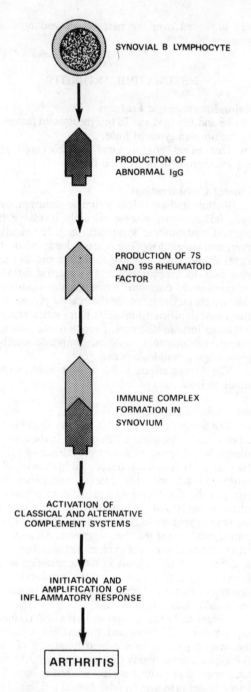

SYNOVIAL B LYMPHOCYTE

PRODUCTION OF
ABNORMAL IgG

PRODUCTION OF 7S
AND 19S RHEUMATOID
FACTOR

IMMUNE COMPLEX
FORMATION IN
SYNOVIUM

ACTIVATION OF
CLASSICAL AND ALTERNATIVE
COMPLEMENT SYSTEMS

INITIATION AND
AMPLIFICATION OF
INFLAMMATORY RESPONSE

ARTHRITIS

Figure 26–2. Hypothetical immunopathogenesis in rheumatoid arthritis.

rheumatoid factor complexes results in activation of the classic complement system. Breakdown products of complement accumulate within the joint and amplify the activation of complement by stimulation of the alternative (properdin) system. Activation of the complement system results in a number of inflammatory phenomena, including histamine release, the production of factors chemotactic for polymorphonuclear

leukocytes and mononuclear cells, and membrane damage with cell lysis (see Chapter 11). There is a marked influx of white cells into the synovial space. Prostaglandins produced by immunocytes are thought to play a major role in mediation of the inflammatory process. In addition, activated lysosomes and enzymes released into the synovial space by leukocytes further amplify the inflammatory and proliferative response of the synovium. The mononuclear infiltrate characteristically seen within the synovium includes perivascular collections of small lymphocytes, lymphoblasts, plasma cells, and macrophages. The lymphocytic infiltrate is made up of both T and B cells. The immunologic interaction of these cells leads to the liberation of lymphokines responsible for the accumulation of macrophages within the inflammatory synovium and to continued immunoglobulin and rheumatoid factor synthesis.

Rheumatoid factor may play a role in the causation of extra-articular disease. Patients with rheumatoid vasculitis have high titers of 19S and 7S IgM and 7S IgG rheumatoid factors. Antigen-antibody complexes infused into experimental animals in the presence of IgM rheumatoid factor induce necrotizing vasculitis. Theoretically, immune complexes initiate vascular inflammation by the activation of complement. Pulmonary involvement is associated with the deposition of 11S and 15S protein complexes containing IgG in the walls of pulmonary vessels and alveoli. 19S IgM rheumatoid factor has also been detected in arterioles and alveolar walls adjacent to cavitary nodules. Rheumatoid factors do not initiate the inflammatory process that causes rheumatoid disease, but they probably perpetuate and amplify that process by their effects on complement activation.

Clinical Features

A. Symptoms and Signs:

1. Onset–The usual age at onset is 20–40 years. In most cases the disease presents with joint manifestations; however, some patients first develop extra-articular manifestations, including fatigue, weakness, weight loss, mild fever, and anorexia.

2. Articular manifestations–Patients experience stiffness and joint pain which are generally worse in the morning and improve throughout the day. These symptoms are accompanied by signs of articular inflammation, including swelling, warmth, erythema, and tenderness on palpation. The arthritis is symmetric, involving the small joints of the hands and feet, ie, the proximal interphalangeals, metacarpophalangeals, the wrists, and the subtalars. Large joints (knees, hips, elbows, ankles, shoulders) commonly become involved later in the course of the disease. Although the cervical spine may be involved, the thoracic and lumbosacral spine is usually spared.

Periarticular inflammation is common, with tendonitis and tenosynovitis resulting in weakening of tendons, ligaments, and supporting structures. Joint pain leads to muscle spasm, limitation of motion, and, in advanced cases, muscle contractions and ankylosis with permanent joint deformity. The most characteristic deformities in the hand are ulnar deviation of the fingers, the "boutonniére" deformity (flexed proximal interphalangeal joints are forced through the extensor hood), and the "swan neck" deformity (hyperextension of proximal interphalangeal joints and flexion of the distal interphalangeal joints resulting from contractures of intrinsic hand muscles).

3. Extra-articular manifestations–Twenty to 25% of patients (particularly those with severe disease) have subcutaneous or subperiosteal nodules, the so-called rheumatoid nodules. These are usually present over bony eminences and may be difficult to distinguish clinically from gouty tophi. The most common sites of nodule formation are the olecranon bursa and the extensor surface of the forearm. Nodules are firm, nontender, round or oval masses which can be movable or fixed. They may be found in the myocardium, pericardium, heart valves, pleura, lungs, sclera, dura mater, spleen, larynx, and synovial tissues.

Lung involvement includes pleurisy, interstitial lymphocytic pneumonitis or fibrosis, and Caplan's syndrome (development of large nodules in the lung parenchyma in patients with rheumatoid arthritis who also have pneumoconiosis). The manifestations of rheumatoid cardiac disease include pericarditis, myocarditis, valvular insufficiency, and conduction disturbances.

Several types of vasculitis are associated with rheumatoid arthritis. The commonest form is an obliterative vasculitis due to intimal proliferation which leads to peripheral neuropathy. Less common is a subacute vasculitis associated with ischemic ulceration of the skin. The rarest form of rheumatoid vasculitis is a necrotizing vasculitis of medium and large vessels indistinguishable from polyarteritis nodosa. The major neurologic abnormalities in rheumatoid arthritis involve peripheral nerves. In addition to the peripheral neuropathy associated with vasculitis, there are a number of entrapment syndromes due to impingement of periarticular inflammatory tissue or amyloid on nerves passing through tight fascial planes that allow little room for inflammatory swelling. The carpal tunnel syndrome is a well-known complication of wrist disease; however, entrapment can also occur at the elbow, ankle, and knee. Destruction of the transverse ligament of the odontoid results in atlantoaxial subluxation. This generally causes no symptoms but may be associated with cord or nerve root impingement.

Sjögren's syndrome (keratoconjunctivitis sicca and xerostomia) may occur in up to 30% of patients. Myositis with lymphocytic infiltration of involved muscle is rarely seen. Ocular involvement ranges from benign inflammation of the surface of the sclera (episcleritis) to severe inflammation of the sclera, with nodule formation. Scleronodular disease can lead to weakening and thinning of the sclera (scleromalacia). A catastrophic but rare complication of scleromalacia is perforation of the eye with extrusion of vitreous (scleromalacia perforans).

4. Felty's syndrome–Felty's syndrome is the association of rheumatoid arthritis, splenomegaly, and neutropenia. The syndrome almost always develops in patients with high rheumatoid factor titers and rheumatoid nodules. Other features of hypersplenism and lymphadenopathy may also be present. These patients are at increased risk of developing bacterial infections.

B. Laboratory Findings: A normochromic, normocytic anemia, lymphocytosis, and thrombocytosis are common among patients with active disease. The sedimentation rate is elevated, and the degree of elevation correlates roughly with disease activity.

The synovial fluid is more inflammatory than that seen in degenerative osteoarthritis or systemic lupus erythematosus. The synovial fluid protein concentration ranges from 2.5 g/dL to over 3.5 g/dL. The white cell count is usually 5000–20,000/μL (rarely over 50,000/μL). Two-thirds of the cells are polymorphonuclear leukocytes that discharge lysosomal enzymes into the synovial fluid, leading to depolymerization of synovial hyaluronate, decreased viscosity, and a poor mucin clot. The glucose level may be low or normal. Rheumatoid factor can be found in synovial fluid, and complement is often depressed.

The rheumatoid pleural effusion is an exudate containing less than 5000 mononuclear or polymorphonuclear leukocytes per microliter. Protein exceeds 3 g/dL, and glucose is often reduced below 20 mg/dL. Rheumatoid factors can be detected, and complement levels are usually low.

There are 2 basic pathologic findings. The first is a recurrent or chronic inflammation of the joints leading to an inflammatory thickening of the synovium called pannus. The pannus may erode the articular cartilage and underlying bone, causing destruction and deformity of the joint.

The second finding, the rheumatoid nodule, consists of an irregularly shaped central zone of fibrinoid necrosis surrounded by a margin of large mononuclear cells. This core is surrounded in turn by an outer zone of granulation tissue containing plasma cells and lymphocytes.

C. X-Ray Findings: The first detectable x-ray abnormalities are soft tissue swelling and juxta-articular demineralization. The destruction of articular cartilage leads to joint space narrowing. Bony erosions develop at the junction of the synovial membrane and the "bare area" (unprotected cortical bone just adjacent to articular cartilage). Destruction of the cartilage and laxity of ligaments lead to maladjustment and subluxation of articular surfaces. Spondylitis is usually limited to the cervical spine, with osteoporosis, joint space narrowing, erosions, destruction, and finally subluxation of the involved articulations.

Immunologic Diagnosis

In rheumatoid arthritis, serum protein electrophoresis may show an increased α_2-globulin, a polyclonal hypergammaglobulinemia, and hypoalbuminemia. Cryoprecipitates composed of immunoglobulins are often seen in rheumatoid vasculitis. Serum complement levels are usually normal but may be low in the presence of active vasculitis. Five to 10% of patients have a false-positive VDRL; 8–27% have a positive LE cell preparation; and 20–70% have antinuclear antibodies. The most important serologic finding is the elevated rheumatoid factor titer, present in over 75% of patients. Rheumatoid factors are immunoglobulins with specificity for the Fc fragment of IgG. Most laboratory techniques detect 19S IgM rheumatoid factor, but rheumatoid factor properties are also seen in 7S IgM, IgG, and IgA immunoglobulins. 19S IgM rheumatoid factor may combine with IgG molecules to form a soluble circulating 22S immunoglobulin complex in the serum.

Several tests are available in the laboratory to detect rheumatoid factor. The earliest test, now rarely used, was the streptococcal agglutination reaction. The latex fixation test is now the most commonly used method for detection of rheumatoid factor. Aggregated γ-globulin (Cohn fraction II) is adsorbed onto latex particles, which will then agglutinate in the presence of rheumatoid factor. The latex fixation test is not specific but is very sensitive, resulting in a high incidence of false-positive results. The sensitized sheep red cell test (Rose-Waaler test) depends on specific antibody binding and is the most specific test in common use. Sheep red blood cells are coated with rabbit antibody against sheep red blood cells, and the sensitized sheep cells will then agglutinate in the presence of rheumatoid factor. More complicated tests include a radioimmunoassay for IgM rheumatoid factor and an immunodiffusion assay, which provides better quantification and more precise information on the immunoglobulin classes of rheumatoid factor.

It is important to emphasize that a negative rheumatoid factor by routine laboratory procedures does not exclude the diagnosis of rheumatoid arthritis. The so-called seronegative patient may have 7S IgG or IgM rheumatoid factor or circulating IgG-anti-IgG complexes. Conversely, rheumatoid factors are not unique to rheumatoid arthritis. Rheumatoid factor is also present in patients with systemic lupus erythematosus (30%), in a high percentage (90%) of patients with Sjögren's syndrome, and less often in patients with scleroderma or polymyositis. Positive agglutination reactions with the latex or bentonite tests also occur in patients with hypergammaglobulinemia associated with liver disease, kala-azar, sarcoidosis, and syphilis. The sensitized sheep red cell test is usually negative in these conditions. In some chronic infectious diseases such as leprosy and tuberculosis, both the latex and the sensitized sheep red cell tests may be positive. In subacute bacterial endocarditis, both tests may be positive during active disease and revert to negative as patients improve. The transient appearance of rheumatoid factor has been noted following vaccinations in military recruits. Epidemiologic studies have shown that a small number of normal people also have rheumatoid factors. A large proportion of old people have a positive latex test, though the sensitized sheep red cell test is generally negative.

Differential Diagnosis

In the patient with classic articular changes, bony erosions of the small joints of the hands and feet, and rheumatoid factor in serum or synovial fluid, the diagnosis of rheumatoid arthritis is not difficult. Early in the disease, or when extra-articular manifestations dominate the clinical picture, other rheumatic diseases (including systemic lupus erythematosus, Reiter's syndrome, gout, psoriatic arthritis, degenerative osteoarthritis, and the peripheral arthritis of chronic inflammatory bowel disease) or infectious processes may mimic rheumatoid arthritis. Patients with systemic lupus erythematosus can be distinguished by their characteristic skin lesions, renal disease, and diagnostic serologic abnormalities. Reiter's syndrome occurs in young men, generally affects joints of the lower extremity in an asymmetric fashion, and is often associated with urethritis and conjunctivitis. Gouty arthritis is usually an acute monoarthritis with negatively birefringent sodium urate crystals present within the white cells of inflammatory synovial fluid. Psoriatic arthritis often involves distal interphalangeal joints and produces nail changes. Degenerative arthritis is characterized by Heberden's nodes, lack of symmetric joint involvement, and involvement of the distal rather than the proximal interphalangeal joints. The peripheral arthritis of bowel disease usually occurs in large weight-bearing joints and is often associated with bowel symptoms. The polyarthritis associated with rubella vaccination, HBsAg antigenemia, or infectious mononucleosis can mimic early rheumatoid arthritis.

Treatment

A. Physical Therapy: A rational program of physical therapy is vital in the management of patients with rheumatoid arthritis. Such a program should consist of an appropriate balance of rest and exercise and the judicious use of heat or cold therapy. The patient may require complete or intermittent bed rest on a regular basis to combat inflammation or fatigue. In addition, specific joints may have to be put at rest through the use of braces, splints, or crutches. An exercise program emphasizing active range of motion movements must be initiated to maintain strength and mobility. Heat is valuable in alleviating muscle spasm, stiffness, and pain. Many patients need a hot shower or bath to loosen up in the morning, and others cannot perform their exercises adequately without prior heat treatment. Heating pads or paraffin baths are often used to apply heat to specific joints. Physical and occupational therapists can help the physician devise an appropriate physical therapy program.

B. Drug Treatment:

1. Salicylates–Salicylates are the mainstay of medical therapy of rheumatoid arthritis. Aspirin is an anti-inflammatory as well as an antipyretic and analgesic agent. Although its exact mechanism of action is uncertain, it may act in part by inhibiting the production of prostaglandins. The doses used in patients with rheumatoid arthritis range from 3.6–5.4 g (12–18 tablets) per day in divided doses. High-dosage aspirin therapy is associated with numerous side-effects. Tinnitus—with or without hearing loss—can be bothersome but is usually reversible with a minor decrease in dosage. Gastric upset is almost universal but can be partly alleviated by liberally using antacids and by encouraging patients to take their aspirin with meals. Some patients can avoid gastric irritation by using enteric-coated aspirin. Microscopic blood loss from the gastrointestinal tract is common and is not an indication for stopping aspirin therapy. Since aspirin does decrease platelet adhesiveness, it should be used cautiously in patients receiving coumarin anticoagulants.

2. Other nonsteroidal agents–Several other nonsteroidal anti-inflammatory agents have found limited use in the treatment of rheumatoid arthritis. Phenylbutazone may be used temporarily in acute flare-ups; it is not useful on a long-term basis because of its multiple severe side-effects (agranulocytosis, peptic ulceration, salt and water retention). Indomethacin may benefit some patients, but it too has serious side-effects (gastric intolerance, peptic ulceration, psychic disturbances, marrow depression). Other newer preparations (fenoprofen, ibuprofen, naproxen, sulindac, tolmetin, and mefenamic acid) may be useful in patients who cannot tolerate aspirin.

Many rheumatologists advocate the use of antimalarial drugs for prolonged periods in patients with severe disease. The antimalarials act slowly, often requiring 1–6 months of treatment for maximum therapeutic benefit. The preparations and dosages most often used are chloroquine, 250 mg orally daily, and hydroxychloroquine, 200–400 mg orally daily. The toxic side-effects of these agents include skin rashes, nausea and vomiting, and both corneal and retinal damage. The incidence of eye toxicity is rare at the low doses used in rheumatoid arthritis, but patients should have ophthalmologic examinations every 4–6 months while on antimalarial therapy.

3. Parenteral gold salt therapy–Although associated with a high incidence of toxic side-effects, parenteral gold salt therapy is of significant benefit to many patients. It is one of the few therapeutic agents that is believed to alter the long-term course of the disease. Gold acts as a lysosomal membrane stabilizer, but the relationship of this action to its therapeutic benefit is unclear. It is administered intramuscularly, with an initial test dose of 10 mg of gold salt. If no toxic reactions occur after the test dose, the patient receives 50 mg of gold salt intramuscularly every week for 10–14 weeks, every other week for 16 weeks, and then every 3–4 weeks indefinitely until the patient experiences clinical remission or toxicity develops. Toxic side-effects occur in 40% of patients and include dermatitis, photosensitivity, stomatitis, thrombocytopenia, agranulocytosis, hepatitis, aplastic anemia, peripheral neuropathy, nephritis with nephrotic syndrome, ulcerative enterocolitis, and

keratitis. Before each dose, the patient should be evaluated for possible toxic side-effects. A urinalysis, complete blood count, and platelet count should be obtained. Liver function tests should be performed periodically. Toxic side-effects may necessitate temporary or permanent withdrawal of the drug. Corticosteroids and dimercaprol or penicillamine may be of benefit if life-threatening toxicity occurs.

4. Penicillamine–Penicillamine has been found to be useful in the treatment of rheumatoid arthritis. The mechanism of action is unknown. Like gold, penicillamine is a slow-acting nonsteroidal anti-inflammatory agent, and it may take up to 6 months for a therapeutic response to become apparent. The incidence of drug toxicity is similar to that of gold, so during the initiation of therapy patients should be seen every other week for evaluation, including a complete blood count, platelet count, and urinalysis. The initial dose of 250 mg orally daily is increased by 125–250 mg every 4–12 weeks until improvement occurs or until the patient is receiving a maximum dose of 750 mg daily. Toxic side-effects include rash, loss of sense of taste, nausea and vomiting, anorexia, proteinuria, agranulocytosis, aplastic anemia, and thrombocytopenia. Less commonly, myasthenia, myositis, Goodpasture's syndrome, bronchiolitis, and a lupus-like syndrome may be seen. Since penicillamine is a chelating agent, it cannot be used simultaneously with gold salt therapy.

5. Corticosteroids–Corticosteroids can be used locally or systemically. Intermittent intra-articular injection of corticosteroids is useful for the patient with only a few symptomatic joints. Relief may last for months. However, multiple intra-articular corticosteroid injections of weight-bearing joints should be avoided, since multiple injections may lead to an increased incidence of degenerative arthritis. Systemic corticosteroids may induce a dramatic clinical response, but they should be used with extreme caution because of the many side-effects associated with long-term use. Usually, no more than 5–10 mg of prednisone daily is required. It is difficult to withdraw corticosteroids, since attempts to do so often result in clinical exacerbation of arthritis. Long-term systemic corticosteroid treatment results in hyperadrenocorticism and disruption of the pituitary-adrenal axis. Manifestations of corticosteroid toxicity include weight gain, moon facies, ecchymoses, hirsutism, diabetes mellitus, hypertension, osteoporosis, avascular necrosis of the femoral head, cataracts, myopathy, mental disturbances, activation of tuberculosis, and infections.

6. Immunosuppressive agents have been known to induce dramatic improvement in patients with severe disease and, like gold, may alter the course of the disease. Alkylating agents (eg, chlorambucil, cyclophosphamide) and purine analogs (eg, mercaptopurine, azathioprine) have been used in the treatment of rheumatoid arthritis. However, these drugs are associated with major toxic side-effects, may be teratogenic, and may be associated with an increased incidence of lymphoma and infection. The routine use of these agents in the treatment of rheumatoid arthritis is to be strongly discouraged.

C. Orthopedic Surgery: Surgery is often an essential part of the general management of the patient with rheumatoid arthritis. Surgical procedures can correct or compensate for joint damage. Arthroplasty is employed to maintain or improve joint motion. Arthrodesis can be used to correct deformity and alleviate pain, but it results in loss of motion. Early synovectomy might prevent joint damage or tendon rupture. Synovectomy will decrease pain and inflammation in a given joint, but the synovium often grows back and symptoms return.

Complications & Prognosis

Several clinical patterns of rheumatoid arthritis are apparent. Spontaneous remission may occur, usually within 2 years after the onset of the disease. Other patients have brief episodes of acute arthritis with longer periods of low-grade activity or remission. Rare patients will have sustained progression of active disease resulting in deformity and death. The presence of active disease for more than 1 year, an age of less than 30 at onset of disease, and the presence of rheumatoid nodules and high titers of rheumatoid factor are unfavorable prognostic factors.

Follow-up of patients after 10–15 years shows that 50% are stationary or improved, 70% are capable of full-time employment, and 10% are completely incapacitated. Death from vasculitis or atlantoaxial subluxation is rare. Fatalities are more often associated with sepsis or the complications of therapy.

JUVENILE RHEUMATOID ARTHRITIS

Juvenile rheumatoid arthritis is probably not a single disease but a group of disorders that cause arthritis in individuals under 16 years of age. It commonly presents as a systemic illness (Still's disease) or as a seronegative polyarthritis. The prognosis in these instances is good. The incidence of the disease peaks in boys at 2 and again at 9 years of age, while in girls it peaks between 1 and 3 years of age. Less commonly, juvenile rheumatoid arthritis presents as a pauciarticular process involving 4 or fewer joints. The outlook for girls with pauciarticular disease is excellent, whereas boys with pauciarticular disease may eventually develop ankylosing spondylitis. In older children, juvenile rheumatoid arthritis occasionally presents as a seropositive polyarticular disease that follows a course identical to that of adult rheumatoid arthritis. Although upper respiratory infections and trauma have both been implicated as precipitating factors, the roles of infection, trauma, and heredity in the pathogenesis of the disease are unclear. Although the onset of the disease may be as early as 6 weeks of life, most children are between 2 and 5 or between 9 and 12 years of age at onset. Juvenile rheumatoid arthritis is a major cause of fever of undetermined origin in children.

Immunologic Pathogenesis

The basic immunopathogenic mechanisms in juvenile rheumatoid arthritis are unknown. However, both humoral and cellular defects occur in these patients. Diffuse hypergammaglobulinemia, involving IgG, IgA, and IgM, is present. Rheumatoid factors of all immunoglobulin classes have been detected. Approximately 10% of children with juvenile rheumatoid arthritis have a positive latex fixation test for 19S IgM rheumatoid factor. The sera from some patients with negative latex fixation tests may actually contain IgM rheumatoid factors. Two major theories have been offered in an attempt to explain the presence of these "hidden" rheumatoid factors in juvenile rheumatoid arthritis. First, IgM rheumatoid factor may bind avidly to native IgG in the patient's serum and therefore may not be able to bind IgG coating the latex particles. Second, an abnormal IgG may be present which preferentially binds IgM, thereby blocking latex fixation. Cold-reacting (4 °C) 19S IgM rheumatoid factors (cryoglobulins) are associated with severe disease.

Serum components of both the classic and alternative (properdin) complement systems are elevated, although this elevation is less in patients who have rheumatoid factors or severe disease. CH_{50}, C3, and C4 in the synovial fluid tend to be low, particularly in patients with a positive serum latex fixation or with IgG rheumatoid factor in the synovial fluid. Elevation of serum complement may reflect a secondary overcompensation in response to increased consumption, or possibly a general increase in protein synthesis. Studies of the metabolism of complement actually demonstrate hypercatabolism. The depression of complement in synovial fluid is probably secondary to complement activation by the immune complexes, similar to that seen in rheumatoid arthritis.

A defect in cellular immunity may contribute to the immunopathogenesis of juvenile rheumatoid arthritis, since decreased delayed hypersensitivity has been demonstrated in some patients. Transfer factor therapy has been used in a few patients, with improvement in their in vivo skin test responses as well as their in vitro responses to mitogens. The improvement in cellular immunity has been associated with clinical improvement, although a causal relationship is not established.

Preliminary studies suggest that patients with juvenile rheumatoid arthritis possess certain HLA tissue types with greater than expected frequencies. Thus, patients with early-onset pauciarticular disease tend to be HLA-DR5- or HLA-DRw8-positive, while those with late-onset pauciarticular disease tend to be HLA-B27-positive. Patients with polyarticular disease tend to be HLA-Dw3-positive, and those with systemic disease tend to be HLA-Bw35- or HLA-B8-positive.

Clinical Features
A. Symptoms and Signs:
1. Onset–
a. Twenty percent of children, usually under age

4, present with high, spiking fever, an evanescent rash, polyserositis, hepatosplenomegaly, and lymphadenopathy (Still's disease).

b. Forty percent of patients present with polyarthritis (more than 4 joints involved), sometimes accompanied by low-grade fever and malaise. In 25% of this group, the onset is in late childhood and is associated with rheumatoid factor.

c. Forty percent of patients present with few systemic manifestations and asymmetric involvement of only one or 2 joints. Slightly more than 50% of these patients are young girls particularly likely to develop iridocyclitis.

2. Joint manifestations–Even in the presence of severe arthritis, young children may not complain of pain but may instead limit the use of an extremity. The knees, wrists, ankles, and neck are common sites of initial involvement. Older children occasionally develop symmetric involvement in the small joints of the hands (metacarpophalangeal, proximal interphalangeal, and distal interphalangeal) similar to that seen in adults. With severe hand involvement, children are more likely to develop radial rather than ulnar deviation. Involvement of the feet may lead to hallux valgus or hammer toe deformity. Achillobursitis and achillotendinitis may cause tender, swollen heels. Ankylosing spondylitis occurs most commonly.

3. Systemic manifestations–Fever, often with a high evening spike, is seen in the majority of children. Anorexia, weight loss, and malaise are common. Most children develop an evanescent, salmon-colored maculopapular rash that coincides with periods of high fever. Occasional patients manifest cardiac involvement. Pericarditis is the most common cardiac manifestation but rarely leads to dysfunction or constriction. Myocarditis is an unusual manifestation of the cardiac disease, but heart failure occurs occasionally.

Cases of acute pneumonitis or pleuritis have been described. However, chronic rheumatoid lung disease is rarely seen in juvenile rheumatoid arthritis.

Iridocyclitis occurs most commonly in young girls with pauciarticular disease. This manifestation rarely precedes articular involvement, but it often persists even when joints become quiescent. The iridocyclitis often runs an insidious course and is best monitored by frequent slit lamp examinations, at least through the teens.

Lymphadenopathy and hepatosplenomegaly are associated with severe systemic disease and are uncommon in patients with chiefly articular manifestations.

Subcutaneous nodules occur in children with polyarticular disease, usually in association with a positive test for rheumatoid factor.

4. Complications–The major complication of juvenile rheumatoid arthritis is impairment of growth and development secondary to early epiphyseal closure. This is particularly common in the mandible, causing micrognathia, and in the metacarpals and metatarsals, leading to abnormally small fingers and toes. The extent of growth impairment usually corre-

lates positively with the severity and duration of disease but may also reflect the growth-inhibiting effects of steroids. Vasculitis and encephalitis are occasionally observed in patients with juvenile rheumatoid arthritis. Secondary amyloidosis occurs rarely.

B. Laboratory Findings: The synovial lesion of juvenile rheumatoid arthritis is a nonspecific synovitis with increased vascularity, synovial hypertrophy, and infiltration of synovial fluid with lymphocytes, plasma cells, and macrophages. Mild leukocytosis (15–25 thousand/μL) is the rule, but some patients develop leukopenia. A normochromic microcytic anemia, an elevated erythrocyte sedimentation rate, and an abnormal C-reactive protein occur commonly. Because an elevated ASO titer is so frequently encountered, this test cannot be used to differentiate juvenile rheumatoid arthritis from rheumatic fever. Positive tests for rheumatoid factor occur in older children with polyarticular disease, while antinuclear antibodies are found both in patients with polyarticular disease and in young patients with pauciarticular disease. Antinuclear antibodies almost never occur in Still's disease. Serum protein electrophoresis shows an increase in acute phase reactants (alpha globulins) and a polyclonal increase of γ-globulin. The synovial fluid in active juvenile rheumatoid arthritis is exudative, with a white count of 5–20 thousand/μL (mostly neutrophils), a poor mucin clot, and decreased glucose compared to serum glucose.

C. X-Ray Findings: Radiographic changes early in the disease include periosteal bone accretion, premature closure of the epiphyses, cervical zygapophyseal fusion (particularly at C2–3), and osseous overgrowth of the interphalangeal joints, resembling Heberden's or Bouchard's nodes. Late findings include juxta-articular demineralization and erosion and narrowing of the joint space. Carpal arthritis with ankylosis is seen as a late manifestation of Still's disease.

Immunologic Diagnosis

Currently, the diagnosis of juvenile rheumatoid arthritis is based on clinical criteria. Although certain abnormalities of immunoglobulins, complement, and cellular immunity are compatible with the diagnosis of juvenile rheumatoid arthritis, no specific immunologic test is available.

Differential Diagnosis

The diagnosis of juvenile rheumatoid arthritis is extremely difficult, since the disease can present with nonspecific constitutional signs and symptoms in the absence of arthritis. Other causes of fever, particularly infections and cancer, must be considered. Leukemia can present in childhood with fever, lymphadenopathy, and joint pains. Rheumatic fever closely resembles juvenile rheumatoid arthritis, particularly early in the disease. However, the patient with juvenile rheumatoid arthritis tends to have higher spiking fevers, lymphadenopathy and hepatosplenomegaly in the absence of carditis, and a more refractory, long-lasting arthritis. Rheumatic fever patients are more likely to have evidence of recent streptococcal infection, including elevated titers of antihyaluronidase, antistreptokinase, and antistreptodornase. In addition, patients with rheumatic fever tend to have a less intense leukocytosis and respond more dramatically to low doses of salicylates. Rheumatic diseases that may begin in childhood, such as systemic lupus erythematosus or dermatomyositis, can be differentiated by their different clinical course, different organ system involvement, and characteristic serologic abnormalities.

When juvenile rheumatoid arthritis presents primarily with arthritis, examination of synovial fluid is of paramount importance in excluding infection.

Treatment

The major goals of therapy are to relieve pain, prevent contractures and deformities, and promote normal emotional and physical development. These goals are best achieved by a comprehensive program of physical, medical, and, when necessary, surgical therapy.

A. Physical Therapy: As in the treatment of adult rheumatoid arthritis, rest is an important part of physical therapy. Complete rest is indicated during exacerbations and may be necessary for short afternoon periods on a routine basis. Specific joints can be put at rest by the use of splints, collars, and braces which support the joint and help prevent deformity. Judiciously used heat will decrease pain and muscle spasm and is particularly useful before exercising. Exercises tend to promote muscle strength and prevent deformity.

B. Medical Therapy:

1. Aspirin – The disease responds to aspirin at a dosage level of 90–130 mg/kg/d given in 4–6 divided doses. Tinnitus and decreased hearing are poor indicators of aspirin toxicity in children. Drowsiness and intermittent periods of hyperpnea are early signs of salicylate intoxication. Therefore, it is essential to monitor blood salicylate levels during aspirin therapy. Acidosis and ketosis may develop in infants. Respiratory alkalosis, due to primary stimulation of the respiratory center, occurs in older children.

2. Gold salts – Gold salts should be used only in children who are unresponsive to salicylates. If a test dose of 10 mg intramuscularly does not result in toxic signs, 1 mg/kg/wk intramuscularly should be given. Best results are obtained when the drug is used early in the course of the disease.

3. Corticosteroids – Intra-articular corticosteroid injections are useful in pauciarticular disease. Systemic corticosteroids are reserved for patients with myocarditis, vasculitis, refractory iridocyclitis, or Still's disease that is unresponsive to aspirin therapy. Patients with iridocyclitis may require prolonged corticosteroid therapy. In children, the major toxic effects of corticosteroid therapy include subcapsular cataract formation, vertebral osteoporosis and collapse, infection, premature skeletal maturation with diminished growth, and pseudotumor cerebri with intracranial hypertension.

C. Surgical Treatment: The aims of surgery in juvenile rheumatoid arthritis are to relieve pain and maintain or improve joint function. Synovectomy may diminish pain due to chronic synovitis, but long-term effectiveness is questionable. Synovectomy for severe extensor tenosynovitis of the hand may prevent tendon rupture. Tendon release procedures help relieve joint contractures. Hip replacement is of benefit in selected cases but should be delayed as long as possible, since in some children hip cartilage may regenerate with continued weight-bearing.

Complications & Prognosis

Seventy percent of patients experience a spontaneous and permanent remission by adulthood. Patients with Still's disease tend to have 1–10 recurrences per year. Patients presenting with oligoarthritic disease, particularly if they are female, tend to remain oligoarthritic, while those presenting with polyarthritis remain polyarthritic. Rarely, the disease persists into adulthood. This usually occurs in children with symmetric polyarthritis similar to that seen in adults. Sometimes a patient with juvenile rheumatoid arthritis in apparent remission develops rheumatoid arthritis as an adult. In an occasional unfortunate case, the disease becomes a prolonged crippling polyarthritis. Small joint involvement, positive serum rheumatoid factor, and onset in later childhood all portend a poor prognosis.

SJÖGREN'S SYNDROME

Major Immunologic Features

- Lymphocyte and plasma cell infiltration of involved tissues.
- Hypergammaglobulinemia, rheumatoid factor, and antinuclear antibodies, including a specific anti-extractable nuclear antigen.
- Autoantibodies against salivary duct antigens.

General Considerations

Sjögren's syndrome is a chronic inflammatory disease of unknown cause characterized by diminished lacrimal and salivary gland secretion resulting in keratoconjunctivitis sicca and xerostomia. There is characteristic dryness of the eyes, mouth, nose, trachea, bronchi, vagina, and skin. Half of patients have rheumatoid arthritis, and a small percentage have other connective tissue diseases. Ninety percent of patients with Sjögren's syndrome are female. Although the mean age at onset is 50 years, the disease has been detected in children.

Immunologic Pathogenesis

The strong association of Sjögren's syndrome with rheumatoid arthritis and systemic lupus erythematosus suggests that immunologic processes play a role in the pathogenesis of this disease. It has been hypothesized that patients with Sjögren's syndrome respond abnormally to one or more unidentified antigens, perhaps a virus or a virus-altered autoantigen. This abnormal response is characterized by excessive B cell and plasma cell activity, manifested by polyclonal hypergammaglobulinemia and the production of rheumatoid factor, antinuclear factors, cryoglobulins, and anti-salivary duct antibodies. Immunofluorescence studies have shown both B and T lymphocytes and plasma cells infiltrating involved tissues. Large quantities of IgM and IgG are synthesized by these infiltrating lymphocytes. In patients with coexisting macroglobulinemia, monoclonal IgM may be synthesized in the salivary glands.

It has been suggested that excessive B cell activity may not be due to a primary B cell defect but rather to defective T lymphocyte regulation. A subpopulation of T lymphocytes exists whose normal physiologic role is the suppression of excessive B cell proliferation and synthesis of autoantibodies. In Sjögren's syndrome, this "suppressor" T cell population may fail to adequately control B cell responses to an antigenic challenge, leading to excessive B cell activity. However, about one-third of patients have decreased in vitro responsiveness to mitogens (such as PHA) and decreased numbers of peripheral blood T lymphocytes, as measured by E rosettes (see Chapter 23).

Clinical Features

A. Symptoms and Signs:

1. Oral–Dryness of the mouth is usually the most distressing symptom and is often associated with burning discomfort and difficulty in chewing and swallowing dry foods. Polyuria and nocturia develop as the patient drinks increasing amounts of water in an effort to relieve these symptoms. The oral mucous membranes are dry and erythematous, and the tongue becomes fissured and ulcerated. Severe dental caries is often present. Half of patients have intermittent parotid gland enlargement with rapid fluctuations in the size of the gland.

2. Ocular–The major ocular finding is keratoconjunctivitis sicca. Symptoms include burning, itching, decreased tearing, ocular accumulation of thick mucoid material during the night, photophobia, pain, and a "gritty" or "sandy" sensation in the eyes. Decreased tearing is demonstrated by an abnormal Schirmer test. Slit lamp examination reveals punctate rose bengal or fluorescein staining of the conjunctiva and cornea, strands of corneal debris, and a shortened tear film break-up time. Severe ocular involvement may lead to corneal ulceration, vascularization with opacification, or perforation.

3. Miscellaneous–Dryness of the nose, posterior oropharynx, larynx, and respiratory tract may lead to epistaxis, dysphonia, recurrent otitis media, tracheobronchitis, or pneumonia. The vaginal mucosa is also dry, and women commonly complain of dyspareunia. Active synovitis is a common finding, particularly in patients who also have rheumatoid arthritis. Twenty percent of patients with Sjögren's syndrome complain of Raynaud's phenomenon. Ten percent of patients have extraglandular lymphocytic infiltrates, particularly in the kidneys, lungs, lymph nodes, and muscles. A few such patients may develop lymphoma.

B. Laboratory Findings: Anemia, leukopenia, and an elevated erythrocyte sedimentation rate are common features. Parotid salivary flow is less than the normal 5 mL/10 min/gland. Secretory sialography with radiopaque dye demonstrates many findings of glandular disorganization. Salivary scintigraphy with technetium Tc 99m pertechnetate reveals decreased parotid secretory function. Histologically, a lymphocytic infiltrate involves exocrine glands of the respiratory, gastrointestinal, and vaginal tracts as well as glands of the ocular and oral mucosa. Histologic demonstration of lymphocytic infiltration in a biopsy specimen taken from the minor labial salivary glands may be the most specific and sensitive single diagnostic test for Sjögren's syndrome.

Immunologic Diagnosis

No immunologic test is diagnostic for Sjögren's syndrome. However, a myriad of nonspecific immunologic abnormalities occur in these patients.

A. Humoral Abnormalities: Hypergammaglobulinemia is seen in half of patients. Although serum protein electrophoresis usually shows a polyclonal hypergammaglobulinemia, occasional patients develop monoclonal IgM paraproteinemia, usually of the kappa type. Patients who develop lymphoma sometimes become severely hypogammaglobulinemic and show disappearance of autoantibodies. With latex agglutination, rheumatoid factor is present in 90% of patients. ANA in a speckled or homogeneous pattern is present in 70% of patients. Many of these antinuclear antibodies are directed against acid-extractable nuclear antigens. Antibodies against one such antigen, termed SS-B, are relatively specific for patients with primary Sjögren's syndrome. Antibodies against a second acid-extractable nuclear antigen, SS-A, may be found in Sjögren's syndrome alone or in Sjögren's syndrome associated with systemic lupus erythematosus. Patients with Sjögren's syndrome and rheumatoid arthritis have neither anti-SS-A nor anti-SS-B antibodies. They tend, instead, to develop antibodies against the Epstein-Barr virus–associated nuclear antigen called rheumatoid arthritis nuclear antigen (RANA). Autoantibodies against salivary duct antigens have been detected in 50% of patients.

B. Cellular Abnormalities: Thirty percent of patients with Sjögren's syndrome have decreased lymphocyte responses to mitogenic stimulation. A few patients also have decreased numbers of circulating T lymphocytes in the peripheral blood (see Immunologic Pathogenesis, above).

C. Beta$_2$-Microglobulin: Beta$_2$-microglobulin is a normal cell membrane component present on all human cells and linked to the HLA surface antigen complex. It is elevated in the synovial fluid of patients with active rheumatoid arthritis and in the saliva of patients with Sjögren's syndrome (as measured by radioimmunoassay). The concentration in saliva correlates directly with the content of lymphocytic infiltration as graded on lip biopsy. Elevated serum β_2-microglobulin levels may be seen in severe Sjögren's syndrome, particularly when associated with pseudolymphoma or lymphoma.

D. HLA Associations: Although the frequency of HLA-B8 is increased in Sjögren's syndrome, there is an even stronger association between Sjögren's syndrome and HLA-Dw3. These HLA associations indicate that there is a genetic predisposition to the development of Sjögren's syndrome.

Differential Diagnosis

The diagnosis of Sjögren's syndrome can be made on the basis of 2 of the 3 classic manifestations (xerostomia, keratoconjunctivitis sicca, and rheumatoid arthritis). However, the varied and multisystemic nature of the disease may obscure the diagnosis. Certainly, any patient with a rheumatic disease—eg, systemic lupus erythematosus, rheumatoid arthritis, or scleroderma—should be observed for Sjögren's syndrome; likewise, any patient with Sjögren's syndrome should be examined for the purpose of ruling out other rheumatic diseases. Parotid gland cancer must always be considered in a patient with unilateral parotid swelling.

Treatment

A. Symptomatic Measures:

1. Oral–Patients must be urged to maintain fastidious oral hygiene, with regular use of fluoride toothpaste, mouthwashes, and regular dental examinations. Frequent sips of water and the use of sugarless gum or candy to stimulate salivary secretion are sometimes helpful in relieving xerostomia.

2. Ocular–Methylcellulose artificial tears alleviate ocular symptoms and protect against ocular complications. Shielded glasses offer protection against the drying effects of wind.

B. Systemic Measures: Sjögren's syndrome can usually be adequately controlled with symptomatic therapy only. In severe or life-threatening disease, corticosteroids or immunosuppressive agents have been used. These drugs are indicated primarily in patients with lymphoma, Waldenström's macroglobulinemia, or massive lymphocytic infiltration of vital organs (such as the lung).

Complications & Prognosis

In the vast majority of patients, significant lymphoproliferation is confined to salivary, lacrimal, and other mucosal glandular tissue, resulting in a benign chronic course of xerostomia and xerophthalmia. Rarely, patients develop significant extraglandular lymphoid infiltration or neoplasia.

Splenomegaly, leukopenia, and vasculitis with leg ulcers may occur even in the absence of rheumatoid arthritis. Hypergammaglobulinemic purpura, often associated with renal tubular acidosis, has been described and may be a presenting complaint. Five per-

cent of patients with Sjögren's syndrome develop chronic autoimmune thyroiditis. Other associations include primary biliary cirrhosis, chronic active hepatitis, gastric achlorhydria, pancreatitis, renal and pulmonary lymphocytic infiltration, cryoglobulinemia with glomerulonephritis, and adult celiac disease. Neuromuscular complications include polymyositis, peripheral or cranial (particularly trigeminal) neuropathy, and cerebral vasculitis. Rarely, patients with Sjögren's syndrome develop lymphoid malignancy, immunoblastic sarcoma, or Waldenström's macroglobulinemia. The lymphoma is often a monoclonal B cell neoplasm containing intracellular IgM-κ immunoglobulin.

PROGRESSIVE SYSTEMIC SCLEROSIS

Major Immunologic Features

- Antinuclear antibodies with a speckled or nucleolar pattern.
- Antibodies against the ribonuclease-sensitive component of extractable nuclear antigen (ENA) in patients with mixed connective tissue disease.

General Considerations

Progressive systemic sclerosis is a disease of unknown cause characterized by abnormally increased collagen deposition in the skin. The course is usually slowly progressive and chronically disabling, but it can be rapidly progressive and fatal because of involvement of internal organs. It commonly begins in the third or fourth decade of life. Children are rarely affected. The incidence of the disease is 4–12.5 cases per million population. Women are affected twice as often as men, and there is no racial predisposition.

Immunologic Pathogenesis

Progressive systemic sclerosis has many clinical features in common with other rheumatic diseases (systemic lupus erythematosus, rheumatoid arthritis, polymyositis). The association of progressive systemic sclerosis with Sjögren's syndrome and, less often, with thyroiditis—and the serologic abnormalities seen in the majority of cases (presence of ANA, rheumatoid factor, polyclonal hypergammaglobulinemia)—are suggestive of an immunologic aberration in these patients. At present, there is scanty evidence for a humoral mechanism in the pathogenesis of the disease, although a serum factor toxic to vascular endothelium has been identified. Immunoglobulins have not been found at the dermal-epidermal junction in scleroderma, although examination of the fibrinoid lesions seen in the walls of renal arterioles has revealed the presence of γ-globulin and complement. The ability of lymphocytes to destroy embryonic fibroblasts in tissue cultures may indicate an alteration in cellular immunity in these patients. However, in contrast to other autoimmune diseases, cellular infiltration in scleroderma is minimal or absent in all organs except the synovium, where impressive collections of lymphocytes and plasma cells can be seen. Unfortunately, research on the pathogenesis of progressive systemic sclerosis is severely hampered by the absence of an animal model.

Clinical Features

A. Symptoms and Signs:

1. Onset–In more than half of cases, Raynaud's phenomenon heralds the onset of the disease. Progressive systemic sclerosis frequently begins with skin changes, but in one-third of patients polyarthralgias and polyarthritis are the first manifestations. Initial visceral involvement without skin manifestations is very unusual.

2. Skin abnormalities–There are 3 stages in the clinical evolution of scleroderma. In the edematous phase, symmetric nonpitting edema is present in the hands and, rarely, in the feet. The edema can progress to the forearms, arms, upper anterior chest, abdomen, back, and face. In the sclerotic phase, the skin is tight, smooth, and waxy and seems bound down to underlying structures. Skin folds and wrinkles disappear. The hands are involved in two-thirds of patients, with painful, slowly he...ing ulcerations of the fingertips in half of those cases. The face appears stretched and masklike, with thin lips and a "pinched" nose. Pigmentary changes and telangiectases are frequent findings at this stage. The skin changes may stabilize for prolonged periods and then either progress to the third (atrophic) stage or soften and return to normal. It should be emphasized that not all patients pass through all the stages. Subcutaneous calcifications, usually in the fingertips (calcinosis circumscripta), occur more often in women than in men. The calcifications vary in size from tiny deposits to large masses and may develop over bony prominences throughout the body.

3. Raynaud's phenomenon–Raynaud's phenomenon occurs in 30% of patients. In the so-called CREST syndrome—*c*alcinosis, *R*aynaud's phenomenon, *e*sophageal dysmotility, *s*clerodactyly, and *t*elangiectases—the disease may remain confined to the skin for prolonged periods. Pulmonary fibrosis, often associated with pulmonary hypertension, is a recognized complication of CREST syndrome.

4. Joints and muscles–Articular complaints are very common in progressive systemic sclerosis and may begin at any time during the course of the disease. The arthralgias, stiffness, and frank arthritis seen in progressive systemic sclerosis may be difficult to distinguish from those of rheumatoid arthritis, particularly in the early stages of the disease. Involved joints include the metacarpophalangeals, proximal interphalangeals, wrists, elbows, knees, ankles, and small joints of the feet. Flexion contractures, due to changes in the skin or joints, are common. Muscle involvement is usually mild but may be clinically indistinguishable from that of polymyositis, with muscle weakness, tenderness, and pain of proximal muscles of the upper and lower extremities.

5. Lungs–The lungs are frequently involved in progressive systemic sclerosis, either clinically or at autopsy. A low diffusion capacity is the earliest detectable abnormality, preceding alterations in ventilation or clinical and radiologic evidence of disease. Dyspnea on exertion is the most frequently reported symptom. Orthopnea and paroxysmal nocturnal dyspnea are seen in advanced cases. Chronic cough with variable production of sputum is also seen in scleroderma lung disease. Hemoptysis, fever, chest pain, and hoarseness are infrequent manifestations of pulmonary involvement. Pleurisy (with associated pleural friction rub) can also occur. Patients with diffuse pulmonary involvement have an intense bronchiolar epithelial proliferation.

6. Heart–Because of the frequency of pulmonary fibrosis, cor pulmonale is the commonest cardiac finding in progressive systemic sclerosis. Myocardial fibrosis, leading to digitalis-resistant left-sided heart failure, is a poor prognostic sign. Cardiac arrhythmias and conduction disturbances are common manifestations of myocardial fibrosis. The pericarditis of progressive systemic sclerosis is usually asymptomatic and is found incidentally at autopsy. Although 40% of patients have pericardial effusion by electrocardiography, tamponade is extremely rare.

7. Kidneys–Renal involvement is an uncommon but life-threatening development in progressive systemic sclerosis. It presents as rapidly progressive oliguric renal failure with or without malignant hypertension.

8. Gastrointestinal tract–The gastrointestinal tract is commonly affected in progressive systemic sclerosis. The esophagus is the most frequent site of involvement, with dysphagia or symptoms of reflux esophagitis occurring in 80% of patients. Gastric and small bowel involvement presents with cramping, bloating, and diarrhea alternating with constipation. Hypomotility of the gastrointestinal tract with bacterial overgrowth may result in malabsorption. Colonic scleroderma is associated with chronic constipation.

9. Sjögren's syndrome–Keratoconjunctivitis sicca is seen in 5–7% of patients.

10. Uncommon clinical manifestations–Biliary cirrhosis or mononeuropathy, either cranial or peripheral, may rarely be associated with progressive systemic sclerosis.

11. Mixed connective tissue disease–Mixed connective tissue disease is a recently described syndrome with features of scleroderma, rheumatoid arthritis, systemic lupus erythematosus, and polymyositis-dermatomyositis. The manifestations of the disease include arthritis, Raynaud's phenomenon, scleroderma of the fingers, muscle weakness and tenderness, interstitial lung disease, and a skin rash resembling that of systemic lupus erythematosus. These patients have a high-titer speckled pattern of ANA and antibody to the ribonuclease-sensitive component of extractable nuclear antigen. Renal disease is unusual in these patients, and they appear to respond to corticosteroid treatment.

B. Laboratory Findings: The normochromic normocytic anemia of chronic inflammatory disease is usually seen in progressive systemic sclerosis. Microangiopathic anemia can also occur. Eosinophilia is rare. An elevated erythrocyte sedimentation rate and polyclonal hypergammaglobulinemia are common. A positive speckled or nucleolar pattern ANA is frequently encountered, even in the absence of anti-ENA antibody.

Biopsy of clinically involved skin reveals thinning of the epidermis with loss of the rete pegs, atrophy of the dermal appendages, hyalinization and fibrosis of arterioles, and a striking increase of compact collagen fibers in the reticular dermis.

Synovial tissue findings range from an acute inflammatory lymphocytic infiltration to diffuse fibrosis with relatively little inflammation.

The histologic changes seen in muscle tissue include interstitial and perivascular inflammatory infiltration followed by fibrosis and myofibrillar necrosis, atrophy, and degeneration.

In patients with renal involvement, the histologic appearance of the kidney is similar to that of malignant hypertensive nephropathy, with intimal proliferation of the interlobular arteries and fibrinoid changes in the intima and media of more distal interlobular arteries and of afferent arterioles.

There is increased collagen deposition in the lamina propria, submucosa, and muscularis of the gastrointestinal tract. With loss of normal smooth muscle, the large bowel is subject to development of the characteristic wide-mouthed diverticula and to infiltration of air into the wall of the intestine (pneumatosis intestinalis).

C. X-Ray Findings:

1. Bone x-rays–Thickening of the periarticular soft tissues and juxta-articular osteoporosis are seen in involved joints. Erosions may be seen on the distal phalangeal tufts and at the joint margins of the proximal and distal interphalangeal joints. Absorption of the terminal phalanges is often associated with soft tissue atrophy and subcutaneous calcinosis.

2. Chest x-rays–Characteristically, a diffuse increase in interstitial markings is seen in the lower lung fields of patients with moderate to severe pulmonary involvement. "Honeycombing," nodular densities, and disseminated pulmonary calcifications may also be seen.

3. Gastrointestinal x-rays–Upper gastrointestinal series will often reveal decreased or absent esophageal peristaltic activity, even in patients without symptoms of dysphagia. Long-standing disease leads to marked dilatation of the lower two-thirds of the esophagus. Gastrointestinal reflux is present in the majority of cases, and ulcers or strictures of the lower esophagus due to peptic esophagitis are commonplace. With gastrointestinal involvement, barium is often retained in the second and third portions of the duodenum. Intestinal loops become dilated and atonic, with irregular flocculation and hypersegmentation.

The barium enema may reveal large, wide-mouthed diverticula along the antimesenteric border of the transverse and descending colon.

4. Renal arteriography–Marked changes are seen on renal arteriography in patients with scleroderma kidney. Irregular arterial narrowing, tortuosity of the interlobular arterioles, persistence of the arterial phase, and absence of a nephrogram phase are typical findings.

Immunologic Diagnosis

Polyclonal hypergammaglobulinemia is a frequent serologic abnormality in progressive systemic sclerosis. Rheumatoid factors are found in 25–30% of patients. The fluorescent antinuclear antibody test shows a speckled or nucleolar pattern in 70% of cases. A specific antinuclear antibody found only in patients with scleroderma (Scl-1) has been identified.

Differential Diagnosis

When classic skin changes and Raynaud's phenomenon are associated with characteristic visceral complaints, the diagnosis is obvious. In patients presenting with visceral or arthritic complaints and no skin changes, the diagnosis is difficult. In many cases, only the presence or absence of antibodies to ribonuclease-sensitive extractable nuclear antigen makes it possible to differentiate scleroderma from mixed connective tissue disease. Patients with eosinophilic fasciitis present with marked thickening of the skin similar to that seen in the edematous phase of scleroderma. The 2 entities can be distinguished histologically because, in eosinophilic fasciitis, fibrosis and inflammatory cell infiltration are seen in the deep fascial layers, whereas in scleroderma the fibrosis occurs predominantly in the dermis. The differential diagnosis also includes scleromyxedema, carcinoid syndrome, phenylketonuria, porphyria cutanea tarda, amyloidosis, Werner's syndrome, and progeria.

Treatment

There is at present no cure for progressive systemic sclerosis. Sympathectomy has resulted in only transient relief of vascular symptoms. Corticosteroids have no effect on the visceral progression of the disease, though they are beneficial in scleroderma with myositis and in mixed connective tissue disease. Colchicine has limited efficacy in treatment of the cutaneous manifestations of the disease. Penicillamine is often effective in the treatment of cutaneous scleroderma, and there is evidence that it may be of benefit in slowing the progression of visceral disease.

Patients should avoid exposure to cold and should wear gloves to protect their hands. Tobacco should be avoided. Skin ulcers require careful antiseptic care. Cor pulmonale and left-sided heart failure may be treated with diuretics and digitalization, although the response is often poor. Antibiotics may be beneficial in decreasing intestinal bacterial overgrowth that leads to malabsorption.

Hypertensive crisis in renal disease associated with progressive systemic sclerosis is very difficult to control even with potent hypotensive agents. The arthritis can often be controlled with aspirin and other analgesics. Lotions can be used for skin lubrication to alleviate dryness and cracking.

Complications & Prognosis

Spontaneous remissions occur in progressive systemic sclerosis, but the usual course of the disease is one of relentless progression from dermal to visceral involvement. Involvement of the heart, lung, or kidney is associated with a high mortality rate. Aspiration pneumonia resulting from esophageal dysfunction is a complication in advanced disease.

Although the prognosis for any given patient is extremely variable, the overall 5-year survival rate for progressive systemic sclerosis is approximately 40%.

POLYMYOSITIS–DERMATOMYOSITIS

Major Immunologic Features
- Focal deposition of complement, IgG, and IgM in vessel walls of involved tissue.
- Production of cytotoxin by lymphocytes incubated with autologous muscle.
- Lymphocytic and plasma cell infiltration of involved muscle.

General Considerations

Polymyositis-dermatomyositis is an acute or chronic inflammatory disease of muscle and skin that may occur at any age. Women are affected twice as commonly as men. There is no racial preponderance. The incidence of the disease is 1 per 200,000 population.

Polymyositis-dermatomyositis can be subclassified into 5 categories: (1) idiopathic polymyositis, (2) idiopathic dermatomyositis, (3) polymyositis-dermatomyositis associated with cancer, (4) childhood polymyositis-dermatomyositis, and (5) polymyositis-dermatomyositis associated with other rheumatic diseases (Sjögren's syndrome, systemic lupus erythematosus, progressive systemic sclerosis, mixed connective tissue disease).

Immunologic Pathogenesis

Although the precise pathogenetic mechanisms are unknown, there is a great deal of evidence that autoimmunity may play a role in disease causation. Experimental polymyositis has been induced in rats and guinea pigs by the injection of allogeneic muscle tissue in Freund's complete adjuvant. Polymyositis-dermatomyositis may coexist with other autoimmune diseases. An infectious cause (viral or bacterial) has been suggested, but no microorganism has ever been conclusively implicated.

A. Humoral Factors: Polyclonal hypergammaglobulinemia is common in patients with polymyositis-dermatomyositis, and rheumatoid factors and antinuclear antibodies occur in 20% of cases. In children, focal deposits of complement, IgG, and IgM have been seen in vessel walls of involved skin and muscle. Some patients with polymyositis-dermatomyositis have been shown to produce antibodies both against a component of the extractable nuclear antigen and against purified human skeletal muscle myoglobin.

B. Cellular Factors: There is evidence that cellular immunity plays a role in the pathogenesis of polymyositis-dermatomyositis. Polymyositis has been induced in rats and guinea pigs by the transfer of sensitized lymphoid cells. Lymphocytes from patients with polymyositis-dermatomyositis, after incubation with normal autologous muscle, produce a lymphokine that is toxic to monolayers of human fetal muscle cells. The lymphocytes in the muscle infiltrate of patients with polymyositis-dermatomyositis produce this lymphotoxin upon simple incubation of involved muscle. Thus, the lymphocytes of patients with polymyositis-dermatomyositis may respond to their own muscle antigens as if they were foreign (Fig 26–3). It is not known whether this is a primary defect in antigen recognition by the lymphocytes or whether these muscle antigens are cross-reactive with an unidentified foreign antigen.

Clinical Features

A. Symptoms and Signs:

1. Onset–Although the symptoms may begin abruptly, the onset of the disease is usually insidious.

2. Muscle involvement–The commonest manifestation is weakness of involved striated muscle. The proximal muscles of the extremities are most often affected, usually progressing from the lower to the upper limbs. The distal musculature is involved in only 25% of patients. Weakness of the cervical muscles with inability to raise the head and weakness of the posterior pharyngeal muscles with dysphagia and dysphonia are also seen. Facial and extraocular muscle involvement is unusual. Muscle pain, tenderness, and edema may be seen in acute polymyositis-

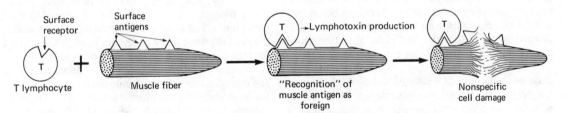

Figure 26–3. Defective "recognition" in polymyositis.

dermatomyositis but are uncommon in the chronic form of this disease.

3. Skin involvement–The characteristic rash of dermatomyositis, present in approximately 40% of patients, consists of raised, smooth or scaling, dusky red plaques over bony prominences of the hands, elbows, knees, and ankles. An erythematous telangiectatic rash may appear over the face and sun-exposed areas. Less commonly seen is the pathognomonic "heliotrope" rash of the face (a dusky, lilac suffusion of the upper eyelids). One-fourth of patients have various dermatologic manifestations ranging from skin thickening to scaling eruptions to erythroderma. Raynaud's phenomenon is occasionally seen.

4. Malignancy–Some patients with polymyositis-dermatomyositis are found to have a concomitant malignant tumor. In men over 40 years of age, the association between polymyositis-dermatomyositis and cancer appears to be more common. Removal of the tumor may result in a dramatic improvement in the polymyositis-dermatomyositis.

5. Miscellaneous features–A mild transitory arthritis is not unusual. Sjögren's syndrome occurs in 5–7% of cases. Gastrointestinal ulceration with abdominal pain, hematemesis, and melena occurs in children. Patients with severe muscle disease are particularly susceptible to the development of interstitial pneumonia and pulmonary fibrosis.

B. Laboratory Findings: An elevated erythrocyte sedimentation rate and a mild anemia are very common. Half of patients have elevated α_2- and γ-globulins on serum protein electrophoresis. Myoglobinemia and myoglobinuria are often seen. Up to 20% of patients with acute polymyositis have nonspecific T wave abnormalities on their electrocardiograms.

1. Muscle enzymes–When muscle cells are injured, a number of muscle enzymes, including glutamic-oxaloacetic transaminase, creatine phosphokinase, and aldolase, are released into the blood. The serum enzyme elevation reflects the severity of muscle damage as well as the amount of muscle mass involved.

2. Urinary creatine–Creatine is normally produced in the liver and transported via the circulatory system to the musculature. After attaching to receptor sites on the muscle cell surface, it is carried into the cell where it is converted to creatinine. Polymyositis-dermatomyositis and other myopathies lead to a decrease in the number of cell surface receptors, causing an increase in circulating creatine which is quickly cleared by the kidneys. An increase in the urine creatine concentration is the most sensitive laboratory test for muscle damage and is a valuable indicator of disease activity. It is the first detectable laboratory abnormality in relapse of disease.

3. Muscle biopsy–Biopsy of involved muscles is diagnostic in only 50–80% of cases. Therefore, a normal muscle biopsy does not rule out the diagnosis of polymyositis-dermatomyositis in a patient with a characteristic clinical picture, muscle enzyme eleva-

tions, and an abnormal electromyogram. The histologic findings in acute and subacute polymyositis-dermatomyositis include (1) focal or extensive primary degeneration of muscle fibers, (2) signs of muscle regeneration (fiber basophilia, central nuclei), (3) necrosis of muscle fibers, and (4) a focal or diffuse lymphocytic infiltration. Chronic myositis leads to a marked variation in the cross-sectional diameter of muscle fibers and a variable degree of interstitial fibrosis.

4. Electromyography–When involved muscles are examined, 70–80% of patients will demonstrate myopathic changes on electromyography. These changes are nonspecific but can point to the diagnosis of myositis. They include (1) spontaneous "sawtooth" fibrillatory potentials and irritability on insertion of the test needle; (2) complex polyphasic potentials, often of short duration, indicative of involuntary fiber contraction; and (3) salvos of repetitive high-frequency action potentials (pseudomyotonia).

Immunologic Diagnosis

There is no known immunologic test that is pathognomonic for polymyositis-dermatomyositis. The diagnosis must be based on the nonimmunologic clinical and laboratory data discussed above.

Differential Diagnosis

The 5 major criteria for the diagnosis of polymyositis-dermatomyositis are (1) weakness of the shoulder or pelvic girdle, (2) biopsy evidence of myositis, (3) elevation of muscle enzymes, (4) electromyographic findings of myopathy, and (5) typical skin changes. A number of diseases can affect muscles and lead to clinical and laboratory abnormalities that are identical to those seen in polymyositis-dermatomyositis. The diagnostic criteria outlined above cannot be strictly applied in patients with these diseases, which include infection, sarcoidosis, muscular dystrophy, systemic lupus erythematosus, progressive systemic sclerosis, mixed connective tissue disease, drug-induced myopathy (alcohol, clofibrate), rhabdomyolysis, and various metabolic and endocrine disorders (McArdle's syndrome, hyperthyroidism, myxedema). A diligent search for occult cancers should be made in any patient who develops polymyositis-dermatomyositis as an adult.

Treatment

A. Corticosteroids: Prednisone, 60–80 mg orally daily, will usually decrease muscle inflammation and improve strength. The dose is tapered slowly, with clinical and laboratory monitoring. Creatinuria is the most sensitive index of disease activity and is often the first indication of relapse as corticosteroid dosage is reduced. However, assessment of muscle strength and determination of serum enzyme levels are usually sufficient indicators of disease activity. Some patients require chronic prednisone therapy (5–20 mg daily) to control the disease.

B. Cytotoxic Agents: Methotrexate or azathioprine has been used with success in patients who do not respond to corticosteroids or who develop life-threatening complications of corticosteroid therapy.

Complications & Prognosis

Polymyositis-dermatomyositis is a chronic disease characterized by spontaneous remissions and exacerbations. Most patients respond to corticosteroid therapy. Patients with severe muscle atrophy show little response to either corticosteroid or other immunosuppressive therapy. When the disease is associated with cancer, improvement often occurs following treatment of the neoplasm.

POLYARTERITIS NODOSA, WEGENER'S GRANULOMATOSIS, & OTHER VASCULITIDES

The vasculitides represent a spectrum of pathologic and clinical disease ranging from acute, overwhelming necrotizing vasculitis to chronic, indolent vascular inflammation. Granuloma formation is present to a greater or lesser degree in most of these entities, but the basic lesion is vascular. It is important to classify and to differentiate the vasculitides because the course, treatment, and prognosis are different for each disease.

Immunologic Pathogenesis & Diagnosis

No unifying pathogenetic mechanism has yet been defined for the vasculitides, but most are probably hypersensitivity disorders. Many inciting antigens which could induce specific clinical responses may exist. Alternatively, there may be relatively few causative antigens, with the type of clinical response being determined by host factors (heredity).

A. Humoral Pathogenesis:

1. Polyarteritis nodosa—Several animal experiments suggest that humoral factors may play a role in the pathogenesis of polyarteritis nodosa. Repeated intravenous injections of horse serum into rabbits will induce an arteritis similar to that seen in polyarteritis nodosa. Bovine albumin serially administered intravenously into rabbits will also induce a vasculitis. (Bovine γ-globulin administration induces immune complex renal disease with only minor inflammatory vascular changes.) The intravenous injection of immune complexes, particularly in the presence of rheumatoid factor, will induce vasculitis in rats. Immunofluorescence studies in humans have demonstrated immunoglobulin and complement in vessel walls during active disease. Hepatitis B antigen (HBsAg), either alone or with immunoglobulin and complement, has been demonstrated in the vessel walls of patients with polyarteritis nodosa who have circulating HBsAg (Fig 26–4). HBsAg or anti-HBsAg antibodies can be detected in the serum of over half of patients with polyarteritis nodosa.

2. Hypersensitivity angiitis—Vascular deposition of IgG, IgM, IgA, and complement in patients with hypersensitivity angiitis has been documented by immunofluorescence studies.

3. Wegener's granulomatosis—Ultrastructural and immunofluorescence studies of renal biopsies from patients with Wegener's granulomatosis have demonstrated subepithelial basement membrane deposition of IgG and complement in a lumpy-bumpy pattern in glomerular tufts, characteristic of immune complex disease. Circulating autoantibodies against smooth muscle have been detected in a few patients, and circulating immune complexes have occasionally been detected by complement consumption techniques.

4. Henoch-Schönlein purpura—Examination of renal biopsies reveals subendothelial granular and nodular deposition of IgA, IgG, and complement along the glomerular basement membrane. Circulating IgA-containing immune complexes have been identified in two-thirds of patients, and skin biopsy studies have demonstrated a preponderance of IgA deposited in the walls of involved vessels.

5. Takayasu's disease—Patients with Takayasu's disease commonly have elevated serum IgG, IgA, and IgM levels. False-positive VDRL and rheumatoid factors are not uncommon. Rarely, patients will have the LE cell phenomenon. Circulating autoantibodies against vascular antigens have been demonstrated by sheep cell agglutination, complement fixation, and tanned red cell agglutination.

6. Giant cell arteritis—Immunofluorescence studies have revealed IgG, IgA, IgM, and complement deposition in the cytoplasm of cells and along the elastic tissue within vessel walls. Antinuclear antibodies against nuclei of vessel wall cells occur in patients with serum antinuclear antibody.

B. Cellular Pathogenesis: Decreased delayed cutaneous hypersensitivity to various antigens (PPD, mumps, streptokinase-streptodornase, keyhole limpet hemocyanin), as well as decreased in vitro lymphocyte mitogenic responsiveness, has been documented in patients with **Wegener's granulomatosis.** However, most studies have been done on patients being treated with corticosteroids or cytotoxic drugs.

C. Antigens Associated With the Vasculitides:

1. Streptococcal antigens—Antecedent upper respiratory infections, occasionally streptococcal in origin, have been associated with Henoch-Schönlein purpura, hypersensitivity angiitis, and polyarteritis nodosa. A necrotizing arteritis can be induced in the coronary arteries of rats receiving repeated injections of hemolytic streptococcal antigens.

2. Viral antigens—Various viral infections (upper respiratory infections, influenza, influenza vaccination) are known to occasionally precede Henoch-Schönlein purpura, hypersensitivity angiitis, and polyarteritis nodosa. Serum HBsAg and circulating HBsAg-anti-HBsAg complexes are present in some patients with polyarteritis nodosa. HBsAg, IgG, IgM, and complement have also been detected in the vessel

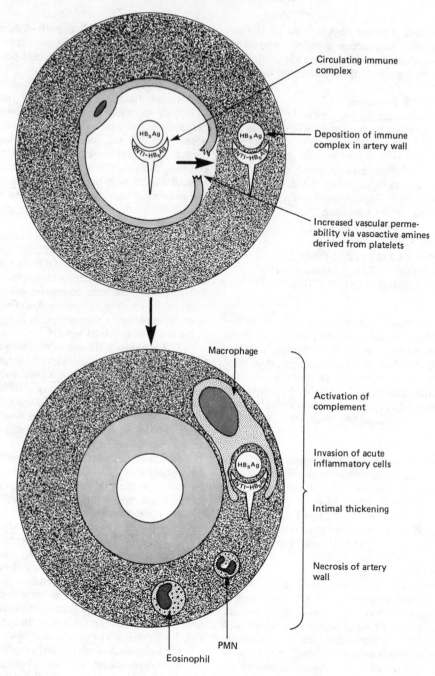

Circulating immune complex

Deposition of immune complex in artery wall

Increased vascular permeability via vasoactive amines derived from platelets

Macrophage

Activation of complement

Invasion of acute inflammatory cells

Intimal thickening

Necrosis of artery wall

PMN

Eosinophil

Figure 26–4. Hypothetical immunopathogens in HBsAg-associated polyarteritis nodosa.

walls of patients with polyarteritis nodosa who have circulating HBsAg.

3. Drugs–Drugs have been implicated as causes of polyarteritis nodosa, hypersensitivity angiitis, and Henoch-Schönlein purpura. Suspected agents include sulfonamides, penicillin, phenytoin, arsenicals, thiouracil, iodides, and thiazides. There is a very high incidence of polyarteritis nodosa in parenteral methamphetamine abusers, although there is controversy over the role of HBsAg in these patients.

4. Autoantigens–Anti-vessel wall antibodies have been detected in some patients with Takayasu's disease. However, such antibodies could result from the vascular inflammatory process. Lymphocyte activation by homologous muscle has been demonstrated in patients with polymyalgia rheumatica.

Clinical Features

A. Symptoms and Signs:

1. Polyarteritis nodosa–Polyarteritis nodosa is

a necrotizing vasculitis of small muscular arteries (0.5–1 mm in diameter). Involved vessels contain a segmental perivascular inflammatory infiltrate that consists predominantly of polymorphonuclear leukocytes and eosinophils. Segmental fibrinoid necrosis of the media and adventitia and weakening of the vessel wall with aneurysm formation occur. As the lesion evolves, intimal proliferation results in luminal obliteration and ischemia of involved tissues. Finally, as inflammation subsides, the vessel is replaced by fibrous tissue. Biopsy of involved tissue from patients with classic polyarteritis nodosa will show lesions at all stages of development.

Polyarteritis nodosa usually occurs in men, who present with fever, malaise, and weight loss. The protean manifestations of polyarteritis nodosa reflect the multisystemic organ involvement of the disease.

a. Kidney–The kidneys are involved in 70% of patients, and renal insufficiency is the commonest cause of death. Renovascular hypertension develops in 50% of patients.

b. Heart–Sixty percent of patients have cardiac involvement, with congestive heart failure being the commonest manifestation. Myocardial infarction may be seen in up to 20% of patients.

c. Gastrointestinal tract–Half of patients develop vasculitis of the gastrointestinal tract, manifested by pancreatitis, hepatitis, cholecystitis, bowel infarction or perforation, and gastrointestinal bleeding.

d. Lungs–The lung may be involved pathologically in 25% of cases. Typical clinical manifestations include asthma, bronchitis, and pneumonia. Pulmonary infection complicates the course of half of patients with polyarteritis nodosa.

e. Muscles–Twenty percent of cases show signs of myositis such as pain, weakness, and tenderness.

f. Central nervous system–Eight to 25% of patients have some central nervous system abnormality. The major complication is infarction.

g. Skin–One-fourth of patients have a variety of skin manifestations, including livedo reticularis, subcutaneous nodules, and pyoderma gangrenosum. In a small group of patients, skin disease may be the only manifestation of necrotizing vasculitis.

h. Testis–Although the testis is a favorite site for biopsy, only 19% of autopsy cases show testicular involvement. In the absence of signs or symptoms of testicular involvement, biopsy will probably be unproductive.

Polyarteritis nodosa was once thought to have only a 10% 5-year survival rate. With better diagnosis and therapy, a number of investigators report 5-year survival rates of 80% or greater.

2. Hypersensitivity angiitis–Hypersensitivity angiitis can be a more fulminant disease than classic polyarteritis nodosa. It occurs with equal frequency in both sexes, at any age, and often begins after infections or drug treatment. Pathologically, hypersensitivity angiitis differs from classic polyarteritis nodosa in that smaller vessels (including capillaries) are involved and

individual lesions appear to be at the same stage of development. Clinically, the lungs, spleen, and skin are commonly involved, and gastrointestinal involvement is unusual. Hypertension is uncommon. Cases associated with a known antigen may go into remission when the offending agent is removed.

3. Henoch-Schönlein purpura (allergic purpura)–Henoch-Schönlein purpura usually occurs in boys. The histopathologic features by light microscopy are virtually identical to those of hypersensitivity angiitis, with involvement of venules and capillaries as well as small arterioles. Henoch-Schönlein purpura also frequently follows antigenic exposure, eg, infection or drugs, and some patients have a history of food allergies.

Patients with Henoch-Schönlein purpura demonstrate a fairly characteristic clinical picture, with nonthrombocytopenic purpura, colicky abdominal pain, arthralgias of the knees and ankles, and glomerulonephritis. Nephrotic syndrome and renal failure have been described, but these complications are more likely to occur in adults than in children. There is a high incidence of intestinal hemorrhage and intussusception. The disease is usually limited to a single episode lasting 4–6 weeks, but recurrences can occur up to 2 years thereafter.

4. Wegener's granulomatosis–Wegener's granulomatosis is a necrotizing granulomatous angiitis affecting arteries and veins. The 3 major areas of involvement are the upper respiratory tract, the lung parenchyma, and the kidneys. Men and women are affected with equal frequency. With involvement of the upper and lower respiratory tract, patients develop sinusitis, rhinitis, septal perforation, tracheobronchitis, asthma, and pneumonia. With the onset of renal involvement, the patient progresses rapidly to renal failure. Renal findings include necrotizing angiitis, glomerulitis with thrombosis of glomerular capillaries, adhesions of the glomerular tuft to Bowman's capsule, glomerular and interstitial necrosis, and granuloma formation. As in hypersensitivity angiitis, hypertension is uncommon. Other manifestations of Wegener's granulomatosis include arthralgias, polyneuropathy, parotitis, prostatitis, pericarditis, myocarditis (occasionally with infarction), skin involvement, and ocular disease (exophthalmos, episcleritis, conjunctivitis, and corneal erosion).

Before modern methods of therapy became available, patients with Wegener's granulomatosis almost always died in renal failure, and even today a patient's renal status still determines the long-range outlook. Survival with current treatment regimens approaches 90%.

5. Takayasu's arteritis (pulseless disease, aortic arch syndrome, giant cell arteritis of the aorta)–Takayasu's disease is a disease of females, age 10–50, described most often in Japanese women. It is an indolent inflammatory process involving the thoracic aorta and large arteries. The inflammation, which can be diffuse or focal, is characterized by mononuclear cell infiltration and giant cell formation in the media and adventitia. Degeneration of the media with disruption of the elastic layer leads occasionally to aneurysm formation. Proliferation of fibrous tissue may lead to narrowing and obliteration of the lumen of any involved vessel. Extensive vascular calcification resembling that seen in atherosclerosis develops in patients with long-standing disease. Takayasu's disease has been described in patients with other rheumatic diseases such as systemic lupus erythematosus or rheumatoid arthritis.

Constitutional symptoms of fever, night sweats, and weight loss are universal among patients with Takayasu's disease. Erythema nodosum and pyoderma gangrenosum may be seen. Carotid and vertebral arterial involvement leads to cerebrovascular insufficiency with transient ischemic attacks, vertigo, and intermittent visual disturbances. Takayasu's disease of the renal artery is associated with renovascular hypertension. Involvement of the femoral and iliac arteries leads to peripheral claudication. Either the coronary ostia or the coronary arteries themselves may become involved, leading to angina pectoris or infarction. The case fatality rate is 25–75% within 5 years, with a high incidence of sudden death.

6. Giant cell arteritis (temporal arteritis)– Giant cell arteritis is a disease of the elderly, being very unusual in patients under 55 years of age. Women are affected twice as often as men. Pathologically, the disease is characterized by nonsuppurative granulomatous inflammation (either focal or diffuse) of the aorta and large vessels. Giant cells are conspicuous on histologic examination.

Constitutional findings include fever, weight loss, and malaise. Patients characteristically complain of symmetric arthralgias, myalgias, morning stiffness, and weakness of pelvic and shoulder girdles. The characteristic morning headache, which is described as constant and "boring," may be limited to the temporal areas or radiate widely over the head. The complications of the disease depend on the vessels involved. The temporal arteries may become warm, red, and tender, with or without painful nodules. With ocular vessel involvement, visual symptoms (ranging from intermittent blurring to diplopia to blindness) may result. Without treatment, blindness may occur in up to 30% of patients with acute giant cell arteritis. The manifestations of cerebrovascular involvement include transient ischemic attacks, stroke, and cranial nerve palsies. With involvement of the aorta and other large vessels, peripheral claudication or myocardial ischemia can be seen. Giant cell arteritis is usually a self-limited disease that lasts for approximately 2 years. Because of the high incidence of blindness, it is crucial to make the diagnosis and treat the disease. The definitive diagnostic technique is temporal artery biopsy, but a large segment of one or both temporal arteries is required because of the focal nature of the disease. The relationship of giant cell arteritis to polymyalgia rheumatica is a matter of some controversy. The 2 diseases have the same age and sex distribution, and the systemic symptoms are virtually identical. Forty percent of patients with polymyalgia rheumatica have giant cell arteritis on biopsy even in the absence of signs of temporal arteritis. At this time, polymyalgia rheumatica should be considered a clinical syndrome often, but not always, associated with giant cell arteritis.

B. Laboratory Findings: Eighty percent of patients with vasculitis have leukocytosis (20–50 thousand/μL). Eosinophilia—often up to 1500/μL—occurs most commonly in patients with systemic necrotizing vasculitis with lung involvement. Anemia is very common and may be due to blood loss, autoimmune hemolytic anemia (in Wegener's granulomatosis), microangiopathic damage, or chronic disease.

Proteinuria, hematuria, and granular or cellular casts may be seen with renal involvement. Azotemia is a common complication of the disseminated vasculitides. Nonspecific laboratory tests indicating inflammation, such as the erythrocyte sedimentation rate and the "acute phase reactants" (eg, C-reactive protein), are almost universally abnormal. Polyclonal hypergammaglobulinemia is a common finding. Cryoglobulinemia, macroglobulinemia, rheumatoid factor, and a false-positive VDRL may all occur.

C. X-Ray Findings: With active pulmonary involvement, the chest film may reveal multiple infiltrates with interstitial fibrosis (polyarteritis nodosa) or nodular densities with or without cavitation (Wegener's granulomatosis). Patients with Takayasu's disease may show diffuse vascular calcifications similar to those seen in atherosclerosis. On angiography, a high percentage of patients with polyarteritis nodosa, particularly those with abdominal or renal manifestations, will have microaneurysms in small arteries throughout the visceral circulation. Angiography may show beading and irregularity of involved arteries in patients with giant cell arteritis.

Treatment

A. Corticosteroids: Corticosteroids are useful in polyarteritis nodosa and hypersensitivity angiitis. They may result in rapid clinical improvement and have been shown to increase the 12-month survival rate in these 2 diseases. Carefully controlled studies of the effects of corticosteroids on long-term survival in these diseases have not been done. The suggested therapeutic regimen is prednisone, 60–80 mg orally daily, using clinical and laboratory parameters to determine the duration of therapy. Corticosteroids are also the major mode of therapy in giant cell arteritis. In patients with polymyalgia rheumatica without temporal arteritis, the recommended treatment is prednisone in moderate doses, using the erythrocyte sedimentation rate and clinical symptoms to determine how fast to taper the drug. When temporal arteritis is suspected, the artery should be biopsied immediately and the patient begun on prednisone, 60 mg orally daily, to forestall the possibility of blindness. These patients usually respond dramatically within 4 days. Corticosteroids should be tapered to the lowest dose required to control symptoms and therapy continued for 2 years, after which attempts should be made to withdraw corticosteroids completely. The use of corticosteroids in Takayasu's disease has been shown to control acute inflammatory reactions and probably to stop the progression of the disease. Prednisone is begun in a dosage of 30 mg orally daily and, after 9 weeks, is tapered to a maintenance dose of 5–10 mg daily. The duration and the long-term effectiveness of therapy have not been determined.

Corticosteroids are of little benefit in Henoch-Schönlein purpura. Although they decrease acute inflammatory symptoms and can be used when the response to aspirin is inadequate, they have no effect on the severity or progression of the renal disease.

B. Cytotoxic Agents: Cytotoxic drugs have dramatically improved the prognosis in Wegener's granulomatosis. Cyclophosphamide, starting at 1–2 mg/kg daily (orally or intravenously, depending on the severity of the clinical situation), has been employed most commonly. The drug is administered until there is a clinical response or until signs of toxicity develop (marrow suppression, gastrointestinal intolerance, alopecia, hemorrhagic cystitis). The duration of therapy required is unknown. Long-term remissions have been induced, so periodic attempts should be made to withdraw this potentially dangerous drug. Corticosteroids are used concurrently only with severe inflammatory disease. Cytotoxic agents have also been shown to increase significantly the survival of patients with polyarteritis nodosa.

SERUM SICKNESS

Serum sickness is an adverse immunologic response to a foreign antigen, usually a heterologous protein. The incidence of the disease has declined with the decreasing therapeutic use of heterologous antisera; however, it still occurs following the administration of various heterologous antitoxins, including those for rabies, diphtheria, snake venom, and clostridia, and following administration of certain drugs (eg, penicillin, sulfonamides).

Signs and symptoms begin 7–15 days after exposure to the offending antigen and include fever, myalgias, arthralgias, arthritis, urticaria, lymphadenopathy, and splenomegaly. The arthritis may involve large or small joints, and although pain, swelling, and effusions are common, heat and erythema are seldom reported.

Laboratory evaluation reveals leukocytosis (occasionally with eosinophilia), hematuria, proteinuria, and decreased complement levels (CH_{50}). The synovial fluid white count is over 20,000/μL, mostly polymorphonuclear leukocytes, and the complement level is decreased. The disease is usually self-limited, with no residua. Rare complications include laryngeal edema, mononeuritis, glomerulonephritis, and vasculitis.

Serum sickness is the prototype immune complex disease. During the initial immune response, there is antigen excess leading to the formation of soluble antigen-antibody complexes which diffuse into involved tissues, activate complement, and initiate the inflammatory response that causes the disease. As antibody titers rise and approach equivalence, insoluble complexes are formed which are quickly cleared by the reticuloendothelial system. Precipitating antibodies that fix complement can be demonstrated in most patients with serum sickness. Hemagglutinating antibodies against sheep red blood cells can be detected in virtually 100% of patients. Titers of hemagglutinating antibody rise following the onset of clinical manifestations and peak with clinical recovery.

The urticaria responds to epinephrine and antihistamine therapy, and salicylates are effective in controlling constitutional symptoms and the arthritis. A short course of corticosteroids may be required in severely ill patients.

BEHÇET'S DISEASE

Behçet's disease is a chronic recurrent inflammatory disease affecting adults of both sexes. The major manifestations of the disease are aphthous stomatitis, iritis, and genital ulcers. Other findings include vasculitis (particularly of the skin), arthritis, meningomyelitis, enterocolitis, erythema nodosum, thrombophlebitis, and epididymitis. The differential diagnosis includes viral (herpes simplex) or chlamydial (inclusion conjunctivitis, lymphogranuloma venereum) infections, Reiter's syndrome, inflammatory bowel disease, Stevens-Johnson syndrome, and systemic lupus erythematosus. A pustular lesion appearing after needle puncture of the skin is highly suggestive of Behçet's disease.

Genetic and environmental factors probably play a role in pathogenesis. The prevalence of HLA-B5 is increased in patients with Behçet's disease, but there is some evidence suggesting that a virus may play a role in disease causation. Cerebrospinal fluid from patients with Behçet's disease will produce encephalitis, optic neuritis, uveitis, keratitis, and conjunctivitis in rabbits. A viral agent cultured from the eye, blood, and urine of one patient has produced encephalitis in mice. Antibodies against various human mucosal antigens have been detected, and indirect immunofluorescence has demonstrated vascular deposition of immunoglobulins as well as circulating anticytoplasmic antibodies. Furthermore, lymphocytes and plasma cells are prominent in the perivascular infiltrate of Behçet's vasculitis. Amyloidosis may develop in these patients.

Local corticosteroids are useful in the treatment of mild ocular and oral disease. Systemic corticosteroids are helpful in the treatment of systemic manifestations, but chlorambucil is thought to be the most useful agent when dealing with ocular disease. Unproved remedies include whole blood transfusions, transfer factor, levamisole, and colchicine.

ANKYLOSING SPONDYLITIS

Ankylosing spondylitis is a chronic progressive inflammatory disorder involving the sacroiliac joints, spine, and large peripheral joints. Ninety percent of cases occur in males, with the usual age at onset being the second or third decade of life.

The disease begins with the insidious onset of low back pain and stiffness, usually worse in the morning. Symptoms of the acute disease include pain and tenderness in the sacroiliac joints and spasm of the paravertebral muscles. Findings in advanced disease include ankylosis of the sacroiliac joints and spine, with loss of lumbar lordosis, marked dorsocervical kyphosis, and decreased chest expansion. Peripheral arthritis, particularly of axial joints, may be seen. Twenty-five percent of patients will also have iritis or iridocyclitis. Carditis with or without aortitis is seen in 10% of patients, with 1–4% progressing to insufficiency of the aortic valves. Rare complications include pericarditis and pulmonary fibrosis.

Patients with ankylosing spondylitis are seronegative for rheumatoid factor. Hypergammaglobulinemia and antinuclear antibodies are not seen in ankylosing spondylitis. An elevated erythrocyte sedimentation rate and a mild anemia are almost universal during active disease. Electrocardiographic abnormalities, such as atrioventricular block, left or right bundle branch block, and left ventricular hypertrophy reflect cardiac involvement. X-rays of the sacroiliac joints reveal osteoporosis and erosions early in the disease and sclerosis with fusion in advanced disease. Calcification of the anterior longitudinal ligament of the spine and squaring of the vertebrae are seen on lateral x-ray. Ossification of the outer margins of the intervertebral disk (syndesmophyte formation) eventually leads to fusion of the spine.

On pathologic examination, these patients have a chronic proliferative synovitis very similar to that of rheumatoid arthritis. The characteristic skeletal change in advanced disease is ossification of the sacroiliac joints and interspinous and capsular ligaments. Pathologic cardiac findings include focal inflammation and fibrous thickening of the aortic wall and valve cusps.

The physical findings in patients with severe osteoarthritis of the spine may resemble those of patients with end-stage ankylosing spondylitis. However, degenerative osteoarthritis begins much later in life, does not involve the sacroiliac joints, and is characterized radiographically by osteophytes rather than syndesmophytes. The differentiation of ankylosing spondylitis from other diseases associated with sacroiliitis and spondylitis, such as psoriatic arthritis, Reiter's syndrome, regional enteritis, and ulcerative colitis, depends upon the presence or absence of the clinical and radiologic characteristics of those diseases.

The basic pathogenesis of ankylosing spondylitis is unknown. Although the presence of mononuclear cells in acutely involved tissue and the histologic similarity of the synovitis to rheumatoid arthritis suggest a possible immunologic mechanism, there are no real data to support an autoimmune pathogenetic mechanism. There is a strong genetic component. Several members of the same family are often involved, and twin concordance for ankylosing spondylitis has been described. Furthermore, 90% of patients with ankylosing spondylitis have HLA-B27. The gene that determines this specific cell surface antigen may be linked to other genes that determine pathologic autoimmune phenomena or that lead to an increased susceptibility to infectious or environmental agents. There is no specific immunologic diagnostic test.

The treatment of ankylosing spondylitis consists of giving anti-inflammatory agents to decrease acute inflammation and relieve pain and of instituting physical therapy to maintain muscle strength and flexibility. Therapy is designed to maintain a position of function even if ossification and ankylosis progress. The anti-inflammatory agents suggested are indomethacin, 75–100 mg orally daily in divided doses, or one of the newer nonsteroidal agents such as ibuprofen, naproxen, or fenoprofen. Posturing exercises (lying flat for periods during the day, sleeping without a pillow, breathing exercises), the judicious use of local heat, and job modification are all part of a rational physical therapy program. Total hip replacement may offer considerable relief to patients with ankylosis of the hips, although recurrent ankylosis is sometimes a problem.

REITER'S SYNDROME

Reiter's syndrome is classically defined as a clinical triad consisting of arthritis, urethritis, and conjunctivitis. Although it usually affects men, it may also occur in women and children. The arthritis is recurrent or chronic, migratory, asymmetric, and polyarticular, involving primarily joints of the lower extremity. Fever, malaise, and weight loss occur commonly with acute arthritis. The urethritis is nonspecific and often asymptomatic. The conjunctivitis is mild, but 20–50% of patients develop iritis. Balanitis circinata, painless oral ulcerations, and keratoderma blennorrhagicum (thick keratotic lesions of the palms and soles) are frequent mucocutaneous manifestations. Complications include spondylitis and carditis.

Most patients have a leukocytosis of 10–18 thousand/μL. The urethral discharge is purulent, and smear and culture are negative for *Neisseria gonorrhoeae*. Synovial fluid is sterile, with a white count of 2000–50,000/μL, mostly polymorphonuclear neutrophils. The classic radiographic finding is fluffy periosteal proliferation of the heels, ankles, metatarsals, phalanges, knees, and elbows. Bony erosions may be seen in severe cases.

Major diseases in the differential diagnosis include gonococcal arthritis, psoriatic arthritis, ankylosing spondylitis, and the arthritis of inflammatory bowel disease. Patients with psoriatic arthritis also develop urethritis or conjunctivitis. The differentiation of psoriatic arthritis and Reiter's syndrome is difficult to make on the basis of the skin lesion, since keratoderma blennorrhagicum is histologically indistinguishable from pustular psoriasis. Reiter's syndrome can be differentiated from ankylosing spondylitis by the presence of the urethritis and conjunctivitis, the prominent involvement of distal joints, and the radiologic characteristics of the spine disease.

The cause of Reiter's syndrome is not known. Some cases have been associated with sexual contact. Several infectious agents, including shigellae, gonococci, mycoplasmas, chlamydiae, yersiniae, and *Campylobacter* have been associated with Reiter's syndrome, but there is no consensus on the significance of these associations. Ninety percent of patients with Reiter's syndrome have HLA-B27. It is not known whether this antigenic marker imparts an increased susceptibility to environmental or infectious agents or is associated with an unusual immune response gene. The presence of lymphocytes and plasma cells in the inflammatory synovial fluid of patients with Reiter's syndrome suggests a persistent immune response.

Salicylates, indomethacin, or one of the newer nonsteroidal agents (ibuprofen, naproxen, or fenoprofen) may be used to control acute inflammation. Although the acute attack usually subsides in a few months, recurrences are common and some patients develop a chronic deforming arthritis.

PSORIATIC ARTHRITIS

Psoriatic arthritis is a chronic, recurrent, erosive polyarthritis seen in 5–7% of patients with psoriasis. The onset of the arthritis may be acute or insidious and is usually preceded by skin disease. It characteristically involves the distal interphalangeal joints of the fingers and toes, the hips, the sacroiliac joints, and the spine. Distal interphalangeal joint disease is frequently accompanied by nail pitting or onycholysis secondary to psoriasis of the nail matrix or nail bed. Constitutional signs and symptoms, such as fever and fatigue, are common. Severe erosive disease may lead to marked deformity of the hands and feet (arthritis mutilans), and marked vertebral involvement can result in ankylosis of the spine.

An elevated erythrocyte sedimentation rate and a mild anemia are extremely common. Hyperuricemia is occasionally seen in patients with severe skin disease. Serum immunoglobulin levels are normal, and rheumatoid factor is absent. Synovial fluid examination reveals a white cell count of 5–40 thousand/μL, mostly polymorphonuclear leukocytes. Characteristic x-ray findings include "pencil cup" erosions, fluffy periosteal proliferation, and bony ankylosis of peripheral joints. Sacroiliac changes, including erosions, sclerosis, and ankylosis similar to that in ankylosing spondylitis, occur in 10–30% of patients.

The major diseases that must be differentiated from psoriatic arthritis include rheumatoid arthritis, ankylosing spondylitis, and Reiter's syndrome. Psoriatic arthritis is differentiated from rheumatoid arthritis by the absence of rheumatoid factor and subcutaneous nodules, the involvement of distal interphalangeals, the characteristic x-ray findings of psoriatic arthritis, and the presence of psoriasis. The presence of the skin lesion, the involvement of distal interphalangeals, and differences in the radiologic appearance of the spine help differentiate psoriatic arthritis from ankylosing spondylitis. The differentiation of psoriatic arthritis from Reiter's syndrome is particularly difficult, since both diseases are associated with HLA-B27 and involve the sacroiliac joints and spine and since keratoderma blennorrhagicum is histologically indistinguishable from pustular psoriasis. The diagnosis of psoriatic arthritis rests on the absence of urethritis, conjunctivitis, and oral ulcers.

The cause of psoriasis and psoriatic arthritis is unknown. Genetic factors appear to play a role in disease causation. Psoriasis and rheumatic diseases are found in family members of 12–13% of patients. Furthermore, 20% of patients with peripheral arthritis and 45% of patients with spondylitis have HLA-B27. HLA-B13 and HLA-Bw17 are increased in psoriasis without arthritis. The high prevalence of genetic markers might be associated with an increased susceptibility to unknown infectious or environmental agents or to primary abnormal autoimmune phenomena. However, no immunologic pathogenetic mechanism has yet been demonstrated.

Skin and arthritic manifestations require therapy. Corticosteroids, coal tar and ultraviolet light, or immunosuppressive agents can be used to treat the skin disease. Treatment of arthritis is similar to that of rheumatoid arthritis.

RELAPSING POLYCHONDRITIS

Relapsing polychondritis is a rare disease characterized by recurrent episodes of inflammatory necrosis involving cartilaginous tissues of the ears, nose, upper respiratory tract, and peripheral joints. The disease begins abruptly with swollen, painful, erythematous lesions of the nose or ears, usually associated with fever. The inflammation destroys supporting cartilaginous tissues, and patients are left with characteristic "floppy ear" and "saddle nose" deformities. Involvement of the upper respiratory tract leads to collapse of the trachea with recurrent bronchitis and pneumonia; the commonest cause of death in these patients is airway obstruction. Recurrent episcleritis, cataract formation, auditory and vestibular defects, and arthritis are common manifestations of relapsing polychondritis. Aortic insufficiency due to destruction and dilatation of the aortic valve ring occurs rarely.

Laboratory abnormalities include an elevated erythrocyte sedimentation rate, increased serum immunoglobulins, a false-positive VDRL, and mild anemia. Pathologic examination reveals infiltration of the cartilage–connective tissue interface with lymphocytes, plasma cells, and polymorphonuclear leukocytes. As the lesion evolves, the cartilage loses its basophilic stippling and stains more acidophilic. Eventually, the cartilage becomes completely replaced by fibrous tissue.

The pathogenesis of this disease is unknown. However, there is some evidence that autoimmune phenomena play a role. Indirect immunofluorescence has revealed the presence of anticartilage antibodies in the serum of a few patients. Electron microscopy reveals electron-dense deposits of unknown origin in involved cartilage. In some patients with relapsing polychondritis, cartilage antigen will induce lymphocyte activation and lymphocyte production of MIF. These observations must be verified and expanded before definitive statements on the immunopathogenesis of relapsing polychondritis can be made.

Corticosteroids and dapsone have been used with success in the treatment of relapsing polychondritis, presumably because both inhibit lysosomal activity.

RELAPSING PANNICULITIS
(Weber-Christian Disease)

Relapsing panniculitis is a rare syndrome characterized by recurrent episodes of discrete nodular inflammation and nonsuppurative necrosis of subcutaneous fat. Most patients are women. Painful, erythematous nodules usually appear over the face, trunk, and limbs and progress to local atrophy and fibrosis. Occasionally, they may undergo necrosis with the discharge of a fatty fluid. Constitutional signs, including fever, usually accompany an acute episode. Histologically, one sees edema, mononuclear cell infiltration, fat necrosis, perivascular inflammatory cuffing, and endothelial proliferation. The differential diagnosis includes superficial thrombophlebitis, polyarteritis nodosa, necrotizing vasculitis, erythema induratum, erythema nodosum, and factitious disease.

The cause of relapsing panniculitis is not known. The syndrome has been associated with a number of environmental factors, including trauma, cold, exposure to toxic chemicals, and infection. It has been seen in patients with systemic lupus erythematosus, rheumatoid arthritis, diabetes mellitus, sarcoidosis, tuberculosis, withdrawal from corticosteroid therapy, and acute and chronic pancreatitis. In some patients, it appears to be a hypersensitivity phenomenon, since it follows repeated injections of various drugs. An autoimmune mechanism is suggested by the association of relapsing panniculitis with several autoimmune diseases and with numerous phenomena that could conceivably expose or alter autoantigens in fatty tissue. However, the only autoantibodies demonstrated to date are circulating leukoagglutinins.

Acute episodes respond to corticosteroid therapy.

HEREDITARY COMPLEMENT DEFICIENCIES & COLLAGEN VASCULAR DISEASES

The past decade has seen the development of techniques for the evaluation and characterization of complement and complement inhibitors (see Chapter 11). The use of these techniques has revealed hereditary deficiencies of various components of the complement system. Complement deficiency is seen in one in a million normal adult males and is much more common in patients with various rheumatoid diseases.

Deficiencies of a number of complement components have been associated with several rheumatic disorders. Deficiencies of C1r, C2, C4, C5, C8, and C1 esterase have all been associated with lupuslike syndromes. Other autoimmune phenomena have been associated with deficiencies of specific complement components.

The significance of complement deficiency in collagen vascular disease has yet to be clarified. However, it is hypothesized that complement deficiency may lead to an increased susceptibility to infectious agents, particularly viruses, which may then stimulate the autoimmunity that results in disease.

At present there is no specific treatment for most complement deficiencies. Therapy is directed at the associated disease.

HYPOGAMMAGLOBULINEMIA & ARTHRITIS

Hypogammaglobulinemia is an acquired or congenital disorder that may involve all or any one of the specific classes of immunoglobulin (see Chapter 25). Hypogammaglobulinemia is associated with infections, chronic inflammatory bowel disease, sarcoidosis, a number of rheumatic diseases (systemic lupus erythematosus, scleroderma, Sjögren's syndrome, polymyositis-dermatomyositis), an increased incidence of malignancy, and a seronegative rheumatoidlike arthritis. Patients with classic adult and juvenile rheumatoid arthritis may develop hypogammaglobulinemia.

Hypogammaglobulinemia patients may develop a seronegative, symmetric arthritis, with morning stiffness, occasional nodule formation, and radiographic evidence of demineralization and joint space narrowing. Bony erosions are rarely seen. Biopsy of the synovium reveals chronic inflammatory changes without plasma cells. Despite the reduction of serum immunoglobulins, immunoglobulin may be detected in the inflammatory synovial fluid. Total hemolytic complement is commonly depressed in the synovial fluid, suggesting immune complex formation.

Hypogammaglobulinemia may result in an increased susceptibility to infection by unidentified viruses that may induce the autoimmune phenomena (including arthritis) in these patients.

Hypogammaglobulinemic arthritis may improve after the administration of gamma globulin.

• • •

References

Systemic Lupus Erythematosus

Appel AR et al: The effect of normalization of serum complement and anti-DNA antibody on the course of lupus nephritis: A two year prospective study. *Am J Med* 1978;**64**:274.

Aptekar RG, Lawless A, Decker JL: Deforming nonerosive arthritis of the hand in SLE. *Clin Orthop* 1974;**100**:120.

Baldwin DS et al: Lupus nephritis: Clinical course as related to morphologic forms and their transitions. *Am J Med* 1977;**62**:12.

Bennett K et al: Neuropsychiatric problems in SLE. *Br Med J* 1972;**4**:342.

Bulkley BH, Roberts CS: The heart in systemic lupus erythematosus and the changes induced in it by corticosteroid therapy: A study of 36 necropsy patients. *Am J Med* 1975;**58**:243.

Castro O, Farber LR, Clyne LP: Circulating anticoagulants against factors IX and XI in systemic lupus erythematosus. *Ann Intern Med* 1972;**77**:543.

Decker JL et al: Systemic lupus erythematosus: Evolving concepts. *Ann Intern Med* 1979;**91**:587.

Donadio JV et al: Treatment of diffuse proliferative lupus nephritis with prednisone and combined prednisone and cyclophosphamide. *N Engl J Med* 1978;**299**:1151.

Eisenberg H, Dubois EL, Sherwin RP: Diffuse interstitial lung disease in SLE. *Ann Intern Med* 1973;**79**:37.

Fish AJ et al: Systemic lupus erythematosus within the first two decades of life. *Am J Med* 1977;**62**:99.

Keeffe EB et al: Antibody to DNA and DNA–anti-DNA complexes in cerebrospinal fluid. *Ann Intern Med* 1974;**80**:58.

Notman DD, Kurata N, Tan EM: Profiles of antinuclear antibodies in systemic rheumatic diseases. *Ann Intern Med* 1975;**83**:464.

Pekin TJ, Zvaifler NJ: Synovial fluid findings in SLE. *Arthritis Rheum* 1970;**13**:777.

Reichlin M, Mattioli M: Antigens and antibodies characteristic of SLE. *Bull Rheum Dis* 1973–1974;**24**:756.

Reinersten JL et al: B-lymphocyte alloantigens associated with systemic lupus erythematosus. *N Engl J Med* 1978;**299**:515.

Rothfield NF, Stollar BD: The relation of immunoglobulin class, pattern of antinuclear antibody and complement fixing antibodies to DNA in sera from patients with SLE. *J Clin Invest* 1967;**46**:1785.

Spriggs B, Epstein W: Clinical and laboratory correlates of L-chain proteinuria in systemic lupus erythematosus. *J Rheum* 1974;**1**:287.

Talal N: Immunologic and viral factors in the pathogenesis of SLE. *Arthritis Rheum* 1970;**13**:887.

Trimble RB et al: Preliminary criteria for the classification of SLE. *Arthritis Rheum* 1974;**17**:184.

Ziff M: Viruses and the connective tissue diseases. *Ann Intern Med* 1971;**45**:951.

Rheumatoid Arthritis

Abruzzo JL, Heimer R: IgG anti-IgG antibodies in rheumatoid arthritis and certain other conditions. *Ann Rheum Dis* 1974;**33**:256.

Feigenbaum SL, Masi AT, Kaplan SB: Prognosis in rheumatoid arthritis: A longitudinal study of newly diagnosed younger adult patients. *Am J Med* 1979;**66**:377.

Franco AE, Schur PH: Hypocomplementemia in rheumatoid arthritis. *Arthritis Rheum* 1971;**14**:231.

Goldman JA, Hess EV: Treatment of rheumatoid arthritis—1970. *Bull Rheum Dis* 1970;**21**:609.

Hurd ER: Extra-articular manifestations of rheumatoid arthritis. *Semin Arthritis Rheum* 1979;**8**:151.

Morgan ES et al: A study of the relation of seronegative and seropositive rheumatoid arthritis to each other and to necrotizing vasculitis. *Am J Med* 1969;**47**:23.

O'Sullivan JB, Cathcart ES: The prevalence of rheumatoid arthritis: Follow-up evaluation of the effect of criteria on rates in Sudbury, Massachusetts. *Ann Intern Med* 1972;**76**:573.

Pope RM, Teller DC, Mannik M: The molecular basis of self-association of antibodies to IgG (rheumatoid factors) in rheumatoid arthritis. *Proc Natl Acad Sci USA* 1974;**71**:517.

Schmid FR et al: Arteritis in rheumatoid arthritis. *Am J Med* 1961;**30**:56.

Srinivasan R, Miller BL, Paulus HE: Long-term chrysotherapy in rheumatoid arthritis. *Arthritis Rheum* 1979;**22**:105.

Stage DE, Mannik M: 7S M-globulin in rheumatoid arthritis: Evaluation of its clinical significance. *Arthritis Rheum* 1971;**14**:440.

Stastny P: Association of the B-cell alloantigen DRw4 with rheumatoid arthritis. *N Engl J Med* 1978;**298**:869.

Ziff M: Relation of cellular infiltration of rheumatoid synovial membrane to its immune response. *Arthritis Rheum* 1974;**17**:313.

Zvaifler NJ: Rheumatoid synovitis: An extravascular immune complex disease. *Arthritis Rheum* 1974;**17**:297.

Juvenile Rheumatoid Arthritis

Bianco NE et al: Immunologic studies of juvenile rheumatoid arthritis. *Arthritis Rheum* 1971;**14**:685.

Brewer EJ, Giannini EH, Barkley E: Gold therapy in the management of juvenile rheumatoid arthritis. *Arthritis Rheum* 1980;**23**:404.

Bywaters EGL: The management of juvenile chronic polyarthritis. *Bull Rheum Dis* 1977;**27**:882.

Calabro JJ, Katz RM, Maltz BA: A critical reappraisal of juvenile rheumatoid arthritis. *Clin Orthop* 1971;**74**:101.

Moore T, Dorner RW, Zuckner J: Hidden rheumatoid factor in seronegative juvenile rheumatoid arthritis. *Ann Rheum Dis* 1974;**33**:255.

Schaller JG, Wedgwood RJ: Juvenile rheumatoid arthritis: A review. *Pediatrics* 1972;**50**:940.

Schaller JG et al: The association of antinuclear antibodies with the chronic iridocyclitis of juvenile rheumatoid arthritis. *Arthritis Rheum* 1974;**17**:409.

Sjögren's Syndrome

Anderson LG, Talal N: The spectrum of benign to malignant lymphoproliferation in Sjögren's syndrome. *Clin Exp Immunol* 1971;**9**:199.

Bloch KJ et al: Sjögren's syndrome: A clinical, pathological, and serological study of sixty-two cases. *Medicine* 1965;**44**:187.

Fye KH et al: Relationship of HLA-Dw3 and HLA-B8 to Sjögren's syndrome. *Arthritis Rheum* 1978;**21**:337.

Moutsopoulos HM et al: Sjögren's syndrome (sicca complex): Current issues. *Ann Intern Med* 1980;**92**:212.

Talal N, Zisman E, Schur PH: Renal tubular acidosis, glomerulonephritis and immunologic factors in Sjögren's syndrome. *Arthritis Rheum* 1968;**11**:774.

Talal N et al: T and B lymphocytes in peripheral blood and tissue lesions in Sjögren's syndrome. *J Clin Invest* 1974; **53**:180.

Zulman J, Jaffe R, Talal N: Evidence that the malignant lymphoma of Sjögren's syndrome is a monoclonal B-cell neoplasm. *N Engl J Med* 1978;**299**:1215.

Progressive Systemic Sclerosis

Cannon PJ et al: The relationship of hypertension and renal failure in scleroderma (progressive systemic sclerosis) to structural and functional abnormalities of the renal cortical circulation. *Medicine* 1974;**53**:1.

LeRoy EC, Fleischmann RM: The management of renal scleroderma: Experience with dialysis, nephrectomy, and transplantation. *Am J Med* 1978;**64**:974.

Medscer TA et al: Skeletal muscle involvement in progressive systemic sclerosis. *Arthritis Rheum* 1968;**11**:554.

Rodnan GP: When is scleroderma not scleroderma? *Bull Rheum Dis* 1981;**31**:7.

Rodnan GP, Myerowitz RL, Justh GO: Morphologic changes in the digital arteries of patients with progressive systemic sclerosis (scleroderma) and Raynaud's phenomenon. *Medicine* 1980;**59**:393.

Sharp GC et al: Mixed connective tissue disease. *Am J Med* 1972;**52**:148.

Subcommittee for Scleroderma Criteria of the American Rheumatism Association Diagnostic and Therapeutic Criteria Committee: Preliminary criteria for the classification of systemic sclerosis (scleroderma). *Arthritis Rheum* 1980;**23**:581.

Weaver AL, Divertie MD, Titus JL: The lung in scleroderma. *Mayo Clin Proc* 1967;**42**:754.

Polymyositis-Dermatomyositis

Bohan A, Peter JB: Polymyositis-dermatomyositis. (2 parts.) *N Engl J Med* 1975;**292**:344, 403.

Bohan A et al: A computer-assisted analysis of 153 patients with polymyositis and dermatomyositis. *Medicine* 1977; **56**:255.

Johnson RL, Fink CW, Ziff M: Lymphotoxin formation by lymphocytes and muscle in polymyositis. *J Clin Invest* 1972;**51**:2435.

Vignos PJ, Goldwyn J: Evaluation of laboratory tests in diagnosis and management of polymyositis. *Am J Med Sci* 1972;**263**:291.

Vasculitides

DeShazo RD et al: Systemic vasculitis with coexistent large and small vessel involvement: A classification dilemma. *JAMA* 1977;**238**:1940.

Fauci AS, Haynes BF, Katz P: The spectrum of vasculitis: Clinical, immunologic, and therapeutic considerations. *Ann Intern Med* 1978;**89**:660.

Fauci AS et al: Cyclophosphamide therapy of severe systemic necrotizing vasculitis. *N Engl J Med* 1979;**301**:235.

Fraga A et al: Takayasu's arteritis: Frequency of systemic manifestations (study of 22 patients) and favorable response to maintenance steroid therapy with adrenocorticosteroids (12 patients). *Arthritis Rheum* 1972;**15**:617.

Fye KH et al: Immune complexes in hepatitis B antigen–associated periarteritis nodosa. *Am J Med* 1977;**62**:783.

Goodman BW: Temporal arteritis. *Am J Med* 1979;**67**:839.

Huston KA et al: Temporal arteritis: A 25-year epidemiologic, clinical, and pathological study. *Ann Intern Med* 1978; **38**:162.

Leib ES, Restivo C, Paulus HE: Immunosuppressive and corticosteroid therapy of polyarteritis nodosa. *Am J Med* 1979;**67**:941.

Meadow SR et al: Schönlein-Henoch nephritis. *Q J Med* 1972; **41**:241.

Travers RL et al: Polyarteritis nodosa: A clinical and angiographic analysis of 17 cases. *Semin Arthritis Rheum* 1979; **8**:184.

Wolff SM et al: Wegener's granulomatosis. *Ann Intern Med* 1974;**81**:513.

Serum Sickness

Dixon FJ et al: Immunology and pathogenesis of experimental serum sickness. Page 354 in: *Cellular and Humoral Aspects of Hypersensitivity States*. Lawrence HS (editor). Hoeber, 1959.

Vaughan JH et al: Serum sickness. *Ann Intern Med* 1967; **57**:596.

Weigle WO, Dixon FJ: Relationship of circulating antigen-antibody complexes, antigen elimination and complement fixation in serum sickness. *Proc Soc Exp Biol Med* 1958; **99**:226.

Behçet's Disease

Gamble CN et al: The immune complex pathogenesis of glomerulonephritis and pulmonary vasculitis in Behçet's disease. *Am J Med* 1979;**66**:1031.

O'Duffy JD: Suggested criteria for the diagnosis of Behçet's disease. VI Pan-American Congress on Rheumatic Diseases. *J Rheum* 1974; **(Suppl) 18.**

Shimizu T et al: Behçet's disease (Behçet syndrome). *Semin Arth Rheum* 1979;**8**:223.

Ankylosing Spondylitis

Calabro JJ, Maltz BA: Ankylosing spondylitis. *N Engl J Med* 1970;**282**:606.

Dick HM et al: Inheritance of ankylosing spondylitis and HL-A antigen W27. *Lancet* 1974;**1**:24.

McEwen C et al: Ankylosing spondylitis and spondylitis accompanying ulcerative colitis, regional enteritis, psoriasis, Reiter's disease: A comparative study. *Arthritis Rheum* 1971;**14**:291.

Moll JMH et al: Associations between ankylosing spondylitis, psoriatic arthritis, Reiter's disease, the intestinal arthropathies, and Behçet's syndrome. *Medicine* 1974; **53**:343.

Schlosstein L et al: High association of an HL-A antigen, W27, with ankylosing spondylitis. *N Engl J Med* 1973; **288**:704.

Reiter's Syndrome

Ford DK: Reiter's syndrome. *Bull Rheum Dis* 1970;**20**:588.

Fox R et al: The chronicity of symptoms and disability in Reiter's syndrome: An analysis of 131 consecutive patients. *Ann Intern Med* 1979;**9**:190.

Morris R et al: HL-A W27: A clue to the diagnosis and pathogenesis of Reiter's syndrome. *N Engl J Med* 1974; **290**:554.

Wilkens RF et al: Reiter's syndrome: Evaluation of preliminary criteria for definite disease. *Arthritis Rheum* 1981; **24**:844.

Psoriatic Arthritis

Brewerton DA et al: HL-A 27 and arthropathies associated with ulcerative colitis and psoriasis. *Lancet* 1974;**1**:956.

Dorwart BB et al: Chrysotherapy in psoriatic arthritis: Efficacy and foxicity compared to rheumatoid arthritis. *Arthritis Rheum* 1978;**21**:513.

Kammer GM et al: Psoriatic arthritis: A clinical, immunologic, and HLA study of 100 patients. *Semin Arth Rheum* 1979;**9**:75.

Polychondritis

Barranco VP, Minor DB, Solomon H: Treatment of relapsing polychondritis with dapsone. *Arch Dermatol* 1976; **112**:1286.

Herman JH, Dennis MV: Immunopathologic studies in relapsing polychondritis. *J Clin Invest* 1973;**52**:549.

McAdam LP et al: Relapsing polychondritis: Prospective study of 23 patients and a review of the literature. *Medicine* 1976;**55**:193.

Panniculitis

Fayemi AO, Williams J, Cuttner J: Systemic Weber-Christian disease and thrombocythemia terminating in reticulum cell sarcoma. *Am J Clin Pathol* 1974;**62**:88.

Förström L, Winkelmann RK: Factitial panniculitis. *Arch Dermatol* 1974;**110**:747.

MacDonald A, Fiewel M: A review of the concept of Weber-Christian panniculitis with a report of five cases. *Br J Dermatol* 1968;**80**:355.

Hereditary Complement Deficiency

Agnello V: Complement deficiency states. *Medicine* 1978; **57**:1.

Gewurz A et al: Homozygous C-2 deficiency with fulminant lupus erythematosus: Severe nephritis via the alternative complement pathway. *Arthritis Rheum* 1978;**21**:28.

Shaller JG et al: Severe systemic lupus erythematosus with nephritis in a boy with deficiency of the fourth component of complement. *Arthritis Rheum* 1977;**20**:1519.

Hypogammaglobulinemia & Arthritis

Ammann AJ, Hong R: Selective IgA deficiency: Presentation of 30 cases and a review of the literature. *Medicine* 1971; **50**:223.

Grayzel AI et al: Chronic polyarthritis associated with hypogammaglobulinemia: A study of two patients. *Arthritis Rheum* 1977;**20**:887.

Talal N: Connective tissue disease and other immunologic disorders. Page 589 in: *Arthritis and Allied Conditions*, 8th ed. Hollander JL, McCarty DJ (editors). Lea & Febiger, 1972.

27 | Hematologic Diseases

J. Vivian Wells, MD, FRACP, FRCPA, & Curt A. Ries, MD

There are few areas in hematology that are not significantly affected by immunologic processes. A large group of hematologic disorders—the plasma cell dyscrasias, lymphocytic leukemias, and lymphomas—represent abnormal proliferations of primary cells of the immune system. Another important group of disorders—the autoimmune hemolytic anemias, autoimmune neutropenias, and immune thrombocytopenias—are characterized by immunologic destruction of circulating blood cells. Even hematopoietic precursor cells in the bone marrow may be destroyed or suppressed by immunologic mechanisms, as seen in pure red cell aplasia and some cases of aplastic anemia.

This chapter will be devoted primarily to hematologic disorders in which immunologic cells or mechanisms play a major role. The chapter will also review other selected hematologic disorders in which immunologic observations have contributed significantly to the basic understanding or diagnosis of the disorder. Finally, bone marrow transplantation will be discussed since it is an area of major hematologic and immunologic importance.

I. WHITE BLOOD CELL DISORDERS

Since many of the cells of the lymphoid system in peripheral blood and in tissues are included in the general category of white blood cells, it is not surprising that many diseases affecting these cells involve immunologic processes. These include the lymphoid malignancies—the plasma cell dyscrasias, leukemias, and lymphomas—and the nonmalignant disorders of infectious mononucleosis and some forms of leukopenia.

Traditionally, malignant cells in leukemias, lymphomas, and related disorders have been distinguished from their normal counterparts by morphologic, histochemical, and cytogenetic differences. Recently, immunologic techniques have been applied to cells in these disorders in an attempt to increase our understanding and improve our classification of these disorders. Immunologic classification has already shown clinical usefulness in acute lymphocytic leuke-

Table 27–1. Diseases of the lymphoid system classified by cell surface markers.

T cell
Acute lymphocytic leukemia (20%)
Lymphoblastic lymphoma
Some other non-Hodgkin lymphomas
Sézary syndrome
Mycosis fungoides
B cell
Chronic lymphocytic leukemia
Waldenström's macroglobulinemia
Multiple myeloma
Burkitt's lymphoma
Most other lymphocytic lymphomas
Null cell
Acute lymphocytic leukemia (80%)
Some non-Hodgkin lymphomas
Histiocyte-monocyte
Acute monocytic leukemia
Malignant histiocytosis
Histiocytosis X
Controversial
Hodgkin's disease
Hairy cell leukemia

mia, where prognosis and therapy depend partly on lymphocyte type. However, much additional basic and clinical work must be done before the full potential of immunologic classification of leukemias, lymphomas, and related disorders can be realized. Table 27–1 lists lymphoid disorders classified according to cell surface markers (see Chapter 23).

PLASMA CELL DYSCRASIAS

These diseases are also called the **paraproteinemias** or **monoclonal gammopathies.** They comprise a heterogeneous group of diseases characterized by the presence in serum or urine of a monoclonal immunoglobulin. This protein is also called a paraprotein, M protein (factor), or myeloma protein. It is the product of a single clone of lymphoid cells, is of restricted electrophoretic mobility, and appears in serum elec-

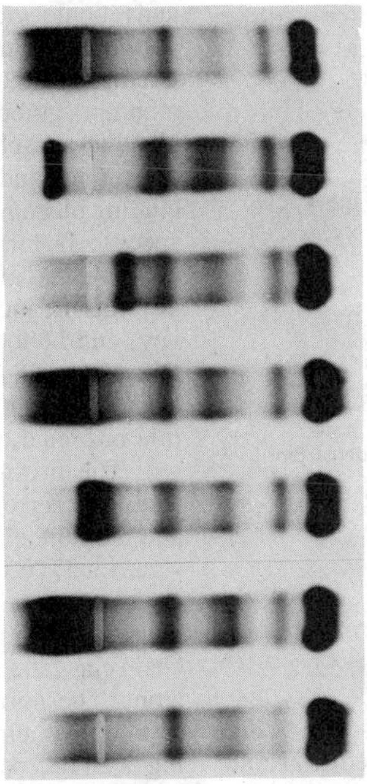

SOURCE OF SPECIMEN	PATTERN	INTERPRETATION
Rheumatoid arthritis—serum		A broad polyclonal increase in γ-globulin
IgG-λ multiple myeloma—serum		A narrow, intensely staining monoclonal IgG-λ band in cathodal end of γ-globulin zone with little normal γ-globulin
IgG-κ benign monoclonal gammopathy—serum		A monoclonal IgG-κ band in anodal part of γ-globulin zone with normal γ-globulin staining
SLE—serum		A broad polyclonal increase in γ-globulin zone
IgM-κ Waldenström's macro-globulinemia—serum		An intense broad monoclonal IgM-κ band with very little migration of macroglobulin from application trough
Benign hypergammaglobuli-nemic purpura—serum		The monoclonal IgG-κ paraprotein forms a complex with normal IgG, producing a broad appearance midway between monoclonal and polyclonal
Normal human serum		Normal pattern

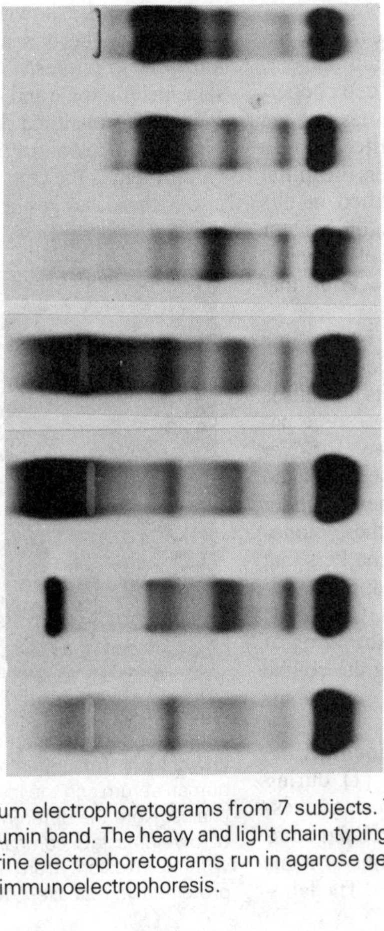

SOURCE OF SPECIMEN	PATTERN	INTERPRETATION
IgA-κ multiple myeloma—urine		Heavy proteinuria, IgA-κ paraprotein, κ Bence Jones L chains
IgA-κ multiple myeloma—serum		Monoclonal IgA aggregates in β_2 region
κ-Light chain myeloma—serum		Narrow β_1 peak consists of κ Bence Jones L chains
Chronic liver disease—serum		Very broad polyclonal increase in γ-globulin
Benign hypergammaglobulinemic purpura—serum		Monoclonal IgG-κ complexes with normal IgG to give broader appearance
IgG-κ multiple myeloma—serum		Narrow cathodal monoclonal IgK-κ band, very little normal γ-globulin
Normal human serum		Normal pattern

Figure 27–1. *Top:* Patterns of serum electrophoretograms from 7 subjects. They were run on agarose gel with the anode (on the right side) showing the albumin band. The heavy and light chain typing was determined by immunoelectrophoresis. *Bottom:* Patterns of serum and urine electrophoretograms run in agarose gel. The anode (albumin) is on the right. H and L chain types were determined by immunoelectrophoresis.

Table 27–2. Classification of plasma cell dyscrasias.

Malignant monoclonal gammopathy
  Multiple myeloma
  Waldenström's macroglobulinemia
  Solitary plasmacytoma
  Amyloidosis
  Heavy chain diseases
  Malignant lymphoma
  Chronic lymphocytic leukemia
Secondary monoclonal gammopathy
  Cancer (nonlymphoreticular)
  Monocytic leukemia
  Hepatobiliary disease
  Rheumatoid disorders
  Chronic inflammatory states
  Cold agglutinin syndrome
  Benign hyperglobulinemic purpura of Waldenström
  Papular mucinosis
  Immunodeficiency
Benign monoclonal gammopathy
  Transient
  Persistent

trophoretograms as a narrow band or "spike" (Fig 27–1). The paraproteinemias are classified in Table 27–2.

Immunologic Pathogenesis

Despite intensive study over many years, the actual causes of plasma cell dyscrasias remain unclear. The recent clarification of several areas of cell cooperation in regulation of immune responses has not yet included control of monoclonal B cell proliferation. In particular, the presumed antigen that triggers the initial B cell proliferation is generally unidentified in this group of disorders. Rarely, a possible etiologic factor is observed, such as multiple myeloma developing in a mink handler chronically exposed to the virus that causes Aleutian disease of mink.

Another major unresolved problem is the time that elapses between the stimulus and the development of clinical disease. Recent research suggests that this is 2–3 years in multiple myeloma. However, some patients with a paraprotein have been followed for over 30 years with no clinical evidence of disease associated with their paraprotein. Attempts are presently under way to analyze the long-term behavior of these monoclonal tumors by using specific antigenic markers that are unique to a particular tumor in an individual patient. Thus, the idiotype of the paraprotein (Chapter 4) is used as a tumor marker to study the distribution of lymphoid cells bearing that marker during the course of the disease.

Laboratory Investigation of Paraproteinemias

Serum paraproteins may be found (1) during routine screening of serum samples, (2) during investigation of a patient with an apparently unrelated complaint, and (3) when a patient has symptoms or signs suggesting malignant plasma cell dyscrasia. The labo-

ratory investigations should include **hematologic tests,** including complete blood count with differential and reticulocyte count, erythrocyte sedimentation rate, and bone marrow examination; **routine clinical chemistry,** including serum levels of total protein, albumin, globulin, calcium, phosphate, electrolytes, alkaline phosphatase, uric acid, blood urea nitrogen, creatinine, and cholesterol; **hemostatic profile,** including bleeding and clotting tests, platelet count, and specific factor assays if indicated; **serum viscosity** measured in an Ostwald viscosimeter; **radiologic examination,** including chest x-ray, skeletal bone survey, and bone scan if indicated; and **renal function tests,** including urinalysis, 24-hour protein, creatinine clearance, and measurement of renal acidification to rule out renal tubular acidosis.

The **immunologic tests** (see Chapter 22) that should be performed are serum protein electrophoresis and immunoelectrophoresis after separation of the serum at 37 °C to avoid loss of a serum paraprotein as a cryoprecipitate. Fig 27–1 demonstrates the various patterns of paraproteins and the inability to predict H chain class and L chain type from zone electrophoresis alone. The amount of paraprotein is measured by densitometric tracing (see Chapter 22). Immunologic typing of an IgG paraprotein by immunoelectrophoresis is demonstrated in Fig 27–2. This is routinely performed with antisera to detect γ, α, μ, κ, and λ chains. If no abnormality is shown with these antisera and other evidence suggests a malignant paraproteinemia, immunoelectrophoresis should be performed with antisera specific for δ and ϵ chains to detect rare cases with IgD or IgE myeloma proteins. The main feature in the immunoelectrophoretic pattern which identifies a paraprotein is the change in the shape of the precipitin arc. Other changes are the reduction in amount of

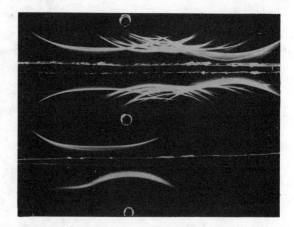

Figure 27–2. Immunoelectrophoresis of normal human serum (upper and center wells) and IgG myeloma serum (lower well). The upper trough contains antiserum to whole human serum and the lower trough antiserum specific to γ chains. Note the different shape and shorter precipitin line of myeloma IgG compared to normal IgG. (Reproduced, with permission, from Wells JV, Fudenberg HH: Paraproteinemia. *Disease-A-Month* [Feb] 1974.)

normal immunoglobulin of the same class as the paraprotein and localized splitting of the precipitin lines. Almost all paraproteins show an abnormal precipitin arc for either κ or λ chains which is similar in electrophoretic mobility to the H chain. The only exception is in H chain disease (see below).

All patients with paraproteins and suspected plasma cell dyscrasias without serum paraproteins must be tested for the presence of Bence Jones protein in the urine. Bence Jones protein consists of either monoclonal κ or λ light chains (see Chapter 4) which are excreted in significant amounts in about half of patients with multiple myeloma. They are best detected by zone electrophoresis and immunoelectrophoresis of the concentrated urine.

Immunofluorescence microscopy on specimens of bone marrow with fluorescein-labeled specific antisera to various H and L chains can confirm the intracellular location of a monoclonal immunoglobulin in rare cases of nonsecretory myeloma (see below).

Ancillary investigations include tests for euglobulin (protein which precipitates at low ionic strength), cryoglobulin, rheumatoid factor, and cold agglutinins. In special cases it is necessary to perform analytic ultracentrifugation of the serum to measure the molecular size of a paraprotein.

1. MULTIPLE MYELOMA

Major Immunologic Features

- Serum paraprotein (80%).
- Urinary paraprotein (50%).
- Reduced serum levels of nonmyeloma immunoglobulins.
- Recurrent infections.
- Presence of immature plasma cells in bone marrow.

General Considerations

Multiple myeloma is a disease characterized by the presence of a serum or urine paraprotein, anemia, and lytic bone lesions. It is the result of malignant transformation of a single clone of plasma cells. The diagnosis depends on the typical finding of large numbers of malignant plasma cells in the bone marrow, characteristic lytic bone lesions, and an associated serum or urine monoclonal protein.

Clinical Features

A. Symptoms and Signs: Bone pain and tenderness are common presenting features of multiple myeloma. Spontaneous pathologic fractures are not infrequent. Other major presenting features are anemia (weakness, pallor), recurrent infections (especially of the sinuses and respiratory tract), and occasionally renal failure or hypercalcemia.

B. Laboratory Findings: There is normocytic, normochromic anemia, with normal to slightly decreased white blood count and platelet count, and an elevated erythrocyte sedimentation rate. Azotemia and hypercalcemia are common complications. The bone marrow shows increased numbers of plasma cells with many abnormal forms which often completely replace the marrow. The plasma cells may be arranged in sheets; many are large immature cells with large or multiple nuclei and nucleoli.

C. X-Ray Findings: X-rays show characteristic punched-out lytic bone lesions throughout the skeleton in most patients. Generalized osteoporosis is also common.

Immunologic Diagnosis

Serum or urine paraproteins detected by zone electrophoresis (Fig 27–1) are typed by immunoelectrophoresis (see Chapter 22). Of all patients with multiple myeloma, about 50% have IgG paraproteins and 25% have IgA paraproteins. Serum levels of immunoglobulins other than the myeloma class are significantly lower than normal in almost all patients. Bence Jones protein is detected in the urine in about half of these patients. About 20% of patients have only Bence Jones proteinuria. These findings have important clinical and prognostic correlations.

IgD myeloma comprises 2% of cases of multiple myeloma but differs from the main group in several ways. A review of 133 cases in the literature disclosed that patients with IgD myeloma are generally younger than patients with other forms of multiple myeloma; over 50% had marked lymphadenopathy, hepatomegaly, or splenomegaly; and that extraosseous lesions, amyloidosis, severe anemia, and azotemia were more common. The serum levels of total protein and monoclonal protein are usually not very high, but Bence Jones proteinemia is common and Bence Jones proteinuria almost invariable. The L chain type is λ in 90% of cases of IgD myeloma compared to approximately 30% in IgG and IgA myelomas. The survival time in IgD myeloma is short—approximately 14 months after diagnosis.

In Bence Jones or L chain myeloma, the only detectable paraprotein occurs in the patient's urine as monoclonal κ or λ chains. This group comprises approximately 20% of myeloma patients. These patients are more likely to present with severe renal failure. The absence of an obvious serum paraprotein may present diagnostic difficulty in some cases, but Bence Jones proteinemia (monoclonal light chains in the serum) occurs in 80% and hypogammaglobulinemia and lytic bone lesions in over 60% of patients. Patients with λ type Bence Jones myeloma have more protein in the urine, poorer renal function and shorter overall survival. Amyloidosis is more frequent in Bence Jones myeloma and may dominate the clinical course. Bence Jones myeloma has a poorer overall prognosis than IgG or IgA myeloma.

Nonsecretory myeloma refers to otherwise typical multiple myeloma with no paraprotein detectable in blood or urine; this accounts for approximately 1% of myeloma patients. The plasma cell tumor is incapable of secreting the synthesized intracellular monoclonal protein. This protein can be detected either by immunofluorescence microscopy of bone marrow or immunochemical analysis of a lysate of the tumor cells.

Differential Diagnosis

It is necessary to confirm by means of immunoelectrophoresis that the heavily stained band in the serum electrophoretogram is an immunoglobulin rather than fibrinogen, transferrin, or another protein.

Lytic bone lesions in an anemic patient may be metastases from a tumor of the breast, prostate, thyroid, kidney, or other primary site. The main distinguishing features are confirmation of a primary tumor or a history of its removal, the histopathologic features of the lytic lesion, abnormal plasma cells in bone marrow, and paraproteinemia. However, there are many reports of coexisting paraproteinemia and primary malignant nonlymphoid tumor.

Differentiation between clinically malignant and benign monoclonal gammopathies is discussed below with the latter group.

Treatment

A. General Measures: Supportive management is essential. Control pain with analgesics, provide adequate fluid intake, and give blood transfusions for symptomatic anemia. Ambulation should be maintained whenever possible to avoid further bone loss and hypercalcemia; adequate analgesics and mechanical support with corsets and braces often allow early ambulation, especially when the vertebral column is affected.

B. Irradiation: Local radiation therapy is very useful for relief of pain and reduction of tumor mass for isolated plasmacytoma or myeloma with localized painful bony lesions. Care must be taken to avoid large-scale radiation of active bone marrow sites since this may cause severe pancytopenia and limit chemotherapy.

C. Chemotherapy: Cytotoxic chemotherapy, together with improved general management, will achieve good therapeutic responses in about 70% of patients with multiple myeloma and will produce increased median survival with improved quality of life. Response is gauged by clinical and laboratory observations such as general status and pain relief, hemoglobin concentration, serum or urine paraprotein levels, and plasma cell counts in the bone marrow.

Melphalan with or without prednisone is the drug regimen of choice for the initial treatment of myeloma. The most popular schedule for the use of melphalan is intermittent high-dose melphalan-prednisone for 4 days every 4–6 weeks. The alternative is to give a loading dose of melphalan for 7–10 days followed by a continuous low maintenance dose, usually given daily. This approach is now used less commonly. The white cell and platelet count must be checked frequently to avoid toxicity. Prednisone should probably not be used when patients present with renal failure or serious infection. Poor-risk patients, ie, patients who present with renal failure, serious infection, hypercalcemia, leukopenia, thrombocytopenia, extensive lytic bone disease, and very large amounts of M protein, have a significantly shorter mean survival than patients who do not have these abnormalities.

Cyclophosphamide is also a widely used alkylating agent for the treatment of myeloma. It is probably as effective as melphalan but has additional adverse side-effects. It is sometimes useful for patients who have become refractory to melphalan.

Multiple drug regimens are currently being assessed in patients who fail to respond to a single alkylating agent initially or who respond and then relapse. Combination chemotherapy may also be used for initial therapy for patients with high-risk disease (see above). The drugs used include melphalan, cyclophosphamide, carmustine (BCNU), procarbazine, vincristine, doxorubicin, and other agents in various combinations. Occasional favorable responses result.

D. Surgery: Emergency laminectomy followed by local radiation therapy is indicated for acute spinal cord compression. Internal fixation of long bone fractures and prosthetic hip replacement may allow early return to ambulation after pathologic fractures. Occasionally, surgical cure of a solitary plasmacytoma may be successful.

E. Complications:

1. Infections–Recurrent bacterial infections, especially with pneumococci and sometimes with gram-negative organisms, are a major problem in some patients. Timely evaluation of fevers and other symptoms of infection, with appropriate cultures and prompt coverage with appropriate antibiotics, is essential in these patients. Gamma globulin may also be useful in the treatment of established bacterial infection. Prophylactic administration of antibiotics, γ-globulin, or both is not warranted as a routine measure.

2. Hypercalcemia–This may present as an emergency with vomiting, dehydration, azotemia, coma, and cardiac arrhythmias. Rapid rehydration is essential. Patients usually respond to rehydration, diuretics, and high doses of corticosteroids; refractory cases may require phosphate infusion or mithramycin.

3. Renal failure–Both acute and chronic renal failure are common. Etiologic factors include precipitation of the paraprotein in tubules, amyloidosis, hypercalcemia, hyperuricemia, invasion of the kidney by malignant plasma cells, precipitation of cryoimmunoglobulins, hyperviscosity syndrome, pyelonephritis, and nephrotoxic antibiotics. Renal disease appears more frequently and often is more severe in patients with light chain myeloma (Bence Jones paraproteins). Prevention of dehydration is very important in those patients. Fluid restriction should be avoided, especially fluid restriction for intravenous urography. Rapid treatment of complications such as hypercalcemia and hyperuricemia will help to avoid irreversible renal damage. Successful chemotherapy of multiple myeloma will prevent most of the factors leading to renal failure. Hemodialysis may be lifesaving and allow time for chemotherapy in patients with acute renal failure due to Bence Jones paraproteinemia.

4. Spinal cord compression–Acute spinal cord compression is fortunately an uncommon initial presentation of myeloma but requires emergency laminectomy when it occurs. Treatment for cord compression of gradual onset includes localized radiotherapy, chemotherapy, and supportive physiotherapy, including a brace. Despite the frequent radiologic evidence of widespread involvement of the vertebral column and frequent vertebral compression fractures, cord compression is not a frequent complication. Continued ambulation with adequate analgesia must be maintained if at all possible.

5. Hyperviscosity syndrome–This occurs occasionally in multiple myeloma and is discussed below with Waldenström's macroglobulinemia.

6. Acute leukemia–Many cases of acute leukemia have now been reported developing 1–10 years after a diagnosis of malignant paraproteinemia has been made, especially multiple myeloma. Almost invariably the leukemia is of the acute monocytic or myelomonocytic type. This is a serious complication; there are no reports of survivals beyond 6 months after diagnosis. It is not yet known if the leukemia is part of the natural history of multiple myeloma which only becomes obvious with prolonged survival or if it is due to chromosomal or other abnormalities induced by cytotoxic therapy. Dyserythropoietic anemia and chromosomal abnormalities may sometimes be detected prior to overt leukemia.

Plasma cell leukemia is a variant of multiple myeloma where abnormal plasma cells are found not only in the bone marrow but also in the peripheral blood. Plasma cell leukemia may be acute or chronic. Acute plasma cell leukemia presents as acute leukemia, and a mistaken diagnosis of acute lymphocytic or acute myelogenous leukemia may be made. The true nature of the leukemic cell is recognized when a paraprotein is detected in blood or urine, lytic bone lesions develop, severe hypercalcemia is noted, or renal failure supervenes. The correct diagnosis can also be confirmed by electron microscopic or immunofluorescence techniques. Plasma cell leukemia also occurs in patients with known multiple myeloma; such patients have a much higher incidence of hepatosplenomegaly, more severe anemia and thrombocytopenia, more renal failure, and a poorer prognosis than myeloma patients without plasma cell leukemia. Occasionally, plasma cell leukemia occurs as a terminal event in multiple myeloma, with a rapidly rising plasma cell count and death from infection and renal failure.

Therapy of plasma cell leukemia should be directed at the underlying multiple myeloma, although cell cycle–specific drugs, similar to those used in other acute leukemias, may be more useful than alkylating agents. The overall prognosis of plasma cell leukemia is poor, with a mean survival of well under a year.

Prognosis

Seventy percent of patients with multiple myeloma respond to therapy and have a mean overall survival of more than 30 months. Patients presenting with serious infection, thrombocytopenia, leukopenia, hypercalcemia, or azotemia have a poorer prognosis. A large amount of paraprotein and a low serum albumin indicate a large plasma cell tumor mass and are associated with a poorer prognosis. Patients with IgG-type myeloma proteins tend to do better than those with IgA-type or Bence Jones proteins. The rate of response to chemotherapy also appears to be useful in predicting prognosis. Patients who do not respond to chemotherapy at all and those that respond very rapidly to initial chemotherapy have a poorer prognosis. The "fast responders" quickly relapse and often are resistant to further chemotherapy. The prognosis appears to be best for the "slow responders," ie, patients who show a slow but gradual and steady response to chemotherapy.

Radiologically proved bone healing occurs in approximately 30% of patients who respond to treatment, generally after a fall in serum paraprotein concentration. Serial observations of lytic lesions in the skull, ribs, and pelvis provide an index of disease activity in long-term management. However, bone healing is not a prognostic sign, since patients who respond to therapy and show bone healing do not have longer remissions or longer overall survival times than those who respond without bone healing.

2. WALDENSTRÖM'S MACROGLOBULINEMIA

The main clinical and laboratory features of Waldenström's macroglobulinemia are listed in Table 27–3 and compared to those of multiple myeloma. Most of the clinical manifestations of this disease can be directly attributed to the excess monoclonal IgM in the blood. Patients frequently present with hyperviscosity syndrome (Table 27–4). A relative serum viscosity of > 3.0 may be associated with symptoms, although severe symptoms do not usually occur until

Table 27–3. Comparison of clinical and laboratory features of Waldenström's macroglobulinemia and multiple myeloma.

	Macro-globulinemia	Multiple Myeloma
Recurrent bacterial infections		+++
Bone pain		+++
Lytic bone lesions		+++
Bleeding from mucosal areas	+++	+
Hepatosplenomegaly	+++	+
Lymphadenopathy	+++	+
Neuropathy		+
Changes in visual state	+++	+
Abnormalities in optic fundus	+++	+
Anemia	++	+++
Leukopenia		+
Thrombocytopenia		+
Hypercalcemia		++
Serum hyperviscosity	+++	+
Renal insufficiency		++

Table 27–4. Symptoms and signs of hyperviscosity syndrome.

System	Findings
General	Weakness, fatigue, malaise, anorexia.
Cardiovascular	Congestive heart failure, hypervolemia.
Neurologic	Headache, dizziness, vertigo, nystagmus, deafness, somnolence, stupor, coma, generalized seizures, electroencephalographic abnormalities.
Hematologic	Recurrent epistaxis, bleeding from oral mucosa, hematuria, hematemesis, melena, prolonged postoperative bleeding, anemia.
Ocular	Loss of visual acuity (may be total), retinal hemorrhages, distention and tortuosity of retinal veins, papilledema.

the viscosity is > 7.0–10.0 (see Chapter 22). Severe hyperviscosity is a medical emergency and requires prompt treatment. There is marked variation in the level of viscosity that causes symptoms in patients, but each patient tends to develop the same symptoms at the same viscosity level. Several factors contribute to hyperviscosity, including the serum concentration of monoclonal IgM, polymer or aggregate formation, cryoprecipitation, antibody activity against serum proteins, and red cell and vascular factors.

Monoclonal IgM mainly exists in the pentamer 19S form or aggregates thereof, but many patients also have monomeric 7S IgM. A biosynthetic abnormality often exists in which the malignant clone is not always able to assemble all of the synthesized IgM in the pentamer form. Bence Jones proteinuria is found in approximately 10% of patients.

Plasmapheresis is the treatment of choice for most patients with Waldenström's macroglobulinemia to remove the excess IgM and restore the plasma volume to normal. It is performed either with sterile plastic bags in a closed system which permits readministration of the patient's red cells after centrifugation or with an automatic continuous flow centrifuge. The latter can remove a much greater amount of paraprotein in one treatment period, but patients treated in this way usually have to be given normal plasma to prevent hypovolemia. Standard plasmapheresis using plastic bags is less efficient but still very effective. Patients with severe hyperviscosity need as many as 4–6 units per day of plasmapheresis for several days. Subsequently, plasmapheresis is given on a maintenance basis to keep the patient free of hyperviscosity symptoms with a serum viscosity preferably under 3.0. Plasmapheresis of 2 units every 2–4 weeks is often sufficient for maintenance. Chemotherapy is necessary if plasmapheresis is required more frequently than every 2 weeks. Chlorambucil is usually given in low doses on a daily basis, with frequent monitoring of blood counts to prevent bone marrow depression. Intermittent high-dose chlorambucil and prednisone — or cyclophosphamide, vincristine, and prednisone — can be used if there is no response to low-dose chlorambucil.

3. SOLITARY PLASMACYTOMA

Solitary plasmacytoma is an isolated malignant plasma cell tumor that can occur as a solitary plasmacytoma of bone or an extramedullary plasmacytoma. The patient has no other clinical or bone marrow features of multiple myeloma. Solitary plasmacytoma may be discovered on routine x-ray or may be diagnosed in a patient who complains of local pain or pressure on adjacent structures, eg, the spinal cord. In one study, 63% of patients with solitary plasmacytomas had a circulating or urinary monoclonal protein. Solitary plasmacytoma of bone and extramedullary plasmacytoma probably represent different diseases. Extramedullary plasmacytoma often has an indolent course, is commonly nonsecretory, and occasionally progresses to multiple myeloma. Solitary plasmacytoma of bone has a higher incidence of paraproteins, frequently progresses to multiple myeloma, has a poorer prognosis, and may represent an early form of multiple myeloma.

Solitary plasmacytoma is generally treated by excision (depending on the site) or high-dose local radiotherapy. The role of chemotherapy is disputed. Despite treatment, a significant number of patients will develop local recurrence or generalized multiple myeloma. Close follow-up and regular evaluation of serum and urine protein is essential, since multiple myeloma may develop many years after the diagnosis of solitary plasmacytoma.

4. AMYLOIDOSIS

Amyloidosis has proved an enigma to clinicians and pathologists ever since the 19th century, when Rokitansky and Virchow argued about its nature and origin. Its relationship to chronic infection and prolonged antigenic stimulation are well known. Amyloid has a complex structure, and several distinct components can produce amyloid fibrils with comparable biophysical properties. Solubilization of amyloid fibrils and amino acid sequence analysis show that in most cases a major component of amyloid is a fragment of an immunoglobulin L chain, especially the V region. This explains the negative results of earlier tests with antisera to detect immunoglobulins in amyloid tissue, since such antisera are made against C region and not V region determinants. Antiserum prepared against V region determinants of a Bence Jones protein from a patient with Bence Jones proteinuria and amyloidosis reacted with a component in that patient's amyloid tissue. Identical amino acid sequences in a patient's Bence Jones protein V region and a peptide component of his amyloid tissue have also been described.

Possible mechanisms which might account for the deposition of immunoglobulin components in amyloid tissue are as follows: (1) Catabolism by macrophages of deposited antigen-antibody complexes. (2) De novo synthesis in situ of whole immunoglobulins or of L chains with reduced solubility. (3) Genetic deletions in the L chain gene, producing an anomalous protein of reduced solubility. (4) Separate synthesis of discrete regions of the L chain.

The major nonimmunoglobulin component of amyloid is known as nonimmunoglobulin protein of unknown origin, amyloid of unknown origin, or protein "A." It has a molecular weight of approximately 8000 (76 amino acids), and it may be derived by proteolytic digestion of an unidentified protein precursor. Approximately 10% of amyloid tissue consists of doughnut-like structures 8–10 nm in diameter composed of 5 globular subunits surrounding a central cavity. The "P" or plasma component may aggregate into "periodic rods" with a periodicity of 4 nm. It is a glycoprotein, unrelated to fibril protein but related antigenically to an α_1-globulin present in small amounts in normal human plasma. This protein may be measured by radioimmunoassay.

Clinically suspected amyloidosis must be confirmed by biopsy of appropriate tissues. Light microscopy of H&E-stained sections shows amyloid as an eosinophilic material. Typical birefringence occurs when stained sections are examined under polarized light. Electron microscopy shows characteristic nonbranching fibrils 8.5 nm wide and of varying lengths.

The classification of amyloidosis as primary or secondary is of little benefit etiologically or clinically. Amyloid fibrils of L chain origin can occur in both primary and secondary forms, as can the nonimmunoglobulin protein of unknown origin. The Third International Symposium on Amyloidosis recommended adoption of a system of nomenclature for the chemical composition of amyloid of different types, and this is incorporated into Table 27–5. The first of the 2 letters ("A") denotes amyloid fibril protein. The second letter indicates the nature of the protein, the tissue or organ, or the disorder in which it is found. Thus, AA indicates the main nonimmunoglobulin component (and SAA its serum-related protein); AL, the L chain amyloid protein; AS, senile amyloid; etc.

The clinical features reflect the particular site and extent of amyloid deposition, especially in the gastrointestinal tract, nervous system, and kidneys. Renal involvement is often a poor prognostic sign. Treatment is mainly symptomatic since no chemotherapy has been shown to consistently benefit patients with established amyloidosis. Patients with amyloidosis and plasma cell dyscrasia occasionally respond to melphalan or other drugs; rarely, full remission may be achieved.

5. HEAVY CHAIN DISEASES

These relatively rare diseases are characterized by a serum paraprotein composed of incomplete H chains without L chains. The 3 types are γ, μ, and α, with α chain disease the most prevalent. The paraprotein is generally in relatively low concentration in blood and shows broad zone electrophoretic pattern, but it is frequently excreted in urine in measurable amounts. Immunoelectrophoresis confirms the diagnosis, with demonstration of a paraprotein that reacts with antiserum to γ, μ, or α chains but not to κ or λ chains. No cases of δ or ϵ disease have been reported.

Much information on the genetic aspects of immunoglobulin biosynthesis has come from analysis of the paraproteins in H chain diseases. The abnormalities include partial deletion in the Fd portion of the H chain (with a normal amino acid sequence from residue 216), deletion in the hinge region (see Chapter 4), or a combination of the 2 findings.

Clinical Features
A. Gamma Chain Disease: The clinical features in γ chain disease vary markedly—from a malignant process with death within weeks of presentation to a course extending over 20 years. The most common presentation is a lymphoproliferative disorder with hepatosplenomegaly, lymphadenopathy, and uvular and palatal edema. Recurrent febrile episodes are not uncommon. Infection is the most common cause of death. The peripheral blood generally shows anemia, leukopenia, and atypical lymphocytes or plasma cells. Remission was obtained in one such patient

Table 27–5. Classification of amyloidosis.

	Clinical Type	Sites of Deposition	Chemical Type of Fibril*
Familial	Amyloid polyneuropathy (Portuguese, dominant inheritance)	Peripheral nerves Viscera	AF_p (prealbumin)
	Familial Mediterranean fever (recessive)	Liver, spleen, kidneys, adrenals	AA
Generalized	Primary	Tongue, heart, gut, skeletal and smooth muscles, nerves, skin, ligaments	AL
	Associated with plasma cell dyscrasia	Liver, spleen, kidneys, adrenals	AL
	Secondary (infection, inflammation)	Any site	AA
Localized	Lichen amyloidosis	Skin	AD
	Endocrine-related (eg, thyroid carcinoma)	Endocrine organ (thyroid)	AE (AE_t)
Senile		Heart, brain	AS_c AS_b

*See text for explanation of abbreviations in this column.

treated with intermittent cyclophosphamide and prednisone.

B. Alpha Chain Disease: The clinical features in α chain disease are those of a severe malabsorption syndrome with chronic diarrhea, steatorrhea, weight loss, hypocalcemia, and lymphadenopathy. Biopsy of bowel shows infiltration of the small bowel with plasma cells, lymphocytes, and reticulum cells. Initially, the plasma cell infiltration of the lamina propria and mesenteric lymph nodes appears benign, suggesting an early premalignant phase. Patients at this stage may show regression of their abnormalities with oral antibiotic therapy. With disease progression, the plasma cells become more immature and extend beyond the lamina propria. Abdominal lymphoma and α chain disease are closely associated in the area of the Mediterranean Sea, and a recent study confirmed that they share identical etiologic, clinical, pathologic, and immunologic features. The diseases also occur in many more geographical areas. Two reported cases of α chain disease involved the respiratory tract instead of the gastrointestinal tract. Improved diagnosis of α chain disease is now achieved by immunodiffusion techniques with an antiserum specific for the Fab fragment.

C. Mu Chain Disease: The clinical features in 3 cases of μ chain disease were those of long-standing chronic lymphocytic leukemia with progressive hepatosplenomegaly.

6. BENIGN MONOCLONAL GAMMOPATHY

Benign monoclonal gammopathy is defined as the presence of a monoclonal serum or urine protein without any of the other manifestations of malignant plasma cell dyscrasia. Monoclonal protein spikes have been found in approximately 5% of all persons over 50 years of age and 8% of those over 70 years. Some of these people will ultimately develop multiple myeloma, but most will not.

Clinically, the problem is deciding whether a patient found to have a small monoclonal immunoglobulin spike has early multiple myeloma or benign monoclonal gammopathy. The following laboratory features tend to support a diagnosis of malignant paraproteinemia: serum paraprotein level > 2 g/dL, reduced serum levels of nonmonoclonal immunoglobulins, presence of immunoglobulin fragments in serum, increased serum or urine light chains, presence of radiographic bone lesions, presence of increased and abnormal plasma cells in the bone marrow, and, most importantly, increasing serum or urine paraprotein levels with time. Thus, the patient with a high and increasing serum paraprotein level, low serum levels of normal immunoglobulins, and significant amounts of Bence Jones protein in the serum and urine is likely to develop the full clinical picture of multiple myeloma within a relatively short period of time. Decreased total numbers of circulating B lymphocytes are present in

malignant but not benign monoclonal gammopathies.

It is essential to review all patients with monoclonal gammopathies until the benign or malignant nature of the disease is established. Even in patients with proved benign monoclonal gammopathy, follow-up is required for a prolonged period since multiple myeloma may supervene after an interval of as long as 24 years.

7. CRYOGLOBULINEMIA

A number of serum and plasma proteins precipitate at low temperature, including cryofibrinogen, C-reactive protein–albumin complex, heparin-precipitable protein, and immunoglobulins. The first step in evaluating a suspected cryoimmunoglobulin, therefore, is to rule out nonimmunoglobulin cryoproteins (see Chapter 22). The following points should be kept in mind when testing for a cryoglobulin: (1) Some monoclonal cryoglobulins may precipitate at temperatures as high as 35 °C. Adequate precautions such as prewarming of syringes, containers, etc and centrifugation at 37 °C should therefore be taken to avoid loss of the cryoprotein from the supernate on centrifugation. (2) Some cryoglobulins rapidly precipitate in the cold, while others may take days. The serum should therefore be observed at 4 °C for at least 72 hours. (3) Most normal people have a small amount of polyclonal serum cryoglobulin—up to 80 μg/mL.

Cryoglobulinemias can be classified into the following 3 immunologic and clinical types:

Type I (25%) cryoglobulins are monoclonal proteins, most commonly IgM, occasionally IgG, and rarely IgA or Bence Jones protein.

Type II (25%) are mixed cryoglobulins with a monoclonal component. The monoclonal protein is usually IgM but is occasionally IgG or IgA, and it complexes with autologous normal IgG in the cryoprecipitate.

Type III (50%) are mixed polyclonal cryoglobulins, with a mixture of polyclonal IgM and IgG being by far the most frequent combination.

The clinical features in patients with cryoglobulins depend largely on the type of cryoglobulin involved. Patients with monoclonal cryoglobulins (type I) suffer primarily from the symptoms of their underlying disease process, eg, multiple myeloma or Waldenström's macroglobulinemia. Patients with "mixed cryoglobulins" (types II and III) often have "immune complex disease," with vascular purpura, arthritis, and nephritis. These immune complexes often fix complement in vivo and in vitro.

Treatment of cryoglobulinemias is generally directed toward treatment of the underlying disorder if it is recognized. General measures such as avoidance of cold objects or weather are often helpful. Management of the idiopathic mixed cryoglobulinemias may be difficult. Cytotoxic drugs, with or without prednisone, are generally used. Excellent remissions with reduction of serum cryoglobulin levels and control of nephritis, arthritis, and purpura can sometimes be achieved. Plasmapheresis is generally not very useful for the chronic control of patients with cryoglobulins, but may be useful for short-term control of serious complications.

8. BENIGN HYPERGAMMAGLOBULINEMIC PURPURA

This relatively rare disease was described by Waldenström and occurs especially in young and middle-aged women who present with a dependent purpuric rash precipitated by exercise or alcohol. Some of these women have autoimmune disorders, especially SLE and Sjögren's syndrome.

The characteristic immunologic finding is a monoclonal IgG-κ paraprotein that acts as a rheumatoid factor and complexes autologous normal IgG to produce a broad appearance in the γ region on electrophoresis (Fig 27-1). Serum levels of IgA and IgM are normal or increased. There are no findings to support a diagnosis of multiple myeloma (no Bence Jones protein, no lytic bone lesions, no abnormal plasma cells).

Treatment is directed mainly at correction of any underlying autoimmune disorder (eg, corticosteroid for SLE) and avoidance of factors that obviously exacerbate the purpuric rash, such as excessive alcohol consumption and dancing. Rarely, the symptoms may be severe enough to warrant more active treatment such as plasmapheresis.

9. BICLONAL GAMMOPATHY

More patients are being recognized whose serum contains 2 distinct paraproteins. This does not include the combination of a paraprotein and its corresponding Bence Jones protein. The most common combinations are 2 different monoclonal IgM proteins or monoclonal IgM and IgG proteins. Rarely, one may find 3 monoclonal serum proteins in one patient. Some of these patients are of great interest because their paraproteins show sharing of identical parts of their primary structure, and this fact supports the **genetic switch hypothesis.**

The clinical features are most frequently those of macroglobulinemia or lymphoma, and IgM is generally the monoclonal protein in highest concentration. Plasmapheresis is frequently required in these patients.

LEUKEMIAS

The leukemias are characterized by abnormal maturation and accumulation of white blood cells. They are classified as acute or chronic on the basis of clinical and hematologic features. The main types of leukemias are acute lymphocytic leukemia, acute myelogenous leukemia (and subtypes acute myelomonocytic, monocytic, and promyelocytic leukemia), chronic lymphocytic leukemia, chronic myelogenous leukemia, and hairy cell leukemia (leukemic reticuloendotheliosis).

ACUTE LEUKEMIAS

The acute leukemias are characterized by a block in maturation of lymphoid or granulocytic cells at the primitive blast stage. The immature leukemic cells are no longer cleared in a normal fashion and accumulate in the bone marrow, the peripheral blood, and at times in other tissues. This results in a loss of normal hematopoietic function of the bone marrow, with development of anemia, thrombocytopenia, and granulocytopenia. Patients with large leukemic cell masses and high peripheral blood blast cell counts develop tissue infiltration and damage in the brain, lungs, liver, spleen, and other organs. The acute leukemias are usually rapidly progressive, death often occurring in a few weeks to a few months in untreated patients. Modern combination chemotherapy has dramatically improved survival in these diseases, especially in acute lymphocytic leukemia in children; a significant number of patients are now being permanently cured of what was formerly an invariably fatal disease.

Immunologic Features

The cause of leukemia in humans is unknown. Accumulating evidence continues to implicate RNA viruses. Other factors may also be important. Acute leukemia develops in a significant number of individuals exposed to ionizing radiation and some chemicals. Genetic factors are also involved since leukemia is more frequent in some individuals with chromosomal abnormalities. Improved techniques for the analysis of chromosomes in cultured specimens of bone marrow have yielded results suggesting that all leukemic cells have an abnormal karyotype.

Both human and animal leukemia cells possess cell surface antigens not found in normal cells of the same type. These human leukemia–associated antigens have been isolated and partially characterized. Antibodies to leukemia-associated antigens can be detected in the blood or on the leukemia cells of many patients with acute leukemia. Antibodies to these antigens can also be prepared by immunization of laboratory animals, eg, rabbits and nonhuman primates. Serum leukemia-associated antigens and antibodies can be detected by radioimmunoassay (see Chapter 22). Some laboratories have developed antisera that react with antigens common to all forms of leukemia or just acute leukemia; others have developed antisera that react with only a single type of leukemia. In some cases, the human antibodies function in cytotoxicity tests. About 15% of acute leukemia patients have serum antibodies that are cytotoxic for acute lymphocytic or acute myelogenous leukemia cells and long-term human cultured lymphoid cell lines, but not for normal bone marrow cells, chronic myelogenous leukemia cells, or lymphocytes transformed by exposure to PHA.

Membrane-bound immunoglobulins have been detected on the surface of human leukemia cells. In acute myelogenous and acute lymphocytic leukemia, they may represent adsorbed serum antibodies which can be eluted and characterized. Leukemia-associated antigens can also be demonstrated on human leukemia cells by immunofluorescence techniques with antisera prepared in laboratory animals, although these antisera are not yet routinely available.

Foreign antigens on leukemia cells can also be demonstrated by the ability of leukemia cells to stimulate lymphocytes from patients or normal subjects. To eliminate the problem of different histocompatibility antigens (see Chapter 6), leukemia cells from a patient are isolated at diagnosis, stored deep-frozen, and subsequently tested against lymphocytes of the same patient during the course of the disease. Patients in remission can demonstrate stimulation of their lymphocytes by their own stored leukemia cells.

The leukemic cells in acute lymphocytic leukemia (ALL) can be characterized by T and B cell markers (see Chapter 23) and by results of testing with heterologous or monoclonal antisera against T cells, B cells, and non-T, non-B (common) ALL cells. Human T cells are recognized by their ability to form spontaneous rosettes with sheep red blood cells and their reactivity with antisera specific for T cells. Pre-T cells do not form rosettes with sheep red blood cells but react with antisera against early T cell determinants. Human B cells are recognized by the presence of readily detectable membrane immunoglobulins and the presence of membrane receptors for C3. Pre-B cells have cytoplasmic but not membrane-bound immunoglobulins and react with antisera against early B cell determinants. Null cells lack all of the above T and B cell markers and also fail to react with common-ALL antisera (CALLA).

Acute leukemia cells can also be characterized by the presence of Ia antigen on the cell surface and the presence of the cytoplasmic enzyme marker terminal deoxynucleotidyl transferase (TdT) (see Chapter 23). The latter is found in immature T cells, in most acute lymphocytic leukemia cells, and in the cells of patients with acute lymphoid transformation of chronic myelogenous leukemia but not in nonlymphoid leukemias or acute myeloid transformation of chronic myelogenous leukemia (see following section on chronic myelogenous leukemia). Using a combination of these immunologic techniques, acute lymphocytic leukemia can be classified as shown in Table 27–6. Most patients have common-ALL (50–65%) and null-ALL (15–40%), although about 30% of these have pre-B cell characteristics and a lesser percentage have pre-T cell characteristics. About 20% of patients have T-ALL; these patients are important to recognize clinically, because they have a higher incidence of mediastinal tumors and central nervous system involvement and generally have more aggressive disease and a worse prognosis. B-ALL is the least common type of acute lymphocytic leukemia (2–5%) and has a worse prognosis than common-ALL.

The understanding of the immunologic heterogeneity of acute lymphocytic leukemia has led to a better understanding of the biology of acute lymphocytic leukemia and has contributed to the development of better treatment strategies. For example, the propensity of T cells to migrate to extramedullary sites, such as the meninges and testes, explains the increased frequency of central nervous system and other extramedullary relapses in patients with T-ALL. Also, patients with T-ALL and B-ALL do poorly when treated with standard chemotherapy when compared to patients with common-ALL, and these patients required more intensive chemotherapy. Patients with common-ALL and favorable prognoses, on the other hand, may actually require less intensive therapy than they are now receiving.

Several immunologic tests may indicate the overall prognosis in acute leukemia. A poorer prognosis is suggested by abnormalities in specific immunity, eg, greater amounts of antileukemia antibody and leukemia-associated antigens, and abnormalities in general immune function, eg, reduced lymphocyte activation by PHA or reduced skin test reactivity. Patients with T-ALL have a high T lymphocyte blood count and a poor prognosis. However, patients with acute lymphocytic leukemia and a markedly reduced normal residual T cell count also have a poor prognosis, probably reflecting a reduction in cellular immunity.

Clinical Features

A. Symptoms and Signs: Acute leukemia is typically manifested by weakness, fatigue, fever, weight loss, petechiae, purpura or bleeding, sternal tenderness, lymphadenopathy, and splenomegaly.

Table 27–6. Immunologic classification of acute lymphocytic leukemia (ALL).

Type of Acute Lymphocytic Leukemia	Surface Immunoglobulins	Sheep Red Blood Cell Rosettes	Anti-T Antisera	Anti–Common-ALL Antisera	Ia Antigen	TdT
Common-ALL	−	−	−	+	+	+
Null-ALL	−	−	−	−	+/−	+
T-ALL	−	+/−	+	−	−	+
B-ALL	+	−	−	−	+	−

B. Laboratory Findings: The principal laboratory findings are either leukocytosis or leukopenia (occasionally normal white blood cell count), with immature abnormal white cells in peripheral blood and bone marrow, and anemia and thrombocytopenia. About 25% of patients present with leukopenia rather than leukocytosis, but the bone marrow shows a marked increase in blast cells. Specialized staining techniques are used to characterize the leukemia cell type in blood and bone marrow since there is a significant correlation between the type of leukemia and response to treatment.

Treatment

A. Chemotherapy: Treatment of acute leukemia relies on chemotherapy to destroy as many of the leukemic cells as possible. More effective chemotherapeutic agents for acute leukemia have become available during the past 2 decades. Use of multiple agents in combination with variations in drug scheduling and dosages are all designed to achieve maximal destruction of the tumor mass of approximately 10^{12} leukemia cells at the time of diagnosis. The goal of initial therapy is to reduce this to less than 10^9 leukemia cells, resulting in complete clinical and hematologic remission. This is the stage of remission induction, and a primary remission can be achieved in over 95% of children with acute lymphocytic leukemia and 50–75% of adults with acute myelogenous leukemia.

Patients who achieve a complete remission may subsequently be given "consolidation" or "intensification" chemotherapy to further reduce the total number of leukemic cells present. Patients with acute lymphocytic leukemia are also treated with central nervous system "prophylaxis" to prevent central nervous system relapse; such treatment usually consists of cranial irradiation and a series of intrathecal injections of methotrexate. Patients are then treated with maintenance chemotherapy, usually for 2–3 years, after which chemotherapy is discontinued.

B. Immunotherapy: Numerous clinical trials of immunotherapy in both acute myelogenous and acute lymphocytic leukemia have been conducted in recent years. The immune system is best equipped to deal with a tumor load of 10^5–10^6 leukemic cells or less, so "cytoreduction" of the tumor mass must first be accomplished with chemotherapy. Immunotherapy can therefore not be expected to produce remissions of leukemia in relapse but may be able to prolong remissions and survivals and may perhaps contribute to permanent cures when used in the maintenance phase of treatment.

Two types of immunotherapy have been used in acute leukemias. Some groups have attempted to stimulate specific tumor immunity by immunizing with irradiated or otherwise altered autologous or pooled heterologous leukemic cells. Other groups have attempted to stimulate nonspecific tumor immunity by immunization with BCG or its derivative, methanol extraction residue (MER; see Chapter 40).

The results of specific and nonspecific immunotherapy trials in acute lymphocytic and acute myelogenous leukemia are contradictory. Early reports of improved remission duration and survival in the acute leukemias following immunotherapy with BCG and MER have not been confirmed by large controlled studies. Similarly, studies with irradiated or otherwise altered leukemic cells have shown variable results. These studies have generally been smaller because of the logistic difficulties of collecting and storing large numbers of leukemic cells for active immunization. Additional carefully controlled clinical trials using presently available methods of immunotherapy are needed in both acute myelogenous and acute lymphocytic leukemia—and new methods of immunotherapy must be developed—before final recommendations for the use of immunotherapy in these diseases can be established.

C. Bone Marrow Transplantation: Bone marrow transplantation following otherwise lethal radiation and chemotherapy has been successfully used to achieve complete remissions—and a substantial number of permanent cures—in patients with acute leukemia. Bone marrow transplantation is discussed in detail in section V of this chapter.

CHRONIC LEUKEMIAS

The chronic leukemias are also disorders of cell maturation, resulting in accumulation of abnormal leukemic cells in the bone marrow, peripheral blood, spleen, liver, lymph nodes, and occasionally other organs. Chronic leukemia cells are, however, morphologically and functionally better differentiated than acute leukemia cells, and in general the chronic leukemias are clinically much less aggressive, at times requiring little or no treatment.

1. CHRONIC MYELOGENOUS LEUKEMIA

Chronic myelogenous leukemia is characterized by the presence of abnormal myeloid cells in the blood, bone marrow, spleen, and other organs. The clinical and hematologic features include weakness, fatigue, weight loss, sweats, splenic pain, splenomegaly, anemia, leukocytosis, and occasionally thrombocytosis.

The peripheral blood contains myeloid cells of variable maturity but relatively few myeloblasts. The bone marrow shows intense myeloid hyperplasia. The immature myeloid cells characteristically contain the Philadelphia chromosome (Ph^1). It arises as an abnormal chromosome by translocation from the long arm of chromosome 22, most commonly to chromosome 9. The Ph^1 chromosome is a specific cytogenetic marker for chronic myelogenous leukemia.

Leukemia-associated antigens on chronic myelogenous leukemia cells usually cross-react with antigens on acute myelogenous leukemia cells. This is consistent with the observation that within a mean of 3 years from diagnosis, over half of patients with chronic myelogenous leukemia undergo transformation to acute leukemia, which in most cases is indistinguishable from acute myelogenous leukemia. However, about one-third of patients with typical Philadelphia chromosome–positive chronic myelogenous leukemia appear to undergo transformation to ALL. Evidence for this is based on morphologic, histochemical, and biochemical criteria, particularly the finding of terminal deoxynucleotidyl transferase, an enzyme previously found only in ALL and some normal lymphocytes. The presence of terminal transferase in some of these blast cells was also found in one study to correlate with the ability of these cells to react with antiserum to human ALL cells, further supporting the concept of lymphoblastic transformation. Because of the marked heterogeneity of blast transformation in chronic myelogenous leukemia, it has been suggested that this may be a disorder involving a primitive stem cell which is capable of differentiation into both myeloid and lymphoid cell lines. This theory is in conflict with the cytogenetic data, which indicate the presence of the Philadelphia chromosome in myeloid, erythroid, and megakaryocytic bone marrow precursor cells but not lymphoid cells, indicating that chronic myelogenous leukemia is a disease involving the pluripotent hematopoietic stem cell.

The early stages of chronic myelogenous leukemia are often asymptomatic and no therapy is indicated. Generally, however, symptoms of anemia, hypermetabolism, or splenomegaly develop and treatment is initiated.

The chronic phase of chronic myelogenous leukemia is usually easily controlled with single chemotherapeutic agents. Aggressive combination chemotherapy of patients with frank blast crisis of chronic myelogenous leukemia, however, is usually not effective. Patients with the lymphoblastic form of transformation may respond to treatment with vincristine and prednisone (treatment for acute lymphocytic leukemia), but responses are usually of short duration. Attempts to prevent the development of acute blastic transformation of chronic myelogenous leukemia by permanent eradication of the Philadelphia chromosome–positive clone of cells from the bone marrow by aggressive early chemotherapy or by early splenectomy have not been successful.

2. CHRONIC LYMPHOCYTIC LEUKEMIA

Chronic lymphocytic leukemia is characterized by the progressive accumulation of small lymphocytes of abnormally long life span in blood, bone marrow, liver, spleen, lymph nodes, and other tissues. The leukemia cell in chronic lymphocytic leukemia most often appears as a small but otherwise normal lymphocyte with a low mitotic rate. Occasionally, larger cells with more abundant cytoplasm are seen resembling those in infectious mononucleosis. Chronic lymphocytic leukemia increases in frequency with age and is often diagnosed by examination of a routine blood film. In many cases it is a relatively benign, slowly progressive disease, causing no symptoms for years. In other patients, however, it may be a serious illness, causing recurrent infections and early death.

The leukemia cell in chronic lymphocytic leukemia is a B lymphocyte in about 95% of cases. In the remainder, the cell is usually a T cell. In most B cell cases there is evidence that the abnormal cells come from a single clone. Not only do some patients have a circulating serum monoclonal protein, but the surface immunoglobulin on the B cells is restricted to a single L chain type and H chain class. IgM is the most common monoclonal surface immunoglobulin. However, more than one H chain class may be detected on lymphocytes in approximately 15% of cases of chronic lymphocytic leukemia. IgD and IgM occur frequently on cells from these patients.

Deficiency of serum immunoglobulins may develop with resultant recurrent infections. A reduction in the serum IgM level often occurs first, followed by reduction of serum IgG and IgA. Abnormalities of both B and T cell function have been found in these patients.

A serum monoclonal immunoglobulin, most frequently IgM, is a relatively common finding. Generally, however, the concentration of IgM monoclonal protein is not great, and the clinical features of Waldenström's macroglobulinemia do not occur. There may be biclonal gammopathy. Two patients have been reported whose chronic lymphocytic leukemia terminated as multiple myeloma; one had an IgA-κ paraprotein and the other κ monoclonal light chains.

Hemolytic anemia develops in some patients with chronic lymphocytic leukemia and frequently is clinically severe. Over half of the patients who become anemic have autoimmune hemolytic anemia with a positive Coombs test. Some patients with chronic lymphocytic leukemia have autoimmune thrombocytopenia as well.

Patients with chronic lymphocytic leukemia have an increased tendency to develop malignancies of other types. In one series, 16% of patients with chronic lymphocytic leukemia had malignant solid tumors and 7% had other lymphoreticular malignancies.

Many asymptomatic patients with chronic lymphocytic leukemia do not require treatment. The onset of symptoms, bulky lymphadenopathy, marked splenomegaly, a rapidly rising lymphocyte count, or a falling red cell and platelet count generally warrants treatment. Chemotherapy usually consists of intermittent or continuous administration of chlorambucil in low doses, although intermittent high doses of chlorambucil-prednisone in combination are also employed. The development of complications requires special treatment, eg, increased prednisone dosage for autoimmune hemolytic anemia or thrombocytopenia. Injections of therapeutic human γ-globulin (ISG) may be necessary in patients with secondary hypogamma-globulinemia and significant recurrent bacterial infections.

3. HAIRY CELL LEUKEMIA
(Leukemic Reticuloendotheliosis)

Hairy cell leukemia is being diagnosed with increased frequency. It affects mainly older adult males, who present with fatigue, malaise, infection, abdominal discomfort, pancytopenia, splenomegaly, and at times, lymphadenopathy. The main pathologic findings are in peripheral blood, bone marrow, spleen, and liver. Pancytopenia is often due to hypersplenism. The number of abnormal cells in the peripheral blood is variable and may be quite low when the white blood cell count is low. The characteristic cell in blood and tissue is shown in Figs 27–3 and 27–4. Routine light microscopy shows the irregular fingerlike projections of cytoplasm that give rise to the term hairy cell leukemia, and these are confirmed by transmission electron microscopy. Scanning electron microscopy further emphasizes the presence of these projections and shows the rufflelike ridges on the surface. The origin of these cells remains controversial. Studies of lymphocyte surface markers, phagocytosis, glass adherence, surface immunoglobulin production, metabolism, in vitro growth, ability to produce colony stimulating factor, and support of growth of normal bone marrow in vitro have led different groups of investigators to the conclusion that hairy cells are either of B lymphocyte or monocyte-histiocyte origin. Since results have differed among different patients studied, it is possible that the cell of origin in hairy cell leukemia is a primitive stem cell with the capacity to differentiate into both B lymphocyte and monocyte-histiocyte.

The prognosis in hairy cell leukemia is quite variable, but median survival is at least 5 years. Patients with splenomegaly and pancytopenia should be treated by splenectomy. Splenectomy often provides long remissions. Chemotherapy should be reserved for patients who fail to respond to splenectomy or who relapse after a transient response to splenectomy.

LYMPHOMAS

Lymphomas are malignant tumors derived from lymphoid stem cells, their lymphocytic and histiocytic derivatives, or a combination of these cell types. They represent solid tumors of the immune system, and immunologic abnormalities are common. Lymphomas have been traditionally studied by conventional clinical and histologic methods, and only recently have immunologic principles and techniques been applied.

Etiology
There are several examples of viruses causing lymphomas in animals, including nonhuman primates. A viral etiology has been proposed for human lymphomas, but causative viruses have not been isolated nor infectivity confirmed. The best-studied example is Epstein-Barr virus (EBV) in Burkitt's lymphoma (discussed below with infectious mononucleosis). It may be that viruses exist in lymphomas not as infectious virions but only as part of the viral genome incorporated into the DNA of host cells.

A current hypothesis is that a lymphoma represents the result of imbalance between homeostatic control mechanisms and immune responses. Specifically, it is suggested that a suppressor lymphocyte population is absent or ineffective and the immune response to a virus or other agent is abnormal, permitting development of malignant lymphoid transformation.

Classification & Immunologic Features
Standardized histologic classification of the lymphomas has led to improved understanding of the natural history and treatment of these diseases. The presently accepted histologic classifications of Hodgkin's disease and non-Hodgkin lymphomas are shown in Table 27–7. More recently, immunologic classification has been proposed (Table 27–8). Immunologic studies have shown the vast majority of nodular and diffuse non-Hodgkin lymphomas to be malignant monoclonal tumors of B lymphocytes, in which degrees of differentiation represent degrees of lymphocyte transformation. It now seems clear that the majority of "histiocytes" in histiocytic lymphomas are transformed B lymphocytes and that true malignancies of the macrophage-histiocytic system are rare. With continued immunologic, histologic, functional, ultrastructural, and biochemical studies of the

Table 27–7. Histologic classifications and relative frequencies of Hodgkin's disease and non-Hodgkin lymphomas.

Histologic Classification	Relative Frequency (%)
Hodgkin's disease classification (Rye Conference)	
Lymphocyte predominance	10–15
Nodular sclerosis	40–70
Mixed cellularity	20–40
Lymphocyte depletion	5–10
Non-Hodgkin lymphoma classification (Rappaport)	
Nodular	
Lymphocytic, well differentiated	2
Lymphocytic, poorly differentiated	17
Mixed lymphocytic-histiocytic	18
Histiocytic	7
Diffuse	
Lymphocytic, well differentiated	3
Lymphocytic, poorly differentiated	11
Mixed lymphocytic-histiocytic	10
Undifferentiated	3
Histiocytic	29

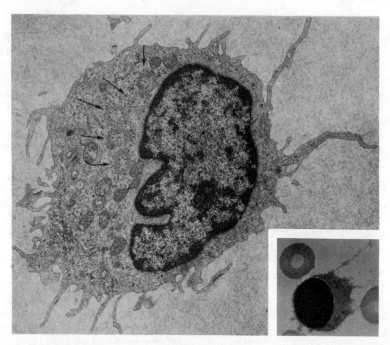

Figure 27–3. Electron micrograph of the neoplastic hairy cell in peripheral blood in leukemic reticuloendotheliosis. (Original magnification × 10,000.) Note the long cytoplasmic projections and multiple ribosome-lamella complexes in the cytoplasm (arrows). The inset is a light photomicrograph of a hairy cell from a peripheral blood smear. (Wright-Giemsa stain; original magnification × 1300.) (Reproduced, with permission, from Katayama I, Li CY, Yam LT: Ultrastructural characteristics of the "hairy cells" of leukemic reticuloendotheliosis. *Am J Pathol* 1972;**67**:361.)

Figure 27–4. Scanning electron micrograph of 2 hairy cells in leukemic reticuloendotheliosis, demonstrating the exaggerated ruffled membranes, ridgelike profiles, and occasional microvilli, resembling monocyte-macrophage cells. A spherical lymphocyte with microvilli is seen in the upper left corner. (Original magnification × 9025.) (Reproduced, with permission, from Polliack A, De Harven E: An interpretative review. Surface features of normal and leukemic lymphocytes as seen by means of scanning electron microscopy. *Clin Immunol Immunopathol* 1975;**3**:412.)

Table 27–8. Immunologic classification of lymphomas (Lukes & Collins).

Undefined cell type

T cell types

Convoluted lymphocyte

Small lymphocyte

Mycosis fungoides and Sézary's syndrome

Immunoblastic sarcoma (of T cells)

B cell types

Small lymphocyte (chronic lymphocytic leukemia)

Plasmacytoid lymphocyte (Waldenström's macroglobuline-mia)

Follicular center cell (FCC) types:

Small cleaved

Large cleaved

Small transformed (Burkitt's lymphoma)

Large transformed

Immunoblastic sarcoma (of B cells)

Histiocytic types

lymphomas, it is likely that further revisions in classification will occur. Since most clinical information relevant to prognosis and treatment of the lymphomas has been based on histologic classification, this system must be retained for clinical purposes at the present time.

A. Hodgkin's Disease: Hodgkin's disease is a malignant lymphoma of mixed cell type. The origin of the characteristic Reed-Sternberg cell and its mononuclear variants remains controversial, thereby excluding immunologic classification at present. Different investigators have presented evidence implicating both B and T lymphocytes and the macrophage-monocyte as the cell of origin in Hodgkin's disease. Current evidence favors the macrophage-monocyte as the primary malignant cell.

All clinical studies of Hodgkin's disease continue to rely on the histologic classification of Lukes and Butler as modified at the Rye Conference (Table 27–7) and accurate pathologic staging to determine the extent of disease. About 80% of patients with Hodgkin's disease have histologic findings of nodular sclerosis or mixed cellularity. The nodular sclerosing type of Hodgkin's disease is frequently seen in young women, often associated with a mediastinal mass. Mixed cellularity type is seen in older patients, as is lymphocyte depletion. Lymphocyte predominance type is seen in younger patients, is usually limited in extent, and has an excellent prognosis. Lymphocyte depletion type is at the opposite end of the spectrum, usually presenting with widespread disease and constitutional symptoms and having a poor prognosis. Most investigators feel that the lymphocytic infiltrate present in Hodgkin's disease lesions represents host cellular immune response against the tumor and correlates with a more favorable prognosis. Patients with lymphocyte predominance and nodular sclerosing Hodgkin's disease therefore have a strong host immune response to the tumor, patients with mixed cellularity have an intermediate response, and patients with lymphocyte depletion show a failure of response of the immune system to the tumor.

Defects in cell-mediated immunity occur in Hodgkin's disease, even in early stage I or stage II patients. This can be demonstrated by skin testing and in vitro lymphocyte transformation in response to mitogens, antigens, and allogeneic cells. The patients must be tested before chemotherapy or radiotherapy, which are themselves immunosuppressive. Analysis of dose-response curves for PHA stimulation in 27 patients revealed that 16 had significantly depressed responses. The depression may be more severe and occur at all PHA concentrations (5–800 μg/mL), or it may be less severe and occur only at low PHA concentrations. Anergy was found in 13 of these 27 patients.

MLC tests performed with lymphocytes from patients with Hodgkin's disease showed that 53% produced abnormally low levels of stimulation of normal leukocytes. This was due to suppressive action of some patients' lymphocytes, and the defect disappeared when the patient achieved remission. The defect in advanced Hodgkin's disease includes a disproportionate excess of suppressor lymphocytes despite overall lymphocyte depletion with frequent lymphopenia.

Tissue cultures from lymph nodes or spleen of Hodgkin's disease have been used to isolate an antigen and prepare antisera in rabbits. The antigen is specifically associated with Hodgkin's disease but requires an initial period of in vitro culture. However, the antiserum does not react with tumor tissue from patients with Hodgkin's disease. Measurement of in vitro IgG synthesis by splenic tissue showed increased total IgG synthesis in 91% of cases of Hodgkin's disease. The IgG synthesized showed significant binding to lymphocytes from patients with Hodgkin's disease. This suggests that in Hodgkin's disease the spleen is responding with humoral antibody to an antigen associated with lymphocytes. It is not yet known if this is identical to the antigen detected in cultures and if it is a viral component, a tumor-associated or oncofetal antigen (see Chapter 17), or a normal tissue component.

B. Non-Hodgkin Lymphomas: Until recently, non-Hodgkin lymphomas were classified solely by standard histologic methods. The Rappaport classification (Table 27–7) continues to be used for clinical purposes. Under this system, lymphomas originating in lymph nodes are classified as lymphocytic, histiocytic (previously reticulum cell sarcoma), or mixed and are further subdivided according to degree of differentiation and whether there is a nodular or diffuse histologic pattern. The histologic patterns of the majority of patients with non-Hodgkin lymphomas are nodular poorly differentiated lymphocytic or nodular mixed lymphocytic-histiocytic (both with good prognosis), or diffuse poorly differentiated lymphocytic, histiocytic, or mixed (all with poor prognosis).

Although the standard histologic classification has great clinical relevance, it provides little information regarding the origin or biology of these tumors. Immunologic classification (Table 27–8), as recently proposed by Lukes and Collins, emphasizes the principal immunologic cell type in the lymphoma as well as considering standard histologic features. The degrees of differentiation of cells are viewed as stages in transformation of B lymphocytes. Some comments are necessary regarding this classification.

1. Undefined cell type–This type consists of lymphoma due to lymphoid stem cells lacking T and B cell markers. It is not yet known if cells of this type correspond to stem cells or null cells.

2. T cell types–These may be acute or chronic.

a. Lymphoblastic lymphoma (convoluted T cell lymphoma)–This is an acute, aggressive, poorly differentiated lymphocytic lymphoma often associated with an anterior mediastinal mass. It has a high propensity for bone marrow and central nervous system involvement. It most commonly affects children and young adults, and appears to be closely related to T cell acute lymphocytic leukemia. The prognosis with conventional lymphoma therapy is very poor; therefore, current treatment protocols call for aggressive combination chemotherapy, similar to that used for treatment of high-risk acute lymphoblastic leukemia, including central nervous system prophylaxis.

b. Cutaneous T cell lymphomas–Mycosis fungoides and Sézary syndrome are 2 closely related chronic T cell malignancies that originate in the skin but may subsequently spread to regional lymph nodes and occasionally terminate in visceral or disseminated lymphoma. In mycosis fungoides, the skin lesions classically progress through the 3 stages of eczema, plaque, and tumor and may include a mixture of eczema, exfoliative erythroderma, macules, nodules, tumors, ulcers, and psoriatic dermatitis. Progression is often slow, over many years. Once more advanced skin lesions occur, however, and regional lymphadenopathy is present, the prognosis is poor. Sézary syndrome is characterized by generalized erythroderma and the presence of typical Sézary cells in the peripheral blood. These are usually large mononuclear cells, often with cytoplasmic vacuoles which are PAS-positive. They have been identified as abnormal T cells that may retain "helper" activity with regard to immunoglobulin synthesis by B cells. The skin biopsies are indistinguishable between mycosis fungoides and Sézary syndrome, the classic earliest diagnostic feature being the Pautrier intraepidermal microabscesses, which are aggregates of the malignant T cells. Later, there is progressive bandlike dermal infiltration with the abnormal cells; subsequently, the cells can be found in regional lymph nodes, and, in fatal cases, diffuse infiltration of internal organs may be found.

Patients are now recognized with generalized erythroderma and exfoliation and increased numbers of lymphocytes in the dermis but normal peripheral blood differential counts. Long-term studies will determine if these patients represent the first clinical stage in the spectrum of T cell lymphomas which progress through Sézary syndrome and mycosis fungoides.

3. B cell types–The subtypes are at present classified according to the microscopic features of the cells, especially the nuclei. These are thought to represent different stages of differentiation of B cells between stem cells and plasma cells. Some malignant diseases of certain stages of B cell differentiation have already been discussed, ie, chronic lymphocytic leukemia and the monoclonal gammopathies, especially multiple myeloma and Waldenström's macroglobulinemia.

a. Burkitt's lymphoma–In Africa, this B cell lymphoma frequently presents with facial or jaw tumors, occurs in tropical areas of malarial endemicity, has a constant association with EBV, and is extremely sensitive to radiotherapy or chemotherapy. American Burkitt's lymphoma has similar histologic findings, but the disease seems much more aggressive, with a high incidence of abdominal and bone marrow involvement and a poor prognosis.

b. Angioimmunoblastic lymphadenopathy–This recently recognized disorder presents clinically with fever, sweats, weight loss, and often rash, lymphadenopathy, and hepatosplenomegaly. There is consistent polyclonal hypergammaglobulinemia and a high incidence of autoimmune hemolytic anemia. The histologic diagnosis is based on the triad of proliferation of arborizing small blood vessels, proliferation of immunoblasts, and amorphous acidophilic interstitial material (Fig 27–5). It is thought to represent an abnormal hyperimmune response of B cells rather than a true lymphoma, but it usually has a progressive course with a median survival of only 15 months. Moreover, it may terminate as immunoblastic sarcoma.

c. Immunoblastic sarcoma–This disease may arise de novo or secondary to a previously diagnosed immunologic disorder, eg, angioimmunoblastic lymphadenopathy, Sjögren's syndrome, α chain disease, congenital immunodeficiency, or chronic allograft rejection. The main cell is now termed an **immunoblast** (Fig 27–6). It is similar to the large noncleaved follicular center cell or transformed lymphocyte. Lymphomas with this appearance are generally clinically aggressive.

Immunologic Pathogenesis

Some specific examples of abnormalities in immune function were given above with individual diseases.

A. Serum Immunoglobulins: The presence of monoclonal proteins is of course one of the diagnostic requirements in multiple myeloma and Waldenström's macroglobulinemia. However, serum monoclonal proteins are also found in chronic lymphocytic leukemia and in various forms of lymphoma. Monoclonal IgM peaks were found in 5% of lymphomas with a diffuse infiltration of lymph nodes. In some cases the monoclonal protein is a cryoglobulin.

Polyclonal hypergammaglobulinemia is a feature of angioimmunoblastic lymphadenopathy but may occur occasionally in other subjects as a response to infection.

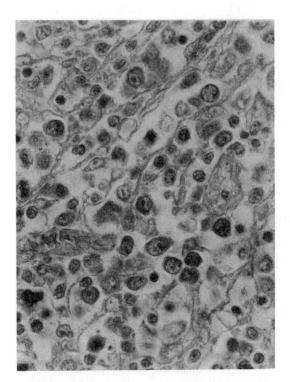

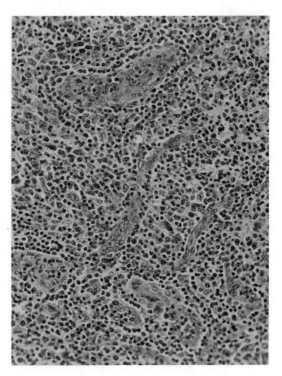

Figure 27–5. Histologic findings in lymph node biopsy of angioimmunoblastic lymphadenopathy. (Giemsa stain, original magnification × 250.) Note the arborizing thick-walled small blood vessels, the amorphous interstitial material, and the mixed cell population, including immunoblasts, plasmacytoid cells, mature plasma cells, and lymphocytes with different intermediate forms. (Reproduced, with permission, from Lukes RJ, Tindle BH: Immunoblastic lymphadenopathy. *N Engl J Med* 1975;**292**:1.)

Figure 27–6. Histologic findings in lymph node biopsy of angioimmunoblastic lymphadenopathy which transformed to immunoblastic sarcoma. (Giemsa stain, original magnification × 1000.) Note the cells and numerous immunoblasts. The latter are 15–25 μm in diameter and have large oval nuclei with freely dispersed, pale, basophilic fine chromatin, with one large or 2–3 smaller nucleoli close to the nuclear membrane. (Reproduced, with permission, from Lukes RJ, Tindle BH: Immunoblastic lymphadenopathy. *N Engl J Med* 1975;**292**:1.)

Hypogammaglobulinemia implies a poor prognosis in chronic lymphocytic leukemia or lymphoma, generally indicating advanced disease. It not infrequently leads to death from infection.

B. Cellular Immunity: Anergy is a common finding in Hodgkin's disease, but it can occur with any type of lymphoma at an advanced stage. It is more frequent in later than earlier stages but does not always correlate positively with the stage of disease. Other tests such as lymphocyte activation also commonly indicate defects in cellular immunity. This is expressed clinically as infection with fungi, viruses, or uncommon organisms such as *Pneumocystis carinii*.

C. Autoimmunity: Lymphoma is recognized as a late complication in patients with autoimmune manifestations, eg, systemic lupus erythematosus or Sjögren's syndrome. Moreover, some patients with lymphoma may subsequently develop autoimmune abnormalities, eg, autoimmune hemolytic anemia in chronic lymphocytic leukemia or angioimmunoblastic lymphadenopathy, immune thrombocytopenic purpura, or other rheumatoid diseases such as dermatomyositis.

Treatment

The patient with Hodgkin's disease or non-Hodgkin's lymphoma must be fully evaluated before treatment can be logically planned. This evaluation, called staging, is used to determine the extent of involvement by lymphoma. Since radiation therapy is often curative when disease is limited to lymph nodes, it is particularly important to evaluate nonnodal tissues such as bone marrow, liver, spleen, etc for possible involvement. This often requires a "staging laparotomy" with resection of multiple lymph nodes from various intra-abdominal and retroperitoneal areas, splenectomy, open liver biopsy, and open bone marrow biopsy. If after such a full evaluation no tumor can be found outside of lymph nodes (stages I, II, and III), the patient most often is treated with "extended field" or "total nodal" radiation to 4000–4500 R with curative intent. If tumor is found in bone marrow, liver, lung, etc (stage IV), the patient is not a candidate for radiation therapy and should be treated with chemotherapy. Patients with unfavorable histologic types are often treated with chemotherapy in addition to radiation therapy even when their disease appears to be confined to lymph nodes, since they often have undetected microscopic extranodal disease.

Extended field or total nodal radiation therapy is curative for 90% of patients with stage I and II Hodgkin's disease with favorable histologic types. Stage III patients also may be cured. Patients with non-Hodgkin lymphomas more frequently have involvement of extranodal tissues and therefore are less likely to be candidates for radiation. However, selected patients have been cured with local or extended field radiation therapy.

Advanced Hodgkin's disease responds very well to multiple drug combination chemotherapy. Complete remission rates of over 80% can be achieved with current multiple drug therapy. About a third of patients who achieve complete remission appear to be permanently cured. Well-differentiated and nodular lymphocytic lymphomas also respond very well to chemotherapy; diffuse histiocytic and poorly differentiated lymphocytic lymphomas respond less well and have a poorer prognosis.

The typing of lymphomas as T or B cell lymphomas may have therapeutic applications. For example, cytotoxic monoclonal antibodies have been used experimentally to treat T cell lymphomas.

INFECTIOUS MONONUCLEOSIS

Major Immunologic Features
- Acute EBV infection of B lymphocytes.
- Absolute T cell and B cell lymphocytosis.
- Lymphadenopathy and splenomegaly.
- Sheep cell agglutinin > 1:100.
- Antibodies to EBV antigens.
- Antibodies to other viruses and autoantigens.

General Considerations
Infectious mononucleosis is a common acute, usually self-limited infectious disease caused by Epstein-Barr virus (EBV). It may occur at any age, though the highest incidence is in teenagers and young adults. It is usually spread by respiratory droplet infection in epidemic or sporadic epidemiologic distribution.

Immunologic Pathogenesis
Infectious mononucleosis has traditionally been considered to be a lymphoproliferative disease distinguished from lymphoma only by its tendency to spontaneous regression. Several observations testify to the intense lymphoproliferation. The peripheral blood contains atypical lymphoid cells with a high rate of turnover and DNA synthesis. Histologic examination shows marked lymphoproliferation in almost all lymphoid tissues. Lymph nodes show marked hyperplasia, especially in the T-dependent paracortical areas. Distortion of normal architecture by lymphoproliferation and the presence of occasional Reed-Sternberg

Table 27–9. List of antibodies produced in infectious mononucleosis.

Heterophil antibody
Antibodies to i antigen on red blood cells
EBV-associated antibodies:
Early antigen
Membrane antigen
Viral capsid (cytoplasmic) antigen
Nuclear antigen
Virus-neutralizing antibody
Antibodies to Newcastle disease virus
Rheumatoid factor
Antinuclear antibody (ANA)
Syphilis reagins

cells rarely leads to an incorrect diagnosis of lymphoma. Lymphocytes taken during the acute phase proliferate in continuous in vitro cultures and will produce lymphomalike lesions if injected into immunosuppressed animals. These lesions can also be produced by fresh noncultured lymphocytes, and human immunoglobulins may be synthesized.

The lymphoproliferation in infectious mononucleosis is secondary to the entry of EBV into B cells. This induces a small and short-lived increase in B cells, which is followed by a marked, prolonged T cell response. This accounts for the variable findings of T and B cell typing of the atypical lymphocytes at different stages of the disease. These responses produce detectable changes in both cellular and humoral immunity. Decreased delayed skin hypersensitivity to antigens is found during the acute phase. Humoral changes include a polyclonal increase in IgG and synthesis of several antibodies (Table 27–9).

Recent studies suggest that the T cell lymphocytosis that occurs in response to primary EBV infection of B cells is a suppressor T cell response, thereby limiting the B cell proliferation and possibly preventing malignant transformation.

A. Antibodies: The heterophil antibody is the IgM antibody in the diagnostic Paul-Bunnell test. It agglutinates sheep red blood cells and can be absorbed by preincubation with beef red blood cells but not guinea pig kidney. A slide spot test is now used for screening purposes, and positive reactions are confirmed by means of the Paul-Bunnell test. The antibody titer generally rises after day 3 of the illness, reaches a maximum at 2 weeks, and remains high for approximately 6 weeks.

Low-titer IgM antibodies to i blood group antigen are present in 20–90% of patients. Occasionally, a high-titer response to i is associated with autoimmune hemolytic anemia as a complication.

Serum antibodies to EBV capsid antigen appear de novo within 7 days of clinical disease, increase in titer, fall gradually, and then remain positive at a low level indefinitely. Antibodies to other EBV antigens appear later and are more transient.

B. Epstein-Barr Virus (EBV): The association of this herpesvirus with Burkitt's lymphoma was reported in 1964, and intensive study has provided compelling but not fully confirmatory evidence for the oncogenicity of EBV.

There is a high incidence of antibodies to EBV antigens, especially the early antigen, in Burkitt's lymphoma. High titers of antibodies to early antigen are found in all patients. However, up to 30% of patients with American Burkitt's lymphoma do not have EBV antibodies. Furthermore, antibodies to EBV capsid antigen have been detected in some patients with sarcoidosis, systemic lupus erythematosus, and Guillain-Barré syndrome. Efforts to demonstrate enveloped viral particles, nucleocapsids, or early antigens in Burkitt's lymphoma biopsies are generally negative. The continued production of EBV antibodies might be a general indication of B cell overactivity, somehow induced nonspecifically by the lymphoma, or might indicate that viral replication is continuing elsewhere in the body, as happens with Marek's lymphoma in chickens. Fluorescence studies have now demonstrated EBV membrane antigen on tumor cells.

The application of RNA-DNA hybridization techniques to tumor cells, long-term human lymphoblastoid cell lines, and tissues from animals with lymphomas has demonstrated the wide distribution of the EBV genome. The genome may be detected in cells that do not produce infectious virions, and the relevance of this fact to EBV oncogenicity has yet to be explained. Another major paradox is the association of EBV with at least 3 distinct entities, ie, a lymphoid malignancy (Burkitt's lymphoma), a self-limited lymphoproliferative disease (infectious mononucleosis), and an epithelial malignancy (nasopharyngeal carcinoma). These differences may be due to other etiologic agents in these 3 diseases.

Recent reports of 3 families clearly demonstrate the role of genetic factors in determining the outcome of exposure of an individual to EBV. In one family several male members were affected by successive, progressive, combined variable X-linked immunodeficiency (Duncan's disease). A fatal lymphoproliferative disease occurred in 6 of the 18 boys in the kindred, and laboratory evidence confirmed infectious mononucleosis in at least 3 cases. A second family was characterized by fulminant infectious mononucleosis in previously normal male children, with replacement of T cells by atypical B cells. Normal or increased serum immunoglobulins were observed, but antibodies to EBV were not produced. The third family also showed a predilection for fulminant infectious mononucleosis in male children; in 2 cases the children survived, but with severe acquired hypogammaglobulinemia.

Clinical Features

A. Symptoms and Signs: The most frequent presentation is with fever and sore throat, tender lymphadenopathy, anorexia, malaise, headache, and myalgia. There is discrete, moderately tender lymphadenopathy which often is generalized but may be limited to the neck. Splenomegaly occurs in most patients. A macular, maculopapular, or petechial rash occurs in half of cases, but such rashes occur in almost all patients with infectious mononucleosis who have been given ampicillin.

Symptoms may be referable to specifically involved organ systems: myocarditis, manifested by arrhythmias and congestive heart failure; hepatitis, manifested by hepatomegaly and jaundice; central nervous system involvement, manifested by headache, photophobia, neck stiffness, or, rarely, transverse myelitis; and respiratory involvement, manifested by cough, pain, and dyspnea.

B. Laboratory Findings: There is initial granulocytopenia followed by an absolute lymphocytosis. The lymphocytes include many atypical forms which are often larger, with abundant cytoplasm, and show nuclear and cytoplasmic vacuolization. The atypical lymphocytes are not specific for infectious mononucleosis and occasionally are confused with lymphoblasts of acute lymphocytic leukemia.

Liver function tests usually show evidence of mild hepatocellular dysfunction.

The cerebrospinal fluid may show increased pressure and protein and atypical lymphocytes.

The sheep cell agglutination test is discussed above.

Differential Diagnosis

Viral and streptococcal tonsillitis must be excluded as causes of the exudative tonsillitis. Rubella, toxoplasmosis, and infection with cytomegalovirus may resemble some of the manifestations of infectious mononucleosis.

Treatment

There is no specific treatment. Short-term corticosteroids may be useful for acutely ill patients who are very toxic and for some complications such as myocarditis and central nervous system involvement.

Complications & Prognosis

The complications of infectious mononucleosis include secondary bacterial pharyngitis, rupture of the spleen, autoimmune hemolytic anemia, autoimmune thrombocytopenia, myocarditis, hepatitis, and central nervous system involvement with meningoencephalitis or transverse myelitis. Rarely, one may see fatal fulminant infectious mononucleosis or acquired hypogammaglobulinemia.

Fever generally subsides within 10 days and the lymphadenopathy and splenomegaly within 4 weeks. Occasionally, symptoms may last for up to 3 months, and lethargy and malaise may persist for 6–12 months. The mortality rate is negligible.

LEUKOPENIA

Leukopenia is defined as a reduction in the number of circulating leukocytes below 4000/μL.

Granulocytopenia or neutropenia occurs more commonly than lymphopenia. Granulocytopenia may be caused either by decreased granulocyte production by the bone marrow or by increased granulocyte utilization or destruction. Decreased granulocyte production occurs in aplastic anemia, leukemia, and other diseases marked by bone marrow infiltration; many drugs also cause leukopenia by this mechanism. Increased granulocyte utilization or destruction occurs in hypersplenism, autoimmune neutropenia, and some forms of drug-induced leukopenia.

AUTOIMMUNE NEUTROPENIA

Autoimmune neutropenia may occur as an isolated disorder or secondary to an underlying autoimmune disease. These patients may be asymptomatic or may have recurrent infections. Antigranulocyte antibodies have been detected by a variety of procedures, including the utilization of anti-immunoglobulin antisera with fluorescent or antiglobulin consumption techniques, functional assays, and cytotoxicity assays. The presence of leukoagglutinins does not correlate well with leukopenia. A recent report described 2 patients with autoimmune neutropenia in which the mechanism of granulocyte destruction appeared to be antibody-dependent lymphocyte-mediated cytotoxicity against granulocytes. Bone marrow function is generally normal in autoimmune neutropenia, with myeloid hyperplasia and a shift to the left in maturation often observed, presumably in response to increased peripheral granulocyte destruction. Rare cases have been described in which the autoantibody also suppressed bone marrow myeloid cell growth in vitro and in vivo. Autoimmune neutropenia often responds to splenectomy and treatment with corticosteroids or immunosuppressive drugs.

Autoimmune neutropenia may also be seen in systemic lupus erythematosus, Felty's syndrome (rheumatoid arthritis, splenomegaly, and severe neutropenia), and other autoimmune disorders. There is some evidence that immune neutropenia in these disorders may be caused by adsorption of immune complexes onto the neutrophil membrane with premature cell destruction rather than by an antibody directed at specific neutrophil antigens. Some patients with Felty's syndrome also appear to have depressed granulocyte production by the bone marrow, probably also on an immunologic basis.

DRUG–INDUCED IMMUNE
NEUTROPENIA

Although most drugs produce neutropenia by bone marrow suppression, some may cause neutropenia by the attachment of drug-antibody immune complexes to the surface of the granulocytes, with premature cell destruction. This so-called "innocent bystander" mechanism is known to occur in drug-induced immune hemolytic anemia and thrombocytopenia. Cephalothin causes granulocytopenia in approximately 0.1% of patients given the drug, probably by this mechanism.

AGRANULOCYTOSIS

Agranulocytosis is characterized by the total absence of granulocytes and granulocyte precursors from the peripheral blood and bone marrow. This most often results from exposure of the patient to certain drugs, eg, aminopyrine, dipyrone, and phenylbutazone. Patients with agranulocytosis usually present with infections—often serious, life-threatening ones. Prior to the antibiotic era, agranulocytosis was almost invariably fatal. Patients now usually recover with intensive antibiotic treatment and granulocyte transfusions when necessary. Unlike drug-induced aplastic anemia, agranulocytosis usually resolves spontaneously within a few days to a few weeks after discontinuing the offending drug.

Although antigranulocyte antibodies or leukocyte drug-dependent antibodies generally have not been demonstrated in agranulocytosis, there is circumstantial evidence that immunologic damage to peripheral blood and bone marrow granulocytic cells is the mechanism of cell destruction, at least in some cases. Such patients often develop agranulocytosis after taking the responsible drug for weeks or months. If they recover from the agranulocytosis after the drug is discontinued and later are rechallenged with a small test dose of the same drug, acute agranulocytosis occurs immediately, associated with the acute onset of fever, chills, and hypocomplementemia. In 2 cases of drug-induced agranulocytosis due to phenytoin, a non-complement-dependent antibody capable of suppressing granulopoiesis and also of causing dysfunction of circulating granulocytes was found. Additionally, recent studies of several patients with non–drug-induced agranulocytosis demonstrated inhibition of in vitro bone marrow colony formation by peripheral blood lymphocytes from these patients, suggesting suppression or lymphocytotoxic destruction of the early granulocytic precursor cells in the bone marrow.

II. RED CELL DISORDERS

The red cell disorders in which immune processes play an important role are the immune hemolytic anemias, paroxysmal nocturnal hemoglobinuria, and aplastic anemia and related disorders.

IMMUNE HEMOLYTIC ANEMIAS

The immune hemolytic disorders are classified in Table 27–10. The classification is based on the type of

Table 27-10. Classification of immune hemolytic anemias.

Autoimmune hemolytic anemias
  A. Warm antibody types
    1. Idiopathic warm autoimmune hemolytic anemia (AIHA)
    2. Secondary warm autoimmune hemolytic anemias
      a. Systemic lupus erythematosus and other autoimmune disorders
      b. Chronic lymphocytic leukemia, lymphomas, etc
      c. Hepatitis and other viral infections
  B. Cold antibody types
    1. Idiopathic cold agglutinin syndrome
    2. Secondary cold agglutinin syndrome
      a. *Mycoplasma pneumoniae* infection; infectious mononucleosis and other viral infections
      b. Chronic lymphocytic leukemia, lymphomas, etc
    3. Paroxysmal cold hemoglobinuria
      a. Idiopathic
      b. Syphilis, viral infections
Drug-induced immune hemolytic anemias (partial list of drugs)

Aminosalicylic acid (PAS)	Methyldopa
Antihistamines	Penicillin
Carbromal	Phenacetin
Cephalothin	Pyramidon
Chlorinated hydrocarbons	Quinidine
Chlorpromazine	Quinine
Dipyrone	Rifampin
Insulin	Stibophen
Isoniazid	Sulfonamides
Levodopa	Sulfonylureas
Mefenamic acid	Tetracyclines
Melphalan	

Alloantibody-induced immune hemolytic anemias
  A. Hemolytic transfusion reactions
  B. Hemolytic disease of the newborn

ered as a series of questions: (1) Are the red cells of the patient coated with IgG, complement components, or both? (2) How heavily are the red cells sensitized? (3) What antibodies are eluted from the red cells of the patient? (4) What antibodies are present in the serum?

Routine screening is performed by means of the direct antiglobulin (Coombs) test by tube or slide agglutination (see Chapter 22) using antisera with broad specificity. Subsequent evaluation requires testing the red cells with dilutions of monospecific antisera, especially antisera to IgG and C3. The activity of the antibody is examined at different temperatures to see if the temperature of maximal activity identifies it as a "warm" or "cold" antibody.

False-negative and false-positive results can be obtained in direct antiglobulin tests. Approximately 20% of all patients with immune hemolytic anemias will have a negative or only weakly positive direct antiglobulin test unless the antiserum contains adequate titers of antibodies to complement components, especially C3. This inability to detect complement on red cells was probably the cause of many early reported cases of Coombs-negative autoimmune hemolytic anemia. A positive direct antiglobulin test may be seen in situations other than autoantibodies on red cells and does not necessarily mean autoimmune hemolytic anemia. Causes of such reactions include the following: (1) antibody formation against drugs rather than intrinsic red cell antigens (see below); (2) damage to the red cell membrane due to infection or cephalosporins, leading to nonimmunologic binding of proteins; (3) in vitro complement sensitization of red blood cells by low-titer cold antibodies (present in many normal individuals) in clotted blood samples stored at 4 °C prior to separation; (4) delayed transfusion reactions; and (5) unknown mechanisms. The above reactions are generally weak and can be differentiated by clinical and detailed serologic studies.

Serologic investigations of the patient's serum and red cell eluates should then answer another series of questions: (1) Are antibodies present? (2) Do they act as agglutinins, hemolysins, or incomplete antibodies? (3) What is their thermal range of activity? (4) What is their specificity?

The patient's serum is tested both undiluted and with fresh added complement against untreated and enzyme-treated pools of red cells. Enzyme treatment enhances the sensitivity of the system. The tests are run at 37 °C and 20 °C and examined at 1 hour for agglutination and lysis. Cold agglutinin titration at 4 °C is also performed. Red cell eluate is similarly tested.

Specialized tests may be performed to detect antibodies to drugs in cases of drug-induced immune hemolytic anemia.

The specificity of the antibodies is tested at different temperatures with a panel of red cells of different Rh genotypes and with cells of different types in the Ii blood group system (see below).

The results of the serologic investigations are then correlated with clinical and other laboratory investigations to establish a definitive diagnosis.

antibodies involved and whether there is a demonstrable underlying disease or not. Since correct identification of the type of antibody is essential to correct diagnosis in patients with suspected immune hemolytic anemia, the immunologic laboratory investigation of such patients will be discussed before the individual diseases.

Immunologic Laboratory Investigations

There are 2 basic groups of immunologic tests necessary to properly investigate patients with suspected immune hemolytic anemias: (1) tests to detect and characterize antibodies involved in the hemolytic process, and (2) tests to aid in diagnosis of possible underlying disease processes. Tests which define underlying disorders include detection of anti-DNA antibodies and ANA in systemic lupus erythematosus, rheumatoid factors in rheumatoid arthritis, and monoclonal B cells in chronic lymphocytic leukemia.

The serologic tests used to characterize antibodies in serum and on red cells are basic blood-banking procedures, with the addition of monospecific antisera to identify specific proteins on red cells and titration techniques to precisely quantitate antibody activity. Laboratory evaluation of such patients can be consid-

1. WARM AUTOIMMUNE HEMOLYTIC ANEMIA

Major Immunologic Features
- Positive direct antiglobulin (Coombs) test.
- Associated lymphoreticular malignancy or autoimmune disease may be present.
- Splenomegaly common.

General Considerations
Warm antibody autoimmune hemolytic anemia is the most common type of immune hemolytic anemia. It may be either idiopathic or secondary to chronic lymphocytic leukemia, lymphomas, systemic lupus erythematosus, or other autoimmune disorders or infections (Table 27–10). The idiopathic form may follow overt or subclinical viral infection.

Clinical Features
A. Symptoms and Signs: Patients usually present with symptoms of anemia, congestive heart failure, angina pectoris, and hemolysis (fever, jaundice, splenomegaly). There may also be manifestations of an underlying disease, eg, lymphadenopathy, hepatosplenomegaly, or manifestations of autoimmune disease.

B. Laboratory Findings: Normochromic normocytic or slightly macrocytic anemia is usually present; spherocytosis is common, and nucleated red cells may occasionally be found in the peripheral blood. Leukocytosis and thrombocytosis are often present, but occasionally (especially in systemic lupus erythematosus) leukopenia and thrombocytopenia are seen. There is usually a moderate to marked reticulocytosis.

The bone marrow shows marked erythroid hyperplasia with plentiful iron stores. There is an increase in the serum level of indirect (unconjugated) bilirubin. Stool and urinary urobilinogen may be greatly increased. Transfused blood has a short survival time.

Immunologic Diagnosis
The results of the serologic tests discussed above are summarized in Table 27–11. The most common pattern is IgG and complement on red cells, with IgG in the eluate. The eluate generally has no activity if the red cells are sensitized only with complement.

Warm hemolysins active against enzyme-treated red cells occur in 24% of sera, but warm serum agglutinins or hemolysins against untreated red cells are rare. The indirect antiglobulin test (Chapter 22) is positive in approximately 40% of patients' sera tested with untreated red cells but in 80% of serum samples tested with enzyme-treated red cells. This warm antibody is usually IgG but rarely may be IgM, IgA, or both.

The specificity of antibodies in warm antibody autoimmune hemolytic anemia is very complex, but the main specificity is directed against determinants in the Rh complex (see below). Identification is generally performed by blood banks or hematology laboratories with reference panels of red cells of rare types.

Differential Diagnosis
Congenital nonspherocytic hemolytic anemia, hereditary spherocytosis, and hemoglobinopathies can usually be differentiated by the family history, routine hematologic tests, hemoglobin electrophoresis, and a negative direct antiglobulin test.

Table 27–11. Summary of serologic findings in patients with autoimmune hemolytic anemia.*

Disease Group	Red Cells			Serum		
	Direct Antiglobulin Test	Eluate	Immunoglobulin Type	Serologic Characteristics		Specificity
Warm antibody type	IgG 30% IgG + complement 50% Complement 20%	IgG IgG No activity	IgG (rarely also IgA or IgM)	Positive indirect antiglobulin test 40% Agglutination enzyme-treated red cells 80% Hemolysis enzyme-treated red cells 24% Agglutination of untreated red cells (20 °C) 20% Agglutination or hemolysis of untreated red cells (37 °C) Very rare		Rh system (often with a "nonspecific" component)
Cold agglutinin syndrome	Complement	No activity	IgM (rarely IgA)	High-titer cold agglutinin (usually 1:1000 at 4 °C) up to 32 °C; monoclonal IgM-κ in chronic disease		Anti-I usually (can be anti-i or anti-Pr)
Paroxysmal cold hemoglobinuria (very rare)	Complement	No activity	IgG	Potent hemolysin also agglutinates normal cells. Biphasic (usually sensitizes cells in cold up to 15 °C and hemolyzes them at 37 °C)		Anti-P blood group

*Modified from Petz LD, Garratty G: Laboratory correlations in immune hemolytic anemias. Page 139 in: *Laboratory Diagnosis of Immunologic Disorders.* Vyas GN, Stites DP, Brecher G (editors). Grune & Stratton, 1975.

Treatment

A. General Measures: Treatment of the primary disease is necessary when autoimmune hemolytic anemia is secondary to an underlying disease process. Blood transfusions may be necessary for life-threatening anemia but should be avoided when possible since the transfused cells are rapidly destroyed. Careful serologic studies are needed to minimize the risks of serious hemolytic transfusion reactions, and successful cross-matching can be difficult or impossible in this situation.

B. Specific Measures: Hemolysis can be controlled with relatively high doses of corticosteroids in most patients. The steroids are fairly rapidly tapered and then slowly reduced until the clinical state, hemoglobin level, and reticulocyte count indicate the appropriate maintenance dose. Occasionally it is possible to gradually withdraw steroids completely. Regular monitoring is necessary since relapses often occur in patients in remission.

Monitoring generally includes serologic studies, eg, direct and indirect antiglobulin tests, and these may show improvement with reduced amounts of IgG and complement on red cells and lower antibody titers or a negative antibody test. However, there is no consistent correlation between clinical response and serologic tests; prednisone often induces clinical remissions in patients with warm antibody autoimmune hemolytic anemia in spite of persistently positive direct antiglobulin tests.

If prednisone therapy fails or if unacceptable side-effects occur, splenectomy is usually performed. Since splenectomy often produces long-term remissions in patients with idiopathic autoimmune hemolytic anemia, splenectomy is the treatment of choice if hemolysis persists after 2–3 months of corticosteroids. ^{51}Cr-labeled red cell survival studies can be used to identify abnormal splenic red cell sequestration prior to splenectomy; however, clinical remissions may occur after splenectomy even when abnormal splenic sequestration cannot be documented. Continued significant hemolysis or late relapse sometimes occurs after splenectomy and requires therapy with steroids with or without other immunosuppressive agents.

Prognosis

The prognosis of idiopathic warm antibody autoimmune hemolytic anemia is fairly good; however, relapses are not infrequent, and death sometimes occurs. The prognosis of secondary warm autoimmune hemolytic anemia is determined by the underlying disease, eg, systemic lupus erythematosus or lymphoma.

2. COLD AGGLUTININ SYNDROMES

These diseases may also be primary or may be secondary to infections or the lymphomas (Table 27–10). The infections include mycoplasmal pneumonia and infectious mononucleosis and other viral infections.

The clinical features are often those of the underlying disease. Cold-reactive symptoms such as Raynaud's phenomenon or vascular purpura are seen in some patients. Hemolysis is generally mild but may occasionally be severe, especially in cases secondary to lymphoreticular malignancy. The onset may be acute in cases secondary to infection. The idiopathic form is generally slow in onset and runs a chronic course in older patients.

These diseases are characterized by very high serum titers of agglutinating IgM antibodies which react optimally in the cold. Some, however, may have a thermal range reacting up to 37 °C. These patients have cold agglutinin titers in the thousands or millions, while normal individuals may have low-titer IgM cold agglutinins, and patients with chronic parasitic infections and most patients with *Ancylostoma* infection have titers up to 1:500. The specificity of the IgM is generally anti-I in the Ii system, but occasionally it is anti-i or anti-Pr (Table 27–11). In chronic idiopathic cases or cases associated with lymphoreticular malignancy, the cold agglutinin is generally a monoclonal IgM-κ paraprotein. The direct antiglobulin test is always positive using antiserum to C3.

Treatment consists of keeping the patient warm and waiting for spontaneous resolution in acute cases. Chronic cases sometimes respond to chlorambucil in low doses. Corticosteroids and splenectomy are probably not helpful.

The prognosis is generally good except for patients with severe underlying disease such as malignant lymphoma.

3. DRUG–INDUCED IMMUNE HEMOLYTIC ANEMIA

Many cases of immune hemolytic anemia have been reported in association with drug administration; the most common examples are included in Table 27–10. There are 3 stages in the investigation of a patient with suspected drug-induced hemolytic anemia: a history of intake of the drug, confirmation of hemolysis, and serologic tests. Detailed serologic tests are necessary to confirm the diagnosis since different drugs produce hemolysis by different mechanisms. The immunopathologic mechanisms and clinical and laboratory features are summarized in Table 27–12. The mechanisms are classified as **immune complex formation, hapten adsorption, nonspecific adsorption,** and **other unknown mechanisms.**

(1) Immune complex formation: Circulating preformed immune complexes between the drug and antibody to the drug sensitize the red cell ("innocent bystander" phenomenon). Quinine in low doses is a typical example. There is great variability in clinical features and serologic findings.

(2) Drug (hapten) adsorption: The drug acts as a hapten in that it is bound to the red cell membrane and stimulates the production of a high titer of antidrug antibodies.

Table 27—12. Summary of immunopathologic mechanisms and clinical and laboratory features in drug-induced immune hemolytic disorders.*

Mechanism	Drugs	Clinical Findings	Serologic Evaluation	
			Direct Antiglobulin Test	Antibody Characterization
Immune complex formation (drug + antidrug antibody)	Quinine, quinidine, phenacetin	History of small doses of drugs. Acute intravascular hemolysis and renal failure. Thrombocytopenia occasionally found.	Complement (IgG occasionally also present).	Drug + patient's serum + enzyme-treated red cells → Hemolysis, agglutination, or sensitization. Antibody often complement-fixing IgM. Eluate generally nonreactive.
Drug adsorption to red cell membrane (combination with high-titer serum antibodies to drug)	Penicillins, cephalosporins	History of large doses of drugs. Other allergic features may be absent. Usually subacute extravascular hemolysis.	IgG (strongly positive if hemolysis occurs). Rarely, weak complement sensitization also present.	Drug-coated red cells + serum → Agglutination or sensitization (rarely hemolysis). High-titer antibody. Eluate reacts only with antibiotic-coated red cells.
Membrane modification (nonimmunologic adsorption of proteins to red cells)	Cephalosporins	Hemolytic anemia rare.	Positive with reagents with antibodies to a variety of serum proteins.	Drug-coated red cells + serum → Sensitization to antiglobulin antisera in low titer.
Unknown	Methyldopa	Gradual onset of hemolytic anemia. Common.	IgG (strongly positive if hemolysis occurs).	Antibody sensitizes normal red cells without drug. Antibody in serum and eluate identical to warm antibody. No in vitro tests demonstrate relationship to drug.

*Adapted from Garratty G, Petz LD: Drug-induced immune hemolytic anemia. *Am J Med* 1975;58:398.

(3) Nonspecific adsorption: The drug affects the red cells so that various nonimmunologic proteins are adsorbed onto red cells and give a positive Coombs test. This does not result generally in marked hemolysis.

(4) Unknown mechanisms: This type is exemplified by the positive Coombs test that develops within 3 months in 20% of patients treated with methyldopa. The IgG that coats red cells in these patients does not have antibody activity against the drug, and the drug is not required in in vitro tests.

The hemolysis may be acute and severe, but only rarely is blood transfusion required. The main treatment is to stop the offending drug and monitor the patient to be sure the hemolysis disappears. The prognosis is therefore excellent.

4. PAROXYSMAL COLD HEMOGLOBINURIA

This rare disease may be transient or chronic. It may occur as a primary idiopathic disease or secondary to syphilis or viral infection. It is characterized clinically by signs of hemolysis and hemoglobinuria following local or general exposure to cold. Symptoms may include combinations of fatigue, pallor, aching and pain in the back, legs, or abdomen, chills and fever, and the passing of dark-brown urine. The symptoms may appear from within a few minutes to a few hours after exposure to cold.

The disease is characterized by the presence of the classic biphasic Donath-Landsteiner antibody. This IgG antibody sensitizes red cells in the cold (usually below 15 °C), so that complement components are detected on the red cells by the direct antiglobulin test after rewarming. Heavily sensitized cells are hemolyzed when warmed to 37 °C.

Acute attacks are treated symptomatically, and postinfectious cases generally resolve spontaneously.

5. HEMOLYTIC DISEASE OF THE NEWBORN

Immunologic Pathogenesis

During pregnancy, very small amounts of fetal blood are leaked into the maternal circulation, especially during the last trimester. However, this is usually not enough to trigger antibody formation in the mother. During delivery, when the placenta is detached, bleeding of cord blood into the mother's circulation can elicit an immune response to fetal red cell alloantigens.

Hemolytic disease of the newborn results from mother's antibodies crossing the placenta and destroying fetal red cells. This leads to hemolytic anemia and hyperbilirubinemia in the newborn infant, since the hematopoietic tissue may not be able to compensate for the increased red cell destruction and the immature liver does not conjugate bilirubin efficiently enough to be excreted with bile.

The first child is seldom affected by the hemolytic disease, but the chances for alloimmunization increase with each incompatible pregnancy. The primary stimulus for immunization can also be a previous incompatible blood transfusion or abortion.

Formation of Rh antibodies is the most common form of alloimmunization to give rise to clinically important disease. Antibodies to blood groups A and B (Chapter 24) may also cause hemolysis of fetal cells if the maternal antibodies are IgG and thus capable of crossing the placenta. In these cases, the mother belongs usually to group O and the baby to group A. In fact, ABO immunization during pregnancy occurs more often than Rh immunization, but it seldom results in serious problems. If the fetus secretes soluble A or B substances, the maternal antibodies become neutralized before they cause damage to red cells. A or B substances are present not only on red cells but also on other tissues, including the placental endothelium. Therefore, many of the antibodies are consumed by these cells.

Clinical Features

The most frequent signs in the newborn are anemia and rapidly developing jaundice, which is usually present within the first 24 hours (in contrast to the physiologic icterus which occurs later). The infant's response to the anemia is marked reticulocytosis and even erythroblastosis—hence the older name erythroblastosis fetalis. As bilirubin accumulates in the plasma, it may cross the blood-brain barrier and cause damage to the nervous system (kernicterus). Severe alloimmunization causes fetal hydrops, and the fetus may die in utero. In these cases, if the father is homozygous for the relevant blood group, the prognosis is very poor for future babies.

Immunologic Diagnosis

Since the cause of the disease is antibody on red cell membrane, the direct Coombs test is usually positive. In ABO incompatibility, it is often negative. The reason for this is somewhat unclear, but the relatively small amount of IgG antibody and the adsorption by other tissues may result in so few antibody molecules on the red cell surface that the conventional Coombs method is not able to detect them. Thus, a negative direct Coombs test does not rule out an immunologic cause for neonatal icterus. If antibodies are not found in the mother's serum, however, immune hemolysis is unlikely.

Alloimmunization should be detected during pregnancy. In many countries, all Rh-negative women are screened for the presence of blood group antibodies during pregnancy. As the number of D immunizations decreases, the relative proportion of immunizations to other blood groups has increased. Consequently, antibody screening should not be restricted to Rh-negative women. No reliable screening test is available for ABO disease, although several assays for detection of clinically important IgG anti-A or anti-B have been used.

When unexpected antibodies are found in the mother's serum, the father's blood groups should be determined. If the father is negative for the relevant blood group, there is no risk; if he is heterozygous, the baby has only a 50% chance of being affected. Increasing antibody titer or a history of previously ill children increases suspicion that the fetus can be affected, and amniocentesis is done to determine the concentration of bile pigments and possibly antibodies in the amniotic fluid. With these procedures, the presence and seriousness of the hemolytic disease can be assessed. Detectable amounts of antibodies sometimes develop in the serum so late in the pregnancy that they remain unnoticed until the time of delivery. Alloimmunization should always be suspected if the bilirubin level starts rising rapidly in an anemic newborn infant.

Treatment & Prevention

Treatment can be started during the last trimester of pregnancy if the results of amniocentesis and antibody determinations indicate that the fetus has serious disease. Compatible blood is injected into the abdominal cavity of the fetus and is rapidly absorbed into the circulation. These intrauterine transfusions may help the fetus to survive until mature enough to live outside the uterus. The last weeks of pregnancy are the most critical time for the fetus. Careful monitoring of clinical data by the obstetrician and neonatologist may prompt a decision to deliver the affected baby prior to term.

Immediately after delivery, the infant's blood group is determined and the cord cells are tested by the direct Coombs technique. If the baby is affected, exchange transfusions are usually needed, although in mild cases phototherapy with ultraviolet light or close supervision of bilirubin levels may be sufficient.

Women who have antibodies to the fetal red cells should deliver in hospitals that have facilities and experience in exchange transfusion. Despite modern advances in the treatment of hemolytic disease of the newborn, the mortality rate in severe intrauterine cases remains high.

Over 90% of Rh-negative women having Rh-positive offspring do not form anti-D antibodies. The immunization of the rest can be prevented by giving the mother concentrated anti-D (Rh$_0$) immunoglobulin within 72 hours of delivery if she does not have any preexisting anti-D antibodies. Since it is not possible to predict who will make antibodies, all Rh-negative women with an Rh-positive baby must be given prophylaxis. Since Rh antigens are detectable in an embryo a few weeks postconception, anti-D immunoglobulin should also be given to Rh-negative women who have aborted.

The mechanism of inhibition of antibody synthesis is unclear, but rapid destruction and clearance of Rh-positive cells from the circulation seem to play a role. In experimental conditions, Rh-positive cells coated with blood group antibodies other than anti-D are quickly destroyed and anti-D antibodies are not formed. This idea is supported by the clinical observation that mothers with anti-A or anti-B antibodies reacting with fetal cells produce Rh antibodies less often than in ABO-compatible pregnancies.

Systematically applied anti-D prophylaxis has reduced the number of immunized women from about 7–8% to a little over 1% if measured by the number of Rh-negative women with antibodies after 2 consecutive Rh-positive babies. Several reasons have been suggested for the few failures: immunization early during the pregnancy (not starting at the time of delivery); abnormally large volume of fetal blood leaking into the maternal circulation with insufficient anti-D immunoglobulin; and unusual sensitivity of the maternal immune system to the antigen D.

PAROXYSMAL NOCTURNAL HEMOGLOBINURIA

This rare disease occurs in adults as a chronic hemolytic anemia with acute exacerbations. It may follow other hematologic disorders such as idiopathic or drug-induced bone marrow aplasia and may terminate in acute myelogenous leukemia. The intravascular hemolysis causes intermittent hemoglobinemia and hemoglobinuria. This activity fluctuates throughout the day; the classic timing with nocturnal hemoglobinuria is seen in only 25% of cases.

The diagnosis is suggested by the findings of intermittent or chronic intravascular hemolysis, a low leukocyte alkaline phosphatase value, and frequently pancytopenia. The diagnosis of paroxysmal nocturnal hemoglobinuria is confirmed by any of the following tests: the acid hemolysis (Ham) test, the sugar water test, and the inulin test. These tests are presumably expressions of the 2 presently known abnormalities in paroxysmal nocturnal hemoglobinuria, ie, the exquisite sensitivity of paroxysmal nocturnal hemoglobinuria red cells to complement lysis and the abnormally low acetylcholinesterase activity in the red cell membrane. Patients' cells are lysed by approximately 4% of the amount of complement required to lyse normal red cells. These tests demonstrate the sensitivity to complement lysis of paroxysmal nocturnal hemoglobinuria red cells but do not elucidate the fundamental underlying cause of paroxysmal nocturnal hemoglobinuria. The alternative complement pathway may well be involved in this disease, as suggested by the inulin test, since inulin activates this pathway. However, serum complement studies are normal, no antibody has been identified either in the serum or on red cells, and no abnormalities have been defined in membrane lipids and phospholipids. Electron microscopy shows a pitted surface on red cells, but this has not been correlated with the functional complement abnormalities.

Treatment is mainly symptomatic. Transfusions are often required. Androgens may be useful if there is underlying bone marrow hypoplasia. Corticosteroids and splenectomy are probably not useful.

APLASTIC ANEMIA & RELATED DISORDERS

Recently there has been growing interest in the possibility that aplastic anemia and certain other disorders characterized by lack of normal hematopoiesis by the bone marrow may be immunologic in origin. Reports have confirmed immunologic mechanisms in pure red cell aplasia and some patients with aplastic anemia.

Pure Red Cell Aplasia

This rare form of anemia is characterized by a marked reduction or absence of bone marrow erythroblasts and blood reticulocytes, with normal granulopoiesis and thrombopoiesis. It occurs as an acquired disorder in adults, either in an idiopathic form or associated with thymoma, lymphoma, other tumors, or certain drugs. Patients usually present with progressive anemia, generally requiring transfusion support. Bone marrow examination confirms the diagnosis. Thymoma is present in a small number of patients, and other immunologic abnormalities, such as hypogammaglobulinemia, monoclonal gammopathy, autoimmune hemolytic anemia, and features of systemic lupus erythematosus, may also be present.

Many patients with pure red cell aplasia, with or without thymoma, have been found to have serum antibodies which react with bone marrow erythroblasts. These IgG antibodies have been demonstrated by immunofluorescence microscopy, with staining of nuclei of bone marrow erythroblasts. These antibodies fix complement and are specifically cytotoxic for erythroblasts. It has also been demonstrated that plasma from patients with pure red cell aplasia suppresses erythropoiesis by normal bone marrow when cultured in vitro, while bone marrow from patients with pure red cell aplasia shows normal erythropoiesis when cultured in vitro in normal plasma. This plasma factor suppressing erythropoiesis in pure red cell aplasia is an IgG antibody.

Patients with pure red cell aplasia usually require total red blood cell transfusion support. Patients with thymomas should have these tumors removed; this will produce a remission in about 30% of these patients. Patients with idiopathic pure red cell aplasia and those that do not respond to thymectomy should be treated with immunosuppressive drugs. Corticosteroids are usually used first, but few patients respond, and most are subsequently treated with cyclophosphamide plus prednisone. This combination produces remissions in 30–50% of patients, but relapses may occur when drugs are discontinued. Splenectomy has also been advocated for refractory patients with pure red cell aplasia, as has plasmapheresis.

Diamond-Blackfan Syndrome

This disorder, also known as congenital hypoplastic anemia, represents the congenital form of pure red cell aplasia seen in infants. Anemia is usually noted in the first year of life but may occur later. These patients must be distinguished from patients with transient erythroblastopenia of infancy and childhood, which is a less serious self-limited disorder.

Two recent reports indicated that peripheral blood lymphocytes from patients with Diamond-Blackfan syndrome suppress erythropoiesis of normal bone marrow when cultured in vitro. However, in a subsequent study, no evidence was found of suppression of erythrogenesis by lymphocytes; to the contrary, it was found that T lymphocytes even from patients with Diamond-Blackfan syndrome had helper activity in erythropoiesis. Children with Diamond-Blackfan syndrome often respond dramatically to treatment with corticosteroids, rarely requiring treatment with cytotoxic immunosuppressive drugs.

Aplastic Anemia

Aplastic anemia is defined as pancytopenia due to bone marrow aplasia. Patients with severe aplastic anemia have no hematopoietic precursor cells present in their bone marrow and must be supported with red cell and platelet transfusions and antibiotics. Even with optimal supportive care, severe aplastic anemia rarely undergoes spontaneous remission, and there is a 75–90% mortality rate. Treatment with high doses of androgens may benefit some patients, but few patients with severe aplasia respond. Bone marrow transplantation produces long-term remissions in about 50% of patients with severe aplastic anemia, and early bone marrow transplantation is currently considered the treatment of choice for younger patients with a histocompatible matched sibling (see section V of this chapter).

In the past, aplastic anemia was usually associated with exposure to toxic drugs or chemicals (benzene, chloramphenicol, arsenicals, gold, anticonvulsants, etc). Recent series, however, indicate that most patients have no such exposure and no other associated illness, and these patients are classified as having idiopathic aplastic anemia. Although it is possible that these patients have been exposed to unknown or inapparent environmental toxins, recent studies indicate that at least some of these cases are due to immunologic causes. Lymphocytes from the bone marrow of about one-third of patients with aplastic anemia have been shown to suppress the growth of granulocyte colonies from normal bone marrow in vitro. When these abnormal suppressor lymphocytes are separated from the marrow granulocytic stem cells or killed with a specific cytotoxic antilymphocyte serum, increased granulocyte colony formation occurs. Other investigators found that peripheral blood lymphocytes from 5 of 7 patients with aplastic anemia suppressed erythropoiesis of normal bone marrow when cultured in vitro—a result similar to the findings reported in some patients with Diamond-Blackfan syndrome.

Aplastic anemia, therefore, may result from at least 3 different defects involving the stem cells, the hematopoietic environment, or suppressor cells. A review of 14 patients with aplastic anemia studied by in vitro bone marrow cultures found evidence that 8 patients had defects in their stem cells. One patient had a defective hematopoietic environment, and 5 patients had increased suppressor cell activity. Characterization of the nature of the defects would permit more rational management of patients with aplastic anemia, since those afflicted with evidence of increased suppressor cell activity would be considered for treatment with immunosuppressive drugs or antithymocyte globulin (ATG) and those with obvious stem cell defects would be considered for early bone marrow transplantation.

III. PLATELET DISORDERS

Thrombocytopenia may be due to decreased platelet production, increased platelet destruction, or abnormal platelet pooling. Immunologic thrombocytopenias, the subject of this section, are caused by increased platelet destruction, usually following platelet sensitization with antibody. Thrombocytopenias due to decreased platelet production (aplastic anemia, leukemias, etc) have already been discussed with regard to immunologic features. Thrombocytopenia due to abnormal platelet pooling in an enlarged spleen (hypersplenism) is generally not associated with immunologic abnormalities.

Immunologic Mechanisms of Platelet Destruction

Several immunologic mechanisms of platelet damage leading to thrombocytopenia have been described. Platelet autoantibodies sensitize circulating platelets in idiopathic thrombocytopenic purpura and related disorders, leading to premature destruction of these cells in the spleen and other parts of the monocyte-macrophage system (see following section). Platelet alloantibodies may develop after multiple transfusions with blood products, or maternal sensitization can occur during pregnancies. Such platelet alloantibodies are becoming a major problem in long-term platelet support for patients with bone marrow failure. Alloantibodies may cause shortened platelet survival after transfusion or produce immediate platelet lysis with severe fever and chill reactions. Shortened platelet survival appears to be mediated by non–complement-dependent IgG or IgM antibodies similar to autoantibodies seen in idiopathic thrombocytopenic purpura. Platelet lysis, on the other hand, appears to be mediated by complement-dependent cytotoxic antibodies. These alloantibodies are directed primarily at HLA antigens, but non-HLA platelet antigens may also be involved. Alloantibody-dependent lymphocyte-mediated cytotoxicity has also been described in some patients. Neonatal thrombocytopenia due to passive transfer of maternal alloantibody or autoantibody is fortunately rare but may be life-threatening when it occurs.

Table 27–13. Classification of immune thrombocytopenias.

Idiopathic (autoimmune) thrombocytopenic purpura (ITP)
Secondary autoimmune thrombocytopenias
  Systemic lupus erythematosus and other autoimmune
    disorders
  Chronic lymphocytic leukemia, lymphomas, some nonlym-
    phoid malignancies
  Infectious mononucleosis and some other infections
Drug-induced immune thrombocytopenias (partial list of drugs)

Acetazolamide	Meprobamate
Allymid	Methyldopa
Aminosalicylic acid (PAS)	Novobiocin
Antazoline	Phenolphthalein
Apronalide	Phenytoin
Aspirin	Quinidine
Carbamazepine	Quinine
Cephalothin	Rifampin
Chlorothiazide	Spironolactone
Digitoxin	Stibophen
Hydrochlorothiazide	Sulfamethazine
Imipramine	Thioguanine

Posttransfusion purpura
Neonatal immune thrombocytopenias
  Due to autoantibodies (ITP)
  Due to alloantibodies (maternal sensitization)
Due to alloantibodies (destruction of transfused platelets)
  Sensitization from previous transfusions
  Maternal sensitization during pregnancies

Other immunologic mechanisms of platelet de-struction include development of antibodies to drugs or other antigenic substances (haptens) adsorbed to the platelet membrane and adsorption of preformed antigen-antibody complexes onto the platelet mem-brane, with rapid removal of these sensitized cells from the circulation (''innocent bystander'' phenom-ena). The reactions are often complement-dependent. These mechanisms are seen in drug-induced immune thrombocytopenia, in some infections, and in autoim-mune disorders such as systemic lupus erythematosus. It has been suggested that cell-mediated immunity, ie, lymphocyte activation, may alone be able to cause platelet damage and thrombocytopenia. Lymphocyte activation has been observed in response to autologous platelets in some patients with idiopathic thrombocy-topenic purpura. Whether this represents a true cellular immune response or whether the lymphocytes are reacting to immune complexes or otherwise altered platelets remains uncertain. Finally, it is known that bacterial endotoxin can cause thrombocytopenia di-rectly, usually involving activation of the complement system. Antibodies are not required for this reaction.

Table 27–13 shows a classification of im-munologic thrombocytopenias that are discussed in more detail in the following section.

IDIOPATHIC THROMBOCYTOPENIC PURPURA

Major Immunologic Features
- Antiplatelet antibodies demonstrable on platelets and in serum.
- Shortened platelet survival.
- Therapeutic response to prednisone and splenec-tomy.

General Considerations

Idiopathic thrombocytopenic purpura is an au-toimmune disorder characterized by increased platelet destruction by antiplatelet autoantibody. IgG autoan-tibodies sensitize the circulating platelets, leading to accelerated removal of these cells by the macrophages of the spleen and at times the liver and other compo-nents of the monocyte-macrophage system. Although there is a compensatory increase in platelet production by the bone marrow (total platelet turnover may be 10–20 times the normal rate), thrombocytopenia oc-curs, and, depending on the severity, gives rise to the 2 typical clinical features of the disease: purpura and bleeding.

Idiopathic thrombocytopenic purpura most often occurs in otherwise healthy children and young adults. Childhood idiopathic thrombocytopenic purpura often occurs within a few weeks following a viral infection, suggesting possible cross-immunization between viral and platelet antigens, or adsorption of immune com-plexes, or a hapten mechanism. Adult idiopathic thrombocytopenic purpura is less often associated with a preceding infection. An identical form of autoim-mune thrombocytopenia can also be associated with systemic lupus erythematosus, chronic lymphocytic leukemia, lymphomas, nonlymphoid malignancies, infectious mononucleosis, and other viral and bacterial infections. Certain drugs can also cause immune thrombocytopenia and these can produce a clinical picture that is indistinguishable from idiopathic thrombocytopenic purpura.

Although adult and childhood idiopathic throm-bocytopenic purpura appear to have similar basic pathophysiologic features, there are significant differ-ences in their course and therefore their treatment. Most children have spontaneous remissions within a few weeks to a few months, and splenectomy is rarely necessary. Adult patients, on the other hand, rarely have spontaneous remissions and usually require splenectomy within the first few months after diag-nosis. Although some authors have attempted to sepa-rate acute and chronic idiopathic thrombocytopenic purpura into 2 distinct entities, current clinical, im-munologic, and kinetic findings provide little justifica-tion for this distinction.

Immunologic Diagnosis

Harrington and co-workers first showed in 1951 that the plasma from most patients with idiopathic thrombocytopenic purpura contained a factor that caused thrombocytopenia when transfused into normal

Table 27–14. Tests for platelet autoantibodies in idiopathic thrombocytopenic purpura (ITP).

Methods	Percent Positive
Standard immunologic tests (agglutination, complement fixation, etc)	0
Transfusion of plasma from patients with ITP into normal donors	63–75
Platelet factor 3 release	65–70
^{14}C-serotonin release	60
Lymphocyte activation by autologous platelets	70
Lymphocyte activation by platelet-antibody immune complexes	90+
Phagocytosis of platelet-antibody immune complexes by granulocytes	90+
Measurement of platelet-associated IgG by competitive binding assays	90+
Radiolabeled Coombs antiglobulin test	90+
Enzyme-linked immunosorbent assay (ELISA)	90+

human recipients. Although the plasma factor was suspected of being an antibody, immunologic tests to detect serum antibodies (agglutination, complement fixation, etc) did not demonstrate the factor, since these tests are too insensitive to detect platelet autoantibody in idiopathic thrombocytopenic purpura and similar disorders. More sophisticated techniques have been developed for detection of antiplatelet antibodies in the past decade (Table 27–14). The so-called "immuno-injury" techniques (platelet factor 3 release, ^{14}C-serotonin release) detect antiplatelet antibodies in the serum of 60–70% of adult patients with idiopathic thrombocytopenic purpura. Recent methods for detecting platelet-autoantibody complexes by lymphocyte activation or ingestion by granulocytes, or competitive binding assays or antiglobulin tests for the measurement of antiplatelet antibodies on the platelet surface have shown positive results in almost all patients with idiopathic thrombocytopenic purpura. Unfortunately, all of these latter methods are generally too complex for routine clinical laboratory use, so in most cases the diagnosis of immune thrombocytopenia must be made without the benefit of a specific immunologic diagnosis.

Platelet Kinetics

^{51}Cr-platelet kinetic studies show that all patients with idiopathic thrombocytopenic purpura and other types of autoimmune thrombocytopenia have markedly shortened platelet survival times (T½ 0.1–30 hours; normal T½ 100–120 hours) and have normal or only slightly subnormal platelet recoveries at T_0 (40–80%; normal 60–80%). About 75% of patients have splenic platelet sequestration, and 25% have both splenic and hepatic sequestration. Patients with thrombocytopenia due to an enlarged splenic platelet pool can be easily distinguished from patients with autoimmune thrombocytopenia by these kinetic methods. Although it was felt initially that determination of the sites of platelet sequestration might be

useful in predicting the response to splenectomy, a recent report shows no significant difference in response rates based on presplenectomy platelet sequestration patterns. Both groups in this report had an 85–90% complete remission rate at 2 years' follow-up postsplenectomy.

Clinical Features

A. Symptoms and Signs: The onset may be acute, with sudden development of petechiae, ecchymoses, epistaxis, and gingival, gastrointestinal, or genitourinary tract bleeding. Alternatively, the disease may be gradual in onset and chronic in course. Often, however, chronic idiopathic thrombocytopenic purpura is slowly progressive or suddenly becomes acute.

B. Laboratory Findings: The platelet count is usually less than 20–30 thousand/μL in acute cases, and 30–100 thousand/μL in chronic cases. There may be moderate anemia due to blood loss and iron deficiency. The white blood count is normal or slightly increased but may be low in systemic lupus erythematosus. Platelets are often larger than normal on peripheral blood smear, and no immature white cells are present. The bone marrow shows normal or increased numbers of megakaryocytes and is otherwise normal. The megakaryocytes may be normal or immature in appearance but at times are larger than normal with increased numbers of nuclei.

Differential Diagnosis

All causes of thrombocytopenia must be considered when evaluating a patient with suspected idiopathic thrombocytopenic purpura (Table 27–15). Patients with idiopathic thrombocytopenic purpura characteristically feel and look well, and all physical and laboratory findings are normal except for thrombocytopenia and the associated purpura and possible

Table 27–15. Differential diagnosis of thrombocytopenic purpuras.

Thrombocytopenias due to increased platelet destruction
  Immune thrombocytopenias
    Idiopathic thrombocytopenic purpura
    Secondary autoimmune thrombocytopenias
    Drug-induced immune thrombocytopenias
    Posttransfusion purpura
    Neonatal immune thrombocytopenias
  Consumptive thrombocytopenias
    Thrombotic thrombocytopenic purpura
    Hemolytic-uremic syndrome
    Disseminated intravascular coagulation
    Vasculitis
    Sepsis
  Hypersplenism
Thrombocytopenias due to decreased platelet production
  Bone marrow suppression by drugs, alcohol, toxins, infections
  Aplastic anemia
  Leukemias and other bone marrow malignancies
  Megaloblastic anemia
  Refractory anemias, preleukemia, hematopoietic dysplasia

bleeding. Patients with "consumptive" thrombocytopenias, on the other hand, tend to be acutely ill, often with fever and evidence of multisystem disease, especially renal disease. These patients generally have microangiopathic hemolytic anemia, the fragmented red cells being a critical diagnostic finding on the peripheral blood smear. Abnormalities of clotting function are also often present. Patients with acute leukemia, aplastic anemia, and other serious bone marrow disorders are also often acutely ill, and bone marrow examination is diagnostic. Patients with hypersplenism sufficient to cause thrombocytopenia usually have an easily palpable spleen; hypersplenism alone rarely causes a platelet count of less than 50,000/μL.

Secondary causes of autoimmune thrombocytopenia, such as systemic lupus erythematosus, must be ruled out by appropriate laboratory tests. If a patient with apparent idiopathic thrombocytopenic purpura has been taking any suspicious drugs, the possibility of drug-induced thrombocytopenia must be considered.

Treatment

Splenectomy is the treatment of choice for adult patients with idiopathic thrombocytopenic purpura who have persistent symptomatic thrombocytopenia. Corticosteroids are usually able to increase the platelet count temporarily but probably do not alter the course of the underlying disease, and most patients relapse when steroids are tapered or discontinued. Adults rarely have spontaneous remissions. Splenectomy is therefore usually necessary in adults with idiopathic thrombocytopenic purpura within the first few months after diagnosis. Large doses of steroids over long periods of time should be avoided in these patients, as 75–90% will have prolonged complete remissions following splenectomy. Immunosuppressive therapy with cytotoxic drugs should generally not be used until the patient has had the benefit of splenectomy; this is particularly true for younger patients, since these drugs may cause serious late adverse effects.

Vincristine now seems to be the drug of choice for patients with autoimmune thrombocytopenia who do not respond to splenectomy, who relapse after an initial response to splenectomy, or in whom the risk of splenectomy is unacceptable. A significant increase in platelet count occurs in 70–80% of patients with refractory autoimmune thrombocytopenia treated with vincristine. Vincristine appears to be more effective, less toxic, and better tolerated than cyclophosphamide or other standard immunosuppressive drugs. Its mechanism of action in increasing the platelet count in autoimmune thrombocytopenia remains uncertain; it appears to work by a different mechanism than other immunosuppressive drugs.

Children with mild or moderately severe idiopathic thrombocytopenic purpura should be observed without therapy. Corticosteroids should be given when severe thrombocytopenia and bleeding occur, although the platelet count does not respond as consistently to steroids in children as in adults. Splenectomy should be considered in children only when severe thrombocytopenia persists for 3–6 months, since most children will have had a spontaneous remission by that time. The postsplenectomy state is much more likely to predispose to serious or overwhelming infection in young children than in adults. Immunosuppressive drugs should generally not be used in children.

DRUG–INDUCED IMMUNE THROMBOCYTOPENIAS

The principal drugs that may cause immune thrombocytopenic purpura are listed in Table 27–13. The best-studied example is the sedative apronalide (Sedormid) (no longer in use); the drugs most commonly used in clinical practice that can produce immune thrombocytopenic purpura are sulfonamides, thiazide diuretics, chlorpropamide, quinidine, and gold. A syndrome resembling acute drug-induced immune thrombocytopenia has also been observed in heroin addicts, although the mechanism of this kind of thrombocytopenia has not been proved.

There is a variable period of sensitization after initial exposure to the drug, but subsequent drug reexposure is rapidly followed by thrombocytopenia. Patients therefore usually give a history of having taken the drug in the past for at least several weeks if this is their first exposure. A very small plasma concentration of the drug and very small amounts of antibody may induce severe thrombocytopenia. The drug itself generally shows only weak and reversible binding to the platelet; the thrombocytopenia in most cases appears to be caused by adsorption of the drug-antibody complexes to the platelet membrane with complement activation.

Treatment consists mainly of withdrawal of the offending drug (or all drugs) and monitoring for return of normal platelet counts, generally within 7–10 days. Thrombocytopenia may persist if the drug is excreted slowly. When a patient who is taking a number of suspicious drugs is first seen, it is often impossible to tell whether he has drug-induced immune thrombocytopenia or idiopathic thrombocytopenic purpura. In vitro tests can now be used in some centers to confirm drug-antibody reactions involving platelets. In vivo drug challenges of sensitized patients for confirmation of drug-induced immune thrombocytopenia should be avoided as they are too hazardous.

POSTTRANSFUSION PURPURA

Posttransfusion purpura is an acute severe thrombocytopenic state appearing about 1 week after transfusion of a blood product. It occurs almost exclusively in women. It is mediated by an alloantibody, usually directed against the platelet PL_A^1 antigen. Platelets both with and without the PL_A^1 antigen are destroyed.

The diagnosis is suspected when acute thrombocytopenia occurs 7–10 days after blood transfusion.

Coagulation studies are normal, and the bone marrow shows abundant megakaryocytes. The anti-PL_A^1 antibody is often difficult to detect. Platelet aggregation of PL_A^1 platelets, inhibition of ADP aggregation of such platelets, and ^{51}Cr release from PL_A^1 platelets from patients with paroxysmal nocturnal hemoglobinuria have all been successful in detecting the antibody in some patients.

Gradual recovery from posttransfusion purpura usually occurs in 1–6 weeks. Corticosteroids do not appear to alter the course of the disease. Massive exchange transfusions have been associated with more rapid recovery, but severe transfusion reactions often occur. Aggressive plasmapheresis has also been shown to be effective without the risks of severe transfusion reactions.

IV. COAGULATION DISORDERS

HEMOPHILIA & VON WILLEBRAND'S DISEASE

Classic hemophilia and von Willebrand's disease are both congenital bleeding disorders caused by abnormalities of the factor VIII molecule complex. Hemophilia is an X-linked disorder characterized by severe deficiency of factor VIII procoagulant activity (VIII:C), which is measured in clotting assays. Von Willebrand's disease is an autosomally inherited disorder also characterized by a deficiency of VIII:C, but it is also associated with defective platelet function, resulting in a prolonged bleeding time. The abnormal platelet function in von Willebrand's disease is due to a deficiency of factor VIII–related protein (VIIIR), which is also known as von Willebrand factor (vWF). vWF activity is measured by testing the ability of plasma to support platelet agglutination by the antibiotic ristocetin or ristocetin cofactor (VIIIR:RC) activity.

The factor VIII/vWF complex consists of a heterogeneous population of glycoprotein multimers with molecular weights of 850,000 to 12×10^6. This heterogeneity can be demonstrated, and the different-sized multimers can be separated by SDS-agarose gel electrophoresis and crossed immunoelectrophoresis. It now seems clear that factor VIII procoagulant activity (VIII:C) is a basic property of the smaller subunits of the factor VIII molecule, while von Willebrand factor (vWF) activity is present only in the larger polymeric forms of the molecule.

Heterogeneous antibodies made to purified factor VIII detect antigenic determinants on VIIIR (VIIIR:Ag). VIIIR:Ag has been found to be normal in patients with classic hemophilia, indicating that these patients have a normal amount of the basic factor VIII molecule but that they lack the portion of the molecule necessary for normal procoagulant activity. The heter-

ologous antibodies therefore appear to recognize antigenic determinants distinct from the functional site responsible for procoagulant activity. Patients with von Willebrand's disease, on the other hand, have reduced levels of both VIII:C and VIIIR:Ag, indicating a true deficiency of factor VIII complex molecules. Measurement of VIII:C and VIIIR:Ag can therefore be used to differentiate between classic hemophilia and von Willebrand's disease and in most cases can differentiate between female carriers of hemophilia (heterozygotes) and normal individuals. Measurement of ristocetin cofactor (VIIIR:RC) can also be used to identify patients with von Willebrand's disease.

Human antibodies to factor VIII, unlike heterologous antibodies, are usually directed at antigenic determinants at the functional procoagulant site of factor VIII (VIII:CAg), and these antibodies are capable of blocking factor VIII clotting activity. These antibodies sometimes develop in patients with severe hemophilia after they have been transfused with factor VIII–containing blood products and sometimes develop spontaneously in otherwise healthy individuals. When present in high titer, they cause a severe hemorrhagic disorder that is difficult to correct with factor VIII transfusions since the transfused factor VIII is simply inactivated by the factor VIII antibodies (see next section).

CIRCULATING INHIBITORS OF COAGULATION

Abnormal bleeding is occasionally due to circulating inhibitors which block one or more plasma coagulation factors. These inhibitors, also called endogenous circulating anticoagulants, have in most cases been shown to be IgG antibodies. Inhibitors against factor VIII and against the prothrombin activator complex ("lupus inhibitor") occur most often, but inhibitors directed against factors V, IX, and XIII have also been reported. There are rare reports of human monoclonal proteins (especially IgM) with antibody activity directed against clotting components, eg, factor VIII, phospholipid. Inhibitors may appear abruptly and be associated with life-threatening hemorrhage or may be chronic and associated with little or no bleeding.

Factor VIII inhibitors develop in 5–20% of patients with classic hemophilia after they have been transfused with factor VIII–containing blood products; genetic factors appear to determine which patients develop inhibitors. Factor VIII inhibitors also occasionally occur spontaneously in women postpartum, in patients with autoimmune disorders such as systemic lupus erythematosus, and in older patients without demonstrable underlying disease. Rarely, the paraprotein in a monoclonal gammopathy has specific inhibitor activity against factor VIII or other clotting factors. High titer factor VIII inhibitors (antibodies) often cause serious bleeding and require aggressive treatment. Patients with serious bleeding can be given several times the calculated amount of factor VIII to saturate the inhibitor, provided the inhibitor titer is not too high. When bleeding cannot be stopped, even after giving large amounts of factor VIII, activated pro-thrombin complex concentrates should be given, as these will often stop the bleeding by providing acti-vated clotting factors which bypass the factor VIII step. If this is unsuccessful, aggressive large-volume plasmapheresis can be used to remove the inhibitor. Treatment of factor VIII inhibitors with immunosup-pressive drugs has also been successful in some cases.

The ''lupus inhibitor'' or ''lupus anticoagulant'' is seen in 5–10% of patients with systemic lupus ery-thematosus as well as in patients with a variety of other disorders. This inhibitor is characteristically directed against the prothrombin activator complex. Although patients with the ''lupus inhibitor'' often have signifi-cant prolongation of the partial thromboplastin time (and sometimes the prothrombin time), they do not have abnormal bleeding and do not require treatment. When patients with systemic lupus erythematosus who have inhibitors are treated with steroids, the inhibitors usually disappear.

V. BONE MARROW TRANSPLANTATION

Extensive studies with different species over a period of 25 years provided the experimental back-ground for bone marrow transplantation in humans. However the great majority of the initial human bone marrow transplants failed, in some cases due to the moribund condition of the recipient before grafting, but primarily as a result of histoincompatibility. More recently, these problems have been partly overcome, and improved results have been obtained in selected patients undergoing bone marrow transplantation.

The diseases for which bone marrow transplanta-tion has been performed are aplastic anemia, acute leukemia, immunodeficiency disorders, and occasion-ally miscellaneous disorders, including radiation acci-dents, solid malignant tumors sensitive to chemother-apy and radiotherapy, genetic disorders such as sickle cell disease and thalassemia, and malignant his-tiocytosis.

DONOR SELECTION FOR BONE MARROW TRANSPLANTATION

The critical factor in selection of an appropriate donor is histocompatibility. Syngeneic transplantation from an identical donor may be performed with either autologous bone marrow obtained from the patient before radiation or chemotherapy or with bone marrow from a genetically identical twin. The great majority of bone marrow transplants are obtained from allogeneic donors, which implies 2 possible major problems of histoincompatibility: graft rejection and graft-versus-host (GVH) disease. Rejection of the graft by the recipient is also known as failure of engraftment. GVH disease is a reaction against host tissues by immuno-competent lymphoid cells in the graft. The donor is chosen by HLA typing and MLC matching to reduce the likelihood of these complications of histoincom-patibility. HLA typing is performed on various mem-bers of the patient's family, and HLA-identical mem-bers are tested in MLC to determine whether reactions occur between their cells and the patient's cells. Unfor-tunately, many patients who might be candidates for bone marrow transplantation have no suitable donor. The chances are 25% that a full-blooded sibling will be HLA-identical. MLC tests are particularly important since there are rare examples of successful bone mar-row transplantation between donors and recipients who were HLA-nonidentical but MLC-nonreactive.

TECHNIQUES OF BONE MARROW TRANSPLANTATION

Bone marrow transplantation does not involve complicated surgery. The marrow is obtained by mul-tiple aspirations from the iliac crests of the donor under sterile conditions using spinal or general anesthesia. Multiple bone marrow sites are aspirated, with 1–3 mL of bone marrow being taken from each site. Up to 800 mL of bone marrow diluted with blood may be ob-tained during the procedure. The bone marrow is trans-ferred into tissue culture medium, passed through stainless steel mesh screens, and examined mi-croscopically to exclude potentially lethal marrow fat emboli. The marrow preparation containing $5–30 \times 10^9$ nucleated marrow cells is then infused intrave-nously into the recipient.

CLINICAL FEATURES

Preparation of Patient

This includes correction of severe anemia and thrombocytopenia by transfusion of red blood cells and platelets and vigorous treatment of infection if present. Excessive transfusion of blood products should be avoided since sensitization of the recipient will occur, increasing the risk of rejection of the bone marrow graft. Patients with severe combined immunodefi-ciency disease or immunosuppression may develop GVH disease from viable immunocompetent stem cells in transfused blood or plasma; it is therefore necessary to irradiate all blood products with 1500 rads before administration to the patient. The marrow donor should never be used prior to transplantation as a blood donor in order to avoid sensitization of the recipient.

Recipients with immunocompetent cells must be treated to suppress those cells and prevent rejection of the graft. This is usually not necessary for syngeneic grafts between identical twins. Current regimens use cyclophosphamide with or without total body irradiation immediately prior to engraftment. Failure of bone marrow engraftment after pretreatment with cyclophosphamide alone may be followed by successful engraftment if the recipient is reprepared with cyclophosphamide, procarbazine, and antithymocyte globulin for 4 days prior to transplantation.

Cyclosporin A is an antilymphocyte agent that appears to inhibit mitosis in the early stages of T cell differentiation but has little activity against unstimulated lymphocytes or hematopoietic cells. Several trials are currently assessing its role in clinical transplantation. It appears to enhance engraftment, diminish episodes of rejection, and significantly reduce GVH disease. These trials are also assessing the reported complication of nephrotoxicity in the short term and the possibility of lymphoma in the long term.

Supportive Care

It is essential to support the patient with platelet, red cell, and granulocyte transfusions and antibiotics as indicated pending evidence of engraftment and maintenance of satisfactory blood counts. Prophylactic granulocyte transfusions and germ-free protected environments reduce the number of serious infections in these patients.

Engraftment

Successful engraftment is shown by the recovery of hematopoietic and (later) immunologic functions. Hematopoietic function is indicated by a rising platelet, granulocyte, and reticulocyte count. This generally occurs in 2–4 weeks, well before evidence of establishment of immunocompetence. Assessment of immunologic status must be based on several tests since various aspects of cellular and humoral immunity may become functional at variable periods after engraftment.

DISEASES IN WHICH BONE MARROW TRANSPLANTATION MAY BE USEFUL

Aplastic Anemia

Severe aplastic anemia carries a grave prognosis, with a mortality rate of 80–90% in spite of treatment by means of transfusions, antibiotics, and androgens. Survival can be significantly improved with bone marrow transplantation. The patient with aplastic anemia should be observed for evidence of spontaneous recovery for a 3–4 week period after diagnosis. Continuing severe aplasia after this time interval increases the likelihood of fatal complications and decreases the chances for successful engraftment. Patients who have an identical twin should be transplanted as early as possible using the normal twin as marrow donor, since engraftment usually occurs easily, immunosuppressive therapy is not usually necessary, GVH disease does not occur, and patients usually have a normal survival after transplantation. Other patients are transplanted using HLA-identical MLC-compatible siblings as donors, when these are available. For al-

logeneic grafting, the recipient is given large doses of cyclophosphamide prior to bone marrow infusion to diminish the chances of graft rejection. GVH disease occurs in about 50% of patients who receive allogeneic bone marrow grafts and is severe or life-threatening in about 15% of patients. Long-term survival of transplanted children and young adults with aplastic anemia is close to 100% for identical twins, about 70% for HLA-identical siblings when the patient has not been sensitized by previous transfusions, and about 40% for HLA-identical siblings when the patient has been heavily transfused.

Acute Leukemia

In patients with acute leukemia, the abnormal population of leukemic cells in the bone marrow and the rest of the body must first be eradicated by intensive chemotherapy and whole body radiation before transplantation. Failure of bone marrow transplantation in acute leukemia in the past was often due to the advanced state of the disease and the poor condition of the patient by the time transplantation was undertaken. Patients are now receiving transplants earlier, often when they are in complete remission following initial chemotherapy. These patients are in much better condition to undergo bone marrow transplantation and have a much lower number of leukemia cells that must be eradicated prior to transplantation. Recent reports from several bone marrow transplantation centers indicate a 50–60% long-term survival rate for acute leukemia patients who have been transplanted in complete remission, as compared to only 15% when they are transplanted in relapse. These improved results appear to reflect better control of the leukemia, with fewer relapses after transplantation. GVH disease, however, continues to be an important problem, as it is in aplastic anemia.

Immunodeficiency

The principal indication for early bone marrow transplantation is severe combined immunodeficiency disease (see Chapter 25). Data from the NIH Organ Transplant Registry in January 1975 showed that 95 bone marrow transplants had been performed in 52 patients with immunodeficiency and that 22 patients had survived with functioning grafts in 18. Most survivors had received grafts from HLA-identical, MLC-nonreactive siblings. The causes of failure included lack of engraftment and death from infection.

COMPLICATIONS OF BONE MARROW TRANSPLANTATION

Failure of Engraftment

The graft fails to "take" or is rejected in about 15% of recipients with aplastic anemia. Engraftment rarely fails in patients with leukemia. Factors that may contribute to failure of engraftment include infusion of insufficient numbers of nucleated stem cells; reduced viability of the cells due to the handling procedures;

inadequate bone marrow "space" because of residual tumor or leukemic cells; and rejection by functioning immunocompetent host cells possibly sensitized by prior transfusion and not destroyed by preparatory immunosuppressive therapy. Finally, a potentially successful graft may fail because the recipient is in a terminal stage of illness and dies from preexisting infection before the graft becomes established. Careful selection of donors for histocompatibility, attention to the techniques of transplantation, and the clinical status of the recipient should reduce the incidence of failure of engraftment.

Graft-Versus-Host (GVH) Disease

This denotes the clinical and pathologic sequelae produced by immunocompetent cells in the graft against the histoincompatible cells of the recipient (see Chapter 6). Fatal GVH disease occurs in approximately 15% of grafted patients. In several studies significant GVH disease was found in about half of patients given an allogeneic bone marrow graft from an HLA-identical, MLC-nonreactive donor. Thus, there are biologically important genetically determined antigenic determinants on lymphoid cells, and some of these are not yet fully understood or characterized and may lead to GVH disease.

The clinical and pathologic findings of GVH disease occur mainly in the skin, gut, liver, and lymphoid system. The skin shows a fine maculopapular erythematous rash resembling measles, with maximal localization on the trunk. It has a fine "sandpaper" feel and may become confluent, hemorrhagic, and grossly exfoliative. The main gastrointestinal symptoms are diarrhea, malabsorption, and weight loss. Severe diarrhea may be associated with abdominal cramps and melena. Abnormalities in liver function include increases in serum bilirubin, alkaline phosphatase, and glutamic-oxaloacetic transaminase. The

effects on the lymphoid system are defects in cellular immunity with resulting infection, especially certain viral infections. A grading system for the severity of GVH disease is presented in Table 27–16.

Recently, more and more patients have been seen with **chronic GVH disease.** This is a chronic debilitating syndrome seen in long-term survivors following allogeneic bone marrow transplantation. Chronic GVH disease is characterized by progressive sclerodermalike skin involvement, sicca syndrome, and frequent infections, especially interstitial pneumonia and viral infections. Immunologic abnormalities are often seen, with hypergammaglobulinemia, autoimmune hemolytic anemia, monoclonal gammopathy, circulating immune complexes, etc. Chronic GVH disease appears to be a syndrome of disordered immune regulation, with features of immunodeficiency and autoimmunity.

Management of GVH disease is difficult. Most centers now give methotrexate routinely after marrow grafting to attempt suppression of immunocompetent cells in the graft, thereby preventing GVH reactions. Life-threatening exacerbations of GVH disease are usually treated with corticosteroids and antithymocyte globulin. Chronic GVH disease is treated with corticosteroids and immunosuppressive drugs.

Experimental approaches have been attempted, such as pregrafting immunosuppression of the graft. The cells in donor bone marrow responsible for GVH disease may be partly separated by fractionation on discontinuous albumin gradients before transplantation or eliminated by exposing them to foreign cells in vitro and inducing them to "commit suicide" by incorporating highly radioactive DNA precursors into their nuclei during blast transformation. Donors may be treated with soluble HLA antigens, or children with immunodeficiency disorders may be treated with alloantibodies of maternal origin.

Table 27–16. Clinicopathologic grading of the severity of human GVH disease.*

Parameter	Grade I	Grade II	Grade III	Grade IV
Skin rash	Mild	Moderately severe	Moderately severe	Severe
Gastrointestinal tract abnormalities	Nil	Mild	Moderately severe	Severe
Liver dysfunction	Nil	Mild	Moderately severe	Severe
Overall clinical status	Unchanged	Unchanged	Significant impairment	Marked impairment
Microscopic findings				
Skin	Focal or diffuse vacuolar degeneration of epidermal basal cells and acanthocytes	Basal vacuolar degeneration; spongiosis; dyskeratosis and degeneration of epidermal cells	Spaces from necrosis of basal cells and acanthocytes; separation at dermal-epidermal junction	Loss of entire epidermal layer
Gut	Focal dilatation and degeneration of the mucosal glands	Changes in mucosal and intestinal glands	Focal mucosal denudation	Diffuse mucosal denudation.
Liver	Degeneration and necrosis of parenchyma and epithelium of small bile ducts (<25% bile ducts affected)	25–49% bile ducts affected	50–74% bile ducts affected	>75% bile ducts affected.

*Compiled from data in Storb R et al: Treatment of established human graft-versus-host disease by antithymocyte globulin. *Blood* 1974;44:47.

GVH disease can also have a beneficial effect. Transplanted acute leukemia patients who develop GVH disease have a lower incidence of recurrent leukemia, suggesting that GVH disease may help suppress the host leukemic cells.

Infection

Infection is the most common fatal complication of aplastic anemia, acute leukemia, and immunodeficiency disorders; infection also is a common cause of death after bone marrow transplantation. The increased susceptibility to infection following bone marrow transplantation is partly due to the cytotoxic and immunosuppressive therapy given before and after transplantation, but it is also due to immunosuppression due to GVH reactions and inadequate immunologic reconstitution.

Bacterial infections are most frequent during the marked granulocytopenia that occurs just before and after transplantation. The patient may survive these initial infections, but, if engraftment is not successful or if GVH disease progresses, infection with fungi (eg, *Candida, Aspergillus*) and other opportunistic organisms is more likely. Mixed or bacterial and fungal infections are not uncommon.

Severe interstitial pneumonitis occurs in 25–50% of patients in the first 6 months after transplantation, with cytomegalovirus found in 30% and *Pneumocystis carinii* in 10% of patients. In the remaining cases, the cause is not clear. However, there is a positive correlation between interstitial pneumonia and GVH disease and previous total body irradiation. Approximately half of the cases run a fatal course.

Relapse of Malignancy

Recurrent leukemia in transplanted patients is less frequent now that leukemia patients are receiving transplants while in remission. Relapses are infrequent beyond 1 year posttransplantation, so most disease-free survivors for more than 1 year are probably cured of their leukemia.

It will be necessary to monitor long-term bone marrow transplantation survivors for the development of other malignancies, especially lymphoreticular ones. Both human and experimental subjects with chronic allograft rejection and long-term immunosuppression show an increased incidence of malignancy. Total body irradiation and cyclophosphamide in high doses might also predispose to the development of malignancy.

CONCLUSION

Bone marrow transplantation is a highly specialized investigational procedure which should be performed only in referral centers with facilities for the necessary investigatory work and full patient support. At present, the 3 main indications for allogeneic bone marrow transplantation are aplastic anemia, acute leukemia, and severe immunodeficiency. Successful long-term uncomplicated engraftment is most likely with a syngeneic identical twin. GVH disease and infection remain major factors in determining patient survival following allogeneic transplantation, even in those who appear compatible by present methods of HLA and MLC testing. Recurrent leukemia also limits survival in patients transplanted for leukemia. Effective methods to circumvent or treat these complications are necessary before bone marrow transplantation can be used more widely as a therapeutic procedure.

• • •

References

Plasma Cell Dyscrasias

Bataille R, Sany J: Solitary myeloma: Clinical and prognostic features in a review of 114 cases. *Cancer* 1981;**48**:845.

Brouet J-C & others: Biologic and clinical significance of cryoglobulins. *Am J Med* 1974;**57**:775.

Cohen AS, Wegelius O: Classification of amyloid: 1979–1980. *Arthritis Rheum* 1980;**23**:644.

Grey HM, Kohler PF: Cryoimmunoglobulins. *Semin Hematol* 1973;**10**:87.

Isobe T, Osserman EF: Patterns of amyloidosis and their association with plasma cell dyscrasia, monoclonal immunoglobulins and Bence Jones proteins. *N Engl J Med* 1974;**290**:474.

Jancelewicz Z & others: IgD multiple myeloma: Review of 133 cases. *Arch Intern Med* 1975;**135**:87.

Kyle RA, Bayrd ED: *The Monoclonal Gammopathies: Multiple Myeloma and Related Plasma-Cell Disorders.* Thomas, 1976.

Kyle RA, Greipp PR, Banks PM: The diverse picture of gamma heavy-chain disease: Report of seven cases and review of the literature. *Mayo Clin Proc* 1981;**56**:439.

Kyle RA, Robinson RA, Katzmann JA: The clinical aspects of biclonal gammopathies: Review of 57 cases. *Am J Med* 1981;**71**:999.

Mackenzie MR, Fudenberg HH: Macroglobulinemia: An analysis of 40 patients. *Blood* 1972;**39**:874.

McIntyre OR: Multiple myeloma. *N Engl J Med* 1979;**301**:193.

Merlini G, Waldenström JG, Jayakar SD: A new improved clinical staging system for multiple myeloma based on analysis of 123 treated patients. *Blood* 1980;**55**:1011.

Ritzmann SE & others: Idiopathic (asymptomatic) monoclonal gammopathies. *Arch Intern Med* 1975;**135**:96.

Stone MJ, Frenkel EP: The clinical spectrum of light chain myeloma. *Am J Med* 1975;**58**:601.

Wiltshaw E: The natural history of extramedullary plasmacytoma and its relationship to solitary myeloma of bone and myelomatosis. *Medicine* 1976;**55**:217.

Leukemias

Berard CW et al: Current concepts of leukemia and lymphoma: Etiology, pathogenesis, and therapy. *Ann Intern Med* 1976; **85**:351.

Bowman WP, Mauer A: The role of cell markers in the management of leukemia. *Prog Hematol* 1981; **12**:165.

Bradstock KF et al: Immunofluorescent and biochemical studies of terminal deoxynucleotidyl transferase in acute leukemia. *Br J Haematol* 1981; **47**:121.

Cline MJ & others: Acute leukemia: Biology and treatment. *Ann Intern Med* 1979; **91**:758.

Foon KA et al: Immunologic classification of acute lymphoblastic leukemia: Implications for normal lymphoid differentiation. *Blood* 1980; **56**:1120.

Golomb HM et al: Hairy cell leukemia: A clinical review based on 71 cases. *Ann Intern Med* 1978; **89**:677.

Greaves MF et al: Immunologically defined subclasses of acute lymphoblastic leukaemia in children: Their relationship to presentation features and prognosis. *Br J Haematol* 1981; **48**:179.

Jansen J et al: Splenectomy in hairy cell leukemia: A retrospective multicenter analysis. *Cancer* 1981; **47**:2066.

Koeffler HP, Golde DW: Chronic myelogenous leukemia: New concepts. (2 parts.) *N Engl J Med* 1981; **304**:1201, 1269.

Koziner B et al: Characterization of B-cell leukemias: A tentative immunomorphological scheme. *Blood* 1980; **56**:815.

Leventhal BG et al: Immune reactivity to tumor antigens in leukemia and lymphoma. *Semin Hematol* 1978; **15**:157.

Metzgar RS, Mohanakumar T: Tumor-associated antigens of human leukemic cells. *Semin Hematol* 1978; **15**:139.

Murphy S, Hersh E: Immunotherapy of leukemia and lymphoma. *Semin Hematol* 1978; **15**:181.

Nadler LM et al: Diagnosis and treatment of human leukemias and lymphomas utilizing monoclonal antibodies. *Prog Hematol* 1981; **12**:187.

Nadler LM et al: A unique cell surface antigen identifying lymphoid malignancies of B cell origin. *J Clin Invest* 1981; **67**:134.

Naeim F et al: Hairy cell leukemia: A heterogenous chronic lymphoproliferative disorder. *Am J Med* 1978; **65**:479.

Rowley JD: Do all leukemic cells have an abnormal karyotype? *N Engl J Med* 1981; **305**:164.

Thiel E et al: Multimarker classification of acute lymphoblastic leukemia: Evidence of further T subgroups and evaluation of their clinical significance. *Blood* 1980; **56**:759.

Lymphomas

Berard CW et al: A multidisciplinary approach to non-Hodgkin's lymphomas. *Ann Intern Med* 1981; **94**:218.

Bernard A et al: Cell surface characterization of malignant T cells from lymphoblastic lymphoma using monoclonal antibodies: Evidence for phenotypic differences between malignant T cells from patients with acute lymphoblastic leukemia and lymphoblastic lymphoma. *Blood* 1981; **57**:1105.

Bloomfield CD et al: Clinical utility of lymphocyte surface markers combined with the Lukes-Collins histologic classification in adult lymphoma. *N Engl J Med* 1979; **301**:512.

Cullen MH et al: Angio-immunoblastic lymphadenopathy: Report of 10 cases and review of the literature. *Q J Med* 1979; **48**:151.

Hansen H, Koziner B, Clarkson B: Marker and kinetic studies in the non-Hodgkin's lymphomas. *Am J Med* 1981; **71**:107.

Kaplan HS: Review: Hodgkin's disease: Biology, treatment, and prognosis. *Blood* 1981; **57**:813.

Lukes RJ, Tindle BH: Immunoblastic lymphadenopathy: A hyperimmune entity resembling Hodgkin's disease. *N Engl J Med* 1975; **292**:1.

Lukes RJ et al: Immunologic approach to non-Hodgkin's lymphomas and related leukemias. *Semin Hematol* 1978; **15**:322.

Lutzner M et al: Cutaneous T-cell lymphomas: The Sézary syndrome, mycosis fungoides, and related disorders. *Ann Intern Med* 1975; **83**:534.

Miller RA, Levy R: Response of cutaneous T cell lymphoma to therapy with hybridoma monoclonal antibody. *Lancet* 1981; **2**:226.

Rosen PJ et al: Convoluted lymphocytic lymphoma in adults. *Ann Intern Med* 1978; **89**:319.

Rosenberg SA: Non-Hodgkin's lymphomas: Selection of treatment on the basis of histologic type. *N Engl J Med* 1979; **301**:924.

Ziegler JL: Burkitt's lymphoma. *N Engl J Med* 1981; **305**:735.

Infectious Mononucleosis

Britton S et al: Epstein-Barr-virus immunity and tissue distribution in a fatal case of infectious mononucleosis. *N Engl J Med* 1978; **298**:89.

Haynes BF et al: Characterization of thymus-derived lymphocyte subsets in acute Epstein-Barr-virus-induced infectious mononucleosis. *J Immunol* 1979; **122**:699.

Horwitz CA et al: Clinical and laboratory evaluation of infants and children with Epstein-Barr virus-induced infectious mononucleosis. *Blood* 1981; **57**:933.

Schnipper LE: The Epstein-Barr virus and human lymphoproliferative disorders. *Prog Hematol* 1981; **12**:275.

Schooley RT et al: Development of suppressor T lymphocytes for Epstein-Barr virus-induced B-lymphocyte outgrowth during acute infectious mononucleosis: Assessment by two quantitative systems. *Blood* 1981; **57**:510.

Tosato G et al: Activation of suppressor T cells during Epstein-Barr virus-induced infectious mononucleosis. *N Engl J Med* 1979; **301**:1133.

Leukopenias

Abdou NI et al: Suppressor cell-mediated neutropenia in Felty's syndrome. *J Clin Invest* 1978; **61**:738.

Blumfelder TM, Logue GL, Shimm DS: Felty's syndrome: Effects of splenectomy upon granulocyte count and granulocyte-associated IgG. *Ann Intern Med* 1981; **94**:623.

Harmon DC, Weitzman SA, Stossel TP: A staphylococcal slide test for detection of antineutrophil antibodies. *Blood* 1980; **56**:64.

Kelton JG et al: The use of in vitro technics to study drug-induced pancytopenia. *N Engl J Med* 1979; **301**:621.

Lightsey AL et al: Immune neutropenia. *Ann Intern Med* 1977; **86**:60.

Linch DC et al: Abnormalities of T-cell subsets in patients with neutropenia and an excess of lymphocytes in the bone marrow. *Br J Haematol* 1981; **48**:137.

Logue GL, Shimm DS: Autoimmune granulocytopenia. *Annu Rev Med* 1980; **31**:191.

Logue GL et al: Antibody-dependent lymphocyte-mediated granulocyte cytotoxicity in man. *Blood* 1978; **51**:97.

Starkebaum G et al: Autoimmune neutropenia in systemic lupus erythematosus. *Arthritis Rheum* 1978; **21**:504.

Taetle R et al: Drug-induced agranulocytosis: In vitro evidence for immune suppression of granulopoiesis and a cross-reacting lymphocyte antibody. *Blood* 1979; **54**:501.

Red Cell Disorders

Abdou NI et al: Heterogeneity of pathogenetic mechanisms in

aplastic anemia: Efficacy of therapy based on in-vitro results. *Ann Intern Med* 1981;**95**:43.

Applebaum FR, Fefer A: The pathogenesis of aplastic anemia. *Semin Hematol* 1981;**18**:241.

Bacigalupo A et al: Severe aplastic anaemia: Correlation of in vitro tests with clinical response to immunosuppression in 20 patients. *Br J Haematol* 1981;**47**:423.

Gale RP et al: Aplastic anemia: Biology and treatment. *Ann Intern Med* 1981;**95**:477.

Garratty G, Petz LD: Drug-induced immune hemolytic anemia. *Am J Med* 1975;**58**:398.

Kagan WA et al: Studies of the pathogenesis of aplastic anemia. *Am J Med* 1979;**66**:444.

Krantz SB: Diagnosis and treatment of pure red cell aplasia. *Med Clin North Am* 1976;**60**:945.

Messner HA et al: Control of antibody-mediated pure red cell aplasia by plasmapheresis. *N Engl J Med* 1981;**304**:1334.

Petz LD, Garratty G: *Acquired Immune Hemolytic Anemias.* Churchill Livingstone, 1980.

Young N: Aplastic anemia: Research themes and clinical issues. *Prog Hematol* 1981;**12**:227.

Platelet Disorders

Abramson N et al: Post-transfusion purpura: Immunologic aspects and therapy. *N Engl J Med* 1974;**291**:1163.

Cimo PL & others: Detection of drug-dependent antibodies by the ^{51}Cr lysis test: Documentation of immune thrombocytopenia induced by diphenylhydantoin, diazepam, and sulfisoxazole. *Am J Hematol* 1977;**2**:65.

Cines DB, Schrieber AD: Immune thrombocytopenia: Use of Coombs antiglobulin to detect platelet IgG and C3. *N Engl J Med* 1979;**300**:106.

Dixon R, Rosse W, Ebbert L: Quantitative determination of antibody in idiopathic thrombocytopenic purpura. *N Engl J Med* 1975;**292**:230.

Gudino M, Miller WV: Application of the enzyme-linked immunospecific assay (ELISA) for the detection of platelet antibodies. *Blood* 1981;**57**:32.

Handin RI, Stossel TP: Effect of corticosteroid therapy on the phagocytosis of antibody-coated platelets by human leukocytes. *Blood* 1978;**51**:771.

Handin RI, Stossel TP: Phagocytosis of antibody-coated platelets by human granulocytes. *N Engl J Med* 1974;**290**:989.

Karpatkin S: Review: Autoimmune thrombocytopenic purpura. *Blood* 1980;**56**:329.

Kelton JG et al: Comparison of two direct assays for platelet associated IgG (PAIgG) in assessment of immune and nonimmune thrombocytopenia. *Blood* 1980;**55**:424.

Kelton JG et al: Drug-induced thrombocytopenia is associated with increased binding of IgG to platelets both in vivo and in vitro. *Blood* 1981;**58**:524.

Kernoff LM, Blake KCH, Shackleton D: Influence of the amount of platelet-bound IgG on platelet survival and site of sequestration in autoimmune thrombocytopenia. *Blood* 1980;**55**:730.

Kim HD, Boggs DR: A syndrome resembling idiopathic thrombocytopenic purpura in ten patients with diverse forms of cancer. *Am J Med* 1979;**67**:371.

Luiken GA et al: Platelet-associated IgG in immune thrombocytopenic purpura. *Blood* 1977;**50**:317.

McMillan R: Chronic idiopathic thrombocytopenic purpura. *N Engl J Med* 1981;**304**:1135.

McMillan R, Tani P, Mason D: The demonstration of antibody binding to platelet-associated antigens in patients with immune thrombocytopenic purpura. *Blood* 1980;**56**:993.

Morse BS, Giuliani D, Nussbaum M: Quantitation of platelet-associated IgG by radial immunodiffusion. *Blood* 1981;**57**:809.

Coagulation Disorders

Acquired hemophilia. (Editorial.) *Lancet* 1981;**1**:255.

Herbst KD et al: Syndrome of acquired inhibitor of factor VIII responsive to cyclophosphamide and prednisone. *Ann Intern Med* 1981;**95**:575.

Hoyer LW et al: Review: The factor VIII complex: Structure and function. *Blood* 1981;**58**:1.

Hultin MB et al: Heterogeneity of factor VIII antibodies: Further immunochemical and biological studies. *Blood* 1977;**49**:807.

Kasper CK: Management of inhibitors of factor VIII. *Prog Hematol* 1981;**12**:143.

Schleider MA et al: A clinical study of the lupus anticoagulant. *Blood* 1976;**48**:499.

Slocombe GW et al: The role of intensive plasma exchange in the prevention and management of haemorrhage in patients with inhibitors to factor VIII. *Br J Haematol* 1981;**47**:577.

Switzer ME, McKee PA: Immunologic studies of native and modified human factor VIII/von Willebrand factor. *Blood* 1979;**54**:310.

Bone Marrow Transplantation

Bortin MM, Rimm AA: Treatment of 144 patients with severe aplastic anemia using immunosuppression and allogeneic marrow transplantation: A report from the International Bone Marrow Transplant Registry. *Transplant Proc* 1981;**13**:227.

Fefer A et al: Bone marrow transplantation for refractory acute leukemia in 34 patients with identical twins. *Blood* 1981;**57**:421.

Graze PR, Gale RP: Chronic graft versus host disease: A syndrome of disordered immunity. *Am J Med* 1979;**66**:611.

Hows J et al: Immunosuppression with cyclosporin A in allogeneic bone marrow transplantation for severe aplastic anaemia: Preliminary studies. *Br J Haematol* 1981;**48**:227.

Storb R et al: Bone marrow transplantation for the treatment of hematologic malignancy and of aplastic anemia. *Transplant Proc* 1981;**13**:221.

Storb R et al: Marrow transplantation in thirty untransfused patients with severe aplastic anemia. *Ann Intern Med* 1980;**92**:30.

Sullivan KM et al: Chronic graft-versus-host disease in 52 patients: Adverse natural course and successful treatment with combination immunosuppression. *Blood* 1981;**57**:267.

Thomas ED et al: Marrow transplantation for acute nonlymphoblastic leukemia in first remission. *N Engl J Med* 1979;**301**:597.

Thomas ED et al: Marrow transplantation for patients with acute lymphoblastic leukemia in remission. *Blood* 1979;**54**:468.

Weiden PL et al: Antileukemic effect of chronic graft-versus-host disease: Contribution to improved survival after allogeneic marrow transplantation. *N Engl J Med* 1981;**304**:1529.

28 | Allergic Diseases

Abba I. Terr, MD

Allergy accounts for a substantial number of human diseases with significant morbidity. The immune response in allergic diseases involves the same process of antigen recognition and the same humoral and cellular effector mechanisms as in immunologic defense against infectious microorganisms, toxins, neoplasms, and tissue grafts. In allergy, however, disease results from the deleterious effect of the resultant inflammatory reaction to environmental antigens ("allergens") that are often not intrinsically harmful. Allergic diseases have been classified by Gell and Coombs into 4 types based on the nature of the immunologic reaction:

Type I: IgE antibodies fixed to mast cells react with antigen, triggering release of histamine and activation of slow-reacting substance (SRS-A) and eosinophil chemotactic factor (ECF-A). This is the mechanism responsible for atopy, anaphylaxis, urticaria, and angioedema (Chapter 18).

Type II: IgG or IgM antibodies react with antigen on target cells and activate complement, causing cell lysis. This occurs in certain types of drug reactions.

Type III: IgG or IgM antibodies form complexes with antigen and complement, generating neutrophil chemotactic factors, with resultant local tissue inflammation. The Arthus reaction, serum sickness, and hypersensitivity lung diseases involve this mechanism.

Type IV: Sensitized T lymphocytes react with antigen, producing inflammation through the action of lymphokines. The principal example is allergic contact dermatitis.

Certain allergic diseases may be expressions of 2 or more types. This chapter will deal primarily with type I allergy, whereas the remaining types are discussed throughout the clinical immunology chapters.

ATOPY

About one out of every 10 persons in the USA suffers from symptomatic atopic disease. The most common form of the disease is allergic rhinitis, usually seasonal pollen allergy (hay fever). Less frequently, atopic disease is expressed as bronchial asthma or atopic dermatitis, and rarely as gastrointestinal food allergy. The patient may have 2 or more manifestations of the atopic state, but not necessarily at the same time.

Atopic allergy is a type I hypersensitivity reaction to environmental antigens (allergens) in genetically susceptible individuals who produce IgE antibodies to allergens such as pollens, molds, house dust, animal danders, or foods. Exposure to the offending allergen results in the release of mediators, including histamine, SRS-A, and ECF-A, in the target organ. The action of these mediators on blood vessels, smooth muscle, and secretory glands and the accompanying edema and cellular infiltrate are responsible for the clinical manifestations and pathologic features of the disease. Individual allergic sensitivities can usually be identified accurately, but the clinical manifestations are modified and influenced by many nonimmunologic factors such as infections, emotions, and drugs.

Genetic factors have long been suspected in atopy and are complex. There is a strong familial clustering of cases. IgE antibody responses occur in normal persons, so the phenotypic expression of atopy may be an enhanced absorption or processing of antigen prior to its exposure to IgE antibody–forming cells. There is evidence that specificities of IgE antibodies in hay fever are determined by immune response (Ir) genes closely linked to the HLA histocompatibility gene complex. Total serum IgE concentration, which is typically elevated in atopy, is controlled by a separate non-HLA gene.

Atopic Allergens

The patient with atopic disease may be sensitive to one or many allergens, and the success of treatment frequently depends on their identification.

A. Inhalants: Plant pollens, fungal spores, animal danders, and certain airborne particles in the home are the most common inhalant allergens.

Wind-pollinated (anemophilous) plants discharge large numbers of light-weight buoyant pollen grains into the air that can be dispersed by wind currents over a wide area. Within each geographic location, the common allergenic trees, grasses, and weeds pollinate each year during a specific and predictable season. For example, in the midwestern USA the important allergenic trees—maple, elm, oak, and birch—pollinate for 6 or 8 weeks beginning with the spring thaw; grass pollen appears principally during June and

July; and the weeds pollinate from the middle of August until the first frost. Pollinating seasons in the Far West are long and overlapping. In the San Francisco Bay Area, for example, there are about 12 important allergenic trees with pollen seasons covering the period from December through September; this overlaps with the grass and weed pollen season, which begins in April and continues through October. Allergists must be familiar with the allergenic plants and pollinating seasons in their area. Air-sampling devices for identifying and quantitating pollen are available, but their use requires knowledge of pollen morphology.

Plants with attractive flowers are generally insect-pollinated, producing small amounts of heavy pollen that do not become airborne and are thus not usually inhaled.

Spores of fungi in soil and on decaying vegetation are important aeroallergens and are found in air samples in significant quantities throughout the year except when there is snow cover on the ground. Although sensitivity to fungi is less common than pollen allergy, the spores of *Alternaria, Hormodendrum, Helminthosporium, Aspergillus, Pullularia, Mucor, Rhizopus, Penicillium,* and others are important allergens for some patients. Rusts and smuts that infect certain crops and grasses also produce allergenic spores.

In certain localities, insect debris has been identified as the cause of allergic symptoms.

House dust is the most common indoor allergen. For many dust-sensitive patients, the allergen is a house dust mite, *Dermatophagoides farinae* or *Dermatophagoides pteronyssimus*. These mites flourish on human skin scales and are found especially in dust from pillows and mattresses. Feathers in down pillows, quilts, comforters, sleeping bags, or jackets may be allergenic. Danders or excretions from household pets (cats, dogs, hamsters, guinea pigs) or from horses, farm stock, or zoo animals also cause allergy.

The patient's occupation is sometimes responsible for atopic allergy, as in "baker's asthma," where chronic inhalation of wheat flour causes allergic rhinitis or asthma.

B. Ingestants: Absorption of allergens from the alimentary tract can lead to IgE antibody production with subsequent allergic symptoms to foods, food additives, and drugs.

C. Contactants: Direct skin contact with a pollen or food can cause localized urticaria or systemic allergic symptoms in a patient highly sensitive to the allergen.

SKIN TESTING FOR IMMEDIATE HYPERSENSITIVITY

Skin testing is the method generally used to confirm specific sensitivity in patients with atopic disease or anaphylaxis after the history has suggested the relevant allergens for testing. Within minutes after introduction of the allergen, histamine released from skin mast cells causes vasodilatation (erythema), localized edema from increased vascular permeability (wheal), and pruritus. The skin reacts to allergen in almost all patients with type I allergy, even though their symptoms occur in other target organs, such as the nose, conjunctiva, lungs, or gastrointestinal tract. Many tests with different allergens can be performed simultaneously. Skin testing is convenient, safe, and reliable, and experience over many years has shown it to be useful for diagnosis in most patients with suspected allergic disease if care is taken to correlate the findings with the history and other clinical information.

Antihistaminic drugs inhibit or diminish skin test responses and so must be discontinued 24 hours or more before testing. Hydroxyzine is inhibitory for as long as 1 week. Xanthines, sympathomimetic drugs, corticosteroids, and cromolyn sodium do not inhibit immediate skin test reactions and need not be withdrawn prior to testing.

Best results are obtained by using a combination of cutaneous and intracutaneous methods, and each test series should include the diluent as a control. Some allergists also include histamine or a nonspecific histamine liberator (or both) as positive controls, although these are not necessary for routine use.

Cutaneous Tests

Cutaneous tests should always be done first. Either prick or scratch testing can be used. The tests are applied to the back or to the volar surfaces of the forearms, depending upon the number of tests. The skin is cleansed with a sterile alcohol pledget and then wiped dry. In prick testing, a drop of concentrated extract is applied and a needle prick of the skin is made through the drop. After 20 minutes, the drop is wiped off and the reaction is quantitated and recorded as indicated in Table 28–1. When properly done, the control is negative, and a result 2+ or greater is significant. Allergens giving a negative or 1+ prick test should be retested intracutaneously.

Scratch tests are done by making a short linear scratch in the skin to which the allergen is then applied.

Table 28–1. Wheal and erythema skin tests.

	Reaction	Appearances
Prick	Neg	No wheal or erythema.
	1+	No wheal; erythema < 20 mm in diameter.
	2+	No wheal; erythema > 20 mm in diameter.
	3+	Wheal and erythema.
	4+	Wheal with pseudopods; erythema.
Intracutaneous	Neg	Same as control.
	1+	Wheal twice as large as control; erythema < 20 mm in diameter.
	2+	Wheal twice as large as control; erythema > 20 mm in diameter.
	3+	Wheal 3 times as large as control; erythema.
	4+	Wheal with pseudopods; erythema.

This method is more likely to produce nonspecific irritant reactions, causes more discomfort to the patient, and occasionally leaves scars.

Intracutaneous Tests

Negative or questionable prick tests can be further evaluated by the intracutaneous test. This is a more sensitive technique but has the disadvantage of being more likely to produce a systemic reaction in a highly sensitive subject. Intracutaneous tests should always be done on the extremities. The lateral aspect of the upper arm is the preferred site, but the volar aspect of the forearm may be used. The number of intracutaneous tests should be limited to about 12 at one sitting even though the allergens have been shown to be prick test–negative for that patient.

The skin is wiped with a sterile alcohol pledget as for any injection. No more than 0.01 mL (preferably 0.005 mL) of sterile extract is injected intracutaneously and the reaction read in 20 minutes as indicated in Table 28–1. A 2+ or greater reaction is considered a positive test. Some allergens give false-positive irritant reactions if a high concentration is injected, so the proper concentration is important and must be determined for each allergen. A 1:500 (w/v) dilution of pollens and fungi is generally satisfactory for routine use. Some allergists use serial dilution titrations for each allergen, but this is time-consuming and rarely provides more diagnostic information than a single properly selected dilution, except in Hymenoptera insect venom allergy testing.

Selection of Tests

The specific allergens to be tested should be determined by the history. Table 28–2 lists the important pollen and mold allergens for patients living in the San Francisco Bay Area. Extracts of pollens, fungi, house dust, feathers, danders from various animals, and other common inhalant allergens are readily available commercially, but occasionally it is necessary to test material obtained from the patient's home or place of work.

Skin testing in patients with suspected food allergy is discussed elsewhere.

The intensity of the skin test reaction is also influenced by a number of factors not directly related to the patient's symptoms, such as the potency of the extract and reactivity of the skin. The size of the skin test response therefore should not be used to indicate how "allergic" the patient is to that particular allergen, although it should be considered in assessing the possible risk of a systemic reaction in immunotherapy.

The radioallergosorbent test (RAST) as described in Chapter 18 semiquantitatively measures IgE antibodies in serum, avoiding the potential risk or discomfort of skin testing. While valuable for research purposes, the test has limited use clinically because it is applicable only to those allergens that can be chemically coupled to the immunosorbent and is less sensitive than skin testing. Furthermore, results are influenced by high levels of total serum IgE and by IgG blocking antibody in patients who have received immunotherapy.

Table 28–2. Allergenic plant pollens and mold spores in the San Francisco Bay Area.*

Trees and Shrubs	Weeds	Grasses	Fungi
Acacia	Beach sandbur	Bermuda	*Alternaria*
Alder	Cocklebur	Bluegrass	*Aspergillus*
Ash	English	Brome	*Cephalothecium*
Birch	plantain	Orchard	*Fusarium*
Box elder	Lamb's	Perennial rye	*Helminthospo-*
Cottonwood	quarters	Sweet vernal	*rium*
Cypress	Mugwort	Velvet	*Hormodendrum*
Elm	Pickleweed	Wild oat	*Mucor*
Juniper	Pigweed		*Penicillium*
Live oak	Ragweed,		*Rhizopus*
Mulberry	false		
Olive	Ragweed,		
Privet	western		
Sycamore	Russian thistle		
Walnut	Sheep sorrel		
	Wingscale		

*Example of one area's allergenic pollens. For further details regarding other geographic areas, see Samter M, Durham OC: *Regional Allergy of the US, Canada, Mexico and Cuba.* Thomas, 1955; and Roth A: *Allergy in the World.* Univ Press of Hawaii, 1978.

IMMUNOTHERAPY
(Hyposensitization)

Treatment of allergic disease requires long-term use of a variety of measures, including avoidance of allergens, drug therapy, and immunotherapy. It must be individualized and periodically reassessed.

The offending allergen should be avoided if possible. In food or drug allergy, this can be accomplished once the offending allergen is identified. Elimination of inhalant allergens is generally more difficult. Removal of the animal pet from the household, dust control measures, synthetic materials in pillow stuffing, and a dehumidifier to inhibit molds are all helpful when indicated, but it is difficult to control airborne pollens or mold spores. Avoidance of pollens and molds from outdoor sources is possible only if the patient can remain indoors in an air-conditioned environment.

Immunotherapy is effective in reducing symptoms of allergic rhinitis in patients with seasonal pollen allergy and is probably effective also in mold or dust allergy. Several immunologic changes occur during the course of immunotherapy in atopic patients. Circulating IgE antibody increases slightly during the initial months of treatment and then gradually falls below pretreatment levels over a period of several years. However, it is rarely eliminated completely; ie, a true state of desensitization is seldom achieved.

Blocking antibody, which is an IgG antibody with specificity for the injected allergen that binds circulating allergen without initiating a type I reaction, appears in the serum of most treated patients. The normal postseasonal rise in IgE antibody to pollens is diminished, suggesting that treatment may induce a form of partial immunologic tolerance.

Clinical improvement during immunotherapy correlates better with blocking antibody response than with other immunologic changes, but a combination of several mechanisms might be required for optimal results. This treatment is effective, but a better understanding of the mechanism of immunotherapy should lead to improvements in methods of treatment.

Methods of Treatment

Several types of injection schedules have been devised, but only 2 are in current general use: perennial and preseasonal. In the perennial method, the patient receives injections containing a mixture of the relevant allergens continuously. Treatment is begun at a dosage low enough to avoid any local or systemic reactions, and frequent injections, usually once or twice a week, are administered at increasing dosages until the highest dose the patient can tolerate without excessive local or systemic reactions is reached. This is the maintenance dose, which is then continued at less frequent intervals, usually every 2–6 weeks depending upon the patient's response. If treatment is begun during a pollen season, the starting dose must be quite low to avoid reactions.

In the preseasonal method, frequent injections of increasing dosages are administered beginning 3–6 months before the anticipated start of the pollen season, and the treatment is stopped just before the season begins. The same procedure is repeated each year. This is a more cumbersome method to use in patients with multiple seasonal allergies.

Because of the large number of injections required in immunotherapy of atopic disease, several attempts have been made to use immunologic adjuvants to reduce the number of injections to as few as one for each season. Freund's incomplete adjuvant, an emulsion of aqueous allergen extract suspended in mineral oil and administered intramuscularly, was given extensive trials in the 1960s but is rarely used today because of concern about possible adverse effects of mineral oil in tissues. Alum-adsorbed allergen extracts are available commercially, but studies have not yet shown that they are superior to aqueous allergens. Chemical modification or polymerization of the allergen molecule to render it less allergenic while retaining or enhancing its immunogenicity for treatment is currently under study with the aim of achieving good blocking antibody levels in all patients without risk of adverse reactions.

Technique of Administering Allergy Injections

The success of immunotherapy using conventional aqueous extracts requires proper technique. Injections are given subcutaneously using a tuberculin syringe for accurate measurement of the dose and a 26- or 27-gauge needle. The preferred site is the lateral or dorsal aspect of the upper arm, about midway between the shoulder and elbow. Excess allergen on the needle should be wiped away and the injection given slowly. The patient should be observed for 20 minutes afterwards so that a systemic reaction can be treated immediately if it occurs. In the event of a systemic reaction, the next dose should be decreased. Swelling up to 3 or 4 cm in diameter lasting less than 24 hours and accompanied by erythema and itching is to be expected at the maintenance dose level. Local reactions greater than this indicate the need to reduce the dose.

Duration of Treatment

The optimum length of treatment differs for each patient. When injections are continued for several years, most patients report that symptoms lessen with each succeeding year. After 2 full years with few or no allergic symptoms, it is probably desirable to discontinue the injections, although many patients want to continue on a maintenance dose even longer.

Adverse Effects of Immunotherapy

Immunotherapy of atopic disease is effective, and the risk of discomfort or serious reaction is relatively low if treatment is done properly. The principal danger is the immediate systemic reaction, an anaphylactic response to an excessively high dose or inadvertent administration into a blood vessel. The symptoms and treatment of anaphylaxis are discussed below. Reactions to allergy injections can be minimized by scrupulous record-keeping, questioning the patient each time about local reactions from the previous dose, and proper technique of administration. Anaphylactic deaths have occurred from allergy injections, but in most cases this has been attributed to an incorrect dose or improper procedure.

There is no evidence that repeated administration of allergens to atopic patients induces other forms of immunologic disease.

ALLERGIC RHINITIS
(Hay Fever)

Major Immunologic Features
- Allergic rhinitis is the most common clinical expression of atopic hypersensitivity.
- Allergic rhinitis is type I allergy localized in the nasal mucosa and conjunctiva.
- Pollens, fungal spores, dust, and animal danders are the usual atmospheric allergens.

General Considerations

Allergic rhinitis is the most common manifestation of an atopic reaction to inhaled allergens. At least 20 million persons in the USA suffer from this disease. The disease can begin at any age, but the onset is usually during childhood or adolescence.

The immunologic pathogenesis of allergic rhinitis is discussed above in the section on atopy.

Clinical Features

A. Symptoms and Signs: A typical attack consists of symptoms of profuse watery rhinorrhea, paroxysmal sneezing, and nasal obstruction. Itching of the nose and palate is common. There is frequently an accompanying allergic blepharoconjunctivitis, with intense itching of the conjunctiva and eyelids. In some patients, conjunctivitis may occur in the absence of nasal symptoms. The disease occurs seasonally in patients with pollen allergy, year-round if the sensitivity is to a perennial allergen such as house dust, or there may be perennial symptoms with seasonal exacerbations in patients with multiple allergies. Severe attacks are often accompanied by systemic symptoms of malaise and sometimes muscle soreness after intense periods of sneezing. Fever is absent. Swelling of the nasal mucosa may lead to headache because of obstruction of the ostia of the paranasal sinuses.

Physical examination shows a pale, swollen nasal mucosa with watery secretions. The conjunctiva is suffused or injected, and the lids are frequently swollen. These changes revert to normal when there is no allergen exposure and the patient is asymptomatic.

B. Laboratory Findings: Eosinophils are numerous in the nasal secretions, but blood eosinophilia is slight. Serum IgE is modestly elevated but may be normal.

Immunologic Diagnosis

The diagnosis of allergic rhinitis is based on the history, physical findings during a symptomatic phase, and nasal eosinophilia. Wheal and erythema skin tests will detect the specific sensitivities. (See section on skin testing.)

Differential Diagnosis

Chronic vasomotor rhinitis is a common disorder of unknown cause in which the primary complaint is nasal congestion, usually associated with postnasal drainage. It differs from allergic rhinitis by the absence of sneezing paroxysms, minimal rhinorrhea, and lack of eye symptoms. The congestion may be unilateral or bilateral and often shifts with position. Symptoms occur year-round and are generally worse in cold weather or in dry climates. The nasal mucosa is unusually sensitive to irritants such as tobacco smoke, fumes, and smog. Symptoms usually begin in adult life, and the disease is more common among women. It may begin during pregnancy. Examination shows swollen, erythematous nasal mucosa and strands of thick mucoid postnasal discharge in the pharynx. Allergy skin tests are negative or unrelated to the symptoms. In nonallergic vasomotor rhinitis, the nasal secretions may or may not contain eosinophils, so nasal eosinophilia is not a reliable sign of allergy but may indicate a preasthmatic state. There is a good response to decongestants and humidification, but antihistamines are usually not effective.

Rhinitis medicamentosa denotes the severe congestion that occurs from the rebound effect of sympathomimetic nasal sprays or nose drops used excessively. In this disease, the mucosa is often bright red and swollen, but these changes are reversible with complete avoidance of nose drops or sprays even if they have been used excessively for many years.

Infectious rhinitis is almost always due to a virus, and most patients with allergic rhinitis can distinguish their allergic symptoms from those of a common cold, which usually produces fever, an erythematous nasal mucosa, and polymorphonuclear rather than eosinophilic exudate in the nasal secretions. Primary bacterial or fungal infections of the nasal passages are rare.

Treatment

Treatment consists of environmental measures to avoid allergen exposure, drugs, and immunotherapy.

A. Avoidance of Allergen: In any allergic disease, avoidance of the allergen is the ideal method of treatment. Elimination of household pets, control of house dust exposure by frequent cleaning and avoidance of dust-collecting toys or other objects in the bedroom, and dehumidification and repair of leaking pipes or roofs to prevent mold growth are indicated where these are appropriate to the patient's allergy. Avoidance of pollen and outdoor molds is not possible unless the patient is able to stay in an air-conditioned home or office. In some cases, the patient might arrange a vacation trip to a pollen-free area during the peak pollen season at home.

B. Drug Treatment: Antihistaminics are the most useful drugs in allergic rhinitis, although they have drawbacks. They act as competitive inhibitors of histamine and so must be used repeatedly and regularly to be effective. Their usefulness is restricted by their sedative property. Antihistaminics also have anticholinergic activity, producing dryness of the mouth which may be unacceptable to some patients, and they occasionally cause nausea, dizziness, or blurred vision. Nasal decongestants may be helpful, either alone or in combination with antihistaminics. Sympathomimetic eye drops are useful for allergic conjunctivitis. Cromolyn by nasal or conjunctival drops is beneficial for some patients but is not currently available in the USA.

Corticosteroids can be extremely effective in relieving symptoms of allergic rhinitis, but since the disease is a chronic, recurrent, benign condition, these drugs should be used with extreme care. The patient with very severe symptoms lasting for only a few days or several weeks each year who does not respond to antihistaminics can be given oral prednisone or nasal dexamethasone or beclomethasone spray for 1 or 2 weeks in a dosage just high enough to repress symptoms for that patient. Dexamethasone spray is readily absorbed and can lead to systemic effects and adrenocortical suppression.

C. Immunotherapy: Immunotherapy has been shown to be effective in allergic rhinitis. Because of the length of treatment required and the potential danger of serious systemic reactions, injection treatment is used in patients whose symptoms are uncontrolled in spite of appropriate environmental measures and symptomatic medications. This is discussed in detail above.

Complications & Prognosis

Bronchial asthma may develop in patients with allergic rhinitis, but this is another atopic manifestation rather than a complication per se. Secondary purulent sinusitis and otitis media can result from obstruction of the sinus ostia or auditory (eustachian) tubes, respectively. The development of nasal polyps is not directly related to the severity of the allergic disease.

Although no definitive studies have been done on the course of untreated allergic rhinitis, symptoms can be expected to recur or persist for many years if not for life, although the severity of the symptoms is dependent upon the degree of exposure to the allergen. A patient with pollen allergy who moves to an area devoid of that particular plant will no longer be symptomatic.

ASTHMA

Major Immunologic Features

- Allergic asthma is a manifestation of type I allergy localized in the bronchus.
- Immunologically released or activated mediators are histamine, SRS-A, and ECF-A.
- Hyperirritability of bronchial mucosa amplifies the bronchoconstricting effects of mediators.

General Considerations

Bronchial asthma is a chronic disease characterized by hyperirritability of the bronchial mucosa and eosinophilia. It may begin at any age and results in attacks of wheezing and dyspnea which can range in severity from mild discomfort to life-threatening respiratory failure. Some patients are symptom-free between attacks, whereas others are never entirely free of airway obstruction.

Extrinsic asthma (allergic, atopic, or immunologic asthma). About 50% of asthmatics have evidence of atopic allergy. As a group, they generally develop the disease early in life, usually in infancy or childhood. Other manifestations of atopy—eczema or allergic rhinitis—often coexist. A family history of atopic disease is common. Attacks of asthma occur during pollen seasons, in the presence of animals, or on exposure to house dust, feather pillows, or other allergens, depending upon that patient's particular allergic sensitivities. Skin tests give positive wheal and flare reactions to the suspected allergens. Total serum IgE concentration is frequently elevated but is sometimes normal.

Intrinsic asthma (nonallergic or idiopathic asthma). It is characteristic of this type of asthma to appear first during adult life, usually after an apparent respiratory infection, so that the term "adult-onset asthma" is sometimes applied to this disorder. This term is misleading because in some cases the disease first appears during childhood, and some allergic asthmatics become symptomatic for the first time as adults because they have not previously been exposed to the relevant allergen. Intrinsic asthma pursues a relentless course with chronic or recurrent bronchial obstruction unrelated to pollen seasons or exposure to other allergens. Skin tests are negative to the usual atopic allergens. Serum IgE concentration is normal. The personal and family histories are usually negative for other atopic diseases.

Approximately 10% of asthmatic patients have aspirin sensitivity. In these patients, ingestion of aspirin is followed in 20 minutes to 3 hours by an asthmatic attack, which is caused by an idiosyncratic pharmacologic response to the drug. In some cases, other nonsteroidal anti-inflammatory drugs and certain food and drug additives, particularly tartrazine yellow, cause a similar reaction. Nasal polyposis is common in aspirin-sensitive patients.

Immunologic Pathogenesis

The cause of asthma is unknown. There is evidence that bronchoconstriction is mediated by an autonomic reflex mechanism involving afferent receptors in the bronchial mucosa or submucosa which respond to irritants or chemical mediators and efferent cholinergic (vagal) impulses causing bronchial muscle contraction and hypersecretion of mucus. In the asthmatic patient, the afferent receptors appear to be sensitized to respond to a low threshold of stimulation. It has been proposed that the hyperirritable state of the bronchial mucosa results from defective functioning or blockade of its beta-adrenergic receptor, preventing a homeostatic bronchodilating response from endogenous catecholamines.

The abnormality is presumably the same in all asthmatics, differing only in degree. In allergic asthma, allergen-induced attacks can be initiated by direct reaction between inhaled allergen and IgE antibody on bronchial mast cells, releasing histamine and SRS-A to stimulate local bronchial receptors, or indirectly by allergen or mediators reaching the site via the circulation if the allergen is ingested or injected.

The mechanism of aspirin-sensitive asthma is idiosyncratic and not immunologic. Since aspirin and related compounds normally inhibit the cyclooxygenase pathway of biosynthesis of prostaglandin E_2 (a bronchodilator) from arachidonic acid, it is suspected that in this disease an aberrant response to these drugs favors the local synthesis of prostaglandin $F_{2\alpha}$ (a bronchodilator) or leukotrienes (SRS-A) via the lipoxygenase pathway.

Clinical Features

A. Symptoms and Signs: The asthmatic attack causes shortness of breath, wheezing, and tightness in the chest, with difficulty in moving air during both inspiration and expiration. Coughing is usually present, and with prolonged asthma the cough may produce thick, tenacious sputum that can be either clear or yellow. Physical examination during the attack shows tachypnea, audible wheezing, and use of the accessory muscles of respiration. The pulse is usually rapid, and blood pressure may be elevated. Pulsus paradoxus indicates severe asthma. The lung fields are hyperresonant, and auscultation reveals diminished breath sounds, wheezes, and rhonchi but no rales.

B. Laboratory Findings: Blood and sputum eosinophilia are characteristic of asthma, whether or not allergy is present. The chest x-ray may be normal during the attack or may show signs of hyperinflation, and there may be transient scattered parenchymal densities indicating focal atelectasis caused by mucous plugging in scattered portions of the airway.

Pulmonary function tests show the abnormalities of airway obstructive disease. Flow rates and FEV_1* are decreased, vital capacity is normal or decreased, and total lung capacity and functional residual capacity are increased over normal values. Diffusing capacity is usually normal or slightly increased but may be decreased with extreme bronchospasm. Following administration of a bronchodilator, such as isoproterenol in aerosol form, ventilation improves, with significant increase in flow rates and FEV_1, indicating the reversible nature of the bronchial obstruction. The lack of response to isoproterenol in a patient already receiving large doses of sympathomimetic drugs does not rule out reversibility, and the test should be repeated at a later date after additional treatment such as hydration, corticosteroids, and chest physical therapy.

Repeated tests of ventilatory function are helpful in the long-term management of the asthmatic patient. Serial determinations of FEV_1, maximal expiratory flow rate (MEFR), or peak flow rates are easily done in the office or clinic, and they will often detect airway obstruction that may not be apparent to the patient or on auscultation of the chest.

Increased total eosinophil count in the peripheral blood is almost invariably present unless suppressed by corticosteroids or sympathomimetic drugs. Sputum examination reveals eosinophils, Charcot-Leyden crystals, and Curschmann's spirals.

Immunologic Diagnosis

The diagnosis of bronchial asthma is based on the history, physical examination, and pulmonary function tests. The history is the primary diagnostic tool for evaluating the presence of allergy and identifying the relevant allergens. In general, those inhalant allergens that are important in allergic rhinitis are also implicated in allergic asthma: pollens, fungi, animal danders, house dust, and other household and occupational airborne allergens. In young children and infants, allergy to foods may also cause asthma. If atopic allergy is suggested by the history, skin testing for wheal and flare reactions will verify the specific sen-

sitivities to inhalant allergens but is less reliable for detection of food allergens.

Bronchial inhalation challenge testing with allergenic extracts has been proposed as more definitive than skin tests, but this procedure has a number of inherent drawbacks. Aqueous allergen extract in aerosol form is not deposited in the same portion of the airway as are naturally inhaled pollen grains, mold spores, or other allergenic particles. Some extracts may be irritating and therefore may give nonspecific irritant responses. The testing procedure is cumbersome and time-consuming compared to skin testing. A positive bronchial challenge may provoke severe bronchospasm, causing discomfort and danger to the patient, so the procedure must be done in a hospital with appropriate measures for immediate control of the severe asthmatic reaction. It is not practical for routine evaluation but may be useful for definitive testing of occupational allergens.

Differential Diagnosis

Chronic bronchitis and emphysema (chronic obstructive lung disease) produce airway obstruction that does not respond to sympathomimetic bronchodilators or corticosteroids, and there is no associated eosinophilia in the blood or sputum. In children, acute bronchiolitis, cystic fibrosis, aspiration of a foreign body, and airway obstruction caused by a congenital vascular anomaly must be considered. Benign or malignant bronchial tumors or external compression from an enlarged substernal thyroid, thymus enlargement, aneurysm, or mediastinal tumor may cause wheezing. Acute viral bronchitis may produce enough bronchial inflammation with symptoms of obstruction and wheezing to be called asthmatic bronchitis. Cardiac asthma is a term used for intermittent dyspnea (resembling allergic asthma) caused by left ventricular failure. Carcinoid tumors may occasionally cause attacks of wheezing because of release of serotonin or activation of kinins by the neoplasm.

Treatment

Since the cause of asthma is unknown, correction of the basic defect, the hyperirritable bronchial mucosa, is not possible. The aim of treatment is symptomatic control. Drugs, environmental measures, and immunotherapy may be required.

A. Drug Treatment:

1. Sympathomimetics–Adrenergic bronchodilator drugs are effective treatment and are used in the acute attack or for long-term management. Epinephrine, 0.2–0.5 mL of 1:1000 aqueous solution given subcutaneously, acts rapidly and is the first drug to be used for the acute attack. Its duration of action is short, so that if repeated injections are required, long-acting epinephrine 1:200 (Sus-Phrine), epinephrine in oil (2 mg/mL), or terbutaline can be used. Epinephrine can also be given by inhalation as an aerosol, but albuterol, metaproterenol, or isoetharine is preferable because these drugs have a predominantly β-adrenergic activity. They are available as solutions to be administered

---

*FEV_1 = forced expiratory volume in 1 second, the greatest amount of air that can be expelled in that time, beginning with full inspiration.

by a hand-held nebulizer or in an intermittent positive pressure breathing (IPPB) device. They are also dispensed in convenient metered-dose pressurized inhalers, but these may be dangerously overused. Patients must be cautioned that overuse can lead to paradoxic bronchial constriction and worsening of the asthma. Deaths from isoproterenol aerosol abuse have been reported.

Beta-adrenergic drugs—terbutaline, metaproterenol, and albuterol—have largely supplanted ephedrine as oral sympathomimetic drugs for achieving sustained bronchodilation in chronic asthma. Side-effects of nervousness, muscle twitching, palpitations, tachycardia, and insomnia can occur with all of these.

2. Xanthines–Aminophylline and related compounds are bronchodilators especially effective when used in combination with sympathomimetic drugs. Intravenous aminophylline, 250–500 mg, can be administered fairly rapidly in the acute asthmatic attack, and various oral forms of theophylline are available for long-term oral use. Absorption of theophylline varies with the drug preparation, the age of the patient, and other factors such as smoking and heart failure. Serum theophylline determinations should be utilized to obtain a therapeutic level of 10–20 μg/mL.

3. Corticosteroids–Glucocorticoids are remarkably effective in the treatment of asthma. Even when all other forms of treatment have failed, the response to adequate steroid treatment is so dependable that failure of response might be considered grounds for questioning the diagnosis of asthma. The mechanism of action is unknown, and these drugs are just as effective in reversing asthma in nonallergic patients as in patients suffering allergen-induced attacks.

In spite of their effectiveness, however, corticosteroids should not be considered primary agents in the treatment of asthma, and in actual practice are usually given when other forms of treatment prove inadequate. The dangers of long-term steroid usage must be kept in mind by any physician using these drugs.

Treatment is started in high dosage and continued until the obstruction is alleviated, with return of physical findings and flow rates to normal. The dose necessary to achieve this varies with the individual patient, but 30–60 mg of prednisone daily are usually sufficient. An occasional steroid-resistant patient may require a much higher dose because of an abnormally accelerated rate of drug catabolism. After complete clearing of the attack, the daily dose is reduced by slow tapering over many days or weeks to avoid a flare-up. Long-term maintenance therapy is required by some patients, using a dose as low as possible to maintain symptomatic control, usually at a level of 10–15 mg of prednisone daily. Single-dose alternate-day maintenance therapy minimizes adrenocortical suppression, but not all steroid-dependent asthmatic patients can be controlled in this fashion.

Beclomethasone dipropionate, a highly potent corticosteroid drug available in aerosolized form for inhalation, is effective for long-term maintenance therapy for many steroid-dependent asthmatic patients. When beclomethasone is used in a daily dosage of less than 1000 μg, adrenocortical suppression and systemic side-effects are virtually absent. The starting dose is 400 μg daily, with subsequent dosage adjustment to meet the patient's requirement, but the previously used systemic steroid drug must be tapered very slowly to avoid adrenal insufficiency. Inhaled beclomethasone is not useful for treatment of an acute attack.

4. Cromolyn sodium–This drug is available as a powder administered in 20 mg doses by inhalation using a specially designed inhaler. It is not a bronchodilator but is believed to inhibit release of mediators of immediate hypersensitivity in the lung. It is administered as long-term prophylactic treatment. It is more effective in younger patients with allergic asthma than in adults, and it frequently prevents exercise-induced bronchospasm. Cromolyn has no effect in the acute attack.

5. Other drugs–Antibiotics are used if secondary bacterial bronchitis or pneumonia occurs. Expectorants and hydration are helpful for thick, tenacious sputum.

B. Environmental Control: Irritants such as smoke, fumes, dust, and aerosols should be avoided. If the diagnostic evaluation indicates allergy to animal danders, feathers, molds, or house dust, these should be eliminated from the house.

C. Immunotherapy: The effectiveness of injection treatment in pollen hay fever has been shown in several controlled studies, and most allergists feel that allergic asthma responds just as well. (See section on immunotherapy, below.)

D. Treatment of Status Asthmaticus and Respiratory Failure: A severe attack of asthma unresponsive to repeated injections of epinephrine or other sympathomimetic drugs, termed status asthmaticus, is a medical emergency requiring immediate hospitalization and prompt treatment. Factors leading to this condition include respiratory infection, excessive use of respiratory depressant drugs such as sedatives or opiates, overuse of aerosolized bronchodilators, rapid withdrawal of corticosteroids, and ingestion of aspirin in an aspirin-sensitive asthmatic patient.

Immediate determination of arterial blood gases and pH with repeated measurements until the patient responds satisfactorily is necessary for optimal treatment. Injections of epinephrine, Sus-Phrine, or epinephrine in oil are continued. Aminophylline, 250–500 mg, is given intravenously over a period of 10–30 minutes initially, followed by slow intravenous drip, but careful attention must be paid to toxic symptoms of nausea, vomiting, or headache. Serum theophylline determinations are useful in maintaining the optimal therapeutic level of 10–20 μg/mL of serum. Intravenous corticosteroids are indicated if the patient has previously received steroids, if the attack was caused by aspirin, if excessive aerosolized isoproterenol was a factor in the attack, or if significant CO_2 retention exists. Intravenous hydrocortisone, 4 mg/kg, or methylprednisolone, 1 mg/kg, repeated every 2–4 hours, should be given until the patient can be maintained on oral prednisone, 60–80 mg daily in divided doses.

Dehydration usually accompanies status asthmaticus and may give rise to inspissated mucous plugs which further impair ventilation. During the first 24 hours, up to 3–4 L of intravenous fluid may be necessary for rehydration. Oxygen should be supplied by tent, face mask, or nasal catheter to maintain arterial P_{O_2} at about 90–100 mm Hg. Expectorants and chest physical therapy are helpful adjuncts to eliminate mucous plugs. Sedatives should be avoided even in the anxious patient because of the danger of respiratory depression. Antibiotics are used only for concomitant bacterial infection.

Respiratory failure, indicated by an arterial P_{CO_2} level of 65 mm Hg or more and arterial blood pH below 7.25, may require mechanical assistance of ventilation in addition to all the measures listed above. This should be performed by a team of physicians, nurses, and technicians experienced in respiration therapy.

Complications & Prognosis

The disease is chronic, and its severity may change in an unpredictable fashion. Some children apparently "outgrow" asthma in the sense of becoming asymptomatic, but they will continue to show evidence of bronchial lability, and symptoms can reappear later in life. The acute attack can be complicated by pneumothorax, subcutaneous emphysema, rib fractures, atelectasis, or pneumonitis. There is no evidence that emphysema, bronchiectasis, pulmonary hypertension, or cor pulmonale results from longstanding asthma.

ATOPIC DERMATITIS

Major Immunologic Features

- Often accompanies atopic respiratory allergy.
- Clinical course often independent of allergen exposure.
- There may be an accompanying partial T cell defect.

General Considerations

Atopic dermatitis is associated with allergic rhinitis and asthma in families and frequently in the same patient, suggesting that it is a cutaneous form of atopic hypersensitivity. Furthermore, serum IgE is usually very high. However, it is often difficult to prove that allergy plays a role, because the dermatitis infrequently flares on exposure to allergens to which the patient reacts positively on skin testing, and immunotherapy is not effective in this disease. There is evidence for an underlying target organ (skin) abnormality which might be a metabolic or biochemical defect, possibly linked genetically to the high level of serum IgE. Recent studies also suggest a partial deficiency in cell-mediated immunity.

Atopic dermatitis may begin at any age. Onset at 3–6 months is typical, but it may appear during childhood or adolescence and occasionally during adult life.

Immunologic Pathogenesis

A. The Role of Allergy in Atopic Dermatitis: Atopic respiratory diseases with hypersensitivity to environmental allergens, eosinophilia, elevated serum IgE levels, and a family history of allergy are frequently associated with atopic dermatitis. Nevertheless, it is often difficult to attribute the dermatitis to allergy. The skin lesions rarely flare during pollen seasons, although in some patients there is an association with exposure to house dust, animals, or other environmental allergens. More commonly, food allergy in children can be demonstrated. Milk, corn, soybeans, fish, nuts, and cereal grains are frequently implicated, but other foods may occasionally be important.

B. Association With Systemic Disorders: Eczema indistinguishable from atopic dermatitis is found in children with phenylketonuria. The skin lesions of Letterer-Siwe disease are also very similar. Atopic dermatitis without allergy is a feature of several immunologic deficiency disorders, especially Wiskott-Aldrich syndrome, ataxia-telangiectasia, and X-linked hypogammaglobulinemia.

Clinical Features

Dry skin and pruritus are the essential abnormalities in the skin. This leads to chronic scratching and rubbing, producing the characteristic features of eczema. In infancy, the forehead, cheeks, and extensor surfaces of the extremities are usually involved, but later the lesions show a flexural pattern of distribution, with predilection for the antecubital and popliteal areas and the neck. The face, especially around the eyes and ears, is often affected when distribution is more widespread. The skin is excessively dry. Active lesions are initially erythematous and pruritic. This leads to scratching, which results in excoriations, papules, and scaling. If treated promptly, these changes revert to normal; but with prolonged scratching the skin becomes lichenified and pigmentation is altered. The disease often improves spontaneously during the summer months.

Differential Diagnosis

Generalized neurodermatitis, localized neurodermatitis (lichen simplex chronicus), and contact dermatitis produce similar eczematous changes of the skin. Seborrhea and dermatophytoses are occasionally confused with atopic dermatitis.

Treatment

Atopic dermatitis is a chronic disease requiring constant attention to proper skin care, environmental control, drugs, and avoidance of allergens when indicated. Dry skin enhances the tendency to itch, so frequent application of nonirritating topical lubricants is the most important preventive measure. Areas involved with active eczema respond well to topical corticosteroids, but acute involvement of large areas of skin may warrant a brief course of systemic corticosteroids beginning with a high dose initially and tapering slowly after the acute eruption clears. Oral antihistaminics help to control itching. Even if their sedative effect precludes use during the daytime, a bedtime dose will help to control involuntary scratching during sleep. Frequent bathing or washing, irritating fabrics such as wool, and harsh detergents should be avoided. The hands and fingernails must be kept clean to prevent secondary infection, and if infection does occur an appropriate antibiotic should be prescribed.

Complications & Prognosis

Atopic dermatitis has an unpredictable tendency to remit spontaneously, even after years of involvement, and this is not related to the severity of involvement, the presence or absence of allergy, or treatment. Allergic rhinitis and asthma are not complications but rather additional manifestations of the underlying atopic disease.

The most frequent complication is secondary infection from scratching. In the past, the most serious complication was eczema vaccinatum from exposure to vaccinia virus by inadvertent vaccination or contact with a recently vaccinated person in the family or classroom. Eczema herpeticum is a similar condition caused by the virus of herpes simplex. Topical antibiotics or antihistaminics may cause secondary contact dermatitis. Cataracts occur in a small number of cases; the cause is unknown.

ANAPHYLAXIS

Major Immunologic Features

- Systemic anaphylaxis is the simultaneous occurrence of a type I reaction in multiple organs.
- The usual causative allergen is a drug, insect venom, or food.
- The reaction can be evoked by a minute quantity of allergen and is potentially fatal.

General Considerations

Anaphylaxis is a systemic form of immediate hypersensitivity affecting several organ systems simultaneously. The reaction occurs rapidly and may cause death through respiratory obstruction or irreversible vascular collapse. Systemic anaphylaxis is usually mediated by IgE antibodies, with release of histamine and SRS-A, but IgG- or IgM-mediated complement-dependent mechanisms generating anaphylatoxins or kinins may account for some anaphylactic reactions.

In most cases, anaphylaxis is a systemic effect of type I allergy. The allergen combines with IgE antibodies on mast cells, releasing histamine from its stores within mast cell granules and generating SRS-A from arachidonic acid in membrane phospholipid. The vasodilating, permeability-increasing, and smooth

Table 28–3. Common causes of anaphylaxis.

Drugs
  Proteins (presumably complete antigens)
    Foreign serum
    Vaccines
    Allergen extracts
    Enzymes
  Nonprotein drugs (presumably haptens)
    Penicillin and other antibiotics
    Sulfonamides
    Local anesthetics
    Salicylates
Foods
  Legumes (especially peanuts)
  Nuts
  Berries
  Seafoods
  Egg albumin
Stinging insects
  Honeybees
  Wasps
  Hornets
  Yellow jackets
  Fire ants

muscle-constricting properties of these chemical mediators account for most of the pathophysiologic changes in anaphylaxis.

Histamine release may also occur in the absence of IgE antibody, but the clinical significance is uncertain. IgG or IgM antibodies which activate the complement system can generate anaphylatoxins, C3a and C5a, which are cleavage products of C3 and C5 capable of stimulating mast cell release of histamine. In cases of profound vascular collapse, it is likely that kinins—oligopeptides with vasodilating activity—are activated from plasma kininogen.

The allergen–IgE antibody–mast cell–mediator pathogenesis of anaphylaxis is the same mechanism responsible for atopy, but the allergens and route of exposure differ, and genetic factors and target organ hyperresponsiveness are not present in anaphylaxis.

The most common sources of allergens causing anaphylaxis are drugs, foods, and insect stings (Table 28–3).

Clinical Features

The reaction begins within seconds or minutes after exposure to the allergen. There may be an initial fright or sense of impending doom, followed rapidly by symptoms in one or more target organs: cardiovascular, respiratory, cutaneous, and gastrointestinal.

The cardiovascular response may be peripheral or central. Hypotension and shock are symptoms of generalized arteriolar vasodilatation and increased vascular permeability producing decreased peripheral resistance and leakage of plasma from the circulation to extravascular tissues, thereby lowering blood volume. In some patients without previous heart disease, cardiac arrhythmias may occur. Death can result from blood volume depletion and irreversible shock or from a cardiac arrhythmia.

The respiratory tract from the nasal mucosa to the bronchioles may be involved. Nasal congestion from swelling and hyperemia of the nasal mucosa and profuse watery rhinorrhea with itching of the nose and palate simulate an acute hay fever reaction. The hypopharynx and larynx are especially susceptible, and obstruction of this critical portion of the airway by edema is responsible for some of the respiratory deaths. Bronchial obstruction from bronchospasm, mucosal edema, and hypersecretion of mucus results in an asthma-like paroxysm of wheezing dyspnea. Obstruction of the smaller airways by mucus may lead to respiratory failure.

The skin is a frequent target organ in anaphylaxis, with generalized pruritus, erythema, urticaria, and angioedema occurring. Occasionally, urticaria may persist for many weeks or months after all other symptoms have subsided.

Gastrointestinal involvement occurs because of contraction of intestinal smooth muscle, resulting in crampy abdominal pain and sometimes nausea or diarrhea. Similarly, uterine muscle contraction may cause pelvic pain.

Immunologic Diagnosis

A history of symptoms and signs of anaphylaxis immediately after an insect sting, after parenteral administration of a drug or vaccine, or following the ingestion of a drug or food likely to cause anaphylaxis is sufficient to make the diagnosis.

Occasionally, a reaction occurs after injection of 2 agents with high anaphylactic potential (eg, penicillin and horse serum) or after a meal which included suspicious foods such as fish, legumes, nuts, or berries. A positive immediate skin test to the suspected drug or food is probably diagnostic, but a negative test to these allergens never excludes sensitivity. Prick testing should always be done first, followed by serial-dilution intradermal tests if the prick test is negative. If the cause of the reaction is obvious from the history, skin testing should not be done.

Differential Diagnosis

Urticaria, angioedema, shock, and bronchospasm from intravenous radiographic contrast media are "anaphylactoid" reactions, possibly caused by nonimmunologic activation of complement with generation of vasoactive and inflammatory mediators in certain susceptible individuals.

Cardiogenic, hypovolemic, septic, and neurogenic causes of shock must be considered. Acute respiratory obstruction may occur in asthma, pulmonary edema, mechanical obstruction by foreign body or tumor, or adult respiratory distress syndrome. Some patients experience vasovagal syncope after injections, particularly local anesthetics.

Prevention

Once an episode of anaphylaxis has occurred, every effort should be made to identify the allergen so that the patient can avoid further exposure. Any physician or nurse who administers drugs by injection should be prepared to treat a possible anaphylactic reaction by having appropriate drugs available, and patients should remain under observation for 15–20 minutes after any injection.

Treatment

Speed is essential, but treatment must be individualized according to organ involvement. Always give epinephrine as soon as anaphylaxis is suspected, then examine carefully to determine what further measures are needed. The severity of the reaction is inversely related to the interval between exposure to the allergen and the onset of symptoms.

A. Immediate Treatment: Give epinephrine, 1:1000 aqueous solution, 0.2–0.5 mL intramuscularly into the deltoid muscles. Repeat every 30–60 minutes as necessary, or use a long-acting preparation, such as Sus-Phrine (1:200) or epinephrine in oil, 2 mg/mL. If the reaction was caused by an injected drug or insect sting, give 1:1000 aqueous epinephrine, 0.1–0.2 mL subcutaneously at the injection site, to slow down absorption. If the injection was into an extremity, apply a tourniquet proximally.

B. Hypotension and Shock: Restoration of circulating fluid volume is definitive, but initial vasopressors such as levarterenol bitartrate or metaraminol bitartrate given intravenously may be used. Monitor blood pressure. Give 1000–2000 mL physiologic saline or 5% glucose in saline rapidly intravenously. If there is no response, use plasma or other plasma expanders. If the patient is in profound shock, give whole blood while monitoring central venous pressure.

C. Laryngeal Edema: Maintain the airway. Passage of an endotracheal tube may be difficult because of the swelling, in which case tracheostomy should be performed. Continue epinephrine and give diphenhydramine, 50–100 mg intravenously.

D. Bronchospasm: Treat as for status asthmaticus. Aminophylline, 250–500 mg intravenously, should be administered over a 10-minute period while observing carefully for signs of gastrointestinal or central nervous system toxicity. An aerosolized beta-adrenergic bronchodilator can be administered by hand nebulizer or intermittent positive pressure breathing.

E. Urticaria, Angioedema, and Gastrointestinal, Genitourinary, or Uterine Symptoms: These respond well to antihistaminic drugs. If severe, inject diphenhydramine, 50–100 mg intravenously or intramuscularly. For milder symptoms, oral antihistaminics are satisfactory.

F. Other Measures: Oxygen therapy must be given to correct hypoxia caused by respiratory obstruction or shock. Cardiopulmonary resuscitation should be administered in case of cardiac arrest. Corticosteroids have no known "antianaphylactic" property, and there is no rationale for their use in the critical initial stages of treatment. However, they may be helpful in refractory shock, persistent urticaria or angioedema after subsidence of the acute reaction, and bronchospasm in the asthmatic patient previously treated with corticosteroids.

Complications & Prognosis

Death from laryngeal edema, respiratory failure, shock, or cardiac arrhythmia usually occurs within minutes after onset of the reaction, but in occasional cases irreversible shock persists for hours. Permanent brain damage may result from the hypoxia of respiratory or cardiovascular failure. Urticaria or angioedema may recur for months after penicillin anaphylaxis.

STINGING INSECT HYPERSENSITIVITY

Anaphylactic sensitivity to Hymenoptera venom can be easily identified, and patients can be protected from future potentially fatal reactions by desensitization and simple protective measures. The venom of these insects contains protein allergens in addition to the pharmacologically active chemicals responsible for the usual local inflammation. In honeybee (family Apidae) venom, the major allergen is phospholipase A, and minor allergens are hyaluronidase and melittin. In vespids (family Vespidae), which include hornets, yellow jackets, and wasps, the venom allergens have not yet been identified but are different from those found in the honeybee.

The sting of a single insect is sufficient to produce a severe, even fatal anaphylactic reaction in sensitive patients. Sensitization occurs from prior stings, and if patients are allergic to a common or cross-reacting antigen they may have an anaphylactic reaction should they be stung by any species of Hymenoptera insect. There is no evidence that other allergic disease, including atopy and drug anaphylaxis, predisposes to Hymenoptera anaphylaxis.

The normal response of erythema, itching, and localized swelling from a Hymenoptera sting is caused by vasoactive and irritant chemical substances in the venom. In some patients, this localized reaction is unusually large and persistent, possibly indicating type III (immune complex) or type IV (cellular) hypersensitivity. Such reactions are not related to anaphylactic sensitivity.

The diagnosis is made by history and skin testing. Anaphylaxis begins immediately after an insect sting, although mild reactions may not begin until several hours after the sting. Precise insect identification is possible only if the insect is caught and saved for study by an expert.

The diagnosis is confirmed by positive wheal and erythema intradermal test to the specific venom at a dilution of 1:100 or greater. RAST is less sensitive but may be substituted for skin testing if exquisite sensitivity is suspected.

Treatment

The management of anaphylaxis from a Hymenoptera sting is the same as for any anaphylactic reaction (see above). In the case of honeybee sting, the venom sac and stinger usually remain in the skin and should be removed promptly by scraping with a knife or fingernail.

Local reactions require only cold compresses to ease pain and reduce swelling.

A. Hyposensitization: The effectiveness of immunotherapy in this disease is now accepted on the basis of recent clinical studies. Patients with systemic anaphylactic reactions by history and positive skin test to the corresponding Hymenoptera venom should receive injection therapy using the specific venom. Injections of whole body insect extracts are ineffective.

B. Anaphylaxis Kit: The patient should carry at all times a small kit containing a preloaded syringe of epinephrine and an antihistamine tablet. Epinephrine or isoproterenol in a pressurized-aerosol hand nebulizer is not a reliable means of protection for anaphylactic shock.

C. Protective Measures: Avoid using strong scents such as perfumes and hair sprays when outdoors. Wear shoes outdoors. Avoid garbage cans. Do not tamper with beehives or with wasp or hornet nests.

URTICARIA & ANGIOEDEMA

Major Immunologic Features

- These are cutaneous forms of anaphylaxis.
- Allergens causing acute urticaria are usually foods or drugs.
- Chronic urticaria is usually related to nonimmunologic causes or is idiopathic.

General Considerations

Urticaria affects many people at some time, usually as an acute self-limited episode but occasionally in a chronic or recurrent form. The lesion—a localized area of increased vascular permeability—appears as multiple areas of well-demarcated swelling of the skin usually accompanied by pruritus. It can result from a variety of causes, some of which are immunologic. Angioedema is a similar condition in which the affected blood vessels are deeper, resulting in diffuse swelling, usually without pruritus. Urticaria and angioedema may appear together in the same patient. When an allergic cause can be found, the disease is actually a localized cutaneous form of anaphylaxis, since the immunologic mechanism and the causative allergens are similar.

Causes of urticaria and angioedema. Allergy, infections, physical factors, certain systemic diseases, and emotional stress have all been associated with urticaria.

Ingestant allergens are much more frequent causes of urticaria than are inhalants. Any food or drug can cause hives. Occult sources of drugs such as penicillin in milk and proprietary medications such as laxatives, headache remedies, and vitamin preparations must be considered. Food and drug additives are occasionally responsible.

A localized or systemic infection may provoke urticaria concomitant with the immune response to the infecting organism. This is particularly true with parasitic diseases, which are often associated with eosinophilia and a prominent IgE immune response. Urticaria may appear during the prodromal phases of certain viral infections, especially HBsAg-associated hepatitis and infectious mononucleosis. Bacterial infections are much less likely to cause urticaria.

"Physical allergy" refers to a type of urticaria in which external physical stimuli cause hives or swelling. The most frequent type is cold urticaria, in which exposure to cold temperature results in hives and angioedema, either during the cold exposure or after rewarming. In some cases, the sensitivity to cold can be passively transferred by serum to normal skin, suggesting an antibody mechanism, but the nature of the antigen is unknown. It is assumed that cold alters a normal skin protein in such a way as to make it antigenic. Occasional patients have been described with urticaria or angioedema on exposure to heat, sunlight ("actinic"), water ("aquagenic"), and vibratory stimulation of the skin. The localization of urticaria to areas of the skin subjected to mild pressure or trauma is characteristic of urticaria in general.

Cholinergic urticaria is a condition in which small wheals with a large area of surrounding flare appear after exercise, being overheated, or emotional stress.

Urticaria occasionally is a sign of an underlying systemic disease. Neoplasms—especially Hodgkin's disease and lymphomas—and connective tissue disorders—particularly systemic lupus erythematosus—have been reported to cause hives.

Emotional trauma can precipitate acute urticaria or angioedema or aggravate the chronic form of the disease.

Immunologic Pathogenesis

Several different mechanisms are capable of effecting cutaneous vascular permeability with expression as urticaria and angioedema. IgE antibodies to foods, drugs, or insect venoms sensitize cutaneous mast cells for release of histamine, which results in acute hives on exposure to the allergen. IgG or IgM antibodies complexed to antigen—or aggregated immunoglobulin without antigen—may activate the classic pathway of complement, generating anaphylatoxins C5a or C3a, which can stimulate mast cells for mediator release. Activation of the alternative complement pathway might also generate these anaphylatoxins, since they arise from the final effector pathway in the complement sequence. However, the clinical relevance of complement-dependent mechanisms in urticaria is uncertain. Physical agents or trauma might release histamine from mast cells by mechanical stimulation. Aspirin and nonsteroidal anti-inflammatory drugs have a nonspecific potentiating effect on urticaria and angioedema, suggesting a

possible role for the leukotrienes, products of the lipoxygenation of arachidonic acid that have SRS-A activity.

Immunologic Diagnosis

As in any allergic diagnosis, a thorough medical history and complete physical examination are essential in order to interpret the significance of any subsequent test. Skin testing with the usual inhalant allergens is warranted only in those unusual cases in which the history suggests a relationship of such allergens to the patient's urticaria.

Food allergy is diagnosed by careful dietary history, use of elimination diets, and appropriate food challenges. Drug allergy requires close scrutiny of the patient's recent drug history, elimination of suspected drugs, and occasionally deliberate challenge, although skin testing is helpful for certain drugs such as penicillin. The diagnosis of cold urticaria is made by application of an ice cube to the forearm for 5 minutes and the appearance of localized urticaria after the skin has been rewarmed. Similar tests with heat, ultraviolet light, or water to a test area of skin are appropriate if the history suggests these causes.

Appropriate tests for parasitic or other infections, lymphomas or other neoplasms, or connective tissue diseases are generally indicated only if the history and physical examination would have suggested such diseases in the absence of urticaria. It should be emphasized that in most cases of chronic recurrent urticaria, no cause is found even with the most diligent search.

Differential Diagnosis

Multiple insect bites may evoke wheals, but careful inspection will show the bite punctum at the center of the lesion. Angioedema can be distinguished from ordinary edema or myxedema by its absence from dependent areas of localization and its evanescent appearance. Hereditary angioedema is discussed below.

Treatment

Urticaria caused by foods or drugs is treated by avoidance of the offending agents, although hyposensitization to a drug might be attempted in rare instances in which no alternative drug is available. Urticaria associated with infection is self-limited if the infection is adequately treated. In cases of physical allergy, protective measures to avoid heat, sunlight, or cold must be advised.

Drug treatment is a useful adjunct in the management of all patients whether or not the cause has been found, but a good response to symptomatic treatment should not deter the physician from efforts to find an underlying cause. Antihistaminic drugs are the principal method of treatment, but they must be given in adequate dosage. Epinephrine injections may relieve hives transiently and should be used in treating angioedema involving the pharynx or larynx. Corticosteroids are usually ineffective and should not be used to treat urticaria of unknown cause.

HEREDITARY ANGIOEDEMA
(Hereditary Angioneurotic Edema)

This rare form of angioedema is inherited as an autosomal mendelian dominant deficiency of C1 inactivator (C1 esterase inhibitor). The defect produces an uncontrolled activation of the early components of the complement system, with generation of a kininlike substance in the plasma causing recurrent episodes of angioedema in the skin, the gastrointestinal and genitourinary tracts, and the larynx.

Patients with this disorder have a lifelong history of repeated episodes of swellings without urticaria and a family history of the disease. Attacks of abdominal or pelvic pain from visceral angioedema may mimic acute surgical conditions. Death can occur from laryngeal angioedema.

The history alone is usually sufficient to suggest the diagnosis, which can then be confirmed by laboratory tests. Measurement of serum C4 by functional or immunologic assay is the best screening test, because C4 levels are markedly diminished in almost all patients, even during symptom-free intervals. Levels of other complement components are normal. The diagnosis can be confirmed by measurement of C1 inactivator protein by immunoassay and its functional activity by hemolytic assay. There are 2 variants of the disease: In about 85% of kindreds, the C1 inactivator is absent from the serum, and in the remaining 15% it is present in normal amount but is functionally inactive. The disease was once thought to be extremely rare, but the availability of a specific laboratory diagnosis has made possible identification of a significant number of affected families.

Several modes of treatment have been advocated. Plasmin inhibitors such as aminocaproic acid (EACA, Amicar) and tranexamic acid (Amstat) orally have been helpful in preventing or ameliorating attacks in some patients, possibly by inhibiting fibrinolytic generation of the active kinin peptide. Androgen therapy using methyltestosterone or attenuated sex hormones such as oxymetholone and danazol has not only prevented attacks but coincidentally significantly increased the serum concentrations of C1 inactivator and C4, suggesting that these hormones may correct the inherited deficiency. Administration of fresh plasma to supply the missing inactivator has also been advocated to prevent attacks that might be precipitated by trauma such as dental surgery, but this approach has not been evaluated critically. Any attack of laryngeal edema occurring in a patient with this disease demands close observation—even hospitalization if necessary—in case tracheostomy is required.

Rarely, acquired C1 esterase inhibitor deficiency and angioedema can arise in a patient with lymphoma. Unlike the hereditary form of the disease, serum levels of C1 as well as C4 are low.

DRUG ALLERGY

Major Immunologic Features

- Any of the 4 types of hypersensitivity can cause an allergic drug reaction.
- An immunogenic response to a drug usually requires covalent binding of haptenic drug determinant to host carrier protein.
- The allergenic determinant may be a drug metabolite.

General Considerations

Drugs cause allergic reactions by virtue of the ability of the drug or a metabolite of the drug to evoke an immune response. Most drugs function immunologically as haptens and must couple in vivo to a host carrier protein before they become immunogenic. Protein drugs such as sera, vaccines, biologicals, and allergen extracts are antigenic per se and carry a high risk of allergic sensitization.

Many factors influence the allergic potential of a drug. Topical administration is more likely to induce sensitization than the oral or parenteral routes. Infection may increase the risk of drug allergy, but atopy and other immunologic diseases do not. Certain patients are multiple drug reactors, possibly on a genetic basis. Children are much less susceptible than adults. Allergy to a particular drug is independent of its pharmacologic properties but highly dependent upon the ease with which the drug or its metabolite binds covalently to carrier protein.

Type I allergic reactions to drugs include anaphylaxis, urticaria, and angioedema. These can occur with any drug, but systemic anaphylaxis is most likely to result if the drug is given by injection, although severe reactions and even death have occurred from oral administration of penicillin.

Type II allergic reactions are complement-dependent and therefore involve IgG or IgM antibodies. The drug-antibody-complement complex is fixed to a target cell, usually a circulating blood cell, resulting in complement-dependent cell lysis. Such reactions may involve erythrocytes, leukocytes, or platelets.

There are 4 mechanisms by which drugs can induce immunologic damage to cells: (1) The drug first fixes to the cell membrane, followed by reaction of the antibody to the cell-fixed drug antigen, resulting in a cell-antigen-antibody complex. The complex then activates the complement sequence, with lysis of the cell. Immunohemolytic anemia from penicillin is an example of this mechanism. (2) The drug-antibody-complement complex is formed first in the plasma, and the complex secondarily fixes to the cell, after which lysis occurs. In these reactions, the direct antiglobulin (Coombs) test is positive. Autoimmune hemolytic anemia, leukopenia, and thrombocytopenia from quinidine, sulfonamides, and stibophen are examples of this type of drug reaction. (3) The membrane of red blood cells may be modified by drugs so that the cells adsorb proteins nonspecifically and give positive antiglobulin tests. However, disease from this mechanism is rare. (4) Methyldopa causes hemolytic anemia by inducing autoantibody formation. The drug damages normal red cells to expose erythrocyte auto-antigens which induce an autoimmune hemolytic anemia that can persist even after the drug has been withdrawn. It is possible that some drugs may produce type II reactions by more than one of these 4 mechanisms.

Type III drug reactions are exemplified by serum sickness, a term applicable to the reaction whether caused by heterologous serum or by a haptenic drug such as penicillin. The disease is a multi-system complement-dependent vasculitis in which immune complexes are deposited along the endothelial surfaces of blood vessels, stimulating inflammation and vascular wall damage. There is a latent period of several days after administration of the drug before sufficient antibody is produced to generate immune complexes capable of activating the complement system. The classic symptoms of serum sickness are fever, arthralgias, lymphadenopathy, and a skin eruption which is often urticarial. The serum sickness caused by penicillin is generally mild, although the urticaria may persist for many weeks.

Type IV (cell-mediated) allergy is the mechanism of allergic contact dermatitis from topically applied drugs. Topical antibiotics, antihistamines, local anesthetics, and certain additives found in topical medications, including parabens and lanolin, are frequent causes of this type of allergy.

In many adverse drug reactions, allergy is strongly suspected but the immunologic mechanism is difficult to prove. Allergy is suggested by (1) a reaction occurring in a small proportion of persons exposed to the drug, (2) a latent period between exposure to the drug and the appearance of a reaction which is of shorter duration with succeeding exposures to the drug, (3) elicitation of the reaction by very small doses, and (4) an association with other signs suggesting allergic disease, such as eosinophilia. Erythematous, morbilliform, or other skin eruptions, drug fever, and cholestatic liver disease induced by certain drugs belong to the category of suspected allergic reactions.

Certain drug reactions can be caused by allergic or nonallergic means. Urticaria and angioedema may be produced either by type I allergy to a drug or by nonspecific liberation of mast cell histamine by drugs such as morphine.

Clinical Features

An allergic reaction to a drug occurs after sufficient exposure to induce an immune response, so some patients may react even though the drug had been used frequently in the past without incident. A reaction on first exposure suggests prior sensitization by a cross-reacting drug or antigen. Once a reaction occurs, any subsequent use of the drug, sometimes even in trace amounts, can cause a recurrence of symptoms.

All 4 types of allergy have occurred from drugs, and these can produce a variety of clinical manifestations (Table 28–4).

Table 28–4. Clinical manifestations of drug allergy.

Systemic anaphylaxis

Serum sickness

Fever

Cutaneous eruptions
  Urticaria
  Angioedema
  Erythema multiforme, Stevens-
    Johnson syndrome
  Pruritus
  Allergic contact dermatitis,
    photoallergic dermatitis
  Purpura
  Morbilliform, erythematous,
    exfoliative rash
  Fixed drug eruption

Hematologic abnormalities
  Hemolytic anemia
  Leukopenia
  Thrombocytopenia
  Eosinophilia

Hepatic cholestasis

Acute interstitial nephritis

Immunologic Diagnosis

A high index of suspicion and a careful history to uncover all sources of drugs the patient might have taken are the most important means of diagnosis. In addition to prescribed drugs, the patient must be asked about the use of proprietary medications such as aspirin, cold tablets, headache remedies, laxatives, vitamins, and nose drops.

Tests for diagnosis of allergy to a specific drug are available for only certain drugs and certain types of reactions. Protein drugs causing type I allergy will give an immediate wheal and flare skin test reaction, but a proper dilution of the drug must be used to avoid a nonspecific irritant reaction. Haptenic drugs will usually not give a positive test, but penicillin is an important exception. For suspected type II allergy, in vitro agglutination of erythrocytes, leukocytes, and platelets in the presence of the drug and the patient's serum, or lysis with the addition of complement, can be diagnostic provided adequate controls are included. In type III reactions, antibodies may be found by gel precipitation tests if the antigen is a protein, by passive hemagglutination, or by Arthus-type skin tests, in which the response to intradermal injection of antigen is a localized swelling and inflammation maximal at 5–8 hours. Patch testing is the appropriate procedure in allergic contact dermatitis.

Many other in vitro tests have been proposed for diagnostic use in drug allergy, including the basophil degranulation test, lymphocyte activation test, radioallergosorbent test, and others, but at present their usefulness is questionable. In each case, the selection of the test must be appropriate to the drug and to the type of immune response suspected from the clinical picture. Furthermore, the fact that the patient has an antibody to a particular drug is not proof that the antibody is the cause of the allergic reaction.

In vivo testing by readministration of a small test dose of the drug after the initial reaction has subsided may prove that the reaction is drug-associated. This should not be attempted with serious reactions such as anaphylaxis or exfoliative dermatitis.

Differential Diagnosis

Nonallergic drug reactions are adverse pharmacologic, chemical, and physical effects of the drug which are not immunologically mediated. These include toxicity, idiosyncrasy, intolerance, and side-effects.

Treatment

Proved or even suspected drug reactions require withdrawal of the drug. If a substitute drug is given, it should be one which is unlikely to cross-react antigenically. Symptomatic treatment is used where indicated. The patient must be advised to avoid use of the same drug in the future, but there are instances in which desensitization may be attempted.

PENICILLIN ALLERGY

The haptenic determinants of type I penicillin allergy are metabolic degradation products. Penicilloic acid is the major determinant and is responsible for late urticarial reactions and probably other skin eruptions. Anaphylaxis and immediate urticaria or angioedema are caused by other minor determinants that have not yet been fully characterized. The source of the protein carrier is unknown. The nature of the antigenic determinant in type II, III, and IV reactions has not been studied.

The antibodies, cell types, mediators, and tissue responses in each type of allergic drug reaction have been described in the preceding sections.

Clinical Features

Penicillin can cause almost every known type of allergic reaction. Anaphylaxis occurs about once in every 10,000 patient courses of the drug and accounts for about 300 deaths in the USA each year. Urticaria or angioedema appearing within an hour after administration of the drug is a form of anaphylaxis. Urticaria which begins days to weeks after the drug is administered has less serious implications and in some cases may disappear even if penicillin treatment is continued. The most common manifestation of penicillin allergy is a diffuse erythematous or morbilliform skin eruption. Serum sickness occurs occasionally, and immunohemolytic anemia may complicate high-dosage intravenous therapy. Allergic contact dermatitis is common after topical penicillin. It is estimated that some type of adverse reaction to penicillin occurs in 3% of patient courses of the drug.

Immunologic Diagnosis

IgE antibodies to major and minor penicillin al-lergy determinants are detected by wheal and flare skin tests. Penicilloyl-polylysine 6×10^{-5} M solution elicits a positive skin test in most patients with a history of late urticaria and many of those with exanthematous reactions. A "minor determinant mixture" for testing suspected anaphylactically sensitive patients is not presently marketed, but a skin test using penicillin G, 1000 units/mL, is usually positive in persons with documented anaphylaxis. The tests are performed by injecting 0.005 mL intradermally and reading for wheal and erythema at 20 minutes.

Skin testing with these 2 reagents has predictive value if used in relation to the patient's history. If there is a history of penicillin anaphylaxis, the diagnosis is certain, and no tests should be done, since anaphylaxis can be produced by the test. If late urticaria or other skin eruptions are suspected on the basis of the history, negative reactions to both determinants strongly suggest that the patient is not allergic to penicillin and the drug can be administered with no greater risk of reaction than in those patients who had not received penicillin before. If the minor determinant test is positive, the risk of anaphylaxis is almost certain, and if the major determinant test is positive the chance of a skin eruption is very high. However, the appearance of late-onset urticaria does not always signify that the drug must be withdrawn or withheld, since continued treatments may result in the appearance of IgG blocking antibody, causing the urticaria to disappear without interfering with the therapeutic effect of the drug. Hemagglutination tests may be used to detect serum IgG or IgM antibody. The former can function as a blocking antibody, but either might produce type II hemolytic anemia if the drug is given in high dosage intravenously.

Differential Diagnosis

Penicillin toxicity is exceedingly low, so the appearance of an adverse reaction during therapy almost always indicates allergy to the drug. Exanthematous eruptions, however, frequently complicate those infections for which penicillin is prescribed and may be erroneously diagnosed as penicillin allergy. This is particularly true in children given penicillin for viral or streptococcal respiratory infections.

Treatment

As with any drug allergy, the reaction will subside when penicillin is discontinued. In some cases, hives persist for many months afterward, occasionally traceable to small amounts of penicillin in dietary milk. Avoidance of milk products may be helpful.

Patients with a history of late urticaria and major (but not minor) determinant skin test reactivity may be given penicillin if no alternative antibiotic is available. The drug will stimulate IgG blocking antibody and should be started at a low dose subcutaneously, followed by increasing dosage at frequent intervals until a therapeutic level is achieved. This is not "desensitization" but rather an immunization procedure to stimulate blocking antibody. Immunization should not be attempted in any other type of penicillin allergy. Semisynthetic penicillins, eg, methicillin, nafcillin, oxacillin, and cloxacillin, all cross-react with the parent compound and should be used with the same precautions discussed for penicillin itself.

Symptomatic treatment of anaphylaxis, urticaria, and angioedema is discussed above.

Penicillinase to eliminate residual drug in tissues is rarely effective and frequently causes allergic reactions.

FOOD ALLERGY

Major Immunologic Features

- Type I reactions to foods include systemic anaphylaxis, urticaria, and exacerbation of atopic symptoms.
- Prevalence is inversely proportional to age because of maturation of gastrointestinal digestion of food allergens.
- Current diagnostic techniques, including skin testing, must correlate with history to be meaningful.

General Considerations

Food allergy is too often used to explain subjective complaints without proper documentation. The diagnosis should be reserved for patients whose symptoms occur reproducibly after ingestion of a certain food and in whom an immunologic basis is proved or suspected. This will prevent needless elimination of foods and delay in making a correct diagnosis of a different disorder responsible for the symptoms.

Allergic reactions to foods occur more commonly in children than in adults, are usually type I, and frequently accompany other manifestations of atopic disease.

Immunologic Pathogenesis

These are type I reactions in which the allergen is a food protein or a partially digested product. Carbohydrates, fats, additives such as preservatives or flavoring and coloring agents, and contaminating drugs are other potential allergens in foodstuffs. Closely related foods may contain common or cross-reacting allergens; for example, some patients react to all legumes, including beans, peas, and peanuts. Some food allergens are heat-labile, so that sufficient cooking may render the food nonallergenic. Less commonly, the reaction occurs to the cooked food only.

In gastrointestinal allergy, the allergen reacts locally with IgE antibodies in the intestinal mucosa, with subsequent mediator release. The respiratory and cutaneous manifestations are initiated by absorbed allergen which reaches the target organs via the bloodstream.

Delayed-onset reactions to foods have occasionally been ascribed to a type III allergy, but there has been no convincing proof of this. Type IV allergic contact perioral dermatitis, stomatitis from ingestion, or hand dermatitis from handling a food can occur.

Clinical Features

Systemic anaphylaxis, urticaria, angioedema, eczema, and respiratory and gastrointestinal symptoms are the usual manifestations of food allergy.

A. Anaphylaxis: The reaction typically appears promptly after the food is ingested, so the patient is generally aware of the causative food. Peanuts and other legumes, nuts, seafoods (especially shellfish), and berries are frequent offenders. However, any food can potentially sensitize a person and then cause anaphylaxis. In most cases the diagnosis is apparent; if there is doubt or confusion about which of several foods might have been responsible, skin testing for wheal and flare reaction is appropriate, since the test would generally be positive in this disease. Skin tests to highly potent allergens such as peanuts or cottonseed protein should be avoided if the diagnosis is certain on the basis of the history.

B. Urticaria and Angioedema: Food allergy is a common cause of acute urticaria. In chronic or recurrent urticaria, a food or food additive is occasionally responsible.

C. Atopic Dermatitis: Food allergies may exacerbate the disease in infants and children but less frequently in adults. Milk, wheat, eggs, corn, fish, and legumes are most frequently suspected, but other foods must also be considered.

Immunologic Diagnosis

Diagnosis begins with a careful dietary history to note the association of symptoms with specific foods. If necessary, this is supplemented with a diet-symptom record. Careful examination of the record may reveal previously unsuspected food allergens or eliminate previously suspected ones. Where the record is inconclusive, trial elimination diets are used.

Elimination diets are for short-term diagnostic use only. They are frequently deficient in essential nutrients or vitamins, so that their prolonged use may cause nutritional problems. While on the diet, the patient keeps a diet-symptom record and avoids medications that might suppress symptoms.

Several types of diets are suitable. If the list of suspect allergens is short, these foods alone can be eliminated and then reintroduced separately if the symptoms disappear. If there are no strong suspicions, an arbitrary group of "highly allergenic foods" such as wheat, milk, eggs, corn, legumes, fish, and nuts can be eliminated. In extreme cases, a synthetic diet can be used. In any case, the elimination period should be continued no longer than 7 days. If symptoms clear completely, the avoided foods are then reintroduced one at a time, usually every other day, to determine which one actually precipitates symptoms. Successful challenge will provoke an allergic reaction within minutes or several hours but rarely more than 24 hours if the reaction is a type I allergic response. Once a positive response occurs, the food is again eliminated and later rechallenged. The diagnosis can be made if symptoms occur on several such challenges.

Skin testing in food allergy. Wheal and erythema skin testing in the diagnosis of food allergy has been a confusing issue for years. The test will be positive in cases of bona fide type I allergy, provided the testing material is active, since some food allergens are labile. False-positive reactions are common because of irritant or histamine-releasing chemicals in certain foods. Furthermore, the presence of IgE antibody to a food—or to an inhalant—as determined by positive skin test is frequently associated with absence of any symptoms on natural exposure to that allergen. In some instances, this can be explained as the loss of allergenicity in cooking or in the alimentary digestive process. For these reasons, skin testing results must be interpreted in the light of the clinical history and, if appropriate, dietary trials. The radioallergosorbent test (RAST), which detects IgE antibodies in serum, has not been shown to be reliable in the diagnosis of food allergy.

Differential Diagnosis

Adverse reactions to foods can result from a variety of gastrointestinal diseases or psychologic or cultural aversions. Gastrointestinal milk allergy may be confused with intestinal lactase deficiency, which can be ruled out by lactose tolerance testing or enzyme assay from a jejunal biopsy specimen.

Treatment

The treatment of food allergy is avoidance. This is usually not difficult, since patients are rarely allergic to more than one or at most a small number of foods, permitting them to eat an adequate diet without difficulty. In the case of anaphylactic sensitivity, avoidance must be complete and scrupulous, since severe reactions can occur from minute amounts of the allergen.

An antihistamine tablet taken before a meal may occasionally prevent an attack. Some studies suggest that oral cromolyn sodium can inhibit symptoms of food allergy in some patients, but use of the drug for this purpose is still experimental in the USA.

Complications & Prognosis

Allergy to foods tends to diminish with age. Infants and children with bona fide food sensitivities frequently tolerate these foods without difficulty later in life. It is not known whether this is acquired immunologic tolerance or physiologic maturation of the digestive process preventing absorption of intact food proteins.

Anaphylactic sensitivity does not remit and is potentially lethal throughout life.

●　　●　　●

References

General

Bierman CW, Pearlman DS (editors): *Allergic Diseases of Infancy, Childhood and Adolescence.* Saunders, 1980.

Gell PGH, Coombs RRA, Lachmann PJ (editors): *Clinical Aspects of Immunology,* 3rd ed. Blackwell, 1975.

Middleton E, Reed C, Ellis E (editors): *Allergy: Principles and Practice.* 2 vols. Mosby, 1978.

Patterson R (editor): *Allergic Diseases: Diagnosis and Management,* 2nd ed. Lippincott, 1980.

Samter M (editor): *Immunological Diseases,* 3rd ed. Little, Brown, 1978.

Sheldon JM, Mathews KP, Lovell RG: *Manual of Clinical Allergy,* 2nd ed. Saunders, 1967.

Atopy

Blumenthal MN, Mendell N, Yunis E: Immunogenetics of atopic disease. *J Allergy Clin Immunol* 1980;**65:**403.

Broder I, Barlow PP, Horton RJ: The epidemiology of asthma and hay fever in a total community, Tecumseh, Michigan. 2. The relationship between asthma and hay fever. *J Allergy Clin Immunol* 1962;**33:**524.

Butcher BT, Salvaggio JE, Leslie GA: Secretory and humoral immunologic response of atopic and nonatopic individuals to intranasally administered antigen. *Clin Allergy* 1975; **5:**33.

Ishizaka K, Ishizaka T: Mechanisms of reaginic hypersensitivity: A review. *Clin Allergy* 1971;**1:**9.

Skin Testing for Immediate Hypersensitivity

Adkinson NF: The radioallergosorbent test in 1981: Limitations and refinement. *J Allergy Clin Immunol* 1981; **67:**87.

Adkinson NF: The radioallergosorbent test: Uses and abuses. *J Allergy Clin Immunol* 1980;**65:**1.

Bock SA et al: Appraisal of skin tests with food extracts for diagnosis of food hypersensitivity. *Clin Allergy* 1978; **8:**559.

Bruce CA et al: Diagnostic tests in ragweed-allergic asthma: A comparison of direct skin tests, leukocyte histamine release, and quantitative bronchial challenge. *J Allergy Clin Immunol* 1974;**53:**230.

Curran WS, Goldman G: The incidence of immediately reacting allergy skin tests in a "normal" adult population. *Ann Intern Med* 1961;**55:**777.

Immunotherapy (Hyposensitization)

Johnstone DE, Dutton A: The value of hyposensitization therapy for bronchial asthma in children: A 14-year study. *Pediatrics* 1968;**42:**793.

Lichtenstein LM, Norman PS, Winkenwerder WL: Clinical and in vitro studies on the role of immunotherapy in ragweed hay fever. *Am J Med* 1968;**44:**514.

Lowell FC, Franklin W: A double-blind study of the effectiveness and specificity of injection therapy in ragweed hay fever. *N Engl J Med* 1965;**273:**675.

Norman PS: An overview of immunotherapy: Implications for the future. *J Allergy Clin Immunol* 1980;**65:**87.

Norman PS: Specific therapy in allergy. *Med Clin North Am* 1974;**58:**111.

Patterson R: Clinical efficacy of allergen immunotherapy. *J Allergy Clin Immunol* 1979;**64:**155.

Sherman WB, Connell JT: Changes in skin-sensitizing antibody titer (SSAT) following two to four years of injection (aqueous) therapy. *J Allergy Clin Immunol* 1966;**37:**123.

Terr AI: Immunologic basis for injection therapy of allergic diseases. *Med Clin North Am* 1969;**53**:1257.

Allergic Rhinitis (Hay Fever)

Chan JCM, Logan GN, McBean JB: Serous otitis media and allergy: Relation to allergy and other causes. *Am J Dis Child* 1967;**114**:684.

Connell JT: Quantitative intranasal pollen challenges. 3. The priming effect in allergic rhinitis. *J Allergy Clin Immunol* 1969;**43**:33.

Mullarkey MF, Gill JS, Webb DR: Allergic and nonallergic rhinitis: Their characterization with attention to the meaning of nasal eosinophilia. *J Allergy Clin Immunol* 1980; **65**:122.

Patterson R: Rhinitis. *Med Clin North Am* 1974;**58**:43.

Solomon WR: Comparative effects of transient body surface cooling, recumbency, and induced obstruction in allergic rhinitis and control subjects. *J Allergy Clin Immunol* 1966; **37**:216.

Asthma

Beall GN (moderator): Asthma: New ideas about an old disease. *Ann Intern Med* 1973;**78**:405.

Falliers CJ: Interpretation of consecutive lung function tests for asthma. *Ann Allergy* 1972;**30**:443.

Franklin W: Current concepts: Treatment of severe asthma. *N Engl J Med* 1974;**290**:1469.

Middleton E: Autonomic imbalance in asthma with special reference to beta adrenergic blockade. *Adv Intern Med* 1972;**18**:177.

Nadel JA: Mechanisms of airway response to inhaled substances. *Arch Environ Health* 1968;**16**:171.

Rebuck AS, Pengelly LD: Development of pulsus paradoxus in airways obstruction. *N Engl J Med* 1973;**288**:66.

Reed CW: Abnormal autonomic mechanisms in asthma. *J Allergy Clin Immunol* 1974;**53**:34.

Samter M, Beers RF: Intolerance to aspirin. *Ann Intern Med* 1968;**68**:975.

Spector S, Farr RS: Bronchial inhalational procedures in asthmatics. *Med Clin North Am* 1974;**58**:71.

Szentivanyi A: The beta adrenergic theory of the atopic abnormality in bronchial asthma. *J Allergy Clin Immunol* 1971;**47**:23.

Terr AI: Bronchial asthma. Page 421 in: *Textbook of Pulmonary Diseases*. Baum G (editor). Little, Brown, 1974.

Terr AI: Occupational asthma. Chap 15, pp 257–274, in *Bronchial Asthma*. Gershwin ME (editor). Grune & Stratton, 1981.

Atopic Dermatitis

Baer RL: *Atopic Dermatitis*. New York Univ Press, 1955.

Brunsting LA, Reed WB, Baer HL: Occurrence of cataracts and keratoconus with atopic dermatitis. *Arch Dermatol* 1962;**85**:17.

Conference on infantile eczema. *J Pediatr* 1965;**66**:163.

Hanifin JM, Lobitz WC Jr: Newer concepts of atopic dermatitis. *Arch Dermatol* 1977;**113**:663.

Lobitz WC, Honeyman SF, Winkler NW: Suppressed cell-mediated immunity in two adults with atopic dermatitis. *Br J Dermatol* 1972;**86**:317.

Norins AL: Atopic dermatitis. *Pediatr Clin North Am* 1971; **18**:801.

Peterson RDA: Immunologic responses in infantile eczema. *J Pediatr* 1965;**66**:24.

Sedlis E: Natural history of infantile eczema: Its incidence and course. *J Pediatr* 1965;**66**:161.,

Stone SP, Muller SA, Gleich GJ: IgE levels in atopic dermatitis. *Arch Dermatol* 1973;**108**:806.

Anaphylaxis

Austen KF: Systemic anaphylaxis in the human being. *N Engl J Med* 1974;**291**:661.

Bacal E, Patterson R, Zeiss CR: Evaluation of severe (anaphylactic) reactions. *Clin Allergy* 1978;**8**:295.

James LP, Austen KF: Fatal systemic anaphylaxis in man. *N Engl J Med* 1964;**270**:597.

Kelly JF, Patterson R: Anaphylaxis: Course, mechanisms and treatment. *JAMA* 1974;**227**:1431.

Stinging Insect Hypersensitivity

Lichtenstein LM, Valentine MD, Sobotka AK: Insect allergy: The state of the art. *J Allergy Clin Immunol* 1979;**64**:5.

Mueller JL: Further experiences with severe allergic reactions to insect stings. *N Engl J Med* 1959;**261**:374.

Parrish HM: Analysis of 460 fatalities from venomous animals in the United States. *Am J Med Sci* 1963;**245**:35.

Urticaria & Angioedema

Beall GN: Urticaria: A review of laboratory and clinical observations. *Medicine* 1964;**43**:131.

Beck P et al: Hereditary angioneurotic edema. *Q J Med* 1973; **42**:317.

Mathews KP: A current view of urticaria. *Med Clin North Am* 1974;**58**:185.

Mathews KP: Management of urticaria and angioedema. *J Allergy Clin Immunol* 1980;**66**:347.

Soter NA, Wasserman SI: Physical urticaria/angioedema: An experimental model of mast cell activation in humans. *J Allergy Clin Immunol* 1980;**66**:358.

Tas J: Chronic urticaria: A survey of one hundred hospitalized cases. *Dermatologica* 1967;**135**:90.

Drug Allergy

Amos HE: *Allergic Drug Reactions*. Arnold, 1976.

Dash CH, Jones HEH: *Mechanisms in Drug Allergy*. Williams & Wilkins, 1972.

Gralnick HR et al: Hemolytic anemia associated with cephalothin. *JAMA* 1971;**217**:1193.

Levine BB, Redmond AP: Immune mechanisms of penicillin-induced Coombs positivity in man. *J Clin Invest* 1967; **46**:1085.

LoBuglio AF, Jandl JH: The nature of the alpha-methyldopa red-cell antibody. *N Engl J Med* 1967;**276**:658.

Neely CL, Kraus AP: Mechanisms of drug-induced hemolytic anemia. *Adv Intern Med* 1972;**18**:59.

Parker CW: Drug allergy. (3 parts.) *N Engl J Med* 1975; **292**:511, 732, 957.

Weinstein L, Weinstein AJ: The pathophysiology and pathoanatomy of reactions to antimicrobial agents. *Adv Intern Med* 1974;**19**:109.

Penicillin Allergy

Bierman CW, Van Arsdel PP Jr: Penicillin allergy in children: The role of immunological tests in its diagnosis. *J Allergy Clin Immunol* 1969;**43**:267.

Fellner MJ et al: Mechanisms of clinical desensitization in urticarial hypersensitivity to penicillin. *J Allergy Clin Immunol* 1970;**45**:55.

Green GR, Rosenblum AH, Sweet LC: Evaluation of penicillin hypersensitivity: Value of clinical history and skin testing with penicilloyl-polylysine and penicillin G. A cooperative prospective study of the Penicillin Study Group of the American Academy of Allergy. *J Allergy Clin Immunol* 1977;**60:**339.

Levine BB: Immunologic mechanisms of penicillin allergy: A haptenic model system for the study of allergic diseases of man. *N Engl J Med* 1966;**275:**1115.

Levine BB, Zolov DM: Prediction of penicillin allergy by immunologic tests. *J Allergy Clin Immunol* 1969;**43:**231.

Sullivan TJ et al: Skin testing to detect penicillin allergy. *J Allergy Clin Immunol* 1981;**68:**171.

Van Dellen RG et al: Differing patterns of wheal and flare skin reactivity in patients allergic to penicillins. *J Allergy Clin Immunol* 1971;**47:**230.

Food Allergy

Bahna SL, Heiner DC: *Allergies to Milk.* Grune & Stratton, 1980.

Bock SA et al: Studies of hypersensitivity reactions to foods in infants and children. *J Allergy Clin Immunol* 1978;**62:**327.

Goldman AS, Heiner DC: Clinical aspects of food sensitivity: Diagnosis and management of cow's milk sensitivity. *Pediatr Clin North Am* 1977;**24:**133.

Goldstein GB, Heiner DC: Clinical and immunological perspectives in food sensitivity. *J Allergy Clin Immunol* 1970;**46:**270.

Waldmann TA et al: Allergic gastroenteropathy: A cause of excessive gastrointestinal protein loss. *N Engl J Med* 1967; **276:**761.

Walker WA, Hong R: Immunology of the gastrointestinal tract. (2 parts.) *J Pediatr* 1973;**83:**517, 711.

29 | Gastrointestinal & Liver Diseases

Keith B. Taylor, MD, & Howard C. Thomas, MD, PhD

The mammalian gastrointestinal system, including the liver, contributes to the total immune responsiveness of the body. In both qualitative and quantitative terms, this contribution is no better defined than that of other organs, including the thymus, which is itself derived from the foregut. Knowledge of what and how the digestive system contributes to total immune activity is incomplete, as is our understanding of how the immune functions of the digestive organs and of the body as a whole serve to maintain homeostasis of the gastrointestinal tract. Transient or chronic failure of any of these functions may underlie or contribute to human gastroenterologic diseases. The pathogenesis of almost all such diseases except those associated with infection by recognized pathogenic microorganisms is unknown. Immunologic phenomena are associated with many of them.

STRUCTURAL & FUNCTIONAL COMPONENTS OF THE IMMUNE SYSTEM PECULIAR TO THE GASTROINTESTINAL TRACT

The lymphoreticular components of the mature gastrointestinal tract consist of plasma cells, Peyer's patches, and intraepithelial lymphocytes (theliolymphocytes).

Plasma Cells

Plasma cells are distributed rather homogeneously throughout the lamina propria of the large and small gut and in much smaller numbers in the lamina propria of the stomach. They are not present before birth, and their appearance coincides with population of the alimentary tract with microorganisms. It has been shown experimentally that sterile fetal small bowel implanted autologously under the skin or renal capsule will also become populated with plasma cells, demonstrating that exogenous antigens may not be necessary for this phenomenon to occur. Plasma cells are derived from large B lymphocytes. They contain immunoglobulins of classes A, G, M, E, and D. IgA-containing cells predominate (A, 80%; M, 15%; G, < 5%; D and E, 2%) and contribute part of the total circulating 7S IgA. IgA-containing cells occur in higher proportion in small than in large intestine, and the reverse is true of IgG cells. Approximately 60% of IgA- and IgM-containing cells are found within 200 μm of the surface epithelium; the majority of IgG-containing cells are found farther basally.

Peyer's Patches

Peyer's patches are groups of subepithelial lymphoid follicles located in the mucosa of the small intestine, being more numerous in the ileum than the jejunum. They are recognizable in humans by the 24th week of gestation, becoming larger and more numerous by puberty. Each patch is only one follicle thick, and the overlying epithelium is devoid of villi and consists of a single layer of cells. These cells in humans have the appearance of transporting cells and have been called microfold, or M, cells. Serial studies in animals have shown that Peyer's patches are initially populated predominantly by thymus-derived cells but that numbers of marrow-derived B cells later accumulate, so that in adult animals the population is approximately 70% T cells and 30% B cells.

The function of Peyer's patches is not known. It has been suggested that they are the mammalian analog of the avian bursa of Fabricius, the central lymphoid organ responsible for the generation of B cells in birds. However, repopulation of irradiated Peyer's patches by peripheral lymphocytes has been observed—in contrast to the absence of repopulation of the irradiated mammalian thymus, which is unequivocally a central lymphoid organ. It has also been observed that the rate of cell proliferation in Peyer's patches in young animals is not sufficiently high to account for the appearance of B cells in other organs.

Peyer's patches are not capable of mounting a primary immune response in vivo. This appears to be due to lack of an antigen-trapping mechanism. Experiments using cells from mouse Peyer's patches in vitro have shown that antigen-sensitive T and B cells are present but that exogenous accessory adherent cells are required for generation of a primary immune response. There is a paucity of IgA plasma cells as well as those of other immunoglobulin classes in Peyer's patches. However, cells from Peyer's patches in the rabbit repopulate the irradiation-depleted lamina propria with predominantly IgA plasma cells, a few IgG and IgM cells being found as well.

One theory holds that Peyer's patches are a source

of large lymphocytes found in thoracic duct lymph, which circulate and populate the intestinal mucosa with immunoglobulin-containing plasma cells, of which the great majority are IgA. Recent experimental evidence suggests that Peyer's patches constitute the afferent limb of the local immune response to antigens present in the intestinal lumen.

Intraepithelial Lymphocytes or Theliolymphocytes

These are mainly T lymphocytes, whose function and fate are unknown. They lie in contiguity with intestinal epithelial cells. The isolation, characterization, and quantification of lymphoid cells from the intestinal wall of the rabbit have unexpectedly revealed that of the whole population of lymphoid cells, excluding those of Peyer's patches, immunoglobulin-containing cells (plasma cells) constitute only 1% and the theliolymphocytes more than one-third of the total population. Although theliolymphocytes have not been found either in the blood or in thoracic duct lymph, experimental studies have shown that the majority do not persist more than 3–4 days in the epithelium.

IMMUNOGLOBULINS IN THE INTESTINAL TRACT
(See Chapter 15.)

All classes of immunoglobulin are found in gastric and intestinal secretions, but IgA predominates. Similarly, immunofluorescence studies reveal all classes of immunoglobulins in the intercellular spaces of the lamina propria, but IgG predominates.

The IgA in gastrointestinal (and other) secretions is largely in the form of an 11S dimer designated secretory IgA. This differs from the predominant type of IgA in serum by the addition of a so-called J piece, a polypeptide of about MW 15,000, which appears to be necessary for the dimeric IgA to combine with a glycoprotein of approximately MW 60,000 called secretory piece or secretory component (SC) (Fig 29–1). SC is synthesized within the endoplasmic reticulum of the epithelial cells of the mucosa, transported to the Golgi complex, where it is found in unbound form, and then acts as a receptor, at the basal surface of the epithelial cell, for the dimeric J chain–containing IgA. The resulting complex is taken into the epithelial cell by pinocytosis, passes across the cell, and is discharged into the intestinal lumen. IgM is also secreted by plasma cells as a J chain–containing polymer and is transported similarly to secretory IgA, being bound to SC. In intestinal secretions, more than two-thirds is present as secretory complex.

Secretory IgA therefore contains 4 types of polypeptide chains: four L, four H, one J, and one SC. It is more resistant than 7S IgA to proteolysis. It possesses specific antibody activity. Both 7S and secretory IgA activate complement by the alternative pathway and are not, therefore, involved in Arthus-type reactions.

Secretory IgA constitutes the major part of the coproantibodies found in the feces of humans and animals following natural, therapeutic, or experimental infection, including immunization. Similar antibody production in response to ingested antigens unrelated to microorganisms and to autoantigens of the gastrointestinal tract itself has been demonstrated. Immunoglobulin-containing plasma cells in the lamina propria of stomach or gut have been shown to contain specific antibodies to such antigens, and IgA predominates. It is therefore clear that the gut is capable of mounting a local primary immune response. Such a response could be (1) protective, (2) regulatory of the gut flora, or (3) pathogenic.

In humans and other species, it has been shown that oral administration of antigen also results in the

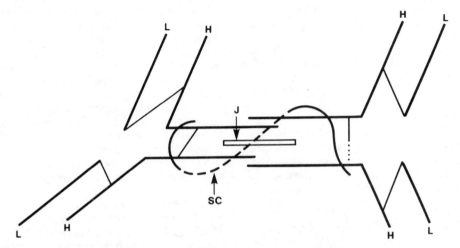

Figure 29–1. Model for secretory IgA. (SC, secretory component; H, heavy chain; L, light chain; J, J chain.) (Modified from Heremans JS: The IgA system in connection with local and systemic immunity. In: *The IgA System.* Mestecky J, Lawton AR [editors]. Plenum Press, 1974.)

production of **circulating** antibodies. The class of serum antibodies formed as a consequence of oral administration of antigen varies. In mice fed ferritin, it is predominantly IgA, whereas in humans administration of live attenuated poliovirus is followed by a response initially of IgM followed by IgG, similar to that seen after parenteral inoculation. Systemic lymphoid tissue acquires the capacity to produce antibodies to ingested antigens. Thus, antigen must reach this lymphoid tissue across the mucosal and vascular structures, or lymphoid cells which are committed to specific antibody production migrate to systemic lymphoid tissue from the gut.

THE GASTROINTESTINAL TRACT AS A SITE OF IMMUNOLOGIC REACTIONS

The gut possesses the capacity to mount a primary immunologic response, a rich vascular supply, and mast cells and other cells capable of releasing substances associated with immediate allergic reactions and contraction of smooth muscle. Theoretically, it could be involved in any type of allergic reaction:

Type I: Anaphylactic reactions involving specific IgE and allergen. The IgE (reagin) is bound to mast cells and other cell surfaces through a specialized part of the Fc fragment. The allergen-reagin reaction damages cell membranes, releasing pharmacologically active amines such as histamine.

Type II: Cytotoxic reactions. Interaction of IgG and IgM antibodies with antigens attached to cell surfaces, causing phagocytosis of the cells or death by K (killer) cells or lysis by activation of the complement system.

Type III: Reaction of antigen with antibody in antigen excess to form soluble complexes which activate the complement system. Cells are damaged by direct toxic effect or secondarily as a consequence of damage to vascular endothelium.

Type IV: Delayed reactions involving interaction of allergen and sensitized T lymphocytes to release lymphokines. The result is a subacute or chronic inflammatory response, with cell damage or destruction.

The primary antigen may be extrinsic (microorganism, dietary constituent) but may share antigenic determinants with autoallergens of the gastrointestinal tissues, or a disturbance of immune responsiveness may allow primary autoimmunization to occur.

CHASE–SULZBERGER PHENOMENON

This eponym is applied to the induction of a state of partial or complete low-zone tolerance to antigens or haptens such as dinitrochlorobenzene by their inges-

tion. An immune response in the intestinal wall may be partly responsible, or low concentrations of IgA antibody-antigen complexes formed in antigen excess may act as tolerogens. The hyporesponsive state is believed to be due to antigen-specific suppressor T cells. The importance of the intestinal wall in subserving this phenomenon is diminished and that of the liver emphasized by experimental evidence that injection of antigen into the portal vein produces a similar tolerance. Venous portasystemic bypassing of the liver prevents occurrence of the phenomenon in response to oral ingestion of antigens, as does experimental cirrhosis.

Following ingestion of a food protein, specific IgG and IgA complexes containing the protein appear transiently in the circulation of both healthy and atopic subjects. In the former, it is assumed that a state of tolerance exists as a consequence of prolonged ingestion of an antigen or that blocking antibodies are present that prevent activation of tissue-damaging immune reactions. In the atopic subject, specific circulating IgE complexes to a dietary antigen occur following its ingestion, and these have been shown to be capable of activating complement by the classic pathway.

ACUTE GASTROINTESTINAL ALLERGY

Major Immunologic Features
- Acute reactions of type I.
- Involves reaction of specific IgE antibody and alimentary antigens.
- Subsequent release of histamine and other mediators of immediate hypersensitivity.

General Considerations
Acute and subacute allergic reactions occurring in the gastrointestinal tract as a consequence of ingestion of allergens are well documented. It has been estimated that in the USA 0.3–0.7% of infants are sensitive to cow's milk protein. The β-lactoglobulin component is an important allergen. It is absent from human milk, which usually does not evoke a reaction in an infant intolerant to cow's milk. Tolerance develops with maturity in most subjects. Hypersensitivity to other dietary proteins occurs less frequently. What may be interpreted as allergy to milk is sometimes an expression of intestinal lactase deficiency and lactose intolerance. This may be primary, or secondary to intestinal damage associated with an allergic response. Reactions to small amounts of milk or to lactose-free milk products such as cheeses are not due to alactasia and are probably allergic.

Immunologic Pathogenesis
The reason why some individuals are atopic is unknown. The atopic child appears to have the same exposure to ingested antigens as the normal child. Some data suggest that hypersensitivity occurs significantly more often in subjects who are deficient in IgA. Absence of secretory IgA in the intestinal mucosa or

lumen may impair the physiologic mechanisms responsible for excluding potential allergens from the body without involvement of tissue-damaging or exciting reactions. The consequence might be the recruitment of more vigorous immune reactions involving other classes of antibody. Stimulation of normally responsive precommitted IgE plasma cells during a transient IgA-deficient period at the age of about 3 months has been proposed as a cause of the development of subsequent type I allergy or atopy to dietary proteins. An apparently—though not necessarily—conflicting view is that acute allergic disease occurs as a consequence of early contact with allergens and a genetically favored IgE pathway of antibody formation.

The sequence of events following presentation of an allergen to the intestinal tract has been studied by serial mucosal biopsy in infants sensitive to cow's milk. At 6 hours after challenge, edema and a small excess of plasma cells are noted in the jejunal lamina propria. By 12 hours, the numbers of mast cells and plasma cells, eosinophils, and neutrophils have greatly increased. The increase of plasma cells consists mainly of those containing IgE and IgM.

Experimental studies of passive anaphylaxis in intestine and skin have shown that the magnitude and timing of responses at both sites are the same whether the antigen is administered orally, intravenously, or locally. This suggests that allergen does not reach mast cells in the mucosa directly from the lumen but via the bloodstream. Thus, inhaled or injected allergens may produce reactions in the intestinal tract.

Clinical Features

A. Symptoms and Signs: Abdominal discomfort, nausea and vomiting, watery and sometimes bloody diarrhea, and, in severe cases, prostration and fever may occur. Extraintestinal responses such as bronchospasm, skin eruptions, and migrainous headaches may complicate or dominate the clinical picture. Severe gastrointestinal allergy to cow's milk is seen much more frequently than acute gastrointestinal allergy. The former is a more insidious subacute reaction occurring in infants 2–3 months old typically 1 month after introduction of cow's milk into the diet and characterized by vomiting, prolonged diarrhea, failure to thrive, and sometimes atopic asthma and recurrent respiratory infection.

B. Laboratory Findings: A transient eosinophilia may be the only objective finding, but it may be short-lived and is often missed. Thus, in clinical practice, the diagnosis often depends solely on the history, and objective evidence is rarely obtained. Lacking evidence, many clinicians regard the whole subject skeptically.

Immunologic Diagnosis

The results of skin tests with suspected allergens correlate poorly with the clinical history. The presence of IgG and IgM serum antibodies to dietary proteins detected by standard techniques such as gel diffusion and passive hemagglutination does not correlate positively with clinical sensitivity.

Studies by Ishizaka and others have established that reagins are immunoglobulins of the class designated IgE. IgE-containing plasma cells are found in relatively small numbers in the mucosa of the small intestine, which may be the site of sensitization to dietary allergens. Increased numbers of IgE plasma cells have been reported in the jejunum of children with food allergy. Elevated serum IgE concentrations are found in some but not all subjects with gastrointestinal allergy.

The Prausnitz-Küstner (PK) test, which requires intradermal injection of the possibly allergic subject's serum into a healthy human recipient followed by injection of the suspected antigen at the same site, provides good evidence of specific circulating IgE antibodies, but the test is positive in only two-thirds of subjects with unequivocal acute gastrointestinal and alimentary allergy. The risk of transmitting viral hepatitis has eliminated the use of this test in humans. The response can be elicited in other primates.

Confident diagnosis of gastrointestinal allergy is difficult. Tests other than the PK are required. Human skin from cadavers has been used successfully in vitro as a site for the anaphylactic reaction. It is unlikely to be more discriminating than the PK test. Radioallergosorbent techniques may provide sensitive methods for detecting specific reagins with high concordance with provocative tests. At present, tests involving dietary exclusion and challenge, sometimes combined with jejunal biopsy, are the diagnostic tools most often employed. Valid blind tests have not been reported. There is a need for such studies, since there is often a psychogenic component to the complaints of sufferers from gastrointestinal allergy.

Differential Diagnosis

Acute gastrointestinal allergy may be mistaken for lactase deficiency, infectious gastroenteritis, or the onset of chronic nonspecific ulcerative colitis. Persistence of symptoms despite exclusion of cow's milk or other protein components of the diet prior to the clinical attack points to some other cause of the symptoms and requires thorough fecal examination and proctosigmoidoscopy.

Treatment

Appropriate clinical tests, including fecal examinations and proctosigmoidoscopy, should be done before embarking on exclusion diets. Treatment consists of identifying the allergen and excluding it from the diet. If it is an important item nutritionally, a substitute must be found.

Recent trials of cromolyn sodium, administered orally to atopic children, have been encouraging.

Complications & Prognosis

Complications of an acute attack are vomiting and diarrhea, resulting sometimes in serious dehydration and circulatory collapse. Bronchospasm may rarely be fatal, as may acute laryngeal edema.

Malabsorption and failure to thrive, atopic eczema, and recurrent respiratory infections are seen in less severely affected children until the specific allergen is excluded from their diet. Available data suggest that the hypersensitivity abates with age in most children and that in some cases full recovery is possible.

CHRONIC OR RELAPSING INFLAMMATORY DISEASES OF THE GASTROINTESTINAL TRACT

1. APHTHOUS ULCERATION OF THE BUCCAL CAVITY

This distressing condition is often dismissed by nonsufferers as trivial. The lesions consist of painful, recurrent ulcers on the tongue and buccal mucosa, lasting several days. About one in 10 otherwise healthy subjects suffers from the condition. In some, exposure to chocolate, nuts, or other foodstuffs is the precipitating cause. The lesions begin as tender red swellings and on histologic examination show acute inflammatory change with some mononuclear cell infiltration. The surface sloughs and becomes secondarily infected; healing with fibroblast activity occurs over days or weeks, usually leaving no scar.

The pathogenesis is unknown. The disease is not associated with herpes simplex. In some patients, a specific allergen can be identified. Serum antibodies to crude extracts of buccal mucosa have been demonstrated by complement fixation in subjects suffering from recurrent aphthous ulceration, although their significance is uncertain.

In sprue, Crohn's disease, ulcerative colitis, and intestinal lymphoma, more severe aphthous ulceration may occur, causing anorexia and providing a site for candidal and other infection. It is not known whether this more severe type of lesion is an expression of poor nutrition or of an abnormal immune response, possibly of an immune complex disease, as has been suggested in the case of pyoderma gangrenosum associated with inflammatory bowel disease. The lesions respond when the bowel disease is treated successfully.

2. SJÖGREN'S SYNDROME
(See Chapter 26.)

The complete Sjögren's syndrome consists of conjunctival and buccal dryness, recurrent swelling of lacrimal and salivary glands, rheumatoid arthritis, and a higher incidence of malignant lymphoma than in the normal population. Salivary glands show plasma cell and lymphocyte infiltration.

Humoral antibodies to salivary tissue occur; in a large proportion of patients, antibodies to thyroid and nuclear antigens may also be found (Table 29-1).

3. CHRONIC ATROPHIC GASTRITIS & PERNICIOUS ANEMIA

Major Immunologic Features
- Evidence for both humoral and cellular immunity to gastric mucosal antigens.
- High incidence of anti-parietal cell antibodies—one to canaliculi and the other to intrinsic factor.
- Autoantibodies found in gastric mucosal plasma cells and in secretions (IgA).

General Considerations
The primary pathologic feature of pernicious

Table 29-1. Autoantibodies in gastrointestinal and hepatic disease.

Disease	Antigen	Detection of Antibody
Aphthous ulceration	Buccal mucosa	Complement fixation
Sjögren's syndrome	Salivary ducts	Immunofluorescence
	Nuclei	Immunofluorescence and complement fixation
	Thyroid	Immunofluorescence and complement fixation
Pernicious anemia	Parietal cell canalicular lipoprotein	Immunofluorescence on gastric mucosa
		Complement fixation
	Thyroid	Immunofluorescence and complement fixation
	Intrinsic factor	Inhibition of biologic activity
		Blocking B_{12} binding
		Coprecipitation
Chronic antral gastritis	Gastrin-secreting G cells	Immunofluorescence
Gluten-sensitive enteropathy	Reticulin	Immunofluorescence
Chronic inflammatory bowel disease	Colonic epithelial lipopolysaccharide	Immunofluorescence
		Passive hemagglutination
Chronic active hepatitis	Smooth muscle ("actomyosin")	Immunofluorescence
Primary biliary cirrhosis	Nuclei	Immunofluorescence
	Mitochondria	Immunofluorescence and complement fixation (kidney or other tissue)

anemia is progressive destruction of the normal glands of the body of the stomach. This is associated with partial or complete loss of acid, pepsinogen, and intrinsic factor secretion. When the last is complete, failure of vitamin B_{12} absorption occurs. In an undetermined number of subjects, complete loss of intrinsic factor secretion may require many years or may never occur. The gastric mucosa is infiltrated, homogeneously or in patchy distribution, with variable numbers of polymorphonuclear and mononuclear leukocytes—predominantly the latter. Atrophy of the mucosa is a consequence of destruction and failure of regeneration of gastric parietal and chief cells. Often the gastric body mucosa is partly or wholly replaced by antral or small intestinal mucosa, a phenomenon known as metaplasia.

Immunologic Pathogenesis

The evidence of immunologic pathogenesis in pernicious anemia is indirect. Experimentally, chronic inflammatory lesions of the gastric mucosa, glandular atrophy, and loss of gastric secretory function have been produced in dogs by immunization using gastric mucosal material and Freund's complete adjuvant. Other species, such as rabbits, rats, mice, and guinea pigs, are resistant to these procedures. In dogs, the appearance of gastric lesions is associated more with development of cell-mediated immunity than with humoral antibodies. However, repeated injection of human gastric antibodies into rats has reduced gastric secretory cells after several weeks.

In pernicious anemia, humoral antibodies are found to 2 antigens of the gastric parietal cell. One is a glycoprotein, Castle's intrinsic factor, and the other a lipoprotein of the microvilli of the parietal cell canalicular system also present on the cell surface (parietal cell canalicular antibody). Neither antigen is species-specific; both are completely cell-specific. Serum parietal cell canalicular antibody is present, as determined by immunofluorescence, in about 90% of patients with pernicious anemia, and intrinsic factor antibody in 60–70%.

There are 2 types of intrinsic factor antibody: type I blocks the attachment of vitamin B_{12} to the intrinsic factor molecule, and type II attaches to intrinsic factor or the intrinsic factor-B_{12} complex (Fig 29–2). Type II intrinsic factor antibody occurs with about half the frequency of type I and only rarely occurs in the absence of type I. Experimentally, the immunogenicity of the intrinsic factor antigenic site for type I antibody is greater than that for type II. Evidence suggests that antibodies to intrinsic factor are capable of inhibiting intrinsic factor-mediated vitamin B_{12} absorption in vivo, and parietal cell canalicular antibody may inhibit acid secretion by the parietal cell.

Gastric antibodies in serum are mainly of the IgG class, with some IgA and rarely IgM. In chronic atrophic gastritis of the body of the stomach without the lesion of pernicious anemia, serum parietal cell canalicular antibody occurs less frequently than in pernicious anemia, and intrinsic factor antibodies are found so rarely that their presence requires further diagnostic work-up which almost always reveals pernicious anemia. They rarely occur in the absence of severe gastritis, but a group of patients with thyroid disease has been described in which humoral intrinsic factor antibodies were present despite some acid and intrinsic factor secretion which persisted during many years of follow-up. Recently, serum antibodies to the gastrin-secreting G cells of the antral mucosa have been described in a small percentage of patients with chronic antral gastritis whose sera are negative for parietal cell canalicular or intrinsic factor antibodies.

Parietal cell canalicular antibodies—but not intrinsic factor antibodies—are found in some first-order relatives of patients with pernicious anemia. They are also present with significantly increased frequency in iron deficiency anemia, thyroid disease, idiopathic Addison's disease, diabetes mellitus, and vitiligo in association with chronic gastritis (Table

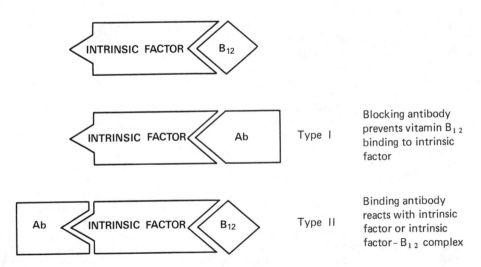

Figure 29–2. The 2 types of intrinsic factor antibody.

Table 29–2. Frequency of circulating parietal cell canalicular antibody in pernicious anemia and other diseases.

Patient Group	Approximate Positive Parietal Cell Canalicular Antibody (%)
Pernicious anemia	86
Normal population*	11
Vitiligo	20
Thyroiditis	30
Thyrotoxicosis	25
Addison's disease	24
Diabetes mellitus	21
Iron deficiency anemia	20

*Chronic gastritis not excluded.

29–2). The infrequency of parietal cell canalicular antibody increases in apparently healthy subjects with age. This antibody is rarely or never found unless chronic gastritis is present, and the prevalence of this condition increases with age.

Thyroid microsomal and thyroglobulin antibodies are also found in some pernicious anemia subjects, though in lower frequency than in subjects with thyroid diseases.

Gastric autoantibodies are not detectable in patients with chronic gastritis associated with gastric and duodenal ulcer disease or following partial gastrectomy for ulcer disease, or in gastric carcinoma, except in subjects with preexisting pernicious anemia. In these, the presence or absence of circulating gastric antibodies apparently has no significance with regard to development of gastric carcinoma. The gastritic lesions in these conditions are histologically indistinguishable from those in pernicious anemia, but gastric functional changes are usually less severe.

Gastric antibodies in gastric secretions. Both parietal cell canalicular antibody and intrinsic factor antibody are present in the gastric juice of the majority of pernicious anemia patients. Intrinsic factor antibodies may form complexes with any residual intrinsic factor secreted. The antibodies are IgG and IgA, and some activity is present in 11S (secretory) IgA. This, together with demonstration of the presence of both parietal cell canalicular antibody and intrinsic factor antibody in plasma cells in the inflamed mucosa and the absence of thyroid antibodies from gastric juice in subjects with thyroid antibodies in their sera, attests to gastric antibody formation in the gastric mucosa. By immunofluorescence, complement fixation has been demonstrated at the site of parietal canalicular antigen when it reacts with antibody.

Cell-mediated immunity in pernicious anemia. Cellular immunity to intrinsic factor and gastric parietal cell canalicular antigen has been measured by lymphocyte activation and MIF production. Positive responses have been detected in patients with pernicious anemia, in patients with pernicious anemia and immunoglobulin deficiency, and in a few normal individuals.

Response of the gastric lesion of pernicious anemia to corticosteroids and immunosuppressive drugs. Improved vitamin B_{12} absorption, enhanced intrinsic factor secretion, some regeneration of gastric parietal cells, and decreased titers of circulating gastric antibodies have been reported in pernicious anemia subjects treated with corticosteroids. Achlorhydria usually persists. However, there is a lack of correlation in treated individuals between improved vitamin B_{12} absorption, improved gastric structure and function, and changes of intrinsic factor antibody titers in either serum or gastric juice, and the mode of action of corticosteroids remains uncertain.

Parietal cell regeneration and restoration of gastric acid secretion have been reported in patients with pernicious anemia treated with azathioprine, but no immunologic studies were performed. No direct effect of immune cells or of gastric antibodies on human gastric mucosa has been observed. Until this is achieved, evidence of an immunologic pathogenesis in pernicious anemia is only presumptive.

Clinical Features

A. Symptoms and Signs: Atrophic gastritis without pernicious anemia is frequently undiagnosed, since the gastric lesion is usually asymptomatic. Mild to severe dyspepsia may occur together with impairment of appetite. Pernicious anemia is the expression of vitamin B_{12} deficiency. It is characterized by increasing weakness, fatigability, loss of appetite, and pallor. Loss of weight is common, but wasting is rare. Involvement of the nervous system, which is quite variable, may include peripheral neuropathy, damage to pyramidal tract and posterior column neurons, and disturbance of higher cortical functions.

Pernicious anemia displays a strong familial association, but how much is environmentally and how much genetically determined is still unknown. No specific HLA genotype has been unequivocally associated with the disease. There is an association between pernicious anemia and thyroid disease, especially thyrotoxicosis, which occurs frequently in close relatives of pernicious anemia patients. Less strong associations have been claimed with diabetes mellitus and idiopathic Addison's disease. Pernicious anemia also occurs in acquired immunoglobulin deficiency, most commonly of IgA but sometimes of IgG or IgM also.

B. Laboratory Findings: Macrocytic anemia and hypersegmentation of the nuclei of the neutrophil granulocytes are the morphologic findings in the peripheral blood. Bone marrow aspirates show megaloblastosis. Serum vitamin B_{12} values below 120 pg/mL are found (normal, 200–1500 pg/mL). Serum lactate dehydrogenase activity is markedly elevated owing to excessive intramedullary destruction of red blood cells. The excretion of methylmalonate in the urine is increased. Vitamin B_{12} therapy corrects all of these abnormalities except that some damage to the central nervous system may be irreversible.

Immunologic Diagnosis

The finding of circulating parietal canalicular antibodies by complement fixation or immunofluorescence almost certainly indicates chronic gastric disease, though negative serologic findings do not exclude this diagnosis. Antibodies to intrinsic factor indicate the lesion of pernicious anemia, with the rare exceptions of a few patients with thyroid disease. Cell-mediated immune tests are not yet generally available.

Differential Diagnosis

Clinically, other anemias and untreated myxedema and pituitary hypofunction may be confused with pernicious anemia. The finding of megaloblastic anemia reduces the possibilities to three—namely, deficiency of vitamin B_{12}, deficiency of folic acid, or both. Unequivocal involvement of the nervous system points to the former. However, a deficiency of vitamin B_{12} may occur as a consequence of dietary deficiency (an unsupplemented vegetarian diet) or of malabsorption due to pancreatic or small intestine disease as well as a lack of intrinsic factor. Correction of vitamin B_{12} malabsorption by administration of intrinsic factor provides unequivocal evidence of the basic lesion of pernicious anemia. Impaired absorption of vitamin B_{12} is demonstrable by a variety of tests using tracer doses of radioactive cobalt-labeled vitamin B_{12} without and with intrinsic factor (eg, the Schilling test, in which urinary excretion of labeled vitamin B_{12} is the index of intestinal absorption). Aspirated gastric juice contains negligible intrinsic factor activity and no hydrochloric acid, even in response to powerful stimulants of secretion. The presence of serum antibodies to gastric antigens may provide confirmatory evidence.

Treatment

Intramuscular injections of vitamin B_{12} will maintain remissions in pernicious anemia. Corticosteroids and immunosuppressive agents have only been used experimentally. There is no practicable means at present of recognizing the gastric lesion sufficiently early to offer any hope of instituting therapy at a reversible stage of the disease.

Complications & Prognosis

The only important complication is gastric carcinoma, which is probably 3 times more common in patients with pernicious anemia than in the population at large. No immunologic or other test has yet been devised which reliably identifies subjects prone to develop gastric carcinoma or provides early recognition of such a lesion.

GLUTEN–SENSITIVE ENTEROPATHY; CELIAC SPRUE

Major Immunologic Features
- Genetic association with HLA-B8 and HLA-Dw3.
- Infiltration of jejunal lamina propria with lymphocytes and plasma cells when untreated.
- Possible local IgA deficiency with production of IgM antigluten antibodies.

General Considerations

This disease, also termed nontropical sprue and, in adults, idiopathic steatorrhea, is a disease of the small intestine characterized by functional disturbances causing malabsorption of food and nutrients and structural changes of partial or complete villous atrophy. The normally columnar jejunal epithelial cells become stunted and cuboid, and distortion of their microvilli occurs. The lamina propria becomes infiltrated with inflammatory cells, of which the majority are mononuclear in type. In contrast, the ileal mucosa is relatively or completely normal.

Dicke showed more than 25 years ago that ingestion of wheat gluten was the causative factor, and the term gluten-sensitive enteropathy has now been adopted. α-Gliadin is the noxious component of gluten, and some polypeptide products of α-gliadin hydrolysis as small as MW 8000 have been shown to produce mucosal damage in susceptible individuals.

Immunologic Pathogenesis

Two theories have been advanced to explain the damaging effect of wheat protein in this condition and the improvement in jejunal structure and function that follows dietary gluten exclusion. The enzymatic hypothesis holds that the intestinal mucosa in gluten-sensitive enteropathy congenitally lacks a peptidase necessary for hydrolysis of a toxic partial breakdown product of wheat gluten and that accumulation of this material, apparently of low molecular weight (1000), produces damage to the intestinal mucosa. However, in gluten-sensitive enteropathy in remission, jejunal mucosal biopsies have revealed no peptidase deficiency.

The second, immunologic theory is supported by the following observations:

(1) In a small number of gluten-sensitive enteropathy patients maintained on gluten-exclusion diets, ingestion of small amounts of wheat gluten results in what clinically appears to be an acute (type I) allergic reaction. This has been termed gluten shock.

(2) In untreated gluten-sensitive enteropathy, the jejunal lamina propria is heavily infiltrated with lymphocytes and plasma cells and an increase of theliolymphocytes which have the ultrastructure of immunoblasts, which are not seen in healthy mucosa. In treated gluten-sensitive enteropathy, the histologic appearances are partially or wholly restored to normal. The events in the jejunal mucosa following oral challenge with wheat gluten are as follows: (a) eosinophilic infiltration within 4–5 hours; (b) polymorphonuclear infiltration and vascular endothelial swelling at 10–16 hours; and (c) plasma cell increase of predominantly IgM-containing cells, this IgM being largely antibody-specific for gluten. IgA and IgM immune

complexes appear in the basement membrane region, with variable complement fixation.

(3) Anti-inflammatory doses of corticosteroids correct the clinical and histologic abnormalities of gluten-sensitive enteropathy and effectively suppress gluten shock. Of itself, this clearly does not imply an immune basis for gluten-sensitive enteropathy.

(4) Humoral and secretory antibodies to gluten are present in many patients with untreated gluten-sensitive enteropathy. However, antibodies to other dietary antigens also occur in excess in such patients, suggesting an enhanced immune responsiveness, probably at the mucosal level, due to either increased access of antigens in the lumen as a result of mucosal damage or a quantitative increase in immune-responsive tissue. The latter seems more likely.

(5) Immunoglobulin disturbances occur in untreated gluten-sensitive enteropathy, including elevated or depressed levels of serum IgA, depressed serum IgM, and a significantly more frequent absence of IgD than in normal subjects. Following successful treatment, the IgA levels return to normal limits. A subgroup of subjects have the lesion of gluten-sensitive enteropathy and a persistent IgA deficiency. The jejunal lesion responds to gluten exclusion. An isolated IgA deficiency is found in approximately one in 700 normal individuals and in one in 70 subjects with gluten-sensitive enteropathy. The reason for this discrepancy is unknown.

In the jejunal mucosa, the most constant finding in untreated gluten-sensitive enteropathy is an increased number of IgM plasma cells, though IgA cells still predominate. There is a corresponding increase in IgM in jejunal secretions. In IgA-deficient subjects, IgM and IgG plasma cells are found in the lamina propria, compensating to a variable degree for absence of IgA cells. A relative failure of jejunal IgA antibody response might be pathogenetically significant, since an IgM and IgG compensatory antibody response might result in tissue-damaging immune reactions.

(6) Reticulin antibodies are found in the sera of 60% of untreated gluten-sensitive enteropathic children, 30% of gluten-sensitive enteropathic adults, and 25% of patients with dermatitis herpetiformis. Following treatment by gluten exclusion, the antibody titer may fall or disappear. There is no validated explanation for this phenomenon. The occurrence of similar reticulin antibodies in subjects with small bowel inflammation due to other causes (eg, Crohn's disease) suggests a nonspecific response. Others have claimed that gluten and reticulin share antigenic determinants. The problem has still to be resolved.

(7) Circulating antigen-antibody complexes occur. A relatively simple method of demonstrating the presence of circulating immune complexes depends on the property of a component of the complement system, C1q, to precipitate soluble complexes in agar gel (see Chapter 22). This technique has revealed circulating antigen-antibody complexes in untreated gluten-sensitive enteropathy. That the antigen involved is gluten or a derivative is still speculative.

(8) There is a relative and absolute reduction of circulating T cells in intestinal celiac disease, restored by gluten exclusion.

In summary, it is possible that the intestinal damage of gluten-sensitive enteropathy is a consequence of an Arthuslike immune reaction and that it occurs because of a tendency for local production in the jejunum of IgM rather than IgA antibodies in response to a gluten challenge. This might result from abnormal handling of the antigen by the intestinal epithelium or other structures or an inherent immune abnormality. The fact that only a minority of IgA-deficient subjects have gluten-sensitive enteropathy is unexplained.

Clinical Features

A. Symptoms and Signs: Malabsorption is associated with stunting of growth in the child, loss of weight in the adult, various deficiency states, and greasy, bulky stools of high fat content. The disease expresses itself at any age, but most frequently in childhood.

B. Laboratory Findings: In the untreated subject there may be electrolyte depletion, reflected in abnormally low serum potassium and calcium values. Hypoalbuminemia may reflect protein depletion. Anemia is often present and may be due to iron deficiency, folic acid deficiency, or both. Analysis of the stools reveals increased excretion of fat and nitrogen, and tests of absorption of glucose and xylose reveal malabsorption. The diagnosis is established on the basis of an abnormal jejunal biopsy and response to gluten exclusion.

Recent studies have revealed an association of the disease with the HLA-B8 histocompatibility antigens, suggesting a genetic basis for the previously noted familial association of the disease. The frequency of HLA-B8 in celiac disease is 80% compared with 20–25% in the population at large. (HLA-A1 is also much more frequent, but this gene is associated with HLA-B8 as a consequence of linkage disequilibrium.) An association with the HLA-Dw3 haplotype has recently been demonstrated, and that with HLA-B8 is thought to be secondary. It has also been noted that a skin disease, dermatitis herpetiformis, is associated with small bowel malabsorption and that the latter responds like uncomplicated gluten-sensitive enteropathy to a gluten-exclusion diet, though the skin disease is not affected. HLA-Dw3 and HLA-B8 occur in dermatitis herpetiformis in an abnormal frequency similar to that in gluten-sensitive enteropathy. Thus, as in the case of ankylosing spondylitis, tissue histocompatibility typing may have diagnostic value in the future.

Immunologic Diagnosis

There are no clinically useful immunologic tests. The finding of circulating gluten antibodies has not been applied diagnostically, but the presence of reticulin antibodies has proved to be helpful in the diagnosis of celiac disease in children. Arthus-type reactions to intradermal injection of a subfraction of gluten known to be pathogenic have been reported in subjects with celiac sprue, control subjects being uniformly negative. The same subfraction induces transformation in lymphocytes from celiac sprue subjects. Quantitative serum immunoglobulin levels may reveal an underlying immunoglobulin deficiency.

Differential Diagnosis

The list of causes of small intestinal malabsorption in both children and adults is very large. In infants and children, sensitivity to cow's milk or dietary proteins other than gluten, lactase deficiency, cystic fibrosis of the pancreas, parasitic infestations, Crohn's disease, and congenital anatomic abnormalities of the gastrointestinal tract must be considered. In the adult, the consequences of upper gastrointestinal surgery, chronic pancreatitis, intestinal lymphoma, Crohn's disease, and Whipple's disease may present in a manner that makes these disorders indistinguishable from gluten-sensitive enteropathy.

Treatment

Exclusion of even traces of wheat gluten from the diet almost always results in restoration of small bowel structure and function to normal. This may take weeks or months, and until it is accomplished, dietary supplements and even parenteral administration of some essential nutrients are required. In initially refractory patients, corticosteroids may sometimes induce significant improvement.

Complications & Prognosis

Failure to recognize and treat the disease may result in severe malnutrition, the most important expression of which is irreversible stunting of growth. Delays in initiating treatment may result in a refractory state of malnutrition which does not respond to gluten exclusion and standard oral supplementation. Parenteral nutrition techniques may have to be used.

There is an increased risk of developing intestinal lymphoma (6–10% after a mean duration of the disease of 21 years). Malignancies of the foregut also occur in significantly higher incidence in subjects with celiac disease. A variable degree of splenic atrophy and immune deficiency may occur when the disease is of long duration. Otherwise it appears that rigorous dietary control can achieve a prognosis of normal health and longevity.

CROHN'S DISEASE
(Intestinal Granulomatous Disease)

Major Immunologic Features

- Granulomatous response in intestinal lesions and regional lymph nodes.
- No consistently demonstrable alterations in humoral immunity.
- Abnormalities in cellular immunity may be secondary.

General Considerations

This condition may affect any part of the gastrointestinal tract, most frequently the terminal ileum. The inflammatory lesion is primarily submucosal but ultimately involves the whole thickness of the gut wall. Ulceration of the mucosa occurs and may extend deeply to reach the serosa and cause local perforation and the development of fistulas. Obstructive lymphedema and lymphadenoid hyperplasia occur. In 50–70% of such lesions, noncaseating granulomas are found.

Granulomas are also frequently present in regional mesenteric lymph nodes. The affected bowel becomes thickened and rigid. Two or more diseased segments may be separated by relatively normal bowel (skip lesions).

Immunologic Pathogenesis

The cause of Crohn's disease is not known. Granulomatous lesions have been induced in the footpads and bowel walls of experimental animals, using cell-free and ultrafiltered extracts of Crohn's lesions. Recently, a virus was cultured consistently from the lesions of Crohn's disease, different in appearance and characteristics from one derived similarly from the lesions of ulcerative colitis. Further support for the infectious nature of Crohn's disease (and nonspecific ulcerative colitis) is the finding of RNA antibodies in sera of some affected individuals and their spouses with significant concordance. However, the nonspecific nature of granulomas and the failure to demonstrate any epidemiologic evidence of infectivity make resolution of the infectious nature of the disease at present uncertain. The disease displays some familial tendency but no pattern that suggests a genetic determinant. No satisfactory experimental analog has been produced. Immune phenomena are not well substantiated in Crohn's disease. Experimentally, the granulomatous response appears to be a delayed hypersensitivity reaction, but there are many inciting agents, inorganic or organic, living or dead, which produce the same lesions. Immunosuppressive agents inhibit the production of experimental granulomas but have not been shown to be of substantial therapeutic value in Crohn's disease.

A. Humoral Factors: There is no consistent alteration of any class of circulating immunoglobulin in Crohn's disease. Low plasma protein concentrations occasionally occur as a consequence of protein-losing enteropathy.

Turnover studies reveal increased synthesis and catabolism of IgG, IgM, and C3, and breakdown products of C3 activation occur in the serum of patients with active Crohn's disease. Antibodies to a colonic epithelial lipopolysaccharide and to a similar antigen derived from *E coli* O14 but not to any small intestinal antigen are demonstrable in the blood of some patients with Crohn's disease.

Antigen-antibody complexes have been demonstrated by at least 2 techniques in the sera of some patients with Crohn's disease. The nature of the antigen or antigens involved and the significance of these findings are unknown. Some of the extraintestinal diseases might be due to immune complex deposition. The cytotoxic effect on colonic epithelial cells of normal lymphocytes incubated with the sera of some patients with Crohn's disease might be due to the presence of circulating colonic antibodies. Recently, lymphocytotoxicity has been demonstrated in some Crohn's sera, the effect being more marked on lymphocytes from healthy subjects than from Crohn's subjects. This is not HLA-associated.

B. Delayed Hypersensitivity:

1. Skin tests–No consistent pattern of response to standard antigens such as PPD or DNCB is evident to suggest either anergy or hypersensitivity.

Some discrepant results may be a consequence of nutritional deficiencies secondary to severe Crohn's disease or to quantitative differences in peripheral lymphocyte populations. Reports of positive Kveim tests in patients with Crohn's disease suggest a link with sarcoidosis (as do the successful attempts to transmit granulomatous changes experimentally). Other reports are negative, and variations in Kveim reagents are currently being examined.

2. Tests of lymphocyte activation and MIF production using lymphocytes of patients with Crohn's disease in vitro and antigens of adult and fetal human and rat small and large intestine reveal no abnormal responses.

3. Peripheral lymphocytes of some patients with Crohn's disease exert a cytotoxic effect on human rectal epithelial cells but not on the mucosa of small intestine. There is a relative deficiency of circulating T cells in Crohn's disease, possibly as a consequence of selective lymphocytotoxic factor present in Crohn's sera.

In summary, there is no evidence of primary immunologic pathogenesis in Crohn's disease. The factors involved in the formation of the typical granulomatous lesions remain obscure. At present, conclusive evidence for or against involvement of a transmissible agent is awaited. An unexplained observation of healing of the granulomatous lesion following surgical diversion of the fecal stream may favor the theory that some dietary constituent plays a role in causing or perpetuating the disease.

Clinical Features

A. Symptoms and Signs: The disease is clinically manifested by fever, abdominal colic, diarrhea, malabsorption with loss of weight, and consequences of specific nutritional deficiencies of iron, folic acid, and vitamin B_{12}. Frank intestinal bleeding is rare, but the presence of fecal occult blood is common. The lesion may present as a palpable and often tender mass, most commonly in the right lower quadrant of the abdomen. Surgery may be required to resect or bypass stenosed segments of bowel, fistulous involvement of the body wall and skin, or other viscera such as the urinary bladder; occasionally, surgery is needed to resect bleeding ulceration.

Extraintestinal disease. The skin, eyes, liver, and joints may be involved in Crohn's disease, but the reason is not known. There is little or no correlation with the apparent severity of the bowel disease. (1) Lesions of skin and buccal mucosa: erythema nodosum, pyoderma gangrenosum, and aphthous ulceration. (2) Lesions of the eye: uveitis (including iritis) and episcleritis. (3) Liver: fatty infiltration and portal triaditis (pericholangitis); possibly cirrhosis and biliary tract carcinoma. (4) Ankylosing spondylitis. (5) Episodic polysynovitis.

There is a strong association between ankylosing spondylitis in Crohn's disease (and nonspecific ulcerative colitis; see p 529) and HLA-B27, and the same is true in uncomplicated ankylosing spondylitis, whereas neither Crohn's disease nor ulcerative colitis has been associated with any HLA genotype.

B. Laboratory Findings: Some degree of anemia, usually due to chronic blood loss and iron deficiency, is common. There may be hematologic evidence of vitamin B_{12} deficiency.

An elevated erythrocyte sedimentation rate is often a valuable indication of active Crohn's disease.

Immunologic Diagnosis

No reliable methods are available.

Differential Diagnosis

Nonspecific ulcerative colitis, lymphoma of the small intestine, Whipple's disease, giardiasis, gluten-sensitive enteropathy, tuberculous enteritis, and small bowel neoplasms are some of the conditions which may clinically resemble Crohn's disease.

Treatment

Treatment of this disease remains quite unsatisfactory. No controlled therapeutic trials have established clear superiority of any regimen. Corticosteroids, sulfasalazine (salicylazosulfapyridine), and azathioprine are used in various combinations. Surgery is never curative but may be required to relieve the complications of obstruction and fistula formation.

Complications & Prognosis

The major complications have been described as part of the clinical features. The prognosis can only be characterized as extremely uncertain. The disease varies in its activity. In some patients the course is relentless and may lead to death as a consequence of repeated resections of bowel and ultimately uncorrectable malnutrition. In others the disease is self-limiting or may require a single surgical resection, with no recurrence over a period of many years.

Another complication, recently recognized, is a high incidence of malignant change in both affected large and small bowel.

NONSPECIFIC CHRONIC ULCERATIVE COLITIS

Major Immunologic Features

- Increased turnover of IgG, IgM, and C3 in active ulcerative colitis.
- Lymphocytes are cytotoxic for colonic epithelial cells.
- Antibodies detected against intestinal epithelial antigens do not seem pathogenic.
- Antibody to intestinal lipopolysaccharide cross-reacts with *E coli* O14.

General Considerations

Ulcerative colitis is a chronic inflammatory disease of the colonic mucosa. The early changes are confined to the mucosa, which is diffusely inflamed and ulcerated to a variable degree. Inflammatory changes in the submucosa are seen only in long-standing chronic disease. Infiltration of the lamina propria with mononuclear inflammatory cells is an invariable feature. Eosinophilic infiltration is at times marked, and in severe disease polymorphonuclear leukocytes abound. The mucosal vessels are dilated. The crypt abscess, a focal collection of polymorphonuclear leukocytes in the deepest part of the lamina propria, contiguous with dilated crypts of Lieberkühn, is found in more severe disease. Ulcers may be superficial or may involve the entire thickness of mucosa, which may then be lost and replaced by granulation tissue. Granuloma formation rarely occurs.

Immunologic Pathogenesis

The cause of ulcerative colitis is unknown. Specific infections and psychologic, nutritional, and immunologic theories have been entertained without solid evidence. In a recent study, a virus was isolated consistently from affected tissue. It has been classified as a reovirus but has a different appearance and different properties from the virus isolated in Crohn's disease. Its significance is uncertain. The immunologic theory of causation received limited support from studies of the disease, including convincing evidence in some patients of beneficial effects of dietary exclusion of cow's milk or other proteins and of immediate and severe relapse following oral challenge with the same protein. A higher than normal frequency of atopic eczema, asthma, and hay fever in persons with chronic ulcerative colitis has been reported but has not been confirmed by recent studies.

A. Humoral Immunity: No consistent differences in circulating immunoglobulins are found, but rates of turnover of IgG, IgM, Clq, and C3 are increased. This may reflect increased protein loss from the inflamed gut, but there is some evidence of extravascular sequestration of the complement components. The presence and titer of circulating antibodies to cow's milk and other dietary proteins do not correlate positively with the severity or extent of chronic ulcerative colitis, though there may be some correlation with its chronicity and tendency to relapse. Re-sponses to dietary exclusion of cow's milk do not correlate positively with milk antibody titers. No reaginic activity to suspected allergens has been convincingly demonstrated in chronic ulcerative colitis.

Antibodies of IgG, IgA, or IgM classes against an intestinal epithelial lipopolysaccharide are found in the sera of patients with chronic ulcerative colitis with variable frequency and more often in children than in adults with the disease. They have been reported in some healthy relatives of patients with chronic ulcerative colitis. Other immunologic features can be summarized as follows: (1) Antibody titers are independent of duration, extent, severity, or complications of chronic ulcerative colitis. (2) Antibodies persist following colectomy. (3) Antibodies are not cytotoxic to colonic epithelial cells even in the presence of complement. (4) Attempts to demonstrate antibody bound to colonic epithelial cells in chronic ulcerative colitis have been unsuccessful. (5) Antibodies cross-react with lipopolysaccharide antigen of *E coli* O14. It has been concluded that coliform antigens may break tolerance to intestinal epithelial antigen. A pathogenetic role cannot be substantiated. Chronic ulcerative colitis has been described in patients with hypogammaglobulinemia.

B. Immune Complexes in Chronic Ulcerative Colitis: These have been demonstrated in the sera of some patients by several techniques. The antigen or antigens have not been identified, but the antibody is IgG. Theoretically, their presence might be responsible for extracolonic complications of chronic ulcerative colitis, some of which strongly resemble those seen in serum sickness, but no association has been demonstrated. They might also serve to "arm" K cells, rendering them cytotoxic (see below).

C. Cellular Immunity:

1. Skin tests–Patterns of response in chronic ulcerative colitis to standard tests do not differ from those of healthy controls. Delayed cutaneous hypersensitivity to DNA is reported in one-third of the patients. This may explain observed reactions to intradermal autologous leukocytes.

2. Tests of lymphocyte activation and MIF production using lymphocytes from patients with chronic ulcerative colitis have given inconclusive results. PHA, PPD, colonic antigen, and *E coli* O14 antigen resulted in no differences in these 2 tests using chronic ulcerative colitis lymphocytes and normal lymphocytes in many studies. One study showed some depression using cells from patients with chronic ulcerative colitis during attacks.

There is a single report of leukocyte migration inhibition using lymphocytes from patients with chronic ulcerative colitis in the presence of extracts of human fetal colon. Colectomy abolished this abnormal response.

3. Cytotoxicity–Lymphocytes from patients with chronic ulcerative colitis and with Crohn's disease are specifically cytotoxic to allogeneic colonic epithelial cells in vitro, gastric and ileal cells being unaffected. This phenomenon persists in remissions of chronic ulcerative colitis but not following colectomy, is specific for chronic ulcerative colitis and Crohn's disease, is inhibited by preincubation of lymphocytes with horse anti-human thymus serum, is inhibited by preincubation of lymphocytes with serum from other patients with chronic ulcerative colitis and Crohn's disease but not by autologous serum, is inhibited by preincubation with *E coli* O119:B14 lipopolysaccharide, and does not require the presence of complement.

Furthermore, cytotoxicity is conferred on lymphocytes of healthy subjects by preincubation with *E coli* O119:B14 lipopolysaccharide (but not with PHA) and by preincubation with serum from patients with chronic ulcerative colitis or Crohn's disease. This effect is due to IgM in the sera.

These findings suggest the possible involvement of either sensitized T cells binding to epithelial cells through specific surface receptors or K cells coated with immune complex recognizing target epithelial cells through free antibody valencies in the complex.

Clinical Features

A. Symptoms and Signs: Patients have symptoms that range from mild diarrhea without systemic upset to a severe illness—with sustained fever, prostration associated with dehydration, and passage of more than 8–10 bloody stools daily—which may be life-threatening. The complications may be local or remote. Local ones occur around the large bowel and anus; perforation is the most dangerous. Fistula formation is less common than in Crohn's disease. The remote complications are similar to those of Crohn's disease, involving predominantly the skin, eyes, liver, and joints.

B. Laboratory Findings: Disease of abrupt onset is distinguished from *Shigella* and amebic dysentery by the absence of specific pathogens in the stool and negative serologic findings for these organisms. The peripheral blood may exhibit eosinophilia and neutrophilia. There may be variable anemia due to acute or chronic blood loss. The erythrocyte sedimentation rate may be elevated. The stool contains no pathogens.

Immunologic Diagnosis

At present no immunologic tests have demonstrated diagnostic value.

Differential Diagnosis

Nonspecific ulcerative colitis of acute onset must be distinguished from *Shigella* and amebic dysentery by the history of potential infection and fecal and serologic examinations. In older subjects, abrupt infarction of the colon or small bowel may present a diagnostic problem. Occasionally, sigmoid diverticulitis and even a colonic carcinoma may present with bloody diarrhea and lower abdominal pain. Crohn's disease when it involves the colon may be almost indistinguishable from ulcerative colitis.

Treatment

As in Crohn's disease, treatment of the first attack or relapse of chronic ulcerative colitis includes general supportive measures. Glucocorticoids and sulfasalazine (salicylazosulfapyridine) have been shown to be effective in controlled trials. Azathioprine may be useful in allowing reduction of corticosteroid dosage.

Complications & Prognosis

One complication of the acute attack is colonic perforation. Anal fissures and fistulas may occur. The extraintestinal complications may rarely be so severe as to warrant colectomy when the severity of the colonic disease would not do so. The gravest problem is the indisputable association of chronic ulcerative colitis with cancer of the colon occurring 10 years or more after the onset of colitis.

THE LIVER

Many of the immunologic phenomena associated with both acute and chronic liver disease are secondary to liver damage and have no primary pathogenetic significance. Changes of diagnostic and possibly pathogenetic significance in each disease state will be emphasized.

HEPATITIS A VIRUS (HAV) INFECTION

Major Immunologic Features

- Presence of IgM antibody to HAV is diagnostic of acute infection.
- Serum IgM increased.
- Presence of IgG anti-HAV alone indicates past infection and confers protective immunity.
- Chronic infection and chronic liver disease do not occur.

General Considerations

This viral infection, which is common in childhood, is enterally transmitted, with an incubation period of 4–6 weeks. The virus is an RNA (picorna) virus that replicates within the liver, is excreted in the stools, and evokes a strong antibody response. The rapid rise in IgM antibody titer occurs at onset and is diagnostic. IgG antibodies are present in high titer from the clinical onset and remain for life, conferring protective immunity.

The disease is often asymptomatic. In North America and Western Europe, by middle age, approximately 40% of people have immunity. The prevalence of infection increases by 10% per decade of life. The infection rate is greater in developing countries.

Fulminant hepatitis is rare, and the virus does not result in either chronic infection or chronic hepatitis.

Immunologic Pathogenesis

During the acute phase, serum IgM concentration increases and large amounts of circulating immune complexes are present. The composition of these complexes is unknown. Low-titer smooth muscle antibody is often present.

Prevention

Household contacts can be protected by administering immune serum globulin, 0.02 mL/kg intramuscularly, within 10 days.

HEPATITIS B VIRUS (HBV) INFECTION

Major Immunologic Features

- The virus is not cytopathic, and it is the host's immune response to the virus that causes liver damage.
- Infection may result in acute hepatitis, chronic active or persistent hepatitis, a carrier state with normal histologic features on liver biopsy, or extrahepatic disorders including polyarteritis nodosa and membranoproliferative glomerulonephritis.
- Diagnosis is dependent on the presence of HBsAg or IgM anti-HBc.
- There are 2 phases of chronic infection: (1) the phase of active viral replication, when the patient is HBeAg-positive; and (2) the phase of HBsAg production in the absence of detectable viral replication, when the patient is anti-HBe–positive.

General Considerations

Hepatitis B virus is parenterally transmitted, usually during therapeutic use of blood or blood products, sexual contact, or sharing of needles during drug abuse. The incubation period is 3–6 months. This infection may result in asymptomatic, symptomatic, or fulminant hepatitis, and in 10% of cases, chronic infection with chronic hepatitis (Fig 29–3). More rarely, extrahepatic syndromes, including polyarteritis nodosa, membranoproliferative glomerulonephritis, polyneuropathy, papular acrodermatitis (Gionotti-Crosti syndrome), and essential mixed cryoglobulinemia may occur. In some patients, particularly those infected at birth or in the neonatal period, chronic infection may be associated with only minimal inflammatory liver disease. Chronic infection may be terminated by the development of primary liver cell cancer.

Immunologic Pathogenesis

The virus itself is not directly cytopathic, and the diversity of lesions described in infected patients has been attributed to variation in the capacity of the host's immune response to eliminate or suppress the infective agent. In acute hepatitis, the mononuclear cell infiltrate in the liver is composed chiefly of cytotoxic T cells. The lysis of infected hepatocytes, in association with production of virus-neutralizing antibody, is probably responsible for recovery. The humoral immune response during this acute phase has been studied in detail and is summarized in Fig 29–4. The appearance of anti-HBe and an HBV-reactive antibody is associated with the disappearance of HBeAg and of

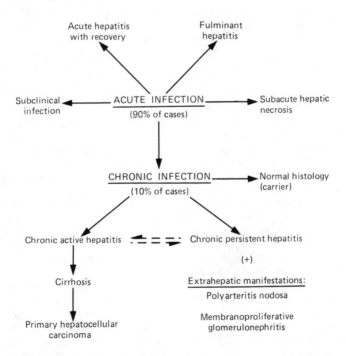

Figure 29–3. Clinical syndromes associated with acute and chronic HBV infection.

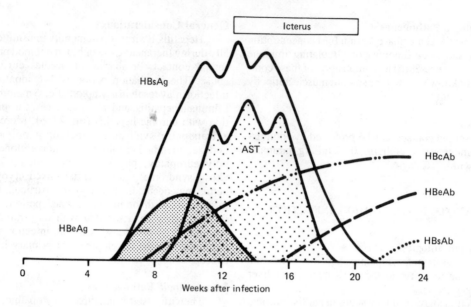

Figure 29–4. Acute type B hepatitis. Viral antigens and host immune response. *Note:* During the phase of HBe antigenemia, HBV particles are present in blood.

HBV particles from the serum. The antibody conferring protective immunity is anti-HBs. This develops late in the illness, sometimes 1–2 months after disappearance of HbsAg. IgM anti-HBc is present from the first 2 weeks after onset of the infection and is useful diagnostically. Less is known about the cell-mediated immune response to the virus and its role in destruction of infected liver cells.

A major enigma in this field is the mechanism by which the virus persists and why chronically infected subjects develop lesions varying from severe chronic active hepatitis to minimal hepatitis and extrahepatic syndromes. Defects in the mechanism of elimination of infected hepatocytes and in neutralization of infectious virus particles have been postulated to underlie the chronic infection, but satisfactory data to support these hypotheses have not been forthcoming. It seems clear, however, that the heterogeneity of hepatic and extrahepatic lesions is dependent on variation in the immune response to the virus. A useful analogy can be drawn to the tuberculoid and lepromatoid responses to *Mycobacterium leprae*. Thus, there is evidence that chronic active hepatitis is the result of a dominant cell-mediated (tuberculoid) response to the virus, while the extrahepatic diseases (polyarteritis nodosa and membranoproliferative glomerulonephritis) represent a dominant humoral (lepromatoid) response. The carrier state associated with only minimal hepatitis has been postulated to represent a state of partial tolerance to the virus, perhaps occurring because of infection in the neonatal period, when the host's immune system is relatively immature.

The presence in the serum of HBeAg, a low-molecular-weight component of the nucleocapsid of the virus, usually indicates the presence of virus particles in the circulation and therefore a state of relatively high

infectivity. These patients readily transmit infection to sexual contacts, and even small amounts of their blood used in transfusion will cause infection. During this stage of infection, IgM anti-HBc is present in high titer.

After several years of chronic infection, HBeAg will disappear from the serum and HBeAb can be demonstrated. Although most of these patients have no virus particles in their serum and are therefore of low or zero infectivity, when HBV-DNA hybridization techniques are used to detect viral DNA, small numbers of virus particles can be detected in 20% of cases. Thus, HBeAg-positive patients and a small proportion of HBeAb-positive patients are infectious. The majority of HBeAb-positive patients are noninfectious.

The continued secretion of the viral coat protein (HBsAg), in the absence of active viral replication, probably represents a phase of infection in which the viral DNA has become integrated into the host DNA, so that the viral genome is transcribed and translated as if it were a part of the host. This integration event may explain why, late in the infection, patients develop primary liver cell cancer.

Low-titer antibodies to smooth muscle are present and are a reflection of the immune response to partially denatured antigens released from necrotic liver cells. Antibodies to single-stranded and double-stranded DNA are present for similar reasons.

Treatment of Chronic HBV Infection

Patients who are actively replicating the virus (HBeAg positive) may be treated with either interferon or vidarabine (adenine arabinoside; Vira-A). Both of these agents will reproducibly inhibit viral replication, but in only one-third of cases is this long-lasting. In patients with prolonged responses, inhibition of viral replication is associated with falling HBsAg titers and ultimately with reduced hepatic inflammatory activity. It is anticipated that this therapy will be associated with an increased survival. Modified regimens, particularly those using the more water-soluble vidarabine monophosphate, hold greater promise and are currently under evaluation. Immunostimulants have been tried to enhance the endogenous immune response, thus increasing the chance of clearance of the virus. Attempts at immunotherapy have been largely unsuccessful, but immunotherapy has the theoretic advantage of perhaps destroying clones of cells containing integrated HBV-DNA.

NON–A NON–B INFECTION

Major Immunologic Features
- Both parenteral (short [2–4 weeks] and long [6–12 weeks] incubation) and enteral (6–8 weeks incubation) transmission may occur.
- Chronic hepatitis occurs in 20–80% of cases of parenterally transmitted disease, but rarely after enteral non-A non-B hepatitis.
- Diagnosis is dependent on exclusion of hepatitis A, hepatitis B, Epstein-Barr virus, and cytomegalovirus infection and drug-induced hepatitis.
- Immunoglobulin concentrations are normal, and auto-antibodies (smooth muscle antibodies, antinuclear antibodies) are absent.

General Considerations

The non-A non-B viruses are an important cause of sporadic (presumably enterally transmitted) and posttransfusion (parenterally transmitted) hepatitis. The diagnosis depends on the exclusion of hepatitis A and B virus infection by demonstrating the absence of IgM anti-HAV and HBsAg, respectively. Epstein-Barr virus (EBV) and cytomegalovirus infection must also be excluded by serologic tests. The acute illness is often mild, and many individuals are asymptomatic. The disease, however, has considerable importance in that between 20% and 80% of parenterally infected individuals develop chronic infection and chronic hepatitis. This disease is also relatively benign in its course, but some patients do progress to cirrhosis. The importance of these viruses as etiologic factors in the causation of cryptogenic cirrhosis remains to be determined.

Serum transaminases fluctuate rapidly in the course of the chronic disease, and this pattern has been useful diagnostically.

The complexity of the problem has been increased by the knowledge that there are probably at least 3 non-A non-B viruses. One, which is enterally transmitted and responsible for epidemic and probably sporadic non-A non-B hepatitis, does not result in chronic liver disease. There are, in addition, 2 parenterally transmitted viruses which can be characterized by the duration of their incubation periods (2–4

and 6–12 weeks) and which commonly cause chronic hepatitis.

Immunologic Features

Low-titer smooth muscle antibody occurs, but hyperglobulinemia is not evident until cirrhosis is present.

Serologic methods for the positive identification of this group of viruses are not yet available.

Treatment & Prevention

There is no proved method of therapy. Immune serum globulin may confer protection if given before blood transfusion. Its value in preventing infection in needlestick victims is unproved. The dosage and use are under investigation at this time, and, therefore, no definitive recommendation can be made.

AUTOIMMUNE CHRONIC ACTIVE HEPATITIS

Major Immunologic Features
- Autoantibodies to liver membrane, smooth muscle, and nuclear antigens.
- Genetic association with HLA-B8 and HLA-Dw3.
- A defect in nonspecific immunoregulation associated with polyclonal hypergammaglobulinemia.

General Considerations

Chronic hepatitis is defined as chronic hepatic inflammation continuing without improvement for longer than 6 months. Inflammation of the intrahepatic biliary tree is usually excluded from this group of diseases. Several etiologic factors may initiate chronic hepatitis (Table 29–3). These include a primary defect in regulation of the immune response (autoimmune), persistent viral infection (type B and non-A non-B hepatitis viruses), prolonged administration of drugs (oxyphenisatin, methyldopa, isoniazid, nitrofurantoin), alcohol, and Wilson's disease. In a substantial number of cases, no etiologic factor has been identified.

The distribution of the inflammatory infiltrate in the portal tracts and hepatic lobules, established by hepatic biopsy, allows a further classification (Fig 29–5) that is justifiable on prognostic grounds. These lesions may be seen with any of the etiologic factors.

Table 29–3. Etiologic classification of chronic active hepatitis.

Autoimmune (lupoid)
Hepatitis B virus
Non-A non-B virus (short incubation)
Non-A non-B virus (long incubation)
Drug exposure (oxyphenisatin, methyldopa, isoniazid)
Alcohol exposure
Wilson's disease
Unknown cause

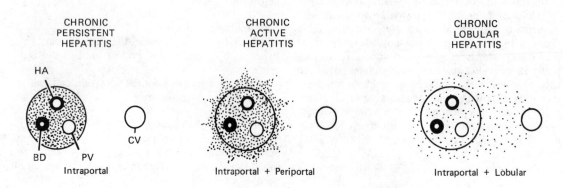

Figure 29–5. Anatomic classification of chronic hepatitis, dependent on the distribution of the inflammatory infiltrate within the hepatic lobule. HA, hepatic artery; BD, bile duct; PV, portal vein; CV, central vein. Clear circles represent limiting plate of portal tract. Black dots represent inflammatory cells.

In autoimmune chronic active hepatitis, there is a mononuclear and plasma cell infiltration of the portal and periportal areas of the liver. Groups of mononuclear cells surround hepatocytes, some of which appear to be damaged, in a lesion called piecemeal necrosis. Three-quarters of the patients are female, and although all ages may be affected, peak incidences are seen between 10 and 25 years and 50 and 65 years. The disease has an insidious onset in most cases but occasionally presents abruptly with features suggestive of acute viral hepatitis. In these cases, acute symptoms that call attention to chronic hepatitis probably represent intercurrent (new) infections with type A, B, or non-A non-B virus. Patients usually complain of general malaise for several months before jaundice is noted.

The clinical signs include mild to moderate jaundice and stigmas of chronic liver disease, including spider nevi and palmar erythema. The liver is usually of normal size or even smaller than normal. The spleen is enlarged. Seventy percent of patients have established cirrhosis at the time of diagnosis. Additional features are abdominal striae, acne, gynecomastia, and amenorrhea. About half of patients have other immunologic disorders, including arthralgia or arthritis, vasculitis, ulcerative colitis, glomerulonephritis, fibrosing alveolitis, Hashimoto's thyroiditis, autoantibody-positive hemolytic anemia, leukopenia, thrombocytopenia, and diabetes mellitus.

The biochemical picture shows predominantly an elevation of aminotransferases with normal alkaline phosphatase. Hepatic synthetic function is reduced, manifested as a low serum albumin and prolongation of the prothrombin time. There is often hematologic evidence of hypersplenism secondary to portal hypertension. Serum IgG is usually markedly elevated, with smaller changes in IgM and IgA levels. Antinuclear antibodies and antibodies to double-stranded DNA and to smooth muscle are present in high titer, usually greater than 1:40 by immunofluorescence. The term

lupoid chronic active hepatitis was given to this syndrome because of the presence of antinuclear factor. More recently, additional autoantibodies have been described, including the liver-kidney microsomal and mitochondrial antibodies. Whether these antibodies define separate subgroups of differing origin remains to be determined.

Differential Diagnosis

Differential diagnosis involves exclusion of other causes of chronic active hepatitis (Table 29–3). Additional problems may lie in differentiating the disease from primary biliary cirrhosis: approximately 20% of these patients have mild piecemeal necrosis. These patients, however, also have cholestatic features and are mitochondrial antibody–positive.

Most patients with sclerosing cholangitis also exhibit piecemeal necrosis. Cholangiography usually establishes the cholangitic component and makes the diagnosis. These patients are clinically and biochemically cholestatic.

Immunologic Pathogenesis

Both the number and function of suppressor cells are diminished in these patients, and this defect may be responsible for the development of autoantibodies reacting with liver membrane antigens. These antibodies are found in high titer only in autoimmune chronic active hepatitis. A reflection of the diminished activity of nonspecific suppressor cells is the high serum immunoglobulin concentration, particularly IgG. These patients also manifest autoimmune diseases affecting other organs, and it is suggested that the defect of the regulatory system is generalized. That this defect may be genetically determined is suggested by the finding of an increased incidence of autoantibodies and raised γ-globulin levels in the relatives of these patients and of a state of linkage disequilibrium of the disease with the human leukocyte antigens HLA-B8 and Dw3. The latter association suggests that the inheritance of a gene or genes close to the B and D loci of the MHC on chromosome 6 predisposes to the development of the disease, either spontaneously or in response to some environmental trigger factor.

Treatment

Until we are able to correct the defect in the immunoregulatory system, immunosuppression represents the mainstay of therapy. Controlled trials have demonstrated that corticosteroids produce a prolongation of survival over a period of 10 years. Azathioprine may occasionally be added to allow maintenance with lower doses of steroids. The defect in immunoregulatory function returns to normal during steroid therapy. In most cases, relapse will occur on cessation of therapy. It seems probable that therapy must be continued for life.

PRIMARY BILIARY CIRRHOSIS

Major Immunologic Features

- Ninety-nine percent of patients are mitochondrial antibody-positive.
- Diminished suppressor cell function.
- Increased serum concentrations of polymeric and monomeric IgM.
- Inability to convert from IgM to IgG antibody synthesis.
- Complement-activating immune complexes.
- Granulomatous infiltrate of intrahepatic biliary tree.

General Considerations

In this disease, a chronic granulomatous inflammatory process results in destruction of the intrahepatic biliary tree. These patients also exhibit lesions of the salivary, lacrimal, and pancreatic glands, scleroderma, rheumatoid arthritis, and thyroid disease. The finding of mitochondrial antibody in the serum of these patients led to the conclusion that the disease was probably of autoimmune origin.

The disease occurs commonly in middle-aged women, who present with symptoms of cholestasis. Liver function tests show an elevated alkaline phosphatase, often with normal transaminases and bilirubin. The most prominent symptom is pruritus. The rate of progression of the disease is slow, and jaundice occurs late. Many patients remain anicteric for 10–20 years. Once jaundice develops, life expectancy is considerably reduced.

Immunologic Features

Recently, evidence of an abnormality in the immunoregulatory system in these patients has been obtained. Both the concentrations and functions of suppressor T cells are markedly reduced. It is hypothesized that this abnormality allows the expansion of a clone of autoreactive lymphocytes with the potential to mount an immune response to both hepatic and nonhepatic ductular antigens. Similarity of the syndrome to chronic graft-versus-host disease, in which transplanted bone marrow cells attack the tissues of the body bearing a high density of HLA antigens, has led to the suggestion that the target antigen in primary biliary cirrhosis may be either a native or denatured HLA protein.

One result of the reduced suppressor cell activity is an increased rate of synthesis of IgM with failure of polymerization, leading to release of monomeric IgM. An additional effect on the humoral immune system is failure to convert from IgM to IgG antibody production. The protracted IgM response may be the result of failure of feedback inhibition because of the poor IgG antibody response.

Mitochondrial antibody is found in 99% of cases and is therefore a useful diagnostic test. The antibody binds to a nonenzymatic determinant on a lipoprotein component of the ATPase complex on the inner mitochondrial membrane. The role of this antibody in the pathogenic process is at present unclear.

These patients have large amounts of immune complexes in their serum that result in activation of the classic and alternative pathways of complement. These complexes are responsible for some of the extrahepatic manifestations of the disease, including, in some cases, arthritis, arteritis, and glomerulonephritis. Their role in the genesis of hepatic granulomas is unknown.

Patients with primary biliary cirrhosis are severely anergic in delayed hypersensitivity skin tests. Serum factors appear to be important, and of late evidence has focused on the role of abnormal high- and low-density lipoproteins in the anergic state.

Treatment

Penicillamine, a copper chelating and anti-inflammatory compound, has been shown to produce biochemical and histologic improvement and also to increase survival. This drug has been shown to reduce the ratio of helper to suppressor T cells, and this may be one factor responsible for improvement.

ALCOHOL– & DRUG–INDUCED HEPATITIS

Major Immunologic Features

- Direct toxic damage is followed by an immunologically mediated response to altered or denatured membrane and intracellular antigens (eg, alcohol and halothane hepatitis).
- Immune responses to altered antigens may be genetically determined (linkage of florid alcohol-induced hepatitis with HLA-B genes).
- Polyclonal hyperglobulinemia, particularly of IgA, in alcohol-induced liver disease.
- Depressed cell-mediated immune reactions.

1. ALCOHOL–INDUCED LIVER DISEASE

Several factors contribute to the liver damage that occurs in patients consuming large amounts of alcohol. The alcohol or its metabolites are undoubtedly directly hepatotoxic, producing ultrastructural changes within a few hours after ingestion.

Since persons with similar exposure histories may respond with widely different degrees of liver damage, it is suspected that other factors than simply amount of alcohol consumed influence susceptibility. It seems likely that alcohol ingestion induces steatosis in all subjects, but progression to hepatitis and cirrhosis does not always occur. Some authors suggest that all patients with alcohol-induced cirrhosis have gone through a stage of hepatitis, but in other studies this march of events is less clear. The factors that determine the rate of development of the disease are not understood.

Recent studies have revealed an increased incidence of HLA-B8 in a group of patients with alcohol-induced hepatitis. The incidence in patients with steatosis is similar to that found in the normal population, and subjects who have established cirrhosis without obvious hepatitis exhibit a low incidence of this phenotype. The authors suggest that in subjects who have progressed to cirrhosis with or without hepatitis, the mechanism of liver damage may be similar, but that the presence of the gene or genes linked to HLA-B8 predisposes the subject to a more florid hepatitic component of the disease.

Immunologic Pathogenesis

A. Immune Response to Live Cell Antigens: The histologic picture of liver biopsy in alcohol-induced liver disease has some features that may be compatible with an immunologically mediated component of the disease process. Although a major feature is central necrosis and polymorphonuclear cell infiltration, in some cases the portal zones reveal a mononuclear cell infiltrate and stellate fibrosis. This periportal infiltrate is similar to that seen in chronic active hepatitis and may represent an immunologic reaction to hepatocytes at the point of entry of lymphocytes to the hepatic lobule. This possibility is supported by the observation that lymphocytes from patients with alcohol-induced hepatitis are sensitized to liver cell antigens and are cytotoxic for rabbit hepatocytes.

The involvement of immune mechanisms in alcohol-induced liver disease is further supported by studies of the hepatic cellular infiltrate. Eighty percent of the cells in the liver of patients with alcoholic hepatitis are T lymphocytes and 20% are B lymphocytes. This contrasts with other forms of liver disease, in which the ratio of T to B lymphocytes is nearer 50/50. These findings are consistent with the suggestion that T lymphocytes have become sensitized to liver antigens and are mediating a tissue-damaging reaction.

The role of an immune response to Mallory's hyaline stain in the pathogenesis of alcohol-induced hepatitis is more difficult to determine. Hyalin is found in about 50% of cirrhotic patients with a history of alcohol abuse, but it is also found in Indian childhood cirrhosis, Wilson's disease, and primary biliary cirrhosis. The material is a highly refractile, eosinophilic, cytoplasmic inclusion that probably represents a condensation of intracellular contractile filaments. Interest in this material has increased following the demonstration that patients with alcohol-induced hepatitis and cirrhosis are sensitized to the purified material. These patients also exhibit low-titer antibodies to smooth muscle and aggregated albumin, and it seems probable that all are a reflection of an immune response to intracellular proteins released from degenerating hepatocytes.

More recently, antibodies to alcohol-altered hepatocytes have been found in sera of patients with alcohol-induced hepatitis.

B. Altered Humoral Immunity: Although many of the immunologic features of alcohol-induced disease are common to other types of liver injury and presumably result from changes in hepatic phagocyte function, some features are peculiar to the disease. In alcohol-induced disease, one of the earliest changes is an increase in serum IgA concentration. This occurs at a stage when the liver is either normal or exhibits only a mild degree of steatosis. Since this class of antibody is produced in the intestinal wall, one explanation of this increase would be that alcohol exposure results in an increase in permeability of the mucosa, thereby allowing increased access of intestinal antigens to the IgA immunocytes of the lamina propria and mesenteric lymph nodes. This change may merely represent an epiphenomenon, but it also seems possible that the change in permeability allows absorption of factors that contribute to the induction of hepatic damage. Increased titers of antibody to E coli occur at this early stage, indicating that endotoxin is absorbed and may be one of the intestine-derived factors contributing to the ongoing liver damage.

C. Altered Cell-Mediated Immunity: Cell-mediated immunity is altered in patients with alcohol-induced liver disease. Since many of the changes are also found in other types of liver disease and in animal models of cirrhosis, it seems probable that they are the result of liver damage rather than the chemical effect of alcohol.

Eighty percent of patients with alcohol-induced liver disease fail to develop a delayed hypersensitivity reaction to a challenge with dinitrochlorobenzene and exhibit a significant decrease in responsiveness to streptokinase and to mumps, antigens to which the subjects are likely to have been already sensitized. This demonstrates a defect in the efferent part of the delayed hypersensitivity response but does not exclude a coexisting defect in the afferent limb. The normal response to croton oil rules out a defect in the inflammatory response. A normal in vitro response to T cell mitogens excludes an intrinsic T cell defect, but serum inhibitors of this response can be demonstrated.

Treatment & Prognosis

Withdrawal of alcohol is the main goal of therapy. In florid alcohol-induced hepatitis, corticosteroid therapy has been tried without significant beneficial effect. In poorly nourished alcoholics, some of the immunologic abnormalities may respond to improved diet.

The response to abstinence is variable and partly dependent on the degree of damage and subsequent hepatic cirrhosis.

2. DRUG–INDUCED LIVER DISEASE

An increasing number of widely used and generally well-tolerated drugs can cause hepatic injury, ranging from a transient asymptomatic elevation of serum transaminases to clinically overt acute or chronic liver disease. These drug-induced states are often clinically, biochemically, and histologically indistinguishable from virally induced forms of liver injury, and this makes it difficult to establish a causal relationship between the drug and the disease. For this reason, the list of drugs suspected of inducing liver injury is much longer than that of drugs which are of proved relationship.

Most drugs that injure the liver do so by one of 2 mechanisms. Some drugs or their metabolites are hepatotoxic by a chemical interaction with an essential structural component or metabolic enzyme system of the liver cell, whereas others involve a hypersensitivity reaction. In both cases, host factors may influence the probability of a significant adverse reaction. The rate of generation and detoxification of a toxic metabolite will influence both types of reaction, and immune response genes may be involved in determining whether or not a patient manifests an idiosyncratic hypersensitivity response.

Direct Hepatotoxins

Drugs toxic to liver usually cause acute hepatic necrosis. Prolonged administration causes protracted or repeated episodes of necrosis and may ultimately lead to the development of chronic liver disease. Salicylates and acetaminophen are 2 such drugs.

The onset of liver damage is immediate in all subjects exposed to sufficient dosage if direct toxicity is the mechanism. Such drugs also produce liver damage in animals, and are usually identified as hepatotoxic in preliminary animal toxicology studies. A causal relationship between the drug and the adverse reaction is readily established in an individual case by studying the effect of drug withdrawal on recovery.

Drugs Inducing Hypersensitivity Responses

A drug or its metabolite may induce liver damage by immunologic mechanisms. The drug may alter either the regulatory system of the immune response, so that reactions to self antigens are no longer suppressed; or it may alter hepatocyte antigens, so that they are no longer recognized as self components. In

Table 29–4. Characteristics of toxic and hypersensitivity reactions.

	Direct Hepatotoxins	Hypersensitivity Reactions
Susceptibility	All subjects	Minority of subjects
Onset	Immediate	Delayed
Severity	Dose-related	Not dose-related
Animals affected?	Yes	No
Associated features	Other organs affected (renal damage)	Fever, arthralgia, rash, eosinophilia

the former case, the ensuing disease may be multisystemic, whereas the alteration of liver antigens would be expected to produce an autoaggressive assault solely on the liver.

One can approach the problem from 2 directions. The first is to define the host factors that determine susceptibility; the second is to define the mechanism by which the drug produces liver damage.

The involvement of host factors is suggested by the observation that only a small minority of exposed subjects develop hepatic injury. This is in contrast to the high susceptibility rates to hepatotoxins (Table 29–4). The factors involved are poorly understood. The increased incidence in atopic subjects and the occurrence of identical reactions in several generations of a family suggest that hereditary factors exist. Genetic factors may influence the rate and form of metabolism of the drug, thereby influencing the rate of formation of immunogenic complexes of drug metabolite with cellular macromolecules. Some progress has been made by the demonstration that microsomal enzyme activity is genetically determined. In the field of immunology, evidence suggests that HLA phenotypes may be linked to immune response genotypes.

The mechanism by which the drug initiates an autoaggressive immune response is also unknown. The drug may act as a hapten and combine with a membrane component of the hepatocyte, or it may denature a self antigen. This will result in a response to either the drug or a native or denatured liver cell antigen. Successful attempts to demonstrate these humoral and cellular responses are rare. When responses have been found, they are usually of the delayed hypersensitivity type. The paucity of positive data may in part be attributed to the insensitivity of the test systems but also probably stems from failure to test with both the drug and its metabolites complexed to the appropriate carrier molecule.

Although it is theoretically possible that the autoimmune reaction may continue after removal of the offending drug, this does not usually occur. Thus, for chronic liver disease to develop, prolonged exposure over several months would be necessary. Establishing a causal relationship between the drug and the liver lesion is a major problem. Withdrawal of the suspected drug usually results in clinical and biochemical improvement, and in a clinical setting, this is all that can be done. Rechallenge may be permissible in mild reactions, but in more severe cases it carries the risk of a severe exacerbation. Very little help can be derived from biochemical, histologic, or serologic studies. For example, chronic active hepatitis induced by methyldopa, oxyphenisatin, or isoniazid is indistinguishable on biochemical and histologic grounds from other forms of the disease, and in many cases the autoimmune markers (antinuclear antibody, LE cells) are also present.

The type of liver injury may be classified on histologic and biochemical grounds as hepatocellular or cholestatic and, in some cases, as a mixture of the two. There are no specific features that incriminate one drug rather than another. The history usually points to exposure to a specific drug.

Hepatitic Reactions

This type of reaction has been reported with monoamine oxidase inhibitors, oxyphenisatin, methyldopa, halothane, aminosalicylic acid (PAS), and sulfonamides (not discussed here). If exposure is prolonged, the patient may develop chronic liver disease.

A. Monoamine Oxidase Inhibitors: Monoamine oxidase inhibitors produce a predominantly hepatitislike picture. Iproniazid was the first recorded example, and this was followed by phenelzine, pheniprazine, and isocarboxazid—all hydrazine derivatives. The reaction may be severe, and fulminant cases have been reported.

Isoniazid is a member of this group used mainly in tuberculosis chemotherapy. Ten percent of patients show increased transaminase levels during the first 2 months of therapy, and liver biopsy shows a mild hepatitis. Only a minority of patients (less than 1%) develop symptomatic liver disease, and fatalities are rare. The reaction is usually mild, and the transaminases return to normal when the drug is stopped. It is possible, however, that continued administration may occasionally induce chronic active hepatitis.

B. Oxyphenisatin: A constituent of many laxatives, oxyphenisatin has been associated with hepatocellular damage. Only a minority of exposed persons react adversely, usually after at least 6 months of continual use. Most patients develop an acute hepatitic illness, but some present with chronic active hepatitis indistinguishable from the lupoid variety. The LE test and antinuclear factor are often positive, and hyperglobulinemia develops. The illness subsides when the drug is stopped, and challenge leads rapidly to worsening liver function as disclosed by appropriate tests.

C. Methyldopa: This drug produces mild subclinical abnormalities in transaminases in 5% of recipients. The frequency of this reaction and its occurrence early after ingestion suggest a direct toxic mechanism. In a minority of patients, a more severe hepatic reaction occurs 3–16 weeks after starting treatment. The prodromal symptoms are similar to those of acute viral hepatitis, and the patient becomes jaundiced. The Coombs test and tests for antinuclear factor and

smooth muscle antibody may be positive. The patient usually recovers uneventfully when the drug is stopped, but occasionally the course is fulminant or a stage of subacute hepatic necrosis proceeds to chronic active hepatitis and then cirrhosis.

D. Halothane: Halothane is now established in controlled trials as a cause of postoperative jaundice. Many of the features of the hepatitis strongly suggest a hypersensitivity mechanism. The reaction occurs 8–13 days after the first operation, and earlier after subsequent exposures. Pyrexia usually precedes the development of jaundice by 2–3 days and may be accompanied by eosinophilia. The outcome is good in the majority of cases. However, if the patient becomes icteric, the mortality rate is very high—up to 20%. Of particular interest is the observation that tolerance to the drug develops after numerous (more than 4) exposures. It is not known whether this indicates the development of immunologic tolerance or whether it is due to enzyme induction resulting in a faster handling of the toxic metabolite.

Early reports of mitochondrial antibodies in these patients' sera have not been confirmed, but a recent study did demonstrate that 40% of cases were positive for liver-kidney microsomal antibody. Demonstrations of cell-mediated immunity to the drug by lymphocyte transformation or leukocyte migration inhibition are also conflicting. Sensitization was demonstrated by some authors but not by others.

The mechanism of the reaction to this drug is unexplained. Once again, it seems likely that the reaction occurs to a metabolite of the native drug and therefore the rate of metabolism and the degree of sensitization will determine the severity of the reaction. Furthermore, the drug may produce damage as a result of both direct toxicity and hypersensitization.

E. Aminosalicylate (PAS): PAS reactions involving the liver are common and are usually part of a generalized reaction. Pyrexia, rashes, and arthralgias accompany the hepatitis. Cholestatic features are common.

Cholestatic Reactions

This type of reaction occurs in association with phenothiazines, oral hypoglycemics (chlorpropamide), and antithyroid drugs (thiouracil). Only chlorpromazine will be discussed here.

Chlorpromazine-induced reactions are often of a mixed hepatitic/cholestatic type. The reaction occurs 1–3 weeks after starting treatment in approximately 0.5% of patients receiving the drug. The reaction is unrelated to the dose and may occur several weeks after stopping the drug. If chlorpromazine is given a second time, approximately 40% suffer a relapse; it is postulated that the remaining subjects, who do not respond to challenge, are desensitized by subsequent doses.

Prodromal symptoms of fever and rash and blood and tissue eosinophilia all support a hypersensitivity mechanism as the cause of the syndrome. Liver biopsy shows cholestasis and a marked portal mononuclear and eosinophilic infiltrate. There is variable hepatitis. The prognosis is good. There are 2 reports of progression to biliary cirrhosis.

Granulomatous Reactions

Granulomatous reactions are seen in patients treated with phenylbutazone and sulfonamides. Although clinical and histologic features suggest an immunologic basis for the lesion, serologic tests and tests for lymphocyte sensitization have been unrewarding.

INFLUENCE OF LIVER DISEASE ON THE IMMUNE RESPONSE

Hyperglobulinemia and depressed cell-mediated immunity are common to most forms of chronic liver disease, and it seems probable that these changes are a result of liver damage. This is supported by the observation that similar changes can be induced in rats when they are rendered cirrhotic.

Phagocytic Function

Phagocytic function is markedly altered in patients with hepatic cirrhosis. This results in changes in antigen distribution, which is a major factor in determining the characteristics of the ensuing humoral and cellular immune responses.

Antigens enter the circulation from the gastrointestinal tract, the larger ones via the mesenteric lymphatics and the smaller ones via the mesenteric venous circulation. The liver, which is an important phagocytic organ, may therefore receive intestinally derived antigen either directly, via the portal circulation when it acts as a filter interposed in series with the rest of the body, or it may receive antigen from the systemic circulation via its arterial supply and in this situation acts as a filter in parallel. The hepatic phagocytes render antigens nonimmunogenic, while splenic and lymph node–derived macrophages serve to enhance immunogenicity. The distribution of antigen between liver and spleen (and other lymphoid organs) will therefore influence the magnitude of the immune response. Diversion of antigen from the liver to the spleen will enhance the immune response. Changes in the phagocytic function of the liver have an effect on both portal and systemic routes of immunization.

Immune complexes are cleared from the portal and systemic blood by the hepatic sinusoidal phagocytes. Large complexes that fix complement are avidly cleared by the liver, whereas smaller complexes, which do not fix complement, are cleared by the spleen. In hepatic cirrhosis, these functions are impaired, and complexes accumulate in the plasma. In most cases these complexes do not result in significant activation of C3 and do not cause tissue damage. The composition of such complexes is unknown, but it seems probable that many will contain food and bacterial antigens derived from the gut.

Endotoxins are phagocytosed and detoxified by the liver: they can be demonstrated in portal blood but not in systemic blood in normal subjects. Endotoxinemia has been demonstrated during fulminant hepatic failure and in some subjects with established cirrhosis, presumably as a result of impaired hepatic clearance of this substance. It is suggested that it plays a significant role in the renal malfunction that often accompanies these diseases.

Humoral Immunity

The altered handling of antigen in subjects with hepatic cirrhosis has a significant effect on the humoral immune response. This is seen most clearly in the response to putative thymus-independent antigens, which are not influenced by changes in cell-mediated immunity that accompany the development of chronic liver disease. It seems probable that the increased *E coli* titers found in patients with alcohol-induced cirrhosis, chronic active liver disease, and primary biliary cirrhosis are the result of this phenomenon.

The response to thymus-dependent antigens is more complex, involving the cooperation not only of macrophages and B lymphocytes but also of T lymphocytes. When patients with alcohol-induced cirrhosis, chronic active liver disease, and primary biliary cirrhosis were immunized intravenously with the bacteriophage OX174, a thymus-dependent antigen, the primary and secondary responses were significantly decreased when compared with the responses of normal subjects. In the presence of increased responses to thymus-independent antigens, this implies that the cooperating functions of T cells are reduced, so that B cells challenged with thymus-dependent antigens cannot respond to the increased antigenic stimulus. Recent studies indicate that $T\mu$- and OKT4-positive cells (helper T cells) are diminished in patients with cirrhosis.

In addition to the quantitative changes in the humoral response of subjects with hepatic cirrhosis, there are also qualitative changes. In normal subjects, during a secondary response, more than 90% of the antibody is IgG, whereas in patients with primary biliary cirrhosis, chronic active hepatitis, and alcohol-induced cirrhosis, the percentage of IgM antibody is much increased. This relative failure to change from IgM to IgG antibody production during the evolution of the immune response is also compatible with a defect in helper T cell function.

The relationship of the increased viral antibody titers, which have been described in chronic liver disease, to altered mononuclear phagocytic function is more vexed. Small increases in titer to lipoprotein-coated viruses such as herpes simplex, cytomegalovirus, influenza A, rubella, and measles are seen in HBsAg-positive and HBsAg-negative chronic active hepatitis, alcohol-induced cirrhosis, and primary biliary cirrhosis, but the sixfold increase in titer to measles and rubella viruses seen in lupoid chronic active liver disease is peculiar to this disease. It seems probable that the one- to twofold increase in titer to several viruses, which is common to all types of chronic liver disease, is a reflection of the altered immune function that occurs in any type of chronic liver injury but that the specific association of a high-titer response to measles and rubella with lupoid chronic active liver disease is an indication of the presence of an additional diathesis in the immune system of these patients.

The cumulative effect of these increased humoral responses is readily seen in the hypergammaglobulinemia that accompanies any form of experimental or natural chronic liver disease. The fact that this change is probably secondary to alterations in the mononuclear phagocytic system of the liver should not be allowed to direct attention away from the increased IgM of primary biliary cirrhosis and IgA of alcohol-related disease—changes specific to these diseases that may therefore give further clues to their pathogenesis.

Cell-Mediated Immunity

The incidence of positive delayed hypersensitivity skin tests to common bacterial and viral antigens is decreased in alcohol-related liver disease, chronic active hepatitis, and primary biliary cirrhosis. This occurrence in all types of liver disease suggests that this is in part secondary to the chronic liver disease.

The delayed hypersensitivity response involves the cooperation of macrophages and T cells in the presence of various serum factors that may enhance or inhibit the response. The afferent limb of the system, whereby cells become sensitized to the antigen concerned, has not been evaluated in patients with chronic liver disease because of the limitations of the test systems.

The efferent limb requires that T lymphocytes be present in adequate concentrations; that they be sensitized to and recognize the antigen under test; and that they be capable of producing the lymphokine mediators of the delayed hypersensitivity reaction. The concentration of peripheral blood T lymphocytes measured by rosetting techniques is diminished in HBsAg-positive and HBsAg-negative chronic active liver disease, alcohol-related disease, and primary biliary cirrhosis, and concentrations of null cells are increased. The demonstration that some null cells can be converted into E-rosetting mature T lymphocytes suggests that some null cells are either immature T cells or T cells that are altered because of the biochemical changes associated with chronic hepatocellular and, to a lesser extent, cholestatic liver disease. The presence of plasma or serum inhibitors of T lymphocyte function may also contribute to the anergy seen in patients with chronic liver disease. Serum factors that inhibit mitogen transformation of lymphocytes have been demonstrated in primary biliary cirrhosis, chronic active hepatitis, and alcohol-induced liver disease, as well as in an animal model of hepatic cirrhosis. Increased macrophage suppressor cell activity, which is dependent on the level of antigen stimulation of the spleen, has also been described in animals and patients with hepatic cirrhosis. Although the humoral and cellular inhibitors of T lymphocyte function are readily demonstrated in vitro, their functional importance in vivo remains uncertain. Many of the inhibitors appear to be common to several types of liver disease and are therefore probably a reflection of the altered metabolic state in these conditions.

Immunologically Active Plasma Proteins

The liver is the major site of synthesis for many plasma proteins, some of which have either a regulator or effector role in the immune response.

A. Alpha-Fetoprotein (AFP): Alpha-fetoprotein is produced by the entodermal cells of the foregut, particularly the liver. It is present in high concentration in the plasma of the fetus and mother. Within a few hours after birth, the concentration starts to fall, and by 1 year, adult levels are attained (10–20 ng/mL).

Increased concentrations of AFP have been demonstrated in 90–95% of primary hepatocellular carcinomas. Smaller increases (< 500 ng/mL) are seen following acute hepatic necrosis, acute viral hepatitis, and in patients with chronic liver disease, particularly those with macronodular cirrhosis. In these circumstances, the increase is believed to be a reflection of an increased rate of liver cell division (ie, regeneration). Thus, this protein is synthesized at an increased rate during hyperplastic and neoplastic growth.

The immunosuppressant properties of AFP were shown to be dependent on the induction of a suppressor cell. The presence of sialic acid residues on the protein appears to be essential for these biologic effects. More recently, other workers have failed to confirm these observations.

B. Alpha Globulins: These are a complex group of proteins that are produced by the liver and have immunoregulatory properties. Pregnancy-associated globulin inhibits T cell functions. It is increased mainly in pregnancy but also in patients with chronic liver disease and in cancer. Alpha$_2$ macroglobulin is an important inhibitor of both the complement and coagulation systems. It has recently been suggested that it has immunoregulatory properties in relation to K cell function. Increased concentrations are found in primary biliary cirrhosis and also HBsAg-negative chronic active hepatitis.

C. Complement Components: Complement components are produced by either the mononuclear phagocytes or hepatocytes and are often reduced in acute and chronic liver disease.

• • •

References

General

Immunology of the Gut. CIBA Foundation Symposium 46. (New Series.) Elsevier, 1977.

Thomas HC, Jewell DP: *Clinical Gastrointestinal Immunology*. Blackwell, 1979.

Tomasi TB: Secretory immunoglobulins. *N Engl J Med* 1972;**287**:500.

Sjögren's Syndrome

Whaley K et al: Sjögren's syndrome. 2. Clinical associations and immunological phenomena. *Q J Med* 1973;**42**:513.

Chronic Atrophic Gastritis & Pernicious Anemia

Strickland RG: Gastritis. *Front Gastrointest Res* 1975;**1**:12.

Taylor KB: Immune aspects of pernicious anaemia and atrophic gastritis. *Clin Haematol* 1976;**5**:497.

Gluten-Sensitive Enteropathy; Celiac Sprue

Crabbé PA, Heremans JF: Selective IgA deficiency with steatorrhea: A new syndrome. *Am J Med* 1967;**42**:319.

Douglas AP: The immunological basis of coeliac disease. *Front Gastrointest Res* 1975;**1**:49.

Hekkens WTJM, Pena AS (editors): *Coeliac Disease*. Stenfert Kroese, 1974.

Crohn's Disease

Thayer WR Jr: The immunopathology of intestinal granulomatous disease. *Front Gastrointest Res* 1975;**1**:74.

Ulcerative Colitis

Hammarström S et al: Immunological studies in ulcerative colitis. *J Exp Med* 1965;**122**:1075.

Kirsner JB, Shorter RG (editors): *Inflammatory Bowel Disease*, 2nd ed. Lea & Febiger, 1980.

Shorter RG et al: Inflammatory bowel disease: Cytophilic antibody and the cytotoxicity of lymphocytes for colonic cells in vitro. *Am J Dig Dis* 1971;**16**:673.

The Liver

Berk PD, Chalmers TC: Primary biliary cirrhosis. Pages 242–304 in: *Frontiers in Liver Disease*. Thieme-Stratton, 1981.

Sherlock S, Scheuer P: The presentation and diagnosis of 100 patients with primary biliary cirrhosis. *N Engl J Med* 1973; **289**:673.

Thomas HC, Miescher PA, Mueller-Eberhard HJ: *Immunological Aspects of Liver Disease*. Springer-Verlag, 1982.

Thomas HC, Jewell DP: *Clinical Gastrointestinal Immunology*. Blackwell, 1979.

Thomas HC, Bamber M: Clinical aspects of non-A, non-B hepatitis. *Advanced Medicine* 1981;**17**:159.

Zuckerman AJ, Howard CR: *Hepatitis Viruses of Man*. Academic Press, 1979.

30 | Pulmonary & Cardiac Diseases

Joseph L. Caldwell, MD, & H. Benfer Kaltreider, MD

IMMUNOLOGIC DISEASES OF THE LUNG

The immune system normally serves a protective role against pathogenic organisms in the lung. However, exaggerated immune mechanisms or hypersensitivity reactions can result in clinically important lung disease. The various hypersensitivity reactions involved in the production of tissue damage have been classified into 4 basic types, I–IV. These 4 immune mechanisms are described in detail in Chapter 12. This system of classification has been applied to certain diseases of the lung. Table 30–1 summarizes a classification of lung diseases according to the major immunologic mechanism proposed for their pathogenesis. Type I hypersensitivity diseases are discussed in Chapter 28. Major examples of other immunologic lung diseases are discussed in this chapter.

Our knowledge of the details of the humoral and cellular immune mechanisms contributing to the pathogenesis of these diseases is relatively limited. This is due largely to the inaccessibility of lung tissue for repeated laboratory examination during the course of the disease. Transbronchial lung biopsy and diagnostic pulmonary lavage have recently opened the possibility of serial sampling of tissue, fluid, and cells from the lower respiratory tract for morphologic and functional analysis. While diagnostic bronchopulmonary lavage is currently considered to be primarily a clinical investigative tool, more widespread clinical applicability is anticipated in the near future. Several laboratories have demonstrated distinct alterations in

Table 30–1. Immunologic diseases of the lung.

Reaction Type	Immunologic Mediators	Clinical Examples
Type I	IgE	Extrinsic allergic asthma.
Type II	IgG or IgM antibody against basement membrane and complement.	Goodpasture's syndrome.
Type III	IgG- or IgM-soluble or precipitating antigen-antibody complexes and complement.	Extrinsic allergic alveolitis; lung disease associated with connective tissue disorders.
Type IV	Sensitized T lymphocytes. Lymphokines.	Granulomatous diseases. Tuberculosis; perhaps sarcoidosis.

the relative concentrations of immunoglobulins and in the composition of bronchoalveolar cells in pulmonary lavage fluids from patients with a variety of interstitial lung diseases (Table 30–2). Serial analysis of these parameters may prove useful in monitoring interstitial disease activity.

GOODPASTURE'S SYNDROME

Major Immunologic Features
- Serum anti-GBM antibodies.
- Linear deposition of Ig and complement in basement membranes of renal glomerulus and pulmonary alveoli.

Table 30–2. Alterations in cellular composition and in IgG content of bronchopulmonary lavage fluids in patients with interstitial lung diseases.

Disease	Ratio of IgG:Albumin	Total Cells	Percentage Of		
			Lymphocytes	PMNs	Macrophages
Hypersensitivity pneumonitis	↑↑↑	↑	↑↑↑	↓	↓↓
Idiopathic pulmonary fibrosis	↑↑	↑↑	N	↑↑	↓
Sarcoidosis	↑↑	↑↑	↑↑	↑	↓↓

↑ = Slightly increased, ↑↑ = increased, ↑↑↑ = markedly increased, N = normal, ↓ = slightly decreased, ↓↓ = decreased.

General Considerations

Goodpasture's syndrome is a clinical disorder of unknown cause characterized by recurrent pulmonary hemorrhage, hematuria, severe anemia, and progressive glomerulonephritis. The disease principally affects young adult males, follows a rapidly progressive course, and usually terminates in death within several months after onset.

Immunologic Pathogenesis

The pathogenesis of Goodpasture's syndrome involves circulating antibodies directed toward some basement membranes. These antibodies react with and disrupt the basement membanes of both the glomerulus of the kidney and the alveoli of the lung. Histologic examination of renal tissue regularly shows linear deposits of immunoglobulin (usually IgG, though IgM and IgA have also been reported) and complement components on the basement membranes. (For a discussion of the immune aspects of the renal features, see Chapter 31.) Similar deposits frequently, but not always, appear on alveolar epithelial and capillary endothelial basement membranes of the lung. Antibodies to glomerular basement membranes have been eluted from diseased kidneys and the eluted antibody reacted with normal kidney tissue but not with normal lung tissue. In contrast, antibody eluted from lung tissue can bind to glomerular basement membranes of normal human kidney. Hence, it appears that there is at least some degree of cross-reactivity of these antibodies between lung and kidney. It may be that viral or chemical modification of basement membrane antigens leads to production of autoantibody.

Clinical Features

Pulmonary hemorrhage, hemoptysis, and necrotizing glomerulitis with hematuria suggest the possibility of Goodpasture's syndrome. Chest x-rays show fluctuating pulmonary infiltrates depending on the degree of hemorrhage in the lung. Histologic examination of lung tissue shows alveolar spaces filled with hemosiderin-laden macrophages and blood.

Immunologic Diagnosis

The diagnosis can be established by measurement of serum antibodies to glomerular basement membrane antigens and by immunofluorescent demonstration of linear deposits of immunoglobulin and complement in glomerular basement membranes and alveolar septa of lung tissue.

Differential Diagnosis

Goodpasture's syndrome may be confused with uremic pneumonitis accompanying more common forms of nephritis, polyarteritis nodosa, Wegener's granulomatosis, or infective endocarditis. In addition, fluid overload and pulmonary edema in a uremic patient may mimic pulmonary hemorrhage.

Treatment & Prognosis

The prognosis is poor, and death often occurs within a few months from uremia or pulmonary hemorrhage. Treatment with corticosteroids and cytotoxic drugs alone does not appear to prolong survival. Exchange transfusion, plasmapheresis, or bilateral nephrectomy will decrease circulating anti-glomerular basement membrane antibodies. When plasmapheresis, corticosteroids, and cytotoxic drugs are combined, remission of the disease and prolonged survival have been reported. Hemodialysis and subsequent renal transplantation have been used in a few cases with beneficial results.

HYPERSENSITIVITY PNEUMONITIS
(Allergic Alveolitis)

Major Immunologic Features

- Onset of symptoms 4–8 hours after inhalation of antigen.
- Serum precipitating IgG antibodies to inhaled organic antigens.
- Chronic granulomatous interstitial pneumonitis.
- Probable combined immune complex and cell-mediated immunopathogenesis.

General Considerations

Ambient air contains a variety of organic particles which can act as antigens when inhaled into the respiratory tract. While susceptible individuals can develop acute or chronic interstitial lung disease after repeated inhalation of certain organic antigens, most people fail to develop pulmonary disease following similar exposure. The prototype of this group of disorders is farmer's lung. This disease results from repeated inhalation of spores from thermophilic actinomycetes which are present in abundance in moldy hay. Many related syndromes have also been described (Table 30–3).

Table 30–3. Selected causes of hypersensitivity pneumonitis.

Disease	Exposure	Antigen Source
Farmer's lung	Moldy hay	*Micropolyspora faeni*
Bagassosis	Moldy sugar cane	Thermophilic actinomycetes
Air conditioner pneumonitis	Humidifiers, air conditioners	Thermophilic actinomycetes
Redwood, maple, red cedar pneumonitis	Moldy bark, moldy sawdust	Thermophilic actinomycetes, *Cryptostroma corticale,* sawdust
Mushroom worker's lung	Mushrooms, compost	Thermophilic actinomycetes
Cheese worker's lung	Moldy cheese	*Penicillium casei*
Malt worker's lung	Malt dust	*Aspergillus clavatus*
Bird fancier's lung	Bird excreta and serum	Avian serum proteins
Enzyme lung	Enzyme detergents	Alcalase derived from *Bacillus subtilis*
Drug-induced hypersensitivity pneumonitis	Drugs, industrial materials	Nitrofurantoin, cromolyn, hydrochlorothiazide, toluene diisocyanate

The exotic names applied to these disorders reflect the epidemiologic conditions under which they develop. However, these diseases present a similar clinical picture, share a common immunopathogenesis regardless of the source of antigen, and thus may be considered as a single group of diseases.

Immunologic Pathogenesis

A. Properties of Antigens Responsible for Initiation of Lung Disease: While a wide variety of foreign materials stimulate detectable immune responses after deposition in the lung, it appears that only some antigens produce hypersensitivity pneumonitis. These are predominantly fungal spores and certain proteins. Characteristics of these organic materials which may contribute to their pathogenicity include their particulate nature, chemical composition, resistance to intracellular degradation, ability to activate complement, and ability to induce inflammation.

B. Susceptibility of the Host: A minority of individuals (3–5%) regularly exposed to the etiologic agents responsible for hypersensitivity pneumonitis will develop disease. Possible determinants are the genetic constitution of the individual and the presence of preexisting lung disease. No clear association appears to exist between HLA antigens and the development of lung disease. Experimental and clinical evidence suggests that pulmonary inflammation enhances the host's immune responses to pathogenic organic antigens.

C. Immunopathogenetic Mechanisms: Classically, the type III hypersensitivity reaction (immune complex; Chapter 12) has been considered to be the major mechanism contributing to the pathogenesis of hypersensitivity pneumonitis. Strong evidence for a type III reaction includes high levels of precipitating serum antibody, the time course of tissue reactivity after antigenic challenge, and the demonstrable Arthus skin reaction to intradermal testing. A major immune reaction to inhaled organic antigens is the appearance in serum of high levels of complement-fixing, precipitating IgG antibodies. The sera of virtually all patients with clinically evident hypersensitivity pneumonitis display such antibodies if the appropriate reagents are used for their detection. In addition, a large proportion of exposed individuals can have demonstrable circulating antibody but be asymptomatic and disease-free. The absolute concentration of specific IgG antibody does not correlate well with the presence or severity of disease.

Inhalation exposure of a susceptible and previously sensitized individual results in the development of acute hypersensitivity pneumonitis after 4–6 hours. It is postulated that antigen-antibody complexes form and precipitate in the interstitium of the lung. The complexes activate the complement sequence and result in the evolution of acute inflammation and tissue injury (see Chapter 12). Intradermal challenge with the appropriate antigen results in necrotizing vasculitis of the skin whose kinetics are identical to those of lung disease. Controlled inhalation of extracts of antigen can reproduce all features of the clinical syndrome.

Recent evidence strongly suggests an important role for type IV (cell-mediated) reactions in the pathogenesis of hypersensitivity pneumonitis. The strongest evidence is derived from histopathologic observations, from in vitro tests for T lymphocyte sensitivity to antigen, and from analogy with experimental animal models.

Lung biopsies from patients with advanced hypersensitivity pneumonitis consist of interstitial infiltrations with mononuclear inflammatory cells and granuloma. Such material has been obtained from patients with chronic hypersensitivity pneumonitis late in the course of the disease. The few patients biopsied early after antigenic exposure have displayed vasculitis and deposition of immunoglobulin, C3, and fibrin in and around interstitial blood vessels. Hence, histopathologic evidence exists for both cell-mediated immune mechanisms (type IV) and immune complex–mediated tissue injury (type III) contributing to hypersensitivity pneumonitis.

Specifically sensitized lymphocytes may be demonstrated in the blood of patients with hypersensitivity pneumonitis. Lymphocytes from lungs of patients with pigeon breeder's disease have been shown to elaborate migration inhibition factor (MIF) when exposed to the appropriate antigens in vitro.

Data obtained from animal models of hypersensitivity pneumonitis suggest strongly that type IV reactions result in the production of histologic lesions which resemble those in the chronic form of human disease. Since the relevance of these animal models to human disease is not known, extrapolation of results to naturally occurring disease is difficult.

Clinical Features

A. Acute Hypersensitivity Pneumonitis: The acute illness is characterized clinically by fever, chills, dry cough, malaise, and profound dyspnea 4–8 hours after exposure of a previously sensitized individual to the antigen. Physical examination reveals an ill-appearing patient with tachypnea, cyanosis, and basilar rales. Leukocytosis with or without eosinophilia is usually present. Chest x-ray shows fine micronodular and linear interstitial markings at the lung bases. Physiologic alterations include reduced lung volumes (vital capacity, total lung capacity), lung compliance, and carbon monoxide diffusion capacity. There is moderate hypoxemia without hypercapnia. Airway obstruction is usually not present unless the patient is also atopic. In such patients an acute asthmatic attack can occur within minutes of antigen inhalation and subside before the onset of the late reaction. Acute attacks usually clear in 1–4 days after cessation of exposure to antigen. Recurrent acute attacks result in chronic interstitial fibrosis.

B. Chronic Hypersensitivity Pneumonitis: The chronic form of hypersensitivity pneumonitis may result either from repeated acute episodes or from chronic exposure. In up to 50% of cases, the disease progresses insidiously to far-advanced pulmonary fibrosis. The chronic form may be clinically and physiologically indistinguishable from idiopathic pulmonary fibrosis (see below). Such patients present clinically with chronic respiratory failure and pulmonary fibrosis. The severity of physiologic abnormalities correlates best with the duration of exposure to antigen.

Immunologic Diagnosis

The clinical suspicion that a patient with acute or chronic interstitial pneumonitis has been exposed to organic particulates demands that a meticulous historical search be made for environmental clues to specific antigen exposure (moldy hay, bird droppings, etc). The immunologic hallmark of hypersensitivity pneumonitis is the presence of precipitating antibody to the inhaled antigen. Precipitins are present in over 50% of exposed individuals and are detectable in over 90% of patients with clinical disease. These are minimal estimates, since the accuracy of detection depends on the sensitivity of the methods employed and the diversity of antigenic preparations available for testing. The presence of precipitating antibody denotes exposure to antigen; it does not establish its role in the pathogenesis of disease. Patients with hypersensitivity pneumonitis frequently display a polyclonal elevation of serum IgG. Serum IgE is not elevated unless the patient is also atopic.

A positive Arthus skin reaction to intradermal testing provides potent biologic evidence that the host is capable of mounting a type III hypersensitivity response to the antigen. Unfortunately, with certain exceptions (eg, *Aspergillus* species), most antigenic extracts are useless for testing because they contain impurities which cause nonspecific inflammation of the skin. Inhalation provocation has been used to simulate conditions of natural exposure. Patients with hypersensitivity pneumonitis will manifest clinical symptoms and physiologic abnormalities 4–8 hours after inhalational challenge. While such studies are definitive in establishing the diagnosis, they are generally clinically unavailable except in specialized research centers. In practice, the patient is returned to the suspect environment and the physician observes for exacerbation of disease.

Experimental studies have focused on characterizing the cells and fluids obtained from diseased lungs by bronchopulmonary lavage. The total yield of lymphocytes retrieved from bronchoalveolar spaces is markedly increased over normal, and this increase correlates positively with disease activity. It appears that the majority of these bronchoalveolar lymphocytes are T cells. Concentration of IgG in alveolar washes is also increased (Table 30–2). Peripheral blood lymphocytes from patients with pigeon breeder's lung undergo activation when cultured with components of avian serum.

Differential Diagnosis

Differential diagnosis of the acute form of hypersensitivity pneumonitis includes such interstitial diseases as viral pneumonitis, interstitial pulmonary edema, toxic drug reactions, sarcoidosis, acute idiopathic interstitial pneumonitis (see below), and lymphangitic carcinomatosis. Associated clinical features and the evolution of these diseases usually serve to differentiate them from hypersensitivity pneumonitis.

Treatment & Prognosis

The mainstay of treatment is prevention. In the acute form of hypersensitivity pneumonitis, avoidance of the offending environment should reverse the disease process with no permanent sequelae. If the acute illness is severe, a short course of corticosteroids will effect prompt resolution of symptoms. Exposure to antigen may be avoided by such simple measures as wearing a face mask while working in heavily contaminated environments. Patients may suffer severe economic loss attempting to avoid antigen exposure, and physicians should securely establish the diagnosis before suggesting major changes in a patient's vocation. Neither hyposensitization nor the use of antifungal agents is indicated.

ALLERGIC BRONCHOPULMONARY ASPERGILLOSIS

Major Immunologic Features

- Atopic host.
- Blood and sputum eosinophilia.
- Episodic wheezing and pulmonary infiltrates.
- Positive skin reactions, both type I and type III, to extracts of *Aspergillus* species.
- Precipitating serum antibody to *Aspergillus* extracts.
- Elevated serum IgE levels.

General Considerations

Allergic bronchopulmonary aspergillosis, originally described as a common cause of pulmonary infiltration with eosinophilia in the United Kingdom, is being recognized increasingly in the USA as an adult complication of childhood asthma. The clinical syndrome presents in early adulthood with episodic wheezing associated with noninfective pulmonary infiltrates, proximal bronchiectasis, mucus plugging of airways, and eosinophilia of sputum and blood. Recognition of the syndrome is of importance because of its prompt response to corticosteroid therapy, which appears to delay or prevent pulmonary fibrosis.

Immunologic Pathogenesis

The immunopathogenesis of allergic bronchopulmonary aspergillosis is thought to involve at least type I and type III reactions. Predisposition of the host to develop both reactions is necessary for full expression of the disease. Colonization of mucous secretions of the bronchopulmonary tree with *Aspergillus* species occurs initially. Saprophytic growth of the organism with concomitant release of antigenic materials stimulates sensitization of the host.

Because of their atopic status, these patients are prone to manifest type I hypersensitivity. They have elevated serum levels of IgE, IgE antibody to *Aspergillus* antigens, and positive immediate hypersensitivity skin reactions, and they develop bronchospasm within minutes after inhalation exposure to the antigen. Type I hypersensitivity accounts for the acute bronchospastic component of their disease.

The sera of patients with allergic bronchopulmonary aspergillosis contain precipitating IgG antibody against antigens present in extracts of *Aspergillus* species. Intradermal skin testing with such extracts results in positive Arthus skin reactivity in the majority of patients. On the basis of these observations, it has been suggested that type III hypersensitivity contributes to the pathogenesis of the characteristic transient pulmonary infiltrates by mechanisms analogous to those producing the interstitial lung disease of hypersensitivity pneumonitis (see previous section). Type III reactions also produce inflammatory injury to the walls of major bronchi, resulting in bronchiectasis. Circulating T lymphocytes sensitized to *Aspergillus* antigens have been described. Whether type IV reactions play an important role in immunopathogenesis remains to be determined.

Clinical Features

A. Symptoms and Signs: Typically, a young adult with a history of childhood asthma develops frequent exacerbations of episodic bronchospasm. Patients are in acute distress, with dyspnea, labored respiration, and audible wheezes. Fever is often present. The asthmatic diatheses are accompanied by pulmonary parenchymal infiltrates, cough, and expectoration of rusty-brown mucus plugs. The bronchospasm is unusually resistant to conventional bronchodilator therapy but may respond promptly to corticosteroids. Patients continue to produce large amounts of sputum between episodes of asthma and may develop bronchiectasis of proximal airways.

B. Laboratory Findings: Leukocytosis is usually present with intense blood and sputum eosinophilia. Serum IgE levels are markedly increased. Sputum culture may be positive for *Aspergillus* species. Serum IgG precipitating antibody against extracts of *Aspergillus* is present. Both immediate (type I) and intermediate (type III; Arthus) skin reactivity to *Aspergillus* extracts may be present if the patient is not receiving antihistamines or steroids, respectively. Type I skin hypersensitivity is detectable in over 95% of patients with this syndrome, whereas type III can be detected in only 40–60%.

Acutely, the chest x-ray shows evidence of hyperinflation of the lungs, with fleeting, ill-defined pulmonary infiltrates. The infiltrates may represent segments of atelectasis secondary to mucus plugging of airways or may be due to an inflammatory process in the parenchyma itself. Early in the course of the disease, the chest x-ray will clear completely between episodes of bronchospasm. As the disease progresses, irregular pulmonary fibrosis will develop and bron-

chography will demonstrate bronchiectasis of proximal airways in the upper lobes.

During the acute illness, airway obstruction is the predominant physiologic abnormality. The vital capacity is reduced, residual volume is increased, and total lung capacity is either normal or slightly increased. The forced expiratory volume in 1 second (FEV_1) is markedly reduced. With time, physiologic correlates of interstitial fibrosis appear. These include a restrictive ventilatory defect characterized by a reduced vital capacity, total lung capacity, and single breath carbon monoxide diffusing capacity.

Immunologic Diagnosis

The diagnosis of allergic bronchopulmonary aspergillosis is based on a complex of clinical and laboratory abnormalities and should be considered in any adult patient who suffers a relapse of childhood asthma. The following criteria should be fulfilled to confidently establish the diagnosis: (1) history of atopy, (2) episodes of bronchospasm, (3) pulmonary infiltrates, (4) blood and sputum eosinophilia, (5) presence of serum precipitins, and (6) positive immediate and intermediate skin reactions to antigens of *Aspergillus* species. Additional features which will help establish the diagnosis include (1) elevated serum IgE, (2) sputum cultures positive for *Aspergillus*, (3) demonstration of proximal bronchiectasis, and (4) positive response after inhalation provocation with *Aspergillus* antigens.

Strict adherence to these criteria is important. Many of these features, including type I hypersensitivity (positive immediate skin reactivity), elevated IgE levels, eosinophilia, and bronchospasm may be present in uncomplicated extrinsic asthma. It is the additional evidence of type III reactions which distinguishes allergic bronchopulmonary aspergillosis from uncomplicated asthma. These include pulmonary infiltrates, bronchiectasis, positive serum precipitating antibody, and positive Arthus skin reactivity (40–60%) to *Aspergillus* extracts. A positive delayed response to inhalation provocation demonstrates the biologic potential for airway hypersensitivity. It is presumed that these distinguishing immunologic features contribute to the pathogenesis of pulmonary infiltrates, interstitial fibrosis, and bronchiectasis.

Differential Diagnosis

In practice, the only difficult differentiation lies between extrinsic allergic asthma and the superimposition of the complication of allergic bronchopulmonary aspergillosis. Strict adherence to the above criteria will establish the correct diagnosis.

Treatment & Prognosis

The aims of therapy are to prevent the development of irreversible fibrosis or bronchiectasis and to reduce the frequency and severity of bronchospasm. A maximal regimen of standard bronchodilators should be employed. When allergic bronchopulmonary aspergillosis develops as a complication of extrinsic asthma, corticosteroid therapy should be instituted promptly. The major effect of corticosteroids appears to be to hasten the elimination of *Aspergillus* from the respiratory tract, thereby removing the antigen load. The bronchodilator and anti-inflammatory actions of corticosteroids promote mucociliary clearance of contaminated mucous secretions. The therapeutic response of acute episodes to short courses of corticosteroids is often dramatic. It appears that prompt corticosteroid treatment of acute episodes will prevent the development of pulmonary fibrosis and respiratory failure. With aggressive management of such patients, the long-term prognosis should be good.

IDIOPATHIC INTERSTITIAL PULMONARY FIBROSIS
(Fibrosing Alveolitis)

Major Immunologic Features
- High frequency of nonspecific autoantibodies, including rheumatoid factor and antinuclear antibody (ANA).
- Elevated serum immunoglobulin levels.
- Elevated IgG levels in bronchoalveolar fluids.
- Elevated levels of circulating immune complexes.

General Considerations
Idiopathic pulmonary fibrosis is a progressive interstitial lung disease of unknown cause. Originally, the interstitial inflammatory and fibrotic processes were thought to be invariably and rapidly progressive, resulting in pulmonary insufficiency and death within weeks of onset (Hamman-Rich syndrome). It is now evident that there is wide variation in the natural course of this disease, with patients surviving for months to 15 or more years. The disease begins as an alveolitis and progresses to interstitial fibrosis. Idiopathic pulmonary fibrosis displays certain histopathologic and serologic features which are similar to those found in rheumatic (collagen-vascular) disorders. By analogy, it has been suggested that immune mechanisms also play some role in the pathogenesis of idiopathic pulmonary fibrosis.

Immunologic Pathogenesis
At present, evidence implicating immune mechanisms in the pathogenesis of idiopathic fibrosis is circumstantial. Pulmonary fibrosis indistinguishable from the idiopathic variety does occur in association with rheumatoid arthritis and systemic lupus erythematosus, which have been attributed to circulating immune complexes (eg, rheumatoid factor, antinuclear antibody). Since there is a high incidence of nonspecific autoantibodies in idiopathic pulmonary fibrosis, the implication has been that these disorders may all share common mechanisms of pathogenesis. Experimental animal models have been described in which high levels of circulating antigen-antibody complexes resulted in diffuse interstitial lung disease.

Recently, immune complexes have been reported to be present in the circulation of some patients with idiopathic pulmonary fibrosis.

Clinical Features
A. Symptoms and Signs: Clinically, the disease is characterized by the insidious onset of dyspnea on exertion. It may occur at any age but is most frequent between ages 40 and 70 years. The sex incidence is equal. Physical examination reveals finger clubbing, cyanosis, tachypnea, basilar rales, and signs of pulmonary hypertension. Progression of the disease is highly variable, ranging from a few months to 10–15 years from the time of initial symptoms until death (mean survival, 50 months). The course is characterized by increasing dyspnea, pulmonary hypertension, and respiratory failure.

B. Laboratory Findings: Chest x-ray shows diffuse interstitial infiltrates, most prominent in the lower lung zones. These may range from faint reticular-nodular infiltrates to a honeycomb appearance, depending on the stage and chronicity of the disease. Early, there are hypocapnia and hypoxemia; late, CO_2 retention occurs. Pulmonary function shows a restrictive ventilatory defect, with reductions in vital capacity, total lung capacity, compliance, and diffusing capacity for carbon monoxide. The histopathology is characterized by fibrotic thickening of alveolar septa, accompanied by variable degrees of interstitial cellular infiltrate. In addition, desquamation of large mononuclear cells into alveolar spaces and cuboidal transformation of alveolar epithelium are present.

Immunologic Diagnosis
There are no specific diagnostic techniques currently available. Rheumatoid factor and ANA are present in the serum in as many as 60% of cases. These are usually present in low titers. Serum immunoglobulin levels are nonspecifically increased. Analysis of cells and fluids retrieved by bronchopulmonary lavage reveal that the total number of cells and the numbers of neutrophils and eosinophils are substantially greater than normal. The content of IgG in lavage fluids exceeds that of normal subjects (Table 30–2).

Differential Diagnosis
The differential diagnosis involves consideration of the extraordinarily large number of disease processes affecting the interstitium of the lung. Prominent among these are granulomatous processes such as sarcoidosis and hypersensitivity pneumonitis, drug reactions, infectious processes, interstitial edema, neoplastic disease, and collagen-vascular disorders. In practice, the diagnosis of idiopathic pulmonary fibrosis is largely one of exclusion.

Treatment & Prognosis
The natural history of idiopathic pulmonary fibrosis is variable, but the long-term prognosis is uniformly poor. The extent of radiographic abnormality and the presence of rheumatoid factor and ANA corre-

late poorly with prognosis. A favorable response to corticosteroids appears to improve the overall prognosis. The more cellular the infiltrative process as determined by biopsy, the more likely the patient is to derive therapeutic benefit from corticosteroid therapy.

SARCOIDOSIS

Major Immunologic Features
- Depression of cell-mediated immune responses.
- Elevated serum immunoglobulin levels.
- Granuloma formation characteristic but not diagnostic of sarcoidosis.
- Positive Kveim test in about 80% of cases.

General Considerations
Sarcoidosis is a systemic granulomatous disorder of unknown cause. It varies greatly in reported incidence and clinical severity both among various geographic regions and among different ethnic groups. Many agents have been suspected but not proved as the cause of sarcoidosis: viruses, organic dusts, pine pollen, fungi, beryllium, mycobacteria, etc. The contribution of any of these agents remains unclear. Clinically, sarcoidosis initially involves the mediastinal lymph nodes and the interstitium of the lung. Acutely, bilateral hilar lymphadenopathy is prominent and is accompanied by constitutional symptoms and variable degrees of pulmonary infiltration. As the disease becomes chronic, progressive pulmonary fibrosis dominates the clinical picture. There is a variable but high incidence of extrathoracic involvement of any organ in the body.

Immunologic Pathogenesis
A. Systemic Immune Reactivity: Although numerous abnormalities of the systemic immune system can be demonstrated in sarcoidosis, the exact role of immune mechanisms in the pathogenesis of this disease is not known. Immunologic abnormalities of systemic cell-mediated and humoral immunity are outlined in Table 30–4.

Table 30–4. Systemic immunologic abnormalities in sarcoidosis.

Cell-mediated immunity
Complete or partial anergy to delayed hypersensitivity skin tests
Lymphopenia with decreased proportions of T cells
Depressed proliferative responses of lymphocytes to mitogens, antigens, and allogeneic cells
Inhibitory factors (soluble and cellular) for lymphocyte activation present in blood.
Humoral immunity
Elevated levels of immunoglobulins
High levels of serum antibodies and enhanced humoral responses to certain antigens
Presence of autoantibodies in serum
Detectable levels of circulating immune complexes

Delayed hypersensitivity skin reactions to recall antigens (tuberculin, mumps, *Candida, Trichophyton,* etc) and to novel antigens (DNCB) all may be greatly reduced or absent. Anergy, particularly to tuberculin, tends to parallel disease activity, being present during activity and disappearing during remission of disease. It is of note that the presence of active tuberculosis results in positive tuberculin skin reactivity even in the face of anergy to other antigens.

During active disease, lymphopenia is evident, with a concomitant reduction in T lymphocyte numbers and functional capacities. Peripheral blood lymphocytes from patients with active sarcoidosis respond poorly to stimulation with PHA and ConA (see Chapter 30). A wide variety of inhibitory factors, both cellular and soluble, have been implicated as accounting for the reduced functional capacities of these lymphocytes. There appears to be a general correlation between reduced lymphocyte number and function and the activity (acute or chronic) of sarcoidosis. Monitoring these parameters may be a useful adjunct to clinical management.

Patients with sarcoidosis have a polyclonal increase in serum immunoglobulins, presumably as a result of nonspecific activation of B cells. Elevation of IgG is most prominent, but IgM and IgA levels may also be increased. There is no apparent correlation between the serum immunoglobulin levels and the extent or activity of the sarcoidosis. IgG levels in bronchial washings of lungs of patients with sarcoidosis are increased, but such increases occur also in other interstitial lung diseases (Table 30–2). Patients with sarcoidosis may display unusually high levels of antibody against bacteria such as *Mycoplasma* and viruses such as Epstein-Barr, rubella, and herpes simplex virus. Low titers of autoantibodies may be found in sarcoidosis, and these include rheumatoid factor, antinuclear antibody, and antibodies to T lymphocytes. Recently, the presence of circulating immune complexes has been demonstrated in patients with sarcoidosis; however, their significance is presently unknown.

Peripheral blood T lymphocytes are reduced in sarcoidosis as measured by the E rosette technique. The proportion of B cells in circulating blood appears to be increased, as detected by measured surface immunoglobulin and complement receptors.

B. Pulmonary Immune Reactivity: Recent studies have been directed toward characterizing the cell types and functional characteristics of populations of cells retrieved by pulmonary lavage from lungs of patients with sarcoidosis. Lavage cells appear to constitute a reasonably accurate sample of intra-alveolar and interstitial inflammatory cells present in lung parenchyma.

In contrast to systemic lymphopenia, the relative proportions and total numbers of lymphocytes in lavage samples are increased (Table 30–2), and the increase appears to be directly proportionate to disease activity (alveolar interstitial inflammation). Most lymphocytes recovered by lavage are T cells that appear by morphologic and functional criteria to be "activated." The relative proportions of T helper to T suppressor cells is greatly increased, as assessed by the monoclonal antisera OKT4 and OKT8. Lung lavage T cells spontaneously elaborate monocyte chemotactic factor and appear to promote immunoglobulin synthesis by peripheral blood B cells. Because the lymphocytosis, increased proportion of T cells, and enhanced lymphocyte activity in lung lavage populations contrasts markedly with findings in the blood (see above), the concept has emerged that focusing and concentration of active T cell effectors occurs in the lung at the expense of the peripheral circulation. Such recruitment of cells to the lung might be important in the pathogenesis of the granuloma of pulmonary sarcoidosis.

The relative concentration of IgG in lavage fluid is increased in sarcoidosis (Table 30–2). Populations of lymphocytes obtained by pulmonary lavage in patients with sarcoidosis contain increased concentrations of cells spontaneously producing IgG and IgM but not IgA—as compared with cells obtained from normal controls. It has been suggested that the increased proportions of T helper cells in lungs of patients with sarcoidosis contribute to enhanced immunoglobulin synthetic activity of lung B cells. The pathogenetic significance of these findings remains to be elucidated.

Despite the conflicting immunologic data, it appears likely that the sarcoid granuloma results from immunologic reactions. Currently, there is no direct evidence for this postulate. Detailed studies of the immune function of cells derived from sarcoid granuloma should help in the understanding of the immunopathogenesis of this disease.

Clinical Features

A. Symptoms and Signs: The disease most often presents before age 40 and affects both sexes equally. Most patients have asymptomatic sarcoidosis and the disease is first noticed on a routine chest x-ray. The principal findings in symptomatic disease are respiratory, dermatologic, or ocular in origin; and dyspnea, erythema nodosum, acute iritis, splenomegaly, peripheral lymphadenopathy, or cardiac arrhythmias may be present at the time of initial examination. Radiographic findings vary from prominent bilateral hilar lymphadenopathy to extensive pulmonary infiltrates with fibrosis. Skin nodules are present in about one-fifth, peripheral lymphadenopathy in about one-third, and splenomegaly in slightly over one-tenth of patients. It should be emphasized that sarcoidosis is a protean disease which can present with involvement of almost any organ system.

B. Laboratory Findings: Radiographic findings vary from prominent hilar lymphadenopathy to extensive pulmonary infiltrates with fibrosis (Table 30–5). The routine blood count is usually normal. Polyclonal hypergammaglobulinemia may be present and usually represents increased IgG, but IgM and IgA may also be increased. Hypercalcemia is present in about 15% of

Table 30–5. International convention for staging chest roentgenograms of patients with sarcoidosis.

Stage 0: Clear chest roentgenogram.
Stage 1: Bilateral hilar lymphadenopathy.
Stage 2: Bilateral hilar lymphadenopathy plus parenchymal pulmonary infiltration.
Stage 3: Advanced parenchymal pulmonary infiltration with nodular densities.

patients, but this percentage has varied considerably in different clinical series. The Kveim test (see below) is positive in about 60–80% of patients. The clinical diagnosis is supported most commonly by the demonstration that tissue obtained by transbronchial lung biopsy or hilar node biopsy contains noncaseating granulomas and is negative after culture for bacteria and fungi.

Immunologic Diagnosis

The only immunologic assay clinically useful for establishing the diagnosis of sarcoidosis has been the Kveim skin test. The original test antigen was prepared by extracting human spleen tissue obtained from a patient with active sarcoidosis. A small quantity (0.15 mL) of the preparation is injected intradermally, and the site is observed for 6 weeks to note the development of a nodule. The nodule is biopsied, and the test is considered positive if the nodule contains a typical granulomatous reaction. Initial studies with this test reagent demonstrated selectivity for sarcoidosis, being positive in up to 80% of patients with the disease, with only 2% false-positive results. Unfortunately, the test antigen is not available commercially. The specificity of preparations is highly variable and the practical usefulness of Kveim testing is at present in question. Bronchopulmonary lavage, with analysis of cell differentials, can be helpful in following the course of the disease in an investigative setting. However, its routine clinical use in initial diagnosis is not yet indicated.

Differential Diagnosis

The ability of sarcoidosis to involve multiple organ systems can result in considerable difficulty in establishing the diagnosis when the disorder has an atypical presentation. The major points in the differential diagnosis of acute pulmonary sarcoidosis are tuberculosis, other granulomatous lung diseases, and mediastinal lymphoma. Chronic pulmonary sarcoidosis is indistinguishable radiographically from any other interstitial fibrotic process (see above). The tissue diagnosis of both acute and chronic disease requires the demonstration of noncaseating granuloma in mediastinal lymph nodes or pulmonary parenchymal tissue.

Treatment & Prognosis

The prognosis in sarcoidosis associated with bilateral hilar lymphadenopathy and erythema

Table 30—6. Prognosis and treatment of sarcoidosis.

Chest X-Ray	Prognosis	Corticosteroid Therapy
Stage 1	Resolves in 60% of cases.	No corticosteroid therapy.
Stage 2	Resolves in 46% of cases.	Corticosteroids to decrease pulmonary fibrosis and relieve symptoms.
Stage 3	Resolves in 12% of cases.	Same as stage 2.

nodosum is favorable. In other stages of sarcoidosis, the prognosis depends on the extent of lung involvement and the presence of extrathoracic lesions. Corticosteroid therapy may be given to decrease clinical symptoms and prevent extensive pulmonary fibrosis (Table 30—6). Ocular and cardiac involvement, extensive skin lesions, and central nervous system, renal, and bone lesions usually require intensive corticosteroid therapy and have a poorer prognosis. The disease is fatal in about 5% of cases.

PULMONARY DISEASE RESULTING FROM DRUGS

Idiosyncratic or allergic reactions to medications can result in pulmonary injury. The incidence of pulmonary complications of drug therapy is unknown, but there are several compounds now reported as producing pulmonary interstitial disease, pleural effusions, bronchospasm, or paralysis of respiratory muscles

Table 30—7. Types of pulmonary reactions produced by drugs.*

Diffuse pulmonary disease	Pleural effusion
Chemotherapeutic agents	Nitrofurantoin (acute)
Nitrofurantoin (acute and chronic reactions)	Drug-induced SLE
	?Methysergide
Heroin, methadone, propoxyphene	Radiation
Methysergide	**Bronchospasm**
Drug-induced SLE	Aspirin
Oxygen	Propranolol
Corticosteroids (opportunistic infection)	Aerosolized drugs
	Isoproterenol
Radiation (acute and chronic)	Polymyxin B
Drug-induced PIE (pulmonary infiltrations with eosinophilia)	Cromolyn sodium
	Acetylcysteine
Mineral oil aspiration	Pituitary snuff
Blood	**Respiratory muscle paralysis**
Cromolyn sodium	Gentamicin
Salicylate (overdose)	Neomycin
Pituitary snuff	Kanamycin
Mediastinal and hilar changes	Streptomycin
Corticosteroids (lipomatosis)	Polymyxin B
Phenytoin	Colistin

*Modified slightly from Rosenow EC: Drug-induced pulmonary disease. *Clin Notes Respir Dis* 1977;**16**:3.

(Table 30—7). The interstitial lung disease associated with the administration of nitrofurantoin is considered a typical example of this type of disorder. An acute illness develops 3–10 days after initiation of therapy, characterized by fever, chills, dyspnea, and in some cases peripheral blood eosinophilia. Symptoms can also appear on the first day of treatment, even in patients without prior exposure to the drug. Physical examination may disclose rales, and the chest x-ray demonstrates interstitial infiltration. Symptoms clear within several days after cessation of the drug and will return upon administration of the same medication. Patients receiving long-term nitrofurantoin therapy can develop chronic interstitial pulmonary fibrosis without fever or eosinophilia.

The evidence implicating immune mechanisms in these pulmonary responses is limited. Circulating antibodies reacting with these compounds have been demonstrated in only a few cases. Attempts to induce transformation of specifically sensitized lymphocytes isolated from peripheral blood have been unsuccessful in almost all cases. Thus, the relationship between these disorders and immunologic reactions against the administered medication must remain unclear until additional patients have been investigated. Treatment of acute illness is largely symptomatic once the offending medication has been discontinued.

PULMONARY REACTIONS TO LEUKOAGGLUTININS

The infusion of blood incompatible for leukocyte antigens can result in fever, chills, cough, transient pulmonary infiltrates, and high-permeability pulmonary edema. These reactions have an immunologic basis and are associated with leukoagglutinins either in the transfused blood or in the recipient's plasma. These are not anti-HLA antibodies.

When blood containing leukoagglutinins is infused, the donor plasma contains an antibody that reacts with recipient white cells and produces an acute clinical syndrome of fever, dyspnea, cough, and pulmonary infiltrates. In severe cases, cyanosis and hypertensive episodes have also been described. Corticosteroids appear to relieve some of the symptoms, but several days may be required for clearing of the chest x-ray. Laboratory studies may demonstrate the presence of the agglutinating antibody in the donor plasma.

When the agglutinating antibody is in the recipient's plasma, although febrile reactions are common, no pulmonary manifestations occur when incompatible leukocytes are infused. These reactions are more common in patients with a history of multiple transfusions. The febrile reactions can be prevented by separating the white cells from the blood prior to transfusion.

IMMUNOLOGIC DISEASES
OF THE HEART

POSTPERICARDIOTOMY SYNDROME
(Postmyocardial Infarction Syndrome; Dressler's Syndrome)

Major Immunologic Features
- Circulating anticardiac antibodies.
- Possible activation of classic complement pathway.
- Circulating immune complexes.

General Considerations

Extensive damage to myocardial and pericardial tissues can result from trauma, from surgical procedures, or from myocardial infarctions. Several days to several months after the initial injury, about 10% of postthoracotomy patients and 1% of postmyocardial infarction patients will develop a syndrome of recurrent fever, pericarditis, and effusions. The cause of this syndrome is unknown, but the temporal relationship to cardiac damage, the high frequency of anticardiac antibodies, and prompt clinical response to corticosteroid therapy suggest that this syndrome may result from autoimmune responses to antigens released from damaged cardiac tissue.

Immunologic Pathogenesis

Circulating antibodies against cardiac antigens can frequently be demonstrated following traumatic, surgical, or vascular injury to cardiac or pericardial tissue. Hemagglutination, immunofluorescence, and complement fixation assays have detected circulating antibodies in up to 80–90% of patients who have had cardiac surgery. The immunofluorescence studies demonstrated 3 main patterns of staining of cardiac muscle fibers: (1) diffuse sarcoplasmic, (2) sarcolemmal-subsarcolemmal, and (3) intermyofibrillar. The sarcolemmal-subsarcolemmal pattern of staining was present in both cardiac and skeletal muscle but not in other organs.

Hemagglutination and complement fixation assays have employed saline and alcoholic extracts of cardiac tissue as antigen, and results have been variable. These antigen extracts are complex preparations and have been incompletely defined in terms of antigen specificity. In patients known by immunofluorescence studies to be positive for circulating anticardiac antibodies, hemagglutination or complement fixation studies have given only a 10–45% frequency of positive responses.

The relationship between circulating anticardiac antibody and the development of clinical symptoms is poorly defined. The lack of clear correlation may be partly the result of the particular antigen preparation or assay system used in clinical studies. Many patients develop anticardiac antibodies without demonstrating any symptoms of Dressler's syndrome, and the quantitative levels of antibody do not appear to correlate well with either the onset or severity of symptoms.

More recently, total hemolytic complement levels and C3 and C4 inactivation products were studied in a group of patients several weeks after myocardial infarction. Although serum complement levels normally rise slightly after myocardial infarction, in a few cases there was evidence for activation of complement via the classic pathway. Some of these patients developed symptoms suggestive of Dressler's syndrome, and, although the evidence is limited, this suggests that Dressler's syndrome (and similar clinical disorders) might result from circulating immune complexes of cardiac antigen and anticardiac antibody.

Clinical studies measuring only the serum antibody response to cardiac antigens frequently ignore the contribution to clinical symptoms resulting from cell-mediated immune reactions to heart tissue. Studies of cardiac transplantation in humans and other animals clearly show that cardiac cells are sensitive to the cytolytic effect of activated lymphocytes, and myocardial injury may produce sufficient alterations in the tissue to induce autoimmune pathologic changes. However, no clinical studies have been performed to assess the importance of cell-mediated cardiac damage in such patients. Clearly, much additional work will be required to define the manner in which immune reactions contribute to the pathogenesis of these post-injury disorders.

Clinical Features

A. Symptoms and Signs: The disease is characterized by intermittent fever and episodes of mild to severe chest pain. The chest pain is usually mild to moderate in intensity, made worse by deep inspiration, and persists for days to weeks. Sometimes, however, the pain can be very severe and can resemble the crushing pain of myocardial ischemia. Pericardial or pleural effusions may be present, and a pericardial friction rub may be heard.

B. Laboratory Findings: The laboratory findings are nonspecific and are usually of little help in diagnosis of the syndrome. There may be leukocytosis, an increased red cell sedimentation rate, and a positive test for C-reactive protein. The ECG can show changes of pericarditis as well as the findings associated with the underlying cardiac disease, such as myocardial infarction, which preceded the onset of the syndrome. Circulating immune complexes and anticardiac antibodies have been demonstrated in a high percentage of patients (see above), but their relationship to the clinical onset of symptoms remains unclear.

Differential Diagnosis

If the chest pain is severe and abrupt in onset, it must be differentiated from additional ischemia or infarction of myocardial tissue. Interval changes in the ECG or changes in serum levels of cardiac muscle enzymes may be helpful. The presence of chest pain and pleural effusions may suggest pulmonary emboli, and a distinction between emboli and this syndrome is important. Anticoagulant therapy is not recommended in Dressler's syndrome because of the risk of hemo-pericardium.

Treatment & Prognosis

Most patients with this disease require no treatment beyond a simple analgesic. Normally, the symptoms and fever can be controlled and will clear spontaneously over several weeks. At times, however, the patient will become sufficiently ill to require corticosteroid therapy for symptomatic relief. The clinical response to corticosteroids is usually prompt, but the symptoms may reappear after cessation of therapy. The ultimate outcome is related to the underlying cardiac disease and not to the development of Dressler's syndrome. Tamponade from pericardial effusions is rare.

ACUTE RHEUMATIC FEVER

Major Immunologic Features

- Occurs after group A streptococcal infection, with antibodies against various group A streptococcal antigens.
- Presence of circulating autoantibodies directed at cardiac tissues and group A streptococcal antigens.
- Deposition of immunoglobulin and complement in myocardial and valvular tissues.

General Considerations

Rheumatic fever is a multisystemic inflammatory disease associated with a recent history of group A streptococcal infection. The disease usually occurs in children between 5 and 15 years of age. It only develops after repeated oropharyngeal streptococcal infections and is usually not associated with streptococcal skin infections. The incidence, which varies from 0.4% to 2–3% of patients with streptococcal oropharyngitis, is falling, probably as a result of an improved standard of living in the industrialized world.

The Jones criteria (revised) for the diagnosis of rheumatic fever are often helpful (Table 30–8). The presence of 2 major or one major and 2 minor criteria, along with clinical or laboratory evidence of recent streptococcal infection, is highly suggestive of rheumatic fever. Sydenham's chorea is diagnostic of rheumatic fever even in the absence of any other criteria.

Table 30–8. Jones criteria (revised) for the diagnosis of rheumatic fever.

Major Criteria	Minor Criteria
Carditis	Fever
Polyarthritis	Arthralgia
Erythema marginatum	Previous rheumatic fever
Subcutaneous nodules	Prolonged P–R interval on ECG
Sydenham's chorea	Elevated erythrocyte sedimentation rate; elevated C-reactive protein; leukocytosis (any of these)

Immunologic Pathogenesis

Several theories on the pathogenesis of rheumatic fever have been proposed.

A. Infection Theory: It has been suggested that the disease is caused by the direct invasion of involved tissue either by group A streptococci or their "L" forms. However, neither of these has been isolated from involved tissues.

B. Streptococcal Toxin Theory: It has been hypothesized that the manifestations of rheumatic fever are secondary to the action of streptococcal toxins. Group A streptococci produce a number of potent toxins which could, either singly or in combination, cause some manifestations of rheumatic fever.

1. Streptolysin S (SS)–Streptolysin S is a nonantigenic hemolysin responsible for the hemolytic zones characteristically produced by group A streptococcal cultures on blood agar. The action of streptolysin S is inhibited by a nonspecific serum lipoprotein, the "serum inhibitor of streptolysin S." Since serum inhibitor of streptolysin S is decreased in patients with rheumatic fever, such patients may have an increased susceptibility to the action of streptolysin S. However, serum inhibitor of streptolysin S is also depressed in juvenile and adult rheumatoid arthritis and several other rheumatoid diseases.

2. Streptolysin O (SO)–Streptolysin O is an antigenic protein found in low or moderate titer in most human sera. Although streptolysin O is not as effective a hemolysin as streptolysin S, it is known that streptococcal strains associated with rheumatic fever produce more streptolysin O than non–rheumatic fever-associated strains. It has been postulated that serum complexes of streptolysin O–antistreptolysin O circulate in rheumatic fever patients and that specific myocardial substrates compete with the immunoglobulin for the toxin, which is then deposited in the heart, where it leads to rheumatic carditis.

3. Streptococcal proteinase (SP)–Streptococcal proteinase is an antigenic enzyme produced by streptococci of low virulence. When injected into rabbits, streptococcal proteinase produces myocardial lesions similar to those seen in acute rheumatic carditis.

4. C-polysaccharide and protein complexes–High-molecular-weight preparations of fragmented streptococci injected into animals induce chronic inflammatory changes in various organs, including the heart. This reaction is not a typical immune response, since it begins within 3 hours of administration and is not affected by repeated injections.

C. Allergic Theory: Because of the clinical similarity of rheumatic fever to serum sickness, it has been suggested that rheumatic fever is an allergic reaction to components of products of group A streptococci. There are several arguments against this hypothesis. First, recurrent allergic reactions manifest a progressively shorter latent period, which does not occur in rheumatic fever. Second, patients with serum sickness have decreased serum complement owing to increased consumption by immune complexes. In rheumatic fever, serum complement is often elevated. Third, it is

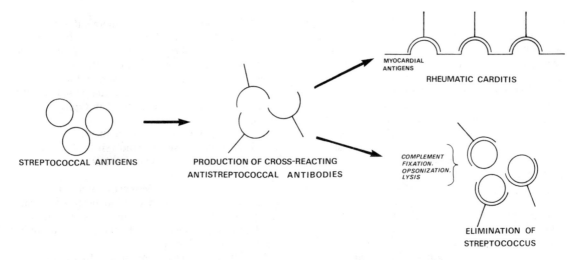

Figure 30-1. Autoantibodies as mediators of carditis in rheumatic fever.

difficult to explain the characteristic Aschoff body on the basis of an allergic reaction.

D. Autoimmune Theory: (Fig 30–1.) At present this is the most widely accepted theory of the pathogenesis of rheumatic fever.

1. Humoral mechanism–In up to 80% of patients with acute rheumatic fever, autoantibodies against cardiac tissue have been demonstrated. Those with acute carditis or recurrences tend to have the highest titers of autoantibody, but 60% of patients with inactive rheumatic heart disease also have significant titers. Immunofluorescent staining demonstrates that serum from rheumatic fever patients contains autoantibodies against cardiac myofibrils, smooth muscle of cardiac vessels, and endocardium. These autoantibodies cross-react with group A streptococcal antigens, many of which are closely associated with M protein. Half of patients with rheumatic fever or inactive rheumatic heart disease have anticardiac autoantibodies that cross-react with streptococcal cell wall or cell membrane preparations. Immunofluorescence techniques reveal that 18% of patients with inactive rheumatic heart disease have focal deposits of immunoglobulin throughout the myocardium. Patients with active rheumatic carditis have diffuse myocardial deposition of γ-globulin and complement as well as valvular deposition of IgG, but not IgA, IgM, or complement. It is not known whether the immunoglobulin deposited in the myocardium cross-reacts with streptococcal antigens.

2. Cellular mechanism–Streptococcal cell wall antigens present in streptolysin S preparations are lymphocyte mitogens. Patients with rheumatic fever show a decreased mitogenic response during the first attack, but mitogenic response is normal during subsequent attacks. Streptococcal M protein can induce delayed hypersensitivity in humans or animals, as measured by in vivo skin testing and in vitro lymphocyte activation and MIF production. However, lymphocytes of normal children, as well as of patients

with rheumatic fever, are stimulated by streptococcal cell wall antigens. This suggests that cellular hypersensitivity to these antigens is not a major immunologic determinant of disease.

Clinical Findings

A. Symptoms and Signs:

1. Preceding streptococcal infection–Almost half of patients recall having had a sore throat prior to their first attack of rheumatic fever, whereas only 30% of recurrences are preceded by symptomatic infections. The latent period between the infection and the onset of rheumatic fever is approximately 18 days.

2. Arthritis–The arthritis of rheumatic fever is an acute migratory polyarthritis, with only transient involvement of each joint. The large joints of the legs and arms are usually involved. Soft tissue swelling without bony erosions is seen radiographically.

3. Carditis–One-third of patients develop carditis with the first attack, and the incidence of cardiac involvement increases with each recurrence. Carditis, which is often asymptomatic, involves the myocardium, endocardium, and pericardium. Myocarditis may be present with or without overt congestive heart failure. Mitral valve regurgitation with a resultant pansystolic murmur is the commonest manifestation of endocardial involvement. Aortic valvulitis with regurgitation is less common. Pericarditis is commonly associated with pain and transitory friction rubs but rarely leads to pericardial effusion or tamponade.

4. Chorea (Sydenham's chorea, St. Vitus' dance)–Chorea is a neurologic disorder characterized by purposeless, nonrepetitive, spasmodic movements of any voluntary muscle. It occurs in only 5% of patients with rheumatic fever, most commonly in females. Chorea may last for up to 14 weeks; recovery without residual neurologic deficit is the invariable rule.

5. Subcutaneous nodules–The subcutaneous nodules of rheumatic fever are firm, painless, transient, "pea-sized" nodules that develop over bony prominences. When present, there are usually only 3 or 4 of these nodules. They occur in 5% of rheumatic fever patients and are often associated with severe carditis.

6. Erythema marginatum–Patients with rheumatic fever may have an evanescent, painless, nonpruritic, nodular or raised rash over the trunk or proximal limbs. Erythema marginatum occurs in 5% of patients, is usually associated with carditis, and may appear, migrate, and then disappear over the course of a few hours.

7. Nonspecific manifestations–Fever, anorexia, and nausea and vomiting are almost universal. A vague periumbilical pain of unknown cause may occur. Epistaxis, previously present in up to 48% of patients, now occurs in only 4–9%.

B. Laboratory Findings: Elevations in acute phase reactants, including erythrocyte sedimentation rate, C-reactive protein, complement, mucoproteins, α- and γ-globulins, and fibrinogen, are almost universal. Leukocytosis and mild anemia are common. A transient microscopic hematuria rarely occurs.

The subcutaneous nodules of rheumatic fever are composed largely of edema fluid and strands of fibrinoid material. The cellular infiltrate consists of fibroblasts, histiocytes, lymphocytes, and a few polymorphonuclear leukocytes.

Histologic findings in acute myocarditis include swelling and necrosis of muscle cells and fibrinoid degeneration of collagen tissue. The classic myocardial lesion in rheumatic fever is the Aschoff body, which consists of a central focus of degeneration and necrosis surrounded by mononuclear cells and by large, multinuclear cells (Anitschkow cells) with a "banded" or serrated appearance of their nuclear chromatin and with a clear area adjacent to the nuclear membrane.

C. Electrocardiographic Findings: The ECG shows prolongation of the P–R interval in 25% of all cases. T wave inversions may also be seen. However, electrocardiographic changes correlate poorly with clinical carditis.

Immunologic Diagnosis

There is no specific immunologic test for the diagnosis of rheumatic fever. Evidence of prior streptococcal infection can be obtained serologically. Virtually all rheumatic fever patients have antibodies to streptococcal antigens, although the height of the antibody titer bears no relationship to the severity of the disease. Most normal individuals also have low titers of antistreptococcal antibodies. Therefore, decisive evidence of recent infection rests on showing a rise in antibody titers. There are 2 basic classes of streptococcal antigens that stimulate the production of antibodies used in the diagnosis of rheumatic fever.

A. Typing Antigens:

1. The C-carbohydrate component of the cell wall forms the basis of the Lancefield classification of streptococcal groups A–O.

2. M protein is a cell wall component that inhibits phagocytosis and therefore increases virulence. It forms the basis of the precipitin test used for specific typing within the major Lancefield groups. M protein stimulates both a cellular and a humoral response.

3. T substance is an antigen that stimulates the production of an agglutinin useful in typing streptococcal strains.

B. Antigenic Streptococcal Products:

1. Streptokinase (fibrinolysin)–Streptokinase is a streptococcal enzyme that converts plasminogen to plasmin.

2. Streptodornase (deoxyribonuclease)–Streptodornase depolymerizes deoxyribonucleoprotein and deoxyribonucleotide. Antistreptodornase remains elevated longer than other antibodies and is very useful in the diagnosis of chorea.

3. Hyaluronidase (spreading factor)–Hyaluronidase splits the hyaluronic acid of ground substance and aids in the spread of microorganisms through infected tissues. Antihyaluronidase is most useful in the diagnosis of acute infection.

4. Erythrogenic factor, which causes the rash of scarlet fever, is produced only by streptococci infected with a temperate phage.

5. Hemolysins–Two hemolysins are produced by streptococci. Streptolysin O is an antigenic hemolysin whose antibody, antistreptolysin O (ASO), blocks the hemolytic activity and forms the basis for the most commonly used serologic test for the diagnosis of rheumatic fever. High antistreptolysin O titers may represent either recent infection or persistence of antibody from an earlier infection. Eighty percent of patients with rheumatic fever have a significant antistreptolysin O titer rise within 2 months after an attack. Since antistreptolysin O is so common among the normal population, only high titers—250 Todd units in adults and 333 units in children—constitute evidence of recent infection.

Differential Diagnosis

The clinical manifestations of fever, arthralgia or arthritis, and a heart murmur, in association with mild leukocytosis and anemia, are compatible with infective endocarditis, juvenile rheumatoid arthritis, systemic lupus erythematosus, and acute leukemia. In many instances the differentiation between these diseases rests entirely on laboratory data. Patients with rheumatic fever have negative blood cultures, no erosive joint disease, no ANA in their sera, a negative LE cell test, and nonleukemic bone marrow. Sometimes the diagnosis remains in doubt despite intensive laboratory evaluation. The diagnosis of rheumatic fever cannot be made in the absence of evidence of streptococcal infection; however, its presence obviously does not exclude other diseases.

Treatment

A. General Measures: The aim of therapy is to decrease morbidity and mortality rates. Despite the dictates of traditional therapy, no specific benefit is achieved by prescribing bed rest. Patients with carditis and chorea will limit their activities voluntarily. More than anything else, patients with chorea need reassurance and the understanding of family and friends. It must be emphasized that the course is self-limited and that there are no neurologic residuals. Barbiturates and tranquilizers are of benefit in patients with severe chorea. Congestive heart failure should be treated with salt restriction, diuretics, and digitalis preparations as appropriate.

B. Specific Measures:

1. Antibiotics–Even though throat cultures are negative, antibiotics should be administered. Organisms may be present in areas inaccessible to culture, and the persistence of organisms presumably means the continued presence of streptococcal antigens cross-reactive to the myocardium. Either a single intramuscular injection of 1.2 million units of benzathine penicillin G or 600,000 units of procaine penicillin G intramuscularly daily for 10 days is adequate.

2. Anti-inflammatory agents–Patients often show a dramatic symptomatic response to salicylates. Aspirin, 0.1 g/kg orally daily, is the drug of choice. If no improvement is seen with salicylate therapy or if the patient has severe carditis, corticosteroids—usually prednisone, 10–15 mg orally every 6 hours, or its equivalent—may be used.

Course & Prognosis

If no exacerbations occur within 2 months following an attack of rheumatic fever, the disease is considered to have resolved. If carditis is absent, full recovery without residuals occurs in 95% of patients. Patients with carditis should limit their activity for 6 months after an attack. In patients with a residual murmur, the dynamics of cardiac function will determine the level of activity.

The most important sequelae are those involving the heart. The incidence of residual heart disease is directly correlated with the severity of the acute attack. Half of patients with a pathologic murmur during an attack of rheumatic fever develop residual heart disease. Seventy percent of patients with rheumatic fever who develop pericarditis or congestive heart failure will have a murmur 5 years later. Of the total number of patients with rheumatic fever, 1.4% have mitral stenosis at 5 years and 5% have mitral stenosis 10 years later. The mortality rate of rheumatic fever is related to the severity of the heart disease. The overall mortality rate for first attacks is less than 1%; for subsequent attacks, 3%.

Recurrences are a major problem in rheumatic fever, since anyone who has had one attack has an increased susceptibility to subsequent attacks. Because the incidence of cardiac involvement increases with each recurrence, it is important to prevent recurrent rheumatic fever. This is accomplished by preventing streptococcal infections by the use of prophylactic antibiotics. Acceptable prophylactic regimens include 1.2 million units of benzathine penicillin G intramuscularly every month; sulfadiazine, 1 g orally daily; or potassium penicillin, 200,000 units orally twice daily. There is some controversy over the duration of prophylactic therapy. One view is that prophylaxis should be continued for at least 5 years after the last attack of rheumatic fever and until the patient is 25 years of age. The other major view is that anyone under 18 who develops rheumatic fever or anyone with rheumatic heart disease should be continued on prophylaxis indefinitely.

• • •

References

General

Crystal RG et al: Interstitial lung disease: Current concepts of pathogenesis, staging and therapy. *Am J Med* 1981;**70**:542.

Hunninghake GW, Fauci AS: Pulmonary involvement in the collagen vascular diseases. *Am Rev Respir Dis* 1979; **119**:471.

Kaltreider HB: Expression of immune mechanisms in the lung. *Am Rev Respir Dis* 1976;**113**:347.

Schatz M, Patterson R, Fink J: Immunologic lung disease. *N Engl J Med* 1979;**300**:1310.

Bronchopulmonary Lavage

Hunninghake GW et al: Inflammatory and immune processes in the human lung in health and disease: Evaluation by bronchoalveolar lavage. *Am J Pathol* 1979;**97**:149.

Weinberger SE et al: Bronchoalveolar lavage in interstitial lung disease. *Ann Intern Med* 1978;**89**:459.

Goodpasture's Syndrome

Bergrem H et al: Goodpasture's syndrome: A report of seven patients including long-term follow-up of three who received a kidney transplant. *Am J Med* 1980;**68**:54.

Rosenblatt SG et al: Treatment of Goodpasture's syndrome with plasmapheresis: A case report and review of the literature. *Am J Med* 1979;**66**:689.

Hypersensitivity Pneumonitis

Kaltreider HB: Hypersensitivity pneumonitis: Immunologically mediated lung disease resulting from the inhalation of organic antigens. *J Occup Med* 1973;**15**:949.

Richerson HB: Varieties of acute immunologic damage to the rabbit lung. *Ann NY Acad Sci* 1974;**221**:340.

Roberts RC, Moore VL: Immunopathogenesis of hypersensitivity pneumonitis. *Am Rev Respir Dis* 1977; **116**:1075.

Schatz M, Patterson R, Fink J: Immunopathogenesis of hypersensitivity pneumonitis. *J Allergy Clin Immunol* 1977; **60**:27.

Allergic Bronchopulmonary Aspergillosis

Glimp RA, Bayer AS: Fungal pneumonias: Allergic bronchopulmonary aspergillosis. *Chest* 1981;**80**:85.

Rosenberg M et al: The assessment of immunologic and clinical changes occurring during corticosteroid therapy for allergic bronchopulmonary aspergillosis. *Am J Med* 1978; **64**:599.

Rosenberg M et al: Clinical and immunologic criteria for the diagnosis of allergic bronchopulmonary aspergillosis. *Ann Intern Med* 1977;**86**:405.

Idiopathic Pulmonary Fibrosis

Crystal RG et al: Idiopathic pulmonary fibrosis (NIH Staff Conference). *Ann Intern Med* 1976;**85**:769.

Stack BHR, Choo-Kang YFJ, Heard BE: The prognosis of cryptogenic fibrosing alveolitis. *Thorax* 1972;**27**:535.

Sarcoidosis

Crystal RG et al: Pulmonary sarcoidosis: A disease characterized and perpetuated by activated lung T lymphocytes. *Ann Intern Med* 1981;**94**:73.

Daniele RP, Dauber JH, Rossman MD: Immunologic abnormalities in sarcoidosis. *Ann Intern Med* 1980;**92**:406.

Leukoagglutinins

Thompson JS et al: Pulmonary "hypersensitivity" reactions induced by transfusion of non-HLA leukoagglutinins. *N Engl J Med* 1971;**284**:1120.

Postpericardiotomy Syndrome

Engle MA et al: The postpericardiotomy syndrome and anti-heart antibodies. *Circulation* 1974;**49**:401.

Rheumatic Fever

Kaplan MH, Frengley JD: Autoimmunity to the heart in cardiac disease: Current concepts of the relation of autoimmunity to rheumatic fever, postcardiotomy and postinfarction syndromes and cardiomyopathies. *Am J Cardiol* 1969; **24**:459.

McLaughlin JF et al: Rheumatic carditis: In vitro responses of peripheral blood leukocytes to heart and streptococcal antigens. *Arthritis Rheum* 1972;**5**:600.

Read S, Zabriskie JB (editors): *Streptococcal Disease and the Immune Response.* Rockefeller Univ Press, 1979.

Read SE et al: Cellular reactivity studies to streptococcal antigens: Migration inhibition studies in patients with streptococcal infections and rheumatic fever. *J Clin Invest* 1974; **54**:439.

Renal Diseases | 31

Curtis B. Wilson, MD, Edward H. Cole, MD,
Maurizio Zanetti, MD, & Francisco M. Mampaso, MD

GLOMERULONEPHRITIS

Immunologically induced glomerulonephritis is estimated to be responsible for over one-half of instances of end stage renal failure and its consequent mortality, morbidity, and expense. Antibody-associated mechanisms of glomerular injury can be broadly divided in terms of the physical state of the antigen involved: insoluble (tissue-fixed) and soluble (present in the body fluids) (see Table 31–1). Antibodies can form that react with fixed antigens in the kidney, present as a structural component or trapped there from some outside source. In humans, the major nephritogenic antigen or antigens identified to date are in the glomerular basement membrane (GBM), and antibodies reactive with them are responsible for up to 5% of cases of human glomerulonephritis. Experimental models of nephritis induced by anti-GBM antibody have allowed investigation of this mechanism of injury. Antibodies reactive with other glomerular antigens have not been implicated as yet in human glomerulonephritis; however, in some rabbits with spontaneous glomerulonephritis, an antibody to one or more non–basement membrane glomerular antigens has been found. Fixed structural glomerular antigens have been incriminated in the active and passive models of Heymann's nephritis in rats. Also, renal injury can be induced by binding of antibody to "planted" antigens such as the lectin (concanavalin A) or other materials that have been previously bound to the GBM. To exclude concomitant circulating immune complex formation from residual circulating soluble antigens in these models, selective perfusion or transplantation of the kidney and planted antigens to a naive host is often necessary. The experimental observation about fixed or "planted" antigens has renewed interest in determining if some facet of what is now regarded as immune complex disease may be related to glomerular trapping of antigen and subsequent local interaction with antibody. In most instances, the additional presence of circulating antigen and the dynamic immune complex equilibrium make clear distinctions between these 2 modes of immune reactant accumulation quantitatively difficult to separate.

Glomerular injury can also occur when antibodies react with soluble antigens in the circulation to form immune complexes, which subsequently accumulate in the glomerulus. Since immune complex formation is a dynamic process, continual modification of the deposited complexes by ongoing interaction with antibody and antigen or immune complexes from the circulation is to be expected. This continuing interaction with tissue deposits demonstrates the overlap or concomitant role of soluble and tissue-fixed antigens (as well as antibodies) in some forms of glomerulonephritis. Based on identification of nonglomerular exogenous and endogenous antigens and their antibodies in general, most cases of human glomerulonephritis ap-

Table 31–1. Immunopathogenesis of renal disease classified by the solubility of the antigen.

Solubility	Mechanism	Antigen	Condition
Insoluble or tissue-fixed antigens	Antibodies react with structural components of the kidney.	Glomerular basement membrane.	Glomerulonephritis.
		Tubular basement membrane.	Tubulointerstitial nephritis.
		Other glomerular wall antigens.	Experimental glomerulonephritis.
	Antibodies react with antigens trapped or "planted" in the glomerulus.	Mesangial deposits, immunoglobulin, complement, lectins; possibly bacterial antigens, DNA.	Experimental glomerulonephritis. May contribute to human glomerulonephritis as well.
Soluble antigens	Antibodies react with antigens in the vascular compartment to form circulating immune complexes.	Exogenous antigens: drugs, products of infectious agents, etc.	Glomerulonephritis. Tubulointerstitial nephritis. Vasculitis.
		Endogenous antigens: nuclear antigens, tumor antigens, etc.	
	Antibodies react with antigens in the extravascular fluid near the site of antigen release.	Tubular antigens.	Experimental tubulointerstitial nephritis.

pear to be caused by the immune complex mechanism, and this mechanism also appears to cause many spontaneous and experimentally induced cases of glomerulonephritis in animals. Antibodies reactive with soluble and insoluble antigens can cause tubulointerstitial renal injury as well as glomerulonephritis.

The glomerular injury caused by glomerular antibody accumulation results from the action of immunologic mediation systems. The best-studied mediation systems in experimental glomerulonephritis are the complement and neutrophil systems. In experimental glomerulonephritis and most types of human glomerulonephritis, antibody deposition is followed by activation of the complement sequence, and complement components can be shown to be present in glomeruli by immunofluorescence microscopy, although the functional importance of these deposited components is not clear in all situations. Circulating immune complexes often contain activated complement components, and this feature is utilized in the detection of complexes in many current assay systems. Congenital deficiencies of the complement system may be associated with recurrent infections, the development of connective tissue disorders, or glomerulonephritis. Neutrophils attracted by products of complement activation accumulate in the glomerular capillary loops in many forms of glomerulonephritis. There they displace the endothelium and release enzymes and other materials that damage the basement membrane and induce proteinuria. In experimental animals, some types of glomerulonephritis have been shown to occur independently of complement and neutrophils, implicating other as yet undefined mediation pathways.

In addition to neutrophils and the complement system, fibrin, macrophages, platelets, and humoral factors—including prostaglandins and the Hageman factor systems—have been suggested as mediators of glomerular injury. Glomerular fibrin deposits have been found in glomerulonephritis, particularly in association with extracapillary crescent formation. In anti-GBM antibody and circulating immune complex–induced experimental glomerulonephritis, defibrination with ancrod (Malayan pit viper venom) has prevented glomerular fibrin deposition, crescent formation, and renal failure. However inflammatory infiltrates, endocapillary proliferation, proteinuria, and complement deposition were unaffected.

Macrophages have recently been found in the glomeruli in experimental anti-GBM nephritis and acute and chronic experimental immune complex disease. The number of macrophages present correlates directly with the timing and extent of proteinuria and glomerular hypercellularity and the presence of crescent formation. Sensitized cell transfer experiments have shown that mononuclear cells can accumulate in glomeruli following the glomerular planting of the specific antigen. Morphologic evidence suggests that macrophages participate in glomerulonephritis in both experimental animal models and in humans. Antimacrophage antisera have been used successfully to inhibit glomerular macrophage accumulation and in

turn prevent some forms of experimental anti-GBM and immune complex–induced experimental glomerular injury. There is little experimental evidence for a major role for platelets in the mediation of immunologic glomerular injury, although this has not been fully evaluated. Extensive studies are in progress on the involvement of the Hageman factor system and prostaglandins in experimental glomerulonephritis, but no proven role for the former has yet emerged, and insufficient data are available regarding the involvement of prostaglandins.

The immune complex and anti-GBM antibody mechanisms of glomerular disease may be indistinguishable from each other unless the patient is studied by immunopathologic means. In renal biopsy tissue, antibodies reactive with GBM have a characteristic linear configuration by immunofluorescence microscopy, whereas randomly deposited immune complexes have a granular pattern. In experimental models of other types of anti-glomerular antibody disease (involving nonclassic GBM antigen[s]) noted earlier, the irregular distribution of the reactive antigen can result in irregular, granular antibody deposits that could be confused with those previously thought to be indicative of immune complex disease. Anti-GBM antibodies in the serum can now be detected by radioimmunoassay in almost all patients with the disease. In contrast, circulating immune complexes may be detectable easily only in acute cases of apparent immune complex glomerulonephritis or in patients whose glomerulonephritis is part of a systemic immune complex disorder such as lupus erythematosus.

When immunofluorescence is used to study renal biopsies from patients with glomerulonephritis, perhaps 10% of them show complement deposits in the absence of immunoglobulin. This observation, coupled with the finding of persistent hypocomplementemia in some patients with membranoproliferative histologic forms of glomerulonephritis, raises the possibility of yet another mechanism of glomerular injury. Such a mechanism could involve the "nonimmunologic" activation of immunologic mediator systems such as complement, a possibility that will be discussed in a subsequent section.

1. ANTI–GLOMERULAR BASEMENT MEMBRANE ANTIBODY–INDUCED GLOMERULONEPHRITIS

Major Immunologic Features
- Linear deposition of immunoglobulin and complement occurs along GBM.
- Anti-GBM antibodies usually detectable in serum by radioimmunoassay; less often by immunofluorescence.

General Considerations
The nephritogenicity of antikidney antisera was noted in 1900 by Lindemann. Subsequent studies by Masugi et al amplified these early observations, and in

the 1950s Krakower and Greenspon convincingly demonstrated that the major nephritogenic antigens of the kidney were in the GBM. Thereafter, the old term nephrotoxic antiserum was largely replaced by the more specific term anti-GBM antibody.

In humans, anti-GBM antibodies are now implicated in the production of glomerulonephritis, glomerulonephritis and pulmonary hemorrhage (Goodpasture's syndrome), and occasionally clinical presentations indistinguishable from those of idiopathic pulmonary hemosiderosis. The possibility of central nervous system involvement caused by an interaction of these antibodies with the choroid plexus basement membrane has also been raised. In addition, some patients present with arthritic manifestations.

Immunologic Pathogenesis

Two forms of experimental anti-GBM antibody-induced glomerulonephritis have been demonstrated. First, anti-GBM antibodies can be induced by immunizing animals with GBM in adjuvant. The antibody can then be used to induce anti-GBM nephritis in normal recipients. For example, rabbit, sheep, or duck anti-rat GBM antibodies are often used to induce anti-GBM glomerulonephritis in rats. The resulting glomerular injury occurs in 2 phases. If sufficient quantities of anti-GBM antibodies are given (75 μg of kidney-fixing antibody per gram of kidney in the rat), immediate injury and proteinuria occur. If insufficient antibody is given to cause immediate injury, overt glomerulonephritis does not develop until the recipient has produced antibody reactive with the foreign immunoglobulin already bound to its GBM. The foreign immunoglobulin fixed to the GBM in this phase acts as a "planted" antigen. Quantitative differences in the numbers of antibody molecules required to induce immediate glomerular injury as well as the severity of the resultant glomerulonephritis have been equated with the antibody's ability to activate complement and to involve neutrophils. This situation has led to designation of the antibody as "dependent on" or "independent of" complement and polymorphonuclear leukocytes and indicates that separate mediators of immunologic injury must be utilized by the complement-independent antibodies. Similarly, one-fourth to one-third of patients with anti-GBM antibodies have no detectable complement fixed in the glomeruli, suggesting the possibility of complement-independent processes.

In the second form of experimental anti-GBM nephritis, some animals immunized with GBM in adjuvant (sheep are particularly susceptible) develop anti-GBM antibodies that cross-react with their own GBM. Severe glomerulonephritis follows which can prove fatal to the sheep within 2–3 months. This lesion is similar in many ways to that of spontaneous anti-GBM glomerulonephritis in humans. Circulating anti-GBM antibodies are clearly pathogenic because they can be used to transfer glomerular injury to normal lambs.

In research done in the mid 1960s, immunofluorescence of kidney sections from occasional patients with glomerulonephritis showed anti-GBM antibodies bound in a smooth linear pattern along the GBM. In 1967, Lerner and others demonstrated anti-GBM antibodies in the circulations of such patients. These investigators also isolated anti-GBM antibodies from the sera of these patients or eluted them from the nephritic kidneys and showed the antibodies' pathogenicity by using them to transfer anti-GBM glomerulonephritis to subhuman primates. The most convincing evidence of similar pathogenicity in humans came when glomerulonephritis was accidentally transferred to a renal transplant placed in a patient who had circulating anti-GBM antibodies.

In patients with Goodpasture's syndrome, anti-GBM antibodies can be found bound to the alveolar basement membranes, and antibodies cross-reactive with the GBM can be eluted from the involved lung tissue. Experimentally, anti-GBM antibodies appear to cross-react with both the glomerular and alveolar basement membranes; however, lung injury is difficult to induce. Recently, it has been shown in rabbits that the binding of anti-GBM antibodies to alveolar basement membrane is enhanced by prior lung injury, presumably by increasing endothelial cell permeability. The evidence, then, suggests that anti-basement membrane antibodies are responsible for both the pulmonary and the renal injury in patients with Goodpasture's syndrome.

Little is known about the events responsible for the induction of spontaneous anti-GBM responses in humans. Materials cross-reactive with the GBM have been identified in the urine of animals and humans. Similar materials accumulate in the circulation after nephrectomy, suggesting that they represent basement membrane fragments released during basement membrane metabolism throughout the body and excreted in the urine. Immunization of rabbits with basement membrane antigens from their own urine can induce anti-GBM glomerulonephritis, suggesting the same potential in humans. In addition, noxious environmental or infectious insults to basement membranes (eg, in the lung) could induce anti-GBM antibody responses. Both hydrocarbon solvent inhalation and influenza A2 infections have been associated with anti-GBM antibody-associated Goodpasture's syndrome in a few patients. The lung damaged in this way might also react more easily with anti-GBM antibodies formed for unrelated reasons. Development of anti-GBM antibody has also occasionally been associated with immunologic or ischemic renal injury, and has occurred in patients with Hodgkin's disease. Differences in basement membrane antigens occur between individuals. Some individuals with hereditary glomerulonephritis lack the usual GBM antigens reactive with anti-GBM antibodies. Sometimes, anti-GBM antibodies can be induced in such individuals by transplantation of kidneys containing antigens lacking in the recipient.

In virtually all instances, the spontaneous production of anti-GBM antibodies is self-limited (weeks to 1 or 2 years), suggesting that the immunologic stimulus is also transient and potentially identifiable. Most affected individuals have only one episode; however, one interesting patient had 3 distinct episodes of hemoptysis and mild glomerulonephritis over an 11-year period, with evidence of anti-GBM antibodies detected during the first and last episodes. The nature of the nephritogenic antigens within the GBM is at present only partially defined but appears to be a non-collagenous glycoprotein of heterosaccharide content. Much current research, some utilizing basement membrane–producing tumors, is in progress at this area. It is interesting, as noted above, that anti-GBM antibodies do not react with the GBM from some patients with hereditary nephritis (some kindreds of Alport's syndrome), indicating that these patients have an abnormal noncollagenous GBM component.

Clinical Features

Less than 5% of cases of glomerulonephritis in humans appear to be caused by anti-GBM antibodies, which most commonly induce proliferative crescent-forming histologic types of glomerular injury with rapidly progressive clinical courses. About two-thirds of these patients with glomerulonephritis also have pulmonary hemorrhage and often respiratory failure, a condition referred to as Goodpasture's syndrome. It should be noted that although anti-GBM antibodies are probably the most frequent cause of Goodpasture's syndrome, immune complex mechanisms can induce a similar clinical picture; therefore, immunopathologic investigation is essential for correct diagnosis.

Anti-GBM antibody–induced diseases are more commonly identified in males in the second to fourth decades of life; however, either sex can be involved, and the disease affects children under 5 through adults of advanced age. Indeed, a second grouping of cases occurs particularly in women over 50. The first symptoms may be either renal or pulmonary or both, with onset occurring simultaneously or separated by as much as a year. In many patients, particularly those with Goodpasture's syndrome, flulike symptomatology precedes the onset of renal or pulmonary symptoms. It is unclear if this is a true infectious illness or merely prodromal symptoms. Arthritis has also been a prominent early complaint in some (less than 10%) patients. Overall, about 75% of patients develop renal failure necessitating dialysis, although the outlook seems to be improving somewhat, probably as a result of more aggressive treatment. As experience with the disease increases and better diagnostic methods evolve, it has become evident that a milder form does occur. This milder form, however, probably accounts for fewer than 15% of cases. In a few patients, the pulmonary features of the disease predominate or are the sole clinical manifestation. Anti-GBM antibodies may be responsible for an as yet undetermined percentage of cases of so-called pulmonary hemosiderosis. Nephrotic syndrome is unusual in anti-GBM glomerulonephritis, probably because renal failure supervenes before sufficient urinary protein spillage has occurred.

Immunologic Diagnosis

Patients with rapidly progressive glomerulonephritis or Goodpasture's syndrome should be suspected of having anti-GBM antibodies. However, immune complex disease and other undetermined causes are responsible for half or more cases of rapidly progressive glomerulonephritis. A diagnosis of anti-GBM glomerulonephritis is based on identifying anti-GBM antibodies by at least 2 of the 3 following means: (1) linear deposits of immunoglobulin along the GBM seen by immunofluorescence, (2) elution of anti-GBM antibodies from renal tissue, and (3) detection of circulating anti-GBM antibodies.

By immunofluorescence, anti-GBM antibodies appear as linear deposits of IgG and infrequently IgA or IgM along the GBM (Fig 31–1). Irregular IgM deposits along the GBM are present in less than half of the kidneys studied. Linear deposits of immunoglobulin are also frequently present along the tubular basement membrane (TBM) (see later section). The linear deposits of immunoglobulin are accompanied by linear or irregular deposits of C3 in about two-thirds of these kidneys. Fibrin-related antigens may be striking in areas of extracapillary proliferation and crescent formation. When C3 is present, it is usually accompanied by deposits of other components of the classic complement pathway. Care must be taken in basing the diagnosis on immunofluorescence study alone.

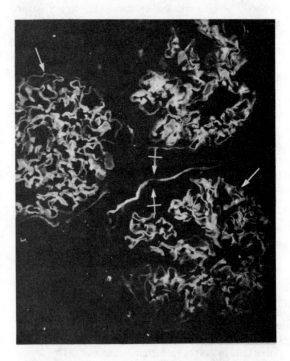

Figure 31–1. Smooth linear deposits of IgG (arrows) representing anti-GBM antibodies are seen outlining the GBM of 3 glomeruli from a young man with Goodpasture's syndrome. The antibody also had reactivity with Bowman's capsule (opposed hatched arrows). (Original magnification × 160.)

Nonimmunologic accumulations of IgG are sometimes observed in a linear pattern along the GBM, particularly in kidneys from patients with diabetes mellitus, in kidneys obtained at autopsy, in kidneys perfused in preparation for transplantation, and in some reasonably normal kidneys. These occasional "false-positive" kidneys indicate the need for confirming diagnoses by eluting anti-GBM antibodies or detecting them in the circulation.

Anti-GBM antibodies can be dissociated from renal or lung tissue by elution in acid buffers or buffers containing chaotropic ions (KI, KSCN, etc), which can dissociate hydrophobic and ionic bonds. The eluted immunoglobulin can then be recovered and tested for anti-GBM reactivity in vitro by indirect immunofluorescence or radioimmunoassay or in vivo by injection into subhuman primates. The ability to elute GBM-reactive antibodies from renal tissue confirms the specificity of immunofluorescence observations and establishes a clear-cut diagnosis.

Anti-GBM antibodies can be sought in the circulation by using indirect immunofluorescence, hemagglutination, or, more recently, radioimmunoassay. About 80% of patients with anti-GBM antibody-induced Goodpasture's syndrome and 60% of patients with anti-GBM antibody-induced glomerulonephritis alone have anti-GBM antibodies detectable by indirect immunofluorescence. By radioimmunoassay, almost all of both groups are positive when serum is available early in the course of the disease. Patients may have pulmonary hemorrhage at any time during the period of their anti-basement membrane antibody production, apparently unrelated to the amount of circulating anti-GBM antibody detected by radioimmunoassay. This suggests that nonimmunologic factors such as fluid overload and infection may contribute to the lung injury. Nephrectomy has no immediate effect on the levels of circulating anti-GBM antibodies in most patients, which suggests that damaged kidneys have little or no residual immunoabsorptive properties.

A group of patients with rapidly progressive, crescentic glomerulonephritis exists in whom neither anti-GBM antibodies nor immune complexes are detected. These patients may share clinical features with anti-GBM antibody-induced glomerulonephritis, including flulike prodromes, arthralgia, and occasionally hemoptysis. Diffuse endocapillary proliferation and extensive crescent formation are observed without the detection of immunoglobulin or complement by fluorescence microscopy or evidence of electron-dense deposits by electron microscopy. However, extensive deposition of fibrin can be found in relation to the crescents. The pathogenesis of this lesion is unknown.

Treatment

No immunologically specific treatment is available. Corticosteroids are thought to be helpful in the management of acute pulmonary hemorrhage in patients with anti-GBM antibody-associated Goodpasture's syndrome. The variable duration and intensity of the transient anti-GBM response must be considered in evaluating any therapeutic regimen, and occasional patients have recovered adequate renal function "spontaneously" even after being on dialysis for short periods of time. Approaches have recently been employed to hasten the disappearance of antibodies as a therapeutic modality. Repeated and intensive plasmaphereses in conjunction with immunosuppression are employed to remove circulating anti-GBM antibodies and to impair their production. Initial results are promising if the combined therapy is instituted before irreversible renal damage has taken place, in those patients without oliguria, and in patients with fewer circumferential crescents. The longest-running controlled trial has shown only modest improvement in patients undergoing plasmapheresis and immunosuppression compared to similarly immunosuppressed controls. Initial improvement is not sustained in all patients, so that long-term follow-up will also be needed.

Nephrectomy has been advocated by some as being helpful—even lifesaving—in the management of severe pulmonary hemorrhage in Goodpasture's syndrome. The results of nephrectomy are by no means clear-cut, and several nephrectomized patients have continued to manifest pulmonary hemorrhage, sometimes leading to death. Nephrectomy is also not essential to terminate production of anti-GBM antibody. Nephrectomy obviously precludes the occasional spontaneous recovery and should be considered only as a last resort.

Circulating anti-GBM antibodies can transfer glomerulonephritis to a transplanted kidney. The severity with which the anti-GBM disease recurs in the transplant seems to relate in a general way to the level of antibody present at the time of transplantation and is certainly influenced and modified by the intensive immunosuppression the transplant recipient receives. Quantities of anti-GBM antibodies insufficient to cause histologic change may be detected by immunofluorescence in some recipients. It is therefore advisable to postpone transplantation in patients with anti-GBM antibody-associated glomerulonephritis until circulating anti-GBM antibodies are absent or greatly reduced. The mean duration of the anti-GBM antibody response measured with today's sensitive radioimmunoassays is about 12 months (range, a few weeks to 3 years). Immunosuppression, plasmapheresis, or nephrectomy—or all 3—appear to hasten the disappearance of the anti-GBM antibody response.

2. IMMUNE COMPLEX–INDUCED GLOMERULONEPHRITIS

Major Immunologic Features

- Granular deposition of immunoglobulins and complement occurs in the glomeruli.
- Circulating immune complexes may be detectable.

General Considerations

In 1911, von Pirquet recognized the relationship between the immune response and the symptoms of serum sickness. Dixon and others demonstrated, in the 1950s, that immune complexes composed of antigen and antibody were the toxic products responsible for the tissue injury of individuals with serum sickness. It has become widely accepted that the demonstration by immunofluorescence of granular deposits of immunoglobulin in the glomerulus can usually be interpreted as evidence of immune complex–mediated nephritis. It must be kept in mind that the direct reaction of antibody with irregularly deposited fixed or "planted" antigens, as noted earlier in animal models, could be confused with immune complex deposits by immunofluorescence, thereby stressing the need for identification of the antigen-antibody systems involved.

Immunologic Pathogenesis

The principles of immune complex–induced renal injury are best understood by examining the events that accompany acute and chronic serum sickness in rabbits. To induce acute serum sickness, one gives rabbits large amounts of foreign proteins such as bovine serum albumin (BSA), 250 mg/kg. The BSA rapidly equilibrates with the intra- and extravascular fluids and then disappears at a rate governed by its catabolic half-life. Antibody production is initiated, and after 4–5 days, sufficient antibody is present to combine with the circulating antigen to be detected in circulating immune complexes. Since antigen is present in great excess, the complexes remain small and continue to circulate. As antibody production increases, the complexes increase in size and after 10–12 days are eliminated by the mononuclear phagocytic system. During the process of eliminating the immune complexes, small amounts (mean, 18 μg) of BSA in immune complex form are deposited in the kidney, inducing a severe but transient endocapillary proliferative glomerulonephritis with macrophage accumulation manifested clinically by heavy proteinuria. Immune complexes are also deposited in other vascular beds, inducing conditions such as arteritis, a feature of experimental acute serum sickness, and synovitis.

Evidence for deposition of circulating immune complexes is substantial in this model. There is no evidence that BSA is handled differently than the rabbit's own albumin by the kidney before immune complexes form. Since antigen excess is present, all antibody is immediately complexed and must reach the kidney in immune complex form. In addition, only complexes of a certain size (larger than 19S) are deposited in the kidney, and then only if vasoactive amine release has occurred. After antigen has been eliminated from the circulation, free antibody appears, combining with and masking the antigen complexed within the glomerulus. This demonstrates that tissue-bound immune complexes are in equilibrium with antibody and with antigen from the circulation; the composition of the glomerular-bound immune complexes is then determined at any point in time by the relative concentrations of antigen or antibody in the circulation.

The mechanisms responsible for mediating injury in acute serum sickness have been poorly understood until recently. Depleting an animal of complement and of polymorphonuclear leukocytes prevents arteritis but does not prevent glomerular injury. Antimacrophage serum, however, does abrogate the histologic and functional lesion.

If the rabbits are given BSA repeatedly in amounts to balance antibody production, chronic serum sickness glomerulonephritis can be induced. A spectrum of glomerulonephritis develops in this model which resembles many of the histologic types of glomerulonephritis found in humans. During the 6–8 weeks of daily intravenous BSA injection required for the development of chronic serum sickness glomerulonephritis, only small amounts of radiolabeled BSA accumulate in the glomerular immune deposits in the kidney. When viewed by immunofluorescence, the deposition is confined largely to the mesangium, where it induces hypercellularity and macrophage accumulation. After this time, the deposition increases to about 0.5% of the daily injected dose (10–200 mg), and localization of the deposits changes from the mesangium to the peripheral GBM, with occasional deposits observed in extraglomerular renal structures (TBM, interstitium, and peritubular capillaries) and other tissues as well. A wide variety of glomerular histologic changes are induced by the immune complex accumulation, apparently governed in part by the quantity and rate of this deposition. Rabbits with poor immune responses and with low levels of antibody are given correspondingly small amounts of antigen; as a result, they form only minimal amounts of immune complexes. Such rabbits tend to develop membranous glomerulonephritis with prolonged immunization. In contrast, active antibody producers given large amounts of antigen form large amounts of circulating immune complexes and have more proliferative (often crescent-forming) histologic changes.

The half-life for disappearance of the bound antigen from the kidneys of rabbits with chronic serum sickness glomerulonephritis is about 5 days. It has been possible to hasten the disappearance of the renal-bound immune complexes by deliberately creating huge antigen excess in a rabbit's circulation. This treatment dissolves the glomerular-bound immune complexes (detected by immunofluorescence and electron microscopy), and recovery follows if the excess antigen is given before irreversible glomerular changes develop. Administration of a huge antigen excess also terminates the antibody response, preventing formation of additional immune complexes. The multiple therapeutic benefits of this treatment may eventually be useful in humans.

Although still incompletely understood, several factors have been identified that may influence the tissue localization of immune complexes. In thinking about these factors, it must be remembered that the dynamics of immune complex formation render the complex subject to continual modification as shifts in the relative concentration of either antigen or antibody occur. Once localization has begun, antigen, antibody, or their complexes can interact at the site. This local interaction has made it very difficult to quantitate the exact contribution of the several factors that have been recognized. The glomerulus seems to be a uniquely susceptible site for immune complex accumulation, probably related in part to its function as an arterial capillary filter with a fenestrated endothelial lining. Changes in blood flow caused, for example, by vascular bifurcations, aortic coarctation, or hypertension may predispose the vessels to immune complex deposition and may contribute to the accumulation of deposits in glomeruli. Vasoactive substances released as part of the immune response—in particular that involving mast cell-bound or basophil-bound IgE—may enhance vascular permeability and, potentially, immune complex localization. Indeed, antihistamines and antiserotonins have been suggested to decrease immune complex deposition in rabbits with acute serum sickness. Immune complex size is also an important determinant of deposition, with complexes around 19S being the most nephritogenic. Immune complex size is influenced by the relative antigen-antibody ratio. The avidity of the antibody may also influence the stability of the immune complex. The size of the antigen as well as the class of the antibody would also be expected to alter immune complex size. Recently, evidence has accumulated to suggest that differences in physicochemical properties of the antigen, antibody, and presumably the immune complex formed may alter the site of accumulation. Cationic antigens, for example, seem to preferentially accumulate at the anionic sites present at the subepithelial aspect of the GBM. An excess of either antigen or antibody causes formation of immune complexes that are too small to lodge in the kidney or so large that the complexes are rapidly cleared from the circulation by the mononuclear phagocytic system. Impairment of the way in which the systemic mononuclear phagocytic system handles circulating immune complexes could conceivably lead to glomerular deposition by increasing the amount of complex presented to the glomerulus. Uptake and catabolism of immune complexes by the glomerular mesangium may be a mechanism for removal of potentially injurious immune complexes from the glomerulus. Endocapillary hypercellularity and a quantitative increase in glomerular uptake of administered aggregated immunoglobulin system are noted in the development of chronic serum sickness glomerulonephritis. Temporally, this increased uptake of phagocytosable probes coincides with an increase in the number of macrophages present in the glomerulus. The recent identification of complement receptors on human glomerular epithelial cells led to speculation about the role of these receptors in the glomerular trapping of immune complexes. No such receptors have been identified in the glomeruli of experimental animals, but in humans, receptor activity (measured by in vitro techniques) has been reported to

decrease in some forms of immune complex glomerulonephritis associated with complement deposition. Their precise role, if any, in immune complex glomerulonephritis requires further detailed study.

Many chronic infectious processes, exemplified by viral infections, provide sufficient exogenous antigens to eventually provoke circulating and potentially nephritogenic immune complex formation. The response of mice to chronic lymphocytic choriomeningitis virus is considered the prototype of viral immune complex mechanisms. Mice infected at birth with lymphocytic choriomeningitis virus maintain lifelong infection and have been thought by some to be immunologically unresponsive to the virus. Antibodies bound to circulating viral antigens can be detected, however, by immunoprecipitation. The antibody is completely complexed with the antigen and is undetectable by commonly employed immunologic techniques. The complexes lodge in the glomeruli, beginning shortly after birth in mice infected in utero. Similarly, antigens from murine leukemia virus, Aleutian mink disease virus, and infectious equine anemia virus lead to immune complex glomerulonephritis in mice, mink, and horses, respectively.

Endogenous or self antigens that are involved in producing autoimmune antibody may also cause immune complex diseases. At least 3 strains of mice, of which the New Zealand black and the New Zealand black-white hybrid are the best known, develop antibodies reactive with nuclear materials such as DNA. These antibody responses are associated with the development of a systemic lupus erythematosus-like immune complex disease. The mice have various abnormalities in their immune systems that can be influenced by different accelerating factors, resulting in loss of the usual resistance to autoantibody formation. The immune complex deposits are not confined to the glomeruli but may involve extraglomerular renal sites (TBM and interstitium) and extrarenal structures such as the choroid plexus and coronary vessels as well. Antibodies also form that are reactive with retroviral antigens such as gp70, forming circulating and deposited immune complexes. Other endogenous antigens, such as thyroglobulin, erythrocyte surface antigens, and histocompatibility antigens can cause immune complex glomerulonephritis in experimental animals.

An ever-increasing number of antigen-antibody systems are being identified in immune complex glomerulonephritis in humans (Table 31–2). As in animals, the antigens in humans can be divided into exogenous or foreign and endogenous or self antigens. Administration of foreign proteins used for passive immunization as well as inoculations and drugs can result in serum sickness-like immune complex diseases. Infectious agents provide the largest number of antigens identified to date in humans. Streptococcal antigens have been identified in some patients with poststreptococcal glomerulonephritis, staphylococcal antigen in children with infected ventriculoatrial shunts, enterococcal antigen in glomerular immune complex deposits of a patient with subacute bacterial

Table 31–2. Antigen-antibody systems known to cause or strongly suspected of causing immune complex glomerulonephritis in humans.

Antigens	Clinical Condition
Exogenous or foreign antigens	
Iatrogenic agents	
Drugs, toxoids, foreign serum	Serum sickness, heroin nephropathy(?), gold nephropathy(?), etc
Infectious agents	
Bacterial: Nephritogenic streptococci, *Staphylococcus albus, Corynebacterium bovis,* enterococci, *Streptococcus pneumoniae, Treponema pallidum, Salmonella typhi*	Poststreptococcal glomerulonephritis, infected ventriculoatrial shunts, endocarditis, pneumonia, syphilis, typhoid fever
Parasitic: *Plasmodium malariae, Plasmodium falciparum, Schistosoma mansoni, Toxoplasma gondii, Loa loa*	Malaria, schistosomiasis, toxoplasmosis, filarial loiasis
Viral: Hepatitis B, oncornavirus-related antigen, measles, Epstein-Barr virus, cytomegalovirus	Hepatitis, leukemia, subacute sclerosing panencephalitis, Burkitt's lymphoma, cytomegalovirus infection
Perhaps others as yet undetermined	Endocarditis, leprosy, kala-azar, dengue, mumps, varicella, infectious mononucleosis, Guillain-Barré syndrome
Endogenous or self antigens	
Nuclear antigens	Systemic lupus erythematosus
Immunoglobulin	Cryoglobulinemia
Tumor antigens	Neoplasms
Thyroglobulin	Thyroiditis
Renal tubular antigen (?)	Membranous glomerulonephritis in Japan, sickle cell anemia, renal carcinoma

endocarditis, and *Salmonella* antigen in glomerulonephritis associated with typhoid fever. In some instances, the bacterial antigens have been formed only early in disease and are not clearly associated with antibody, suggesting some element of local trapping for subsequent antibody interaction. *Treponema pallidum* antigens were recently identified in a patient with syphilis-associated glomerulonephritis. Chronic parasitic infections also provide antigens for immune complex formation. Both *Plasmodium malariae* and *P falciparum* antigens have been found in patients with malaria and glomerulonephritis, and patients with congenital toxoplasmosis and glomerulonephritis have immune complexes containing *Toxoplasma gondii* antigens. Filariasis and schistosomiasis are also associated with immune complex glomerulonephritis—again presumably related to antigens from these parasitic infections. Hepatitis B, measles, and EB viral antigens in patients with hepatitis, subacute sclerosing panencephalitis, and Burkitt's lymphoma, respectively, can also contribute to nephritogenic immune

complex formation. Oncornaviral antigens related to feline leukemia retrovirus have been tentatively identified in glomerular immune complex deposits in human leukemia.

Endogenous antigens leading to immune complex formation are best exemplified in the glomerulonephritis of patients with systemic lupus erythematosus, who form antibodies reactive with a variety of nuclear materials. Their immune responses can lead to nephritogenic immune complex formation, and their disease activity most clearly relates to the presence of native DNA antigen-antibody complexes. Recent studies in animals have suggested that DNA can bind to GBM, leading to the speculation that some deposits may form locally. Circulating immune complex localization, however, remains the favored immunopathogenic mechanism for this disease. Rheumatoid factors and cryoglobulins may contribute to the phlogogenic glomerular accumulations in systemic lupus erythematosus.

Immunoglobulin aggregates or complexes such as those seen in essential cryoglobulinemia may also cause glomerular injury. Thyroglobulin-antithyroglobulin immune complexes have been identified in glomeruli of patients with thyroiditis, and radiation-induced thyroid damage can release sufficient thyroglobulin to shift the ratio of circulating antigen and antibody so that nephritogenic immune complexes form. Renal tubular brush border antigen has been reported in a few patients in Japan with membranous glomerulopathy and in patients in the USA with sickle cell anemia or renal carcinoma and glomerulonephritis. The tubular antigen system remains controversial. We have occasionally found circulating anti-brush border antibodies in nephritic patients and have recovered anti-brush border antibodies in the eluates of one infant with membranous nephropathy; however, in our experience the tubular antigen-antibody system appears to be rare. Finally, antigens associated with neoplasms have also been identified in glomerular immune complex deposits of patients with neoplasia.

Clinical Features

Immune complex accumulation, both in the glomerular capillary wall and in the mesangium, appears to be responsible for over 75% of cases of human glomerulonephritis and encompasses a wide range of histologic and clinical presentations (Table 31–3). Primary immune complex glomerulonephritis (ie, patients without identifiable systemic disease) is usually classified histologically into diffuse, focal, and crescent-forming proliferative types; membranoproliferative (mesangiocapillary) glomerulonephritis; membranous glomerulonephritis; focal glomerulosclerosis; and chronic glomerulonephritis. The glomerulonephritis associated with systemic diseases such as Henoch-Schönlein purpura, systemic lupus erythematosus, and subacute infective endocarditis is often of a proliferative type, though several histologic variants occur.

Table 31–3. Generalizations regarding morphologic and clinical features of presumed immune complex–induced glomerulonephritis in humans.

Morphology	Clinical Features
Proliferative glomerulonephritis	
Diffuse proliferative glomerulonephritis; diffuse hypercellularity, electron-dense glomerular deposits.	Proteinuria, hematuria; nephrotic syndrome hypertension may be present. Onset and course variable but often progressive to renal failure.
Postinfectious glomerulonephritis; as above with subepithelial electron-dense "humps."	Generally poststreptococcal; acute onset of edema, oliguria, hypertension, with proteinuria, hematuria, and red blood cell casts in urinary sediment. Usually resolves in children. Hypocomplementemia usual, lasting 6–8 weeks.
Diffuse proliferative, crescent-forming glomerulonephritis; diffuse hypercellularity with extracapillary crescent formation; electron-dense deposits in the GBM or mesangium (or both).	Rapidly progressive renal failure, or may be anuric or oliguric from onset. Proteinuria, hematuria, red blood cell casts in urinary sediment. Nephrotic syndrome unusual. Sometimes microangiopathic hemolytic anemia.
Focal or segmental proliferative glomerulonephritis; focal and segmental hypercellularity; often confined to the mesangium; electron-dense deposits in the GBM or mesangium (or both).	Proteinuria or hematuria frequent; episodes of gross hematuria may accompany intercurrent respiratory infections (syndrome of "benign recurrent hematuria"); otherwise may be asymptomatic. Progresses slowly if at all.
Membranous glomerulonephritis	
Thickening of the GBM with few or no proliferative changes; subepithelial "spikes" with silver stains; diffuse subepithelial electron-dense deposits.	Proteinuria, often with nephrotic syndrome. Slow progression to renal failure with remission in one-third.
Membranoproliferative glomerulonephritis	
Mesangial proliferation and hypertrophy with interposition between endothelium and thickened GBM; at least 2 electron microscopic variants on the basis of dense deposits: subendothelial (type I) and intramembranous (type II).	Proteinuria, hematuria; often nephrotic syndrome or hypertension. Persistent hypocomplementemia in most cases. Common in children and young adults; usually progresses to renal failure.
Focal glomerulosclerosis (?)	
Segmental glomerular sclerosis progressing to hyalinization; appears first in juxtamedullary glomeruli.	Proteinuria, corticosteroid-unresponsive nephrotic syndrome common. Frequently progresses to renal failure.
End stage glomerulonephritis	
End stage renal architecture, hyalinized glomeruli, extensive tubulointerstitial damage; electron-dense GBM deposits may be present.	Proteinuria, hypertension frequent. Renal failure progressing to uremia. End stage of many morphologic forms of glomerulonephritis.

The clinical features of these various forms may include any or all of the possible manifestations of glomerular damage. Proteinuria may be mild, moderate, or severe; nephrotic syndrome occurs when urinary protein loss exceeds the body's capacity to completely replace it, after which serum oncotic pressure decreases and edema develops. Nephrotic syndrome most frequently accompanies focal glomerulosclerosis and membranous or membranoproliferative glomerulonephritis. Hematuria is more common in patients with proliferative or membranoproliferative histologic findings. The presence of red blood cell casts in the urinary sediment suggests an acute phase of glomerular inflammation. Hypertension can be present from the outset of any of these diseases or may appear later if the nephritis progresses.

The factors responsible for progression of immunologically induced glomerulonephritis are unclear. Although they may relate in part to continuing immunologic insult, features such as the hemodynamic effects of reduced renal mass, hypertension, and calcium and phosphorus metabolism need to be considered. Chronic glomerulonephritis may follow any form of immune complex glomerular injury, although the likelihood of such progression can be related to the particular histologic type. For instance, the acute diffuse proliferative lesion of poststreptococcal glomerulonephritis frequently appears to resolve completely, especially in children, even though chronic glomerulonephritis sometimes develops later after many years of apparent good health. A fluctuating course with exacerbations and remissions may occur in systemic lupus nephritis, Henoch-Schönlein nephritis, and focal proliferative and membranous glomerulonephritis, whereas in membranoproliferative and some other forms of proliferative glomerulonephritis a steady progression to chronic renal failure is typical, sometimes taking many years. Crescent-forming proliferative lesions are usually associated with rapidly progressive glomerulonephritis, which destroys the kidneys within a few weeks to months; this form of immune complex disease in particular may be clinically and morphologically indistinguishable from anti-GBM-mediated nephritis. Similarly, immune complex mechanisms can induce a clinical picture much like that of anti-GBM antibody–induced Goodpasture's syndrome.

Hypocomplementemia is a frequent clinical finding in immune complex–induced glomerulonephritis,

Table 31–4. Generalizations regarding immunofluorescence findings in presumed immune complex glomerulonephritis in humans.

Morphologic Type of Glomerulonephritis	Immunofluorescence Findings		
	Granular Immunoglobulin	Granular C3	Fibrinogen-Related Antigen
Proliferative glomerulonephritis			
Diffuse proliferative glomerulonephritis, including poststreptococcal glomerulonephritis	IgG, variable IgA and IgM scattered along the GBM	Similar to immunoglobulin (may be seen when immunoglobulin minimal or absent in poststreptococcal glomerulonephritis)	Usually minimal
Diffuse proliferative, crescent-forming glomerulonephritis	IgG, variable IgA and IgM scattered along the GBM	Similar to immunoglobulin (may be seen when immunoglobulin minimal or absent in poststreptococcal glomerulonephritis)	Heavy in areas of crescents
Focal or segmental proliferative glomerulonephritis	IgG, often prominent IgA, sometimes IgM in a mesangial (or segmental) pattern	Similar to immunoglobulin	Usually absent
Membranous glomerulonephritis	IgG, variable IgA and IgM diffusely along the GBM	Similar to immunoglobulin	Usually minimal
Membranoproliferative glomerulonephritis	IgG, variable IgA and IgM along the GBM in type I; in type II immunoglobulin deposits may be present	In type I, may overshadow immunoglobulin; in type II, present in the GBM, mesangium, and TBM	Variable
Focal glomerulosclerosis	Minimal IgG and prominent IgM in areas of sclerosis	Similar to immunoglobulin	Usually minimal
End stage of glomerulonephritis	Variable, IgG, IgA, and IgM, usually most prominent in least damaged glomeruli	Similar to immunoglobulin, may also be present in absence of immunoglobulin	Usually minimal
Systemic diseases with glomerulonephritis			
Systemic lupus erythematosus	IgG, IgA, and IgM distributed segmentally to diffusely along the GBM or mesangium and frequently in the tubulointerstitium	Similar to immunoglobulin	Variable, heavy when crescents present
Henoch-Schönlein purpura	IgG, often prominent IgA, variable IgM may be confined to the mesangium	Similar to immunoglobulin	Frequently prominent

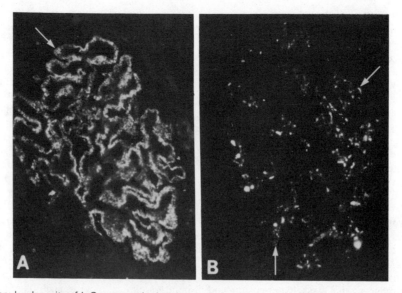

Figure 31–2. Granular deposits of IgG are seen in the glomeruli of patients with immune complex–induced glomerulonephritis. *A:* Heavy diffuse deposits (arrow) are present in a patient with membranous glomerulonephritis and nephrotic syndrome. *B:* Focal granular deposits (arrows), largely confined to the mesangium, are present in a patient with focal proliferative glomerulonephritis and mild proteinuria. (Original magnification × 250.)

particularly that associated with systemic lupus erythematosus or infections (streptococcal, endocarditis, infected ventricular atrial shunts, etc). A particular form of glomerulonephritis of probable immune complex origin called membranoproliferative glomerulonephritis deserves additional discussion. This condition is most frequently identified in children. It is characterized by glomerular capillary wall thickening with varying degrees of mesangial cell hyperplasia and interposition between the endothelium and the GBM. At least 2 morphologic subtypes exist. Type I shows subendothelial deposits by electron microscopy, and type II has such a distinctive electron density throughout the basement membrane that it is also called "dense deposit disease." Chemical analysis of the basement membrane does not suggest the accumulation of a non–basement membrane component but rather an increase in sialic acid–rich basement membrane glycoproteins. Evidence suggests that type I is an immune complex disease with immunoglobulin deposits and complement component deposits consistent with classic complement activation. In type II, immunoglobulin deposits are usually undetectable, but complement component accumulations consistent with alternative complement pathway activation are seen. Circulating immune complexes have, however, been detected in the sera of patients with both forms of membranoproliferative nephritis. In about 10% of cases, type II is associated with partial lipodystrophy.

A serum factor capable of activating the alternative complement pathway is present in many patients with membranoproliferative glomerulonephritis. This factor, termed nephritic factor (NF), has recently been shown to be an immunoglobulin with immunoconglutinin properties capable of reacting with activated components of the alternative complement pathway—specifically, the bimolecular complex of C3b and activated factor B, stabilizing its C3 convertase activity. A similar factor has been found in patients with partial lipodystrophy with or without membranoproliferative glomerulonephritis. Occasionally, other C3 activation factors have been noted. No immunopathogenic role for NF has been established, and experiments to purposefully activate complement chronically in animals have not caused glomerular injury. Finnish Landrace sheep develop a histologic lesion similar to membranoproliferative glomerulonephritis in the absence of NF. Placental transfer of NF has occurred. NF at 5 months was associated with mild glomerulonephritis in one infant studied in our laboratory. NF is relatively species-specific, so that attempts to transfer disease to subhuman primates have not been successful. Membranoproliferative glomerulonephritis, particularly type II, frequently recurs in renal allografts but is unrelated to levels of NF.

Immunologic Diagnosis

The diagnosis of immune complex glomerulonephritis is based on finding granular deposits of immunoglobulin, usually accompanied by complement, in the glomeruli. This is, of course, only presumptive evidence until the antigens can be identified. The immunoglobulin most commonly found in these deposits is IgG, with IgA or IgM occasionally predominating (Table 31–4). The glomerular immune complex deposition may diffusely involve all capillary loops in membranous or diffuse proliferative glomerulonephritis (Fig 31–2A). In focal glomerulonephritis, the deposits tend to involve only segments of the glomerular capillary wall but may be more widespread than expected from the focal nature of the histologic change. In some patients, the immune complex deposition appears to be confined to the mesangium, usually causing only mild histologic and clinical evidence of glomerular damage (Fig 31–2B).

The class of immunoglobulin identified in glomerular deposits may be of value in classification. For example, predominant IgA (usually associated with IgG) deposits are seen in patients with focal glomerulonephritis and recurrent benign hematuria. The association has been so striking in some series that the term "IgG-IgA nephropathy" has been coined to denote the condition. IgM may be the predominant immunoglobulin in patients with similar clinical courses, often manifested by recurrent hematuria. The rapidity with which hematuria follows an infectious episode in patients with "IgG-IgA nephropathy" suggests that the immune complexes may be forming during antibody excess, possibly with preformed antibody to a common infectious agent of the oropharynx. The large antibody excess complexes would preferentially accumulate in the mesangium. Alternative explanations for the IgA accumulation have been offered, including IgA aggregates or "antimesangial antibodies."

In systemic lupus erythematosus, the immune complex deposits may be widespread, involving glomeruli and, in 70% of instances, extraglomerular renal tissues as well. Indeed, granular deposits of immunoglobulin and complement in TBM or peritubular capillaries should suggest the diagnosis of systemic lupus erythematosus. IgA and Clq deposits are prominent in kidneys of patients with systemic lupus erythematosus—particularly when present diffusely along the GBM—and also suggest this diagnosis.

The identity of the antigen in the glomerular immune complex deposits can be sought either by detection of the antigen with fluoresceinated specific antisera or by elution of antibody from the kidney, with subsequent detection of its reactivity. The immunofluorescence technique may be enhanced by partial elution of the kidney sections with buffers that dissociate immune complexes to uncover antigen sites. Alternatively, the sections can be preincubated with the antigen itself to bind to unoccupied binding sites, increasing the amount and accessibility of the antigen for detection by the fluoresceinated antiserum. Successful elution and recovery of antibody from glomerular immune complex deposits require optimal conditions to recover maximal amounts of functional antibody. Losses can occur through recombination with antigen. Finally, it must be shown that more antibody is present in the eluate than would be expected by simple serum contamination alone.

The patient's physician plays an important part in helping the immunopathologist identify antigen-antibody systems in individuals with immune complex glomerulonephritis. Careful environmental histories may narrow the field of possible antigenic exposures to a few testable systems, with emphasis placed upon detection of chronic, possibly subclinical infective processes. Recent streptococcal infections should be excluded. Serologic testing can be helpful in some cases. Antinuclear and anti-DNA antibodies should be sought, since the nephritis of systemic lupus erythematosus can occur without other overt organ involvement. Similarly, the presence of rheumatoid factors or cryoglobulins may provide additional insight into the pathogenic process. Antithyroid antibodies, anti-smooth muscle antibody, or other autoantibodies may be an indication of an immune complex system involving endogenous antigens. Screening of sera for antibodies to common viruses or for hepatitis B antigens may be fruitful, particularly when clinical symptomatology suggests viral infection. Abnormalities in serum complement levels, (see above), should also be noted.

Several sensitive methods for the detection of circulating immune complexes are now available. These include assays based on the altered Fc reactivity of complexed immunoglobulin, which causes complement fixation, binding of Clq, and binding of rheumatoid factor, or on the special properties of immune complex-bound complement components, which cause binding to bovine conglutinin and the production of serum immunoconglutinins. Other assays exploit the cellular reactivities of immune complexes: immune complex-induced platelet aggregation, phagocytosis of immune complexes by peritoneal macrophages, and binding of immune complexes to the surface complement receptors of certain lymphoblastoid cell lines. Each assay is distinctive in reactivity, sensitivity, and idiosyncrasies, and no single assay is infallible. The use of a combination of assays with different reactivities, therefore, offers the best approach to determining the presence of immune complexes in test sera. Several studies of sera from patients with glomerulonephritis have now been reported. In general, the assays detect large amounts of circulating immune complexes in patients with systemic lupus erythematosus and with glomerulonephritis associated with other systemic immune complex diseases. In primary (presumed immune complex-induced) glomerulonephritis, the frequency of detection is lower than in the systemic disease, and the quantities of immune complexes detected are also less. Immune complexes are present more frequently in acute than chronic glomerulonephritis and in patients with low levels of complement.

The inability of the assays to detect circulating immune complexes in all patients with glomerular immune complex deposits requires careful consideration. Quantitative differences in the load of circulating immune complexes may account for these discrepancies. Thus, large amounts of immune complexes are present in systemic diseases and acute or fulminant glomerulonephritis, and it is possible that the more indolent forms of glomerulonephritis (membranous, membranoproliferative, etc) are mediated by much smaller quantities of circulating immune complexes. The limited sensitivity of the assays certainly could preclude the detection of small quantities. In addition, such patients may have inherent abnormalities causing them to handle more or less physiologic amounts of circulating immune complexes in a nephritogenic manner. Such variations might include the amount and quality of antibody produced or the efficiency of systemic removal of immune complexes from the circulation. The proposed role of low affinity or non-precipitating antibody in the pathogenesis of membranous forms of glomerulonephritis in patients with systemic lupus erythematosus is a possible example of this concept. Alternatively, circulating immune complexes may be present only intermittently or with changing composition in some forms of glomerulonephritis. The detection of circulating immune complexes would then be influenced by the timing of such determinations. Thus, circulating immune complexes may be present only during the acute phase of poststreptococcal glomerulonephritis or during exacerbations in IgG-IgA nephropathy. Finally, it is possible that the glomerular immune deposits in some forms of glomerulonephritis in fact represent immune complexes formed in situ, and in this situation immune complexes would be present in the glomeruli but not in the circulation. It is clear that serologic immune complex determination cannot yet replace diagnostic renal immunofluorescence. The assays do, however, provide the opportunity for serial studies that may prove to be of clinical and prognostic value and may provide a way of isolating immune complexes for subsequent determination of their antigenic makeup.

Treatment

Nonspecific antiphlogistic and immunosuppressive types of treatment have been widely used, mostly in uncontrolled trials for patients with immune complex-induced glomerulonephritis. The most commonly used agents are corticosteroids, cyclophosphamide, and azathioprine, or occasionally other "immunosuppressive" agents used singly or in combination. The results of these trials are difficult to interpret because of problems with classification, variable treatment regimens, and failure to establish the natural course of the form of immune complex glomerulonephritis under consideration. In general, membranous or membranoproliferative glomerulonephritis does not respond to immunosuppressive treatment, although some investigators believe that corticosteroids may be beneficial. A recent prospective randomized controlled trial demonstrated a beneficial effect of short-term alternate-day prednisone in preserving renal function in membranous nephritis. The true value of this treatment will need to be evaluated in large numbers of patients. Proliferative forms of immune complex glomerulonephritis are usually also unresponsive to immunosuppressive therapy, but occasional apparent success continues to encourage its usage. In contrast, the glomerulonephritis of Wegener's granulomatosis seems to respond favorably to cyclophosphimide. Patients with systemic lupus erythematosus often show similar benefit from corticosteroid therapy, and the addition of azathioprine treatment may sometimes be appropriate. However, the long-term value of such treatments is still somewhat controversial.

Attempts have also been made to modify the effects of the mediators of immune complex-induced glomerulonephritis, eg, by using antihistamines and antiserotonins. There has also been some enthusiasm for anticoagulant and antiplatelet drugs in the management of immune complex glomerulonephritis, but one must await carefully controlled trials to judge their true value.

Ideally, management of immune complex-induced glomerulonephritis should either eradicate the source of the antigen or inhibit production of the specific antibody. These approaches stress the need for identification of the antigen-antibody systems in each patient. Acute infections, such as streptococcal pharyngitis, should be treated to eradicate the infectious agent. For example, removal of antigen by treating *T pallidum* has been beneficial to individuals with syphilitic immune complex glomerulonephritis, as has removal of malignant tissue in immune complex glomerulonephritis associated with neoplasia. The use of plasmapheresis and of specific immunoadsorbents to remove circulating antibody, antigen, or immune complexes is under investigation.

Many forms of immune complex nephritis progress to renal failure, necessitating renal transplantation. As with anti-GBM antibody-induced glomerulonephritis, immune complex-induced glomerulonephritis may recur in the transplanted kidney. It seems prudent to delay renal transplantation in patients whose renal failure is from rapidly progressive immune complex glomerulonephritis until the production of nephritogenic immune complexes is minimal.

TUBULOINTERSTITIAL NEPHRITIS

Immune processes that cause injury to the glomerulus also injure extraglomerular renal structures. Just as they do in the glomerulus, anti-basement membrane antibodies and immune complexes can produce tubulointerstitial nephritis. Immunologic tubulointerstitial renal damage can then accompany glomerulonephritis or occur as a primary event. Animal models of anti-basement membrane antibody and immune complex-induced tubulointerstitial nephritis have been developed, and similar processes are beginning to be identified in humans. The role of sensitized cells in tubulointerstitial nephritis is not clearly defined. Evidence exists that sensitized cells may contribute to tubulointerstitial injury in experimental animals, but in

humans, although interstitial mononuclear cell infiltration may be conspicuous, their pathogenetic role is not established.

1. TUBULOINTERSTITIAL INJURY & ANTI–BASEMENT MEMBRANE ANTIBODIES

Major Immunologic Features
- Linear deposits of immunoglobulin, usually accompanied by complement, are found along the TBM.
- Circulating anti-TBM antibodies are often detectable.

General Considerations
The occurrence and pathogenic significance of anti-TBM antibodies has been recognized only recently. Anti-TBM antibodies occur in about 70% of patients with anti-GBM glomerulonephritis. The incidence of these antibodies is perhaps greater in the Goodpasture syndrome type of anti-basement membrane antibody-induced glomerulonephritis, reflecting the broader basement membrane reactivity of the antibody in Goodpasture's syndrome. When present, the anti-TBM antibodies are associated with increased tubulointerstitial injury, indicating their immunopathologic potential. Other situations in which anti-TBM antibodies have occasionally been found are drug-induced interstitial nephritis, primary interstitial nephritis following immune complex-induced glomerulonephritis, and renal transplants.

Immunologic Pathogenesis
The phlogogenic effect of anti-TBM antibodies has been well demonstrated in animal models. Rats or guinea pigs immunized with homologous or heterologous TBM in adjuvant develop anti-TBM antibodies that bind to their TBMs (primarily of proximal tubules) and induce interstitial nephritis. In rats immunized with bovine TBM, antibodies form and react with the TBM, after which complement becomes fixed and polymorphonuclear leukocytes infiltrate. The polymorphonuclear infiltrate is rapidly replaced by a persisting mononuclear infiltrate, the characteristic cell type in tubulointerstitial nephritis. Using monoclonal anti–immune cell antibodies, the infiltrate in rats consists largely of helper T lymphocytes, with fewer numbers of suppressor T cells, B cells, and monocytes. Depending on the animal and type of immunization, the subject may develop azotemia, proteinuria, glycosuria, and lysozymuria, singly or in combination. The importance of the antibody in the pathogenesis of experimental tubulointerstitial nephritis is clearly shown by the ability to transfer the disease to normal rats or guinea pigs by the passive administration of anti-TBM antibody recovered from the sera of diseased animals. In contrast, transfer of lymphoid cells from diseased to normal animals is relatively ineffective in producing disease. The role of the often

prominent mononuclear cell infiltrate in tubulointerstitial nephritis remains to be defined. Experimentally
delayed hypersensitivity can be produced in renal
structures with exogenous antigens. The best characterized is that caused by transfer of cells sensitized to
bovine gamma globulin into kidneys with aggregated
bovine gamma globulin introduced in their renal cortex. A mononuclear infiltrate and injury ensue. Transfer of cells sensitized to glomerular-bound heterologous anti-GBM antibody also causes mononuclear cell
accumulation. Finally, passive transfer of anti-TBM
antibody fails to cause injury in animals depleted of
radiosensitive circulating leukocytes.

It is of interest that the TBM antigens against
which these antibodies react are strain-specific in rats,
ie, some inbred strains possess the antigen and others
do not. When rats lacking the TBM antigen are given a
TBM antigen–positive kidney, they form anti-TBM
antibodies reactive with the graft but not with their own
kidneys. Such antibodies may contribute to transplant
failure in these rats. In humans, similar variability in
the occurrence of TBM antigens may account for the
fact that anti-TBM antibodies develop in some renal
allograft recipients. In other patients, anti-TBM antibodies develop as part of the rejection process. Immune responses to the TBM antigens appear to be
genetically influenced. Passive transfer of anti-TBM
antibodies in strain XIII guinea pigs has been reported
to induce host production of anti-TBM antibodies. To
what extent this mechanism operates in humans is
unknown.

Anti-TBM antibodies have also arisen in a few
patients with methicillin-associated tubulointerstitial
nephritis. Experimental studies have shown that native
proteins can be made immunogenic to a host animal by
conjugation with a foreign hapten. Methicillin derivatives (and those of other penicillin analogs) can form
stable conjugates with proteins, and it has been demonstrated that methicillin derivatives can bind to the
TBM. The drug-TBM conjugate may induce a
humoral immune response with subsequent development of anti-TBM antibodies. Since anti-TBM antibodies are an unusual finding in drug-induced
tubulointerstitial nephritis, other mechanisms such as
unidentified cellular immune responses may play a
role in the tubulointerstitial injury.

Anti-TBM antibodies have been found in occasional patients with immune complex-induced glomerulonephritis, particularly children. In some of
these patients, the immune complex glomerular injury
preceded the formation of anti-TBM antibodies,
suggesting that immunologic damage to the kidney
may on rare occasions trigger subsequent autoantibody
formation. Anti-TBM antibodies have also been identified in a few children with suspected primary
tubulointerstitial nephritis.

Clinical Features

When anti-TBM antibodies occur with anti-GBM
or immune complex-induced glomerulonephritis, the
clinical course is generally that of the underlying glo-

merulonephritis. In transplant recipients it is difficult
to distinguish the effects of anti-TBM antibodies from
the rejection process itself. Since anti-TBM antibodies
can induce severe tubulointerstitial nephritis in animals, one can hardly discount their importance in
patients with glomerulonephritis or transplant rejection. Some patients with anti-TBM antibody-induced
tubulointerstitial nephritis may manifest complete or
partial Fanconi's syndrome.

Drug-induced interstitial nephritis is usually
characterized by the relatively sudden onset of azotemia in a patient receiving large doses of antibiotics,
particularly methicillin, for at least 1 week. Flank
pain, fever, rash, and eosinophilia often herald its
development; and pyuria, white cell casts, hematuria,
and proteinuria are the usual findings on urinalysis.

Immunologic Diagnosis

Diagnosis of anti-TBM antibody-associated
tubulointerstitial nephritis is based on the detection by
immunofluorescence of linear deposits of immunoglobulin and complement along the TBM (Fig 31-
3A). As in anti-GBM antibody-induced disease, the
specificity of the reaction should be confirmed by
elution studies or by detection of circulating anti-TBM
antibodies. Serum is usually tested by indirect immunofluorescence on normal kidney targets for the presence of circulating anti-TBM antibodies. Radioimmunoassays are also available. In cases of suspected
drug-induced interstitial nephritis, the renal biopsy
specimen should be tested for drug deposition along
basement membranes by using specific fluoresceinated antiserum to the drug. The patient's reactivity to
the drug can be tested by hemagglutination assay to
detect antibodies and by in vitro assays of cellular
sensitivity performed with peripheral blood lymphocytes.

Treatment

The associated glomerulonephritis is treated as
outlined in previous sections. In cases of drug-induced
tubulointerstitial nephritis, the offending drug should
be immediately discontinued and replaced as needed
by a suitable structurally unrelated alternative drug.

2. TUBULOINTERSTITIAL INJURY & IMMUNE COMPLEXES

Major Immunologic Features

• Immunoglobulin and complement are present in a
  granular pattern along the TBM, in the interstitium, or in the walls of peritubular capillaries.
• Circulating immune complexes may be detected.

General Considerations

In some patients, the tubulointerstitial damage
associated with glomerulonephritis may be due in part
to extraglomerular renal deposition of immune complexes. Granular deposits of immunoglobulin and

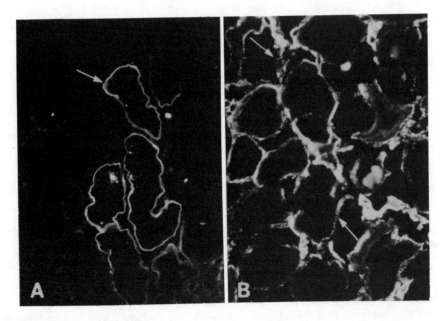

Figure 31–3. *A:* Linear deposits of IgG (arrow) are present along the TBM of focal renal tubules in the renal biopsy of a patient with anti-GBM glomerulonephritis. *B:* Diffuse granular deposits of IgG (arrows) are seen along the TBM of most renal tubules in the renal biopsy of a patient with systemic lupus erythematosus and immune complex glomerulonephritis. (Original magnification × 250.)

complement are seen along the TBM, peritubular capillaries, or in the interstitium of 50–70% of patients with lupus nephritis. The deposits' presence generally correlates positively with the severity of the tubulointerstitial histopathology. Extraglomerular deposits have also been found, though with much lower frequency, in cases of cryoglobulinemia and in membranoproliferative and rapidly progressive glomerulonephritis, Sjögren's syndrome, and primary idiopathic interstitial nephritis. Prominent immune complex localization in extraglomerular renal sites in the absence of glomerular immune complex deposits is uncommon. A few patients with systemic lupus erythematosus have been noted to have predominant or exclusive localization in the interstitium.

Immunologic Pathogenesis

The role of interstitial immune complex deposition in inducing tubulointerstitial injury has been determined by studying chronic serum sickness in rabbits. Rabbits having active immune responses and forming large amounts of immune complexes accumulate these complexes on TBM, in peritubular capillaries, and in interstitial spaces in addition to the GBM. Along with such deposits, these rabbits have prominent tubulointerstitial histopathologic injury that is much more severe than that in rabbits with glomerular immune complex deposition alone. Extraglomerular renal deposits of immune complexes and consequent interstitial damage are frequent in systemic lupus erythematosus (Fig 31–3B). In some patients with systemic lupus erythematosus (just as in some rabbits with chronic serum sickness), circulating immune com-

plexes may be unique in quantity—or quality—which may allow these complexes to become deposited in the renal interstitium in addition to the glomerulus.

In experimental animals, immune complexes may form locally in the renal interstitium. Rabbits given repeated injections of a soluble basement membrane-poor extract of renal cortex develop tubulointerstitial lesions and sometimes glycosuria and aminoaciduria. Immunofluorescence studies reveal granular deposition of IgG and C3 along proximal TBMs. Sera from the injected rabbits contain antibodies reactive with antigens normally present in the cytoplasm of proximal tubular cells. It is postulated that the deposits along the TBM result when circulating autoantibodies complex with autologous antigens as they move out of tubular cells. In another model, rats immunized with urinary Tamm-Horsfall glycoprotein develop immune deposits along the ascending thick limbs of the loop of Henle, macula densa, and portions of the distal tubule, sites of production of the protein. Only mild interstitial infiltration of mononuclear cells occurs, but these models demonstrate that in situ tubulointerstitial immune complex formation has a potential for injury in humans.

Clinical Features

The clinical course is usually that of the associated glomerulonephritis. Evidence of tubular dysfunction may be present.

Immunologic Diagnosis

The tubules, vessels, and interstitium should be examined with particular care during study of renal biopsies by immunofluorescence. Interstitial deposits of immunoglobulin and complement are usually focal and less intense than glomerular deposits and may easily be overlooked. Prominent or widespread tubulointerstitial deposits suggest systemic lupus erythematosus.

Treatment

The underlying glomerulonephritis is treated as outlined in previous sections.

3. TUBULOINTERSTITIAL INJURY OF POSSIBLE IMMUNE PATHOGENESIS

Renal tubular acidosis, particularly distal type I, either latent or clinically overt, is a frequent finding in certain "autoimmune" disorders and hypergammaglobulinemic syndromes such as Sjögren's syndrome, chronic active hepatitis, and essential cryoglobulinemia. Although an exact immunopathologic cause has not been demonstrated, the association of renal tubular acidosis with these probable "autoimmune" conditions suggests that an immune mechanism may be responsible for the renal tubular dysfunction as well. Antibodies to salivary duct epithelium and nucleoprotein have been identified in some patients with Sjögren's syndrome. Judging from limited studies of sera from such patients (as well as some normals), antibodies reactive with the cytoplasm of renal distal tubular epithelial cells may be present. A few biopsies from patients of this sort have contained a peritubular interstitial lymphocytic infiltrate. Renal allograft rejection, a good example of immunologic renal injury, has occasionally been associated with acute renal tubular acidosis. It seems likely that some form of autoimmunity to renal tubular cells is active in patients who have Sjögren's syndrome and other hypergammaglobulinemic conditions and develop renal tubular acidosis.

OTHER GLOMERULAR DISEASES OF SUSPECTED OR UNCERTAIN IMMUNE PATHOGENESIS

In addition to those nephritides already discussed, which clearly are due to immunologic disorders, there is a group of glomerular diseases in which the role of immune mechanisms is uncertain. These diseases include minimal change disease, focal glomerulosclerosis, vasculitides, diabetes mellitus, some disorders of coagulation, amyloidosis, and plasma cell dyscrasias. With the exception of minimal change disease and diabetes mellitus, these disorders account for only a small percentage of cases of glomerular injury.

Minimal Change Disease & Focal Glomerulosclerosis

Minimal change disease is the commonest cause of the nephrotic syndrome in children and also occurs, though less commonly, in adults. The glomerular lesion is characterized by minimal or no histologic changes at the light microscopic level, no immune reactants demonstrable by immunofluorescence microscopy, but diffuse effacement of the epithelial cell foot processes observed on ultrastructural examination. Typically, these patients have selective proteinuria and a good response to corticosteroid or cyclophosphamide therapy. This condition is not thought to be mediated by immune complexes or anti-kidney antibodies; however, a few investigators have been able to demonstrate circulating complexes in the sera of such patients. There remains a large number of interesting observations that might suggest a possible immunologic origin of minimal change disease. Lymphocytotoxic antibodies have been demonstrated in the sera of minimal change patients, as have high levels of immunoconglutinin, especially during relapse. High levels of circulating IgM and IgE and depressed levels of IgG and IgA have been noted, and a relative lymphocytopenia is a frequent observation. A number of findings suggest a possible cell-mediated mechanism of injury. Remission can be induced by an intercurrent measles infection, which is known to be associated with depressed cell-mediated immunity. A minimal change lesion is sometimes seen in Hodgkin's disease in adults, and lymphocytes from minimal change disease patients can be shown to have been sensitized to fetal kidney antigens in migration inhibition experiments. A blastogenesis-inhibiting factor has been described in the sera of minimal change patients, and recent studies suggest that while there is a normal T cell count there is discordance between those cells possessing surface immunoglobulin and those with C3b receptors. This has been ascribed either to the presence of double-marked cells or to diminished null cell levels. It is possible that some cellular immune mechanism is instrumental in producing glomerular protein leakage in minimal change disease, either alone or in concert with an undisclosed humoral mechanism.

Another common cause of nephrotic syndrome in childhood is focal glomerulosclerosis. Clinically, in contrast to minimal change disease, the condition is usually steroid-resistant. In areas of sclerosis, immunofluorescence studies show coarse granular accumulations of IgM, often with C3 and fibrin, consistent with immune complex deposits. Some investigators suggest that the immunofluorescence findings are due to nonimmunologic trapping in the areas of sclerosis. Assays for immune complexes are positive only in a minority of patients. An experimental model of focal glomerulosclerosis has been reported in rats repeatedly subjected to the nephrotoxic effects of the aminonucleoside of puromycin. Heroin users may exhibit the same pathologic feature.

Vasculitis

The vasculitides are made up of syndromes with a spectrum of clinicopathologic features with the essential common component of vasculitis, an inflammatory reaction in vessel walls, leading to ischemia of the supplied tissues. Increasing evidence points to an immunologic pathogenesis of the vascular lesions—in particular, the deposition of circulating immune complexes triggering the inflammatory process. The mediation of injury is brought about by the action of neutrophils, complement, and mononuclear cells as well as platelets and vasoactive amines. Cellular immunity is also involved, and true granulomatous reactions may be observed in some of these conditions. The vasculitides are classified according to several different features, including the type and size of the vessels affected, the involvement of specific organs such as skin, lung, or kidneys, the characteristics of the inflammatory reaction—in particular granuloma formation—and the clinical features. Utilizing pathologic, clinical, and immunopathogenic criteria, several distinct disorders can be identified. Several of the vasculitides commonly involve the renal vessels.

Polyarteritis nodosa is characterized by a necrotizing vasculitis of small and medium-sized muscular arteries. Aneurysmal dilatations may be produced, and the lesions are usually segmental. Hepatitis B antigenemia has been detected in up to 50% of cases, occasionally with immunofluorescence evidence of vascular deposition of hepatitis B antigen and antibody in vessel walls. Widespread involvement of vessels leads to diffuse organ involvement, with the kidney being frequently affected. Renal injury is primarily brought about by vasculitis of the arcuate and interlobular vessels, with resulting ischemic glomerular changes.

The syndromes collected under the heading of hypersensitivity vasculitis have the common feature of involvement of smaller vessels, in contrast to those affected in the polyarteritis nodosa groups. Typically, the skin is involved with a characteristic leukocytoclastic vasculitis involving postcapillary venules. Endogenous and exogenous antigens are being associated with the syndromes with increasing frequency, and immune complex deposition has been shown to trigger the vasculitis in many cases. The syndromes commonly involving the kidney include serum sickness, Henoch-Schönlein purpura, and essential mixed cryoglobulinemia. Henoch-Schönlein purpura may be associated with preceding infections (often respiratory) and food and drug allergies. Abdominal pain, fever, malaise, arthralgia, edema, and a characteristic nonthrombocytopenic purpuric skin rash are seen Glomerulonephritis occurs in a significant proportion of patients. Diffuse mesangial IgA, C3, and fibrin are found on immunofluorescent examination of biopsy tissue. The syndrome usually occurs in children and follows a relapsing course, but with progression of renal disease in a minority of patients. Essential mixed cryoglobulinemia is produced by the deposition of immune complexes made up of monoclonal IgM, rheumatoid factor, and polyclonal IgG. Purpura, arthralgia, fever, and hepatosplenomegaly are the typical clinical features. A rapidly progressive glomerulonephritis with diffuse endocapillary proliferation associated with endomembranous deposits and crescents can occur. IgG, IgM, and C3 can be demonstrated in the glomeruli by immunofluorescence microscopy. Hepatitis B antigen has also been found in association with this syndrome.

Wegener's granulomatosis is a syndrome comprised of granulomatous vasculitis involving the upper and lower respiratory tracts, disseminated small vessel vasculitis, and glomerulonephritis. The renal lesion consists of a segmental necrotizing glomerulonephritis with associated granulomatous vasculitis. The underlying antigens remain unidentified, but circulating immune complexes have been detected in some patients. Immune reactants including IgG and complement have been inconsistently seen in the glomeruli of renal biopsy specimens and electron-dense deposits occasionally seen on electron microscopy. This vasculitis is particularly responsive to cyclophosphamide therapy.

Diabetes Mellitus

Although the renal involvement in diabetes is variable, a large number of patients develop proteinuria within 20 years after the onset of diabetes and frequently die from renal failure within 5 years. It is still controversial whether good control of blood glucose levels can prevent this progression. The primary renal insult is microangiopathic. There is little evidence that immunologic mechanisms contribute to renal impairment of persons with diabetes. The striking linear accumulations of IgG, albumin, and other major plasma proteins found in the basement membranes of diabetics (both glomerular and tubular) are not thought to have immunologic specificity. Glomerular trapping of circulating beef insulin antigen-antibody immune complexes in patients receiving beef insulin has been observed, but only infrequently. During experimentally induced diabetes, rats not given exogenous insulin accumulate IgG and C3 in their renal mesangia, suggesting alterations of mesangial function. There is currently no evidence that similar deposits contribute to renal dysfunction in humans.

Coagulopathies

Several systemic coagulation syndromes can cause acute renal failure, including hemolytic-uremic syndrome, thrombotic thrombocytopenic purpura, and postpartum renal failure. Disseminated intravascular coagulation may occur as a secondary if not the primary event in all 3 syndromes. The lesions have certain similarities to those seen in immunologically induced hyperacute rejection in renal allograft recipients, a lesion that has striking glomerular fibrin accumulation. In the 3 syndromes mentioned here, infectious agents (or a retained product of conception) may act, perhaps through immunologic mechanisms, to cause intravascular platelet aggregation as the triggering event. When immunoglobulin and complement deposits accompany the glomerular fibrin deposits, an immunologic basis for the coagulopathy is suggested.

A "localized" coagulopathy, renal vein thrombosis, can also affect the kidney. This diagnosis is suggested when back pain is associated with the nephrotic syndrome and can be confirmed by renal venography. Renal vein thrombosis is usually seen in association with the nephrotic syndrome and glomerulonephritis, with heavy granular IgG and C3 deposits. The diagnosis is suggested by observation of margination of polymorphonuclear leukocytes in the glomerular capillary. The relationship between glomerulonephritis and renal vein thrombosis has been elusive and controversial. Currently, it is thought that most instances of thrombosis are secondary to the underlying disease state; however, the suspicion remains that in isolated cases primary renal vein thrombosis might induce renal injury, releasing renal antigens and thereby initiating a nephritogenic immune reaction.

Amyloidosis & Plasma Cell Dyscrasias

Renal amyloid deposition may occur in association with plasma cell dyscrasias and may also be seen in conditions characterized by chronic or recurrent infection or inflammation. Examples are rheumatoid arthritis or familial Mediterranean fever. Clinical features include proteinuria, the nephrotic syndrome, and renal failure. Underlying systemic disease, particularly multiple myeloma, should be sought when a diagnosis of amyloidosis is confirmed. Renal amyloidosis is usually diagnosed by demonstrating abnormal accumulations of proteins in a renal biopsy with special histochemical stains. In primary amyloidosis, which has an associated plasma cell proliferation and often multiple myeloma, the deposited protein has features of immunoglobulin light chains. Immunofluorescence studies with light chain–specific reagents may be a useful diagnostic approach. In amyloidosis secondary to chronic inflammation, amyloid protein A is identified in the deposits. This protein is related to a serum protein that acts as an acute phase reactant. Another component of amyloid, the P component, is quite similar to C-reactive protein. This P component has recently been shown to be a constituent of normal human GBM. Additional types of amyloid protein are being recognized, and it is anticipated that further definition of this group of diseases may develop on a biochemical basis.

Acute renal failure is often associated with multiple myeloma (the so-called myeloma kidney). Many different factors are present to induce renal damage. They include hypercalcemia, hyperuricemia, and fluid depletion, as well as the toxic effects of Bence Jones proteins (immunoglobulin light chains) found inspissated within the lumens of the tubules. In addition, diffuse renal deposition of amyloid proteins may produce chronic renal injury. Monoclonal IgG cryoimmunoglobulins may be found in multiple myeloma and may be deposited within glomeruli; however, this is not a frequent cause of renal injury in this disease. Cryoimmunoglobulinemia is more commonly found in Waldenström's macroglobulinemia (plasma cell dyscrasia producing IgM). Uncommonly, glomerular disease can be produced acutely by the deposition of occlusive thrombi of IgM. However, renal involvement in macroglobulinemia occurs less frequently than renal disease in myeloma.

•   •   •

References

Andres GA, McCluskey RT: Tubular and interstitial renal disease due to immunologic mechanisms. *Kidney Int* 1975;**7**:271.

Beaufils M, Morel-Maroger L: Pathogenesis of renal disease in monoclonal gammopathies: Current concepts. *Nephron* 1978;**20**:125.

Brentjens JR et al: Classification and immunopathologic features of human nephritis. Page 214 in: *Contemporary Issues in Nephrology*. Vol 3. Wilson CB, Brenner BM, Stein JH (editors). Churchill Livingstone, 1979.

Churg J, Grishman E: Ultrastructure of glomerular disease: A review. *Kidney Int* 1975;**7**:254.

Cochrane CG: Mediation systems in neutrophil-independent immunologic injury of the glomerulus. Page 106 in: *Contemporary Issues in Nephrology*. Vol 3. Wilson CB, Brenner BM, Stein JH (editors). Churchill Livingstone, 1979.

Cochrane CG, Koffler D: Immune complex disease in experimental animals and man. *Adv Immunol* 1973;**16**:185.

Couser WG, Salant DJ: In situ immune complex formation and glomerular injury. (Editorial.) *Kidney Int* 1980;**17**:1.

Fish AJ, Michael AF: Immunopathogenesis of renal disease. In: *Strauss and Welt's Diseases of the Kidney*, 3rd ed. Earley LE, Gottschalk CW (editors). Little, Brown, 1979.

Germuth FG Jr, Rodriguez E: *Immunopathology of the Renal Glomerulus: Immune Complex Deposit and Antibasement Membrane Disease.* Little, Brown, 1973.

Glassock RJ, Cohen AH: Secondary glomerular diseases. Page 1493 in: *The Kidney*, 2nd ed. Vol 2. Brenner BM, Rector FC Jr (editors). Saunders, 1981.

Glassock RJ et al: Primary glomerular diseases. Page 1351 in: *The Kidney*, 2nd ed. Vol 2. Brenner BM, Rector FC Jr (editors). Saunders, 1981.

Golbus SM, Wilson CB: Experimental glomerulonephritis induced by in situ formation of immune complexes in glomerular capillary wall. *Kidney Int* 1979;**16**:148.

Holdsworth SR, Neale TJ, Wilson CB: Abrogation of macrophage-dependent injury in experimental glomerulonephritis in the rabbit: Use of an antimacrophage serum. *J Clin Invest* 1981;**68**:686.

Levy M et al: Immunopathology of membranoproliferative glomerulonephritis with subendothelial deposits (Type I MPGN). *Clin Immunol Immunopathol* 1978;**10**:477.

McCluskey RT, Colvin RB: Immunologic aspects of renal tubular and interstitial diseases. *Annu Rev Med* 1978;**29**:191.

Schreiber RD, Müller-Eberhard HJ: Complement and renal disease. Page 67 in: *Contemporary Issues in Nephrology*. Vol 3. Wilson CB, Brenner BM, Stein JH (editors). Churchill Livingstone, 1979.

Theofilopoulos AN, Dixon FJ: The biology and detection of immune complexes. *Adv Immunol* 1979;**28**:89.

Unanue ER, Dixon FJ: Experimental glomerulonephritis: Immunologic events and pathogenetic mechanisms. *Adv Immunol* 1967;**6**:1.

Wilson CB: Nephritogenic antibody mechanisms involving antigens within the glomerulus. *Immunol Rev* 1981;**55**:257.

Wilson CB, Dixon FJ: Diagnosis of immunopathologic renal disease. *Kidney Int* 1974;**5**:389.

Wilson CB, Dixon FJ: Renal injury from immune reactions involving antigens in or of the kidney. Page 35 in: *Contemporary Issues in Nephrology*. Vol 3. Wilson CB, Brenner BM, Stein JH (editors). Churchill Livingstone, 1979.

Wilson CB, Dixon FJ: The renal response to immunological injury. Page 1237 in: *The Kidney*, 2nd ed. Brenner BM, Rector FC Jr (editors). Saunders, 1981.

32 | Dermatologic Diseases

Thomas T. Provost, MD

Advances in immunologic laboratory methods and a better understanding of the basic immunologic mechanisms of tissue injury, including autoantibody formation, immune complexes, and cell-mediated immunity, are making valuable contributions to research in the pathogenesis of skin disease. Immunofluorescence techniques have demonstrated the deposition of various immunoglobulins, complement components, and alternative pathway components of complement activation at the site of lesions in various bullous diseases, including dermatitis herpetiformis and bullous pemphigoid. In addition, direct immunofluorescence techniques have demonstrated the presence of immunoglobulins and complement, presumably in the form of immune complexes, in the blood vessel walls of patients with various forms of vasculitis. Immunoelectronmicroscopic studies have provided important new information suggesting the existence of epidermolysis bullosa acquisita and IgA "bullous pemphigoid" as distinct entities. At present, immunologic data also indicate an important immunopathologic role of cell-mediated immunity in allergic contact dermatitis and photoallergic contact dermatitis. Preliminary data suggest an important role of normal host cell–mediated immunity in the defense against cutaneous fungi. Absence of this cell-mediated immunity may result in widespread cutaneous fungal diseases as well as mucocutaneous candidiasis.

ALLERGIC CONTACT DERMATITIS

Major Immunologic Features
- T cell–mediated eczematous disease.
- Characterized by a 48-hour delayed eczematous response to the epicutaneous application of the allergen.

General Considerations
Allergic contact dermatitis is an example of a disease involving cell-mediated immunity. Although the exact incidence of allergic contact dermatitis in the general population is unknown, it is certainly the most common immunologic disease encountered by dermatologists. In fact, about 3–5% of patients seen by dermatologists are evaluated for possible allergic contact dermatitis. The potential contact sensitizing antigens to which humans are exposed are multitudinous and include drugs, dyes, plant oleoresins, preservatives, and metals. The 5 most common contact sensitizing antigens encountered in clinical practice are *Rhus* species of plants (poison ivy, oak, or sumac), paraphenylenediamine, nickel compounds, rubber compounds, and the dichromates.

Immunologic Pathogenesis
The exact underlying immunologic basis of allergic contact dermatitis is unknown. Much has been learned by experimental application of simple chemicals such as dinitrochlorobenzene (DNCB) to the skin of guinea pigs. It is hypothesized that these chemicals react with skin components to form hapten-carrier molecules. The precise identification of the hapten-carrier molecule responsible for sensitization has been difficult, since DNCB is a highly reactive substance which can form dinitrophenyl-protein bonds with a variety of tissue substances. Early experiments showed that induction of sensitization to a topically applied antigen required an intact local lymphatic system and regional lymph node. Severing the local lymphatics or excising the regional lymph node prevented active cutaneous sensitization but did not interfere with a secondary response once sensitization was established. The participation of regional lymph nodes was demonstrated by the observation of their proliferation (predominantly in the thymus-dependent paracortical area) following the experimental induction of allergic contact dermatitis in animals.

The primary role of the regional lymph node and lymphatic system has been made doubtful by the suggestion that the "training ground" for actively sensitizing the lymphocytes occurs at the site of antigen deposition. When radiolabeled antigen was injected intradermally, much of this antigen rapidly disappeared from the injection site. Subsequently, the antigen could not be identified in the local lymphatic system or regional lymph node. However, a small quantity of antigen remained at the site of injection, and the intensity of the cell-mediated response could be directly correlated with the persistence of this local antigen depot. These data suggest that peripheral sensitization at the site of antigen deposition can occur and that regional lymph node proliferation may occur as sensitized lymphocytes recruit other lymphocytes. It is not known whether these 2 sets of experiments, one demonstrating peripheral sensitization and the other the need for an intact regional lymph node and lymphatic system in the development of allergic contact dermatitis, are contradictory or represent a difference in experimental design.

The dendritic Langerhans cell, which comprises 2–8% of the epidermal cell population, is a bone marrow-derived macrophage expressing Ia cell surface antigens and Fc and C3 cell surface receptors. The Langerhans cell is capable of binding and presenting antigens to sensitized T cells and participating in allogeneic T cell stimulation. There is also good evidence suggesting that prior exposure of epidermal cells to ultraviolet light results in (1) depletion of ATPase-positive cells (presumably Langerhans cells) and (2) interference with the function of the remaining Langerhans cells. Such treatment blocks optimal sensitization to epicutaneously applied dinitrofluorobenzene and is also capable of inducing antigen-specific unresponsiveness (tolerance). One recent study indicates that the tolerance is due at least in part to the generation of suppressor T cells.

These data relating to Langerhans cells suggest that the immune system at the most peripheral region of the body (ie, the epidermis) has an intact antigen-processing macrophage system capable of providing a "training ground" for the active sensitization of lymphocytes.

One additional fascinating aspect of experimental allergic contact dermatitis is that by prior oral feeding of DNCB one can induce an immunologic specific unresponsiveness to epicutaneous sensitization with DNCB. Recent studies suggest preferential stimulation of T suppressor cells by oral ingestion of antigen as the mechanism for this unresponsiveness. The significance of this intriguing and readily reproducible phenomenon, initially reported by Sulzberger and Chase, is unknown.

The central role of the lymphocyte in the pathogenesis of allergic contact dermatitis was first reported in the classic experiment of Landsteiner and Chase in 1942. These investigators specifically transferred allergic contact dermatitis from a sensitized guinea pig to an unsensitized one by the intraperitoneal injection of peritoneal exudate cells. Similar experiments substituting serum for peritoneal exudate cells failed. Furthermore, lymph node lymphocytes from sensitized animals, placed in tissue culture with the appropriate sensitizing antigen, underwent a proliferative response measured by increased DNA synthesis. In mice, the proliferative response of sensitized lymphocytes to the antigen could be abolished by pretreatment of the lymphocytes with anti-Thy-1 (θ) serum, which suggested that T lymphocytes are involved in the sensitization process.

In addition to these animal studies, in vitro studies in humans have demonstrated that peripheral lymphocytes from some patients with allergic contact dermatitis, cultured with the sensitizing antigen, undergo a proliferative response. In fact, peripheral lymphocytes from a patient suffering from nickel contact dermatitis produced migration inhibitory factor (MIF) on exposure to nickel in tissue culture.

Several years ago, Polak et al presented some evidence to indicate that the spontaneous flare of chromium dermatitis may involve plasma cells. Their experiments in animals failed to detect circulating antibody to chromium. Furthermore, it was possible to specifically transfer this "flare-up" reaction by the intradermal injection of peritoneal exudate cells from sensitized donors into normal recipients followed by the intravenous injection of chromium. However, peritoneal cells from animals permanently desensitized (tolerant) to contact hypersensitivity to chromium continued to produce "flare reactions" when injected into normal animals. These data suggest that small quantities of chromium may be absorbed from a site of inadvertent contact and could be systemically transported to sites of previous eczematous disease. There, the antigen would activate previously sensitized lymphocytes, producing reexacerbation of the eczematous disease.

Clinical Features

Allergic contact dermatitis is an eczematous reaction. Eczema is characterized in the acute form by erythema, edema, and vesiculation and in the chronic form by scaling. Histologically, eczematous lesions are characterized by a perivascular mononuclear infiltrate and varying degrees of dermal and epidermal edema (spongiosis).

The site of allergic contact dermatitis is often a clue to diagnosis. For example, nickel contact sensitization may be manifested by an eczematous reaction on the ear lobes, around the neck, and on the upper mid back, the wrists, and upper thighs. These sites correspond to points of contact with earrings, necklaces, brassiere clasps, bracelets or wrist bands, and girdle clasps, respectively. Paraphenylenediamine sensitivity occurs in individuals using hair dyes or sunscreens that contain PABA, which cross-reacts. Sensitivity to rubber results from chemical additives or antioxidants. Dichromate reactivity occurs in leather tanning workers or wearers of leather.

Immunologic Diagnosis

The diagnosis of allergic contact dermatitis is based on the distribution of the lesions, an exhaustive history, and examination of the patient's home and place of work for possible sensitizing compounds. The diagnosis is confirmed by patch testing, a procedure introduced in 1896 by Jadassohn. Patch testing consists of applying a nonirritating (low) concentration of the suspected contact antigen to the patient's skin, usually the back, and covering with an occlusive dressing. The dressing is removed after 48 hours. An eczematous reaction at the site of the patch test constitutes a positive response.

Differential Diagnosis

An eczematous reaction is not pathognomonic of

allergic contact dermatitis. Similar skin reactions occur with bacterial and fungal diseases (infectious eczematoid dermatitis). Eczema also occurs when the skin is repeatedly traumatized by scratching (neurodermatitis) or following the cutaneous application of harsh chemicals and solvents (primary irritant dermatitis). Eczematous lesions are characteristic features of certain inherited diseases such as atopic dermatitis, X-linked hypogammaglobulinemia (see Chapter 25), and Wiskott-Aldrich syndrome (thrombocytopenia, recurrent infections, and eczema). These conditions can be differentiated from allergic contact dermatitis on the basis of the history and clinical features and by patch testing (see above).

Treatment

Avoidance of exposure to an identified allergen is theoretically curative, but avoiding known allergens may prove difficult. For example, common sensitizers such as benzocaine are employed in a variety of topical medications such as sunburn preparations and antiseptic creams. If individuals with sensitivity to benzocaine fail to read the labels on these preparations, they may inadvertently reexpose themselves to the offending agent. Another example of unwitting exposure to a known allergen such as poison ivy is contact with the smoke from burning leaves. If poison ivy is present in the leaves, the pentadecacatechols, the allergen in poison ivy, will vaporize and can be transmitted to a sensitized individual as an aerosol without direct contact with the plant.

In addition, the patient may exacerbate an allergic contact dermatitis by exposure to cross-reacting chemical compounds that are quite similar to the allergen to which he was originally sensitized. The most common example of a cross-reacting chemical is the para-aminobenzoic acid group (PABA). Para-aminobenzoic acid is used in sunscreens and will cross-react with sulfonamides, sulfonylurea diuretics (eg, chlorothiazides), azo dyes, and topical analgesics (eg, benzocaine).

One valuable clinical tool in the management of persistent allergic contact dermatitis is to have patients bring in the contents of their medicine cabinets. This simple procedure will often lead to prompt identification of the offending agent.

Symptomatic treatment consists of the application of wet dressings employing Burow's solution and a 1% hydrocortisone cream or lotion. Oral or parenteral corticosteroids (eg, triamcinolone, 40 mg intramuscularly per week, or prednisone, 40 mg orally daily) may be needed temporarily in severe cases.

Oral desensitization with poison ivy extracts has been employed with some claims of success. Although data are now available that indicate that one can produce tolerance to DNCB by oral administration, the clinical feasibility of oral desensitization remains unproved.

Prognosis

Most patients with allergic contact dermatitis respond to the procedures mentioned above. In some cases—particularly chromium contact dermatitis—the course is chronic with frequent spontaneous exacerbations.

PHOTOALLERGIC CONTACT DERMATITIS

Major Immunologic Features
- T cell–mediated eczematous disease.
- Ultraviolet light plays an essential role in generating the allergen.

General Considerations

Photoallergic contact dermatitis is characterized by a chronic eczematous reaction in areas of skin exposed to light (the backs of the hands, the face, the V of the neck). Unexposed areas of skin are usually not affected.

This disorder became a prominent dermatologic problem following the introduction of germicidal soaps in the late 1950s and early 1960s. Several chemicals, particularly halogenated salicylanilides and bithionol, were found to be prime offenders in producing sensitization. However, other drugs and chemicals such as chlorpromazine and sulfonamides have also been found to produce photoallergic contact dermatitis when applied topically either intentionally or accidentally. Recent evidence indicates that a component of musk deodorant is capable of inducing a photoallergic contact dermatitis.

The role of ultraviolet light in the production of photoallergic contact dermatitis is controversial. Evidence has been presented that ultraviolet light causes photodecomposition of topically applied chemicals and in the process generates a potent sensitizing contact antigen which, when applied to the skin of a sensitized individual in the absence of ultraviolet light, produces an eczematoid reaction. An alternative hypothesis is that ultraviolet light forms free radicals which generate a strong covalent bond between the chemical contactant and host skin structures and that binding of the chemical to the skin results in formation of the contact antigen.

Although the exact role of ultraviolet light is still unclear, there is little doubt about the immunologic nature of this eczematous disease. Photoallergic contact dermatitis has been passively transferred by the intraperitoneal injection of mononuclear cells from a sensitized guinea pig into an unsensitized one.

Clinically, the diagnosis is made by observation of the characteristic eczematous involvement in areas of skin exposed to light and by a history of exposure to photocontactants. A special form of patch testing is employed to confirm the diagnosis. This procedure consists of applying the suspected agent to the patient's skin and then later—usually within 24 hours—exposing the patch test site to ultraviolet light. A second covered patch test serves as a control. An eczematous eruption at 48 hours at the patch test site represents a positive response. The reaction duplicates the clinical lesion.

Topical and systemic corticosteroids, avoidance of the offending agent, and avoidance of sunlight have all been used with some success, but persistence or recurrence of the eczema is common. There is evidence that persistence of the disease is due to prolonged retention of the offending agent in the skin, but this is controversial. Thus, despite lack of recent exposure to the antigen, patients can develop eczematous disease upon exposure to ultraviolet light.

DERMATOPHYTOSIS

Dermatophytes are saprophytic fungi capable of evoking an eczematous response on infecting the skin. They commonly produce infection in the groin (jock itch), on the fingernails and toenails, and between the toes (athlete's foot). Studies by Jones et al indicate that an intact cell-mediated immune response may play an important role in the normal host's response to dermatophyte infections and may be responsible for the clinical manifestations of the skin lesions. These authors have demonstrated that the experimental inoculation of dermatophytes in the skin of an unsensitized individual results in propagation of the fungal disease (an eczematous lesion). However, within 48 hours the cutaneous fungal infection resolves. This resolution corresponds to the development of delayed hypersensitivity to the fungus. Subsequent infection of the arm of a sensitized individual results in a more intense transient initial eczematous response with persistent failure of the fungal infection to spread.

Fungal infections of the feet can be readily treated by the use of various topical preparations, including undecylenic acid powder, 2% miconazole cream, and tolnaftate solution or cream. Severe cases require the use of microsize griseofulvin, 0.5–1 g orally daily for approximately 3 weeks.

Fungal infections are usually self-limited, involving only the moist areas of the body. However, generalized cutaneous fungal infections, including tinea versicolor, have been reported in immunosuppressed patients, in patients with Hodgkin's disease, and in patients with isolated defects in cell-mediated immunity.

MUCOCUTANEOUS CANDIDIASIS

Major Immunologic Features

- Syndrome of cutaneous candidiasis generally found in the presence of T cell dysfunction.
- T cell defects include lymphocytopenia, the presence of lymphocytotoxin, serum factors inhibiting lymphocyte activation, absence of a 48-hour delayed skin test response to a variety of antigens, and impaired lymphocyte transformation or MIF production.
- Neutrophil chemotactic defects may be present.

General Considerations

Mucocutaneous candidiasis is a rare syndrome associated with skin and mucous membrane infection with *Candida albicans* that occurs most commonly—though not exclusively—in patients with defective cell-mediated immunity. It has been found in patients suffering from Hodgkin's disease and thymomas, in children born with severe combined immune deficiency, and in the DiGeorge and Nezelof syndromes. This form of candidal infection has also been found in children born with ill-defined and subtle profound defects in function of the T lymphocyte system.

C albicans, a saprophytic yeast, is a common inhabitant of the human gastrointestinal tract. Exposure begins in early infancy. During pregnancy, approximately 25% of women have significant yeast vaginitis. Approximately 5% of newborn infants develop oral candidiasis (thrush of mouth). Oral candidiasis generally disappears during the neonatal period. By the end of the first year of life, almost all children have been exposed to *C albicans,* as indicated by the presence of serum *Candida*-agglutinating antibodies. One study also indicates that approximately 60% of children over 1 year of age can mount a 48-hour delayed response to the intradermal injection of *C albicans* skin test antigen.

Children with mucocutaneous candidiasis may also have other fungal infections. However, *C albicans,* by virtue of its colonization of the gut in infancy, is the first potentially pathogenic fungus to challenge children with defective cell-mediated immunity.

Immunologic Pathogenesis (See Chapter 25.)

Extensive immunologic studies of patients with mucocutaneous candidiasis have demonstrated a variety of abnormalities of the cell-mediated immune mechanism. Most patients are unable to respond with a 48-hour delayed skin reaction to a battery of skin tests. This cutaneous "anergy" appears on infrequent occasions to be limited to the *Candida* antigen. These patients also have delayed homograft rejection and an inability to become sensitized with DNCB. Some in vitro studies have demonstrated lymphocyte failure to respond to an antigenic challenge with increased DNA synthesis and migration inhibitory factor (MIF) production. Other patients' lymphocytes appear to have normal MIF production, but lymphocyte proliferation does not occur in response to antigenic challenges. On the other hand, some patients have a normal lymphocyte proliferative response but fail to produce additional MIF.

Mucocutaneous candidiasis has also been reported in association with a serum inhibitory factor that prevents lymphocytes from proliferating in response to antigenic challenge in vitro. One report describes clearance of the inhibitory factor and return of cell-mediated immunity following successful eradication of the *C albicans* infection with amphotericin B. This suggests that this serum inhibitory factor may be secondary to the *Candida* infection.

Recent studies also suggest that some of these

patients may have defective neutrophil and mononuclear chemotaxis in addition to a defective cell-mediated immunity.

Clinical Findings

Mucocutaneous candidiasis generally develops during the first 2 years of life. It commonly presents as persistent oral candidiasis beyond the neonatal period. The candidiasis may spread to involve large areas of skin. Granulomatous lesions may or may not form. The esophagus and nails may be involved. Multiple endocrinopathies and, at times, iron deficiency anemia may also be present.

Immunologic Diagnosis

The diagnosis of mucocutaneous candidiasis is made by culturing *C albicans* from the cutaneous lesions. For information regarding in vitro lymphocyte testing to evaluate the suspected underlying cell-mediated defect, see Chapter 23.

Differential Diagnosis

The granulomatous lesions of mucocutaneous candidiasis must be differentiated from pyodermas, cutaneous coccidioidomycosis, histoplasmosis, blastomycosis, and leishmaniasis.

Treatment

Some children with mucocutaneous candidiasis have been successfully treated by immunologic reconstitution with transfusions of normal homologous leukocytes. Thymic transplantation and amphotericin B, followed by transfer factor therapy, have also been successfully employed. Topically, 2% miconazole cream and clotrimazole have both been successfully employed.

Recent data indicate that some patients with mucocutaneous candidiasis may be treated with the histamine (H_2) antagonist cimetidine. Although the data are preliminary, they suggest that histamine and other inflammatory mediators may—in addition to their phlogistic activity—modulate the immune system. For example, suppressor T cells stimulated by concanavalin A possess H_2 receptors. Further research with cimetidine certainly appears warranted and offers an exciting new approach to the treatment of some defective T cell–mediated responses.

Prognosis

The prognosis is guarded. Theoretically, defective T cell function makes these individuals susceptible to viral, fungal, and protozoal infections as well as autoimmune disorders.

BULLOUS DISEASES

The bullous diseases can only be properly understood if the distinctive anatomic features of the skin are clearly visualized. The epidermis is composed of layers of epidermal cells. These cells originate in the basal layer of the epidermis and then migrate toward the stratum corneum. During this migration, the cells undergo a process of keratinization. Upon reaching the skin surface, these compacted keratinized epidermal cells form the **stratum corneum,** or **horny layer,** of the skin.

Individual epidermal cells, during their upward migration, are held together by cytoplasmic projections ending on desmosomes ("intercellular bridges"). These epidermal cells also interdigitate with one another, and in the intercellular spaces there is an amorphous material called intercellular "cement." Destruction of the intercellular spaces interferes with the cohesion of the epidermis, leading to blister formation.

The epidermis is anatomically anchored to the dermis by a lamellar structure termed **basement membrane.** Extending from the basal layer of the epidermis to this structure are "anchoring" structures termed **half desmosomes.** Destruction of the integrity of the basement membrane and surrounding structures results in separation of epidermis from the dermis and blister formation (Table 32–1).

Table 32–1. Immunofluorescence studies in bullous skin diseases.

Disease	Site of Blister Formation	Location of Ig and C Deposits	Autoantibodies
Pemphigus	Intraepidermal	Epidermal, intercellular	Yes
Bullous pemphigoid	Subepidermal	Basement membrane	Yes
Benign mucous membrane pemphigoid	Subepidermal	Basement membrane	Yes
Herpes gestationis	Subepidermal	Basement membrane	Yes
Dermatitis herpetiformis	Subepidermal	Granular pattern, beneath basement membrane	No
IgA "bullous pemphigoid"	Subepidermal	Basement membrane	Yes (occasionally)
Epidermolysis bullosa acquisita	Subepidermal	Papillary dermis	Yes (occasionally)
Erythema multiforme	Subepidermal	Dermal blood vessels	No
Toxic epidermal necrolysis	Intraepidermal	None	No

TOXIC EPIDERMAL NECROLYSIS

Toxic epidermal necrolysis (Ritter's disease, Lyell's disease, scalded skin syndrome) is a relatively benign acute febrile disease of infancy and early childhood characterized by mucopurulent rhinorrhea, conjunctivitis, mild to moderate toxemia, and a cutaneous response characterized by fragile intraepidermal blister formation and the loss of sheets of epidermis following minimal shearing pressure (Nikolsky's sign). Group II phage 71 *Staphylococcus aureus* can be isolated from the nose or conjunctiva. The cutaneous disease is short-lived, and recovery is complete.

Histologic and electron microscopic studies reveal epidermal cleft formation in the subgranular layer resulting from intraepidermal separation. Epidermal cytotoxic changes are minimal.

Experiments in newborn mice employing a low-molecular-weight protein (MW approximately 25,000), exfoliatin, isolated from group II phage 71 *S aureus* filtrates, have demonstrated that the intradermal injection of this protein produces epidermal denudation similar to if not identical with that seen in human infants and small children. Further studies in humans have demonstrated the presence of a detectable serum antibody to the exfoliatin found in the recovery phase of the disease. This antibody then appears to confer host immunity against subsequent toxic epidermal necrolysis cutaneous response to staphylococcal group II infections.

On rare occasions the exfoliatin (epidermolysin) toxin may be found in non–group II staphylococcal infections.

A second form of toxic epidermal necrolysis unassociated with a staphylococcal infection is found as part of a severe erythema multiforme cutaneous reaction. This reaction histologically demonstrates cleft formation deep in the epidermis and pronounced epidermal cell cytotoxicity. In contrast to the toxic epidermal necrolysis associated with group II staphylococcal infections, this syndrome has a guarded prognosis.

PEMPHIGUS VULGARIS

Major Immunologic Features
- Immunoglobulin and complement deposition found in the squamous intercellular spaces.
- Serum antibody directed against intercellular substance of stratified squamous epithelium.
- Increased incidence of HLA-A10 and HLA-B13.
- In vitro induction of acantholysis.

General Considerations

Pemphigus vulgaris is a chronic bullous disease which formerly was reported almost exclusively in Jews. It has now been documented in all races and ethnic groups. Pemphigus vulgaris has been reported in association with bullous pemphigoid, thymoma,

myasthenia gravis, and systemic lupus erythematosus. Before the corticosteroid and antibiotic drugs became available, pemphigus vulgaris was fatal in a large percentage of cases. Patients died of fluid and electrolyte abnormalities, cachexia, and sepsis secondary to the denudation of large areas of skin.

New studies indicate that 91% of Jewish patients with pemphigus possess the HLA-DRw4 phenotype, compared to a 25% prevalence in controls. Furthermore, the A26, Bw38, DRw4 haplotype is almost nonexistent in non-Jewish whites but has a frequency of 11% in the normal Jewish population. However, this haplotype has a 36% prevalence in Jewish pemphigus patients. The Bw38 and DRw4 phenotypes occur jointly in 55% of Jewish pemphigus patients and in 11% of controls.

It is also interesting to note that the DRw4 phenotype was found in 4 of 4 Mexican, 3 of 3 Oriental, and 7 of 17 non-Jewish white pemphigus patients. The meaning of this striking increased prevalence of the DRw4 phenotype in pemphigus patients is unknown.

Immunologic Pathogenesis

Direct immunofluorescence of the skin lesions in pemphigus vulgaris has demonstrated the deposition of immunoglobulins (predominantly IgG), complement components (C1, C4, C3), properdin factor B (C3 proactivator), and, to a lesser extent, properdin at the site of involvement, the epidermal intercellular spaces. In addition to evidence of complement deposition at the disease site, complement levels in the blister fluid—in contrast to serum complement levels—are markedly decreased. Preliminary evidence also indicates the presence of C1q precipitating material in the blister fluid, suggesting the presence of immune complexes. All of the above studies have been interpreted as suggesting local activation of complement at the site of blister formation.

However, in vitro studies using normal human skin explants show that pemphigus antibody in the apparent absence of complement can also induce acantholytic epidermal lesions. The exact meaning of this striking observation is at present unknown. However, additional in vitro studies suggest that the pemphigus antibody is capable of activating a normal epidermal serine protease. This activation can be blocked by alpha$_2$ macroglobulin and soybean trypsin inhibitor, 2 known inhibitors of this enzyme system. It is conceivable that activation of this enzyme destroys the intercellular substance and produces acantholysis.

Recent reports indicate that a pemphigus foliaceus–like skin disease occurs in 5–10% of rheumatoid arthritis patients receiving penicillamine for 6 or more months. Furthermore, these patients demonstrate classic pemphigus antibodies in perilesional biopsies and in their serum. Discontinuation of penicillamine is generally followed by disappearance of clinical and serologic findings of pemphigus, although some patients require treatment. It is also interesting to note that pemphiguslike antibodies have

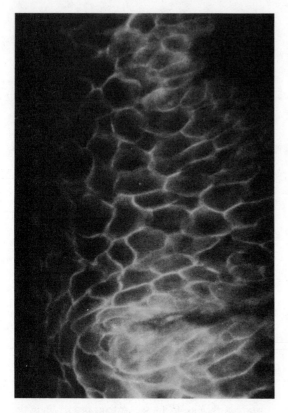

Figure 32–1. Indirect immunofluorescence examination of pemphigus serum, demonstrating the presence of IgG antibody to intercellular substance. The substrate is monkey esophagus.

been described in skin lesions associated with sensitivity to penicillin and ampicillin.

Most (not all) specimens of serum from pemphigus patients contain a circulating IgG antibody (Fig 32–1) directed against a substance in the intercellular spaces of squamous epithelium. Several groups of investigators have attempted to induce pemphigus lesions in animals by the passive transfer of high-titer human pemphigus serum, and one group has claimed success.

Clinical Features

Pemphigus vulgaris is characterized by the development of thin flaccid bullae on normal-appearing skin. The mucous membranes are commonly involved. In fact, the disease commonly begins with extensive oral erosions. Shearing force applied to normal-appearing skin or direct pressure applied to the blister will cause further denudation of the skin and extension of the blister (Nikolsky's sign). The ruptured blisters display little tendency to heal.

Histologic examination of the blister reveals intraepidermal blister formation (the epidermis forms both the roof and base of blisters). In the blister fluid one can see single, unattached, rounded epidermal cells (Tzanck cells). At the margin of the blister, inter-cellular clefts may be seen between the individual epidermal cells (acantholysis).

Electron microscopic studies have demonstrated that destruction of the intercellular "cement" substance is the earliest pathologic finding in pemphigus vulgaris.

Immunologic Diagnosis

The diagnosis is made by the clinical features and histologic demonstration of acantholytic intraepidermal bulla formation. The diagnosis of pemphigus can also be made by the direct immunofluorescence demonstration of immunoglobulin deposition in the intercellular spaces of diseased or normal-appearing skin of the patients. This can also be confirmed by demonstrating the typical pemphigus antibody in the patient's serum by using indirect immunofluorescence techniques that employ heterologous tissue as a substrate. Rarely, pemphiguslike antibodies (Fig 32–1) may be seen in the sera of patients with cutaneous fungal infections or thermal burns. However, pemphigus antibody titers in these sera are usually low, and the clinical and histologic features of these conditions are distinct from those of pemphigus vulgaris.

Differential Diagnosis

This disease must be differentiated from other blistering diseases such as bullous pemphigoid, erythema multiforme, and benign mucous membrane pemphigoid.

Treatment

This disease can be successfully controlled with high doses of corticosteroids. In the past, prednisone in doses as large as 300–500 mg/d was required to control the lesions. In recent years, either azathioprine, 100–150 mg orally daily, methotrexate, 25–50 mg intramuscularly once weekly, or cyclophosphamide, 50–100 mg orally daily, usually in conjunction with corticosteroids, 40–60 mg orally daily, has been employed to treat these patients. The combined use of corticosteroids with immunosuppressive therapy allows one to employ much smaller doses of the former, thus avoiding the objectionable complications of corticosteroid therapy.

Recent evidence also suggests that intramuscular gold therapy is effective in the treatment of pemphigus. This form of therapy appears to be especially helpful in the treatment of patients with complications from corticosteroids or a poor response to corticosteroids.

After prolonged therapy, about 30–40% of pemphigus patients undergo a sustained clinical remission which persists without further therapy. One group has reported successful treatment of pemphigus patients with clinical and serologic remissions for as long as 4 years employing skin and serum pemphigus antibody determinations to monitor corticosteroid and immunosuppressive therapy. This constant monitoring of the pemphigus antibody may prevent unwarranted continuation of corticosteroid and immunosuppressive therapy. In fact, complications of corticosteroid and immunosuppressive therapy are the major clinical problems in the treatment of pemphigus, accounting for 8–10% of deaths in this disease.

Prognosis

The prognosis of this disease has changed radically in the last 2 decades. Death during the first or second year after onset occurred in approximately 50% of patients in the preantibiotic and precorticosteroid era. The mortality rate is now being reported as 8% in several studies. Several groups have also reported long-term (over 2 years) clinical and serologic remission in pemphigus vulgaris patients following completion of high-dose corticosteroid and immunosuppressive therapy. However, morbidity (gastrointestinal bleeding, osteoporosis, diabetes) associated with large doses of corticosteroids is high. The addition of an immunosuppressive agent (azathioprine, methotrexate, and cyclophosphamide) to small doses of corticosteroids shows promise of immunizing the corticosteroid side-effects while still controlling the disease.

BULLOUS PEMPHIGOID

Major Immunologic Features

- Immunoglobulin and complement deposition on the skin basement membrane.
- Serum anti-skin basement membrane antibody found in approximately 80% of patients.
- Neutrophil and eosinophil chemotactic factors in blister fluid.

General Considerations

This is a chronic bullous disease occurring mostly in middle-aged and older people. Like pemphigus vulgaris, this blistering disease had a significant mortality rate prior to the advent of corticosteroids and antibiotics.

Bullous pemphigoid is a self-limited blistering disease characterized by formation of tense bullae on an erythematous base. The flexor areas of the body (axillary, inguinal, and sides of the neck) are the common sites of involvement. The blister forms subepidermally. (The roof is formed by the epidermis, and the base of the blister is the dermis.) The individual bullae are difficult to rupture. Mucous membrane lesions are not a common feature. It has recently been recognized that bullous pemphigoid may occur as isolated bullae localized to one area of the body, especially the lower legs. Patients with isolated bullous lesions demonstrate classic histologic and serologic bullous pemphigoid features.

Immunologic Pathogenesis

Direct immunofluorescence studies have demonstrated the deposition of IgG, IgA, IgM, IgD, IgE, C1q, C4, C3, C5, properdin, properdin factor B, β_1H, and fibrin along the skin basement membrane (the site of bullous formation). Immunoelectronmicroscopic studies demonstrate localization of IgG and C3 in the lamina lucida.

There is no increased incidence of a particular HLA phenotype, nor is there an increased incidence of malignancy associated with bullous pemphigoid.

Complement component levels in the blister fluid are markedly decreased, whereas the total serum complement in these patients is normal. As in pemphigus vulgaris, these studies have been interpreted as suggesting local activation of complement at the site of blister formation.

Eosinophil and neutrophil chemotactic activity has been demonstrated in the blister fluids. One of the neutrophil chemotactic factors is C5, and at least one of the eosinophil chemotactic factors closely resembles eosinophil chemotactic factor of anaphylaxis (ECF-A).

In addition to these studies, indirect immunofluorescence techniques (Fig 32–1) have demonstrated, in the sera of approximately 80% of these patients, a complement-fixing IgG antibody to skin basement membrane. However, attempts to passively transfer this disease to animals by the infusion of high-titer human pemphigoid serum have thus far failed.

Studies by Gammon employing a unique in vitro tissue culture apparatus have demonstrated that human skin cultured in the presence of pemphigoid antibody, complement, and human leukocytes displays a directed migration of the polymorphonuclear leukocytes and attachment to the skin basement membrane zone. This directed migration is an active process requiring viable leukocytes and complement. Following attachment of these leukocytes to the skin basement membrane zone, sequential examination reveals the development of the subepidermal separation at the basement membrane zone. This constitutes the first in vitro evidence that the pemphigoid antibody is indeed responsible for the development of the subepidermal blistering disease so characteristic of bullous pemphigoid.

Anhalt and Diaz have developed a rabbit animal model for bullous pemphigoid utilizing intraocular injection of "purified pemphigoid antibody." This procedure produced inflammation in the eye together with subepidermal blister formation of the corneal epithelium. Similar control experiments with normal serum were without effect.

Immunologic Diagnosis

The diagnosis is made clinically by observing the typical clinical features and by demonstrating a subepidermal bulla on a histologic preparation. The diagnosis may also be established by demonstrating, by direct immunofluorescence, the deposition of immunoglobulins or complement (C3) along the skin basement membrane (Fig 32–2). The serum may also be employed in indirect fluorescence techniques to demonstrate IgG skin basement membrane antibodies.

Differential Diagnosis

This bullous disease must be differentiated from

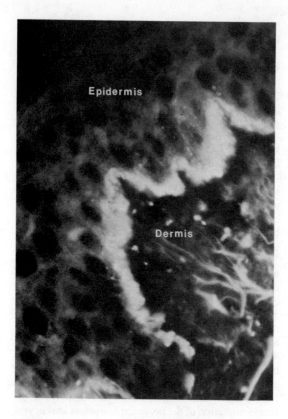

Epidermis

Dermis

Figure 32–2. Direct immunofluorescence examination of the skin of a patient with bullous pemphigoid. Note heavy Ig deposition along the basement membrane.

pemphigus vulgaris and erythema multiforme. The small blisters of an acute onset of bullous pemphigoid may be confused with dermatitis herpetiformis.

Treatment

Like pemphigus vulgaris, bullous pemphigoid responds to high doses of corticosteroids (eg, prednisone, 40–60 mg orally daily). Azathioprine, 100–150 mg orally daily, and methotrexate, 25–50 mg intramuscularly once weekly, have also been successfully employed, along with corticosteroids, in the treatment of bullous pemphigoid. As in pemphigus vulgaris, the combined use of corticosteroids and immunosuppressive agents has allowed use of low doses of corticosteroids, thereby reducing the incidence of severe corticosteroid complications.

Prognosis

The prognosis for life is much improved, although, as in pemphigus vulgaris, large doses of corticosteroids in elderly people involve great risks that can only be undertaken if the probable benefits outweigh the possible hazards.

The great majority of patients with bullous pemphigoid have a self-limited disease. The average course of immunosuppressive or steroid therapy is 4–6 months. Thereafter, most patients have a prolonged

(over 2 years) clinical, immunohistologic, and serologic remission.

BENIGN MUCOUS MEMBRANE PEMPHIGOID

This is a subepidermal blistering disease involving the mucous membranes of the eyes, mouth, and vagina. Scar formation may occur. Few or no blisters appear on the skin. Recent investigations have now firmly established the presence of immunoglobulins and complement components along the basement membrane of the mucous membrane (the site of blister formation). One recent study demonstrated an 80% incidence of immunoglobulin or complement deposition along the basement membrane zone of perilesional biopsies in 25 patients. Serum anti-basement membrane zone antibodies were detected in approximately 10% of patients. These observations suggest a possible relationship between this disease and bullous pemphigoid.

Treatment of this disease is difficult. Local forms of therapy with corticosteroid eyedrops and surgical procedures do not produce lasting benefits. There is some evidence that these lesions respond partially to systemic corticosteroid therapy (eg, prednisone, 40–60 mg orally daily). The benefits of corticosteroid therapy must be weighed against the possible serious side-effects of corticosteroids in elderly persons. Immunosuppressive therapy (azathioprine, 100–150 mg orally) has been used in some of these patients, although its efficacy remains to be proved.

Prognosis

Benign mucous membrane pemphigoid is a chronic scarring disease of mucous membranes. Conjunctival scarring leads to failure to close the eye. Severe dryness and infection follow, and ultimately blindness.

HERPES GESTATIONIS

Major Immunologic Features
• Complement and, at times, immunoglobulin deposition on skin basement membrane.
• Avid complement-fixing serum autoantibody.

General Considerations
Herpes gestationis is a rare subepidermal bullous disease of pregnancy, occurring in one out of every 10–30 thousand pregnancies. The term herpes in this disease does not refer to herpesviruses but to the serpentine appearance of the lesions. It is characterized by an intense burning pruritus and subepidermal blister formation on erythematous papules. Histologically, the blister formation is indistinguishable from that of bullous pemphigoid.

Herpes gestationis may occur at any time during pregnancy but most commonly in the late second or early third trimester. It disappears following the termination of pregnancy, but persistence into the postpartum period and episodic flares with menses have been reported. The disease has also been reported following the use of estrogen-containing birth control pills. It may recur in succeeding pregnancies and may have an earlier and more severe onset. Infants born of affected mothers are generally without evidence of skin disease, but on rare occasions a transient bullous skin disease has been reported.

Direct immunofluorescence studies of the skin of patients with herpes gestationis have demonstrated IgG, IgE, C1, C4, C3, C5, and properdin deposition along the basement membrane. In many cases biopsy shows only heavy C3 deposition. The serum may or may not contain a factor capable of depositing complement components C1, C4, or C3 on the skin basement membrane. While some technical difficulty has been encountered in demonstrating a serum anti-basement membrane autoantibody in some patients, it appears likely that this basement membrane complement-fixing serum factor is an immunoglobulin.

Direct immunofluorescence studies of the skin of infants afflicted with the disease have thus far revealed the deposition of only C4 and C3 on the basement membrane. Immunoelectronmicroscopic studies indicate that immunoreactants are localized to the lamina lucida in a pattern quite similar to that found in bullous pemphigoid.

These studies suggest a role for immunoglobulin and complement in the pathogenesis of the bullous disease of the mother and infant. The relationship between this disease and bullous pemphigoid is unknown, although immunofluorescence staining of specimens of basement membrane gives quite similar results.

Treatment

Treatment of herpes gestationis is difficult. These patients complain of an intense pruritus in addition to the blistering skin disease. The disease can be controlled during pregnancy with low to moderate doses of prednisone (15–30 mg orally daily). The aim is to control the disease and make the patient comfortable until she delivers. One possible complication is that the prednisone may suppress the fetus' adrenals. The neonatologist should be warned of the possibility of adrenal insufficiency in the infant at birth.

Prognosis

Generally, the bullous disease disappears within a few months after termination of pregnancy. Exacerbations may occur with subsequent menses or with the use of birth control pills. The mechanism of induction by birth control pills is completely unknown. Subsequent pregnancies may result in a more acute and earlier onset of the bullous disease. Recent evidence suggests that there may be an increased incidence of neonatal deaths among infants born to mothers with herpes gestationis.

DERMATITIS HERPETIFORMIS

Major Immunologic Features

- Deposition of IgA at the dermal-epidermal junction.
- Increased incidence of HLA-B8 antigen.
- Increased incidence of selected B cell alloantigens.
- IgA immune complexes in serum.

General Considerations

Dermatitis herpetiformis is a chronic bullous disease that may occur at any age. Unlike pemphigus and, to a lesser extent, bullous pemphigoid, untreated dermatitis herpetiformis is not fatal.

Immunologic Pathogenesis

Direct immunofluorescence studies show that granular deposition of IgA is almost always present at the dermal-epidermal junction and IgG and IgM deposition much less commonly so. C3 is often found at sites corresponding to IgA deposition, especially in areas of blister formation. C1q and C4 are only occasionally found. These studies have been interpreted as suggesting activation of complement, predominantly via the alternative pathway, at the site of blister formation. No serum autoantibodies have been demonstrated, and serum complement levels are normal. Immunoelectronmicroscopy demonstrates the sublamina lucida granular deposition of immunoreactants.

Immunologic studies of the gut have demonstrated increased levels of IgA and IgM in the gastrointestinal fluid. Serum IgA levels are increased.

Genetic studies have demonstrated that approximately 90% of patients with dermatitis herpetiformis have HLA-B8 and HLA-Dw3 antigen, compared to a frequency of less than 30% in the general population. About 90% of patients suffering from adult celiac disease also have HLA-B8. These 2 diseases have in common a very high incidence of B cell surface antigens Bw1 and B1.

The relationship between the gut disease and the skin disease is unknown. This may be a hypersensitivity disease in genetically predisposed individuals. Conceivably, antigen—perhaps gluten—is presented to the host via the gastrointestinal tract, preferentially stimulating the secretory immune system (IgA). Combining the antigen with IgA in the gut could produce the patchy duodenal or jejunal atrophy. The damaged mucosa may then permit IgA immune complexes to diffuse into the systemic circulation. For unknown reasons, these IgA complexes may be deposited in the skin, where they activate the complement system via the alternative pathway and produce the skin disease. Another hypothesis is that the inciting antigen and a normal skin structure—perhaps reticulin fibers—may bear antigenic similarities to each other. The IgA directed against the inciting antigen may then cross-react with the skin structure.

Recent evidence indicates the cutaneous manifestations as well as the gut lesions in dermatitis herpetiformis respond to a gluten-free diet. One unconfirmed study has indicated that there is a concomitant disappearance of the skin lesions and IgA deposition following institution of a gluten-free diet.

Dermatitis herpetiformis patients have been shown to possess antigliadin antibodies. Three groups of investigators have demonstrated the presence of serum IgA immune complexes in approximately one-third of the random sera of dermatitis herpetiformis patients. Dermatitis herpetiformis patients contain little or no serum IgG immune complexes. Two groups of researchers using 2 different techniques have demonstrated the presence of wheat antigen in these IgA serum immune complexes. Following wheat ingestion, dermatitis herpetiformis patients—but not normal individuals—without exception develop serum IgA immune complexes. These complexes generally form 90–150 minutes following ingestion of wheat and are generally cleared within 5 hours. These IgA immune complexes have been shown to be 10–12S in size and do not contain secretory component. This suggests that the IgA immune complexes are formed following absorption of the wheat antigen across the gut mucosa.

Clinical Features

Dermatitis herpetiformis is characterized by small groups of tense vesicles on an erythematous base. Symmetric distribution over the extensor surfaces is common, and the buttocks, lower back, and shoulders are most severely affected. An intense burning pruritus accompanies this disease.

Histologically, the lesions demonstrate a subepidermal bullous formation. Eosinophilic microabscesses are seen in the dermal papillae.

Dermatitis herpetiformis also has systemic manifestations. Biopsies of the small intestine have revealed a patchy duodenal or jejunal atrophy indistinguishable from adult celiac disease. Signs and symptoms of a malabsorption syndrome, however, are only occasionally seen (probably because of the patchy involvement of the gut disease).

Immunologic Diagnosis

In addition to the characteristic clinical and histologic features of this disease, the direct immunofluorescence demonstration of granular IgA deposition in the upper dermis of these patients is considered diagnostic of dermatitis herpetiformis. IgA deposits are present in over 95% of patients upon random biopsy of normal skin. Recent evidence indicates that approximately 10% of dermatitis herpetiformis patients have linear rather than granular IgA deposition along the dermal-epidermal junction. The majority of these patients, upon immunoelectronmicroscopic examination, demonstrate sub-lamina lucida deposition of the immunoreactants.

Differential Diagnosis

Dermatitis herpetiformis must be differentiated from other intensely pruritic diseases such as scabies, pediculosis, and neurodermatitis and the blistering disease bullous pemphigoid.

Treatment

Dapsone (diaminodiphenylsulfone), 100 mg daily, and sulfapyridine, 1–3 g daily, are effective in controlling the cutaneous features of this disease. They have no effect on the gastrointestinal lesions. The mechanisms of action of these drugs are unknown. The gut lesions respond to a gluten-free diet, and in one recent report it was claimed that a prolonged gluten-free diet resulted in clearance of the skin lesions.

Prognosis

The prognosis is excellent. Unlike in bullous pemphigoid and pemphigus vulgaris, no deaths occur as a result of this disease. Untreated, it persists for years and is characterized by chronic low-grade activity with acute exacerbations. Patients treated with dapsone and free of disease for years, upon discontinuation of the dapsone, may have recurrence of their disease within 72–96 hours.

IgA "BULLOUS PEMPHIGOID"

This is a newly recognized entity characterized by subepidermal bullous formation on glabrous skin. Direct immunofluorescent studies demonstrate a linear deposition of IgA along the zone of the basement membrane. Immunoelectronmicroscopy shows deposition of IgA in the lamina lucida in a pattern similar to that of bullous pemphigoid. Several of these patients have IgA anti-basement membrane antibody in their serum. These patients—like dermatitis herpetiformis patients—respond to sulfones; unlike dermatitis herpetiformis patients, however, they do not have an increased incidence of HLA-B8 or HLA-Dw3 phenotypes or a patchy duodenojejunal atrophy.

Patients with this peculiar bullous disease have undoubtedly been diagnosed as having linear IgA dermatoses and linear IgA dermatitis herpetiformis.

A similar IgA-associated bullous disease has been reported in children. The exact relationship of this childhood entity to adult IgA bullous disease is unknown.

EPIDERMOLYSIS BULLOSA ACQUISITA

This is an extremely rare subepidermal vesicular bullous disease of the skin and the mucous membranes. Traumatic induction of blister formation and mucous membrane blisters are prominent findings. Recent direct immunofluorescent studies have demonstrated bound immunoglobulin and complement deposited in a linear configuration along the basement membrane zone. In addition, several of these patients have an IgG antibody in their serum which reacts with the basement membrane zone. Electronmicroscopic studies, however, have demonstrated that the blister formation occurs below the lamina lucida. Yaoita et al, employing immunoelectronmicroscopic techniques, have demonstrated that the bound IgG and the circulating IgG antibodies found in some of these patients are reactive against antigens localized to the sub-basal lamina anchoring fibril zone. These authors, utilizing an indirect immunoelectronmicroscopic technique, have observed that the IgG antibody is capable of binding the cytoplasm of the basal cell layer. This suggests that the origin of the sub-basal lamina zone antigen is the epidermal basal cell.

The same authors have also demonstrated in one of their patients the disappearance of serum and in vivo IgG antibody and the concomitant disappearance of the subepidermal blistering disease, suggesting a cause and effect relationship between the autoantibody and the bullous dermatoses.

Most importantly, these studies demonstrate that despite a similarity of this blistering disease with bullous pemphigoid, the 2 diseases represent distinct clinical and pathologic entities. Furthermore, in marked contrast to bullous pemphigoid, this blistering disease is resistant to corticosteroid and immunosuppressive therapy.

ERYTHEMA MULTIFORME

Erythema multiforme is a common cutaneous reaction pattern seen in a variety of disorders, including infections, drug reactions, connective tissue diseases, and malignant or chronic disease of the internal organs. Recent data indicate that biopsies taken from early lesions of erythema multiforme frequently show deposition of granular deposits of C3 or IgM (or both) in blood vessels of the papillary dermis. IgA and IgG are detected only rarely in these specimens. About half of erythema multiforme patients with immunoglobulin and complement deposition in the papillary blood vessels had recurrent herpes simplex (herpesvirus hominis); in the remainder, a definite cause of erythema multiforme could not be found. In addition to these interesting findings, other studies in patients with the bullous form of erythema multiforme have recently demonstrated immune complexes and reduced levels of individual complement components in the blister fluid. Serum immune complexes have also been detected.

These data suggest a role for immunoglobulin and complement, perhaps in the form of immune complexes, in the pathogenesis of erythema multiforme. These data also provide further evidence that cutaneous manifestations interpreted as erythema multiforme are occasionally another cutaneous manifestation of an immune complex-mediated vascular insult.

VASCULITIDES

Major Immunologic Features
- Deposition of immunoglobulin and complement in blood vessel walls.
- Serum complement levels may be decreased.
- Cryoglobulins and rheumatoid factor may be present in serum.

General Considerations

A partial list of vasculitic diseases includes leukocytoclastic angiitis, allergic granulomatosis, polyarteritis nodosa, giant cell arteritis, and Wegener's granulomatosis.

All forms of vasculitis may have significant cutaneous features. The size of the vessel, its anatomic location, and the intensity of the inflammatory insult determine what the cutaneous manifestations will be. Vasculitis may therefore present as pustular, petechial, urticarial, nodular, or ulcerative lesions. Recent studies have demonstrated deposits of various immunoglobulins, complement, and alternative pathway components in the diseased blood vessel walls of patients suffering from various forms of leukocytoclastic angiitis. Electron microscopic studies of blood vessel walls of early lesions of leukocytoclastic angiitis have demonstrated electron-dense deposits (presumably immune complexes). Immunoglobulin and complement are deposited in the temporal arteries of some patients suffering from temporal arteritis. Some patients with polyarteritis nodosa have deposits of HBsAg, immunoglobulins, and complement in the diseased blood vessel walls. In addition, circulating HBsAg antigen has been found in the serum of some of these patients.

These studies suggest that the deposition of immune complexes in the blood vessel walls may play a role in the pathogenesis of several forms of necrotizing vasculitis. Evidence also suggests that circulating immune complexes and complement activation may play a role in the pathogenesis of urticarial and angioneurotic edema-like lesions frequently seen in the prodromal stage of acute viral hepatitis.

Several studies have reported the association of recurrent urticaria, including angioedema, with marked hypocomplementemia involving both the classic and alternative complement pathways. Histologically, the urticarial plaques display a vasculitis. In contradistinction to hereditary angioneurotic edema, these patients have normal C1 esterase inhibitor activity and C1q is low. These patients have been described as having hypocomplementemic vasculitis. It is most important to stress that this is a systemic disease. Although a few patients have developed arthritis and renal disease, a large percentage—perhaps as high as 50%—have developed a rapid onset of progressive, potentially fatal obstructive lung disease. The nature of the lung abnormalities is not known. (See Chapter 26 for further clinical discussions of these disorders.)

A striking statistically significant association exists between Sjögren's syndrome and vasculitis. The vasculitis involves systemic organs, including the central nervous system, as well as the skin. The cutaneous manifestations of vasculitis found in association with Sjögren's syndrome range from urticarialike lesions to infarcts and ulcerations. These Sjögren syndrome patients with vasculitis have a statistically significant increased prevalence of rheumatoid factor, hypergammaglobulinemia, and Ro(SSA) and La(SSB) antibodies. A significant number of patients thought to have Waldenström's hypergammaglobulinemic purpura have been found to have occult Sjögren's syndrome and to possess Ro and La antibody.

The cutaneous vasculitic lesions and the glomerulonephritis which occur in patients with Henoch-Schönlein purpura are characterized by prominent deposits of IgA and terminal complement components. These patients also have been found to have IgA immune complexes in their sera.

Patients with the intestinal bypass surgery syndrome—an entity observed in patients who have undergone ileojejunal bypass surgery for obesity—characterized by deep dermal erythematous plaques and pustules and papules, possess serum IgA immune complexes. Work by Utsinger indicates that these complexes contain antigens related to enteric bacteria, eg, *Escherichia coli*.

Some patients with primary biliary cirrhosis contain small cutaneous pustular lesions and possess in their serum large quantities of IgA immune complexes.

These studies suggest that some of the cutaneous manifestations associated with primary biliary cirrhosis, Henoch-Schönlein purpura, and intestinal bypass surgery syndrome may represent the cutaneous expression of an IgA-mediated immune complex vasculitis.

DISCOID LUPUS ERYTHEMATOSUS

Major Immunologic Features
- Lesions may or may not be associated with systemic lupus erythematosus.
- Immunoglobulins and complement components generally found in the dermal-epidermal junction in old discoid lesions.

General Considerations
The cutaneous lesions of discoid lupus erythematosus may be characterized as sharply demarcated atrophic plaques. Telangiectasia, follicular plugging, and a hyperkeratotic scale are often prominent. These lesions can involve any part of the body but are usually in light-exposed areas, especially the face and scalp. Histologically, the lesions are characterized by a patchy lymphocytic infiltrate at the dermal-epidermal junction. Liquefaction degeneration of the basal layer of the epidermis and epidermal atrophy are common features. These discoid lesions may be seen in the absence of any systemic disease or as

part of the clinical picture of systemic lupus erythematosus.

Direct immunofluorescence study of these lesions has revealed the deposition in a granular pattern of immunoglobulins, complement, and alternative pathway components at the dermal-epidermal junction. Elution studies have demonstrated that these immunoglobulins have antinuclear specificity. Antibodies to skin basement membrane have also been eluted from the granular deposits, which are found in about 90% of the discoid skin lesions. However, the role of these granular deposits in the pathogenesis of discoid lesions is doubtful for 2 reasons: (1) Similar immunoglobulin and complement deposits are found in normal-appearing light-exposed skin in approximately 60% of patients with systemic lupus erythematosus. These deposits have been found in patients who have never had any skin lesions. (2) Ultraviolet light is capable of inducing classic discoid lesions in patients with systemic lupus erythematosus. Direct immunofluorescence studies of these experimental ultraviolet light-induced lesions have failed to consistently demonstrate immunoglobulin or complement deposition. If deposition does occur, it is found only after the lesions are several months old.

Despite the lack of evidence that immune complexes play a role in the pathogenesis of the cutaneous lesions, their presence in the skin of patients with systemic lupus erythematosus that has not been exposed to light appears to be a reflection of the systemic immune complex disease. The presence of these cutaneous deposits is very often associated with severe lupus nephritis (Fig 32–3). Several studies have demonstrated a statistically significant correlation between noninvolved skin, immunoglobulin deposition at the dermal-epidermal junction (lupus band test), and the presence of serum hypocomplementemia, anti-DNA antibodies, and the presence of clinical renal disease. More recent evidence indicates that patients having either a negative lupus band test or a lupus band test composed of pure IgM have a lupus process characterized by a low incidence of renal disease. Patients possessing a lupus band test composed of IgG alone or together with other immunoglobulins, however, have a lupus process characterized by a high incidence of clinical renal disease and demonstrate serum hypocomplementemia and anti-DNA antibodies. Because of this association, the routine examination of the noninvolved and nonexposed skin of patients with systemic lupus erythematosus can provide valuable information regarding the presence or absence of immune complex nephritis.

It has recently been recognized that urticarialike lesions can occur in systemic lupus erythematosus as a manifestation of low-grade necrotizing vasculitis. Direct immunofluorescent examination of the urticarial lesions may reveal Ig and C3 deposition in the diseased blood vessels, and routine hematoxylin and eosin stains demonstrate a leukocytoclastic angiitis. Furthermore, systemic lupus erythematosus patients with these urticarial lesions appear to be acutely ill as well

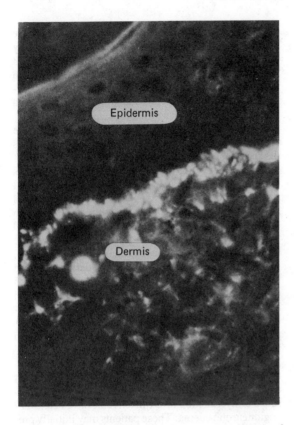

Figure 32–3. Direct immunofluorescence examination of the skin, not exposed to light, of a patient with systemic lupus erythematosus and severe nephritis. Note heavy granular deposition of IgM.

as chronically ill. They frequently manifest overt renal disease and demonstrate anti-DNA and anti-Sm antibodies, hypocomplementemia, and markedly elevated concentrations of immune complexes in their serum.

A good deal of evidence has accumulated demonstrating prominent photosensitive cutaneous lupus lesions in significant numbers of lupus patients who possess serum antibodies directed against the cytoplasmic RNA macromolecule termed Ro(SSA). These patients often fail to demonstrate a significant antinuclear antibody titer when mouse liver is employed as the antinuclear antibody substrate. Despite this failure to demonstrate a significant antinuclear antibody titer, these patients frequently have systemic manifestations, and about 50% satisfy the American Rheumatism Association's preliminary criteria for the diagnosis of systemic lupus erythematosus. Approximately half of these patients possess large annular or psoriasiform lupus lesions to which Sontheimer et al have applied the term subacute cutaneous lupus erythematosus. Other lupus patients with this anticytoplasmic antibody demonstrate classic discoid lesions (coin-shaped, scarring) and widespread photosensitive malar dermatitis. Most systemic lupus patients possessing anti-Ro(SSA) antibodies and subacute cutane-

ous lupus erythematosus patients have a statistically significant increased prevalence of the HLA-DR3 phenotype.

Infants (and mothers of infants) with the rare neonatal lupus syndrome, characterized by cutaneous lupus lesions, organomegaly, and cardiac conduction defects, possess the La(SSB) or Ro(SSA) antibody system (or both). Thus far, 13 of 13 mothers and infants with the neonatal lupus syndrome have been shown to possess these serologic features.

Approximately 75% of C2-deficient lupus patients possess the Ro(SSA) antibody system. In several of these C2-deficient lupus patients, the Ro(SSA) antibody system was the only serologic abnormality detected.

These studies indicate that systemic lupus erythematosus patients make antibodies directed against a variety of nuclear and cytoplasmic antigens. Most lupus patients make predominantly antinuclear antibodies. Approximately 25% of systemic lupus erythematosus patients make both antinuclear and anticytoplasmic antibodies. About 5–10% of classic systemic lupus erythematosus patients make predominantly cytoplasmic antibodies. These latter patients make little (if any) antinuclear antibodies as detected by routine testing. There is a large group of predominantly dermatologic patients previously diagnosed as having discoid lupus (because they failed to demonstrate a significant antinuclear antibody titer) who develop significant systemic features of lupus—including renal disease—who possess anti-Ro(SSA) antibodies.

These studies have provided evidence for the serologic relationship between classic systemic lupus erythematosus and the more atypical, predominantly cutaneous lupus erythematosus patients. Preliminary studies indicate that about 25% of the random sera of patients with chronic coin-shaped (discoid) lesions possess anti–single-stranded DNA antibodies. Approximately 90% of systemic lupus erythematosus patients possess these antibodies. This additional study demonstrates again a serologic link between patients with typical dermatologic discoid lupus and the classic systemic lupus erythematosus.

CUTANEOUS MANIFESTATIONS
OF COMPLEMENT DEFICIENCIES
(See also Chapter 11.)

In recent years, individual deficiencies have been described for all of the 9 complement components. The isolated complement deficiencies are associated with a high incidence of associated cutaneous disease (Table 32–2). Absence of C1r, C1s, C2, C4, and C5 has been associated with the presence of cutaneous (discoid) as well as systemic lupus erythematosus. C2 deficiency, the most common inherited complement deficiency, has been found in normal individuals as well as in patients suffering from lupus erythematosus, anaphylactoid purpura, and dermatomyositis. C2 defi-

Table 32—2. Inherited and acquired deficiencies of the human complement system.

Component	Systemic Disease	Cutaneous Manifestations
C1q	Bacterial infections	?
C1r	LE-like glomerulonephritis	DLE-like lesions
C1s	SLE (not described), ANA positive	?
C4	LE-like syndrome, ANA positive	LE lesions
C2	SLE, glomerulonephritis, vasculitis, dermatomyositis. May be normal.	"Butterfly" rash, heliotrope, anaphylactoid purpura
C3	Recurrent pyogenic infections.	Pyoderma
C5	SLE. May be normal.	?
C6	Disseminated gonococcal disease	Gonococcal cutaneous and arthritis syndromes
C7	Scleroderma. May be normal.	Scleroderma changes
C8	Disseminated gonococcal disease	Xeroderma pigmentosa
C9	None	None
C1s inhibitor (C1 INH)	Hereditary angioneurotic edema, SLE, glomerulonephritis	"Butterfly" rash, DLE lesions, angioedema
C3b inactivator (type 1 hypercatabolism of C3)	Recurrent pyogenic infections	Pyoderma
Properdin	None	None
Acquired C1 INH deficiency	Angioedema, paraproteinemias, lymphoproliferative disorders	Angioedema, diffuse plane xanthomatosis
C3 hypercatabolism (type II hypercatabolism)	Recurrent pyogenic infections, nephritis	Partial lipodystrophy
C5 dysfunction	Failure to thrive, recurrent gram-negative infections	Leiner's syndrome
Opsonic defect in sickle cell disease	Pneumococcal meningitis, osteomyelitis	None

LE = lupus erythematosus; SLE = systemic lupus erythematosus; DLE = discoid lupus erythematosus.

ciency has been associated with an HLA haplotype consisting of A10 and B18.

Isolated deficiencies of the late complement sequence, ie, C3–C9, may also have prominent cutaneous features. A partial lipodystrophy has been described with low C3 concentrations (type II hypercatabolism). These patients have a C3 cleaving serum enzyme which is probably identical to the C3 nephritic factor described in patients with membrano-

proliferative glomerulonephritis. Several patients have now been described who have a partial lipodystrophy and mesangioproliferative glomerulonephritis with C3 nephritic factor in their serum. A single patient with a defect of C7 has been described. This individual appears to have the cutaneous and systemic findings of a mixed connective tissue syndrome.

Isolated deficiencies of properdin and C9 have recently been described. No systemic or cutaneous disease was detected in these patients.

It is interesting to note that a number of patients suffering from isolated deficiencies of various terminal complement components appear to have an increased susceptibility to repeated *Neisseria* infections. Six of 6 patients with a homozygous deficiency of C6, 5 of 10 with C7 deficiency, and 3 of 8 with C8 deficiency have had meningococcal or gonococcal bacteremia. In total, 16 of 30 patients with C6, C7, or C8 deficiency have had disease due to *Neisseria* bacteremia. In addition, 5 of 8 patients with homozygous C5 deficiency have had disease due to meningococcal or gonococcal bacteremia. These studies indicate that patients with repeated *Neisseria* bacteremia are much more likely to have late-acting complement deficiencies.

Defects in the regulatory proteins of the complement system may be associated with prominent cutaneous manifestations. Patients born with an absence or dysfunction of C1 inactivator have hereditary angioneurotic edema. These patients may initially present to the dermatologist with an explosive onset of painless edema of the eyes and lips. Recently, several patients with hereditary angioneurotic edema have also developed systemic lupus erythematosus. At least one of the patients had the classic butterfly rash.

LICHEN MYXEDEMATOSUS
(Papular Mucinosis)

This is a generalized dermal infiltrative process characterized by the presence of large amounts of dermal mucin composed of acid mucopolysaccharides (hyaluronic acid, chondroitin sulfate, and heparin). A fibrotic variant, characterized histologically by fibroblastic proliferation and clinically by firm papules and plaques, is termed scleromyxedema.

This dermal infiltrative process is associated with the consistent presence in the serum of a highly basic, electrophoretically slow IgG paraprotein. This unique paraprotein is almost always composed of λ L chains, but these paraproteins do not share idiotypic specificity with each other. The IgG λ paraprotein has a molecular weight of approximately 110,000, and the Fd portion of the γ heavy chain is partially or completely deleted. The exact relationship of the paraprotein to the cutaneous disease is unknown.

•   •   •

References

Allergic Contact Dermatitis

Fisher AA: *Contact Dermatitis*. Lea & Febiger, 1974.

Landsteiner K, Chase MW: Experiments on transfer of cutaneous sensitivity to simple compounds. *Proc Soc Exp Biol Med* 1942;**49**:688.

Macher E, Chase MW: Studies on the sensitization of animals with simple chemical compounds. 11. The fate of labeled picryl chloride and dinitrochlorobenzene after sensitizing infection. 12. The influence of excision of allergenic depots on onset of delayed hypersensitivity and tolerance. (2 parts.) *J Exp Med* 1969;**129**:81, 103.

Sauder DN et al: Induction of tolerance to topically applied TNCB using TNP-conjugated ultraviolet light–irradiated epidermal cells. *J Immunol* 1981;**127**:261.

Stingl G et al: Analagous functions of macrophages and Langerhans cells in the initiation of the immune response. *J Invest Dermatol* 1978;**71**:59.

Toews GB, Bergstresser PR, Streilein JW: Epidermal Langerhans cells density determines whether contact hypersensitivity or unresponsiveness follows skin painting with DNFB. *J Immunol* 1980;**124**:445.

Photoallergic Contact Dermatitis

Giovinazzo VJ et al: Photoallergic contact dermatitis to musk ambrette. *Arch Dermatol* 1981;**117**:344.

Willis I, Kligman AM: The mechanism of the persistent light reactor. *J Invest Dermatol* 1968;**51**:385.

Willis I, Kligman AM: The mechanism of photoallergic contact dermatitis. *J Invest Dermatol* 1968;**51**:378.

Dermatophytosis

Hanifin JM, Ray LF, Lobitz WC Jr: Immunological reactivity in dermatophytosis. *Br J Dermatol* 1974;**90**:1.

Jones HE, Reinhardt JH, Renaldi MG: Acquired immunity to dermatophytes. *Arch Dermatol* 1974;**109**:840.

Koranda FC et al: Cutaneous complications in immunosuppressed renal homograft recipients. *JAMA* 1974;**229**:419.

Mucocutaneous Candidiasis

Kirkpatrick CH, Rich RR, Bennett JE: Chronic mucocutaneous candidiasis: Model-building in cellular immunity. *Ann Intern Med* 1971;**74**:955.

Levy RL et al: Thymic transplantation in a case of chronic mucocutaneous candidiasis. *Lancet* 1971;**2**:898.

Patterson PY et al: Mucocutaneous candidiasis, anergy and a plasma inhibitor of cellular immunity: Reversal after amphotericin B therapy. *Clin Exp Immunol* 1971;**9**:595.

Snyderman R et al: Defective mononuclear leukocyte chemotaxis: A previously unrecognized immune dysfunction. Studies in a patient with chronic mucocutaneous candidiasis. *Ann Intern Med* 1973;**78**:509.

Toxic Epidermal Necrolysis

Wuepper KD, Dimond RL, Knutson DD: Studies of the mechanism of epidermal injury by a staphylococcic epidermolytic toxin. *J Invest Dermatol* 1975;**65**:191.

Pemphigus Vulgaris

Diaz LA et al: Isolation of pemphigus antigen from human saliva. *J Immunol* 1980;**124**:760.

Farb RM, Dykes R, Lazarus GS: Antiepidermal cell surface pemphigus antibody detaches viable epidermal cells from culture plates by activation of proteinase. *Proc Natl Acad Sci USA* 1978;**75**:459.

Jordon RE et al: Classical and alternate pathway activation of complement in pemphigus vulgaris lesions. *J Invest Dermatol* 1974;**63**:256.

Jordon RE et al: Complement activation in pemphigus vulgaris blister fluid. *Clin Exp Immunol* 1973;**15**:53.

O'Loughlin S, Goldman GC, Provost TT: Pemphigus: Fate of antibody following successful therapy. *Arch Dermatol* 1978;**114**:1769.

Parks MS et al: HLA-DRw4 in 91% of Jewish pemphigus vulgaris patients. *Lancet* 1979;**2**:441.

Pennys NS, Eagelstein WH, Frost P: Management of pemphigus with gold compounds: A long term follow-up report. *Arch Dermatol* 1976;**112**:185.

Schiltz JR, Michel B: Production of epidermal acantholysis in normal human skin in vitro by the IgG fraction from pemphigus serum. *J Invest Dermatol* 1976;**67**:254.

Bullous Pemphigoid

Ahmed AR, Maize J, Provost TT: Bullous pemphigoid: Clinical and immunologic follow-up after successful therapy. *Arch Dermatol* 1977;**113**:1043.

Diaz-Perez JL, Jordon RE: The complement system in bullous pemphigoid. 4. Chemotactic activity in blister fluid. *Clin Immunol Immunopathol* 1976;**5**:360.

Gammon WR et al: Pemphigoid antibody mediated attachment of peripheral blood leukocytes at the dermal epidermal junction of human skin. *J Invest Dermatol* 1980;**76**:334.

Holubar K et al: Ultrastructural localization of immunoglobulins in bullous pemphigoid skin. *J Invest Dermatol* 1975; **64**:220.

Lawley TJ et al: Small intestinal biopsies and HLA types in dermatitis herpetiformis patients with granular and linear IgA skin deposits. *J Invest Dermatol* 1979;**72**:200.

Prystowsky S, Gilliam JN: Benign chronic bullous dermatosis of childhood: Linear IgA and C3 deposition on the basement membrane. *Arch Dermatol* 1976;**112**:837.

Benign Mucous Membrane Pemphigoid

Bean SF et al: Cicatricial pemphigoid: Immunofluorescent studies. *Arch Dermatol* 1972;**106**:195.

Rogers RS III, Jordon RE, Bean SF: Immunopathology of cicatricial pemphigoid: Studies of complement deposition. *J Invest Dermatol* 1977;**68**:39.

Herpes Gestationis

Jordon RE et al: The immunopathology of herpes gestationis: Immunofluorescence studies and characterization of "HG factor." *J Clin Invest* 1976;**57**:1426.

Katz SI, Hertz KC, Yaoita H: Herpes gestationis: Immunopathology and characterization of HG factor. *J Clin Invest* 1976;**57**:1434.

Dermatitis Herpetiformis

Hall RP et al: IgA containing circulating immune complexes in dermatitis herpetiformis, Henoch-Schönlein purpura, systemic lupus erythematosus and other diseases. *Clin Exp Immunol* 1980;**40**:431.

Katz SI, Strober W: The pathogenesis of dermatitis herpetiformis. *J Invest Dermatol* 1978;**70**:63.

Zone JJ, LaSalle BA, Provost TT: Characterization of IgA immune complexes in patients with dermatitis herpetiformis. *Clin Res* 1980;**28**:586A.

Zone JJ, LaSalle BA, Provost TT: Circulating immune complexes of IgA type in dermatitis herpetiformis. *J Invest*

Dermatol 1980;**75**:152.

Zone JJ, LaSalle BA, Provost TT: Induction of IgA immune complexes in dermatitis herpetiformis by wheat ingestion. *J Invest Dermatol.* [In press.]

Erythema Multiforme

Kazmierowski JA, Wuepper KD: Erythema multiforme: Immune complex vasculitis of the superficial cutaneous microvasculature. *J Invest Dermatol* 1978;**71**:366.

Safai E, Good RA, Day NK: Erythema multiforme: Report of two cases and speculation on immune mechanisms involved in the pathogenesis. *Clin Immunol Immunopathol* 1977;**7**:379.

Epidermolysis Bullosa Acquisita

Yaoita H et al: Epidermolysis bullosa acquisita: Ultrastructural and immunological studies. *J Invest Dermatol* 1981; **76**:288.

Vasculitides

Alexander EL et al: The Ro(SSA) and La(SSB) antibody systems in Sjögren's syndrome. *J Rheumatol.* [In press.]

Braverman IM, Yen A: Demonstration of immune complexes in spontaneous and histamine-induced lesions and in normal skin of patients with leukocytoclastic angiitis. *J Invest Dermatol* 1975;**64**:105.

Gocke DJ et al: Vasculitis in association with Australia antigen. *J Exp Med* 1971;**134 (Suppl)**:330S.

Levo Y et al: Association between hepatitis B virus and essential mixed cryoglobulinemia. *N Engl J Med* 1977; **296**:1501.

McDuffie FC et al: Hypocomplementemia with cutaneous vasculitis and arthritis: Possible immune complex syndrome. *Mayo Clin Proc* 1973;**40**:340.

Schroeter AL et al: Immunofluorescence of cutaneous vasculitis associated with systemic disease. *Arch Dermatol* 1971;**104**:254.

Soter NA, Austen KF, Gigli I: Urticaria and arthralgias as manifestations of necrotizing angiitis (vasculitis). *J Invest Dermatol* 1974;**63**:485.

Lupus Erythematosus

Cripps DJ, Rankin J: Action spectra of lupus erythematosus and experimental immunofluorescence. *Arch Dermatol* 1973;**107**:563.

Franco HL et al: Autoantibodies directed against sicca syndrome antigens in neonatal lupus. *J Am Acad Dermatol* 1981;**4**:67.

Gilliam JN et al: Immunoglobulin in clinically uninvolved skin in systemic lupus erythematosus: Association with renal disease. *J Clin Invest* 1974;**53**:1434.

Kephart DC, Hood AF, Provost TT: Neonatal lupus erythematosus: New serologic findings. *J Invest Dermatol* 1981;**77**:331.

Landry M, Sams WM Jr: Systemic lupus erythematosus: Studies of the antibodies bound to skin. *J Clin Invest* 1973; **52**:1871.

Maddison PJ, Provost TT, Reichlin M: Serologic findings in patients with "ANA negative" systemic lupus erythematosus. *Medicine* 1981;**60**:87.

Provost TT et al: Lupus band test in untreated SLE patients: Correlation of immunoglobulin deposition in the skin of the extensor forearm with clinical renal disease and serologic abnormalities. *J Invest Dermatol* 1980;**74**:407.

Provost TT et al: Urticaria-like lesions in SLE. 1. Correlation with clinical and serological abnormalities. *J Invest Dermatol* 1980;**75**:495.

Sontheimer RD, Thomas JR, Gilliam JN: Subacute cutaneous lupus erythematosus: A cutaneous marker for a distinct lupus erythematosus subset. *Arch Dermatol* 1979; **115**:1409.

Tan EM, Kunkel HG: An immunofluorescent study of the skin lesions in systemic lupus erythematosus. *Arthritis Rheum* 1966;**9**:37.

Complement Deficiencies

Agnello V, DeBraco MME, Kunkel HG: Hereditary C2 deficiency with some manifestations of systemic lupus erythematosus. *J Immunol* 1972;**108**:837.

Alper CA, Block KJ, Rosen FS: Increased susceptibility to infection in a patient with type II essential hypercatabolism of C3. *N Engl J Med* 1973;**288**:601.

Fu SM et al: Evidence for linkage between HL-A histocompatibility genes and those involved in synthesis of second component of complement. *J Exp Med* 1974;**140**:1108.

Gelfand EW, Clarkson JE, Minta JO: Selective deficiency of the second component of complement in a patient with anaphylactoid purpura. *Clin Immunol Immunopathol* 1975; **4**:269.

Sissons JGP et al: Complement abnormalities of lipodystrophy. *N Engl J Med* 1976;**294**:461.

Lichen Myxedematosus

James K et al: Studies on a unique diagnostic serum globulin in papular mucinosis (lichen myxedematosus). *Clin Exp Immunol* 1967;**2**:153.

Wells JV, Fudenberg HH, Epstein WL: Idiotypic determinants on the monoclonal immunoglobulins associated with papular mucinosis. *J Immunol* 1972;**108**:977.

Infectious Diseases | 33

David J. Drutz, MD, & John Richard Graybill, MD

Infectious diseases are associated so intimately with the functions of the immune system that it is possible to classify every human infection on the basis of local/systemic, specific/nonspecific, and cellular/humoral immune mechanisms. In essence, any infectious disease implies that the immune defense system has been successfully breached. It was the search for knowledge about protection against infection that yielded much of the basic information underlying the science of immunology today.

In this chapter, representative infectious diseases have been separated into categories based upon broad patterns of interaction between pathogenic microorganisms and the components of the immune system (Table 33–1). Such a classification is by nature arbitrary; clearly, such categories are not mutually exclusive. However, we hope this approach will emphasize some of the common immunologic features of diverse infective processes. Such an approach is not intended to serve as a substitute for the traditional study of specific pathogens and clinical syndromes.

EXTRACELLULAR INFECTIONS IN WHICH OPSONINS & POLYMORPHONUCLEAR NEUTROPHILS ARE DECISIVE IN RECOVERY

Major Immunologic Features

- Microorganisms possess antiphagocytic surface factors.
- Serum opsonins promote phagocytosis.
- Phagocytosis by polymorphonuclear neutrophils (PMNs) is followed by microbial death.
- Infection may progress because of qualitative or quantitative defects of opsonins or PMNs.
- Lymphocytes and macrophages apparently play no decisive role.

General Considerations

Many microorganisms are characterized by the presence of surface factors that retard phagocytosis. Since their presence in tissues stimulates an outpouring of PMNs, they are known as **pyogenic microorganisms.** Because they are highly susceptible to being killed by PMNs, they rely upon evasion of phagocytosis for their survival. Thus, they are also known as **extracellular pathogens.** Opsonins are humoral factors that promote phagocytosis and are needed to overcome antiphagocytic surface factors so that PMNs can ingest these microorganisms. Examples of microorganisms that must evade phagocytosis in order to survive (and the nature of the antiphagocytic surface factors) include *Streptococcus pneumoniae, Neisseria meningitidis, Haemophilus influenzae, Klebsiella pneumoniae, Escherichia coli, Bacteroides fragilis,* and *Pseudomonas aeruginosa*—especially cystic fibrosis strains (capsular polysaccharide); *Streptococcus pyogenes* (hyaluronic acid and M protein); *Staphylococcus aureus* (protein A); *Neisseria gonorrhoeae* (pili composed of protein); *Yersinia pestis* (F1 and VW antigens); and *Bacillus anthracis* (capsular polypeptide).

1. *STREPTOCOCCUS PNEUMONIAE* INFECTION

Streptococcus pneumoniae (pneumococcus) is a gram-positive, lancet-shaped diplococcus that is found normally in the pharynx in 40–70% of adults. Infection is uncommon in comparison with the organism's frequent presence, generally occurring when there is a breach of host defenses such as aspiration, inhalation of irritants, viral upper respiratory infection, or pulmonary edema. An estimated 420,000 cases of pneumococcal pneumonia occur yearly in the USA, and pneumococci rank second to *Haemophilus influenzae* as a cause of bacterial meningitis.

Pneumococci possess a series of 83 antigenically specific capsular polysaccharides that confer type-specific immunity in mice.

The capsules are composed of large polysaccharides which are hydrophilic gels. The complete structures of only a few capsular types (types 3, 6, and 8) are known. Type 3, for example, has a capsule composed of repeating cellobiuronic acid units joined by $\beta(1\rightarrow3)$ glucosidic bonds. Capsular polysaccharide subserves an antiphagocytic function. The mechanisms of host defense against encapsulated bacteria are discussed in Chapter 16.

In general, the amount of capsular material is directly proportionate to the degree of virulence. Types 1, 2, 3, 5, 7, and 8 are all considered highly virulent. Type 3 pneumococci generally have the largest capsules and are the most difficult to phagocytose; infections with these microorganisms are associated with a poor prognosis. Type 3 pneumococci

Table 33–1. Infectious diseases classified by mechanisms of immunity, associated diseases, or causative agents.

Extracellular infections in which opsonins and PMNs are decisive in recovery: Infection due to—
  Streptococcus pneumoniae
  Streptococci of groups A and B
  Staphylococcus aureus
  Haemophilus influenzae
  Neisseria meningitidis
  Neisseria gonorrhoeae
  Enteric gram-negative rods
  Yersinia pestis (plague)
  Bacillus anthracis (anthrax)
Infections in which antibody may be decisive in prevention or in recovery through a mechanism other than opsonization: Diseases in which antibody—
  Neutralizes exotoxins
  Blocks epithelial attachment
  Participates in complement-mediated bacteriolysis
  Neutralizes viruses
Infections in which humoral and cell-mediated immunity collaborate in host defense:
  Syphilis
  Cryptococcosis
  Candidiasis
  Salmonellosis
  Listeriosis
Intracellular infections in which lymphocytes and macrophages are decisive in recovery and humoral mechanisms play no protective role:
  Measurement of antibody not useful in diagnosis and prognosis
  Tuberculosis
  Leprosy
  Measurement of antibody useful in diagnosis and prognosis
  Histoplasmosis
  Coccidioidomycosis
  Brucellosis
  Tularemia
Infections characterized by unique host-parasite relationships:
  Mycoplasma pneumoniae infection
  Bordetella pertussis infection
  Chlamydial infection
  Rickettsial infection
Infections complicated by deposition of circulating immune complexes:
  Infective endocarditis
  Viral hepatitis
  Poststreptococcal glomerulonephritis
  Quartan malaria
  Syphilis
  Typhoid fever
  Leprosy
The spectrum of host-virus immunologic relationships:
  Viral diseases (acute, chronic, latent, slow)
Opportunistic infections: Infections associated with—
  Hypogammaglobulinemia
  Granulocytopenia
  Depressed cellular immunity
  Hemolytic anemia
  Splenectomy
  Foreign bodies
  Gastrectomy

---

may result in pulmonary abscesses, which are extremely rare in infection with other types. There is some evidence that type 14 pneumococci share antigenic determinants with blood group substances. Such infections would theoretically be harder to control, since the host might have difficulty discerning "nonself" from "self."

Pneumococcal polysaccharide dissociates from the surface of microorganisms and may be detectable in the tissues, blood, and urine for some time after recovery from pneumococcal infection. There is evidence that this material may be endocytosed and later extruded from macrophages. A high level of pneumococcal polysaccharide antigenemia is associated with a less favorable prognosis for recovery from pneumococcal pneumonia.

Aside from the capsular antigens of pneumococci, other immunogenic constituents of the microorganisms (C substance, M protein, etc) do not appear to play an important role in virulence or host response. However, C substance, a polysaccharide antigen probably equivalent to the group-specific C substances of *Streptococcus pyogenes,* does have the peculiar ability to precipitate a β-globulin (C-reactive protein) found in the sera of patients with diverse inflammatory diseases. C-reactive protein binds and promotes the phagocytosis of a variety of bacteria by human PMNs. Among these are *S pneumoniae, S aureus,* and *E coli.* In addition, C-reactive protein protects mice against otherwise fatal infection with *S pneumoniae.*

Clinical Features

Pneumococcal pneumonia begins classically with a single hard shaking chill, pleuritic chest pain, and cough productive of bloody (rusty) sputum. Bacteremia is a regular early feature of infection, generally occurring in close temporal relationship to the chill. The bacteremia may be self-limited or may result in metastatic infection of heart valves, meninges, or joints. Patients with ascites due to cirrhosis or the nephrotic syndrome seem particularly prone to pneumococcal peritonitis, often in the absence of any obvious respiratory infection. Prior to the advent of antimicrobial therapy, about two-thirds of patients with pneumococcal pneumonia would spontaneously recover by "crisis," the change in clinical course reflecting the synthesis of specific anticapsular antibody and the resultant enhancement of the phagocytic process after several days of acute illness.

Immunologic Diagnosis

Individual capsular types of pneumococci can be identified by the quellung phenomenon (*Quellung,* swelling). In the presence of type-specific antiserum, polysaccharide capsules undergo refractive changes and swelling that can be detected by light microscopy, especially if the preparation is examined in the presence of India ink. In the era preceding the use of antimicrobial agents, precise identification of capsular type was very important; antisera used in treatment were often selected on the basis of the capsular type of the infecting strain. The capsular types most often associated with infection may vary from time to time and from community to community. Effective therapy with penicillin and other antibiotics has done away with the need for identifying individual capsular types except for epidemiologic purposes.

Some investigators employ a polyvalent omniserum to assist in rapid identification of pneumococci in clinical specimens. This reagent consists of a mixture of antisera to capsules of the common pneumococcal types.

The presence of antibody to a given pneumococcal capsular type can be detected by the Francis skin test. Here, capsular polysaccharide injected into the skin produces a wheal and flare response if antibody is present. This test is rarely if ever employed today; antibody is detected by more sophisticated techniques such as radioimmunoassay.

Pneumococcal capsular polysaccharide antigen can be detected in blood and other body fluids by counterelectrophoresis or radioimmunoassay techniques. Although blood cultures are generally positive when pneumococcal polysaccharide is detectable in the blood, the advantage of immunologic detection of this antigen is the rapidity with which diagnosis may be established (around 30 minutes) so that definitive treatment can be started. A full day may be required before blood cultures show evidence of growth (see Chapter 22).

Differential Diagnosis

Pneumococcal infection must be differentiated from other bacterial and viral pneumonias, from fungal and mycobacterial infections, and from noninfective processes such as pulmonary embolization. The diagnosis is established by isolation and cultivation of the infecting pathogen.

Prevention

Persons 50 years of age and older, patients with underlying immune defects (splenectomy; sickle cell anemia), and those with debilitating illnesses may be unusually susceptible to pneumococcal infection. These persons can be protected by active immunization with specific capsular types of pneumococci. Type-specific antibody to purified pneumococcal polysaccharide readily promotes phagocytosis of encapsulated pneumococci.

A 14-valent polysaccharide vaccine is currently used in the USA. Each dose of the vaccine contains 50 μg of polysaccharide from types 1, 2, 3, 4, 6, 8, 9, 12, 14, 19, 23, 25, 51, and 56 pneumococci—these account for at least 80% of the pneumococcal bacteremic disease seen in this country. Nasopharyngeal acquisition of pneumococcal types included in the vaccine appears to be reduced by vaccination. The duration of protection is as yet unknown, but elevated antibody levels persist at least 2 years following immunization.

Antibody responses to pneumococcal vaccine in infants and very young children are not as reliable as in older persons. Types 6, 9, 14, 19, and 23 seem to be particularly poor immunogens in children below the age of 2 years.

Because the capsular polysaccharides of certain strains of *Klebsiella pneumoniae* and *S pneumoniae* are quite similar, polyvalent pneumococcal vaccine may provide a minor degree of cross-protection against *Klebsiella* infections.

Treatment

Penicillin is the drug of choice in the treatment of pneumococcal pneumonia and its local and hematogenous complications. Recent reports of pneumococcal resistance to penicillin may make the issue of pneumococcal vaccination a more urgent one in the future.

Complications & Prognosis

A small percentage of patients with bacteremic pneumococcal pneumonia die regardless of the rapidity with which a diagnosis is established and specific bactericidal antibiotic therapy is begun. The factors responsible for this presently "irreducible minimum" of deaths are uncertain, but it is this group that might be most benefited by prior pneumococcal vaccination. The mortality rate is higher in patients at the extremes of age; in alcoholics; in those with multilobar pulmonary involvement, meningitis, or endocarditis; in those infected with type 3 pneumococci; in those with profound leukocytopenia; and in patients who have been previously splenectomized. Splenectomy often portends a fulminating clinical course, with death in less than a day. There may be associated disseminated intravascular coagulation.

2. STREPTOCOCCI OF GROUPS A & B

The genus *Streptococcus* comprises a heterogeneous group of microorganisms with a broad range of animal hosts. They can be divided into a number of immunologically specific groups (A–O) based upon the presence of group-specific carbohydrate antigens in their cell walls. The group-specific carbohydrate of group A streptococci is N-acetylglucosamine. The most common etiologic agents of streptococcal infection in humans are from groups A, B, and D.

Group A Streptococcal Disease

Group A streptococci (with *S pyogenes* as the prototype species) are the commonest streptococcal pathogens of humans, accounting for more (and more clinically distinct) disease than groups B and D. Group A strains produce complete (beta) hemolysis when streaked on sheep blood agar. Group B and D strains are usually nonhemolytic but may produce beta or alpha (incomplete, or "green") hemolysis.

Disease caused by *S pyogenes* may be suppurative (respiratory disease, impetigo, etc), toxigenic (scarlet fever; see Table 33–2), or nonsuppurative (acute rheumatic fever, acute glomerulonephritis; see Chapters 30 and 31).

Group A streptococci can be divided into 60 or more immunologic types based upon the presence of specific M proteins in the cell wall. Immunity to group A streptococci is type-specific; thus, several streptococcal infections can occur in the same person. Two other protein antigens (T and R) are not directly related to virulence but provide an important additional serologic scheme for subclassifying group A strains.

Group A streptococci possess 2 antiphagocytic surface components: **hyaluronic acid** (which is not immunogenic, presumably because of its close structural relationship to the ground substance of human connective tissue) and **M protein.** The M protein is a readily accessible surface antigen, not blocked by the hyaluronic acid envelope of encapsulated strains, and is displayed as surface fimbriae. M proteins are necessary for virulence; non–M-typable group A strains are avirulent and are phagocytosed and killed in the absence of type-specific antibody. Although M protein was once considered the structure that mediated streptococcal attachment to epithelial surfaces, it is now known that this function is subserved by lipoteichoic acid (repeating units of polyglycerophosphate attached to lipids).

Group A streptococcal strains produce at least 20 distinct antigens, many of which have strong clinical diagnostic relevance. Streptolysins are responsible for the beta hemolysis observed in sheep blood agar. Streptolysin S (oxygen-stable) produces surface hemolysis by a nonenzymatic surface-active mechanism. Streptolysin O (oxygen-labile) produces subsurface hemolysis by altering membrane sterols of the red blood cells. Except for streptolysin S, all known extracellular products of group A streptococci are antigenic. Antibodies directed against one or more of these antigens are useful markers of recent streptococcal infections but are not protective.

The most commonly measured antibody has been antistreptolysin O. Three weeks after streptococcal pharyngitis, 80% of children will have a 4-fold increase in titer. In contrast, patients with impetigo, even when this is associated with acute glomerulonephritis, will have a feeble or absent antistreptolysin O response. This finding is not due to absence of streptolysin O production. Instead, skin cholesterol binds streptolysin O and appears to prevent the enzyme from serving as an effective antigen.

The "streptozyme" test was devised to measure antibodies to streptolysin O, deoxyribonuclease B, hyaluronidase, nicotinamide deaminase, streptokinase, and other unspecified antigens with a single reagent: sheep erythrocytes coated with streptococcal "extracellular products." The current lack of standardization between different lots of the streptozyme reagent may limit the comparability of results of tests at different times and in different laboratories. In some cases (children under age 2 years; patients with acute glomerulonephritis), the streptozyme test may be insufficiently accurate; individual enzyme assays may have to be performed.

Antibodies to group A carbohydrate appear at about the same time as the antistreptolysin O and anti–DNase B titers but are less sensitive indicators of infection. The M proteins are poor antigens in humans; type-specific antibodies may not be detectable until 30–60 days after onset of infection. Their presence correlates positively with the duration of the convalescent carrier state. However, type-specific protective antibodies may persist in serum for many years, and a small booster dose of homologous M antigen may produce a rapid increase in antibody titer.

Notwithstanding the rich immunologic potential of this microorganism, it is possible that none of the diverse sequelae of streptococcal infection would be encountered if prompt phagocytosis and killing were to take place. Previous attempts to develop M protein vaccines have been thwarted by the occurrence of local inflammatory reactions and even acute rheumatic fever. Recent studies with a highly purified polypeptide vaccine prepared from streptococcal M24 protein show promise that previous problems with M protein vaccines may now be overcome.

Group B Streptococcal Disease

Within the past decade, *S agalactiae* (the group B streptococcus) has been identified as a major cause of infection in the newborn. Common manifestations of illness include bacteremia, meningitis, and pneumonia. The pneumonia is more common in newborns than in infants over 10 days of age.

The principal human reservoir of group B streptococci is the female genital tract. Infants may become infected during birth or as a result of nosocomial spread in the nursery.

Human isolates of group B streptococci can be divided into 5 capsular serotypes (Ia, Ib, Ic, II, and III). Type III accounts for 60% of all group B streptococcal infections in neonates and infants. These organisms can be killed by PMNs in the presence of complement and anticapsular antibody, whereas the classic complement pathway in the absence of antibody suffices for the phagocytosis of type Ia.

Recent studies suggest that infants who develop type III meningitis are those whose mothers lack antibody to this microorganism. Thus, immunization of adult women should be an effective means of preventing infant disease by transplacental passage of antibody. Preliminary studies indicate that a safe and immunogenic type III capsular polysaccharide vaccine can be developed.

Group D Streptococcal Disease

Group D streptococci (particularly enterococci) are encountered most frequently as causes of urinary tract infection or endocarditis in humans. There are currently no useful immunodiagnostic or immunopreventive measures relative to these illnesses.

3. *STAPHYLOCOCCUS AUREUS* INFECTION

Staphylococcus aureus is a gram-positive coccal microorganism that grows in grapelike clusters. Our knowledge of the immunopathology of this common microorganism is incomplete.

There is probably no other human pathogen that produces as many candidate virulence factors ("aggressins") as *S aureus*. Among the best-characterized are alpha toxin (one of 4 known hemolysins), coagulase, lipase, leukocidin, enterotoxin, exfoliatin, and protein A. The toxic moieties responsible for toxic shock syndrome are still unknown. Coagulase production and virulence are so closely (although probably coincidentally) linked that coagulase positivity is often considered to be synonymous with staphylococcal virulence. Enterotoxin and exfoliatin will be considered elsewhere in this chapter.

The cell walls of most *S aureus* strains are composed of teichoic acids (40% of cell wall weight), peptidoglycan (50%), and protein A (5%). Teichoic acids are charged polymers of ribitol phosphate linked to muramic acid residues of the peptidoglycan. They may serve as attachment ligands, allowing *S aureus* to adhere to mucosal receptor sites. The peptidoglycan component is a linear polymer composed of repeating β-1,4- linked N-acetylglucosamine and N-acetylmuramic acid. Recent studies suggest that peptidoglycan is the key cell wall component involved in staphylococcal opsonization and that it not only binds to IgG but is capable of activating both the classic and alternative complement pathways. Protein A is distributed evenly on the outermost layer of the cell wall of most *S aureus* strains. Protein A has the unique ability to bind to the Fc portion of IgG1, IgG2, and IgG4, leading to the production of "pseudoimmune complexes"; this phenomenon provides a powerful tool with which to investigate the biologic mechanisms of antigen-antibody reactions. Protein A can also bind to the Fc receptors on PMNs, thereby interfering with opsonization and phagocytosis.

Although some special staphylococcal strains will demonstrate capsule formation under highly defined in vitro conditions, staphylococci are not generally considered to possess antiphagocytic capsules.

Staphylococcal infection is highly destructive and produces prominent abscess formation. Most staphylococci appear to be killed once they are ingested by PMNs, although a few may survive under experimental conditions. Whether escape from PMN bactericidal activity is an important virulence mechanism in staphylococcal disease is presently uncertain. There is evidence that cell-mediated immunity may play a role in host defense against staphylococcal infection, although granuloma formation is distinctly unusual in this disease.

The detection of teichoic acid antibodies in the blood may occasionally be useful in estimating the duration and degree of antigenemia in patients with *S aureus* infection. Staphylococcal antigen has also been detected directly in the blood, pleural fluid, pericardial fluid, and cerebrospinal fluid by radioimmunoassay and counterimmunoelectrophoresis. Its detection is sufficiently infrequent that it has been suspected of being complexed with previously existing antistaphylococcal antibody. Detection of staphylococcal antigen currently serves no useful diagnostic purpose.

4. *HAEMOPHILUS INFLUENZAE* INFECTION

Haemophilus influenzae is a small pleomorphic gram-negative rod with fastidious growth requirements. Six types of *H influenzae* (a–f) have been identified on the basis of capsular polysaccharides. Invasive infection with *H influenzae* (meningitis, arthritis, cellulitis, epiglottitis) is virtually always due to type b strains. However, otitis media generally results from nontypable strains.

H influenzae is the most common cause of bacterial meningitis in the first few years of life and is responsible for many deaths as well as mental retardation. It is also extremely important as a cause of otitis media and epiglottitis. Until recently, *H influenzae* was considered predominantly a pathogen of children. Protective antibody acquired as a result of experience with this microorganism in childhood appeared to prevent infections later in life. However, it is now apparent that the common use of antibiotics in childhood infections may attenuate development of protective antibody titers. Thus, more frequent episodes of *H influenzae* pneumonia, bacteremia, and even meningitis are being encountered in adults.

The nasopharynx is considered to be the principal site for carriage and dissemination of *H influenzae* strains. Most strains are nontypable, but up to 38% of children have had nasopharyngeal carriage experience with type b strains by 5 years of age.

The capsular polysaccharides of *H influenzae* are considered to subserve an antiphagocytic function. The specific carbohydrates of types a, b, and c are polysugarphosphates; capsular polysaccharide of the clinically important type b strain is composed of polyribophosphate. Individual *H influenzae* types are readily identified with agglutination, precipitation, and quellung tests performed with specific antisera.

There has been much debate about the relative importance of opsonization and phagocytosis versus antibody- and complement-mediated bacteriolysis of *H influenzae* in protection against type b disease. In 1933, Fothergill and Wright noted an inverse relationship between the bactericidal activity of blood for *H influenzae* and susceptibility to meningeal infection. The period of peak susceptibility between 6 months and 3 years of age was considered to represent the gap reflecting loss of transplacental bactericidal antibody on the one hand and acquisition of active immunity on the other. There is now serious question about whether direct bactericidal activity of blood (ie, antibody- and complement-mediated bacteriolysis) plays any real role in protection or whether it is more important as an in vitro indicator of immunity. The preponderance of data suggests that opsonic antibody, directed principally against polyribophosphate of type b strains (and to some extent against somatic antigens), is the principal protective system.

Because not all persons become nasopharyngeal carriers of type b *H influenzae,* it is not clear why hematogenous infection (meningitis, etc) is so rarely encountered beyond 4 or 5 years of age in the absence of an immunizing event. It has been suggested that immunity may take place through colonization of body surfaces with microorganisms possessing cross-reactive surface antigens. For example, certain strains of *Escherichia coli* and *S pneumoniae* stimulate production of antibody which cross-reacts with type b *H influenzae* strains.

Clinical Features

The principal clinical manifestations of *H influenzae* infection in children are meningitis and otitis media. Unencapsulated species are also found in the respiratory secretions of adults with chronic obstructive pulmonary disease and may be responsible for intermittent infective exacerbations of chronic bronchitis or frank pneumonia.

Immunologic Diagnosis

The measurement of antibodies to *H influenzae* is not of practical diagnostic importance. Circulating type b polyribophosphate capsular antigen can be detected by a variety of techniques including counterelectrophoresis and latex particle agglutination. Rapid diagnosis of *H influenzae* meningitis has been made possible by examination of cerebrospinal fluid by counterelectrophoresis.

Differential Diagnosis

H influenzae must be considered in the differential diagnosis of a variety of pyogenic infective processes but may usually be suspected on clinical grounds as a cause of otitis, meningitis, or epiglottitis in children of susceptible age.

Prevention

Despite the availability of potent antibiotics, *H influenzae* meningitis is still an important cause of illness and death in children. There are an estimated 10,000 cases of *H influenzae* meningitis yearly, with 400–500 deaths and 3000–5000 survivors who have residual central nervous system damage. Recent studies have concentrated upon development of a vaccine against type b *H influenzae* based upon immunization with purified polyribophosphate. Adults respond to such a vaccine with long-lived bactericidal and opsonic antibody production. Side-effects are minimal. Unfortunately, children under age 2 years (and especially under age 6 months)—the population at risk—respond poorly to polyribophosphate vaccination in terms of antibody response. *H influenzae* infections are transmissible to close personal contacts,

especially in households or day care centers. Antibiotic prophylaxis with rifampin is currently recommended for close personal contacts (especially children) of patients with documented *H influenzae* infection.

Treatment

The drug of choice for *H influenzae* infection depends upon local patterns of antibiotic resistance. With the increasing frequency of ampicillin resistance among *H influenzae* strains, a variety of other antibiotics are now being used.

5. NEISSERIA MENINGITIDIS INFECTION

Neisseria meningitidis (meningococcus) is a gram-negative diplococcus with fastidious growth requirements. Meningococci possess 8 group-specific capsular polysaccharides with antiphagocytic activity (A, B, C, X, Y, Z, 29E, and 135). These antigens are major determinants of virulence, since nonencapsulated strains are incapable of producing progressive disease. Groups A, B, and C have been the most clinically important of the meningococci to date. Group A antigen consists of N-acetyl-O-acetyl-mannosamine phosphate. The B and C antigens both consist of N-acetylneuraminic acid (sialic acid), which is partially O-acetylated in the C antigen. Meningococci belonging to groups A and C differ from other meningococci in that capsular swelling (quellung phenomenon) can be demonstrated with specific antisera. Groups A and C capsular polysaccharides induce specific IgG or IgM antibody formation, whereas purified group B polysaccharide stimulates a pure IgM response. Because group B polysaccharide is relatively nonimmunogenic, it has been postulated that group B meningococcal neuraminic acid is so similar to that present on host cell membranes that the microorganism is not recognized as foreign. Alternatively, host neuraminidase might break down group B capsular polysaccharide too rapidly to allow potent immunity to develop. Recent studies suggest a strong correlation between the presence of the Km(1) allotype and the immune response to meningococcal group B vaccine.

Meningococci also possess type-specific antigens based upon the composition of their outer membrane proteins. The precise number of serotypes is a function of the method used in their demonstration (10 types by serum bactericidal reaction; 10 by SDS-polyacrylamide gel electrophoresis [SDS-PAGE]; 15 by double immunodiffusion; 18 by solid phase radioimmunoassay). Serotypes are important determinants of virulence, but even ''virulent'' serotypes are capable of producing only nasopharyngeal carriage in the absence of encapsulation. Thus, disease pathogenesis appears to be related to specific combinations of serogroups and serotypes. Serotypes are shared among serogroups and are independent of serogroup. Meningococcal groups B, C, Y, and 135 share several serotype determinants, and over 50% of infections produced by these organisms are attributable to serotype 2 (immunodiffusion method). Serotype 2 is not found among meningococcal groups A, X, Z, or 29E, perhaps because these organisms have in common an absence of sialic acid in their capsules. Group A meningococci contain very few protein serotypes, and the one predominant serotype found is distinct from those in groups B and C meningococci.

Meningococci also possess a lipopolysaccharide-endotoxin complex (8 serotypes) that is thought to play an important role in the fulminating course of acute meningococcemia.

Meningococci are transmitted by airborne droplets. Adherence to nasopharyngeal epithelium appears to be mediated by pili (for encapsulated strains) or by outer membrane proteins (for unencapsulated strains). The antigenicity of meningococcal pili has not been explored in detail.

Meningococcal carriers rapidly develop elevated humoral antibody levels in response to capsular and noncapsular antigens. The antibody produced is both opsonic and bactericidal. Despite the prompt humoral immune response, the antibody produced has no effect on the nasopharyngeal carrier state. This may be partially related to the ability of meningococci to produce IgA protease, an enzyme that cleaves and inactivates the IgA molecule (see Chapter 15).

The factors that lead to benign nasopharyngeal carriage of encapsulated strains for some meningococcal contacts and rapidly progressive infection for the others are uncertain. However, the presence of circulating meningococcal antibody (specifically, antibody that participates with complement in direct meningococcal bacteriolysis in vitro) appears to be an important indicator of protection. Whether actual bacteriolysis occurs in vivo or whether opsonic antibody alone is important in protection under clinical circumstances is uncertain. However, the susceptibility to hematogenous neisserial infections of patients lacking complement components C6, C7, or C8 suggests that direct serum bacteriolysis may indeed play a direct role in protection against meningococcal infection. Antimeningococcal IgA antibody has been shown to block the bactericidal activity of serum for meningococci.

Protective serum antibody may be stimulated in a number of ways: (1) nonencapsulated, nonvirulent meningococcal strains may colonize the nasopharynx and stimulate protection via antibodies to serotype antigens shared with encapsulated strains; (2) colonization by encapsulated strains of low virulence (such as group B serotypes 4 and 6) may elicit anticapsular antibody without producing disease; and (3) some *E coli* and *Bacillus* species possess capsular polysaccharides closely related to those of meningococci and may be responsible for natural immunity to *N meningitidis*.

Factors determining the occurrence of epidemics of meningococcal disease are not fully understood. However, it is clear that overall group-specific carrier rates are not the important determinant. What is important in the prediction of meningococcal outbreaks is information on strain-specific acquisition rates. Identification of strains requires determination of serogroup, serotype, and SDS-PAGE type (the last of these being useful in characterization of otherwise nontypable strains).

Clinical Features

Meningococcal infection arising from the nasopharynx (or possibly from meningococci aspirated into the lungs) may produce a spectrum of clinical manifestations ranging from transient asymptomatic bacteremia to fulminating and rapidly fatal septicemia characterized by disseminated intravascular coagulation or Waterhouse-Friderichsen syndrome. Metastatic infection may involve joints, heart valves, and a wide variety of other loci, but the most common targets are the skin (infective vasculitis) and the meninges.

The meningococcal lipopolysaccharide-endotoxin complex may be responsible for the fulminating nature of meningococcemia and the production of disseminated intravascular coagulation, peripheral vascular collapse, and shock. Meningococci are known to "shed" endotoxin blebs in vitro, and they presumably do the same thing in vivo.

The rash of meningococcemia is typically widespread and purpuric. **Chronic meningococcemia** is a rare manifestation of meningococcal infection characterized by episodes of fever of a few days' duration recurring at daily, weekly, or monthly intervals. Rash is uncommon, but the occurrence of erythema nodosum–like lesions around the joints suggests that this disease may be partially due to the deposition of circulating immune complexes.

Immunologic Diagnosis

The measurement of antibodies to meningococci is not of practical diagnostic importance. However, the measurement of free capsular polysaccharide antigen by counterelectrophoresis and other techniques may have practical significance in rapidly establishing the diagnosis and prognosis of patients with meningococcal disease. In studies of group C meningococcal infection, the presence of meningococcal antigen in serum portended a severe clinical course; pretreatment levels were directly related to the degree of subsequent leukopenia, thrombocytopenia, and hypofibrinogenemia. High level of antigen in the cerebrospinal fluid were associated with prolonged coma and elevated intracranial pressure.

Differential Diagnosis

A variety of pyogenic microorganisms (particularly pneumococci and *H influenzae*) can produce purulent meningitis. Skin rash and the occurrence of disseminated intravascular coagulation are suggestive but not diagnostic of meningococcal infection. The diagnosis is established by isolating *N meningitidis* on appropriate bacteriologic media.

Prevention

Until 10 years ago, the danger of meningococcal spread could be minimized by the simple expedient of treating close personal contacts of patients and carriers with prophylactic sulfonamides. The advent of sulfonamide-resistant meningococci prompted a search for alternative chemoprophylactic agents, none of which have been fully satisfactory. At present, rifampin is the drug of choice for meningococcal prophylaxis.

Three meningococcal vaccines composed of purified meningococcal polysaccharide (monovalent A, monovalent C, and bivalent A and C vaccine) have been released for use. These vaccines are highly effective in preventing meningococcal infection; side-effects are negligible. The vaccines induce protective opsonic and bactericidal antibodies. It has been suggested that vaccination should be considered an adjunct to antibiotic chemoprophylaxis for household contacts of patients with meningococcal disease, since half of the secondary family cases occur more than 5 days after the onset of the primary case; this is considered long enough to yield potential benefit from vaccination in case antibiotic prophylaxis is not successful.

There remain a number of problems with meningococcal vaccines. Of major concern is the apparent lack of immunogenicity of group B polysaccharides and the poor antibody responses of infants and young children to group C polysaccharides.

The nonimmunogenicity of the purified group B polysaccharide has caused a renewed interest in the vaccine potential of major outer membrane proteins of *N meningitidis*, especially serotype 2. Although purified type 2 outer membrane protein is poorly immunogenic when given alone, recent studies involving immunization of a small number of volunteers with a noncovalent complex of meningococcal group B polysaccharide and type 2 outer membrane proteins demonstrate that both components of the complex are immunogenic when presented in this form.

Another approach to vaccination is suggested by the fact that the K1 capsular polysaccharide antigen of *E coli* is practically identical to that of group B meningococci. (More than 80% of neonatal meningitis cases attributable to *E coli* possess the K1 antigen.) Antibody is formed to the K1 antigen in experimental animals.

Treatment

Meningococcal meningitis and other complications of meningococcemia are best treated with penicillin. Because disseminated intravascular coagulation often complicates meningococcemia, anticoagulation with heparin has been suggested as a therapeutic adjunct. This cannot currently be considered of definite benefit.

Complications & Prognosis

Acute meningococcemia carries a high mortality rate, and meningococcal meningitis may be followed by neurologic defects and impaired learning. Speed in establishing the diagnosis and initiating specific therapy is essential. There is virtually no other acute infectious disease that can kill with the rapidity of meningococcemia. The occurrence of meningitis is, paradoxically, a good prognostic sign, since it indicates that the patient has survived the initial bacteremia long enough to develop symptomatic secondary metastatic infection.

The occurrence of bilateral adrenal hemorrhage during acute meningococcemia (as part of the Waterhouse-Friderichsen syndrome) has often prompted the use of corticosteroid therapy on the grounds that death occurs from acute adrenal insufficiency. In fact, direct measurements of adrenal corticosteroids in the blood indicate no such deficiency. Adrenal hemorrhage presumably reflects the general occurrence of vasculitis and disseminated intravascular coagulation.

6. NEISSERIA GONORRHOEAE INFECTION

Neisseria gonorrhoeae (gonococcus) is a gram-negative diplococcus with fastidious growth requirements. Despite considerable knowledge concerning gonococcal pili, principal outer membrane protein, and lipopolysaccharide, there exists no acceptable immunologic typing scheme for the gonococcus. Gonococcal capsules have recently been demonstrated, but the significance of this discovery for classification purposes remains unclear. Gonococci can, however, be classified according to auxotype (ie, nutritional requirements).

Only gonococci that possess pili are virulent under clinical and experimental circumstances. Also, gonococci from transparent colonies appear to be more invasive than those from opaque colonies. Colony transparency or opacity is a function of the composition of outer membrane proteins of the gonococcus.

Gonorrhea is currently epidemic throughout the world, with an estimated 100 million new cases occurring yearly. Factors predisposing to this epidemic include a short incubation period, high infectivity, widespread asymptomatic carriage (at least 80% of uterine cervical infections; up to 40% of male urethral infections; and perhaps the majority of pharyngeal and rectal infections in both sexes are asymptomatic), transmissibility of infection from asymptomatic carriage sites, absence of a reliable serologic test for infection, relaxed sexual mores, and greater resistance of current strains of gonococci to antimicrobial agents.

The upsurge in gonorrhea has rekindled interest in the immunologic pathogenesis of this disease, since it is now apparent that bactericidal antibiotics have not been the key to control.

The first step in the production of a gonococcal infection is attachment of the microorganism to a susceptible mucosal surface. Adherence appears to be mediated by pili (fimbriae), hairlike proteinaceous appendages found on virulent gonococci. Pili cannot be the only determinant of local invasiveness, however, because many nonpathogenic *Neisseria* species (such as *Neisseria flavescens*) are also piliated. Local immune response to the gonococcus is manifested by the prompt appearance of IgG and secretory IgA antibody in genital secretions. Both antibody classes appear capable of inhibiting gonococcal attachment to mucosal cells in a strain-specific manner in vitro. Clinical observations suggest that local IgA antibody is not protective against reinfection. This may be *partially* attributable to the ability of gonococci to elaborate IgA protease, which cleaves and inactivates IgA-1 molecules (see Chapter 15). In addition, seminal plasma interferes with the progress of normal immune responses. Once gonococci have become attached to epithelial cells, they are endocytosed. Intracellular and extracellular gonococcal multiplication results in spread to contiguous cells and to the subepithelial tissues. In the uterine tubes, gonococci attach to nonciliated epithelial cells, but the release of gonococcal lipopolysaccharide results in the detachment and sloughing of neighboring ciliated epithelium, with presumed resultant adverse effects on oviduct function.

It is widely accepted that either the pili of gonococci or a component of the outer membrane protein ("leukocyte association factor") subserves an antiphagocytic function. Recently, some strains of gonococci have been shown to possess capsules. If gonococci truly possess antiphagocytic surface factors, then the question arises why gonococci in urethral exudates generally appear to be intracellular. One possible explanation is surface phagocytosis, the process whereby phagocytosis is enhanced by crowding together of microorganisms and phagocytic leukocytes, bypassing the need for opsonic antibody. In general, gonococci which are phagocytosed by polymorphonuclear leukocytes are considered to be rapidly killed. However, experimental data relating to this question are contradictory, and the extent to which intracellular gonococci are killed remains uncertain.

Serum antibody against *N gonorrhoeae* may be both opsonic and bactericidal. Patients with deficiencies of complement components C6, C7, or C8 appear to be at especially increased risk for hematogenous gonococcal infection.

Clinical Features

The principal clinical manifestations of gonorrhea are urethral exudate (males) and vaginal discharge. However, as noted above, mucosal carriage is asymptomatic in most sites in the majority of cases.

In approximately 1% of patients, gonococci gain access to the bloodstream and produce the syndrome of disseminated gonococcal infection (DGI), characterized by suppurative arthritis (often monoarticular), tenosynovitis, and metastatic skin lesions reflecting a frank infective vasculitis. Strains of gonococci producing DGI are highly resistant to serum bactericidal activity and may have other unique attributes as well, including the AHU- (argenine-hypoxanthine-uracil-) requiring auxotype, high susceptibility to penicillin,

and unique principal outer membrane protein (POMP) type. Serum resistance is apparently attributable to the ability of DGI strains to absorb a blocking IgG antibody that precludes the binding of bactericidal antibody. DGI strains are less often associated with symptomatic mucosal infection than strains that produce disease exclusively at mucosal sites. This may be attributable to the fact that DGI strains have reduced ability to activate the alternative complement pathway. Thus, elaboration of chemotactic factors necessary for generation of the inflammatory response is hindered.

Immunologic Diagnosis

There currently is no reliable serologic test for gonorrhea. Attempts to develop such tests have been frustrated by the use of impure antigens and by unreproducible tests based on detection of small differences in antibody levels between patients and controls. The gonococcal complement fixation test and a more recent test based upon the agglutination of latex particles coated with crude gonococcal antigen lack apparent specificity and sensitivity. The development of techniques for detecting antibody to gonococcal pili holds promise that a means may become available for the detection of asymptomatic carriers, especially women, in whom antibody titers tend to be relatively high. At present, the most useful immunologic test for clinical purposes is probably detection of gonococcal antigens in skin lesions by immunofluorescence.

Differential Diagnosis

Gonococcal urethritis is easily diagnosed in males by the presence of typical gonococci in Gram-stained smears of urethral exudate. Nongonococcal urethritis (or nonspecific urethritis) also produces purulent urethral discharge. About half of these infections are due to *Chlamydia trachomatis* types D–K.

Prevention

Although there are significant cellular, humoral, and mucosal immune responses to infection with *N gonorrhoeae*, gonorrhea can occur repeatedly in sexually active populations. Lack of apparent solid immunity may be based on the likelihood that the immune response is specific to the infecting microorganism and that subsequent infections occur with gonococci of differing "serotype." Indeed, there is great diversity of cell surface antigens among various strains of gonococci: over 20 antigenically distinct types of pili; 16 type-specific outer membrane proteins; 4 distinct polysaccharides; and at least 5 or 6 distinct lipopolysaccharides. Furthermore, the precise chemical composition of the gonococcal capsule and the numbers of antigenically distinct capsular types are not yet known.

Development of gonococcal vaccine is considered to be of high priority, and 2 major structural components are under active investigation as potential immunogens: pili and POMP. Pilus-mediated attachment of gonococci to epithelial cells is inhibited by antibodies to pili, and maximal inhibition occurs when antibodies are directed to pili antigenically identical to those mediating attachment. In recent clinical trials, pilus vaccine has stimulated both mucosal and opsonic antibody with specificity for the immunizing strain. A pilus-based vaccine would seem to provide the best hope for preventing mucosal infection.

In recent studies in guinea pigs, isolated POMP complex proved to be a better protective immunogen than pili from the same gonococcal strains. POMP appears to react in antibody-complement–mediated killing of gonococci, whereas antibodies to pili are only weakly bactericidal. Protective immunity to gonococcal infection in the chimpanzee correlates best with bactericidal antibody in the serum of vaccinated chimpanzees. Thus, POMP also appears promising as an immunogen adaptable to a vaccine, with the advantage of stimulating bactericidal antibodies. Such a vaccine might be of value in the prevention of DGI.

Treatment

Penicillin, tetracycline, and spectinomycin are the antibiotics most commonly used to treat all forms of gonorrhea.

Complications & Prognosis

The most serious complication of untreated gonococcal infection is salpingitis—a major cause of involuntary sterility, especially in underdeveloped countries. Disseminated gonococcal infection complicates approximately 1% of local mucosal infections and has been discussed above.

7. GRAM–NEGATIVE RODS
(Enteric & Environmental)

There is one episode of gram-negative bacteremia for every 100 hospital admissions in the USA today. Antibiotics have failed to alter this situation in a meaningful way; 30–60% of patients with gram-negative sepsis continue to die despite antibiotic therapy—perhaps because of irreversible effects of endotoxin.

Immunization is successful for the prevention of disease due to exotoxin-producing bacteria or infections caused by certain specific serologic types of infecting microorganisms. In the case of the common hospital-acquired gram-negative rod infection, however, the situation is more complex; multiple species and serotypes of Enterobacteriaceae and Pseudomonadaceae are commonly involved. For example, 103 K, 164 O, and 75 H antigen types are recognized in *E coli,* and 80 capsular types of *Klebsiella* are known. As a result, immunization based upon type-specific antigens does not appear to be a realistic goal.

Because the core portions of lipopolysaccharide from most of these diverse microorganisms are of nearly identical chemical constitution, the possibility has been raised that antibody to rough mutants might be protective against infections caused by heterologous gram-negative bacilli. Support for this concept comes from studies that have shown an improved

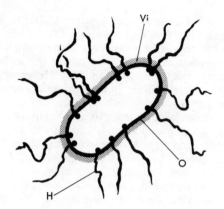

Figure 33–1. Schematic diagram of cellular locations of H, O, and Vi antigens of enteric bacilli. H, flagellar antigens (Ger *Hauch* breath; named for the flagellar-induced swarming of *Proteus* species on agar, which resembles the appearance of a breath on cold glass). O, lipopolysaccharide somatic antigen (Ger *ohne* without, ie, without flagella). Vi, an additional surface polysaccharide antigen of *S typhi* originally thought to be responsible for virulence. It is probably a special example of a K (Ger *Kapsel* capsule) antigen which is itself too thin to be seen as a capsule. (Reproduced, with permission, from Davis BD et al: *Microbiology,* 2nd ed. Harper & Row, 1973.)

prognosis for survival in patients with gram-negative septicemia who possess high hemagglutinating antibody titers to core glycolipid. An understanding of the surface antigens of enteric bacilli and of the composition of bacterial lipopolysaccharide may be gained by examination of Figs 33–1 and 33–2, respectively.

Rough (R) strains are mutants that are blocked in biosynthesis of the complete O antigen (region I). There can also be mutations of the core polysaccharide (region II). Lipid A (region III) serves as the primer or membrane carrier upon which core polysaccharide is built. Ketodeoxyoctonate (KDO), one of the core sugars of region 2, is unique to bacterial lipopolysaccharide and links the core to lipid A. In the biosynthesis of the core region, each sugar is added by a specific enzyme. Hence, the potential exists for a series of core mutants, each dependent upon the absence of a specific enzyme. Ra mutants contain the

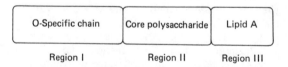

O-Specific chain	Core polysaccharide	Lipid A
Region I	Region II	Region III

Figure 33–2. Structural diagram of bacterial lipopolysaccharides. Lipopolysaccharide (endotoxin) is composed of O-specific side chains consisting of repeating (oligosaccharide) units attached to a basal core polysaccharide which is attached in turn to lipid A. Rough mutants are blocked in biosynthesis of the complete O antigen. (Reproduced, with permission, from Davis BD et al: *Microbiology,* 2nd ed. Harper & Row, 1973.)

complete core, whereas Rb through Rd mutants are deficient in one or more basal sugars. The Re mutant of lipopolysaccharide is composed solely of KDO and lipid A; these "extreme rough" mutants have the most incomplete lipopolysaccharide compatible with bacterial viability.

Antisera prepared from animals immunized with the Re mutant of *Salmonella minnesota* are able to provide passive protection to mice with *Klebsiella pneumoniae* bacteremia. The J-5 mutant (Heath) of *E coli* O111 has been impressive in active and passive immunization studies involving both heterologous Enterobacteriaceae and Pseudomonadaceae. (J-5 lacks the enzyme uridine diphosphate glucose 4-epimerase and therefore produces an incomplete lipopolysaccharide containing only lipid A, KDO, heptose, and glucose—a composition equivalent to that of the Rc mutants of *Salmonella*.)

The mechanism of protection of core antibody appears to involve both antiendotoxic and direct opsonic effects. Even in patients without circulating granulocytes, core antisera may be protective by enhancing phagocytosis of blood-borne gram-negative bacilli by the fixed mononuclear phagocytes of the liver and other reticuloendothelial tissues.

Studies with core glycolipid provide hope that immunotherapeutic approaches may be of value in the management of nosocomial gram-negative rod infection. There are already data to suggest that normal human gamma globulin has significant activity against *Pseudomonas aeruginosa* infections in both experimental animals and in humans. Studies of the value of specific *Pseudomonas* antiserum in passive protection against *P aeruginosa* sepsis are currently in progress. Recent studies indicate that high antibody titers against *P aeruginosa* lipopolysaccharide and exotoxin A are associated with survival in patients with septicemia. Both antibodies may have therapeutic or prophylactic potential, whereas serum antiexotoxin A antibodies may be particularly beneficial in immunocompromised patients.

8. PLAGUE

Plague is caused by a gram-negative rod *(Yersinia pestis)*. Its pathophysiology and immunology are somewhat unique: It behaves in some respects as a facultative intracellular pathogen (multiplication in macrophages) and in others as an extracellular pathogen (killed by PMNs in the presence of opsonic antibody).

Plague is a natural disease of rodents and is transmitted by the bites of fleas. In the fleas, bacilli proliferate in the intestinal tract and produce obstruction. When the fleas next bite, they regurgitate bacilli and aspirated blood into the new host. If rodents are not available as hosts, humans may become involved by default. Bacilli enter dermal lymphatics and produce severe regional lymphadenitis (buboes; *bubonic* plague). Infection may disseminate hematogenously.

When metastatic pneumonia occurs, infection may be spread by airborne droplets (*pneumonic* plague). This is a particularly contagious and malignant form of infection.

Bacilli contained in the gut of the flea have no antiphagocytic surface factors. Consequently, they are promptly ingested and destroyed by PMNs and monocytes. When ingested by macrophages, however, they survive, multiply, and emerge containing 2 new antigens: a capsular glycoprotein antigen (fraction 1; F1; Fra^+) and the VW antigen system consisting of protein (V) and a lipoprotein (W). Apparently the low body temperature of the flea (25 °C) blocks development of these virulence factors. The ability to survive and multiply in macrophages is a key factor in virulence of *Y pestis*. Nevertheless, specific antibodies do promote phagocytosis and killing by PMNs. Effective plague vaccines must include both antiphagocytic antigens (F1 and VW).

9. ANTHRAX

Bacillus anthracis is a large gram-positive, spore-forming microorganism possessing an antiphagocytic capsule composed of a gamma polypeptide of D-glutamic acid. Although important in the initiation of infection, evasion of phagocytosis is a less critical pathogenetic factor than toxin production once disease becomes established. Hence, virulence of the anthrax bacillus is due to both capsule formation and toxin production. Anticapsular antibody alone is not sufficient to prevent anthrax; vaccines must stimulate antitoxin immunity as well.

INFECTIONS IN WHICH ANTIBODY MAY BE DECISIVE IN PREVENTION OR IN RECOVERY THROUGH A MECHANISM OTHER THAN OPSONIZATION

1. DISEASES RESULTING FROM EXOTOXIN PRODUCTION
(Table 33–2)

Major Immunologic Features

- Microorganisms are generally poorly invasive.
- Important disease manifestations are based predominantly upon toxin-related effects.
- Antitoxins may prevent the disease or ameliorate its course.

General Considerations

The diffusible toxins produced by certain grampositive and gram-negative microorganisms are referred to as **exotoxins** because they are by-products of living bacteria and are not intrinsic to the bacterial cell walls (as are **endotoxins**). Exotoxins may be actively excreted by growing microorganisms in which no appreciable autolysis has occurred, or they may be re-

Table 33–2. Diseases resulting from exotoxin production.

Bacterial Species	Occurrence in Nature	Disease Produced	Tissue Invasion	Toxin and Mechanisms of Action	Role of Antibody and Vaccines	Comments
Vibrio cholerae (gram-negative bacillus)	Human cases and carriers	Cholera	No, but intestinal mucosal attachment appears critical (via flagella? pili? other?)	Enterotoxin (choleragen), a chromosomal (ie, intrinsic) toxin. Toxin binds to GM_1 gangliosides in target cell membrane → ADP ribosyl transferase activity with activation of adenylate cyclase → production of cyclic AMP → hypersecretion of chloride, HCO_3^-, and water → severe diarrhea.	Presently unclear. Vaccines: (1) Parenteral killed bacterial vaccine: limited protection. (2) Parenteral toxoid: very limited protection. (3) Live attenuated oral vaccine still a research goal; should stimulate secretory IgA to block *V cholerae* attachment to bowel as well as stimulate local antitoxic activity in gut.	Noncholera vibrios (nonagglutinating [NAG] vibrios) have also been described that secrete enterotoxin and produce a similar clinical syndrome. ADP ribosyl transferase activation is a mechanism common to cholera, enterotoxigenic *E coli*, diphtheria, and *P aeruginosa* exotoxins.
Escherichia coli (gram-negative bacillus)	Human cases and carriers; animals	Diarrhea (enterotoxigenic *E coli* diarrhea)	No, but intestinal mucosal attachment via a pilus-like colonization factor (Cf) appears critical	Two enterotoxins (transmitted by extrachromosomal plasmids). Mechanism of heat-labile toxin (LT) similar to that of cholera toxin (GM_1 ganglioside binding; ADP ribosyl transferase → cyclic AMP, etc). Mechanism of heat-stable toxin (ST) not defined. Since toxin production is plasmid-mediated, enterotoxin production is not serotype-specific.	Presently unclear. No available vaccines. Because of the transmissibility of plasmids among *E coli* of various serotypes, a vaccine prepared against *E coli* somatic antigens would be of little value. Vaccine directed against toxin or Cf of theoretic value.	Must be differentiated from invasive *E coli* syndrome which reflects actual epithelial invasion by *E coli* (enteropathogenic *E coli*). LT or ST activity (or both) has also been found in species of *Aeromonas, Enterobacter,* and *Klebsiella.*
Shigella dysenteriae type I (Shiga's bacillus) (gram-negative bacillus)	Human cases and carriers	Dysentery	Epithelial cells of gastrointestinal tract; rarely beyond submucosa	Neurotoxin (producing motor ataxia in rabbits and meningismus in humans). May be identical to enterotoxin (produces diarrhea). Common mechanism of action seems to be capillary endothelial cell damage.	Presently unclear. No available vaccines. Parenteral toxoid immunization fails to prevent diarrhea in monkeys despite high antibody titers in serum.	Virulent *Shigella* species are both invasive and toxigenic. Stimulation of local gut immunity may be the key to protection.
Clostridium botulinum (gram-positive sporulating bacillus)	Soil. Rarely, gastrointestinal tract.	Botulism	No	Neurotoxin (released by cellular autolysis, ie, an intracellular toxin). Eight type-specific toxins known (A, B, C_1, C_2, D, E, F, G); only A, B, E, and F common in humans. Spores germinate in foods → ingestion of preformed toxin. Spores may rarely germinate in wounds. Toxin binds at neuromuscular junction; blocks presynaptic release of acetylcholine, resulting in impaired breathing and swallowing, diplopia, and flaccid paralysis.	No immunity conferred by infection; enough botulinus toxin to immunize is enough to kill. Active immunization: toxoid. Passive immunization: antitoxin (polyvalent A, B, E; equine); critical in treatment of botulism.	Botulism is less an infection than an intoxication. Botulinus toxin may enter the body in 3 ways: (1) preformed, in food (most common); (2) germination of spores in a contaminated wound; (3) germination of spores in the gastrointestinal tract (infants may present with "floppy infant syndrome").
Clostridium tetani (gram-positive sporulating bacillus)	Soil and gastrointestinal tract of humans and animals	Tetanus	No	Tetanospasmin (released by cellular autolysis, ie, an intracellular toxin). Acts pre- or post-synaptically to block inhibition mediated by internuncial neurons in the spinal cord → spasmodic muscle contractions (spastic paralysis). May also interfere with muscle relaxation.	No immunity conferred by infection. The lethal dose is insufficient to immunize. Active immunization: toxoid. Passive immunization: tetanus antitoxin (human).	Tetanolysin (a hemolysin) is also produced but plays no apparent role in neuromuscular problems.

Organism	Reservoir/source	Disease	Invasiveness	Toxins/mechanism	Immunity/vaccine	Comments
Clostridium difficile (gram-positive sporulating bacillus)	Intestinal tracts of humans and animals; environment	Diarrhea; pseudomembranous colitis	No, but toxins produce focal and diffuse necrosis	Cytotoxin (toxin B): direct cytotoxic effect on cell membranes of diverse cell lines; mechanism of action may involve stimulation of cGMP and suppression of cAMP. Enterotoxin (toxin A): causes fluid accumulation in rabbit ileal loop assay and death when injected intracecally in hamsters (neither occurs with toxin B).	No vaccine available. Cytotoxicity is blocked by *Clostridium sordellii* antitoxin (reversible cross-reaction) and *C difficile* antitoxin (specific).	The most common cause of diarrhea following antibiotic administration (especially clindamycin, ampicillin, cephalosporins). Diarrhea may be mild or severe; secretory and/or hemorrhagic; benign or fatal. Treatment: oral vancomycin (to kill *C difficile*) or anionic chelating agents (to bind toxins).
Clostridium perfringens (gram-positive sporulating bacillus)	Soil and gastrointestinal tract of humans and animals	Gas gangrene (clostridial myonecrosis)	Minimal	Eleven soluble toxins produced that may be active in various aspects of disease (including phospholipase C, collagenase, hemolysin, proteinase, and DNase). The chief lethal component is α toxin (phospholipase C; lecithinase). In some cases (especially clostridial myonecrosis of the uterus), sufficient α toxin may be liberated to produce massive intravascular hemolysis.	Highly questionable (although polyvalent equine antitoxin is often used in gas gangrene, even in the absence of the massive hemolysis syndrome). Commercially available antisera neutralize only a small portion of the spectrum of toxins.	*C novyi* and *C septicum* may also produce gas gangrene. Mainstays of treatment are surgical excision, antibiotics, and, probably, hyperbaric oxygen.
		Clostridial enterotoxin–mediated diarrhea	No	Enterotoxin: released by sporulating microorganisms in gastrointestinal tract which lyse to → toxin → diarrhea.	Systemic vaccination in animals without effect on toxin production in gut. No information in humans.	Perhaps due to ingestion of preformed toxin as well.
Corynebacterium diphtheriae (gram-positive bacillus)	Human cases and carriers	Diphtheria	No	Diphtheritic toxin (produced only by corynebacteria which are themselves infected by a tox⁺ temperate phage). Blocks protein synthesis by ADP ribosyl transferase–mediated binding of the ADP ribose moiety of NAD to elongation factor 2 (EF 2), an enzyme necessary for peptide chain elongation in protein synthesis. Toxin has diffuse effects but is principally manifested by cardiotoxicity (cardiomyopathy) and neurotoxicity (motor paralysis; cranial nerves generally first).	Antibody to toxin prevents toxin-related death but has no effect on epithelial cell attachment or production of pseudomembrane by *C diphtheriae*. Active immunization: toxoid. Passive immunization: equine antitoxin; critical in management of suspected diphtheria.	Can measure presence of circulating antitoxin by intradermal injection of diphtheria toxin (Schick test). Lack of response demonstrates immunity. Possibility of nonspecific reactivity requires multiple controls.

Table 33–2 (cont'd). Diseases resulting from exotoxin production.

Bacterial Species	Occurrence in Nature	Disease Produced	Tissue Invasion	Toxin and Mechanisms of Action	Role of Antibody and Vaccines	Comments
Streptococcus pyogenes (gram-positive coccus)	Human cases and carriers	Scarlet fever	Yes	Erythrogenic toxin (produced by *S pyogenes* strains infected by a tox⁺ temperate phage). Any *S pyogenes* can be converted to toxigenicity. Mechanism of action may be direct skin toxicity or hypersensitivity reaction.	Antibody can prevent rash but has no effect on streptococcal infection. Three immunologically distinct rash-producing toxins have been identified, explaining the occasional occurrence of several episodes of scarlet fever in the same patient.	An incidental complication of *S pyogenes* infection; clinically dramatic, but with no real pathogenic significance. Historically an important illness; not common in USA today. Can measure presence of circulating antitoxin by intradermal injection of erythrogenic toxin (Dick test). Lack of response demonstrates immunity. Can also use a skin test to establish diagnosis (Schultz-Charlton reaction). Here a scarlet fever rash is blanched by locally injected serum from a convalescent patient. Large numbers of other toxins are also produced by *S pyogenes* but without clear clinical syndromes.
Staphylococcus aureus (gram-positive coccus)	Human cases and carriers	Scalded skin syndrome (Ritter's disease; toxic epidermal necrolysis; generalized exfoliative dermatitis; pemphigus neonatorum)	No	Exfoliatin (often due to phage group 2 *S aureus*) produces disruption of desmosomes between granular cells of epidermis → epidermal cleavage plane. Intense erythema about mouth and nose spreads to neck, trunk, and extremities. Followed by loosening of epidermis, bulla formation, and peeling. Bullous impetigo and scarlatiniform rash (erythema without exfoliation) may be variants. More common in young children. Often no clear site of infection apparent.	Unclear. Immunization with exfoliatin will prevent its effects in mice.	Exfoliatin-positive strains appear unique in their ability to → subcutaneous infection in mice without the intervention of a foreign body. Since experimental skin infection with *S aureus* is ordinarily difficult to establish using bacteria alone, exfoliatin may be an important virulence factor.
		Staphylococcal food poisoning	No	Preformed enterotoxin (6 types) → vomiting and diarrhea (toxin absorbed → stimulation of vomiting center).	Unclear.	Ingestion of preformed toxin.
		Toxic shock syndrome	No	Candidate toxins include pyrogenic exotoxin C and staphylococcal enterotoxins. The mechanism of toxicity is unknown.	Unknown.	Syndrome is most frequently encountered in women who use tampons and is associated with intravaginal colonization with *S aureus*. Manifestations include fever, hypotension, vomiting, diarrhea, and scarlatiniform rash with subsequent desquamation.

leased by microbial autolysis (intracellular toxins). All characterized exotoxins are proteins and thus are capable of stimulating antibody formation. In many of the diseases to be discussed, active immunization against exotoxins is carried out by preparing **toxoids** through the introduction of substituent groups such as formaldehyde or iodine. Toxoids are antigenic but essentially nontoxic.

Many of the diseases in Table 33–2 rely solely upon toxin production for their clinical manifestations (eg, tetanus). In others, production of toxin is coincidental and not essential to disease production (eg, erythrogenic toxin elaborated by *Streptococcus pyogenes*). In some diseases (eg, anthrax, pertussis, plague, *P aeruginosa* infection), exotoxins are suspected of playing important pathogenetic roles, but data are not sufficient to permit their inclusion in the table. Many fungi produce poisonous substances (mycotoxins). For example, aflatoxin from *Aspergillus flavus* may be important in hepatic neoplasia and may also impair antibody formation, complement activation, phagocytosis, and blastogenesis under diverse experimental circumstances. A discussion of mycotoxins is beyond the scope of this chapter.

2. INFECTIONS IN WHICH EPITHELIAL CELL ATTACHMENT IS THE CRITICAL FIRST STEP IN ESTABLISHMENT OF INFECTION

Secretory IgA as well as IgG may be critical in preventing the attachment to epithelial cells of potential pathogens (*Vibrio cholerae, Shigella* species, *Salmonella* species, etc). The physiologic role of secretory antibody and the activity of microbial IgA proteases are discussed elsewhere in this book (see Chapters 15 and 16).

3. COMPLEMENT–MEDIATED BACTERIOLYSIS

Many gram-negative microorganisms are lysed by complement in the presence of specific antibody. As already noted, measurement of such bactericidal antibody in meningococcal infections is an important means for assessing immunity to infection. Bactericidal antibody may play a protective role in gonococcal and meningococcal infection. There is considerable question, however, about whether this mechanism is operative in other infections. Part of the confusion arises because microorganisms that have been passaged in vitro are commonly used in tests of the serum bactericidal mechanism. Such microorganisms may be more susceptible to membrane damage than microorganisms encountered in vivo during actual infections. Further, patients with granulocytopenia do not appear to be protected from sepsis with antibody- and complement-susceptible gram-negative rods even when their humoral immune mechanisms are apparently intact.

Antibody- and complement-mediated bacteriolysis may be augmented by lysozyme. The practical significance of this interaction remains uncertain.

4. VIRAL NEUTRALIZATION

As noted in Chapter 16, direct inhibition of viral infectivity by interaction of antibody with viral surface antigens is a critically important host defense mechanism. Antibody prevents attachment and host cell penetration by susceptible viruses. Not all viruses are susceptible to the effects of antibody.

INFECTIONS IN WHICH HUMORAL & CELL–MEDIATED IMMUNITY COLLABORATE IN HOST DEFENSE

Major Immunologic Features
- An etiologically heterogeneous group.
- Infecting microorganisms may be extracellular or facultatively intracellular pathogens.
- The dominant protective immune mechanism varies with each pathogen.

General Considerations

The microorganisms in this group are extremely diverse. The justification for grouping them together at all is partially negative; they do not fit easily into the other groups. None of these microorganisms are considered to be either strictly extracellular (and under the control of opsonins and PMNs) or strictly intracellular (and under the sole control of lymphocytes and macrophages). Some of them are characterized by an apparent immunologic paradox: *Cryptococcus neoformans* possesses an antiphagocytic capsule, and yet PMNs do not appear to be the critical host defense; *Treponema pallidum* appears to function as an extracellular pathogen, and yet cell-mediated immunity is unquestionably important in its control.

1. SYPHILIS

Treponema pallidum is a noncultivable, motile, highly infectious spirochete that appears to function predominantly as an extracellular pathogen. The organism attaches in vitro to receptor sites on host cells exclusively by its tapered ends, meanwhile retaining active motility. Ingestion by macrophages in vitro may be facilitated by the provision of specific antibody, but this point is unclear.

T pallidum is extremely susceptible to heat and drying, so that direct transfer by intimate contact, preferably in the presence of moisture, is essential for its survival. Sexual contact is therefore an ideal mode of transmission of syphilis. Syphilis occurs naturally only in humans.

Three clinically identifiable stages of syphilis are traditionally described. The first 2 (**primary** and **secondary** syphilis) both occur early in the infectious, spirochetemic stage of disease. The third stage (**tertiary** syphilis) occurs much later, following a period of prolonged latency, and reflects a tissue-damaging immunologic response to previously deposited microorganisms (bystander cell injury).

Syphilis is an unusual infection in that there is evidence for both humoral and cell-mediated immunity. However, the relative importance of each is unclear, and protective immunity against rechallenge is incomplete. Evidence for the participation of humoral immunity in syphilis is as follows:

(1) A variety of nonspecific ("reaginic") and specific antibodies are regularly present in the serum of patients who have syphilis.

(2) *Treponema pallidum*–immobilizing antibodies (TPIA) are regularly present in the serum of patients who have syphilis.

(3) The frequency with which TPIA are found increases as syphilis progresses to latent and tertiary infection.

(4) Partial immunity can be conferred in rabbits by passive transfer of serum from syphilis-immune animals. This protection is apparent when *T pallidum* is injected intracutaneously into rabbits. Chancres may be either prevented or delayed by passive immunization.

Interestingly, humans who have been experimentally infected with *T pallidum* also develop increased local resistance to rechallenge at a cutaneous site. This local resistance is referred to as **chancre immunity.** Chancre immunity persists if primary infection remains untreated and syphilis progresses to a latent stage. Although chancre immunity is indicative of heightened local resistance, it does not prevent the systemic spread of *T pallidum* from the site of initial challenge. Chancre immunity may be attributable to antibody, as both the immunity and reaginic antibodies wane after treatment of primary syphilis. The time required depends on the titer of antibody and the severity of the illness. For several reasons, it is not likely that the antibodies are completely protective:

(1) Treponemes from the initial infection persist during latent syphilis, even though there is resistance to a second challenge. This suggests that the organism has found sanctuary in some sort of priveleged residence where it is immune from host defense.

(2) Some antibodies are nonspecific and are found in other diseases such as lupus erythematosus. They might even be directed against host rather than treponemal antigens.

(3) By preventing attachment of treponemes to cells in tissue culture, antibodies might in fact aid the organisms in escaping host defense mechanisms.

(4) Circulating immune complexes are formed during infection with *T pallidum*. They are demonstrable in sera of both rabbits and patients with syphilis. They may be composed of cardiolipin-anticardiolipin as well as of treponemal antigen–antitreponemal antibody. They may act to depress synthesis of IgG against independent antigens, such as sheep erythrocytes. It is conceivable that circulating immune complexes may prevent the host from synthesizing treponemicidal antibody during primary syphilis or from synthesizing antitreponemal antibody that might act in concert with cell-mediated immunity against *T pallidum*.

(5) The patterns of antibody production change during the course of untreated syphilis. Patients with secondary syphilis have antitreponemal antibody as well as anticardiolipin antibody. These antibodies are of both IgG and IgM classes. As the disease enters latency, antitreponemal IgM antibody production ceases and patients are left with antitreponemal IgG and anticardiolipin IgM and IgG. The clinical significance of this sequence of events is uncertain.

Recent investigations in animal models have increasingly implicated cell-mediated immunity as a critical element in host response to *T pallidum*. Evidence for the participation of cell-mediated immunity in syphilis is as follows:

(1) Passive transfer of syphilis immune serum is only partially protective and does not follow classic models of humoral immunity.

(2) Syphilis progresses through primary and secondary stages despite the presence of antibodies that immobilize the infecting organism.

(3) Delayed hypersensitivity to treponemal antigens is absent in primary and early secondary syphilis but develops late in secondary infection and is regularly present in latent and tertiary syphilis.

(4) Granulomatous lesions characterize tertiary syphilis.

(5) Immunization with killed microorganisms is usually unsuccessful, whereas immunization with live attenuated organisms has produced immunity.

(6) In vitro lymphocyte reactivity to treponemal and nontreponemal antigens and T lymphocyte counts are suppressed during primary and secondary syphilis.

(7) Infecting rabbits with *T pallidum* stimulates acquired cellular resistance to *Listeria;* this reaction is mediated by T lymphocytes.

It is puzzling why so much time is required for patients to develop humoral and cellular immunity to syphilis. One theory holds that the mucoid envelope of *T pallidum* renders it highly resistant to phagocytosis; only after the treponemes have remained in the host for some time is the mucoid coat broken down enough for phagocytosis to occur. (Treponemal mucopolysaccharides also suppress lymphocyte blastogenic response to ConA.) As a result, treponemal proliferation outstrips the rate of antigenic processing for stimulation of humoral and cellular immune mechanisms; a condition of "antigen overload" then occurs, with production of secondary immunosuppression. An alternative explanation is that sensitization with treponemal antigen leads primarily to generation of antibodies that then "block" antigenic sites, thereby inhibiting an appropriate cell-mediated immune response.

These proposed immunologic mechanisms are highly speculative.

Clinical Features

The first clinically apparent manifestation of syphilis (**primary** syphilis) is an indurated, circumscribed, relatively avascular and painless ulcer (**chancre**) at the site of treponemal inoculation. Spirochetemia with secondary metastatic distribution of microorganisms occurs within a few days after onset of local infection, but clinically apparent secondary lesions may not be observed for 2–4 weeks. The chancre lasts 10–14 days before healing spontaneously.

The presence of metastatic infection (**secondary** syphilis) is manifested by highly infectious mucocutaneous lesions of extraordinarily diverse description as well as headache, low-grade fever, diffuse lymphadenopathy, and a variety of more sporadic phenomena. The lesions of secondary syphilis ordinarily go on to apparent spontaneous resolution in the absence of treatment. However, until solid immunity develops—a matter of about 4 years—25% of untreated syphilitic patients may be susceptible to repeated episodes of spirochetemia and metastatic infection.

Following the resolution of secondary syphilis, the disease enters a period of **latency,** with only abnormal serologic tests to indicate the presence of infection. During this time, persistent or progressive focal infection is presumably taking place, but the precise site remains unknown in the absence of specific symptoms and signs. One site of potential latency, the central nervous system, can be evaluated by examining the cerebrospinal fluid, where pleocytosis, elevated protein, and a positive serologic test for syphilis are indicative of asymptomatic neurosyphilis.

Only about 15% of patients with untreated latent syphilis go on to develop symptomatic **tertiary** syphilis. Serious or fatal tertiary syphilis in adults is virtually limited to disease of the aorta (aortitis with aneurysm formation and secondary aortic valve insufficiency), the central nervous system (tabes dorsalis, general paresis), or the eye (interstitial keratitis). Less frequently, the disease becomes apparent as localized single or multiple granulomas known as **gummas.** These lesions are typically found in skin, bones, liver, testes, or larynx. The histopathologic features of the gumma resemble those of earlier syphilitic lesions except that the vasculitis is associated with increased tissue necrosis and often frank caseation.

Immunologic Diagnosis

In its primary and secondary stages, syphilis is best diagnosed by darkfield microscopic examination of material from suspected lesions. Diagnostic serologic changes do not begin to occur until 14–21 days following acquisition of infection. Serologic tests provide important confirmatory evidence for secondary syphilis but are the only means of diagnosing latent infection. Many forms of tertiary syphilis can be suspected on clinical grounds, but serologic tests are important in confirming the diagnosis. Spirochetes are notoriously difficult to demonstrate in the late stages of syphilis.

Two main categories of serologic tests for syphilis (STS) are available: tests for reaginic antibody and tests for treponemal antibody.

A. Tests for Reaginic Antibody: (This is an unfortunate and confusing designation. There is no relationship between this antibody and IgE reaginic antibody.)

Patients with syphilis develop an antibody response to a tissue-derived substance (from beef heart) that is thought to be a component of mitochondrial membranes and has been called **cardiolipin.** Antibody to cardiolipin antigen is known as Wassermann, or reaginic, antibody. Numerous variations (and names) are associated with tests for this antigen. The simplest and most practical of these is the VDRL test (Venereal Disease Research Laboratory of USPHS), which employs a slide microflocculation technique and can provide qualitative and quantitative data. Positive tests are considered to be diagnostic of syphilis when there is a high or increasing titer or when the medical history is compatible with primary or secondary syphilis. The test may also be of prognostic aid in following response to therapy, since the antibody titer will revert to negative within 1 year of treatment of seropositive primary syphilis or within 2 years for secondary syphilis.

Biologic false-positive tests. Since cardiolipin antigen is found in the mitochondrial membranes of many mammalian tissues as well as in diverse microorganisms, it is not surprising that antibody to this antigen should appear in other diseases. A positive VDRL test may be encountered, for example, in infectious mononucleosis, leprosy, hepatitis, and systemic lupus erythematosus. Although the VDRL test lacks specificity for syphilis, its great sensitivity makes it extremely useful nonetheless.

B. Tests for Treponemal Antibody: The first test employed for detecting specific antitreponemal antibody was the *Treponema pallidum* immobilization test (TPI). Although highly reliable, it proved to be too cumbersome for routine use. A major test employed today is the fluorescent *T pallidum* antibody test (FTA). If virulent *T pallidum* from an infected rabbit testicle is placed on a slide and overlaid with serum from a patient with antibody to treponemes, an antigen-antibody reaction will occur. The bound antibody can then be detected by means of a fluoresceinated anti-human γ-globulin antibody. Specificity of the test for *T pallidum* is enhanced by first absorbing the serum with nonpathogenic treponemal strains. This modification is referred to as the FTA-ABS test. (If specific anti-IgM antibody to human γ-globulin is employed, the acuteness of the infection or the occurrence of congenital syphilis can be assessed. However, this test may sometimes be falsely positive or negative in babies born of mothers with syphilis.)

The FTA-ABS test is reactive in approximately 80% of patients with primary syphilis (versus 50% for the VDRL test). Both tests are positive in virtually 100% of patients with secondary syphilis. Whereas the VDRL test shows a tendency to decline in titer with successful treatment, the FTA-ABS test may remain positive for years. The FTA-ABS test is especially useful in confirming or ruling out a diagnosis of syphilis in patients with suspected biologic false-positive reactions to the VDRL test. However, even the FTA-ABS test may be susceptible to false positives, especially in the presence of lupus erythematosus.

The microhemagglutination-*T pallidum* (MHA-TP) test, a simple passive hemagglutination test, appears to be a satisfactory substitute for the FTA-ABS test. Its principal advantages are economy of technician time and money. Its results correlate closely with FTA-ABS except during primary and early secondary syphilis, when both the VDRL and FTA-ABS are more likely to show reactivity.

The interpretation of serologic data in syphilis may be extremely complex in some cases. For example, a prozone phenomenon may be encountered in secondary syphilis; serofastness may characterize late syphilis; and the VDRL test may be negative in up to one-third of patients with late latent syphilis.

Differential Diagnosis

Syphilis produces sufficiently diverse clinical manifestations that a discussion of its differential diagnosis should be sought in a textbook of general internal medicine.

Prevention

Early treatment with antibiotics is the only way known to prevent the later ravages of syphilis.

Treatment

Penicillin is the drug of choice for syphilis in all its stages. Since the lesions of tertiary syphilis may be irreversible, it is crucial to identify and treat the disease before tertiary lesions begin.

Complications & Prognosis

The most frequent complication of treatment is the **Jarisch-Herxheimer reaction,** which occurs in up to half of patients with early syphilis and is manifested by fever, headache, myalgias, and exacerbation of cutaneous lesions. It has been suggested that this reaction may be mediated by IgE. The intensity of a Jarisch-Herxheimer reaction reflects the intensity of local inflammation prior to treatment and is thought to

result from the release of antigenic material from dying microorganisms. The reaction is of short duration (2–4 hours) and generally not harmful, although shock and death have been attributed to this reaction in tertiary forms of the disease. (The Jarisch-Herxheimer reaction has also been described in the treatment of louse-borne borreliosis, brucellosis, and typhoid fever.)

Other immunologic complications of syphilis include paroxysmal cold hemoglobinuria and nephrotic syndrome.

In patients who fail to receive any treatment for syphilis, it is estimated that one in 13 will develop cardiovascular disease; one in 25 will become crippled or incapacitated; one in 44 will develop irreversible damage to the central nervous system; and one in 200 will become blind.

2. CRYPTOCOCCOSIS

Cryptococcus neoformans is a yeastlike fungus that reproduces by budding. A mycelial form, *Filobasidiella neoformans,* has recently been described. Parent and daughter cells are surrounded by a thick polysaccharide capsule, and a characteristic "halo" is produced by the capsule in the presence of India ink.

Humans are thought to acquire cryptococcosis from inhalation of fungi. Person-to-person transmission has not been documented. It is likely that many are exposed to *C neoformans,* but few develop the disease. There are an estimated 300 new cases of symptomatic cryptococcosis per year in the USA.

Among the major systemic mycoses, the interaction between the host and *C neoformans* is perhaps the least well understood. One problem in dissecting the immune response has been the absence of potent and specific antigens to use as immunologic tools. Poor antigenicity of *C neoformans* may also be a practical problem for the host during natural infection.

Once established in the tissues, cryptococci evoke 2 principal histopathologic patterns. In the first, fungi proliferate largely unchecked, forming large gelatinous masses of capsular polysaccharide surrounding clumps of yeasts. There is little tissue reaction, and no necrosis occurs. In the second, there is granuloma formation with macrophages, lymphocytes, and plasma cells. Cryptococci may be found in centrally located giant cells. Again, there is no necrosis. Reactive lymphadenopathy is not common in lymph nodes draining cryptococcal pulmonary lesions. Healing is not associated with the intense scarring and calcification that characterize histoplasmosis, tuberculosis, and other infections evoking an intense delayed hypersensitivity reaction (ie, there is no "bystander" tissue injury).

The most important pathogenic cryptococcal constituent identified thus far is capsular polysaccharide. Capsular polysaccharide contains a backbone of α-1,3-linked D mannopyranoside residues. There are 4 serotypes of *C neoformans;* all are virulent. Capsular polysaccharide is poorly immunogenic, a problem that is reflected in the difficulties in immunizing laboratory animals and the low antibody titers in patients with cryptococcosis.

Capsular polysaccharide subserves an antiphagocytic function. Nonencapsulated cryptococcal mutant strains that are easily phagocytosed are avirulent for mice; the encapsulated parent strains are highly lethal. Addition of capsular polysaccharide to in vitro systems impairs phagocytosis by PMNs. In vivo inoculation of capsular polysaccharide shortens survival of mice when they are later challenged with encapsulated cryptococci.

Both antibody and complement appear to be important in potentiating phagocytosis of cryptococci. Guinea pigs and mice decomplemented in vivo have enhanced susceptibility to cryptococcosis. Mice of C5-deficient inbred strains are exquisitely susceptible to cryptococcosis. Complement and antibody may interact protectively in that only mice with normal complement activity can be passively immunized with high-titer rabbit anticryptococcal antibody. Complement activation appears to follow the alternative pathway.

Thus, it has been postulated that antibody- and complement-dependent opsonization may be the crucial factor in limiting cryptococcal infection in most tissues and that the prominence of central nervous system infection may represent an "escape" of fungi to a milieu in which complement components penetrate in low titer or not at all. However, this is speculative and deemphasizes the unquestionably important role of cell-mediated immune mechanisms in cryptococcosis. Without invoking an important role for lymphocytes and macrophages, it would be difficult to explain (1) the virtual absence of PMNs from nonneurologic lesions; (2) the classic granulomatous response present in many tissues; (3) the apparent lack of undue susceptibility of hypogammaglobulinemic patients to cryptococcosis; and (4) the susceptibility to cryptococcosis of patients with Hodgkin's disease.

There is now evidence that some polysaccharide- or protein-containing extracts prepared from cryptococci are able to elicit cell-mediated immune responses. The skin test response in sensitized humans and nonprimates is of the delayed type. Lymphocyte activation and MIF have been demonstrated in lymphocyte cultures from healthy subjects exposed to *C neoformans*. These responses appear to be defective in patients with active and even resolved cryptococcosis.

Animal models of infection also support a role for cell-mediated immunity. Immunization of mice with cryptococcal extracts elicits a delayed cutaneous hypersensitivity response that correlates with increased protection on challenge. Treatment with anti–mouse thymocyte globulin enhances susceptibility to cryptococcosis and ablates both the skin test reaction and protective effects of vaccination. The congenitally athymic (nude) mouse is exquisitely susceptible to cryptococcosis. Finally, activated macrophages have increased killing capacities against *C neoformans* and

may be able to kill them by some mechanism other than phagocytosis.

From these bits of information, we are gradually gaining insight into the pathogenesis of cryptococcosis.

Clinical Features

The first encounter between humans and fungus is probably in the lung. In persons with intact immune defenses, cryptococci may reside saprophytically in the respiratory tract or produce pulmonary disease. In patients with sufficient immunity to develop symptomatic pulmonary cryptococcosis, clinically apparent dissemination to other sites is not common. However, with host immunosuppression, cryptococci can readily spread from a primary pulmonary focus.

Extrapulmonary dissemination accounts for 90% of all clinically apparent cases of cryptococcosis and is characteristically (although not exclusively) seen in patients with underlying immune deficiency. Half of these patients either have primary lymphoreticular disease or are receiving immunosuppressive medications for other disorders.

Without treatment, cryptococcal meningitis runs an irregular course of months to years, ending with seizures, hydrocephalus, dementia, coma, and death.

Immunologic Diagnosis

The diagnosis of cryptococcosis has traditionally depended upon the demonstration of microorganisms in cerebrospinal fluid by India ink staining, together with their isolation on appropriate artificial media. Attempts to establish a diagnosis of cryptococcosis on the basis of elevated antibody titers have been frustrated by the absence of reliable tests, reflecting perhaps the poor antigenicity of *C neoformans* and the fact that many infected patients have underlying immune disorders that might compromise antibody synthesis.

Unfortunately, some patients with cryptococcal meningitis have negative India ink preparations of the spinal fluid, negative cultures, and an absence of demonstrable antibody. In many of these patients, a diagnosis can be made using a recently developed test for free cryptococcal polysaccharide antigen. The test uses high-titer rabbit anticryptococcal antibody adsorbed onto latex beads. In the presence of even minute amounts of cryptococcal antigen, a suspension of the beads agglutinates. A positive test in either serum or cerebrospinal fluid is considered diagnostic of cryptococcosis. In addition to its diagnostic value, the latex cryptococcal agglutination test has prognostic value. Falling titers are associated with improvement, and many physicians use an end-titer of 1:4 or less to terminate therapy.

Tests for cell-mediated immunity are presently of little help, as "cryptococcin" is poorly defined, and many patients are anergic to skin test antigens during active disease. Some regain skin test reactivity as they improve, but others do not.

Prevention

There is no commercially available cryptococcal vaccine. Experimental models have failed to show a benefit from passive immunization with "immune" serum. On the other hand, prior infection of mice with low numbers of cryptococci appears to confer immunity against later challenge with high numbers of the same strain. Immunization of mice with cryptococcal extracts or intact cells in Freund's complete adjuvant also provides protection. However, use of live vaccines would be hazardous to immunosuppressed humans, and Freund's complete adjuvant cannot be used in humans.

Treatment

The mainstay of treatment is amphotericin B given with or without flucytosine (5-fluorocytosine).

A few patients have been treated with transfer factor; however, the value of transfer factor in cryptococcosis remains controversial.

3. CANDIDIASIS
(See also Chapters 25 and 32.)

Candida albicans is the prototype for the *Candida* group of fungi and is responsible for the overwhelming majority of infections with this genus. However, *C tropicalis* is responsible for an increasing number of infections in immunosuppressed hosts. *C albicans* colonizes mucosal surfaces in its yeast form, whereas tissue invasion is characterized by the formation of pseudomycelia. The fungus grows readily on most media as a yeast. *C albicans* produces several distinctive syndromes that reflect the immune capacities of the host. Chronic mucocutaneous candidiasis (see Chapter 25) is associated with selective congenital defects in cell-mediated immunity.

Recent studies indicate that mucosal candidal infection is one feature of the gay-related immunodeficiency (GRID) syndrome. Certain homosexual men have markedly depressed CMI, with evidence of increased Leu 2^+, suppressor T lymphocyte populations. These men show increased susceptibility to a variety of opportunistic pathogens, including *C albicans, Pneumocystis carinii,* and atypical mycobacteria, and are predisposed to Kaposi's sarcoma. There is some suggestion that these susceptibilities may result from underlying cytomegalovirus infection.

C albicans can adhere to and penetrate intact mucosal surfaces of even the healthy host. In the presence of saliva, *Candida* will also undergo germ tube formation, which may be important in their invasiveness. Normally, the skin and mucosa are not exposed to high concentrations of *Candida,* and one function of the host defenses is to keep these numbers low. Factors considered to have a regulatory effect upon the presence of *Candida* in external secretions include local glucose concentration and pH, the availability of iron as mediated by transferrin or lactoferrin, and the presence of other microorganisms.

Alteration of these factors is responsible for overgrowth of *Candida* on mucosal surfaces, including the mouth, esophagus, lower gastrointestinal tract, vagina, and respiratory tract. With a high *Candida* burden, it is not surprising that some of the organisms penetrate into the circulation.

Once in the bloodstream, *Candida* organisms are not free to proliferate unchecked. Serum anti-*Candida* "clumping factors" cause *Candida* agglutination and may facilitate uptake of *Candida* by phagocytic cells. The alternative complement pathway and late complement components are very important in *Candida* opsonization. *Candida* yeast forms are more readily killed by PMNs than pseudomycelia and mycelia, which are too large to be ingested. The host deals with such forms by a coordinated attack of PMNs and monocytes, which attach to and spread over hyphal surfaces, generate oxidative intermediates, degranulate, and kill the hyphal forms.

When PMNs ingest *Candida* species, both oxidative and nonoxidative antifungal mechanisms are activated. Unlike the situation in chronic mucocutaneous candidiasis, the PMN is a critical cell in defense against hematogenous dissemination of *Candida.* In animal models, cell-mediated immunity seems to play no protective role in systemic candidiasis.

Disseminated candidiasis usually develops in patients who are "preconditioned." Preconditioning includes factors such as elevated blood glucose, corticosteroid therapy, broad-spectrum antibiotics, and disruption of the integument with either open wounds or indwelling vascular catheters. Once in the bloodstream, fungi disseminate to certain preferred target tissues, including the eyes, kidneys, meninges, skin, and myocardium. The renal tubule is an immunologically protected focus for *C albicans* replication. By budding into the renal tubules, fungi are able to transiently escape phagocytosis by PMNs, permitting them a temporal advantage in the course of infection. Mycelia enter the interstitial tissues and reseed the blood in a self-perpetuating mechanism. The susceptibility of a patient and the speed with which *Candida* disseminates are dramatically increased by the presence of leukopenia, especially in patients with myelotoxic cancer chemotherapy.

Immunologic Diagnosis

Despite the dramatic clinical picture, the diagnosis of disseminated candidiasis is often quite difficult. This is caused by the difficulty in distinguishing common superficial from less common deep infection. Skin testing is of no value because of the high incidence of positive tests in healthy populations and possible anergy in those with overwhelming infections. A number of serologic tests have been developed to detect circulating candidal antibody. Of these, the precipitin technique appears to be the most useful. However, desperately ill patients may not form adequate antibody. When they do, it may be complexed to candidal antigens and thus not be detectable as free antibody. Recently, a radioimmunoassay has been developed to detect circulating **mannan,** a major cell-surface antigen of *Candida* species. Antigenemia was detected in 5 of 11 patients with systemic candidiasis but not in patients with superficial candidiasis or other fungal infections. An alternative diagnostic method has been direct nonimmunologic demonstration of candidal cell constituents by gas-liquid chromatography.

Prevention

There is no available *Candida* vaccine.

Treatment

Systemic candidiasis is usually treated with amphotericin B, occasionally in combination with flucytosine. Mucosal disease responds well to ketoconazole, 200–400 mg orally daily.

4. SALMONELLOSIS

Salmonellae are gram-negative, aerobic, non-spore-forming rods that are found in the gastrointestinal tracts of humans and animals. The microorganisms may survive for variable periods of time in the environment. There are 3 principal *Salmonella* species: *Salmonella enteritidis* (humans and animals), *Salmonella choleraesuis* (swine), and *Salmonella typhi* (humans). More than 1800 serotypes of *S enteritidis* have been described. *S choleraesuis* and *S typhi* have only one serotype each.

Three principal syndromes result from *Salmonella* infection in humans: (1) gastroenteritis, the most common form of salmonellosis; (2) enteric fever; and (3) extraintestinal focal infections such as osteomyelitis, infected aortic aneurysms, etc.

In the gastroenteritis syndrome, salmonellae invade and destroy the bowel mucosa. The mechanism whereby *Salmonella* species attach to mucosal cells is unknown. PMNs appear to play at least some role in the host response. PMNs not only can kill many *Salmonella* species in vitro but are also prominent in the intestinal lesions and stools of patients with gastroenteritis. *Salmonella* gastroenteritis is generally self-limited.

The lymphoid follicles of Peyer's patches provide a formidable first line of defense. After oral infection of mice, low numbers of salmonellae appear in Peyer's patches, multiply in 3 days to 10^5 organisms, but then decline to scarcity by 10 days after challenge. This does not appear to represent a passthrough to other target organs. Local immunity may be a consequence of chronic stimulation by gram-negative enteric bacilli and thus nonspecific.

In enteric fever (usually due to *S typhi*), the host-parasite relationship is dramatically different. After ingestion, the microorganisms multiply asymptom-atically in the gastrointestinal tract and result in a transient bacteremia. However, salmonellae appear susceptible to the complement-mediated bactericidal activity of normal human serum. This occurs through initial C1 binding, probably to the sugar portion of the core of lipopolysaccharides and is independent of antibody. Perhaps the salmonellae are protected within phagocytes and carried to the fixed macrophages of the reticuloendothelial system. The subsequent intracellular multiplication of *S typhi*, with production of a secondary sustained bacteremia, constitutes an essential pathophysiologic feature of enteric fever. Invasion of the biliary system results in the reentry of microorganisms into the gastrointestinal tract in massive numbers. Involvement of lymphoid tissue in the intestinal tract, principally Peyer's patches in the terminal ileum, leads to necrosis and ulceration. Typical clinical manifestations of typhoid fever include fever, headache, apathy, cough, prostration, splenomegaly, skin rash ("rose spots"), and leukocytopenia. The course of the disease is prolonged; relapses are common.

Factors that suggest the involvement of cell-mediated immune mechanisms in *Salmonella* enteric fever include the following:

(1) The occurrence of intracellular parasitism.
(2) The demonstrated ability to transfer immunity to normal animals adoptively with lymphocytes of immune animals.
(3) The absence of significant participation by PMNs in the infective process.
(4) When killed salmonellae or their extracts are administered to animals in Freund's complete adjuvant, solid immunity is established which is comparable to the immunity achieved by infection with attenuated microorganisms. This is a pattern characteristic of cell-mediated immunity. Conversely, administration of killed vaccines alone will generate high-titer antibodies and delay (but not prevent) infection. Passive immunization with immune serum is of no benefit.
(5) Delayed hypersensitivity skin tests with protein extracts of salmonellae convert to positive after animals are immunized with salmonellae in Freund's complete adjuvant.

The macrophage is important in host defense as well. Peritoneal exudate cells from immunized mice are far more active against *S enteritidis* than those from nonimmunized mice. This bactericidal activity depends in part on heat-stable opsonizing antibody. It is highly specific in that nonspecifically activated macrophages (*Listeria* infection) are no more effective than normal macrophages in reducing *S enteritidis* growth.

Immunologic Diagnosis

An increase in titer of agglutinins against the somatic (O) and flagellar (H) antigens of *S typhi* (Widal test) usually occurs during the course of typhoid fever, reaching a peak during the third week of illness. A 4-fold titer increase is held to be significant. Unfortunately, the test is far less specific than is generally appreciated, and titers may be elevated in many hyperglobulinemic states (chronic liver disease is one example). Furthermore, progressive increases in titer occur in association with many diseases not due to *Salmonella*. The use of the agglutination reaction as a diagnostic test should always be subordinated to direct cultural demonstration of the infecting microorganism. There are no commercial tests for cell-mediated immune responses to *Salmonella* extracts.

Prevention

Commercial typhoid vaccines consist of acetone-killed *S typhi;* they appear capable only of raising the minimum infecting dose of *S typhi* in vaccinated subjects. New vaccines made from Vi antigen (a simple homopolymer of N-acetylgalactosaminuronic acid expressed as a surface antigen; Fig 33–1) or from *Salmonella* ribosomes are controversial and of uncertain clinical benefit. From the preceding discussion, it would appear that a live attenuated vaccine should offer the best chance of protection.

Treatment

Chloramphenicol and ampicillin are the major agents used to treat enteric fever or bacteremic salmonellosis. Prolonged therapy is required, since microorganisms are sequestered in macrophages and presumably protected from the entry of antibiotics.

5. LISTERIOSIS

Listeria monocytogenes is a small, pleomorphic gram-positive rod that may be confused with nonpathogenic "diphtheroids" or with beta-hemolytic streptococci. It produces sporadic infections in humans, usually in the form of bacteremia and meningitis. Two features have elevated listeriosis to a position of prominence in the fields of infectious disease and immunology. First, it is clear that patients with depressed cell-mediated immunity resulting from lymphoreticular malignancy or the use of immunosuppressive drugs have an increased susceptibility to listeriosis. Second, infection with *L monocytogenes* has become an important model for studies of cell-mediated immune mechanisms in experimental animals. An important observation made with *L monocytogenes*—since confirmed with other intracellular pathogens—is that immunity can be adoptively transferred to noninfected animals by means of lymphocytes from animals that have recovered from listeriosis.

In mice infected with *Listeria,* initial reduction in tissue counts is due to sequestration and killing by macrophages. PMNs play a prominent role somewhat later in the course of infection.

In humans, the infection appears to be self-limited and usually does not produce prolonged granulomatous disease. Indeed, listeriosis often presents as an acute purulent meningitis with a predominance of PMNs and a low cerebrospinal fluid glucose concentration. Nevertheless, there appears to be no question that cell-mediated immune mechanisms are critically important in control of this infection. The precise factors that dictate the virulence of this pathogen are unknown. There has been some suggestion that the complement system which readily opsonizes *Listeria* may actually "protect" the bacilli by facilitating their transport to a "protected" environment within monocytes.

INTRACELLULAR INFECTIONS IN WHICH LYMPHOCYTES & MACROPHAGES ARE DECISIVE IN RECOVERY & HUMORAL IMMUNE MECHANISMS PLAY NO PROTECTIVE ROLE

Major Immunologic Features

- Facultative or obligate intramacrophagic parasitism.
- Lymphocyte-macrophage interaction regulates immunity but may simultaneously mediate destruction of host tissues (bystander cell injury).
- Granulomas and giant cells characteristic of immune response.
- PMNs and opsonins inconsequential in protection.

General Considerations

Infections due to *Mycobacterium tuberculosis* and *Mycobacterium leprae* fulfill the above criteria particularly well. Although there may be considerable antibody synthesis in many mycobacterial infections (to the point of marked hypergammaglobulinemia in lepromatous leprosy), the antibody is broadly cross-reactive. Hence, its measurement is not of current practical significance. Mycobacteria are easily phagocytosed in the absence of specific opsonins, perhaps because of an affinity between their lipid-rich cell walls and the lipids of macrophage cell membranes.

The second group of diseases in this section—histoplasmosis, coccidioidomycosis, brucellosis, and tularemia—are distinguished from diseases due to mycobacteria in that measurement of antibody is of definite practical value in diagnosis, prognosis, or both.

Diseases in Which Measurement of Antibodies Is Not Useful in Diagnosis or Prognosis

1. TUBERCULOSIS

Mycobacterium tuberculosis is a facultatively intracellular, aerobic, acid-fast bacillus naturally pathogenic only for humans. It produces no known toxins, and its virulence relates to its ability to survive and proliferate in mononuclear phagocytes. Recent studies suggest that *M tuberculosis* may evade the bactericidal activity of macrophages by preventing the fusion of enzyme-containing lysosomes with phagosomes containing the bacilli. Dead tubercle bacilli do not demonstrate this phenomenon.

Several microbial constituents appear to influence the pattern of host response: (1) **Cord factor** (trehalose-6,6'-dimycolic acid), the material responsible for the in vitro serpentine cordlike growth of *M tuberculosis,* inhibits migration of leukocytes and stimulates granuloma formation. (2) High-molecular-weight **lipids** and **waxes** are probably responsible for much of the tissue reaction to this microorganism. Up to 60% of the dry weight of the cell wall of *M tuberculosis* is composed of lipid—which may account for the relative impermeability to stains, acid-fastness, unusual resistance to killing by acid and alkali, resistance to the bactericidal activity of complement, and resistance to intracellular macrophage digestion of this microorganism. (3) **Wax D** and **tuberculoproteins** may be largely responsible for the production of tuberculin hypersensitivity and skin test positivity. Wax D has been detected for up to 56 days in experimentally induced skin lesions and may account for the chronicity of tuberculous lesions.

The clinical manifestations of tuberculosis are clearly a function of the immune status of the host. The immune status appears to be at least in part genetically controlled. Recent studies have strongly suggested an increased susceptibility to tuberculosis infection and subsequent dissemination in persons with HLA-Bw15 antigen. The development of a sensitized T lymphocyte population is a double-edged sword. On the one hand, macrophages are stimulated (activated) to enhanced antimicrobial activity with limitation of mycobacterial growth. On the other hand, normal (bystander) tissues are seriously damaged by the violence of the immune (hypersensitivity) response to the infective agent. Tissue damage may reflect the discharge of hydrolytic enzymes from dying macrophages as well as direct inflammatory effects of lymphocyte mediators such as lymphotoxin, MIF, and others.

During the early course of tuberculosis in experimental animals, there is suppression of delayed hypersensitivity and other indices of cell-mediated immunity. This has been associated with suppressor T lymphocytes and macrophages. More recently, arabinogalactan in the sera of tuberculous patients has been shown to suppress lymphocyte responses of normal subjects to PPD and phytohemagglutinin. These phenomena may account for the anergy seen in some patients with tuberculosis.

Some investigators believe that immunity and tuberculin hypersensitivity are not inextricably linked. For example, macrophages may act to control *M tuberculosis* through nonphagocytic mechanisms by the secretion of antimycobacterial fatty acids. Furthermore, animals can be rendered tuberculin-sensitive by injecting them with wax D and tuberculoprotein; such animals are still entirely susceptible to

infection with *M tuberculosis.* Conversely, certain RNA-protein complexes isolated from mycobacterial cells will induce high degrees of increased resistance to tuberculous infection without inducing tuberculin hypersensitivity. Finally, animals immunized against tuberculosis with a mycobacterial RNA–protein complex do not show increased resistance to infection with other intracellular parasites. These data suggest that the general phenomenon of macrophage activation with enhanced nonspecific killing of any intracellular microorganism may not be as important as specific, lymphocyte-mediated immunity, however that specificity is mediated.

Clinical Features

Tuberculosis is predominantly a pulmonary disease transmitted by aerosol. Hematogenous dissemination may allow secondary infection to develop in virtually any organ system. Major sections of standard textbooks are devoted to the clinical features of tuberculosis. This discussion will be limited to the immunologic perspective.

Pulmonary tuberculosis in the nonimmune patient is characterized initially by relatively unrestricted bacillary multiplication, with the development of infiltrative disease of the lower lobes or lower segments of the upper lobes. The inflammatory response is "exudative," being composed mainly of PMNs and monocytes. Tissue destruction and cavitation are not seen, and there may be remarkably few symptoms of infection, particularly in children. Bacilli spread via the lymphatics to regional lymph nodes and often reach the bloodstream. Infection is well tolerated for several weeks, during which time active immunity develops with resultant enhanced macrophage antimicrobial activity, curtailment of bacillary multiplication, resolution of the pneumonic process, and healing of extrapulmonary lesions. Simultaneously, a positive tuberculin skin test develops, reflecting the presence of specifically sensitized T lymphocytes. A hallmark of healed primary pulmonary tuberculosis is the **Ghon complex,** which generally consists of a calcified node in the lung parenchyma and enlarged, often calcified hilar nodes. It is crucial to realize that virulent tubercle bacilli may persist for years, or even a lifetime, in such "healed" lesions. These organisms are different from replicating *M tuberculosis* in that they have unique antigens not shared with dividing *M tuberculosis.* In some cases, primary tuberculosis does not heal but goes on to produce cavitation (especially in adults). Patients may also develop fulminating disseminated (miliary) tuberculosis, typically associated with meningitis.

The pattern of infection in the immune (tuberculin skin test–positive) patient results in a totally distinct disease process in which there is extensive tissue destruction. **Postprimary,** or **reinfection, tuberculosis** may occur as a result of exogenous reinfection but more often reflects a recrudescence of old infection (**endogenous reinfection**) in response to intercurrent debilitating illness, advanced age, or immunosuppression. Lesions are located typically in apical or subapical pulmonary segments. Regional lymph node involvement is not conspicuous; disease is far more localized. Lesions are more likely to excavate and spread by bronchogenic dissemination within the lung rather than by lymphohematogenous spread beyond the lung. The inflammatory response is characterized by granuloma formation with giant cells and **caseation necrosis** (in which the necrotic tissue remains semisolid, with the consistency of cheese). Tissue destruction is profound; pulmonary fibrosis is common, and calcification may occur.

Reinfection tuberculosis may occur at any of the sites of original hematogenous dissemination resulting from primary tuberculosis. Renal, meningeal, genitourinary, and skeletal tuberculosis are beyond the scope of this discussion.

Immunologic Diagnosis

The diagnosis of tuberculosis is established by isolating and identifying the infective etiologic agent on bacteriologic media and not by immunologic means. Recent studies suggest that tuberculostearic acid, a fatty acid characteristic of microorganisms in the order Actinomycetales, may be identifiable in the sputum of patients with pulmonary tuberculosis by gas chromatography/mass spectrometry with selected ion monitoring. If these findings are confirmed, it may be possible to diagnose tuberculosis more rapidly than by current bacteriologic techniques.

Tuberculin skin test. (See Chapter 23.) The tuberculin skin test provides no diagnostic information relative to a given acute illness unless it can be established that the skin test has converted from negative to positive in temporal relation to that illness. Otherwise, a positive skin test indicates only that the patient has experienced tuberculosis or a closely related mycobacterial infection at some time in the past. A positive tuberculin skin test indicates the presence of specifically sensitized T lymphocytes. A strongly positive skin test is thought to represent greater liability to active infection, since a larger mass of latent tuberculous disease would theoretically have to be present to maintain strong tuberculin hypersensitivity.

The principal tuberculin skin test preparation is **purified protein derivative (PPD)**. PPD is prepared by ammonium sulfate precipitation of culture filtrate and is standardized in terms of biologic reactivity as "tuberculin units" (TU). One TU is the activity contained in a specific weight of Seibert's PPD lot No. 49608 in a specified buffer (PPD-S). First strength tuberculin has 1 TU, intermediate strength 5 TU, and second strength 250 TU of activity.

Of several ways to administer intradermal PPD, only the Mantoux procedure is reliable and reproducible. First strength tuberculin is no longer used. Second strength tuberculin is frequently cross-reactive with mycobacteria other than *M tuberculosis* (atypical mycobacteria) and thus lacks specificity. Intermediate strength tuberculin is the material used for most skin-testing procedures. A positive response consists of 10 mm or more of erythema and induration and should be read between 48 and 72 hours after the skin test is applied. A negative skin test signifies either no tuberculosis infection or else the presence of anergy due to overwhelming infection or associated immunosuppressive illness (sarcoidosis, Hodgkin's disease). (See Chapter 23.) Anergy may be specific to PPD or broad to all antigens. It may be associated with depressed in vitro tests for cell-mediated immunity, such as lymphocyte blastogenesis. Anergy is frequently associated with increased numbers of T suppressor lymphocytes. Tuberculin sensitivity develops 2–10 weeks after infection. Patients with persistent anergy frequently convert their skin tests and in vitro tests to positive after a few weeks of treatment. Unfortunately, such "conversions" can be confused with "boosting" reactions in healthy people. Boosting occurs when a person with low-grade PPD reactivity is retested a week later and responds with a significantly larger reaction in the second test. This is due to the stimulus of the PPD antigen of the first test. The original infection may have been due to *M tuberculosis* occurring many years before or to nontuberculous mycobacteria that cross-react with PPD. To avoid mistaking boosting for real conversion, it is recommended that persons participating in regular skin testing programs who, within a period of 2 years, exhibit an increase in diameter of induration of at least 6 mm, with a resultant change in the diameter of skin test reactivity from < 10 mm to > 10 mm of induration, be considered newly infected.

Other Tests

There has been recent interest in using in vitro tests to diagnose tuberculosis. The rationale is that these tests may be positive at a time when skin tests are negative. A recent study has cast doubt on the use of lymphocyte transformation assay. In 58 children with active tuberculosis, suspected tuberculosis, or no tuberculosis, there was complete correlation of the skin test reaction with the lymphocyte transformation reaction. Thus, the lymphocyte transformation test represented no improvement over the simpler skin test. There has also been interest in the use of antibody assays to diagnose tuberculosis. Hemagglutinating antibody, radioimmunoassay, and other techniques have been used. The issue of testing is controversial, and there is still no convincing evidence that techniques other than the skin test will aid in diagnosis.

Differential Diagnosis

Infiltrative and cavitary pulmonary tuberculosis must be considered in the differential diagnosis of a plethora of pulmonary diseases. Weight loss, night sweats, and hemoptysis are common clues to reinfection tuberculosis. Discussion should be sought in standard medical textbooks.

Prevention

Living avirulent tubercle bacilli—especially BCG, an attenuated strain of *Mycobacterium bovis*—have been used to stimulate resistance to infection in persons at greater than normal risk of exposure to tuberculosis. Such immunization may provide many years of protection from tuberculosis infection, the principal disadvantage being conversion of the tuberculin skin test and hence unavailability of the test as a clue to exposure to *M tuberculosis*. BCG vaccine has never achieved popularity in the USA.

An alternative method of providing protection against tuberculosis is to treat all patients with recent skin test conversions with isoniazid for 1 year. The numbers of infecting microorganisms are low; thus, multiple drug regimens are not required. Recent data indicating the hepatotoxicity of isoniazid have led to greater care in selection of patients for isoniazid prophylaxis so that only those who definitely require the drug will be treated in this way. It is no longer suggested that anyone with a positive skin test, regardless of age or of the duration of the reaction, receive isoniazid as a matter of course.

Treatment

Cavitary pulmonary tuberculosis and disseminated forms of tuberculosis require treatment with combinations of drugs (isoniazid plus rifampin or other combinations) to retard the ascendency of naturally occurring drug-resistant mutants found in small numbers in any large population of *M tuberculosis*. Other texts should be consulted for more detailed discussions of the complicated problem of the treatment of tuberculosis.

Complications & Prognosis

Some of the complications of tuberculosis have already been mentioned. Meningitis, renal infection, etc, are discussed in other texts. Rarely—but especially in Scandinavian countries—tuberculosis may be complicated by the occurrence of erythema nodosum. This presumably reflects the presence of circulating immune complexes. Amyloidosis is an immunologic complication that may occur in patients with long-standing infection.

2. LEPROSY

Mycobacterium leprae is an obligate intracellular acid-fast bacillus which has a unique ability to invade nerves and a preference for growth in cool areas of the body. *M leprae* has never been cultivated successfully in vitro but will multiply to a limited extent in the footpads of mice. More widespread infection occurs in animals thymectomized at birth, emphasizing the crucial role of thymus-mediated immunity in this infection. Armadillos are susceptible to disseminated infection without the necessity for prior immunosuppression.

M leprae produces a remarkably broad spectrum of clinical disease ranging from **tuberculoid leprosy** at one extreme to **lepromatous leprosy** at the other. The pattern of infection is intimately related to the underlying degree of cell-mediated immunity. Like *M tuberculosis*, the leprosy bacillus elaborates no destructive enzymes or toxins; disease production is related directly to the ability to survive macrophage residence. Recent electron microscopic studies suggest that *M leprae* may evade macrophage antimicrobial activity by escaping from phagolysosomes to lie free in macrophage cytoplasm. The significance of these observations remains to be established.

Lepromatous leprosy is characterized by the virtual absence of a specific cellular immune response to *M leprae*. Thus, bacillary infiltration of tissues is extensive, and tissue destruction is minimal until very late in the disease. In tuberculoid leprosy, the converse is true: the immune response is severe enough to damage or destroy bacilli and the nerves they infect at the outset. Borderline leprosy refers to the broad sweep of intervening disease between the lepromatous and tuberculoid "poles" and accounts for most clinical infections. Borderline leprosy is characterized by clinical and immunologic instability.

M leprae is traditionally regarded as a feeble pathogen, requiring intimate and prolonged contact for transmission. However, there are so many exceptions that leprosy has also been considered an easily transmissible infection in populations where only a few persons are sufficiently susceptible to permit development of clinically apparent disease. Unfortunately, there is no diagnostic skin test to assist in identifying persons who have experienced asymptomatic infection. Recent studies based upon examination of *M leprae*-specific lymphocyte activation in asymptomatic leprosy contacts suggest that acquisition of infection (sensitization) is relatively common despite the rarity of symptomatic disease. (Whether the blastogenesis test is specific for *M leprae* is unclear.)

The factors that dictate susceptibility to clinical infection remain uncertain. However, it is clear that inability to respond to the lepromin skin test (see below) is characteristic of patients with lepromatous leprosy and that lepromin anergy often persists despite apparent cure of disease. Thus, in a patient susceptible to lepromatous leprosy, an immune defect related to impaired recognition of *M leprae* is present. Whether the defect is predominantly one of macrophages or of lymphocytes remains contested.

Clinical Features

A. Lepromatous Leprosy: Lepromatous leprosy is manifested by widespread bacillary invasion of the integument (except in warm skin folds) and of the cooler mucous membranes (especially the nose, which may be a source of infective aerosols). Diffuse bacillary invasion of the facial tissues results in the characteristic leonine facies of advanced disease. There is continuous heavy bacteremia (10^5–10^6 bacilli/mL), which is well tolerated; liver, spleen, and bone marrow are loaded with microorganisms. Although peripheral nerves are heavily invaded by *M leprae*, nerve destruction does not occur until late in the illness, reflecting the poor immunologic response to infection. Histologic findings reflect the lack of immune response. Macrophages are packed with acid-fast bacilli; neither lymphocytes nor giant cells are present; there is no granuloma formation.

B. Tuberculoid Leprosy: This form of the disease is characterized by the presence of no more than one or 2 extremely well demarcated skin lesions with anesthetic atrophic centers and erythematous, raised edges. A palpable nerve trunk can often be found in the vicinity of the skin lesion. Histologic findings resemble those of sarcoidosis (epithelioid cell foci surrounded by well-defined zones of lymphocytes); however, the cutaneous nerves are destroyed by the tuberculoid leprosy granuloma, whereas nerves are spared in sarcoidosis. Rare acid-fast bacilli may be found in nerve remnants by careful serial sectioning of skin lesions. Caseation necrosis occurs very rarely in leprosy but may be seen in the nerves of patients with tuberculoid leprosy when there is a particularly vigorous immune response.

C. Borderline Leprosy: So-called borderline leprosy accounts for a broad spectrum of clinical disease. The more nearly lepromatous a case of borderline leprosy is, the more plentiful the bacilli, the more numerous the skin lesions, the less well defined their edges, and the less pronounced the anesthesia. The more nearly tuberculoid a case of borderline leprosy is, the fewer the number of lesions (and bacilli), the sharper their edges, the more pronounced the degree of anesthesia, the greater the chances for finding enlarged peripheral nerves, and the more lymphocytes on histologic examination.

Immunologic Diagnosis

There is no immunologic test for leprosy.

Lepromin skin test. Lepromin has no diagnostic usefulness; lepromin skin test reactivity is common in normal persons by virtue of sensitivity to crossreacting mycobacterial antigens and foreign skin proteins. Lepromin is prepared from a homogenate of lepromatous skin nodules; the extracted leprosy bacilli are variably purified. In a person who is *known* to have leprosy, lepromin reactivity is diagnostic of tuberculoid or near-tuberculoid disease, whereas lepromin anergy carries the prognosis for progression to lepromatous leprosy in the absence of treatment. Treated patients who fail to recover lepromin reactivity are at risk of relapse and should receive antileprosy chemotherapy for life.

Differential Diagnosis

Leprosy should be suspected whenever an anesthetic skin lesion is found. Skin biopsies with stains for mycobacteria should be used to seek histologic proof of diagnosis since even apparently fullblown lepromatous leprosy may be confused with post-kala azar dermal leishmaniasis. (The striking immunologic similarities between leishmaniasis [see Chapter 37] and leprosy are noteworthy as well.) The essential histologic criterion for a diagnosis of leprosy is the presence of acid-fast bacilli in nerves. More specialized sources should be sought for details of the diagnosis of leprosy.

Prevention

About 10% of untreated household contacts of lepromatous patients eventually develop leprosy; the risk is higher for children than adults. Prophylactic dapsone therapy may be of value in blocking disease transmission within families. The efficacy of BCG vaccine in the prevention of leprosy has not been established.

Treatment

The mainstay of leprosy treatment is dapsone (diaminodiphenylsulfone, DDS). Rifampin is bactericidal for *M leprae* and promises to be very useful in treatment; its principal problem is one of expense. Clofazimine, a phenazine dye, has direct anti–*M leprae* activity but also appears capable of stimulating macrophage bactericidal activity (at least for *Listeria monocytogenes*). In high doses, clofazimine also suppresses erythema nodosum leprosum activity (see below).

Immunologic Complications

There are 5 principal immunologic complications of leprosy:

A. "Antigen Overload": In patients with lepromatous leprosy, lepromin anergy permits the accumulation of astounding numbers of *M leprae* (10^9/g of skin, 10^5–10^6/mL of blood, 10^7/mL of nasal secretions, 10^{12} total body). Associated with the massive accumulation of foreign antigen are a variety of immunologic aberrations. Humoral abnormalities include polyclonal hypergammaglobulinemia, cryoglobulinemia, rheumatoid factor, biologic falsepositive syphilis serology, and hyperglobulinemia-related latent distal renal tubular acidosis. Cellular abnormalities include depletion of paracortical (T) lymphocytes from lymph nodes, decreased numbers of circulating T cells, anergy to skin tests with recall antigens, impaired skin graft rejection, and impaired lymphocyte activation. All abnormalities are reversible with treatment, with the general exception of lepromin anergy.

The relationships that exist among antibody production, delayed type hypersensitivity, and cellmediated immunity in patients with leprosy are shown in Fig 33–3. In localized (tuberculoid) disease, serum antibody titers are low and delayed hypersensitivity and cell-mediated immunity maximal. In disseminated (lepromatous) disease, the opposite relationships obtain.

This precise relationship can be applied without significant modification to a broad variety of other intracellular infections including coccidioidomycosis, histoplasmosis, leishmaniasis, and tuberculosis. The factors underlying depression of cell-mediated immunity and delayed hypersensitivity in disseminated infection are unclear but may relate to interruption of normal lymphocyte (predominantly T cell) traffic by granulomatous involvement of the periarteriolar lymphocytic sheaths of splenic white pulp and paracortical areas of lymph nodes. In addition, serum or plasma

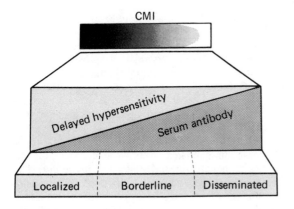

Figure 33-3. A schematic representation of the relationships among antibody production, delayed hypersensitivity, and cell-mediated immunity (CMI) as related to severity of intracellular infection. (Reproduced, with permission, from Bullock WE: Anergy and infection. *Adv Intern Med* 1976; 21:158.)

factors may be present that impair the response of lymphocytes to microbial antigens. Finally, there is evidence that intense stimulation of suppressor T cell function in certain intracellular disease processes may result in apparent deficiency of cell-mediated immune mechanisms.

B. Erythema Nodosum Leprosum: Erythema nodosum leprosum is a complication of lepromatous leprosy and results from an Arthus-type immune reaction in the skin and from the deposition of circulating immune complexes in the joints and kidneys. Nearly 50% of lepromatous patients will acquire erythema nodosum leprosum; it may occur spontaneously but more often follows initiation of chemotherapy. Erythema nodosum leprosum is characterized histologically by vasculitis and panniculitis and clinically by recurrent crops of up to hundreds of red, hot, tender skin lesions occurring all over the body. This complication is associated with severe systemic symptoms. The recent discovery that erythema nodosum leprosum is rapidly eradicated by thalidomide has revolutionized the therapeutic approach to this difficult problem.

C. Lucio Phenomenon (Erythema Necroticans): The Lucio phenomenon is a complication of certain forms of lepromatous leprosy. Necrotizing vasculitis produces crops of large polygonal lesions characterized by ulceration and sloughing of large areas of skin. It may be peculiar to specific ethnic groups.

D. Reversal and Downgrading Reactions: These "reactions" are characteristic of borderline forms of leprosy and represent abrupt shifts in cell-mediated immunity, often with striking nerve damage. Preexisting quiescent skin lesions become abruptly red, hot, and tender. Granulomas may break up and lymphocytes become sparse (downgrading reaction), or skin lesions may show evidence of acquisition of immunologic activity with influx of lymphocytes (re-

versal reaction). These immunologic complications may be very severe, necessitating treatment with corticosteroids. Thalidomide is not effective.

E. Amyloidosis: Secondary amyloidosis is an important cause of renal failure and death in patients with advanced leprosy. Curiously, this complication appears to be far more common in Caucasians than other ethnic groups.

Diseases in Which Measurement of Antibody Is Useful in Diagnosis or Prognosis

The diseases in this group share many of the immunopathologic features of the mycobacterial infections, particularly tuberculosis; a major difference is that antibodies, though subserving no protective function, may assist in establishing a diagnosis or prognosis.

3. HISTOPLASMOSIS

Histoplasma capsulatum is a dimorphic fungus that exists in mycelial form in nature and as an intracellular yeast in humans and susceptible animals. Despite its name, this fungus is not encapsulated.

In the USA, the midwestern portion of the country, especially the Mississippi and Missouri River valleys, is the area of highest endemicity.

Exposure to *H capsulatum* in the endemic areas is usually frequent and often heavy. Avian droppings of chickens, starlings, and other birds provide a compost for luxuriant growth. When infected soil is disturbed, spores are aerosolized and inhaled. These are distributed throughout the lungs and presumably enter macrophages, where they convert to the parasitic yeast form. In the first few weeks after exposure, cell-mediated immune responses develop. The results are a positive histoplasmin skin test, lymphokine production, death or cicatrization of the intracellular yeast, and fibrocalcific healing at the site of primary infection. This last process is expressed by "buckshot" calcifications in the lung and spleen (fungemia is part of the initial process).

Cell-mediated immunity is critical to host defense. If there is failure of cell-mediated immunity, the yeasts proliferate unchecked in macrophages. This results in uncontrolled disseminated histoplasmosis with diffusely enlarged reticuloendothelial organs such as the liver, spleen, and lymph nodes. Athymic ("nude") mice develop this form of disease. They can be protected by thymus transplantation or provision of T lymphocytes. Further, in murine histoplasmosis there is activation of splenic suppressor macrophage activity. This depresses cell-mediated immune responses. Activity of these cells is maximal in the first weeks after infection. Their role in host defense is not known. As with other fungi, transferrin may inhibit the growth of *H capsulatum* by sequestering iron from the fungus.

It is of note that the healing process may be more

destructive of tissue than the disseminated disease. If extensive fibrosis occurs, the buckshot calcification may enlarge into a histoplasmoma, or mediastinal fibrosis may occur. There is much granuloma and inflammatory reaction with few fungi seen. In disseminated disease, granuloma formation is poor; macrophages are loaded with yeasts, but there is little necrosis.

Clinical Features

Several distinctive syndromes of histoplasmosis are recognized:

A. Primary Histoplasmosis: Primary histoplasmosis is generally asymptomatic or attributed to an episode of "flu"; it is recognized in retrospect only by the acquisition of histoplasmin skin test reactivity. In heavy exposures, patients are more likely to manifest cough, malaise, and fever. In most cases, the disease is self-limited, with calcified granulomas representing the residue.

B. Acute Disseminated Histoplasmosis: In the patient who fails to contain the infection at the outset, the result may be acute disseminated histoplasmosis. This complication occurs typically but not exclusively in children. It is characterized by fever, hepatosplenomegaly, anemia, and leukopenia. Untreated, it is highly lethal; death occurs in days to weeks.

C. Acute Reinfection Histoplasmosis: The patient with histoplasmin sensitivity who continues to reside in a histoplasmosis-endemic area is subject to reexposure to the fungus. Mild reexposures may be asymptomatic, serving only as "boosters" to maintenance of histoplasmin skin test reactivity. In patients possessing cell-mediated immunity to *H capsulatum,* the course of illness resulting from a subsequent massive reexposure is characterized by a severe pulmonary inflammatory response. Acute reinfection pulmonary histoplasmosis is thus related more closely to host hypersensitivity than to fungal invasiveness and is usually self-limited.

There is no event comparable to massive exogenous histoplasmosis reexposure in patients with tuberculosis, since neither the environment nor infected patient contacts harbor mycobacteria in the concentrations necessary to produce this intense immunologic reaction.

D. Chronic Pulmonary Histoplasmosis: Chronic pulmonary histoplasmosis bears a striking resemblance to pulmonary tuberculosis (with which it was historically confused and with which it may coexist). It occurs predominantly in middle-aged white cigarette smokers, especially those with chronic obstructive pulmonary disease and, undoubtedly, recurrent exposure to *H capsulatum.* At the outset, one or more areas of infiltration or cavitation usually develop in the peripheral apical-posterior segments of the lungs. The lesions may slowly heal, contracting into a scarred band; or they may cavitate, with progressive cavitary enlargement and attendant pulmonary destruction. New lesions may appear as old ones are resolving, which suggests that breakdown of old lesions may lead to antigenic spillover into new sites, with development of secondary inflammatory processes.

Chronic pulmonary histoplasmosis is not associated with extrapulmonary dissemination, as cellular immunity is basically intact. The disease appears to persist because of the presence of underlying abnormal pulmonary anatomy and perhaps aberrantly increased immune response.

E. Chronic Disseminated Histoplasmosis: Chronic disseminated histoplasmosis occurs in patients with defective cell-mediated immunity. This syndrome reflects generalized *Histoplasma* invasion of the reticuloendothelial system. Clinical findings thus include fever, anemia, leukopenia, hepatosplenomegaly, lymphadenopathy, and wasting. Childhood forms include widespread dissemination with signs of marrow suppression and splenic involvement. Adult forms are usually chronic, with little marrow dysfunction and more focal lesions, particularly in the oral mucosa. The most serious (and surprisingly common) complication of this form of histoplasmosis is adrenal gland invasion and destruction.

Immunologic Diagnosis

Despite the close correlation of immunologic and clinical status, immunologic tools are of little help in establishing a clinical diagnosis. There are several reasons for this: (1) The histoplasmin skin test is so frequently positive in endemic areas that a positive skin test is meaningless in an individual patient and merely reflects a prior infective encounter with the fungus. (2) The serologic titers are often boosted artifactually by a previous positive skin test. Improved skin test antigens are now being prepared from yeast phase fungi. These have less cross reactivity and apparently do not influence the serologic assays. Other efforts have been made to circumvent problems of skin testing by measuring complement fixation titers against yeast phase antigens (since histoplasmin is prepared from mycelial phase microorganisms). This is done in the hope that the yeast phase titer will rise only in worsening disease, in contrast to the false mycelial phase elevation from skin testing. This works better in theory than in practice, since both titers often rise after skin testing. Even a coccidioidin skin test may produce an elevation of *Histoplasma* yeast phase complement-fixing antibody titers. (3) Other serologic assays, such as precipitins and agar gel diffusion, have been used in an attempt to identify the patient with active histoplasmosis. None of these are thoroughly reliable. (4) The histoplasmin complement fixation antibody is elevated in only about half of patients with disseminated histoplasmosis. Many are therefore missed by this test. (5) There is frequent serologic cross-reaction with antigens of *Blastomyces dermatitidis.* Because blastomycosis occurs in the histoplasmosis-endemic areas, this could lead to misdiagnosis. (6) Antigens of these 3 fungi cross-react extensively in tests of cell-mediated immunity such as lymphocyte blastogenesis.

One might ask whether there is any value at all in immunologic testing. The response is a qualified "yes" for serology and a very limited "yes" for the skin test. The serologic titer might conceivably be helpful in a very ill patient with clinical findings suggesting histoplasmosis, one in whom it may be inappropriate to withhold treatment for up to 4 weeks pending culture results. If strongly elevated, and if not complicated by a preceding skin test, the high titer may be grounds for a presumptive diagnosis of histoplasmosis pending the results of cultures.

Histoplasmin skin tests are most useful (1) in epidemiologic surveys, (2) in evaluating a patient for skin test anergy as part of a general immunologic evaluation for a reason unrelated to histoplasmosis, and (3) to assess cell-mediated immunity in a mycologically confirmed histoplasmosis patient. This is rarely necessary and should be done for prognostic purposes, not for diagnosis. Immunohistochemical tissue staining may also be helpful in detecting *H capsulatum*.

Marked elevation of IgE occurs in active histoplasmosis. The cause of this phenomenon and its possible diagnostic value, if any, have not been determined.

In summary, many physicians use immunologic methods to diagnose histoplasmosis. Because of the pitfalls outlined above, many of these diagnoses are incorrect. The best and most absolute method is to culture *H capsulatum* from tissue of the infected patient.

Prevention

Animals can be immunized with *Histoplasma* extracts in Freund's complete adjuvant or by sublethal infections with virulent *H capsulatum*. However, there are no suitably attenuated strains for human use. Furthermore, it is conceivable that immunization could adversely affect patients in whom hypersensitivity may play the major role in disease production.

Treatment

Prolonged amphotericin B has been the mainstay of medical therapy. Ketoconazole appears effective and less toxic. Several patients with histoplasmosis, both pulmonary and disseminated, have been treated with transfer factor. Results are inconclusive.

Complications & Prognosis

These may include bronchial obstruction by calcified *Histoplasma* granulomas that become broncholiths. Destruction of lung by chronic pulmonary histoplasmosis may lead to secondary bacterial infection and respiratory insufficiency as a late complication, and even treated patients should be followed chronically for this problem.

The prognosis for spontaneous recovery from acute pulmonary histoplasmosis is excellent, whereas patients with chronic cavitary pulmonary histoplasmosis are prone to relapse even after treatment with amphotericin B. Surgical resection is often beneficial. Indications for surgery are unclear. Disseminated forms of histoplasmosis are fatal in more than 80% of instances in the absence of treatment with amphotericin B.

4. COCCIDIOIDOMYCOSIS

Whereas histoplasmosis is endemic in the midwestern USA, coccidioidomycosis is its counterpart in the southwestern states. Like *H capsulatum*, the fungus *Coccidioides immitis* is dimorphic, with a sporulating mycelial form in nature and a separate spherule form in humans. Infectious arthrospores survive long periods in the desert and travel miles on the gentlest breeze. Shortly after inhalation, the "barrel-shaped" arthrospores convert to spherules, probably within alveolar macrophages. Over the next 4–7 days, the spherules progressively enlarge to reach a total diameter of up to 30 μm, with a chitinous outer wall 1–2 μm in thickness. At maturity, the outer wall thins and ruptures, liberating numerous small endospores. Endospores are chemotactic for PMNs, which attempt to ingest and destroy them. However, the PMNs are unsuccessful and are themselves destroyed, leaving necrotic cell debris and maturing spherules in their wake. If not interrupted, endospores mature into successive generations of spherules and the cycle repeats itself. Thus, in early coccidioidomycosis, there are focal areas of pulmonary consolidation, with alveoli full of spherules, necrotic debris, PMNs, and few mononuclear cells.

Macrophages are unable to immediately kill all spherules, but the development, in 2–3 weeks, of cell-mediated immunity to *C immitis* results in macrophage activation and in enhancement of their ability to wall off or kill infecting fungi. The exact mechanism of killing is unknown. Cell-mediated immunity can be demonstrated by conversion of the coccidioidin (mycelial antigen) or spherulin (spherule antigen) skin test and by lymphocyte activation and MIF responses to these antigens.

There are at least 2 critical immunologic events that, if interrupted, might influence the clinical course of coccidioidomycosis. The first involves a block of macrophage processing of *C immitis* and of subsequent T cell instruction. Without an effective processing step, the unsuccessful PMN cycle would repeat itself and the fungi would grow essentially uninterrupted. The clinical picture that is compatible with this sort of immune defect consists of fulminating coccidioidal pneumonia with metastatic spread through the body and the dramatic appearance of dermal and subcutaneous abscesses filled with spherules and PMNs. Tests for cell-mediated immunity are negative. The second defect involves a failure of production or function of lymphokines. The defect is surprisingly subtle, as are its clinical consequences. There may be a selective defect of lymphocyte responsiveness to coccidioidin, with preservation of responses to other antigens such as PPD and *Candida*. There may be an even milder defect, manifested solely by deficient MIF response. Many patients with coccidioidomycosis have circulating immune complexes bound to *C immitis* antigens. These have been shown to depress lymphocyte transformation and may block other manifestations of cell-mediated immunity as well. Patients with this immunologic pattern often have chronic cutaneous coccidioidal granulomas, with a few spherules demonstrable within Langhans giant cells. They restrain but do not eradicate the spherules. While a spherule is unable to free itself of these immunologic talons, the grip can be loosened by steroids or other immunosuppressive chemotherapy. Under these circumstances, a minimal impairment of immunity is vastly aggravated, and the fungus can spread to other parts of the body, with either poorly structured granulomas or an ultimate reversion to the PMN-abscess pattern indicating serious immune failure. Even without the intervention of exogenous immunosuppression, some patients may run a spontaneous course of remission and relapse over many decades.

Clinical Features

Coccidioidomycosis may present as a pulmonary problem with pneumonia, abscesses, and thin-walled cysts or as a disseminated disease process. The most devastating form of the disease is represented by meningeal involvement, which is almost invariably complicated by obstructive hydrocephalus. There is a remarkable propensity for black and Filipino patients and pregnant women of any race to develop coccidioidal dissemination when exposed to the fungus. Recently, estradiol-17β has been shown to directly stimulate the growth of *C immitis* in vitro. This may help to explain the heightened risk in pregnant women.

Immunologic Diagnosis

A. Skin Tests and In Vitro Correlates of Cell-Mediated Immunity: A positive coccidioidin skin test indicates only that coccidioidal infection has occurred in the past. Thus, the skin test is seldom useful diagnostically unless interim skin test conversion can be documented. In contrast, the close correlation between the intensity of the skin test response and immunologic competence has permitted the coccidioidin skin test to be used as a direct immunologic index of clinical prognosis in patients known to have coccidioidomycosis. Most patients with pulmonary disease or limited disseminated disease will have a positive reaction (over 5 mm induration at 24 or 48 hours) to 1:100 coccidioidin. Patients with more severe disease will react only to the concentrated 1:10 antigen or not at all.

Interpretation of the skin test reactions has become more difficult with the introduction of **spherulin.** Spherulin has been considered sensitive enough to detect almost all persons who are skin test–reactive to coccidioidin. In some reports, it also detects an additional group of healthy persons who have been exposed to *C immitis* and coccidioidomycosis patients who react only to this antigen. This raises the question of whether *C immitis*-infected patients with positive spherulin and negative coccidioidin skin tests are immunologically depressed or are responding normally, but selectively, to only the invasive form of the fungus. This is consistent with recent studies showing that spherulin contains antigens distinct from those in coccidioidin. However, recent studies have found identical sensitivity for both spherulin and coccidioidin, so the question remains open. Spherulin reactions, like reactions to coccidioidin, tend to be negative in extensive active disease. Neither coccidioidin nor spherulin skin testing has an effect upon coccidioidal serologic tests.

In vitro parameters of cell-mediated immunity also correlate with disease activity but are less helpful. The MIF is negative in most patients with active disease and is therefore not a helpful index of severity. The lymphocyte transformation reaction is negative in the most severe cases; in milder cases, lymphocyte transformation often does not correlate well with other tests of immune response. In vitro test responses, like the skin test, may convert to positive with clinical improvement, though they do not always do so simultaneously.

Expressions of cell-mediated immunity are also related to serologic changes. Serum blocking factors (probably immune complexes) have been described which can depress skin test or lymphocyte transformation reactivity. Their relationship to clinical disease, severity, or prognosis is uncertain.

B. Serologic Tests: Primary coccidioidomycosis is detected by the precipitin and latex agglutination tests, which appear to reflect the appearance of IgM antibody response to infection. In 80% of infections, the precipitin test is positive within 2 weeks of the onset of symptoms. A precipitin response is considered nearly pathognomonic of infection with *C immitis*. Over 90% of positive reactions revert to negative within 6 months, although a few patients with disseminated disease will have persistent or late positive precipitins. The latex agglutination test may become positive even before the tube precipitin test, but false-positive reactions occur in up to 10% of cases.

The complement fixation test appears to reflect the presence of IgG antibody response and is positive in only 10% of patients by the second week of symptoms; it is positive in most patients by 2 months. The immunodiffusion test is technically simpler than the complement fixation test. It becomes positive at about the same time as the latter but can only be used for screening purposes, since it is not quantitative as usually performed.

The sequence of immunologic responses during primary coccidioidomycosis is indicated in Fig 33–4. A positive precipitin test coupled with a negative complement fixation test indicates early primary disease. As the precipitin antibody titer falls, the complement fixation titer rises, especially in the presence of long-active disease. Therefore, a positive complement fixation test with or without precipitin reactivity indicates chronic disease.

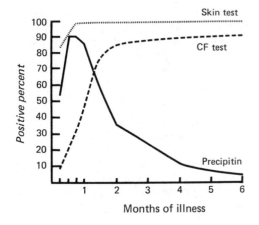

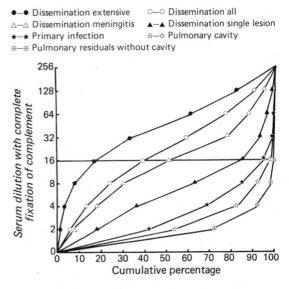

Figure 33–4. Relationships among immunologic reactions in symptomatic primary coccidioidomycosis, relating time of appearance and duration to the frequency of positive reactions. (Reproduced, with permission, from Huppert M: Serology of coccidioidomycosis. *Mycopathol Mycol* [Appl] 1970;**41**:108. Courtesy of W. Junk N.V., Publishers, The Hague.)

Figure 33–5. Relationship of coccidioidal complement-fixing antibody titer to various clinical forms of the disease. Note that the majority of patients with multi-lesion dissemination develop a complement fixation titer that exceeds 1:16. (Reproduced, with permission, from Smith CE et al: Pattern of 39,500 serologic tests in coccidioidomycosis. *JAMA* 1956;**160**:550. Copyright © 1956, American Medical Association.)

The relationship between complement fixation titer and severity of illness is shown in Fig 33–5. The complement-fixing antibody titer correlates inversely with the competence of cell-mediated immunity. In one study, 80% of patients with a coccidioidin complement fixation titer of 1:32 or less had a positive coccidioidin skin test, compared to only 41% of those with higher serologic titers. Furthermore, DNCB sensitization, another index of cell-mediated immune function, was markedly depressed in those with high complement-fixation titers.

Serologic tests are particularly important in diagnosing coccidioidal meningitis. *C immitis* is difficult to recover from cerebrospinal fluid, and there may be no other identifiable foci of disease. Unfortunately, 10–25% of patients with coccidioidal meningitis have a negative complement fixation test in the cerebrospinal fluid. Diagnosis may rest upon finding lymphocytosis and hypoglycorrhachia in patients with coccidioidal lesions documented elsewhere on their bodies.

Prevention

A number of efforts have been made to develop vaccines against *C immitis*. Inactivated vaccines have been prepared from mycelia or spherule extracts or from whole cells, administered to mice in oil-base adjuvants. Vaccination with formalin-killed spherules increases the LD_{50} for mice from 50 to 3000 arthrospores. Killed vaccines prepared from mycelia or spherules apparently do not prevent infection, although they do minimize dissemination and fungal replication and prolong survival of challenged animals. A large-scale placebo-controlled vaccine trial is now in progress in California. The vaccine is prepared from spherules of *C immitis*.

Attenuated strains have also been used as live vaccines. These have been protective in animal studies. However, attenuated strains are not eliminated by the host and persist for long periods in granulomas. Also, attenuation has proved somewhat unstable, with gradual reversion to virulent forms. Therefore, live vaccines are still considered unacceptable for use in humans.

Treatment

Amphotericin B is the only drug with proved efficiency in coccidioidomycosis. Miconazole may be a useful alternative drug, but frequent posttreatment relapses may limit its value. Recent large trials with ketoconazole have suggested efficacy comparable to amphotericin B. Doses up to 1200 mg/d have been used. This oral agent has much less toxicity than amphotericin B, but few patients were treated at the maximum dose.

Because many patients with severe disease are refractory to amphotericin B and have defective cell-mediated immune responses to coccidioidin, a number of investigators have attempted immune reconstitution with transfer factor. Approximately 60 patients with a variety of lesions (including 11 with meningitis) have been treated. Immune conversions were dramatic, especially for MIF activity. Conversions were transient, requiring administration of more transfer factor to be sustained. Clinical improvement followed transfer factor administration in 60% of patients. These changes cannot be attributed to transfer factor with confidence at present, because (1) coccidioidomycosis is characterized by spontaneous remissions and relapses; (2) most patients were receiving concurrent amphotericin B; and (3) it is often difficult to distinguish subjective from objective improvement in this disease.

Complications & Prognosis

Erythema nodosum with or without erythema multiforme occurs in a varying proportion of patients with primary coccidioidomycosis. Such patients exhibit violently positive reactions to coccidioidin or spherulin skin tests. A negative coccidioidin skin test in a person with erythema nodosum or erythema multiforme is thought to rule out the diagnosis of coccidioidomycosis. The immunologic basis of the reaction is unknown.

Disseminated coccidioidomycosis should be considered an incurable illness in large numbers of patients, particularly in those who fail to recover coccidioidin reactivity following treatment. As in leprosy, therapy may have to be continued intermittently for life in patients whose immunologic status predisposes them to relapse. The toxicity of amphotericin B may directly produce renal failure or, when the drug is withdrawn because of toxicity, allow the disease to progress to fatal outcome.

5. BRUCELLOSIS

Brucellosis is an acute or chronic illness manifested principally by chills, fever, and weakness. Occasionally, chronic relapsing febrile episodes occur, giving rise to the popular name "undulant fever." Brucellosis is endemic in many animal species; humans are infected incidentally, by either the oral or percutaneous route. Pregnant animals are especially susceptible to brucellosis and may abort. The growth of microorganisms in the placenta is apparently greatly stimulated by the local presence of erythritol in high concentration.

Once introduced into the body, brucellae quickly pass from lymph to regional nodes to bloodstream, where they are transported by PMNs and monocytes to sinusoids of the liver, spleen, bone marrow, and lymph nodes. The microorganisms multiply locally and are secondarily phagocytosed by fixed macrophages of these reticuloendothelial tissues. Brucellae are relatively resistant to macrophage killing, and small numbers may survive the peak of heightened macrophage activity after an acute infection. It is not known whether brucellae survive because of innate resistance or because "incompetent" macrophages are unable to kill them. The subsequent appearance of clinical illness is apparently dependent upon host ability to restrain brucellar multiplication. In some cases the incubation period may be quite prolonged. The pathogenicity of Brucella organisms is at least partially related to differences in the composition of lipopolysaccharide in smooth virulent strains. It is possible that these may contribute to the slowed degranulation of specific granules in PMNs that have ingested Brucella abortus.

The usual histologic response to infection is granuloma formation, but in some tissues, especially spleen and bones, frank abscesses may develop. Abscesses are also more likely to occur when the infecting microorganism is Brucella suis or Brucella melitensis; B abortus more commonly produces granulomas. In mice, the formation of abscesses with B melitensis is associated with short-lived "acquired cellular resistance" and also with rapid elimination of all brucellae. On the other hand, B abortus produces granulomas, with evidence of prolonged hepatic infection.

The immunologic response to brucellar infection is both cellular and humoral. The importance of cell-mediated immunity is suggested by the successful use of viable attenuated Brucella species for vaccinating cattle and by the development of delayed skin test reactivity and in vitro lymphocyte transformation responses to Brucella antigens in persons who have had brucellosis. The Brucella skin test underwent a period of popularity in the USA but was withdrawn from commercial use because of nonspecificity. Protection conferred by vaccination for brucellosis, like that for salmonellosis, is only partial and can be overwhelmed by massive challenge doses.

Infection with Brucella species generates a vigorous antibody response. Although the antibody is not protective, rises in antibody titer may be used diagnostically. Both agglutinating and complement-fixing antibodies can be measured. Nearly all cases of acute brucellosis will show an agglutinin titer of 1:160 or greater within 3 weeks after infection; titers may persist at low levels for months or years, especially in patients with chronic infection. There is a problem of serologic cross-reaction with Francisella tularensis, Vibrio cholerae, and certain strains of Yersinia enterocolitica. In addition, a blocking factor has been described in some chronic cases. This results from the presence of IgA or IgG antibody, which produces spuriously negative agglutinins at low dilutions and, when added to high titer serum, depresses agglutinin levels. The prozone phenomenon can be avoided by carrying agglutinin titers out to a 1:320 dilution. Another way to serologically diagnose brucellosis is to mix the brucellae and the serum to be tested, wash the brucellae, and then add antihuman globulin. This equivalent of the Coombs test will cause brucellae to agglutinate even if a prozone phenomenon is present. Furthermore, a technique for passive hemagglutinating antibody is very sensitive and does not have the problem of cross-reaction with Yersinia. Serologic titers are very important in the diagnosis of brucellosis because the organisms are fastidious and require Castaneda's medium and CO_2 enrichment for optimal recovery from blood. Treatment (generally streptomycin plus tetracycline) may be complicated by the Jarisch-Herxheimer reaction. Relapses are common.

6. TULAREMIA

Francisella (Pasteurella) tularensis is a small gram-negative coccobacillus that requires special culture media for isolation. Infection occurs by inhalation or by invasion through abrasions in the skin. The organism is spread by contact with infected animals or by insect vectors such as ticks. Tularemia is an occupational hazard of trappers, sheepherders, mink ranchers, hunters, and butchers.

Tularemia may present in different ways depending upon the site of inoculation, but the most common clinical features are local ulcer formation and regional lymphadenopathy in association with symptoms of systemic febrile illness.

Host defense mechanisms are not fully understood. However, immunity is associated with the appearance of delayed hypersensitivity to tularemia skin test antigen. Also, in vitro responses of cell-mediated immunity can develop to the skin test antigen in sensitized persons. Immunity is associated with increased ability of rabbit macrophages to kill *F tularensis*. Inactivated vaccines are of no benefit, but a live attenuated strain has been successful in vaccinating humans and lower animals. This provides further evidence supporting the protective role of cell-mediated immunity. Finally, because the organisms are fastidious and highly infective, serologic responses are generally used to confirm the diagnosis. Tularemia agglutinins usually rise after the first 2 weeks of illness but may take much longer. The test is relatively specific, with some cross-reactions with brucellae. As in brucellosis, there is no evidence that antibody formation is protective. Treatment is with streptomycin or gentamicin.

INFECTIOUS DISEASES CHARACTERIZED BY UNIQUE HOST–PARASITE RELATIONSHIPS

A number of infectious diseases do not fit easily into the preceding categories because of particularly unique aspects of their relationship to the host. Among these are syndromes resulting from infection with *Mycoplasma, Chlamydia,* and *Rickettsia* species and *Bordetella pertussis.*

Mycoplasma pneumoniae

Mycoplasmas, members of the class Mollicutes, are the smallest known free-living microorganisms and differ from bacteria in lacking cell walls. They have been recognized as etiologic agents of disease in humans, animals, insects, and plants. *Mycoplasma* species have unique morphologic, growth, and metabolic characteristics beyond the scope of this discussion.

The only *Mycoplasma* species with an unquestioned ability to regularly produce human infection is *Mycoplasma pneumoniae.* This microorganism, like *Bordetella pertussis,* appears to produce its major disease manifestations at the surface of epithelial cells. Unlike *Corynebacterium diphtheriae* and *Vibrio cholerae,* which also occupy an extraepithelial position, *M pneumoniae* produces no definite exotoxins. However, several nonhuman mycoplasmas are known to produce exotoxins.

Presumably, *M pneumoniae* is phagocytosed and killed by leukocytes, although inhibition of macrophage function has been observed in vitro. The details of *Mycoplasma*-host interaction are outlined in Table 33–3.

Chlamydiae

These microorganisms are obligate intracellular parasites with a unique reproductive cycle. The infectious particle is a 0.3 μm structure termed the "elementary body" (EB); it is specialized for extracellular survival. Following endocytosis, a "reticulate body" (RB) is formed that multiplies intracellularly by binary fission to produce a large intracellular inclusion. Innumerable elementary bodies are secondarily formed that are then released by rupture of the host cell. Within macrophages, nonopsonized chlamydiae can apparently avoid lysosomal enzyme activity.

In addition to a unique developmental cycle, chlamydiae possess common morphologic characteristics and a common protoplasmic family antigen. Type-specific antigens are found in the cell wall. *Chlamydia trachomatis* and *Chlamydia psittaci* differ in 4 major respects: (1) *C trachomatis* is susceptible to sulfonamides, (2) *C trachomatis* forms rigid (as opposed to diffuse) microcolonies; (3) intracellular inclusions of *C trachomatis* are glycogen-positive, and stainable with iodine; and (4) *C trachomatis* and *C psittaci* show little DNA homology.

Chlamydial diseases often run a protracted and relapsing course (especially trachoma). Chronicity of infection has led to the suggestion that chlamydial infection does not evoke an effective immune response. On the other hand, the host ordinarily restrains and localizes chlamydial disease without serious sequelae. Cell-mediated immune mechanisms appear to be important in chlamydial immunity. However, antibodies that combine with cell wall antigens of the parasite appear to prevent penetration of susceptible host cells, thus limiting the spread of infection.

Details of *Chlamydia*-host interaction are outlined in Table 33–3.

Rickettsiae

Rickettsial species are small pleomorphic coccobacilli which function as obligate intracellular parasites. With the exception of *Coxiella burnetii,* the etiologic agent of Q fever, members of this group share a number of important characteristics: (1) failure to survive in the environment; (2) dependence upon arthropods as vectors and reservoirs; (3) transmission by arthropod bites; and (4) multiplication in the endothelial cells of blood vessels, with production of vasculitis, thrombosis, hematogenous dissemination, and rash.

Table 33–3. Host-parasite relationships in mycoplasmal, chlamydial, and rickettsial infections.

Microorganism	Disease	Principal Manifestations	Pattern of Illness	Host-Parasite Interaction*	Serologic Tests	Comments
Mycoplasmas *Mycoplasma pneumoniae*	Primary atypical pneumonia	Pneumonia. Central nervous system and hepatic abnormalities, occasionally noted, may be due to antimycoplasmal antibody with shared antigens in brain and liver or to actual metastatic infection. Myringitis and Stevens-Johnson syndrome also reported.	Acute infection. Clinical disease may not occur until after several preceding asymptomatic infections. Thus, clinical illness may reflect the development of cellular hypersensitivity to the organism.	Extracellular. Attaches to neuraminic acid cell receptor via a specialized tip structure. Metabolic, cytopathic, and ciliostatic epithelial cell damage results, due partially to H_2O_2. Macrophages with attached mycoplasmas are immobile. Mycoplasmas evade phagocytosis perhaps because of shared antigens with host cell membranes. Organisms rapidly ingested and degraded in presence of specific antiserum.	CF (most commonly used). Many others available (indirect hemagglutination; immunofluorescence, etc). The sera of about 50% of patients with *M pneumoniae* infection contain antibodies to I antigen that cause nonspecific agglutination of human type O Rh-negative red blood cells at 4 °C. Cold agglutinins tend to be present as a function of the severity of mycoplasma infection.	*M pneumoniae* infection stimulates antibodies cross-reactive with red cell membrane and can cause an acute hemolytic response. Another cross-reactive antibody is able to agglutinate streptococci of species MG. Disease usually self-limited, but antibiotics (tetracycline, erythromycin) may shorten course without eliminating organisms. Inactivated vaccine may accentuate subsequent infection.
Chlamydiae *Chlamydia psittaci*	Psittacosis (ornithosis)	Pneumonia. Occasionally hepatitis, myocarditis, encephalitis, skin rash.	Broad spectrum of disease ranging from acute infection to latency. Immunity may be incomplete following infection; prolonged shedding of microorganisms sometimes occurs (especially in birds).	Obligate intracellular pathogen. EBs rapidly endocytosed by nonprofessional phagocytes and macrophages via interaction of a heat-labile surface factor with a protein cell surface receptor. Phagolysosomal fusion fails to occur in macrophage, and normal EB → RB → EB life cycle ensues in all cell types. In the presence of specific antibody, endocytosis by nonprofessional phagocytes is impaired; that by macrophages is enhanced; and phagolysosomal fusion occurs, apparently by antibody neutralization of the heat-labile surface factors. Chlamydial destruction ensues. Host cell damage may be partially attributable to poorly defined "chlamydial toxins."	CF (a group-specific test that measures antibodies to an antigenic determinant common to all chlamydiae [2-keto-3-deoxyoctanoic acid]). Cross-reacts with LGV and *Chlamydia trachomatis* D → K (see below). Rising CF titers assist in diagnosis, especially if titer > 1:16, but do not differentiate from LGV.	Frei skin test may be positive following psittacosis (see below).

Organism	Disease	Clinical	Course	Biology	Diagnosis	Comments
Chlamydia trachomatis Serotypes A, B, Ba, C	Trachoma	Chronic follicular conjunctivitis, pannus, scarring.	Characterized by chronicity, latency, and relapse. Hypersensitivity response due to repeated exposure may play an important pathogenic role. Scarring may reflect "bystander" cell injury due to a vigorous immune response.	Obligate intracellular pathogen (predominantly epithelial cells of the eye). Infections limited to humans.	Microimmunofluorescence (micro-IF; measures specific antibodies to antigenic determinants in EB cell walls that are not detected by the CF test used for psittacosis/LGV). Can identify diverse serotypes of *C trachomatis* (A → K; see below) and can determine Ig class of the antibody.	The single greatest cause of blindness in the world. No skin test. No available vaccine (inactivated vaccine may accentuate subsequent infection).
Serotypes D → K	Nongonococcal (nonspecific) urethritis; NGU; NSU	Subacute purulent urethral discharge (males); asymptomatic carriage (females); purulent conjunctivitis and pneumonia (neonates).	Broad range; asymptomatic to acute.	Obligate intracellular pathogen (epithelial cells). Natural habitat is genitourinary tract.	Micro-IF (see above). CF titers commonly < 1:16 and cross-react with psittacosis/LGV.	A common cause of urethritis, salpingitis, perihepatitis, ophthalmia neonatorum, and neonatal pneumonia. Identical to the inclusion conjunctivitis agent.
Serotypes L1, L2, L3	Lymphogranuloma venereum (LGV)	Anogenital infection; lymphadenitis (buboes). Infection initially generalized.	Acute or chronic illness. May be considerable mucosal scarring. Latency common.	Obligate intracellular pathogen (epithelial cells and beyond). Much more invasive than other *C trachomatis* serotypes. Multiplies more readily in nonimmune macrophages than other serotypes.	CF (see psittacosis). Titers > 1:16 are most suggestive of LGV or psittacosis.	Sexually transmitted. Frei skin test (like CF antibody) measures a group antigen and may be positive in LGV or psittacosis. Frei test becomes positive well beyond changes in serologic tests; it is of little diagnostic value and is no longer available commercially.
Rickettsiae *Rickettsia prowazekii*	Epidemic typhus	Headache, fever, rash.	Acute illness. Mild to severe, depending on specific microorganism. Immunity is usually long-lasting, with some exceptions: (1) Epidemic typhus may relapse 10—20 years after apparent recovery (Brill-Zinsser disease). Clinically milder. (No rash. No OX19 antibody titer rise.) (2) Trench fever is characterized by relapses.	Obligate intracellular pathogen (epithelial cells). Naturally pathogenic for arthropods. Bites → endothelial cell invasion → acute vasculitis → thrombosis (and DIC). Rickettsiae may actively enter macrophages but escape phagolysosomal fusion. If opsonic antibody is present, macrophages actively ingest rickettsiae → phagolysosomal formation → rickettsial death.	Weil-Felix, CF, Micro-IF.	*All* can be diagnosed by CF test using yolk sac antigen or micro-IF, which is the best test available. *Many* can be diagnosed by their ability to stimulate formation of antibodies cross-react with strains of *Proteus vulgaris* (Weil-Felix reaction). *Examples:* Epidemic typhus → OX19 antibody. Scrub typhus → OXK antibody. Rocky Mountain spotted fever → antibody to OX19 and OX2. (Must eliminate any possibility of a concurrent *Proteus* infection). No skin test. RMSF vaccine available, but efficacy uncertain.
Rickettsia typhi (mooseri)	Endemic typhus					
Rickettsia rickettsii	Rocky Mountain spotted fever					
Rickettsia tsutsugamushi	Scrub typhus					
Rickettsia quintana	Trench fever					
Rickettsia akari	Rickettsialpox					
Coxiella burnetii	Q fever	Headache, fever, pneumonia, hepatitis.	Acute or subacute illness.	Obligate intracellular pathogen. Can be acquired by inhalation.	CF	Vaccination effective but not practical.

*Antibody and CMI responses demonstrable, but protective role unclear. No apparent role for PMNs or opsonins, except as noted.

Abbreviations used: CMI, cell-mediated immunity; CF, complement fixation test; DIC, disseminated intravascular coagulation; EB, elementary body; PMN, polymorphonuclear neutrophil; RB, reticulate body.

C burnetii is more often transmitted by the respiratory route, seldom involves biting arthropods, produces no rash, and is manifested principally by pneumonia.

The details of *Rickettsia*-host interaction are outlined in Table 33–3.

Bordetella pertussis

B pertussis is a short, ovoid, encapsulated, gram-negative rod which produces the clinical syndrome known as pertussis (whooping cough). Apparently other *Bordetella* species, as well as some viruses (especially adenoviruses), can also produce this syndrome. However, *B pertussis* infection is epidemic, whereas the others are sporadic. *B pertussis* acquisition is associated with a very high clinical attack rate; asymptomatic carriage is not common.

B pertussis possesses pili-like surface factors and 4 "phases" of in vitro growth (phases I and II are smooth and virulent; phases III and IV are rough and avirulent). In these and other respects, there is a striking resemblance to *N gonorrhoeae*. *B pertussis* multiplies only in association with the ciliated epithelium of the respiratory tract and does not invade epithelial cells. An important element of protection is surface antibody, probably IgA, which prevents adherence of *B pertussis* to epithelial cells. The microorganism is presumed to be killed by PMNs; its surface capsule is apparently not antiphagocytic. Many of the pathophysiologic manifestations of *B pertussis* infection have been attributed to one or more toxins that produce a necrotizing inflammatory response of the tracheobronchial mucous membrane and ciliary paralysis.

B pertussis is rich in a variety of potentially pathogenic factors (surface components, endotoxin, histamine-sensitizing factor, lymphocytosis-producing factor) the importance of which is unsettled in human infections. One of the most striking clinical accompaniments of pertussis is leukocytosis with an absolute lymphocytosis. This is accompanied by depletion of small lymphocytes in the thymus, spleen, and lymph nodes and reflects a failure of lymphocyte traffic back to the lymph nodes. Increased lymphocyte production is not considered to play a role. In vitro and animal studies indicate a variety of contradictory alterations of cell-mediated immune responses in pertussis (immune enhancement with increased or decreased tumor growth, increased or decreased infection susceptibility, etc). The precise role of cell-mediated immune mechanisms in pertussis is unclear. Successful immunization with a killed vaccine has reduced the threat of pertussis enormously in this country. Presumably, this indicates that systemic humoral immune mechanisms may be more important than cell-mediated immunity in protection. The role of cell-mediated immunity in recovery from established infection is unsettled, however.

The use of pertussis vaccine in Great Britain is being seriously questioned because of a high incidence of neurologic sequelae.

INFECTIONS COMPLICATED BY DEPOSITION OF CIRCULATING IMMUNE COMPLEXES

Major Immunologic Features

- Infections often characterized by persistence or chronicity.
- Complications include glomerulonephritis, arthritis, or skin lesions.
- Immunologic manifestations may include hypergammaglobulinemia, cryoglobulinemia, hypocomplementemia.
- Immune complex deposition in target tissues triggers vasculitis.

General Considerations

The production of antigen-antibody complexes is probably quite common in a majority of infectious diseases, but symptoms rarely result from their presence. Ordinarily, they possess physicochemical characteristics that permit their asymptomatic clearance from the bloodstream by the reticuloendothelial system. In some circumstances, however, antigens and antibodies combine under conditions that predispose to their deposition in the walls of blood vessels. As a result of such deposition, complement is activated locally and results in the establishment of an inflammatory response through the release of soluble mediators, including chemotactic factors. The result of the inflammatory response is dependent upon the site of immune complex deposition; glomerulonephritis, arthritis, and skin lesions are common clinical manifestations of this process.

Table 33–4 deals with infectious diseases known to be complicated by immune complex deposition. There seems to be little question that more examples will be found in the near future.

The familiar "proteinuria of fever" is very likely a manifestation of subclinical glomerulonephritis in a broad variety of infectious diseases. Acute nephritis has been described in infectious mononucleosis, mumps, variola, varicella, adenovirus (type 7) and echovirus (type 9) infection, and following vaccination.

Erythema nodosum complicates many infectious diseases (leprosy, coccidioidomycosis, histoplasmosis, tuberculosis, and streptococcal infection, to name but a few). It is likely that the cause of this complication will prove to be immune complex deposition (as does seem to be the case in leprosy) when appropriate studies are performed.

The natural history of many virus infections (and of leptospirosis) is biphasic, and the development of gross clinical phenomena is often preceded by a nonspecific febrile illness. Whereas the nonspecific illness is often the direct result of the virus infection, the more specific manifestations of the disease such as the exanthems are probably due to the presence of immune complexes formed by virus and antibody in the circulation. The mechanism of development of the rash may be similar to that in serum sickness.

Table 33—4. Immune complex complications of infectious diseases.

Disease	Etiologic Agent	Immunologic Predisposition	Immunologic Complications	Comments
Infective endocarditis	Bacteria (*Streptococcus viridans; Staphylococcus aureus,* enterococci; many others). Fungi (*Candida albicans* and others). Miscellaneous (*Coxiella burnetii* and others; rare).	Continuous discharge of microorganisms or their antigens into the bloodstream. Infecting microorganisms protected from phagocytes by overlying fibrin network and by the avascular nature of cardiac valve tissue. High levels of rheumatoid factor may impair opsonic capacity of IgG which is specifically bound to microorganisms. Immunologic complications are directly proportionate to duration of infection (ie, more common in "subacute" than acute endocarditis).	Immune complex glomerulonephritis characterized by proteinuria, microscopic hematuria, and red cell casts in urine. Antibody, complement, and specific bacterial antigen present in renal vasculature. Nephritis may be focal or diffuse. Focal nephritis may occur in 50—90% with few sequelae. Diffuse nephritis occurs in < 10%; may produce uremia. Osler's nodes (painful nodular lesions in fingertips and elsewhere), Roth spots in ocular fundi (white center with surrounding hemorrhagic zone), petechiae, splinter hemorrhages beneath nails—all may reflect hypersensitivity angiitis characterized by intimal proliferation. "Embolic" complications (especially central nervous system) may often represent hypersensitivity angiitis. Splenomegaly and presence of circulating histiocytes (especially in earlobe blood) reflect chronic stimulation of reticuloendothelial system. Other immunologic accompaniments include hyperglobulinemia, rheumatoid factor, cryoproteinemia, and, perhaps, myocarditis and anemia.	Endocarditis is a disease of heart valves; valves may be destroyed by infection. Similar immunologic sequelae may be encountered in infected arteriovenous shunts, infective endarteritis, and infected central nervous system ventriculoatrial shunt devices (usually due to *S epidermidis*). Common feature to all is continuous discharge of microorganisms into blood. Treatment consists of antibiotics. Immunologic complications currently handled expectantly; corticosteroids may exacerbate infection and are usually contraindicated.
Viral hepatitis	Hepatitis B	Persistent antigenemia due to HBsAg stimulates production of anti-HBs; results in circulating immune complexes. If HBsAg is eliminated, resultant illness is similar to "one shot serum sickness" with only transient clinical manifestations. If there is continual production of HBsAg, HBsAg-Ab complexes are continually present, resulting in an illness resembling chronic serum sickness in animals and expressed as a generalized necrotizing vasculitis. Why most patients who acquire HBsAg do not develop these syndromes but only subclinical or clinical hepatitis probably relates to poorly understood "host immune factors."	The syndrome equivalent to "one shot serum sickness" is characterized by migratory, additive, or simultaneous polyarthralgias and arthritis together with skin rash which is often urticarial. Hepatitis may be subclinical or associated with jaundice. Serum and joint complement may be decreased; cryoglobulins composed of HBsAg, anti-HBs, and complement may be found. Occasionally associated with glomerulonephritis. The syndrome equivalent to "chronic serum sickness" is characterized by multisystem disease with a prolonged course. Manifested by arthritis, renal disease, heart disease, etc, with the features of polyarteritis or hypersensitivity angiitis. Only by finding HBsAg can viral etiology be established. Otherwise, will be considered a "collagen vascular disease of unknown etiology." May need to test repeatedly for these viral factors. No apparent relationship between appearance of vasculitis and liver disease (if present).	"One shot" syndrome often self-limited; usually preicteric. Hepatitis A may produce a similar transient syndrome. Necrotizing vasculitis syndrome is potentially life-threatening but may evolve as a chronic debilitating disorder requiring immunosuppressive therapy.
Poststreptococcal acute glomerulonephritis	*Streptococcus pyogenes*	May follow either pharyngeal or skin infection. Related to specific M types of *S pyogenes:* pharyngeal (types 1, 4, 12, and 18; perhaps 3, 6, and 25), skin (types 2, 31, 49, 52—55, 57, 60). Seven- to 14-day latent period between infection and onset of glomerulonephritis (similar to interval in experimental serum sickness).	Immune complex glomerulonephritis characterized by proteinuria, hematuria. May progress to hypertension, renal functional impairment, and edema of face and legs. All glomeruli diffusely involved. Antibody, complement deposited in renal vasculature. Hypocomplementemia during first 2 to 6 weeks of illness.	Usually heals; especially in children.

Table 33–4 (cont'd). Immune complex complications of infectious diseases.

Disease	Etiologic Agent	Immunologic Predisposition	Immunologic Complications	Comments
Quartan malaria	*Plasmodium malariae*	High level of parasitemia. High malaria antibody titers.	Immunoglobulins and complement in glomerular capillary walls. Nephrotic syndrome.	Poor response to corticosteroids. Most common in children 4–8 years of age.
Syphilis	*Treponema pallidum*	Congenital or secondary syphilis.	Nephrotic syndrome. "Hemorrhagic glomerulonephritis" has also been described.	Responds to penicillin.
Typhoid fever	*Salmonella typhi*	Persistent infection with prolonged bacteremia.	Antibody, complement, and *Salmonella* "Vi" antigen in glomerular capillary walls → glomerulonephritis.	Probably a common complication of typhoid fever but rarely appreciated because renal biopsies are seldom done (or justified).
Leprosy	*Mycobacterium leprae*	Erythema nodosum leprosum (see description elsewhere in chapter).		

In a simple exanthematous disease such as rubella, other signs due to circulating immune complexes, such as arthritis, may be seen occasionally.

THE SPECTRUM OF HOST–VIRUS IMMUNOLOGIC RELATIONSHIPS

Major Immunologic Features

- Disease may be acute, latent, chronic, or delayed ("slow virus") in onset.
- Altered disease presentation may result from prior immunization with inactivated virus.

General Considerations

Viral diseases can be divided into 2 main categories with respect to the ultimate fate of the virus in the tissues:

(1) Virus may be eliminated from the body: This is the pattern encountered in the vast majority of human viral infections, ranging from smallpox to influenza to poliomyelitis. Appropriate secretory and systemic, cellular and humoral immune defenses are mobilized, and the virus is dealt with appropriately. Subsequent immunity is solid and usually persists for life. (Some investigators regard the firm persistence of immunity as evidence that the virus may continue to be sequestered in the tissues for life, serving to chronically boost the host immunologic response. Even if this is the case, the viruses in this group never manifest themselves clinically beyond the initial acute illness.)

(2) Virus may persist in the body and produce disease: An uneasy immunologic balance between virus and host may obtain in certain viral infections, giving rise to patterns of latency, chronicity, or extremely delayed ("slow") onset. Examples of acute and persistent host-virus relationships are outlined in Table 33–5.

A third category of viral illness may be encountered in patients who have previously received certain inactivated vaccines. Here, vaccine-modified host defenses accentuate to a greater or lesser degree the characteristics of subsequent natural infection, while failing to provide adequate protection. Examples of these vaccine-activated illnesses are discussed briefly below.

Measles

Recipients of formaldehyde-inactivated measles vaccine, upon subsequent natural exposure to measles, may develop a hyperacute "atypical measles" syndrome characterized by an inordinate febrile response, pneumonia with pleural effusion, and a severe hemorrhagic rash in atypical distribution. Severe local skin reactions may also occur when previous recipients of inactivated measles vaccine receive an inoculation with live vaccine.

It has been suggested that the prior vaccination results in augmentation of delayed hypersensitivity to measles virus. Alternatively, there is evidence that "atypical measles" may reflect immune complex deposition. According to the latter explanation, inactivated vaccine produces serum IgG antibody titers, which then wane. Upon subsequent exposure to the live virus, a marked anamnestic IgG response occurs, producing antibody that complexes with viral antigen and precipitates a subsequent Arthus response in the respiratory tract and skin.

Respiratory Syncytial Virus

Recipients of formaldehyde-treated, alum-precipitated respiratory syncytial virus (RSV) vaccine may develop clinically typical but much more severe illness upon subsequent natural exposure to the virus. Bronchiolitis and pneumonia, in particular, are accentuated. Again, augmented delayed hypersensitivity or Arthus-type immune complex deposition in the bronchiolar walls has been held responsible.

Immunologic exacerbation of infection by prior vaccination is not unique to viral diseases. Local ocu-

Table 33—5. The spectrum of host-virus immunologic relationships.*

Fate of Virus in Tissues	Type of Infection	Characteristic Host-Virus Relationships	Specific Examples	Comments
Eliminated	Acute	Short incubation periods (2 days to 2 or 3 weeks). Virus recoverable before but not after onset of disease. Recovery common. Recovered host is immune to same or closely related viruses.	Smallpox (high clinical attack rate; usually results in disease). Poliomyelitis (rarely results in clinical disease). Innumerable others.	The vast majority of the acute viral infections of humans fall into this immunologic category. Immunity is solid and persistent.
Not eliminated; persists in host tissues for months, years, or a lifetime	Latent	Acute primary infection followed by recovery and subsequent relapses and remissions. Virus recoverable during primary and relapsing phases of infection; not recoverable from target tissues during remissions. Host immune response demonstrable but ineffective in preventing relapse.	Herpes simplex ("fever blisters"). Varicella-zoster ("shingles").	These viruses apparently persist in nerve ganglions during periods between attacks. Humoral antibody is demonstrable but not protective. Cell-mediated immunity is critical but not sufficient to prevent relapses. Immunosuppressive diseases or drugs may permit dissemination of these otherwise well-localized recurrent illnesses.
	Chronic	Variable incubation period, outcome, and course. Virus persists and is regularly recoverable. Host immune response demonstrable but does not influence pattern of disease.	Congenital rubella syndrome.	Infection of fetus occurs during second or third month of gestation. Persistent viral infection produces congenital abnormalities and vasculitis. Brisk IgM antibody response; depressed cell-mediated immunity.
			Cytomegalovirus infection.	May produce mental retardation, hepatitis when acquired in utero. Hepatitis, rash, and "mononucleosis-like" syndrome in older persons. Commonly asymptomatic but becomes apparent (variably symptomatic) in the presence of immunosuppression. High antibody titers are not protective.
			Hepatitis B infection.	Eighty-five percent of patients with acute hepatitis show HBsAg for 1—13 weeks; 5% for up to 6 months; some carry HBsAg chronically. Persistence of carriage is associated with suppression of T cell function.
	Slow	Incubation period of months to years. Relentless progress and lethal course of disease.	Kuru; Creutzfeldt-Jakob disease (humans); scrapie (sheep); transmissible mink encephalopathy (mink).	Progressive demyelinating syndromes characterized by "subacute spongiform encephalopathy." Kuru and Creutzfeldt-Jakob disease are transmissible to chimpanzees. Virus (or viroid) not identified.
			Progressive multifocal leukoencephalopathy.	Due to a conventional virus (SV40 or similar DNA virus) which may constitute part of the "normal brain flora." Disease emerges under immunosuppression. Virus recoverable throughout course of disease. Minimal inflammation or other evidence of host immune response.
			Subacute sclerosing panencephalitis (SSPE) (Dawson's inclusion body encephalitis).	Due to a conventional virus (measles virus) which produces persistent infection. Abnormally high titers of measles antibody present (depressed cell-mediated immunity). High IgG levels. Epidemiologic evidence suggests very early measles infection (< 2—3 years of age) with manifestations of SSPE in early teens (= "slow"). Might be classified with the "chronic" group.

*Adapted from Youmans GP, Paterson PY, Somers HM (editors): *The Biological and Clinical Basis of Infectious Diseases*, 2nd ed. Saunders, 1980.

lar immunization with *C trachomatis* vaccine has been shown to predispose to more intense ocular infection upon subsequent challenge with a wild type heterologous trachoma strain. Immunity to the homologous strain, in contrast, is intact. Delayed hypersensitivity is an important immune mechanism in trachoma and is presumably intensified by prior immunization. Similarly, *M pneumoniae* infection is intensified by prior immunization, but only in those patients who fail to develop growth-inhibitory *Mycoplasma* antibody. These patients appear to be sensitized by the prior vaccination. This phenomenon is of particular interest because the occurrence of *M pneumoniae* pneumonia (typically in young adults) is considered to reflect an immune response to an agent encountered frequently (and asymptomatically) throughout early childhood.

OPPORTUNISTIC INFECTIONS

These diseases are the consequence of defective functioning of the normal immune system, predisposing the patient to infections characteristic for the compromised immune function. The infecting pathogen may be either common or rare, in the latter case emerging only under circumstances of defective immunity. Restoration of normal immune status may be of greater importance in recovery than antimicrobial drug therapy.

Nothing is more revelatory of the normal functional capacity of the immune system than the infectious diseases that result when immunity is suppressed. In a sense, every infectious disease represents an opportunistic infection. (For example, pneumococcal

Table 33–6. Opportunistic infections.

Immunologic Setting	Commonly Associated Pathogens	Comments
Hypogammaglobulinemia (congenital or acquired)	Pyogenic extracellular bacteria. Some viruses.	Loss of opsonic or neutralizing antibody. (*S pneumoniae* infection is especially common in multiple myeloma.)
Granulocytopenia (< 1000 circulating granulocytes/μL; often due to cancer chemotherapy; bone marrow failure)	Pyogenic extracellular bacteria. Gram-negative enteric bacteria (*E coli*, etc). Environmental gram-negative bacteria (*P aeruginosa; S marcescens*). *Candida albicans.*	Inadequate circulating phagocytic cells (qualitative granulocyte defects give rise to similar infections).
Depressed cell-mediated immunity due to basic illness (Hodgkin's disease) or drug therapy (cancer chemotherapy; organ transplantation)	Intracellular pathogens (*M tuberculosis, H capsulatum*, etc). Rare "unusual" pathogens *(N asteroides; L monocytogenes, Legionella pneumophila, Pneumocystis carinii, Toxoplasma gondii).* DNA-type viruses (varicella-zoster, cytomegalovirus, wart virus, progressive multifocal leukoencephalopathy).	Defective lymphocyte function. (*T gondii* is actually a very common pathogen; immunosuppression permits reactivation of quiescent cysts, especially in the brain). (*P carinii* is a protozoan parasite of the pulmonary alveolar space, where it replicates in a proteinaceous coagulum. There are no useful immunologic tests for its presence. It produces an alveolar capillary block [arterial shunt] syndrome.)
Hemolysis (chronic, severe) (especially with sickle cell disease, malaria, bartonellosis)	Salmonellosis with bacteremia and secondary local abscess formation.	*Salmonella* species may compete with red cell breakdown products for macrophage membrane receptor sites, resulting in impaired phagocytosis. In sickle cell disease, *Salmonella* may infect bone infarcts, leading to high incidence of *Salmonella* osteomyelitis.
Splenectomy	Pyogenic encapsulated extracellular bacteria (especially *S pneumoniae*). Rarely, malaria, piroplasmosis (babesiosis).	Fulminating and rapidly fatal bacterial infection, often complicated by disseminated intravascular coagulation. Risk of infection far greater when there is an underlying disease of the reticuloendothelial system or when the patient is very young (eg, adolescent splenectomy for trauma carries less risk than childhood splenectomy for thalassemia). Spleen is critically important in the early control of bacteremia, prior to the synthesis of specific opsonic antibody. Impaired synthesis of IgM, tuftsin, and complement shunt pathway components may follow splenectomy. Loss of "pitting" function for malaria and similar protozoa.
Foreign bodies (intravascular, intra-articular, etc)	Pyogenic extracellular bacteria (especially *S aureus* and *S epidermidis*). *Candida albicans* (especially during total parenteral nutrition, hyperalimentation).	Direct vascular portal from the skin (intravascular catheters). High *Candida* incidence in hyperalimentation may reflect glucose-rich material infused. Arteriovenous shunts (as from dialysis) may predispose to infective endocarditis by changing flow characteristics across heart valves, leading to predisposition to incidental infection.
Gastrectomy	Pulmonary tuberculosis. *Salmonella* gastroenteritis. Cholera.	Malnutrition due to excessive stomach removal (tuberculosis reactivation). Loss of gastric acidity barrier (salmonellosis and cholera).

pneumonia occurs because of the opportunity afforded by aspiration of secretions and the absence of circulating type-specific opsonic antibody.)

The diseases summarized in Table 33–6, however, result when there is a more flagrant disruption of the functional capacity of the immune system. There is no attempt to list every potential opportunistic pathogen; major relationships are stressed.

•   •   •

References

General

Braude AI, Davis CE, Fierer J (editors): *Medical Microbiology and Infectious Diseases*. Saunders, 1981.

Dick G (editor): *Immunological Aspects of Infectious Diseases*. University Park Press, 1979.

Mims CA: *The Pathogenesis of Infectious Disease*. Academic Press, 1977.

Rose NR, Friedman H (editors): *Manual of Clinical Immunology*, 2nd ed. American Society for Microbiology, 1980.

Voller A, Friedman H: *New Trends and Developments in Vaccines*. University Park Press, 1978.

Streptococcus pneumoniae Infection

Amman AJ et al: Polyvalent pneumococcal-polysaccharide immunization of patients with sickle cell anemia and patients with splenectomy. *N Engl J Med* 1977;**297**:897.

Austrian R: Random gleanings from a life with the pneumococcus. *J Infect Dis* 1975;**131**:474.

Kass EH (editor): Assessment of the pneumococcal polysaccharide vaccine. *Rev Infect Dis* 1981;**3(Suppl)**:1.

Mold C et al: C-reactive protein is protective against *Streptococcus pneumoniae* infection in mice. *J Exp Med* 1981; **154**:1703.

Quie PG, Giebink GS, Winkelstein JA (editors): The pneumococcus. *Rev Infect Dis* 1981;**3**:183.

Streptococci of Groups A & B

Anthony BF, Okada D: The emergence of group B streptococci in infections of the newborn infant. *Annu Rev Med* 1977;**28**:355.

Baker CJ et al: Antibody-independent classical pathway-mediated opsonophagocytosis of type Ia, group B streptococcus. *J Clin Invest* 1982;**69**:394.

Baker CJ et al: Immunogenicity of polysaccharides from type III, group B streptococcus. *J Clin Invest* 1978;**61**:1107.

Peter G, Smith AL: Group A streptococcal infections of the skin and pharynx. (2 parts.) *N Engl J Med* 1977;**297**:311, 365.

Stollerman GH: Streptococcal immunology: Protection versus injury. *Ann Intern Med* 1978;**88**:422.

Staphylococcus aureus Infection

Kaplan MH, Tenenbaum MJ: *Staphylococcus aureus*: Cellular biology and clinical application. *Am J Med* 1982; **72**:248.

Peterson PK et al: The key role of peptidoglycan in the opsonization of *Staphylococcus aureus*. *J Clin Invest* 1978; **61**:597.

Schlievert PM et al: Identification and characterization of an exotoxin from *Staphylococcus aureus* associated with toxic-shock syndrome. *J Infect Dis* 1981;**143**:509.

Wheat LJ et al: Circulating staphylococcal antigen in humans and immune rabbits with endocarditis due to *Staphylococcus aureus*: Inhibition of detection by preexisting antibodies. *J Infect Dis* 1979;**140**:54.

Yotis WW (editor): Recent advances in staphylococcal research. *Ann NY Acad Sci* 1974;**236**:1.

Haemophilus influenzae Infection

Anderson P et al: Immunization of humans with polyribophosphate, the capsular antigen of *Haemophilus influenzae*, type b. *J Clin Invest* 1972;**51**:39.

Bradshaw M et al: Bacterial antigens cross-reactive with the capsular polysaccharide of *Haemophilus influenzae*, type b. *Lancet* 1971;**1**:1095.

Smith DH et al: Responses of children immunized with the capsular polysaccharide of *Hemophilus influenzae*, type b. *Pediatrics* 1973;**52**:637.

Neisseria meningitidis Infection

Edwards EA: Immunologic investigations of meningococcal disease. 2. Some characteristics of group C antigen of *Neisseria meningitidis* in the sera of patients with fulminant meningococcemia. *J Infect Dis* 1974;**129**:538.

Pandey JP et al: Immunoglobulin allotypes and immune response to meningococcal group B polysaccharide. *J Clin Invest* 1981;**68**:1378.

Zollinger WD et al: Complex of meningococcal group B polysaccharide and type 2 outer membrane protein immunogenic in man. *J Clin Invest* 1979;**63**:836.

Neisseria gonorrhoeae Infection

Brooks GF et al: Human seminal plasma inhibition of antibody complement-mediated killing and opsonization of *Neisseria gonorrhoeae* and other gram-negative organisms. *J Clin Invest* 1981;**67**:1523.

Brooks GF et al (editors): *Immunobiology of Neisseria gonorrhoeae*. American Society for Microbiology, 1978.

Danielsson D, Normark S (editors): *Genetics and Immunobiology of Pathogenic Neisseria*. European Molecular Biology Organization Workshop, June 16–19, 1980, Hemavan, Sweden. Norrlandstryck i; Umea AB.

Koransky JR, Jacobs NF: Serologic testing for gonorrhea. *Sex Transm Dis* 1977;**4**:27.

Tramont EC et al: Gonococcal pilus vaccine: Studies of antigenicity and inhibition of attachment. *J Clin Invest* 1981; **68**:881.

Gram-Negative Rods

Braude AI et al: Antibody to cell wall glycolipid of gram-negative bacteria: Induction of immunity to bacteremia and endotoxinemia. *J Infect Dis* 1977;**136(Suppl)**:167.

Young LS et al: Gram-negative rod bacteremia: Microbiologic, immunologic, and therapeutic considerations. *Ann Intern Med* 1977;**86**:456.

Pseudomonas aeruginosa Infection

Pier GB: Safety and immunogenicity of high molecular weight polysaccharide vaccine from immunotype I *Pseudomonas aeruginosa*. *J Clin Invest* 1982;**69**:303.

Pollack M, Young LS: Protective activity of antibodies to exotoxin A and lipopolysaccharide at the onset of *Pseudomonas aeruginosa* septicemia in man. *J Clin Invest* 1979;**63**:276.

Reynolds HY et al: *Pseudomonas aeruginosa* infections: Persisting problems and current research to find new therapies. *Ann Intern Med* 1975;**82**:819.

Yersinia pestis (Plague)

Brubaker RR: Expression of virulence in yersiniae. Page 168 in: *Microbiology–1979*. Schlessinger D (editor). American Society for Microbiology, 1979.

Bacillus anthracis (Anthrax)

Brachman PS: Anthrax. *Ann NY Acad Sci* 1970;**174**:577.

Exotoxin Production & Disease

Chang T-W et al: *Clostridium difficile* toxin. *Pharmacol Ther* 1981;**13**:441.

Collier RJ: Genetic approaches to structure and activity in ADP-ribosylating exotoxins. Page 242 in: *Microbiology–1979*. Schlessinger D (editor). American Society for Microbiology, 1979.

Exotoxins. Pages 236–301 in *Microbiology–1975*. Schlessinger D (editor). American Society for Microbiology, 1975.

Simpson LL: The action of botulinal toxin. *Rev Infect Dis* 1979;**1**:656.

Vesely DL et al: Purified *Clostridium difficile* cytotoxin stimulates guanylate cyclase activity and inhibits adenylate cyclase activity. *Infect Immun* 1981;**33**:285.

Epithelial Cell Attachment & Disease

Interactions at body surfaces. Page 106 in: *Microbiology–1975*. Schlessinger D (editor). American Society for Microbiology, 1975.

Penetration. Page 158 in: *Microbiology–1975*. Schlessinger D (editor). American Society for Microbiology, 1975.

Viral Neutralization

Johnson TC: Host-virus interaction: General properties of animal viruses. Chapter 4 in: *The Biological and Clinical Basis of Infectious Diseases*. Youmans GP, Paterson PY, Somers HM (editors). Saunders, 1975.

Syphilis

Baseman JB et al: Virulence determinants among the spirochetes. Page 203 in: *Microbiology–1979*. Schlessinger D (editor). American Society for Microbiology, 1979.

Baughn RE et al: Detection of circulating immune complexes in the sera of rabbits with experimental syphilis: Possible role in immunoregulation. *Infect Immun* 1980;**29**:575.

Bey RF, Johnson RC, Fitzgerald TJ: Suppression of lymphocyte response to concanavalin A by mucopolysaccharide material from *Treponema pallidum*–infected rabbits. *Infect Immun* 1979;**26**:64.

Bos JD, Hamerlinck F, Cormane RH: Antitreponemal IgE in early syphilis. *Br J Vener Dis* 1980;**56**:20.

Bryceson ADM: Clinical pathology of the Jarisch-Herxheimer reaction. *J Infect Dis* 1976;**133**:696.

Hardy PH: Death knell for the *Treponema pallidum* immobilization test. *Sex Transm Dis* 1980;**7**:145.

Lukehart SA, Baker-Zander SA, Sell S: Characterization of lymphocyte responsiveness in early experimental syphilis. 1. In vitro response to mitogens and *Treponema pallidum* antigens. *J Immunol* 1980;**124**:454.

Musher DM, Schell RF: The immunology of syphilis. *Hosp Pract* (Dec) 1975;**10**:45.

Schell RF et al: Endemic syphilis: Passive transfer of resistance in the serum and cells in hamsters. *J Infect Dis* 1979; **140**:378.

Shannon R et al: Immunological responses in late syphilis. *Br J Vener Dis* 1980;**56**:372.

Wozniczko-Orlowska G et al: Immune complexes in syphilis sera. *J Immunol* 1981;**127**:1048.

Cryptococcosis

Bennett JE: Cryptococcal skin test antigen: Preparation variables and characterization. *Infect Immun* 1981;**32**:373.

Diamond RD, Bennett JE: Prognostic factors in cryptococcal meningitis: A study in 111 cases. *Ann Intern Med* 1974; **80**:176.

Goodman JS et al: Diagnosis of cryptococcal meningitis: Value of immunologic detection of cryptococcal antigen. *N Engl J Med* 1971;**285**:434.

Graybill JR, Alford RH: Cell-mediated immunity in cryptococcosis. *Cell Immunol* 1974;**14**:12.

Kerkering TM, Duma RJ, Shadomy S: The evolution of pulmonary cryptococcosis: Clinical implications from a study of 41 patients with and without compromising host factors. *Ann Intern Med* 1981;**94**:611.

Kozel TR et al: Opsonization of encapsulated *Cryptococcus neoformans* by specific anticapsular antibody. *Infect Immun* 1981;**31**:978.

Rhodes JC et al: Genetic control of susceptibility to *Cryptococcus neoformans* in mice. *Infect Immun* 1980;**29**:494.

Candidiasis

Diamond RD: Mechanisms of host resistance to *Candida albicans*. Page 200 in: *Microbiology–1981*. Schlessinger D (editor). American Society for Microbiology, 1981.

Elin RJ, Wolff SM: Effect of pH and iron concentration on growth of *Candida albicans* in human serum. *J Infect Dis* 1973;**127**:705.

Gelfand JA et al: Role of complement in host defense against experimental disseminated candidiasis. *J Infect Dis* 1978; **138**:9.

Gottlieb MS et al: *Pneumocystis carinii* pneumonia and mucosal candidiasis in previously healthy homosexual men: Evidence of a new acquired cellular immunodeficiency. *N Engl J Med* 1981;**305**:1425.

Hurtrel B et al: Absence of correlation between delayed-type hypersensitivity and protection in experimental systemic candidiasis in immunized mice. *Infect Immun* 1981;**31**:95.

Kaufman L: Laboratory diagnosis of candidiasis. Page 205 in: *Microbiology–1981*. Schlessinger D (editor). American Society for Microbiology, 1981.

Morrison RP et al: In vitro studies of the interaction of murine phagocytic cells with *Candida albicans*. *J Reticuloendothel Soc* 1981;**29**:23.

Richardson MD et al: Resistance of virulent and attenuated strains of *Candida albicans* to intracellular killing by human and mouse phagocytes. *J Infect Dis* 1981;**144**:557.

Rogers TJ et al: Immunity to *Candida albicans*. *Microbiol Rev* 1980;**44**:660.

Weiner MH, Coats-Stephen M: Immunodiagnosis of systemic candidiasis: Mannan antigenemia detected by radioimmunoassay in experimental and human infections. *J Infect Dis* 1979;**140**:989.

Salmonellosis

Collins FM, Carter PB: Cellular immunity in enteric disease.

Am J Clin Nutr 1974;**27**:1424.

Grady GF, Keusch GT: Pathogenesis of bacterial diarrheas. (2 parts.) *N Engl J Med* 1971;**285**:831, 891.

Hohmann AW: Intestinal colonization and virulence of salmonellae in mice. *Infect Immunol* 1978;**22**:763.

Hornick RB et al: Typhoid fever: Pathogenesis and immunologic control. (2 parts.) *N Engl J Med* 1970;**283**:686, 739.

Marneeruschapisal V et al: Local cell-associated immunity in the Peyer's patches of mouse intestines. *Infect Immun* 1981;**33**:338.

Melendez M et al: Immunity to antigenically related salmonellae: Effects of humoral factors on the bactericidal activity of normal and immune peritoneal exudate cells. *Infect Immunol* 1978;**22**:640.

Listeriosis

Medoff G et al: Listeriosis in humans: An evaluation. *J Infect Dis* 1971;**123**:247.

van Kessel KPM et al: Interactions of killed *Listeria monocytogenes* with the mouse complement system. *Infect Immun* 1981;**34**:16.

Tuberculosis

Al-Arif LI et al: HLA-Bw15 and tuberculosis in a North American black population. *Am Rev Respir Dis* 1979;**120**:1275.

Bass JB Jr et al: The use of repeat skin tests to eliminate the booster phenomenon in serial tuberculin testing. *Am Rev Respir Dis* 1981;**123**:394.

Cox RA et al: Lymphocyte transformation assays as a diagnostic tool in tuberculosis of children. *Am Rev Respir Dis* 1981;**123**:627.

Daniel TM et al: The immune spectrum in patients with pulmonary tuberculosis. *Am Rev Respir Dis* 1981;**123**:556.

Higuchi S et al: Persistence of protein, carbohydrate and wax components of tubercle bacilli in dermal BCG lesions. *Am Rev Respir Dis* 1981;**123**:397.

Kaplan M et al: Antibodies to mycobacteria in human tuberculosis. 2. Response to nine defined mycobacterial antigens with evidence for an antibody common to tuberculosis and lepromatous leprosy. *J Infect Dis* 1980;**142**:835.

Kleinhenz ME et al: Suppression of lymphocyte responses by tuberculous plasma and mycobacterial arabinogalactan: Monocyte dependence and indomethacin reversibility. *J Clin Invest* 1981;**68**:153.

Reggiardo Z et al: Hemagglutination tests for tuberculosis with mycobacterial glycolipid antigens: Results in patients with active pulmonary tuberculosis before and during chemotherapy and in healthy tuberculosis contacts. *Am Rev Respir Dis* 1981;**124**:21.

Snider DE: The tuberculin skin test. *Am Rev Respir Dis* 1982;**125(Suppl)**:102.

Winters WD et al: Serodiagnosis of tuberculosis by radioimmunoassay. *Am Rev Respir Dis* 1981;**124**:582.

Leprosy

Abe M et al: Immunological problems in leprosy research. (2 parts.) *Bull WHO* 1973;**48**:345, 482.

Bullock WE: Leprosy: A model of immunological perturbation in chronic infection. *J Infect Dis* 1978;**137**:341.

Bullock WE et al: The evaluation of immunosuppressive cell populations in experimental mycobacterial infection. *J Immunol* 1978;**120**:1709.

Drutz DJ et al: Leukocyte antimicrobial function in patients with leprosy. *J Clin Invest* 1974;**53**:380.

Sansonetti P, Lagrange PH: The immunology of leprosy: Speculations on the leprosy spectrum. *Rev Infect Dis* 1981;**3**:422.

Stoner GL et al: Antigen-specific suppressor cells in subclinical leprosy infection. *Lancet* 1981;**2**:1372.

Histoplasmosis

Anderson KL, Marcus S: Immunity to histoplasmosis induced in mice by components of *Histoplasma capsulatum*. *Am Rev Respir Dis* 1970;**102**:614.

Buechner HA et al: The current status of serologic, immunologic, and skin tests in the diagnosis of pulmonary mycoses. *Dis Chest* 1973;**63**:259.

Goodwin RA Jr, Des Prez RM: State of the art: Histoplasmosis. *Am Rev Respir Dis* 1978;**117**:929.

Nickerson DA et al: Immunoregulation in disseminated histoplasmosis: Characterization of splenic suppressor cell populations. *Cell Immunol* 1981;**60**:287.

Sutcliffe MC et al: Transferrin-dependent growth inhibition of yeast-phase *Histoplasma capsulatum* by human serum and lymph. *J Infect Dis* 1980;**142**:209.

Williams DM et al: Adoptive transfer of immunity to *Histoplasma capsulatum* in athymic nude mice. *Sabouraudia* 1981;**19**:39.

Coccidioidomycosis

Ajello L (editor): *Coccidioidomycosis: Current Clinical and Diagnostic Status*. Symposia Specialists, 1977.

Drutz DJ, Catanzaro A: Coccidioidomycosis, state of the art. (2 parts.) *Am Rev Respir Dis* 1978;**117**:559, 727.

Drutz DJ et al: Human sex hormones stimulate the growth and maturation of *Coccidioides immitis*. *Infect Immun* 1981;**32**:897.

Gifford J et al: A comparison of coccidioidin and spherulin skin testing in the diagnosis of coccidioidomycosis. *Am Rev Respir Dis* 1981;**124**:440.

Gunby P: Coccidioidomycosis vaccine trial planned with 3,000 volunteers. *JAMA* 1981;**245**:1711.

Harvey RP et al: In vitro assays of cellular immunity in progressive coccidioidomycosis: Evaluation of suppression with parasitic-phase antigen. *Am Rev Respir Dis* 1981;**123**:665.

Huppert M et al: Antigenic analysis of coccidioidin and spherulin determined by two-dimensional immunoelectrophoresis. *Infect Immunol* 1978;**20**:541.

Smith CE et al: Pattern of 39,500 serologic tests in coccidioidomycosis. *JAMA* 1956;**160**:546.

Yoshinoya S et al: Circulating immune complexes in coccidioidomycosis: Detection and characterization. *J Clin Invest* 1980;**66**:655.

Brucellosis

Birmingham JR et al: Characterization of macrophage functions in mice infected with *Brucella abortus*. *Infect Immun* 1981;**32**:1079.

Cheers C et al: Macrophage activation during experimental murine brucellosis: A basis for chronic infection. *Infect Immun* 1979;**23**:197.

Renoux M: A passive hemagglutination test for the detection of *Brucella* infection. *J Immunol Methods* 1980;**32**:349.

Young EJ et al: Comparison of *Brucella abortus* and *Brucella melitensis* infections of mice and their effect on acquired cellular resistance. *Infect Immun* 1979;**26**:686.

Tularemia

Hornick RB: Tularemia. Pages 1043–1049 in: *Infectious*

Diseases: A Modern Treatise of Infectious Processes. Hoeprich PD (editor). Harper & Row, 1977.

Mycoplasma

Clyde WA Jr: Pathogenic mechanisms in *Mycoplasma* diseases. Page 143 in: *Microbiology–1975.* Schlessinger D (editor). American Society for Microbiology, 1975.

Collier AM: Virulence determinants of mycoplasmas, with emphasis on *Mycoplasma pneumoniae.* Page 198 in: *Microbiology–1979.* Schlessinger D (editor). American Society for Microbiology, 1979.

Bordetella pertussis

Olson LC: Pertussis. *Medicine* 1975;**54**:427.

Pittman M: Pertussis. *Rev Infect Dis* 1979;**1**:401.

Chlamydiae

Kuo C-C: Interaction of *Chlamydia trachomatis* and mouse peritoneal macrophages. Page 116 in: *Microbiology–1979.* Schlessinger D (editor). American Society for Microbiology, 1979.

Manire GP, Wyrick PB: Cell envelopes of chlamydiae: Adaptation for intracellular parasitism. Page 111 in: *Microbiology–1979.* Schlessinger D (editor). American Society for Microbiology, 1979.

Moulder JW: Interaction of chlamydiae with host cells. Page 105 in: *Microbiology–1979.* Schlessinger D (editor). American Society for Microbiology, 1979.

Schachter J, Dawson CC: *Human Chlamydial Infections.* PSG, 1978.

Rickettsiae

Murray ES et al: Brill's disease. 1. Clinical and laboratory diagnosis. *JAMA* 1950;**142**:1059.

Philip RN et al: A comparison of serologic methods for diagnosis of Rocky Mountain spotted fever. *Am J Epidemiol* 1977;**105**:56.

Zdrodowskii PF, Golinevich HM: *The Rickettsial Diseases.* Pergamon Press, 1960.

Circulating Immune Complexes & Disease

Barnett EV (moderator): Circulating immune complexes: Their immunochemistry, detection, and importance. *Ann Intern Med* 1979;**91**:430.

Duffy J et al: Polyarthritis, polyarteritis and hepatitis B. *Medicine* 1976;**55**:19.

Gutman RA et al: The immune complex glomerulonephritis of bacterial endocarditis. *Medicine* 1972;**51**:1.

Nissenson AR (moderator): Poststreptococcal acute glomerulonephritis: Fact and controversy. *Ann Intern Med* 1979;**91**:76.

Sergent JS et al: Vasculitis with hepatitis B antigenemia: Long-term observations in nine patients. *Medicine* 1976;**55**:1.

Sitprija V et al: Glomerulitis in typhoid fever. *Ann Intern Med* 1974;**81**:210.

Host-Virus Relationships

Craighead JE: Report of a workshop: Disease accentuation after immunization with inactivated microbial vaccines. *J Infect Dis* 1975;**131**:749.

Opportunistic Infections

Barrett-Connor E: Bacterial infection and sickle cell anemia: An analysis of 250 infections in 166 patients and a review of the literature. *Medicine* 1971;**50**:97.

Bisno AL, Freeman JC: The syndrome of asplenia, pneumococcal sepsis and disseminated intravascular coagulation. *Ann Intern Med* 1970;**72**:389.

Dilworth JA, Mandell GL: Infections in patients with cancer. *Semin Oncol* 1975;**2**:349.

Merigan TC, Stevens DA: Viral infections in man associated with acquired immunological deficiency states. *Fed Proc* 1971;**30**:1858.

Saravolatz LD et al: The compromised host and Legionnaire's disease. *Ann Intern Med* 1979;**90**:533.

Endocrine Diseases | 34

Noel R. Rose, MD, PhD, Mara Lorenzi, MD, & Mark Lewis, PhD

Some of the best-studied examples of organ-specific autoimmune disease are found among the endocrine disorders. Organ-specific autoimmunity primarily affects a single organ of the body. The target antigen of the immunologic response is unique for the affected organ, ie, it is an organ-specific antigen. Such antigens arise during embryonic differentiation and are often associated with the unique function of the organ. Organs of internal secretion, with their highly specialized physiologic functions, possess distinctive organ-specific antigens. Thus, organs with distinctive, specific antigens, like the endocrine glands, frequently induce autoimmune responses (see Table 34–1).

CHRONIC THYROIDITIS

Major Immunologic Features
- Produced experimentally by injection of thyroglobulin in adjuvants.

- Thyroid function tests may be elevated, depressed, or normal.
- Autoantibodies to thyroglobulin or thyroid microsomes (or both) present.
- Self-limited or responsive to thyroid hormone treatment.

General Considerations
The thyroid gland has certain unusual structural and functional properties that seem to predispose to the development of autoimmune responses. It is made up of a series of saclike follicles lined with cuboid epithelium. Within the follicles is found the homogeneously stained colloid, the principal constituent of which is a glycoprotein, thyroglobulin. This high-molecular-weight protein (about 650,000) contains iodinated amino acids, ie, mono- and diiodotyrosine, triiodothyronine (T_3), and thyroxine (T_4). The latter 2 amino acids are the active thyroid hormones. Similar proportions of each hormone (99.9% T_4,

Table 34–1. Endocrine diseases with autoimmune phenomena.

Disease	Antigen(s)	Methods for Detection of Antibody
Chronic thyroiditis and primary hypothyroidism	Thyroglobulin	Precipitation Hemagglutination Radioassay Immunofluorescence
	Microsomes of thyroid epithelium	Complement fixation Immunofluorescence Hemagglutination
	Second colloid antigen	Immunofluorescence
	Membranes	Cytotoxicity Mixed agglutination Immunofluorescence
Hyperthyroidism (Graves' disease)	TSH receptor of thyroid cell surface	Bioassay (LATS) Radioreceptor assay In vitro thyroid stimulation assays
Adrenal insufficiency (Addison's disease)	Microsomes of adrenal cortex Heat-stable antigen of adrenal cortex Steroid-producing cells of adrenal, ovary, testis, and placenta	Immunofluorescence Complement fixation Precipitation
Primary hypoparathyroidism	Oxyphil cells Chief cells	Immunofluorescence
Diabetes mellitus	A, B, D cells of pancreatic islets	Immunofluorescence
Ovarian failure	Cells of theca interna of corpus luteum	Immunofluorescence

99.5% T_3) are bound to plasma proteins, but the binding affinity for T_3 is much lower; its distribution volume is greater; and a greater proportion of the extrathyroidal hormone is located within cells. The synthesis of thyroglobulin in the follicle-lining cells is usually balanced by its resorption and splitting by thyroid proteolytic enzymes or cathepsins. Thyroglobulin is essentially a molecular storage form of the thyroid hormones. Thyroglobulin breakdown is enhanced by one of the peptides secreted by the anterior pituitary, termed thyroid-stimulating hormone (TSH) or thyrotropin, and decreased by iodide.

As might be expected of a large glycoprotein, thyroglobulin is a good antigen. Injected into foreign species, it readily elicits antibody formation. A large proportion of the antibodies produced to thyroglobulin are organ-specific. They react with thyroglobulin and not with other antigens of the body, such as glycoproteins isolated from other organs. In contrast, antibodies to thyroglobulin of one species partially cross-react with thyroglobulins of other mammals. This lack of strict species-specificity is a characteristic of some of the most potent organ-specific antigens.

It was formerly believed that thyroglobulin is anatomically sequestered from the vascular and lymphatic pathways. More recent information indicates that low levels of thyroglobulin are found in the lymphatics draining the thyroid and in the bloodstream. Plasma thyroglobulin is elevated in many cases of hypertension and some cases of thyroid carcinoma and subacute thyroiditis; thyroglobulin concentrations are less often elevated in toxic nodular goiter and lymphocytic thyroiditis. By itself, thyroglobulin does not generally evoke formation of antibodies in the same animal. However, injection of an animal's own thyroglobulin, combined with certain adjuvants, elicits production of specific autoantibodies. If given with Freund's complete adjuvant (an emulsion with mineral oil, acid-fast microorganisms, and an emulsifying agent) or with bacterial lipopolysaccharide, thyroglobulin injections elicit lymphocytic infiltration of the thyroid gland of the immunized animal. This process of chronic inflammation is referred to as thyroiditis.

Injection of foreign thyroglobulins also causes thyroiditis without the need for adjuvants. Thyroglobulin molecules of the same species can be rendered antigenic by inserting foreign chemical determinants such as arsenilic or sulfanilic groups. These apparently provide immunologic handles similar to those supplied by the foreign determinants of cross-reacting thyroglobulins. It is also possible to make thyroglobulin antigenic by incomplete proteolytic digestion. Perhaps this procedure exposes unfamiliar sites of the molecule that act like foreign determinants.

The immunologic reaction to thyroglobulin is determined in part by the innate, genetically determined responsiveness of the injected animal. For example, among mice, some inbred strains are excellent responders to their own thyroglobulin while other strains are very poor responders. It is probable that several genes are involved in determining the response. The ability to produce circulating antibody to thyroglobulin can sometimes be separated from the ability to develop autoimmune lesions in the thyroid. One of the main genes controlling recognition is linked to the major histocompatibility (H-2) complex of the mouse and is probably an Ir gene coding response to a particular determinant or small number of determinants on the thyroglobulin molecule.

Some animals have a strong tendency to develop thyroiditis spontaneously, such as certain strains of beagle dogs and of rats. A closed colony of chickens called OS (for obese strain) has been established by selective breeding, and these birds have severe thyroid inflammation with typical clinical and biochemical evidence of thyroid failure. Study of these hereditary models of thyroiditis provides valuable clues about the cause, pathogenesis, and genetic predisposition to autoimmune disease of the thyroid in humans.

Immunologic Pathogenesis

The similarity of chronic thyroiditis in the human to experimentally induced or hereditary thyroiditis in animals is striking. The principal antigen is thyroglobulin. Under experimental conditions, this purified protein can be shown to be autoantigenic. Immunization results in production of autoantibodies reactive with antigen from the immunized animal itself. Lesions arise simultaneously in the thyroid gland of the animal, and these lesions are quite similar to those of the human disease. Human chronic thyroiditis fulfills these minimal criteria for diseases of autoimmune origin (Table 34–2).

Defining the precise pathogenic mechanisms of thyroiditis has proved to be difficult. In some species, such as the rabbit and mouse, it has been possible to transfer the disease from immunized to normal animals by injecting antibody-containing serum. The mechanism by which antibodies induce lymphocytic inflammation of the thyroid is uncertain. Antibodies may interact with thyroglobulin in the follicles or along the basement membrane of the thyroid gland. A localized immune complex tissue injury would result. On the other hand, the antibodies may cooperate with normal lymphocytes to produce tissue damage.

In other species, such as the guinea pig or rat, thyroiditis has thus far been transferred only with living, histocompatible lymph node cells. The histologic features of thyroiditis are more suggestive of cell-

---

Table 34–2. Criteria for establishing the autoimmune etiology of an organ-specific human disease.*

(1) Autoantibodies reactive at body temperature, or evidence of cell-mediated immunity
(2) Isolation and purification of the organ-specific antigens
(3) Production of autoantibodies to analogous antigen in experimental animals
(4) Development of similar lesions in autosensitized animals

*Modified from Witebsky E et al: Chronic thyroiditis and autoimmunization. *JAMA* 1957;**164**:1439.

mediated than of antibody-mediated immunologic re-actions. It is possible to demonstrate delayed hypersensitivity by skin tests in immunized guinea pigs and rats. In vitro indicators of cell-mediated immunity such as production of macrophage migration inhibitory factor (MIF) and lymphocyte transformation have also been shown in some species.

In the test tube, it can be shown that normal lymphocytes of the human can cooperate with thyroid antibody to damage thyroid cells or lyse carrier cells coated with thyroglobulin or thyroid microsomes. These findings support the view that antibody-dependent cell-mediated lymphotoxicity is responsible for the induction of pathologic changes in the thyroid. Immune complexes have also been found in the thyroid basement membrane of a few patients with thyroiditis. Complexes of appropriate size may adhere to the stroma of the thyroid gland, activate complement, and provoke inflammation. Obviously, more work must be done to define the pathogenetic mechanisms in thyroiditis both in humans and in experimental animals.

Clinical Features

Chronic lymphocytic thyroiditis is most common in the age group from 30 to 60 years, although juvenile thyroiditis may cause sporadic goiter in children and adolescents. The female-to-male ratio is about 5:1, an indication that sex hormones may influence expression of the disease. The incidence of thyroiditis in monozygotic twins is about 6 times greater than in dizygotic twins of the same sex, suggesting a strong genetic predisposition. A number of studies have pointed to a relationship of thyroiditis and chromosomal aberrations, especially Down's syndrome. Although unpredictable in its occurrence, the disease is found more frequently in persons who have relatives with a thyroid disorder, such as thyroiditis, hyperthyroidism, or myxedema. The relatives may have thyroid antibodies without overt disease or may have autoimmune disease of another endocrine gland, pernicious anemia, or atrophic gastritis. This immunologic overlap among the organ-specific autoimmune disorders has been taken as tentative evidence that there is some genetic fault in the immunologic regulatory mechanisms that normally control self-reactive lymphocytes.

The subacute and silent (painless) forms of thyroiditis sometimes occur in small outbreaks following viral infections. Mumps has been reported to predispose to thyroiditis. It may be that respiratory tract infections can trigger autoimmunity to thyroid, but this relationship has not been clearly demonstrated in cases of chronic thyroiditis. In some cases, postpartum thyroiditis may be autoimmune in nature. There may be lymphocytic infiltration of the thyroid and serologic evidence of thyroid autoantibodies. Some patients have repeated postpartum episodes of thyroiditis and show increasing antibody titers as the disease progresses.

The clinical features of chronic thyroiditis in humans are relatively mild. The thyroid gland may be diffusely enlarged to produce a goiter. It is usually firm to hard in consistency, only rarely tender, and smooth or scalloped without distinct nodules. Severe symptoms of neck pain with upward radiation may be present.

Most chronic thyroiditis patients are clinically euthyroid even though uptake of radioactive iodine by the thyroid is high. About 20% are hypothyroid when first seen, and occasionally hyperthyroidism is present initially in the disease. During the later phases of chronic thyroiditis, patients may develop signs of diminished thyroid function, suggesting failure of regeneration of the epithelial cells. The skin is dry and the hair coarse, and myxedema is sometimes present. These patients show lowered values of circulating thyroid hormones, decreased thyroidal radioiodine uptake, high serum TSH levels, and high serum cholesterol levels. Their basal metabolic rates are low.

Immunologic Diagnosis

The cornerstone of immunologic diagnosis of human thyroiditis is the demonstration of autoantibodies to thyroid-specific antigens. In humans, as in animals, thyroglobulin is the major autoantigen of the thyroid (Table 34–1). Approximately 60–75% of patients with various forms of chronic thyroiditis (depending upon the histologic type) show positive reactions in an indirect hemagglutination test (Tables 34–3 and 34–4). About a third of these patients have elevated hemagglutination titers of 600–1000 or more. Titers in this elevated range are strongly indicative of autoimmune thyroiditis or a related autoimmune process. Patients with primary adult myxedema may also demonstrate high titers of antibody to thyroglobulin in the same high prevalence as thyroiditis (Table 34–3). About a third of patients with hyperthyroidism due to Graves' disease and one-fourth of patients with carcinoma of the thyroid (especially papillary adenocarcinoma) have antibodies to thyroglobulin, usually with titers of less than 600 (Table 34–3). In many cases of

Table 34–3. Incidence of thyroglobulin autoantibodies in various thyroid diseases and controls (tanned cell hemagglutination method).

Histologic Diagnosis	Approximate Percentage of Positive Reactions
Thyroiditis	
Acute	10%
Subacute (granulomatous or de Quervain's)	35%
Fibrotic (Riedel's)	50%
Chronic	
Lymphocytic	60%
Fibrous	75%
Mixed (nonspecific)	75%
Primary hypothyroidism (adult myxedema)	75%
Graves' disease (hyperthyroidism; thyrotoxicosis)	40%
Carcinoma	25%
Control hospital population	5%

Table 34—4. Incidence of autoantibodies to thyroglobulin and thyroid microsomes in 546 patients with various forms of thyroiditis.

Antibodies to Thyroglobulin (Tanned Cell Hemagglutination)	Antibodies to Thyroid Microsomes (Complement Fixation)	Percentage Positive
+	+	37
+	−	27
−	+	33
−	−	3

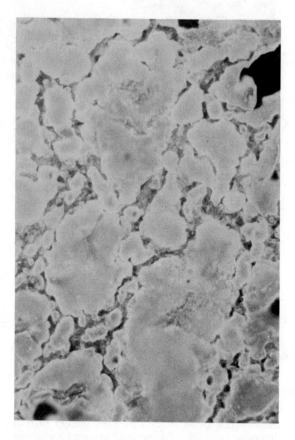

Figure 34–1. Immunofluorescent staining of thyroglobulin. Monkey thyroid tissue was frozen rapidly, thin-sectioned with a cryostat (4 μm), and fixed in methanol at 56 °C for 10 minutes. It was covered with serum from a patient with chronic thyroiditis (diluted 1:10), washed, covered with fluorescein-labeled anti–human globulin goat serum, washed, and examined with the ultraviolet microscope. A floccular pattern of fluorescence is seen within the thyroid follicles, indicating staining of the colloid. (Original magnification, × 180.)

hyperthyroidism or of thyroid cancer, localized lymphocytic infiltrates are found. The presence of antibodies in these 2 diseases may be indicative of a secondary process of autoimmunization.

Autoantibodies to thyroglobulin may be found in a few other diseases. Patients with pernicious anemia or atrophic gastritis frequently have antibodies to thyroid antigens. Patients with idiopathic adrenal insufficiency or parathyroid failure sometimes have autoantibodies to thyroid. In Sjögren's syndrome, autoantibodies to thyroglobulin are sometimes found in the same high titers characteristic of thyroiditis and hypothyroidism.

Autoantibodies to thyroglobulin are reported in about 3–18% of individuals with no clinical evidence of thyroid disease. This figure depends to a great extent upon the age and sex of the group being sampled. For example, the normal reactor group is much higher if made up of female subjects 40–60 years of age. It is quite plausible that the appearance of autoantibodies in these individuals actually signifies a subclinical focal thyroiditis, which has been frequently reported in middle-aged women. Almost one-fifth of older women were reported to have lymphocytic thyroiditis in one postmortem study.

The autoantibodies to thyroglobulin found in human thyroiditis provide the usual reactions in precipitation and agglutination techniques. By immunofluorescence, they localize in the colloid of methanol-fixed sections, producing a floccular appearance (Fig 34–1). The antibodies may be found in any of the major immunoglobulin classes, IgG, IgM, or IgA. However, they do not fix complement. Sera from patients with thyroiditis sometimes produce complement fixation when mixed with suspensions of thyroid. The antigen involved, however, is not thyroglobulin. It is associated with a lipoprotein of the microsomal membrane. The reaction is thyroid-specific. About 70% of patients with thyroiditis demonstrated this antibody (Table 34–4).

Since the group of patients with antibodies to thyroid microsomes does not correspond precisely with the group that has thyroglobulin antibodies, the total of patients in whom complement-fixing or hemagglutinating antibodies can be measured is about 97% (Table 34–4). Thus, the immunologic diagnosis of chronic thyroiditis using these 2 independent tests is more successful than with either test alone. Like hemagglutinating antibodies, the incidence of complement-fixing antibodies differs in the different forms of thyroiditis, being greatest in the mixed and fibrous varieties of chronic thyroiditis and least in the lymphocytic form of thyroiditis. About 2% of healthy male blood donors and 6% of female donors have autoantibodies to thyroid microsomes as shown by complement fixation method.

Indirect immunofluorescence provides a convenient method for demonstrating antibodies to the microsomal antigen. Fixed tissues cannot be used because the antigen is easily destroyed. Fresh frozen human or monkey thyroids are sectioned, flooded with patient's serum, washed, and treated with a fluorescent antiglobulin reagent. In the UV microscope, fluorescence is found in the apical cytoplasm of the thyroid epithelial cells (Fig 34–2). Nuclei are unstained. During the procedure, most of the thyroglobulin is washed

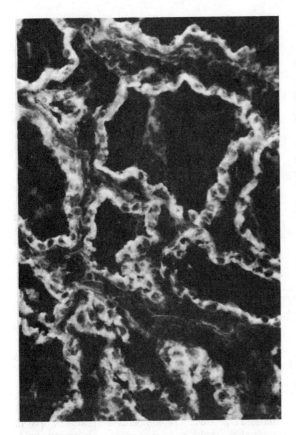

Figure 34–2. Immunofluorescent staining of thyroid microsomal antigen. Monkey thyroid tissue was prepared in the same manner as that described for Fig 34–1 except that it was not fixed in methanol. Immunofluorescent staining is seen in the cytoplasm of the thyroid epithelial cells lining the follicles. Note that the nuclei of the epithelial cells and the interstitial cells are unstained. (Original magnification, × 180.)

out of the follicles, so that no reaction occurs that can be attributed to thyroglobulin antibodies. A test for antibodies to thyroid microsomes has also been devised using the tanned cell hemagglutination technique. A third type of antibody will occasionally be found. This type reacts with the colloid in a homogeneous pattern but cannot be absorbed with thyroglobulin. The reaction is attributed to a second colloid antigen. The antigen, which is not well characterized, is a noniodinated colloid protein (Table 34–1).

When serum of certain thyroiditis patients is mixed with viable thyroid cell suspensions in the presence of complement, it will prevent the thyroid cells from attaching to the surface of the glass vessel and generating a monolayer. Control sera do not have this cytotoxic action. These cytotoxic antibodies are the only ones to have an injurious effect on thyroid cells in vitro. The antigen is a component of the thyroid epithelial cell membrane. Its presence also seems to be demonstrated on the surface of the thyroid cell by means of a mixed agglutination reaction using thyroglobulin-coated erythrocytes and a bridging antibody. The cytotoxic antigen is distinct from microsomal antigen. Many patients with positive complement fixation tests have no evidence of a cytotoxic reaction and are negative in mixed agglutination, and vice versa. Cytotoxic antibodies can be found in a large proportion of patients with thyrotoxicosis and the juvenile form of thyroiditis.

Positive assays for TSH receptor antibodies are sometimes encountered in patients with lymphocytic thyroiditis. This is particularly apt to be the case where there is an initial hyperthyroid phase. It is possible that in some instances where radioreceptor techniques are used, the antibodies measured are in fact receptor-blocking rather than stimulating.

Cell-mediated immunity to thyroid antigens has also been described. Some thyroiditis patients develop typical delayed hypersensitivity reactions when injected intradermally with thyroid extracts. Positive leukocyte, lymphocyte, and T lymphocyte migration inhibition and lymphocyte transformation have been obtained using crude thyroid extract, thyroglobulin, thyroid microsomes, and thyroid mitochondria. The clinical significance of these assays has not yet been established, but correlation of these studies with disease course and comparison with results obtained using tissue from relatives suggest that they may provide insights into the cause of autoimmune disease.

Patients with one particular form of chronic thyroiditis—the atrophic or fibrous variant of Hashimoto's thyroiditis—have a significantly higher prevalence of the HLA-DRw3 when compared with control populations. It is of interest that this specificity, which is in strong linkage disequilibrium with HLA-B8, has now been found to be associated with the many autoimmune disorders.

Differential Diagnosis

Chronic lymphocytic thyroiditis must be distinguished from nontoxic goiter, subacute thyroiditis, Graves' disease, and several types of cancer of the thyroid. The first distinction can be difficult, but nontoxic goiter is usually less firm than thyroiditis, and the presence of distinct nodularity favors the diagnosis of nontoxic goiter. In adults, high titers of thyroid autoantibodies will favor a diagnosis of thyroiditis. In adolescents, however, thyroiditis may be present in the absence of high antibody titers. Evidence of hypothyroidism favors a diagnosis of thyroiditis over that of either nontoxic goiter or thyroid cancer. Thyroid cancer would be suggested by the finding of very firm or hard nodules, adherence to skin or underlying structures, hoarseness due to invasion of the recurrent laryngeal nerve, and regional lymphadenopathy, all of which are unusual signs in thyroiditis and nontoxic goiter. A thyroid scintiscan is of critical importance in the evaluation of the nodular thyroid. Areas of nonfunction ("cold" nodules) are unusual in thyroiditis as compared to nontoxic goiter and cancer. A needle biopsy can be done if thyroiditis is suspected but should not be relied upon if cancer is more likely. In the latter instance, if a tissue diagnosis is desired, excisional biopsy is necessary.

Patients with subacute thyroiditis may complain of sore throat occurring coincident with or before the onset of thyroiditis. Perhaps the most significant statement a patient with subacute thyroiditis makes is that the throat is "sore on the outside rather than the inside." In contrast to chronic thyroiditis, the goiter of subacute thyroiditis may be accompanied by early elevations of serum thyroxine, probably as a result of release of hormone from the damaged gland, but these values usually return to normal after an intervening hypothyroid phase.

Acute thyroiditis is usually due to infection with pyogenic or mycobacterial strains. It is occasionally associated with autoantibody production; and, although lymphocytic infiltration may occur, histologic resolution of the disease is usually rapid and complete.

Histologically, several forms of thyroiditis can be differentiated (Table 34–3). Some thyroids show granulomas containing typical giant cells and epithelioid cells. This form of thyroiditis, referred to as de Quervain's type, corresponds to the subacute disease, the most common type following viral infection. The patients show systemic evidence of inflammation, such as fever, a rapid pulse, and an elevated sedimentation rate. Radioiodine uptake may be low even though circulating thyroid hormone is high.

Sometimes the gland is largely replaced by dense hyaline connective tissue, with extension of the fibrotic process beyond the thyroid capsule. In this invasive form of fibrotic thyroiditis (Riedel's struma), the thyroid gland is woody hard and fixed. Esophageal constriction and dysphagia may be major complications of fibrotic thyroiditis.

The most common form of chronic thyroiditis is associated with enlargement of the gland and infiltration by lymphocytes. Lymphoid nodules with germinal centers are sometimes found. Often one sees a mixed process of inflammation. There are many small and large lymphocytes, plasma cells, and macrophages which are prominent especially within the colloid. The colloid appears thin and foamy. Phagocytosis of the colloid can sometimes be demonstrated by proper staining. Eosinophils may be seen with special stains. Fibrosis may be evident in some portions of the gland. The follicular basement membrane may appear fragmented when viewed in the electron microscope. The thyroid is usually moderately enlarged but may be small in size and weight. If inflammation is extensive, it may invade the surrounding capsular tissue.

In the fibrous variant of chronic lymphocytic thyroiditis, the gland contains prominent strands of fibrous connective tissue. In contrast to Riedel's struma, this form of fibrosis does not invade the surrounding muscle. Between the bands of fibrous tissue, the thyroid parenchyma shows epithelial degeneration and chronic inflammation with infiltration of lymphocytes and plasma cells. These cases are the ones most often associated with depressed thyroid function.

In chronic thyroiditis, thyroid epithelial cells show evidence of regeneration and proliferation, appearing as oxyphilic or eosinophilic (Askanazy, or Hürthle) cells. The inflammatory process is commonly multifocal, so that some portions of the gland appear relatively normal while other areas are intensely infiltrated, with consequent degeneration of the epithelium. Often one can find neighboring sections in which there is evidence of an active process of regeneration. The follicular epithelium may be hypercellular, suggesting an effort to respond to thyroid-stimulating hormone.

Although the term Hashimoto's disease, or **struma lymphomatosa,** is often given to all the goitrous forms of the disease, the simple designation chronic thyroiditis describes the broad spectrum of pathologic and clinical variants. In all forms of the disease, evidence of an immunologic response is found, but frequencies of antibodies may vary greatly (Table 34–3).

Treatment, Complications, & Prognosis

In most instances, the thyroid enlargement may persist if active treatment is not given. Administration of synthetic thyroxine usually relieves the distressing symptoms and reduces the size of the gland, probably by suppressing pituitary thyrotropin production. The neck pain may require treatment with analgesics such as aspirin. Corticosteroids reduce local inflammation and often produce a rapid decrease in titers of thyroid antibodies. In the cases that progress to hypothyroidism, chronic replacement therapy with thyroxine or some other thyroid preparation is necessary. In theory, immunosuppressive drugs should be effective, as demonstrated in experimental animals. However, their use is rarely warranted in this disease.

Surgery of the thyroid and use of radioactive iodine are not generally indicated in chronic thyroiditis. Therefore, the differentiation of thyroiditis from thyroid carcinoma and hyperthyroidism, respectively, is a matter of great practical importance. As a matter of fact, therapeutic doses of radioactive iodine may intensify thyroiditis. Patients with preexisting antibody seem to develop more autoantibody following radioiodine treatment. An elevation in antibody to the thyroid microsomes is especially prominent.

The patient with subacute thyroiditis generally recovers complete thyroid function, and any thyroid enlargement which may appear during the course of the disease generally disappears. The antibodies fall to undetectable levels when the inflammation has subsided. The hyperthyroidism that may accompany subacute thyroiditis does not require treatment.

PRIMARY HYPOTHYROIDISM
(Adult Myxedema)

Insufficiency of circulating thyroid hormones leads to symptoms of hypothyroidism. The signs and symptoms depend greatly on the age at onset. Cretinism results from thyroid deficiency during fetal life and is characterized by irreversible arrest in development of the musculoskeletal and central nervous systems. There is no evidence that this disease is immunologic in origin. It occurs no more frequently in children of mothers with thyroid autoantibodies than in children of normal mothers, which means that thyroid antibody alone does not damage a normal thyroid gland.

Primary adult myxedema occurs without known cause, though it is reasonable to assume that immunologic processes play a role in the development of the disease. Patients typically have cold, dry skin; dry, coarse hair; constipation; intolerance to cold; and loss of vigor. The face is puffy and the complexion yellow as a result of carotenemia. Speech is slowed and thought processes retarded. In some cases, the heart rate is slowed and the heart is enlarged, with pericardial effusion. Deep tendon reflexes are characteristically slowed, with delayed recovery return. Firm myxedema is apparent under the skin. Laboratory findings usually include a decreased radioiodine uptake and low thyroxine (T_4) and triiodothyronine (T_3) levels. Serum cholesterol is high.

Primary hypothyroidism must be differentiated from thyroid failure due to pituitary insufficiency. The thyroid in pituitary insufficiency usually responds well to administration of thyrotropic hormone.

In severe primary hypothyroidism, the thyroid gland is usually atrophic, with fibrosis and only a few isolated islets of acinar tissue. The appearance is quite different from the fibrous variant of chronic thyroiditis.

Immunologically, hypothyroidism closely resembles chronic thyroiditis. Circulating antibodies and cell-mediated immunity to thyroid antigen are present. Antibodies are found in the same high titers characteristic of thyroiditis (Table 34–3).

HYPERTHYROIDISM

Major Immunologic Features

- Presence of thyroid-stimulating antibody (TSab) in about 80% of patients.
- TSab is present in the γ-globulin fraction and may be stimulatory antibody directed to the thyrotropin receptor on the surface of the thyroid cell.
- Autoantibodies to thyroid can be identified in most patients by a combination of hemagglutination, cytotoxicity, complement fixation, or immunofluorescence tests.

General Considerations

In older individuals, hyperfunction of the thyroid is often insidious in onset and therefore difficult to recognize clinically. Hyperthyroidism may be due to diffuse hyperplasia (diffuse toxic goiter or Graves' disease), nodular goiter, or localized autonomous adenoma. Graves' disease is linked to thyroiditis by familial clustering; ie, patients with thyroiditis often have family members with hyperthyroidism, and vice versa. In some patients, the 2 diseases may coexist.

Because of the difficulty in recognizing mild forms of the disease, the prevalence of hyperthyroidism is not definitely known. It is clear, however, that women develop the disease 4–5 times as often as men and that the greatest incidence is in the fourth and fifth decades. In these respects also, hyperthyroidism resembles thyroiditis.

Study of the involvement of autoimmunity in Graves' disease is hampered by the lack of a well-defined experimental model. In the human disease, a relative increase of lymphocytes has been reported, with the increase in absolute numbers of peripheral B cells correlating positively with disease severity indicated by thyroid hormone levels. The thymus may be larger than normal. As mentioned previously, about one-third of patients with hyperthyroidism have autoantibody to one or another thyroid antigen. However, these antibodies might signify the simultaneous occurrence of thyroiditis and hyperthyroidism in the same patient rather than an immunologic cause of hyperthyroidism itself.

The first indication of an immunologic basis for hyperthyroidism came from studies of long-acting thyroid stimulator (LATS). The serum of patients with diffuse hyperplasia of the thyroid produced a prolonged stimulation of guinea pig or mouse thyroids, measured as an increase in radioiodine uptake. In contrast, thyrotropin causes only a brief increase in iodine uptake.

Following standard fractionation techniques, LATS was isolated from human serum in the γ-globulin fraction. It was also precipitated by anti-IgG. After cleavage of IgG with papain, LATS activity appeared in the Fab fragment. Moreover, antisera to human IgG neutralized the biologic action of LATS. Crude extracts of normal human thyroid tissue also inhibited or neutralized LATS activity. The active fraction was localized at the cell surface on the plasma membrane. It was destroyed by treatment with proteolytic enzymes but not by lipases or deoxycholate. Purified human thyroglobulin did not neutralize LATS.

Although LATS seems to react specifically with the surface of thyroid cells and possibly with the thyrotropin (TSH) receptor, the autoimmune pathogenesis of Graves' disease cannot be established solely upon the basis of this antibody. In fact, LATS was detected in only about 50% of patients with active Graves hyperthyroidism, and its presence correlated poorly with thyroid function (ie, degree of hyperthyroidism and nonsuppressibility). It was later observed that IgG from patients with no demonstrable LATS activity stimulates the human thyroid gland in vitro and protects LATS from inhibition by human but not by mouse thyroid extracts. For this reason, these non-LATS thyroid-stimulating immunoglobulins have been named "LATS protectors." When sensitive methods are used, the great majority of sera from patients with active Graves' disease are found to stimulate the human thyroid gland. The antibodies responsible for the stimulation have been shown to compete with TSH for receptor sites on the thyroid cell membrane and mimic TSH activity by stimulating adenylate cyclase. It should be noted, however, that not all antibodies measured by radioreceptor assay are stimulatory. There is convincing evidence that many sera contain antibodies that compete for binding sites at the TSH receptor but lack the ability to stimulate it either in vitro or in vivo. These assays are therefore said to measure thyrotropin binding–inhibiting immunoglobulins (TBII) rather than TSAb. In Graves' disease, the pathologic immunoglobulins (LATS and LATS protectors) are antireceptor antibodies that perform the function of the hormone they displace (TSH). The general term thyroid-stimulating antibody (TSab) is now applied to both LATS and LATS protector.

Exophthalmos

Exophthalmos in Graves' disease is encountered in 2 forms. The staring expression commonly present in hyperthyroid patients is caused by increased sensitivity of the sympathetic innervation of the extraocular muscles to circulating catecholamines. It is alleviated by drugs such as guanethidine and specific beta-blockers. This is clearly distinct from infiltrative ophthalmopathy, or endocrine exophthalmos, which is thought to be autoimmune in nature and is found in a small proportion of patients with Graves' disease (and a smaller proportion of patients with chronic lymphocytic thyroiditis). It may be very severe, progressive, and sight-threatening. Recently, cellular immunity to retro-orbital antigens was demonstrated in patients with exophthalmos by using leukocyte migration inhibition. Furthermore, retro-orbital muscle has affinity for both thyroglobulin and thyroglobulin-antibody complexes. Retro-orbital tissue may actually share a carbohydrate moiety of thyroglobulin. Other researchers have traced tenuous lymphatic connections between the thyroid region and the retro-orbital area. They suggested that thyroid antigens, antibodies, or immune complexes may flow from the thyroid to the orbital space and set up an immunologic reaction.

Immunologic Pathogenesis

One theory of an immunologic origin of hyperthyroidism rests on the demonstration of TSab. The evidence that this factor represents a stimulating autoantibody has been outlined above. However, lack of an experimental model has hampered the definition of stimulatory antibodies.

Important new information about the pathogenesis of Graves' disease has come from studies of HLA associations. Several studies in Caucasian populations have shown an increased frequency of the HLA-B8 antigen. The relative risk of Graves' disease in persons with HLA-B8 compared with persons lacking this antigen is about 2.5. An even closer association has been reported with HLA-Dw3, which suggests that a gene influencing susceptibility to Graves' disease is close to the D locus. HLA-Dw3 and HLA-B8 are in linkage disequilibrium.

In the Japanese, HLA-B8 is rare, and other alleles, HLA-Bw35 and HLA-Dw12, are significantly associated with Graves' disease. Among Chinese people, a significant association with HLA-Bw46 has been reported.

Clinical Features

A. Symptoms and Signs: Hyperthyroidism or Graves' disease results from overproduction of thyroid hormone. It is marked by an increased metabolic rate in most tissues of the body. It may occur in all grades of severity. Occasionally the onset is sudden, but more commonly the symptoms develop so slowly that the patient is unaware of the disease. Symptoms may be aggravated and noticeable following physical or emotional trauma. The most common symptoms are restlessness, heat intolerance, weight loss, and palpitations. The principal signs include smooth, warm, and moist skin resulting from vasodilatation and excessive sweating, a diffuse goiter, tachycardia, a wide pulse pressure, fine tremor of the hands, and proximal muscle weakness. The heart rate in hyperthyroidism is typically rapid, with an elevated systolic pressure and wide pulse pressure. In other individuals, tachycardia, arrhythmia, or evidence of congestive heart failure may first bring the patient to the physician. A striking feature of many cases of hyperthyroidism is unilateral or bilateral ophthalmopathy (also called exophthalmos) consisting of widened palpebral fissures, retro-orbital edema, proptosis, conjunctivitis, and sometimes loss of vision due to optic nerve ischemia.

B. Laboratory Findings: The histologic counterpart of Graves' hyperthyroidism is a diffusely enlarged thyroid gland with increased vascularity and varying degrees of infiltration by lymphocytes and plasma cells, often arranged to form lymphoid follicles.

Laboratory studies of patients with hyperthyroidism usually show that blood levels of protein-bound iodine, thyroxine, and triiodothyronine are high, and uptake of radioactive iodine by the thyroid gland is increased. Serum cholesterol may be low.

Immunologic Diagnosis

The demonstration of LATS requires a complex bioassay based on the release of radioiodine from the thyroid of a mouse following administration of patient's serum. About 45% of patients with diffuse hyperplasia of the thyroid have detectable amounts of LATS in their serum. Slightly higher positive reactions (62%) are found if the concentrated γ-globulin fraction is employed. LATS is not usually found in patients with autonomous adenoma or multinodular goiter. Some individuals with normal thyroid function have LATS in their serum. It has been found that their thyroids do not respond normally to thyrotropin, suggesting that the gland is insensitive to thyroid stimulation.

Instead of LATS, patients with hyperthyroidism may have LATS protector in their circulation. This

Table 34–5. Incidence of thyroid autoantibodies to any thyroid antigen in patients with hyperthyroidism.*

Histologic Diagnosis	Percentage of Sera Positive By		
	Hemagglu-tination	Complement Fixation	Cytotoxicity
Diffuse hyperplastic goiter	38	25	61
Nodular toxic goiter	57	14	71
Chronic thyroiditis	75	67	75

*Modified from Kite JH Jr et al: *Ann NY Acad Sci* 1965;124: 626.

substance has the property of blocking the binding of LATS to the human thyroid microsomal fraction which absorbs LATS activity. It is an antibody, perhaps one that combines only with human thyroid cells. LATS and LATS protector may both be found in the serum of a few patients with hyperthyroidism. The general term thyroid-stimulating antibody (TSab) is now applied to both LATS and LATS protector.

At least 3 reliable methods for demonstrating thyroid-stimulating antibodies are now available. They measure (1) the increase in colloid droplets intracellularly, (2) increased metabolic activity of cAMP, or (3) competition with radiolabeled thyrotropin for the thyroid cell membrane. Using the thyrotropin displacement assay, about 80% of patients with untreated Graves' disease have significantly elevated values.

A certain proportion of patients with hyperthyroidism associated with either diffuse or nodular goiters have antibodies in their sera to thyroid microsomal antigen, thyroid surface antigen, and thyroglobulin. These antibodies can be demonstrated by complement fixation, cytotoxicity, or hemagglutination (Table 34–5). Hemagglutination and complement fixation reactions are less frequently positive—and the antibodies are found in lower titers—in hyperthyroidism than in thyroiditis. These antibodies are sometimes accentuated after radioiodine therapy, but after a short time they decrease in titer.

Differential Diagnosis

If symptoms are prominent, the diagnosis of hyperthyroidism usually presents no difficulty. Often, however—particularly in the early stages—the disease is mild. It may be confused with emotional anxiety states or tachycardia associated with infection or other causes. The tremor may resemble that of chronic alcoholism or parkinsonism. The diagnosis is usually based on appropriate laboratory tests. Unfortunately, the results of radioiodine uptake and serum hormone determinations may be invalidated by the use of drugs such as iodides, radiopaque contrast media, or estrogens unless the clinical situation is fairly obvious.

Treatment

The treatment of hyperthyroidism includes surgical removal of the thyroid, administration of radioac-

tive iodine, or therapy with antithyroid drugs with adjunctive use of iodide or adrenergic blocking agents. Iodide is rarely used alone for the treatment of hyperthyroidism. It is useful in reducing the size of the gland in preparation for surgery or for promoting prompt cessation of thyroid hormone release before administration of the slower-acting antithyroid drugs. Although the reduction in size and vascularity of the thyroid gland following iodide treatment is remarkable, it is generally temporary. Antithyroid drugs such as methimazole or propylthiouracil do not prevent release of preformed hormone, so their effectiveness is slower than that of iodide. After several weeks, however, they can be quite effective in alleviating the major symptoms of hyperthyroidism. The drugs may be given continuously for control of the disease or as preparation for surgical removal of the gland.

Radioiodine (^{131}I) is widely used for the treatment of hyperthyroidism. The effectiveness of the isotope depends upon its preferential localization in the thyroid and emission of beta particles that damage the thyroid cells. The main problem in its use is to determine a dose that will alleviate symptoms without producing hypothyroidism. Part of the difficulty in determining the proper dose of radioiodine may reside in its tendency to increase sensitization. After ^{131}I treatment, patients show a transient elevation in the titer of thyroid microsomal and cytotoxic antibodies. Patients with autonomous toxic nodules rarely develop hypothyroidism or thyroid autoantibodies after radioiodine treatment. Thus, it seems that in the absence of some predisposing condition, injury to the thyroid is not sufficient to induce autosensitization.

Subtotal thyroidectomy is an effective way of treating hyperthyroidism in a properly prepared patient. Without adequate preparation, the complications of surgery are significant. In addition, removal of a hyperfunctioning gland can lead to thyroid crisis. Following surgery, it is often necessary to provide some measure of replacement with thyroid hormone. If exophthalmos is severe, treatment with anti-inflammatory corticosteroids or surgical decompression may be necessary. Radiation has also been found to be useful in treating exophthalmos.

Complications & Prognosis

Untreated hyperthyroidism can produce irreversible problems in several organ systems. There may be gradual deterioration of the cardiovascular system leading to congestive heart failure. Stressful situations, including infection, may precipitate thyrotoxic crisis or "storm." Generally, infections are not well handled by thyrotoxic patients. Infectious hepatitis may be a serious hazard. The exophthalmos may lead to keratitis and corneal scarring or, worse, optic neuritis and blindness. Although the course of the disease may be irregular, untreated patients are always subject to recurrence and complications.

Irvine and his colleagues have shown that patients with Graves' disease who relapsed after a prolonged course of antithyroid drugs had a much higher prevalence of HLA-B8 than those who remained in remission. Similar observations have now been made with HLA-Dw3. HLA typing may eventually be useful in designing a plan of treatment in cases of hyperthyroidism.

THYROGASTRIC DISEASE & AUTOIMMUNE POLYENDOCRINOPATHY

The autoimmune response to thyroid antigens of patients with thyroiditis is strikingly analogous to the response to gastric mucosal antigens that occurs in patients with pernicious anemia. Antibodies that bind with or block the action of intrinsic factor are found in many adult patients with pernicious anemia (see Chapter 29). By immunofluorescence, antibodies to a cytoplasmic antigen of the gastric parietal cell can be demonstrated in pernicious anemia sera. These reactions are comparable to the reactions of thyroiditis patients with soluble thyroglobulin or thyroid microsomal antigen.

In addition, there is considerable overlap in the occurrence of circulating gastric and thyroid antibodies. One-fourth of patients with chronic thyroiditis were found in one study to have antibodies to the gastric parietal cell. One-third of myxedema patients were also positive. Conversely, about 30% of patients with pernicious anemia have antibody to one or another thyroid antigen in their serum. Equally interesting relationships emerge when the asymptomatic relatives of patients are studied. Forty-seven percent of relatives of patients with thyroiditis have antibody to thyroid antigens, and 18% have antibody to parietal cells. Of the relatives of patients with pernicious anemia, 45% showed antibody to the gastric parietal cells and 67% to thyroid antigens. When proper allowance is made for age and sex, patients with these organ-specific autoimmune disorders show little or no increase in the anticipated occurrence of systemic lupus erythematosus or of antinuclear antibodies.

In addition to the concurrence of autoimmunity with thyroid and gastric antigens, considerable clinical and serologic overlap has been found with other idiopathic endocrine deficiencies. Examples are adrenocortical insufficiency, hypoparathyroidism, pituitary failure, and the insulin-dependent form of diabetes mellitus. A higher incidence of myasthenia gravis, vitiligo, and alopecia totalis has also been reported in this group of patients. The basis of this clustering is unclear, since no single autoantigen common to these diverse cells has been discovered. However, many of these conditions, including Graves' disease, adrenocortical insufficiency, pernicious anemia, and myasthenia gravis, are associated with the HLA haplotype HLA-A1, HLA-B8, HLA-Dw3 (or DRw3).

An association of chronic mucocutaneous candidiasis with hypofunction of one or more endocrine organs has also been described, including hypoparathyroidism or adrenocortical insufficiency and other lesions in the thyrogastric group. IgA deficiency is also encountered in these disorders.

The simultaneous presence of several independent autoimmune processes and immunodeficiency suggests that these patients have some underlying defect in immunologic regulation; a deficiency in suppressor T cell capacity has been proposed. It may be that a fundamental genetic defect in suppression of autoimmune clones of lymphocytes underlies all of these abnormalities. The expression of the HLA-A1, HLA-B8, HLA-Dw3 haplotype may serve as a useful marker of this hypothetical abnormality.

CHRONIC ADRENOCORTICAL INSUFFICIENCY

Adrenal antibodies have been produced in experimental animals following injection of adrenal homogenate plus Freund's complete adjuvant. However, the reports with regard to the development of lesions have been variable in different species. Guinea pigs were found to develop lymphocytic and histiocytic infiltration and necrosis of the adrenal cortex following immunization with guinea pig adrenal extract. Cell-mediated immune reactions to adrenal microsomes were also present. Rabbits developed adrenalitis after injection of foreign but not rabbit adrenal homogenate. In inbred rats, disease could be induced by injection of syngeneic adrenal extract with Freund's complete adjuvant and pertussis vaccine. Adrenalitis was transferred from actively immunized donors to normal recipients by means of living lymph node cells. Lesions could be seen as early as 5 days after transfer. They seemed to be initiated by the arrival in the adrenal of a few specially sensitized lymphocytes which migrated by chance from the bloodstream. Their local stimulation by adrenal antigen may have caused the lymphocytes to produce mediators that attracted and activated macrophages and trapped additional nonsensitized lymphocytes at the site.

Patients with adrenocortical failure (Addison's disease) are recognized by typical symptoms of postural hypotension, weight loss, anorexia, weakness, and hyperpigmentation of folds of the skin. Acute adrenal failure sometimes leads to hypovolemic shock. It is necessary to distinguish secondary adrenal insufficiency caused by anterior pituitary failure from the primary form of the disease. In the latter instance, circulating corticotropin (ACTH) levels are usually high. Confirmatory diagnosis depends upon demonstrating low serum and urinary levels of cortisol unresponsive to ACTH stimulation. High plasma ACTH levels and low plasma and urinary cortisol levels are also indications of primary disease. Functional tests of the adrenal medulla are usually normal.

Two etiologic forms of primary Addison's disease are distinguished: exogenous and idiopathic. Tuberculous adrenal failure is now rare in countries where tuberculosis is well controlled. Systemic mycoses, metastatic tumors, irradiation, infarction, or amyloidosis may produce similar adrenocortical insufficiency. More common in Western countries is idiopathic adrenocortical failure. It occurs at any age, with a peak incidence in the fourth and fifth decades. It is seen more often in females in a ratio of approximately 2:1 or 3:1.

Histologically, in adrenocortical insufficiency, the adrenal cortex loses its normal 3-layered structure so that the cortical cells are reduced to disorganized islets. Lymphocytic and monocytic infiltration and fibrosis are prominent. The medulla is usually normal in appearance.

There is considerable overlap of idiopathic adrenocortical insufficiency with other autoimmune diseases, including primary myxedema, chronic thyroiditis (Schmidt's syndrome), thyrotoxicosis, pernicious anemia, primary hypoparathyroidism, and diabetes mellitus. In addition to antibodies to adrenal tissue, patients with idiopathic Addison's disease frequently show antibodies to gastric parietal cells, thyroid epithelial cells, thyroglobulin, and intrinsic factor. On the other hand, the occurrence of antinuclear

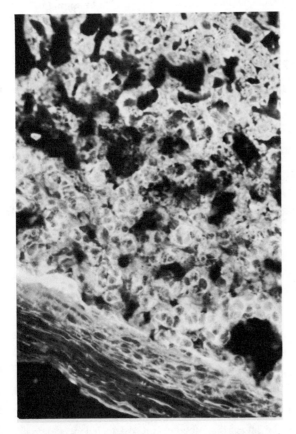

Figure 34–3. Immunofluorescent staining in adrenal insufficiency. Monkey adrenal tissue was prepared in the same manner as the thyroid tissue described in Figs 34–1 and 34–2. The tissue was not fixed and was tested with serum from a patient with adrenocortical insufficiency (diluted 1:5). Fluorescent staining of cells in the glomerulosa and fasciculata layers can be seen. (Original magnification, × 180.)

antibody is not unusually high in this group of patients when one takes into account their age and sex.

Antibodies to adrenal microsomes can be demonstrated by means of immunofluorescence (Table 34–1). By this method, antibodies can be found in approximately 50% of patients (38–64% in various series) with idiopathic adrenal insufficiency. The incidence of positive reactions reported in sera of patients with the tuberculous form of insufficiency varies from none to 18% in different series. Antibodies persist for many years despite replacement therapy in which adrenal hormones are used. The incidence of adrenocortical antibodies in the general population is below 5%. Normal individuals with these autoantibodies tend to have reduced adrenocortical functional reserve and sometimes progress to frank insufficiency.

In indirect immunofluorescence microscopy, localization is usually found in the secretory cells of the zona glomerulosa, zona fasciculata, and zona reticularis. Some sera stain only one or 2 layers of the adrenal (Fig 34–3). A relatively small proportion of patients show antibodies specific for the zona fasciculata which cross-react with steroid hormone–secreting cells of the theca interna of the corpus luteum of the ovary as well as with interstitial cells of the testes and placental trophoblasts. There is said to be a correlation between the presence of these antibodies to steroid-producing cells and a clinical history of ovarian failure in addisonian patients. In young women, delayed menarche or unexplained amenorrhea has been associated with these antibodies to steroid-secreting cells. The observations support the hypothesis that ovarian disorders are related by an autoimmune pathogenetic mechanism involving antigens shared by the adrenals and ovary.

PRIMARY OVARIAN FAILURE

Ovarian failure is often associated clinically with multiple features of endocrinopathy such as adrenal insufficiency, thyroiditis or thyrotoxicosis, hypoparathyroidism, and diabetes mellitus, as well as chronic candidiasis. The patients have symptoms of primary or secondary amenorrhea or premature menopause, with elevation of serum and urinary pituitary gonadotropins. A high proportion of ovarian failure patients with associated autoimmune endocrinopathy have antibodies that are reactive with human ovarian tissue. Fluorescence is seen mainly on the cells of the theca interna, a pattern similar to that seen with antibodies to steroid-producing cells of the adrenal (Table 34–1). The antibodies can be absorbed by extracts of adrenal gland, which suggests that antigens are shared by the adrenal cortex and the gonads. Some of the sera from patients with ovarian failure are cytotoxic to luteinized human granulosa cells in the presence of complement. Antibodies are rare in patients with premature ovarian failure due to a genetic or developmental defect not associated with adrenal or other endocrine autoantibodies.

DIABETES MELLITUS

The symptomatology of diabetes mellitus is primarily a consequence of decreased production of insulin or of reduced insulin effect at peripheral target tissues, ie, insulin resistance. Both situations may occur as a consequence of autoimmune phenomena. Although by far the most common cause of insulin-resistant diabetes is obesity—approximately 80% of all diabetic patients in Western societies are in this category—in a small number of patients, hyperglycemia and striking resistance to the glucose-lowering effect of exogenous insulin occur on the basis of autoantibodies competing with insulin for binding to tissue receptors (antireceptor antibodies). In most sera studied, activity resided in polyclonal molecules of the IgG class, although IgM activity was also detected. These antibodies may act in vitro as potent insulin agonists, although chronic exposure to them in vivo mostly results in an insulin-resistant diabetic condition. Occurrence of anti-insulin receptor antibodies has thus far been described as part of the syndrome that includes the skin condition acanthosis nigricans and a number of autoimmune features ranging from well-defined autoimmune diseases to combinations of elevated sedimentation rate, leukopenia, hypocomplementemia, and antinuclear antibodies. The syndrome is quite rare, has been seen mostly but not exclusively in females, and appears not to be age-related.

More intriguing—and epidemiologically more important—is the relationship between the pathogenesis of insulin deficiency in type I diabetes (juvenile-onset, insulin-dependent) and autoimmune phenomena. Gepts reported in 1965 that 68% of patients with juvenile diabetes who died soon after the clinical onset of disease had peri-insular and intra-insular inflammatory infiltrates consisting of macrophages, neutrophils, lymphocytes, and rare plasma cells. More recently, the same author has again reported "insulitis" in 11 of 16 cases of recent onset, and in one case the lymphocytic infiltration was found only in islets containing insulin-secreting cells (B cells—formerly called β [beta] cells) but was strikingly absent in the islets composed of glucagon, somatostatin, and pancreatic polypeptide cells.

The recognition that some cases of insulin-dependent diabetes are clinically associated with Addison's disease, certain thyroid disorders, and pernicious anemia—all diseases characterized by organ-specific autoimmunity—prompted a search for pancreatic islet cell autoimmunity in diabetic patients. And indeed, antibodies against islet cells (ICAs) first identified in female patients with Addison's disease were then found in 38% of individuals with at least one other manifestation of autoimmune disease besides diabetes and in variable proportions of type I diabetics without other autoimmune manifestations. It is now known that variations in prevalence of ICA, especially in diabetics without other organ-specific autoimmune disorders, are related to the duration of diabetes: detectable in 70–85% of cases at the time of diagnosis,

Table 34–6. Types of diabetes mellitus.

	Type I	Type II
Usual age at onset	< 30	> 40
Peak age	< 15	> 50
Onset	Often rapid	Insidious
Obesity	Uncommon	Common
Ketoacidosis	Common	Uncommon
Insulin dependence	Common	Uncommon
B islet cell decrease	Usually present	Usually absent
Insulitis	Common	Uncommon
Prevalence in population	< 0.5%	2%
Twin concordance	Low	High
HLA association	A1, B8, DR3	None known
	A2, B15, DR4	
Islet cell antibodies	Common early	Rare
Other endocrine autoanti-	Relatively common	Rare
bodies		

these antibodies tend to disappear from the serum after about a year. ICAs are demonstrable with the technique of indirect immunofluorescence using fresh group O human pancreas either quick-frozen in liquid nitrogen and then used unfixed or fixed in acetone; or fixed in Bouin's solution and then embedded in paraffin in the usual manner. These antibodies react against cytoplasmic antigens present in all islet cells, not just B cells, and they are not species-specific, since positive sera react also with rat, guinea pig, and rhesus monkey islets. The titer of ICA is generally much lower than that of thyroid or gastric antibodies in patients with autoimmune thyroid disease or in pernicious anemia. They are exclusively IgG, mostly of subclasses IgG2 and IgG4. Approximately 70% of the ICA present at the time of diagnosis are complement-fixing, but this proportion declines to less than 50% in long-standing cases. Because of their ability to fix complement, substantial representation at the time of diagnosis, and occasional selective staining of portions of the islets, complement-fixing antibodies to islet cells may be considered plausible agents of B islet cell damage.

Another technique used for detection of humoral autoimmunity in type I diabetes has employed dispersed rat islet cells isolated by collagenase treatment. This technique identifies antibodies against the islet cell surface (ICSAs) which are organ-specific but obviously not species-specific. In the original study by Lernmark, such antibodies (again exclusively IgG) were detected in 38% of patients at the time of diagnosis; in a subsequent study, such antibodies were detected in approximately 50% of patients with type I diabetes and in 25% of nondiabetic first-degree relatives. ICSAs are most likely different from ICAs, since the 2 types of antibodies can be detected independently of each other in diabetic sera. Moreover, in the presence of complement, ICSAs are cytotoxic against newborn rat B cells whereas ICAs are not. The presence of ICSAs in nondiabetic relatives suggests that they might not be the only determinant of B islet cell failure, although progressive damage may be occurring while clinical diabetes has not yet appeared.

Still using indirect immunofluorescence, a third substrate has been reported by MacLaren to allow detection of humoral autoimmunity in diabetic patients: tissue cultured human insulinoma cells. Antibodies reacting in this system are both IgM and IgG and were found in 87% of type I diabetics, apparently independently of disease duration. These antibodies too were present in patients with multiple autoimmune endocrinopathies but with no clinical evidence of diabetes.

Islet cell cytotoxicity has also been observed in incubating sera from type I diabetics with pancreatic islets of golden hamster in the presence of guinea pig complement, but the serum factors responsible for such complement-mediated cytotoxicity were not isolated. A positive correlation was found between cytotoxic activity and the presence of ICA in the sera tested. Although the relationships between the antibodies detected by various techniques are not presently defined and their pathogenetic role in B islet cell damage is not established, the consistent absence of such antibodies in type II diabetic patients and the low prevalence (0.5–2%) in the general population confers on them some predictive value for an event which is unique to type I diabetes.

Cell-mediated autoimmunity has also been observed. Nerup reported inhibition of migration of leukocytes specific for the endocrine pancreas in type I diabetics; Huang and MacLaren have observed that lymphocytes of patients with variable duration of type I diabetes but not of normal controls adhere to cultured insulinoma cells and exert some degree of cell-mediated or antibody-dependent cytotoxicity. Lymphocytes obtained from peripheral blood of newly diagnosed type I diabetics were reported to induce diabetes in some athymic nude mice transplanted with such cells, but these results could not be confirmed in subsequent studies. Suppressor T cell activity appears decreased at the clinical onset of diabetes but returns to normal within 6 months after diagnosis. The best evidence for an essential role of cell-mediated autoimmune processes in the development of diabetes has been provided in experimental models. The striking "insulitis" and clinical diabetes that result in laboratory animals from the administration of multiple subdiabetogenic doses of streptozocin do not develop in athymic nude mice, whose susceptibility to the lesion and the disease are, however, restored by thymus graft. Moreover, splenic lymphocytes from euthymic littermates previously made diabetic induced transient glucose intolerance in the nude mice. The spontaneous diabetes that develops in approximately 30% of a colony of Bio Breeding/Worcester rats has been, in some cases, prevented or partially reversed by administration of antiserum to rat lymphocytes. In this latter model of spontaneous diabetes, which is phenotypically very similar to human type I diabetes—hypoinsulinemia, hyperglucagonemia, ketoacidosis, mononuclear infiltration of pancreatic islets with destruction of B cells, B cell-specific ICSAs—the immunologic abnormalities responsible for B cell damage appear to remain operative for some time after onset of the disease, since transplanted islets from histocompatible donors become heavily infiltrated by mononuclear cells. Inoculation of bone marrow from normal rats into neonates of the diabetes-susceptible colony substantially reduced the incidence of diabetes; although the mechanism is unclear, the phenomenon points to disturbances in immune regulation as contributory to this model of human type I diabetes.

Further support for an autoimmune contribution to human type I diabetes is provided by the association of this disease with HLA haplotypes highly prevalent in disorders of well-established autoimmune etiology. Both HLA-DR3 and HLA-DR4 show a strong positive association with insulin-dependent diabetes in Caucasians, American blacks, and Mexican-Americans. The associations with HLA-B specificities (B8, B15, and B18) are clearly secondary to the linkage disequilibrium existing between these latter specificities and DR3/DR4. At least in Caucasians, the diabetes risk conferred by DR3/DR4 heterozygosity is much higher than the simple summation of the relative risk computed for individual DR3 or DR4 positivity. Studies of families with 2 or more siblings with juvenile-onset diabetes have disclosed that affected patients share identical HLA haplotypes with significantly higher frequency than expected (55% concordance observed versus 25% expected).

The individual's genetic patrimony, while it appears to be an important determinant of susceptibility to type I diabetes, does not exhaust the etiologic possibilities, since concordance for the disease both in identical twins and in siblings sharing both HLA haplotypes does not exceed 50%. Environmental factors whose diabetogenic potential is perhaps expressed or magnified through autoimmunity must then be postulated. It is likely that viruses may represent environmental contributions—and indeed, in humans, correlation between viral infections and development of juvenile-onset diabetes has been reported in cases of mumps, rubella, and infection with coxsackie B viruses and encephalomyocarditis virus. Particular strains of the latter 2 viruses have been found to have a selective tropism for pancreatic B cells in animals and to elicit mononuclear infiltration of pancreatic islets. A type 4 coxsackie B virus has been isolated from the pancreas of a child with recent acute onset of diabetes and found capable of causing B cell necrosis in recipient animals. The failure to find IgM antibodies against coxsackieviruses in recently diagnosed cases of juvenile-onset diabetes, however, militates against a close temporal relationship between coxsackievirus infection and development of diabetes in the average case.

Attempts to modify a viral or autoimmune pathogenetic process of B cell damage with therapeutic agents have thus far been either unsuccessful or inconclusive. Human leukocyte interferon has been administered to 2 children without sustained therapeutic benefit; a trial of levamisole, used in doses expected to stimulate T suppressor function, has resulted in no improvement in a few newly diagnosed patients. A

12-month course of prednisone in doses of 0.25 mg/kg/d has been reported to maintain urinary C-peptide (possibly reflecting insulin secretion) at higher levels for 24 months after diagnosis—without, however, changing the prevalence of positivity for ICA and without decreasing the amount of exogenous insulin required for metabolic control.

IDIOPATHIC HYPOPARATHYROIDISM

Parathyroid failure is predominantly a disease of childhood and adolescence. Idiopathic hypoparathyroidism in association with adrenocortical failure is found most often in younger individuals. Histologically, idiopathic hypoparathyroidism is characterized by lymphocytic infiltration of the parathyroid glands and atrophy of glandular secretory cells. Antibodies specific for parathyroid have been demonstrated by indirect immunofluorescence in about a third of patients with idiopathic hypoparathyroidism (Table 34–1). Many of these patients also had antibodies to adrenal or thyroid tissues. Another feature of many cases of primary hypoparathyroidism is the occurrence of refractory mucocutaneous candidiasis.

Experimentally, it has been demonstrated that repeated injection of homologous parathyroid tissue into dogs may induce the characteristic biochemical changes of hypoparathyroidism. Histologic damage to the gland can be demonstrated, and parathyroid autoantibodies are found in low titer in dog serum by complement fixation.

PITUITARY FAILURE

Serologic and histologic evidence of autoimmunity to pituitary tissue has been found in a few patients. Antibodies to prolactin-secreting cells have been found most frequently in the sera of patients with multiple autoimmune endocrinopathies, especially those with idiopathic hypoparathyroidism. A second antibody has been identified that reacts with the growth hormone–producing cells of the anterior pituitary. This antibody may have diagnostic value, because several of the positive sera were taken from children with growth retardation. Lymphoplasmacytic infiltration of the hypophysis, which has recently been demonstrated by biopsy, seems to be confined to women and mostly to those who are pregnant or just postpartum. The patients presented with space-occupying lesions of the pituitary, causing visual field disturbances, but there was no histologic evidence of adenoma. In only one of 10 cases, antibodies to pituitary cells were also detectable. Two animal models of the disease have been established, but passive transfer by cells or serum has not yet been demonstrated.

GUT–RELATED ENDOCRINE CELLS

The importance of the gut as an endocrine organ has only recently been fully appreciated. With the advent of immunocytochemistry in the early 1970s, it was recognized that the "clear cells" scattered among the intestinal epithelial cells are the source of several important peptide hormones. By the use of indirect immunofluorescence, antibodies have been demonstrated in patient's sera that react specifically with the cells secreting secretin, gastric inhibitory peptide (GIP), somatostatin, and enteroglucagon. In one study by Doniach and Bottazzo, 26 of 173 (15%) serum samples from patients with celiac disease gave positive reactions with the cytoplasm of single cells located in the epithelium of the duodenal villi or crypts of Lieberkühn. These antibodies were shown to be directed to cells containing secretin or GIP. Other investigators demonstrated antibodies to GIP-producing or somatostatin-producing cells in sera of patients with the non-insulin-dependent type of diabetes mellitus. Sera of patients with inflammatory bowel diseases such as Crohn's disease and ulcerative colitis sometimes react with cells containing GIP, somatostatin, or enteroglucagon. These findings suggest that the diffuse endocrine system that coordinates the functions of the digestive tract may sometimes come under autoimmune attack.

• • •

References

Chronic Thyroiditis & Primary Hypothyroidism

Beall GN, Solomon DH: Hashimoto's disease and Graves' disease. Pages 1261–1277 in: *Immunological Diseases,* 3rd ed. Vol 2. Samter M (editor). Little, Brown, 1978.

Bigazzi PE, Rose NR: Spontaneous autoimmune thyroiditis in animals as a model for human diseases. *Prog Allergy* 1975; **19**:245.

Doniach D, Bottazzo GF: Thyroid autoimmunity. Pages 22–34 in: *The Menarini Series on Immunopathology: First Symposium on Organ Specific Autoimmunity.* Miescher PA et al (editors). Schwabe, 1978.

Doniach D, Roitt IM: Thyroid auto-allergic disease. Chap 47, pp 1355–1386, in: *Clinical Aspects of Immunology,* 3rd ed. Gell PGH, Coombs RRA, Lachmann PJ (editors). Blackwell, 1975.

Rose NR: Autoimmune diseases. Chap 8, pp 347–499, in: *The Inflammatory Process,* 2nd ed. Vol 3. Zweifach B, Grant L, McCluskey R (editors). Academic Press, 1974.

Rose NR: The autoimmune diseases. Chap 28 in: *Principles of Immunology,* 2nd ed. Rose N, Milgrom F, van Oss C (editors). Macmillan, 1978.

Rose NR, Bigazzi P: The autoimmune diseases. In: *Handbook of Immunology.* Baumgarten A, Richards R (editors). CRC Press, Inc., 1977.

Hyperthyroidism

Adams DD: Thyroid-stimulating autoantibodies. Pages 218–223 in: *The Menarini Series on Immunopathology: First Symposium on Organ Specific Autoimmunity.* Miescher PA et al (editors). Schwabe, 1978.

Bonnyns M et al: Lymphocytic thyroiditis and thyrotoxicosis. Page 171 in: *Thyroiditis and Thyroid Function.* Bastenie PA, Ermans AM (editors). Pergamon Press, 1972.

Volpé R: *Autoimmunity in the Endocrine System.* Vol 20 of: *Monographs in Endocrinology.* Springer-Verlag, 1981.

Volpé R: The genetics and immunology of Graves' and Hashimoto's diseases. Pages 43–56 in: *Genetic Control of Autoimmune Disease.* Rose NR, Bigazzi PE, Warner NL (editors). Elsevier/North Holland, 1978.

Thyrogastric Disease and Autoimmune Endocrinopathy

Doniach D, Roitt IM: Thyroid auto-allergic disease. Chap 47, pp 1355–1386, in: *Clinical Aspects of Immunology,* 3rd ed. Gell PGH, Coombs RRA, Lachmann PJ (editors). Blackwell, 1975.

Irvine WJ: The association of atrophic gastritis with autoimmune thyroid disease. *Clin Endocrinol Metabol* 1975; **4**:351.

Irvine WJ: The immunology and genetics of autoimmune endocrine disease. Pages 77–100 in: *Genetic Control of Autoimmune Disease.* Rose NR, Bigazzi PE, Warner NL (editors). Elsevier/North Holland, 1978.

Chronic Adrenocortical Insufficiency

Irvine WJ: Adrenalitis, hypoparathyroidism and associated diseases. Pages 1278–1295 in: *Immunological Diseases,* 3rd ed. Vol 2. Samter M (editor). Little, Brown, 1978.

Irvine WJ, Barnes EW: Addison's disease, ovarian failure and hypoparathyroidism. *Clin Endocrinol Metabol* 1975; **4**:379.

Ovarian Failure

Irvine WJ, Barnes EW: Addison's disease and associated conditions. Chap 46, pp 1301–1354, in: *Clinical Aspects of Immunology,* 3rd ed. Gell PGH, Coombs RRA, Lachmann PJ (editors). Blackwell, 1975.

Diabetes Mellitus

Irvine WJ: *The Immunology of Diabetes Mellitus.* Teviot, 1978.

Cahill GF, McDevitt HO: Insulin-dependent diabetes mellitus: The initial lesion. *N Engl J Med* 1981; **304**:1454.

Flier JS et al: Receptors, antireceptor antibodies and mechanisms of insulin resistance. *N Engl J Med* 1979; **300**:413.

Platz P et al: HLA-D and -DR antigens in genetic analysis of insulin-dependent diabetes mellitus. *Diabetologia* 1981; **21**:108.

Svejgaard A et al: HLA and autoimmune disease with special reference to the genetics of insulin-dependent diabetes. Pages 101–112 in: *Genetic Control of Autoimmune Disease.* Rose NR, Bigazzi PE, Warner NL (editors). Elsevier/North Holland, 1978.

Idiopathic Hypoparathyroidism

Irvine WJ, Barnes EW: Addison's disease and associated conditions. Chap 46, pp 1301–1354, in: *Clinical Aspects of Immunology,* 3rd ed. Gell PGH, Coombs RRA, Lachmann PJ (editors). Blackwell, 1975.

Pituitary Failure

Asa SL et al: Lymphocytic hypophysitis of pregnancy resulting in hypopituitarism; a distinct clinicopathological entity. *Ann Intern Med* 1981; **95**:166.

Bottazzo GF, Doniach D: The detection of autoantibodies to discrete endocrine cells in anterior pituitary and pancreatic islets. Pages 50–63 in: *The Menarini Series on Immunopathology: First Symposium on Organ Specific Autoimmunity.* Miescher PA et al (editors). Schwabe, 1978.

Topliss DJ, Volpé R: Lymphocytic hypophysitis. (Editorial.) *Ann Intern Med* 1981; **95**:227.

Gut-Related Endocrine Cells

Bottazzo GF, Vandelli C, Mirakian R: The detection of autoantibodies to discrete endocrine cells in complex endocrine organs. Pages 367–377 in: *Autoimmune Aspects of Endocrine Disorders.* Doniach D, Fenzi GF, Baschieri L (editors). Academic Press, 1980.

35 | Neurologic Diseases

Paul M. Hoffman, MD

The role of immunologic mechanisms in diseases of the nervous system has recently become the focus of increased interest and investigation. In diseases such as acute idiopathic polyneuropathy (Guillain-Barré syndrome) and postinfectious encephalomyelitis, the host response to an infectious agent may trigger the immune system to make a direct auto-aggressive assault on the nervous system. The role of immune mechanisms in the pathogenesis of multiple sclerosis is much less clear, but evidence from immunogenetic studies, the response to viral antigens, the oligoclonal nature of immunoglobulins found in cerebrospinal fluid, and changes that have been observed in immunoregulatory subpopulations of T lymphocytes during the course of the disease suggest that the immune response is involved in the pathogenesis of the disease. In myasthenia gravis, an auto-aggressive antibody response directed against acetylcholine receptor protein at the myoneural junction is directly involved in disease pathogenesis. In other diseases such as subacute sclerosing panencephalitis (SSPE), myotonic dystrophy, amyotrophic lateral sclerosis (ALS), and some chronic neuropathies, abnormal immune responses are known to occur; however, their pathogenetic role is unclear. In the subacute spongiform encephalopathies—a group of diseases of the nervous system in which a transmissible agent or agents different from known conventional human and animal viruses have been found—immune responses have for the most part been normal. However, strain differences in production and onset of experimental disease and the possibility that factors which effect the immune response may influence disease outcome have stimulated interest in the role of the host immune response in these conditions.

DEMYELINATING DISEASES

The demyelinating diseases of the central and peripheral nervous systems have unique pathologic, epidemiologic, and clinical features which suggest that immunologic mechanisms may play a role in the etiology and pathogenesis of some of these disorders. The commonly accepted pathologic criteria for a demyelinating disease are destruction of myelin sheaths of nerve fibers and relative sparing of axis cylinders and other elements of the nervous system. These lesions are frequently perivenous in location and are accompanied, at least in the acute phase, by an inflammatory infiltrate that is primarily of a mononuclear cell type. Two diseases of the central nervous system—acute disseminated encephalomyelitis and multiple sclerosis—and one disease of the peripheral nervous system—idiopathic polyneuritis (Guillain-Barré syndrome)—meet these criteria.

ACUTE DISSEMINATED ENCEPHALOMYELITIS (ADEM)

Major Immunologic Features
- Follows infectious diseases or immunization against them.
- Animal model is experimental allergic encephalomyelitis.
- Cellular but not humoral immunity to basic protein of myelin is present during the illness.

General Considerations

Although acute disseminated encephalomyelitis is a relatively uncommon disease of the nervous system, it has become important because of the widespread practice of vaccination for prevention of infectious diseases throughout the world. The incidence is not related to race, age group, or sex. The onset of clinical illness can be several days to weeks following vaccination, or, in the case of natural infection with viruses such as measles, rubella, varicella, mumps, and influenza, it can occur concomitantly with the illness (parainfectious) or following the acute phase of the illness (postinfectious). The lesions of acute disseminated encephalomyelitis are markedly inflamed; polymorphonuclear leukocytes and hemorrhage as well as mononuclear cell infiltrates are frequently seen in perivascular areas of white matter throughout the brain. As the lesions age, they tend to become less inflamed and more sclerotic, with proliferation of astrocytes and formation of gliotic scars in the center. The lesions of acute disseminated encephalomyelitis are pathologically all of the same age, which reflects the monophasic clinical character of the illness.

Immunologic Pathogenesis

The major arguments favoring an immunologic explanation of this disorder are that multiple infectious agents produce a single stereotyped lesion in the central nervous system and that this same lesion can be produced in several animal species by inoculation of brain material. Experimental allergic encephalomyelitis (EAE) is a reproducible autoimmune disease in which an animal is immunized with homologous or heterologous extracts of whole brain, the basic protein of myelin, or certain polypeptide sequences within the basic protein together with Freund's complete adjuvant. Ten to 21 days following immunization, an illness will ensue characterized by lethargy, weight loss, tremor, hind limb paresis, loss of sphincter control, and (frequently) death. The lesions are all of the same age and consist of perivascular mononuclear cell infiltrates in white matter with varying degrees of demyelination. As early as 9 days following immunization, cellular immunity to the immunizing antigens can be demonstrated by skin testing as well as by in vitro tests of cellular immunity such as inhibition of leukocyte and macrophage migration and lymphocyte activation (see Chapter 23). Antibodies to basic protein and to myelin can be demonstrated but do not correlate positively with disease production. The disease can be transferred by adoptive transfer of lymphocytes but not by serum.

Cellular immunity to basic protein has been demonstrated in acute disseminated encephalomyelitis by measuring the activation of peripheral blood or spinal fluid lymphocytes (see Chapter 23). The response tends to be highest during the acute phase of the illness and decreases as the disease progresses. No antibodies to basic protein or myelin can be demonstrated. Cerebrospinal fluid may be abnormal in acute disseminated encephalomyelitis, with mild to moderate pleocytosis and mildly elevated total protein. The proportion of γ-globulin in the cerebrospinal fluid may also be increased, but there is no evidence that this represents local immunoglobulin production in the central nervous system as occurs in multiple sclerosis.

Clinical Features

Systemic symptoms such as fever, malaise, headache, myalgia, nausea, and vomiting generally precede neurologic symptoms by 24–48 hours. Neurologic symptoms develop rapidly thereafter and include pain, numbness, paresthesias, motor weakness, incoordination, and bulbar symptoms such as dysarthria, dysphagia, pooling of pharyngeal secretions, and respiratory distress. Spasticity, extrapyramidal signs, and pathologic reflexes are commonly seen. Visual defects can occur if the optic nerve is involved, and widespread lesions in the brain can lead to stupor and coma. Seizures are common, though not early in the illness.

Differential Diagnosis

Acute disseminated encephalomyelitis must be differentiated from other diseases that can acutely and diffusely affect the central nervous system. Acute multiple sclerosis without a history of neurologic dysfunction can be difficult to differentiate from acute disseminated encephalomyelitis. The presence of fever and a preceding viral illness or vaccination favors the latter diagnosis. Allergic vasculitis such as occurs in systemic lupus erythematosus and polyarteritis nodosa can affect the nervous system primarily, although neurologic symptoms generally tend to occur during the course of the systemic illness and tend to be more focal than in acute disseminated encephalomyelitis. Evidence of vasculitis in other organs is helpful in distinguishing these diseases from acute disseminated encephalomyelitis. Primary infections of the nervous system with measles, mumps, and rubella viruses as well as with the arboviruses tend to involve gray matter as well as white and produce more evidence of neuronal dysfunction such as seizures, stupor, coma, and extrapyramidal signs early in the illness. Direct isolation of viruses from cerebrospinal fluid as well as a rise in serum antibody titer is helpful in differentiating viral encephalitides from acute disseminated encephalomyelitis. Toxoplasmosis can also directly infect the central nervous system and present as an acute disseminated encephalitis. Positive serologic tests for *Toxoplasma* will differentiate it from acute disseminated encephalomyelitis.

Treatment

Although the course of acute disseminated encephalomyelitis is unpredictable, it appears that corticosteroids are of value in treatment. The successful suppression of experimental allergic encephalomyelitis and clinical recovery of animals after receiving injections of basic protein, encephalitogenic peptides, or even some basic copolymers offer hope that by manipulating the immune system a state of immune paralysis or tolerance can be produced, resulting in cessation of the attack of sensitized lymphocytes on the nervous system.

Complications & Prognosis

The mortality rate from acute disseminated encephalomyelitis varies from 1–27%, with a higher rate reported in cases associated with measles. Major and minor neurologic sequelae persist in 25–40% of survivors.

MULTIPLE SCLEROSIS

Major Immunologic Features

- Inflammatory demyelination in central nervous system.
- Increased frequency of HLA-A3, HLA-B7, HLA-Dw2 in European and North American patients.
- Increased level of cerebrospinal fluid IgG containing oligoclonal bands.
- Alterations in immunoregulatory cells during the course of the disease.

General Considerations

Multiple sclerosis is a relapsing disease in which there are signs and symptoms of multiple areas of central nervous system involvement both in time and in space. It is one of the most prevalent diseases of the central nervous system, and, because young adults are frequently affected with debilitating symptoms lasting many years, it represents a serious public health problem. Epidemiologic studies have uncovered important clues about multiple sclerosis, but the cause remains unknown. Low-risk areas of the world have a prevalence of 5–10 cases per 100,000 population; high-risk areas have a prevalence of 50–100 per 100,000 population. Populations migrating from the areas of their birth have the same risk of acquiring the disease as others born in the same region who remain there— particularly if they move after age 15. These studies, in addition to the age at onset curve, in which there is a peak onset at age 30 with few cases before age 15 or after age 55, have suggested to many that some critical event in determining the risk of acquiring multiple sclerosis occurs in adolescence. Familial cases are not uncommon, and the risk of a first-degree living relative having the disease is 10–15 times higher than the risk in the rest of the population. The disease is rare among Orientals and Africans. A consistent finding in several large studies of multiple sclerosis patients has been slightly but persistently elevated serum and cerebrospinal fluid antibody titers to measles and, less commonly, to other viruses such as vaccinia, mumps, herpes simplex, and parainfluenza viruses. These findings have suggested the possibility that a latent viral infection may play a role in the etiology of multiple sclerosis. Several studies of histocompatibility antigens in multiple sclerosis patients have indicated a statistically significant but low-level association with HLA-A3 and HLA-B7 in Northern European and North American populations. A higher level association has been demonstrated with HLA-Dw2, which is linked to HLA-A3 and HLA-B7 and may be more closely linked to a multiple sclerosis–susceptibility gene.

Immunologic Pathogenesis

The lesions of multiple sclerosis are confined to the central nervous system and involve primarily the white matter in the periventricular areas of the cerebrum, cerebellum, brain stem, and spinal cord. In early active disease the lesions consist of inflammatory demyelination with mononuclear exudates; older lesions consist of plasma cells, mature lymphocytes, and astrocytes. Unlike the lesions of acute disseminated encephalomyelitis, these lesions appear to be of different ages and correlate positively with the appearance of clinical signs and symptoms at different times during the illness. The lesions of multiple sclerosis, termed plaques, contain increased proportions of immunoglobulin, suggesting local production. This finding is reflected in the cerebrospinal fluid, where increased concentration of γ-globulin can be found in 60–80% of multiple sclerosis patients, depending upon the method used. This is helpful information for the diagnosis of multiple sclerosis but is not pathognomonic, since elevated spinal fluid γ-globulin occurs in many inflammatory central nervous system processes. The immunoglobulin present in the cerebrospinal fluid of multiple sclerosis patients has an abnormal kappa to lambda chain ratio. The ratio of cerebrospinal fluid to serum immunoglobulin is reduced and the cerebrospinal fluid IgG index is elevated in over 85% of patients with active multiple sclerosis.

$$\frac{CSF\ IgG \div Serum\ IgG}{CSF\ albumin \div Serum\ albumin} = CSF\ IgG\ index$$

This index is also elevated in inflammatory nervous system disease and indicates that local IgG synthesis is occurring within the nervous system. The immunoglobulin has an oligoclonal pattern on electrophoresis, which is further evidence for local central nervous system production. A small portion of the oligoclonal immunoglobulin has been shown to react with measles antigen and myelin basic protein; the reactivity of the remaining immunoglobulin is still unknown.

The similarities between the lesions of multiple sclerosis and the inflammatory demyelination seen in experimental allergic encephalomyelitis have suggested that immune mechanisms may be involved in the pathogenesis of multiple sclerosis. In experimental allergic encephalomyelitis, disease induction requires that a species-specific encephalitogenic determinant be presented to the immune system. The cellular immune response that results includes, in some cases, inflammatory demyelination. It is clear from studies of several different animal species with differing encephalitogenic presentations (ie, as a purified peptide, as a sequence within basic protein, or as a component of myelin) that demyelination is not an invariable component of the response. Furthermore, inflammatory demyelination may be nonspecific in that a response to a nonneural antigen such as PPD can produce sensitized and activated lymphocytes which, when in contact with myelinated tissue, will produce demyelination. This bystander effect has relevance to multiple sclerosis, where it has been postulated that a distant and ongoing immune response to an as yet unidentified pathogen could result in inflammatory demyelination within the central nervous system. Candidate agents have included paramyxolike viruses in brain, jejunum, and bone marrow, herpes virus latent in sensory ganglia, and an unidentified agent that behaves like a virus in in vitro and in vivo mouse assays. At this time, the role of these or other proposed agents in the etiology of multiple sclerosis is still unproved.

Although inflammatory demyelination may be nonspecific, its occurrence in response to a known encephalitogenic challenge may be genetically determined. Inbred strain 13 guinea pigs and inbred Lewis rats are more susceptible to experimental allergic encephalomyelitis and develop more severe disease, including inflammatory demyelination, than do other strains. This response in rats may be controlled by an immune response gene closely linked to the major histocompatibility locus. A multiple sclerosis susceptibility gene may be closely associated with HLA-Dw2 and less closely associated with HLA-A3 and HLA-B7. Evidence of altered immune functions in multiple sclerosis patients in the form of changes in the numbers and functional capabilities of immunoregulatory T cells during exacerbation has been described. While these studies suggest that multiple sclerosis patients have a tendency toward aberrant immune reactions, the genetic control of such reactions and their association with the lesions of multiple sclerosis remain unproved.

Clinical Features

Since the lesions of multiple sclerosis tend to involve many areas of the central nervous system white matter, the symptoms of the disease are extremely varied. The most common manifestations are the development of motor weakness, paresthesias, impairment of visual acuity, and diplopia. These symptoms usually occur gradually—though rapid onset has been reported—and, following an initial attack, the patient may return to a normal functional status. Subsequent exacerbations occur at widely varying intervals and tend to subside with less complete recovery of function and more chronic disability as the disease progresses. Ataxia of gait, urinary bladder dysfunction, impotence, spasticity, mental aberrations (particularly euphoria), and seizures are common.

Differential Diagnosis

Acute episodes of multiple sclerosis must be differentiated from other structural lesions of the central nervous system. Spinal cord compression due to tumors or spondylosis usually presents with evidence of partial or complete intraspinal subarachnoid block, and the cerebrospinal fluid protein is elevated to much higher levels than in multiple sclerosis. Central nervous system tumors, both primary and metastatic, can mimic multiple sclerosis and must be ruled out with appropriate neurodiagnostic procedures. The symptoms of neurosyphilis, particularly tabes dorsalis, may mimic multiple sclerosis. The presence of Argyll Robertson pupils, hypotonic limbs, and areflexia in the lower extremities in tabes dorsalis as well as a history of syphilitic infection or the presence of a positive serologic test for syphilis are helpful in differentiating syphilis from multiple sclerosis. Vasculitides such as systemic lupus erythematosus and polyarteritis nodosa have been mentioned previously in the discussion of acute disseminated encephalomyelitis. Finally, degenerative spinal and cerebellar disorders such as Friedreich's ataxia, parenchymatous cerebellar degeneration, and olivopontocerebellar degeneration can all mimic multiple sclerosis. These disorders tend to be familial, chronically progressive, and not associated with the elevation of spinal fluid γ-globulin that occurs in the majority of cases of multiple sclerosis.

Treatment

While experimental allergic encephalomyelitis can be successfully suppressed with specific, nonspecific, and related antigens as well as with immunosuppressive agents such as corticosteroids and cytotoxic drugs, patients with multiple sclerosis have shown less clear benefit from such treatment. Corticosteroids may shorten the duration of acute exacerbations, particularly when optic neuritis is present, but the long-term benefits of corticosteroid therapy are not striking. A completed therapeutic trial using daily injections of myelin basic protein was ineffective in suppressing disease, while trials of immunosuppression with cytotoxic agents, immunomodulation with transfer factor or interferon, and plasmapheresis are still in progress.

Complications & Prognosis

The prognosis of multiple sclerosis is difficult to predict because of the extremely variable nature of the disease. Benign cases in which patients have functioned normally or with little deficit after initial episodes are not uncommon. At the other extreme, fulminant cases of acute multiple sclerosis have resulted in death during the initial episode. Most patients fall between these extremes and continue to have exacerbations and remissions for many years. The average duration of life after onset of symptoms is at least 25 years and was said to be more than 35 years in a follow-up study of multiple sclerosis among a Veterans Administration Hospital population.

The late complications of multiple sclerosis include recurrent urinary tract infections and respiratory infections and decubiti in debilitated and bedridden patients.

ACUTE IDIOPATHIC POLYNEURITIS
(Guillain-Barré Syndrome)

Major Immunologic Features

- Commonly follows viral infections.
- Inflammatory demyelination of peripheral nerves.
- Marked similarity to experimental allergic neuritis in animals.
- Cellular immunity to nerve proteins present.

General Considerations

Acute idiopathic polyneuritis, like acute disseminated encephalomyelitis, frequently occurs following an infectious illness. Upper respiratory infections, exanthems, vaccinations, and specific viral illnesses such as measles, infectious mononucleosis, and hepatitis commonly precede acute idiopathic polyneuritis by 1–3 weeks. Fever therapy and surgery have also preceded episodes of acute idiopathic polyneuritis in some patients. The disease affects all age groups, and incidence is not related to sex or race.

Immunologic Pathogenesis

Acute idiopathic polyneuritis is a demyelinating disease of the peripheral nervous system characterized by a perivascular mononuclear cell infiltrate with segmental demyelination of peripheral nerves in the areas of inflammation. The inflammatory response is present even in the earliest stages. In areas of most severe involvement there is some axonal destruction and wallerian degeneration. These areas often show infiltration of polymorphonuclear leukocytes as well as mononuclear cells early in the course of the disease. Later, the lesions frequently have plasma cells in the exudate. Experimentally, an identical clinical and pathologic entity can be produced in many animal species by the injection of peripheral nerve myelin, the P_2 protein of myelin, or peptides of P_2 protein together with Freund's complete adjuvant. This illness, experimental allergic neuritis (EAN), begins as weakness and later leads to paralysis 10–24 days after immunization. The immunopathologic nature of the illness can be demonstrated by the fact that lymphocytes from animals with experimental allergic neuritis are sensitive to extracts of peripheral nerve and purified proteins of peripheral nerve myelin and undergo activation or produce lymphokines in the presence of these antigens. Sensitivity to the immunizing antigen parallels the course of the illness. The disease can be passively transferred with sensitized cells but not with serum. Antinerve antibodies are present but are not considered pathogenic, since their appearance does not parallel the appearance of clinical signs or histopathology. Lymphocytes from animals with experimental allergic neuritis have the capacity to produce demyelination in tissue culture; serum from such animals does not. However, antibody to galactocerebroside can produce a demyelinating neuropathy when injected locally into peripheral nerve or systemically into rabbits as a result of repeated injections of galactocerebroside in Freund's complete adjuvant. In chickens, infection with Marek's disease virus, a chicken herpesvirus with oncogenic properties, frequently results in the development of a demyelinating neuropathy similar to acute idiopathic polyneuritis. In this disease, a latent infection of nonneuronal ganglion cells stimulates a host immune response to both viral and peripheral nerve antigens.

Immunologic abnormalities have also been described in acute idiopathic polyneuritis. An increased number of spontaneously transformed circulating lymphocytes has been described, as well as lymphocytes that show sensitivity to extracts of peripheral nerve and peripheral nerve myelin proteins by activation or lymphokine production. This sensitivity appears to be specific, since there is no sensitivity to central nervous system antigens in these patients. Antinerve antibodies have been described in acute idiopathic polyneuritis and in several other types of neuropathy and may reflect immune reactions to nerve tissue destruction. There is no specific immunologic test that is diagnostic of acute idiopathic polyneuritis.

Clinical Features

The onset of acute idiopathic polyneuritis is generally characterized by a rapidly progressing weakness first of the lower extremities, then the upper extremities, and then the respiratory musculature over a period of 3–7 days. Weakness and paralysis are frequently preceded by paresthesias and numbness of the limbs, but objective sensory loss is generally mild and transient. Cranial nerves, most commonly the facial nerve, can be involved. The tendon reflexes are decreased or lost early in the course of the illness, and nerve conduction velocities in affected limbs are moderately to markedly slowed, consistent with a demyelinating peripheral neuropathy. Cerebrospinal fluid protein is increased in all cases, but frequently not during the first few days of the illness. Cerebrospinal fluid white cell counts are commonly normal or slightly elevated. The most common clinical course is one of rapid evolution of symptoms over a period of 1–3 weeks with improvement thereafter and return to normal function over a period of 6–9 months. However, other patterns such as a more gradual onset, a more prolonged period of complete paralysis, recovery with severe residual deficits, and a relapsing course have also been described. Whether these latter patterns represent different illnesses has been a topic of debate for many years, but, in the absence of clearly different causes and pathologic features, it seems more likely that they represent different clinical variants of the same underlying process.

Differential Diagnosis

Acute idiopathic polyneuritis can be differentiated from porphyric polyneuropathy by the demonstration of porphyrins in the urine of such patients. Heavy metal intoxication with lead, thallium, and arsenic can all be ruled out by appropriate blood or urine tests. Acute transverse myelitis in the early stages may resemble acute idiopathic polyneuritis, but pathologically increased reflexes and spasticity occur several days to weeks after initial flaccidity, and hyporeflexia and bowel and urinary bladder involvement are more common in transverse myelitis. Vasculitides such as systemic lupus erythematosus and polyarteritis nodosa can produce peripheral neuropathies, but these tend to present as asymmetric involvement of one or more nerves. The weakness of skeletal muscles involved in myasthenia gravis may resemble acute idiopathic polyneuritis, but the former is more likely to be associated with ocular muscle involvement and will generally respond to anticholinesterase drugs.

Treatment

The use of anti-inflammatory agents in treating acute idiopathic polyneuritis is controversial. Some patients show no beneficial effects from corticosteroids; others respond favorably and tend to relapse when these drugs are discontinued. A third group will respond to cytotoxic drugs such as cyclophosphamide or azathioprine after failing to respond to corticosteroids. Patients with recurrent and severe idiopathic polyneuropathy may respond to plasmapheresis. This diversity of responses may indicate a heterogeneous population of patients based on cause, host immune responses, or stage of disease when treatment was begun. A controlled study of these methods using disease staging based on clinical and immunologic criteria is needed before their value in the treatment of Guillain-Barré syndrome can be determined.

Complications & Prognosis

The widespread availability of modern methods for assisting and maintaining respiration has resulted in a marked decrease in the number of fatalities from acute idiopathic polyneuritis. However, the incidence of residual neurologic deficits is higher than previously recognized and may occur in as many as 50% of cases. Persistent deficits such as weakness and loss of reflexes are understandable, since irreversible axonal disruption and wallerian degeneration occur in severely affected nerves. The mechanical problems of clearing respiratory secretions in patients with respiratory muscle and pharyngeal weakness favor the development of respiratory infections, which are the most severe threat to life in hospitalized patients.

• • •

MYASTHENIA GRAVIS

Major Immunologic Features

- Commonly associated with thymoma or thymic hyperplasia.
- Pathogenic autoantibodies directed against acetylcholine receptor protein and immune complexes at the myoneural junction present in serum.
- Other autoantibodies are common.
- Often associated with other autoimmune diseases.

General Considerations

Myasthenia gravis is a disease of unknown cause in which there is motor weakness due to a disorder of neuromuscular transmission. The disease tends to affect young adults, more commonly women, but onset in childhood as well as onset beyond age 40 is not uncommon. Familial cases are known, but there is no racial predilection. The occurrence of myasthenia gravis with thymomas, thymic hyperplasia, autoantibodies, and certain autoimmune diseases strongly suggests that an abnormality of the immune system is involved in the pathogenesis of this disorder. Recent studies have shown that the abnormality is the production of anti–acetylcholine receptor antibody, which binds at the myoneural junction, interrupts neuromuscular transmission by increasing endocytosis of acetylcholine receptors, and forms immune complexes that bind complement and cause additional destruction of the myoneural junction.

Immunologic Pathogenesis

Immunologic abnormalities are common in myasthenia gravis. Antibodies to striated muscle that cross-react with thymic epithelial cells have been described, as have antinuclear and antithyroid antibodies. Cellular immunity to crude muscle antigen and purified muscle protein, measured by inhibition of leukocyte migration, has been demonstrated. These abnormalities, as well as the association of myasthenia gravis with systemic lupus erythematosus, rheumatoid arthritis, Sjögren's syndrome, and thyroiditis (more commonly than would be expected by chance alone), have focused attention on the immune system. Abnormalities are present in the thymus in 80% of myasthenics, either as true thymomas (10%) or in the form of thymic hyperplasia with increased numbers of germinal centers (70%) that contain increased numbers of B lymphocytes. The fact that two-thirds of all myasthenics who undergo thymectomy show complete or partial remission also suggests that the thymus may be the site of production of a neuromuscular blocking agent.

The immunoglobulin nature of the blocking agent and its further characterization as anti–acetylcholine receptor antibody have greatly elucidated the pathogenesis of myasthenia gravis. The abnormalities in neuromuscular transmission, the immunopathologic features, and the response to treatment in clinical practice are quite similar to what is seen in experimental allergic myasthenia gravis produced in rabbits and rats by the injection of heterologous and homologous acetylcholine receptor protein. In both diseases, anti-acetylcholine receptor antibody is present at the myoneural junction, in the peripheral blood, and in the thymus, where it may be directed against acetylcholine receptors present on thymic epithelial cells. The antibody binds to acetylcholine receptors, which then become endocytosed, depleting the membrane of receptor. Immunoglobulin and complement can be identified at the myoneural junction in myasthenia gravis and in chronic experimental allergic myasthenia gravis. Phagocytes can be seen in the acute stages of the latter but not in myasthenia gravis. The consequences of the autoimmune attack in severe and advanced cases of myasthenia gravis are that the remaining receptor is complexed with antibody and there is a simplification and unfolding of the myoneural junction. The loss of acetylcholine receptors is responsible for the decrease in the amplitude of the miniature end plate potential in myasthenia gravis. Cellular and humoral immunity to acetylcholine receptor protein occurs in both diseases. However, it appears that the antibody response is most closely associated with disease symptoms. Serum from patients with myasthenia gravis and from animals with experimental allergic myasthenia gravis will produce disease in recipient animals, and—while cells from experimental allergic myasthenia gravis animals will produce disease in recipients—the time course of disease production suggests that the cells responsible are antibody-producing cells.

Clinical Features

Myasthenia gravis is an abnormality of muscles. The muscles may be weak or normal at rest but become increasingly weaker with repetitive use. The weakness is often first noted in the extraocular muscles and manifested as diplopia or ptosis. Pharyngeal and facial muscle weakness, resulting in dysphagia, dysarthria, and difficulty in chewing, commonly occurs. Skeletal muscle weakness is more often proximal than distal, and difficulty in climbing stairs, rising from chairs, combing the hair, or even holding up the head results. All of these symptoms show fluctuations in intensity and are more severe late in the day. The neurologic examination is normal except for the muscle weakness. The disease is said to remit spontaneously in 25% of cases within the first 2 years. Serious exacerbations of the illness, including respiratory impairment—especially in elderly patients who have other complicating diseases—account for the majority of the deaths from myasthenia gravis. Modern methods of assisted respiration and constant monitoring of cardiac and respiratory function have greatly reduced the mortality rate in myasthenia gravis, which previously was about 20–30%.

The abnormality in neuromuscular transmission in myasthenia gravis, which includes a decrease in the amplitude of the miniature end-plate potential, can usually be overcome by anticholinesterase drugs such as edrophonium (Tensilon) and neostigmine. The improvement in myasthenic weakness after injection of these drugs is helpful both in diagnosis and treatment.

Immunologic Diagnosis

Anti-acetylcholine receptor antibodies can be found in 90% of myasthenia gravis patients and occasionally in thymoma patients without muscle weakness. Their presence in patients with symptoms suggestive of myasthenia gravis can be considered diagnostic.

Differential Diagnosis

Myasthenia gravis can usually be differentiated from other myopathies on the basis of its response to anticholinesterase drugs. The various forms of periodic paralysis do not show the ocular muscle involvement seen in myasthenia. The myasthenic syndrome (Eaton-Lambert syndrome) is seen in association with a remote cancer and can be differentiated by electrodiagnostic studies as well as by its response to guanidine.

Treatment

Anticholinesterase drugs such as pyridostigmine (Mestinon) and neostigmine in combination with atropine are the most commonly used form of long-term therapy. Beneficial effects from thymectomy are seen in the majority of cases, and all patients with myasthenia gravis except those with nondisabling ocular myasthenia should be considered for thymectomy. The response to corticosteroids and immunosuppressive agents such as cyclophosphamide and azathioprine has been encouraging. These agents frequently can bring about remission and long-term control of symptoms in patients who have not responded to anticholinergic medication or thymectomy. Dramatic effects have been described in severely ill patients who have been treated with plasmapheresis or thoracic duct drainage. The beneficial effect of both of these therapies may consist of removal of large quantities of anti-acetylcholine receptor antibody. Plasmapheresis has been found to be more effective if patients are simultaneously given immunosuppressive drugs to diminish the rapid increase in anti-acetylcholine receptor antibody that follows plasma exchange.

The costs, technical difficulties, and morbidity involved in plasmapheresis and thoracic duct drainage have limited their use to severely ill patients who have failed to respond to other treatments. Remission or improvement can be induced with such treatment, which can be maintained using anticholinergic or immunosuppressive drug therapy.

Complications & Prognosis

The course of myasthenia gravis prior to the widespread practice of thymectomy and the use of corticosteroids was one of remission in 25% of cases during the first 2 years and a course of chronic, persistent weakness with a 20–30% mortality rate in the remainder. Improvement and remission within 5 years can now be anticipated in up to 90% of patients undergoing thymectomy, and further improvement with reduction of the dosage of anticholinesterase drugs can be expected with the use of corticosteroids. Cholinergic crisis with weakness resulting from overdosage of anticholinesterase drugs, pulmonary infections resulting from pooling of pharyngeal secretions, and lowered resistance to invading organisms resulting from corticosteroid therapy are persistent hazards for the myasthenic patient.

IMMUNOLOGIC ABNORMALITIES IN OTHER NEUROLOGIC DISEASES

In addition to the decreased levels of IgA noted in ataxia-telangiectasia (Chapter 25), abnormalities of the major immunoglobulin classes and abnormal immune responses have been described in several seemingly unrelated neurologic diseases. The relationships of the immune abnormalities and the neurologic deficits are still unclear, but there is little evidence for a causal relationship in most of these conditions.

MYOTONIA DYSTROPHICA

Myotonia dystrophica is an autosomal dominant disease in which there are dystrophic changes in muscle tissue leading to a syndrome of muscle weakness and atrophy in addition to the characteristic "myotonia," which is a delayed relaxation of the muscle after contraction. In addition to the changes in muscle, abnormalities in several other organ systems have been described, including testicular atrophy, early frontal balding and skull abnormalities, cataracts in adults, low basal metabolic rates, and impaired tolerance to glucose, with excessive release of insulin. Serum levels of IgG are low in this disease because of increased catabolism of IgG. Poor antibody responses to bacterial antigens have also been described in several patients who had normal immunoglobulin levels. The basic immunologic defect in this disease remains to be defined.

AMYOTROPHIC LATERAL SCLEROSIS

Amyotrophic lateral sclerosis (ALS) is a degenerative disease of anterior horn cells (motor neurons) and the motor system, resulting in weakness, muscle wasting, hyperreflexia, and progressive debilitation leading to death in 3–5 years. The cause is unknown, but a viral infection or virus-immune mechanism has been suspected. Immunologic and immunogenetic studies on small numbers of patients have produced inconsistent results. Occasional defects in cellular immunity, increased levels of circulating immune complexes containing unidentified antigens, and altered levels of serum immunoglobulins have been reported. HLA-A3, HLA-A2 + HLA-A28, and HLA-Bw35 have been overrepresented in some groups of ALS patients but not in others. On Guam, where a focus of ALS has been studied for many years, moderate immunodeficiency including skin test anergy, low numbers of total lymphocytes (particularly T cells), and poor functional responses of lymphocytes tested in vitro occurred in many ALS patients. The most severe immunodeficiency was associated with HLA-Bw35 and shortened survival. Serum immunoglobulin levels (IgA and IgG) were elevated and immune complexes were present in some, but a specific antiviral or autoimmune response associated with the altered serum immunoglobulin levels, the deficient cellular immune response, or differences in survival could not be identified. Therefore, while aberrant immune responses do occur during the course of ALS, it appears that neither immunodeficiency nor a specific autoimmune or antiviral immune response is a major feature of the disease.

CHRONIC POLYNEUROPATHIES

In addition to the neuropathies that have been described with amyloidosis, Waldenström's macroglobulinemia, multiple myeloma, and benign monoclonal gammopathy, a large group of patients with sporadic and familial chronic or relapsing polyneuropathic diseases have immunologic abnormalities. Patients with hereditary sensory neuropathies

were found to have increased levels of serum IgA as well as increased production of IgA in jejunal biopsy specimens. Recently, demyelination in the peripheral nerves of a patient with a plasma cell dyscrasia was associated with a monoclonal IgM protein that had antineural activity. While demonstration of binding to peripheral nerve by immunoglobulins may not occur in all cases, autoimmune antibody may play a direct role in some cases. In still other patients in whom no immunoglobulin abnormalities can be identified, a remission of disease has been accomplished by the use of immunomodulating drugs such as polyinosinate:polycytidylate:poly L-lysine stabilized with carboxymethyl cellulose or the use of plasmapheresis. This suggests that aberrant immune responses may be involved in the pathogenesis of neuropathy in these patients, but the nature of the immune abnormality remains unclear.

SLOW, CHRONIC, & LATENT VIRAL INFECTIONS OF THE NERVOUS SYSTEM

Several subacute and chronic degenerative diseases of human and animal nervous systems have been shown to be related to persistent or chronic infection of the nervous system with viruses and other less well defined transmissible agents. Subacute sclerosing panencephalitis in humans and a similar disorder produced experimentally in hamsters are related to persistent infection of the central nervous system with measles virus. Progressive multifocal leukoencephalopathy in humans has been associated with the recovery of 2 different papovaviruses previously thought not to be pathogenic for humans. A third group of diseases, referred to as the subacute spongioform encephalopathies, including kuru and Jakob-Creutzfeldt disease in humans and scrapie and mink encephalopathy in animals, have been shown to be caused by small transmissible agents which are present in affected brain material and will produce an identical disease when inoculated into susceptible primate or nonprimate hosts after a relatively long disease-free latent period. Although the role of the host immune response is unclear in most of these disorders, the infectious nature of these diseases has directed research toward understanding the host response in both the treatment and possible prevention of these diseases.

Subacute Sclerosing Panencephalitis (SSPE)

Subacute sclerosing panencephalitis is a subacute degenerative central nervous system disease which affects mainly school-age children. Personality changes, dementia, seizures, and myoclonus are all common symptoms which progress rapidly to death over a period of 12–18 months in most cases. Pathologically, intranuclear and intracytoplasmic inclusion bodies had been noted for many years before electron microscopic studies revealed paramyxoviruslike structures in infected brain material. Later, measles virus antigen was demonstrated by fluorescent antibody staining and measles virus was recovered from infected brain material by co-cultivation techniques.

The persistence of measles virus in the presence of high titers of locally produced antimeasles antibody suggested that an underlying defect in immunity was present in patients with SSPE. However, consistent abnormalities in in vitro assays of cellular and humoral immunity could not be demonstrated. The possibility that measles virus associated with SSPE was different from wild type measles virus was also entertained, but to date no biochemical or biologic marker that will differentiate an SSPE strain from a wild-type measles virus strain has been identified. More recently, the use of sensitive immunoprecipitation techniques has shown that although SSPE patients have high titers of antibody against most measles virus proteins, they have a relative lack of antibody against the M protein, a protein essential for virus assembly. Current evidence suggests that measles virus M protein is not synthesized in infected brain cells of SSPE patients. This results in an abortive infection in which mature virions are not produced but exposed surface glycoproteins are capable of stimulating an antibody response. The internal components of measles virus accumulating within brain cells may ultimately result in cell death and the appearance of the neurologic signs and symptoms associated with SSPE.

Progressive Multifocal Leukoencephalopathy (PML)

Progressive multifocal leukoencephalopathy is a disease of adults which presents as a widespread disease of the nervous system with ataxia, spasticity, visual disturbances, difficulty with speech and swallowing, and rapid progression to coma and death over a period of 1 year. The disease occurs most frequently in patients with debilitating illnesses, most of which produce some form of immunosuppression. These include lymphomas, leukemia, sarcoidosis, systemic lupus erythematosus, and exogenous immunosuppression for renal transplantation. Papovaviruses of 2 types, JC virus and SV40 virus, have been isolated and identified immunologically by the reaction of these viruses with specific antisera produced in rabbits. How these viruses are introduced into humans is unknown, but there was definite inadvertent introduction of SV40 virus by contaminated killed poliovirus vaccines in a large number of people inoculated subcutaneously between 1955 and 1961, and some evidence of antibodies to SV40 virus in USA residents with no history of receiving contaminated poliovirus vaccine. Recently, a variable decrease in mitogen responsiveness and a specific absence of production of leukocyte inhibitory factor (LIF) in response to JC virus has been described in patients with progressive multifocal leukoencephalopathy. The added insult of generalized immunosuppression coupled with an absent or diminished response to latent papovaviruses may be involved in the pathogenesis of this disease.

Subacute Spongioform Encephalopathies

The neuropathologic similarities of kuru and Jakob-Creutzfeldt disease in humans and scrapie and mink encephalopathy in animals, as well as the fact that all are transmissible to other animals, have led to the suggestion by Gajdusek and Gibbs that these diseases should be considered similar types of subacute viral encephalopathies. They are chronic illnesses which proceed relentlessly to death after a long illness-free latent period. None of the signs of acute viral encephalopathy are present. Clinically, there is no elevation of cerebrospinal fluid protein or γ-globulin and no detectable cellular response. Pathologically, there is no inflammatory reaction in the central nervous system. The pathologic changes consist of severe gliosis, loss of neurons in affected areas, and vacuolization within neuroglia. These changes are similar in naturally occurring illness and in experimentally transmitted disease.

Kuru was first described in 1957 by Gajdusek and Zigas in the Fore linguistic group of the New Guinea highlands. The disease presented as a subacute degenerative disorder characterized by progressive ataxia, tremor, dysphagia, and death within 3–18 months following the onset of symptoms. It had been noted that cannibalism was extensively practiced in this area, but its significance in terms of this disease was not appreciated until 1966, when it was demonstrated that kuru could be transmitted to chimpanzees by intracerebral inoculation of brain tissue from affected patients. It was later demonstrated that transmission could also occur by inoculation via the intradermal, intravenous, and oral routes not only with brain material but occasionally by inoculation of kidney, spleen, and lymph node material from affected patients. Since cannibalism was suppressed in this area in the 1950s the incidence of kuru has decreased.

Jakob-Creutzfeldt disease has been known clinically and pathologically for many years. The striking neuropathologic similarity to kuru and the rapid clinical course led to the attempted transmission of the disease to monkeys, which was successful after an incubation period of 13 months. Since the original transmission experiment Gibbs and Gajdusek have successfully transmitted the disease to several subhuman primates.

Scrapie, a naturally occurring disease of sheep and occasionally of goats, has been known since 1732. It was first described as transmissible in 1896, and this was confirmed in 1936. Later, the disease was transmitted to mice as well as monkeys after prolonged latent periods. The fact that the disease can be transmitted to mice makes it readily accessible to experimental study.

The natural course of scrapie in the mouse has been well characterized. The agent multiplies and reaches a relatively high titer in the spleen and lymphoid tissue 3–4 weeks after intracerebral and intravenous inoculation. The titer begins to fall thereafter in these organs but increases in the brain, where it reaches its peak at 6 months. The animals succumb to the disease 6–10 months following inoculation. There are no pathologic changes in the spleen or lymph nodes, but the nervous system does show spongioform changes prior to the onset of clinical symptoms.

The role of the host immune response to these agents is unknown. Specifically, no antibodies to the infecting agents, no evidence of immune paralysis as shown by a number of tests of humoral and cellular immune function, and no alteration of the immune system have resulted in any significant changes in the course of these disorders. The fact that there is some difference in the susceptibility of different strains of mice to scrapie and of monkeys to kuru, scrapie, and Jakob-Creutzfeldt disease suggests that certain genes may enhance the expression of the disease, but this has not yet been clearly linked to specific immune response genes.

Spongiform pathologic changes in the nervous systems of wild and laboratory mice can be associated with the expression of murine leukemia virus (MuLV) antigen and lymphomas. This **murine motor neuron disease** pathologically resembles scrapie and clinically resembles amyotrophic lateral sclerosis. In this disease, age-specific exposure to a potentially neurotropic virus, an immature immunologic system, and genetic susceptibility controlled by loci that permit or restrict the growth of MuLV must all be present, or the mouse will not develop progressive neurologic disease as an adult. Some or all of these factors may be important in the slow virus diseases of humans and may explain the extremely low incidence of these rare human infectious diseases involving the nervous system.

● ● ●

References

Acute Disseminated Encephalomyelitis (ADEM)

Adams RD, Kubik CS: The morbid anatomy of the demyelinative diseases. *Am J Med* 1952;**12**:510.

Lisak RP, Zweiman B: In vitro cell-mediated immunity of cerebrospinal fluid lymphocytes to myelin basic protein in primary demyelinating diseases. *N Engl J Med* 1977;**297**:850.

Multiple Sclerosis

Antel JP, Arnason BGW, Medof ME: Suppressor cell function in multiple sclerosis: Correlation with clinical disease activity. *Ann Neurol* 1979;**5**:338.

Jersild C et al: Histocompatibility determinants in multiple sclerosis with special reference to clinical course. *Lancet* 1973;**2**:1221.

Kurtzke JF et al: Studies on the natural history of multiple sclerosis. 5. Long-term survival in young men. *Arch Neurol* 1970;**22**:215.

McFarlin DE et al: The immune response against myelin basic protein in two strains of rat with different genetic capacity to develop experimental allergic encephalomyelitis. *J Exp Med* 1975;**141**:72.

Olsson JE, Link H: Immunoglobulin abnormalities in multiple sclerosis. *Arch Neurol* 1973;**28**:392.

Wisniewski H, Bloom BR: Primary demyelination as a nonspecific consequence of a cell-mediated immune reaction. *J Exp Med* 1975;**141**:346.

Acute Idiopathic Polyneuritis (Guillain-Barré Syndrome)

Arnason BGW: Inflammatory polyradiculoneuropathies. Chapter 56, pages 1110–1148, in: *Peripheral Neuropathy*. Vol 2. Dyck PJ, Thomas PK, Lambert EH (editors). Saunders, 1975.

Brostoff SW, Levit S, Powers JM: Induction of experimental allergic neuritis with a peptide from myelin P₂ basic protein. *Nature* 1977;**268**:752.

Pepose JS et al: Marek's disease as a model for the Landry-Guillain-Barré syndrome. *Am J Pathol* 1981;**103**:309.

Rocklin RE et al: The Guillain-Barré syndrome and multiple sclerosis. *N Engl J Med* 1971;**284**:803.

Myasthenia Gravis

Almon RR, Andrew CG, Appel SH: Serum globulin in myasthenia gravis: Inhibition of α-bungarotoxin binding to acetylcholine receptors. *Science* 1974;**186**:55.

Dau PC et al: Plasmapheresis and immunosuppressive drug therapy in myasthenia gravis. *N Engl J Med* 1977;**297**:1134.

Drachman DB: Myasthenia gravis. (2 parts.) *N Engl J Med* 1978;**298**:136, 186.

Lindstrom JM et al: Pathological mechanisms in experimental autoimmune myasthenia gravis. *J Exp Med* 1976;**144**:726.

Papatestas AE et al: Thymectomy in myasthenia gravis: Pathologic, clinical, and electrophysiologic correlations. *Ann NY Acad Sci* 1976;**274**:555.

Patrick J, Lindstrom J: Autoimmune response to acetylcholine receptors. *Science* 1973;**180**:871.

Other Neurologic Diseases

Hoffman PM et al: Cellular immunity in Guamanians with amyotrophic lateral sclerosis and parkinsonism-dementia. *N Engl J Med* 1978;**299**:680.

Hoffman PM et al: Humoral immunity in Guamanians with amyotrophic lateral sclerosis and parkinsonism-dementia. *Ann Neurol* 1981;**10**:193.

Latov N et al: Plasma cell dyscrasia and peripheral neuropathy with a monoclonal antibody to peripheral nerve myelin. *N Engl J Med* 1980;**303**:618.

Whitaker JN et al: Hereditary sensory neuropathy: Association with increased synthesis of immunoglobulin A. *Arch Neurol* 1974;**30**:359.

Wochner RD et al: Accelerated breakdown of immunoglobulin G in myotonic dystrophy: A hereditary error of immunoglobulin catabolism. *J Clin Invest* 1966;**45**:321.

Slow, Chronic, & Latent Viral Infections of the Nervous System

Brooks BR et al: Slow viral infections. *Annu Rev Neurosci* 1979;**2**:309.

Choppin PW et al: The functions and inhibition of the membrane glycoproteins of paramyxoviruses and myxoviruses and the role of the measles virus M protein in subacute sclerosing panencephalitis. *J Infect Dis* 1981;**143**:352.

Gajdusek DC: Unconventional viruses and the origin and disappearance of kuru. *Science* 1977;**197**:943.

Hoffman PM, Ruscetti SK, Morse HC III: Pathogenesis of paralysis and lymphoma associated with a wild mouse retrovirus infection. 1. Age and dose related effects in susceptible laboratory mice. *J Neuroimmunol* 1981;**1**:275.

Prusiner SB, Hadlow WJ: *Slow Transmissible Diseases of the Nervous System*. 2 vols. Academic Press, 1979.

Weiner LP et al: Isolation of virus related to SV40 from patients with progressive multifocal leukoencephalopathy. *N Engl J Med* 1972;**286**:385.

Willoughby EW et al: Progressive multifocal leukoencephalopathy (PML): In vitro cell-mediated immune responses to mitogens and JC virus. *Neurology* 1980;**30**:256.

Eye Diseases | 36

G. Richard O'Connor, MD

The eye is frequently considered to be a special target of immunologic disease processes, but proof of the causative role of these processes is lacking in all but a few disorders. In this sense, the immunopathology of the eye is much less clearly delineated than that of the kidney, the testis, or the thyroid gland. Because the eye is a highly vascularized organ and because the rather labile vessels of the conjunctiva are embedded in a nearly transparent medium, inflammatory eye disorders are more obvious (and often more painful) than those of other organs such as the thyroid or the kidney. The iris, ciliary body, and choroid are the most highly vascularized tissues of the eye. The similarity of the vascular supply of the uvea to that of the kidney and the choroid plexus of the brain has given rise to justified speculation concerning the selection of these 3 tissues, among others, as targets of immune complex diseases (eg, serum sickness).

Immunologic diseases of the eye can be grossly divided into 2 major categories: antibody-mediated and cell-mediated diseases. As is the case in other organs, there is ample opportunity for the interaction of these 2 systems in the eye.

ANTIBODY–MEDIATED DISEASES

Before it can be concluded that a disease of the eye is antibody-dependent, the following criteria must be satisfied: (1) There must be evidence of specific antibody in the patient's serum or plasma cells. (2) The antigen must be identified and, if feasible, characterized. (3) The same antigen must be shown to produce an immunologic response in the eye of an experimental animal, and the pathologic changes produced in the experimental animal must be similar to those observed in the human disease. (4) It must be possible to produce similar lesions in animals passively sensitized with serum from an affected animal upon challenge with the specific antigen.

Unless all of the above criteria are satisfied, the disease may be thought of as *possibly* antibody-dependent. In such circumstances, the disease can be regarded as antibody-mediated if only one of the following criteria is met: (1) if antibody to an antigen is present in higher quantities in the ocular fluids than in the serum (after adjustments have been made for the total amounts of immunoglobulins in each fluid); (2) if abnormal accumulations of plasma cells are present in the ocular lesion; (3) if abnormal accumulations of immunoglobulins are present at the site of the disease; (4) if complement is fixed by immunoglobulins at the site of the disease; (5) if an accumulation of eosinophils is present at the site of the disease; or (6) if the ocular disease is associated with an inflammatory disease elsewhere in the body for which antibody dependency has been proved or strongly suggested.

HAY FEVER CONJUNCTIVITIS

This disease is characterized by edema and hyperemia of the conjunctiva and lids (Fig 36–1) and by itching and watering of the eyes. There is often an associated itching sensation in the nose and rhinorrhea. The conjunctiva appears pale and boggy because of the intense edema, which is often rapid in onset. There is a distinct seasonal incidence, some patients being able to establish the onset of their symptoms at precisely the same time each year. These times usually correspond to the release of pollens by specific grasses, trees, or weeds.

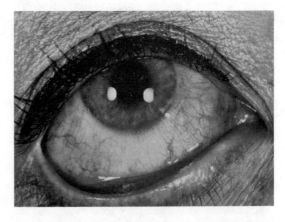

Figure 36–1. Hay fever conjunctivitis. Note edema and hyperemia of the conjunctiva. (Courtesy of M Allansmith and B McClellan.)

Immunologic Pathogenesis

Hay fever conjunctivitis is one of the few inflammatory eye disorders for which antibody dependence has been definitely established. It is recognized as a form of atopic disease with an implied hereditary susceptibility. IgE (reaginic antibody) in its dimeric form is believed to be attached to mast cells lying beneath the conjunctival epithelium. Contact of the offending antigen with IgE triggers the release of vasoactive amines, principally histamine, in this area, and this in turn results in vasodilatation and chemosis.

The role of circulating antibody to ragweed pollen in the pathogenesis of hay fever conjunctivitis has been demonstrated by passively transferring serum from a hypersensitive person to a nonsensitive one. When exposed to the offending pollen, the previously nonsensitive individual reacted with the typical signs of hay fever conjunctivitis.

Immunologic Diagnosis

Victims of hay fever conjunctivitis show many eosinophils in Giemsa-stained scrapings of conjunctival epithelium. They show the **immediate** type of response, with wheal and flare, when tested by scratch tests of the skin with extracts of pollens or other offending antigens. Biopsies of the skin test sites have occasionally shown the full-blown picture of an **Arthus reaction,** with deposition of immune complexes in the walls of the dermal vessels. Passive cutaneous anaphylaxis can also be used to demonstrate the presence of circulating antibody.

Treatment

Systemically administered antihistaminics such as diphenhydramine or tripelennamine are effective, particularly when given prophylactically during the season of greatest exposure. Sustained release capsules of antihistaminics such as Ornade (chlorpheniramine maleate) are preferred by some. Locally applied antihistaminics such as Prefrin-A drops contain both an antihistaminic agent (pyrilamine) and a vasoconstrictor (phenylephrine). Where conjunctival edema is severe and of sudden onset, epinephrine drops (1:100,000) instilled into the conjunctival sac may help to reduce the edema quickly. Corticosteroids applied locally offer some relief. Topical use of cromolyn (disodium cromoglycate; Cromoptic), a stabilizer of the mast cell, is still being evaluated but appears to be a promising method of treatment.

Hyposensitization with gradually increasing doses of subcutaneously injected pollen extracts or other suspected allergens appears to reduce the severity of the disease in some individuals if started well in advance of the season. The mechanism is presumed to be production of blocking antibodies in response to the injection of small, graded doses of the antigen. This procedure cannot be recommended routinely, however, in view of the generally good results and relatively few complications of antihistamine therapy. Acute anaphylactoid reactions have occasionally resulted from overzealous hyposensitization therapy.

VERNAL CONJUNCTIVITIS & ATOPIC KERATOCONJUNCTIVITIS

These 2 diseases also belong to the group of atopic disorders. Both are characterized by itching and lacrimation of the eyes but are more chronic than hay fever conjunctivitis. Furthermore, both ultimately result in structural modifications of the lids and conjunctiva.

Vernal conjunctivitis characteristically affects children and adolescents; the incidence decreases sharply after the second decade of life. Like hay fever conjunctivitis, vernal conjunctivitis occurs only in the warm months of the year. Most of its victims live in hot, dry climates. The disease characteristically produces giant ("cobblestone") papillae of the tarsal conjunctiva (Fig 36–2). The keratinized epithelium from these papillae may abrade the underlying cornea, giving rise to complaints of foreign body sensations.

Atopic keratoconjunctivitis affects individuals of all ages and has no specific seasonal incidence. The skin of the lids has a characteristic dry, scaly appearance. The conjunctiva is pale and boggy. Both the conjunctiva and the cornea may develop scarring in the later stages of the disease. Atopic cataract has also been described. Staphylococcal blepharitis, manifested by scales and crusts on the lids, commonly complicates this disease.

Immunologic Pathogenesis

Reaginic antibody (IgE) is fixed to subepithelial mast cells in both of these conditions. Contact between the offending antigen and IgE is thought to trigger degranulation of the mast cell, which in turn allows for the release of vasoactive amines in the tissues. It is unlikely, however, that antibody action alone is responsible, since—at least in the case of the papillae of

Figure 36–2. Giant papillae ("cobblestones") in the tarsal conjunctiva of a patient with vernal conjunctivitis.

vernal conjunctivitis—there is heavy papillary infiltration by mononuclear cells. Hay fever and asthma occur much more frequently in patients with vernal conjunctivitis and atopic keratoconjunctivitis than in the general population. Of the criteria outlined above (see p 663) for demonstration of *possible* antibody-mediated diseases, (2), (5), and (6) have been met by atopic keratoconjunctivitis.

Immunologic Diagnosis

As in hay fever conjunctivitis, patients with atopic keratoconjunctivitis and vernal conjunctivitis regularly show large numbers of eosinophils in conjunctival scrapings. Skin testing with food extracts, pollens, and various other antigens reveals a wheal-and-flare type of reaction within 1 hour of testing, but the significance of these reactions is not reliably established.

Treatment

Local instillations of corticosteroid drops or ointment relieve the symptoms. However, caution must be observed in the long-term use of these agents because of the possibility of steroid-induced glaucoma and cataract. Corticosteroids produce less dramatic relief in vernal conjunctivitis than in atopic keratoconjunctivitis, and the same can be said of the antihistamines. Cromolyn is currently being investigated for its usefulness in both vernal conjunctivitis and atopic disease. The initial results of clinical testing are encouraging.

Avoidance of known allergens is helpful; such objects as duck feathers, animal danders, and certain food proteins (egg albumin and others) are common offenders. Specific allergens have been much more difficult to demonstrate in the case of vernal disease, although some workers feel that such substances as rye grass pollens may play a causative role. Installation of air conditioning in the home or relocation to a cool, moist climate is useful in vernal conjunctivitis if economically feasible.

RHEUMATOID DISEASES AFFECTING THE EYE

The diseases in this category vary greatly in their clinical manifestations depending upon the specific disease entity and the age of the patient. Uveitis and scleritis are the principal ocular manifestations of the rheumatoid diseases. **Juvenile rheumatoid arthritis** affects females more frequently than males and is commonly accompanied by iridocyclitis of one or both eyes. The onset is often insidious, the patient having few or no complaints and the eye remaining white. Extensive synechia formation, cataract, and secondary glaucoma may be far-advanced before the parents notice that anything is wrong. The arthritis generally affects only one joint (eg, a knee) in cases with ocular involvement.

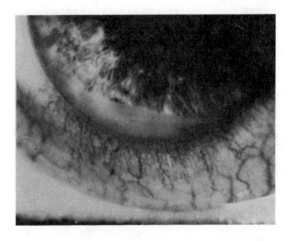

Figure 36–3. Acute iridocyclitis in a patient with ankylosing spondylitis. Note fibrin clot in anterior chamber.

Ankylosing spondylitis affects males more frequently than females, and the onset is in the second to sixth decades. It may be accompanied by iridocyclitis of acute onset, often with fibrin in the anterior chamber (Fig 36–3). Pain, redness, and photophobia are the initial complaints, and synechia formation is common.

Rheumatoid arthritis of adult onset may be accompanied by acute scleritis or episcleritis (Fig 36–4). The ciliary body and choroid, lying adjacent to the sclera, are often involved secondarily with the inflammation. Rarely, serous detachment of the retina results. The onset is usually in the third to fifth decade, and women are affected more frequently than men.

Reiter's disease affects men more frequently than women. The first attack of ocular inflammation usually consists of a self-limited papillary conjunctivitis. It follows, at a highly variable interval, the onset of nonspecific urethritis and the appearance of inflammation in one or more of the weight-bearing joints. Subsequent attacks of ocular inflammation may

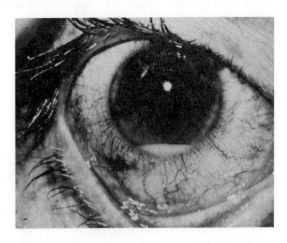

Figure 36–4. Scleral nodules in a patient with rheumatoid arthritis. (Courtesy of S Kimura.)

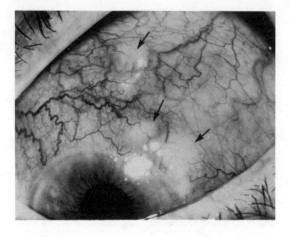

Figure 36–5. Acute iridocyclitis with hypopyon in a patient with Reiter's disease.

consist of acute iridocyclitis of one or both eyes, occasionally with hypopyon (Fig 36–5).

Immunologic Pathogenesis

Rheumatoid factor, an IgM autoantibody directed against the patient's own IgG, may play a major role in the pathogenesis of rheumatoid arthritis. The union of IgM antibody with IgG is followed by fixation of complement at the tissue site and the attraction of leukocytes and platelets to this area. An occlusive vasculitis, resulting from this train of events, is thought to be the cause of rheumatoid nodule formation in the sclera as well as elsewhere in the body. The occlusion of vessels supplying nutriments to the sclera is thought to be responsible for the "melting away" of the scleral collagen that is so characteristic of rheumatoid arthritis (Fig 36–6).

While this explanation may suffice for rheumatoid arthritis, patients with the ocular complications of juvenile rheumatoid arthritis, ankylosing spondylitis, and Reiter's syndrome usually have negative tests for

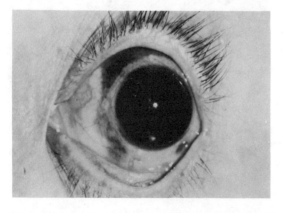

Figure 36–6. Scleral thinning in a patient with rheumatoid arthritis. Note dark color of the underlying uvea.

rheumatoid factor, so other explanations must be sought.

Outside the eyeball itself, the lacrimal gland has been shown to be under attack by circulating antibodies. Destruction of acinar cells within the gland and invasion of the lacrimal gland (as well as the salivary glands) by mononuclear cells result in decreased tear secretion. The combination of dry eyes (keratoconjunctivitis sicca), dry mouth (xerostomia), and rheumatoid arthritis is known as Sjögren's syndrome (see Chapter 38).

A growing body of evidence indicates that the immunogenetic background of certain patients accounts for the expression of their ocular inflammatory disease in specific ways. Analysis of the HLA antigen system shows that the incidence of HLA-B27 is significantly greater in patients with ankylosing spondylitis and Reiter's syndrome than could be expected by chance alone. It is not known how this antigen controls specific inflammatory responses.

Immunologic Diagnosis

Rheumatoid factor can be detected in the serum by a number of standard tests involving the agglutination of IgG-coated erythrocytes or latex particles. Unfortunately, the test for rheumatoid factor is not positive in the majority of isolated rheumatoid afflictions of the eye.

The HLA types of individuals suspected of having ankylosing spondylitis and related diseases can be determined by standard cytotoxicity tests using highly specific antisera. This is generally done in tissue typing centers where work on organ transplantation necessitates such studies. X-ray of the sacroiliac area is a valuable screening procedure that may show evidence of spondylitis prior to the onset of low back pain in patients with the characteristic form of iridocyclitis.

Treatment

Patients with uveitis associated with rheumatoid disease respond well to local instillations of corticosteroid drops (eg, dexamethasone 0.1%) or ointments. Orally administered corticosteroids must occasionally be resorted to for brief periods. Salicylates given orally in divided doses with meals are thought to reduce the frequency and blunt the severity of recurrent attacks. Atropine drops (1%) are useful for the relief of photophobia during the acute attacks. Shorter-acting mydriatics such as phenylephrine 10% should be used in the subacute stages to prevent synechia formation. Corticosteroid-resistant cases, especially those causing progressive erosion of the sclera, have been treated successfully with immunosuppressive agents such as chlorambucil.

OTHER ANTIBODY–MEDIATED EYE DISEASES

The following antibody-mediated diseases are infrequently seen by the practicing ophthalmologist.

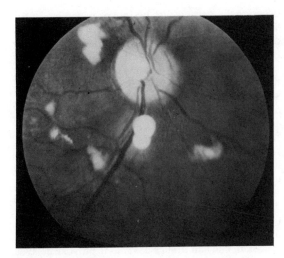

Figure 36–7. "Cotton wool" spots (cytoid bodies) in the retina of a patient with lupus erythematosus.

Systemic lupus erythematosus, associated with the presence of circulating antibodies to DNA, produces an occlusive vasculitis of the nerve fiber layer of the retina. Such infarcts result in cytoid bodies or "cotton wool" spots in the retina (Fig 36–7).

Pemphigus vulgaris produces painful intraepithelial bullae of the conjunctiva. It is associated with the presence of circulating antibodies to an intercellular antigen located between the deeper cells of the conjunctival epithelium.

Cicatricial pemphigoid is characterized by subepithelial bullae of the conjunctiva. In the chronic stages of this disease, cicatricial contraction of the conjunctiva may result in severe scarring of the cornea, dryness of the eyes, and ultimate blindness. Pemphigoid is associated with local deposits of tissue antibodies directed against one or more antigens located in the basement membrane of the epithelium.

Lens-induced uveitis is a rare condition that may be associated with circulating antibodies to lens proteins. It is seen in individuals whose lens capsules have become permeable to these proteins as a result of trauma or other disease. Interest in this field dates back to Uhlenhuth (1903), who first demonstrated the organ-specific nature of antibodies to the lens. Witmer showed in 1962 that antibody to lens tissue may be produced by lymphoid cells of the ciliary body.

CELL–MEDIATED DISEASES

This group of diseases appears to be associated with cell-mediated immunity or delayed hypersensitivity. Various structures of the eye are invaded by mononuclear cells, principally lymphocytes and macrophages, in response to one or more chronic antigenic stimuli. In the case of chronic infections such as tuberculosis, leprosy, toxoplasmosis, and herpes simplex, the antigenic stimulus has clearly been identified as an infectious agent in the ocular tissue. Such infections are often associated with delayed skin test reactivity following the intradermal injection of an extract of the organism.

More intriguing but less well understood are the granulomatous diseases of the eye for which no infectious cause has been found. Such diseases are thought to represent cell-mediated, possibly autoimmune processes, but their origin remains obscure.

OCULAR SARCOIDOSIS

Ocular sarcoidosis is characterized by a panuveitis with occasional inflammatory involvement of the optic nerve and retinal blood vessels. It often presents as iridocyclitis of insidious onset. Less frequently, it occurs as acute iridocyclitis, with pain, photophobia, and redness of the eye. Large precipitates resembling drops of solidified "mutton fat" are seen on the corneal endothelium. The anterior chamber contains a good deal of protein and numerous cells, mostly lymphocytes. Nodules are often seen on the iris, both at the pupillary margin and in the substance of the iris stroma. The latter are often vascularized. Synechiae are commonly encountered, particularly in patients with dark skin. Severe cases ultimately involve the posterior segment of the eye. Coarse clumps of cells ("snowballs") are seen in the vitreous, and exudates resembling candle drippings may be seen along the course of the retinal vessels. Patchy infiltrations of the choroid or optic nerve may also be seen.

Infiltrations of the lacrimal gland and of the conjunctiva have been noted on occasion. When the latter are present, the diagnosis can easily be confirmed by biopsy of the small opaque nodules.

Immunologic Pathogenesis

Although many infectious or allergic causes of sarcoidosis have been suggested, none has been confirmed. Noncaseating granulomas are seen in the uvea, optic nerve, and adnexal structures of the eye as well as elsewhere in the body. The presence of macrophages and giant cells suggests that particulate matter is being phagocytosed, but this material has not been identified.

Patients with sarcoidosis are usually anergic to extracts of the common microbial antigens such as those of mumps, *Trichophyton, Candida,* and *Mycobacterium tuberculosis.* As in other lymphoproliferative disorders such as Hodgkin's disease and chronic lymphocytic leukemia, this may represent suppression of T cell activity such that the normal delayed hypersensitivity responses to common antigens cannot take place. Meanwhile, circulating immunoglobulins are usually detectable in the serum at higher than normal levels.

Immunologic Diagnosis

The diagnosis is largely inferential. Negative skin

tests to a battery of antigens to which the patient is known to have been exposed are highly suggestive, and the same is true of the elevation of serum immunoglobulins. Biopsy of a conjunctival nodule or scalene lymph node may provide positive histologic evidence of the disease. X-rays of the chest reveal hilar adenopathy in many cases. Elevated levels of serum lysozyme or serum angiotensin converting enzyme may be detected.

Treatment

Sarcoid lesions of the eye respond well to corticosteroid therapy. Frequent instillations of dexamethasone 0.1% eyedrops generally bring the anterior uveitis under control. Atropine drops should be prescribed in the acute phase of the disease for the relief of pain and photophobia; short-acting pupillary dilators such as phenylephrine should be given later to prevent synechia formation. Systemic corticosteroids are sometimes necessary to control severe attacks of anterior uveitis and are always necessary for the control of retinal vasculitis and optic neuritis. The latter condition often accompanies cerebral involvement and carries a grave prognosis.

SYMPATHETIC OPHTHALMIA & VOGT–KOYANAGI–HARADA SYNDROME

These 2 disorders are discussed together because they have certain common clinical features. Both are thought to represent autoimmune phenomena affecting pigmented structures of the eye and skin, and both may give rise to meningeal symptoms.

Clinical Features

Sympathetic ophthalmia is an inflammation in the second eye after the other has been damaged by penetrating injury. In most cases, some portion of the uvea of the injured eye has been exposed to the atmosphere for at least 1 hour. The uninjured or "sympathizing" eye develops minor signs of anterior uveitis after a period ranging from 2 weeks to several years. Floating spots and loss of the power of accommodation are among the earliest symptoms. The disease may progress to severe iridocyclitis with pain and photophobia. Usually, however, the eye remains relatively quiet and painless while the inflammatory disease spreads around the entire uvea. Despite the presence of panuveitis, the retina usually remains uninvolved except for perivascular cuffing of the retinal vessels with inflammatory cells. Papilledema and secondary glaucoma may occur. The disease may be accompanied by vitiligo (patchy depigmentation of the skin) and poliosis (whitening) of the eyelashes.

Vogt-Koyanagi-Harada syndrome consists of inflammation of the uvea of one or both eyes characterized by acute iridocyclitis, patchy choroiditis, and serous detachment of the retina. It usually begins with an acute febrile episode with headache, dysacusis, and occasionally vertigo. Patchy loss or whitening of the scalp hair is described in the first few months of the disease. Vitiligo and poliosis are commonly present but are not essential for the diagnosis. Although the initial iridocyclitis may subside quickly, the course of the posterior disease is often indolent, with long-standing serous detachment of the retina and significant visual impairment.

Immunologic Pathogenesis

In both sympathetic ophthalmia and Vogt-Koyanagi-Harada syndrome, delayed hypersensitivity to melanin-containing structures is thought to occur. Although a viral cause has been suggested for both disorders, there is no convincing evidence of an infectious origin. It is postulated that some insult, infectious or otherwise, alters the pigmented structures of the eye, skin, and hair in such a way as to provoke delayed hypersensitivity responses to them. Soluble materials from the outer segments of the photoreceptor layer of the retina have recently been incriminated as possible autoantigens. Patients with Vogt-Koyanagi-Harada syndrome are usually Orientals, which suggests an immunogenetic predisposition to the disease.

Histologic sections of the traumatized eye from a patient with sympathetic ophthalmia may show uniform infiltration of most of the uvea by lymphocytes, epithelioid cells, and giant cells. The overlying retina is characteristically intact, but nests of epithelioid cells may protrude through the pigment epithelium of the retina, giving rise to **Dalen-Fuchs nodules.** The inflammation may destroy the architecture of the entire uvea, leaving an atrophic, shrunken globe.

Immunologic Diagnosis

Skin tests with soluble extracts of human or bovine uveal tissue are said to elicit delayed hypersensitivity responses in these patients. Several investigators have recently shown that cultured lymphocytes from patients with these 2 diseases undergo transformation to lymphoblasts in vitro when extracts of uvea or rod outer segments are added to the culture medium. Circulating antibodies to uveal antigens have been found in patients with these diseases, but such antibodies are to be found in any patient with longstanding uveitis, including those suffering from several infectious entities. The spinal fluid of patients with Vogt-Koyanagi-Harada syndrome may show increased numbers of mononuclear cells and elevated protein in the early stages.

Treatment

Mild cases of sympathetic ophthalmia may be treated satisfactorily with locally applied corticosteroid drops and pupillary dilators. The more severe or progressive cases require systemic corticosteroids, often in high doses, for months or years. An alternate-day regimen of oral corticosteroids is recommended for such patients in order to avoid adrenal suppression. The same applies to the treatment of patients with Vogt-Koyanagi-Harada disease. Occasionally, patients with long-standing progressive disease become resistant to corticosteroids or cannot take additional corticosteroid medication because of pathologic fractures, mental changes, or other reasons. Such patients may become candidates for immunosuppressive therapy. Chlorambucil has been used successfully for both conditions.

OTHER DISEASES OF CELL–MEDIATED IMMUNITY

Giant cell arteritis (temporal arteritis) (see Chapter 26) may have disastrous effects on the eye, particularly in elderly individuals. The condition is manifested by pain in the temples and orbit, blurred vision, and scotomas. Examination of the fundus may reveal extensive occlusive retinal vasculitis and choroidal infarcts. Atrophy of the optic nerve head is a frequent complication. Such patients have an elevated sedimentation rate. Biopsy of the temporal artery reveals extensive infiltration of the vessel wall with giant cells and mononuclear cells.

Polyarteritis nodosa (see Chapter 26) can affect both the anterior and posterior segments of the eye. The corneas of such patients may show peripheral thinning and cellular infiltration. The retinal vessels reveal extensive necrotizing inflammation characterized by eosinophil, plasma cell, and lymphocyte infiltration.

Behçet's disease (see Chapter 26) has an uncertain place in the classification of immunologic disorders. It is characterized by recurrent iridocyclitis with hypopyon and occlusive vasculitis of the retinal vessels. Although it has many of the features of a delayed hypersensitivity disease, dramatic alterations of serum complement levels at the very beginning of an attack suggest an immune complex disorder. Furthermore, high levels of circulating immune complexes have recently been detected in patients with this disease.

Contact dermatitis of the eyelids represents a significant though minor disease caused by delayed hypersensitivity. Atropine, perfumed cosmetics, materials contained in plastic spectacle frames, and other locally applied agents may act as the sensitizing hapten. The lower lid is more extensively involved than the upper lid when the sensitizing agent is applied in drop form. Periorbital involvement with erythematous, vesicular, pruritic lesions of the skin is characteristic.

Phlyctenular keratoconjunctivitis (Fig 36–8) represents a delayed hypersensitivity response to certain microbial antigens, principally those of *Mycobacterium tuberculosis*. It is characterized by acute pain and photophobia in the affected eye, and perforation of the peripheral cornea has been known to result from it. The disease responds rapidly to locally applied corticosteroids. Since the advent of chemotherapy for pulmonary tuberculosis, phlyctenulosis is much less of a problem than it was 30 years ago. It is still encountered

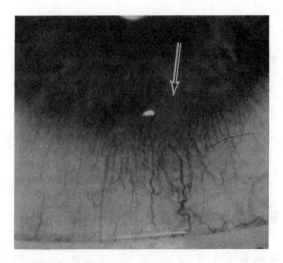

Figure 36–8. Phlyctenule (arrow) at the margin of the cornea. (Courtesy of P Thygeson.)

occasionally, however, particularly among American Indians and Alaskan Eskimos. Rarely, other pathogens such as *Staphylococcus aureus* and *Coccidioides immitis* have been implicated in phlyctenular disease.

CORNEAL GRAFT REACTIONS

Blindness due to opacity or distortion of the central portion of the cornea is a remediable disease. If all other structures of the eye are intact, a patient whose vision is impaired solely by corneal opacity can expect great improvement from a graft of clear cornea into the diseased area. Trauma, including chemical burns, is one of the most common causes of central corneal opacity. Others include scars from herpetic keratitis, endothelial cell dysfunction with chronic corneal edema (Fuchs's dystrophy), keratoconus, and opacities from previous graft failures. All of these conditions represent indications for penetrating corneal grafts, provided the patient's eye is no longer inflamed and the opacity has been allowed maximal time to undergo spontaneous resolution (usually 6–12 months). It is estimated that approximately 10,000 corneal grafts are performed in the USA annually. Of these, about 90% can be expected to produce a beneficial result.

The cornea was one of the first human tissues to be successfully grafted. The fact that recipients of corneal grafts generally tolerate them well can be attributed to (1) the absence of blood vessels or lymphatics in the normal cornea and (2) the lack of presensitization to tissue-specific antigens in most recipients. Reactions to corneal grafts do occur, however, particularly in individuals whose own corneas have been damaged by previous inflammatory disease. Such corneas may have developed both lymphatics and blood vessels, providing afferent and efferent channels for immunologic reactions in the engrafted cornea.

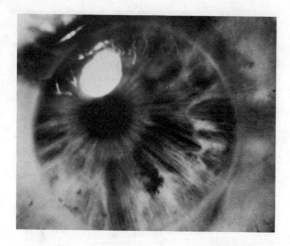

Figure 36–9. A cornea severely scarred by chronic atopic keratoconjunctivitis into which a central graft of clear cornea has been placed. Note how distinctly the iris landmarks are seen through the transparent graft.

Although attempts have been made to transplant corneas from other species into human eyes (xenografts), particularly in countries where human material is not available for religious reasons, most corneal grafts have been taken from human eyes (allografts). Except in the case of identical twins, such grafts always represent the implantation of foreign tissue into a donor site; thus, the chance for a graft rejection due to an immune response to foreign antigens is virtually always present.

The cornea is a 3-layered structure composed of a surface epithelium, an oligocellular collagenous stroma, and a single-layered endothelium. Although the surface epithelium may be sloughed and later replaced by the recipient's epithelium, certain elements of the stroma and all of the donor's endothelium remain in place for the rest of the patient's life. This has been firmly established by sex chromosome markers in corneal cells when donor and recipient were of opposite sexes. The endothelium must remain healthy in order for the cornea to remain transparent, and an energy-dependent pump mechanism is required to keep the cornea from swelling with water. Since the recipient's endothelium is in most cases diseased, the central corneal endothelium must be replaced by healthy donor tissue.

A number of foreign elements exist in corneal grafts that might stimulate the immune system of the host to reject this tissue. In addition to those mentioned above, the corneal stroma is regularly perfused with IgG and serum albumin from the donor, although none—or only small amounts—of the other blood proteins are present. While these serum proteins of donor origin rapidly diffuse into the recipient stroma, these substances are theoretically immunogenic.

Although the ABO blood antigens have been shown to have no relationship to corneal graft rejection, the HLA antigen system probably plays a sig-

nificant role in graft reactions. HLA incompatibility between donor and recipient has been shown by several authors to be significant in determining graft survival, particularly when the corneal bed is vascularized. It is known that most cells of the body possess these HLA antigens, including the endothelial cells of the corneal graft as well as certain stromal cells (keratocytes). The epithelium has been shown by Hall and others to possess a non-HLA antigen that diffuses into the anterior third of the stroma. Thus, while much foreign antigen may be eliminated by purposeful removal of the epithelium at the time of grafting, that amount of antigen which has already diffused into the stroma is automatically carried over into the recipient. Such antigens may be leached out by soaking the donor cornea in tissue culture for several weeks prior to engraftment.

Both humoral and cellular mechanisms have been implicated in corneal graft reactions. It is likely that early graft rejections (within 2 weeks) are cell-mediated reactions. Cytotoxic lymphocytes have been found in the limbal area and stroma of affected individuals, and phase microscopy in vivo has revealed an actual attack on the grafted endothelial cells by these lymphocytes. Such lymphocytes generally move inward from the periphery of the cornea, making what is known as a "rejection line" as they move centrally. The donor cornea becomes edematous as the endothelium becomes compromised by an accumulation of lymphoid cells.

Late rejection of a corneal graft may occur several weeks to many months after implantation of donor tissue into the recipient eye. Such reactions may be antibody-mediated, since cytotoxic antibodies have been isolated from the serum of patients with a history of multiple graft reactions in vascularized corneal beds. These antibody reactions are complement-dependent and attract polymorphonuclear leukocytes, which may form dense rings in the cornea at the sites of maximum deposition of immune complexes. In experimental animals, similar reactions have been produced by corneal xenografts, but the intensity of the reaction can be markedly reduced either by decomplementing the animal or by reducing its leukocyte population through mechlorethamine therapy.

Treatment

The mainstay of the treatment of corneal graft reactions is corticosteroid therapy. This medication is generally given in the form of frequently applied eye drops (eg, prednisolone acetate, 1%, hourly) until the clinical signs abate. These clinical signs consist of conjunctival hyperemia in the perilimbal region, a cloudy cornea, cells and protein in the anterior chamber, and keratic precipitates on the corneal endothelium. The earlier treatment is applied, the more effective it is likely to be. Neglected cases may require systemic corticosteroids (80–150 mg prednisone daily) in addition to local eye drop therapy. Occasionally, vascularization and opacification of the cornea occur so rapidly as to make corticosteroid therapy useless, but even the most hopeless-appearing graft reactions have occasionally been reversed by corticosteroid therapy.

Patients known to have rejected many previous corneal grafts are managed somewhat differently, particularly if disease affects their only remaining eye. An attempt is made to find a close HLA match between donor and recipient. Pretreatment of the recipient with immunosuppressive agents such as azathioprine has also been resorted to in some cases. Although HLA testing of the recipient and the potential donor is indicated in cases of repeated corneal graft failure or in cases of severe corneal vascularization, such testing is not necessary or practicable in most cases requiring keratoplasty.

•   •   •

References

Allansmith MR, O'Connor GR: Immunoglobulins: Structure, function, and relation to the eye. *Surv Ophthalmol* 1970; **14:**367.

Cogan DG: Immunosuppression and eye diseases. *Am J Ophthalmol* 1977;**83:**777.

Friedlaender MH: *Allergy and Immunology of the Eye.* Harper & Row, 1979.

Godfrey WA et al: The use of chlorambucil in intractable idiopathic uveitis. *Am J Ophthalmol* 1974;**78:**415.

Helmsen RJ et al: *Immunology of the Eye. Workshop II: Autoimmune Phenomena and Ocular Disorders.* Information Retrieval, Inc., Washington, DC, 1981.

O'Connor GR (editor): *Immunologic Diseases of the Mucous Membranes.* Masson Publishing USA, 1980.

O'Connor GR: Uveitis and the immunologically compromised host. *N Engl J Med* 1978;**299:**130.

Silverstein AM, O'Connor GR (editors): *Immunology and Immunopathology of the Eye.* Masson Publishing USA, 1978.

Smolin G, O'Connor GR: *Ocular Immunology.* Lea & Febiger, 1981.

Witmer R: Phaco-antigenic uveitis. *Doc Ophthalmol* 1962; **16:**271.

Wong VG, Anderson RR, McMaster PRB: Endogenous immune uveitis. *Arch Ophthalmol* 1971;**85:**93.

37 | Parasitic Diseases

Donald Heyneman, PhD

Parasitic diseases such as malaria, schistosomiasis, and trypanosomiasis are among the most important causes of morbidity and mortality in developing countries. Because vector control and chemotherapy have failed to eradicate these diseases, WHO/UNDP/World Bank are undertaking a long-term Special Programme for Research and Training in Tropical Diseases, in which development of immunization procedures plays an important role. Rapid and frequent travel to all parts of the globe now makes the solution to the problem of parasitic disease imperative. However, better understanding of the immune response to parasites must precede any program intended to develop effective immunization procedures. At present, technologic limits preclude any program for immunologic control of parasites except for local and largely experimental efforts.

Immune responses to the complex antigenic structures of parasites have diverse manifestations. For example, immunity with specific protection to reinfection occurs after primary infection with cutaneous leishmaniasis; in falciparum malaria, partial protection against recurrent infection results from persistent low levels of parasitemia, which stimulate production of protective antibody. Disease can result from the immune response itself, as in the cellular response which produces hepatic granulomas in schistosomiasis (Boros, 1978)*, antigen-antibody complex glomerulonephritis in quartan malaria, or antibody-mediated anaphylactic shock from a ruptured hydatid cyst. Alternatively, protection can be subverted by the ability of a parasite to disguise itself as "self" with host antigens, as occurs in schistosomiasis, or to produce successive waves of progeny with different surface antigens, as in African trypanosomiasis. The ability of parasites to adapt to the host environment is the essence of successful parasitism, but it increases immeasurably the difficulty of developing immunization procedures against parasitic infection (Wakelin, 1978).

These varied host or parasite responses require that the host-parasite relationship be elucidated in order to detect when in the life cycle of the parasite the immune responses of the host may be exploited in the host's favor. Some progress in this area has already been made as a consequence of the increased interest of immunologists in parasitic disease and of parasitologists in immune phenomena. However, parasite antigens are exceedingly complex, and the immune responses to them form complicated mosaics. When animals respond to the multiple determinants present in these antigens, it is difficult to distinguish which determinants induce humoral or cellular responses, which produce protection, which cause disease in the host, and which possess little or no clinical significance but are of importance in diagnosis.

Substantial new interest and research by immunologists and parasitologists give promise of significant advances in parasite immunology within the next few years. Particular efforts are under way in malaria and schistosomiasis to develop prophylactic or therapeutic vaccines (Taylor et al, 1976). The latter disease has also yielded important new knowledge on the role of the eosinophil and humoral factors in the destruction of invading schistosomules (Kassis et al, 1979; McLaren et al, 1979; von Lichtenberg et al, 1976). Serodiagnostic techniques have also undergone significant recent improvement in specificity and sensitivity. For specific tests and procedural details, readers are referred to Kagan (1980), Kagan and Norman (1979), and Walls and Smith (1979). Many of these tests are available for physicians' use from the Centers for Disease Control, Division of Parasitic Diseases, Atlanta, GA 30333. Methodology and findings in the development of new survey tools in seroepidemiology have been reviewed by Lobel and Kagan (1978). A chart of available serodiagnostic procedures is shown in Table 37–1 and the routine tests run at Centers for Disease Control in Table 37–2. An extremely useful epidemiologic tool, blood sampling on filter paper, is now well developed (Matthews, 1981).

THE IMMUNE RESPONSE TO PROTOZOA

Protozoa are important agents of worldwide disease. Falciparum malaria, for example, is still thought to be one of the most lethal diseases in hu-

*Writings referred to in the text are grouped by subject on p 686.

Table 37—1. Immunodiagnostic tests for parasitic diseases.*

Parasitic Diseases	Complement Fixation	Agglutination Tests				Indirect Immunofluorescence	Immunodiffusion	Immunoelectrophoresis	Countercurrent Electrophoresis	ELISA	Intradermal
		Bentonite Flocculation	Indirect Hemagglutination	Latex	Special Agglutination						
Amebiasis	■	▲	■	▲	O^A	■	■	■	▲	O	▲
Chagas' disease	■		■	▲	▲^A	■	O	▲	O	▲	O
African trypanosomiasis	▲		O		O^C	▲	▲			O	
Visceral leishmaniasis	■		■	O	▲^A	▲	O	O			■
Malaria	▲		■	▲		■	■	O	O	O	
Pneumocystosis	■			O		■					
Toxoplasmosis	■		■	O		■	O			O	▲
Ancylostomiasis	O		■	▲		O		O			▲
Ascariasis	O	■	■			▲	▲	O		O	▲
Clonorchiasis	■		■					O			■
Cysticercosis	▲		▲	▲		▲	▲	O	O		O
Echinococcosis	■	■	■	▲		■	▲	■	O	O	■
Fascioliasis	■	O	■	▲		▲	O	O	O		▲
Filariasis	▲	■	■	O		■		O			▲
Paragonimiasis	■	O	O				O	O			■
Strongyloidiasis			■			▲					
Schistosomiasis	■	▲	■	O	■^C	■	▲	O		O	▲
Toxocariasis	O	■	■			▲	O	O		O	▲
Trichinellosis	■	■	■	■	■^B	■	▲	▲	O	▲	■

*Reproduced, with permission, from Kagan IG, Norman LG: Immune response to infection: Parasitic. Pages 165–185 in: Immunology. Section F, Vol 1, Part 2 of: *CRC Handbook Series in Clinical Laboratory Science.* Seligson D (editor). ©The Chemical Rubber Co., CRC Press, Inc.

Legend:

■ = Evaluated test   ▲ = Experimental test   O = Reported in the literature

Special agglutination tests:

A = Direct agglutination   B = Cholesterol agglutination   C = Charcoal agglutination

Table 37—2. Serologic tests for the diagnosis of parasitic diseases performed in the Parasitology Division of the Centers for Disease Control.*

Diseases	Tests	Diagnostic Titers
Amebiasis	IHA	≥1:128
Chagas' disease	CF, DA, IHA	≥1:32, ≥1:128, ≥1:128
Leishmaniasis	IHA, DA	≥1:64, ≥1:64
Malaria	IIF	≥1:64
Pneumocystosis	DIF	≥1:16
Toxoplasmosis	DIF, (IgM-IIF), IHA	≥1:256, ≥1:16, ≥1:128
Ascariasis	IHA, BF	≥1:128, ≥1:5
Filariasis	IHA, BF	≥1:128, ≥1:5
Toxocariasis	IHA, BF	≥1:128, ≥1:5
Strongyloidiasis	IHA	≥1:64
Trichinellosis	BFT	≥1:5
Paragonimiasis	CF	≥1:16
Schistosomiasis	CF, IIF	≥1:8, ≥1:16
Cysticercosis	IHA, BF	≥1:128, ≥1:5
Echinococcosis	IHA, BF	≥1:128, ≥1:5

IHA = indirect hemagglutination; CF = complement fixation; DA = direct agglutination; DIF = direct immunofluorescence; IIF = indirect immunofluorescence; BF = bentonite flocculation.

*Reproduced, with permission, from Desowitz RS: *Ova and Parasites. Medical Parasitology for the Laboratory Technologist.* Harper & Row, 1980.

mans, in spite of massive efforts at its eradication and control. These parasites also offer unlimited immunologic challenges, the immune responses induced being as diverse as the protozoa themselves. In developing countries, especially in Africa, malaria and trypanosomiasis take enormous tolls of life and are significant barriers to development, survival of domestic animals, and human occupation of vast grazing lands. Amebiasis, giardiasis, and toxoplasmosis are widespread even in highly developed countries. The use of immunosuppressive drugs to treat cancer and to prevent rejection of transplanted organs has resulted in activation of otherwise subclinical infections with protozoa such as *Toxoplasma* and *Pneumocystis*. In some instances, deaths have been caused by these infections rather than by the underlying illness for which treatment was being given.

MALARIA

Major Immunologic Features

- Species-specific protective IgG antibody produced against merozoites after multiple infections.
- High serum immunoglobulin levels in endemic areas due only partly to malaria itself.
- Immunosuppression of other antigens during course of disease.
- Parasites display antigenic variation.
- Great variety of humoral antibodies elicited as well as increased reticuloendothelial activities.
- Complex state of partial immunity induced after many years and multiple exposures, involving humoral and cellular, specific and nonspecific, hereditary and acquired characteristics, as well as the effect of a current low-level infection on a challenge infection: premunition.

Human malaria is caused by species of the genus *Plasmodium*. It is transmitted by female anopheline mosquitoes that ingest the sexual forms of the parasite in blood meals. The infective sporozoites develop in the mosquito and are injected into the definitive host when bitten by the insect. In the definitive host, the parasites first develop in an exoerythrocytic form, multiplying within hepatic cells without inducing an inflammatory reaction. The resulting merozoites invade host erythrocytes to begin the erythrocytic cycle and initiate the earliest phase of clinical malaria. Destruction of red cells occurs on a 48-hour cycle with *Plasmodium vivax, Plasmodium ovale,* and *Plasmodium falciparum* and every 72 hours with *Plasmodium malariae*. The characteristic chills-fever-sweat malarial syndrome follows this cyclic pattern, being induced by synchronous rupture of infected red cells by the mature asexual forms (schizonts), releasing merozoites that quickly invade new red cells. In contrast to the exoerythrocytic stage, these erythrocytic merozoites induce an array of humoral responses in the host, as demonstrated by complement fixation, precipitation, agglutination, and fluorescent antibody reactions.

Relapse results from periodic (perhaps genetically determined) release of infective merozoites from the liver, which lacks an immune response to the intracellular parasites. When the erythrocytic cellular and humoral protection is deficient (from concurrent infection, age, trauma, or other debilitating factors), relapse of clinical malaria occurs until the erythrocytic cycle is again controlled by a humoral and thymus-dependent cell-mediated host response. True relapse, as opposed to a delayed exoerythrocytic cycle or a recrudescence of erythrocytic infection, generally will occur for up to 5 years with *P vivax* and possibly 2–3 years for *P ovale*. *P malariae* appears to recur only as a recrudescent erythrocytic infection, sometimes lasting 30 or more years after the primary infection. *P falciparum* may have a short-term recrudescence and also does not develop a true relapse from liver-developed merozoites.

Blackwater fever, formerly a common and highly fatal form of falciparum malaria among colonists in Africa, has declined in frequency with reduction in quinine therapy. It is associated with repeated falciparum infection, inadequate quinine therapy, and possibly genetic factors more frequently found in whites. The resulting rapid, massive hemolysis of both infected and uninfected red cells is thought to result from autoantibodies from previous infections that react with autoantigens (perhaps a red cell–parasite–quinine combination) derived from a new infection with the same falciparum strain. With increased use of quinine to prevent or treat chloroquine-resistant falciparum malaria, blackwater fever may increase in frequency in coming years.

Quartan malaria in African children has been associated with a serious antigen-antibody immune complex glomerulonephritis and nephrosis, resulting in edema and severe kidney damage unless the disease is arrested early. After loss of the edema, persistent symptomless proteinuria or slowly deteriorating renal function is common. Stable remission with corticosteroid therapy occurs when proteinuria is restricted to only a few classes of protein and histologic changes are minimal. But patients with poorly controlled generalized proteinuria are probably not benefited by antimalarial or immunosuppressive therapy. According to Allison and Houba (in Cohen and Sadun, 1976), chronic *P malariae* infection probably triggers an autoimmune mechanism perpetuating the immune complex glomerulonephritis, but the antigen involved is not yet identified.

Innate, nonacquired immunity to malaria is well demonstrated. African or American blacks lacking Duffy blood group antigen are immune to *P vivax*, as this genetic factor appears to be necessary for successful merozoite penetration of the human red cell by this plasmodial species (Miller et al, 1976). Intracellular growth of the malaria parasites is also affected by the hemoglobin molecular structure. Sickle cell (SS) hemoglobin inhibits growth of *P falciparum*.

This genetic factor is widespread in areas of Africa hyperendemic for falciparum malaria. Though prevalence of infection appears unaffected by the sickling trait, *severe* infections are very much reduced compared with those in nonsickling homozygote individuals. Similarly, *P falciparum* growth is retarded in red cells with the fetal hemoglobin (F)—hence the selective advantage of β-thalassemia heterozygotes, in whom postnatal hemoglobin F declines at a lower than normal rate. Other red cell abnormalities such as glucose-6-phosphate dehydrogenase deficiency appear on epidemiologic grounds to be protective of the red cell and reduce the severity of plasmodial infection.

Both acquired and innate specific or nonspecific resistance to malaria is influenced by a number of genetic traits that reflect strong selective pressure in areas with specific mosquito-human-*Plasmodium* combinations. Though we have much to learn about expressions and mechanisms of malaria resistance from rodent and monkey malaria studies, direct application to humans or broad generalizations about acquired or natural immunity cannot be readily drawn from these host-parasite experiments. A very gradual long-term resistance to hyperendemic falciparum malaria is acquired in African populations. The resistance develops years after the onset of severe disease among nearly all children over 3 months of age. Initial passive protection is present owing to transplacental maternal IgG. There are estimates of a million malaria deaths a year in Africa, chiefly among children under 5. Nonetheless, even after surviving this, a large proportion of adults remain susceptible to infection and show periodic parasitemia, while their serum contains antiplasmodial antibodies, some with demonstrated protective action. Susceptibility to low-level infection provides the population with a protective **premunition** or prevention of subsequent infection during the course of a chronic asymptomatic current infection. In these hyperendemic areas of Africa, it is believed that nearly all residents harbor throughout their lives a continuous series of falciparum infections of low to moderate pathogenicity. The immune response that leads to protection is thought to be production of complement-independent antibody that inhibits entry of merozoites into the host erythrocytes. All immunoglobulin classes are elevated in the serum of malaria patients, but IgG levels appear to correlate best with the degree of malaria protection (or control of acute manifestations).

By various protective adaptations (eg, antigenic variability), the parasites survive and—by reason of a limited level of red cell destruction—elicit only a mild host response. Therefore, innate and acquired protective host responses (specific and nonspecific) and parasite counteradaptations to these host characteristics occur. In addition, vector biology and population fluctuation, as well as the parasite's response to varied ecologic conditions (such as a required ambient temperature for successful development of the sporogonic cycle in the mosquito), add to the vagaries of differential host/parasite survival. They combine to determine the host-parasite-environment balance in which each of the many patterns of human malaria exists.

Immunization has become a major focus of malaria research, accelerating with Trager and Jensen's breakthrough in 1976 of a continuous culture method for producing red cell asexual stages in vitro (Reese et al, 1978). Two approaches have been followed: (1) induction of immunity using sporozoites inactivated by ultraviolet light, formalin, or mechanical disruption; and (2) the use of frozen or stored merozoites (which are spontaneously inactivated in 1 hour, so that special treatment is unnecessary). The first method induces a short-term thymus-dependent species- and strain-specific immunity active only against the sporozoite-induced infection. Recent development of this approach (by Nussenzweig and co-workers) involves use of sporozoites dissected from irradiated mosquitoes or by inoculation through the bite of irradiated mosquitoes. Only mature infective sporozoites are immunogenic; adjuvants appear to be unnecessary. This method is limited by the difficulty in storing the vaccine; inability to culture and therefore obtain large amounts of immunizing antigen; the requirement of intravenous administration of the vaccine; and the continuing susceptibility of the immunized person to a merozoite infection (should any sporozoites succeed in developing in the liver).

The second approach—a killed or inactivated merozoite vaccine—induces an antibody that reacts with the red cell surface and selectively agglutinates infected red cells to produce a strain- and species-specific clinical cure. New infections can still develop, since there is no protection against sporozoites or the exoerythrocytic cycle. So long as the humoral titer is high, however, merozoites (but not gametocytes) will be destroyed, and symptoms will not develop. Rhesus monkeys vaccinated with *P knowlesi* merozoites, which normally are quickly killed by this form of malaria, were fully protected for 18 months. Freund's complete adjuvant is required—a major deterrent to development of a human vaccine. More recent studies (Reese et al, 1978), using karyotype-selected *Aotus* monkeys infected with human *P falciparum*, showed significant prolongation of life in owl monkeys vaccinated with parasite material cultivated in vitro for over a year when the synthetic adjuvant muramyl dipeptide was used instead of Freund's adjuvant. In the rhesus monkey immunization studies, helper T cells, other cell-mediated effector mechanisms, and humoral antibody are involved. Extracellular merozoites are specifically inhibited by IgG and IgM in the absence of complement. Immunization in rhesus monkeys induces complete elimination of parasites after 1–3 weeks, whereas natural immunity following repeated infection and drug cure is associated with chronic relapsing parasitemia. Immunization probably is associated with far fewer soluble circulating antigens than natural infection, which preferentially stimulates suppressor cells or lymphocyte mitogens, all of which favor parasite survival. Difficulties of immunization with a merozoite vaccine even with a nontoxic adjuvant include the risk of contamination of the merozoite vaccine with blood group substances acquired during its cultivation, and substantial potential problems of vaccine delivery, cost, and acceptance. Nonetheless, the possibility of a prophylactic or therapeutic merozoite vaccine is most promising, and the extraordinarily complex immunity induced by malaria remains an instructive and important challenge (Miller, 1977; Cohen, 1977; Cohen and Mitchell, 1978; Cohen, 1979). An excellent volume of reviews of malaria immunology is presented in Kreier (1980).

AMEBIASIS

Major Immunologic Features
- Specific antibody detectable following tissue infection.
- Skin tests for immediate and delayed hypersensitivity indicate past or present disease.
- Delayed hypersensitivity depressed with liver abscess.

Immunity to amebiasis in humans remains unproved, though acquired immunity has been demonstrated in experimental animals, including dogs, hamsters, and guinea pigs—all unnatural hosts. Cases of repeated infection and repeated intestinal lesions in humans are common, even in the presence of high titers of circulating antibody. Antibodies of the IgG and IgM classes can be demonstrated by passive hemagglutination, precipitation, latex agglutination, and fluorescent antibody techniques. These antibodies can be used for diagnosis. However, the presence of specific antibody does not necessarily indicate active infection but rather an exposure to the organism at some time. Skin tests give immediate responses in many patients, indicating IgE production, and Arthus reactions can also be demonstrated. To date, there is little direct evidence that immunoglobulin is protective.

Cell-mediated immunity to *Entamoeba histolytica* antigens can be demonstrated by delayed hypersensitivity skin tests in many patients who do not have clinically evident disease, and recent evidence indicates that patients with amebic abscess of the liver have depressed cell-mediated immunity to amebic antigens while retaining their ability to respond to other skin test antigens such as streptokinase-streptodornase. Cell-mediated immunity returns after treatment for liver abscesses, and there is usually no recurrence of infection. It is not known whether this is due to protective immunity. Other normally nonpathogenic amebas such as *Naegleria* or *Acanthamoeba* can invade the central nervous system and cause rapid death due to meningoencephalitis *(Naegleria)* or local lesions in the throat or on the skin which may finally involve the central nervous system and produce death *(Acanthamoeba)*. Probably little immune response to *Naegleria* occurs, owing to the short lives of infected patients; however, *Acanthamoeba* may induce an immune re-

sponse because of the duration of infection. No protective immune mechanisms to these parasites have been demonstrated. Diagnosis can be made from infected tissues by fluorescent antibody staining of the parasites. Amebiasis serodiagnosis can be performed by a number of techniques, including newer procedures such as counterelectrophoresis (Hillyer and Kagan, 1980) and gel diffusion precipitin (Patterson et al, 1980). The 11 serodiagnostic tests currently available are reviewed by Kagan and Norman (1979) and Kagan (1980).

LEISHMANIASIS

Leishmania is a genus of obligate intracellular parasites that infect macrophages of the skin and viscera to produce disease in both animals and humans (Lewis and Peters, 1977). Sandflies, the principal vector, introduce the parasites into the host while taking blood meals.

A range of host responses interact with a number of parasite leishmanial species and strains to produce a panoply of pathologic and immunologic responses. Only in recent years have some of the factors responsible for the variety of disease manifestations and degrees of immunity to leishmaniasis been elucidated in experimental and clinical studies. For an excellent review of this complex topic, the reader is referred to Preston and Dumonde's comprehensive review (in Cohen and Sadun, 1976).

1. CUTANEOUS LEISHMANIASIS

Major Immunologic Features
- Delayed hypersensitivity present.
- Little or no specific antibody.

Old World cutaneous leishmaniasis, or tropical sore, which is caused by various distinct strains of *Leishmania tropica,* results in an immune response characterized by little antibody but strong cell-mediated immunity. In cutaneous leishmaniasis, it is the patient's immune response to the infection that primarily determines the form taken by the clinical disease; however, the strain of parasite may also determine part of the host response. If the patient mounts an adequate but not excessive cell-mediated immune response to the parasite, healing of the lesions and solid protection result. However, if cell-mediated immunity to the parasite is inadequate, the result may be diffuse cutaneous leishmaniasis, a disseminated disease in which there is little chance of spontaneous cure. On the other hand, an excessive cell-mediated immune response produces lupoid or recidiva leishmaniasis, in which nonulcerated lymphoid nodules form at the edge of the primary lesion; these lesions persist indefinitely, although parasites are not easily demonstrated. Thus, a spectrum of host responses to cutaneous leishmaniasis exists, as in leprosy, ranging from multiple disseminated parasite-filled ulcers (anergic response), to single, spontaneously cured immunizing sores, to recidiva hyperactive host responses with few or no parasites (allergic response). Parasite strain differences in virulence and other characteristics add to the complexity of the host-parasite interaction, resulting in prolonged disease or cure with immunity.

Delayed hypersensitivity ordinarily occurs early during the course of cutaneous leishmaniasis; nevertheless, new lesions can develop for several months. Secondary lesions quickly assume the histologic picture of the early lesions (the isophasic reaction) and usually heal at the same time as the primary lesion or shortly thereafter. Protection appears to be permanent after a primary infection has terminated naturally, although immunosuppressive treatment of patients residing in endemic areas has resulted in reinfection in previously protected individuals. It is not known whether this is due to new infection or to recrudescence of the old disease. If excision is used to terminate the primary infection before spontaneous healing has taken place, protection against reinfection may not occur. Animal experiments indicate that sensitized lymphocytes are widely distributed when the lesion heals. Thereafter, new disease cannot occur, presumably because immune lymphocytes are generally distributed in lymph nodes and spleen. Reinfection is usually manifested by a prolonged delayed hypersensitivity response at the site of the sandfly bite, but ulceration does not follow. Vaccination with virulent strains of the parasite is a common practice for cosmetic protection and to assure uninterrupted work in highly endemic areas, as in parts of southern USSR and Israel. "Vaccination" against these forms of *L tropica* is a full, lesion-producing infection in a selected skin area. Avirulent, modified, or dead parasites will not induce a protective response. In fact, only the most virulent strains will protect against the same and other strains; less virulent forms protect only against reexposure to the same strain.

Cell-mediated and humoral immune responses may act together to produce protection after initial infection.

2. VISCERAL LEISHMANIASIS

Major Immunologic Features
- Delayed hypersensitivity only after spontaneous recovery or chemotherapy.
- Increased nonspecific immunoglobulin levels.

The immune response to visceral leishmaniasis (kala-azar)—caused by various strains of *Leishmania donovani* (considered separate species by some authors)—is remarkably different from that of cutaneous leishmaniasis, although the parasites are morphologically indistinguishable. Massive polyclonal hypergammaglobulinemia with little or no evidence of cell-mediated immunity is the rule in visceral leishmaniasis. There is no quantitative relationship between the elevated serum immunoglobulin and antiparasite antibodies, which are, moreover, not species-specific. The elevated immunoglobulin diminishes rapidly when treatment begins. Delayed cutaneous hypersensitivity to parasite antigens becomes demonstrable only after spontaneous recovery or treatment, which suggests that cell-mediated mechanisms play a role in the resolution of the infectious process. Under certain circumstances, post–kala-azar dermal "leishmanoid" occurs. Nodules containing many parasites form papules as a result of incomplete or defective cell-mediated immunity, or a persistent allergic reaction to parasite antigens. Most cases have been reported from India, developing 6 months to 2 years after cure of kala-azar. Insufficient data are available at this time to establish exact correlation between delayed hypersensitivity and protection. Serodiagnosis is readily available by indirect hemagglutination, immunofluorescence, complement fixation, and direct agglutination.

3. AMERICAN LEISHMANIASIS

Major Immunologic Features
- Positive delayed hypersensitivity.
- Increased immunoglobulin levels.
- Anergic type of host response.

Cutaneous leishmaniasis of the New World is caused by a number of leishmanial pathogens now divided into 2 species complexes: *Leishmania mexicana* (subdivided into 3 or more species) and *Leishmania braziliensis* (subdivided into 3 or more species). The parasite species are distinguished on the basis of growth characteristics, isoenzymes, and DNA buoyant density, and subspecies by geographic factors, hosts, and the disease produced in humans. The most significant clinical distinction in the *L mexicana* complex is the high frequency of ear cartilage lesions (chiclero ulcer) and rare diffuse cutaneous leishmaniasis; in the *L braziliensis* complex, the development of metastatic lesions, usually within 5 years of healing of the initial ulcer, which itself may be large, persistent, and disfiguring. Nasal cartilage and other nasopharyngeal tissues are attacked and destroyed by this subsequent massive ulceration (espundia), which may erode away much of the face and cause death by septic bronchopneumonia, asphyxiation, or starvation. This manifestation of American leishmaniasis is frequently nonresponsive to treatment. Parasites are abundant in the early stages of espundia but subsequently are rare, while persistent infiltration of giant cells, plasma cells, and lymphocytes is characteristic. Delayed and perhaps immediate hypersensitivity and circulating antibody levels are higher in espundia than in cases of the primary lesion alone. The mucocutaneous form is thought to be an allergic or abnormal immunologic manifestation of infection with the type subspecies *L b braziliensis*. Both host and parasite genetic factors—

as well as vector characteristics—appear to be involved in this additional example of the interaction between immunogenicity of the parasite and immunologic response of the host.

A skin test (Montenegro test) is rapidly positive with cutaneous leishmaniasis, particularly the New World forms. Dermal response to kala-azar is slower, becoming positive only after cure of the visceral infection.

TOXOPLASMOSIS

Major Immunologic Features
- Sabin-Feldman dye test positive.
- Specific antibody present.
- Nonspecific increase in serum immunoglobulins.
- Natural acquired immunity widespread; cell-mediated immunity probably the major means, aided by humoral factors.

Toxoplasma infection in humans is generally asymptomatic; it has been estimated that as much as 40% of the adult population in the world is infected, as well as all species of mammals that have been tested for the presence of this ubiquitous parasite. Clinical disease, which develops in only a small fraction of those infected, ranges from benign lymphadenopathy to an acute and often fatal infection of the central nervous system. The developing fetus and the aged or otherwise immunologically compromised host are most vulnerable to the pathologic expression of massive infection and resulting encystation in the eye or brain. Damage to the neonate is greatest during the first trimester, when the central nervous system is being organized, and nearly all such instances end in fetal death. Infection of the mother during the second trimester may produce hydrocephaly, blindness, or varying lesser degrees of neurologic damage. Most cases of neonatal infection occur during the third trimester, resulting in chorioretinitis or other ophthalmic damage, reduced learning capacity or other expression of central nervous system deficit, or asymptomatic latent infection that may become clinically apparent years later. Women exposed *before* pregnancy—as indicated by a positive indirect immunofluorescent or Sabin-Feldman dye test—are thought to be unable to transmit the infection in utero.

Many potential sources of infection have been proposed, including partially cooked infected meat or oocysts shed from infected cats, but these cannot account for such large numbers of infections. The major reservoirs of infection are as yet unknown. *Toxoplasma* infection usually occurs through the gastrointestinal tract, and the protozoa can apparently penetrate and proliferate in virtually every cell in the body, though very rarely in mature red cells, forming cysts that remain viable for long periods. Following a cellular and humoral immune response, only encysted parasites can survive.

Toxoplasma infection results in production of IgA, IgG, and IgM antibodies, which can readily be demonstrated by hemagglutination, complement fixation, indirect fluorescent antibody techniques, and the Sabin-Feldman dye test (see Tables 37–1 and 37–2). The mere presence of antibody is not sufficient for protection, as shown by the ability of the parasite to persist in the presence of high antibody titers and by the fact that passive transfer of antibody is not protective.

Recent work has shown that the ability of macrophages to kill infective trophozoites is greatly increased if the parasites are first exposed to antibody and complement. This mechanism may be one way that parasite numbers are reduced in the infected host. It has been shown that the parasite can multiply only to a certain number within macrophages before the host cells are destroyed and that when this occurs, extracellular trophozoites come into contact with antibody and may be more efficiently killed by macrophages than before.

Cell-mediated immunity is also involved in protection against *Toxoplasma* because delayed hypersensitivity and its in vitro correlates such as production of migration inhibitory factor (MIF) develop early in toxoplasmosis, and protection results only from infection with *living* organisms. Interferon is also produced, and activated macrophages can be demonstrated that kill or inhibit the multiplication of the parasite, which would effectively reduce the parasite burden. In such cellular immunity, macrophage activation is probably affected by the action of antigen upon specifically sensitized T lymphocytes, which in turn produce lymphokines that activate the macrophages (see Chapter 9).

An intact immune system is necessary for protection against *Toxoplasma;* thus, immunosuppression to control transplant rejection or malignancies may result in active toxoplasmosis. This phenomenon may result either from the elimination of sensitized lymphocytes previously limiting an inapparent infection or from the inability of the immunosuppressed host to mount an adequate protective response to new infection.

Vaccination of the population with strains of low virulence would probably be effective in establishing protection to *Toxoplasma*, but because most persons develop adequate protection after natural infection, this procedure is probably not worthwhile, except for previously uninfected women of childbearing age in order to prevent intrauterine transmission.

TRYPANOSOMIASIS

1. AFRICAN TRYPANOSOMIASIS

Major Immunologic Features
- Increase in nonspecific IgM.
- Succession of parasite populations in bloodstream, each with a different antigenic coating.

Trypanosoma brucei gambiense, also called *T gambiense,* is the agent of chronic Gambian or West

African sleeping sickness. *Trypanosoma brucei rhodesiense*, also called *T rhodesiense*, is the agent of acute Rhodesian or East African sleeping sickness. Both cause human disease, and the Rhodesian form is most responsible for denying vast areas of Africa to human occupation, chiefly in the flybelt regions where the tsetse fly vectors are found. Tsetse-borne trypanosomes (*Trypanosoma b brucei* as well as several other species) infect domestic animals with similar or even greater virulence. The impact of this dual threat—one to humans and the other to domestic animals, especially cattle—has had an enormous effect on human history in Africa and the occupation of vast regions across the tropical belt from West African forests to the savannahs of East and South Africa. The great herds of wild herbivores, once abundant everywhere, have survived in this region because of their natural tolerance to heavy infections. The trypanosomes multiply extracellularly in successive waves in the human and animal bloodstream but produce very little disease in spite of their numbers. Only when the parasites enter the central nervous system does the ravaging disease sleeping sickness develop. It is this pathologic phase of an otherwise harmless chronic or recurrent infection to which humans and domestic animals succumb and which most native antelope and other herbivores resist, presumably as a result of association over millions of years accompanied by a continuing strong natural selection process.

Greatly increased levels of immunoglobulins, especially of the IgM class, are regularly present in infected humans and animals. The increased immunoglobulin levels, which do not correlate positively with protection, may result from B cell mitogens produced by the trypanosomes themselves or by the increased IgG production of helper T cells which act nonspecifically to increase immunoglobulin levels. The validity of this suggestion is supported by the observation that a large proportion of the immunoglobulin in infected hosts is nonspecific in nature.

Specific antibodies do arise in trypanosomal infections. In experimental animals, the *T brucei* group of trypanosomes produces an interesting immunologic phenomenon. Antigenic variants of the parasite appear in the blood in successive waves, each being removed by host antibody, only to be replaced by another peak of trypanosomes (Gray and Luckins, 1976). More than 20 variants have been shown to develop sequentially in experimental animals. Antigenic variation seems to be a property of the surface coat of the trypanosome, which can be shed into the ambient medium and is thought to be under genetic control of the parasite and not induced by the host response. Organisms taken from culture or from vectors do not possess this coat. The ability of the host to respond to multiple antigenic variants with such specificity could account in part for the increased immunoglobulin levels reported during infections.

The specific antibodies can either lyse the parasites or clump them. Clumping allows for more efficient removal of the parasites by the reticuloendothelial system. It is controversial whether humans or domestic animals living in endemic areas develop resistance to infection, although epidemiologic observations suggest that resistance does arise. The fact that there are healthy human carriers of *T rhodesiense*—which usually produces a fatal infection—implies that some protective mechanism must exist. However, the precise immunologic nature of this protection is at present obscure (Mansfield, 1978).

Suppression of immune responses to other unrelated antigens may be observed during trypanosomal infections. It is not known whether the suppression results from exhaustion of B cell clones, the presence of suppressor T cells, a lack of helper T cells, or the availability of fewer T cells to interact with new antigens.

Vaccines specific for antigenic variants can be developed, although few common antigens have been demonstrated. The multiplicity of antigenic variants observed during field studies in bovines makes vaccination an unlikely solution to trypanosomiasis unless common antigens can be found.

2. AMERICAN TRYPANOSOMIASIS

Major Immunologic Features
- Specific antibody not necessarily indicative of active infection.
- Delayed hypersensitivity present.
- No antigenic variation.

An estimated 10 million people in Central and South America are infected with *Trypanosoma cruzi*, and 30 million more are at risk. The resulting chronic debilitating affliction, Chagas' disease, has no cure and is a major factor in premature death from heart disease in Latin America—especially in rural areas where housing and nutrition are inadequate. The disease is transmitted to humans when fecal contamination from infected bloodsucking triatomine bugs occurs in fresh bites, mucous membranes, or abraded skin, frequently from nighttime scratching that rubs the vector's liquid feces into the bite or causes it to be taken into the mouth or rubbed into the eyes. The parasites actively penetrate host cells and multiply intracellularly. The acute form of the disease is characterized by myocardiopathy, lymphadenopathy, hepatosplenomegaly, parasitemia, fever, and malaise. Colonies of intracellular amastigotes develop in striated muscles, smooth muscles, and the reticuloendothelial system. The disease is often fatal in infants or children, but in adults a chronic form usually follows the initial infection, sometimes after a considerable interval, producing a disease characterized by cardiac enlargement, megacolon, megaesophagus, and degeneration of the peripheral and central nervous systems. In chronic disease, nests of intracellular parasites can be found but parasitemia accompanied by fever is infrequent.

Antibody that can be detected by complement

fixation, latex agglutination, indirect hemagglutination, counterimmunoelectrophoresis, or enzyme-linked immunosorbent assay (ELISA) is produced during disease. This can be a guide to diagnosis, although the antibody cross-reacts with other flagellates such as leishmaniae. Antibody may persist after infection and therefore does not indicate active disease. High titers of antibody do not appear to limit the infection in humans; however, complement-dependent lysis of the parasites can be demonstrated in vitro with sera from experimentally infected hosts. This lysis may be an important mechanism for parasite control in vivo. However, lytic antibody does not afford complete protection against reinfection because passive transfer of hyperimmune serum is not always effective. For this reason, the lytic action of antibody may need cooperation with cells such as macrophages to eliminate or lower the parasite burden (Williams and Remington, 1977). Animals can be protected against virulent strains of the organism by infection with avirulent or partially virulent strains or by passive transfer of sensitized lymphocytes. Acquired resistance to virulent strains is probably the result of previous inapparent infection with strains of low virulence. Therefore, progress toward chemically attenuated vaccines is being made.

Activated macrophages can be demonstrated in *T cruzi* animal infections. Although their role in protection in humans has yet to be fully explored, there is some evidence from animal experiments that activated macrophages play the major role in protection against this infection. Delayed hypersensitivity, lymphocyte activation, and MIF production can be documented during infection, but the role of cell-mediated immunity has not been fully elucidated. Additionally, transfer factor made from the leukocytes of immunized monkeys can apparently induce certain new cell-mediated functions. Cardiac damage in infected rabbits may be the result of an immune response to cross-reacting antigens of *T cruzi* and rabbit cardiac muscle, since *T cruzi*–sensitized lymphocytes are cytotoxic for unparasitized cardiac muscle cells in vitro as well as for parasitized cells. Antibody may also participate in immune destruction of normal cells. Attempts to vaccinate against disease might do more harm than good if such sensitized lymphocytes against shared antigens should develop.

A valuable review by Goble of the immunologic features of *T cruzi* appears in *Immunity to Parasitic Animals* (Jackson, 1970).

THE IMMUNE RESPONSE TO HELMINTHS

From the foregoing, it is obvious that the immune response to unicellular parasites is complex. Multicellular parasites, by reason of their size, more complex tissue and organ structure, and varied and active metabolism induce even more complex host responses. A continuing problem in working with immunity to metazoan parasites is the difficulty in separating *functional* immune responses from production of antibody or activated cells with no discernible protective effect. This may be due to parasite evasion of these deleterious effects (see Bloom, 1979); to motility of the parasite, permitting escape from a host response; to wide distribution of host antibody without sufficient local concentration; or to inappropriate host response, in which antibodies or cell-mediated immune reactions may develop against structural antigens, with no harm to the worms, but not against worm growth factors, reproductive factors, or metabolic mechanisms essential to worm life. In general, the primary antigens of helminths are metabolic by-products, enzymes, or other secretory products rather than structural components. For this reason, excretory and secretory products usually are far more immunogenic than are nonliving substances, killed worms, or processed products (Clegg and Smith, 1978). For example, the eggs of *Schistosoma mansoni* have been shown to secrete unique antigens that induce granuloma formation; the various stages of developing nematodes have stage-specific antigens, often molting fluids, to which the host responds in various ways; and the granules in the stichocytes, special cells located in the "neck" of *Trichinella spiralis,* elicit specific antibody.

Nematodes, cestodes, and trematodes all share common antigens. The 2 most frequent responses to helminths — eosinophilia and reaginic antibody (IgE) — are both T cell–dependent (see Chapters 8 and 18). In addition, certain helminths have been shown to potentiate the immune response to other antigens, perhaps by common metabolic by-products acting as nonspecific adjuvants. In addition, helminth infection often induces strong and sometimes self-destructive immunopathologic reactions, such as the excessive granulomatous response to schistosome eggs caught in host tissues (see reviews by Warren, 1976; Boros, 1978, p 208; and Phillips and Colley, 1978, p 115).

TREMATODES

Trematodes are important pathogens of humans and domestic animals. Fascioliasis debilitates and kills domestic animals in large numbers, and schistosomiasis is a major disease of humans. The lung flukes of the genus *Paragonimus* cause central nervous system complications in humans if they encyst in the brain rather than in the lung, where considerable mechanical damage results. The fish-borne Chinese liver fluke *(Clonorchis sinensis)* causes much morbidity both in the Orient and among recent emigrants from endemic areas, producing infection that may last the lifetime of the host in spite of all attempts at chemotherapy, though recent studies in China with praziquantel may change this picture.

1. SCHISTOSOMIASIS

Major Immunologic Features

- Immediate and delayed hypersensitivity are present.
- Diagnostic antibody formed.
- Antigenic mimicry of host tissues (concomitant immunity).

Schistosomiasis in humans is caused by *Schistosoma mansoni, Schistosoma japonicum, Schistosoma haematobium,* and *Schistosoma mekongi.* The advent of new high dams in many areas of the world, especially Africa, has increased the incidence of schistosomiasis because the additional irrigation made possible by the dams has vastly enlarged the habitat of the freshwater snails that serve as intermediate hosts to the worms. The life cycle of this parasite depends upon skin penetration of the definitive host by infective forms produced in the snail. Because attempts to reduce snail populations have largely failed, infection has become rampant in these areas. *S mansoni,* now widespread in Africa and the Middle East, has also spread extensively in South America. *S haematobium* is found in all watered areas of Africa and the Arabian peninsula. *S japonicum* is found in the Yangtze River watershed in China, where it has been subjected to a vast control effort but is still common in Szechwan province and may be returning to the main river valley. It is also common in the central Philippines. A purely animal-infecting (zoophilic) form is found in Taiwan. A newly described species similar to *S japonicum, S mekongi,* causes human disease in Thailand, Laos, and Cambodia, with a scattering of cases in Malaysia. There is also a focus of *S japonicum* in Sulawesi (Celebes) that may prove to be a distinct species.

In brief, the life cycle of the schistosomes which infect humans is as follows: Infected humans and animals excrete eggs that hatch in water, releasing miracidia; these actively penetrate snails in which several generations of multiplying larvae (sporocysts) develop that eventually produce great numbers of free-swimming infectious larvae (cercariae) which leave the host snail at the rate of 300–3000/d. The cercariae penetrate the skin of the definitive host, shed the ciliated epidermal plates, and enter the bloodstream as minute motile immature schistosomes or **schistosomules,** which migrate in 3–8 days to the lungs and then by an uncertain route to the liver, where further development and adult worm pairing take place about 5 weeks after skin penetration. The paired mature schistosomes then migrate against the venous flow into the mesenteric venules, where eggs are deposited. Initially, the larvae (miracidia) within the spined eggs digest their way through the blood vessel and adjacent tissue into the lumen of the intestine (bladder in the case of *S haematobium*). Ultimately, inflammatory and then granulomatous reactions induced by soluble egg antigens passed from the miracidia through the eggshells entrap increasing numbers of eggs. This sets in motion the immunopathogenic processes that characterize clinical schistosomiasis (Bout et al, 1977). Eggs are also retained within the blood vessels and eventually are carried into the hepatic portals, inducing inflammatory lesions that give rise to hepatic disease such as portal hypertension, granulomatosis, and ultimately more advanced disorders such as Symmers's clay pipestem fibrosis, which is associated with severe loss of liver function.

It is generally agreed that the protective immune response to schistosomes is probably mediated by antibody during the time they spend in the skin. The antigens that induce killing of the schistosomules probably come from the adult worm, although—as in other helminth infections—humoral and cellular protective mechanisms are both involved.

In experimental hosts, *S mansoni* is able to coat itself with host materials such as blood group substances and can consequently exist in a host disguised as "self," whereas newly invading schistosomules are rapidly killed or immobilized by the action of antibody. This **concomitant immunity** has been established as an important way in which host protection to reinfection may be achieved while allowing the original parasites to persist (Bloom, 1979).

Chronic infection with schistosomiasis, tied to concomitant immunity, serves as an excellent example of functional tolerance; cases lasting 30 years or longer without reinfection have been reported. Though biologic and ecologic factors are almost impossible to separate from evidence of acquired immunity to schistosomiasis, the evidence is nonetheless persuasive that such an immunity does develop over a period of years. The immunity induced is effective, since *acute* schistosomiasis is rare among older residents in endemic areas but common among newcomers to such regions—eg, among American troops in the Philippine liberation in World War II.

The mechanism of host immunity to schistosome reinfection is entirely uncertain and is a continuing subject of active research. Nevertheless, a broad range of humoral and cell-mediated reactions involving every known class and subclass of antibody have been demonstrated in human schistosomiasis by a variety of techniques: complement fixation, flocculation test, soluble antigen precipitation, cholesterol-lecithin and indirect fluorescent antibody reactions, and cell-bound antigen agglutination. The binding of eggs (circumoval test), of intact larval worms (cercarienhullen test), or of worm fragments has been demonstrated. Direct cytotoxicity in vitro and mediation of adherence and cytotoxic reactions using a variety of cell types are possible. Yet none provides a reliable index of the state of disease, of its activity, of the results of treatment, or of prognosis. All one can reliably infer is a reasonable assurance of past infection.

Tests in experimental animals also vary greatly and must be evaluated separately in terms of each host-parasite system under study. Chimpanzees show little or no evidence of an acquired immunity, and the disease produced is strikingly like that in humans. Baboons develop a slowly acquired immunity, while the rhesus monkey develops a spontaneous "self-cure" several weeks after infection and a strong delayed hypersensitivity after treatment with transfer factor. The grivet monkey develops both an acute illness *and* a strong resistance to reinfection.

A similar broad range of responses can be demonstrated in rodents. The rat is an excellent model for high natural resistance, spontaneous decrease of worm burden in about 1 month, and increased resistance from initial stimulation of T cell-dependent mechanisms and then of B cell-dependent mechanisms. There is an anamnestic response to normal or irradiated cercariae or to worm homogenates, but intact viable parasites are most immunogenic, and immunity is especially strong against younger stages (concomitant immunity). Strong adoptively transferred resistance using cells or serum can also be demonstrated. The mouse is the principal host for maintenance of the worms, as it is considerably more susceptible, produces a less active immunity, and demonstrates far more disease—rather like the human response. The effects of IgG and polymorphonuclear leukocytes against young schistosomules are strongly evident in the rat, whereas IgE and eosinophil effects are especially prevalent in the mouse and in humans. Antieosinophil serum has been used in recent experiments by Mahmoud and colleagues to demonstrate ablation of resistance in mice to schistosome reinfection with cercariae, whereas antisera against mouse lymphocytes, macrophages, or neutrophils did not reduce the host's resistance. Antieosinophil serum also blocked passive transfer of immunity with mouse antischistosome serum. There is evidence from in vitro studies that S mansoni schistosomules are damaged by a complement- and IgG-dependent cell-mediated reaction by the eosinophils acting as killer cells. It has also been established that the eosinophil represents about 50% of the cells in S mansoni egg-induced lung granulomas in mice, and antieosinophil serum reduces the size of these lesions by about 50%. In vitro studies have shown that eosinophils from schistosome-infected mice—but not uninfected mice—specifically damaged schistosome eggs. It is now suggested that eosinophils function within schistosome granulomas containing mature eggs (which in turn have miracidia that produce soluble egg antigen) and that this activity is antibody-directed, probably a cell-antibody attachment mechanism rather than an opsonization process. It must be emphasized, however, that the actual in vivo mechanism of egg destruction remains unknown. A full and timely discussion of this fast-moving research area has been prepared by Phillips and Colley (1978).

Cell-mediated immune responses mounted by the host against the parasites produce many of the lesions of schistosomiasis. In S mansoni and S japonicum infections, fibrosis of the liver is the main cause of death. This fibrosis may be the result of delayed hypersensitivity reactions to antigens produced by secretions from the eggs. Extensive work has shown conclusively that granulomas induced by S mansoni eggs in the lungs of mice are delayed hypersensitivity reactions, and evidence in humans would not contradict the hypothesis that fibrosis results from granuloma formation. The action of antibodies in the immunopathology of this disease is not completely clear.

In S haematobium infections, a florid granulomatous reaction early in the disease may spontaneously subside. It has been suggested that this abatement results from desensitization by blocking antibody or antigen-antibody complexes produced within the granuloma itself. Diminishing egg production by the worms has not been shown to be a factor in the remission because the worms live and continue egg production for long periods in the absence of reinfection.

Four to 6 weeks after infection with certain schistosomes, humans may develop Katayama fever, thought to be an immunologic response that occurs at the onset of egg production by the worms. Whether this is an anaphylactic response (IgE) or a type of serum sickness (IgG) is still a subject of debate, but it is generally agreed that antibodies formed to the developing worms induce the reaction. As might be expected, hypersensitivity and protective and irrelevant antibodies are all produced to the complex worm antigens.

Immunodiagnosis of schistosome infection in the absence of egg excretion by the host can be accomplished in various ways, both humoral and cellular. Stage-specific humoral responses can be used to produce circumoval precipitation, schistosomule growth inhibition or death, and complement fixation, hemagglutination, and various precipitation reactions. It must again be noted that none of these reactions can be positively correlated with protection. Immediate and delayed cutaneous hypersensitivity develop in most individuals during the course of the disease, although the specificity of these reactions is often suspect because of cross-reaction with other worms. However, the isolation of novel antigenic fractions and sensitive radioimmunoassays may help elucidate these responses.

Live attenuated vaccines are being sought to induce protection in humans, but progress has not been great. Ideally, dead vaccines or even purified antigens which induce protection would be more acceptable. Since human schistosomes can be maintained for sustained periods in culture, these aspects are under intensive study.

2. CERCARIAL DERMATITIS
(Swimmer's Itch)

The invasion of a previously sensitized host by the cercariae of schistosomes, particularly those of avian origin, can cause severe 2-stage reactions in the skin. The first stage begins within minutes of contact and consists of a wheal-and-flare reaction. The second stage becomes evident 16–24 hours after contact, with development of papules which are essentially delayed hypersensitivity reactions. These reactions have been shown to be very specific in that persons infected with *S mansoni* did not react to cercariae of an avian schistosome known to cause violent reactions in persons with swimmer's itch.

CESTODES

The immune response to cestodes has 2 distinct modalities: the intestinal lumen–dwelling adult tapeworms such as *Diphyllobothrium latum* or *Taenia saginata,* with minimal immunogenic tissue contact; and the migratory tissue-encysting larval tapeworms such as *Hymenolepis nana* (in its intravillous larval phase) (Ito et al, 1978) or *Echinococcus granulosus* (hydatid cyst). The first of these modalities is essentially a nonimmunogenic infection in which the parasite-to-host contact is limited to scolex attachment to the intestinal mucosa, without penetration or prolonged contact. The second involves intimate and continuous parenteral tissue contact and induces a strong immunogenic host response (Hammerberg and Williams, 1978). Although lumen-dwelling adult cestodes do induce host reactions and are affected by them, the principal immunologic responses are directed against the tissue parasites. Serodiagnostic tests are thus available only for the larval tissue cestode parasites, and humoral responses that protect the challenged host have only been described for this form of cestode parasitism. A summary of recent advances is available in Williams (1979).

Infection with cestodes is usually life-threatening to humans only when they act as unnatural intermediate hosts. *Taenia solium* from swine can develop extraintestinally in humans (cysticercosis) and can be found in any organ of the body. When encysted parasites die in the brain, severe tissue reactions with resultant central nervous system disorders and pressure damage can occur. Death may result, depending upon degree of toxicity and tissues affected.

ECHINOCOCCOSIS

Major Immunologic Features
- IgE elevated.
- Anaphylaxis due to ruptured cyst fluids.
- Casoni skin test of questionable use.
- Diagnostic antibody present.

The most serious human cestode infection is that caused by *Echinococcus.* These tiny tapeworms do not produce pathologic lesions in the definitive host, the dog, but severe complications occur when their eggs are ingested by humans and other animals. The larval form of the tapeworm hatches from the egg in the intestine of the intermediate host; the larva then claws its way through the intestinal mucosa and is transported through the lymphatic and blood vessels to sites in which it is rapidly encapsulated. A heavy cyst wall is laid down both by the host and by the parasite. In

humans, *Echinococcus* normally forms fluid-filled cysts in the liver, but these can also occur in the lungs and other parts of the body. These hydatid cysts are highly immunogenic and result in production of high titers of reaginic antibody (IgE) and other immunoglobulins. If a cyst is ruptured, anaphylactic response to the cyst fluid can cause death. Little or no protection seems to be elicited by this highly immunogenic cestode because the hydatid cysts remain alive for years and in animals can be shown to increase in number as the host ages. Humans are usually a dead-end host for this parasite because the cysts must be eaten by a canid to become sexually mature. There is some evidence that complement-mediated lysis of protoscoleces (hydatid cyst fluid with numerous scoleces; "hydatid sand") might be protective in the infected human or other intermediate host.

The Casoni skin test indicates past or present echinococcosis. The test consists of intradermal injection of hydatid cyst fluid, resulting in both immediate and delayed hypersensitivity. The specificity of this test is in doubt because of cross-reactions with other helminths. Heating the cyst fluid slightly increases the specificity of the test. Serodiagnosis can be made by hemagglutination, complement fixation, and flocculation tests, ELISA, and radioimmunoassay, using serum of the patient and specially fractionated antigenic components made from cyst fluid. These tests are not species-specific. A summary of standardized diagnostic procedures and appropriate techniques was prepared by Kagan and Norman (1979).

NEMATODES

Nematodes are the commonest, most varied, and most widely distributed helminths infecting humans. As with other parasites, immunogenicity is a reflection of degree and duration of parasite contact with the host's tissues. Even with the intestinal lumen dwellers such as *Ascaris* there is a migratory larval phase in which such contact is made—in most cases, in the pulmonary capillaries and alveolar spaces. The hookworms of humans (*Ancylostoma duodenale* and *Necator americanus*) also undergo a migration except that the infective larvae enter via the skin or buccal mucosa rather than as hatchlings in the small bowel. *Strongyloides stercoralis,* the small intestinal roundworm of humans, undergoes a similar hookwormlike migration (as well as a stage of internal autoreinfection or reinvasion via the mucosa of the large intestine). *Trichuris trichiura,* the human whipworm, and *Enterobius vermicularis,* the pinworm, do not undergo parenteral migration; thus, their immunogenicity is limited to direct interchange between worm and host mucosa. In the case of the adult whipworm, its hairlike anterior end contains a row of stichocyte cells whose products are thought to be strongly immunogenic. It becomes deeply embedded in the mucosa of the large intestine, as is also true of the entire bodies of the much smaller *Strongyloides* worms. Only the pinworm lacks a strong or prolonged contact with host tissues, and ready reinfection is the rule rather than the exception among children exposed to the eggs of this ubiquitous parasite. Recent work with rodent pinworms suggests that increasing resistance with age is thymus-dependent.

Living worms characteristically are required to induce functional immunity. The immature stages are particularly immunogenic, probably because of their high production of antigens from secretory glands and of enzymes or other products from these metabolically active stages. Commercially prepared vaccines are available only for nematodes and all are living larval worms, irradiated to arrest their development but not their immunogenic activities. These are the cattle and sheep lungworms *Dictyocaulus viviparus* and *Dictyocaulus filaria* and the dog hookworm *Ancylostoma caninum*.

Serologic studies of human nematodes have focused on *Trichinella spiralis*, the agent of trichinosis. These parasites have a tissue phase both with the developing adult within the intestinal mucosa and with the encysted larva within a muscle cell, which is converted by the parasite's presence into a "nurse cell." Not only is immunogenicity particularly strong with the *Trichinella* worm, but serodiagnosis is the best available diagnostic tool, since eggs or larvae are not routinely passed in the stool. Another parasite receiving special serodiagnostic study is the dog ascarid, *Toxocara canis*, an agent of visceral larva migrans. This organism is acquired, usually by children, as embryonated eggs in contaminated soil. They hatch in the gut, penetrate into the submucosa, enter the bloodstream, and eventually migrate in human viscera until they die or are encapsulated, sometimes 2 years later, as this parasite is not normal to humans and cannot complete its life cycle there as can the human ascarid, *Ascaris lumbricoides*. Serodiagnosis of visceral larva migrans is therefore the only reliable diagnostic tool available.

Ascaris has been the subject of considerable research into hypersensitivity induced by migratory larvae in the lung or even air-borne antigens from adult worms, as occurs in the biology laboratory. Another important group of human parasites are the filariae (chiefly *Wuchereria bancrofti*, *Brugia malayi*, *Loa loa*, *Onchocerca volvulus*, and the related guinea worm, *Dracunculus medinensis*). Diagnosis of these infections is often difficult and various hypersensitivity and even anaphylactoid reactions are common, but serodiagnosis of these infections remains in a very unsatisfactory state — in part because of the presence of common antigens and lack of highly specific immunologic tests.

1. TRICHINOSIS

Major Immunologic Features

- Positive skin tests for immediate and delayed hypersensitivity.
- Diagnostic antibody present.

Trichinosis is acquired by ingestion of the infective larvae of *Trichinella spiralis* in uncooked or partially cooked meat. Pork is the primary source of infection in humans. The larvae are released from their cysts in the meat during digestion and rapidly develop into adults in the mucosa of the host's small intestine. After copulation in the lumen, the males die and the females return to the intestinal mucosa where for about 5–6 weeks they produce 1000–1500 larvae per female, which migrate through the lymphatic system to the bloodstream. These larvae travel in the blood to all parts of the body and develop in voluntary muscles, especially in the diaphragm, tongue, masticatory and intercostal muscles, larynx, and the eye. Within the sarcolemma of striated muscle fibers, the larvae coil up into cysts the outer walls of which are rapidly laid down by host histiocytes. Larvae may remain viable and infective for as long as 24 years even though the cysts calcify. The encysted larvae apparently do not yield protection. The migrating larvae and adult forms of the parasite excrete antigens that appear to be responsible for protection from subsequent challenge infections (James et al, 1977). An important expression of host resistance is active expulsion of developing or adult worms from the gut of a parasitized host — the so-called self-cure phenomenon. This occurs when a new infection initiates a host response, resulting in elimination of the old one — the opposite of concomitant immunity. Much work on this topic has been done with nematodes of veterinary importance, such as the highly pathologic stomach worm of sheep, *Haemonchus contortus*. It has also been reported with *Ascaris* in pigs and humans, *Toxocara* in dogs, and *Brugia pahangi* in cats. The reaction appears to be immediate hypersensitivity induced by antigens released from developing larvae of a new infection, which initiates an anaphylactic reaction resulting in cessation of egg production and even worm expulsion. However, experimental confirmation is lacking, and the inconsistency of this reaction requires explanation. Of special interest is the fact that some of the incoming larvae appear to escape and continue to develop to adult worms in spite of elimination of the preceding generation.

The expulsion of *T spiralis* in humans (Love et al, 1976) appears to follow the mechanism proposed by Ogilvie and co-workers for the *Nippostrongylus brasiliensis* rodent hookworm (Ogilvie et al, 1977). A 2-step mechanism is proposed: antibody-induced metabolic damage that blocks feeding by the worms followed by worm expulsion by activated lymphocytes. Active infection initiates a far stronger response than is possible when either lymph node cells or serum is passively transferred. *Both* antibodies and cells are probably required for full expression of intestinal resistance, and the effect is synergistic rather than additive.

Trichinella infection sometimes presents characteristic clinical symptoms such as edema of the eyelids and face but often presents less specific clinical signs such as eosinophilia, which can be suggestive of several other parasitic infections. Specific immunodiagnostic tests may thus be of great importance. The bentonite flocculation test for human trichinosis is of value because of its high degree of specificity. In addition, there are many other immunodiagnostic tests, including complement fixation, hemagglutination, flocculation, immunofluorescence, soluble antigen fluorescent antibody, and a skin test (Bachman intradermal test). Both immediate and delayed responses are seen; the former shows that reaginic IgE is also produced.

In humans, infection with *Trichinella* initially elicits IgM antibody followed by an IgG response. IgA antibody has been reported, which is not surprising because the female worms are in the intestinal mucosa, though the locally produced protective gut antibodies probably are IgG1 rather than IgA or IgM, based on the *Nippostrongylus* studies. This antimetabolite reaction against the feeding worms is complement-independent and, as noted, precedes the rapid expulsion of the antibody-damaged worms by T lymphocytes. The precise mechanism by which these cells act—or their necessary association with other cells such as activated macrophages—remains a matter of dispute (Wakelin and Lloyd, 1976; Wing and Remington, 1978).

Although *Trichinella* is extremely immunogenic in its hosts, it can also exert an immunosuppressive action. Certain viral infections are more severe during infection with this parasite, and skin grafts show delayed rejection. On the other hand, cellular immunity to BCG seems to be potentiated when *T spiralis* is present, and *T spiralis*-infected mice are less susceptible to *Listeria* infections. These seeming contradictions may be explained by recalling that metazoan parasites contain a large complement of antigens, some of which may produce immunosuppression and others potentiation.

2. ASCARIASIS

Major Immunologic Features
- Specific antibody detectable.
- Elevated IgE.
- Responses to unrelated antigens potentiated or suppressed during infection.

Ascaris, the giant roundworm of humans, is a lumen-dwelling parasite as an adult and causes little inconvenience to the host except in the heaviest infections, though even single adult worms may produce mechanical damage by entering the bile or pancreatic ducts or penetrating a weakened gut wall. For example, worm penetration through an amebiasis intestinal lesion produces peritonitis. Ingestion of eggs results in larvae that migrate through the intestinal wall to eventually reach the lung via the bloodstream. In a previously infected host, hypersensitivity reactions in the lung resulting from high levels of IgE can cause serious pneumonitis. Acute hypersensitivity to *Ascaris* antigens often develops in laboratory workers and makes it virtually impossible for them to continue working with the nematode.

Cases of sudden death in Nigeria have been ascribed to *Ascaris*-induced anaphylactic shock, part of what has been termed "a helminth anaphylactic syndrome" heretofore rarely diagnosed or recognized. (See also Carswell et al, 1976.) Death probably resulted from release of a mast cell degranulator by the worms, since degranulated mast cells were found throughout the body tissues in these children, or from a reagin-*Ascaris* allergen interaction at the mast cell surface. Allergy to ascariasis may underlie many of the symptoms of *Ascaris* infection, including abdominal pain.

Antibodies to *Ascaris* are of no diagnostic or protective value, although they are formed during infection; however, hemagglutination tests can be of epidemiologic value (Jones, 1977).

3. TOXOCARA INFECTIONS

Toxocara canis, the dog ascarid, is now known to infect small children who ingest its eggs in dirt. *Toxocara* eggs produce a population of migrating larvae that are immobilized in the tissues of humans and consequently never produce worms in the intestinal tract. Visceral larva migrans is characterized by high peripheral eosinophilia and chronic granulomatous lesions associated with the migrating larvae; such larvae in the eyes of infected children have been confused with retinoblastoma and diagnosed only after enucleation of the affected eyeball. Immunodiagnostic tests for visceral larva migrans have therefore been eagerly sought. Initially, lack of specificity for *T canis* was a great problem, but specific immunodiagnostic methods have recently been developed that should allow prompt diagnosis, and a sensitive ELISA test for antibody to this parasite is in common use in the USA at present. Visceral larva migrans can also be caused by larvae of other nematodes such as the common ascarids of cats (*Toxocara mystax, Toxascaris leonina*) and also some members of the genus *Capillaria*, which migrate in human tissue but do not develop further. Dog and cat hookworms (*Ancylostoma brasiliense, Ancylostoma caninum, Ancylostoma ceylonicum*) produce a similar "lost larva" condition in which skin-invading larvae from pet-contaminated sandy soil tunnel into the skin, where they produce serpiginous, pruritic, tracklike lesions, a condition called **cutaneous larva migrans.**

• • •

References

General

Bloom BR: Games parasites play: How parasites evade immune surveillance. *Nature* 1979;**279**:21.

Boros DL: Granulomatous inflammations. *Prog Allergy* 1978;**24**:183.

Clegg JA, Smith MA: Prospects for the development of dead vaccines against helminths. *Adv Parasitol* 1978;**16**:165.

Cohen S, Sadun EH (editors): *Immunology of Parasitic Infections*. Blackwell, 1976.

Hillyer GV, Kagan IG: New advances in the immunodiagnosis of parasitic infections. 2. Counterelectrophoresis. *Bol Asoc Med PR* 1980;**72**:117.

Jackson GJ, Herman R, Singer I: *Immunity to Parasitic Animals*. Appleton-Century-Crofts, Vol 1, 1969, Vol 2, 1970.

Kagan IG: Serodiagnosis of parasitic diseases. Chap 70, pp 724–750, in: *Manual of Clinical Microbiology*. American Society for Microbiology, Washington DC, 1980.

Kagan IG, Norman LG: Immune response to infection: Parasitic. Pages 165–185 in: *Immunology*. Section F, Vol 1, Part 2 of: *CRC Handbook Series in Clinical Laboratory Science*. Seligson D (editor). CRC Press, 1979.

Lobel HO, Kagan IG: Seroepidemiology of parasitic diseases. *Annu Rev Microbiol* 1978;**32**:329.

Matthews HM: Parasitic disease: Testing with filter-paper blood spots. *Lab Management* 1981;**19**:55.

Wakelin D: Immunity to intestinal parasites. *Nature* 1978;**273**:617.

Walls KW, Smith JW: Serology of parasite infections. *Int J Parasitol* 1979;**10**:329.

Protozoa

Cohen S: Immunity to malaria. *Proc R Soc Lond [Biol]* 1979;**203**:323.

Cohen S: Mechanisms of malarial immunity. *Trans R Soc Trop Med Hyg* 1977;**71**:283.

Cohen S, Mitchell GH: Prospects for immunisation against malaria. *Curr Top Microbiol Immunol* 1978;**80**:97.

Gray AR, Luckins AG: Antigenic variation in salivarian trypanosomes. Chap 12, pp 493–542, in: *Biology of the Kinetoplastida*. Vol 1. Lumsden WHR, Evans DA (editors). Academic Press, 1976.

Kreier JP (editor): *Malaria*. Vol 3: *Immunology and Immunization*. Academic Press, 1980.

Lewis DH, Peters W: The resistance of intracellular *Leishmania* parasites to digestion by lysosomal enzymes. *Ann Trop Med Parasitol* 1977;**71**:295.

Mansfield JM: Immunobiology of African trypanosomiasis. *Cell Immunol* 1978;**39**:204.

Miller LH: Current prospects and problems for a malaria vaccine. *J Infect Dis* 1977;**135**:855.

Miller LH et al: The resistance factor to *Plasmodium vivax* in blacks: The Duffy-blood-group genotype, FyFy. *N Engl J Med* 1976;**295**:302.

Patterson M, Healy GR, Shabot JM: Serologic testing for amoebiasis. *Gastroenterology* 1980;**78**:136.

Reese RT et al: Immunization against malaria with antigen from *Plasmodium falciparum* cultivated in vitro. *Proc Natl Acad Sci USA* 1978;**75**:5665.

Vickerman K: Antigenic variation in trypanosomes. *Nature* 1978;**273**:613.

Williams DM, Remington JS: Effect of human monocytes and macrophages on *Trypanosoma cruzi*. *Immunology* 1977;**32**:19.

Trematodes

Bout D et al: Circulating immune complexes in schistosomiasis. *Immunology* 1977;**33**:17.

Kassis AI, Warren KS, Mahmoud AAF: Antibody-dependent complement-mediated killing of schistosomula in intraperitoneal diffusion chambers in mice. *J Immunol* 1979;**123**:1659.

McLaren DJ, Ramalho-Pinto FJ: Eosinophil-mediated killing of schistosomula of *Schistosoma mansoni* in vitro: Synergistic effect of antibody and complement. *J Immunol* 1979;**123**:1431.

Phillips SM, Colley DG: Immunologic aspects of host responses to schistosomiasis: Resistance, immunopathology, and eosinophil involvement. *Prog Allergy* 1978;**24**:49.

Taylor MG et al: Immunisation of sheep against *Schistosoma matthei* using either irradiated cercariae or irradiated schistosomula. *J Helminthol* 1976;**50**:1.

Von Lichtenberg F et al: Eosinophil-enriched inflammatory response to schistosomula in the skin of mice immune to *Schistosoma mansoni*. *Am J Pathol* 1976;**84**:479.

Warren KS: Schistosomiasis: A multiplicity of immunopathology. *J Invest Dermatol* 1976;**67**:464.

Cestodes

Hammerberg B, Williams JF: Interaction between *Taenia taeniaeformis* and the complement system. *J Immunol* 1978;**120**:1033.

Ito A, Yamamoto M, Ikamoto K: Primary infection with mouse-derived cysticercoids of *Hymenolepis nana* prepared from baby or adult mice and secondary infections with eggs or cysticercoids. *Int J Parasitol* 1978;**8**:149.

Williams JF: Recent advances in the immunology of cestode infections. *J Parasitol* 1979;**65**:337.

Nematodes

Carswell F, Meakins RH, Harland PSEG: Parasites and asthma in Tanzanian children. *Lancet* 1976;**2**:706.

James ER, Moloney A, Denham DA: Immunity to *Trichinella spiralis*. 7. Resistance stimulated by the parenteral stages of the infection. *J Parasitol* 1977;**63**:720.

Jones HI: Haemagglutination tests in the study of *Ascaris* epidemiology. *Ann Trop Med Parasitol* 1977;**71**:219.

Love RJ, Ogilvie BM, McLaren DJ: The immune mechanism which expels the intestinal stage of *Trichinella spiralis* from rats. *Immunology* 1976;**30**:7.

Ogilvie BM et al: *Nippostrongylus brasiliensis* infection in rats, the cellular requirement for worm expulsion. *Immunology* 1977;**32**:521.

Wakelin D, Lloyd M: Immunity to primary and challenge infections of *Trichinella spiralis* in mice: A re-examination of conventional parameters. *Parasitology* 1976;**72**:173.

Wing EJ, Remington JS: Role for activated macrophages in resistance against *Trichinella spiralis*. *Infect Immun* 1978;**21**:398.

Oral & Dental Diseases | 38

John S. Greenspan, BSc, BDS, PhD, MRC Path

The mouth is the portal of entry for a variety of antigens, including numerous microorganisms, into the alimentary and respiratory systems. Normally, these antigens do not cause disease and are flushed away with swallowed saliva into the distal parts of the alimentary tract. Continual desquamation of oral epithelium, toothbrushing, and other forms of mouth cleaning mechanically protect the mouth. Immunologic defense mechanisms, particularly IgA, probably prevent adherence of microorganisms to mucosal and tooth surfaces by aggregating them and possibly rendering them more susceptible to phagocytosis.

Several of the most important oral diseases, including caries, the common forms of gingival and periodontal disease, oral herpes simplex infections, and candidal infections, are due to an imbalance between oral organisms and the host response. This imbalance may be a hypersensitivity phenomenon or may be the result of immunologic deficiency. Alternatively—particularly in the case of dental caries and chronic inflammatory periodontal disease—specific pathogenic microorganisms may directly damage the tissues regardless of the status of the host response.

Another group of oral diseases in which immunologic factors have been implicated are those in which oral tissues are a target for autoimmune reactions. Manifestations may be confined to the mouth or may involve oral tissues as part of a systemic disease. Many are mucocutaneous diseases and several are rheumatoid diseases; others involve mainly the gastrointestinal tract. The role of tumor immune mechanisms in oral homeostasis and the part that defects in these mechanisms play in the etiology and pathogenesis of oral precancerous lesions and mucosal malignancy constitute a rapidly growing field of interest. Tumor immune mechanisms are probably important but must be considered in the context of other factors, including oncogenic viruses and chemical carcinogens.

LOCAL ORAL DISEASE INVOLVING IMMUNOLOGIC MECHANISMS

INFLAMMATORY PERIODONTAL DISEASES: GINGIVITIS & PERIODONTITIS
(See Fig 38–1.)

Major Immunologic Features
- Bacterial dental plaque induces inflammation of tissues immediately surrounding the teeth.
- Host inflammatory responses to plaque microorganisms and to the substances they release cause additional damage to periodontal tissue.
- The local responses of the host are not effective in eliminating the bacteria, which continue to adhere to the tooth surfaces.
- Humoral and cellular immunity are both involved in these responses.
- Local responses include complement activation, infiltration of leukocytes, release of lysosomal enzymes and cytokines, and production of a serous gingival crevicular exudate.
- Inflammatory agents from the bacteria and immunopathologic reactions of the host result in gingivitis and periodontitis.

General Considerations

Almost all individuals have periodontal disease by age 45. Depending on its severity, the destructive process may involve both the gingiva (gingivitis) and the periodontal ligament and alveolar bone surrounding and supporting the teeth (periodontitis). Periodontitis is probably due both to the direct cytotoxic and proteolytic nature of dental plaque and to the indirect pathologic consequences of the host's immune response to the continued presence of bacterial plaque antigens.

Dental plaque is a mass of bacteria which adheres tenaciously to the tooth surfaces. In gingivitis, the plaque generates inflammation of the gingival tissue without affecting the underlying periodontal bone. In periodontitis, attachment between the gingiva and the involved teeth is lost, a subgingival bacterial plaque forms on the root surfaces, and bone loss is clinically

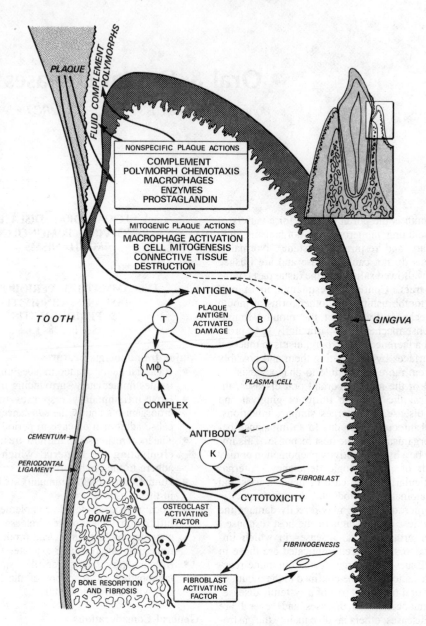

Figure 38–1. The pathogenesis of periodontal disease.

apparent (Figs 38–2 and 38–3). Elimination of the plaque will stop the inflammatory process. In children with poor oral hygiene, gingivitis is common but periodontitis is rarely seen.

The microflora of the dental plaque is complex, comprising many different strains of bacteria (gram-positive rods and cocci and gram-negative rods, cocci, and filamentous forms). In general, as the supragingival plaque develops in the absence of proper oral hygiene, there is a shift from a coccal facultative flora (eg, streptococci) to a more complex flora containing a high proportion of strict anaerobes. The latter population is better suited to survive in the subgingival plaque. No particular organism within the dental

plaque has been conclusively demonstrated to be the sole etiologic agent for any form of periodontal disease. Several different microorganisms isolated from dental plaque are capable of producing alveolar bone loss when inoculated directly into the oral cavity of gnotobiotic rats. These bacteria include *Actinomyces (Actinomyces naeslundii* and *Actinomyces viscosus), Streptococcus (Streptococcus mutans* and *Streptococcus sanguis), Bacteroides melaninogenicus,* and *Eikenella corrodens*. It seems that several types of organisms that can survive under either aerobic or anaerobic environmental circumstances within the plaque can produce gingivitis and periodontitis.

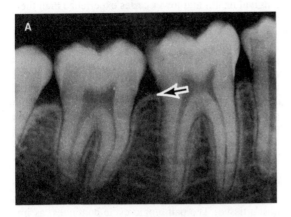
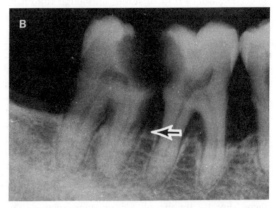

Figure 38–2. X-rays of the lower molars of a 25-year-old man with a normal periodontium *(A)* and a 45-year-old man with advanced periodontitis and severe dental caries *(B)*. In the patient with periodontitis, more than half of the supporting alveolar bone has been destroyed (arrows). (Courtesy of GC Armitage.)

Immunologic Pathogenesis

A delicate balance exists between dental plaque organisms and the host response. In health, the immunologic machinery provides a well-regulated specific defense against infiltration by plaque substances. The tissue-destructive mechanisms thought to be involved in periodontal disease include direct effects of plaque bacteria, PMN-induced damage, complement-mediated damage initiated by both antibody and the alternative pathway, and cell-mediated damage.

Clinically apparent gingivitis is probably the result of an exaggerated response to an uncommonly large amount of bacterial plaque. Individuals with mild gingivitis have, in addition to a continued polymorphonuclear infiltration, a gingival influx of a few lymphocytes believed to be T lymphocytes. However, those with prolonged severe gingivitis and severe periodontitis have an influx composed mainly of B lymphocytes and plasma cells, the latter committed mainly to IgG production. Most noteworthy in severe periodontal disease is the extremely low proportion of the gingival plasma cells committed to IgG2 production, while serum levels of the IgG subclasses are normal. The proportions of IgG3, IgG1, or IgG4 in the gingival tissues with specific antibody activity for plaque antigens are unknown. The unusual local IgG subclass response may indicate a degree of nonspecific activation of B lymphocytes arriving in the inflamed area, possibly caused by a variety of mechanisms involving bacterial mitogens and proteases and continued activation of the alternative complement pathway. Associated with gingivitis is the generation of a serum exudate known as crevicular fluid, which flows from around the teeth and contacts the dental plaque. In individuals with inflammatory periodontal disease, the flow rate of the crevicular fluid is directly proportionate to the severity of disease. This exudate, like serum, contains functional complement components as well as low levels of specific antibodies to the various plaque antigens.

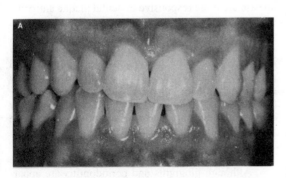
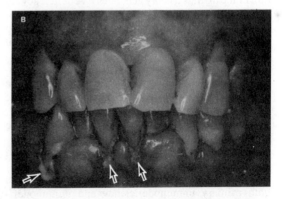

Figure 38–3. Clinical appearance of the anterior teeth and periodontal tissues of a 22-year-old man with healthy gingiva *(A)* and a 48-year-old man with advanced periodontitis *(B)*. In the patient with periodontitis, note the heavy deposits of plaque and calculus (arrows). Marked gingival inflammation is particularly noticeable around the lower anterior teeth. Most teeth have either pocket formation or extensive gingival recession. (Courtesy of GC Armitage.)

The onset of flow of serous crevicular fluid is an important stage in the progression of periodontal disease. Crevicular fluid complement is rapidly activated by a combination of effects. These include activation of the classic pathway by IgG and IgM antibodies to subgingival plaque antigens; activation of the alternative complement pathway by endotoxins and peptidoglycan from gram-negative and gram-positive microorganisms, respectively; and activation of complement components by host and bacterial proteolytic enzymes. Complement activation results first in release of C3a and C5a, which causes additional edema and increases crevicular fluid flow, and subsequently in chemotactic attraction of polymorphonuclear leukocytes. Other chemotactic factors are produced directly by the plaque microorganisms. The release of proteolytic enzymes (eg, collagenaselike and trypsinlike activities) by host cells is believed to damage tissue and activate additional complement components. Complement activation also results in damage to bystander cells by terminal complement components and subsequent release of prostaglandin E. In vitro, prostaglandin E can induce bone resorption through its effect on osteoclasts, but the mechanism of its action is unknown.

Cell-mediated immunity may also play a role in the progression of periodontal disease. Individuals with periodontal disease generally exhibit increased peripheral blood T lymphocyte reactivity to various plaque antigens. Yet, for reasons unknown, in severe gingivitis and severe periodontitis, the local T cell response to the plaque is conspicuously small.

In normal individuals, it is possible that specific secretory IgA-antigen complexes from the oral cavity may penetrate the mucosa and interact with a certain population of lymphocytes, causing those cells to release regulating factors for both cell-mediated immunity and secondary antibody production (particularly the IgA and IgG antibodies, which are highly T cell-dependent). Indeed, it is well established in a variety of animals that early removal of the thymus or dysfunction of the thymus usually generates IgA deficiency, in that T cells are needed for the proper differentiation of IgA-producing B lymphocytes to IgA-producing plasma cells. Normally, the protection of mucosal surfaces is provided by the well-regulated S-IgA system and the T lymphocyte system. However, in individuals with periodontal disease, these systems seem to be replaced by a less well regulated nonspecific inflammatory response.

Bone destruction in periodontal disease may be mediated by lymphokines, including osteoclast-activating factor, as well as by parathyroid hormone and agents such as prostaglandins.

Individuals with reduced immunologic capacity, both primary immunodeficiency and immunodeficiency secondary to treatment associated with kidney transplantation, do not have more gingival and periodontal disease than normal controls. Indeed, in some studies, immunodeficient patients had better gingival health and lower caries experience than their healthy controls.

The rate of the healing process is closely coupled to immunologic responses. In fact, a limited action of proteolytic enzymes can induce, through a complicated sequence, partial regeneration of destroyed host tissues including bone. Older individuals, however, appear to be unable either to specifically control the plaque bacteria or to establish a regulated controlled response to its continued presence. Together with the proteolytic and cytotoxic activity of the plaque, the poorly directed immunopathologic response causes disruption and apical migration of the epithelial gingival attachment to the tooth and thus creates a larger surface area between the bacterial plaque and the host's tissue. The pathologic cycle continues, as immune responses alone are apparently unable to destroy and remove subgingival bacteria.

Clinical Features

In gingivitis, there is generally an accumulation of dental plaque on the tooth adjacent to the inflamed gingiva, which is dark red, especially at the gingival margin. Edematous swelling masks the normal stippled appearance seen in healthy gingiva, and bleeding often occurs, especially after toothbrushing or probing. The flow rate of the crevicular exudate is directly proportionate to the disease severity. In chronic gingivitis, gingival fibrosis may occur, and the inflammatory features may be more difficult to assess.

Chronic inflammatory periodontal disease follows many (not all) cases of gingivitis. (Compare Figs 38–2 and 38–3.) This condition is characterized by progressive inflammatory destruction of periodontal ligament and alveolar bone, apical migration of the epithelial attachment, and pocket formation due to detachment of gingiva from tooth (Figs 38–2 and 38–3). In severe chronic inflammatory periodontal disease where substantial alveolar bone loss has occurred, the teeth become mobile; if the disease progresses, the involved teeth are lost.

Immunologic Diagnosis

Lymphocytes from individuals with periodontal disease are more responsive to dental plaque antigens, but no clear relationships have been found between disease severity and serum or salivary antibody levels. At present, periodontists generally do not use any immunologic test in the diagnosis of gingivitis and periodontitis. Most individuals with inflammatory periodontitis have gingivitis, but the clinical symptoms of the latter may be masked by fibrosis. The flow rate of the crevicular exudate is directly proportionate to the severity of both diseases.

Treatment & Prognosis

Although gingivitis and periodontitis are apparently caused by dental bacterial plaque, there is a reluctance to treat this disease with antibiotics because elimination of one group of organisms by antibiotics may lead to the emergence of antibiotic-resistant strains of organisms. Depending on the severity of the periodontal disease, treatment may range from simply good routine oral hygiene to periodontal surgery. Reducing plaque accumulation to an absolute minimum is essential for the arrest of gingivitis or the reduction of periodontal ligament destruction and bone loss.

JUVENILE PERIODONTITIS

In a small percentage of the population, periodontal bone loss occurs very rapidly, sometimes within 2–5 years. In this condition—juvenile periodontitis, formerly known as periodontosis—conventional periodontal treatment is ineffective. A characteristic gram-negative anaerobic flora, different from that in the more slowly progressive form of periodontitis, is found. Some periodontists feel that short-term antibiotic therapy might be useful in these cases, but there is no evidence that the results of such treatment would be permanent. Several reports suggest that defects in granulocyte or monocyte function may be involved in some instances.

PHENYTOIN–INDUCED GINGIVAL HYPERPLASIA

Individuals who receive phenytoin (Dilantin) often develop severe gingival hyperplasia in response to accumulations of dental plaque, perhaps as a result of an extraordinary local response by fibroblasts and epithelial cells. This response may be due to the effects of phenytoin on fibroblasts and epithelial cells and on the immune system. For example, phenytoin affects salivary and serum immunoglobulin levels and may induce changes in the salivary glands. Induced IgA deficiency has been noted in some individuals who have received phenytoin since infancy. The primary effects of phenytoin may be on the T cells, which are believed to regulate IgA synthesis.

ACUTE NECROTIZING ULCERATIVE GINGIVITIS

Acute necrotizing ulcerative gingivitis is a severe form of gingivitis most commonly seen in adolescents and young adults. The onset is sudden, with pain, gingival bleeding, severe halitosis, and destructive lesions which are most severe in the interdental papillary region. There may be systemic features, including lymphadenopathy, fever, and malaise. The lesions may spread and may also involve other parts of the oral mucous membrane.

Microscopy shows gingival epithelial necrosis with ulceration, a mixed inflammatory cell infiltrate, destruction of the connective tissue in the superficial part of the lesion, and underlying vasodilatation and vascular thrombosis.

A mixed bacterial flora is present that resembles the normal oral flora. There is evidence that spirochetes invade the tissue and penetrate into the connective tissue. There have been few immunologic studies. The only significant finding is increased in vitro lymphocyte activation to certain plaque organisms in patients with this disease as compared with healthy controls. However, the results are very similar to those found in chronic inflammatory periodontal disease and may represent a result rather than the cause of the condition. The lack of significant increases in antibody titers to putative causative organisms during the recovery phase of the condition is evidence against primary infection by one of these organisms.

DENTAL CARIES

Dental caries is a bacterial disease in which the hard structures of the teeth are progressively destroyed by a process involving both the mineral and organic components of enamel and dentin. The principal causative organism of enamel caries is *Streptococcus mutans*, although other organisms may play a role. *S mutans* produces acids which are capable of dissolving enamel. Another important factor is production of a favorable environment through accumulation of bacterial plaque on the tooth surface, partly due to *S mutans* itself, which is capable of manufacturing the dextran bulk of the plaque with its enzyme glucosyltransferase.

One means of caries prevention has involved increasing the resistance of tooth structures through the use of fluoride, either as a public health measure in drinking water or as a topical agent in individual patients. Additional prophylactic measures include attempts to prevent the accumulation of bacterial plaque by measures designed to improve hygiene, by the use of antibacterial agents, and by restriction of fermentable carbohydrates in the diet. Only recently has an immunologic approach been applied to the problem of caries prevention, although the conceptual basis for this approach has been available for over 50 years. The delay was due partly to the difficulty in identifying the causative organisms among the multitude of normal oral flora; partly to the limited availability of acceptable animal models for caries; and partly to the reluctance of many workers to accept the notion that the hard, nonvital enamel surface, which is "outside the body," could be protected by immunologic means. With the establishment of *S mutans* as the probable causative organism and the realization that the gingival sulcus fluid continually brings high concentrations of antibodies to the enamel surface, interest in immunization against dental caries has intensified. Attempts to immunize rodents and monkeys against *S mutans* whole cells or various forms of antigen preparations, including glucosyltransferase, have produced promising results. Significant levels of anti-*S mutans* serum or salivary antibodies and decreased or delayed inception of carious lesions have been reported. Concern has been expressed that antibody to *S mutans* might cross-react with host tissues and possibly produce rheumatic fever, although it is not clear that the bacterial antigen eliciting the anti-caries immune response is also capable of inducing the harmful autoimmune process.

RECURRENT ORAL ULCERATION
(Aphthous Stomatitis)

Major Immunologic Features

- Lymphocyte infiltration present at earliest stage of the lesion.
- Circulating antibodies to oral mucous membrane present in some patients, which cross-react with oral organisms.
- Cellular immunity to the same antigens.
- Circulating immune complexes found in some patients.
- Association with HLA antigens.
- Favorable response to topical or systemic corticosteroids.

General Considerations

After caries and chronic periodontal disease, oral ulceration probably represents the most common lesion of the mouth. Although oral ulcers can be due to a large number of diseases, the most common form is recurrent oral ulceration (aphthous stomatitis). Recurrent oral ulcers usually occur alone but may be a local manifestation of Behçet's syndrome, along with uveitis or genital ulcers and perhaps lesions of other systems. Estimates of the incidence of recurrent oral ulceration vary, but 20% is probably reasonable. The condition may recur only once or twice a year or may be so frequent that a new set of ulcers overlaps a previous group. There is slight evidence of a familial incidence. Emotional and nutritional factors may play a causative role, and an association has been suggested with changes in the hormone status during the menstrual cycle. Extensive searches for specific bacterial or viral causes have been unsuccessful. It must be emphasized that recurrent oral ulceration is not caused by herpes virus, although primary herpetic gingivostomatitis and recurrent herpesvirus lesions are frequently confused with recurrent oral ulceration. One report suggests a role for adenovirus type 1. Somewhat stronger evidence indicates a role for S sanguis, since this organism has been cultured from the ulcers and patients exhibit delayed hypersensitivity reactions to the organism and significant inhibition of leukocyte migration in vitro. However, the organism is a common commensal. Furthermore, another study has shown reduced lymphocyte transformation to the organism in patients as compared with controls. A more likely role for bacterial or viral agents in this disease is that of cross-reacting antigens eliciting host responses to autologous oral mucous membrane antigens.

Immunologic Pathogenesis

Patients have a raised level of circulating antibody to a saline extract of fetal oral mucous membrane. Slightly raised levels of the same antibody have been found in other ulcerative conditions but at lower titers. The antibodies are of the agglutinating and complement-fixing types, suggesting that antibody cytotoxicity might be involved in the tissue destruction. However, other studies show poor correlation between the level of anti-mucous membrane antibody and clinical features of the disease. In addition, 2 other mechanisms could explain the presence of circulating autoantibodies of this type. The antibodies may represent a cross-reaction between antigens of an organism present in the mouth, such as S sanguis or adenovirus, and oral mucous membrane epithelial cells. Alternatively, the antibodies may be produced because ulceration has repeatedly exposed tissue antigens that had previously been protected from the immune system. There have been unsuccessful attempts to show that patients' serum containing significant titers of this antibody has a direct cytotoxic effect against oral epithelial cells. Thus, it is unlikely that the direct action of a cytotoxic anti-oral mucosal antibody is involved in the pathogenesis.

Interest in the role of cellular immune mechanisms in the pathogenesis of recurrent oral ulceration was aroused by the observation that the earliest histologic changes involve the presence of an infiltrate of lymphocytes. Other cells do not appear until a later stage. Furthermore, patients with recurrent oral ulceration were shown to have peripheral blood lymphocytes that were sensitized to oral mucous membrane antigen. These 2 observations support the hypothesis that a cell-mediated hypersensitivity mechanism might be involved in the pathogenesis of the lesion. Lymphocytes from some patients with recurrent oral ulceration are cytotoxic to oral epithelial cells. The antigen eliciting the cytotoxic reaction has not been identified. It might be one or more epithelial cell surface autoantigens, determinants cross-reacting with an infecting organism or organisms, or food or microbial antigens attached to oral epithelial cell surfaces or even produced by a hapten mechanism. Increased antibody-dependent cellular cytotoxicity has been found. The identity of the population of lymphocytes involved in these reactions is also unknown. There is at present no acceptable hypothesis linking oral mucous membrane autoantigen and effector mechanisms, although transient defects in immunoregulation have been postulated.

Patients with Behçet's syndrome and recurrent oral ulceration show elevated levels of serum C9 and of circulating soluble immune complexes. IgG and C3 have also been demonstrated in the basement membrane zone of the lesions. It is not clear whether these observations offer further clues to the immunologic pathogenesis of the disease or represent epiphenomena. There is also some evidence for an increased incidence of HLA-B12 in recurrent oral ulceration.

Clinical Features

Recurrent oral ulceration is a common disease characterized by painful recurrent necrotizing ulcerations of the nonkeratinized oral mucous membrane.

The ulcers are covered with a gray membrane surrounded by an erythematous ring. Ulcers may form singly or in groups and may appear infrequently or be so common that the patient is never free from disease. The current classification recognizes 3 subtypes. Major aphthae are large (> 5 mm in diameter) and are often long-lasting. Minor aphthae (< 5 mm in diameter) are the common form. A rarer subtype known as herpetiform ulceration is characterized by clusters of very small ulcers. Herpetiform ulceration, which bears no relationship to herpesvirus lesions, may represent a different disease.

At the very early stage, prior to fresh ulceration, when the patient first becomes aware of a change in sensation or a small itchy nodule, the microscopic appearance is that of a lymphocytic infiltrate. Once ulceration has occurred, the predominant appearance is that of acute inflammation, with vascular dilatation, polymorphonuclear leukocyte and fluid exudation, and surface necrosis. There may be chronic inflammation, with lymphocytes and plasma cells in the deeper part of the lesion. The smaller ulcers heal at about 4 days, and no scar is produced. Major aphthous ulcers may last several weeks or months, and such lesions extend deeper into the underlying connective tissue, minor salivary glands, and muscle and then heal with scarring. The ulcers may interfere with speech, mastication, and swallowing because of pain and their location. In such cases, the patient may be unable to work and may lose weight.

Differential Diagnosis

The diagnosis is often based on the history of recurrent ulceration in the mouth and on the clinical appearance. The disease must be distinguished from traumatic ulceration, primary herpetic gingivostomatitis, recurrent labial herpes, the oral lesions of vesiculobullous diseases such as pemphigus, pemphigoid, erythema multiforme, and erosive lichen planus, and oral ulcerations associated with ulcerative colitis. Crohn's disease, celiac disease, other malabsorption states, and hematologic abnormalities must also be considered. The last subject is controversial, but several studies indicate a significant incidence of hematologic and malabsorption problems in patients presenting with clinical recurrent oral ulceration. The underlying diseases discovered during these studies include gastric carcinoma, celiac disease, and a variety of inflammatory bowel diseases. The oral ulcers usually resolved when the underlying condition was treated, but they did not respond to local measures. If, as is suggested by some studies, as many as 20% of cases are due to underlying, possibly serious systemic disease, extensive investigation would be indicated, including screening of all patients by means of a complete blood count and determinations of serum iron, vitamin B_{12}, and folic acid.

The oral ulcers of Behçet's syndrome are identical to those in other forms of disease, but the syndrome can usually be diagnosed because of the presence of ocular lesions or genital ulceration or because of the involvement of other systems. Oral ulceration can be a feature of neutropenia or agranulocytosis associated with marrow defects caused by drugs or other factors. The oral ulcers of cyclic neutropenia are very similar and may occur in the absence of other symptoms.

Treatment & Prognosis

Effective treatment depends on identification of any underlying systemic disease. In such cases, treatment of the systemic condition usually leads to cure of the oral ulceration. For the remaining group, uncomplicated by known systemic disease, several treatment forms are available. They involve the use of topical corticosteroids, antibiotics, and immunostimulants. The most effective topical corticosteroids available are 0.1% triamcinolone in Orabase and 2.5 mg tablets of hydrocortisone sodium succinate. Some cases of major aphthous ulceration are sufficiently severe to warrant the use of systemic prednisone. Tetracycline mouth rinses have been used with some success in the herpetiform variety of recurrent oral ulceration. Some reports suggest that systemic therapy with levamisole may be effective in some cases, although this has not been confirmed. The treatment of Behçet's syndrome is dealt with in Chapter 26.

SYSTEMIC DISEASES WITH ORAL MANIFESTATIONS INVOLVING IMMUNOLOGIC MECHANISMS

The cause or causes of the immunologic diseases discussed below that affect oral mucosa have not been determined. However, several recent findings in animals in which autoantibodies have been experimentally induced suggest an association of these diseases with (1) the continued presence of damaged or chemically modified host tissue and (2) genetic factors which affect T lymphocyte suppressor, helper, or recognition functions (see Chapter 8). Deposition of autoantibody on its host antigen will activate the classic complement pathway. In turn, this will activate the alternative complement pathway through C3b and initiate complement-dependent tissue destruction.

PEMPHIGUS

Pemphigus is a rare vesiculobullous disease in which autoantibody to host epithelial intercellular substance is produced (Fig 38–4) (see Chapter 32). No information is available about the cause and little about the nature of the host antigen. Both the mucosal and the skin blisters contain free-floating epithelial cells coated with antibody and complement (Table 38–1). It is not known why lesions commonly appear first on the oral mucosa. However, prompt treatment with systemic corticosteroids may prevent spread of the disease to skin. Direct immunofluorescence should be a

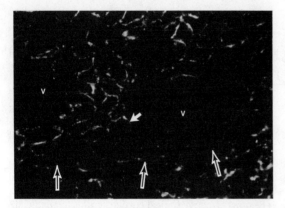

Figure 38–4. Direct immunofluorescence on buccal mucosa from a patient with pemphigus vulgaris. The conjugated antihuman IgG is bound in the intercellular spaces of the epithelial cells and to the surface of the cells undergoing acantholysis (solid arrow). Intraepithelial vesicles (V) form above the row of basal epithelial cells attached to the basement membrane (open arrows). Original magnification × 312. (Courtesy of TE Daniels.)

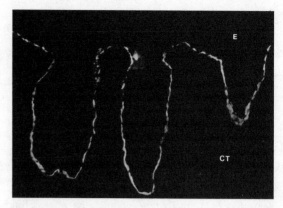

Figure 38–5. Direct immunofluorescence on gingiva from a patient with mucous membrane pemphigoid. The conjugated antihuman C3 forms a continuous linear fluorescent pattern between the epithelium (E) and connective tissue (CT) in the basement membrane zone. Original magnification × 156. (Courtesy of TE Daniels.)

routine procedure in the diagnosis of oral vesiculoerosive disease.

BENIGN MUCOUS MEMBRANE PEMPHIGOID

Benign mucous membrane (cicatricial) pemphigoid is a rare chronic blistering, scarring autoimmune disease with a predilection for mucosal surfaces (see Chapter 32). The host produces autoantibody (IgG, IgA, or IgM) against basement membrane zone

Table 38–1. Immunofluorescence observations in lesions of pemphigus, cicatricial pemphigoid, and chronic discoid lupus erythematosus.

| Antiserum To | Percent With Positive Immunofluorescence* | | |
| | Pemphigus | Cicatricial Pemphigoid | Chronic Discoid Lupus Erythematosus |
	Intercellular Substance†	Basement Membrane Zone	Dermal-Epidermal Junction
IgG	100 (12)	39 (23)	46 (13)
IgA	33 (12)	40 (20)	33 (12)
IgM	25 (12)	29 (21)	46 (13)
C3	100 (12)	81 (21)	57 (41)
C1q	58 (12)	64 (11)	Not done
C4	66 (6)	50 (4)	57 (14)‡
Factor B	50 (12)	50 (10)	Not done
Properdin	25 (12)	64 (11)	71 (13)

*Number of patients tested is shown in parentheses. Data compiled from the following studies: Jordan RE: *J Invest Dermatol* 1976;**67**:366; Rogers RS III et al: *J Invest Dermatol* 1977;**68**: 39; Schrager MA, Rothfield NF: *Arthritis Rheum* 1977;**20**: 637.

†Antigenic substrate used in each disease.

‡Patients with C4 deposition also had C3 deposition.

substances (Fig 38–5). Subsequent complement binding has also been demonstrated in the majority of cases (Table 38–1). The original antigenic stimulus is not known. The T lymphocyte suppressor, helper, and recognition functions are important determinants. The antibody response to human type III collagen, which is found in basement membrane, is highly T lymphocyte–dependent. Circulating antibodies against host basement membrane antigens have been demonstrated in a small percentage of individuals with this disease.

The condition known as **desquamative gingivitis** can be a manifestation of pemphigus, pemphigoid, erythema multiforme, or lichen planus.

The diagnosis of oral vesiculobullous disease involves biopsy and direct immunofluorescence as well as indirect immunofluorescence with the patient's serum. Systemic corticosteroids are used in the treatment of oral pemphigoid.

CHRONIC DISCOID LUPUS ERYTHEMATOSUS

Chronic discoid lupus erythematosus is a disease of unknown cause characterized by skin and oral mucosal lesions that are clinically similar to the chronic scarring lesions seen in 10–20% of patients with systemic lupus erythematosus. Typical histologic changes in oral mucosal lesions consist of hyperkeratosis or atrophy, hydropic degeneration of basal cells, and perivascular lymphocytic infiltrates in the connective tissue. Unlike patients with systemic lupus erythematosus (see Chapters 26 and 32), patients with chronic discoid lupus erythematosus rarely have any systemic manifestations; however, about 5% of the patients ultimately develop systemic lupus erythematosus. In chronic discoid lupus erythematosus, deposition of immunoglobulin and complement usually occurs only in the areas of the visible lesion, whereas in systemic lupus erythematosus deposition occurs even in "normal" mucosa and skin. In both diseases, a granular deposition of immunoglobulin and complement can occur at the mucosal-submucosal interface or in skin at the dermal-epidermal junction (Table 38–1). In chronic discoid lupus erythematosus, serum properdin levels and C3 synthesis may be elevated, whereas in systemic lupus, C3 and often properdin levels are lowered. Significant levels of antinuclear (anti-DNA) antibodies are not found as they are in systemic lupus erythematosus. Elevated serum properdin levels seen in chronic discoid lupus erythematosus may also be seen in systemic lupus erythematosus patients with inactive disease.

ERYTHEMA MULTIFORME

Erythema multiforme is an acute inflammatory disease the manifestations of which range from a few inflamed cutaneous and mucosal lesions to a rare multisystemic and sometimes fatal disorder. The prodromal and inflammatory stages are usually short and the initial erythema usually fades in 3–7 days, leaving hemorrhagic papules. Polymorphous skin lesions form annular or figured patterns, and bullous erosive involvement of the mucous membranes often occurs.

The cause is unknown, but infection and a number of drugs and environmental factors have been suggested as possible causes. Erythema multiforme may be a form of contact dermatitis, though confirmatory evidence is not available. Efforts to identify specific microbial agents have been unsuccessful. Perivascular C3 and IgG have been found in the lesions. If the immune system is involved in the pathogenesis, it is probably at the prodromal stage. Treatment with corticosteroids or other immunosuppressants is not routinely indicated.

LICHEN PLANUS

This relatively common inflammatory disease of the skin often includes oral features, and about one-third of cases of oral lichen planus are associated with skin lesions. The oral lesions vary in character from flat white areas resembling hyperplastic or dysplastic lesions to extensive areas of erosion or ulceration. The latter can be extremely troublesome. Histologically, the lesion is characterized by a tendency to epithelial thickening, with hyperplasia and degenerative changes in the basal area of epithelium. The underlying connective tissue shows a dense infiltrate of round cells that are mostly lymphocytes and macrophages. Several studies have shown that these lymphocytes are predominantly (even exclusively) T cells. The pathogenic mechanism involved in the production of the lesions is unknown. Possibilities include microbial agents or antigens (either bacterial or viral) and autoimmunity. Indirect immunofluorescence does not reveal any characteristic immunoglobulin deposition, but there is a consistent pattern with binding of antiserum to fibrinogen in the basement membrane and superficial connective tissue zone. Attempts to demonstrate cell-mediated immunologic defects have been disappointing. The oral lesions of the erosive variety respond to topical corticosteroids, but these agents do not cure the disease. There is a potential for malignant transformation in lichen planus, and caution must therefore be exercised in long-term use of corticosteroids in this disease.

INFLAMMATORY BOWEL DISEASES WITH ORAL MANIFESTATIONS

Ulcerative colitis and Crohn's disease (see Chapter 29), which classically involve the intestinal mucosa, may also involve the mouth. In ulcerative colitis and, to a much lesser extent, in Crohn's disease, the host lymphocytes may be cytotoxic for colonic epithelial cells. This may be a primary defect or may be due to low levels of suppressor cell activity. Moreover, in a low percentage of cases, high titers of circulating autoantibodies are detected against colonic mucosal epithelial mucopolysaccharides. These antibodies react with bacterial lipopolysaccharide antigens (*Escherichia coli* O14), and bacteria might be partially responsible for the autoantibody response in genetically susceptible individuals. In both diseases, the intestinal mucosa is damaged; subsequently, one might expect a higher penetration of bacterial antigens and, at the onset of the disease, an elevation of the mucosal antibody response (serum and secretory IgA). There may also be an effect on the local synthesis of C1 and secretory component by the epithelial cells of the affected intestinal mucosa. Indeed, elevations of serum and secretory IgA are seen in some cases of ulcerative colitis, although no work has been done on the effects of the inflammatory bowel diseases on the metabolism of C1 or secretory component.

The cause of the oral mucosal lesions is not known. However, malnutrition, anxiety, and the altered macrophage and lymphocyte functions may occur secondary to these intestinal disorders. Damage to intestinal mucosa may lead to alteration of mucosal cell structures so that they too may become antigenic. Patients with Crohn's disease have serum antibodies that react with their own oral mucosa in an immunofluorescence system.

Crohn's disease can involve the oral mucosa and lips, either in association with the gastrointestinal features of the disease or as its sole manifestation. There may be ulcers of the aphthous type, linear ulcers, raised nodules producing a "cobblestone" appearance on the buccal mucosa, or ridges resembling the fibroepithelial hyperplasia induced by ill-fitting dentures. Lips may show marked enlargement and cracking. Biopsy reveals multiple noncaseating granulomas with no evidence of acid-fast organisms. When the oral features appear alone, local topical corticosteroids may be effective.

SARCOIDOSIS

Sarcoidosis (see Chapter 30) is a granulomatous disorder of unknown cause that most commonly affects middle-aged individuals. Many organs and tissues may become involved, particularly the intrathoracic tissues, hilar and paratracheal lymph nodes, and lung parenchyma. In a minority of cases the peripheral lymph nodes, eyes, skin, spleen, nervous system, and salivary glands may be affected.

About 6% of individuals with sarcoidosis have salivary gland involvement. Swelling of major or minor salivary glands and xerostomia can occur. Labial salivary gland biopsy may be useful in excluding other causes of these signs. Oral mucosal lesions may be seen and include red or brown patches that are firm and painless or may ulcerate.

SJÖGREN'S SYNDROME

Sjögren's syndrome is a chronic inflammatory disease with widespread manifestations. The major features involve the salivary and lacrimal glands, and one of the connective tissue diseases is often present. Sjögren's syndrome can be diagnosed with certainty when 2 out of these 3 components are present. In addition to the dry mouth and dry eyes, patients frequently exhibit dryness of the upper respiratory tract, the ears, and the vaginal mucosa (see Chapter 26).

Oral Signs & Symptoms

Patients may complain of dryness of the mouth, soreness of the oral mucous membranes, otherwise inexplicable difficulties in wearing dentures, changes in taste sensation, or dysphagia. There may be a history of salivary gland swelling, but this is not necessary for the diagnosis. The xerostomia frequently leads to extensive dental caries, with numerous lesions at the cervical margins of the buccal surfaces and on the incisal and smooth occlusal surfaces. The latter finding is pathognomonic of xerostomia.

Heretofore, assessment of xerostomia has usually been subjective, but there are now well-established objective criteria. These include measurement of stimulated parotid flow rate under standardized conditions, salivary scintigraphy, and semiquantitative assessment of chronic inflammatory involvement of the minor salivary glands of the lip. Labial salivary gland biopsy is a readily performed procedure which has revolutionized the diagnosis of this disease. Interdisciplinary cooperation between rheumatologists, ophthalmologists, stomatologists, and immunologists is essential for the proper diagnosis and management of Sjögren's syndrome.

The differential diagnosis includes all other causes of chronic xerostomia and salivary gland swelling, ie, drug-induced xerostomia, irradiation xerostomia, diabetes, tuberculosis or sarcoidosis, and salivary gland involvement in lymphoproliferative disorders. Primary salivary gland neoplasms usually develop in one gland, whereas the swelling in Sjögren's syndrome is frequently, but not always, bilateral. Other causes of salivary gland swelling include acute infection, salivary gland duct stones, mumps and cytomegalovirus infection, cirrhosis, and hypolipoproteinemia.

Pathogenesis & Features of the Salivary Gland Lesion

The characteristic lesion of Sjögren's syndrome in the major salivary glands is an infiltrate of lymphocytes, plasma cells, and macrophages which progressively replaces the acinar cells. Ducts may remain, and islands of epithelial cells, presumably proliferating from these duct remnants, may stand out against a monotonous background of chronic inflammatory cells. Although these islands are often referred to as "epimyoepithelial islands," there is no evidence that myoepithelial cells contribute to them. The progressive replacement of secretory acinar tissue causes the functional failure of the salivary glands and presumably also causes the swelling of the major gland when it occurs. The counterpart of this lesion in the minor salivary glands is focal sialadenitis, again with replacement of acini and survival of ducts. However, in the minor salivary glands, epimyoepithelial islands are not seen.

Some workers have described as a separate entity a histologically identical lesion of the major glands, which they term benign lymphoepithelial lesions. However, most if not all cases of this entity represent examples of Sjögren's syndrome. The benign lymphoepithelial lesion originally described by Mikulicz and identified for many years as Mikulicz's disease probably also is Sjögren's syndrome. Unfortunately, the situation was further confused by the use of the term Mikulicz's syndrome for swelling of major salivary glands due to other causes, including tuberculosis, diabetes, lymphoma, and leukemia.

The salivary gland lesion of Sjögren's syndrome and the benign lymphoepithelial lesion (Mikulicz's disease), which probably represents a variant, are associated with a tendency to develop malignant lymphoma. The risk of transformation into non-Hodgkin's lymphoma has been estimated to be 44 times that of the general population. There also appears to be an increased risk of skin cancer. Sometimes the lymphoma develops within the salivary gland lesion, but more often it occurs elsewhere. An intermediate stage (pseudolymphoma), which may represent a form of immunoblastic lymphadenopathy, has also been described.

The mechanism causing the progressive accumulation of lymphocytes, plasma cells, and macrophages within the salivary glands is unknown. The lymphocytes appear to be of both B and T cell types, and the initial lesion may consist of B cells and plasma cells, with T cells appearing later in the center of large foci within the minor glands. The mechanism of acinar cell destruction is also unknown, although direct cellular cytotoxicity or an antibody-dependent cellular cytotoxic mechanism seems likely. These autodestructive mechanisms may be induced by viral antigens, virally modified autoantigens, or abnormal autoantigens of other types. Conversely, a primary abnormality in the control of lymphocyte autoreactivity might be present because of a regulatory defect involving suppressor or helper T cell abnormalities.

Although autoantibodies to salivary duct epithelium have been described in some cases of Sjögren's syndrome and rheumatoid arthritis, these do not appear to be cytotoxic and are probably not a factor in the pathogenesis of the salivary gland lesion. There is some evidence that the very earliest lesion consists of a perivascular lymphomonocytic infiltrate, but vasculitis is not seen and immune complexes have not been reported. No ready explanation exists for the higher incidence of Sjögren's syndrome in women, although recent findings regarding the effects of sex hormones on the severity of the NZB/NZW mouse model of human lupus and Sjögren's syndrome may throw some light on this problem (see Chapter 13).

Treatment

The treatment of the oral manifestations of Sjögren's syndrome is directed toward symptomatic relief of oral dryness and prevention of dental caries. While salivation may be stimulated by sour drinks or sour candies, sugar-containing or acid preparations must be rigorously avoided. Many patients consume large quantities of water or other liquids, but urinary frequency or nocturia often results. Mouth rinses containing methylcellulose 1% with sugar-free and acid-free flavoring are often helpful. Preventive dental measures include strict oral hygiene instruction and plaque control, topical fluoride applications, fluoride mouth rinses, and regular dental examinations, with restorative dental treatment when required. Oral candidiasis is a common complication of Sjögren's syndrome.

SYSTEMIC LUPUS ERYTHEMATOSUS

The oral mucosa and salivary glands may be involved in 15–50% of patients with systemic lupus erythematosus. The oral lesions include erythematous areas and ulcers on the lips or oral mucosa. Occasionally, oral ulcers may be the presenting feature, in which case biopsy and immunofluorescence microscopy may provide the diagnosis before systemic manifestations are discovered. A few patients with systemic lupus erythematosus have frank Sjögren's syndrome, although the incidence of subclinical involvement of salivary glands is probably much higher.

RHEUMATOID ARTHRITIS

In both adult and juvenile forms of rheumatoid arthritis, approximately 50% of cases involve the temporomandibular joint. Damage to the growth center in the developing mandibular condyle may lead to micrognathia and severe malocclusion. There is significant overlap between rheumatoid arthritis and Sjögren's syndrome.

PROGRESSIVE SYSTEMIC SCLEROSIS

Widening of the periodontal ligament spaces as shown on x-ray is found in about one-third of patients with systemic sclerosis. Furthermore, some patients also show resorption of some part of the mandibular angle or coronoid process. There may be limitation in opening the mouth, tongue rigidity, and dysphagia. This disease sometimes coexists with Sjögren's syndrome.

INFECTIOUS DISEASES

Many infectious diseases with immunologic features affect the mouth. Some, including tuberculosis, syphilis, and the acute viral diseases of childhood, have prominent oral features. Most of these diseases are adequately described elsewhere in this book. The 2 diseases described below—herpes simplex and candidiasis—are notable because the oral manifestations are often the most significant.

HERPES SIMPLEX VIRUS INFECTION

Major Immunologic Features
- Antibodies to herpes simplex virus appear during the primary infection and persist at lower levels throughout life.
- Cell-mediated immunity develops early during the primary infection.
- Cellular immune defects may be associated with recurrent infections.

General Considerations

Clinically detectable initial oral disease due to herpes simplex virus type 1 (HSV-1) takes the form of primary herpetic stomatitis. It is probable that many people acquire the virus without experiencing the disease. Recurrent HSV-1 lesions are due not to exogenous reinfection but to reactivation of latent virus. They involve predominantly the lips (herpes labialis), but a rarer intraoral ulcerative form also occurs. The virus probably resides in neurons and in the cell bodies of the trigeminal ganglion or sensory root ganglia between attacks, although other sites for latent virus residence have not been excluded. Recurrence can be precipitated by sunlight, other viral infection, fever, stress, trauma, menstruation, and section of the sensory root of the trigeminal ganglion. There may be a connection between latent HSV-1 infection and oral squamous cell carcinoma (see below).

Immunologic Pathogenesis

Serum antibodies to HSV-1 reach maximum levels within 3 weeks of primary infection, with IgM preceding IgG. Cellular immune responses are first detectable as lymphocyte activation to herpes simplex virus antigen days before a significant antibody titer is found. Other indications of cell-mediated immunity follow weeks later. Persons prone to recurrent infections do not have higher or lower antibody levels than other individuals but may have a transient T cell–mediated immunodeficiency that encourages the virus. Macrophage activation probably contributes to control of the infection. Primary and secondary immunodeficiencies are associated with severe forms of oral and other herpesvirus infections.

Clinical Features

Primary HSV-1 infections usually occur in children and young adults. When the disease affects older individuals, it is often opportunistic and should suggest immunodeficiency. The early phase is characterized by fever, dehydration, malaise, and nausea. The oral features are swelling and mobility of the gingival and oral mucosa, and crops of vesicles which rupture to form ulcers. There is excessive salivation, halitosis, dysphagia, and local lymphadenopathy. Individual lesions are 2–4 mm in diameter, painful, covered by a yellow pseudomembrane, and surrounded by a red margin. The acute primary phase usually lasts about 2 weeks, and the lesions subside without scar formation. Primary lesions in extraoral sites are occasionally seen as a result of inoculation in dentists and other clinicians and are due to virus in the saliva of patients.

Recurrent Herpes Simplex

This condition is much more common than primary herpetic stomatitis, and the lesions are usually confined to the external surface of the lips (cold sore). The lesion starts as a vesicle or group of vesicles after a short period of tingling or burning sensation. The vesicle usually crusts over and heals within 10 days. Precipitating factors include local trauma, emotional stress, menstruation, exposure to sunlight, fever, and other viral infections.

Immunologic Diagnosis

Diagnosis of the primary disease is usually made on clinical grounds and may be confirmed by cytologic examination of the fluid from an intact vesicle. Viral intranuclear inclusion bodies and giant cells may be seen. Viral culture may be performed, but a positive result is not necessarily diagnostic of the disease because HSV-1 can also be found in healthy controls. A rise in antibody titer and the inception of lymphocyte responses to viral antigen during the disease are occasionally helpful in the diagnosis.

Immunologic methods are not particularly helpful in the diagnosis of recurrent herpes. Antibody is always found in sufferers from recurrent herpes and does not appear to be protective, since titers do not change during recurrent episodes.

Treatment & Prognosis

Treatment is usually directed toward symptomatic relief, with tetracycline mouth rinses occasionally being used to reduce secondary infection. Antiviral agents that have been tried include idoxuridine, cytarabine, vidarabine (adenine arabinoside [Ara-A]), acyclovir, and interferon. There are as yet insufficient data to justify the routine use of these drugs for oral herpes simplex. Several specific antiherpes drugs are now undergoing clinical trials. The use of dyes combined with fluorescent light is contraindicated because of the danger of potentiating the oncogenic properties of HSV-1.

ORAL CANDIDIASIS

Major Immunologic Features

- Oral lesions due to *Candida albicans*.
- Many associated immunologic defects.
- The most significant oral indication of an underlying immunodeficiency.

General Considerations

Oral candidiasis is the most common oral fungal disease. It may occur in acute or chronic form at any age. The disease may be a sign of serious life-threatening systemic disease or may be confined to a small part of the oral mucous membrane and be of no general significance. *Candida* species are frequent oral commensals, and it has not yet been established whether candidiasis is predominantly of endogenous or exogenous origin.

Classification

A valuable classification of oral candidiasis has been provided by Lehner:

A. Acute Pseudomembranous Candidiasis (Thrush): This disease, predominantly found in infants and in adults with malignant disease and diabetes, is characterized by the presence of masses of loose, white, curdlike collections of fungus and exudate on the oral mucosa. These can be detached to leave a red, bleeding surface. The condition can also be caused by immunosuppressive drugs and systemic antibiotics.

B. Acute Atrophic Candidiasis: A rarer complication of broad-spectrum antibiotic therapy, this disease presents as a soft, smooth glossitis and angular cheilitis, sometimes involving other areas of the oral mucous membrane.

C. Chronic Atrophic Candidiasis (Denture Stomatitis): This disease is sufficiently common to warrant separate discussion (see below).

D. Chronic Mucocutaneous Candidiasis: Four clinical subtypes are described.

1. Chronic oral hyperplastic candidiasis (candidal leukoplakia)–Lesion limited to the mouth, taking the form of a firm, white area of mucosa that is clinically difficult to distinguish from other forms of leukoplakia.

2. Chronic localized mucocutaneous candidiasis–Long-lasting oral candidiasis, usually starting in childhood and spreading to involve the nails and other areas of skin.

3. Chronic localized mucocutaneous candidiasis with granuloma–Similar to (2) above, starting in infancy and characterized by candidal granuloma of face and scalp.

4. Chronic localized mucocutaneous candidiasis with endocrinopathy–Mucocutaneous candidiasis with, for example, hypoparathyroidism, Addison's disease, pernicious anemia or hypothyroidism, or a combination of endocrine disorders.

Immunologic Pathogenesis

The immunologic features of generalized candidiasis are discussed elsewhere (see Chapters 25, 32, and 33). A wide range of immunologic defects have been found, including defects in cytotoxicity to *Candida,* reduced lymphokine production, failure of anticandidal antibody response of one or more classes, generalized cytotoxicity defects, failure of lymphocyte activation to candidal antigen, absence of delayed hypersensitivity skin test to *Candida* or to many antigens, and presence of an abnormal suppressor cell population. However, immunologic defects alone do not explain the pathogenesis of candidiasis. High glucose levels in diabetics and low levels of serum iron transferrin and blood folate are also important factors. Granulocyte defects have been shown in some patients, as have defects in leukocyte myeloperoxidase. A few patients have been described in whom antibody production to *Candida* and other antigens was raised while cellular immune function was depressed.

Clinical Features of Some Oral Candidal Lesions

A. Pseudomembranous Candidiasis (Thrush): Thrush can be seen in infants, in debilitated patients, and in patients treated with antibiotics, corticosteroids, and immunosuppressive drugs. Creamy whitish-yellow patches cover variable areas of the oral mucous membrane and can be rubbed or lifted off, leaving an erythematous bleeding base. The patient may not notice the lesion or may complain of soreness or dryness.

B. Acute Atrophic Candidiasis: This lesion is painful and presents as smooth, depapillated tongue with localized erosions. It may follow thrush or may occur de novo. It is particularly associated with antibiotic therapy.

C. Chronic Hyperplastic Candidiasis (Candidal Leukoplakia): Persistent white areas are found on the buccal mucous membrane and other areas of the oral mucosa. These may be soft or firm and cannot be readily detached. They may closely resemble other forms of leukoplakia, but it is important that they be diagnosed because of the potential for successful treatment with antifungal drugs. Since the question of malignant transformation in candidal leukoplakia has not been settled, for the moment it is best to assume long-term malignant potential for the untreated lesion.

The clinical features of mucocutaneous candidiasis, candidal granuloma, and mucocutaneous candidiasis with endocrinopathy are discussed elsewhere (see Chapters 25, 32, and 33).

Immunologic Diagnosis

The diagnosis of thrush is based upon the clinical appearance and history. The immunologic approach is directed toward establishing the nature of the immunologic defect, if any. The same remarks apply to acute atrophic candidiasis. Although immunologic investigation of patients with oral candidiasis is still predominantly a research tool, it is likely that subtypes will be identified and that specific immunologic treatment will be directed toward the correction of localized defects in cell-mediated immunity. The differential diagnosis of candidal leukoplakia from other white oral lesions involves smear, culture, and biopsy.

Treatment & Prognosis

Treatment of localized oral candidiasis consists of elimination of predisposing factors, where known, and administration of topical antifungal therapy. This may be prolonged in the case of chronic forms of oral candidiasis. Systemic therapy is used in cases that are resistant to local measures and in generalized mucocutaneous candidiasis. The treatment of denture stomatitis is discussed below.

DENTURE STOMATITIS

Major Immunologic Features

- Inflammation of mucous membrane under dentures.
- Associated with *Candida albicans*.
- Some evidence of impaired cell-mediated responses to *Candida*.
- Restoration of impaired cell-mediated responses with antifungal treatment.

General Considerations

Inflammation of the mucous membrane under dentures is a common problem. The condition can occur with any form of intraoral prosthesis, but removable maxillary full dentures produce the largest number of cases. The mucous membrane is bright red, soft, and somewhat spongy. It is not always possible to isolate *Candida* from the mucous membrane by smear, scraping, or biopsy, but the fungus can usually be cultured from the plaquelike material covering the fitting surface of the denture. It is not clear whether the inflammatory reaction is due to tissue invasion by a small number of organisms, the effects of toxins released by the fungus, or a hypersensitivity reaction to *Candida* antigens.

Immunologic Pathogenesis

Dentures cause a continual mild trauma to the mucous membrane that may facilitate the entry of candidal antigens into the tissues. This effect may be aggravated by the denture-induced obstruction to salivary flow across the mucosa and by reduced elimination of affected epithelial cells. Another factor could be competition by microbial species under the denture for the limited nutrients available in this location. Thus, the condition can be exacerbated by long-term treatment with antibiotics. Salivary IgA antibodies to *C albicans* may be involved in the normal defense mechanism to this organism, and dentures could prevent access of this immunoglobulin to its target. Serum anticandidal antibodies are associated with denture stomatitis but are apparently not protective. On the other hand, cell-mediated immune mechanisms seem to be important in the normal response to *Candida*. There is some evidence that the incidence of positive skin reaction to *Candida* extract is lower in denture stomatitis patients than in controls. Furthermore, defective cellular hypersensitivity to *C albicans* can be restored after successful antifungal treatment. This suggests that *Candida*-induced denture stomatitis might be the cause of the suppression of the cellular immune response rather than the converse. However, the apparent decrease in cell-mediated immunity to candidal antigen could be due to the withdrawal of sensitized lymphocytes from the circulation into the lesion.

Clinical Features

Denture stomatitis consists of inflammation on the denture-bearing surface of the oral mucous membrane and appears more frequently in the maxillary than in the mandibular area. The severity ranges from a localized area of tiny red dots through diffuse erythema to a proliferative response which may result in papillary hyperplasia. The condition may be associated with angular cheilitis and glossitis. There may be no symptoms, or the patient may complain of a burning sensation under the denture.

Immunologic Diagnosis

The diagnosis is usually afforded by the location of the lesion and the clinical appearance; immunologic techniques are not used on a routine basis. However, as with other forms of oral candidiasis, it is always wise to bear in mind the possibility of an underlying immunodeficiency, particularly when the lesion arises in an otherwise previously healthy mouth.

Treatment

Local treatment is usually effective and consists of sterilization of the denture in antiseptic solution and administration of nystatin troches (500,000 units 3 times daily). It is usually necessary to ask the patient not to wear the denture during the period of antifungal therapy, and it may be necessary to replace the ill-fitting denture with a more satisfactory prosthesis. The condition is frequently recurrent and may be intractable. Systemic spread of denture candidiasis has not been documented.

ORAL TUMOR IMMUNOLOGY

Cancer of the mouth is one of the more common forms of malignant disease. Approximately 24,000 new cases are reported each year in the USA. About 3% of cancer deaths in men and 1% of cancer deaths in women have been attributed to cancer of the mouth, pharynx, and larynx.

The most important factors contributing to oral squamous cell carcinoma appear to be tobacco habits, particularly smoking. Alcohol consumption may play a part, though this is less clearly defined. Recently, attention has turned to 2 other groups of factors that may contribute to the cause and pathogenetic development of oral cancer: cell-mediated immune deficiency and herpesvirus infection.

Impaired cellular immunity, as indicated by DNCB sensitization and mitogen activation of lymphocytes, has been found in patients with squamous cell carcinoma of the head and neck as well as other sites. Decreased percentages and numbers of circulating T cells have also been shown in these patients, as have increases in T cell numbers in comparison with pretreatment values in patients who respond to radiotherapy. Furthermore, there is evidence that T cell numbers fall at the development of metastasis. The reduced cell-mediated immune responses may be due, at least in part, to the presence of suppressor cells, probably macrophages.

Preliminary reports suggest that cell-mediated immune responses to HSV-1 are depressed in patients with oral leukoplakia who show only benign hyperkeratosis, whereas in patients in whom the histologic changes suggest a premalignant state (epithelial atypia) the lymphocyte activation response to HSV-1 is raised to levels comparable to those seen in active primary or recurrent herpetic infection. Evidence has been advanced to suggest that a fall in lymphocyte response to HSV-1 may precede the development of carcinoma in situ in a preexisting benign hyperkeratosis. However, the series of patients studied was very small, and these results await confirmation. Other studies indicate that smokers have higher levels of antibody to HSV-1 than nonsmokers, and this may be important since oral cancer is more common in smokers. A possible pathogenesis for oral cancer is that cigarette smoke reactivates latent HSV-1 and then assists integration of transforming genes into epithelial cells. Patients with oral cancer have IgM antibody to HSV-1, possibly directed against a T-independent antigen. Efforts are being made to identify such an antigen, although with only partial success so far. In view of the rapidly accumulating evidence for oncogenic potential of herpes and other viruses and the relationship between host responses and the development and progress of cancer, this field of study can be expected to grow and to yield new methods of assessing prognosis and progress of head and neck cancer.

● ● ●

References

General

Brandtzaeg P: Transport models for secretory IgA and secretory IgM. *Clin Exp Immunol* 1981;**44**:221.

Johnston RB Jr, Stroud RM: Complement and host defense against infection. *J Pediatr* 1977;**90**:169.

Ofek I: Adherence of *Escherichia coli* to human mucosal cells mediated by mannose receptors. *Nature* 1977;**265**:623.

Strober W et al: Secretory component deficiency: A disorder of the IgA immune system. *N Engl J Med* 1976;**294**:351.

Tomasi TB et al: Mucosal immunity. *J Allergy Clin Immunol* 1980;**65**:12.

Periodontal Disease

Allison AC et al: Activation of complement by the alternative pathway as a factor in the pathogenesis of periodontal disease. *Lancet* 1976;**2**:1001.

Courts FJ et al: Detection of functional complement components in gingival crevicular fluid from humans with periodontal disease. *J Dent Res* 1976;**55**:1049.

Genco RB, Mergenhagen SE: Summary of a workshop on leukocyte function in bacterial diseases with an emphasis on periodontal disease. *J Infect Dis* 1979;**139**:604.

Horton JE et al: Relationship of transformation of newborn human lymphocytes by dental plaque antigen to the degree of maternal periodontal tissue. *Cell Immunol* 1976;**21**:153.

Johnson RL, Ziff M: Lymphokine stimulation of collagen accumulation. *J Clin Invest* 1976;**58**:240.

Mackler BF et al: IgG subclasses in human periodontal disease. *J Periodont Res* 1978;**13**:109.

Page RC, Schroeder HE: Pathogenesis of inflammatory periodontal disease. *Lab Invest* 1976;**33**:235.

Robertson PB et al: Periodontal status of patients with abnormalities of the immune system. *J Periodont* 1980;**51**:70.

Seymour GJ, Greenspan JS: The phenotypic characterization of lymphocyte subpopulations in established human periodontal disease. *J Periodont Res* 1979;**14**:39.

Seymour GJ et al: The immunopathogenesis of progressive chronic inflammatory periodontal disease. *J Oral Pathol* 1979;**8**:249.

Juvenile Periodontitis

Ciancola LJ et al: Defective polymorphonuclear leukocyte function in a human periodontal disease. *Nature* 1977;**265**:445.

Lavine WS et al: Impaired neutrophil chemotaxis in patients with juvenile and rapidly progressing periodontitis. *J Periodont Res* 1979;**14**:10.

Vardesteen GE et al: Peripheral blood leukocyte abnormalities and periodontal disease. *J Periodontol* 1980;**52**:174.

Acute Necrotizing Ulcerative Gingivitis

Harding J et al: Salivary antibodies in acute gingivitis. *J Periodontol* 1980;**51**:63.

Jimenez LM, Baer PN: Necrotising ulcerative gingivitis in children. *J Periodontol* 1975;**46**:715.

Wilton JMA, Ivanyi L, Lehner T: Cell-mediated immunity and humoral antibodies in acute ulcerative gingivitis. *J Periodont Res* 1971;**6**:9.

Dental Caries

Cohen B et al: Immunisation against dental caries: Further studies. *Br Dent J* 1979;**147**:9.

McGhee JR et al (editors): *Secretory Immunity and Infection.* Plenum Press, 1978.

Scully C: Dental caries: Progress in microbiology and immunology. *J Infection* 1981;**3**:107.

Recurrent Oral Ulceration

Donatsky O: Cell-mediated and humoral immunity against oral streptococci, neisseria, staphylococci, and adult human oral mucosa antigens in recurrent aphthous stomatitis. *Scand J Dent Res* 1978;**86**:25.

Graykowski E, Hooks JJ: Aphthous stomatitis: Behçet's syndrome workshop. *J Oral Pathol* 1978;**7**:347.

Greenspan JS et al: Antibody-dependent cellular cytotoxicity in recurrent aphthous ulceration. *Clin Exp Immunol* 1981;**44**:603.

Hutcheon AW et al: Clinical and haematological screening in recurrent aphthae. *Postgrad Med J* 1978;**54**:779.

Lehner T: Progress report: Oral ulceration and Behçet's syndrome. *Gut* 1977;**18**:491.

Lehner T, Barnes GC (editors): *Behçet's Syndrome.* Academic Press, 1979.

Pemphigus, Pemphigoid, & Erythema Multiforme

Daniels TE, Quadra-White C: Direct immunofluorescence in oral mucosal disease. *Oral Surg* 1981;**51**:38.

Diaz LA et al: Isolation of pemphigus antigen from human saliva. *J Immunol* 1980;**124**:760.

Jordon RE: Complement systems in the skin. *J Invest Dermatol* 1976;**67**:633.

Rasmussen JE: Erythema multiforme in children. *Br J Dermatol* 1977;**95**:181.

Rogers RS, Jordon RE: Immunopathology of oral mucosal inflammatory disease. *Clin Exp Dermatol* 1977;**2**:97.

Wuepper KD et al: Immune complexes in erythema multiforme and the Stevens-Johnson syndrome. *J Invest Dermatol* 1980;**74**:368.

Lichen Planus

Dockrell H, Greenspan JS: Histochemical identification of T cells in oral lichen planus. *Oral Surg* 1979;**48**:42.

Holmstrup P, Soborg M: Cellular hypersensitivity to oral lichen planus lesions *in vitro. Acta Allergol* 1977;**32**:304.

Chronic Discoid Lupus Erythematosus

Prystowsky SD, Gilliam JN: Antinuclear antibody studies in chronic cutaneous discoid lupus erythematosus. *Arch Dermatol* 1977;**113**:183.

Shklar G, McCarthy PL: Histopathology of oral lesions of discoid lupus erythematosus. *Arch Dermatol* 1978; **114**:1031.

Inflammatory Bowel Diseases

Bernstein ML, McDonald JS: Oral lesions in Crohn's disease. *Oral Surg* 1979;**46**:234.

Hodgson HJF et al: C3 metabolism in ulcerative colitis and Crohn's disease. *Clin Exp Immunol* 1977;**28**:490.

Hodgson HJF et al: Decreased suppressor cell activity in inflammatory bowel disease. *Clin Exp Immunol* 1978; **32**:451.

Walker JEG: Possible diagnostic test for Crohn's disease by use of buccal mucosa. *Lancet* 1978;**2**:759.

Sarcoidosis

Fernandez B et al: Distribution and function of T- and B-cell populations in sarcoidosis. *Ann NY Acad Sci* 1976;**278**:80.

Tannenbaum H et al: Immune function in sarcoidosis: Studies on delayed hypersensitivity, B and T lymphocyte serum immunoglobulin and serum complement components. *Clin Exp Immunol* 1976;**26**:511.

Tarpley TM et al: Minor salivary gland involvement in sarcoidosis. *Oral Surg* 1972;**33**:755.

Sjögren's Syndrome

Daniels TE et al: An evaluation of salivary scintigraphy in Sjögren's syndrome. *Arthritis Rheum* 1979;**22**:809.

Daniels TE et al: The oral component of Sjögren's syndrome. *Oral Surg* 1975;**39**:875.

Greenspan JS, Chisholm DM: Connective tissue disorders. Chap 6, pp 191–210, in: *Oral Manifestations of Systemic Disease.* Jones JH, Mason DK (editors). Saunders, 1980.

Greenspan JS et al: The histopathology of Sjögren's syndrome in labial salivary gland biopsies. *Oral Surg* 1974;**37**:217.

Kassan SS, Gardy M: Sjögren's syndrome: An update and overview. *Am J Med* 1978;**64**:1037.

Miyasaka N et al: Decreased autologous mixed lymphocyte reaction in Sjögren's syndrome. *J Clin Invest* 1980;**66**:928.

Systemic Lupus Erythematosus

Daniels TE, Quadra-White C: Direct immunofluorescence in oral mucosal disease. *Oral Surg* 1981;**51**:38.

Urman JD et al: Oral mucosal ulceration in systemic lupus erythematosus. *Arthritis Rheum* 1978;**21**:58.

Rheumatoid Arthritis

Barriga B, Lewis TM, Law DB: An investigation of the dental occlusion in children with juvenile rheumatoid arthritis. *Angle Orthod* 1974;**44**:329.

Ogus H: Rheumatoid arthritis of the temporomandibular joint. *Br J Oral Surg* 1975;**12**:275.

Sullivan S et al: Improvement of lachrymal and salivary secretion and cellular immune responses to salivary antigens in rheumatoid arthritis. *Ann Rheum Dis* 1978;**37**:164.

Systemic Sclerosis

Weisman RA et al: Head and neck manifestations of scleroderma. *Ann Otol* 1978;**87**:332.

White SC et al: Oral radiographic changes in patients with progressive systemic sclerosis (scleroderma). *J Am Dent Assoc* 1977;**94**:1178.

Herpes Simplex Virus Infection

Bierman SM: The mechanism of recurrent infection by *Herpesvirus hominis. Arch Dermatol* 1976;**112**:1459.

Field HJ, Darby GK: Strategies of drug resistance in herpes simplex. *Nature* 1980;**286**:842.

Moller-Larsen A et al: Cellular and humoral immune responses to herpes simplex virus during and after primary gingivostomatitis. *Infect Immun* 1978;**22**:44.

Rand KH et al: Cellular immunity and herpesvirus infection in cardiac transplant patients. *N Engl J Med* 1977;**296**: 1372.

Shillitoe EJ, Wilton JMA, Lehner T: Responses to herpes simplex virus of unfractionated lymphocytes and T and B lymphocytes in man. *Scand J Immunol* 1978;**7**:357.

Shillitoe EJ et al: Sequential changes in cell-mediated immune responses to herpes simplex virus following primary herpetic infection in man. Page 753 in: *Oncogenesis and Herpesviruses.* Vol 3. De Thé G, Henle W, Rapp F (editors). IARC Scientific Publications, No. 24, 1978.

Steele RW et al: Cellular immune responses to herpes viruses during treatment with adenine arabinoside. *J Infect Dis* 1977;**135**:593.

Oral Candidiasis & Denture Stomatitis

Aronson IK, Soltani K: Chronic mucocutaneous candidiasis: A review. *Mycopathologia* 1976;**60**:17.

Budtz-Jörgensen E: The significance of *Candida albicans* in denture stomatitis. *J Dent Res* 1974;**82**:151.

Lehner T: Classification and clinico-pathological features of Candida infections in the mouth. In: *Symposium on Candida Infections.* Winner HI, Hurley RE (editors). Livingstone, 1966.

Mackie RM et al: The relationship between immunological parameters and response to therapy in resistant oral candidiasis. *Br J Dermatol* 1978;**98**:34.

Stobo JD et al: Suppressor thymus derived lymphocytes in fungal infection. *J Clin Invest* 1976;**57**:319.

Twomey JJ et al: Chronic mucocutaneous candidiasis with macrophage dysfunction, a plasma inhibitor, and co-existent aplastic anemia. *J Lab Clin Med* 1975;**85**:968.

Walker SM, Urbaniak SJ: A serum-dependent defect of neutrophil function in chronic mucocutaneous candidiasis. *J Clin Pathol* 1980;**33**:370.

Oral Tumor Immunology

Berlinger NT et al: Deficient cell-mediated immunity in head and neck cancer patients secondary to autologous suppressive immune cells. *Laryngoscope* 1978;**88**:470.

Broweder JP, Chretien PB: Immune reactivity in head and neck squamous carcinoma and relevance to the design of immunotherapy trials. *Semin Oncol* 1977;**4**:431.

Deegan MJ, Coulthard SW: Spontaneous rosette formation and rosette inhibition assays in patients with squamous cell carcinoma of the head and neck. *Cancer* 1977;**39**: 2137.

Shillitoe EJ, Silverman S: Oral cancer and herpes simplex virus: A review. *Oral Surg* 1979;**48**:216.

Shillitoe EJ et al: Neutralizing antibody to herpes simplex virus type 1 in patients with oral cancer. *Cancer* 1982; **49**:2315.

Silverman NA et al: Correlation of tumor burden with in vitro lymphocyte reactivity and antibodies to herpesvirus tumor-associated antigens in head and neck squamous carcinoma. *Cancer* 1976;**37**:135.

Smith HG et al: Humoral immunity to herpes simplex viral-induced antigens in smokers. *Cancer* 1976;**38**:1155.

Immunization | 39

Stephen N. Cohen, MD

IMMUNIZATION AGAINST INFECTIOUS DISEASES

It has been recognized for centuries that individuals who recover from certain diseases are protected from recurrences. The moderately successful but hazardous introduction of small quantities of fluid from the pustules of smallpox into the skin of uninfected persons (variolation) was an effort to imitate this natural phenomenon. Jenner's introduction of vaccination with cowpox (1796) to protect against smallpox was the first documented use of a live attenuated viral vaccine and the beginning of modern immunization. Koch demonstrated the specific bacterial cause of anthrax in 1876, and the etiologic agents of several common illnesses were rapidly identified thereafter. Attempts to develop immunizing agents followed (Table 39–1).

Table 39–1. Historical milestones in immunization.

Variolation	1721
Vaccination	1796
Rabies vaccine	1885
Diphtheria toxoid	1925
Tetanus toxoid	1925
Pertussis vaccine	1925
Viral culture in chick embryo	1931
Yellow fever vaccine	1937
Influenza vaccine	1943
Viral tissue culture	1949
Poliovaccine, inactivated (Salk)	1954
Poliovaccine, live, attenuated (Sabin)	1956
Measles vaccine	1960
Tetanus immune globulin (human)	1962
Rubella vaccine	1966
Mumps vaccine	1967
Hepatitis B vaccine	1975

Types of Immune Response

Immunization results in the production of antibodies directed against the infecting agent or its toxic products; it may also initiate cellular responses mediated by lymphocytes and macrophages. The most important protective antibodies include those which inactivate soluble toxic protein products of bacteria (antitoxins), facilitate phagocytosis and intracellular digestion of bacteria (opsonins), interact with the components of serum complement to damage the bacterial membrane with resultant bacteriolysis (lysins), or prevent proliferation of infectious virus (neutralizing antibodies). Newly appreciated are those antibodies that interact with components of the bacterial surface to prevent adhesion to mucosal surfaces (antiadhesins). Some antibodies may not be protective, and by "blocking" the reaction of protective antibodies with the pathogen may actually depress the body's defenses.

Antigens react with antibody in the bloodstream and extracellular fluid and at mucosal surfaces. Antibodies cannot readily reach intracellular sites of infection as are found with viral replication. However, they are effective against many viral diseases (1) by interacting with virus before initial intracellular penetration occurs, and (2) by preventing locally replicating virus from disseminating from the site of entry to an important target organ, as in the spread of poliovirus from the gut to the central nervous system or of rabies from a puncture wound to peripheral neural tissue. Lymphocytes acting alone and antibody interacting with lymphoid or monocytic effector K cells may also recognize surface changes in virus-infected cells and destroy these infected "foreign" cells.

Passive Immunization

Immunization may be accomplished passively by administering either preformed immunoreactive serum or cells, or actively by presenting a suitable antigenic stimulus to the host's own immune system.

Antibody—either as whole serum or as fractionated, concentrated immune (gamma) globulin which is predominantly IgG—may be obtained from donors who have recovered from an infectious disease or have been immunized. These antibodies may provide immediate protection to an antibody-free individual. Passive immunization is thus useful for individuals who cannot form antibodies or for the normal host who might develop disease before active immunization could stimulate antibody production, which usually requires at least 7–10 days.

Antibody may be obtained from humans or animals, but animal sera are always less desirable since nonhuman proteins themselves give rise to an immune response which leads to rapid clearance of the protective molecules from the circulation of the recipient and may even result in clinical illness (serum sickness; see Hazards of Passive Immunization, below). Thus, to obtain a similar protective effect, a much greater quantity of animal antiserum must be injected compared to human antiserum, eg, 3000 units of equine tetanus antitoxin versus 300 units of human tetanus immune globulin.

No antiserum of animal origin should be given without carefully inquiring about prior exposure or allergic response to any product of the specific animal source. Patients with an unrelated allergy are probably more prone to develop serum reactions. Whenever a foreign antiserum is administered, a syringe containing aqueous epinephrine 1:1000 should be available, and eye or scratch testing (see Chapter 28) should be followed by intracutaneous testing for hypersensitivity. If allergy is present by history or test and no alternative to serum therapy is possible, a patient may sometimes be given an essential medication to tolerance in repeated fractional doses of progressively increasing size. Simultaneous administration of antihistamines, corticosteroids, and even epinephrine may be necessary during this procedure of "desensitization," which may simply limit the allergic reactions to an acceptably small magnitude.

Persistence of certain human antibodies, eg, to varicella-zoster, is short-lived, and zoster immune globulin (ZIG) must therefore be prepared from the sera of convalescent zoster patients. By contrast, antibody to measles and hepatitis A is so ubiquitous in the population at large that normal immune serum globulin (ISG) will usually prevent or modify clinical illness with these infections if given early in the incubation period. Table 39–2 lists antisera generally available for passive immunization at present.

In the preantibiotic era, passive immunization was administered with some success as therapy for pneumococcal or *Haemophilus* infection. The need to identify the infecting serotype and obtain the appropriate type-specific antiserum, the illness caused by injection of the foreign proteins, and the relatively poor therapeutic response led to the prompt abandonment of this unsatisfactory method of treatment as soon as effective antimicrobial chemotherapy became available. Today, serum therapy for established illness is largely limited to the administration of antivenins and of botulinus, tetanus, and diphtheria antitoxins to block attachment of yet unbound toxin.

In the absence of demonstrably low serum IgG or (rarely) specific antibody deficiencies, the administration of normal immune serum globulin (ISG) is of no value in the prevention of recurrent infections.

Passive Transfer of Cellular Immunity

Antibodies produced following some infections, particularly those due to mycobacteria, fungi, and many viruses, fail to protect against infection. Rather, interaction of immune lymphocytes and macrophages largely determines recovery from these illnesses. Attempts have been made to transmit this cell-mediated immunity, eg, to vaccinia virus in the progressively infected, immunologically incompetent host; to *Coccidioides immitis* in the patient with disseminated coccidioidomycosis; and to *Mycobacterium leprae* in lepromatous leprosy (see Chapter 33). Whole blood, leukocyte-rich buffy coat, and leukocyte-derived "transfer factor" (TF) have been utilized. The value of this type of therapy is uncertain, and these procedures are still experimental (see Chapter 40).

Hazards of Passive Immunization

Illness may arise from a single injection of foreign serum but more commonly occurs in patients who have previously been injected with proteins from the same or a related species. Reactions range in severity from acute anaphylaxis with hives, back pain, dyspnea, cardiovascular collapse, and even death to serum sickness arising hours to weeks following treatment. Typical manifestations of serum sickness include adenopathy, urticaria, arthritis, and fever. Demyelinating encephalopathy has been reported. Rarely, the administration of human γ-globulin is attended by similar allergic reactions, particularly in patients who are congenitally deficient in one or more immunoglobulins but still capable of mounting an immune response. Hepatitis A, B, or "C" (non-A non-B) may be transmitted by whole human plasma or serum, but purified immune (gamma) globulin is free of hepatitis.

Note: Great care must be exercised in administering standard gamma globulin to avoid accidental intravenous injection. Currently, most human and animal γ-globulin preparations are given by the intramuscular route. They all contain high-molecular-weight aggregated IgG, intravenous administration of which will frequently result in moderate to severe anaphylactic reactions with possible vasomotor collapse and death. The standard immune globulin preparation must not be confused with a recently licensed product, immune globulin IV, which *can* be given safely intravenously.

The administration of intact lymphocytes to promote cell-mediated immunity is also hazardous if the recipient is too immunologically depressed to prevent implantation of incompatible donor cells. The engrafted donor cells may "reject" the recipient by a GVH reaction, producing rash, pancytopenia, fever, diarrhea, hepatosplenomegaly, and death (see Chapter 27).

Active Immunization

Primary active immunity develops more slowly than the incubation period of most infections and must therefore be induced prior to exposure to the etiologic agent. One exception (no longer of practical importance) is vaccinia-induced immunity to smallpox, which takes only 10 days as opposed to the 14-day incubation period of the virulent infection. By contrast, "booster" reimmunization in the previously immune individual provides a rapid secondary (anamnestic) increase in serum antibody which outpaces the development—to give one example—of tetanus from a contaminated wound.

Table 39—2. Materials available for passive immunization. (All are of human origin unless otherwise stated.)

Disease	Product	Dosage	Comments
Black widow spider bite	Antivenin widow spider, equine.	1 vial IM or IV.	A second dose may be given if symptoms do not subside in 3 hours.
Botulism	ABE polyvalent antitoxin, equine.	1 vial IV and 1 vial IM; repeat after 2—4 hours if symptoms worsen, and after 12—24 hours.	Available from CDC.* 20% incidence of serum reactions. Only type E antitoxin has been shown to affect outcome of illness. Prophylaxis is not routinely recommended but may be given to asymptomatic exposed persons.
Diphtheria	Diphtheria antitoxin, equine.	20,000—120,000 units IM depending on severity and duration of illness.	Active immunization and (perhaps) erythromycin prophylaxis should be given to nonimmune contacts of active cases rather than antitoxin prophylaxis. Contacts should be observed for signs of illness so that antitoxin may be administered if needed.
Hepatitis A ("infectious")	Immune globulin.	0.02 mL/kg IM as soon as possible after exposure up to 6 weeks. A protective effect lasts about 2 months.	Modifies but does not prevent infection. Recommended for household contacts and other contacts of similar intensity. Not office or school contacts unless an epidemic appears to be in progress. Also recommended for travel to endemic areas.
		For chronic exposure, a dose of 0.1 mL/kg is recommended every 6 months.	Personnel of mental institutions, facilities for retarded children, and prisons appear to be at chronic risk of acquiring hepatitis A, as are those who work with nonhuman primates.
Hepatitis B ("serum")	Hepatitis B immune globulin.	0.06 mL/kg IM as soon as possible after exposure, preferably within 7 days. A second injection should be given 25—30 days after exposure.	Administer to nonimmune individuals as postexposure prophylaxis following either parenteral exposure to or direct mucous membrane contact with HBsAg-positive materials. Should not be given to persons already demonstrating anti-HBsAg antibody. Administration of various live virus vaccines should be delayed for at least a couple of months after this concentrated immune globulin has been given. The administration of 0.5 mL at birth and at 3 and 6 months of age markedly decreases chronic carriage of hepatitis B virus in infants born of mothers who are HBeAg-positive at delivery; this may become routine practice.
Hypogamma-globulinemia	Immune globulin.	0.6 mL/kg IM every 3—4 weeks.	Give double dose at onset of therapy. Immune globulin is of no value in the prevention of frequent respiratory infections in the absence of demonstrable hypogammaglobulinemia.
	Immune globulin IV.	100—150 mg/kg IV.	Ordinary immune globulin cannot safely be given intravenously because of complement-activating aggregates. It is difficult to administer sufficient intramuscular globulin to maintain normal IgG levels in immunodeficient children or to passively protect acutely infected individuals who lack a specific antibody. This chemically modified product appears to be aggregate-free while retaining immunologic potency and the ability to fix complement. The product is licensed and available commercially from Cutter Laboratories.
Measles	Immune globulin.	0.25 mL/kg IM as soon as possible after exposure. This dose may be ineffective in immuno-incompetent patients, who should receive 20—30 mL.	Live measles vaccine will usually prevent natural infection if given within 48 hours following exposure. If immune globulin is administered, delay immunization with live virus for 3 months. Do not vaccinate infants under age 15 months.
Pertussis	Pertussis immune globulin.	1.5 mL IM.	Efficacy doubtful. May also be given for treatment, 1.25 mL IM, with repeat dose 24—48 hours later. No longer manufactured, but may be available.
Rabies	Rabies immune globulin. (Antirabies serum, equine, may be available, but is much less desirable.)	20 IU/kg, 50% of which is infiltrated locally at the wound site, and the remainder given IM. (See also rabies vaccine in Table 39—3.) If the equine product is used, the dose is 40 IU/kg.	Give as soon as possible after exposure. Recommended for all bite or scratch exposure to carnivores, especially bat, skunk, fox, coyote, or raccoon, despite animal's apparent health, if the brain cannot be immediately examined and found rabies-free. Give also even for abrasion exposure to known or suspected rabid animals as well as for bite (skin penetration by teeth) of escaped dogs and cats whose health cannot be determined. Not recommended for individuals with demonstrated antibody response from preexposure prophylaxis.

*See footnotes on next page.

Table 39—2 (cont'd). Materials available for passive immunization.

Disease	Product	Dosage	Comments
Rh isoimmunization (erythroblastosis fetalis)	Rh$_0$ (D) immune globulin.	1 dose IM within 72 hours of abortion, amniocentesis, obstetric delivery of an Rh-positive infant, or transfusion of Rh-positive blood in an Rh$_0$ (D)-negative female.	For nonimmune females only. May be effective at much greater postexposure interval. Give even if more than 72 hours have elapsed. One vial contains 300 μg antibody and can reliably inhibit the immune response to a fetomaternal bleed of 7.5–8 mL as estimated by the Betke-Kleihauer smear technique.
Snakebite	Antivenin coral snake, equine. Antivenin rattlesnake, copperhead, and moccasin, equine.	At least 3–5 vials IV.	Dose should be sufficient to reverse symptoms of envenomation. Consider antitetanus measures as well.
Tetanus	Tetanus immune globulin. (Bovine and equine antitoxins may be available but are not recommended. They are used at 10 times the dose of tetanus immune globulin.)	Prophylaxis: 250–500 units IM. Therapy: 3000–6000 units IM.	Give in separate syringe at separate site from simultaneously administered toxoid. Recommended only for major or contaminated wounds in individuals who have had fewer than 2 doses of toxoid at any time in the past (fewer than 3 doses if wound is more than 24 hours old). (See tetanus toxoid in Table 39–3.)
Vaccinia	Vaccinia immune globulin (VIG). (Available from CDC.*)	Prophylaxis: 0.3 mL/kg IM. Therapy: 0.6 mL/kg IM. VIG may be repeated as necessary for treatment and at intervals of 1 week for prophylaxis.	Give at a different site if used to prevent dissemination in a patient with skin disease who must undergo vaccination. May prevent or modify smallpox if given within 24 hours of exposure. May be useful in treatment of vaccinia of the eye, eczema vaccinatum, generalized vaccinia and vaccinia necrosum, and in the prevention of such complications in exposed patients with skin disorders such as eczema, burns, or impetigo. VIG in prophylactic dosage is also recommended for the pregnant woman who must be vaccinated to prevent fetal vaccinia.
Varicella	Varicella-zoster immune globulin (VZIG).	1 vial/10 kg IM or fraction thereof up to a maximum of 5 vials, given within 96 hours of exposure.	†Available for nonimmune leukemic, lymphomatous, immunosuppressed, or other immunoincompetent children under 15 years of age and with household, hospital (same 2- or 4-bed room or adjacent beds in large ward), or playmate (> 1 hour play indoors) contact with a known case of varicella-zoster, and for neonates whose mothers have developed varicella less than 5 days before or 48 hours after delivery. May be provided for suitable older patients evaluated on an individual basis. VZIG modifies natural disease but may not prevent the development of immunity. Convalescent plasma collected 1–5 weeks after onset of varicella or zoster may be available at local blood banks and is also effective at 7–10 mL/kg IV. If neither VZIG nor convalescent plasma is available, normal immune serum globulin, 0.6–1.2 mL/kg IM, may modify the illness. Not effective for treatment of established infection.

*Centers for Disease Control—Telephone: (404) 329-3311 (main switchboard, day) or (404) 329-3644 (night).
†Contact the regional blood center of the American Red Cross.
Note: Passive immunotherapy or immunoprophylaxis should always be administered as soon as possible after exposure to the offending agent. Immune antisera and globulin are always given intramuscularly unless otherwise noted. Always question carefully and test for hypersensitivity before administering animal sera.

Active immunization may be achieved with either living or dead materials. Nonviable antigens usually are either structural components of the infecting organism which induce antibodies that prevent infection, or detoxified bacterial products (toxoids) which stimulate antitoxins that prevent illness without directly inhibiting the pathogen. Although tetanus toxoid provides a particularly long-lasting immunity of at least 10 years' duration, most nonliving vaccines provide protection for only a limited time. Repeated injections are needed to maintain even a moderate level of protection against influenza, plague, cholera, and typhoid fever. Not even natural infection always results in durable immunity. Examples include repeated, although perhaps milder, attacks of illness with *Mycoplasma pneumoniae* and respiratory syncytial virus as well as chlora.

Previous infection can also substantially alter the

response to an inactivated vaccine. For example, volunteers who have recovered from cholera or who live in a cholera-endemic area respond to parenteral immunization with an increase in anti-cholera secretory IgA. This increase is not seen in immunized control subjects. One of the most interesting experimental prospects for active immunization arises from the recent discovery of cross-reactivity of nonpathogenic bacteria with poorly immunogenic pathogens. Infants, particularly those under 6 months of age, do not reliably develop protective antibody responses to the polysaccharide antigens of *Haemophilus,* meningococcus, and pneumococcus, all important causes of severe illness in this age group. To some extent, this poor response may be overcome by multiple injections. The discovery that cross-reactive protective antibody may be induced by nonpathogenic serotypes of *E coli* and viridans streptococci has opened up the prospect of immunizing this population by colonizing their intestinal and respiratory tracts with carefully selected saprophytic immunizing strains of these antigenic "relatives."

The route of immunization may be an important determinant of successful vaccination, particularly if nonreplicating immunogens are employed. Thus, immunization intranasally or by aerosol often appears more successful than parenteral injection against viral or bacterial challenges to the respiratory tree.

Active immunization with living agents is generally preferable to immunization with killed vaccines because of a superior and long-lived immune response. A single dose of a live, attenuated virus vaccine often suffices for reliable immunization. Multiple immunizations are recommended for polio in case intercurrent enteroviral infection or interference among the 3 simultaneously administered virus types in the trivalent vaccine prevents completely successful primary immunization. The durability of immunity to many viral infections is unexplained and may include repeated natural reexposure to new cases in the community, the unusually large antigenic stimulus that infection with a living agent provides, or other mechanisms such as the persistence of latent virus.

All immunizing materials—but live agents particularly—must be properly stored to retain effectiveness. Serious failures of smallpox and measles immunization have resulted from inadequate refrigeration prior to use. Agents presently licensed for active immunization are listed in Table 39–3.

Hazards of Active Immunization

Active immunization may cause fever, malaise, and soreness at injection sites. Some reactions are relatively specific for the immunizing agent, such as arthralgia/arthritis following rubella vaccine or convulsions following pertussis vaccine, but are much less frequent and less severe than those accompanying unmodified natural illness. Reactions known to be associated with a particular product are described in the manufacturer's package insert, the *Physicians' Desk Reference,* and standard texts.

Repeated immunization, particularly with diphtheria and tetanus toxoids, may result in increasingly severe local reactions. Diphtheria antigen in adult-type combined diphtheria-tetanus toxoid (Td) is therefore 5- to 10-fold less than in childhood DTP, and a lower frequency of booster immunization for tetanus is now recommended than in the past. Although experimentally hyperimmunized animals display a variety of adverse effects, including amyloidosis and malignancy, and immunization has been suspected of precipitating systemic lupus erythematosus in humans, follow-up of intensively immunized individuals over a 15-year period has not shown any clinical sequelae. Antibodies to certain bacteria reportedly cross-react with mammalian tissues, suggesting the potential hazard of autoimmune disease following extensive immunization, but the clinical significance of such experimental observations is unknown.

The careful monitoring system established during the 1976 "swine flu" immunization program revealed a 5-fold increase in postimmunization Guillain-Barré syndrome in comparison with unvaccinated controls. This complication arises within 10 weeks of immunization and has resulted in a 5% mortality rate, with another 5–10% of patients displaying residual weakness. The rarity of this complication (one case per 85,000) would not permit recognition in field trials or in the absence of a surveillance program and demonstrates the difficulty in accurately assessing the risks of immunization. The unexpected complications of the "swine flu" immunization program and the mounting concern about the possible impact of lawsuits for vaccine-related damage upon the present and future availability of old and new vaccines have led to the establishment of an ongoing nationwide Vaccine Adverse Reaction Monitoring System. Episodes determined by the local health department to be (1) more than minor symptoms at the site of injection and (2) sufficiently serious to result in a visit to a physician or hospitalization are reported in detail to the state health departments and hence to the Centers for Disease Control. The latter determines crude reaction rates and investigates unusual types or clusters of reactions. Reports from all sources are encouraged.

Allergic reactions may occur on exposure to egg protein or antibiotics in viral vaccine cell cultures. The quantity of irrelevant antigen in a vaccine is usually insufficient to elicit a response in the allergic individual, but a patient with intense allergy to a vaccine component may be given vaccine from a different source, if available. Improvements in antigenicity and better purification procedures in vaccine production decrease the amount and number of foreign substances injected and result in fewer side-effects.

Unique Hazards of Live Vaccines

Live vaccines should *not* be given to a pregnant woman because of their potential effect upon the fetus. Live vaccines, furthermore, can cause serious or even fatal illness in an immunologically incompetent host. They should not be given to patients receiving cortico-

Table 39—3. Materials available for active immunization.*

Disease	Product (Source)	Type of Agent	Route of Administration	Primary Immunization	Duration of Effect	Comments
Cholera	Cholera vaccine	Killed bacteria	Subcut, IM, intradermal	2 doses 1 week or more apart.	6 months†	50% protective; International Certificate may be required for travel.
Diphtheria	DTP, DT (adsorbed) for child under 6; Td (adsorbed) for all others	Toxoid	IM	3 doses 4 weeks or more apart, with an additional dose 1 year later for a child under 6. (Can be given at the same time as polio vaccine if doses at least 8 weeks apart.)	10 years‡	Use DT if convulsions follow use of DTP. Give school children and adults third dose 6–12 months after second. Need for boosters after age 18 is uncertain.
Hepatitis B	Hepatitis B vaccine (human carriers)	Formalin-treated purified viral antigen	IM	2 doses 1 month apart. A booster dose given 6 months later produces somewhat higher titers.	Uncertain, but probably at least 5 years	A stable, adjuvant-supplemented vaccine from highly purified, formalin-inactivated HBsAg harvested from human carriers. Confers essentially complete protection upon chimpanzees challenged with live virus and has been effective in high-risk populations of homosexuals and patients undergoing hemodialysis. Clinical trials are under way among US medical personnel and in Taiwanese children, whose high natural rate of HBsAg carriage is followed frequently in adulthood by cirrhosis and hepatocellular carcinoma. A similar French vaccine has been shown to be effective in protecting hemodialysis personnel in France and in preventing infected Senegalese children from becoming chronic carriers. The vaccine is licensed and will be commercially available in mid 1982.
Influenza	Influenza virus vaccine, monovalent or bivalent (chick embryo). Composition of the vaccine is varied depending upon epidemiologic circumstances.	Killed whole or split virus A and/or B	IM	1 dose. (Two doses 4 weeks or more apart are preferable in individuals who have not previously received the current antigenic components or been otherwise exposed to the current strain of virus. Two doses of the split virus products should be used in persons under 13 years because of a lower incidence of side-effects.)	1 year	Give immunization by November. Recommended annually for patients with cardiorespiratory disease, diabetes, other chronic diseases, and the elderly. Patients receiving chemotherapy for malignant disease are likely to respond better if immunized between courses of treatment.
Measles§	Measles virus vaccine live (chick embryo)	Live virus	Subcut	1 dose at age 15 months.	Permanent	Reimmunize if given before 15 months of age; may prevent natural disease if given less than 48 hours after exposure.
Meningococcus	Meningococcal polysaccharide vaccine, group A or group C	Polysaccharide	Subcut	1 dose. Since primary antibody response requires at least 5 days, antibiotic prophylaxis with rifampin (600 mg or 10 mg/kg every 12 h for 4 doses) should be given to household contacts.	?Permanent in older children and adults, but transient in children <2 years old	Recommended in epidemic situations, for use by the military to prevent outbreaks in recruits, and possibly as an adjunct to antibiotic prophylaxis in preventing secondary cases in family contacts. Not reliably effective in infants, who require booster injections if antibody is to last for a year (especially antibody to group C). A combination A-C vaccine is also available.
Mumps§	Mumps virus vaccine live (chick embryo)	Live virus	Subcut	1 dose.	Permanent	Reimmunize if given before 1 year of age.
Pertussis	DTP	Killed bacteria	IM	As for DTP.	See‡	Not generally recommended after age 6.

Plague	Plague vaccine	Killed bacteria	IM	3 doses 4 weeks or more apart.	6 months‡	Recommended only for occupational exposure and not for residents of endemic area in the southwest USA.
Pneumococcus	Pneumococcal polysaccharide vaccine, polyvalent	Polysaccharide	Subcut, IM	0.5 mL.	Uncertain—probably at least 5 years	Recommended for patients with cardiorespiratory disease or other chronic illness, for patients with sickle cell disease, and for others with functional, congenital, or post-surgical asplenia. Value in healthy elderly persons is less certain. Only the 14 most common serotypes are represented in the vaccine. Infants, splenectomized children, and some chronically ill patients respond unreliably. *Caution:* Because of a marked increase in adverse reactions following revaccination, booster doses should *not* be given.
Poliomyelitis	Poliovirus vaccine live oral, trivalent (monkey kidney, human diploid)	Live virus types I, II, III	Oral	2 doses 6–8 weeks or more apart, followed by a third dose 8–12 months later. (Can be given at the same time as primary DTP immunization.) A fourth dose before entering school is recommended for children immunized in the first 1–2 years of life.	Permanent	Recommended for adults only if at increased risk by travel to epidemic or highly endemic areas or occupational contact. Individuals who have completed a primary series may take a single booster dose if the risk of exposure is high.
	Poliomyelitis vaccine inactivated	Killed virus types I, II, III	IM	3 doses 1–2 months apart, followed by a fourth dose 6–12 months later and a fifth dose before entering school. A single booster dose should be given every 5 years until age 18, after which the need is uncertain.	5 years, perhaps longer	Killed virus vaccines are licensed but not readily available and are no longer recommended except for immunologically deficient patients or possibly for unimmunized adults who are at risk of exposure to poliomyelitis by reason of travel or immunization of their children.
Rabies	Rabies vaccine (human diploid). (Manufacture of a vaccine derived from infected duck embryo [DEV] has been discontinued, but the product may still be available. DEV is inferior in all respects to the human diploid vaccine and is not recommended.)	Killed virus	IM	**Preexposure:** 2 doses 1 week apart followed by a third dose 2–3 weeks later. **Postexposure:** Always give rabies immune globulin as well. (See Table 39–2.) If not previously immunized, give a total of 5 doses. Give on days 0, 3, 7, 14, and 28 (WHO currently recommends a sixth dose 90 days after the first dose). If the vaccinee is believed to be immunocompromised, a serum specimen should be collected on day 28 or 2–3 weeks after the last dose and tested for rabies antibody.** If the antibody level is insufficient, a booster should be given and the titer determined on a serum specimen collected 2–3 weeks later. *If previously immunized* with diploid vaccine, do not give serum therapy. Give 2 booster doses, one immediately and one 3 days later.	2 years‡ if titer <1:16	Preexposure immunization only for occupational or avocational risk or residence in hyperendemic area. For animal bite, consider antitetanus measures as well. Wounds should be copiously swabbed and flushed with soap and water. (See Table 39—2 regarding use of hyperimmune serum or immune globulin.)

*Dosages for the specific product, including variations for age, are best obtained from the manufacturer's package insert. Immunizations should be given by the route suggested for the product.
†Revaccination interval required by international regulations.
‡A single dose is a sufficient booster at any time after the effective duration of primary immunization has passed.
§Combination vaccines available.
**Arrange rabies antibody testing through state health department. A titer ≥1:16 is considered protective.

Table 39–3 (cont'd). Materials available for active immunization.*

Disease	Product (Source)	Type of Agent	Route of Administration	Primary Immunization	Duration of Effect	Comments
Rubella§	Rubella virus vaccine live (human diploid)	Live virus	Subcut	1 dose (to ensure successful immunization, some experts recommend that a second dose be given to children no later than the fourth or fifth grade).	Permanent	Give after 15 months of age. Do not give during pregnancy. Women must prevent pregnancy for 3 months after immunization. If a female is immunized postpartum and has received blood products or Rh immune globulin, serologic testing should be done 6–8 weeks later to confirm successful immunization.
Smallpox	Smallpox vaccine (calf lymph, chick embryo)	Live vaccinia virus	Intradermal	1 dose.	3 years	Not generally available. Recommended only for laboratory workers exposed to smallpox or related poxviruses. Revaccinate if no jennerian vesicle at 6–8 days postvaccination. If patients with skin disease must be vaccinated or are exposed to a vaccinated household contact, they should receive vaccinia immune globulin. (See Table 39–2.) Travelers to the few remaining countries still requiring smallpox vaccination as a condition of entry should be given a letter waiving the vaccination as contraindicated for health reasons.
Tetanus	DTP, DT (adsorbed) for children under age 6; Td, T (adsorbed) for all others	Toxoid	IM	3 doses 4 weeks or more apart.	10 years‡**	Give school children and adults a third dose 6–12 months after second. (See Table 39–2 regarding use of hyperimmune globulin.)
Tuberculosis	BCG vaccine	Live attenuated *Mycobacterium bovis*	Intradermal, subcut	1 dose.	?Permanent††	Recommended in USA only for PPD-negative contacts of ineffectively treated or persistently untreated cases and for other unusually high-risk groups.
Typhoid	Typhoid vaccine	Killed bacteria	Subcut	2 doses 4 weeks or more apart or 3 doses 1 week apart (less desirable).	3 years‡	70% protective. Recommended only for exposure from travel, epidemic, or household carrier and not, eg, because of floods.
Yellow fever	Yellow fever vaccine (chick embryo)	Live virus	Subcut	1 dose.	10 years†	Certificate may be required for travel. Recommended for residence in or travel to endemic areas of Africa and South America.

*Dosages for the specific product, including variations for age, are best obtained from the manufacturer's package insert. Immunizations should be given by the route suggested for the product.
†Revaccination interval required by international regulations.
‡A single dose is a sufficient booster at any time after the effective duration of primary immunization has passed.
§Combination vaccines available.
**For contaminated or severe wounds, give booster if more than 5 years have elapsed since full immunization or last booster.
††Test for PPD conversion 2 months later and reimmunize if there is no conversion.

steroids, alkylating drugs, and other immunosuppressive agents, nor to individuals who exhibit congenital or acquired defects in cell-mediated immunity, as seen in severe combined immunodeficiency disease or Hodgkin's disease. Patients with pure hypogammaglobulinemia but no defect in cell-mediated immunity usually tolerate viral infections and vaccines well but have a 10,000-fold excess of paralytic complications over the usual one case per million vaccinees, perhaps because of the frequent reversion of attenuated polio strains to virulence in the intestinal tract.

Even if not administered to immunoincompetent hosts, live vaccines may result in mild and, rarely, severe disease.

The early measles vaccines caused high fever and rash in a significant proportion of recipients. Subacute sclerosing panencephalitis, a rare complication of natural infection, has occurred following administration of live attenuated measles vaccine (see Chapter 35), but the rate of perhaps one case per million vaccinees is one-tenth to one-fifth the rate following natural measles, and the number of cases of measles encephalitis has fallen 100-fold since the introduction of the vaccine.

Because passage through the human intestinal tract occasionally results in reversion of oral attenuated poliovirus vaccine (particularly type III) to neurovirulence, paralytic illness has occurred in recipients or their nonimmune contacts, especially adults. The success of live polio vaccines in preventing widespread natural infection has resulted in the paradox that the vaccine itself now causes most of the few cases of paralytic poliomyelitis seen each year in the USA. This fact and the apparent success of a few countries in abolishing polio by the use of inactivated vaccine alone has reopened the question of replacing live (Sabin) with killed (Salk) vaccine some 15 years after the live vaccine displaced the killed virus on grounds of greater potency, ease of administration, and the advantages of "intestinal" immunity.

Vaccinia is not virulent for normal humans at its usual site of administration in the skin but may cause severe local illness if accidentally administered to a child with eczema or if rubbed into the eye.

Live vaccines may contain undetected and undesirable passengers. Epidemic hepatitis has resulted from vaccinia and yellow fever vaccines containing human serum. More recently, millions of people received SV40, a simian papovavirus, along with inactivated poliovirus vaccine prepared in monkey kidney tissue culture. It is disconcerting that a virus closely related to SV40 has been isolated from the brain of patients with the lethal degenerative disease progressive multifocal leukoencephalopathy although there is no known history of polio immunization in these cases. An increased incidence of malignancy in the children of mothers who received inactivated polio vaccine during pregnancy has, however, been suggested in 2 studies. The true extent of risk can only be established by elaborate prospective studies. SV40 can now be detected and excluded from human viral vaccines, but it is possible that presently undetected agents might be transmitted to humans with uncertain consequences, particularly by vaccines grown in nonhuman cell lines. Bacteriophages and, probably, bacterial endotoxins have also been shown to contaminate live virus vaccines, although without known hazard thus far.

Live viral vaccines probably do not interfere with tuberculin skin testing, although they depress some measurements of lymphocyte function.

Legal Liability for Untoward Reactions

It is the physician's responsibility to inform the patient of the risk of immunization and to employ vaccines and antisera in an appropriate manner. Certain of the risks described above are, however, currently unavoidable; on balance, the patient is better off for accepting them.

Manufacturers should be held legally accountable for failure to adhere to known production safeguards. However, the filing of large liability claims by the statistically inevitable victims of good public health practice could lead manufacturers to abandon efforts to develop and produce low-profit but medically valuable therapeutic agents to the detriment of society as a whole. "Strict product liability" (liability without fault) is an inappropriate legal standard when an article could not have been regarded as defective by the "state of the art" when it was sold and where use and sale are subject to careful review by government bodies such as the Surgeon General's Advisory Committee on Immunization Practices and the Food & Drug Administration.

The cost of unpredictable untoward reactions not involving substandard manufacturing practices should logically be borne by the same public that reaps the benefits of control of disease (eg, paralytic poliomyelitis) and could be met through a national compensation scheme of the type recently established in the United Kingdom and Japan to cover vaccine-related injuries incurred during immunization under the National Health Service.

Nonspecific Active Immunization

Immunization with vaccinia has been employed in attempts to nonspecifically improve the immune response and thereby decrease the frequency of recurrences of herpes labialis (cold sores). Careful evaluation has shown that this practice is ineffective—and indeed has occasionally resulted in severe illness due to uncontrolled spread of vaccinia in a patient with unsuspected immunoincompetence.

Under some circumstances, specific activation of cell-mediated immunity may lead to enhanced nonspecific ability of "activated" macrophages to deal with other antigens. Such an interaction has been demonstrated experimentally for tuberculosis, *Salmonella*, *Brucella*, *Listeria*, and *Toxoplasma* infection of animals. The apparent effectiveness of BCG immunization in the prevention of leprosy may be related to this phenomenon as well as to an antigenic similarity between *Mycobacterium tuberculosis* and

Mycobacterium leprae. The possibility that non-specific stimulation of the immune system with *Bordetella pertussis, Corynebacterium parvum (Propionibacterium acnes),* endotoxins, or mycobacterial products can enhance the ability of the body to reject tumor cells is now being studied (see Chapters 17 and 40).

Combined Passive-Active Immunization

Passive immunization has been combined with active immunization to minimize untoward effects of certain active immunizing agents. Low-dose gamma globulin decreased the side-effects of the early attenuated measles vaccines, leading to greater patient acceptance. (Newer "further attenuated" vaccine strains no longer require the modifying effects of gamma globulin.) Similarly, vaccinia immune globulin decreases the likelihood of eczema vaccinatum if an eczematous patient must be vaccinated for travel to the (vanishing) smallpox-endemic area. Passive and active immunization are often simultaneously undertaken to provide both immediate but transient and slowly developing, durable protection against rabies or tetanus. The immune response to the active agent may or may not be impaired by gamma globulin if the injections are given at separate sites. Tetanus toxoid plus tetanus immune globulin may give a response superior to that generated by the toxoid alone, but after antiserum has been given for rabies, the course of immunization is usually extended to ensure an adequate response.

Anomalously Severe Disease in the Immunized Host

Immunization may not limit the spread of infection and may sometimes contribute to the pathogenesis of the disease. A child who has received killed measles virus vaccine (no longer recommended) may not develop protective serum antibody but may develop an exaggerated immune response that results in atypical and unusually severe rubeola upon exposure to wild virus or in an erythematous painful injection site, fever, and eye pain if reimmunization with live vaccine is performed. A poorly antigenic experimental respiratory syncytial virus vaccine increased the intensity of subsequent natural illness in infant recipients. Mice congenitally infected with lymphocytic choriomeningitis virus are clinically well until they begin to produce antibody to the virus; they then develop a fatal disorder resulting from the deposition of antigen-antibody complexes in the central nervous system and kidney. Similar poorly understood problems of intensified disease in immunized subjects have been noted with experimental trachoma and *Mycoplasma pneumoniae* vaccines.

The Decision to Immunize an Individual

Immunizing procedures are among the most effective and economical measures available for preservation and protection of health.

The decision to immunize a specific person against a specific pathogen is a complex judgment based upon an assessment of the risk of infection, the consequences of natural unmodified illness, the availability of a safe and effective immunogen, and the duration of its effect.

The organisms that cause diphtheria and tetanus are ubiquitous and the vaccines have few side-effects and are highly effective, but only the immunized individual is protected. Thus, immunization must be universal.

By contrast, a nonimmune individual who resides in a community which has been well immunized against poliovirus and who does not travel has little opportunity to encounter wild (virulent) virus. Here the immunity of the "herd" protects the unimmunized person since the intestinal tracts of recipients of oral poliovaccine fail to become colonized by or transmit wild virus. If, however, a substantial portion of the community is not immune, introduced wild virus can circulate and cause disease among the nonimmune group. Thus, focal outbreaks of poliomyelitis have occurred in religious communities objecting to immunization.

An intense debate has been in progress in Great Britain for the past few years over the relative risk of pertussis versus the occasional (between 1:300,000 and 1:50,000) neurologic complications of pertussis vaccination, an argument fueled by the discovery that the immunizing material in use prior to 1968 was poorly protective against then-prevalent serotypes of the infecting agent. The vigor of the opposing arguments is an illustration of the extent to which well-informed experts can disagree.

Smallpox vaccine is effective and usually safe, but the immunity it confers is of relatively short duration, declining after about 3 years. The last known case of naturally occurring smallpox was reported from Somalia in October 1977, and the risk from even the low rate of complications significantly exceeds the benefits of vaccination. Thus, vaccination against smallpox is no longer recommended.

Previously available rabies vaccines did, if only rarely, give rise to severe reactions. The risk of exposure is low, and preexposure immunization is thus reserved for travelers to hyperendemic areas or to persons with occupational hazard. The newly available human diploid vaccine may change this risk/benefit assessment: Approximately 30,000 courses of antirabies treatment are given annually in the USA, and perhaps only 20% of these are necessary when the recommended treatment guidelines are carefully followed.

Cholera immunization offers only temporary and incomplete protection. It is of little use to travelers and should only be given where the risk of exposure is high or in fulfillment of local regulations.

Each immunologically distinct viral subtype requires a specific antigenic stimulus for effective protection. Immunization against adenovirus infection has not benefited civilian populations subject to many differing types of virus—in contrast to the demonstrated value of vaccine directed against a few epidemic adenovirus types in military recruits. Similarly, immunity to type A influenza virus is transient because of major mutations in surface chemistry of the virus every few years (antigenic shifts). These changes render previously developed vaccines obsolete and may prevent sufficient production, distribution, and utilization of new antigen in time to prevent epidemic spread of the altered strain. Major antigenic changes have been detected in visna virus recovered 1 year after experimental inoculation, suggesting a mechanism of persisting infection as well as a profound barrier to developing a successful vaccine. Antigenic variation may also be an important impediment to immunization against trypanosomes.

Age at Immunization

The natural history of a disease determines the age at which immunization is best undertaken. Pertussis, polio, and diphtheria often strike in infancy; immunization against these diseases is therefore begun shortly after birth. Serious consequences of pertussis are uncommon beyond early childhood, and pertussis vaccination is not usually recommended after 6 years of age. Since the major hazard of rubella is the congenital rubella syndrome, and since nearly half of congenital rubella occurs with the first pregnancy, it is very important to immunize as many females as possible prior to puberty. One thereby also avoids the theoretic hazard of vaccinating a pregnant female and endangering the fetus, although inadvertently immunized fetuses have thus far not been found to be damaged by their exposure to the attenuated virus.

The efficacy of immunization may also be age-related. Failure may occur because of the presence of interfering antibodies or an undeveloped responsiveness of the immune system. Infants cannot be reliably protected with live measles, mumps, or rubella vaccines until maternally derived antibody has disappeared. Because of the reported failure of measles vaccination in a proportion of children immunized as late as 1 year of age, the age recommended for measles vaccine administration has recently been changed to 15 months, and some workers have made the same suggestion for rubella vaccine administration. Children (now teenagers) who were vaccinated at an earlier age in accordance with recommendations in effect at that time should be revaccinated. Infants frequently develop severe infections with *Haemophilus influenzae* type b, but injecting them with purified

capsular polysaccharide has failed to reliably yield a good antibody response despite the excellent activity of the same antigen in older children and adults. Indeed, one study has shown that several children with early severe disease due to *H influenzae* did not develop active immunity and also failed to show a good antibody response to vaccine administered after 2 years of age. This failure to respond raises the question of a possible immune defect in the patients most in need of protection.

Simultaneous Immunization With Multiple Antigens

Simultaneous immunization with several antigenic stimuli might be expected to result in interference by the immune response to one antigen with the development of immunity to other antigens. Actually, the simultaneous inoculation of the nonliving antigens of diphtheria, tetanus, and pertussis gives a response equal to that seen with their separate injection; the endotoxic components of *Bordetella pertussis* may even act as an adjuvant, providing a superior immune response against the additional antigens.

Similarly, the single injection of a mixture of live, attenuated measles, rubella, and mumps viruses or the simultaneous administration of live measles, smallpox, and yellow fever vaccines gives good responses to each component of the mixture. However, between 2 and 14 days following the administration of one live virus vaccine, there is a period of suboptimal response to a **subsequently injected** live virus vaccine. It is best to administer multiple immunizing agents according to a schedule which has been demonstrated to yield an effective response.

Recommendations for Childhood Immunization

A rational program of immunization against infectious diseases begins in childhood, when many of the most damaging and most preventable infections normally appear. Table 39–4 summarizes the current guidelines for immunization in childhood as compiled by the Expert Committee on Infectious Diseases of the American Academy of Pediatrics. The need for childhood immunization is actually increased since unimmunized individuals in a partially immune population will be less exposed to and will therefore develop later than they otherwise would such typically childhood diseases as measles and mumps. When these illnesses do occur in adolescence or adulthood, they are often

Table 39–4. Guidelines for routine immunization of normal infants and children.

Disease	Vaccine	Schedule of Doses				
		First	Second	Third	Fourth	Fifth
Diphtheria-tetanus-pertussis	DTP, adsorbed	2 months	4 months	6 months	1½ years	4–6 years*
Poliovirus I, II, and III	Oral trivalent	2 months	4 months	6 months†	1½ years	4–6 years
Measles-mumps-rubella	MMR or singly	15 months	...	...	...	...

*Adult-type combined tetanus-diphtheria toxoid (Td) is recommended at 10-year intervals thereafter.
†Optional in nonendemic areas.

much more severe than in childhood as well as being diagnostically bewildering to the physician unprepared for such illnesses in this age group. Epidemic measles is thus being reported in college students for the first time. The 1976 USA immunization survey disclosed immunization rates of 70%, 75%, 72%, and 78% for 5- to 9-year-olds against rubella, measles, polio, and DTP, respectively. Where school attendance requirements mandate immunization, however, the rates are well over 90% (eg, California, 1979).

Physicians can improve immunization rates by using the occasion of a visit for intercurrent illness to investigate and augment a patient's immune status. It is *not* necessary to restart an interrupted series of vaccinations or to add extra doses. If the vaccination history is unknown and there are no obvious contraindications, the child or adult should be fully immunized appropriately for age. Reimmunization poses no significant risk.

Immunization of Adults for Foreign Travel

National health authorities may require an International Certificate of Vaccination against smallpox, cholera, or yellow fever from travelers, usually depending upon the presence of these diseases in countries on their itinerary. Smallpox and cholera vaccinations may be given by any licensed physician. The certificate must be completed in all details and then validated with an approved stamp. Yellow fever vaccination may only be administered and the certificate validated at an officially designated center (these may be located by contacting the state or local health department). In addition to these legal requirements, all adults are advised to be adequately immunized against tetanus and diphtheria and to undergo additional immunizations (polio, typhoid, hepatitis A, plague, typhus) if visiting areas where the frequency of illness in the population or the level of sanitation increases the risk of infection. (Travelers to malaria-endemic areas should also be advised regarding chemoprophylaxis.) Information regarding individual agents may be found in Tables 39–2 and 39–3.

No special immunizations are generally recommended for persons traveling from the USA to Western Europe, Canada, or Australia. Detailed suggestions of the USPHS are given country-by-country in its Health Information for International Travel Supplement (see references).

Vaccines & Antisera of Restricted Availability or Experimental Status

A number of vaccines have been developed that are available for individuals at greatly increased occupational risk but not for the general public. Only a partial listing will be given here.

Adenovirus. Live attenuated oral vaccines have been developed for military use. These are directed against the 2 types of virus—types 4 and 7—that commonly cause severe epidemic disease in recruits. Experimental vaccines have been formulated against additional (civilian) serotypes.

Adjuvants. At least 3 promising synthetic compounds are under active evaluation: muramyl dipeptides, polynucleotides, and liposomes. Adjuvant compounds may allow immunization of infants who respond poorly to the polysaccharide antigens of *Haemophilus influenzae,* pneumococci, and meningococci.

Anthrax. A protein antigen extracted from culture filtrates can protect those who work with imported animal hides and hair and others with occupational exposure.

Arbovirus (various). Vaccines against certain agents causing equine encephalitis are available for persons working with the viruses. Experimental vaccines, either formalin-inactivated or related live, avirulent strains, protect animals against clinically important hemorrhagic fevers in Africa and Argentina. A live attenuated dengue type 2 virus vaccine is undergoing evaluation in humans.

Bacteroides fragilis. It has been observed that rats immunized with capsular polysaccharide of this common participant in intra-abdominal sepsis do not develop early bacteremia or form abscesses after intraperitoneal inoculation of *B fragilis* or *Bacteroides distasonis.*

Cholera. The low level of immunity induced by commercially available whole-cell vaccines has led to the development of experimental vaccines directed against purified heat- and formalin-inactivated toxin. Oral immunization may be more effective than parenteral.

Cytomegalovirus. A live attenuated vaccine grown in a human diploid cell line has been shown to be immunogenic when given subcutaneously but not intranasally. The safety and efficacy of the vaccine, in view of the propensity of herpesviruses to cause latent infections which give rise to disease at the time of reactivation, remain to be demonstrated. There is some evidence that prior infection (or immunization) may modify subsequent disease. For example, transplacental antibody usually (not always) appears to protect the second congenitally infected infant of a chronically infected mother from clinical disease. On the other hand, patients who demonstrate lymphocyte transformation to herpesviruses lose these responses after transplantation, and live virus immunization before transplantation may be no more effective in preventing or modifying infection than natural immunity. Indeed, in one small uncontrolled trial, immunized renal transplant patients developed exogenous cytomegalovirus infections at the same rate as that previously reported in unimmunized patients.

Dental caries. Subcutaneous administration of a purified protein from *Streptococcus mutans* to primates resulted in a 70% decrease in caries and a fall in the numbers of streptococci recovered from the dental plaque. Further studies are required to ensure that antibodies reactive with the heart, which may be induced by whole bacterial vaccines, are not stimulated by the purified antigen as well.

E coli **enterotoxin.** Rats are best protected

against heat-labile toxin by a program of active immunization by the parenteral route, followed by an oral booster. Homologous protection against oral reinfection has also been demonstrated in human volunteers who have recovered from diarrheal illness.

***E coli* K1 neonatal meningitis.** Two-thirds of neonatal meningitis is due to *E coli,* and more than 80% of these strains carry the K1 capsular polysaccharide antigen. Rats that have been suckled by K1-immunized mothers or given oral antiserum to *E coli* K1 have less bacteremia and lower mortality rates following intraperitoneal instillation of *E coli* K1, suggesting a means of preventing and possibly even treating this severe neonatal illness.

Gonococci. Although experimental vaccines have been shown to produce antibody, the role of immunity in protecting against gonococcal infection is not known at this time. A number of differing gonococcal immunotypes have been identified, consistent with the clinical experience of multiple episodes of illness in an individual and suggesting that vaccine development will be difficult. Current attempts to identify common fimbrial antigens are aimed at producing anti-adhesins that would prevent attachment of multiple serotypes.

Gram-negative bacteremia. Vaccines directed against the somatic O antigens of gram-negative bacteria are partially protective against infection with these organisms, eg, pertussis, cholera, plague, and typhoid vaccines. The antigenic heterogeneity of the many serotypes of different species has made a general "anti-O" vaccine impractical. Recent investigations of the structure of the endotoxic lipopolysaccharides of gram-negative organisms have revealed a common "core" antigen shared by nearly all species. A core glycolipid vaccine (J5) was well tolerated by human volunteers. Serum from these volunteers was administered to patients with gram-negative bacteremia and markedly improved the mortality rate in a double-blind controlled trial. Specific "anti-O" vaccines may decrease the extent of renal damage in ineradicable chronic urinary infections.

***Haemophilus influenzae* type b.** The major antigen, capsular polyribophosphate, does not induce protective antibody in infants. Oral immunization with cross-reactive *E coli* appears promising. K100 protected infant rats against bacteremia or meningitis following intranasal inoculation of *H influenzae* and markedly augmented the transient anticapsular antibody response.

Herpesvirus hominis. Exogenous reinfection with a different strain of the same serotype has been clearly documented. Formalinized vaccine has failed to yield protection in 2 separate human trials despite success in animal models. Immunosuppressed recipients of renal transplants, whose cell-mediated immunity is impaired, may develop severe herpetic disease despite very high levels of antibody.

Influenza. Live attenuated vaccines, including mutant strains that replicate poorly at deep body temperature, are being examined as potentially superior immunizing agents compared to currently licensed killed vaccines. Intranasal immunization with live virus is attractive as a means of improving the local barriers to initiating infection, but minor decreases in pulmonary function are detected from 1–3 weeks thereafter, and the hazard to subjects with damaged lungs has not been defined. Other approaches being examined include the use in Russia of orally administered live attenuated strains and the use of recombinant viruses containing only new viral neuraminidase antigens. The latter vaccine is less protective than a vaccine inducing antibody against the new viral hemagglutinin but permits colonization and active immunization by asymptomatic or clinically attenuated illness.

Legionella. Avirulent strains are readily produced on subculture and appear to be effective immunizing agents in guinea pigs.

Leprosy. Cutaneous sensitization to oil-free, killed *M leprae* has been successfully accomplished in guinea pigs, raising the possibility of human vaccination studies.

Malaria. Killed falciparum merozoites given in Freund's complete adjuvant have protected humans against challenge with *Plasmodium falciparum,* and these asexual erythrocyte forms of the parasite have now been successfully cultured in vitro.

Meningococcus. The protection-inducing antigen for group B is a type-specific protein, not a group-defining polysaccharide, as in groups A and C. Vaccines are also under development for groups Y and W135. Because infants respond poorly to meningococcal and other polysaccharides, immunization by feeding cross-reactive *E coli* is also being considered.

Multiple sclerosis. Extracts of myelin basic protein, an extract of neural tissue, are being tested for their potential to absorb antibodies that would otherwise attack the patient's own nervous system.

Mycoplasma pneumoniae. Early killed vaccine may have caused more severe disease in the immunized host. Live, temperature-sensitive mutants that cannot multiply at the temperature of the lower respiratory tract induce protection against experimental challenge with more virulent strains. Experimental vaccination of animals has shown poor correlation of complement-fixing antibody and protection. Live vaccine is superior to inactivated vaccine, and the intranasal route of immunization is more effective than the subcutaneous. Since low levels of mycoplasmacidal antibody are found in a high proportion of children below the age of 5, and since repeat attacks of mycoplasmal pneumonia are well documented, it would appear that antibody is not protective against this infection or that immunity is particularly short-lived, making the long-term value of immunization uncertain. Experimental studies in mice suggest that persistence of intranasal immunity may be more important than serum antibody levels.

Pneumococcus. Temperature-sensitive noninvasive mutants capable of colonizing the upper airways are being studied as possible immunogens, as are antigenically related viridans streptococci.

Pseudomonas aeruginosa. Polyvalent lipopolysaccharide vaccines can stimulate the development of protective opsonizing antibodies, but clinical usefulness in immunosuppressed, neutropenic patients or in patients with cystic fibrosis, 2 of the groups most at risk from this organism, has not been demonstrated. Vaccination may protect the patient with normal humoral immunity and normal white cell count against bacteremia from infected burns. Side reactions to immunization are frequent. Serotype-specific polysaccharide antigens, ribosomal preparations, toxoids of exotoxin A, and other potential immunogens are also being evaluated.

Rabies. Rabies immune globulin is not always readily available in developing countries where the disease is most prevalent. It is thus noteworthy that severely challenged monkeys, given a single dose of a polyI-polyC interferon inducer combined with one dose of the human diploid cell vaccine within 48 hours of exposure, were as well protected as if they had promptly received hyperimmune serum and a course of 3 vaccine doses.

Respiratory syncytial (RS) virus. Recipients of killed vaccines developed more serious illness than unimmunized infants. Live attenuated and temperature-sensitive virus vaccines are being evaluated, as is parenteral administration of wild virus, which appears not to cause illness in young children while inducing neutralizing antibody.

Rhinovirus. Live and inactivated vaccines have been produced. Their use does not appear promising at present because of the multiplicity of serotypes that would be needed and because even natural immunity offers only partial protection.

Rickettsioses. A formalin-inactivated **Q fever** vaccine, produced in chick embryo cell culture, is undergoing clinical trials in humans. The vaccine, produced by the US Army Institute of Infectious Diseases at Fort Detrick, Maryland, could be particularly valuable for animal handlers and researchers utilizing pregnant sheep in experimental surgery, a group with a relatively high incidence of occupationally acquired infection.

A similar investigational vaccine, also produced at Fort Detrick, will protect monkeys against subcutaneous or aerosol challenge with **Rocky Mountain spotted fever.**

Rotavirus. Recent in vitro cultivation of both currently recognized serotypes is an important step toward possible production of a vaccine for a very common infection and, in developing countries, the probable cause of substantial numbers of infant deaths.

Shigella. Live attenuated oral vaccines utilizing either noninvasive hybrid *E coli* modified to carry *Shigella* antigens or streptomycin-dependent shigellae are being evaluated. Lack of immunogenicity and reversion to virulence, respectively, have been problems in the development of these 2 vaccines.

Streptococcus group A. It is now possible to protect human volunteers with type-specific M protein determinants free of contamination with nonspecific antigens. The purified materials do not cause local and systemic reactions, nor do they lead to the production of antibodies reactive with the heart, as did earlier vaccines.

Streptococcus group B. The commonest agent of neonatal meningitis colonizes the female genital tract and causes disease in the absence of transplacentally shared maternal antibody directed against the type-specific antigens. Purified capsular polysaccharide antigen has been prepared from the type III organisms most commonly found in neonatal infection and is under investigation as an immunizing agent for the mother to ensure adequate antibody levels in the neonate at delivery. To avoid the possibility of immunologic paralysis of the fetus, it might be necessary to immunize women of childbearing age before pregnancy. However, protective antibody levels in the mother do not always result in protective levels in cord sera.

Typhoid. Live oral attenuated mutants provide superior protection and decrease enteric carriage of the infective organism.

Varicella. A live attenuated virus is probably effective in inducing antibody and preventing or modifying illness. However, the safety of a live virus vaccine remains to be conclusively demonstrated in the immunoincompetent patients most likely to develop life-threatening complications of wild virus infection. Small numbers of leukemic children and children with solid tumors have been immunized without complications and apparently protected against natural infection. The vaccine virus does not appear to spread readily to contacts.

IMMUNIZATION AGAINST NONINFECTIOUS DISEASES

Prevention of Rh Isoimmunization

Rh-negative females who have not already developed anti-Rh antibodies should receive Rh immune globulin within 72 hours after obstetric delivery, abortion, accidental transfusion with Rh-positive blood, and, probably, amniocentesis, especially if the needle passes through the placenta. This passive immunization suppresses the mother's normal immune response to any Rh-positive fetal cells that may enter her circulation, thus avoiding erythroblastosis fetalis in future Rh-positive fetuses. Even if more than 72 hours has elapsed after exposure, the globulin should be administered, since it will be effective in at least some cases. Three of 6 subjects were protected from the immunogenic effect of 1 mL of Rh-positive red cells given intravenously by 100 μg of anti-Rh globulin given 13 *days* later. Some workers have also suggested the administration of anti-Rh globulin to Rh-negative newborn female offspring of Rh-positive mothers to prevent possible sensitization from maternal-fetal transfusion (see Chapters 21 and 27).

A significant number of Rh isoimmunizations occur during pregnancy rather than at the time of delivery. Published studies suggest that this sensitization can be prevented by administration of anti-Rh globulin throughout pregnancy, despite the theoretic risks of the globulin crossing the placenta and causing erythroblastosis in the fetus.

There is, however, serious disagreement about whether or not antenatal Rh prophylaxis should be widely adopted, because of its marginal improvement on rate of sensitization despite at least a 4-fold increase in costs, the unknown hazards to the fetus of administering other unwanted antibodies, and the strain upon supplies of the Rh immune globulin, with unknown risks to hyperimmunized donors.

Prevention of Diabetes

It is strongly suspected that juvenile-onset diabetes mellitus is often induced by a viral infection, most likely coxsackievirus B4 or mumps virus, particularly in genetically predisposed individuals. If further study confirms this or a similar etiologic relationship, it may be possible for the first time to prevent a chronic progressive noninfectious disease through anti-infective immunization.

Serum Therapy of Poisonous Bites

The toxicity of the bite of the black widow spider, the coral snake, and crotalid snakes (rattlesnakes and other pit vipers) may be lessened by the administration of commercially available antivenins.

Antisera for scorpion stings and rarer poisonous bites, especially of species foreign to North America, may also be available.

A central directory for information on use and availability of antivenins is maintained by the American Association of Zoological Parks and Aquariums at the Antivenin Index Center in Oklahoma City, OK 73126; (405) 271-5454. This service, which is available on a 24-hour basis, should be particularly useful in cases of snakebite by exotic species. The Center should be given the correct scientific name as well as the common name of the biting species; with this information, it can provide information about the availability and location of the nearest supply of antiserum as well as the names and emergency telephone numbers of persons able to supply the antisera and give expert advice.

● ● ●

References

Beachey EH: Bacterial adherence: Adhesin-receptor interactions mediating the attachment of bacteria to mucosal surfaces. *J Infect Dis* 1981;**143**:325.

Chanock RM: Strategy for development of respiratory and gastrointestinal tract viral vaccines in the 1980s. *J Infect Dis* 1981;**143**:364.

Craighead JE: Report of a workshop: Disease accentuation after immunization with inactivated microbial vaccines. *J Infect Dis* 1975;**131**:749.

Edelman R, Hardegree MC, Chedid L: Summary of an international symposium on potentiation of the immune response to vaccines. *J Infect Dis* 1980;**141**:103.

Freestone DS, Knight PA: Preclinical data supporting first clinical trials of new inactivated vaccines. *Lancet* 1976;**2**:786.

General recommendations on immunization. Public Health Service Advisory Committee on Immunization Practices. *MMWR* 1980;**29**:76.

Harrison HR, Fulginiti VA: Bacterial immunizations. *Am J Dis Child* 1980;**134**:184.

Health information for international travel, 1981. *MMWR* 1981;**30 (Suppl)**.

Immunization Abstracts and Bibliography, CDC. [A thrice-yearly serial publication begun in 1978.]

Kass EH (editor): Assessment of the pneumococcal polysaccharide vaccine. (A workshop.) *Rev Infect Dis* 1981;**3 (Suppl):**S1.

Klein JO, Katz SL (editors): Prospects for new viral vaccines: A symposium. *Rev Infect Dis* 1980;**2**:351.

Office of Technology Assessment: *A Review of Selected Federal Vaccine and Immunization Policies*. U.S. Government Printing Office, 1979.

Osborn JE: Cytomegalovirus: Pathogenicity, immunology and vaccine initiatives. *J Infect Dis* 1981;**143**:618.

Rabies prevention. Public Health Service Advisory Committee on Immunization Practices. *MMWR* 1980;**29**:265.

Report of the Committee on Infectious Diseases, 18th ed. American Academy of Pediatrics, 1977.

Riddiough MA, Willems JS: Federal policies affecting vaccine research and production. *Science* 1980;**209**:563.

Robbins JB, Hill JC (editors): Current status and prospects for improved and new bacterial vaccines. *J Infect Dis* 1977;**136 (Suppl):**S8. [Entire issue.]

Voller A, Friedman H (editors): *New Trends and Developments in Vaccines*. University Park Press, 1978.

40 | Experimental Immunotherapy

H. Hugh Fudenberg, MD, & Joseph Wybran, MD

Experimental approaches to immunotherapy have developed along several important lines in recent years. The applications of immunotherapy in current clinical practice include, in addition to immune deficiency diseases, some types of viral infections and some autoimmune disorders. Immunotherapy has a role in cancer treatment when radiation treatment and anticancer drugs have overwhelmed the immune system rendering the patient susceptible to lethal infections. Many adjuvants, immunostimulants, and drugs with specific or nonspecific effects are now being intensively investigated (Table 40–1). Although most are still restricted to a few research centers, others are already widely used in the therapy of cancer and other disorders. In cancer therapy, these agents are usually employed in combination with or after chemotherapy and radiation therapy. The rationale for this approach, called "chemoimmunotherapy" or "immunochemotherapy," is to reduce the antigenic tumor mass in the patient before immunostimulation, since the response of the immune system or its components is limited. In general, all of these immunotherapeutic agents are more effective when the antigenic mass (neoplastic cells, fungus, virus, etc) is small.

There are several approaches to immunotherapy, including the following: (1) Nonspecific systemic immunostimulation with agents such as BCG, with the aim of general stimulation of immunologic responsiveness. (2) Adjuvant contact therapy, where bacterial adjuvants such as BCG and *Cornyebacterium parvum* are administered to become localized in tumor deposits. Such therapy initiates nonspecific as well as probable specific host responses, which can lead to local destruction of tumor cells. (3) Active specific immunotherapy involving immunization with tumor antigen in adjuvant, the objective being to stimulate immune responses to tumor antigens. (4) Adoptive transfer of immunity with sensitized lymphoid cells, subcellular components such as immune RNA or transfer factor, or antisera from immune donors.

All of the various immunomodulators probably function at different levels of the immune system, although the precise target cell is not known except in a very few cases. An obvious need exists for the development of agents that can selectively inhibit or enhance one specific subclass of immunocytes, eg, increase suppressor T cells in systemic lupus erythe-matosus, decrease antigen-specific suppressor T cells in various malignancies, or increase natural killer cell numbers or activity in leukemia and malignancies.

NONSPECIFIC IMMUNOTHERAPY

Nonspecific immunotherapy usually involves the use of immunomodulating agents administered with the aim of general stimulation or suppression of the patient's immune system, without attempting to direct the activity of the stimulated cells toward a given antigen. Nonspecific immunomodulators are of 3 types: (1) those that require a functional immune system; (2) those with maximum effects on a suppressed immune system; and (3) those that act on normal and immunosuppressed systems. Particulate adjuvants (eg, BCG, *C parvum*) are of the first type; ie, they are generally most effective in patients capable of mounting normal immune responses. Agents with restorative effects (eg, levamisole, thymosin) are of the second type; ie, they act by conferring temporary immune competence in patients with suppressed immunity but apparently have little or no effect when administered to patients with normal immune systems. Inosiplex belongs to the third group, because it acts on both normal and suppressed immune systems.

BACILLUS CALMETTE–GUERIN (BCG)

BCG is a viable attenuated strain of *Mycobacterium bovis* obtained by progressive reduction of virulence in a culture medium enriched with beef bile. It is thought that BCG acts mainly by stimulating the reticuloendothelial system, but it is not clear whether this is a primary effect or is secondary to T cell activation and lymphokine production. Since experimental stimulation of the reticuloendothelial system has also been postulated as a mechanism of tumor control, it appeared logical to try BCG in various animal tumor systems. Under various conditions, BCG can delay the appearance, decrease the incidence, inhibit the development, or induce the regression of malignant tumors caused by chemicals and viruses. BCG also

Table 40–1. Experimental immunotherapeutic agents.

Agent	Mechanism of Action	Results in Animals	Results in Humans		Side-Effects
			Disease	Response	
Nonspecific BCG (several types; see text)	Nonspecific adjuvant; cross-reaction with tumor cell antigens (?); augments natural killer cell activity.	Prevention of mammary adenocarcinoma after inoculation of tumor cells in syngeneic mice; prevention of pulmonary metastases from mammary carcinoma in rats; prevention of metastases from intradermally transplanted hepatoma in guinea pigs; prevention of lung metastasis in canine osteosarcoma after resection of primary tumor; occasionally, increase in suppressor T cells and decrease in survival.	Malignant melanoma.	Regression of dermal metastases after intralesional injection; no effect on visceral metastases; effect on survival rates unknown.	Chills, fever, malaise; granulomatous hepatitis; immune complex renal disease; anaphylaxis (rarely) due to antibody formation; persistent BCG infection at injection site in immunodepressed patients; side-effects vary, depending on route of administration (see text).
			Childhood acute lymphoblastic leukemia.	Prolongation of disease-free interval after induction of remission by chemotherapy.	
			Lung carcinoma (intrapleural injection).	Prevention of relapse (?).	
			Lymphoma (after radiotherapy).	Prolongation of remission, prevention of relapse (requires confirmation).	
			Colorectal cancer.	Increase in disease-free interval (in some patients).	
			Metastatic breast cancer.	Increase in survival.	
Muramyl dipeptide	Nonspecific adjuvant; macrophage activation.	Resistance to challenge with infectious agents.	Not effective as an adjuvant in humans (unpublished results).		
MER-BCG	Nonspecific adjuvant.	Preliminary results in animals and humans indicate results comparable to or better than those with whole BCG, but with far fewer complications.			
C parvum (heat-killed and formaldehyde-treated)	Activation of macrophages (augments phagocytosis and cytotoxicity; may involve cellular C3 receptors).	Prevention of tumor growth and metastasis in various animal tumors (eg, rat Moloney sarcoma); best results when injected at tumor site. In mouse mammary carcinoma, sometimes effective when given intradermally but not when given intravenously.	Malignant melanoma (cutaneous metastases).	Regression of lesions after intralesional injection; effects on survival unknown.	Fever (up to 40.5 °C), headache, nausea, vomiting; mild hypertension, peripheral vasoconstriction.
			Lung cancer (intrapleural).	Effects on survival not yet known.	
			Other solid tumors, acute leukemia (in combination with other agents or with irradiated leukemic cells).	Trials in progress.	
Thymic hormones (thymosin fraction V, facteur thymique serique [FTS], thymopoietin, thymosin polypeptides α_1, β_1, α_5, α_7, β_3, β_4, and others)	Differentiation of pre-T cells to mature T cells (eg, increases active and total T cells in patients with low levels). Normalization of increased or decreased suppressor T cell levels.	Prolongation of life span in NZB/NZW mice and aging normal mice.	Hereditary deficiencies of cell-mediated immunity.	Immunologic normalization, clinical improvement.	Allergic reactions (rarely severe).
			Oat cell carcinoma.	Increase in survival.	
			Other malignancies (eg, melanoma, in combination with chemotherapy).	Trials in progress.	
Bone marrow transplants	Replacement of missing component of immune system.	Extensive studies in mice, rats, dogs, etc.	Severe combined immunodeficiency.	Restoration of immune function; reduced infections, increased survival.	Severe GVH disease unless donors are MLC-compatible (HLA-D–matched); mild GVH unless donor is identical twin.
			Aplastic anemia.	Increased survival.	

Table 40–1 (cont'd). Experimental immunotherapeutic agents.

Agent	Mechanism of Action	Results in Animals	Results in Humans		Side-Effects
			Disease	Response	
Nonspecific (cont'd) Fetal thymus (13-week) or fetal liver (8-week) transplants	Replacement of missing component of immune system.	...	DiGeorge syndrome, severe combined immunodeficiency.	Restoration of immune function, reduced infections, increased survival (better success with fetal liver than fetal thymus).	Mild or none.
Cultured thymic epithelium; autologous T cells cultured with fetal thymic epithelium	Replacement of missing component of immune system.	...	Severe combined immunodeficiency.	Restoration of immune function, reduced infections, increased survival.	None reported.
Immunoglobulins (plasma, immune serum globulins, Cohn fraction V)	Replacement of missing component of immune system.	...	Hypogammaglobulinemia, severe combined immunodeficiency, Bruton's disease, complement deficiencies.	Temporary improvement in immune function and clinical course; repeated injections required to maintain humoral immunity.	None reported.
			Malignancies (plasma therapy).	Trials in progress.	
Levamisole	Enhancement of monocyte–T cell interactions; induction of interferon (?); increase in monocyte chemotaxis and phagocytosis.	Restoration of both helper and suppressor cell functions and increased survival in aged mice; modulation of suppressor function in autoimmune mice; increased life span in mice with Lewis lung carcinoma.	Rheumatoid arthritis.	Improvement in some.	Neutropenia (occasionally severe).
			Aphthous stomatitis.	Marked improvement.	
			Bronchogenic carcinoma.	Results controversial.	
			Malignant melanoma.	No significant increase in survival rates.	
			Juvenile periodontitis.	Improvement.	
			SLE.	Trials in progress.	
Interferon	Enhancement of natural killer cell production and activity; inhibition of viral replication; direct effect on tumor cells (reduction in replication rate [?]); increase in macrophage activity (?).	Inhibition of growth of a wide variety of transplantable and ascitic or solid tumors of different origins in mice (spontaneous, viral, chemically induced); inhibition of spontaneous pulmonary metastases of Lewis lung carcinoma injected subcutaneously in mice; delay in appearance and reduced frequency of spontaneous tumors in tumor-prone mice (eg, lymphomas in AKR mice, mammary carcinoma, etc); prevention or delay in appearance of virus-induced tumors (eg, Rous sarcoma, Shope fibrosarcoma, Friend and Rauscher murine leukemias).	Osteosarcoma, Hodgkin's disease (using crude material; see text).	Increase in survival.	Occasional leukopenia.

Agent	Immunologic effect	Effects in experimental animals	Use/trials in humans	Results in humans	Toxicity
Inosiplex	Prevention of virus-induced suppression of cell-mediated immunity; inhibition of viral replication (both RNA and DNA viruses); potentiation of antiviral effects of interferon.	Inhibition of influenza A virus infection in mice, reduction of mortality rate in mice already infected; decrease in mortality rate of hamsters infected with herpes simplex type 2; decrease in mortality rate of hamsters and rabbits infected with herpes simplex virus type 1; increase in survival of tumor-bearing mice also treated with interferon.	Herpes labialis, herpes progenitalis, shingles, rhinovirus infection, influenza A infection, cytomegalovirus infection. Viral hepatitis (both Type A and type B). Subacute sclerosing panencephalitis. Rheumatoid arthritis.	Marked reduction in duration of illness and severity of symptoms. Same as above, and decrease in abnormal liver chemistries. Prevention of further deterioration in stage I and II patients. Rapid response in 60% of patients.	None reported.
Pyrimethamine (antimalarial)	Enhancement of antibody and delayed hypersensitivity responses.	Reversal of immunosuppression in tumor-bearing mice.	No trials in humans.	...	...
Glucan	Increase in activation and proliferation of macrophages, resulting in marked enhancement of both cellular and humoral immunity; increase in granulocyte production (?).	Increased resistance to infection (especially S aureus septicemia) in normal and leukemic mice or cyclophosphamide-treated mice; increased survival in leukemia (rats) and tumors (mice).	Metastatic malignancy (intralesional injection).	Prompt tumor cell necrosis and regression of lesions.	None reported.
Tilorone	Induction of macrophage MIF synthesis (differs from lymphocyte MIF); induction of interferon.	Increase in B cell activity (?).	No trials in humans.	...	...
L-Fucose	Inhibition of action of mediators of cellular immunity both in vitro and in vivo (eg, inhibits guinea pig MIF and delayed hypersensitivity).	Animal experiments in progress.	No trials in humans.	...	...
Synthetic polynucleotides (eg, poly A-U, poly I-C)	Interferon induction for poly I-C.	Inhibition of growth of transplantable tumors in various systems.	Poly A-U, trial in breast cancer.	Increased survival after conventional therapy.	...
Specific Active specific immunotherapy (tumor antigen in Freund's adjuvant)	Increase in specific cell-mediated immunity (?).	Reduction in tumor growth and in some cases elimination of tumors in transplanted guinea pig hepatomas and rat and mouse sarcomas.	Bronchogenic carcinoma (stage I) after chemotherapy. Colon carcinoma, breast carcinoma.	Marked prolongation of survival. Trials pending.	Local ulceration at injection site.

Table 40—1 (cont'd). Experimental immunotherapeutic agents.

Agent	Mechanism of Action	Results in Animals	Disease	Results in Humans Response	Side-Effects
Specific (cont'd) Enzyme-treated (neuraminidase) autochthonous tumor cells	Enhancement of immunogenicity of tumor cells by enzymatic removal of membrane-bound sialic acid (?).	Inhibition of growth of chemically or virally induced and transplantable solid tumors in mice and guinea pigs (and spontaneous mammary tumors in dogs); inhibition of lymphatic leukemia in mice; *tumor must be small.*	Leukemia (in combination with other agents). Stage III breast carcinoma (in combination with BCG). Malignant melanoma (without concomitant therapy).	Increased survival (in some trials). Trials in progress. Apparent cessation of local tumor growth.	None reported.
Irradiated tumor cells	Enhancement of both systemic and tumor-specific immunity in mice.	Prolonged survival in BALB/c x DBA/2 hybrid mice with LSTRA leukemia receiving vaccine containing irradiated LSTRA cells, especially in combination with *C parvum.* Too low a dose may enhance tumor progression and metastasis.	Acute leukemia (in combination with BCG or *C parvum*).	Trials in progress.	...
Immune RNA (xenogeneic)	Information transfer from lymphoid cells of animals immunized with the human tumor type being treated; induction of specific cytotoxic killer cells.	Regression of tumors in various systems; disappearance of pulmonary metastases in murine melanoma.	Metastatic renal cell carcinoma.	Regression or complete disappearance of metastases in some patients.	None reported in phase I studies.
Dialyzable leukocyte extracts (transfer factor)	Induction of antigen-specific cell-mediated immunity; nonspecific adjuvant activity on cell-mediated immunity also present in crude dialysates.	Transfer of antigen-specific cellular immune reactivity from donor to recipient both within and across species lines; prevention of death from parasitic infection in mice and cattle.	Genetically determined immune deficiency.	Dramatic decrease in parasitic, viral, and fungal infections.	Remarkably few: severe pain at site of primary or metastatic bone tumors; occasionally hypersensitivity pneumonia if pulmonary metastases are present.
			Recurrent infections with a single organism unresponsive to antibiotic therapy: fungal (eg, *Candida*), viral (eg, cytomegalovirus, herpes zoster), parasitic (eg, *Leishmania*), mycobacterial (eg, lupus vulgaris, *Mycobacterium fortuitum*, progressive BCG infection).	Excellent clinical results, provided proper donors are used and recipients are monitored by appropriate immunologic tests for frequency and amount of administration.	
			Malignancies (especially those presumed to be of viral origin): eg, epidermodysplasia verruciformis with squamous cell carcinoma and osteosarcoma.	Clinical improvement, prevention of metastases, prolongation of survival.	
			Multiple sclerosis.	Decrease in incidence of relapses, especially in mild disease.	

stimulates natural killer cells, which can nonspecifically and without previous sensitization kill different malignant cells. BCG appears to enhance the production of stem cells, as measured by hematopoietic colony formation. In addition, some investigators have suggested that BCG cross-reacts immunologically with hepatoma, melanoma, and leukemia cells, a finding that may help to explain some apparently specific effects of BCG on these tumors.

Other modes of action for BCG have been proposed. It may be that macrophages activated by BCG are more active killer cells, are more efficient in clearing antigens or antigen-antibody complexes, or are capable of inducing active participation of other cells of the immune system in the struggle against proliferating tumor cells. The formation of granulomas after administration of BCG may reflect this sort of effect. BCG may also affect tumor cells in nonimmunologic ways; eg, it can increase the intracellular content of some enzymes that act on some carcinogens. In some conditions, activation of the immune system after BCG injection appears to be both nonspecific and specific in tumor-bearing animals. Finally, it has been suggested that close contact between BCG and tumor cells is required for an optimal effect (see below).

The use of BCG is not without danger, since in some circumstances it has enhanced tumor growth. This phenomenon has been linked to the presence of serum factors (BCG-anti-BCG antigen-antibody complexes) that block the in vitro cytotoxicity of previously immune lymphocytes and, in animals, stimulation of antigen-specific suppressor cells. Both nonviable extracts of BCG and viable BCG have been shown to be immunostimulatory and to inhibit tumor growth. The chemical structure of the active adjuvant fractions of mycobacterial cell walls has been elucidated. Small molecules such as the monomeric subunit of the peptidoglycan of mycobacteria are still active. The smallest active compound derived from BCG so far identified is N-acetylmuramyl-L-alanyl-D-isoglutamine (muramyl dipeptide), which is an effective nonspecific adjuvant of macrophage activation in mice. Attempts to make analogs active in humans are under intensive investigation (see below).

BCG in Prevention of Human Cancer

Although claims have been made that children immunized with BCG against tuberculosis have a lower incidence of acute leukemia, the statistical methods used in these studies are subject to criticism, and better techniques are required to produce convincing evidence. If further reports continue to be favorable, prospective trials to confirm the efficacy of BCG vaccination in preventing the development of acute leukemia and possibly other tumors would be warranted.

BCG in Treatment of Human Cancer

It has been suggested that BCG can be helpful in the treatment of some types of human cancer. However, the optimal treatment regimen has not yet been clearly defined and indeed may vary depending on the tumor type and the immunologic status of the patient, especially when specific host defense mechanisms for eradication of tumor cells are depressed (as is the case in advanced tumors) by blocking factors such as antigen-antibody complexes, free soluble tumor antigens, and suppressor T cells or macrophages. There are 2 techniques by which BCG can be used for immunotherapy. In the first, immunotherapy is given as adjuvant treatment after cytoreductive treatment of measurable cancer in order to destroy micrometastases. In the second, BCG is used in immunochemotherapy for macrometastatic or disseminated cancer. The immunocompetence of cancer patients is frequently depressed, not only by the developing tumor (see Chapter 17) but also as a consequence of surgery, and more particularly by radiotherapy and chemotherapy. For example, postmastectomy irradiation in breast cancer patients induces a profound T lymphocyte depression for 3–6 months. It is generally considered that immunotherapy should be given during the "immunologic rebound" period, which occurs between day 10 and day 14 of cyclic chemotherapy and not directly before the next cycle of chemotherapy (risk of tolerance).

Types of BCG

Three types of BCG preparations are currently in use: (1) live unlyophilized (Pasteur, Phipps, Tice), (2) live lyophilized (Phipps, Tice, Connaught), and (3) killed lyophilized (Glaxo). Conflicting results of the efficacy of BCG immunotherapy in human tumors reflect the failure of investigators to take into account differences in the immunologic "potency" of these different preparations. For example, administration of viable BCG by scarification (see below) was found to control the development of lymph node metastases from an intradermally transplanted guinea pig hepatoma, but lyophilized BCG was ineffective. Furthermore, the successes of Mathé and co-workers in the treatment of acute lymphoblastic leukemia in children, using Pasteur (live) BCG in a trial begun in 1963, were not repeated by other investigators using Glaxo or Tice BCG preparations.

Routes of Administration

A. Intradermal Injection: BCG, alone or mixed with lymphoid or tumor cells (enzyme-treated or untreated), can be given intradermally, but this causes intense localized reactions.

B. Scarification Technique: The scarification technique is the most widely used method of administering BCG. A standard technique of scarification is to make 20 scratches 5 cm long with an 18-gauge needle on a 5×5 cm area of the upper arm or upper thigh. The scratches should be deep enough to produce some bleeding. BCG containing about 10^8 viable organisms is then applied to the site. Except for the scars, very few complications occur. The Heaf gun makes precise incisions 2 mm deep and is preferred by many immunologists. Usually, BCG is administered once a week. However, when the patient develops confluent papules or other signs of hypersensitization such as pustules and vesicles or induration zones, it is recommended that the dose of BCG be reduced by half and that it be administered only once a month. Finally, it is also advised to give the BCG in a rotating fashion on the upper parts of the 4 limbs, close to the draining lymph nodes.

Some patients, after weekly scarifications with BCG, show an absence of cutaneous reactivity to the treatment. Other tests then indicate that they have become immunosuppressed. In these cases, the therapy should be discontinued for a month and resumed usually on a monthly basis, depending upon restoration of immune function as indicated by various tests.

C. Oral Administration: The efficacy of oral administration is unknown. Only minor side-effects such as intestinal spasms have been noted.

D. Intravenous Injection: Intravenous administration has been attempted in leukemia.

E. Intralesional Injection: BCG (usually 10^7 bacilli) may be injected into skin lesions, but this mode of administration is associated with many side-effects.

F. Intrapleural Administration: Five days after the resection of lung cancer, some workers inject 10^7 organisms into the pleural space.

The first 4 routes of administration above (A-D) represent systemic, nonspecific immunostimulation; the last 2 (E and F) are examples of adjuvant contact therapy (see p 718).

Complications

Complications have been reported mainly with the intralesional and intradermal routes. The most dangerous side-effect of BCG therapy is a severe hypersensitivity reaction and shock. Rarely, patients have died after intralesional therapy. Other complications are listed in Table 40–1.

Complications of BCG therapy administered by scarification or with the Heaf gun are mild, and no fatalities have been reported.

Intravenous therapy has been associated with nonfatal anaphylactic reactions that did not recur when BCG was readministered. In order to avoid systemic tuberculosis as a complication of intrapleural injection of viable organisms, antituberculosis therapy is recommended.

Clinical Applications

A. Malignant Melanoma: BCG injected intralesionally has shown its effectiveness most dramatically in this disease without prolonging the survival of the patients (Table 40–1). BCG has been given by scarification after surgery to patients with stage II, III, or IV melanoma. Especially with only local regional involvement, BCG appears to decrease the recurrence in about 10% of patients compared to patients not receiving BCG, provided it has been given near the site of the tumor. In further studies, patients in stage IV received either chemotherapy alone —dacarbazine (DTIC) —or BCG and dacarbazine. Patients who received chemoimmunotherapy had more remissions, longer remissions, and longer survival than those who received only chemotherapy. In this series, it was also felt that the use of viable organisms and the presence of a soluble antigen in the BCG preparation contributed to maximal efficacy. It has also been reported that an increase in urinary lysozyme excretion is a valid indicator of clinical improvement in such patients after BCG therapy and that no improvement is seen in the absence of such an increase.

B. Acute Lymphocytic Leukemia: BCG was first tried by Mathé and co-workers in patients with acute lymphocytic leukemia. The attempt was based on the experimental observation that drugs were unable to kill all tumor cells and that other means such as immunotherapy were therefore necessary to kill the residual leukemic cells. BCG was found to be effective in leukemic mice if the number of residual malignant cells did not exceed 10^5.

In a clinical trial, a small group of patients received chemotherapy (induction and consolidation) and irradiation (of the central nervous system). After complete remission, the results in various groups receiving or not receiving some form of immunotherapy were compared. The total duration of immunotherapy was 5 years. Patients receiving weekly doses of BCG by scarification with or without irradiated allogeneic tumor cells appear to have responded best, since 7 patients out of 20 are still in remission 19 years after initiation of treatment. Of those who relapsed, the majority (9 patients) did so before 100 days (5 before 30 days). This suggests that the number of tumor cells left after chemotherapy in these patients was greater than the maximum that could be controlled by immunotherapy. In a later trial, using a newer chemotherapeutic combination (prednisone, vincristine, daunorubicin) and replacing total central nervous system radiotherapy (1560 rads) with cranial irradiation (2400 rads), the median duration of survival was more than 10 years, with the remission survival curve flattening out into a "plateau" at about 48 months (Fig 40–1). Addition of *C parvum* to the BCG therapy did not improve the results. In contrast, only 21 of 269 children (17.8%) with acute lymphocytic leukemia receiving maintenance chemotherapy alone survived for more than 5 years. It should, however, be stressed that the current trials with chemotherapy and irradiation achieve remission and perhaps cure in 50% of patients with this disease. These results could not be confirmed by English or American investigators using different therapeutic regimens and different sources of BCG.

Finally, recent data suggest that acute lymphocytic leukemia can now be divided into subgroups according to the histologic appearance of the leukemic cells. Only some histologic forms appear to respond well to immunotherapy. On the other hand, immunologic classifications of acute lymphocytic leukemia now appear to be more reliable than histologic classifications in terms

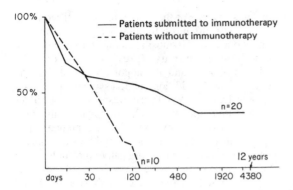

Figure 40–1. Duration of remission in patients of all ages with acute lymphocytic leukemia treated with chemotherapy and active immunotherapy (BCG, leukemic cells, or both). Results shown are for patients treated by Mathé and co-workers in the first controlled active immunotherapy trial in acute lymphoid leukemia, begun in 1963. All 10 of the patients receiving chemotherapy alone relapsed within 130 days. The actuarial curve for the duration of remission for the patients receiving immunotherapy tends to straighten out and continue on a plateau. Six patients were still in remission more than 8 years after chemotherapy had been stopped, and one after more than 12 years. There was no significant difference between the group given BCG alone, the group given leukemic cells alone, and the group given both forms of immunotherapy. Note that the time scale is geometric. (Reproduced, with permission, from Mathé G: *Cancer Active Immunotherapy.* Springer-Verlag, 1976.)

of clinical prognosis. Thus, T, B, pre-B, and "null" cell leukemias have different clinical features and different prognoses. It is conceivable that favorable results may be restricted to one or 2 of the immunologic types of acute lymphocytic leukemia.

C. Acute Myelogenous Leukemia: Various studies have shown that immunotherapy may be a useful adjuvant in this disease. For example, patients have received (1) chemotherapy or (2) chemotherapy plus BCG with or without allogeneic irradiated leukemic cells. Present data indicate that patients receiving immunotherapy have prolonged remissions and live twice as long as those who receive chemotherapy alone. Furthermore, it appeared in an English study that longer remissions were obtained by immunotherapy when the chemotherapy induced incomplete rather than complete remissions. Various trials have confirmed the efficacy of immunotherapy (including BCG or other types of immunotherapy) in acute myelogenous leukemia.

D. Chronic Myelogenous Leukemia: One nonrandomized study indicates that patients receiving a mixture of BCG and cultured allogeneic lymphoid cells intradermally after chemotherapy seem to have significantly longer survival periods than controls receiving chemotherapy only. Some patients in the immunized group have survived more than 7 years.

E. Lymphomas: In a relatively well controlled study, 2 groups of patients with stage IA and stage IIA lymphomas were compared after radiotherapy. Immunotherapy given in one group consisted of intradermal BCG (approximately 10^6 viable bacilli) given when the tuberculin response was not positive or when a positive test reverted to negative (median time to revaccination was 11 months). The immunized group showed a lower incidence of relapses and longer remission. All of these data are impressive, but further confirmation is required, especially since irradiation with or without chemotherapy is highly effective in these diseases.

F. Breast Cancer: A few studies suggest that BCG combined with chemotherapy increases the length of remission in metastatic breast cancer. Further trials are needed before conclusions can be drawn.

G. Head and Neck Tumors: The length of remission was reportedly increased in one study combining BCG and chemotherapy in relapsing tumors.

H. Colon Cancer: In this disease, some studies suggest that the addition of BCG to postoperative chemotherapy may decrease the incidence of relapses, but other reports refute this evidence.

I. Lung Cancer: A pilot study has clearly shown that patients with stage I lung carcinoma who receive intrapleural BCG 5 days after the resection of the tumor have a decreased incidence of relapse. Some trials, repeating this pilot study, have confirmed these results, while other investigators could not confirm the beneficial effect of BCG. Retrospective analysis indicates that the patients responding to BCG are immunosuppressed before treatment since they are skin-tuberculin negative and their lymphocytes do not respond well in mixed lymphocyte culture.

Subfractions of BCG

In view of the sometimes severe side-effects of BCG immunotherapy, various attempts have been made to use purified subfractions of the organism in order to reduce these complications. BCG cell walls have been used in a very limited number of studies. It appears that BCG cell walls attached to oil droplets can produce regression of guinea pig hepatomas. No trials in humans have been reported.

Muramyl dipeptide (MDP) is a substituted monosaccharide (N-acetylmuramyl-L-alanyl-D-isoglutamine) employed to mimic the immunologic activity of BCG cell walls. MDP and related water-soluble analogs have shown potent immunoadjuvant activity both in vitro and in vivo. SM-1213 is a synthetic, substituted monosaccharide very similar in structure to MDP. It has been shown to have immunomodulatory activity in animals. Both MDP and SM-1213 induce macrophage activation, and both have been found to be effective against in vivo challenge with infectious agents to which resistance is highly dependent on the macrophage. Further experimentation is required to determine their therapeutic potential.

MER-BCG (methanol-extractable residue of phenol-treated BCG) has been given in various solid tumors and leukemias in animals. It appears to decrease the size and incidence of the tumors and sometimes prolongs survival. Limited data in humans are available from a few centers, and the results appear promising in solid tumors, acute leukemias, and perhaps melanoma, especially in conjunction with chemotherapy. The use of MER-BCG appears limited because it is relatively poorly tolerated.

CORYNEBACTERIUM PARVUM

Corynebacterium parvum is a gram-positive bacterium. It is used as a heat-killed and formaldehyde-treated suspension, given orally or injected parenterally, either directly into the lesion or at a distant site. It can prevent the growth of tumors in animals. It also inhibits tumor spread by preventing the development of metastases. It appears that *C parvum* acts by activating macrophages. Paradoxically, it depresses T cell function, especially splenic T cells. Nonimmunologic mechanisms can also participate in the antitumor action. *C parvum* has also been injected intralesionally and produces regression of the tumor. Many clinical trials with *C parvum* are under way, and claims have been made of longer remissions in various types of lung cancer and metastatic breast cancer in association with multiple chemotherapy. However, the pronounced toxicity (see Table 40–1) of this substance limits its usefulness.

Recent studies of chemoimmunotherapy in mouse tumor systems indicate that when *C parvum* is used in combination with the cytotoxic drug cyclophosphamide, the onset of both specific and nonspecific antitumor effects is delayed when the adjuvant is administered early during the suppressive phase of the drug's effect, and that the drug increases the susceptibility of mice to the toxic effects of a subsequent high systemic dose of the adjuvant. In contrast, when mice are treated systemically with *C parvum* followed by cyclophosphamide, the drug's antitumor effects are potentiated in a synergistic manner, depending on the interval between the 2 treatments. Combined treatment with BCG and cyclophosphamide has also been shown to be significantly more effective than the drug alone in controlling the growth of a transplantable murine mammary adenocarcinoma only when the immune stimulant is given first but not when the 2 are given in reverse order. Such studies are obviously of major significance in the development of optimal chemoimmunotherapeutic protocols for human cancers.

THYMIC HORMONES

The epithelium of the thymus synthesizes many factors that act as hormones and probably play a major role in the regulation and differentiation of T cells. Multiple factors with thymic activity have already been isolated and described, including thymosin, facteur thymique serique (FTS), and thymopoietin. The structures of some of these have been identified in the past year (eg, thymosin fraction V alpha-1 comprises 28 amino acids). Thymosin has thus far been derived from bovine thymus (presumably from the epithelium); FTS and thymopoietin are of pig and human origin. In addition, TP5, a synthetic pentapeptide (Arg-Lys-Asp-Val-Tyr) corresponding to residues 32–36 of thymopoietin, has been shown to mimic the biologic activity of thymopoietin in a number of in vitro and in vivo (animal) assays and thus probably is related to an active site of the native molecule. Until recently, assays to measure the activities of these factors were based on the induction of specific T cell markers on stem cells and on rosette assays using mouse spleen cells or human peripheral blood lymphocytes. These assays are relatively simple but time-consuming, and it is important to note that fetal calf serum, which itself contains thymosin, should not be employed. However, radioimmunoassays are now becoming available, using antisera prepared against synthesized peptides. Blood levels of thymosin in humans are high throughout childhood and early adulthood, begin to fall in the third or fourth decade, and are low in elderly people. The levels are undetectable in the complete DiGeorge syndrome (Chapter 25), in which the thymus is absent. Thymosin promotes T cell differentiation and possesses other effects. The other thymic hormones appear to be comparable in activity though not in structure. Animal experiments have not disclosed any degree of toxicity. In some patients, reactions to thymosin, presumably to bovine-specific antigens, have been reported (Table 40–1); hence, thymosin should not be given to patients with histories of severe allergy.

Thymic factors have been given in many clinical instances where a congenital or acquired T cell defect is suspected. Dramatic improvement has been reported in a number of patients with congenital T cell defects (Chapter 25).

Thymus extracts have been used in various diseases such as Nezelof's syndrome, Wiskott-Aldrich syndrome, ataxia-telangiectasia, and immunodeficiency with enzyme deficiency. In all of these cases, the thymus extract (mostly thymosin) induced immunologic changes with or without clinical improvement. In some patients with congenital T cell deficiency, combined therapy using both thymosin and dialyzable leukocyte extracts (see below) appears to be beneficial, even though thymosin alone is without effect.

Thymus extracts are now being tried in some autoimmune diseases such as systemic lupus erythematosus, since it appears that thymosin can induce differentiation of "null" cells into suppressor T cells in patients deficient therein, apparently both in vitro and in vivo, and, conversely, can cause reduction in suppressor cells in some hypogammaglobulinemic patients who have an excess thereof (Chapter 25).

Thymus extracts are also under investigation in treating solid tumors. In vitro, thymosin increases the percentage of T cells in cancer patients; apparently, only those in whom such an in vitro increase is produced respond clinically. In one controlled study, patients with lung oat cell carcinoma treated with multiple chemotherapy and thymosin showed increased survival, especially those patients with low levels of peripheral blood T cells before therapy. However, it is still too early to evaluate the clinical results of administration of thymus extracts in other cancer patients.

IMMUNE RECONSTITUTION

A variety of techniques have been used in attempts to reconstitute the immune system of patients with inherited immune deficiency diseases. These include transplantation of bone marrow, fetal thymus, fetal liver, and cultured thymic epithelium; injection of autologous T cells cultured with fetal thymic epithelium; and infusion of normal plasma or immune serum globulins (Table 40–1). The use of these techniques and their results in various immunodeficiencies are described in detail in Chapter 25.

APHERESIS
(Pheresis)

Plasmapheresis, a modified bloodletting procedure in which autologous red cells are returned to the donor in a suitable suspending medium, has been in clinical use for more than 50 years. However, the technique has come into widespread use only in the past decade, with the development of mechanical cell separators. Two types of cell separators are now available, the continuous flow centrifuge and the intermittent flow centrifuge. These machines were originally designed to gather specific populations of normal cells from blood donors (eg, platelets and granulocytes for transfusion into leukemia patients), but they can also be used for therapeutic intensive plasmapheresis.

Most reports available on the use of plasmapheresis as a therapeutic procedure are anecdotal; few controlled studies have been reported. Most of the diseases treated have been associated with immunologic or serologic abnormalities, but no standard protocols are available for patient selection or as a guide to the frequency, intensity (amount of plasma removed), or duration of therapy. The most commonly used replacement fluids are (1) normal serum albumin (5% or 25% isotonic solution), (2) plasma protein fraction, and (3) fresh frozen (homologous) plasma, which is the most physiologic replacement fluid available.

The first use of a semiautomated blood separator for plasma exchange therapy was for the treatment of paraproteinemia, reported in 1971. This procedure is now generally regarded as effective in reducing the serum viscosity characteristic of paraproteinemias (multiple myeloma, macroglobulinemia, cryoglobulinemia). Serum viscosity decreases rapidly after treatment, often accompanied by immediate subjective relief. Side-effects are minimal, and patients have been maintained free of symptoms for as long as 36 months by repeated plasmapheresis without any other supportive therapy.

Other diseases treated by plasmapheresis include hyperlipidemia, endocrinopathies, autoimmune diseases, and immune complex diseases. For example, reversal of an abnormal ratio of suppressor to helper T lymphocytes by therapeutic intensive plasmapheresis has been demonstrated in a hypogammaglobulinemic patient with serum antibody to TH_2 (helper) cells. Similarly, in Graves' disease and in insulin-resistant diabetes, plasmapheresis has been reported to remove circulating antibodies to thyrotropin receptors and insulin receptors, respectively, followed by clinical improvement. Alloimmunization (eg, anti-Rh in mothers, anti-HLA in kidney allograft recipients) has also been treated with apparent beneficial effects. In myasthenia gravis, plasmapheresis has been used to remove antibodies to acetylcholine receptors in the neuromuscular junction of striated muscle, with clinical response reported in about 75% of patients. Some promising results have also been reported in uncontrolled trials of repeated therapeutic plasmapheresis in patients with systemic lupus erythematosus and in patients with rheumatoid arthritis, presumably as a result of removal of circulating immune complexes or autoantibodies. Preliminary trials of plasmapheresis in malignant disease have also produced some encouraging initial observations suggesting that removal of "blocking factors" (eg, circulating tumor antigens, immune complexes, or nonspecific glycoproteins) may restore normal cell-mediated cytotoxicity against resident tumor cells.

In general, intensive plasmapheresis is a relatively safe procedure, although some risk of hypercoagulation has been reported, as well as a small but significant risk of viral hepatitis (non-A non-B) and of diverse reactions to homologous serum proteins (rash, chills, fever, anaphylaxis).

More recently, it has been reported that lymphocyte depletion and immunosuppression can be accomplished by repeated leukapheresis by continuous-flow centrifugation. For example, in 8 patients with active, erosive, seropositive rheumatoid arthritis, repeated leukapheresis with techniques designed to favor the removal of T lymphocytes produced lymphocytopenia and reduced in vitro responses to T cell mitogens, generally accompanied by reduction in disease activity during the first 10 days of treatment, or by the time approximately 3×10^{10} lymphocytes had been removed. Lymphocytopenia ($< 50\%$ of pre-leukapheresis values) persisted for up to 12 months after treatment. The lymphocyte depletion and immunologic changes were analogous to those observed after thoracic duct drainage.

Further refinements in apheresis techniques, especially the development of methods for the selective removal of specific cell populations or plasma components, can be expected in the future. At present, however, apheresis must be regarded as a promising but unproved immunotherapeutic modality.

TOTAL LYMPHOID IRRADIATION

Several recent reports have suggested that total lymphoid irradiation (2000–3000 rads) may be beneficial in the treatment of rheumatoid arthritis refractory to other forms of therapy. Uncontrolled clinical trials have been performed in approximately 20 patients with intractable rheumatoid arthritis, with clinical improvement reported in almost all cases. The treatment produced profound and sustained reductions in total lymphocyte counts and in vitro lymphocyte function, but humoral immunity was not suppressed. These preliminary observations suggest that total lymphoid irradiation may provide an alternative to long-term therapy with cytotoxic drugs such as cyclophosphamide and azathioprine.

LEVAMISOLE

Levamisole, a synthetic derivative of tetramisole, is an established veterinary anthelmintic drug. It has been found that levamisole can increase host resistance to tumor cells in some animal diseases. This has occurred under very restricted conditions, especially when the drug is used with some type of therapy that reduces tumor load. Recent studies suggest that the metabolite DL-2-oxo-3-(2-mercaptoethyl)-5-phenylimidazolidine is the active compound.

In humans, levamisole restores and increases delayed skin hypersensitivity to various antigens in elderly hyporeactors and in patients with malignant and nonmalignant diseases. In addition to the effects noted in Table 40–1, there are claims of clinical improvement in viral diseases such as herpes labialis, herpes genitalis, and warts, in chronic staphylococcal infections, and also in stage IV gastric cancer.

One possible dosage schedule which has been suggested is 2.5 mg/kg/d orally for 2 consecutive days, repeated every week. In fact, however, daily administration of the drug may actually be immunosuppressive, and all investigators employ intermittent administration.

Patients taking levamisole may complain of nausea and a flulike malaise. Cutaneous rashes disappearing after cessation of the therapy have been observed. The most serious side-effect is granulocytopenia, which is reversible after stopping therapy. White cell counts should be monitored in patients taking levamisole. This is especially necessary in rheumatoid arthritis with HLA-B27 (the incidence of leukopenia is around 20% in rheumatoid arthritis), and perhaps when levamisole is given with cytotoxic drugs.

INTERFERON

Interferon was originally described and characterized as a specific antiviral substance. It has also been shown to affect normal cell division and function and to have a marked antitumor effect in experimental animals. Interferon preparations derived from human buffy coat cells of pooled normal blood donors are currently being tested in patients.

Most of the work reported to date in animals and humans has been done with "interferon-containing preparations" of varying purity. Crude preparations from human buffy coat cells probably contain less than 0.5% interferon. It may be that when some of the experiments are repeated with pure interferon, some of the effects described will be found to be due to mediators of cellular immunity and transfer factor (see below) present in the buffy coat extracts rather than to interferon itself.

Virus-induced type I interferons are proteins or glycoproteins with molecular weights varying between 15,000 and 40,000. The specific activity of pure type I interferon may be about 10^{10} units per milligram of protein. Under certain experimental conditions, the antitumor activity of type II interferon has been reported to be greater per antiviral unit of interferon than the type I interferon preparation. Recently it has been shown that type II interferon is far more active in exerting an immunosuppressive effect in vitro than type I interferon. However, the various biologic effects of type II interferons and their activity relative to type I interferons remain to be determined. The major effect of interferon appears to be the potentiation and stimulation of natural killer cell activity.

A clinical trial in Sweden using a crude "interferon preparation" was begun in 1971 on 28 patients with osteosarcoma, receiving daily injections of 3×10^6 units of leukocyte interferon followed by 3 injections per week for 17 months. Although the tumor load was reduced by surgery or irradiation, no other therapy was introduced. The results indicated that at 2.5 years the incidence of pulmonary metastases in the treated group was about 50% of that in concurrent controls, and the mortality rate was less than 50% of that for controls.

Strander and co-workers in Stockholm have also treated patients with several other types of neoplastic disease. Tumor regression was observed in one patient with Hodgkin's disease and in one patient with multiple myeloma, but both patients relapsed with tumor progression after initial improvement. These cases suggest, however, that interferon can be effective even when the total tumor mass is considerable. In preliminary studies, the same group has reported some success in the treatment of laryngeal papilloma and condyloma acuminata. In other countries, a few patients with cervical cancer, basal cell carcinoma, breast cancer, non-Hodgkin's lymphoma, neuroblastoma, and osteosarcoma have been treated with interferon; the preliminary results seem promising in about 10–20% of patients. The tumors usually reappear when treatment with interferon is stopped.

INOSIPLEX

Inosiplex, the *p*-acetamidobenzoic acid salt of N,N-dimethylamino-2-propanol:inosine complex (3:1 molar ratio), is a synthetic drug now in use in Europe but not yet approved for clinical use in the USA. Inosiplex increases in vitro T cell function and macrophage activity. It includes the appearance of T cell markers and enhances the lymphocyte response to mitogens. This property appears to be due to the synthesis of a mitogenic helper factor by inosiplex-treated lymphocytes. In vivo, it will also increase antibody formation, T cell functions, and macrophage activity. It restores T cell immunosuppression in postradiotherapy cancer patients, it potentiates the antiviral and antitumor activity of interferon, and it delays the early appearance of autoimmunity and early tumor development of interferon-treated NZB/NZW mice.

In preliminary clinical studies, inosiplex has been shown to be beneficial in viral diseases such as subacute sclerosing panencephalitis, cutaneous herpes and aphthous stomatitis, cytomegalovirus infection, and possibly warts. Inosiplex also shows promising results in rheumatoid arthritis, where clinical improvement has been observed 2–6 weeks after the onset of treatment. The recommended dose is 50 mg/kg/d orally given daily or 3 times weekly. Immunologic properties are probably either partially or totally responsible for its beneficial effects.

GLUCAN

Yeast glucan, a beta-1,3-polyglucose component of the cell wall of *Saccharomyces cerevisiae*, possesses the property of stimulating the reticuloendothelial system as well as of enhancing humoral and cell-mediated immunity. Recent animal data suggest that it can also potentiate antitumor immunity.

OTHER NONSPECIFIC IMMUNOMODULATORS

Many other agents have been or are being tested as nonspecific immunomodulators. These include microbial extracts (from some strains of *Streptococcus* and *Staphylococcus,* some of which apparently increase the production of suppressor cells), *Bordetella pertussis* vaccines, vitamin A and several of its analogs (retinal, retinol, retinyl acetate, retinoic acid), tilorone, L-fucose, synthetic polynucleotides (poly A-U, poly I-C), lynestrenol (a progesteronelike drug), thiabendazole, tolazoline, lentinen, schizophyllan, picibanil, bestatin (a dipeptide isolated from culture filtrates of *Streptomyces olivoreticuli*, which specifically inhibits aminopeptidase B and leucine aminopeptidase), and a variety of synthetic drugs with immunostimulating activity.

ANTIGEN–SPECIFIC IMMUNOTHERAPY

SPECIFIC ACTIVE IMMUNOTHERAPY

Recent reports of a 5-year trial in 52 patients with lung cancer have indicated a significant increase in survival in 28 stage I patients treated with specific tumor antigen vaccines. The specific vaccines were made by isolating and purifying the antigens present on the surfaces of tumor cells. Following surgical removal of lung tumors, one group of patients received monthly injections of soluble antigen homogenized in Freund's complete adjuvant for 3 months without other therapy, and another group received monthly chemotherapy followed by tumor antigen immunotherapy for 3 months. In both the immunotherapy and chemoimmunotherapy groups, 83% of the patients were still alive after 4 years, compared with only 49% of controls receiving chemotherapy alone or no treatment after surgery. (No control limb with Freund's adjuvant alone was included.) The immunotherapy did not appear to prolong survival in stage II or stage III patients, again indicating the importance of minimizing tumor burden.

Additional trials in some 300 patients with lung cancer have been initiated, and trials in other cancer types (eg, colon adenocarcinoma) are planned. In addition, the possibility of using similar vaccines for prevention of lung cancer in high-risk individuals is being studied.

A vaccine against hepatitis B virus has also been developed recently which may be effective in preventing liver cancer, since there is substantial evidence for a relationship between chronic hepatitis B virus infections and posthepatic liver cancer. Indeed, in mice, immunization with inactivated murine ecotropic type C virus has been found to be effective in inducing immunity to the virus; this should lead to a reduction in the incidence of naturally occurring thymic lymphomas in highly susceptible strains (eg, AKR mice), where an etiologic role of type C virus has been suggested.

ENZYME–TREATED TUMOR CELLS

Animal data have shown that the treatment of tumor cells with the enzyme neuraminidase leads to increased immunogenicity of these cells, even in an autologous system. This effect has led to a trial in human acute myeloblastic leukemia, wherein patients receive, in combination with chemotherapy, multiple intradermal injections of neuraminidase-treated myeloblasts. The results of this trial, which is still in progress, are quite impressive, since significant increases in the duration of remission have already been achieved. In another trial, patients with operated lung cancer who received injections of neuraminidase-treated tumor cells had longer remissions than control patients. It is important to note that the pH of the enzyme treatment must be carefully controlled for optimal immunologic effect.

Similarly, it has been shown that several viruses, such as influenza A and vaccinia, will lyse tumor cells; and such modified cells have been found to produce specific tumor immunity in animals. Results in humans are still preliminary.

CYTOTOXIC DRUGS COUPLED TO ANTITUMOR ANTIBODIES

In some animal experiments, this approach apparently has produced specific destruction of tumor cells, presumably because the drug is delivered directly to the tumor site. Promising results have been obtained in animal osteosarcoma using purified anti-osteosarcoma antibodies coupled to doxorubicin. Similarly, radiolabeled anti-CEA is now being tried for therapy of lung metastases in humans. The future of this approach may be in the use of monoclonal antitumor antibodies produced by hybridomas.

PLASMA THERAPY

The use of fresh frozen plasma in treating patients with isolated complement component deficiencies and with humoral immune deficiencies is outlined elsewhere (Chapter 25). In addition, plasma appears to contain unknown factors capable of retarding tumor growth, and preliminary anecdotal reports of the use of plasma transfusions in the treatment of solid tumors have appeared. Furthermore, the plasma of some normal individuals (household contacts of cancer patients) contains antibodies to specific tumor-associated antigens (osteosarcoma, melanoma, etc) of cancer patients. Infusion of such plasma into patients refractory to conventional therapy and with high levels of immune complexes (presumably in antigen excess) has recently been initiated at a few centers, especially in conjunction with plasmapheresis of the patients. Although this approach seems theoretically sound, the results are still too scanty to be evaluated. Recent reports have described the treatment of several patients with breast or colon carcinoma with autologous or homologous plasma perfused over immobilized protein A. Rapid tumoricidal response and clinical improvement were reported in several cases.

LYMPHOKINES

Nonspecific and specific products of lymphocyte stimulation are currently being tried for their possible effect on malignant tumors. Such products could, by enhancing the immune system, increase the immune resistance to tumors. Their activity is also enhanced by inserting them into liposomes.

IMMUNE RNA

In 1951, it was discovered that antigen fragments complexed with small molecules of RNA were secreted in the urine of immunized rabbits. These complexes, when injected into nonimmunized recipients, were found to have adjuvantlike activity, producing a greater humoral immune response than antigen alone. Later studies indicated that the RNA had an informational role, apparently coding for at least part of the immunoglobulin molecule produced by the recipient, since a portion of the resulting antibodies had allotypic specificities of the donor. In 1964, it was reported that RNA extracts prepared from lymph nodes of rabbits actively rejecting skin allografts could convert nonsensitized lymphoid cells to active cellular immune states, both in vitro and in vivo.

Probably as a result of the complicated experimental systems used in these studies, the apparent fragility of the information-carrying RNA fragments, and the lack of understanding of the mechanisms of action involved, these results remained controversial for many years. In recent years, however, several studies have produced evidence for a therapeutic effect of immune RNA (I-RNA) in animal tumors. For example, after excision of B16 melanoma isografts in C57BL/6J mice, administration of tumor-specific xenogeneic I-RNA was found to prevent the fatal pulmonary metastases that inevitably developed in other murine tumors, as well as in rats and guinea pigs. More recently, clinical trials have been undertaken in a variety of human cancers.

There are 2 potential sources of I-RNA for cancer immunotherapy: (1) allogeneic I-RNA derived from the lymphocytes of "cured" cancer patients, and (2) xenogeneic I-RNA derived from animals specifically immunized with neoplastic cells from the tumor-bearing patient or with tumor cells from another patient with a tumor of the same histologic type. However, repeated removal of lymphocytes from "cured" cancer patients could theoretically produce immunosuppression, leading to exacerbation of disease; in addition, there is evidence that tumor-specific immunity in such patients does not persist for long periods of time (eg, after 5 years free of disease). Therefore, initial clinical trials have been performed with xenogeneic (animal) I-RNA. This approach also eliminates the problems of donor selection and availability.

Two methods have been used for the administration of I-RNA to cancer patients: (1) parenteral injection and (2) collection of peripheral blood lymphocytes from the patient to be treated, incubating them with I-RNA in vitro, and reinjecting intravenously.

In an initial (phase I) trial reported by Pilch and co-workers, 35 cancer patients (15 with malignant melanoma, 12 with hypernephroma, and 8 others) were treated with injections of I-RNA (1–2 mg/mL) extracted from the spleens and lymph nodes of sheep that had received 3 weekly intradermal injections of viable tumor cells in Freund's complete adjuvant. No significant local or systemic toxicity was seen, pain at the injection site was minimal, and there was no evidence of local irritation, febrile reactions, or allergic or anaphylactoid reactions. The immune status of the patients was monitored by in vitro cytotoxicity testing against tumor cells, and substantial increases in cytotoxic activity against the particular type of tumor used to immunize the donor sheep were reported in some of the patients. Signs of clinical improvement or stabilization of disease were reportedly observed in 17 of the 35 patients. The same group later reported promising results in nonrandomized trials of I-RNA therapy for advanced renal cell carcinoma. A more recent phase I trial has been reported by Mannick and coworkers in which 6 patients with metastatic renal cell carcinoma were treated with intravenous transfusions of autologous lymphocytes incubated in vitro with I-RNA extracted from the lymphoid tissues of guinea pigs immunized with the patient's own tumor. Improvement or stabilization was seen in 5 of the recipients.

These results suggest that I-RNA may eventually prove to be a valuable immunotherapeutic agent, especially in view of the complete absence of adverse side-effects. Phase III trials (double-blind, controlled) have been proposed.

In related studies, it has been reported that lymphoid and myeloid cells from tumor-bearing mice, when transferred to normal syngeneic mice never exposed to a tumor, imparted "information" that resulted in the production of tumor-specific cytotoxic cells by the recipients. More recently, similar results have been reported in experiments using tumor-sensitized xenogeneic (eg, rat) cells injected into normal mice. The production of tumor-specific cytotoxic cells in the recipients, which may involve information transfer by immune RNA of the injected cells, suggests the possible usefulness of xenogeneic cells for passive tumor immunotherapy.

DIALYZABLE LEUKOCYTE EXTRACTS
(Transfer Factor)

Dialyzable leukocyte extracts (DLE) are capable of transferring cellular immunity from skin test–positive donors to skin test–negative recipients. The recipient, upon retesting with antigen to which he or she was previously insensitive, will exhibit a specific delayed skin reaction to this antigen. This antigen-specific activity in DLE is currently designated "dialyzable transfer factor" (TFd). (The "transfer factor" originally described by Lawrence in 1955 was a crude DLE preparation containing at least 60 distinct moieties.)

In normal subjects, DLE transfers not only delayed skin reactivity but also the ability to produce various mediators of cellular immunity such as macrophage migration inhibitory factor (MIF) in the presence of the same antigen to which the donor of the leukocytes responded. The exact chemical nature of TFd is not yet known. Moreover, there is evidence that

DLE contains several different moieties that may act on different subpopulations of T cells. In addition, "crude" DLE contains both nonspecific immunostimulatory (adjuvant) activity and one or more inhibitory activities detectable by in vitro assays.

Chemistry & Mode of Action

The antigen-specific TFd moiety of crude DLE has a molecular weight of about 1100–1600. Its exact chemical nature is still undetermined, but it appears to be a small nucleopeptide. Enzymatic inactivation studies indicate that it contains both RNA and protein but not DNA.

The mode of action of TFd remains undetermined. It has been proposed that it acts on a "naive" stem cell to induce specificity for an antigen or a group of antigens. It may assist in recruiting specific antigen-sensitive cells. On the other hand, the adjuvant (non-TFd) activity in DLE acts nonspecifically by enhancing the preexisting reactivity of the recipient's lymphocytes.

Advantages

DLE is a readily available nonantigenic substance that can be lyophilized and stored for long periods without loss of potency. It does not transmit infectious virus disease, and, if properly prepared and tested, it appears to cause no serious side-effects. It does not produce a GVH reaction, a common and often fatal complication of the transplantation of competent lymphocytes (eg, from bone marrow grafts) into immunoincompetent patients, and it does not transfer humoral immunity. This latter advantage could be important in anticancer therapy, since antitumor antibodies are among the blocking factors.

Current Models & Tests

All of these models and tests are still experimental, and in most cases their correlation with the "clinical" activity of DLE is not well defined.

A. Animal Models: Various animal models using guinea pigs, rabbits, mice, cattle, and primates are now available to study the immunologic and clinical properties of DLE.

B. Laboratory Tests: Various in vitro tests reflect the effects of DLE. These include induction of enhanced chemotaxis, increased intracellular cyclic nucleotides, augmented antigen and mitogen responses, and increased active E rosettes in patients with congenital T cell immunodeficiencies, cancer, and other disorders in which the levels of these cells are depressed. Recent studies by several groups have shown that the leukocyte migration inhibition assay in agarose, which measures the production of the mediator leukocyte migration inhibition factor (LIF), can be used to measure both nonspecific and antigen-specific effects of DLE in vitro. The LIF assay is currently the best available test for TFd (antigen-specific) activity, and the results have been shown to correlate well with in vivo skin tests, though LIF assay is far more sensitive.

Problematic Aspects of DLE

A. Selection of Donors: The selection of donors for production of DLE remains a difficult problem. Prior to donating lymphocytes, the donor must be tested for specific cell-mediated immunity. This is an important matter, since the rationale for giving DLE rests on the transfer of known immunologic specificity. For example, it is essential to use a donor with strongly positive *Candida* immunity when DLE is given to patients with chronic mucocutaneous candidiasis. This problem is more difficult in therapeutic trials with cancer patients. Which specificity should be transferred, and how should it be tested? Common sense suggests the use of lymphocytes from a donor who is immune to the type of tumor being treated. Unfortunately, in vitro tests are not completely reliable in establishing the state of antitumor immunity. In the case of osteosarcoma, an in vitro assay for cellular cytotoxicity has been used for this purpose. In other studies, mediator production or leukocyte adherence inhibition assays in the presence of soluble tumor extracts have been used. If there is a quantitative reduction of immunity in cancer patients, injections of specific DLE may increase this immunity.

Furthermore, the selection of donors in the case of malignancies raises several other problems. Despite almost universal belief to the contrary, specific antitumor immunity is not usually found in patients who are "cured" of their disease (eg, 5-year disease-free interval). Furthermore, the possibility exists that removal of "immune" lymphocytes from patients with subclinical micrometastases will be associated with some recurrence of the disease. A practical approach to this problem is provided by the observation that approximately 25–50% of patients' household contacts have specific cell-mediated immunity against the type of tumor borne by the patient. These healthy individuals are more appropriate DLE donors for cancer treatment. However, after repeated leukapheresis of such subjects, their antitumor immunity may disappear, and one must wait for several months without removing leukocytes for reappearance of immunity. Increased susceptibility of these cancer-free contacts to the development of tumors remains a theoretic possibility.

B. Immunologic Monitoring of Recipients: If specificity is the required criterion, then the recipients must be examined to determine if they have acquired donor immunity and how long this immunity persists. Skin tests with tumor antigens remain the most widely used test for this purpose in cancer patients. Other tests such as lymphocyte activation, production of lymphokines, leukocyte adherence inhibition, and cellular cytotoxicity are also used. Lymphocyte activation measured by thymidine incorporation and DNA synthesis now seems generally unsuitable, since it measures nonspecific increases in preexisting low levels of immunity (ie, adjuvant effect) rather than antigen-specific (TFd) activity. As stated above, the LIF assay appears to provide the best correlation with skin test results for measuring antigen-specific cell-mediated

reactivity (and furthermore appears to be more sensitive than skin testing). The counting of T lymphocytes and particularly active T cell rosettes (Chapter 23) appears to be useful for evaluation of therapeutic results in hereditary immunodeficiency diseases. A decrease in active T cells indicates the need for a new injection of DLE.

C. Recipient Specificity: It has been shown that the response to DLE depends to a large extent on the immune status of the recipient. Factors such as previous exposure to antigen, general immune competence, and presumably genetically determined variations in immune responsiveness (ie, "immune response genes") contribute to the variability in responses to DLE. The combined effect of such factors is now referred to as "recipient specificity." The recognition of these influences has reemphasized the need for careful monitoring of DLE recipients by immunologic methods.

Preparations & Administration

One unit of DLE is usually defined as the dialysate of 5×10^8 leukocytes. However, DLE of the same specificity from 2 different donors may vary as much as 10-fold in potency; consequently, in vitro assays (LIF production) are now used to measure "potency units" in DLE preparations. DLE is prepared from isolated leukocytes of peripheral blood, usually obtained by leukapheresis. The dialysate is checked for sterility and for pyrogens after lyophilization. It is diluted in 1 mL of saline prior to use and injected subcutaneously. Recent reports indicate that it is also effective when given orally or intravenously.

Side-Effects & Complications

The injection of DLE is slightly painful and often associated with mild fever and fatigue for 1–4 hours. There are reports of immune reactions (eg, hemolytic anemia) after DLE therapy; however, these complications have occurred in patients in whom such autoimmune phenomena were part of the underlying disease.

A potential cause of reaction to DLE arises from the initiation of a vigorous inflammatory response at the site of antigen load. These reactions can induce pain at the site of the malignant lesion, or hypersensitivity pneumonia if pulmonary metastases are present. The latter can be reversed with small doses of corticosteroids.

Current Applications

DLE has received widespread clinical use owing to its ready availability, its apparent safety, and the need for an immunotherapeutic agent that can reliably alter cellular immunity. Although studies of its efficacy, with a few exceptions, have usually been uncontrolled, the results obtained in some viral, fungal, and other infections using antigen-specific DLE have been striking. Recently, attempts have been made to devise in vitro assays for the potency of DLE preparations; if successful, such assays would permit standardization of dosages in terms of specific activity rather than the number of donor cells used for the preparation.

DLE was first applied as a therapeutic agent in patients with Wiskott-Aldrich syndrome, an X-linked deficiency of cellular and humoral immunity. Impressive results were obtained in about half the patients, including improvement of clinical status (eradication of chronic infections and eczema and amelioration of splenomegaly, thrombocytopenia, and bleeding) and acquisition of lymphokine production (eg, MIF). It was later demonstrated that about half of these patients have a defect in monocyte receptors for IgG and that this subgroup almost always responds well to DLE immunotherapy. Other immunodeficiency diseases treated with DLE include severe combined immunodeficiency disease, ataxia-telangiectasia, rheumatoid arthritis, and others. Conflicting results reported by different investigators probably reflect the use of different methods for selecting donors, preparing the DLE (eg, in some cases leukocytes from a number of donors were pooled to provide larger amounts of material), and monitoring recipients. Moreover, as in the case of Wiskott-Aldrich syndrome, many of the currently defined immunodeficiency "diseases" probably are syndromes consisting of several distinct disease entities that may respond differently to DLE immunotherapy. DLE has been used in multiple sclerosis. The results indicate a beneficial effect, especially when the disease was not severe. The DLE-treated patients showed a lower incidence of relapses.

A wide variety of infections and parasitic diseases have also been treated with DLE. In viral infections, dramatic improvements have been reported by several groups in disseminated vaccinia, measles, pneumonia, congenital herpes simplex, zoster, cytomegalovirus, and other infections treated with antigen-specific DLE. If these results are confirmed, this field of application may soon become a most important area for DLE. In fungal infections, clinical improvement, especially after reduction of antigenic load, has been reported in disseminated mucocutaneous candidiasis, disseminated coccidioidomycosis, and disseminated histoplasmosis refractory to conventional antifungal therapy. In mycobacterial diseases, several cases of miliary tuberculosis refractory to other modes of therapy have responded clinically to DLE. Cutaneous tuberculosis (lupus vulgaris) and progressive BCG infection have also responded to DLE. In lepromatous leprosy, skin test conversion has been reported; clinical trials are under current study, but the overwhelming antigenic burden in most patients suggests that huge amounts of DLE would be required to achieve clinical improvement. One of the few well-controlled double-blind clinical trials of DLE has been reported in the parasitic disease cutaneous leishmaniasis. The results indicated both clinical efficacy and antigenic specificity of DLE prepared from donors with demonstrable cell-mediated immunity to *Leishmania* antigens. In patients with persistent cutaneous leishmaniasis, administration of more than 100 units of specific DLE over a 1-year period was usually required for complete eradication of the lesions.

In cancer, the problems of selection of donors have been discussed above. It is currently not possible to come to a conclusion about the efficacy of DLE in cancer patients, since too few patients have been studied. Osteosarcoma is the tumor in which DLE therapy has been most extensively studied, with encouraging results. In one trial, 5 of 7 patients were treated only with antigen-specific DLE from household contacts with specific cell-mediated reactivity against osteosarcoma cells in vitro after surgical removal of their primary tumor. These 5 individuals have stayed in remission for over 5 years. This is the only tumor in which both lasting clinical and immunologic improvements have been reported after DLE injections. DLE has also been given in breast carcinoma, malignant melanoma, and alveolar cell carcinoma, with reported clinical and immunologic improvement; and in nasopharyngeal carcinoma with no reported improvement. In the latter instance, DLE was prepared from healthy young individuals recovering from infectious mononucleosis, a disease also thought to be due to EB virus; however, retrospective studies showed only humoral immunity and no cell-mediated immunity to EB virus antigens in the donors.

Further trials of DLE therapy in a variety of malignancies are in progress or have been proposed.

• • •

References

Allison AC: Recent developments in adjuvant research. *J Reticuloendothel Soc* 1979;**26**:619.

Amery WK: Final results of a multicenter placebo-controlled levamisole study of resectable lung cancer. *Cancer Treat Rep* 1978;**62**:1677.

Chedid L, Carelli C, Audibert F: Recent developments concerning muramyl dipeptide, a synthetic immunoregulating molecule. *J Reticuloendothel Soc* 1979;**26**:631.

Chedid L (editor): Immunostimulation. *Springer Seminars in Immunopathology* 1979;**2**:1.

Fudenberg HH et al: Dialyzable leukocyte extracts (transfer factor): A review of clinical results and immunological methods for donor selection, evaluation of activities, and patient monitoring. Page 391 in: *Thymus, Thymic Hormones and T Lymphocytes.* Aiuti F, Wigzell H (editors). Academic Press, 1980.

Goldstein AL et al: Current status of thymosin and other hormones of the thymus gland. *Recent Prog Horm Res* 1981; **32**:369.

Gonzalez RL et al: Effect of levamisole as a surgical adjuvant therapy for malignant melanoma. *Cancer Treat Rep* 1978; **62**:1703.

Gresser I, Tovey MG: Antitumor effects of interferon. *Biochim Biophys Acta* 1978;**516**:231.

Hadden J et al: *Advances in Immunopharmacology*. Pergamon Press, 1981.

Holmes EC et al: New method of immunotherapy for lung cancer. *Lancet* 1977;**2**:586.

Jirsch DW, Falk RE: Solid tumour immunotherapy. Page 315 in: *Immunological Engineering*. Jirsch DW (editor). Medical Technical Press, 1978.

Jones F, Bellanti JA: Immunologic reconstitution of patients with immune deficiency. *J Reticuloendothel Soc* 1979;**26**:873.

Krim M: Towards tumor therapy with interferons. (2 parts.) *Blood* 1980;**55**:711, 875.

Mathé G: *Cancer Active Immunotherapy*. Springer, 1976.

Mathé G et al: 1975 current results of first 100 cytologically typed acute patients with lymphoid leukemia submitted to BCG active immunotherapy. *Cancer Immunol Immunother* 1976; **1**:77.

Merigan TC et al: Preliminary observations on the effect of human leukocyte interferon in non-Hodgkin's lymphoma. *N Engl J Med* 1978;**299**:1449.

Milas L, Scott MT: Antitumour activity of *Corynebacterium parvum*. *Adv Cancer Res* 1978;**26**:257.

Oettgen HF et al: Treatment of cancer with immunomodulators. *Med Clin North Am* 1976;**60**:511.

Pardridge DH et al: Chemoimmunotherapy of stage III breast carcinoma with BCG and a live allogeneic tumor cell vaccine. *Cancer Immunol Immunother* 1979;**5**:217.

Sedlacek HH, Seiler FR: Immunotherapy of neoplastic diseases with neuraminidase: Contradictions, new aspects, and revised concepts. *Cancer Immunol Immunother* 1978;**5**:153.

Steele G et al: Results of xenogeneic I-RNA therapy in patients with metastatic renal cell carcinoma. *Cancer* 1981;**47**:1286.

Stewart THM et al: A survival study of specific active immunotherapy in lung cancer. Page 37 in: *Neoplasm Immunity*. Crispen RG (editor). Franklin Institute Press, 1977.

Study Group for Bronchogenic Carcinoma: Immunopotentiation with levamisole in resectable bronchogenic carcinoma. *Br Med J* 1975;**3**:461.

Terman DS et al: Preliminary observations of the effects on breast adenocarcinoma of plasma perfused over immobilized protein A. *N Engl J Med* 1981;**305**:1195.

Trentham DE et al: Clinical and immunological effects of fractionated total lymphoid irradiation in refractory rheumatoid arthritis. *N Engl J Med* 1981;**305**:976.

Wara DW, Ammann AJ: Thymosin treatment of children with primary immunodeficiency disease. *Transplant Proc* 1978; **10**:203.

Wenz B, Barland P: Therapeutic intensive plasmapheresis. *Semin Hematol* 1981;**18**:147.

Wybran J, Famaey JP, Appelboom T: Inosiplex, a novel treatment in rheumatoid arthritis? *J Rheumatol* 1981;**8**:643.

Wybran J, Govaerts A, Appleboom T: Inosiplex, a stimulating agent for normal human T cells and human leukocytes. *J Immunol* 1978;**121**:1184.

Wybran J, Staquet MJ: *Clinical Tumor Immunology*. Pergamon Press, 1976.

Wybran J et al: Rosette-forming cells, immunological disease and transfer factor. *N Engl J Med* 1973;**288**:710.

Glossary of Terms
Commonly Used in Immunology

Abrin: A potent toxin which is derived from the seeds of the jequirity plant and which agglutinates red cells (a lectin).

Absolute catabolic rate: The mass of protein catabolized per day, which is determined by multiplying the fractional turnover rate by the volume of the plasma pool.

Accessory cells: Lymphoid cells predominantly of the monocyte and macrophage lineage that cooperate with T and B lymphocytes in the formation of antibody and in other immune reactions.

Activated lymphocytes: Lymphocytes that have been stimulated by specific antigen or nonspecific mitogen.

Activated macrophages: Mature macrophages in a metabolic state caused by various stimuli, especially phagocytosis or lymphokine activity.

Activation: A process in which the members of the complement sequence are altered enzymatically to become functionally active.

Adenosine deaminase: An enzyme that catalyzes the conversion of adenosine to inosine and is deficient in some patients with combined immunodeficiency syndrome.

Adjuvant: A compound capable of potentiating an immune response.

Adoptive transfer: The transfer of immunity by immunocompetent cells from one animal to another.

Adrenergic receptors: Receptors for various adrenergic agents of either the α or the β class that are present on a variety of cells and from which the action of various adrenergic drugs can be predicted.

Affinity chromatography: A technique in which a substance with a selective binding affinity is coupled to an insoluble matrix such as dextran and binds its complementary substances from a mixture in solution or suspension.

Agammaglobulinemia: See **Hypogammaglobulinemia.**

Agglutination: An antigen-antibody reaction in which a solid or particulate antigen forms a lattice with a soluble antibody. In reverse agglutination, the antibody is attached to a solid particle and is agglutinated by insoluble antigen.

Alexin (also **alexine**): A term coined by Pfeiffer to denote a thermolabile and nonspecific factor that, in concert with sensitizer, causes bacteriolysis.

Allele: One of 2 genes controlling a particular characteristic present at a locus.

Allelic exclusion: The phenotypic expression of a single allele in cells containing 2 different alleles for that genetic locus.

Allergens: Antigens that give rise to allergic sensitization by IgE antibody.

Allergoids: Chemically modified allergens that give rise to antibody of the IgG but not IgE class, thereby reducing allergic symptoms.

Allergy: An altered state of immune reactivity, usually denoting hypersensitivity.

Allogeneic: Denotes the relationship that exists between genetically dissimilar members of the same species.

Allogeneic effect: A form of general immunopotentiation in which specific stimulation of T cells results in the release of factors active in the immune response.

Allograft (also **homograft**): A tissue or organ graft between 2 genetically dissimilar members of the same species.

Allotype: The genetically determined antigenic difference in serum proteins, varying in different members of the same species.

Alpha-fetoprotein (AFP): An embryonic α-globulin with immunosuppressive properties that is structurally similar to albumin.

Alternative complement pathway (also **properdin pathway**): The system of activation of the complement pathway through involvement of properdin factor D, properdin factor B, and C3b, finally activating C3 and then progressing as in the classic pathway.

Am marker: The allotypic determinant on the heavy chain of human IgA.

Amboceptor: A term coined by Ehrlich to denote a bacteriolytic substance in serum that acts together with complement or alexin, ie, antibody.

Anamnesis (also **immunologic memory**): A heightened responsiveness to the second or subsequent administration of antigen to an immune animal.

Anaphylatoxin: A substance produced by complement activation that results in increased vascular permeability through the release of pharmacologically active mediators from mast cells.

Anaphylatoxin inactivator: An α-globulin with a molecular weight of 300,000 that destroys the biologic activity of C3a and C5a.

Anaphylaxis: A reaction of immediate hypersensitivity present in nearly all vertebrates which results from sensitization of tissue-fixed mast cells by cytotropic antibodies following exposure to antigen.

Anergy: The inability to react to a battery of common skin test antigens.

Antibody: A protein which is produced as a result of the introduction of an antigen and which has the ability to combine with the antigen that stimulated its production.

Antibody combining site: That configuration present on an antibody molecule which links with a corresponding antigenic determinant.

Antibody-dependent cell-mediated cytotoxicity (ADCC): A form of lymphocyte-mediated cytotoxicity in which an effector cell kills an antibody-coated target cell, presumably by recognition of the Fc region of the cell-bound antibody through an Fc receptor present on the effector lymphocyte.

Antigen: A substance that can induce a detectable immune response when introduced into an animal.

Antigen processing: The series of events that occurs following antigen administration and antibody production.

Antigen-binding site: The part of an immunoglobulin that binds antigen.

Antigenic competition: The suppression of the immune response to 2 closely related antigens when they are injected simultaneously.

Antigenic determinant (see also **Epitope**): That area of an antigen which determines the specificity of the antigen-antibody reaction.

Antigenic modulation: The spatial alteration of the arrangement of antigenic sites present on a cell surface brought about by the presence of bound antibody.

Antiglobulin test (Coombs test): A technique for detecting cell-bound immunoglobulin. In the direct Coombs test, red blood cells taken directly from a sensitized individual are agglutinated by antigammaglobulin antibodies. In the indirect Coombs test, a patient's serum is incubated with test red blood cells and the sensitized cells are then agglutinated with an anti-immunoglobulin or with Coombs reagent.

Antilymphocyte serum: Antibodies which are directed against lymphocytes and which usually cause immunosuppression.

Antinuclear antibodies (ANA): Antibodies which are directed against nuclear constituents, usually in nucleoprotein, and which are present in various rheumatoid diseases, particularly systemic lupus erythematosus.

Antitoxins: Protective antibodies that inactivate soluble toxic protein products of bacteria.

Apheresis: Process of removing blood or blood element from the body.

Armed macrophages: Macrophages capable of antigen-specific cytotoxicity as a result of cytophilic antibodies or arming factors from T cells.

Arthus phenomenon: A local necrotic lesion resulting from a local antigen-antibody reaction and produced by injecting antigen into a previously immunized animal.

Association constant (K value): The mathematical representation of the affinity of binding between antigen and antibody.

Atopy: A genetically determined abnormal state of hypersensitivity as distinguished from hypersensitivity responses in normal individuals, which are not genetically determined.

Attenuated: Rendered less virulent.

Autoantibody: Antibody to self antigens.

Autoantigens: Self antigens.

Autograft: A tissue graft between genetically identical members of the same species.

Autoimmunity: Immunity to self antigens (autoantigens).

Autoradiography: A technique for detecting radioactive isotopes in which a tissue section containing radioactivity is overlaid with x-ray or photographic film on which the emissions are recorded.

B cell (also **B lymphocyte**): Strictly a bursa-derived cell in avian species and, by analogy, a bursa-equivalent derived cell in nonavian species. B cells are the precursors of plasma cells that produce antibody.

Bacteriolysin: An antibody or other substance capable of lysing bacteria.

Bacteriolysis: The disintegration of bacteria induced by antibody and complement in the absence of cells.

Baseline cellular phagocytosis: Digestion by phagocytic cells and effector mechanisms that have developed for dealing with potential invading pathogens.

BCG (bacillus Calmette-Guérin): A viable attenuated strain of *Mycobacterium bovis* which has been obtained by progressive reduction of virulence and which confers immunity to mycobacterial infection and possibly possesses anticancer activity in selected diseases.

Bence Jones proteins: Monoclonal light chains present in the urine of patients with paraproteinemic disorders.

Beta-lysin: A highly reactive heat-stable cationic protein that is bactericidal for gram-positive organisms.

Biosynthesis: The production of molecules by viable cells in culture.

Blast cell: A large lymphocyte or other immature cell containing a nucleus with loosely packed chromatin, a large nucleolus, and a large amount of cytoplasm with numerous polyribosomes.

Blast transformation: See **Lymphocyte activation.**

Blocking antibody: See **Blocking factors.**

Blocking factors: Substances that are present in the serum of tumor-bearing animals and are capable of blocking the ability of immune lymphocytes to kill tumor cells.

Bradykinin: A 9-amino-acid peptide which is split by the enzyme kallikrein from serum α_2-globulin precursor and which causes a slow, sustained contraction of the smooth muscles.

Bursa of Fabricius: The hindgut organ located in the cloaca of birds that controls the ontogeny of B lymphocytes.

Bursal equivalent: The hypothetical organ or organs analogous to the bursa of Fabricius in nonavian species.

C region (constant region): The carboxyl terminal portion of the H or L chain that is identical in immunoglobulin molecules of a given class and subclass apart from genetic polymorphisms.

Capping: The movement of cell surface antigens toward one pole of a cell after the antigens are cross-linked by specific antibody.

Carcinoembryonic antigen (CEA): An antigen that is present on fetal endodermal tissue and is reexpressed on the surface of neoplastic cells, particularly in carcinoma of the colon.

Cardiolipin: A substance derived from beef heart, probably a component of mitochondrial membranes, that serves as an antigenic substrate for reagin or antitreponemal antibody.

Carrier: An immunogenic substance that, when coupled to a hapten, renders the hapten immunogenic.

Cationic proteins: Antimicrobial substances present within granules of phagocytic cells.

Cell-mediated immunity: Immunity in which the participation of lymphocytes and macrophages is predominant.

Cell-mediated lymphocytolysis: An in vitro assay for cellular immunity in which a standard mixed lymphocyte reaction is followed by destruction of target cells that are used to sensitize allogeneic cells during the MLC.

Central lymphoid organs: Lymphoid organs that are essential to the development of the immune response, ie, the thymus and the bursa of Fabricius.

CH$_{50}$ unit: The quantity or dilution of serum required to lyse 50% of the red blood cells in a standard hemolytic complement assay.

Chase-Sulzberger phenomenon: See **Sulzberger-Chase phenomenon.**

Chemiluminescence: Release of light energy by a chemical reaction usually involving reduction of an unstable intermediate to a stable one. Used as a means of measuring respiratory burst in phagocytic cells.

Chemokinesis: Reaction by which chemical substances determine rate of cellular movement.

Chemotaxis: A process whereby phagocytic cells are attracted to the vicinity of invading pathogens.

Chromatography: A variety of techniques useful for the separation of proteins.

CI genes: Genes located in the I region of the H-2 complex that control cell-cell interaction in the immune response.

Class I antigen: Histocompatibility antigen encoded in humans by A, B, and C loci and in mice by D and K loci.

Class II antigen: Histocompatibility antigen encoded in humans by DR, MB, MT, and Te loci and in mice by I and other loci.

Classic complement pathway: A series of enzyme-substrate and protein-protein interactions that ultimately leads to biologically active complement enzymes. It proceeds sequentially C1, 423 567 89.

Clonal selection theory: The theory of antibody synthesis proposed by Burnet that predicts that the individual carries a complement of clones of lymphoid cells that are capable of reacting with all possible antigenic determinants. During fetal life, clones reacted against self antigens are eliminated on contact with antigen.

Clone: A group of cells all of which are the progeny of a single cell.

Coelomocyte: A wandering ameboid phagocyte found in all animal invertebrates containing a coelom.

Cohn fraction II: Primarily γ-globulin that is produced as the result of ethanol fractionation of serum according to the Cohn method.

Cold agglutinins: Antibodies that agglutinate bacteria or erythrocytes more efficiently at temperatures below 37 °C than at 37 °C.

Complement: A system of serum proteins that is the primary humoral mediator of antigen-antibody reactions.

Complement fixation: A standard serologic assay used for the detection of an antigen-antibody reaction in which complement is fixed as a result of the formation of an immune complex. The subsequent failure of lysis of sensitized red blood cells by complement that has been fixed indicates the degree of antigen-antibody reaction.

Complimentarity: In genetics, the term indicates that more than 1 gene is required for the expression of a particular trait.

Concanavalin A (ConA): A lectin which is derived from the jack bean and which stimulates predominantly T lymphocytes.

Concentration catabolism effect: The direct effect exerted by the serum concentration of a plasma protein on its catabolic rate.

Concomitant immunity: The ability of a tumor-bearing animal to reject a test inoculum of its tumor at a site different from the primary site of tumor growth.

Congenic (originally **congenic resistant**): Denotes a line of mice identical or nearly identical with other inbred strains except for the substitution at one histocompatibility locus of a foreign allele introduced by appropriate crosses with a second inbred strain.

Contact sensitivity: A type of delayed hypersensitivity reaction in which sensitivity to simple chemical compounds is manifested by skin reactivity.

Contrasuppression: Effects of immunoregulatory circuit that inhibit suppressor influences in a feedback loop.

Copolymer: A polymer of at least 2 different chemical moieties, eg, a polypeptide with 2 different amino acids.

Coproantibody: An antibody present in the lumen of the gastrointestinal tract.

Counterimmunoelectrophoresis: See **Electroimmunodiffusion.**

C-reactive protein (CRP): A β-globulin found in the serum of patients with diverse inflammatory diseases.

CREST phenomenon: A phenomenon which consists of calcinosis, *R*aynaud's phenomenon, *e*sophageal dysmotility, *s*clerodactyly, and *t*elangiectasis and which occurs in patients with progressive systemic sclerosis.

Cross-reacting antigen: A type of tumor antigen present on all tumors induced by the same or a similar carcinogen.

Cross-reaction: The reaction of an antibody with an antigen other than the one that induced its formation.

Cryoglobulin: A protein that has the property of forming a precipitate or gel in the cold.

C-terminal: The carboxyl terminal end of a protein molecule.

Cycle-specific drugs: Cytotoxic or immunosuppressive drugs that kill both mitotic and resting cells.

Cytotropic antibodies: Antibodies of the IgG and IgE classes that sensitize cells for subsequent anaphylaxis.

D gene region: Diversity region of genome encoding heavy chain sequences in the hypervariable region of immunoglobulin H chain.

Deblocking factor: An antibody that, when mixed with blocking factors, neutralizes their activity.

Degranulation: A process whereby cytoplasmic granules of phagocytic cells fuse with phagosomes and discharge their contents into the phagolysosome thus formed.

Delayed hypersensitivity: A cell-mediated immune reaction that can be elicited by subcutaneous injection of antigen, with a subsequent cellular infiltrate and edema that are maximal between 24 and 48 hours after antigen challenge.

Determinant groups: Individual chemical structures present on macromolecular antigens that determine antigenic specificity.

Dextrans: Polysaccharides composed of a single sugar.

Diapedesis: The outward passage of cells through intact vessel walls.

Direct agglutination: The agglutination of red cells, microorganisms, or other substances directly by serum antibody.

Direct immunofluorescence: The detection of antigens by fluorescently labeled antibody.

Distribution ratio: The fraction of total body protein located in plasma.

Disulfide bonds: Chemical S–S bonds between sulfhydryl-containing amino acids that bind together H and L chains as well as portions of H–H and L–L chains.

Domains (also **homology regions**): Segments of H or L chains that are folded 3-dimensionally and stabilized with disulfide bonds.

Dysgammaglobulinemia: A term not in common use that refers to a selective immunoglobulin deficiency.

E rosette: A formation of a cluster (rosette) of cells consisting of sheep erythrocytes and human T lymphocytes.

EAC rosette: A cluster of red cells (*e*rythrocytes) sensitized with *a*mboceptor (*a*ntibody) and *c*omplement around human B lymphocytes.

EAE (experimental allergic encephalomyelitis): An autoimmune disease in which an animal is immunized with homologous or heterologous extracts of whole brain, the basic protein of myelin, or certain polypeptide sequences within the basic protein, emulsified with Freund's complete adjuvant.

ECF-A (eosinophil chemotactic factor): An acidic peptide, molecular weight 500, that, when released, causes influx of eosinophils.

Effector cells: A term that usually denotes T cells capable of mediating cytotoxicity suppression or helper function.

Electroimmunodiffusion (counterimmunoelectrophoresis): An immunodiffusion technique in which antigen and antibody are driven toward each other in an electrical field and then precipitate.

Electrophoresis: The separation of molecules in an electrical field.

Encapsulation: A quasi-immunologic phenomenon in which foreign material is walled off within the tissues of invertebrates.

Endocytosis: The process whereby material external to a cell is internalized within a particular cell. It consists of pinocytosis and phagocytosis.

Endotoxins: Lipopolysaccharides that are derived from the cell walls of gram-negative microorganisms and have toxic and pyrogenic effects when injected in vivo.

Enhancement: Improved survival of tumor cells in animals that have been previously immunized to the antigens of a given tumor.

Epitope: The simplest form of an antigenic determinant present on a complex antigenic molecule.

Equilibrium dialysis: A technique for measuring the strength or affinity with which antibody binds to antigen.

Equivalence: A ratio of antigen-antibody concentration where maximal precipitation occurs.

Euglobulin: A class of globulin proteins that are insoluble in water but soluble in salt solutions.

Exotoxins: Diffusible toxins produced by certain gram-positive and gram-negative microorganisms.

F₁ generation: The first generation of offspring after a designated mating.

F₂ generation: The second generation of offspring after a designated mating.

Fab: An antigen-binding fragment produced by enzymatic digestion of an IgG molecule with papain.

F(ab')₂: A fragment obtained by pepsin digestion of immunoglobulin molecules containing the 2 H and 2 L chains linked by disulfide bonds. It contains antigen-binding activity. An F(ab')₂ fragment and an Fc fragment comprise an entire monomeric immunoglobulin molecule.

Fc fragment: A crystallizable fragment obtained by papain digestion of IgG molecules that consists of the C-terminal half of 2 H chains linked by disulfide bonds. It contains no antigen-binding capability but determines important biologic characteristics of the intact molecule.

Fc receptor: A receptor present on various subclasses of lymphocytes for the Fc fragment of immunoglobulins.

Felton phenomenon: Immunologic unresponsiveness or tolerance induced in mice by the injection of large quantities of pneumococcal polysaccharide.

Fetal antigen: A type of tumor-associated antigen which is normally present on embryonic but not adult tissues and which is reexpressed during the neoplastic process.

Fibronectin: A protein that has an important role in the structuring of connective tissue.

Fluorescence: The emission of light of one color while a substance is irradiated with a light of a different color.

Forbidden clone theory: The theory proposed to explain autoimmunity that postulates that lymphocytes capable of self-sensitization and effector function are present in tolerant animals, since they were not eliminated during embryogenesis.

Four locus (4 locus): The second human histocompatibility locus to be described, now called locus B.

Fractional turnover rate: The percentage of plasma pool catabolized and cleared into the urine per day.

Francis skin test: An immediate hypersensitivity test for the presence of antibody on pneumococci in which pneumococcal capsular polysaccharide is injected into the skin and produces a wheal-and-flare response.

Freund's complete adjuvant: An oil-water emulsion that contains killed mycobacteria and enhances immune responses when mixed in an emulsion with antigen.

Freund's incomplete adjuvant: An emulsion that contains all of the elements of Freund's complete adjuvant with the exception of killed mycobacteria.

G cells: Gastrin-secreting cells in mucosa of the gastric antrum.

Gamma globulins: Serum proteins with gamma mobility in electrophoresis that comprise the majority of immunoglobulins and antibodies.

Gammopathy: A paraprotein disorder involving abnormalities of immunoglobulins.

Generalized anaphylaxis: A shocklike state that occurs within minutes following an appropriate antigen-antibody reaction resulting from the systemic release of vasoactive amines.

Genetic switch hypothesis: A hypothesis that postulates that there is a switch in the gene controlling heavy chain synthesis in plasma cells during the development of an immune response.

Genetic theory of antibody synthesis: A theory that predicts that information for synthesis of all types of antibody exists in the genome and that specific receptors are preformed on immunocompetent cells.

Germinal centers: A collection of metabolically active lymphoblasts, macrophages, and plasma cells that appears within the primary follicle of lymphoid tissues following antigenic stimulation.

Gm marker: An allotypic determinant on the heavy chain of human IgG.

Graft-versus-host (GVH) reaction: The clinical and pathologic sequelae of the reactions of immunocompetent cells in a graft against the cells of the histoincompatible and immunodeficient recipient.

Granulopoietin (colony-stimulating factor): A glycoprotein with a molecular weight of 45,000 derived from monocytes that controls the production of granulocytes by the bone marrow.

H chain (heavy chain): One pair of identical polypeptide chains making up an immunoglobulin molecule. The heavy chain contains approximately twice the number of amino acids and is twice the molecular weight of the light chain.

H-2 locus: The major genetic histocompatibility region in the mouse.

Halogenation: A combination of a halogen molecule with a microbial cell wall that results in microbial damage.

Haplotype: That portion of the phenotype determined by closely linked genes of a single chromosome inherited from one parent.

Hapten: A substance that is not immunogenic but can react with an antibody of appropriate specificity.

Hassall's corpuscles (also **Leber's corpuscles** or **thymic corpuscles**): Whorls of thymic epithelial cells whose function is unknown.

HBcAg (also **core antigen**): The 27-nm core of hepatitis B virus which has been identified in the nuclei of hepatocytes.

HBsAg: The coat or envelope of hepatitis B virus.

Heavy chain diseases: A heterogeneous group of paraprotein disorders characterized by the presence of monoclonal but incomplete heavy chains without light chains in serum or urine.

Helper T cells: A subtype of T lymphocytes that cooperate with B cells in antibody formation.

Hemagglutination inhibition: A technique for detecting small amounts of antigen in which homologous antigen inhibits the agglutination of red cells or other particles coated with antigen by specific antibody.

Hematopoietic system: All tissues responsible for production of the cellular elements of peripheral blood. This term usually excludes strictly lymphocytopoietic tissue such as lymph nodes.

Hemolysin: An antibody or other substance capable of lysing red blood cells.

Heterocytotropic antibody: An antibody that can passively sensitize tissues of species other than those in which the antibody is present.

Heterologous antigen: An antigen that participates in a cross-reaction.

High dose (high zone) tolerance: Classic immunologic unresponsiveness produced by repeated injections of large amounts of antigen.

Hinge region: The area of the H chains in the C region between the first and second C region domains. It is the site of enzymatic cleavage into F(ab')$_2$ and Fc fragments.

Histamine: A bioactive amine of MW 111 that causes smooth muscle contraction of human bronchioles and small blood vessels, increased permeability of capillaries, and increased secretion by nasal and bronchial mucous glands.

Histamine releasing factor: A lymphokine released from sensitized lymphocytes or antigenic stimulation that causes basophil histamine release.

Histocompatible: Sharing transplantation antigens.

HLA (human leukocyte antigen): The major histocompatibility genetic region in humans.

Homocytotropic antibody: An antibody that attaches to cells of animals of the same species.

Homologous antigen: An antigen that induces an antibody and reacts specifically with it.

Homopolymer: A molecule consisting of repeating units of a single amino acid.

Homozygous typing cells (HTC): Cells derived from an individual who is homozygous at the HLA-D locus used for MLR typing of the D locus in humans.

Horror autotoxicus: A concept introduced by Ehrlich, proposing that an individual is protected against autoimmunity or immunization against self antigens even though these antigens are immunogenic in other animals.

Hot antigen suicide: A technique in which an antigen is labeled with a high-specific-activity radioisotope (^{131}I). It is used either in vivo or in vitro to inhibit specific lymphocyte function by attachment to an antigen-binding lymphocyte, subsequently killing it by radiolysis.

Humoral: Pertaining to molecules in solution in a body fluid, particularly antibody and complement.

Hybridoma: Transformed cell line grown in vivo or in vitro that is a somatic hybrid of 2 parent cell lines and contains genetic material from both.

Hyperacute rejection: An accelerated form of graft rejection that is associated with circulating antibody in the serum of the recipient and which can react with donor cells.

Hypervariable regions: At least 4 regions of extreme variability which occur throughout the V region of H and L chains and which determine the antibody combining site of an antibody molecule.

Hypogammaglobulinemia (agammaglobulinemia): A deficiency of all major classes of serum immunoglobulins.

I region: That portion of the major histocompatibility complex which contains genes that control immune responses.

Ia antigens (I region–associated antigens): Antigens that are controlled by Ir genes and are present on various tissues.

Idiotype: A unique antigenic determinant present on homogeneous antibody or myeloma protein. The idiotype appears to represent the antigenicity of the antigen-binding site of an antibody and is therefore located in the V region.

IgA: The predominant immunoglobulin class present in secretions.

IgD: The predominant immunoglobulin class present on human B lymphocytes.

IgE: A reaginic antibody involved in immediate hypersensitivity reactions.

IgG: The predominant immunoglobulin class present in human serum.

IgM: A pentameric immunoglobulin comprising approximately 10% of normal human serum immunoglobulins, with a molecular weight of 900,000 and a sedimentation coefficient of 19S.

7S IgM: A monomeric IgM consisting of one monomer of 5 identical subunits.

I-J subregion: Part of mouse I region of the MHC that encodes for antigens present on suppressor cells and their active suppressor factors.

Immediate hypersensitivity: An unusual immunologic sensitivity to antigens that manifests itself by tissue reactions occurring within minutes after the antigen combines with its appropriate antibody.

Immune adherence: An agglutination reaction between a cell bearing $\overline{C4,2,3}$ and an indicator cell, usually a human red blood cell, which has a receptor for C3b.

Immune complexes: Antigen-antibody complexes.

Immune elimination: The enhanced clearance of an injected antigen from the circulation as a result of immunity to that antigen brought about by enhanced phagocytosis of the reticuloendothelial system.

Immune response genes (Ir genes): Genes that control immune responses to specific antigens.

Immune surveillance: A theory that holds that the immune system destroys tumor cells, which are constantly arising during the life of the individual.

Immunocytoadherence: A technique for identifying immunoglobulin-bearing cells by formation of rosettes consisting of these cells and red cells or other particles containing a homologous antigen.

Immunodominant: That part of an antigenic determinant which is dominant in binding with antibody.

Immunoelectrophoresis: A technique combining an initial electrophoretic separation of proteins followed by immunodiffusion with resultant precipitation arcs.

Immunofluorescence: A histo- or cytochemical technique for the detection and localization of antigens in which specific antibody is conjugated with fluorescent compounds, resulting in a sensitive tracer that can be detected by fluorometric measurements.

Immunogen: A substance that, when introduced into an animal, stimulates the immune response. The term immunogen may also denote a substance that is capable of stimulating an immune response, in contrast to a substance that can only combine with antibody, ie, an antigen.

Immunogenicity: The property of a substance making it capable of inducing a detectable immune response.

Immunoglobulin: A glycoprotein composed of H and L chains that functions as antibody. All antibodies are immunoglobulins, but it is not certain that all immunoglobulins have antibody function.

Immunoglobulin class: A subdivision of immunoglobulin molecules based on unique antigenic determinants in the Fc region of the H chains. In humans there are 5 classes of immunoglobulins designated IgG, IgA, IgM, IgD, and IgE.

Immunoglobulin subclass: A subdivision of the classes of immunoglobulins based on structural and antigenic differences in the H chains. For human IgG there are 4 subclasses: IgG1, IgG2, IgG3, and IgG4.

Immunopotency: The capacity of a region of an antigen molecule to serve as an antigenic determinant and thereby induce the formation of specific antibody.

Immunoradiometry: A technique of radioimmunoassay that employs radiolabeled antibody rather than antigen.

Immunotherapy: Either hyposensitization in allergic diseases or treatment with immunostimulants or immunosuppressive drugs or biologic products.

Indirect agglutination (also **passive agglutination**): The agglutination of particles or red blood cells to which antigens have been coupled chemically.

Indirect immunofluorescence (also **double antibody immunofluorescence**): A technique whereby unlabeled antibody is incubated with substrate and then overlaid with fluorescently conjugated anti-immunoglobulin to form a sandwich.

Information theory of antibody synthesis: A theory that predicts that antigen dictates the specific structure of the antibody molecule.

Inoculation: The introduction of an antigen or antiserum into an animal in order to confer immunity.

Interferon: A heterogeneous group of low-molecular-weight proteins elaborated by infected host cells that protect noninfected cells from viral infection.

Interleukin-1: Macrophage-derived factor (previously called LAF or leukocyte activating factor) that promotes short-term proliferation of T cells.

Interleukin-2: Probable lymphocyte-derived factor (previously called TCGF or T cell growth factor) that promotes long-term proliferation of T cell lines in culture.

Inv marker: See **Km marker.**

Ir genes: See **Immune response genes.**

Is genes: Genes that control development of specific suppressor T lymphocytes.

Isoagglutinin: An agglutinating antibody capable of agglutinating cells of other individuals of the same species in which it is found.

Isoantibody: An antibody that is capable of reacting with an antigen derived from a member of the same species as that in which it is raised.

Isohemagglutinins: Antibodies to major red cell antigens present in members of a given species and directed against antigenic determinants on red cells from other members of the species.

Isotype: Antigenic characteristics of given class or subclass of immunoglobulin H and L chains.

J chain: A glycopeptide chain that is normally found in polymeric immunoglobulins, particularly IgA and IgM.

Jarisch-Herxheimer reaction: A local or occasionally generalized inflammatory reaction that occurs following treatment of syphilis and other intracellular infections; it is presumably caused by the release of large amounts of antigenic material into the circulation.

Jones-Mote reaction (cutaneous basophil hypersensitivity): A poorly understood type of delayed hypersensitivity with predominantly basophil infiltrate that occurs transiently 24 hours after cutaneous rechallenge with sensitizing antigen.

K cell: A killer cell responsible for antibody-dependent cell-mediated cytotoxicity.

K and D regions: Genetic loci in the major histocompatibility complex of the mouse, coding for H-2 antigens that are detectable serologically.

Kallikrein system: See **Kinin system.**

Kappa (κ) chains: One of 2 major types of L chains (qv).

Kinin: A peptide that increases vascular permeability and is formed by the action of esterases on kallikreins, which then act as vasodilators.

Kinin system (also **kallikrein system**): A humoral amplification system initiated by the activation of coagulation factor XII, eventually leading to the formation of kallikrein, which acts on an α-globulin substrate, kininogen, to form a bradykinin.

Km marker (also **Inv**): An allotypic marker on the κ L chain of human immunoglobulins.

Koch phenomenon: A delayed hypersensitivity reaction by tuberculin in the skin of a guinea pig following infection with *Mycobacterium tuberculosis.*

Kupffer cells: Fixed mononuclear phagocytes of the reticuloendothelial system that are present within the sinusoids of the liver.

Kveim test: A delayed hypersensitivity test for sarcoidosis in which potent antigenic extracts of sarcoid tissue are injected intradermally and biopsied 6 weeks later in order to observe the presence of a granuloma, indicating a positive test.

L chain: See **Light chain.**

LA locus: The first human histocompatibility locus to be described, now called locus A.

Lactoferrin: An iron-containing compound that exerts a slight antimicrobial action by binding iron necessary for microbial growth.

Lambda (λ) chain: One of 2 major types of L chains (qv).

Langerhans cell: Bone marrow–derived macrophage with Ia cell surface antigens found in the epidermis.

Latex fixation test: An agglutination reaction in which latex particles are used to passively adsorb soluble protein and polysaccharide antigens.

LATS (long-acting thyroid stimulator): A γ-globulin which is present in about 45% of patients with hyperthyroidism and which causes delayed uptake of iodine in an animal assay system.

LATS protector: An immunoglobulin that is present in the circulation of patients with hyperthyroidism and has the property of blocking the binding of LATS to human thyroid microsomes.

LE cell phenomenon: Phagocytic leukocytes that have engulfed DNA, immunoglobulin, and complement and are present as a large homogeneous mass that is extruded from a damaged lymphocyte in systemic lupus erythematosus and other rheumatoid diseases.

Lectin: A substance that is derived from a plant and has panagglutinating activity for red blood cells. Lectins are commonly mitogens as well.

Leukocyte inhibitory factor (LIF): A lymphokine that inhibits the migration of polymorphonuclear leukocytes.

Leukocyte mitogenic factor (LMF): A lymphokine that will induce normal lymphocytes to undergo blast transformation and DNA synthesis.

Levamisole: An anthelmintic drug with possible immunostimulatory capabilities.

Ligand: Any molecule that forms a complex with another molecule, such as an antigen used in a precipitin or radioimmunoassay.

Light chain (L chain): A polypeptide chain present in all immunoglobulin molecules. Two types exist in most species and are termed kappa (κ) and lambda (λ).

Linkage disequilibrium: An unexpected association of linked genes in a population.

Lipopolysaccharide (also **endotoxin**): A compound derived from a variety of gram-negative enteric bacteria that have various biologic functions including mitogenic activity for B lymphocytes.

Local anaphylaxis: An immediate hypersensitivity reaction that occurs in a specific target organ such as the gastrointestinal tract, nasal mucosa, or skin.

Locus: The specific site of a gene on a chromosome.

Low dose (low zone) tolerance: A transient and incomplete state of tolerance induced with small subimmunogenic doses of soluble antigen.

Lucio phenomenon (erythema necroticans): A variant of erythema nodosum leprosum in which necrotizing vasculitis produces crops of large polygonal lesions characterized by ulceration and sloughing of large areas of skin.

Lymphocyte: A mononuclear cell 7–12 μm in diameter containing a nucleus with densely packed chromatin and a small rim of cytoplasm.

Lymphocyte activation (also **lymphocyte stimulation, lymphocyte transformation,** or **blastogenesis**): An in vitro technique in which lymphocytes are stimulated to become metabolically active by antigen or mitogen.

Lymphocyte-defined (LD) antigens: A series of histocompatibility antigens that are present on the majority of mammalian cells and are detectable primarily by reactivity in the mixed lymphocyte reaction (MLR).

Lymphokines (also **mediators of cellular immunity**): Soluble products of lymphocytes that are responsible for the multiple effects of a cellular immune reaction.

Lymphotoxin (LT): A lymphokine that results in direct cytolysis following its release from stimulated lymphocytes.

Lysosomes: Granules that contain hydrolytic enzymes and are present in the cytoplasm of many cells.

Lysozyme (also **muramidase**): The cationic low-molecular-weight enzyme present in tears, saliva, and nasal secretions that reduces the local concentration of susceptible bacteria by attacking the mucopeptides of their cell walls.

Lyt antigens: Differentiation antigens present on thymocytes and peripheral T cells.

Macrophage activation factor (MAF): A lymphokine that will activate macrophages to become avid phagocytic cells.

Macrophage chemotactic factor (MCF): A lymphokine that selectively attracts monocytes or macrophages to the area of its release.

Macrophages: Phagocytic mononuclear cells that derive from bone marrow monocytes and subserve accessory roles in cellular immunity.

Major histocompatibility complex (MHC): An as yet undetermined number of genes located in close proximity that determine histocompatibility antigens of members of a species.

Mast cell: A tissue cell that resembles a peripheral blood basophil and contains granules with serotonin and histamine present.

Matthews' mamillary models: A series of mathematical models that have 3 and 4 compartments and are used to predict the rates of protein metabolism.

β_2 Microglobulin: A protein (MW 11,600) which is associated with the outer membrane of many cells, including lymphocytes, and which may function as a structural part of the histocompatibility antigens on cells.

Migration inhibitory factor (MIF): A lymphokine that is capable of inhibiting the migration of macrophages.

Mithridatism (after Mithridates, king of Pontus): Immunity induced against poisons by the administration of gradually increasing doses of the poison.

Mitogens (also **phytomitogens**): Substances that cause DNA synthesis, blast transformation, and ultimately division of lymphocytes.

Mixed lymphocyte culture (mixed leukocyte culture) (MLC): An in vitro test for cellular immunity in which lymphocytes or leukocytes from genetically dissimilar individuals are mixed and mutually stimulate DNA synthesis.

Mixed lymphocyte reaction (MLR): See **Mixed lymphocyte culture.**

Monoclonal hypergammaglobulinemia: An increase in immunoglobulins produced by a single clone of cells containing one H chain class and one L chain type.

Monoclonal immunoglobulin molecules: Identical copies of antibody that consist of one H chain class and one L chain type.

Monoclonal protein: A protein produced from the progeny of a single cell called a clone.

Monomer: The basic unit of an immunoglobulin molecule that is comprised of 4 polypeptide chains: 2 H and 2 L.

Multiple myeloma: A paraproteinemic disorder consisting typically of the presence of serum paraprotein, anemia, and lytic bone lesions.

Myeloma protein: Either an intact monoclonal immunoglobulin molecule or a portion of one produced by malignant plasma cells.

Myeloperoxidase: An enzyme that is present within granules of phagocytic cells and catalyzes peroxidation of a variety of microorganisms.

Natural antibody: Antibody present in the serum in the absence of apparent specific antigenic contact.

NBT test: A metabolic assay involving the reduction of nitroblue tetrazolium dye during activation of the hexose monophosphate shunt in phagocytic cells.

Neoantigens: Nonself antigens that arise spontaneously on cell surfaces, usually during neoplasia.

Nephelometry: The measurement of turbidity or cloudiness in a suspension or a solution.

Nephritic factor: Serum immunoglobulin with conglutinin activity that can activate the alternative complement pathway. Often present in serum of patients with membranoproliferative glomerulonephritis.

Neutralization: The process by which antibody or antibody in complement neutralizes the infectivity of microorganisms, particularly viruses.

Neutrophil microbicidal assay: A test for the ability of neutrophils to kill intracellular bacteria.

NK cells (natural killer cells): Cytotoxic cells belonging to the cell class responsible for cellular cytotoxicity without prior sensitization.

Nonresponder: An animal unable to respond to an antigen, usually because of genetic factors.

N-terminal: The amino terminal end of a protein molecule.

Nucleoside phosphorylase: An enzyme that catalyzes the conversion of inosine to hypoxanthine and is rarely deficient in patients with immunodeficiency disorders.

Nude mouse: A hairless mouse that congenitally lacks a thymus and has a marked deficiency of thymus-derived lymphocytes.

Null cells: Cells lacking the specific identifying surface markers for either T or B lymphocytes.

NZB mouse: A genetically inbred strain of mice in which autoimmune disease resembling systemic lupus erythematosus develops spontaneously.

Oligoclonal bands: Immunoglobulins with restricted electrophoretic mobility in agarose gels found in cerebrospinal fluid of patients with multiple sclerosis and some other central nervous system diseases.

Oncogenesis: The process of producing neoplasia or malignancy.

Ontogeny: The developmental history of an individual organism within a group of animals.

Opsonin: A substance capable of enhancing phagocytosis. Antibodies and complement are the 2 main opsonins.

Osteoclast activating factor (OAF): A lymphokine that promotes the resorption of bone.

Ouchterlony double diffusion: An immunoprecipitation technique in which antigen and antibody are allowed to diffuse toward each other and form immune complexes in agar.

Paralysis: The pseudotolerant condition in which an ongoing immune response is masked by the presence of overwhelming amounts of antigen.

Paraproteinemia: A condition occurring in a heterogeneous group of diseases characterized by the presence in serum or urine of a monoclonal immunoglobulin.

Paratope: An antibody combining site for epitope, the simplest form of an antigenic determinant.

Passive cutaneous anaphylaxis (PCA): An in vivo passive transfer test for recognizing cytotropic antibody responsible for immediate hypersensitivity reactions.

Patching: The reorganization of a cell surface membrane component into discrete patches over the entire cell surface.

Peripheral lymphoid organs: Lymphoid organs not essential to the ontogeny of immune responses, ie, the spleen, lymph nodes, tonsils, and Peyer's patches.

Peritoneal exudate cells (PEC): Inflammatory cells present in the peritoneum of animals injected with an inflammatory agent.

Peyer's patches: Collections of lymphoid tissue in the submucosa of the small intestine that contain lymphocytes, plasma cells, germinal centers, and T cell–dependent areas.

Pfeiffer phenomenon: A demonstration showing that cholera vibrios introduced into the peritoneal cavity of an immune guinea pig lose their mobility and are lysed regardless of the presence of cells.

Phagocytes: Cells that are capable of ingesting particulate matter.

Phagocytosis: The engulfment of microorganisms or other particles by leukocytes.

Phagolysosome: A cellular organelle that is the product of the fusion of a phagosome and a lysosome.

Phagosome: A phagocytic vesicle bounded by inverted plasma membrane.

Phylogeny: The developmental and evolutionary history of a group of animals.

Phytohemagglutinin (PHA): A lectin which is derived from the red kidney bean (*Phaseolus vulgaris*) and which stimulates predominantly T lymphocytes.

Phytomitogens: Glycoproteins that are derived from plants and stimulate DNA synthesis and blast transformation in lymphocytes.

Pinocytosis: The ingestion of soluble materials by cells.

Plaque-forming cells: Antibody-producing cells capable of forming a hemolytic plaque in the presence of complement and antigenic erythrocytes.

Plasma cells: Fully differentiated antibody-synthesizing cells that are derived from B lymphocytes.

Plasma half-life (half time, T½): The time necessary for 50% of a passively infused protein to disappear from serum.

Plasmin: A fibrinolytic enzyme capable of proteolytically digesting C1.

Pokeweed mitogen (PWM): A lectin that is derived from pokeweed (*Phytolacca americana*) and which stimulates both B and T lymphocytes.

Polyclonal hypergammaglobulinemia: An increase in γ-globulin of various classes containing different H and L chains.

Polyclonal mitogens: Mitogens that activate large subpopulations of lymphocytes.

Polyclonal proteins: A group of molecules derived from multiple clones of cells.

Polymers: Immunoglobulins composed of more than a single basic monomeric unit, eg, an IgA dimer consists of 2 units.

Postcapillary venules: Specialized blood vessels lined with cuboid epithelium located in the paracortical region of lymph nodes through which lymphocytes traverse.

Pre-B cells: Large immature lymphoid cells with diffuse cytoplasmic IgM that eventually develop into B cells.

Precipitation: A reaction between a soluble antigen and soluble antibody in which a complex lattice of interlocking aggregates forms.

Primary follicles: Tightly packed aggregates of lymphocytes found in the cortex of the lymph node or in the white pulp of the spleen after antigenic stimulation. Primary follicles develop into germinal centers.

Primed lymphocyte typing (PLT): A variation on the MLR in which cells are primed by allogeneic stimulation and reexposed to fresh stimulator cells. Used to type for HLA-D determinants.

Private antigen: A type of tumor antigen that is expressed on a particular type of chemically induced tumor.

Procoagulant factor (tissue factor): Lymphokine that can replace factor VIII activity in factor VIII–deficient plasma.

Properdin system: A group of proteins involved in resistance to infection. The 2 main constituents consist of factor A and factor B. Properdin factor A is identical with C3, a β-globulin of MW 180,000. Properdin factor B is a β_2-globulin of MW 95,000. It is also called C3 proactivator, glycine-rich β-glycoprotein (GBG), or β_2-glycoprotein II. Properdin factor D is an α-globulin of MW 25,000 also called C3 proactivator convertase or glycine-rich β-glyco-proteinase (GBGase).

Prostaglandins: A variety of naturally occurring aliphatic acids with various biologic activities, including increased vascular permeability, smooth muscle contraction, bronchial constriction, and alteration in the pain threshold.

Prothymocytes: Immature precursors of mature thymocytes that develop within the thymus gland.

Prozone phenomenon: Suboptimal precipitation that occurs in the region of antibody excess during immunoprecipitation reactions.

Pyogenic microorganisms: Microorganisms whose presence in tissues stimulates an outpouring of polymorphonuclear leukocytes.

Pyrogens: Substances which are released either endogenously from leukocytes or administered exogenously, usually from bacteria, and which produce fever in susceptible hosts.

Pyroglobulins: Monoclonal immunoglobulins that precipitate irreversibly when heated to 56 °C.

Qa locus: Genetic locus mapping between H2-D and TL in mice which encodes Qa antigen found on both Ts and Th cells.

QPt: The percentage of protein-bound plasma activity at time *t*, compared to plasma activity at time *O*.

Quellung: The swelling of the capsules of pneumococci when the organisms are exposed to pneumococcal antibodies.

Radioallergosorbent test (RAST): A radioimmunoassay capable of detecting IgE antibody directed at specific allergens.

Radioimmunoassay: A variety of immunologic techniques in which a radioactive isotope is used to detect antigens or antibodies in some form of immunoassay.

Radioimmunodiffusion (Rowe's method): A modification of immunodiffusion in which a radioactive antibody is incorporated in order to increase the sensitivity by means of autoradiography.

Radioimmunosorbent test (RIST): A solid phase radioimmunoassay that can detect approximately 1 ng of IgE.

Ragocytes (RA cells): Polymorphonuclear leukocytes that have ingested characteristic dense IgG aggregates, rheumatoid factor, complement, and fibrin. They are found in the joints of patients with rheumatoid arthritis.

Raji cell test: An assay for immune complexes using the Raji lymphoblastoid cell line.

Reagin: Synonymous with IgE antibody. Also denotes a complement-fixing antibody that reacts in the Wassermann reaction with cardiolipin.

Recombinant: An animal that has experienced a recombinational event during meiosis, consisting of crossover and recombination of parts of 2 chromosomes.

Recombinatorial germline theory: Theory proposed by Dreyer and Bennett which states that variable region and constant region immunoglobulin genes are separated and rejoined at DNA levels.

Rejection response: An immune response with humoral and cellular components directed against transplanted tissue.

Reticuloendothelial system: A mononuclear phagocytic system located primarily in the reticular connective tissue framework of the spleen, liver, and lymphoid tissues.

Rheumatoid factor (RF): An anti-immunoglobulin antibody directed against denatured IgG present in the serum of patients with rheumatoid arthritis and other rheumatoid diseases.

Ricin: A poisonous substance that derives from the seed of the castor oil plant and agglutinates red blood cells (a lectin).

Rocket electrophoresis (Laurell technique): An electro-immunodiffusion technique in which antigen is electrophoresed into agar containing specific antibody and precipitates in a tapered rocket-shaped pattern. This technique is used for quantitation of antigens.

Rose-Waaler test: A type of passive hemagglutination test for the detection of rheumatoid factor that employs tanned red blood cells coated with rabbit 7S IgG antibodies specific for sheep red blood cells.

S region: The chromosomal region in the H-2 complex containing the gene for a serum β-globulin.

S value: Svedberg unit. Denotes the sedimentation coefficient of a protein, determined usually by ultracentrifugation.

Schultz-Dale test: An in vitro assay for immediate hypersensitivity in which smooth muscle is passively sensitized by cytotropic antibody and contracts after the addition of an antigen.

Second set graft rejection: An immunologic rejection of a graft in a host that is immune to antigens contained in that graft.

Secretory IgA: A dimer of IgA molecules with a sedimentation coefficient of 11S, linked by J chain and secretory component.

Secretory immune system: A distinct immune system that is common to external secretions and consists predominantly of IgA.

Secretory piece (T piece): A molecule of MW 70,000 produced in epithelial cells and associated with secretory immunoglobulins, particularly IgA and IgM.

Sensitized: Synonymous with immunized.

Sensitizer: A term introduced by Pfeiffer to denote a specific thermostable factor capable of bacterial lysis when combined with alexin.

Sequential determinants: Determinants whose specificity is dictated by the sequence of subunits within the determinant rather than by the molecular structure of the antigen molecule.

Serologically defined (SD) antigens: Antigens that are present on membranes of nearly all mammalian cells and are controlled by genes present in the major histocompatibility complex. They can be easily detected with antibodies.

Serology: Literally, the study of serum. Refers to the determination of antibodies to infectious agents important in clinical medicine.

Serotonin (5-hydroxytryptamine): A catecholamine of MW 176 that is stored in murine mast cells and human platelets and has a pharmacologic role in anaphylaxis in most species except humans.

Serum sickness: An adverse immunologic response to a foreign antigen, usually a heterologous protein.

Shwartzman phenomenon: A nonimmunologic phenomenon that results in tissue damage both at the site of injection and at widespread sites following the second of 2 injections of endotoxin.

Side chain theory: A theory of antibody synthesis proposed by Ehrlich in 1896 suggesting that specific side chains that form antigen receptors are present on the surface membranes of antibody-producing cells.

Single radial diffusion (radioimmunodiffusion): A technique for quantitating antigens by immunodiffusion in which antigen is allowed to diffuse radially into agar containing antibody. The resultant precipitation ring reflects the concentration of the antigen.

Skin-reactive factor (SRF): A lymphokine that is responsible for vasodilatation and increased vascular permeability.

Slow virus: A virus that produces disease with a greatly delayed onset and protracted course.

Solid phase radioimmunoassay: A modification of radioimmunoassay in which antibody is adsorbed onto solid particles or tubes.

Spermine: A polyamine present in prostatic secretions that is a pH-dependent inhibitor of gram-positive microorganisms.

Spherulin: A spherule-derived antigen from *Coccidioides immitis* used in delayed hypersensitivity skin testing for coccidioidomycosis.

SRS-A: An acidic lipoprotein, MW about 400, that has a prolonged constrictive effect on smooth muscle.

Sulzberger-Chase phenomenon: Abrogation of dermal contact sensitivity to various chemicals produced by prior oral feeding of the specific agent.

Suppressor T cells: A subset of T lymphocytes that suppress antibody synthesis by B cells or inhibit other cellular immune reactions by effector T cells.

Surface phagocytosis: The enhancement of phagocytosis by entrapment of organisms on surfaces such as leukocytes, fibrin clots, or other tissue surfaces.

Switch: Refers to change in synthesis between heavy chains within a single immunocyte from μ to γ—eg, during differentiation. V regions are not affected by H chain switch.

Syngeneic: Denotes the relationship that exists between genetically identical members of the same species.

T antigens: Tumor antigens, probably protein products of the viral genome present only on infected neoplastic cells.

T cell (T lymphocyte): A thymus-derived cell that participates in a variety of cell-mediated immune reactions.

T cell rosette: See **E rosette.**

T piece: See **Secretory piece.**

Theliolymphocytes: Small lymphocytes that are found in contiguity with intestinal epithelial cells and whose function is unknown.

Theta antigen: An alloantigen present on the surface of most thymocytes and peripheral T lymphocytes.

Thymopoietin (originally **thymin**)**:** A protein of MW 7000 which is derived originally from the thymus of animals with autoimmune thymitis and myasthenia gravis and which can impair neuromuscular transmission.

Thymosin: A thymic hormone protein of MW 12,000 that can restore T cell immunity in thymectomized animals.

Thymus: The central lymphoid organ that is present in the thorax and controls the ontogeny of T lymphocytes.

Thymus-dependent antigen: Antigen that depends on T cell interaction with B cells for antibody synthesis, eg, erythrocytes, serum proteins, and hapten-carrier complexes.

Thymus-independent antigen: Antigen that can induce an immune response without the apparent participation of T lymphocytes.

Tissue factor: See **Procoagulant factor.**

TL antigen: A membrane antigen which is present on prothymocytes in mice with a TL+ gene, but which is lost during thymic maturation.

Tolerance: Traditionally denotes that condition in which responsive cell clones have been eliminated or inactivated by prior contact with antigen, with the result that no immune response occurs on administration of antigen.

Toxoids: Antigenic but nontoxic derivatives of toxins.

Transfer factor: A dialyzable extract of immune lymphocytes that is capable of transferring cell-mediated immunity in humans and possibly in other animal species.

Transplantation antigens: Those antigens which are expressed on the surface of virtually all cells and which induce rejection of tissues transplanted from one individual to a genetically disparate individual.

Trophoblast: Cell layer in placenta in contact with uterine lining. Produces various immunosuppressive substances, eg, hormones.

Tryptic peptides: Peptides produced as a result of tryptic digestion of a protein molecule.

Tuftsin: A γ-globulin that is capable of stimulating endocytosis by neutrophils.

Tumor-associated antigens (TAA): Cell surface antigens that are expressed on malignant but not normal cells.

Tumor-associated rejection antigens (TARA): Antigens on tumor cells that result in initiation of immune rejection when the tumor is transplanted.

Ultracentrifugation: A high-speed centrifugation technique that can be used for the analytic identification of proteins of various sedimentation coefficients or as a preparative technique for separating proteins of different shapes and densities.

Ultrafiltration: The filtration of solutions or suspensions through membranes of extremely small graded pore sizes.

V antigens: Virally induced antigens that are expressed on viruses and virus-infected cells.

V (variable) region: The amino terminal portion of the H or L chain of an immunoglobulin molecule, containing considerable heterogeneity in the amino acid residues compared to the constant region.

V region subgroups: Subdivisions of V regions of kappa chains based on substantial homology in sequences of amino acids.

Vaccination: Immunization with antigens administered for the prevention of infectious diseases (term originally coined to denote immunization against vaccinia or cowpox virus).

Variolation: Inoculation with a virus of unmodified smallpox (variola).

Viscosity: The physical property of serum that is determined by the size, shape, and deformability of serum molecules. The hydrostatic state, molecular charge, and temperature sensitivity of proteins.

Von Krogh equation: An equation that relates complement to the degree of lysis of red blood cells coated with anti–red blood cell antibodies under standard conditions. Used to determine hemolytic complement titers in serum.

Wasting disease (also **runt disease**): A chronic, ultimately fatal illness associated with lymphoid atrophy in mice who are neonatally thymectomized.

Xenogeneic: Denotes the relationship that exists between members of genetically different species.

Xenograft: A tissue or organ graft between members of 2 distinct or different species.

Zone electrophoresis: Electrophoresis performed on paper or cellulose acetate in which proteins are separated almost exclusively on the basis of charge.

Acronyms & Abbreviations Commonly Used in Immunology

ABA Azobenzenearsenate.
ACTH Adrenocorticotropic hormone.
ADA Adenosine deaminase.
ADCC Antibody-dependent cell-mediated cytotoxicity.
AEF Allogeneic effect.
AFC Antibody-forming cells.
AFP Alpha-fetoprotein.
AGN Acute glomerulonephritis.
AHA Autoimmune hemolytic anemia.
AHG Antihemophilic globulin.
AIHA Autoimmune hemolytic anemia.
ALG Antilymphocyte globulin.
ALS Antilymphocyte serum.
Am Allotypic marker on IgA.
AMA Antimitochondrial antibodies.
AMP Adenosine monophosphate.
ANA Antinuclear antibody.
ANF Antinuclear factor.
APSGN Acute poststreptococcal glomerulonephritis.
ASO Antistreptolysin O.
ATG Antithymocyte globulin.
AuAg Australia antigen.

B27 HLA antigen with strong disease association.
BAF B cell activating factor.
BAL Dimercaprol (British anti-Lewisite).
Balb/c Inbred strain of mice.
BCG Bacillus Calmette-Guérin.
BFP Biologic false-positive (tests for syphilis).
BJ Bence Jones.
BPO Benzyl penicilloyl.
BRBC Burro red blood cells.
BSA Bovine serum albumin.
BUDR, BUdR 5-Bromodeoxyuridine.

CAH Chronic active hepatitis.
CALLA Common acute lymphocytic leukemia antigen.
cAMP Cyclic adenosine monophosphate.
CCF Crystal-induced chemotactic factor.
CEA Carcinoembryonic antigen.
CF Complement fixation.
CFA Colonization factor antigens (also Freund's complete adjuvant).
CFU Colony-forming unit.
CGD Chronic granulomatous disease.
cGMP Cyclic guanosine monophosphate.
C$_H$ Constant domain of H chain.
CHS Chédiak-Higashi syndrome.
CI Cell interaction (genes).
C$_L$ Constant domain of L chain.
CMC Chronic mucocutaneous candidiasis.
CMI Cell-mediated immunity.
CML Cell-mediated lympholysis.
CMPGN Chronic membranoproliferative glomerulonephritis.
CMV Cytomegalovirus(es).
C3NeF C3 nephritic factor.
ConA Concanavalin A.
C3PA C3 proactivator.
CPGN Chronic proliferative glomerulonephritis.
CREG Cross-reactive groups of human histocompatibility antigens.
CRP C-reactive protein.
CSA Colony stimulating activity.
CTL Cytotoxic lymphocytes.

DDS Dapsone (diaminodiphenyl-sulfone).
DEAE Diethylaminoethyl.
DGI Disseminated gonococcal infection.

DIC Disseminated intravascular coagulation.
D-L Donath-Landsteiner.
DLE Dialyzable leukocyte extracts; disseminated lupus erythematosus.
DNCB 2,4-Dinitrochlorobenzene.
DNFB Dinitrofluorobenzene.
DNP Dinitrophenyl.
DPO Dimethoxyphenylpenicilloyl.
DR D-related HLA locus in humans.
DSCG Disodium cromoglycate.
DT Diphtheria and tetanus toxoids (containing a larger amount of diphtheria antigens).
DTH Delayed-type hypersensitivity.
DTP Diphtheria and tetanus toxoid combined with pertussis vaccine.

EA Erythrocyte amboceptor (sensitized erythrocytes).
EAC Erythrocyte amboceptor complement.
EAE Experimental allergic encephalitis or encephalomyelitis.
EAN Experimental allergic neuritis.
EB Epstein-Barr.
EBV Epstein-Barr virus.
ECF Eosinophil chemotactic factor.
ECF-A Eosinophil chemotactic factor of anaphylaxis.
EDTA Ethylenediaminetetraacetate.
EIA Enzyme immunoassay.
ELISA Enzyme-linked immunosorbent assay.
EMIT Enzyme multiple immunoassay technique, a homogeneous enzyme immunoassay.
ENA Extractable nuclear antigen.
EP Endogenous pyrogen.
ER Endoplasmic reticulum.
ESR Erythrocyte sedimentation rate.

This list includes many abbreviations and acronyms that are not used in this book either because they have fallen into disuse or because the editors have felt that the modern tendency toward overuse of acronyms—particularly for disease names (SLE, MS, SCID, etc)—should be resisted. The attempt to make the list an extensive one is intended to assist the reader in using other books and journal articles and the older literature.

F₁ First generation.

F₂ Second generation.

FA Fluorescent antibody.

Fab Antigen-binding fragment.

FACS Fluorescent-activated cell sorter.

Fc Crystallizable fragment.

FCR Fractional catabolic rate.

FcRγ Fc receptor specific for IgG.

FcRμ Fc receptor specific for IgM.

FEV Forced expiratory volume in 1 second.

FITC Fluorescein isothiocyanate.

FSH Follicle-stimulating hormone.

FTA-ABS Fluorescent treponemal antibody absorption test.

FUDR, FUAR Fluorodeoxyuridine.

GALT Gut-associated lymphatic (lymphoid) tissue.

GBG Glycine-rich beta-glycoprotein.

GBM Glomerular basement membrane.

GCSA(a) Gross cell surface antigen (a).

GFR Glomerular filtration rate.

GGG Glycine-rich gamma-glycoprotein.

Gm Allotypic marker on human IgG.

GMP Guanosine monophosphate.

gp70 Glycoprotein antigen (MW 70,000) on viral envelope of C type murine viruses

GPA Guinea pig albumin.

GPC Gastric parietal cell.

G6PD Glucose-6-phosphate dehydrogenase.

GRF Genetically related factor or macrophage product.

GVH Graft-versus-host (disease).

GVHR Graft-versus-host reaction.

HAA Hepatitis-associated antigen.

HAE, HANE Hereditary angioneurotic edema.

HAT Hypoxanthine, aminopterin, and thymidine.

HAV Hepatitis A virus.

HbA Adult hemoglobin.

HBcAg Hepatitis B core antigen.

HbF Fetal hemoglobin.

HBsAg Hepatitis B surface antigen.

HBV Hepatitis B virus.

HCD Heavy chain disease.

HCG Human chorionic gonadotropin.

HDL High-density lipoproteins.

HDN Hemolytic disease of newborn.

H&E Hematoxylin and eosin (stain).

HI Hemagglutination inhibition.

HLA Human leukocyte antigen.

(H₂L₂)n General formula for immunoglobulin molecule.

HMP Hexose monophosphate (shunt).

HPRT Hypoxanthine phosphoribosyl transferase.

HSA Human serum albumin.

HSF Histamine-sensitizing factor.

5-HT 5-Hydroxytryptamine (serotonin).

HTC Homozygous typing cells.

ICA Islet cell antibody.

IDU Idoxuridine.

IEP Immunoelectrophoresis.

IF Intrinsic factor (also initiating factor).

IFA Indirect fluorescent antibody.

IL-1 Interleukin-1.

IL-2 Interleukin-2.

INH Isoniazid (isonicotinic acid hydrazide).

Inv Allotypic marker on human kappa chain (κm).

Ir Immune response (genes).

I-RNA Immune RNA.

Is Immune suppressor (genes).

ISG Immune serum globulin.

ITP Idiopathic thrombocytopenic purpura.

J segment Joining segment of DNA encoding immunoglobulins.

JRA Juvenile rheumatoid arthritis.

K (cells) Killer (cells).

KAF Bovine conglutinin: conglutinin activating factor.

KLH Keyhole limpet hemocyanin.

LAF Leukocyte activating factor (see IL–1).

LATS Long-acting thyroid stimulator.

LCM Lymphocytic choriomeningitis.

LD Lymphocyte-defined.

LDH Lactate dehydrogenase.

LDL Low-density lipoproteins.

LE Lupus erythematosus.

Lf Limit flocculation (unit) (1/1000 Lf = 0.0000003 mg).

LH Luteinizing hormone.

LIF Leukocyte inhibitory factor.

LMI Leukocyte migration inhibition.

LPS Lipopolysaccharide.

LT Lymphotoxin or lymphocytotoxin.

Lyb Lymphocyte antigens on murine B cells.

LyNeF Lytic nephritic factor.

Lyt Lymphocyte antigens on murine T cells.

MAF Macrophage activating (arming) factor.

MCA Methylcholanthrene.

MCF Macrophage chemotactic factor.

MCGN Mesangiocapillary (membranoproliferative) glomerulonephritis.

MCTD Mixed connective tissue disease.

MDP Muramyl dipeptide.

MeBSA Methylated bovine serum albumin.

MER Methanol extraction residue (of phenol-treated BCG).

MF Mitogenic factor.

MHC Major histocompatibility complex.

MHD Minimum hemolytic dilution or dose.

MIF Migration inhibitory factor.

MLC Mixed lymphocyte (leukocyte) culture.

MLD Minimum lethal dose.

MLR Mixed lymphocyte (or leukocyte) response or reaction.

MMI Macrophage migration inhibition.

6-MP Mercaptopurine.

MPG Methyl green pyronin.

MPO Myeloperoxidase.

MS Multiple sclerosis.

MTX Methotrexate.

MuLV Murine leukemia virus.

MW Molecular weight.

NBT Nitroblue tetrazolium.

NF Nephritic factor.

NK Natural killer (cells).

NZB New Zealand black (mice).

NZW New Zealand white (mice or rabbits).

OAF Osteoclast activating factor.

OPV Oral poliovirus.

OT Old tuberculin.

PA Pernicious anemia.

PAF Platelet aggregating factor.

PAS p-Aminosalicylic acid; periodic acid–Schiff (reaction).

PBC Primary biliary cirrhosis.

PBI Protein-bound iodine.

PCA Passive cutaneous anaphylaxis.

PCM Protein-calorie malnutrition.

PEC Peritoneal exudate cells.

PF/dil	Permeability factor dilute.	**S**	S value or sedimentation coefficient.	**TdT**	Terminal deoxynucleotidyl transferase.
PFC	Plaque-forming cells.				
PGE	Prostaglandin E (PGE₁, PGE₂, PGE₂α).	**SBE**	Subacute bacterial endocarditis.	**TEBG**	Testosterone-estrogen binding globulin.
PGN	Proliferative glomerulonephritis.	**SC**	Secretory component.	**TF**	Transfer factor.
		SCID	Severe combined immunodeficiency disease.	**TFd**	Dialyzable transfer factor.
PHA	Phytohemagglutinin.			**Th**	Helper T cells.
PIE	Pulmonary infiltration with eosinophilia.	**SCL-I**	Antinuclear antibody found in scleroderma.	**TI**	Thymus-independent.
				TL	Thymic lymphocyte (antigen) on prothymocytes.
PK (P-K)	Prausnitz-Küstner (reaction).	**SD**	serologically defined.		
PLL	Poly-L-lysine.	**SIDS**	Sudden infant death syndrome.	**TLI**	Total lymphoid irradiation.
PLT	Primed lymphocyte typing.	**SK-SD, SKSD**	Streptokinase-streptodornase.	**TMP**	Thymocyte mitogenic protein.
PML	Progressive multifocal leukodystrophy.			**TNP**	Trinitrophenyl.
		SLE	Systemic lupus erythematosus.	**Tp**	Precursor T cells.
PMN	Polymorphonuclear neutrophils.	**SMA**	Smooth muscle antibody.	**TPI**	*Treponema pallidum* immobilization.
		SMAF	Specific macrophage arming factor.		
PNH	Paroxysmal nocturnal hemoglobulinuria.			**Ts**	Suppressor T cells.
		SNagg	Serum normal agglutinator.	**TSA**	Tumor-specific antigen.
PPD	Purified protein derivative (tuberculin).	**SRBC**	Sheep red blood cells.	**TSab**	Thyroid-stimulating antibody.
		SRF	Skin-reactive factor.	**TSH**	Thyroid-stimulating hormone.
PSS	Progressive systemic sclerosis.	**SRS-A**	Slow-reacting substance of anaphylaxis.	**TSI**	Thyroid-stimulating immunoglobulin.
PVP	Polyvinylpyrrolidone.				
PWM	Pokeweed mitogen.	**SS**	Systemic sclerosis.	**TSTA**	Tumor-specific transplantation antigens.
		SSPE	Subacute sclerosing panencephalitis.		
				TU	Tuberculin units.
Qa	Region on 17th mouse chromosome in the MHC that encodes a class of T cell antigens.	**STS**	Serologic test for syphilis.		
				VDRL	Venereal Disease Research Laboratory.
		TA	Transplantation antigens.	**VEA**	Virus envelope antigen.
RA	Rheumatoid arthritis.	**TAA**	Tumor-associated antigens.	**V_H**	Variable domain of heavy chain.
Ragg	Rheumatoid agglutinin.	**TADA**	Tumor-associated developmental antigen.		
RANA	Rheumatoid arthritis nuclear antigen.			**VIG**	Vaccinia immune globulin.
		TAF	T cell activating factor.	**V_L**	Variable domain of light chain.
RAST	Radioallergosorbent test.	**TARA**	Tumor-associated rejection antigens.		
RBC	Red blood cell; red blood count.			**VLDL**	Very low density lipoproteins.
RE	Reticuloendothelial.	**TASA**	Tumor-associated serologic defined antigen.	**VZIG**	Varicella-zoster immune globulin.
RES	Reticuloendothelial system.				
RF	Rheumatic fever; rheumatoid factor.	**TATA**	Tumor-associated transplantation antigen.		
		TAVA	Tumor-associated viral antigen.	**WBC**	White blood cell; white blood count.
RIA	Radioimmunoassay.				
RIST	Radioimmunosorbent test.	**TCGF**	T cell growth factor (see IL-2).		
RSV	Respiratory syncytial virus.	**TD**	Thymus-dependent.		
		Td	Combined tetanus and diphtheria toxoid (adult type).	**ZIG**	Zoster immune globulin.

Index